EX LIBRIS

Name

# MICROECONOMICS

FOURTH EDITION

# MICROECONOMICS
## FOURTH EDITION


**ÅKE BLOMQVIST**
*University of Western Ontario*

**PAUL WONNACOTT**
*University of Maryland*

**RONALD WONNACOTT**
*University of Western Ontario*



**McGraw-Hill Ryerson Limited**
Toronto Montreal New York Auckland Bogotá Caracas Lisbon
London Madrid Mexico Milan New Delhi Paris San Juan
Singapore Sydney Tokyo

**MICROECONOMICS**
**Fourth Edition**



ISBN: 0-07-551538-5

1 2 3 4 5 6 7 8 9 0 RRD 3 2 1 0 9 8 7 6 5 4



Senior Editor: Jennifer Mix

Supervising Editor: Margaret Henderson

Permissions Editor: Norma Christensen

Production Editor: Gail Copeland

Cover & Text Design: Dianna Little

Typeface: Garamond

Printing & Binding: R.R. Donnelly & Sons Company

Cover Photograph: © David Bishop/Phototake NYC/
First Light

**Canadian Cataloguing in Publication Data**

Blomqvist, Åke G., date-
Microeconomics

4th ed.
Previous eds. published under title: An introduction to microeconomics.
Includes index.
ISBN 0-07-551538-5

1. Microeconomics. I. Wonnacott, Paul, date-.
II. Wonnacott, Ronald J., date-. III. Title.
IV. Title: An introduction to microeconomics.

HB172.B56 1994 338.5 C94-930123-X

# SUMMARY OF CONTENTS

Preface xxvii

PART 1 BASIC ECONOMIC CONCEPTS 1

Chapter 1 Economic Problems and Economic Goals 3
Chapter 2 Scarcity and Choice: The Economic Problem 29
Chapter 3 Specialization, Exchange, and Money 43
Chapter 4 Demand and Supply: The Market Mechanism 53
Chapter 5 The Economic Role of the Government 75

PART 2 FOUNDATIONS OF MICROECONOMIC ANALYSIS: THE COMPETITIVE MODEL 99

Chapter 6 Applications of Demand and Supply: The Concept of Elasticity 101
Chapter 7 Demand and Utility 123
Chapter 8 Business Organization and Finance 145
Chapter 9 The Costs of Production 163
Chapter 10 Supply in a Perfectly Competitive Market 183
Chapter 11 Perfect Competition and Economic Efficiency 203

PART 3 THE MARKET MECHANISM: SOME PROBLEMS 227

Chapter 12 Monopoly 229
Chapter 13 Markets Between Monopoly and Perfect Competition 257
Chapter 14 Government Regulation of Business 285

PART 4 FACTOR MARKETS AND INCOME DISTRIBUTION 307

Chapter 15 Wages in a Perfectly Competitive Economy 309
Chapter 16 Wages in Imperfectly Competitive Labour Markets 329
Chapter 17 Other Incomes 353
Chapter 18 Income Inequality 373

PART 5 MICROECONOMIC ISSUES OF OUR TIME 387

Chapter 19 What Are the Gains from International Trade? 389
Chapter 20 International Trade: Policy Debates 411
Chapter 21 Natural Resources: Are We Using Them at the Right Rate? 437
Chapter 22 The Economics of Protecting the Environment 461
Chapter 23 Public Goods and Public Choice 481
Chapter 24 Government Policies to Reduce Inequality: Can We Solve the Poverty Problem? 503

Glossary 525
Index 555

# CONTENTS


**Preface xxvii**

**PART 1 BASIC ECONOMIC CONCEPTS 1**

**1 Economic Problems and Economic Goals 3**

**Economic Progress 3**
**Economic Problems 4**
**Economic Policy 6**
The Controversial Role of Government **6**
**Economic Goals 7**
**Box 1-1: Karl Marx 8**
1. A Low Rate of Unemployment **8**
2. Stability of the Average Price Level **10**
3. Efficiency **11**
4. An Equitable Distribution of Income **12**
5. Growth **13**
**Interrelationships Among the Goals 14**
**A Preview 15**
**Key Points 15**
**Key Terms 16**
**Problems 16**
**Appendix 1-A: Diagrams and Algebra Used in Economics 17**
1. A Simple Comparison of Two Facts **17**
*Things to Watch* **17**
2. Relationships Between Variables **19**
*Straight-Line Relationships* **20**
*Relationships with Diminishing Slopes* **21**
*Diagrams with Two Relationships* **22**
3. Time Series: How Something Changes Through Time **24**
*Should We Measure from Zero?* **24**
*How Should Growth Be Illustrated?* **25**
*Real or Monetary Measures?* **27**
*Relative Measures* **28**

**2 Scarcity and Choice: The Economic Problem 29**

**Unlimited Wants . . . 29**
**. . . Scarce Resources 30**
**Box 2-1: A Tale of Two Dreams 31**
**Scarcity and Choice: The Production Possibilities Curve 33**
The Shape of the Production Possibilities Curve: Increasing Opportunity Costs **33**

**The Production Possibilities Curve is a "Frontier"** **35**
**Growth: The Outward Shift of the Production Possibilities Curve** **36**
**Growth: The Choice Between Consumer Goods and Capital Goods** **37**
Capital Imports and Growth **37**
Economic Development: The Problem of Takeoff **38**
**An Introduction to Economic Theory: The Need to Simplify** **39**
Theory Necessarily Involves Simplification **40**
The Distinction Between Positive and Normative Economics **40**
**Key Points** **41**
**Key Terms** **42**
**Problems** **42**

## 3 Specialization, Exchange, and Money 43

**Exchange: The Barter Economy** **43**
**Exchange with Money** **44**
The Circular Flow of Expenditures and Income **45**
**The Monetary System** **45**
**Box 3-1: Early Money on the Island of Uap** **46**
Monetary Problems in the POW Camp **47**
**Comparative Advantage: A Reason to Specialize** **48**
**Box 3-2: Illustration of Comparative Advantage** **49**
**Economies of Scale: Another Reason to Specialize** **49**
**Living in a Global Economy: Economies of Scale and the Canada/United States Free Trade Agreement** **50**
**Key Points** **51**
**Key Terms** **52**
**Problems** **52**

## 4 Demand and Supply: The Market Mechanism 53

**The Market and the Government** **53**
**The Market Mechanism** **55**
**Perfect and Imperfect Competition** **55**
**The Perfectly Competitive Market: Demand and Supply** **56**
Demand **56**
Supply **57**
The Equilibrium of Demand and Supply **58**
**Shifts in the Demand Curve** **59**
Demand Shifters **60**
*1. Income* **60**
*2. Prices of Related Goods* **60**
*3. Tastes* **60**
***What* is Produced: The Response to a Change in Tastes** **61**
**Shifts in Supply** **61**
Supply Shifters **61**
*1. The Cost of Inputs* **61**
*2. Technology* **62**
*3. Weather* **62**
*4. The Prices of Related Goods* **62**
The Response to a Shift in the Supply Curve **62**
**Shifts in a Curve and Movements Along a Curve** **63**
**Box 4-1: Curve Shifting and Equilibrium: Another View** **63**
**The Interconnected Questions of *What*, *How*, and *For Whom*** **65**
*How?* and *For Whom?* **66**

**The Market Mechanism: A Preliminary Evaluation** **66**
Strengths of the Market **66**
**Box 4-2: The Controversy Over Heroin** **67**
*The Alternative of Price Controls: Some Problems* **68**
The Market Mechanism: Limitations and Problems **69**
**Box 4-3: Supply and Demand in Action: The Market for Big-City Office Space** **70**
**Key Points** **71**
**Key Terms** **72**
**Problems** **72**

## 5 The Economic Role of the Government 75

**The Growth of Government Expenditures** **76**
Government Expenditures in Perspective **76**
Government Purchases versus Transfers **77**
**The Budgets of the Canadian Governments** **79**
Federal Government Expenditures **79**
Provincial and Local Government Expenditures **80**
Government Receipts **80**
Intergovernmental Transfers **82**
**Government Regulation** **82**
**Box 5-1: Federal Transfers to the Provinces** **83**
Problems with Government Regulation **85**
**Public Enterprise** **86**
*Accountability* **86**
*Privatization* **87**
**The Economic Role of the Government: What Should the Government Do?** **87**
1. The Government Provides What the Private Market Can't **87**
2. Externalities **88**
3. Merit Goods **88**
4. Helping the Poor **89**
5. The Government and Economic Stability **89**
**Taxation** **89**
1. Neutrality **89**
2. . . . and Nonneutrality: Meeting Social Objectives by Tax Incentives **89**
3. Simplicity **90**
4. Equity **90**
*The Benefit Principle* **90**
*Ability to Pay* **90**
**The Burden of Taxes: Who Ultimately Pays?** **91**
**Tax Loopholes** **92**
1. Capital Gains **92**
2. Imputed Income from Owner-Occupied Housing **92**
3. Preferences to Some Corporations **93**
**Tax Reform in the 1980s** **93**
*1. The Tax Base Should Be Broadened* **93**
*2. There Should Be a Reduction in Income Tax Rates* **93**
*3. Deductions Should Be Replaced by Tax Credits* **93**
*The 1988 Tax Reforms* **94**

**Box 5-2: The Legacy of Reaganomics 95**
Why Can't We Get Rid of All the Loopholes? **96**
**Key Points 97**
**Key Terms 98**
**Problems 98**

## PART 2 FOUNDATIONS OF MICROECONOMIC ANALYSIS: THE COMPETITIVE MODEL 99

### 6 Applications of Demand and Supply: The Concept of Elasticity 101

**The Price Elasticity of Demand 101**
*Examples* **102**
*Dropping the Minus Sign* **102**
*Elastic and Inelastic Demand* **102**
*The Beginning-point Problem* **102**
*Two Solutions* **103**
The Elasticity of Demand: What Happens to Total Revenue? **103**
Elasticity and Slope **105**
**What Determines Elasticity of Demand? 105**
*1. Substitutability* **105**
*2. Necessities versus Luxuries* **106**
*3. Percentage of Income* **107**
*4. Time* **107**
**The Price Elasticity of Supply 107**
**What Determines Elasticity of Supply? 108**
*1. Time* **108**
*2. Substitutes or Complements in Production?* **108**
*3. The Feasibility and Cost of Storage* **109**
**Significance of Elasticity 109**
Incidence of a Tax: Who Pays? **110**
Elasticity and Tax Revenue **111**
Rent Control **112**
**Living in a Global Economy: How Can Indebted Countries Increase Their Export Earnings? 114**
**Other Elasticity Measures 114**
Income Elasticity of Demand **114**
Cross Elasticity of Demand **115**
**Key Points 115**
**Key Terms 116**
**Problems 116**
**Appendix 6-A: Applying Elasticity: What Are the Special Problems of Agriculture? 118**
Year-to-Year Price Instability **118**
Long-run Downward Trend in Price **119**
Will the Future Bring Food Scarcity? **120**

### 7 Demand and Utility 123

**Market Demand as the Sum of Individual Demands 123**
**Diminishing Marginal Utility 123**
**Marginal Benefit and the Consumer's Equilibrium 125**

**Consumer's Surplus 127**
Changes in Consumer Surplus 128
**The Paradox of Value 128**
**The Consumer's Equilibrium: Another Look 130**
**The Marginal Rate of Substitution: The Slope of the Indifference Curve 131**
**Marginal Utility and the Marginal Rate of Substitution 131**
Diminishing Marginal Rate of Substitution and Diminishing Marginal Utility 131
**Willingness to Pay and the Marginal Rate of Substitution 132**
**Box 7-1: Why Indifference Curves Cannot Cross 133**
**The Budget Limitation 134**
**The Consumer's Equilibrium 134**
The Consumer's Equilibrium When Income Changes 135
**Box 7-2: How the Consumer Chooses Among Many Goods 136**
An Application: Cash Assistance vs. Aid in Kind 137
**Deriving a Demand Curve from an Indifference Map 139**
The Results of a Price Change: Substitution and Income Effects 139
**Extensions of Demand Theory 140**
Transactions Cost 140
How Do Search Costs Influence Market Price? 141
Time Costs in Consumption 141
**Key Points 142**
**Key Terms 142**
**Problems 143**

## 8 Business Organization and Finance 145

**Business Organizations 145**
Sole Proprietorships and Partnerships: Their Advantages and Disadvantages 145
The Corporation 146
Corporation Taxes 147
Double Taxation and the Dividend Tax Credit 147
**How a Corporation Finances Expansion 148**
Common Stock 148
Bonds 148
Convertible Bonds 149
Preferred Stock 149
**Financial Markets 149**
Buyers of Securities: Who Are Canada's Capitalists? 150
**Box 8-1: Who Controls the Corporation? 151**
The Objectives of Buyers of Securities 152
The Objectives of Issuers of Securities 152
The Bond Market 153
The Stock Market 153
**Business Accounting: The Balance Sheet and the Income Statement 155**
The Balance Sheet 155
*The Left-Hand, Asset Side* 156
*The Right-Hand Side, Showing Liabilities and Net Worth* 156
The Income Statement 157
Depreciation 157

**Accounting Cost vs. Opportunity Cost** **158**
**Key Points** **159**
**Key Terms** **160**
**Problems** **160**

## 9 The Costs of Production 163

**The Short Run and the Long** **163**
**Costs in the Short Run** **164**
*1. Fixed Costs or Overhead Costs* **164**
*2. Variable Costs* **164**
Marginal Cost **164**
Average Total Cost **165**
**The Relationship Between Average and Marginal Costs** **166**
**The Short-run Production Function** **166**
Total, Average, and Marginal Product **166**
**Box 9-1: Why a Firm's Costs Are Like a Baseball Player's Average** **167**
The Law of Diminishing Returns **168**
**Marginal Product and Marginal Cost** **168**
The U-Shaped Average Cost Curve **168**
**Costs in the Long Run** **168**
Finding the Least-cost Combination of Inputs **171**
The Envelope Curve and the Best Combination of Inputs **173**
**Box 9-2: If You Have Had Trouble Drawing Curves in Economics, You Are Not Alone** **175**
**Economies of Scale** **176**
The Range of Constant Returns and Minimum Efficient Scale **177**
Economies of Scale and Diminishing Returns **178**
**Living in a Global Economy: The Quest for Lower Costs** **178**
**Key Points** **179**
**Key Terms** **180**
**Problems** **180**
**Appendix 9-A: The Effect of a Change in the Price of Inputs** **182**

## 10 Supply in a Perfectly Competitive Market 183

**Perfect Competition as a Limiting Case** **183**
Perfect Competition: Demand as Seen by an Individual Producer **184**
Marginal Revenue **184**
**Profit Maximization: Marginal Revenue = Marginal Cost** **185**
Another View of Profit Maximization: Total Revenue and Total Cost **186**
**Short-run Supply of a Perfectly Competitive Firm** **187**
The Shutdown Point **187**
**The Short-run Market Supply Curve** **188**
**Supply in the Long Run** **188**
**Box 10-1: Ignoring the Shutdown Principle: The Case of Sysco** **190**
The Importance of Entry and Exit **192**
Case 1: Perfectly Elastic Long-run Supply **193**
*Efficient Scale in the Long Run* **194**
*A Fall in Demand* **195**

Case 2: A Rising Long-run Supply Curve 195
**The Reallocation of Resources: The Role of Profits 197**
**The Gains to Producers from a Higher Price 197**
**Reprise: The Burden of a Tax 198**
**Key Points 198**
**Key Terms 199**
**Problems 199**
**Appendix 10-A: Using the Supply Curve to Measure Producer Gains: Some Complications 201**
*Case 1* **201**
*Case 2* **201**
*Case 3* **201**

## 11 Perfect Competition and Economic Efficiency 203

Two Important Assumptions 203
**How a Perfectly Competitive Market Works 204**
**Demonstrating Why Perfect Competition is Efficient 206**
**Box 11-1: Conditions That Result in an Efficient Solution 206**
**Competition and Efficiency: The Two-good Case 208**
*Producer's Response* **209**
*Market Equilibrium* **209**
**Box 11-2: Pareto and the Elimination of Deadweight Loss 210**
**Efficiency in the Short Run and in the Long Run 211**
**Living in a Global Economy: Freer Entry into the London Financial Market 212**
**Other Types of Efficiency 213**
Technological, or Technical, Efficiency 213
Dynamic Efficiency 214
**Reprise: How the Competitive Market Determines Who Will Produce and Who Will Consume 214**
**Preview: Problems With the Competitive Market 215**
**Reservations About the Perfectly Competitive Outcome 215**
1. It Depends on the Distribution of Income 215
2. The Moral Hazard and Adverse Selection Problems 216
3. Buyers or Sellers May Be Misled By Price Signals 217
**Speculation and Price Instability 218**
Speculation as a Stabilizing Influence 218
Speculation as a Destabilizing Influence 219
The Hunt Brothers: Down at Heel, with Less than a Billion Dollars Left 220
**Government Agricultural Price Supports 220**
**Key Points 221**
**Key Terms 222**
**Problems 222**
**Appendix 11-A: Forms of Farm Assistance 223**
Support Prices and Deficiency Payments 223
*(a) Price Supports* **223**
*(b) Deficiency Payments* **223**
*How do Policies (a) and (b) Compare?* **223**
**Problem 225**

# PART 3 THE MARKET MECHANISM: SOME PROBLEMS 227

## 12 Monopoly 229

**What Causes Monopoly? 229**
**Natural Monopoly: When Economies of Scale Lead to a Single Firm 230**
**The Difference in the Demand Facing a Perfect Competitor and a Monopolist 231**
**What Price Does the Monopolist Select? 233**
What Is the Marginal Revenue of a Monopolist? **233**
Monopoly Output and Price **233**
Monopoly Profit: An Alternative View **235**
Profit Maximization for a Monopolist: Two Remaining Clarifications **236**
*A Monopolist Produces Where Demand is Elastic.* **236**
*A Monopolist Does Not Have a Supply Curve.* **237**
**Is Monopoly Efficient? 237**
Monopoly Resulting from Mergers **238**
**The Transfer Effect of Monopoly 239**
**Box 12-1: The Theory of the Second Best 240**
Agricultural Marketing Boards **241**
**Government Policies to Control Monopoly 242**
**Box 12-2: Unfortunately, Dealing with Natural Monopoly Is Often Not So Simple 244**
1. Average Cost Pricing **245**
2. Government Subsidy plus Marginal Cost Pricing **245**
3. Government Ownership **247**
**The Special Case of Discriminating Monopoly: Letting a Monopolist Act Like a Monopolist—In Spades 247**
**Living in a Global Economy: The World's Largest Firm 249**
**Key Points 250**
**Key Terms 251**
**Problems 251**
**Appendix 12-A: The Paradoxical Case of the Perfectly Discriminating Monopolist 253**
**Appendix 12-B: Public Transit Pricing 255**

## 13 Markets Between Monopoly and Perfect Competition 257

**Monopolistic Competition 257**
**Oligopoly 260**
Measuring the Concentration of an Industry **260**
*The Four-firm and Eight-firm Concentration Ratios* **260**
*The Herfindahl-Hirschman Index* **260**
*Has Concentration Been Increasing or Decreasing Over Time?* **262**
Natural Oligopoly: The Importance of Cost Conditions **262**
Other Influences in Oligopoly Markets **263**
**Barriers to Entry 263**
**The Oligopolist as a Price Searcher 264**
Collusion **264**
**Box 13-1: Competition for Shelf Space 265**
The Breakdown of Collusion: The Incentive to Cheat **267**

**Where Cartels Are Illegal, How Do Oligopolists Determine Price? 267**
The Kinked Demand Curve **268**
**Oligopoly: The Insights of Game Theory 269**
The Prisoner's Dilemma **270**
Duopoly Pricing **270**
A Complication: Repeated Games **271**
Price Leadership **272**
Focal-point Pricing **273**
Cost-plus Pricing **273**
**Non-price Competition 273**
Advertising **273**
Other Non-price Ways in Which Firms Compete **274**
**Don't Just Count Numbers: The Concept of Contestable Markets 275**
**Key Points 275**
**Key Terms 276**
**Problems 276**
**Appendix 13-A: Game Theory: The Concept of Nash Equilibrium 278**
Nash Equilibria and Dominated Strategies **278**
Nash Equilibrium in a Cournot Duopoly Game **278**
**Problem 280**
**Appendix 13-B: The OPEC Story of Collusion and Cheating 281**
The 1970s When Everything Went Right for OPEC **281**
The Key Role of the Saudis **282**
Falling Price in the 1980s: The Attempt to Enforce Production Quotas **282**
**Appendix 13-C: A Market With Elements of Both Competition and Monopoly 283**

## 14 Government Regulation of Business 285

**I. Competition Policy: Some Problems 286**
What Constitutes Collusion? **286**
**Box 14-1: Long Distance: The Next Best Thing to Being There 286**
Are There Advantages to Large Size? **287**
What Is Unfair Competition? **288**
The Difficult Problem of Mergers **289**
**Canada's Competition Law: A Summary 289**
1. Collusive Agreements **290**
2. Mergers and Abuse of Dominant Position **291**
3. Price Discrimination **291**
4. Other Provisions **292**
Final Observations: How to Achieve Workable Competition **292**
**II. Regulation of Price and Entry 292**
A Case History: Regulation of Rail and Truck Transport **293**
**Box 14-2: The Parable of the Parking Lots 293**
The Effects of Trucking Regulation **295**
Regulation in Other Canadian Industries **296**
**Deregulation in the 1980s 296**
**Box 14-3: Airline Deregulation in the United States 297**
**Concluding Observations: Shifts in Economic Decision Making 299**
**Key Points 299**
**Key Terms 300**
**Problems 300**

**Appendix 14-A: Mergers, Takeovers, and Leveraged Buy-outs 302**
Mergers: The Interests of the Acquiring Firm **302**
Mergers: The Interests of the Target Firm **303**
White Knights, Greenmail, and Other Forms of Shark Repellent **303**
Leveraged Buy-outs (LBOs) and Break-up Artists **304**
Conclusions on Mergers: Winners, Losers, and the Interest of Society as a Whole **305**

**PART 4 FACTOR MARKETS AND INCOME DISTRIBUTION 307**

**15 Wages in a Perfectly Competitive Economy 309**
**A Perfectly Competitive Labour Market 309**
**The Demand for Labour 310**
The Value of the Marginal Product of Labour **310**
The Demand Curve for Labour **312**
What Causes a Shift in the Demand for Labour? **312**
The Labour Market for an Industry **313**
**The Demand for Labour and the Division of Income 313**
**An Industry's Supply of Labour in a Perfectly Competitive Economy 314**
**The Invisible Hand in a Perfectly Competitive Economy 315**
**Box 15-1: Does an Invisible Hand Bring Efficiency to the Labour Market? 316**
**Some Complications 318**
**The Minimum Wage 318**
Case 1: Only One Industry Is Covered by the Minimum Wage **318**
Case 2: All Industries Are Covered by the Minimum Wage **318**
The Minimum Wage and Teenage Unemployment **320**
Has the Minimum Wage Been Overrated? **320**
1. *It May Have Less Effect on Efficiency than Figure 15-6(c) Suggests.* **320**
2. *There are Fewer Clear Winners and Clear Losers than the Standard Analysis Implies.* **320**
3. *The Minimum Wage Has Had a Disappointing Equity Effect.* **321**
**Discrimination in the Labour Market: An Introduction 321**
Discrimination Against Women and Minorities: The Equal Pay Debate **322**
**Key Points 324**
**Key Terms 325**
**Problems 325**
**Appendix 15-A: The Economywide Supply of Labour 327**

**16 Wages in Imperfectly Competitive Labour Markets 329**
**Labour Unions: The Benefits of Collective Action 329**
Collective Bargaining **330**
**Labour Unions: Their Historical Development 331**
The Period Before World War II **331**
The Period of Union Growth During and After World War II **332**
The Changing Pattern of Unionism Since the 1960s **333**
**Labour Unions: The Exercise of Market Power 334**
The Economic Effects When a Union Negotiates Higher Wages: A First Approximation **334**
Job Security **336**
**Box 16-1: Problems in the American Union Movement 336**
**How Unions Increase Efficiency: The Other Side of the Coin 337**

**Monopsony: Market Power on the Employers' Side of the Labour Market 338**
**Box 16-2: The Conflicting Objectives of Compassion and Efficiency 338**
**Box 16-3: How Far Does a Monopsonist Try to Reduce the Wage Rate? 339**
Monopsony and Baseball Salaries **340**
The Effects of Unions Reconsidered **340**
A Complication **341**
**Bilateral Monopoly: Relative Bargaining Power 341**
Which Side Has the Stronger Bargaining Position? **342**
**Strikes 342**
The Cost of a Strike **343**
Labour-Management Negotiations to Avoid Strikes **343**
*1. Inept Negotiating* **344**
*2. Irrationality* **344**
*3. Lack of Information* **344**
*4. Either Side May Want a Strike to Establish Its Credibility.* **344**
*5. One Party Has an Extraneous Objective.* **344**
*6. A Positive Contract Zone Does Not Exist.* **344**
Wage Bargaining and Game Theory **345**
**The Impact of Strikes on the Canadian Economy 346**
*Spillover Costs of a Strike* **346**
Last-resort Procedures to Prevent Strikes **347**
Disputes Involving Public Service Employees **348**
**Wage Differences: Why Do They Exist? 349**
**Key Points 350**
**Key Terms 351**
**Problems 351**

## 17 Other Incomes 353
**Interest: The Return to Debt Capital 353**
Investment and the Demand for Investable Funds **353**
Roundabout Production, with Interest as the Reward for Waiting **354**
Risk and Other Influences on the Interest Rate **357**
Effects of an Interest Rate Ceiling **357**
**Normal Profit: A Return to Equity Capital 359**
**The Role of Factor Prices 359**
How Factor Prices Influence Decisions by Individual Firms **359**
*How Factor Prices Influence the Allocation of Scarce Resources Throughout the Economy* **360**
**The Return to Human Capital 360**
The Return on Human Capital: What Is a University Education Worth? **361**
**Box 17-1: Why Private and Social Returns on Education Differ 362**
The Complex Nature of Wages and Salaries **363**
**Rent 363**
**Box 17-2: Rent and Opportunity Cost 364**
Rent on Agricultural Land, Based on Differences in Quality **366**
Another Example of Rent: The Income from Mineral Deposits **367**
Rent on Land Because of Its Location **367**
Above-normal Profit as a Rent **368**
**How Rents Are Capitalized 368**
Taxing Rent **369**
**Key Points 370**
**Key Terms 371**
**Problems 371**

## 18 Income Inequality 373

**Review: Why Do Incomes Differ? 373**
**How Much Income Inequality Is There? 374**
**How Much Inequality Does the Government Now Eliminate? 375**
**What Is an Equitable Income Distribution? 377**
Is the Free Market's Distribution of Income Equitable? **378**
Equality as a Target **378**
**Box 18-1: Rawls on Equality 379**
A Compromise Between the Free Market and Complete Equality **381**
*Make It a Fair Race, . . .* **381**
*. . . but Modify the Rewards.* **382**
Conclusions: Can We Pin Down the Idea of Equity? **382**
**Box 18-2: Kurt Vonnegut on Why Only Horses and Golfers Should Be Handicapped 383**
**Key Points 384**
**Key Terms 385**
**Problems 385**

# PART 5 MICROECONOMIC ISSUES OF OUR TIME 387

## 19 What Are the Gains from International Trade? 389

**With Whom Do We Trade? What Do We Trade? 389**
**Benefits from Trade: Markets Become More Competitive 390**
**Benefits from Trade: Economies of Scale 391**
New Products Become Available **391**
Existing Goods Can Be Produced More Efficiently **392**
**Gains from Trade: Comparative Advantage 392**
Absolute Advantage **392**
Comparative Advantage **393**
Gains from Trade **394**
*Diagrammatic Illustration* **394**
**Box 19-1: Wages and Trade 395**
Trade and Technological Change: Their Similarities **396**
International Trade and Exchange Rates **396**
**Gains from Trade: Illustration Using Demand and Supply 398**
Efficiency Gain on a Typical Export: Wheat **398**
Efficiency Gain on a Typical Import: Woollens **399**
**Winners and Losers from International Trade 400**
**Foreign Investment in Canada: Importing Capital Services 401**
Some Complications **404**
*1. The Taxation of the Return to Capital* **404**
*2. Can We Reduce the Cost of Foreign Capital?* **404**
**Key Points 405**
**Key Terms 405**
**Problems 405**
**Appendix 19-A: The Issue of Foreign Ownership and Control 407**
Direct vs. Portfolio Investment **407**
Foreign Control in the Canadian Economy **407**
Why Do They Come? **408**
**Consequences of Foreign Ownership and Control 409**

## 20 International Trade: Policy Debates 411

**Non-economic Explanation of Trade Barriers 412**
An Industry May Be Essential for National Defence **412**
A Canadian Cultural Industry Should Be Protected to Maintain Our National Identity **412**
People Vote for Their Present Jobs **412**
**Economic Arguments for Protection 412**
1. "Buy Canadian Because It Keeps Our Money at Home." **412**
**Box 20-1: What Happens if the Consumer is Forgotten: Bastiat's Negative Railway 413**
2. "We Can't Compete with Cheap Foreign Labour." **413**
**Box 20-2: The Petition of the Candlemakers 414**
3. "Tariffs Should Be Tailored to Equalize Costs at Home and Abroad." **414**
4. "If We Buy Steel from Hamilton rather than from Tokyo, Employment Will Rise in Hamilton rather than in Tokyo." **414**
5. "Restricting Trade Will Diversify a Nation's Economy." **415**
6. "Restricting Imports May Reduce the Price We Have to Pay for Them." **416**
7. "Restricting Trade Will Make Us Less Dependent on Foreign Supplies." **416**
8. "We Need to Protect Our Infant Industries." **416**
9. "Protection Can Be Used to Engineer a Comparative Advantage." **416**
10. "Industries with Positive Externalities Should Be Protected." **417**
11. "The Existence of Imperfect Competition May Justify Protection." **417**
Free Trade vs. Protection: A Summary **417**
**Non-tariff Barriers (NTBs) 418**
Quotas **418**
Health or Quality Standards **418**
Bureaucracy and Red Tape **418**
**Canadian Tariffs, 1870–1990 418**
The National Policy **418**
**Multilateral Negotiations: The General Agreement on Tariffs and Trade (GATT) 419**
**A Plurilateral Agreement: The European Community (EC) 419**
**A Bilateral Agreement: The Canada/U.S. Free Trade Agreement (FTA) 420**
How is the FTA Working Out? **421**
The Adjustment as Canadian Industry Rationalizes **421**
Trade Liberalization and Jobs **422**
**Box 20-3: How Macroeconomic Pressure from Fighting Inflation Made Canadian Adjustment to the Canada/U.S. FTA More Difficult 423**
The Effect of the FTA on Canadian Trade Performance **423**
Unfinished Business: The FTA Improves, But Doesn't Guarantee, Access into the U.S. Market **424**
**A Trilateral Negotiation: The North American Free Trade Agreement (NAFTA) 425**
Should Canada Have Participated in Negotiating NAFTA? **425**
NAFTA: Fortress North America? **427**
NAFTA's Changes in Rules of Origin **427**
NAFTA and Computer Trade **427**

**Trade and the Environment in NAFTA 427**
**Box 20-4: Rules of Origin: The Preferred Form of Future Protection? 428**
**Imports from the Emerging Less Developed Countries 429**
**Box 20-5: The 1993 GATT Agreement 430**
**Key Points 431**
**Key Terms 432**
**Problems 432**
**Appendix 20-A: The Effects of a Tariff or Quota that Reduces Imports 434**
Effects of a Tariff **434**
Effects of a Quota **434**

## 21 Natural Resources: Are We Using Them at the Right Rate? 437

**Characteristics of Natural Resources: Where Are Conservation Problems Most Likely to Arise? 438**
*1. What is the Supply/Demand Relationship?* **438**
*2. How Substantial are the Costs of Adjustment: Are Users Heavily Dependent on the Resource?* **438**
*3. When the Resource is Used, Does It Disappear?* **439**
*4. Is the Resource Renewable or Non-renewable?* **439**
*5. Is the Resource Common Property or Privately Owned?* **439**
**The Difficulty in Conserving a Common-property Resource: Fish 439**
**The Maximum Sustainable Yield of a Renewable Resource 440**
Why a Free Market Fails to Conserve **440**
Measures to Induce Appropriate Conservation of a Common-property Resource **441**
*1. Place Limits on the Catch.* **441**
*2. Impose a Tax or a Fishing Fee.* **441**
*3. Create Property Rights.* **441**
**Box 21-1: Managing an Offshore Fishery: Two Problems 442**
1. Methods of Regulation **442**
2. International Complications **442**
**A Privately Owned Resource: Timber 443**
Rent and the Reservation Price **446**
**Conservation on Non-renewable Resources 447**
How the Market Conserves the Resource **447**
**Box 21-2: Resource Exploitation and the Environment: Two Cases 448**
1. The Northern Spotted Owl vs. Logging **448**
2. Green vs. Copper: Tatshenshini vs. Windy Craggy **448**
Dynamic Efficiency in a Perfectly Competitive Market for a Resource **449**
Why the Real World Is More Complicated **449**
Market Prices that Promote Conservation and Other Forms of Adjustment **449**
*1. Substitution in Consumption and Production* **449**
*2. Intensified Search for the Resource* **450**
*3. Discovery and Development of Substitutes* **450**
**Oil: A Resource with Very Special Problems 450**
Implications of Keeping the Domestic Canadian Price Below the World Price **451**
**Box 21-3: The International Income Transfer as the World Price of Oil Increased: OPEC as a "Conserving Monopolist"? 452**
Oil Pricing, Conservation, and Energy Security **454**

**Key Points 455**
**Key Terms 455**
**Problems 455**
**Appendix 21-A: Sustainable Yield and the Efficient Rate of Harvesting of a Renewable Resource 457**

## 22 The Economics of Protecting the Environment 461

**Measures to Control Pollution 461**
**Pollution: The Expensive Job of Control 462**
**Pollution: An External Cost 463**
**Box 22-1: Why Not Control Pollution by Ending Economic Growth? 463**
**Pollution and Property Rights 464**
Property Rights in the Environment? **465**
The Problem of Transactions Costs **466**
**Controlling Pollution: The Simple Case 466**
**Controlling Pollution: A More Complex Case 467**
Option 1. A Pollution Tax **468**
Option 2. Command-and-Control: A Physical Limit on the Pollution by Each Firm **468**
Option 3. Physical Limits on Pollution with Trade Allowed in Emissions Permits **468**
How Does Option 1 (Effluent Fees) Compare to Option 3 (Emissions Trading)? **469**
*Tradeable Permits and Property Rights* **469**
How Far Should Pollution Be Reduced? **470**
**Box 22-2: Pollution Control: An Historical Perspective 471**
An Alternative Policy? Subsidizing Pollution-control Equipment **472**
**Pollution Control in Canada: Which Option Does the Government Use? 472**
**Pollution as a Source of Interprovincial and International Conflict 473**
**Box 22-3: Recycling 474**
**Energy and the Environment 476**
Natural Gas **477**
Coal **477**
*1. Problems in Mining* **477**
*2. Problems in Burning Coal in Power Plants* **477**
Fighting the Greenhouse Effect: A Carbon Tax? **477**
Hydroelectric Power **478**
Nuclear Power **478**
**How Do We Protect the Environment?: Concluding Observations 479**
**Key Points 479**
**Key Terms 480**
**Problems 480**

## 23 Public Goods and Public Choice 481

**External Benefits: A Free Market Provides Too Little 482**
One Solution: A Subsidy **483**
Encouraging Private Market Transactions to Internalize the Externality **483**
Government Action as a Way of Dealing with Externalities **484**
**Public Goods 484**
**Problems in Evaluating the Benefits of a Public Good 486**
**The Environment as a Public Good 487**

**Safety and Health in Consumer Products and the Workplace 488**
Safety and Health in Consumer Products **490**
Lack of Information: More Serious for Health than Safety **491**
Benefits of Health and Safety Regulations **491**
**Evaluating a Regulation: Does It Pass the Cost-benefit Test? 491**
Why Cost-benefit Analysis Is Not the Last Word **492**
The Importance of Consistency **492**
**Public Choice: Problems with Government Decision Making 492**
*1. The Difficulty in Reversing a Public Expenditure* **492**
**Box 23-1: The Eternal Puzzle: What Is a Human Life Worth? 493**
*2. Voting Politically for Products is Not Specific Enough* **494**
*3. Short-run, Crisis-oriented Decision Making* **494**
*4. The Incentive for Politicians to Support "Special-interest" Groups* **494**
**Problems in Defining the "Public Interest" 495**
*1. The Problem of the Oppressive Majority* **495**
**Box 23-2: Public Choice in Action: Canada's Free Trade Election of 1988 495**
*2. The Voting Paradox: Why Majority Rule May Lead to No Clear Winner* **497**
*3. Logrolling* **497**
**The Problems of Governing with a Bureaucracy 498**
*1. Difficulties in Controlling a Bureau's Performance and Cost* **498**
*2. The Tendency for the Government Bureau and its Budget to Expand* **499**
*3. Monopoly Inefficiency: Public vs. Private* **499**
**The Public vs. Private Sector: A Review of Microeconomic Markets 499**
**Key Points 501**
**Key Terms 502**
**Problems 502**

## 24 Government Policies to Reduce Inequality: Can We Solve the Poverty Problem? 503

**Poverty 503**
How the Poverty Line Is Defined **504**
Who Are the Poor? **504**
**Government Anti-poverty Policies 504**
Policies to Reduce the Causes of Poverty **505**
*1. Subsidizing Investment in Human Capital* **505**
*2. Dealing With Unemployment and Disability* **506**
*3. Reducing Poverty in One-parent Households* **506**
*4. Other Policies* **506**
**Policies to Reduce the Symptoms of Poverty: Government Programs to Maintain Incomes 506**
Social Insurance Programs **506**
*Old Age Security (OAS)* **506**
*The Canada Pension Plan (CPP) and Quebec Pension Plan (QPP)* **507**
*Unemployment Insurance* **507**
*Health Insurance* **508**

**Box 24-1: The Rising Cost of Health Care 508**
*The OAS and UI Clawback Rules* **510**
Targeted Transfer Programs **510**
*Guaranteed Income Supplement (GIS)* **510**
*The Integrated Child Tax Benefit* **510**
*Social Assistance* **510**
*Other Programs* **511**
**Assessing the Present Welfare Package 511**
How Much Progress Have We Made? **512**
Problems with the Welfare System **512**
*1. Perverse Incentives* **513**
*2. Complexity and Inequity* **513**
**A Guaranteed Minimum Income: A Cure for the Poverty Problem? 513**
Inefficiencies in a Subsidy Program **514**
*Disincentives for Those Paying for the Subsidy* **514**
*Disincentives for Those Receiving the Subsidy* **514**
*Disincentives that Apply to the Non-poor* **515**
*The Implicit Tax Under the Cash Deficit Method* **515**
**Conflicting Views on Welfare 515**
Economic Failure: Is It Cured or Caused by Welfare? **516**
Non-economic Benefits and Costs **517**
**The Key Trade-off: Equity Versus Efficiency 517**
**The Negative Income Tax: Can We Combine Equity and Efficiency? 518**
Design of a Negative Income Tax **518**
Why the Negative Income Tax Should Reduce the Leaks in the "Welfare Bucket" **519**
The Negative Income Tax Does Not Resolve All Conflicts **520**
The Negative Income Tax in Practice: Results of Controlled Experiments **520**
**Where Do We Go from Here? 521**
**Key Points 522**
**Key Terms 522**
**Problems 523**

**Glossary 525**

**Index 555**

# PREFACE

## TO THE STUDENT

Economics is like the music of Mozart. On one level, it holds great simplicity: Its basic ideas can be quickly grasped by those who first encounter it. On the other hand, below the surface, there are fascinating subtleties that remain a challenge — even to those who spend a lifetime in its study. Therefore, we hold out this promise: In this introductory study, you will learn a great deal about how the economy works — the basic principles governing economic life that must be recognized by those in government and business who make policy decisions. At the same time, we also can promise that you won't be able to master it all. You should be left with an appreciation of the difficult and challenging problems of economics that remain unsolved.

## HOW TO USE THIS BOOK

Our objective has been to make the basic propositions of economics as easy as possible to grasp. As each new topic is encountered, essential definitions are printed in coloured type and key terms and concepts in the argument are emphasized with boldface italic type. These highlights should be studied carefully during the first reading and during later review. (A glossary is provided at the end of the book. It contains a list of definitions of terms used in this text plus other common economics terms that you may encounter in class or in readings.) The basic ideas of each chapter and new concepts that are introduced are summarized in the Key Points section at the end of the chapter.

When you read a chapter for the first time, concentrate on the main text. In the first reading, don't worry about the boxes. They are set aside from the text to keep the main line of argument in each chapter as simple and straightforward as possible.

The boxes fall into two broad categories. First, there are the boxes that provide examples or illustrations of the way some of the economic principles discussed in the text show up in the real world (such as the boxes in Chapter 13 on competition for retail shelf space, or in Chapter 21 on the problems of managing an offshore fishery used by both Canadian and foreign fishing crews). Other boxes in this category refer to important historical figures in the economics literature, beyond those discussed in the text (for example, Karl Marx in Chapter 1 and John Rawls in Chapter 18), while some are intended to provide institutional detail on issues briefly referred to in the text, and some are included just because we thought they were interesting (Box 3-1 on primitive money on the island of Uap) or amusing (Bastiat's "negative railway" in Chapter 20).

The second major category consists of boxes with more technical material that supplements the text discussion (Box 3-2 with the illustration of comparative advantage; Box 15-1 on efficiency in the labour market), or introduces new concepts or relationships (Box 12-2 on dealing with natural monopoly). We distinguish between the two categories of boxes by the logo at the top:

and for "general interest" boxes,

and for "technical" boxes.

On first reading, you also may skip starred (*) sections of the text, along with footnotes and appendices; these also tend to be more difficult.

On second reading and in reviewing the material for tests and exams, you should obviously study those boxes and appendices your instructor has told you that you are responsible for. In addition, we encourage you to look, at least briefly, at the other ones as well, for general interest, and to sharpen your understanding of the main concepts.

Economics is not a spectator sport. You cannot learn just from observation; you must work at it. When you have finished reading a chapter, work on the problems listed at the end; they are designed to reinforce your understanding of important concepts. (The starred (*) problems either are based on material in a box, or are more difficult questions designed to provide a challenge to students who want to do more advanced work.) Because each chapter builds on preceding ones and because the solution to some of the problems depends on those that came before it, remember this important rule: Don't fall behind in a problem-solving course. To help you keep up, we recommend the *Study Guide* (Fourth Edition), which is specifically designed to assist you in working through each chapter. It should be available in your bookstore.

## TO THE INSTRUCTOR

The starting point for this book is the Third Canadian edition of *Microeconomics* by Åke Blomqvist, Paul Wonnacott, and Ronald Wonnacott. The revision and updating has been done by Åke Blomqvist, with contributions by Paul Hobson and Peter Townley, both of Acadia University.

In preparing this fourth edition, we have tried hard to maintain what we believe to have been an important strength of earlier editions: An exposition of economic principles that most students find clear and easy to understand. While doing so, however, we have also recognized that with today's large classes in introductory economics, instructors often face a difficult question: How can one teach a course that *both* challenges those students who are well prepared and able to quickly grasp the basic principles, *and* offers useful and interesting insights to those with weaker background preparation, who may have to work harder at understanding these principles? (Another way of describing this conflict that we have often heard, is: How can I teach an introductory course that will appeal both to the student who is planning to go on to advanced work in economics, *and* to the student who doesn't intend to specialize but simply takes economics in order to become a "better informed citizen"?)

In this edition, we have tried to respond to this dilemma by moving a considerable distance in the direction of providing challenging material for the better prepared student, beginning with an extended appendix on the use of diagrams and simple algebra in economics at the end of Chapter 1. However, we have tried to do so in such a way that the book (and its companion volume on macroeconomics) will continue to appeal to those who are looking only for a general introduction to the subject. For example, we have continued to keep the exposition of the central ideas as transparent and readable as possible, even when introducing some relatively advanced concepts. (To reinforce the text, key ideas are frequently repeated in the captions that accompany the diagrams.) We have also continued to devote considerable space to descriptions of real-world examples and events that illustrate "the principle in action," not only in the boxes but also in the main text itself.

In addition, we have tried to structure the presentation in many chapters in such a way that it should be easy for instructors who so prefer to avoid some of the material that students tend to find difficult. For example, although we have brought the indifference curve derivation of the individual demand curve into the main text, a self-contained and complete derivation without indifference curves can still be given by simply omitting a few sections. (To facilitate alternative approaches, the instructor's manual has a number of suggestions for ways in which the material can be "repackaged.")

Moreover, a considerable portion of the supplementary and more challenging material we have added appears in appendices, in a number of "technical boxes," or as end-of-chapter problems. Although we recognize that few instructors will want to take their students through *all* of this material, we hope that at least some of it will be part of the material taught, and perhaps used as supplementary material for interested students.

As we have revised and updated the text, we have continued to keep in mind two major questions (posed in earlier editions) that have long concerned us as teachers of introductory economics.

For microeconomics, what we asked ourselves was this: Does the introductory study of microeconomics lack coherence? To the student, does microeconomics tend to become merely one thing after another — a guided tour through the economist's workshop, introducing as many polished pieces of analytical machinery as possible for later use in more advanced courses? Most students do not continue to advanced economics courses. Even though a comprehensive survey of techniques may give a head start to those who do continue, it also increases the risk that they will be bored by repetition, and will miss some of the forest while concentrating on the trees.

Therefore, although this edition does introduce and explain a number of new technical tools, we have nevertheless tried to continue being guided by the rule of thumb that we followed in earlier editions: Focus on the techniques that most directly relate to contemporary policy issues.

In the Fourth Edition, as in the first three, we have attempted to make microeconomics more interesting by organizing our discussion in Parts 2 to 5 around two continuing themes: efficiency and equity. In Parts 2 and 3, we provide the analytical foundation, leading up to the discussion of the efficiency of a system of competitive markets, and the problems introduced by monopoly and oligopoly. We continue to stress the interpretation of the demand curve as a marginal benefit and the supply curve as a marginal cost curve. In emphasizing marginal concepts, we have tried to give students an appreciation of the meaning of allocative efficiency—why it is desirable to produce the goods that consumers demand. But we have tried to show also why it is not the last word. In particular, we believe that it is possible for first-year students to grasp fairly easily what many in the past discovered only in a graduate school: There is a different efficient solution for each income distribution; hence, a solution that is efficient is not necessarily "best." Directly following the discussion of imperfectly competitive market forms, we provide a discussion of Canadian competition policy.

In Part 4, we turn from product markets to factor markets and the distribution of income. Discussing factor markets at this relatively early stage has the disadvantage of delaying the treatment of microeconomic policy issues. On the other hand, it has the advantage that it draws the students' attention to the idea that overall economic efficiency requires efficiency in *both* product *and* factor markets. It also focuses attention on the fact that the distribution of income is not just a matter of political decisions, but is strongly influenced by market forces as well. The last chapter in Part 4 briefly considers the question of what constitutes an equitable size distribution of income.

In Part 5, the first five chapters deal with a set of microeconomic policy issues that relate primarily to efficiency: The problems and opportunities of international trade policy, both at the multilateral and bilateral levels; the efficient exploitation of natural resources, and the problems caused when a resource is common property; policies to protect the environment (including a brief discussion of the proposals to introduce a "carbon tax"); and the provision of public goods (with a brief introduction to the principles of public choice).

But even though the discussion in these chapters, and in Parts 2 and 3, focuses on efficiency, we emphasize throughout the book that efficiency and equity are interrelated. For example, creating property rights in a common-property resource (Chapter 21) is primarily intended to improve efficiency. However, the way it is done will influence income distribution and, thus, equity. Conversely, as we emphasize in Chapter 24, policies that are intended primarily to improve equity (such as social assistance programs based on the "cash deficit" principle) also may have side-effects on efficiency; we also discuss the idea that a negative income tax may reduce these side-effects.

From a technical point of view, one difference between this and earlier editions is that the analysis of consumption and production using indifference curve or isoquant diagrams has been moved into the main text (in previous editions, brief discussions were provided in appendices), and substantially extended. For example, in Chapter 7 on consumer theory, there is a box explaining why indifference curves can't cross, and the indifference-curve analysis is applied to the problem of showing how transfers in kind may be inferior to cash transfers as a way of helping the poor; in Chapter 17 on savings and the return to capital, it is applied to illustrate the choice between present and future consumption. In Chapter 9 on the costs of production, isoquant analysis is used to explain the relationship between short-run and long-run cost curves; and in Chapter 11, the efficiency of perfect competition is demonstrated in a diagram combining the production possibilities curve and a community indifference curve.

## OTHER POINTS OF INTEREST

Finally, we draw your attention to a number of ways in which our treatment differs from that of many other texts, and also to some changes that we have made in this edition.

- In this edition, the microeconomic material on international economics is treated somewhat differently than in earlier ones. For the benefit of students who take microeconomics before macroeconomics, we have added a section in which we briefly explain the role of foreign exchange markets and foreign exchange rate adjustments in facilitating international trade. Students generally find the concept of comparative advantage and the efficiency gains from hypothetical barter trade relatively easy to understand. However, they need some understanding of exchange rates in order to see how comparative advantage does in fact explain the pattern of international trade even when it does not, in fact, take the form of barter.

The discussion of the potential gains from capital imports has been integrated into the discussion of the gains from trade in Part 5: Since the market for capital services is discussed in Part 4, it is possible to treat the potential efficiency gains from foreign investment (imports of capital services) as simply a special case of the gains from any import.

The trade policy chapter has been extensively updated to reflect the early experience with the Canada/United States Free Trade Agreement, to take into account the most recent developments in the ongoing saga of the Uruguay Round of GATT negotiations, and to discuss the North American Free Trade Agreement (NAFTA). As before, the role of international trade in increasing the intensity of competition in the Canadian economy is discussed in the chapter on competition policy.

- In emphasizing efficiency and the gains from specialization, we continue to give more than usual attention to economies of scale. In Chapters 3 and 19, economies of scale are given billing almost equal to comparative advantage in explaining the efficiency effects of specialization and trade; also, in Chapter 20 we emphasize the potential gains from exploitation of scale economies as an important reason for Canada to enter into international trade agreements. Economies of scale are especially important for a small country such as Canada, and the topic should not be avoided because of the difficult analytical problems that it raises at a more advanced level.
- Although we obviously don't discuss them in detail, we briefly introduce a number of relatively advanced topics and concepts in microeconomics, mostly in appendices or boxes, but occasionally in sections in the main text. Examples include the problems of moral hazard and adverse selection in insurance markets; the efficiency and transfer effects of perfectly discriminating monopoly pricing; a diagrammatic illustration of Nash equilibrium in a simple Cournot-type duopoly game; and the question of what constitutes an optimal rate of exploitation of renewable or non-renewable resources.

## IN ACKNOWLEDGEMENT

First, I wish to acknowledge the contributions by Paul Hobson and Peter Townley of Acadia University, who drafted many of the boxes, appendices, and end-of-chapter problems in this fourth edition, and commented extensively on earlier drafts.

In developing this and earlier editions, I have been helped by many friends and colleagues with whom I have had discussions over the years about Canadian economic problems and policy. Though I cannot list them all, I wish to acknowledge my indebtedness to them. Several persons also helped by commenting on parts of the manuscripts or by providing information on specific matters relating to Canadian institutions and policy. They are:

| | |
|---|---|
| **Barry Barber** | Saskatchewan Institute of Applied Science and Technology |
| **Ronald Bodkin** | University of Ottawa |
| **Michael Bradfield** | Dalhousie University |
| **Jim Brander** | University of British Columbia |
| **Kevin Burley** | University of Western Ontario |
| **Thomas F. Chambers** | Canadore College |
| **Avi J. Cohen** | York University |
| **Don Gilchrist** | University of Saskatchewan |
| **Hugh Grant** | University of Winnipeg |
| **Christopher Green** | McGill University |
| **Morley Gunderson** | University of Toronto |
| **Paul B. Huber** | Dalhousie University |
| **Derek Hum** | University of Manitoba |
| **Ernie Jacobson** | Northern Alberta Institute of Technology |
| **Susan Kamp** | University of Alberta |
| **Nargess Kayhani** | Mount Saint Vincent University |
| **Harvey B. King** | University of Regina |
| **Ronald Kneebone** | University of Calgary |
| **David Laidler** | University of Western Ontario |
| **Chris McDonnell** | Malaspina College |
| **John Palmer** | University of Western Ontario |
| **Tom Powrie** | University of Alberta |
| **David Robinson** | Laurentian University |
| **Gideon Rosenbluth** | University of British Columbia |
| **Nicholas Rowe** | Carleton University |
| **Ronald Shearer** | University of British Columbia |
| **Ian Skaith** | Fanshawe College |
| **George Slazor** | University of Toronto |
| **Larry Smith** | University of Waterloo |
| **Maurice Tugwell** | Acadia University |
| **Robert Will** | University of British Columbia |

| | |
|---|---|
| **Tom Wilson** | University of Toronto |
| **Ronald Wirick** | University of Western Ontario |
| **Edy Wong** | Grant McEwen College |

Furthermore, I would like to acknowledge the research assistance provided by Chris Laundy. The author is also grateful to freelance editor Gail Copeland, and to the editorial and production staff at McGraw-Hill Ryerson in Toronto. In particular, I would like to thank the sponsoring editor, Jennifer Mix, without whose delicate blend of discipline and sympathetic encouragement this book would not have been completed.

Finally, I would like to express my appreciation to the distinguished senior authors of the earlier editions of this book, Paul Wonnacott and Ronald Wonnacott (who drafted the updated version of the chapter on trade policy). Their intense interest in all aspects of economic policy and strong commitment to clear and simple exposition of sometimes difficult material has guided and inspired me in preparing this edition.

Åke Blomqvist
London, Ontario

# MICROECONOMICS

FOURTH EDITION

# PART 1
# BASIC ECONOMIC CONCEPTS

In the first five chapters of this volume, we introduce the basic concepts and issues of economic analysis.

Chapter 1 sets out the most important economic problems that face Canadian society, and discusses the various goals we set for ourselves in conducting economic policy (goals such as low rates of unemployment and inflation, an efficient allocation of economic resources, and an equitable distribution of income). At the end of Chapter 1, a lengthy appendix explains some of the technical tools that are used so extensively in economics: diagrams and simple equations.

Chapters 2 and 3 introduce two very basic concepts that are relevant to all of economic analysis: the necessity to *make choices*, and the advantages and problems of *specialization*. In doing so, we make use of our first two diagrammatic tools, the production possibilities curve, and the circular flow of income and expenditure. Chapter 3 also describes the principle of comparative advantage, a principle that is fundamental to much of economics, including the analysis of international trade, and explains the necessity of having a monetary system if we are to have an efficient economy based on specialization in production.

In Chapter 4, we lay the foundation for much of the analysis of both microeconomics and macroeconomics in free-enterprise and mixed economies, by explaining something most people are at least vaguely familiar with, the concepts of *supply and demand*. We explain how supply and demand in markets for individual products and productive factors interact to answer the questions What?, How?, and For Whom? (What products will be produced? How will they be produced? For whom will they be produced?)

In Chapter 5, we recognize that in every advanced economy, the workings of the market mechanism have to be modified and influenced in important ways by *government*. The chapter describes the various functions of government in modern capitalist economies, and provides statistical and institutional information on Canada's different levels of government.

CHAPTER

1

# ECONOMIC PROBLEMS AND ECONOMIC GOALS

*Economy is the art of making the most out of life.*
*George Bernard Shaw*

Some years ago, a Japanese mass circulation newspaper, the *Mainichi*, conducted a survey of 4000 people, asking them what they thought of first when they heard the word *takai* (high). Twelve percent responded, "Mount Fuji." The overwhelming majority —88%—said: "Prices."

In Canada, as in other countries, economic issues have had centre stage in our political debate. When the short-lived government of Joe Clark lost the 1980 federal election popular dissatisfaction with its budget, which had called for sharp increases in energy prices, was a major contributing factor. The massive swing in the popular vote in 1984, when the Conservatives, led by Brian Mulroney, won a landslide victory over John Turner's Liberals, can in large measure be explained by the record-high unemployment rates that had prevailed in 1982/83 when the Liberals were in power. The 1988 election, in which the Conservatives won their second majority, was almost completely dominated by a single economic question: whether or not Canada should enter into a free-trade agreement with the United States. Economics has played a major part even in the debate about Canadian unity. Estimates of the net cost or benefit that Quebec derives from being part of Canada figured prominently in the debate preceding the 1992 referendum on the Charlottetown Accord.

Issues such as taxes, the cost of living, and job security are of immediate concern to almost all Canadians. With the rare exception of the individual who inherits great wealth, most of us spend a large part of our energy in the struggle to make a living.

In the words of Alfred Marshall, a great teacher and scholar of a century ago, "economics is a study of mankind in the ordinary business of life."

Under this broad definition, economics addresses many specific questions. To list but a few:

- What will be the long-term consequences of the large budget deficits of the federal and some provincial governments in the early 1990s?
- Why is it so difficult to get a job at some times, and so easy at others?
- What jobs will be available when we finish university? What will they pay?
- What determines the relative prices of goods? Why is water cheap, even though it is necessary to life itself? Why are diamonds expensive, even though they are an unessential luxury?
- Will continued economic growth cause the destruction of our environment?
- Why did our economy produce so much more in 1993 than in 1953?

Economics is a study of success, and it is a study of failure.

## ECONOMIC PROGRESS

From the vantage point of the comforts of the late twentieth century, it is easy for us to forget how many people throughout history have found it difficult to make a living. Unvarnished economic history is the story of deprivation, of 80-hour work weeks, of child labour—and of starvation. But it is also the story of the slow climb of civilization toward the goal of relative affluence, where the average person as well as the fortunate few can have a reasonable degree of material well-being and leisure.

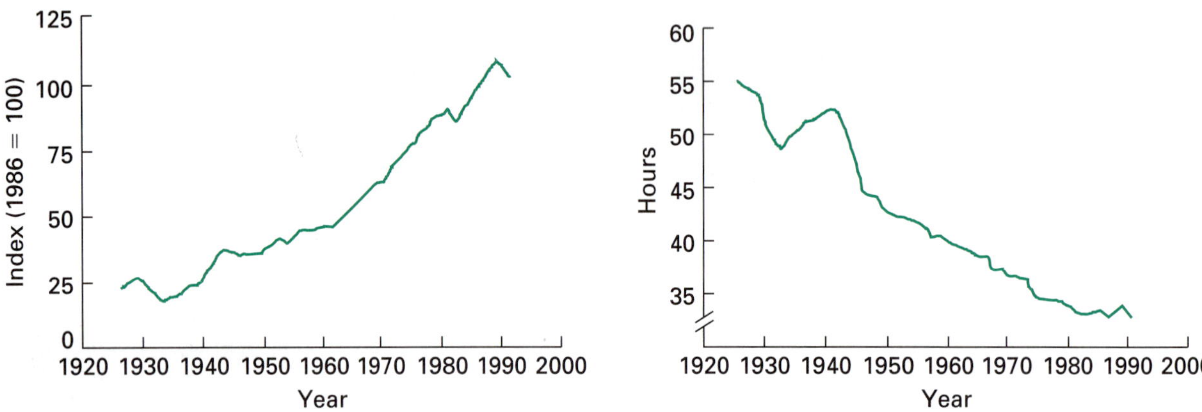


**(a) Production per capita.** **(b) Work week (domestic economy).**

**FIGURE 1-1 Production per person and hours worked per week.**

*Source*: Statistics Canada, *CANSIM Databank,* and K. Buckley and M. Urquhart, eds., *Historical Statistics of Canada,* 1st. ed. (Toronto and Cambridge: Cambridge University Press and Macmillan of Canada, 1965.) Reproduced by permission of the Minister of Supply and Services Canada.

One of the most notable features of the Canadian economy has been its growth. Although there have been interruptions and setbacks, economic progress has been remarkable. Figure 1-1 shows one of the standard measures of success — the increase in total production per person. (The measure of aggregate production in this diagram is gross domestic product, or GDP for short. This concept will be explained in Chapter 6.) The average Canadian now produces nearly three times as much as did the average Canadian just after World War II, and more than six times as much as did the average Canadian at the turn of the century. Furthermore, the higher output is produced with less effort. The duration of the average work week has declined by almost 40% since 1926. Thus, economic progress in Canada has been reflected both in an increase in the goods and services that we produce and enjoy, and in a greater amount of leisure time.

A similar tale of success has occurred in many other countries, as illustrated in Figure 1-2. Between 1965 and 1990, output grew at an average annual rate of 3.1% in the United States, 3.3% in France, 2.8% in Germany, and 3.5% in Italy. Nor has growth been confined to the countries of Europe and North America. Particularly notable has been the growth of the Japanese economy. From the ashes of World War II, Japan has emerged as one of the leading nations. As a result of a rapid growth averaging 5.8% per year between 1965 and 1990, Japan now ranks with Switzerland, the United States, Canada, and Norway as one of the highest-income countries in the world.[1] Other stories of success have come from the middle-income countries of East Asia, such as South Korea, Hong Kong, and Singapore.

## ECONOMIC PROBLEMS

Although rapid growth has occurred in many countries, it has been neither universal nor automatic. In a number of countries, the standard of living remains abysmally low, with an average income per person of less than $300 *per year*. The World Bank — an international institution whose major purpose is to lend to the less developed countries (LDCs) — estimates that between 1965 and 1990, output per person rose at an average annual rate of only 1.7% to 1.8% in the 35 or so poorest countries (excluding China). The rec-

[1] The success of the Japanese economy has made that country the subject of good-natured humour. In a lecture, U.S. economist Paul McCracken of the University of Michigan recalled that on his first trip to Japan in the 1950s, he had gone to offer the Japanese advice on economic growth policy. Added McCracken, "I've been trying to remember ever since what we told them." There are substantial problems in comparing output per person in various countries. See Irving B. Kravis et al., *A System of International Comparisons of Gross Product and Purchasing Power*, United Nations International Comparison Project: Phase One (Baltimore: Johns Hopkins University Press, 1975), p. 231.

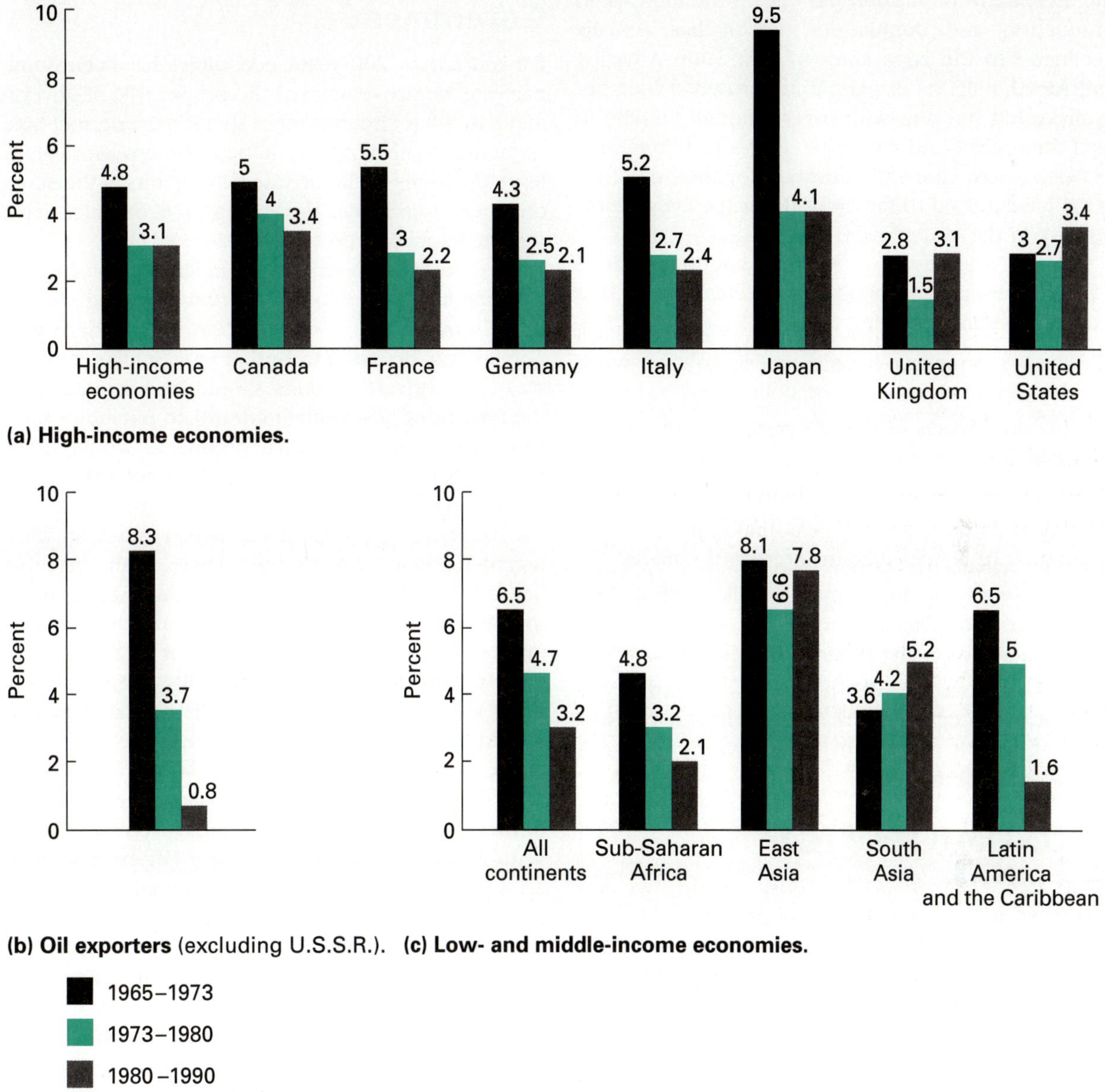


**FIGURE 1-2 Annual rates of increase in output, 1965–1990.**

Growth has been rapid in many countries. Growth was particularly fast in Japan between 1965 and 1973, when output increased at an average annual rate of 9.5%. Note that for most countries, growth slowed down after 1973—with the rapidly developing economies of Asia being an exception. The slower growth may be traced in part to the disruptions caused by the rapid increase in the price of oil.

*Source*: 1965–1973 and 1973–1980 compiled from World Bank, *World Development Report*, 1991, p. 186. 1980–1990 compiled from World Bank, *World Development Report*, 1992, p. 221.

ord is even bleaker in the poorest of the poor, where the increase in population has outrun the increase in production, and output per person has actually declined.[2] In the large cities of Asia, Latin America, and Africa, millions of people are crowded together in makeshift housing, with barely enough income to feed themselves and with little access to things such as basic health care and education for their children. Many have moved to the cities to escape even worse poverty in the countryside.

Even in a relatively prosperous country, such as Canada, substantial economic problems remain. For example, we may wonder:

- Why are so many people unable to find work, when so much needs to be done?
- Why do pockets of poverty remain in an affluent society?
- Why have prices kept marching upward?
- Why is the average income so much lower in the Atlantic provinces than in the rest of Canada?
- Are we really producing the right things? Should we produce more housing and fewer cars? Or more medical services and fewer sports spectaculars?
- Does economic growth necessarily mean that we have to accept an increasingly polluted environment, or is it possible to have *both* more growth *and* less pollution?

## ECONOMIC POLICY

*Why?* and *What should be done?* are the two key questions in economics. The ultimate objective of economics is to *develop policies to deal with our problems*. However, before we can formulate policies, we must first try to understand how the economy has worked in the past, and how it works today. Otherwise, well-intentioned policies may go astray and lead to unforeseen and unfortunate consequences.

When economic policies are studied, the centre of attention is usually the policies of the government—policies in the areas of taxation, government spending programs, international trade, and the regulation of particular industries, such as television and telephone companies, railroads, and farming. However, the policies of private businesses are also important. How should they organize production in order to make their goods at the lowest possible cost? What prices should a business charge? When should a supermarket increase the stocks of goods in its warehouse?

[2] World Bank, *World Development Report*, 1992, pp. 218–19.

### The Controversial Role of Government

For more than 200 years, economics has been dominated by controversy over the proper role of government. In what circumstances should government take an active role? When is it best for government to leave decisions to the private participants in the economy? On this topic, the giants of economics have repeatedly met to do battle.

In 1776, Scottish scholar Adam Smith published his groundbreaking book, *An Inquiry into the Nature and Causes of the Wealth of Nations*.[3] Modern economics may be dated from that year. Smith's message was clear: Private markets should be liberated from the tyranny of government control. In pursuit of their private interests, individual producers would make the goods that consumers want. It is not, said Smith, "from the benevolence of the butcher, the brewer, or the baker that we expect our dinner, but from their regard to their own interest." There is an "invisible hand," he wrote, that causes the producer to promote the interests of society. Indeed, "by pursuing his own interest he frequently promotes that of the society more effectually than when he really intends to promote it." In general, said Smith, the government should be cautious in interfering with the operations of the private market.

According to Smith, the best policy is generally one of ***laissez-faire*** — leave it alone. Government intervention usually makes things worse. For example, government imposition of a tariff is generally harmful. (A tariff or duty is a tax on a foreign-produced good as it enters the country.) Even though a tariff generally helps domestic producers to whom it gives an advantage over foreign producers, the country as a whole loses. Specifically, a tariff increases the cost of goods available to consumers, and this cost to consumers outweighs the possible benefits to domestic producers. Smith's work has been refined and modified during the past 200 years, but many of his laissez-faire conclusions have stood up remarkably well. For example, there is still a very strong economic argument against high tariffs on imported goods. In recent decades, one of the principal areas of international cooperation has been the negotiation of lower tariffs. In the late 1980s, this argument was an important reason

[3] Available in Modern Library edition (New York: Random House, 1937). Smith's book is commonly referred to as *The Wealth of Nations*.

why Canada decided to enter into an agreement with the United States to eliminate all tariffs on trade between the two countries by 1999.

However, during the Great Depression of the 1930s—a century and a half after the appearance of *The Wealth of Nations*—the laissez-faire tradition in economics came under attack. In 1936, John Maynard Keynes published his *General Theory of Employment, Interest and Money* (also known more simply as the *General Theory*). In this book, Keynes (which rhymes with Danes) argued that the government has the duty to intervene in the economy, to put the unemployed back to work. Of the several ways in which this could be done, one stood out in its simplicity. By building public works, such as roads, post offices, and dams, the government could provide jobs directly, and thus provide a cure for the Depression.

With his proposals for a more active role for government, Keynes drew the ire of many business people. They feared that, as a result of his recommendations, the government would become larger and larger and private enterprise would gradually be pushed out of the picture. Keynes, however, did not foresee this result. He believed that, by providing jobs, the government could remove the explosive frustrations caused by the mass unemployment of the 1930s, and could make it possible for Western political and economic institutions to survive. His objective was to modify our economic system and make it better. Unlike Karl Marx, he did not believe that the system would have to be destroyed and then replaced by a different one in order to solve these problems. (For a brief introduction to the revolutionary ideas of Marx, see Box 1-1 on page 8.)[4]

Thus, Smith and Keynes took apparently contradictory positions—Smith arguing for less government, and Keynes for more.[5] It is possible, of course, that each was right. Perhaps the government should do more in some respects, and less in others. Economic analysis does not lead inevitably either to an activist position or to a passive, laissez-faire stance on the part of the government. The economist's rallying cry should not be, "Do something." Rather, it should be, "Think first."

## ECONOMIC GOALS

We have already noted that the ultimate goal of economics is to develop better policies to minimize our problems and to maximize the benefits from our daily toil. More specifically, there is widespread agreement that we should strive for the following goals:

1. *A low rate of unemployment.* People willing to work should be able to find jobs reasonably quickly. Widespread unemployment is demoralizing and it represents an economic waste. Society forgoes the goods and services that the unemployed could have produced.
2. *Price stability.* It is desirable to avoid rapid increases—or decreases—in the average level of prices.
3. *Efficiency.* When we work, we want to get as much as we reasonably can out of our productive efforts.
4. *An equitable distribution of income.* When many live in affluence, no group of citizens should suffer stark poverty.
5. *Growth.* Continuing growth, which would make possible an even higher standard of living in the future, is generally considered an important objective.

The list is far from complete: It is easy to think of other things we might want from our economic system. For example, not only do we want to produce more, but we want to do so without fouling the air we breathe or the water we drink; *environmental protection* should be high on our list of priorities.

*Economic freedom* — the right of people to choose their own occupations, to enter into contracts, and to spend their incomes as they please — is another desirable goal. So, too, is *economic security*—freedom from the fear that chronic illness or some other catastrophe will place an individual or a family in a desperate financial situation. The objective of economic security has played a large and increasingly important part in Canadian policy in the last few decades.

Another long-standing (but more controversial) goal is more *economic independence*. Some people feel that too many decisions that affect the welfare of Canadians are made by foreign firms and that

[4] Throughout this book, the boxes present illustrative and supplementary materials. They can be disregarded without losing the main thread of the discussion.

[5] Conflicting views over the proper role of government may be found in the works of two retired professors: the University of Chicago's Milton Friedman (for laissez-faire) and Harvard's John Kenneth Galbraith (who argues for more government). See John Kenneth Galbraith, *The Affluent Society* (Boston: Houghton Mifflin, 1958), and Milton Friedman and Rose Friedman, *Free to Choose* (New York: Harcourt Brace Jovanovich, 1980). (We strongly recommend that if you read one of these books, you read them both. Each of the books puts forth a convincing case. Nevertheless, they are flatly contradictory.)

## ECONOMICS IN HISTORY — BOX 1-1
### Karl Marx

The main text refers to two towering economists — Adam Smith and John Maynard Keynes. In the formation of the intellectual heritage of most British and North American economists, Smith and Keynes have played leading roles. But, if we consider the intellectual heritage of the world as a whole, Karl Marx is probably the most influential economist of all. For a long time—over 70 years in the former Soviet Union—the economic systems in many countries have been founded on Marx's theories. In countries like China, North Korea, and Cuba, Marxism is still, at least to a substantial extent, the basis of the economic system.

Many business executives viewed Keynes as a revolutionary because he openly attacked accepted economic opinion and proposed fundamental changes in economic policy. But, by revolutionary standards, Keynes pales beside Marx. The Marxist call to revolution was shrill and direct: "Workers of the world, unite! You have nothing to lose but your chains."

Why did they have nothing to lose? Because, said Marx, workers are responsible for the production of all goods. Labour is the sole source of value. But workers get only part of the fruits of their labour. A large—and in Marx's view, unjustified—share goes to the exploiting class of capitalists. (Capitalists are the owners of factories, machinery, and other equipment.) Marx believed that, by taking up arms and overthrowing capitalism, workers could end their exploitation and obtain their rightful rewards.

On our main topic — the role of government in the economy — Marx was strangely ambivalent. Who would own the factories and machines once the communist revolution had eliminated the capitalist class? Ownership by the state — by all the workers as a group — was the obvious solution. And, in fact, this was the path taken by countries such as the former Soviet Union and China: The revolution and subsequent rule by the Communist Party led to state ownership of most means of production. Yet, Marx also believed that after the revolution, the state would ultimately "wither away" and be replaced by a system based on voluntary cooperation. This prediction certainly has not been borne out. In the former Soviet Union and Eastern Europe, the extensive and repressive role of government in the economy, and in society as a whole, ultimately became so resented that the Marxist system was overthrown. In China, the state continues to play a dominant role in the economy.

increased control by Canadians over our own economy is an important objective.

The achievement of our economic goals provides the principal focus of this book. As a background for later chapters, let's look at the major goals in more detail.

## 1. A Low Rate of Unemployment

The importance of the objective of full employment was illustrated most clearly during the Great Depression of the 1930s, when Canada and many other countries conspicuously failed to achieve it. During the sharp contraction from 1929 to 1933, total output in Canada fell by 30% and spending for new buildings, machinery, and equipment declined by more than 85%. As the economy slid downward, more and more workers were thrown out of jobs. By 1933, almost 20% of the labour force was unemployed. (See Figure 1-3.) Long lines of the jobless gathered at factory gates in the hope of work; disappointment was their common fate. Nor was the problem quickly solved. The downward slide into the depths of the Depression went on for a period of four years, and the road back to a high level of employment was even longer. It was not until the beginning of the 1940s, when our industry began working around the clock to produce weapons and war materials, that many of the unem-

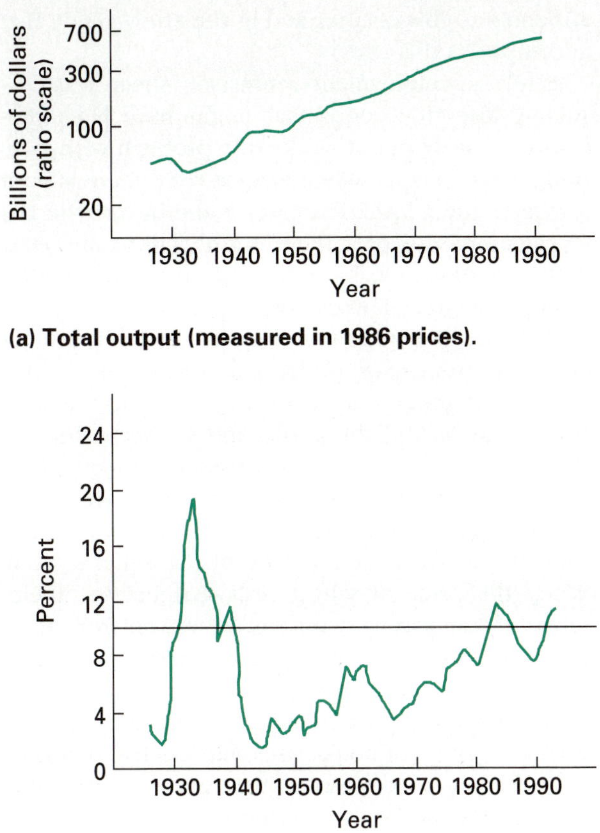


**(a) Total output (measured in 1986 prices).**

**(b) Unemployment rates.**

**FIGURE 1-3 Output and unemployment in Canada, 1926–1992.**

During the Great Depression, output fell and the unemployment rate rose sharply to 20%. In recent decades, the unemployment rate has been much lower, although it did rise above 12% during the recession of 1981/82 and to nearly 12% in 1992.

*Source*: Statistics Canada, *CANSIM Databank*; *Bank of Canada Statistical Summary*; and K. Buckley and M. Urquhart, eds., *Historical Statistics of Canada*, 1st and 2nd ed. (Toronto and Cambridge: Cambridge University Press and Macmillan of Canada). Reproduced by permission of the Minister of Supply and Services Canada.

ployed were able to find jobs. From 1931 to 1940, unemployment averaged above 11% of the labour force in every year except one.

> A *depression* exists when there is a very high rate of unemployment over a long period of time.

Something had clearly gone wrong — disastrously wrong. Large-scale unemployment represents tremendous waste; time lost in involuntary idleness is gone forever. The costs of unemployment go beyond the loss of output; unemployment involves the dashing of hopes. Those unable to find work suffer frustration and a sense of worthlessness, and their skills are lost as they remain idle.

The term ***unemployed*** is reserved for those who are willing and able to work, but are unable to find jobs. Thus, those of you who are full-time university students are not included among the unemployed. Your immediate task is to get an education, not a job. Similarly, the 70-year-old retiree is not included in the statistics of the unemployed. Nor are those in prisons or mental institutions, since they are not available for jobs.

> A person is *unemployed* if he or she is available and looking for work, but has not found it.

The unemployment rate is calculated as a percentage of the total labour force—the labour force being the sum of those who are actually employed, plus those who are unemployed. (Labour force and employment statistics are tied to the traditional definition of "jobs." Thus, for example, a parent who stays at home to raise children is neither "in the labour force" nor "employed," although he or she certainly works.)

At the end of World War II, the Great Depression was still a fresh memory. The public, the politician, and the economist shared a common determination that a repeat of the 1930s could not be permitted. And, so far, we have been largely successful in our efforts to prevent a repetition of the prolonged period of depressed economic activity and very high unemployment of the 1930s.

But the postwar years have certainly not been an unbroken story of success. From time to time, there have been downturns in the economy—much more moderate, it is true, than the slide of 1929 to 1933, but downward movements nonetheless. These more moderate declines, or ***recessions***, have often been accompanied by a substantial increase in the unemployment rate. In December 1982, the unemployment rate rose to a peak of 12.9%, and it rose almost as high during the equally severe recession of 1990/92. While we have been successful in preventing big depressions, the problem of periodic recessions has not been solved.

> A *recession* is a general slowdown of economic activity, usually involving a decline in total out-

put, income, and employment, lasting six months or more, and marked by contractions in many sectors of the economy. (The slowdown is not confined to just one or two industries, such as forest products or car manufacturing.)

## 2. Stability of the Average Price Level

During the Depression of the 1930s, unemployment was the overwhelming problem, and in the early 1990s, joblessness has once again become the dominant economic issue. But, during the late 1970s and again during the second half of the 1980s, ***inflation*** became a major problem.

*Inflation* is an increase in the average level of prices. (Deflation is a fall in the average level of prices.)

Observe in Figure 1-4 how the average of prices paid by consumers has risen through most of our recent history, with the period 1920–1933 being a notable exception. Prices rose most rapidly after World War I and, for a brief period, after World War II. Between 1973 and 1981, inflation was unusually severe for peacetime periods. (Details on how to draw and interpret diagrams may be found in the appendix to this chapter and in the Study Guide that accompanies this text.)

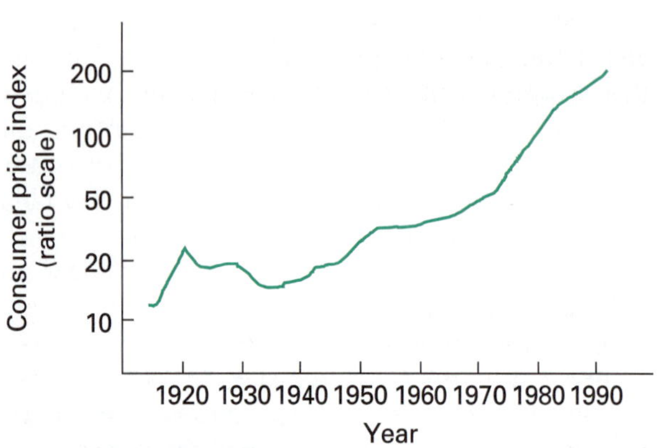


**FIGURE 1-4 Consumer prices.**
Occasionally, prices have fallen—for example, during the early 1930s. In recent decades, however, the trend of prices has been clearly upward. In 1974, and again in 1979 and 1980, Canada suffered from "double-digit" inflation — a rise in the average level of prices by more than 10% per year.

*Source*: Compiled from Statistics Canada, *CANSIM Databank*. Reproduced by permission of the Minister of Supply and Services Canada.

While unemployment represents sheer waste — society loses the goods that might have been produced by those out of work—the problem with inflation is less obvious. When a price rises, there is both a winner and a loser. The loser is the buyer who has to pay more. However, there is a benefit to the seller, who gets more. On balance, it is not clear whether society is better or worse off.

It is true, of course, that there is much resentment against inflation. But, perhaps at least some of this resentment reflects a peculiarity of human nature. When people find the goods and services they *sell* rising in price, they see the increase as perfectly right, normal, and justified. On the other hand, when they find the goods they *buy* rising in price, they often view the increase as evidence of the seller's greed. When the price of wheat rises, farmers see themselves at last getting a reasonable return from their toil. When the price of oil increases, the oil companies argue that they are getting no more than the return necessary to finance the search for more oil. When the price of books rises, authors feel that they are getting no more than a "just" return for their creative efforts and book publishers insist that they are no more than adequately compensated for their risks.

However, when the farmer, the oil company, the author, and the book publisher find that the prices of the goods they buy have increased, they believe they have been cheated by inflation. We all may be the victims of an illusion—the illusion that each of us can and should have a rise in the price of what we sell, but that the price of what we buy should remain stable. For the economy as a whole, this of course is not possible.

This two-sided nature of price increases — a gain to the seller but a loss to the buyer—means that it is difficult to evaluate the dangers of inflation. Indeed, there has been considerable controversy as to whether a low rate of inflation (with prices increasing at a rate of, say, no more than 2% per year) is dangerous or whether, on the contrary, it may actually be beneficial to society. (Some say that a small rate of inflation makes it easier for the economy to adjust to changes and to maintain a high level of employment.)

However, when inflation gets beyond a moderate rate, there is widespread agreement that it becomes a menace. It becomes more than a mere transfer of money from the buyer to the seller; it interferes with the production and exchange of goods. This has most clearly been the situation during very rapid inflations, when economic activity was severely disrupted.

***Hyperinflation***—that is, a skyrocketing of prices at annual rates of 1000% or more—has historically been most common during or soon after a military conflict, when government spending shoots upward; for example, in Germany during the early 1920s, in China during its civil war in the late 1940s, and in the southern states during the U.S. Civil War. More recently, it has happened during times of political crisis, as in Russia following the collapse of the Soviet Union in the early 1990s, or in several Latin American countries in the postwar period. Hyperinflation means that money rapidly loses its ability to buy goods. People are anxious to spend money as quickly as possible while they can still get something for it.

Clearly, hyperinflation of 1000% or more per year is an extreme example. However, lower rates of inflation, amounting to 10% or less per year, can also have serious consequences:

1. Inflation hurts people living on fixed incomes and people who have saved fixed amounts of money for their retirement or for "a rainy day" (future illness or accident). The young couple who put aside $1000 in 1960 for retirement has suffered a rude shock. In 1990, $1000 bought no more than $198 bought in 1960.
2. Inflation can cause business mistakes. To make good decisions, businesses need an accurate picture of what is going on. When prices are rising rapidly, the picture becomes obscured and out of focus. Decision makers cannot see clearly. (For example, business accounting is done in dollar terms. When there is rapid inflation, some businesses may report profits but, using a more accurate calculation, they might actually be suffering losses. Consequently, inflation can temporarily hide problems.) Our economy is complex. It depends on a continuous flow of accurate information. *Prices are an important link in the information chain*. For example, a high price should provide a signal to producers that consumers are especially anxious to get more of a particular product. But, in a severe inflation, producers find it difficult to know whether this is the message, or whether the price of their product is rising simply because all prices are rising. In brief, *a severe inflation obscures the message carried by prices.*

Here, it is important to distinguish between a rise in the ***average level of prices*** (inflation) and a change in ***relative prices***. Even if the average level of prices were perfectly stable (that is, no inflation existed), some *individual* prices would still change as conditions change in specific markets.

For example, new inventions have cut the cost of producing computers and facsimile (FAX) machines, and their prices have come down sharply. At the same time, the price of land in the central business districts of most large North American cities has risen substantially over the last several decades. The resulting fall in the price of computers and FAX machines relative to land in business districts has performed a useful function. It has encouraged businesses to use more of the relatively cheap computers and FAX machines, and to decrease their use of central-city space, by decentralizing some of their operations to the suburbs or smaller cities, or by trying to manage with a smaller number of personnel in downtown offices. (Another way to make more economical use of expensive downtown space has been to increase density by building taller buildings.)

## 3. Efficiency

This illustration—of how consumers and businesses use more computers as they become cheaper—is one example of ***economic efficiency***.

In an economy, both the unemployment rate and the inflation rate may be very low, but performance may still be poor. For example, fully employed workers may be engaged in a lot of wasted effort and the goods being produced may not be those which are most needed. In this case, the economy is inefficient.

> *Efficiency* is the goal of getting the most out of our productive efforts.

Under this broad definition, two types of efficiency can be distinguished: ***technological efficiency*** and ***allocative efficiency***.

To illustrate technological efficiency (also known as technical efficiency), let us consider two bicycle manufacturers. One uses a large number of workers and many machines to produce 1000 bicycles. The other uses fewer workers and fewer machines to produce the same number of bicycles. The second manufacturer is not a magician; he is simply a better manager. He is technologically efficient, whereas the first manufacturer is not. Technological inefficiency exists when the same output could be produced with fewer machines and fewer workers, working at a reasonable pace. (Technological efficiency does not require a sweatshop.) Technological inefficiency involves wasted effort and sloppy management; better management is the solution.

Allocative efficiency, on the other hand, involves the production of the best combination of goods and services, using the lowest-cost combination of inputs. How much food should we produce, and how many houses? Suppose we produce only food, and do so in a technologically efficient way, with no wasted effort. We will still not have achieved the goal of allocative efficiency, because consumers want both food and housing.

Or consider another question: How much newsprint should Canada produce, and how much wine? If we produce just enough of each to meet the demand of Canadian wine drinkers and newspaper readers, we will probably not reach allocative efficiency. A better solution would be to produce more newsprint and less wine, and then to trade newsprint for imported wine in the world market.

Thus, allocative efficiency involves the choice of the right combination of outputs. It also involves using the best (lowest-cost) combination of inputs. Consider our earlier illustration. In recent years, the cost of computers and FAX machines has been coming down while the price of central-city land has been rising. If businesses fail to adjust—that is, fail to make more efficient use of downtown space, and fail to make more use of computers and FAX machines—then there is allocative inefficiency.

*Relative prices* perform a key role in encouraging allocative efficiency. As we have noted, the decrease in the price of computers encourages businesses to use more computers, and fewer other relatively more expensive inputs. And the low cost of producing newsprint in Canada encourages foreigners to buy paper from us, while in turn we are encouraged to buy wine from Italy and Spain because of the low wine prices in those countries. Although it is undesirable to have large changes in the *average* level of prices (inflation or deflation), changes in *relative* prices may perform a very useful function by encouraging businesses and consumers to conserve on scarce goods and use cheaper alternatives.

## 4. An Equitable Distribution of Income

Ours is an affluent society. Yet many people remain so poor that they are barely able to buy the basic necessities of life, such as food, clothing, and shelter. In the midst of plenty, some live in need. The moral question must then be faced: Should some people have so much, while others have so little?

When the question is put this way, the compelling answer must surely be no. Our sense of equity or justice is offended by extreme differences. There is widespread agreement that we should try to bring about a more ***equitable distribution of income***.

Most people think of *equity* as a move toward *reducing inequality*. However, there are widely differing views on how far we should go in this direction. While everyone agrees that the least fortunate should be helped, there is no consensus that the objective of society should be an *equal income* for all—that is, an ***equal distribution of income***. Some individuals are willing to work overtime; it is generally recognized as both just and desirable for them to have a higher income as a consequence. Similarly, few people object to high incomes for those who have devoted long years pursuing an advanced education, or for those who have accumulated assets in the past through savings.

Because there is no agreement on how far we should go toward complete equality of incomes, the "best" division (or distribution) of income is ill defined. Therefore, much of the discussion of income distribution has been focused on narrower questions, such as: What is happening to those at the bottom of the ladder? What is happening to the families who live in poverty?

***Poverty*** is difficult to define in precise dollar terms. For one thing, not everyone's needs are the same. The sickly have the greatest need for medical care. Large families have the most compelling need for food and clothing. Those who live in cities, where the costs of food and shelter are high, need a larger annual income to pay for basic necessities than do those who live on farms, where they can grow some of their own food. There is no simple, single measure of the "poverty line" below which families may be judged to be poor. Reasonable standards may, however, be established by taking into consideration such obvious complications as the number of individuals in a family. For example, the National Council of Welfare, a government advisory body, has defined poverty standards for families in large cities and rural areas. (See Table 1-1.)

There are two ways of raising people above the poverty line. The first is to increase the size of the national "pie." As the level of income rises throughout the economy, the incomes of those at the lower end will also generally rise. In the words of former U.S. president John Kennedy, "A rising tide lifts all boats."

A second way to reduce poverty is to increase the

**TABLE 1-1 Poverty Standards in Large Cities and Rural Areas, 1991 (Annual Family Income)**

| Number of people in the family | Large cities | Rural areas |
|---|---|---|
| 1 | $14,948 | $10,177 |
| 2 | 20,261 | 13,796 |
| 3 | 25,755 | 17,535 |
| 4 | 29,601 | 20,188 |
| 5 | 32,398 | 22,057 |
| 6 | 35,168 | 23,942 |
| 7 or more | 37,824 | 25,751 |

*Source: 1990 Poverty Lines—Estimates by the National Council of Welfare* (Ottawa: Minister of Supply and Services, 1990). The poverty lines were updated to 1991 based on criteria developed from the 1986 *Survey of Family Expenditure.*

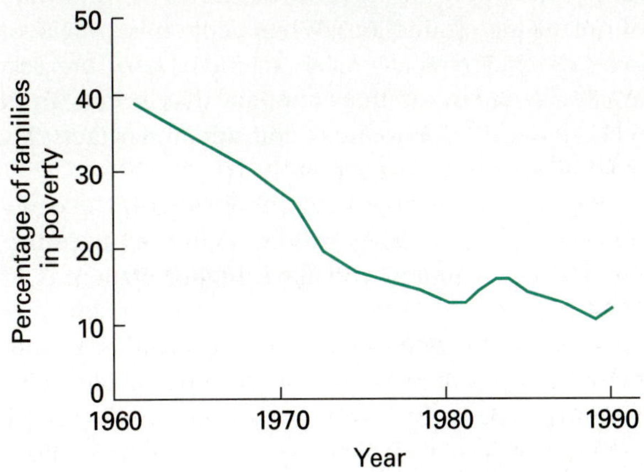


**FIGURE 1-5 The percentage of the population living in poverty.**

By Statistics Canada's poverty standard, the proportion of the population living in poverty declined substantially until 1981. Following an increase in the early 1980s, it fell again to about 11% in 1989.

*Source*: Estimated by authors from data in F. Vaillancourt, *Income Distribution and Economic Security in Canada,* Vol. 1 (Toronto: University of Toronto Press in cooperation with the Royal Commission on the Economic Union and Development Prospects for Canada, 1985) and Statistics Canada, *Income Distribution by Size,* various years. (To account for a change in Statistics Canada's definition of poverty, we have raised earlier estimates relating to years before 1979.)

share of the pie going to people with the lowest incomes. Thus, poverty may be combated by a ***redistribution of income***. For example, the well-to-do may be taxed in order to finance government programs aimed at helping the poor.

Since World War II, Canadian governments have organized or helped finance many major programs designed to raise the incomes of poor families. During the 1960s and 1970s, these programs helped bring about a very substantial reduction in the number of people living in poverty. As Figure 1-5 shows, there was a steady decline in the percentage of Canada's population classified as poor, from over 35% in the early 1960s to a low of 12% in 1981. During 1983/84, under the influence of the deep 1981/82 recession, the percentage rose to as high as 16%. However, as the economy expanded in the later 1980s, the downward trend resumed and by 1989 the figure was down to about 11%.

We are still far short of the objective of eliminating poverty. Why is this task so difficult?

One major reason is unemployment. As unemployment rates rose in the early 1980s and again in the early 1990s, many of those who lost their jobs fell into poverty. Other possible explanations include the tendency for workers to retire early (at which time they tend to drop into the low-income group), and the increased frequency of marriage breakdowns. When one family with an income above the poverty line splits up, it often creates a single-parent family (usually headed by the mother) with an income below the poverty line. In the 1980s and early 1990s, the worsening financial position of the federal and provincial governments has also made it more difficult to further reduce poverty. As rising spending has outstripped growth in revenues, governments have increasingly been forced to go into debt to cover the shortfall. The result has been that a growing portion of revenue has had to be used simply to pay interest on the government debt, leaving less for spending on programs, including those aimed at fighting poverty. Designing policies to combat poverty in a climate of fiscal austerity is a major challenge for the policy makers of the 1990s.

## 5. Growth

In an economy with large-scale unemployment, output can be increased by putting the unemployed back to work. Slack in the economy can be reduced and productive capacity used more fully. Once the economy approaches its capacity, however, additional increases in output require an increase in the productive capacity itself. Capacity can be raised either by an addition to the available resources (for example, an increase in the number of factories and machines), or an improvement in technology (that is, the invention of new, more productive machines or new ways of organizing production). When economists speak of ***growth***, they typically mean an *increase in the productive capacity* of the economy that results from technological improvement and additional factories, machines, or other resources.

The advantages of growth are obvious. If the economy grows, our incomes will be higher in the future. We and our children will have higher standards of material comfort. Moreover, some of the rising production can be used to pay for programs that benefit the poor without reducing the incomes of the rich.

During the early 1960s, growth became a prominent national goal in most Western countries, both because of its economic advantages and because expansion of productive capacity was seen as an important part of Western security; in the Cold War era, the West had to "keep up with the Russians." During the late 1960s and early 1970s, doubts began to develop. While its advantages are obvious, growth comes at a cost. If we are to grow more rapidly, more of our current efforts will have to be directed toward the production of machines and away from the production of consumption goods. In the future, of course, as the new machines begin operating, they will turn out more consumption goods—more clothing, cars, or VCRs. Thus, current policies to stimulate growth will make possible higher consumption *in the future*. But, for the moment, consumption will be lower. Thus, to evaluate a high growth policy, we have to compare the advantage of higher *future* consumption with the sacrifice of lower *current* consumption.

Seen in this light, it is not clear that the faster the rate of growth, the better. Why, for example, should I live modestly, just so my children may at some future date live in luxury? The future generation should be considered, but so should the present one.

Even if we were concerned solely with the welfare of coming generations, it would not be so clear that the more growth, the better. Increasing levels of production require increasing quantities of raw materials. A moderate rate of growth may be in the best interests of future generations because it allows us to conserve raw materials.

Furthermore, during the 1980s and early 1990s, we have become increasingly aware that rapid economic growth may cause serious harm to the environment. As we have produced more paper and chemical products, our lakes, rivers, and even groundwater have become polluted. Burning coal with a high sulphur content has caused acid rain that has damaged lakes and forests. And while progress was made in controlling some forms of pollution during the 1980s, other environmental problems seemed to be worsening. Some were global in scope: the gradual depletion of the atmosphere's ozone layer, and the threat posed by the gradual warming of Earth's climate as a result of the emission of ever larger amounts of carbon dioxide and other "greenhouse gases." For all these reasons, ***environmental protection*** has become an important economic goal.

## INTERRELATIONSHIPS AMONG THE GOALS

The achievement of one goal may help in the achievement of others. As we have noted, growth may make it easier to solve the poverty problem. Additional income may be provided to the poor out of the growth in total income, without reducing the income of those at the top. Thus, social conflicts over the share of the pie may be reduced if the size of the pie is increasing.

Similarly, the poverty problem is easier to solve if the unemployment rate is kept low, so that large numbers of unemployed do not swell the ranks of the poor. When goals are ***complementary*** like this (that is, when achieving one helps to achieve the other), economic policy making is relatively easy. By attacking on a broad front and striving for several goals, we can increase our chances of achieving each.

Unfortunately, however, economic goals are not always complementary. In many cases, they are in conflict. For example, when the unemployment problem is reduced, the inflation problem tends to get worse. There is a reason for this. Heavy purchasing by the public tends to reduce unemployment, but it also tends to increase inflation. It reduces unemployment because, as the public buys more cars, unemployed workers get jobs again in the auto factories; and when families buy more homes, construction workers will have an easier time finding jobs. At the same time, heavy purchasing tends to increase inflation because producers are more likely to raise their prices if buyers are clamouring for their products.

Another example of such ***conflicting goals*** in economic policy making is the relationship between efficiency and economic independence. Allocative efficiency in a relatively small economy such as Canada's, requires a large amount of international trade and investment. But there are many who feel that as our economic relations with foreign countries, particularly the United States, become more extensive, we will ultimately become too dependent on the policies and attitudes in those countries. The price of allocative efficiency may be a partial loss of Canada's political and economic independence. Such conflicts among goals test the wisdom of policy makers, and exacerbate the political controversies over economic policy.

## A PREVIEW

These, then, are the five major objectives of economic policy: *low unemployment*, *price stability*, *efficiency*, an *equitable distribution of income*, and *growth*. The first two goals are related to the *stability* of the economy. If the economy is unstable, moving along like a roller coaster, its performance will be very unsatisfactory. As it heads downhill into recession, large numbers of people will be thrown out of work. Then, as it heads upward into a runaway boom, prices will soar as the public scrambles to buy the available goods. The first two goals may, therefore, be looked on as two aspects of a single objective: that of achieving an *equilibrium* with stable prices and a low unemployment rate. This will be the major topic in Parts 2, 3, 4, and 5 (Chapters 6 through 19) of this book.

Equilibrium is the first of three main "Es" of economics. The second E—*efficiency*—is studied in Parts 2, 3, and 5 of the *Microeconomics* volume that forms a companion to this book. Are we getting the most out of our productive efforts? When does the free market — where buyers and sellers come together without government interference — encourage efficiency? Where the free market does not encourage efficiency, what (if anything) should be done?

Part 4 in *Microeconomics* deals primarily with the third E — *equity*. If the government takes a laissez-faire attitude, how much income will go to workers? To the owners of land? To others? How do labour unions affect the incomes of their members? How can the government improve the lot of the poor? The final objective — growth — cuts across a number of other topics, and thus appears periodically throughout both this book and the *Microeconomics* volume. However, before we get into the meat of policy issues, we must first set the stage with some of the basic concepts and tools of economics. To that task we now turn (in Chapters 2 through 5).

## KEY POINTS

1. During the twentieth century, substantial economic progress has been made in Canada and many other countries. We are producing much more, even though we spend less time at work than did our grandparents.
2. Nevertheless, substantial economic problems remain: problems such as poverty in the less developed countries and at home; high rates of unemployment; rapidly rising government debt; inflation; and environmental deterioration.
3. One of the things we study in economics is how we can deal with our problems, either through private action or through government policies.
4. In the history of economic thought, the role of government has been controversial. Adam Smith in 1776 called for the liberation of markets from the tyranny of government control. By 1936, John Maynard Keynes was appealing to the government to accept its responsibilities and to undertake public works in order to get the economy out of the Depression.
5. Important economic goals include the following:
   (a) An equilibrium with high employment and price stability.
   (b) Efficiency. Allocative efficiency involves the production of the right combination of goods, using the lowest cost combination of inputs. Technological efficiency occurs when goods are produced with the smallest feasible quantity of inputs (while working at a reasonable pace).
   (c) A reduction in poverty and equity in the distribution of income.
   (d) A satisfactory rate of growth.
6. Large changes in the average level of prices are undesirable. However, changes in relative prices may be desirable as a way of encouraging people to conserve scarce goods and use more plentiful, cheaper alternatives.

7. Goals are complementary if the achievement of one helps in the achievement of the other. For example, a reduction in unemployment also generally reduces poverty. However, goals may be in conflict. An increase in spending works to reduce unemployment, but it also can increase the rate of inflation.

## KEY TERMS

**economic policies**
**laissez-faire**
**depression**
**recession**
**unemployment**
**inflation**
**hyperinflation**
**average level of prices**
**relative prices**
**economic efficiency**
**allocative efficiency**
**technological (technical) efficiency**
**poverty**
**equal distribution of income**
**equitable distribution of income**
**redistribution of income**
**growth**
**environmental protection**
**economic freedom**
**economic security**
**economic independence**
**complementary goals**
**conflicting goals**

## PROBLEMS

1-1. According to Smith's "invisible hand," we are able to obtain meat, not because of the butcher's benevolence, but because of his self-interest. Why is it in the butcher's self-interest to provide us with meat? What does the butcher get in return?

1-2. Suppose another depression occurs as severe as the Great Depression of the 1930s. How would it affect you? (Thinking about this question provided a major motivation for a generation of economists. They were appalled at the prospect and determined to play a role in preventing a repeat of the Great Depression.)

1-3. The section on an equitable distribution of income reflects two views regarding the proper approach to poverty:
   (a) The important thing is to meet the basic needs of the poor; that is, to provide at least a minimum income for the purchase of food, shelter, and other necessities;
   (b) The important thing is to reduce inequality; that is, to reduce the gap between the rich and the poor.

   These two views are not the same. For example, if there is rapid growth in the economy, objective (a) may be accomplished without any progress being made toward (b). Which is the more important objective? Why? Do you feel strongly about your choice? Why?

1-4. The introduction of computers in offices has made it possible for many businesses to accomplish their administrative work with less clerical assistance. The introduction of computers, therefore, may have made it more difficult to reach the goal of low unemployment.

   What other economic goal or goals may have been affected by the introduction of computers? Does your answer illustrate economic goals that are complementary or in conflict?

1-5. In Figure 1-1, you saw that the length of the average work week in Canada has declined more or less continuously since the end of World War II. In the United States, the decline has been less sharp, whereas in Sweden the length of the work week has fallen even more than in Canada.
   (a) Can you think of some reason for this difference?
   (b) How would you expect these trends to have affected the growth rates of total production and worker incomes? Is it necessarily true that people in a country where total income is growing rapidly are better off than people in another country where income is growing more slowly?

# APPENDIX 1-A

# DIAGRAMS AND ALGEBRA USED IN ECONOMICS

Chapter 1 contains diagrams that illustrate important points, such as the increase in production per person since 1926 (Figure 1-1), and the fact that economic growth has slowed down in most countries since 1973 (Figure 1-2). In the study of economics, diagrams are frequently used — as you may see by flipping through this book. A picture is often worth a thousand words. Diagrams can fix important ideas in our minds. They present information in a vivid and eye-catching way. But, unfortunately, they can also mislead. The first and lasting impression may be the wrong impression. This appendix explains some of the major types of diagrams used in economics. It also explains some of the ways in which diagrams may be used to impress or mislead, rather than inform.[6]

Three major types of diagrams will be considered:

1. Diagrams that present and compare two facts.
2. Diagrams that show how two variables are related to one another; for example, how an increase in family income (variable 1) results in an increase in spending (variable 2).
3. Diagrams that show how something changes through time. For example, Figure 1-4 illustrates how the average level of prices has usually risen, but has sometimes fallen.

In addition to diagrams, many exercises and illustrations of economic principles use some simple algebra. Some elementary algebraic techniques (for example, how to solve two linear equations in two unknowns) are also considered in this appendix.

[6] For more detail on how readers may be misled, see the sprightly book by Darrell Huff, *How to Lie with Statistics* (New York: Norton, 1954).

## 1. A SIMPLE COMPARISON OF TWO FACTS

The simplest type of diagram brings together two facts for comparison. Often, the best method of presenting two facts — and the least likely to mislead — is to use a bar chart like the one in Figure 1-2. In panel (a) in the top left corner, the first bar shows that the average rate of growth of high-income economies between 1965 and 1973 was 4.8% per year, while the second bar shows that the rate was only 3.1% between 1973 and 1980. By comparing the heights of the two bars, we immediately see how growth rates have changed.

### Things To Watch

Even such a simple diagram may carry a misleading message. There are several "tricks" which an unscrupulous writer can use to fool the reader.

Suppose, for example, that someone wants to present the performance of a country or a corporation in the most favourable light. Consider as an example a country whose steel production rose from 10 million tonnes in 1980 to 20 million tonnes in 1990.

Figure 1-6 is a bar chart illustrating this comparison in the simplest, most straightforward way. Glancing at the height of the two bars in this diagram, the reader gets the correct impression — steel production has doubled.

This is a very good performance, but not a spectacular one. Suppose someone wants to "gild the lily," and make things look even better. Two easy ways of doing so — without actually lying — are illustrated in Figure 1-7.

Panel (a) is designed to mislead because part of the diagram is omitted. The heights of the bars are

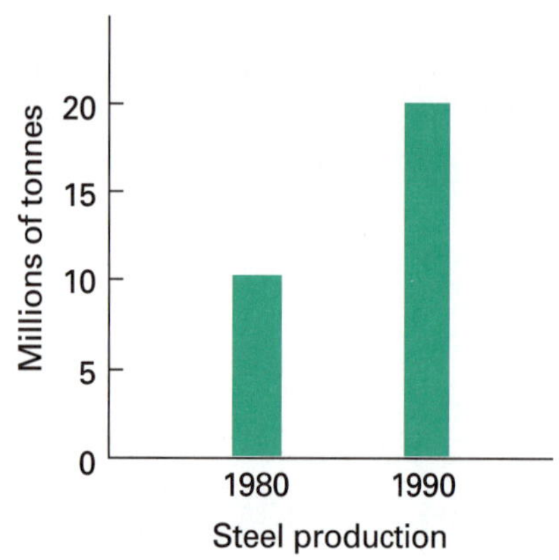


**FIGURE 1-6 A simple bar chart.**

The simplest bar chart provides a comparison of two numbers—in this case, the production of steel in two years. We see correctly that steel production has doubled.

measured from 5 million tonnes rather than zero. Thus, the 1990 bar is three times as high as the 1980 bar, and the unwary reader may be left with the wrong impression—that steel production is three times as high in 1990, whereas, in fact, it is only twice as high. This, then, is the first thing to watch out for: Do the numbers on the vertical axis start from zero? If not, the diagram may give the wrong impression.

Panel (b) shows another way in which the reader may be fooled. The bars of Figure 1-6 are replaced with something more interesting—pictures of steel mills. Because production has doubled, the steel mill on the right is twice as high as that on the left. But notice how this picture gives the wrong impression. The mill on the right is not only twice as high, it is also twice as wide, and we can visualize it as being twice as deep, too. Therefore, it isn't just twice as large as the mill on the left; it is many times as large. Thus, the casual reader again may be left with the wrong impression—that steel output has increased manyfold, when, in fact, it has only doubled. This, then, is the second reason to be wary. Look carefully and sceptically at diagrams using silhouettes or pictures. Do they leave you with an exaggerated impression of the changes that have actually occurred?

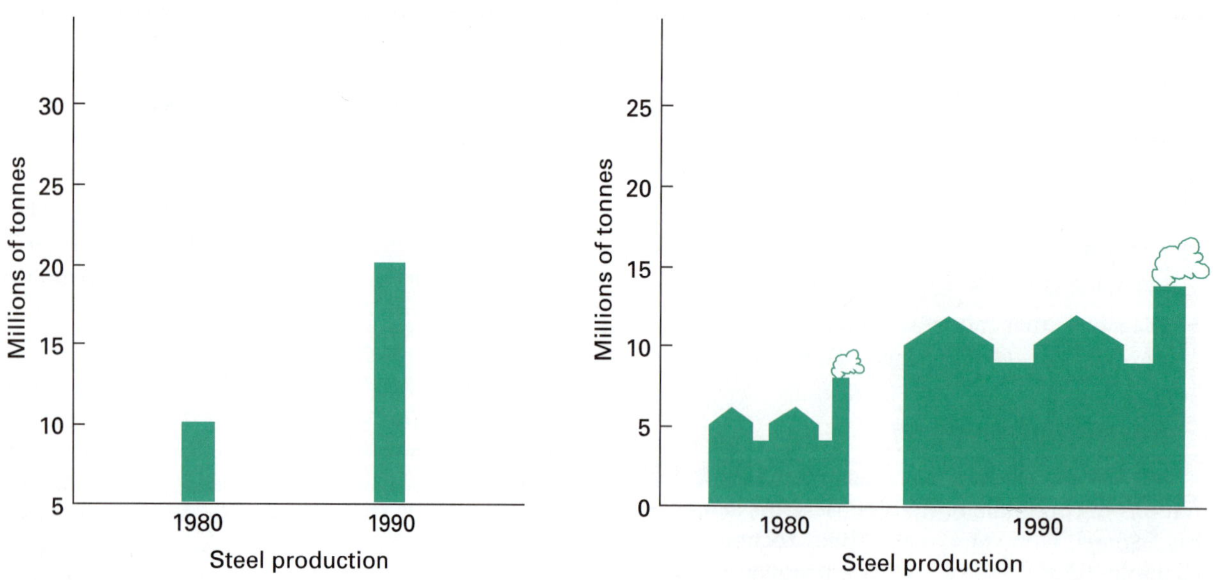


**(a) Starting from a point above zero.**

**(b) Using silhouettes or pictures.**

**FIGURE 1-7 Variations on the simple bar chart.**

Readers may be misled by variations on the simple bar chart. Both of the above panels present the same information as in Figure 1-6. In panel (a), the vertical axis begins with 5 million tonnes, rather than zero. In panel (b), pictures are used instead of bars. In each case, the reader may be left with the erroneous impression that steel production has more than doubled.

A third way to mislead is illustrated in Figure 1-8. In both panels, the facts are correct regarding the average price of common stock in Canada. (Each share of common stock represents part ownership of a company.) Panel (a) shows that between 1929 and 1952, the average price of stocks changed very little. Panel (b) shows facts that are equally true. Between 1932 and 1952—almost the same period of comparison — stock prices increased more than threefold. How can these panels both be correct? The answer: Between 1929 and 1932, the most spectacular stock-market collapse in history occurred, with stocks losing two-thirds of their value. (The bar for 1932 is only one-third as high as the bar for 1929.)

Notice the contrast between the two panels. Panel (a) implies that not much is to be gained by entering the stock market. Panel (b) gives exactly the opposite impression: The stock market is the place to get rich. Thus, an author can give two completely different messages, depending on the choice of the initial "base" year (1929 or 1932). So, beware. In any diagram showing how something has changed over time, ask yourself: Has the author slanted the results by selecting a base year designed to mislead?

## 2. RELATIONSHIPS BETWEEN VARIABLES

Frequently, economists want to keep track of the relationship between two variables. Table 1-2 provides an illustration — the relationship between the incomes of households and their expenditures for the basic necessities (housing, food, and clothing). The top row (Row *A*) indicates that a hypothetical family with an income of $10,000 spent $7000 on the basic necessities. Similarly, Row *B* shows that a family with an income of $20,000 spent $11,000 on these basics.

The data in Table 1-2 may be graphed as Figure 1-9, where income is measured along the horizontal axis and expenditures for basics up the vertical axis. (The lower left corner, labelled "0," is the *origin*—the starting point from which both income and basic expenditures are measured. To plot the data in Row *A* of the table, we measure $10,000 in income along the horizontal axis, and $7000 in spending for basics up the vertical axis. This gives us point *A* in the diagram. Similarly, points *B*, *C*, and *D* represent corresponding rows *B*, *C*, and *D* in Table 1-2.

One question that can be addressed with such a diagram is how expenditures on the basics *change* as

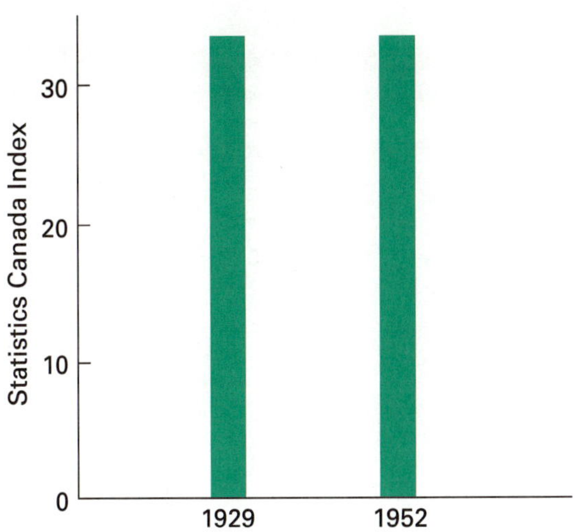


**(a) 1952 compared with 1929.**

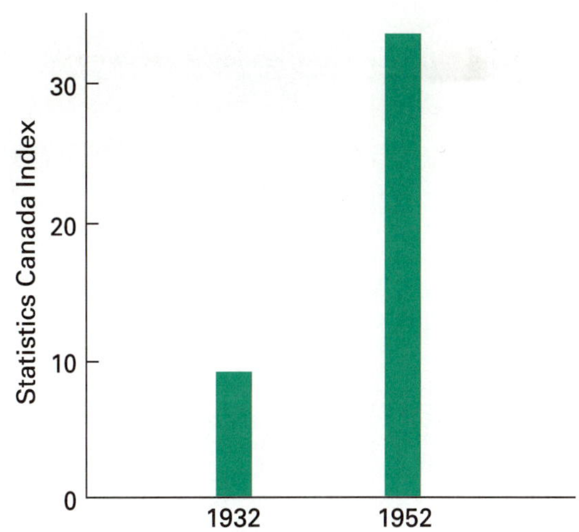


**(b) 1952 compared with 1932.**

**FIGURE 1-8 Comparisons depend on the times chosen.**
Comparisons may change even when seemingly minor changes are made in the dates. In 1952, stock prices were no higher on average than in 1929 (panel (a)). However, they were three times as high in 1952 as they had been in 1932.

*Source*: Statistics Canada, *CANSIM Databank*. Reproduced by permission of the Minister of Supply and Services Canada.

**TABLE 1-2 Household Income and Expenditures for Basics**

| | (1) Household income (after taxes) | (2) Expenditures for basics |
|---|---|---|
| *A* | $10,000 | $ 7,000 |
| *B* | 20,000 | 11,000 |
| *C* | 30,000 | 14,500 |
| *D* | 40,000 | 17,500 |

income increases. For example, as income increases from $10,000 at point *A* to $20,000 at point *B*, basic expenditures rise from $7000 to $11,000. That is, expenditures on the basics rise by $4000 in response to the $10,000 increase in income.

This relation can be illustrated by drawing a line between points *A* and *B*, and looking at its *slope*—the slope being defined as the *vertical change* or *rise* (*HB*) divided by the *horizontal change* or *run* (*AH*). In this example, the slope is $4000/$10,000 = 4/10. As incomes increase from point *A* to point *B*, families spend 40% of the increase on the basics.

Observe in this diagram that the slope becomes smaller and smaller as we go further and further to the right; that is, as we move to larger and larger incomes. Whereas the slope is 4/10 between *A* and *B*, it is only $3000/$10,000, or 3/10, between *C* and *D*. This smaller slope makes sense. Families with high incomes already have good houses, food, and clothing. When their income goes up another $10,000, they don't spend much more on the basics; they have other things to do with their income.

## Straight-Line Relationships

A particularly simple case of a relationship between two variables can be described by a *straight line*. As you may recall from high school algebra, a straight-line (or *linear*) relationship between two variables ($x$ and $y$, say), can be described by an equation such as:

$$y = a + bx \qquad \text{(1-1)}$$[7]

where $x$ and $y$ are the variables measured along the horizontal and vertical axes, and $a$ and $b$ are constant coefficients. In this equation, $a$ is the *intercept* (or

[7] Here and in other places in the book, we follow the convention of numbering the equations that we introduce, for later reference. "(1-1)" means "chapter 1, equation 1", and so on.

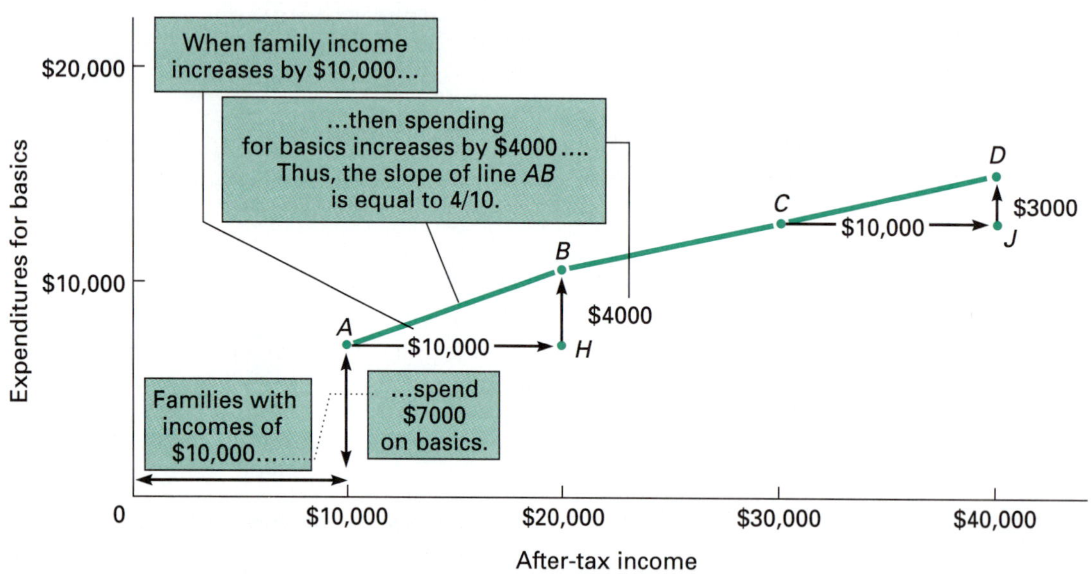


**FIGURE 1-9 How expenditures for basics are related to income.**
As family income increases (along the horizontal axis), the family's expenditures for the basics increase (as measured up the vertical axis). The slope of the line between any two points—such as *A* and *B*—shows how strongly expenditures for basics respond (*HB*) to an increase in income (*AH*).

*y-intercept*) which shows what the value of $y$ would be if $x$ were zero. The constant $b$ is the *slope coefficient*: It describes by how many units $y$ will change (the rise) for a one-unit change in $x$ (the run). When the relationship between $x$ and $y$ is a straight line, the slope $b$ is the same regardless of where you are on the line.

As an example, consider Figure 1-10, where the variable along the vertical axis is $P$, the price of widgets[8]; along the horizontal axis we measure $Q$, the quantity of widgets sold in a particular market during a given period of time. For the curve[9] shown in Figure 1-10, the intercept $a$ is 10 and the slope $b$ is $-0.5$ (that is, if the quantity sold is to increase by one unit (one thousand widgets), the price per widget must fall by 50 cents.

Therefore, the equation for this *demand curve* can be written as:

$$\mathbf{P = 10 - 0.5Q} \qquad \textbf{(1-2)}$$

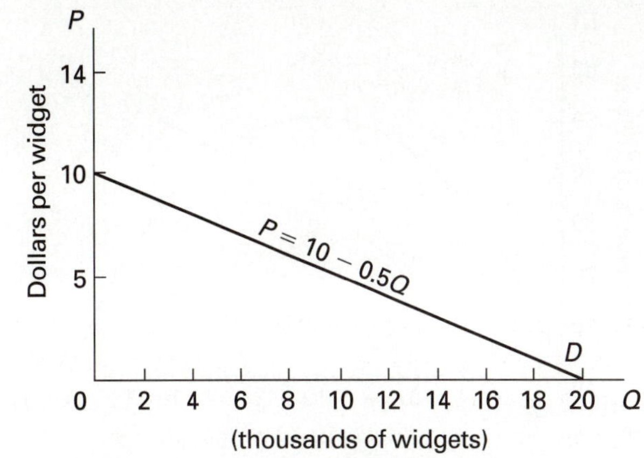


**FIGURE 1-10 The relationship between widgets sold and the price of widgets.**

At a price of $10 per widget, none will be bought. As the price declines more widgets are sold; when the price approaches zero, 20,000 widgets will be bought.

## Relationships with Diminishing Slopes

A demand curve such as that in Figure 1-10 shows the relationship between the number of units that buyers would want to purchase, and the market price per unit. Sometimes we may be interested in the *total amount spent* on a good, or equivalently, in the total revenue received by the seller or sellers of the good. Total revenue $TR$ is simply $P$ multiplied by $Q$; that is, the unit price multiplied by the number of units sold. Multiplying both sides of Equation (1-2) by $Q$, we have:

$$\begin{aligned} \mathbf{TR} &= \mathbf{PQ = Q(10 - 0.5Q)} \\ &= \mathbf{10Q - 0.5Q^2} \qquad \textbf{(1-3)} \end{aligned}$$

The expression to the right of the last equal sign tells us that, since the market price depends on the quantity sold, we can write total revenue as a function of $Q$ alone.

The relation $TR = 10Q - 0.5Q^2$ can be plotted in a diagram such as Figure 1-11. Notice several interesting features in this diagram. First, if the quantity sold is zero, $TR$ is obviously zero too. For small values of $Q$ (such as 1000 widgets at $Q_1$, say), $TR$ is still small; however, as we consider successively larger values of $Q$, $TR$ rises rapidly: The $TR$ curve has a steep positive slope. For example, if we sell 2000 widgets, the market price would be 9 (see Figure 1-10), and $TR$ would be $18,000. If we were to sell another 1000 widgets, on the other hand, the market price would be 8.5, so that $TR$ would be $25,500. Thus in this case, the slope of the $TR$ curve (the rise over the run) would be approximately 7.5; the slope measures the increase in $TR$ (in thousands of dollars) if we were to sell an additional 1000 units.

As we go beyond 3000 to consider larger quantities, $TR$ continues to rise. However, the slope of the $TR$ curve diminishes: The addition to total revenue as we consider larger quantities becomes smaller and smaller. At 10,000 units, $TR$ reaches its maximum (of $50,000). If the total quantity sold goes beyond 10,000 widgets, $TR$ will fall. That is, the curve relating $TR$ to $Q$ has a negative slope beyond this point. Note that precisely at 10,000 widgets, the slope is zero: At this point, the $TR$ curve is neither rising nor falling. The further away we go from 10,000, the more steeply negative the slope becomes. When we reach 20,000, $TR$ once again becomes zero. Looking back at Figure 1-10, the reason is clear. If we want to sell as many as 20,000 widgets, we have to reduce the mar-

[8] A widget is an imaginary good that is sometimes used in economics books to represent "a typical good."

[9] Although it may seem illogical, the term "curve" is used to describe straight lines as well as nonlinear relationships.

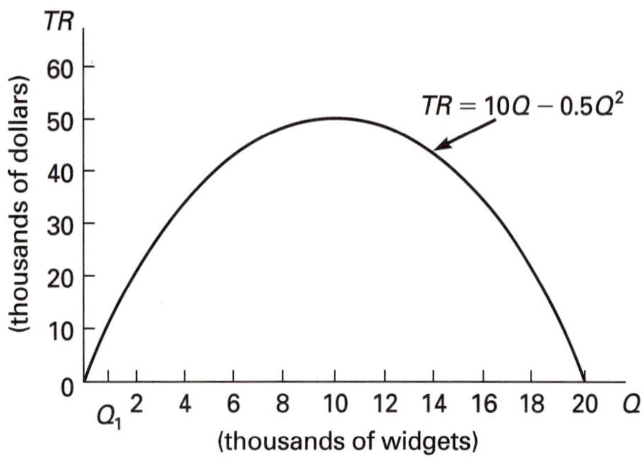


**FIGURE 1-11 The relationship between total revenue and widgets sold.**

As price is reduced from $10 per widget, more units are sold and total revenue rises until 10,000 widgets are sold. If the price is reduced further, the quantity sold increases but total revenue falls until it once again reaches zero when the price is zero.

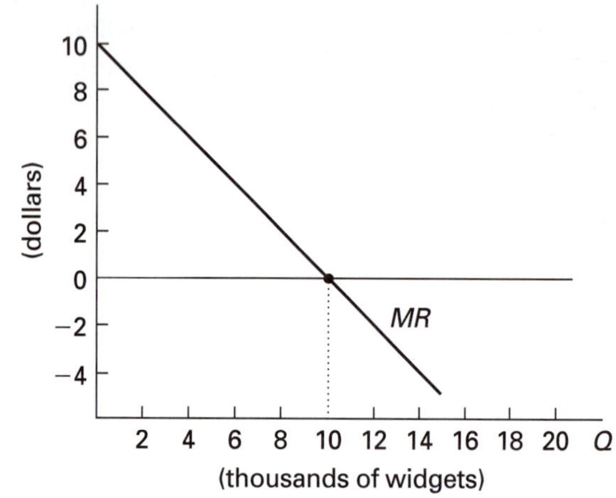


**FIGURE 1-12 The slope of the total revenue curve.**

The height of this curve measures the addition to total revenue (that is, the slope of the total revenue curve in Figure 1-11) as additional units are sold. Note that when 10,000 units are sold, selling additional units will reduce total revenue.

ket price to zero—that is, we have to give the good away. But with a zero price, total revenue is obviously zero, no matter how many units we "sell."

To illustrate how the slope of a curve such as the one in Figure 1-11 changes, it is sometimes helpful to construct a diagram such as in Figure 1-12. In that figure, the vertical axis measures the *change* in total revenue as we consider successive quantities sold. That is, the *height* of the curve labelled *MR* in Figure 1-12 actually measures the *slope* of the *TR* curve in Figure 1-11, at any given quantity sold. Note that the curve in Figure 1-12 has the same vertical intercept (*y*-intercept) as the curve *D* in Figure 1-10. This makes sense. The vertical intercept in Figure 1-10 tells us the market price that can be charged when only a very small number of units are sold. In the limit, it tells us the maximum price that can be charged when only a single widget is sold. But the addition to total revenue—that is, the slope of the *TR* curve—when we go from zero widgets to one, is just the market price of that first widget. In other words, it is the value corresponding to the vertical intercept in Figure 1-10. Also note in Figure 1-12 that the *MR* curve intersects the horizontal axis at 10 (that is, 10,000 widgets). In other words, Figure 1-12 tells us that going from 10,000 to 11,000 or 12,000 units, say, adds nothing to total revenue. In fact, it *decreases* total revenue. But that is also what Figure 1-11 tells us. At 10, the slope of the *TR* curve is zero, meaning that we cannot increase total revenue by selling a larger number of units.[10]

## Diagrams with Two Relationships

Frequently in economics, we consider situations where there is not one but two relationships between the variables that we illustrate in a diagram. For example, in Figure 1-13, the curve *D* shows the quantity (measured along the horizontal axis) that buyers want to purchase at different market prices *P* (measured along the vertical axis), while the curve *S* shows the

[10] When we illustrate the relationships between two variables by smooth curves such as those in Figures 1-10 through 1-12, we are implicitly assuming that both variables can be changed by very small amounts. In some applications in economics, the nature of the relationships between two variables can sometimes be more clearly explained if we consider variables that can only be changed in relatively large steps. In these cases, the relationships we draw will no longer look like smooth curves, but instead will appear as steps, with the height of each step showing how the *y* variable changes for each unit change in the *x* variable. However, the basic principles involved are the same in either case.

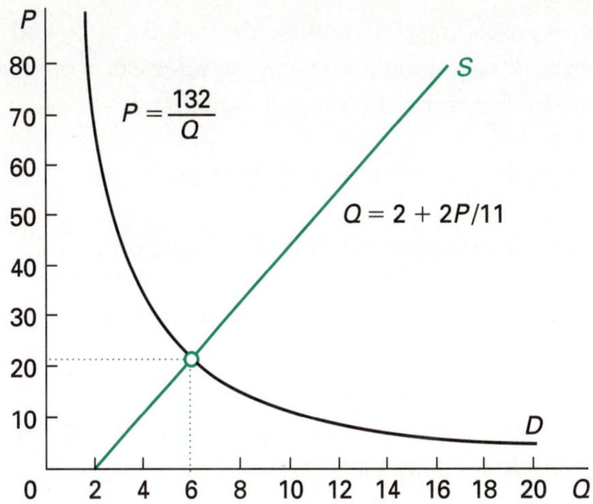


**FIGURE 1-13** **Quantities demanded and supplied at different prices.**
The curve labelled *D* shows the quantities buyers would want to purchase at different prices, while the curve *S* shows the quantities producers would be willing to sell. The point of intersection shows the price where those quantities are equal.

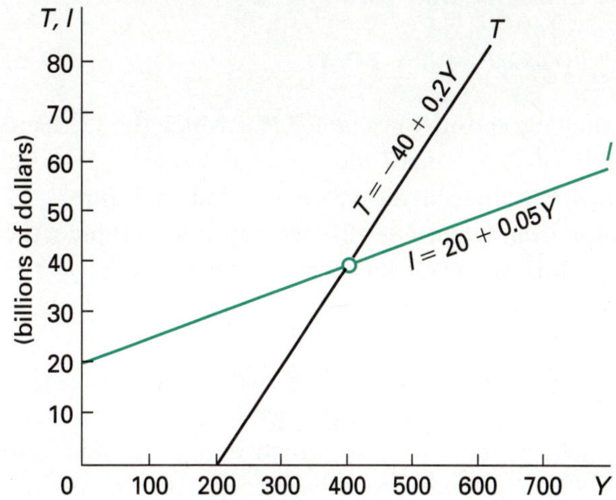


**FIGURE 1-14** **Funds saved and invested at different income levels.**
Here, the height of the *T* curve shows the amounts households want to save, and the height of the *I* curve the amounts firms want to invest, at different levels of income *Y*.

quantity that producers are willing to sell at different prices. In Figure 1-14, the curve $T$ shows the amount of funds (measured in billions of dollars, along the vertical axis), that households are willing to save, at different levels of aggregate income $Y$ (measured along the horizontal axis), while $I$ measures the amount the firms want to invest, at different levels of $Y$.

Typically, economists are interested in the point[11] in a given diagram where the two curves intersect. For example, the point where the $S$ and $D$ curves in Figure 1-13 intersect shows us what the market price has to be in order for the quantity that buyers want to purchase to be equal to the quantity that producers want to sell, and what this quantity is. (In the diagram, the intersection occurs where the price is 22 and the corresponding quantity is 6.) Similarly, in Figure 1-14, the intersection of the $I$ and $T$ curves shows what aggregate income $Y$ has to be in order for the amount that households want to save to be equal to the amount that firms want to invest.

[11] Sometimes, the curves may intersect at more than one point. We disregard that possibility for now, however.

If the curves representing the relationships have been carefully drawn, we can find the approximate point of intersection directly, just by looking at the diagram. Often, however, the information we have about the relationship comes in the form of an equation, rather than as a curve in a diagram. For example, the demand curve in Figure 1-13 has the equation

$$P = 132/Q \qquad (1\text{-}4)$$

and the $S$ curve has the equation

$$Q = 2 + 2P/11 \qquad (1\text{-}5)$$

(You can confirm that these relationships are the correct ones by picking a few specific values for the right-hand side variables and check that the values for the left-hand side variables that you calculate from the equations indeed correspond to the ones you find by inspecting the curves in Figure 1-13.) When we know the equations for two curves, we can often find the point where they intersect by *solving* the two equations. For example, the equation for the $D$ curve in Figure 1-13 can be rewritten $Q = 132/P$. Where the curves intersect, this quantity has to be the same as the quantity that producers are willing to sell. That is, it must be true that

$$132/P = 2 + 2P/11 \qquad (1\text{-}6)$$

The only (positive) value for $P$ at which the left-hand side of (1-6) equals the right-hand side is $P = 22$, which is indeed the value we find in Figure 1-13. Moreover, when $P = 22$, we can also compute the quantity at which the curves intersect; it is $Q = 6$. Note that we can find this quantity either as $Q = 132/P$, or as $Q = 2 + 2P/11$.

A particularly simple case that we will often consider is that where both equations are linear (that is, where the curves to which they correspond are straight lines with constant slopes). In this case, the point where the curves intersect can easily be found through the method of substitution. For example, the equations relating savings and investment to aggregate income in Figure 1-14 are

$$T = -40 + 0.2Y \qquad (1\text{-}7)$$

and

$$I = 20 + 0.05Y \qquad (1\text{-}8)$$

At the point of intersection, it must be true that $T = I$. Substituting the right-hand sides of the two equations into this equality, we obtain:

$$-40 + 0.2Y = 20 + 0.05Y \qquad (1\text{-}9)$$

This equation can be rewritten as:

$$0.2Y - 0.05Y = 20 + 40$$

or

$$0.15Y = 60$$

so that

$$Y = (60/0.15) = 400;$$

at this value of $Y$, you can verify that both $T$ and $I$ are equal to 40.

Sometimes, you may have to rearrange one or both equations in order to use the method of substitution. For example, suppose your equations are

$$y = 5 + 3x; \qquad 20y + 140x - 900 = 0$$

As a simple way of finding the values of $x$ and $y$ where these straight-line curves intersect, you may start by rewriting the second equation as:

$$y = (-140/20)x - (-900/20)$$

and then substitute into the first equation:

$$(-140/20)x - (-900/20) = 5 + 3x.$$

From this equation, you can solve for $x$, and then find the value for $y$ from either the first or the second of the original equations.

## 3. TIME SERIES: HOW SOMETHING CHANGES THROUGH TIME

In the example illustrated by Figure 1-8, we saw how you can get very different impressions about how stock prices changed in the 1930s and 1940s by comparing prices for 1952 with prices for either 1929 or 1932. This problem can be avoided by providing more information to the reader with a *time series* diagram showing stock prices for *each* year, not just a beginning and final year. Even better is to show stock prices for every month. With a more detailed figure, the reader can see a much more complete story, including both the collapse of the stock market in 1929 and the way in which stock prices rose after 1932.

A *time series diagram* shows how something (such as the price of stocks, the output of steel, or the unemployment rate) has changed through time.

However, even when we provide a detailed time series, a number of issues remain. Here are some of the most important.

### Should We Measure from Zero?

In discussing a simple comparison between two facts, we seem to have settled the question of how we

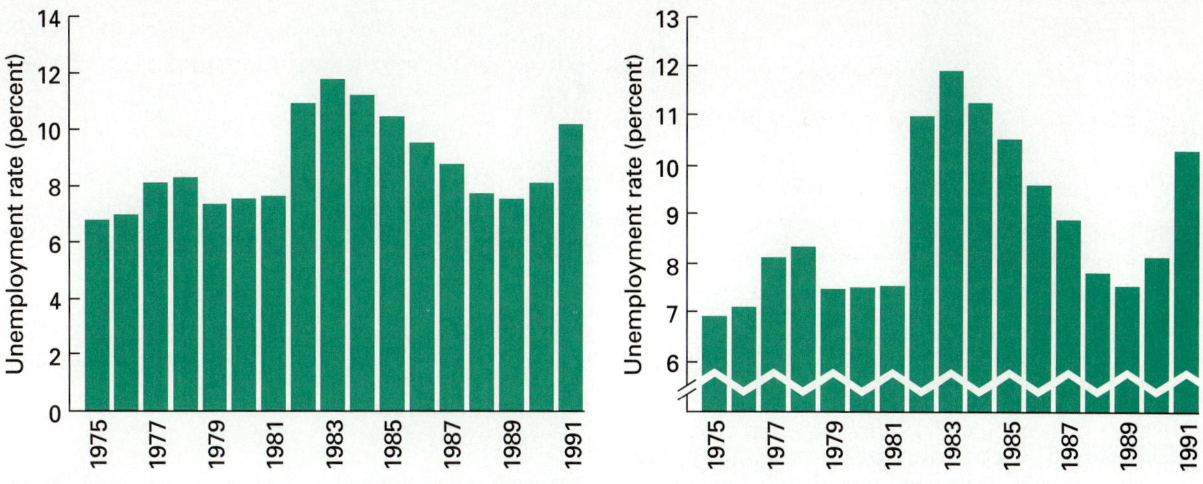


**FIGURE 1-15 A time series: The unemployment rate, 1975–1991.** The reader is provided with much more information with a time series showing every year or every month rather than just two years. In this diagram, there is an advantage in starting the vertical measurement above zero. Observe that the detailed year-to-year changes stand out more clearly in the right panel than in the left. To warn the reader that something has been left out, a gap is left in the vertical bars.

*Source*: Compiled from Statistics Canada, *CANSIM Databank*. Reproduced by permission of the Minister of Supply and Services Canada.

should measure up the vertical axis of a diagram. To start at any figure other than zero can be misleading—as in panel (a) of Figure 1-7, where steel production was measured up from a starting point of 5 million tonnes.

However, once we provide the detailed information of a time series, we should reopen the question of how to measure along the vertical axis. The problem is that we now have two conflicting considerations. We would like to start from zero to avoid misleading the reader. On the other hand, starting from some other point may make the details of a diagram much easier to see.

This is illustrated in Figure 1-15, which shows the rate of unemployment in each year from 1975 to 1991. In the left panel, the unemployment rate is measured vertically, starting from zero. This gives us the best picture of how the overall unemployment rate compares in any two years we might like to choose (for example, 1981 and 1982). Contrast this with the right panel, where the measurement of unemployment starts above zero. As in Figure 1-7, this panel can be misleading. For example, the bars for 1981 and 1982 might leave the impression that the unemployment rate more than doubled between those years, whereas, in fact, it increased by far less.

However, the right panel has a major compensating advantage. It provides a much clearer picture of how the unemployment rate *changes* from year to year; the year-to-year differences are much more conspicuous. These year-to-year changes are very important, since they are one measure of fluctuations in the economy. Consequently, the right-hand diagram can be more informative.

If the right panel is chosen, readers must be warned that we have not started from zero. One way is to leave a gap in the vertical bars, to show that something has been left out. Alternatively, we can leave a gap in the vertical axis itself, as illustrated.

## How Should Growth Be Illustrated?

Some time series—such as a nation's population—have a strong tendency to grow through time. If we measure in the normal way along the vertical axis, the

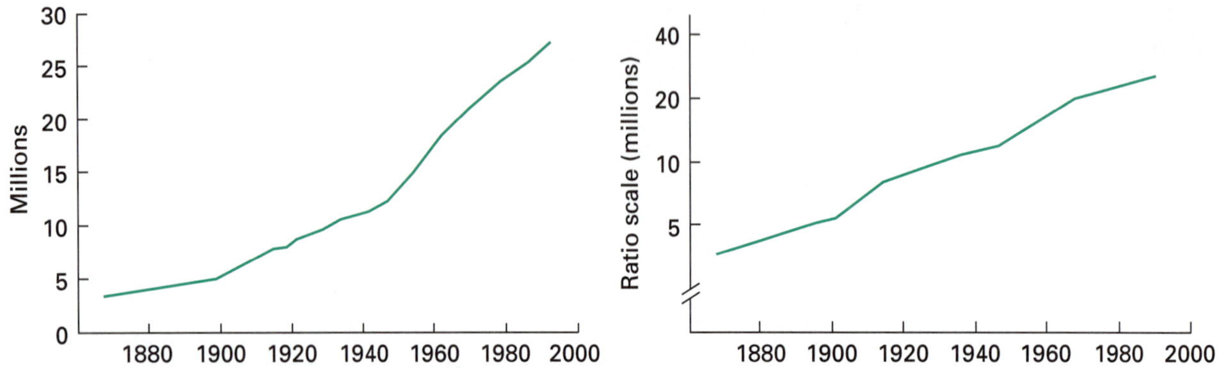


**(a) Standard diagram.** **(b) Using a ratio scale.**

**FIGURE 1-16 Population of Canada, 1867–1991.** By using a ratio scale, we can identify the periods when the rate of population growth was most rapid. It occurred when the slope of the curve in panel (b) was steepest.

*Source*: Statistics Canada, *CANSIM Databank,* and K. Buckley and M. Urquhart, eds., *Historical Statistics of Canada,* 1st. ed. (Toronto and Cambridge: Cambridge University Press and Macmillan of Canada, 1965.) Reproduced by permission of the Minister of Supply and Services Canada.

curve becomes steeper and steeper through time, as shown in panel (a) of Figure 1-16. There is nothing necessarily wrong with this presentation — the increase in the population between 1970 and 1980 (2.7 million) was, in fact, much greater than the increase between 1870 and 1880 (0.6 million).

However, there is a problem with this figure. Suppose we are interested in not just the *absolute numbers*, but the *rate* at which the population is growing. Thus, the 0.6 million increase in population in the 1870s represents a much greater rate of increase (1.8% per year) than the 2.7 million increase of the 1970s (1.2% per year).

To highlight the rate of growth, a *ratio* or *logarithmic* scale is used on the vertical axis (Figure 1-16, panel (b)). On such a scale, equal *percentage* changes show up as equal distances. For example, the distance from 5 million to 10 million (an increase of 100%) is the same as the distance from 10 million to 20 million (also an increase of 100%). In such a diagram, if something grows at a *constant rate* (for example, by 2% per year), it shows up as a *straight line*. By looking for the steepest sections of the time series in panel (b) of Figure 1-16, we can identify the periods when population has grown at the most rapid rate. Similarly, back in Figure 1-4, the steepest parts of the curve show when the most rapid rates of inflation occurred.

A ratio scale is appropriate for a time series such as population, where the emphasis is on proportional rates of growth (or decline). However, it is inappropriate for a series that does not have a strong tendency to grow (or decline) at a proportional rate. For example, there is no reason to expect the unemployment rate in the economy to either grow or decline systematically over time, and there is no particular reason to use a logarithmic scale in a diagram showing the unemployment rate.

Finally, note that when a logarithmic scale is used, the question of whether the vertical axis is measured from zero becomes irrelevant, since zero cannot appear on such a diagram. By looking at Figure 1-16(b), we can see why. Each time we go up 1 cm (one notch on the vertical axis), the population doubles — from 5 to 10 million, and then to 20 million. We can make exactly the same statement the other way around: Each time we go down 1 cm, the population falls by half — from 5 million to 2.5 million, then to 1.25 million, and so on. No matter how far we extend the diagram downward, each additional centimetre will reduce the population by one-half. Therefore, the population can *never* reach zero on such a diagram.

## Real or Monetary Measures?

People often complain that the federal government is getting "too big." Suppose we wanted to look at the size of the government. How would we do so?

The most obvious way is to look at the amount the government spends. Measured in dollars, the growth of government spending has been truly stupendous over the past half century or so (Figure 1-17). But, there are several shortcomings to this simple measure.

The first has to do with prices, which have risen substantially during the past half century. Inflation means that even if the government had remained exactly the same size—building the same number of schools and roads, and keeping the same number of soldiers in the army — it would have spent many more dollars. That is, its expenditures in dollar or *nominal* terms would have gone up rapidly. In order to eliminate the effects of inflation, government statisticians calculate *what government expenditures would have been if prices had not gone up*—that is, if prices had remained at the level existing in a single year. Such a measure of government expenditures—in *constant-dollar* or *real* terms—is shown in panel (a) of Figure 1-18. Observe how much more slowly government expenditures have grown as graphed in Figure 1-18(a) where the effects of inflation have been eliminated as compared to Figure 1-17. (Further

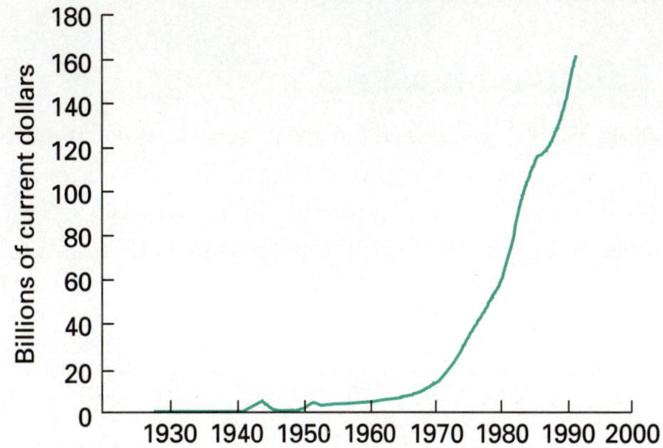


**FIGURE 1-17 Federal government expenditures, measured in dollars.**
As measured by the number of dollars spent, the size of the federal government has expanded very rapidly.

*Source*: Statistics Canada, *CANSIM Databank*. Reproduced by permission of the Minister of Supply and Services Canada.

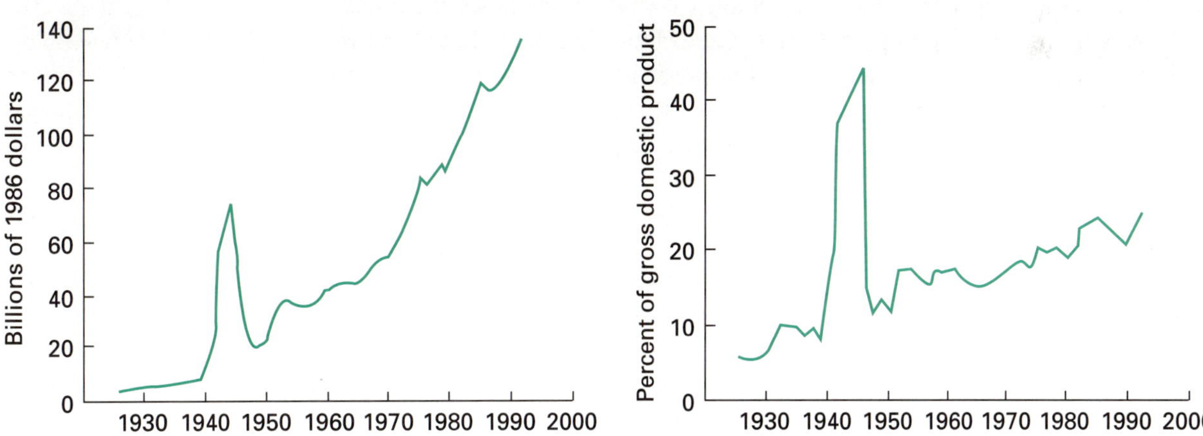


**(a) Measured at 1986 prices.** **(b) As a percentage of gross domestic product.**

**FIGURE 1-18 Federal government expenditures: Alternative representations.**
When the effects of inflation are removed in panel (a), the growth of government spending is much less spectacular than in Figure 1-17. As compared to the overall size of the economy (as measured by gross domestic product), the size of the federal government has grown relatively slowly, as can be seen in panel (b).

*Source*: Compiled from Statistics Canada, *CANSIM Databank*. Reproduced by permission of the Minister of Supply and Services Canada.

details on how real expenditures are calculated will be presented in a later chapter.)

## Relative Measures

Even when measured in real terms, government expenditures have risen substantially. Does this, in itself, mean that the government is "too big"? The answer is, not necessarily. One reason is that, as the government has grown, so has the overall economy. Thus, we may ask the question: Has the government grown *relative to the economy*? (As in Figure 1-1, the size of the economy is measured by gross domestic product or GDP.) In Figure 1-18(b), observe that government expenditures have not grown much relative to the economy (that is, as a percentage of GDP) in recent decades.

CHAPTER 2

# SCARCITY AND CHOICE: THE ECONOMIC PROBLEM

*Economics studies human behaviour as a relationship between ends and scarce means.*

*Lionel Robbins*

In the early 1980s, U.S. president Reagan launched the Strategic Defence Initiative. The SDI (popularly referred to as Star Wars) was a huge program of research and development to create a system of defensive weapons that would make the United States virtually impenetrable to outside attackers. Closer to home, in 1987 the Mulroney government outlined plans to spend some $12 billion on a fleet of nuclear submarines to strengthen Canada's capability to defend our coastal waters and patrol the vast Arctic oceans.

As it turned out, spending on the Star Wars program during Reagan's eight years in office was much less than what was originally planned. In Canada, the nuclear submarine program became a very controversial issue and, in the April 1989 federal budget, the government announced that it had been postponed indefinitely.

The resistance toward these spending proposals did not develop because military officials had a change of heart. Instead, the opposition came from others: from politicians and government officials in charge of other kinds of programs, as well as from the general public. Their concern was with the cost.

How do countries pay for things like Star Wars or a nuclear submarine fleet? The answer: through additional taxes that require the public to give up income that they could otherwise have spent on other things, such as better housing or faster cars; or through cutbacks in other kinds of government spending, such as transfers to help the provinces finance their programs in health care and post-secondary education. These military spending proposals have run directly into the central economic problem: We must make *choices*. We cannot have everything we want because:

1. Our material *wants* are virtually unlimited; and
2. Economic *resources* are *scarce*.

If we use our productive capacity to make nuclear submarines, we will have fewer resources for other things.

> The *economic problem* is the need to make choices among the options permitted by our scarce resources.
>
> *Economics* is the study of how scarce resources are allocated to satisfy alternative, competing, human wants.
>
> To *economize* is to achieve a specific benefit at the lowest cost in terms of the resources used.

## UNLIMITED WANTS . . .

Consider first our wants. If we can survive in a simple one-bedroom apartment, why do we aspire to much larger homes filled with gadgets? Why do our material wants never seem to be satisfied?

Material wants arise for two reasons. First, each of us has basic biological needs: the need for food, shelter, and clothing. But, there is also a second reason. Clearly, we are prepared to work more than is required to meet our minimum needs. We want more than the basic diet of vegetables and water needed to sustain life. We want more than the minimum clothing to protect us from the cold. In other words, we want not only the essential goods and services that make life possible, but also some of the non-essentials that make it pleasant. Of course, the two basic reasons for material wants cannot be sharply separated. When we sit down to a gourmet meal in a restaurant, we are getting the food essential for satisfying our biological requirements. But we are getting something more as well. When we savour exotic foods in a comfortable and stylish atmosphere, we are getting luxuries too. Such non-essentials are sufficiently pleasant that we are willing to work to obtain them.

The range of consumer wants is exceedingly broad. We want ***goods***, such as houses, cars, shirts, and tennis rackets. Similarly, we want ***services***, such as medical care, haircuts, and laundry services. When we get what we want, it may whet our appetites for something more. We may become dissatisfied with the old manual lawnmower and want an electric one instead. After we buy a house, we may wish to replace the carpets and drapes. Furthermore, as new products are introduced, we may want them too. We want video recorders, home computers, and a host of other products that earlier generations never even dreamed of. Even though it is conceivable that, some day, we will say, "Enough," that day seems far away. Our material wants show no sign of being completely satisfied.

## . . . SCARCE RESOURCES

Because of the second fundamental fact (scarcity of economic resources), not all wants can be satisfied. Although our productive capacity is large, it is not without limit. There are only so many workers in the labour force, only a given amount of land, and we have only a certain number of machines and factories. In other words, our resources are limited.

***Resources*** are the basic inputs used in the production of goods and services. Therefore, they are also frequently known as ***factors of production***. They can be categorized under three main headings: land, capital, and labour.

1. *Land*. Economists use the term ***land*** in a broad sense, to include not only the arable land used by farmers and the city land used as building lots, but also the other gifts of nature that come with the land. The abundance of such *natural resources* constitutes an important explanation for the prosperity of the Canadian economy. Early economic development was based to a large extent on our fur-bearing animals and fish resources, as well as on our fertile agricultural land. Other resources, such as minerals, petroleum and natural gas, forestlands, and rivers from which we can produce hydroelectric power, have become more important in the present era. All are classified as part of Canada's vast land resource.
2. *Capital* refers to buildings, equipment, and materials used in the productive process. An automobile assembly plant is "capital," and so are the machines in the plant and the steel with which automobiles will be built. In contrast to land, which has been *given* to us by nature, ***capital*** has been *produced* at some time in the past. This may have been the distant past; the factory may have been built 15 years ago. Or it may have been the recent past; the steel may have been manufactured last month. The process of producing and accumulating capital is known as ***investment***.

   Unlike consumer goods (such as shoes, cars, or food), capital goods or "investment goods" (such as tractors, factories, or machinery in the factories) are not produced to satisfy human wants directly. Rather, they are intended for use in the production of other goods. Capital produced now will satisfy wants only indirectly and only at a later time when it is used in the production of consumer goods. The production of capital, therefore, means that someone has been *willing to wait*. When a machine is produced rather than a car, the choice has been made to forgo the car now in order to produce the machine, thereby making it possible to produce more cars or other goods in the future. Thus, capital formation involves a choice between consumption *now* and more consumption *in the future*.[1] We should emphasize one point of terminology. Unless otherwise specified, economists use the term "capital" to mean *real capital*, not financial capital. In previous paragraphs, we've been referring to real capital — the factories and machinery used to produce other goods. *Financial capital*, on the other hand, consists of financial assets, such as common stocks, bonds, or bank deposits. Such assets are important. The holder of

[1] Note that the one who is willing to wait (forgo present consumption in exchange for an expected future return) may be a foreign capitalist. A substantial proportion of the capital resources used in Canada is indeed owned by foreigners; the implications of this are discussed later in this chapter.

## APPLICATIONS AND ILLUSTRATIONS — BOX 2-1

## A Tale of Two Dreams

One task of the entrepreneur is to identify new opportunities and potential new products. In the business world, it is the entrepreneur who dreams dreams. But, the entrepreneur must also be practical and hard-headed. Will the public share the dream? Will the new product sell? Can the entrepreneur produce it at a price low enough to attract customers?

### Apple Computer

For Steve Jobs and Steve Wozniak, the answer was a resounding "yes."

In the mid-1970s, the two college dropouts were employed in the electronics industry—Wozniak at Hewlett-Packard and Jobs as a designer of video games at Atari. In their spare time, they tinkered. In 1976, Wozniak built the first Apple — a small, easy-to-use computer. Jobs recognized its promise. They put together their available financial resources — $1300 — to start production in Jobs' garage.

For a fledgling electronics company, California's Silicon Valley was the place to be. An early task for the new entrepreneurs was to get funds for expansion by tapping into the local pool of venture capital. They were not immediately successful. One of their first prospects was put off by Jobs' cutoff jeans, sandals, and wispy beard. Then they made contact with A.C. Markkula, a former marketing manager at Intel (a maker of computer chips), who was delighted with the new machine. He put up $250,000, joined the company, and persuaded two venture capital firms to put up more money. Apple Computer was ready to go.

Wozniak quickly redesigned the original model. The trim, attractive Apple II was born. Sales surged: $800,000 in 1977, $7.9 million in 1978, $100 million by 1980, and $500 million by 1982. The pace was frenetic. To Markkula, the problem was to "keep the race car on the track."

Apple's breakneck growth created a major problem: how to keep the creative ferment and raw enthusiasm of a small company while developing the structure and discipline needed in a large business. The team that developed Apple's Macintosh model—mostly young people in their twenties—wore t-shirts with their motto: "Working 90 hours a week, and loving every minute of it." The creativity of that group was remarkable, but the slightly madcap atmosphere exacted a toll. Many of Apple's young engineers burned out and left the company in their thirties. To create a more structured company, in 1983, Apple brought in as president a professional manager and marketing expert, the former president of Pepsi-Cola, John Sculley. In the next two years, both Wozniak and Jobs left Apple.

### The Avro Arrow*

The Apple dream generally has been happy, if somewhat surreal. In contrast, the dream of the pilots, engineers, and executives who, for a short time, put Canada in the spotlight as a world leader in aircraft technology, ended in disappointment.

A.V. Roe of Canada Ltd. was started in 1945 in a Malton, Ontario, plant that had been used to build bombers during World War II. By 1947, the young company had won two important contracts, one to develop a jet-powered transport plane for Trans-Canada Airlines (TCA, which later became Air Canada), the other to build jet fighters for the Canadian Air Force.

* This section is based on material in Greig Stewart's *Shutting Down the National Dream: A.V. Roe and the Tragedy of the Avro Arrow* (Toronto: McGraw-Hill Ryerson Limited, 1988).

*(continued)*

**BOX 2-1 continued**

The transport plane project ended in failure. Even though many international aviation experts were impressed with "the Jetliner," TCA engineers decided its fuel consumption was too high, and none was ever produced beyond the original prototype.

But, on the military side, Avro (as the company was commonly known) was successful. Some 700 of its CF-100 fighters were eventually produced. By the early 1950s, Avro engineers had already designed a successor to the CF-100, a delta-winged fighter capable of flying at one and a half times the speed of sound. The federal government agreed to pay for the development of several prototypes of this plane, the legendary "Avro Arrow."

Under the leadership of its dynamic young president, Crawford Gordon, the company grew rapidly in the 1950s. It diversified its business, and in 1957 had become the third largest company in Canada. But its biggest project by far was the Arrow. In 1958, some $300 million had already been spent on developing the Arrow and the Iroquois engine that would power it, and it was estimated that the cost of just 100 combat-ready planes would bring the total to well over $1 billion. (In relation to Canada's GDP at the time, this was considerably larger than the cost of the nuclear submarine program proposed in the late 1980s.)

By the time the first prototype of the Arrow was flying, however, there was already concern over both the high cost of the program and the need for advanced fighter planes in an age of "unmanned" missiles. After the Conservative election victories in 1957 and 1958, it became clear that the project was in trouble. At Avro, work continued at a frantic pace to get more planes ready, and Gordon went to Ottawa for a personal meeting with Prime Minister Diefenbaker to try to get a commitment to continued funding. But it was too late. In February 1959, Diefenbaker rose in the House of Commons to announce the termination of the project. The six completed Arrows were cut up for scrap, and almost 10,000 people at Avro lost their jobs. A few months later, Crawford Gordon (whose business difficulties had been compounded by a variety of personal problems) was gone from the company. The Avro Arrow dream was dead.

a stock or bond, for example, has a form of wealth that is likely to produce income in the future in the form of dividends on the stock or interest on the bond. But while an individual might consider 100 shares of Hiram Walker stock as part of his or her "capital," these shares are not capital in the economic sense. They are not a resource with which goods and services can be produced.

Similarly, when economists talk of investment, they generally mean *real investment*—the accumulation of machines and other real capital—and not financial investment (such as the purchase of a Canada Savings Bond).

3. *Labour* refers to the human resource—the physical and mental talents that people apply to the production of goods and services. The construction worker provides ***labour***, and so does the university professor and the physician. (The professor produces educational services and the doctor produces medical services.)[2] One particular human resource deserves special emphasis: entrepreneurial ability. ***Entrepreneur*** is a French word that means "someone who undertakes." More specifically, it means someone who

(a) organizes production, bringing together the factors of production—land, labour, and capital—to make goods and services;

(b) makes business decisions, figuring out what goods to produce and how to produce them;

[2] The preceding paragraphs have presented the traditional division of the factors of production into the categories of land, labour, and capital. While still popular, this traditional division is not universally used by present-day economists. In particular, some economists now talk of "human capital." This is the education and training which add to the productivity of labour. Human capital has two of the important characteristics of physical capital: (1) a willingness to wait during the training period, when the trainee does not produce goods or services; and (2) the increase it brings about in the productive capacity of the economy, since a trained worker can produce more than an untrained one.

(c) takes risk. (There is no guarantee that business decisions will turn out to be correct.);

(d) innovates, introducing new products, new technology, and new ways of organizing business.

In order to be successful, an entrepreneur needs to be aware of changes in the economy. Is the market for typewriters declining, while that of computers is expanding? If so, the successful entrepreneur will not build a new assembly line for typewriters, but will instead consider the production of computers. Some entrepreneurs are spectacularly successful: for example, Steve Jobs and Steve Wozniak, who set up Apple Computer while still in their twenties. Their mushrooming sales helped to make the microcomputer a common household appliance—and made them multimillionaires in the process (Box 2-1 on pages 31 and 32). Other entrepreneurs are engaged in much more prosaic, everyday tasks. The mechanic who runs his own garage and filling station is an entrepreneur, as is the university student who runs a house-painting business during the summer months. The key questions facing an entrepreneur are these: Are people willing to pay for what I can produce? Can I sell the good or service for enough to cover costs and have some profit left over?

Because entrepreneurs are the ones who undertake the production of new goods, they play a strategic role in determining the dynamism and growth of the economy.

## SCARCITY AND CHOICE: THE PRODUCTION POSSIBILITIES CURVE

With unlimited wants and limited resources, we face the fundamental economic problem of ***scarcity***. We cannot have everything we want; we must make *choices*.

The problem of scarcity—and the need to make choices—can be illustrated with a *production possibilities curve* (PPC). This curve shows what can be produced with our existing resources (land, labour, and capital) and with existing technology, that is, methods of production. Although our resources are limited and our capacity to produce is likewise limited, we have an option as to what goods and services we produce. We may produce fewer cars and more aircraft, or less wheat and more corn.

In an economy with thousands of products, the choices before us are complex. In order to reduce the problem to its simplest form, consider a very basic economy with only two goods: woollen clothing and wheat. If we decide to produce more food (wheat), then we will have to produce less clothing.

The options open to us are shown in the hypothetical production possibilities table (Table 2-1) and the corresponding production possibilities curve (Figure 2-1) on page 34. Consider first an extreme example, where all our resources are directed toward the production of food. In this case, illustrated by option *A*, we would produce 20 million tonnes of food, but no clothing. This clearly does not represent a desirable composition of output. Although we would be well fed, we would be running around naked. However, no claim has been made that the points on the production possibilities curve are necessarily *desirable*; the only claim is that they are *possible*. And point *A* is possible.[3]

At the other extreme, if we produced nothing but clothing, we would make 5 billion m, as illustrated by option *F*. Again, this is a possible outcome, but not a desirable one. We would be well dressed as we faced starvation.

### The Shape of the Production Possibilities Curve: Increasing Opportunity Costs

More reasonable cases are those in which we produce some of each good. Consider how the economy might move from point *A* toward point *F*. At point *A*, nothing is produced but food. It is grown on all types of arable land throughout the nation. In order to begin the production of clothing, we would raise sheep in the areas which are comparatively best suited for wool production—on hilly meadowland in the Atlantic provinces and British Columbia, say. From these lands, we would get a lot of wool, while giving up just a small amount of food that might have been grown there. This is illustrated as we move from point *A* to point *B* on the production possibilities curve.

[3] It may be advantageous for a country to specialize by devoting most of its resources to producing one good only (wheat, say) when it can sell this good (wheat) to foreign countries in exchange for all other goods (such as clothing). The possibility of specialized production and international trade is likely to be especially important for a relatively small country, such as Canada.

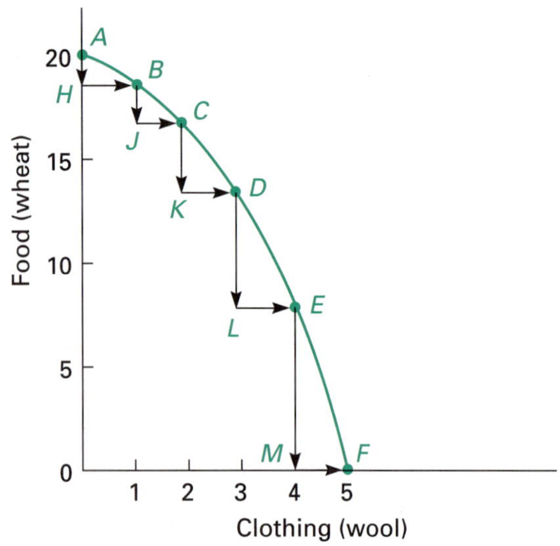


**FIGURE 2-1 The production possibilities curve.**
The curve shows the combinations of two goods that can be produced with limited resources of land, labour, and capital.

**TABLE 2-1 Production Possibilities**

| Options | Clothing (billions of metres) | Food (millions of tonnes) | Units of food that must be given up to produce one more unit of clothing (opportunity cost of clothing) |
|---|---|---|---|
| *A* | 0 | 20 | |
| *B* | 1 | 19 | 1 |
| *C* | 2 | 17 | 2 |
| *D* | 3 | 13 | 4 |
| *E* | 4 | 8 | 5 |
| *F* | 5 | 0 | 8 |

Only one unit of food is given up in order to produce the first unit of clothing.

As we decide to produce more wool, however, we must move to land that is somewhat less suited to wool production. As a result, we do not get the second unit of clothing quite so easily. To produce it, we must give up more than one unit of food. This is illustrated in the move from point *B* to point *C*. As clothing production is increased by one more unit (from one unit to two), food production falls by two units (from 19 to 17). Thus, the ***opportunity cost*** of the second unit of clothing—the food we have to give up to acquire it—is greater than the opportunity cost of the first unit.

The *opportunity cost* of a product is the alternative that must be given up to produce that product. (In this illustration, the opportunity cost of a unit of clothing is the wheat that must be given up when that unit of clothing is produced.)

Further increases in the production of clothing come at higher and higher opportunity costs in terms of lost food. As we move to the third unit of clothing (from point *C* to *D*), we must start grazing sheep on good corn land in Southern Ontario. A lot of food must be given up to produce that third unit of clothing. Finally, as we move from point *E* to point *F*, all our resources are switched into the production of clothing. The last unit of clothing comes at an extremely high opportunity cost in terms of lost output of food. Wheat production is stopped on the farms of Manitoba and Saskatchewan, which are no good at all for producing wool. The wheat lands remain idle, and prairie farmers migrate to the Atlantic region and British Columbia, where they can make only minor contributions to wool production. Thus, the last unit of clothing (the move from point *E* to *F*) comes at a very high cost of eight units of food.

Thus, *the increasing opportunity cost of wool is a reflection of the specialized characteristics of our resources*. Our resources are not completely adaptable to alternative uses. The lands of New Brunswick and Saskatchewan are not equally well suited to the production of wool and wheat. Thus, the opportunity cost of wool rises as its production is increased.

As a result of increasing opportunity cost, the production possibilities curve becomes more and more steeply sloped as we move from point *A*, with all food production, toward points where more clothing is produced. The arrows in Figure 2-1 illustrate this. The horizontal increases in clothing production — from points *H* to *B*, *J* to *C*, *K* to *D*, and so on — are each one unit. The resulting reductions in food production — measured vertically from *A* to *H*, *B* to *J*, *C* to *K*, and so on — become larger and larger, making the curve slope steeper as we move to the right. Another way of describing this is to say that the PPC "bows outward." Technically, a curve with an outward bow is described as *concave to the origin*.

The principle of increasing opportunity cost can also be illustrated in a diagram such as Figure 2-2, where we measure the amounts of clothing and food along the horizontal and vertical axes, respectively, as before, but where the curve labelled *OC* measures the *opportunity cost* of each successive unit of clothing — that is, the number of units of food that have to be given up in order to produce the additional unit of clothing. The outward bow of the PPC in Figure 2-1 must mean that the opportunity cost curve in Figure 2-2 rises as we move to increasing amounts of clothing production: The height of the *OC* curve simply reflects the absolute value — that is, a value that disregards the negative sign — of the slope of the PPC.[4]

While opportunity costs generally increase, as shown in Figure 2-2, it is not logically necessary that they must do so. In some cases, it is possible for opportunity costs to be constant. For example, beef cattle and dairy cattle can graze on similar land; it is possible that the resources used to raise beef are equally suited for dairy cattle. Thus, the opportunity cost of beef in terms of milk may be constant. If so, a production possibilities curve drawn with milk on one axis and beef on the other would be a straight line, and the curve showing the opportunity cost of additional units of milk (in terms of the amount of beef that would have to be given up for each additional unit) would be a horizontal line.

[4] Although our illustration of opportunity cost in Figure 2-1 is based on looking at changing the output of clothing in large steps, when we draw the opportunity cost curve *OC* in Figure 2-2 as a smooth curve, we are implicitly assuming that it is possible to change the output of both food and clothing in very small steps so that we can measure the slope (rise over run) of the PPC between points that are very close together. The reason we illustrate opportunity cost in Figure 2-1 by looking at relatively large changes, of course, is that this makes it easier for the reader to see what is going on in the figure (and also that it keeps Table 2-1 relatively short!).

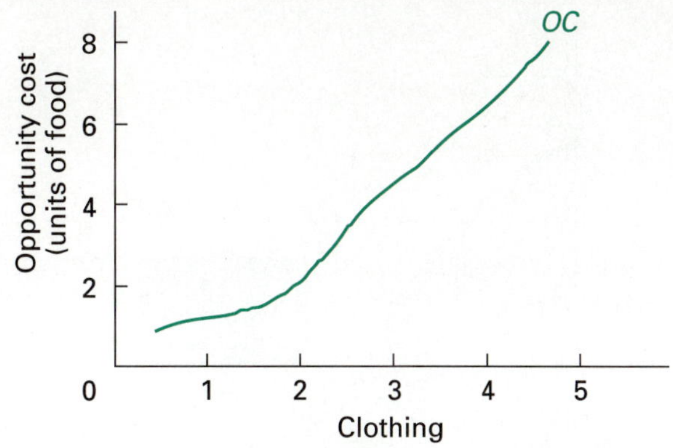


**FIGURE 2-2 The opportunity cost of additional units of clothing.**

As more and more clothing is produced, the opportunity cost (measured in units of food) becomes higher and higher. Note the relation between the height of the opportunity cost curve and the slope of the production possibilities curve (PPC) in Figure 2-1: A steeper slope corresponds to a higher opportunity cost.

## THE PRODUCTION POSSIBILITIES CURVE IS A "FRONTIER"

The production possibilities curve in Figure 2-1 illustrates what an economy is capable of producing. It shows the maximum possible combined output of two goods. In practice, actual production can fall short of our capabilities. Obviously, if there is large-scale unemployment, labour resources are being wasted. The same is true if workers are employed, but are wasting their time on the job. In either case, the result is a point such as *U*, inside the production possibilities curve in Figure 2-3 (page 36). Beginning at such a point, we could produce more food *and* more clothing (and move to point *D*) by putting the unemployed back to work. (With full employment, we alternatively could choose any other point on the production possibilities curve, such as *B*, *C*, or *E*.)

Thus, while the production possibilities curve represents options open to the society, it does not include all conceivable options. The attainable options include not only the points on the curve, but also all points in the shaded area inside the curve.

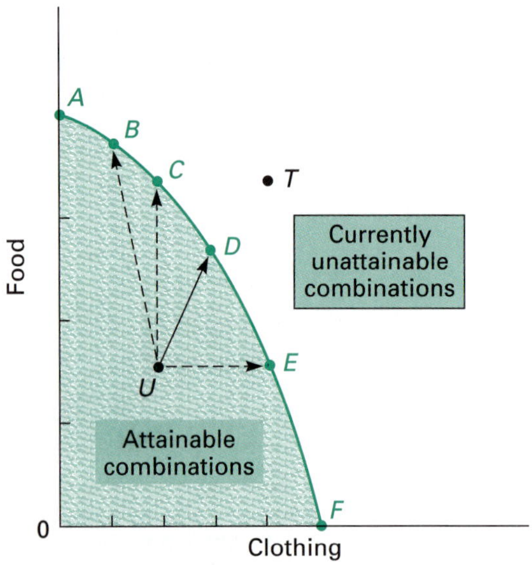


**FIGURE 2-3 Unemployment and the production possibilities curve.**

Point *U* represents a position of large-scale unemployment. If people are put back to work, the economy can be moved to point *D*, with more food and more clothing.

With its limited resources, the society can choose any point along the production possibilities curve, or any point within it. Points in the shaded area within the curve are undesirable; the society could do better by moving out to the curve. Points beyond the curve are unattainable with the resources currently at our disposal.

The production possibilities curve, therefore, traces out a *frontier* or *boundary* of the options open to us. We can pick a point on the frontier if we don't waste resources and maintain a high level of employment. Or we can end up inside the curve if we use resources in a wasteful way or mismanage the economy into a depression. But points outside the curve (such as *T*) are currently unattainable. We cannot reach them with our present quantities of land, labour, and capital, and with our present technology.

In summary, the production possibilities curve illustrates three important concepts: scarcity, choice, and opportunity cost.

1. *Scarcity* is illustrated by the fact that combinations outside the curve cannot be attained. Even though we might want such combinations, we cannot have them with the resources available to us.
2. Because we cannot have combinations outside the curve, we must settle for a *choice* of one of the attainable combinations outlined by the PPC.
3. *Opportunity cost* is illustrated by the downward slope of the production possibilities curve.

## GROWTH: THE OUTWARD SHIFT OF THE PRODUCTION POSSIBILITIES CURVE

As time passes, a point, such as *T* in Figure 2-3 may come within our grasp as our productive capacity increases and the economy grows. There are three main sources of ***growth***:

1. technological improvement, representing new and better ways of producing goods;
2. an increase in the quantity of capital;
3. an increase in the labour force.

Consider a change in technology. Suppose a new type of fertilizer is developed that substantially increases the output of our land, whether wool or wheat is being produced. Then we will be able to produce more wheat and more wool. The production possibilities curve will shift out to the new curve ($PPC_2$) shown in Figure 2-4.

*Growth* is defined as an increase in the productive capacity of the nation. It is illustrated by an

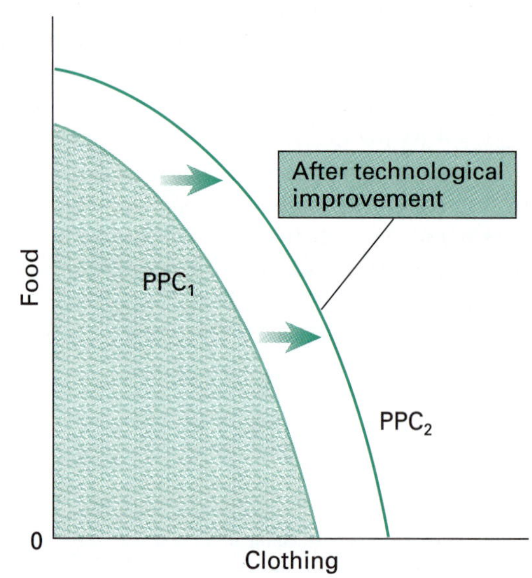


**FIGURE 2-4 Technological improvement.**

As a result of the development of a new fertilizer, our productive capabilities increase. The production possibilities curve moves outward.

outward movement of the production possibilities curve.

Although the new fertilizer illustrated in Figure 2-4 increases our ability to produce both wheat and wool, other types of technological improvement may increase our ability to produce only one of them. For example, the development of a new disease-resistant strain of wheat will increase our ability to produce wheat, but not wool. In this case, illustrated in Figure 2-5, nothing will happen to the place where the production possibilities curve meets the axis for clothing. If we direct all our resources to the production of clothing, we can still produce no more than shown by point *F*. However, if we direct all our resources to wheat, we can produce more; the other end of the PPC moves upward along the food axis, from *A* to *B*. Thus, the development of the new strain of wheat causes the PPC to move upward, from $PPC_1$ to $PPC_3$.

## GROWTH: THE CHOICE BETWEEN CONSUMER GOODS AND CAPITAL GOODS

As an alternative to technological change, consider the second source of growth listed above: an increase in the quantity of capital. The capital we have today is limited. However, capital itself can be produced. The quantity of capital that we will have in the year 2000 will be determined in large part by how much of our resources we choose to devote this year and in coming years to producing capital rather than consumer goods.

In order to study this choice, we must look at a different production possibilities curve — not one showing food and clothing but, rather, one showing the choice between the production of capital goods (such as machines and factories) and the production of consumer goods (such as food, clothing, and TV sets).

In Figure 2-6 on page 38, two hypothetical economies are compared. Starting in 1990, these two countries faced the same initial production possibilities curve ($PPC_{today}$). The citizens of Extravagania (on the left) believe in living for the moment. They produce mostly consumption goods and very few capital goods (at point *A*). As a result, their capital stock will be not much greater in 2000 than it is today, so their PPC will shift out very little. In contrast, the citizens of Thriftiana (on the right) keep down the production of consumer goods in order to build more capital goods (at point *B*). By the year 2000, their productive capacity will be greatly increased, as shown by the large outward movement of the PPC. Because they have given up so much consumption today, their income (and ability to consume) will be much greater in the future. Thus, any society faces a choice: How much consumption should it sacrifice now in order to be able to consume more in the future?

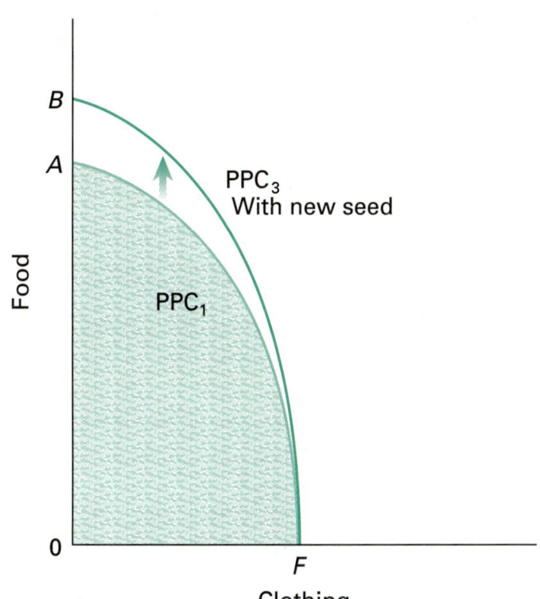


**FIGURE 2-5 Technological improvement in a single good.**

When a new, improved strain of wheat is developed, the production possibilities curve moves out to $PPC_3$.

### Capital Imports and Growth

In the example illustrated by Figure 2-6, we have assumed that the increase in the capital stock of a country is made possible because its citizens are willing to wait—that is, they are willing to forgo a certain amount of present consumption. But, a country's own citizens do not necessarily have to forgo consumption in order for the country's capital stock to increase. For example, an increase in Canada's capital stock may be financed by residents of *foreign* countries, either through their lending money to Canadians, or through direct foreign investment in Canada. (An example of foreign lending to Canadians would be if foreigners bought $10 million worth of bonds issued by B.C. Hydro, with the proceeds being used to finance the building of a new generating station. Direct investment occurs when foreigners control the capital created in Canada, for example, if Suzuki of

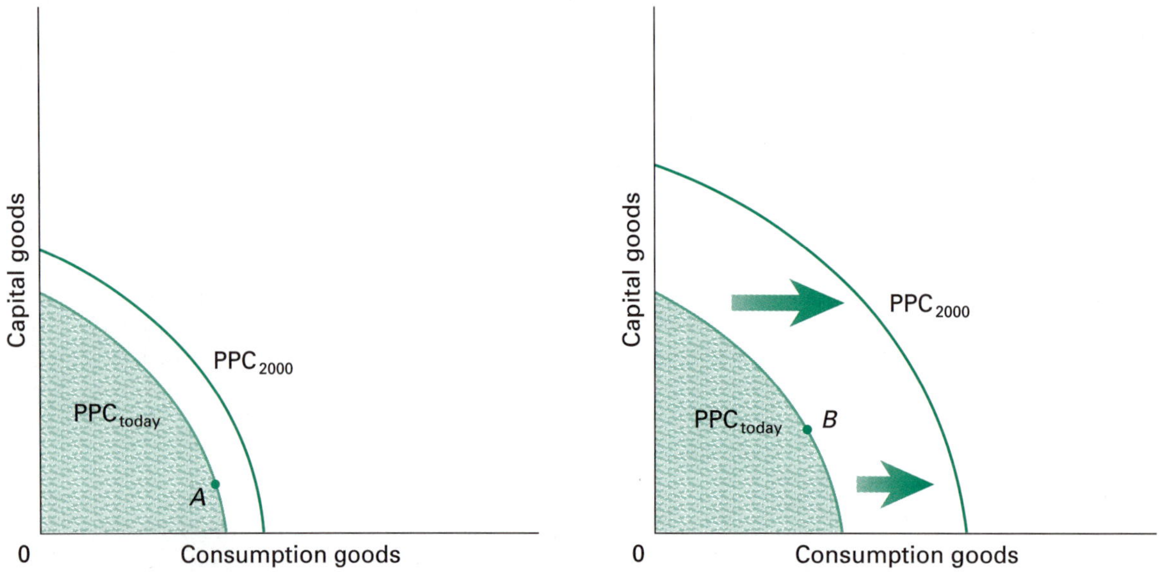


**FIGURE 2-6 Capital formation now helps to determine future productive capacity.**

**(a) Extravagania.** Most productive capacity is directed toward the production of consumer goods (point *A*). Little investment takes place. The result is slow growth.

**(b) Thriftiana.** Much of current (1990) capacity is used to produce capital goods (point *B*). The result is rapid growth, illustrated by a large outward movement of the production possibilities curve by the year 2000.

Japan spends $100 million to construct an assembly plant near Woodstock, Ont.) When increases in Canada's capital stock are financed by foreigners in either of these ways, it is foreigners, not Canadians, who are forgoing present consumption in order to make the increased capital formation possible: This process is referred to as a ***capital inflow*** or ***capital imports*** into Canada.

When foreigners finance a part of the increase in a country's capital stock, the country is said to have a *capital inflow*, or to be *importing capital.*

Although capital inflows can help to move the production possibilities curve outward at a rapid pace, not all of this benefit goes to Canadians. Some goes to the foreigners who have to be paid a return on their investment. To illustrate this, suppose that Canada's production possibilities curve has expanded from $PPC_{today}$ to $PPC_{2000}$ in panel (b) of Figure 2-6 through large-scale capital imports. While it will still be true that the large capital stock in the year 2000 will make it possible for us to produce a large amount of goods and services in that year, some of our output will have to go to the foreign capitalists as a return on their capital.

## Economic Development: The Problem of Takeoff

For some countries, the question of growth may be approached in a relatively relaxed manner. For countries such as Canada or the United States the issue is not a matter of life or death. Even if we consume most of our current output and grow only slowly, we will still be comfortable in the year 2000. The same is true for Japan and for the countries of Western Europe. (However, Japan conspicuously has not taken a relaxed approach to the growth question. Japan has been "Thriftiana" *par excellence*, investing a large share of national output in new plant and equipment, and growing rapidly.)

Some other countries, however, face a much more critical situation. They are so poor that they can scarcely take a relaxed view either of the present or of the future. Unless they can import capital, they face a cruel dilemma (illustrated in Figure 2-7). If they con-

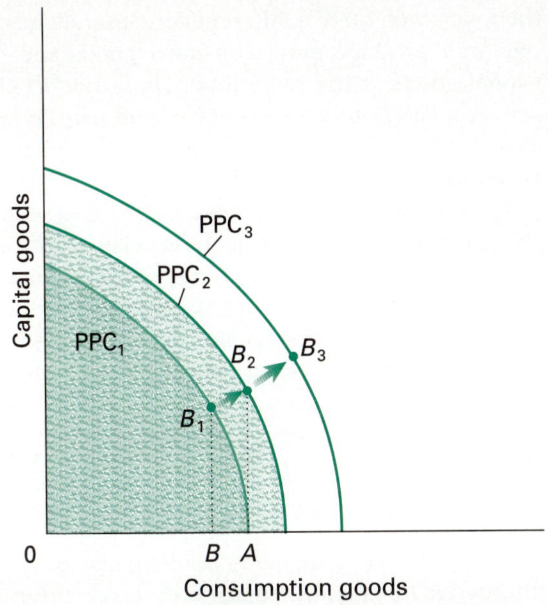


**FIGURE 2-7 "Takeoff" into economic growth.**
If point $B_1$ is initially chosen (on PPC$_1$), then growth will occur. The economy can move progressively to $B_2$, $B_3$, and beyond. However, the initial choice of $B_1$ rather than $A$ will require people to forgo some consumption goods, as measured by the distance $AB$. The problem therefore is: What short-term miseries will be caused by the choice of $B_1$ rather than $A$?

sume all their current output (at point $A$), then they will remain stuck on PPC$_1$. Their future will be just as bleak as the present.[5] On the other hand, if they want to grow, they will have to produce capital, and this means cutting back on their production of consumer goods. If they choose the growth strategy and move initially to point $B_1$, then the production of consumer goods will decrease from $A$ to $B$.) Since the already low level of consumption is depressed further, more people may starve.

In the long run, the growth strategy pays off. Because capital is produced at $B_1$, productive capacity grows. The production possibilities curve shifts out to PPC$_2$. Now the nation can pick point $B_2$, where it not only produces capital goods, but also consumes as much as it originally did at $A$ ($B_2$ is directly above point $A$). The economy has achieved a ***takeoff***. Because it is now producing capital goods, its PPC is continuously moving out. Consequently, the nation can produce ever increasing amounts of both consumer and capital goods.

However, the long-run process does not solve the painful problem of the present: Should consumption be depressed, at the possible risk of starvation, in order to initiate the growth process? How can the economy take off without the danger of a crackup halfway down the runway? (The danger may be political as well as economic. If a government chooses point $B_1$, the population may be unimpressed with "pie in the sky"—the promise of a brighter future. They may vote the government out, or rebel.)

One possible solution to this difficult dilemma lies in capital imports from other countries. Richer countries can provide the resources for the early stages of growth, either by granting aid or through private investment. (For example, a Canadian clothing manufacturer might build a plant in the developing country.) In this way, economic takeoff might occur without the sacrifices that capital formation otherwise requires.

## AN INTRODUCTION TO ECONOMIC THEORY: THE NEED TO SIMPLIFY

The production possibilities curve is the first piece of theoretical equipment that the beginning economics student typically encounters. There will be many more. At this early stage, it is appropriate to address directly a problem that often bothers both beginning and advanced students of economics. The production possibilities curve, like many other theoretical tools that will be introduced in later chapters, represents a gross *simplification* of the real world. When the PPC is drawn, it is assumed that only two types of goods can be produced: food and clothing, or consumer goods and capital goods. (Diagrams are limited to two alternatives because the printed page has only two dimensions.) Yet obviously, there are thousands of goods produced in the modern economy. This raises a question: With our simple approach, can we say anything of relevance to the real world?

[5] In this simplified example, it is assumed that only capital changes, and that technology and population remain constant. In fact, all three major determinants of growth (capital, labour, and technology) may change. If technology improves, growth may occur even in the absence of investment; the outlook is not as bleak as suggested above. On the other hand, population pressures may make the outlook even worse. As population grows, output must grow if the already low standard of living is not to fall even lower. Thus, just to maintain the present standard, some capital formation may be required.

## Theory Necessarily Involves Simplification

If we wished to describe the real world in detail, we could go on without end. A complete description would be useless as a guide to private behaviour or public policy; it would be too complex. In a sense, theory is like a map. A road map is necessarily incomplete. In many ways, it is not very accurate, and, indeed, downright wrong. Towns and villages are not round circles. Roads of various qualities do not really come in different colours. If a road map were more realistic, it would be less useful for its intended purpose. If it tried to show every house and every tree, it would be an incomprehensible jumble of detail. A road map is useful precisely because it *is* a simplification that shows in stark outline the various roads that may be travelled. Similarly, the objective of economic theory is to draw in stark outline the important relationships among producers and consumers.

When details are left out of a road map, it becomes more useful as a guide for the auto traveller. However, it becomes less useful for other purposes. A road map is a poor guide for airplane pilots, for example, who instead need a map with the height of mountains marked clearly. A road map is also a poor guide for sales managers, who need a map showing regional sales targets and staff assignments. The way in which a map is constructed depends on its intended use. Various maps are "true," but they do not represent the "whole truth." An important question for a map user thus becomes: Do I have the best map for my purpose?

The same generalization holds for economic ***theory***. If we wish to study long-run growth, we may use quite different theoretical tools from those we would use to study short-term fluctuations. If we want to study the consequences of price controls on the housing market, we may use different tools from those we would choose to investigate the economic consequences of a cut in Old Age Security benefits. Just as in the case of the map, the "best" theory cannot be identified unless we know the purposes for which it is to be used.

The production possibilities curve is a theoretical tool whose purpose is to illustrate the concept of scarcity. If we begin on the PPC with our resources fully employed, then we can come to a significant conclusion: To produce more of one good, we will have to cut back on the production of some other good or service. The "if" clause is important. It tells us that when we consider points along the PPC, we are making an assumption— that resources are fully utilized. When the "if" clause is violated—when the economy begins with large-scale unemployment—then we reach quite a different conclusion: The economy *can* produce more consumer goods and more capital goods at the same time. Thus, the "if" clause acts as a label on our theoretical road map. It makes clear what assumptions we are making and tells us when the map can be used.

For the novice and old hand alike, it is essential to recognize and remember such "if" clauses. We must pay attention to the assumptions underlying any theory that we use. If we don't, we may use the wrong theory, and make serious policy mistakes—just as the pilot who uses the wrong map may fly a plane into the nearest mountaintop.

## The Distinction Between Positive and Normative Economics

The uses of theory are many, but they may be divided into two main families. ***Positive*** or ***descriptive economics*** aims at understanding how the economy works. It is directed toward explaining the world as it is, and how various forces can cause it to change. In contrast, ***normative economics*** deals with the way the world (or some small segment of it) *ought* to be.

A debate over a positive statement can often be settled by an appeal to the facts. For example, the following is a positive statement: "Canadian newsprint production last year was 100 million tonnes." By looking up the statistics, we can find out whether this was true. A more complicated positive statement is: "There are millions of barrels of oil under the Beaufort Sea." With a geological study, we can discover whether this is likely to be so. A third positive statement is this: "If one cubic metre of tar sands is passed through steam, five litres of oil will flow out of the sand." By experimentation, we can discover whether this is generally true.

A normative statement is more complex: for example, "We ought to extract oil in large quantities from the bottom of the Beaufort Sea." Facts are relevant here. If there is no oil under the Beaufort Sea (a positive conclusion), then the normative statement that we ought to extract oil must be rejected for the very simple reason that it can't be done. However, facts alone will seldom settle a dispute over a normative statement since it is based on something more — on a view regarding appropriate goals or ethical values. A normative statement involves a value judgement, a judgement about what ought to be. It is possible for well-informed individuals of exemplary character to disagree over normative statements, even when they agree completely regarding the facts. For example, they may agree that there is, in fact, a large quantity of oil under the Beaufort Sea. Nevertheless, they may disagree over whether it should be extracted. These differences may develop, perhaps, over the relative importance of a plentiful supply of heating oil as compared with the damage to the Arctic environment that might accompany the extraction of oil; or from a difference of opinion over whether the Canadian taxpayer should be required to provide a subsidy necessary for this development.

Although some positive statements may be easily settled by looking at the facts, others may be much more difficult to judge. This is particularly true of statements making claims about causation. They may be quite controversial because the facts are not easily untangled. For example: "If there is no growth in the money stock next year, then inflation will fall to zero"; or, "If income tax rates are increased by 5%, government revenues will increase by $20 billion next year"; or, "Rent controls have little effect on the number of apartments constructed each year."

In evaluating such statements, economists and other social scientists have two major disadvantages as compared with natural scientists. First, experiments are difficult or impossible in many instances. Society is not the plaything of economists. They do not have the power to conduct an experiment in which one large city is subjected to rent control while a similar city is not, simply to estimate the effects of rent control. Nevertheless, economists do have factual evidence to study. By looking at situations where rent controls have actually been imposed by the government, they may be able to estimate the effects of those controls. Moreover, in special situations, economic experiments are possible, particularly when the government is eager to know the results. For example, experiments have been undertaken to determine whether people work less when they are provided with a minimum income by the government.

The second disadvantage is that the social sciences deal with the behaviour of people, and behaviour can change. Suppose we estimate corporate profits next year to be $35 billion. We might carelessly conclude that, if the profits tax is raised by 10%, the government will receive an additional $3.5 billion in revenues. But this is not necessarily so. With a higher tax rate, businesses may behave differently, in order to reduce the taxes they have to pay. Furthermore, even if we have evidence on how businesses have responded to a 10% tax increase in the past, we cannot be certain that they will respond the same way in the future. They may have become more imaginative in finding ways to avoid taxes. The possibility that people will learn and change their behaviour has been one of the most interesting areas of research in economics in recent years.

In contrast, physical scientists study a relatively stable and predictable universe. Gravity works the same way today as it did in Newton's time.

## KEY POINTS

1. *Scarcity* is a fundamental economic problem. Because wants are virtually unlimited and resources are scarce, we are faced with the need to make *choices*.

2. The choices open to society are illustrated by the *production possibilities curve*. This illustrates the concept of the *opportunity cost* of a good, A, which is the amount of another good, B that must be given up to produce good A.

3. Not all resources are identical. For example, the land of Manitoba is different from the land of Nova Scotia. As a consequence, opportunity cost generally increases as more of a good is produced. For example, as more wool is produced, more and more wheat must be given up for each additional unit of wool. As a result, the production possibilities curve normally bows outward.

4. The production possibilities curve is a frontier, representing the choices open to society if there is full utilization of the available resources of land, labour, and capital. If there is large-scale unemployment, then production occurs at a point *within* this frontier.

5. The economy can grow and the production possibilities curve can move outward if:
   (a) technology improves;
   (b) the capital stock grows;
   (c) and/or the labour force grows.

6. By giving up consumer goods at present, we can produce more capital goods, and thus have a

growing economy. The production of capital goods (investment), therefore, represents a choice of more future production instead of present consumption.

7. Through capital imports, a country may achieve economic growth without reducing its present consumption. However, some of the extra production that results from capital imports has to be used to pay foreign capitalists for the use of their capital.

8. For the poorest countries, a choice between present consumption and growth is particularly painful. If consumption is suppressed in order to grow more rapidly, people may starve. But growth is essential to raise a low standard of living.

9. Like other theoretical concepts, the production possibilities curve represents a simplification. Because the world is so complex, theory cannot reflect the "whole truth." Nevertheless, a theory—like a road map—can be valuable if it is used correctly. In order to determine the appropriate uses of a theory, it is important to identify the assumptions on which the theory was developed.

## KEY TERMS

**goods**
**services**
**resources**
**scarcity**
**factors of production**
**land (natural resources)**
**labour**
**capital**
**willingness to wait**
**investment**
**financial vs. real capital**
**entrepreneur**
**production possibilities curve**
**opportunity cost**
**increasing opportunity cost**
**growth**
**takeoff**
**capital inflow (capital imports)**
**positive (descriptive) economics**
**normative economics**
**theory**

## PROBLEMS

2-1. Some economists like to define economics broadly, as the study of how people make their living, of the problems they encounter in doing so, and of the ways in which they can reduce these problems. Another common definition of economics is tied closely to the idea of scarcity. Economics is "the study of the allocation of scarce resources to satisfy alternative, competing human wants."

Clearly, scarcity is an important part of economics. We cannot have all the goods and services we want. However, one of the central economic problems defined in Chapter 1 cannot be attributed to a scarcity of resources. Which one? Why is this problem not attributable to a scarcity of resources? Is this problem covered by the broader definition of economics?

2-2. "Wants aren't insatiable. The economic wants of Peter Pocklington have been satisfied. There is no prospect that he will spend all his money before he dies. His consumption is not limited by his income." Do you agree? Does your answer raise problems for the main theme of this chapter: that wants cannot all be satisfied with the goods and services produced from our limited resources? Why or why not?

2-3. "The more capital goods we produce, the more the Canadian economy will grow, and the more we and our children will be able to consume in the future. Therefore, the government should encourage capital formation." Do you agree or disagree? Why?

2-4. Does your answer to question 2-3 fall under the heading of "positive" or "normative" economics? Why?

# CHAPTER 3

# SPECIALIZATION, EXCHANGE, AND MONEY

*Money . . . is not of the wheels of trade: it is the oil which renders the motion of the wheels smooth and easy.*

*David Hume*

The early French colony at Quebec was a forbidding place in winter, where temperatures often fell to −30° C. Keeping warm was the first problem. Getting supplies from France was a close second. During the winter, the St. Lawrence River was clogged with ice.

Of the many things that the colony lacked, money was one. Not only did ships have difficulty sailing up the river but, even when they did come, they had little currency; the colony's sponsors in France were reluctant to send money. The colonists found that barter was very cumbersome; even in a simple economy, money was essential. What could they do? They hit upon an ingenious solution. They used playing cards as money. The man with an ace in his pocket often had a smile on his face.

In the modern economy, as in the early colonies, money plays a central role. Over the decades, production has become increasingly specialized with the development of new machinery and equipment. ***Specialization*** contributes to efficiency; often, workers can produce more by specializing. But, specialization necessitates ***exchange***. A farmer who produces only beef wants to exchange some of that beef for clothing, cars, dental care, and a whole list of other products.

This chapter will explain:

- The two types of exchange:
    1. barter
    2. exchange for money
- Why exchange is so much simpler with money than barter.
- How people can gain from specialization and exchange.

## EXCHANGE: THE BARTER ECONOMY

In a ***barter*** system, no money is used: one good or service is exchanged directly for another. The farmer specializing in the production of beef may find a hungry barber and thus get a haircut, or find a hungry tailor and thus exchange meat for a suit of clothes, or find a hungry dentist and thus obtain dental treatment. A simple barter transaction is illustrated in Figure 3-1. In a barter economy, there are dozens of such bilateral (two-way) transactions: between the farmer and the tailor; between the farmer and the dentist; between the dentist and the tailor; and so on.

Clearly, barter is inefficient. Farmers might spend half their time producing beef, and the other half searching for someone willing to make the right trade.

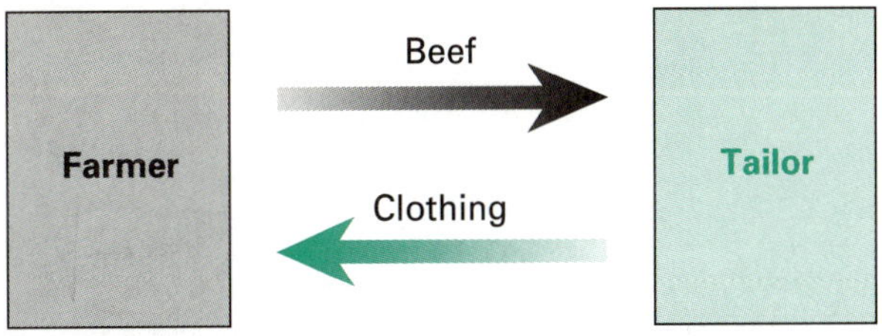


**FIGURE 3-1 Barter.**
With barter, no money is used. The farmer exchanges beef directly for clothing. Transactions involve only two parties—in this case, the farmer and the tailor.

Barter requires a ***coincidence of wants***: Those engaged in barter must each have a product that the other wants. The farmer not only must find someone who wants beef, but that someone must also be able to provide something in exchange that the farmer wants. Furthermore, with barter, there is a problem of ***indivisibility***. A suit of clothes—or an automobile, or a house — should be bought all at once, and not in pieces. To illustrate, suppose that a beef farmer who wants a suit of clothes has been lucky enough to find a tailor who wants meat and is willing to make a trade. The suit of clothes may be worth 50 kg of beef, and the farmer may be quite willing to give up this amount. The problem is that the tailor may not be *that* hungry, perhaps wanting only 25 kg. In a barter economy, what is the farmer to do? Get only the jacket from this tailor, and set out to find another hungry tailor in order to obtain a pair of pants? If the farmer does so, what are the chances that the pants will match?

## EXCHANGE WITH MONEY

With money, exchange is much easier. It is no longer necessary for wants to coincide. In order to get a suit of clothing, the farmer need not find a hungry tailor, but only someone willing to pay money for the beef. The farmer can then take the money and buy the suit of clothes. Money represents ***general purchasing power*** — that is, it can be used to buy any of the goods and services offered for sale. Therefore, complex transactions among many parties are possible with money. Figure 3-2 gives a simple illustration with three parties. Actual transactions in a monetary economy may be very complex, with dozens or hundreds of participants.

Money also solves the problem of indivisibility. The farmer can sell the whole carcass of beef for money, and use the proceeds to buy a complete set of clothes. It doesn't matter how much beef the tailor wants.

In the simple barter economy, there is no clear distinction between seller and buyer, or between producer and consumer. When bartering beef for clothing, the farmer is at the same time both a seller (of beef) and a buyer (of clothing). In a monetary economy, in contrast, there is a *clear distinction between seller and buyer*. In the beef market, the farmer is the seller; the hungry tailor is the buyer. The farmer is the producer; the tailor is the consumer.

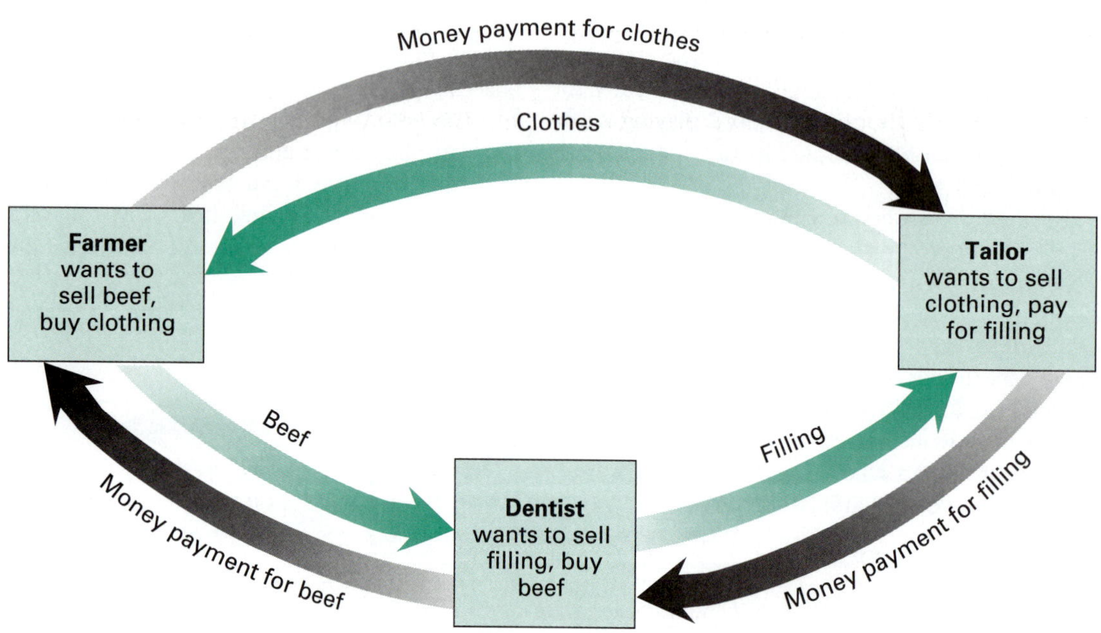


**FIGURE 3-2 Multilateral transactions in a money economy.**
In a money economy, multilateral transactions among many participants are possible. The farmer gets clothing from the tailor, even though the tailor doesn't want to buy the farmer's beef.

## The Circular Flow of Expenditures and Income

The distinction between the producer and consumer in a money economy is illustrated in Figure 3-3. Producers — or *businesses* — are put in the right-hand box; consumers — or *households* — in the left. Transactions between the two groups are illustrated in the loops. In the top loops, consumers' expenditures for goods and services are shown. Beef, clothing, and a host of other products are bought with money.

In the lower loops, transactions in economic resources are shown. In a complex exchange economy, not only are consumer goods bought and sold for money; so are resources. In order to be able to buy food and other goods, households must have money income. They acquire money by providing the labour and other resources that are the inputs of the business sector. For example, workers provide their labour in exchange for wages and salaries, and owners of land provide their property in exchange for rents.

Figure 3-3 is simplified. For example, it does not include government, which is a major purchaser of goods and services. (Remember the purpose of simplification discussed in Chapter 2: to show important relationships in sharp outline.) Figure 3-3 shows the circular flow of payments — that is, how businesses use the receipts from sales to pay their wages, salaries, and other costs of production, while households use their income receipts from wages, salaries, etc., to buy consumer goods.

## THE MONETARY SYSTEM

Because barter is so inefficient, people turn naturally to the use of money. One example was the early colony at Quebec, with its playing card money.

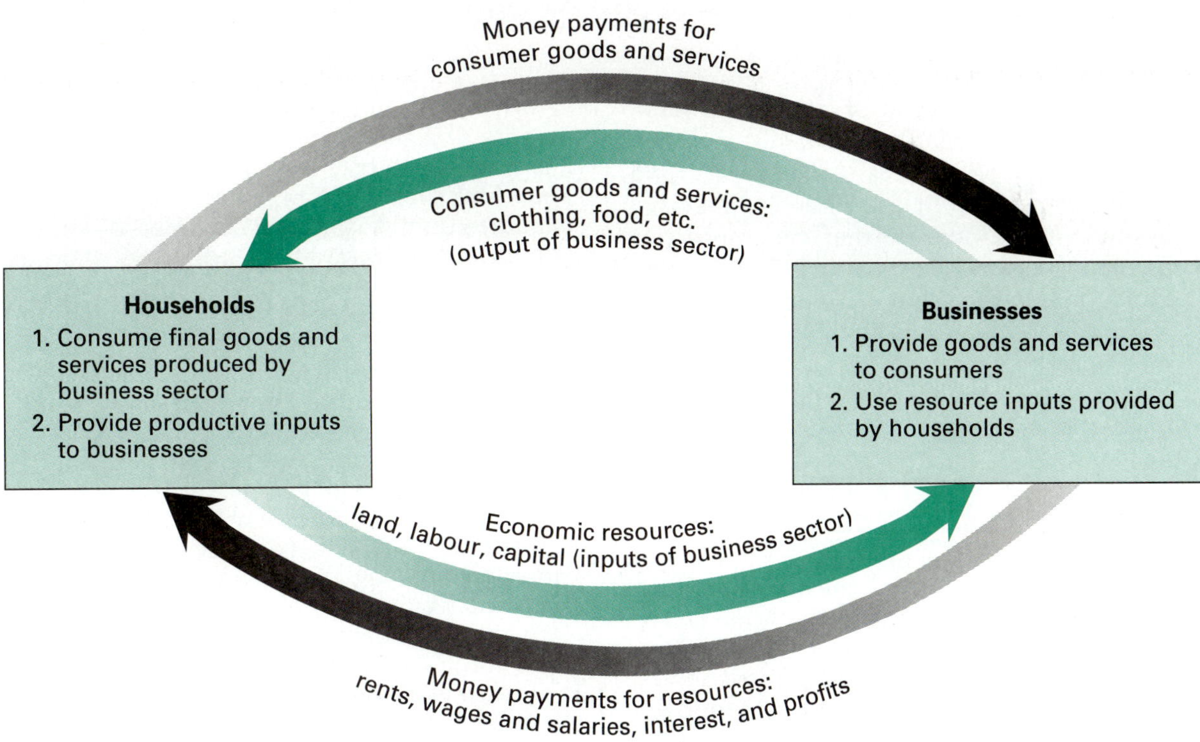


**FIGURE 3-3 The flow of goods, services, resources, and money payments in a simple economy.**
Monetary payments are shown in the outer loop. These pay for the flow of goods and services and resources shown in the inner loop.

The powerful tendency for money to appear may also be illustrated by an example of an economy that began without money: the prisoner-of-war camp of World War II.[1] Economic relations in such a camp were primitive; the range of goods was very limited. But, some things were available: rations supplied by the German captors, and the Red Cross parcels that arrived periodically. These parcels contained a variety of items, such as canned beef, jam, margarine, and cigarettes. Nonsmokers who received cigarettes were eager to trade them for other items. The basis was established for exchange.

At first, trading was rough and ready, with no clear picture of the relative values of the various items. In one instance, a prisoner started around the camp with only a can of cheese and five cigarettes, and returned with a complete Red Cross parcel. He did so by buying goods where they were cheap, and selling them where they were dear. However, as time went by, the relative prices of various goods became more stable, and all prices came to be quoted in terms of cigarettes. For example, a can of cheese was worth seven cigarettes. Not only did cigarettes become the measuring rod for quoting prices, but they were used as the ***common medium of exchange*** — that is, cigarettes were the item used to buy goods. Cigarettes became the money of the POW camp. This was a natural evolution; there was no government to decree that cigarettes were money, and no authority to enforce that choice. At other times and in other societies, other items have been used as money: items as diverse as beads, porpoise teeth, rice, salt, wampum, stones, and even woodpecker scalps. (Box 3-1 describes another example.)

[1] This illustration is based on R.A. Radford, "The Economic Organization of a P.O.W. Camp," *Economica* (November 1945): 189–201.

## APPLICATIONS AND ILLUSTRATIONS — BOX 3-1

### Early Money on the Island of Uap†

On the south-sea island of Uap, the medium of exchange is called fei. This currency consists of large, solid, thick stone wheels ranging in diameter from one to twelve feet, and in the center a hole, so that the stones may be slung on poles and carried. They are not found on Uap itself, but are quarried in Babelthuap, some four hundred miles away. Size is the most important factor, but also the fei must be of a certain fine, white, close-grained limestone. A traveler to Uap described the fei as follows:

> A feature of this stone currency, which is also an equally noteworthy tribute to Uap honesty, is that its owner does not need to actually possess it. After concluding a bargain which involves a fei too large to be conveniently moved, its new owner is quite content to accept the bare acknowledgment of ownership; and without so much as a mark to indicate the exchange, the coin remains undisturbed on the former owner's premises.
>
> There was in a village nearby a family whose wealth was unquestioned — acknowledged by every one, and yet no one, not even the family itself, had ever laid eye on this wealth; it consisted of an enormous fei lying at the bottom of the sea! Many years ago an ancestor of this family, on an expedition after fei, secured this remarkable stone, which was placed on a raft to be towed homeward. A violent storm arose and the party, to save their lives, were obliged to cut the raft adrift, and the stone sank out of sight. When they reached home, they all testified that the fei was of magnificent proportions and extraordinary quality, and that it was lost through no fault of the owners. Thereupon it was universally considered that the mere accident of its loss overboard was too trifling to mention. The purchasing power of the stone remained, therefore, as valid as if it were leaning visibly against the side of the owner's house.

† Abridged, from Norman Angell, *The Story of Money* (New York: Garden City Publishing Co., 1929), pp. 88–89.

## Monetary Problems in the POW Camp

Cigarette money made the primitive economy of the prisoner-of-war camp more efficient. But problems occurred, including problems quite similar to those of more advanced monetary systems. As part of the natural trend toward simplification, distinctions among different brands of cigarettes became blurred. Although all cigarettes were not equally desirable to smokers, all were equal as money. In paying for beef or other items, a cigarette was a cigarette. What was the consequence? Smokers held back the desirable brands for their personal use and spent the others. The less desirable cigarettes, therefore, were the ones used as money; the "good" cigarettes were smoked. This illustrates ***Gresham's Law***. This law, first enunciated by Elizabethan financier Sir Thomas Gresham (1519–1579), is popularly and loosely abbreviated: "Bad money drives out good." In this case, "bad" cigarettes drove "good" cigarettes out of circulation as money. (The good cigarettes were smoked instead.)

> *Gresham's Law:* If there are two types of money whose values in exchange are equal while their values in another use (like consumption) are different, the more valuable item will be retained for its other use while the less valuable item will continue to circulate as money. Thus, the "bad" (less valuable) money drives the "good" (more valuable) money out of circulation.

The tendency for every cigarette to be treated as equal to every other cigarette caused another monetary problem. As a cigarette was a cigarette, prisoners often pulled out a few strands of tobacco before passing a cigarette along. This corresponds precisely to a problem when gold coins circulate: There is a temptation to "clip" coins by chipping off bits of gold. Furthermore, the cigarette currency became "debased": Some enterprising prisoners rolled cigarettes from pipe tobacco or broke down cigarettes and rerolled them, reducing the amount of tobacco in each. Similarly, governments have from time to time given in to the temptation to engage in ***debasement of the currency***: melting down gold and silver coins, and reissuing them with a lower metal content. (Private entrepreneurs have had a strong incentive to do the same, but they have been discouraged throughout history by severe punishments against counterfeiting.)

However, it was not clipping or debasement that led to the greatest monetary problems in the POW camp. As long as there was a balanced inflow of both cigarettes and other goods, the exchange system of the camp worked reasonably well. But, from time to time, the weekly Red Cross issue of 25 or 50 cigarettes per prisoner was interrupted. As the existing stock of cigarettes was consumed by smokers, cigarettes became more and more scarce. Desperate smokers had to offer more and more to get cigarettes; their value skyrocketed. To put the same point another way: Other goods now exchanged for fewer and fewer cigarettes. A can of beef which previously sold for 20 cigarettes dropped in value to 15, 10, or even fewer cigarettes. Thus, there was a ***deflation***—a decline in the prices of other goods, measured in terms of money.

As cigarettes became increasingly scarce and prices continued to fall, prisoners began to revert to barter in exchanging other goods. Smokers who had the few remaining cigarettes were reluctant to give them up to make purchases. Then, from time to time, thousands of cigarettes would arrive at the camp during a brief period. Prices soared; in other words, the value of cigarettes fell. Prisoners became reluctant to accept cigarettes in payment for other goods. Once again, barter became common. Thus, *the monetary system worked smoothly only so long as a reasonable balance was kept between the quantity of money (cigarettes) and the quantity of other goods.*

Several characteristics of a good monetary system may be drawn out of this story of the "cigarette standard":

1. A smoothly operating monetary system should be made up of money whose value is *uniform*. Nonuniform money will set Gresham's law into operation, with "bad" money driving "good" money out of circulation. In our economy, the Bank of Canada has the responsibility to assure that money is uniform. It is the institution that issues paper currency. It matters not whether the bills I have in my pocket are crisp and new, or whether they are tattered and soiled. The Bank of Canada will replace a $2 bill, say, with a new bill of equal value when it becomes excessively worn. This means that it represents $2 in value to anyone. And because the Bank guarantees that I can exchange a $2 bill for coins any time I want to do so, I don't care whether I get a $2 bill or two loonies or eight quarters in change when I make a purchase at the variety store, even though the metal in the coins is more valuable than the paper in the $2 bill.

   This uniformity in the value of each dollar obviously adds to the ease of exchange—and it means that Gresham's law does not operate in our modern economy.

2. A second important characteristic of a good monetary system is that there be the *proper quantity of money*, neither too much nor too little. In Canada, the responsibility for controlling the quantity of money also lies with the Bank of Canada. This important topic will be studied in Parts 3 and 4 of this book.

## COMPARATIVE ADVANTAGE: A REASON TO SPECIALIZE

Money, the development of markets, and — perhaps equally important — the development of a sophisticated transportation and communications system, all make possible a high degree of specialization in production. They make specialization possible and relatively smooth, but they don't provide a reason why specialization is advantageous in the first place. Near the beginning of the chapter, an answer was suggested: Specialization can add to efficiency. Specialization generates *gains*. It is now time to explain just how. A key concept in the explanation is the principle of ***comparative advantage***. To understand this principle, it is useful to look first at the simpler concept of ***absolute advantage***.

A good is often made in the place that is best suited for its production: wood products in British Columbia, corn in Iowa, bananas in the tropical lands of Central America, coffee in the cool highlands of Colombia, and so on. In technical terms, there is some tendency for a good to be produced in the area that has an absolute advantage in its production.

> A country (or region or individual) has an *absolute advantage* in the production of a good if it can produce that good with fewer resources (less land, labour, and capital) than can other countries (or regions or individuals).

Note that this principle applies to specialization among individuals within a city or town. Consider the case of the lawyer and the professional gardener. The lawyer is better at drawing up legal documents and the gardener generally is better at gardening, so it is in the interest of each to specialize in the occupation in which he or she has an absolute advantage.

However, the truth is often more complicated than this. By looking at the complications, we will be led to the idea of comparative advantage. Suppose a certain lawyer is better at gardening than the gardener; she's faster and more effective — in short, she has a "greener thumb." She has an absolute advantage in both the law and gardening. If absolute advantage were the key, she would practise law and do her own gardening as well.

Does this necessarily happen? The answer: No. Unless this lawyer positively enjoys gardening as a recreation, she will leave the gardening to the professional. Why? Even though the lawyer, being an excellent gardener, can do as much gardening in one hour (let us say) as the gardener could in two, she will be better off to stick to law and hire the gardener to work on the flowers and shrubbery. Why? In one hour's work, the lawyer can draw up a will, for which she charges $50. The gardener's time, in contrast, is worth only $5 per hour. By spending the hour on the law rather than gardening, the lawyer comes out ahead. She earns $50, and can hire the gardener for $10 to put in two hours to get the gardening done. The lawyer gains $40 by sticking to law for that one hour. (This is explained in more detail in Box 3-2.)

The gardener also gains through specialization. Although he has to work 10 hours in order to earn the $50 needed to hire the lawyer to draw up his will, it would take him much more time to draw up the will himself. He would have to spend many hours — as many as 100, perhaps — poring over law books just to learn the basic traps to avoid in drawing up a will. (Even after spending the 100 hours, he could not be sure that he might not have missed something very simple that the lawyer learned in her many years of study.) Thus, by spending 10 hours on gardening and using the income to buy the lawyer's time, the gardener gains: He gets a better will than he could have gotten by struggling with legal books for a full 100 hours.

This example leads to two important conclusions:

1. There are *mutual benefits* from specialization and exchange. The lawyer gains by specializing and hiring someone else to do the gardening. The gardener likewise gains, getting a better will in less time than by trying to do it himself.
2. Absolute advantage is *not* necessary for mutually beneficial specialization. The lawyer has an absolute advantage in both gardening and law; the gardener has an absolute disadvantage in both. But, the lawyer has a comparative advantage in law; the gardener has a comparative advantage in gardening. Both gain from specialization.

British economist David Ricardo enunciated the principle of comparative advantage in the early nineteenth century to illustrate how countries gain from international trade. But comparative advantage pro-

## TOOLS AND TECHNIQUES — BOX 3-2
## Illustration of Comparative Advantage

A. Assume the following:
   1. In one hour, the lawyer can plant 20 flowers.
   2. In one hour, the gardener can plant 10 flowers. (Therefore, the lawyer has the absolute advantage in gardening.)
   3. The lawyer's time, in the practice of law, is worth $50 per hour.
   4. The gardener's time, in gardening, is worth $5 per hour.

B. Question: How should the lawyer have 20 flowers planted?

   Option 1: Do it herself, spending one hour.
   Cost: She gives up the $50 she could have earned by practising law for that hour.

   Option 2: Stick to the law, and hire the gardener to plant the 20 flowers.
   Cost: Two hours of gardener's time at $5 per hour, making a total of $10.

C. Decision: Choose option 2.
   Spend the available hour practising law, earning $50. Hire the gardener to do the planting for $10. Net advantage over option 1: $40.

D. Conclusion: The lawyer has the comparative advantage in law.

vides a general explanation of the advantages of specialization; it is just as relevant to domestic as to international trade. Nevertheless, it is customary to follow Ricardo and consider this principle as part of the study of international economics. We follow the custom, and put off our detailed analysis of comparative advantage to the chapter on international trade in the *Microeconomics* volume that forms a companion to this book. For the moment, we note that the concept of comparative advantage is related to opportunity cost.

> If two individuals (or cities or nations) have different opportunity costs of producing a good or service, the individual (or city or nation) with the lower opportunity cost has the *comparative advantage* in that good or service.

The opportunity cost is the alternative forgone. To prepare a will, the lawyer's opportunity cost is the 20 flowers that she could have planted instead. (Details are in Box 3-2.) In contrast, the gardener would have faced a much higher opportunity cost to prepare a will. It would take him 100 hours, in which he alternatively could plant 1000 flowers. Since the lawyer's opportunity cost of drawing up a will is lower than the gardener's (20 flowers versus 1000), the lawyer has the comparative advantage in law. She will specialize in this, leaving the flowers to the gardener. Furthermore, it follows directly that the gardener has the comparative advantage in gardening. To plant a flower, he gives up only one-thousandth of a will, compared to the one-twentieth forgone by the lawyer. Accordingly, the gardener will stick to his gardening, and leave the drafting of the will to the lawyer.

Comparative advantage, then, provides one reason to specialize. It may be considered the first great propellant driving the wheels of commerce, while money acts as the grease, making the machine run with less friction. But, there is also a second fundamental reason to specialize.

## ECONOMIES OF SCALE: ANOTHER REASON TO SPECIALIZE

Consider two small cities that are identical in all respects. Suppose that the citizens of these cities want both bicycles and lawnmowers, but that neither city has any basic advantage in the production of either good. Will each city then produce its own, without any trade existing between the two? Probably not. It is likely that one city will specialize in bicycles, and the other in lawnmowers. Why?

The answer is, ***economies of scale***. To understand what this term means, first assume that there is no specialization. Each city directs half its productive resources into the manufacture of bicycles and half into the manufacture of lawnmowers, thus producing 1000 bicycles and 1000 lawnmowers. But, if either city specializes by directing all its productive resources toward the manufacture of bicycles, it can acquire specialized machinery and produce 2500 bicycles. Similarly, if the other city directs all its productive resources toward the manufacture of lawnmowers, it can produce 2500 lawnmowers. Note that each city, by doubling all inputs into the production of a single item, can *more* than double its output of that item from 1000 to 2500 units. Thus, economies of scale exist.

> *Economies of scale* exist if an increase of $x$% in the quantity of every input causes the quantity of output to increase by more than $x$%. (For example, if all inputs are doubled, then output more than doubles.)

Even though neither city had any fundamental advantage in the production of either product, each can gain by specialization. Before specialization, their combined output was 2000 bicycles and 2000 lawnmowers. After specialization, they together make 2500 bicycles and 2500 lawnmowers.

While Ricardo's theory of comparative advantage dates back to the early nineteenth century, the explanation of economies of scale goes back even further — to Adam Smith's *Wealth of Nations* (1776). In Smith's first chapter, "Of the Division of Labour," there is a famous description of pin-making:

> A workman not educated to this business . . . could scarce, perhaps, . . . make one pin in a day, and certainly not twenty. But, in the way in which this business is now carried on, not only the whole work is a peculiar trade, but it is divided into a number of branches. . . . One man draws out the wire, another straightens it, a third cuts it, a fourth points it, a fifth grinds it at the top for receiving the head. . . . Ten persons, therefore, could make among them upwards of forty-eight thousand pins in a day. Each person, therefore, . . . might be considered as making four thousand and eight hundred pins in a day.[2]

What is the reason for the gain that comes from the division of pin-making into a number of separate steps? Certainly, it is not that some individuals are particularly suited to drawing the wire, while others have a particular gift for straightening it. On the contrary, if two individuals are employed, it matters little which activity each is assigned. Adam Smith's "production line" is efficient because of economies of scale that depend on:

1. The introduction of specialized machinery.
2. Specialization of the labour force on that machinery. Modern corporations also derive economies of scale from a third major source:
3. Specialized research and development, which make possible the development of new equipment and technology.

In the modern word, economies of scale are very important as an explanation of specialization. They are a major reason why the manufacturers of automobiles, aircraft, and mainframe computers are few in number and large in size. It is partly because of economies of scale that the automobile industry is concentrated in central Canada, with cars being shipped to other areas in exchange for a host of other products. And economies of scale help explain why Canada's petrochemical industry is concentrated in the Lake St. Clair region of Southern Ontario.

However, economies of scale explain much more than the trade among the regions, provinces, and cities within a country. They also are an important explanation of trade between countries. For example, economies of scale in the production of large passenger aircraft go on long after the needs of the U.S. market are met. Thus, there is a major advantage to Boeing in producing aircraft for the world market. There are gains to the aircraft buyers, too. For example, Norway can buy a Boeing 747 for a small fraction of the cost of manufacturing a comparable airplane.

## LIVING IN A GLOBAL ECONOMY: ECONOMIES OF SCALE AND THE CANADA/UNITED STATES FREE TRADE AGREEMENT

Even the huge U.S. market is not large enough for some producers to capture all the economies of scale — for example, the manufacturers of aircraft and

[2] Adam Smith, *An Inquiry into the Nature and Causes of the Wealth of Nations* (Modern Library Edition, New York: Random House, 1937), pp. 4-5.

mainframe computers. But it is large enough for the producers of many other goods, such as automobiles. In fact, U.S. auto firms can offer a wide variety of models and still produce most of them at the high volume needed to gain substantially all the economies of scale. Thus, these producers can achieve low cost and at the same time provide a wide choice of models to consumers.

However, the United States is unique, since it is so large. Smaller economies — like Canada's — cannot produce a wide range of cars and at the same time achieve the high volume output necessary to lower costs. Thus, Canada has a choice among three options. It can:

1. Produce a variety of models, each on a small scale and, therefore, at high cost, for the domestic Canadian market. This option would provide car buyers with a choice among models, but at high cost.
2. Produce a small number of models, each at high volume, for the domestic market. This would provide the advantage of low cost, but consumers would not have much choice.
3. Gain both advantages (high-volume, low-cost production and a wide variety of models) by engaging in international trade. (Produce only a few models in Canada, at high volume and low cost. Export many of these cars in exchange for a variety of imported models.)

Historically, up to the early 1960s, Canadian automotive policy was based on the first choice. But, the twin advantages of option 3 are clear, and can come only through international trade. In order to gain these advantages, Canada in 1965 entered a special agreement with the United States, allowing duty-free passage of cars both ways across the border.

The favourable experience with the auto agreement was part of the reason the Canadian government finally decided, in the late 1980s, to negotiate a free trade agreement with the United States. Under the agreement, all tariffs between the two countries will be phased out by 1999. In addition, it provides for more open trade in services (such as banking services) and in energy, and for greater freedom of investment across the border.

For Canada, economies of scale provide one of the main advantages of the free trade agreement. As the treaty came into effect at the beginning of 1989, Canadian businesses had started a process of reorganization, cutting down the number of products and models but increasing the output of the goods they did continue to produce. Much of the output from the longer production runs is destined for the U.S. market. U.S. businesses likewise gain freer access to Canada, which is the most important market for U.S. exports.

The free trade agreement is highly complex, and raises many controversial issues that go beyond economic efficiency. Some of these issues are discussed in detail in the companion *Microeconomics* volume to this book. But, the increase in productivity and the possibility that many new jobs would open up in Canada's export industries were important elements in the debate that took place over free trade in the mid-1980s.

In this chapter, the advantages of specialization and exchange have been studied. Exchange takes place in markets; how markets operate will be the subject of the next chapter.

## KEY POINTS

1. Specialization requires exchange. The most primitive form of exchange is barter. This has the disadvantage that it requires a coincidence of wants.
2. Complex exchange, with many participants, is feasible in an economy with money. Because exchange is so much easier and more efficient with money, money will evolve even in the absence of government action — as happened in the prisoner-of-war camps during World War II.
3. In the prisoner-of-war camps, some cigarettes were more desirable than others. The desirable cigarettes were smoked, leaving the less desirable cigarettes to circulate as money. This illustrated Gresham's Law: "Bad money drives out good." In the modern Canadian economy, the Bank of Canada provides a *uniform* currency. Every dollar is worth the same as every other one; there is no "bad" money to drive "good" money out of circulation.
4. Specialization contributes to efficiency. There are two major reasons why there are gains from specialization and exchange:
   (a) comparative advantage
   (b) economies of scale.

5. If two individuals (or regions or countries) have different opportunity costs of producing a good or service, then the individual (or region or country) with the lower opportunity cost has the *comparative advantage* in that good or service. An example is the lawyer who is better than the gardener at both the law and gardening. Even so, she does not do her gardening herself, because she gains by specializing in the law (her comparative advantage) and hiring the gardener to do the gardening (his comparative advantage).
6. Economies of scale exist if an increase of $x\%$ in the quantity of every input causes the quantity of output to increase by more than $x\%$.
7. Economies of scale is an important argument in favour of freer international trade. Because of scale economies, Canada's auto industry was able to grow rapidly after the 1965 Canada/United States agreement on duty-free trade in autos, and the hope that Canadian industry will be able to take advantage of scale economies was one of the reasons why Canada was willing to enter into a comprehensive free trade agreement with the United States in 1989.

## KEY TERMS

**specialization**
**exchange**
**barter**
**coincidence of wants**
**indivisibility**
**general purchasing power**
**medium of exchange**
**Gresham's Law**
**debasement of the currency**
**deflation**
**uniform money**
**absolute advantage**
**comparative advantage**
**economies of scale**

## PROBLEMS

3-1. (a) Among the goods Canada exports are newsprint and sawn timber, farm machinery, and agricultural products, such as wheat. Why are these goods exported?
(b) Imports include automobiles, computers, oil, and agricultural products, such as wine, coffee, and bananas. Why are these goods imported?
(c) Canada exports some agricultural products, and imports others. Why? Canada exports many cars, but it also imports some. Why are we both exporters and importers of cars?

3-2. Suppose that one individual at your college is outstanding, being the best teacher and a superb administrator. If you were the college president, would you ask this individual to teach or to become the administrative vice-president? Why?

3-3. Most jobs are more specialized than they were 100 years ago. Why? What are the advantages of greater specialization? Are there any disadvantages?

3-4. Draw a production possibilities curve (PPC) for the lawyer mentioned in Box 3-2, putting the number of wills drawn up in a week on one axis and flowers planted on the other. (Assume that the lawyer works 40 hours per week.) How does the shape of this PPC differ from that in Chapter 2?

*3-5. Draw the production possibilities curve of one of the two identical cities described in the section on economies of scale. Which way does the curve bend? Does the opportunity cost of bicycles increase or decrease as more bicycles are produced?

*Problems marked with asterisks are more difficult than the others. They are designed to provide a challenge to students who want to do more advanced work.

# CHAPTER 4

# DEMAND AND SUPPLY: THE MARKET MECHANISM

*Do you know,*
*Considering the market, there are more*
*Poems produced than any other thing?*
*No wonder poets sometimes have to seem*
*So much more business-like than business men.*
*Their wares are so much harder to get rid of.*

*Robert Frost,* New Hampshire

Although some countries are much richer than others, the resources of every country are limited. Choices must be made. Moreover, every economy involves some degree of specialization. In every economy, therefore, some mechanism is needed to answer the fundamental questions raised by specialization and by the need to make choices:

1. *What* goods and services will be produced? (How do we choose among the various options represented by the production possibilities curve?)
2. *How* will these goods and services be produced? For example, will cars be produced by relatively few workers using a great deal of machinery, or by many workers using relatively little capital equipment?
3. *For whom* will the goods and services be produced? Once goods are produced, who will consume them?

## THE MARKET AND THE GOVERNMENT

There are two principal mechanisms by which these questions can be answered. First, answers can be provided by Adam Smith's "invisible hand." If people are left alone to make their own transactions, then the butcher and baker will provide the beef and bread for our dinner. In other words, answers may be provided by transactions among individuals and corporations in the ***market***.

In a *market*, an item is bought and sold. Markets where transactions between buyers and sellers take place with little or no government interference are often referred to as *private* or *free* markets.

The *government* provides the second method for determining what goods and services will be produced, how they will be produced, and for whom. The government affects the economy in four principal ways: by *spending*, by *taxation*, by running *public enterprises*, and by *regulation*.

1. *Spending*. When the government pays Old Age Security benefits to retirees, it influences *who* gets society's output; the recipient of the benefit is able to buy more goods and services. When the government buys ships for the navy, those ships are produced; the government affects *what* is produced. When the government spends money for agricultural research, it influences *how* food will be produced.
2. *Taxes*. When the government collects taxes, it influences *who* gets society's output. When I pay taxes, I have less income left with which to buy

goods and services. Taxes also affect *what* is produced. For example, a tax on gasoline encourages people to buy smaller cars. More small cars are produced, and fewer large ones. Finally, the tax system may also influence *how* goods are produced. Incentives built into the tax law encourage businesses to use more machinery in producing goods. When they buy machinery, their taxes are reduced.

3. *Public enterprises.* The government owns and operates some businesses, including Crown corporations, such as the Canadian Broadcasting Corporation (CBC) or Canada Post. It decides *what* these enterprises will produce, and *how* they will produce it.
4. *Regulation.* Governmental regulations may also influence what, how, and for whom goods and services are produced. For example, the government prohibits the production of some pesticides, and requires seat belts and other safety equipment in cars. It thereby affects *what* is produced. It requires producers of steel to limit their emissions of smoke into the atmosphere, thereby influencing *how* goods are produced. The government also regulates some prices — for example, the price of local telephone and cable TV service. This keeps down the incomes of shareholders, as well as executives and workers, in private phone and cable companies. With less income, these people can buy less. Thus, the government influences *who* gets society's product.

In addition to the market and the government, there are other institutions that play a role in helping to answer the three basic questions: *What? How?* and *For Whom?* For example, when a relief organization collects voluntary contributions of clothing or money for distribution to the poor or to the victims of a natural disaster, it is influencing who gets the output of society. Similarly, within the family, a mechanism other than the market or the government is used to determine how the budget for clothing, etc., is divided among the family members. Nevertheless, economists concentrate on the market and the government when they study the way in which society answers the three basic questions.

Conceivably, a nation might depend almost exclusively on private markets to make the three fundamental decisions. The government might be confined to a very limited role, providing defence, police, the courts, roads, and little else. At the other extreme, the goverment might try to decide almost everything, specifying what is to be produced, and using a system of rationing and allocations to decide who gets the products. But, the real world is one of compromise. Every actual economy is a ***mixed economy*** in which both the markets and government decision making have a role.

In Canada, the United States, Japan, and the Western European nations, most choices are made in the market. In these countries, the government plays a relatively limited role by international standards. This is especially true in the United States, where public enterprise accounts for a very small share of total economic activity, and where there has been a tendency in recent years toward *reduced* regulation of private markets. In Canada, the role of government and public enterprise is more prominent than in the United States. However, in comparison with countries at the other end of the spectrum, this role still appears very limited. Until 1991, responsibility for economic decision making in the former Soviet Union and the nations of Eastern Europe was very heavily concentrated in the government; in a country such as North Korea, it still is.

As *Marxist* nations, these countries rejected the idea that the market should determine *for whom* goods will be produced. Individuals were allowed to own small capital goods, but the major forms of capital — factories and heavy machinery, for example — were owned by the state. Therefore, earnings of the enterprises who used the capital did not flow to private individuals as income that they could use in turn to buy a considerable share of the economy's output. In contrast, most capital in ***capitalist*** or ***free enterprise*** economies such as the United States, Canada, and Japan, is owned — directly or indirectly — by private individuals, and a substantial portion of private consumption is financed out of incomes from capital. (An example is the income paid to retired people from private pension plans.)

In a Marxist nation, not only does the government own most of the capital, it also is involved in detailed decisions as to which products will be produced with this capital. For example, the former Soviet Union had a ***central planning*** agency that issued directives to the various sectors of the economy to produce specific quantities of goods.

Following dramatic political changes, the countries in the former Soviet Union and Eastern Europe were, in the early 1990s, in the process of dismantling their systems of central planning and transforming themselves into market economies. And even in an economy such as China's, which has remained Marxist, there appeared to be a trend toward less reliance on detailed government control over economic decisions, and a correspondingly greater reliance on the market.

> A *capitalist* or *free enterprise* economy is one in which individuals are permitted to own large amounts of capital, and decisions are made primarily in markets, with relatively little government interference.
>
> A *Marxist* economy is one in which the government owns most of the capital, and makes many of the economic decisions. Political power is in the hands of a party pledging allegiance to the doctrines of Karl Marx.

Because the market is relatively important in Canada, it will be our initial concern. (Chapter 5 will deal in detail with the economic role of the government in Canada.) This chapter explains how the market answers the three basic questions: What will be produced? How? For whom?

## THE MARKET MECHANISM

In most markets, the buyer and the seller come face to face. When you buy a suit of clothes, you talk directly to the salesclerk; when you buy groceries, you physically enter the seller's place of business (the supermarket). However, physical proximity is not required to make a market. For example, in a typical stock market transaction, a widow in Medicine Hat puts in a call to her broker to buy 100 shares of Homestake Mining common stock. About the same time, someone in Fredericton calls his broker to sell 100 shares. The transaction takes place on the floor of the Toronto Stock Exchange, where representatives of the two brokerage houses meet. The buyer and the seller of the stock do not leave their respective homes in Alberta and New Brunswick.

Some markets are quite simple. For example, a barbershop is a "market," since haircuts are bought and sold there. The transaction is obvious and straightforward; the service of haircutting is produced on the spot. In other cases, markets are much more complex. Even the simplest everyday activity may be the culmination of a complicated series of market transactions.

As you sat at breakfast this morning drinking your cup of coffee, you were using products from distant areas. The coffee itself was probably produced in Colombia. The brew was made with water that perhaps had been delivered in pipes manufactured in Quebec and purified with chemicals produced in Sarnia, Ontario. The sugar for the coffee may have been produced in the Caribbean. Perhaps you used artificial cream made from soybeans grown in Southern Ontario. Possibly, your coffee was poured into a cup made in Britain, and stirred with a spoon manufactured in Taiwan from Japanese stainless steel which used nickel from Sudbury in its production. All this was for one cup of coffee.

In such a complex economy, something is needed to keep things straight, to bring order out of potential chaos. *Prices* bring order by performing two important, interrelated functions:

1. Prices provide *information*.
2. Prices provide *incentives*.

To illustrate, suppose we start from the example of chaos. Most of the coffee is in Vancouver and most of the sugar in Montreal. Coffee lovers in Montreal would clamour for coffee, even at very high prices. The high price is a signal, providing *information* to coffee owners that there are eager buyers in Montreal. It also provides them with an *incentive* to send coffee to Montreal. In any market, the price provides the focus for interactions between buyers and sellers.

## PERFECT AND IMPERFECT COMPETITION

Some markets are dominated by a few large firms; others have thousands of sellers. The "big three" automobile manufacturers (General Motors, Ford, and Chrysler) make most of the cars sold in Canada and the United States, with the rest provided by Japanese, European, and other foreign firms. Such an industry, which is dominated by a few sellers, is an ***oligopoly***. (The word "oligopoly" means "a few sellers," just as "oligarchy" means "rule by a few.") Some markets are even more concentrated. For example, there is just one supplier of local telephone services to homes in your area; the local telephone company has a ***monopoly***. On the other hand, there are thousands of wheat producers.

> A *monopoly* exists when there is only *one seller*. An *oligopoly* exists when a *few sellers* dominate a market.

The number of participants in a market has a significant effect on the way in which the price is determined. In the wheat market, where there are thousands of buyers and thousands of sellers, no individual farmer produces more than a tiny fraction of the total supply. No single farmer can affect the price of wheat. For each one, the price is given; the individual farmer's decision is limited to the number of bushels of wheat to sell. Similarly, the millers realize that they are each buying only a small fraction of the wheat supplied. They realize that they cannot, as individuals, affect the price of wheat. Each miller's decision is limited to the number of bushels to be bought at the existing market price. In such an environment of ***perfect competition***, *there is no pricing decision* for the individual seller and the individual buyer to make. Each buyer and seller is a *price taker*.

> *Perfect competition* exists when there are so many buyers and sellers that no single buyer or seller has any influence over the price. (Sometimes, this term is shortened simply to "competition.")

In contrast to the sellers in a perfectly competitive market, individual producers in an oligopolistic or a monopolistic market know that they have some control—***market power***—over price. For example, IBM sets the prices of its personal computers. That does not mean, of course, that it can set *any* price it wants and still be ensured of making a profit. It can offer to sell at a high price, in which case it will sell only a few computers. Or it can charge a lower price, in which case it will sell more. A *buyer* may also be large enough to influence price. C.P. Rail is a large enough purchaser of steel to be able to bargain with Canadian steel companies over the price of steel. When individual buyers or sellers can influence price, ***imperfect competition*** exists.

> *Imperfect competition* exists when any buyer or any seller is able to influence the price. Such a buyer or seller is said to have *market power*.

Note that the term "competition" is used differently in economics and in business. Don't try to tell someone from Chrysler that the automobile market isn't competitive; Chrysler is very much aware of the competition from General Motors, Ford, and the Japanese. Yet, according to the economist's definition, the automobile ***industry*** is far *less* competitive than the wheat industry.

> An *industry* refers to all the producers of a good or service. For example, we may speak of the lumber industry, the wheat industry, or the accounting industry. Note that the term "industry" can refer to *any* good or service; it need not be manufactured.
>
> A *firm* is a business organization that produces goods and/or services. A *plant* is an establishment at a single location used in the production of a good or service; for example: a factory, mine, farm, or store. Some firms—such as General Motors—have many plants. Others have only one; for example, the local independent florist.

Because price is determined by impersonal forces in a perfectly competitive market, the competitive market is simplest, and will, therefore, be considered first. The perfectly competitive market is also given priority because competitive markets generally operate more efficiently than imperfect markets (as we show in the *Microeconomics* volume that forms a companion to this book).

# THE PERFECTLY COMPETITIVE MARKET: DEMAND AND SUPPLY

In a perfectly competitive market, price is determined by ***demand*** and ***supply***.

## Demand

Consider, as an example, the market for apples, in which there are many buyers and many sellers, with none having any control over the price. For the buyer, a high price acts as a deterrent. The higher the price, the fewer apples buyers purchase. Why is this so? As the price of apples rises, consumers switch to oranges or grapefruit, or they simply cut down on their total consumption of fruit. Similarly, the lower the price, the more apples are bought. A lower price brings new purchasers into the market, and each purchaser tends to buy more. The response of buyers to various possible prices is illustrated in the demand curve in Figure 4-1. Points *A*, *B*, *C*, and *D* correspond to rows *A*, *B*, *C*, and *D* in the *demand schedule* shown below the figure.

> A *demand curve* and a *demand schedule* show the quantities of a good or service that buyers would be willing and able to purchase at various market prices.

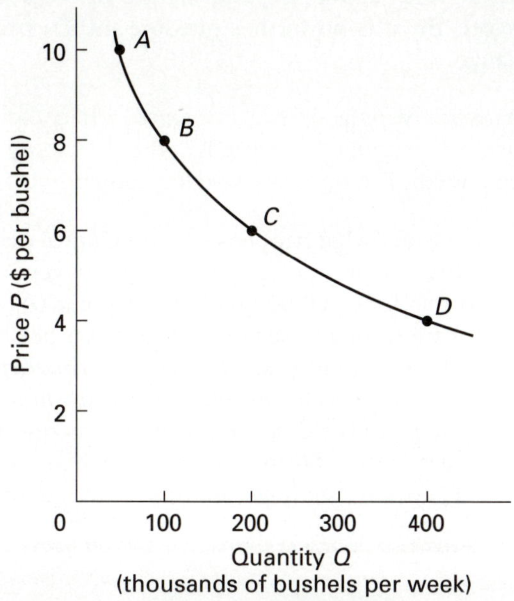


**FIGURE 4-1 The demand curve.**

At each of the possible prices specified, there is a quantity of apples that people would be willing and able to buy. This information is provided in Table 4-1 below and is reproduced in this diagram. On the vertical axis, the possible prices are shown. In each case, the quantity of apples that would be bought is measured along the horizontal axis. Since people are more willing to buy at a low price than at a high price, the demand curve slopes downward to the right.

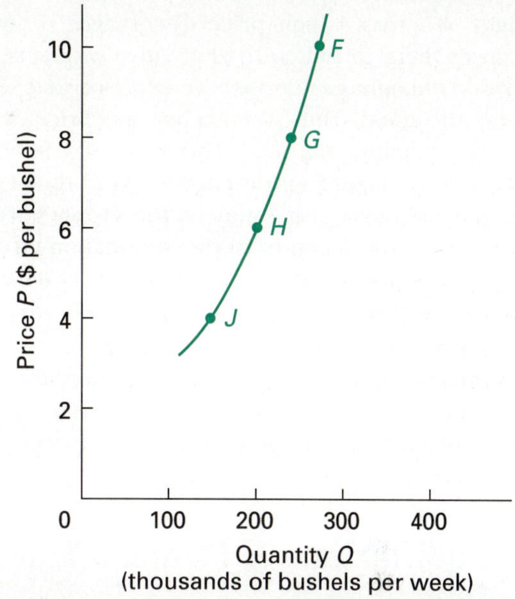


**FIGURE 4-2 The supply curve for apples.**

For each of the possible prices specified, the supply schedule (Table 4-2 below) indicates how many units the sellers would be willing and able to sell. This information is illustrated graphically in this figure, which shows how the supply curve slopes upward to the right. At a high price, suppliers will be encouraged to step up production and offer more apples for sale.

**TABLE 4-1 The Demand Schedule for Apples**

| | (1) Price *P* ($ per bushel) | (2) Quantity *Q* demanded (thousands of bushels per week) |
|---|---|---|
| *A* | 10 | 50 |
| *B* | 8 | 100 |
| *C* | 6 | 200 |
| *D* | 4 | 400 |

**TABLE 4-2 The Supply Schedule for Apples**

| | (1) Price *P* ($ per bushel) | (2) Quantity *Q* supplied (thousands of bushels per week) |
|---|---|---|
| *F* | 10 | 260 |
| *G* | 8 | 240 |
| *H* | 6 | 200 |
| *J* | 4 | 150 |

Note carefully that the demand schedule or demand curve applies to a *specific population* and to a *specific time period*. Clearly, the number of apples demanded during a month will exceed the number demanded during a week, and the number demanded by the people of Nova Scotia will be less than the number demanded in the whole of Canada. In a general discussion of theoretical issues, the population and time framework are not always stated explicitly, but it nevertheless should be understood that a demand curve applies to a specific time and population.

## Supply

While the demand curve illustrates how buyers behave, the supply curve illustrates how sellers behave; it shows how much of a good or service they would be willing to sell at various prices. Needless to say, buyers and sellers look at high prices in a different light. Whereas a high price discourages buyers and causes them to switch to alternative products, a high price encourages suppliers to produce and sell more of the good. Thus, the higher the price, the higher the quantity supplied. This is shown in the *supply curve* in Figure 4-2 on page 57. As in the case of the demand curve, the points on the supply curve (*F*, *G*, *H*, and *J*) are drawn from the information given in the corresponding rows of the *supply schedule* below the figure.

A *supply curve* and a *supply schedule* show the quantities of a good or service that sellers would be willing and able to sell at various market prices.

## The Equilibrium of Demand and Supply

The demand and supply curves may now be brought together in Figure 4-3. (See also Table 4-3.) The ***market equilibrium*** occurs at point *E*, where the demand and supply curves intersect. At this equilibrium, the price is $6 per bushel, and weekly sales are 200,000 bushels.

An *equilibrium* is a situation where there is no tendency to change.

To see why *E* represents the equilibrium, consider what happens if the market price is initially at some other level. Suppose, for example, that the initial price is $10; that is, it is above the equilibrium price. What happens? Purchasers buy only 50,000 bushels (shown by point *A* in Figure 4-3), while sellers want to sell 260,000 bushels (point *F*). There is a large ***excess supply***, or ***surplus***, of 210,000 bushels. Some sellers are disappointed: They sell much less than they wish at the price of $10. Unsold apples begin to pile up. In order to get them moving, sellers now begin to accept a lower price. The price starts to come down—to $9, then $8. Still, there is a surplus, or an excess of the quantity supplied over the quantity demanded. (However, the surplus is now a smaller amount, *BG*). The price continues to fall. It does not stop falling until it reaches $6, the equilibrium. At this price, buyers purchase 200,000 bushels, which is just the amount the sellers want to sell. Both buyers and sellers are now satisfied with the quantity of their purchases or sales at the existing market price of $6. Therefore, there is no further pressure on the price to change.

An *excess supply*, or *surplus*, exists when the quantity supplied exceeds the quantity demanded. (The price is above the equilibrium.)

Now consider what happens when the initial price is below the equilibrium, at, say, $4. Eager buyers are willing to purchase 400,000 bushels (at point *D*), yet producers are willing to sell only 150,000 bushels (at point *J*). There is an ***excess demand***, or ***shortage***, of 250,000 bushels. As buyers clamour for the limited supplies, the price is bid upward. The price continues to rise until it reaches $6, the equilibrium where there is no longer any shortage because the quantity

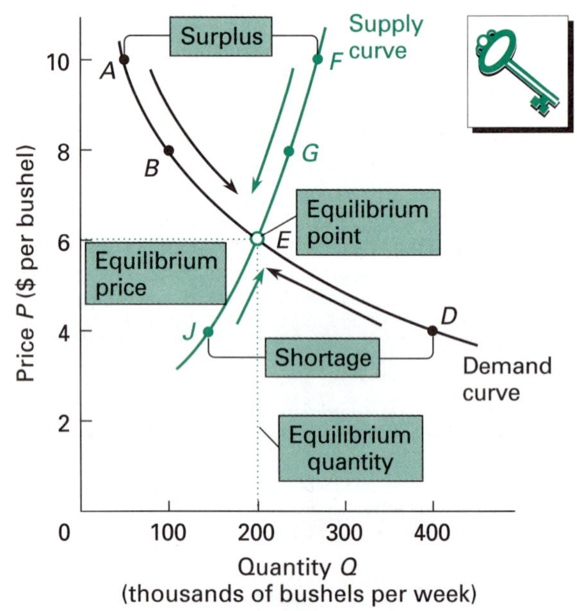


**FIGURE 4-3 How demand and supply determine equilibrium price and quantity.**

Equilibrium exists at point *E*, where the quantity demanded equals the quantity supplied. At any higher price, the quantity supplied exceeds the quantity demanded. Because of the pressure of unsold stocks, competition among sellers causes the price to be bid down to the equilibrium of $6. Similarly, at a price less than the $6 equilibrium, forces are set in motion that raise the price. Because the quantity demanded exceeds the quantity supplied, eager buyers clamour for more apples, and bid the price up to the equilibrium at $6.

**TABLE 4-3 The Equilibrium of Demand and Supply**

| (1) Price *P* ($ per bushel) | (2) Quantity *Q* demanded (thousands of bushels per week) | (3) Quantity *Q* supplied (thousands of bushels per week) | (4) Surplus (+) or shortage (−) (4) = (3) − (2) | (5) Pressure on price |
|---|---|---|---|---|
| 10 | 50 | 260 | Surplus + 210 | Downward |
| 8 | 100 | 240 | Surplus + 140 | Downward |
| **6** | **200** | **200** | **0** | **Equilibrium** |
| 4 | 400 | 150 | Shortage − 250 | Upward |

demanded is equal to the quantity supplied. At point *E*, and only at point *E*, will the price be stable.

An *excess demand*, or *shortage*, exists when the quantity demanded exceeds the quantity supplied. (The price is below the equilibrium.)

## SHIFTS IN THE DEMAND CURVE

The quantity of a product that buyers want to purchase depends on the price. As we have seen, the demand curve illustrates this relationship between price and quantity. But, the quantity that people want to purchase also depends on other influences. For example, if incomes rise, people will want to buy more apples — and more of a whole host of other products, too.

The purpose of a demand curve is to show how the quantity demanded is affected by price, *and by price alone*. When we ask how much people want to buy at various prices, it is important that our answer not be disturbed by other influences. In other words, when we draw a demand curve for a good, we must *hold incomes constant and also everything else that can affect the quantity demanded* — with the sole exception of the price of the good. We make the ***ceteris paribus*** assumption — that other things remain unchanged. (*Ceteris* is the same Latin word that appears in "et cetera," which literally means "and other things." *Paribus* means "equal" or "unchanged.")

Of course, as time passes, other things do not remain constant. Through time, for example, incomes generally rise. When that happens, the quantity of apples demanded at any particular price increases. The whole demand curve shifts to the right, as illustrated in Figure 4-4. Since *economists use the term "demand" to mean the whole demand curve or demand schedule*, we may speak of this rightward shift in the curve more simply as an *increase in demand.*

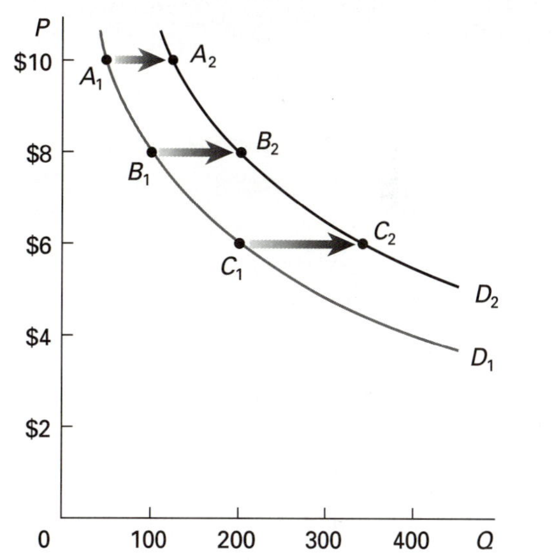


**FIGURE 4-4 A change in the demand for apples.** When incomes rise, there is an increase in the number of apples that people want to buy at any particular price. At a price of $10, for example, the quantity of apples demanded increases from point $A_1$ to $A_2$. At other prices, the increase in incomes also causes an increase in the number of apples demanded. Thus, the whole demand curve shifts to the right, from $D_1$ to $D_2$.

## Demand Shifters

A shift in the demand curve — that is, a change in demand — may be caused by a change in any one of a whole host of "other things." Some of the most important ***demand shifters*** are the following:

### 1. Income

When incomes rise, people are able to buy more. And people do, in fact, buy more of the typical or ***normal good***. For such a good, the number of units demanded at each price increases as incomes rise. Thus, the demand curve shifts to the right with rising incomes, as illustrated in Figure 4-4.

Not all goods are normal, however. As incomes rise, people may buy *less* of a good. For example, they switch away from margarine and buy more butter, which they can afford now. When this happens — when the increase in income causes a leftward shift of the demand curve for margarine — the item is an ***inferior good***.

| If an *increase* in income | Shifts the demand curve for a good to the *right* | It is a *normal* good (or a *superior* good) |
|---|---|---|
| If an *increase* in *income* | Shifts the demand curve for a good to the *left* | It is an *inferior* good |

### 2. Prices of Related Goods

A rise in the price of one good can cause a shift in the demand curve for another good.

For example, if the price of oranges were to double while the price of apples remained the same, buyers would be encouraged to buy apples instead of oranges. Thus, a rise in the price of oranges causes a rightward shift in the demand curve for apples. Goods such as apples and oranges — which satisfy similar needs or desires — are ***substitutes***. Other examples are tea and coffee, butter and margarine, bus and train tickets, and heating oil and insulating materials.

For ***complements*** or ***complementary goods***, exactly the opposite relationship holds. In contrast to substitutes — which are used *instead* of each other — complements are used *together*, as a package. For example, gasoline and automobiles are complementary goods. If the price of gasoline spirals upward, people become less eager to own automobiles. The demand curve for cars, therefore, shifts to the left. So it is with other complements, such as tennis rackets and tennis balls, or formal clothing rentals and tickets to a formal dance.

Finally, many goods are basically *unrelated*, in the sense that a rise in the price of one has no significant effect on the demand curve of the others. Thus, bus tickets and butter are unrelated, as are coffee and cameras.

| If an *increase* in the *price* of *A* | Shifts the demand curve for *B* to the *right* | Then *A* and *B* are *substitutes* |
|---|---|---|
| If an *increase* in the *price* of *C* | Shifts the demand curve for *D* to the *left* | Then *C* and *D* are *complementary* goods |

### 3. Tastes

Tastes change over time. Because of increased interest in physical fitness, more people are jogging. This increases the demand for running shoes. Tastes and, therefore, demand are quite volatile for some products, particularly for fads such as pink flamingo lawn ornaments.

The discussion above covers some of the most important demand shifters, but it is far from complete. To see how it might be extended, consider the following questions:

1. If the weather changes, how will the change affect the demand for skiing equipment? For snow tires?
2. If people expect cars to be priced $2000 higher next year, what effect will this have on the demand for cars this year?
3. As more and more families get videocassette recorders, and thereby become able to skip through the commercials with the fast forward button, how will this affect the demand by companies buying TV ads? (A.C. Nielsen, an American firm that rates TV shows as a service for advertisers, has found that when people watch taped shows half of them do, in fact, "zap" the commercials.)[1]

[1] Answer: It will reduce the demand. It was estimated that this resulted in a yearly loss of $200 million in advertising revenue in the United States in the late 1980s.

## *WHAT* IS PRODUCED: THE RESPONSE TO A CHANGE IN TASTES

At the beginning of this chapter, three basic questions were listed. To see how the market mechanism can help to answer the first of these—What will be produced? — consider what happens when there is a change in tastes. Suppose, for example, that people develop a desire to drink more tea and less coffee. This change in tastes is illustrated by a rightward shift in the demand curve for tea and a leftward shift in the demand curve for coffee.

As the demand for tea increases, the price is bid up by eager buyers. With a higher price, growers in Sri Lanka and elsewhere are encouraged to plant more tea. At the new equilibrium, shown as point $E_2$ in the left panel of Figure 4-5, the price of tea is higher than it was originally (at $E_1$), and the consumers buy a larger quantity of tea. In the coffee market, the results are opposite. At the new equilibrium ($F_2$), the price is lower and a smaller quantity is bought.

Thus, competitive market forces cause producers to "dance to the consumers' tune." In response to a change in consumer tastes, prices change. Tea producers are given an incentive to step up production, and coffee production is discouraged.

## SHIFTS IN SUPPLY

While the market encourages producers to dance to the consumers' tune, the opposite is also true. As we shall now show, consumers "dance to the producers' tune" as well. The market involves a complex interaction: sellers respond to the desires of buyers, and buyers respond to the willingness of producers to sell.

Just as the demand curve reflects the desires of buyers, so the supply curve illustrates the willingness of producers to sell. In an important respect, the two curves are similar. The objective of each is to show *how the quantity is affected by the price of the good, and by this price alone*. Thus, when we draw the supply curve, once again we make the *ceteris paribus* assumption. Everything except the price of the good itself is held constant.

### Supply Shifters

As in the case of demand, the other things that affect supply can change through time, causing the supply curve to shift. Some of these ***supply shifters*** are the following:

#### 1. The Cost of Inputs

For example, if the price of fertilizer goes up, farmers will be less willing to produce wheat at the previ-

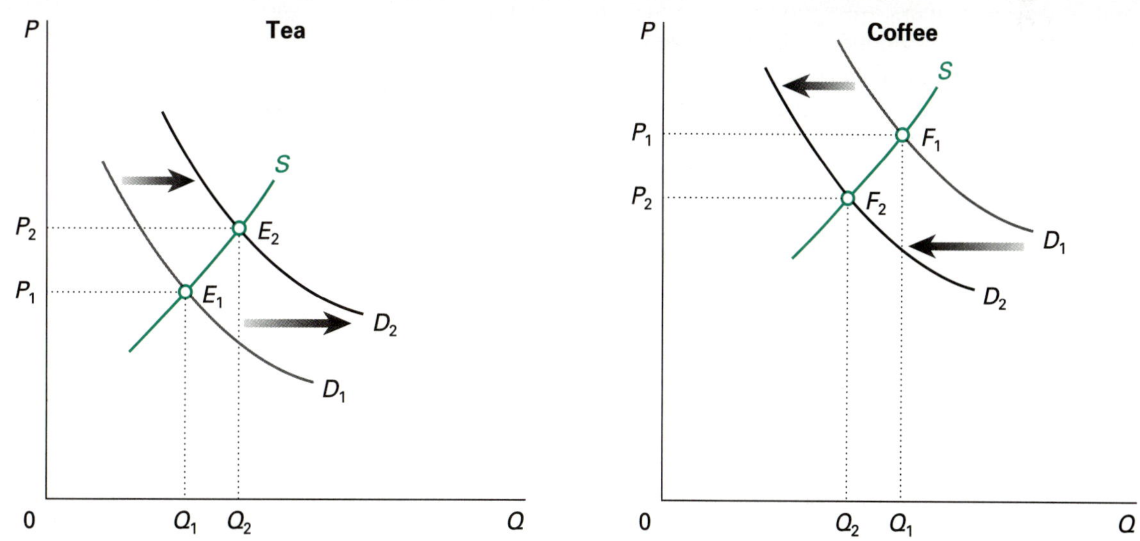


**FIGURE 4-5 A change in tastes.**

A change in tastes causes the demand for tea to increase and the demand for coffee to decrease. As a result, more tea is bought at a higher price. Less coffee is bought, and the price of coffee falls.

ously prevailing price. The supply curve will shift to the left.

## 2. Technology

Suppose that there is an improvement in technology that causes costs of production to fall. With lower costs, producers will be willing to supply more at any particular price. The supply curve will shift to the right.

## 3. Weather

This is particularly important for agricultural products. For example, a drought will cause a decrease in the supply of wheat (that is, a leftward shift in the supply curve), and a freeze in Florida will cause a decrease in the supply of oranges.

## 4. The Prices of Related Goods

Just as items can be substitutes or complements in consumption, so they can be substitutes or complements in production.

We saw earlier that substitutes in consumption are goods that can be consumed as *alternatives* to one another, satisfying the same wants (for example, apples and oranges). Similarly, *substitutes in production* are goods that can be *produced* as alternatives to one another, using the same factors of production. Thus, corn and soybeans are substitutes in production; they can be grown on similar land. If the price of corn increases, farmers are encouraged to switch their lands out of the production of soybeans and into the production of corn. The amount of soybeans they are willing to supply at any given price decreases; the supply curve for soybeans shifts to the left.

We also saw earlier that complements in consumption are used *together* (for example, gasoline and automobiles). Similarly *complements in production* or ***joint products*** are produced together, as a package. Beef and hides provide an example. When more cattle are slaughtered for beef, more hides are produced in the process. An increase in the price of beef causes an increase in beef production that, in turn, causes an increase in the production of hides—that is, a rightward shift of the supply curve of hides.

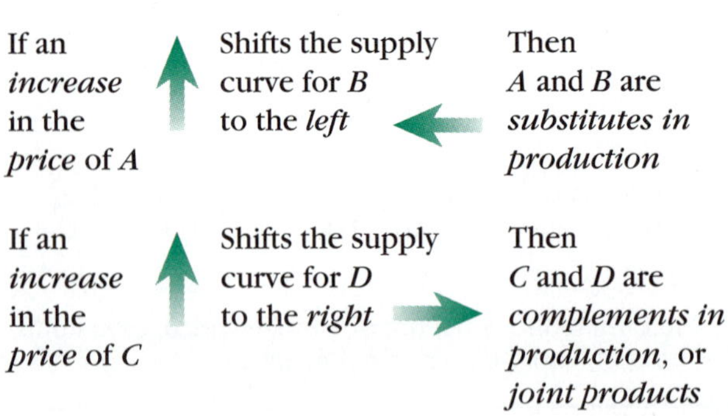


# The Response to a Shift in the Supply Curve

To illustrate how consumers dance to the producers' tune, suppose that there is a frost in Brazil that wipes out part of the coffee crop. As a result, the quantity of coffee available on the market is reduced. That is, the supply curve shifts to the left, as illustrated in Figure 4-6. With less coffee available, the price is bid upward. At the new equilibrium ($G_2$), the price is higher and the quantity sold is smaller.

How do consumers respond to the change in supply? Because of the higher price of coffee, consumers are discouraged from buying. For example, some may decide to drink coffee only once a day, rather than twice. Anyone who is willing and able to pay the high price will get coffee; those who are unwilling or unable to pay the price will not get it. Thus, the *high price acts as a way of allocating the limited supply among buyers*. The coffee goes only to buyers who are sufficiently eager to be willing to pay

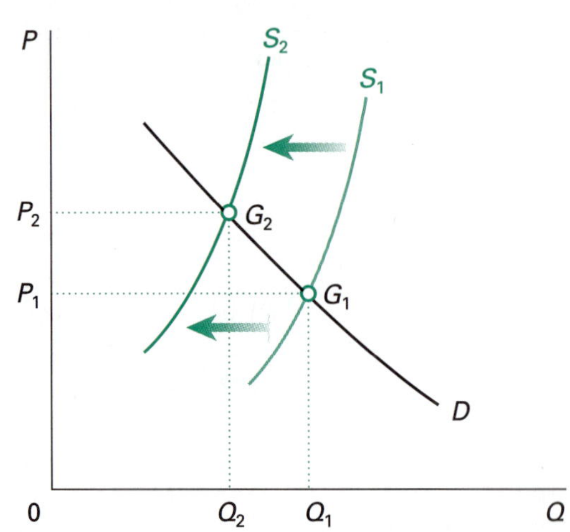


**FIGURE 4-6 A shift in supply.**

A freeze in Brazil causes a leftward shift in the supply curve for coffee. The result is a movement of the equilibrium along the demand curve from $G_1$ to $G_2$. At the new equilibrium, there is a higher price, and a smaller quantity is sold.

the high price, and sufficiently affluent to be able to afford it.

## SHIFTS IN A CURVE AND MOVEMENTS ALONG A CURVE

Because the term "supply" applies to a supply schedule or a supply curve, a "change in supply" means a *shift* in the entire curve. Such a shift took place in Figure 4-6 as a result of a freeze in Brazil.

In this figure, observe that the demand curve has not moved. However, as the supply curve shifts and the price consequently changes, there is a movement *along* the demand curve from $G_1$ to $G_2$. At the second point, $G_2$, less coffee is bought (the quantity of coffee demanded is less) than at the original point, $G_1$.

The distinction between a *shift* in a curve and a *movement along* a curve should be emphasized. What can we say about the move from $G_1$ to $G_2$?

1. It is correct to say that "supply has decreased." Why? Because the entire supply curve has shifted to the left.
2. It is *not* correct to say that "demand has decreased." Why? Because the demand curve has not moved.
3. It is, however, correct to say that "the quantity demanded has decreased." Why? Because a smaller quantity is demanded at $G_2$ than at $G_1$.

A similar distinction should be made when the demand curve shifts. This is shown in Figure 4-7, based on the left panel of Figure 4-5, where the demand for tea increases because of a change in tastes. The rightward movement of the demand curve causes the equilibrium to move *along* the supply curve, from $E_1$ to $E_2$. It is not correct to say that supply has increased, since the supply curve did not move. However, the *quantity supplied* did increase as the price rose. (Quantity $Q_2$ is greater than $Q_1$.) (For another way of looking at the difference between shifts in curves and movements along curves, see Box 4-1.)

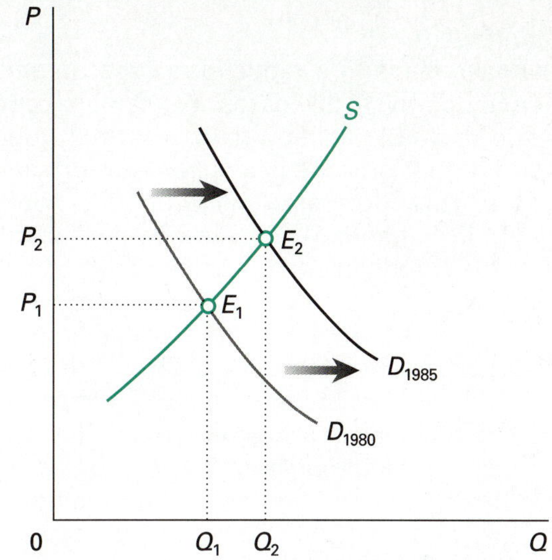


**FIGURE 4-7 A shift in the demand for tea.**
This diagram, based on the left panel of Figure 4-5, shows that there is an increase in the quantity of tea supplied as the equilibrium moves from $E_1$ to $E_2$. However, supply does not change, since the supply curve does not move.

### TOOLS AND TECHNIQUES — BOX 4-1
### Curve Shifting and Equilibrium: Another View

Some simple algebra may be helpful in showing the effects of supply and demand shifters, and how they influence the equilibrium price and quantity in a market.

Suppose we write the demand for cauliflower during the month of August in a particular city, as the following equation:

$$Q^D = 25 - 10P_A + 5Y + 8P_B \qquad (4\text{-}1)$$

where $Q^D$ stands for the quantity demanded (in thousands of cases), $P_A$ is the price of cauliflower per case (in dollars), $Y$ is consumers' total monthly income (in millions of dollars), and $P_B$ is the price of broccoli.

Looking at Equation (4-1), we first see that the demand curve for cauliflower is downward sloping: An increase in its price by $1

*(continued)*

**BOX 4-1 continued**

*(continued)*

per case leads to a reduction in the quantity demanded by 10,000 cases. We can also conclude that (1), cauliflower is a normal good, and (2), that broccoli is a substitute for cauliflower. How do we know? From the coefficients in Equation (4-1): Because the income variable is multiplied by +5, the equation tells us that an increase in consumers' total income by \$1 million increases the demand for cauliflower by 5000 cases. That is, it shifts the demand curve to the right. But that means that cauliflower is a normal good. Similarly, an increase in the price of broccoli by \$1 per case shifts the demand curve for cauliflower to the right by 8000 cases. Thus, broccoli must be a substitute for cauliflower.

Suppose the supply curve for cauliflower is:

$$Q^S = -20 + 30P_A \qquad (4\text{-}2),$$

where $Q^S$ is the quantity supplied.

Equilibrium in this market will occur where the demand and supply curves intersect. Based on what Equation (4-2) tells us, we can graph the supply curve as the curve *S* in the figure. To graph the demand curve, however, we need more information. Specifically, since the position of the demand curve depends on consumer income *Y* and the price of broccoli, $P_B$, we must know what the values of these variables are.

Suppose in particular that *Y* is \$15 million, and that $P_B$ is \$10 per case. Substituting these values into Equation (4-1), we get:

$$Q^D = [\,25 + 5 \cdot 15 + 8 \cdot 10\,] - 10P_A$$
$$= 180 - 10P_A \qquad (4\text{-}3).$$

Graphing this demand curve as curve $D_1$ in the figure, we see that the equilibrium price where the supply and demand curves intersect is $P_A = 5$, and the equilibrium quantity *Q* = 130. Notice that you can also find these equilibrium values by taking into account that in equilibrium, it must be true that $Q^S = Q^D$. Therefore, the right-hand sides of Equations (4-2) and (4-3) must be equal:

$$-20 + 30P_A = 180 - 10P_A \qquad (4\text{-}4)$$

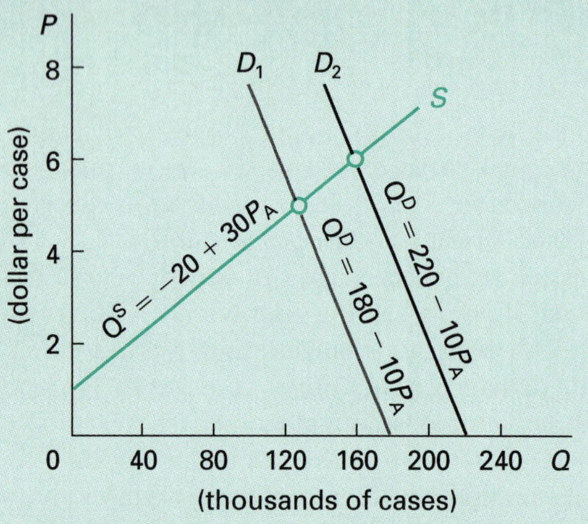


**The supply and demand for cauliflower.**

The position of the demand curve depends on total consumer income and the price of broccoli. As the price of broccoli increases by \$5 per case, the demand curve for cauliflower shifts from $D_1$ to $D_2$, leading to increases in the equilibrium quantities of cauliflower supplied and demanded.

which can be used to solve for the equilibrium value of $P_A$; the equilibrium quantity *Q* can then be found from either (4-2) or (4-3).

Now suppose something makes the demand curve for cauliflower shift. For example, suppose the price of broccoli rises by \$5 per case, to \$15. What will happen? From Equation (4-1), we see that a \$5 increase in the price of broccoli increases the demand for cauliflower by 40,000 cases, at any given price of cauliflower. That is, the demand curve shifts 40 units to the right everywhere, so that the new demand curve will be $Q^D = 220 - 10P_A$ (curve $D_2$ in the figure). As a result, the equilibrium price will rise (to \$6 per case), and the equilibrium quantity goes to 160,000 cases. As before, you can find these solutions either as approximations, by looking at the figure, or exactly, by using the equations for the supply and demand curves to solve for $P_A$ and *Q*. Using the same logic, you could find the effect of a change in consumer income, or, say, a rightward shift in the supply curve (as a result of improved harvesting techniques for cauliflower, for example).

## THE INTERCONNECTED QUESTIONS OF *WHAT, HOW,* AND *FOR WHOM*

We have explored how two tunes are played. Demand is the tune played by consumers, and supply the tune played by producers. We have also seen how each group dances to the tune played by the other.

If we now want to go beyond the question of what will be produced to the other questions—*how*? and *for whom?*—we must recognize that the world is even more complex. We don't merely have two tunes being played. We have a whole orchestra, with the tune played on any one instrument related to the tunes played on all the others.

The major segments of the economy are illustrated in Figure 4-8, which adds detail to Figure 3-3. The *product markets* for apples, coffee, bread, housing, etc., are represented by the upper box; we have concentrated on product markets thus far. The box at the bottom indicates that there are similar *markets for factors of production*, with their own demands and

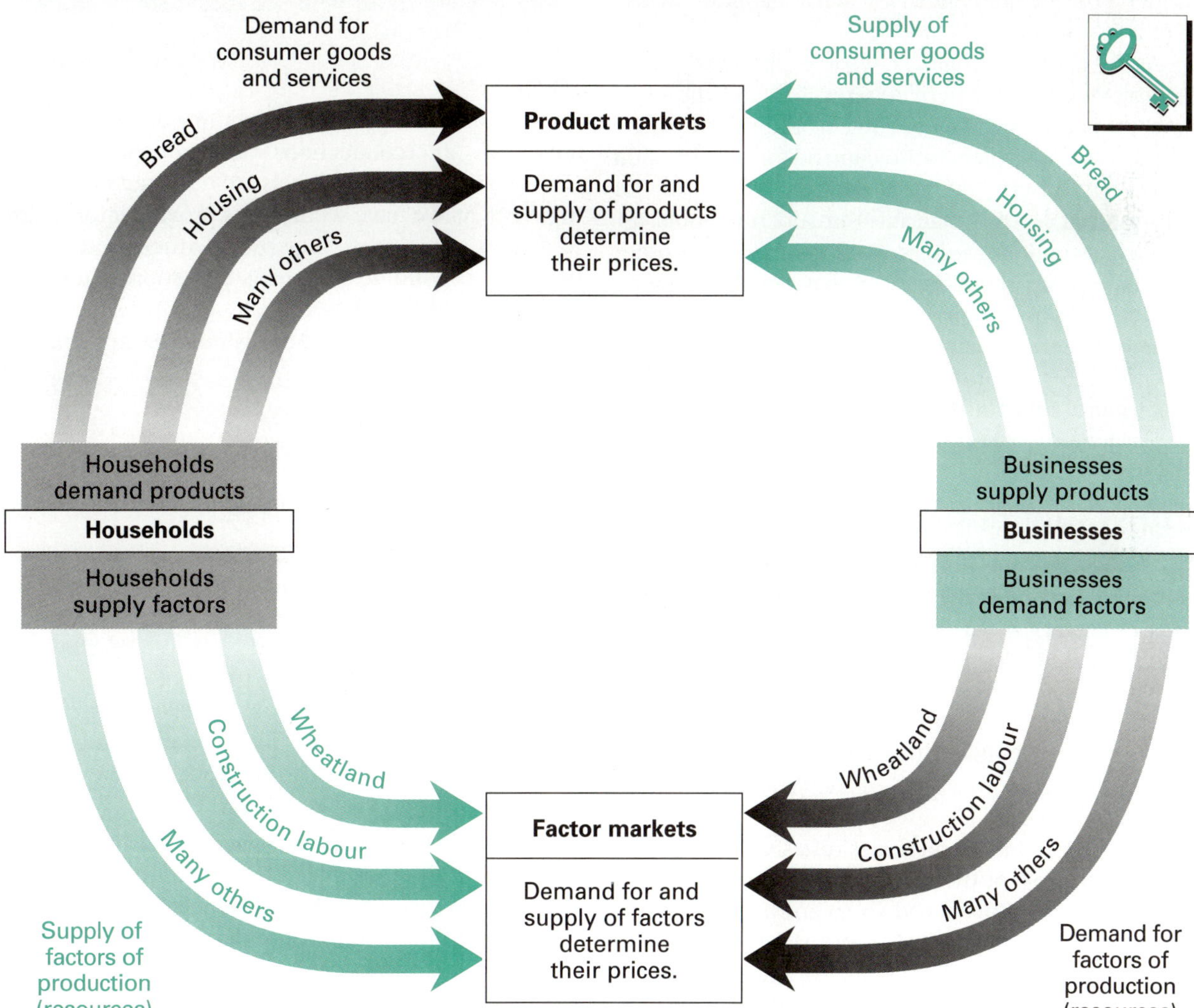


**FIGURE 4-8 Markets answer the basic questions of *what, how,* and *for whom.***

The product markets (upper box) are most important in determining *what* is produced, and the factor markets (lower box) in determining *how* goods are produced, and *for whom*. However, there are many interrelationships among the two boxes. For example, incomes change in response to changing demand and supply conditions in the lower box, and these changing incomes, in turn, influence the demand for products in the upper box.

supplies. For example, to produce wheat, farmers need land; they create a demand for land. At the same time, those with land are willing to sell or rent it if the price is attractive; they create a supply of land.

In answering the question, *What* will be produced?, we begin by looking at the upper box in Figure 4-8, where the demand for and supply of products come together. If there is a large demand for bread, we may expect a lot of it to be produced. But, eventually we will also have to look at the lower box, where the demand for and supply of the factors of production come together. Why are the factor markets relevant? Because the demand and supply in the upper box are influenced by what happens in the factor markets in the lower box.

As an example, consider what happens when oil is discovered in northern Alberta. To build the pipeline needed to get the oil out, workers have to be hired. As a consequence, the demand for construction labour in Alberta increases sharply. The price of labour (that is, the wage rate) in Alberta shoots up, and construction workers flock in from the other provinces. The spiralling wage payments in Alberta (lower box) have repercussions on the demands for goods and services in Alberta (upper box). For example, the demand for housing in Alberta (in the upper box) increases as a result of the higher earnings of construction workers in the lower box.

## *How*? and *For Whom*?

To answer the question, What will be produced?, we began by looking at the product markets in the upper box of Figure 4-8. To answer the questions *How?* and *For whom?*, we begin by looking at the lower box.

The factor prices established in the lower box help to determine *how* goods are produced. During the Black Death of 1348–1350 and subsequent plagues, an estimated quarter to a third of the Western European population died. As a consequence, labour supply was substantially reduced and wages rose sharply—by 30% to 40%. Because of the scarcity of labour and its high price, wheat producers had an incentive to farm their lands with less labour. Wheat was produced in a different way, with a different combination of labour and land. In those days, as today, the market mechanism was the way in which the society conserved its scarce supply of a factor (in this case, labour).

The answer to the question, *For whom* is the nation's output produced?, depends on incomes, which are determined by the interplay of supply and demand in factor markets (lower box in Figure 4-8). For example, the supply of accountants is small compared with the demand for accountants. The price of their "labour" is, therefore, high; accountants generally have high incomes. On the other hand, unskilled labour is in large supply, and is, therefore, cheap. Consequently, the unskilled worker receives a low income.

# THE MARKET MECHANISM: A PRELIMINARY EVALUATION

> Some see private enterprise as a predatory target to be shot, others as a cow to be milked; but few are those who see it as a sturdy horse pulling the wagon.
>
> Winston Churchill

There are thousands of markets in Canada, and millions of interconnections among the markets. Changes in market conditions are reflected in changes in prices. As we have seen, prices provide information to market participants; they provide them with incentives to respond to changing conditions; and they bring order out of a potentially chaotic situation—even though there is no individual or government bureaucracy in control.

## Strengths of the Market

In some ways, the market works very well. Specifically:

1. The market *gives producers an incentive to produce the goods that consumers want.* If people want more tea, the price of tea is bid up, and producers are encouraged to produce more. (However, see Box 4-2 for a special case where producers offer a "bad" rather than a "good," and where a strong case can be made for the government to suppress the product.)
2. The market *provides an incentive to acquire useful skills*. For example, the high incomes that doctors earn give students an incentive to undertake the long, difficult, and expensive training necessary to become a physician.
3. The market *encourages consumers to use scarce goods carefully*. For example, when the coffee crop is partially destroyed by bad weather, the price is driven up, and people use coffee sparingly. Those who are relatively indifferent are encouraged to switch to tea. Even those who feel they must have coffee are motivated to conserve. With

## APPLICATIONS AND ILLUSTRATIONS BOX 4-2

### The Controversy Over Heroin

Kurt Schmoke used to be a prosecutor. He sent hundreds of felons to jail for drug-related crimes. But when he became Mayor of Baltimore, he created a national furor by calling for a debate on the legalization of heroin. The present system, he argued, is a failure. For drug dealers, "going to jail is just part of the cost of doing business. It's a nuisance, not a deterrent."

Proponents of legalization do not condone the use of heroin and other hard drugs. But they pose a question: Why are the social costs of the present system so high? Much of our crime is associated with drugs. Addicts steal to support their habit, and dealers fight over turf. If heroin were legalized, its price would fall, reducing the compulsion of addicts to steal. If drugs were distributed by hospitals or clinics, they would be less attractive; they would be associated with sickness, not with the defiance of authority. Most of the $8 billion spent each year in the United States on the war against drugs could be diverted to treatment, which now receives less than $1 billion.

Proponents of legalization also point out that the drug trade has led to corruption and bribery at home and abroad, because it is both lucrative and illegal. In at least one country—Colombia—the government is engaged in a shooting war with drug barons; two cabinet officers have been assassinated in drug-motivated crimes in recent years.

The undisputed fact that heroin kills people is not sufficient reason to keep it illegal. Tobacco kills people too, and so does alcohol —particularly when used by drivers. Prohibition of alcohol was a failure, and was repealed in the 1930s as a way to reduce the power of organized crime. The same argument can be applied to heroin and many other illegal drugs. So say the advocates of legalization.

Opponents point out that heroin and alcohol are very different. Only 10% of alcohol users become addicts, whereas most heroin users do. If heroin were legalized, its falling price would attract new users. The costs of medical care for addicts would soar. Furthermore, the legalization of heroin, cocaine, and such drugs might lead to a much greater use of new synthetics and derivatives like crack, whose long-term effects are poorly understood. Removing the legal prohibition might be taken as a signal that hard drugs are now socially acceptable.

The British experience underlines just how difficult it is to foresee the long-term consequences of legalization. Beginning in the 1950s, Britain made heroin available to addicts by prescription. Doctors provided small doses—enough to prevent withdrawal symptoms, but not enough to create highs. The objective was to stabilize doses and, if possible, to wean addicts away from the drug. For many years, the program worked; the number of addicts remained about the same. But, the worldwide drug boom of the 1970s created a flood of heroin. Addicts found that they could easily get enough heroin to produce highs, and that, after all, is why they started taking the drug in the first place. Because they could get only limited quantities from doctors, most addicts stopped going. The prescription system virtually died out.

Like many other countries, the Netherlands found drug use increasing in the early 1970s. They responded with a program designed to separate the markets for heroin and marijuana. Jail terms for heroin dealers were tripled. At the same time, the government announced that it would not prosecute people with small amounts of marijuana, although laws against marijuana remained on the books. The idea was to keep a small market in soft drugs, which young people could use in relative safety without going to criminals who might also offer samples of hard drugs. The Dutch were originally concerned that this would lead to an upsurge in the use of mari-

*(continued)*

**BOX 4-2 continued**

*(continued)*
juana, but consumption has actually fallen. And, in the late 1980s, the policy of separating the two markets seemed to be working. The overall use of heroin had fallen, especially among young people. In 1981, 14% of Dutch addicts were under the age of 22; by the end of the decade, less than 5% were.

a high price for coffee, they are careful not to brew three cups when they intend to use only two.

4. Similarly, the price system encourages producers to *conserve scarce resources*. In the pasturelands of Alberta, land is plentiful and cheap; it is used to raise cattle. In Japan, in contrast, land is relatively scarce and expensive; few cattle are raised. At full-size golf courses, fees are astronomical; most golfers have to be content with driving ranges.
5. The market permits a *high degree of economic freedom*. Nobody forces people to do business with specific individuals or firms. People are not directed into specific lines of work by government officials; they are free to choose their own occupations. Moreover, if people save, they are free to use their savings to set themselves up in their own independent businesses.
6. Markets *provide information* on local conditions. For example, if an unusual amount of hay-producing land in a specific county is plowed up to grow corn, then the price of hay in that county will tend to rise. The higher price of hay will signal farmers that they should put some of the land in this county back into hay. No government agency can hope to keep up-to-date and detailed information on the millions of localized markets like this one, each with its own conditions. (Note the amount of information that is relevant, even for this simple decision on whether hay or corn should be planted: the quality of the land, particularly its relative productivity in hay and corn; the number of cattle and horses that eat hay; the cost of fertilizer for hay and for corn; the cost of seed for each; and so on.)

In evaluating how well a market works, we should keep in mind the most important question of all: *Compared to what?* Even a poor market may work better than the alternatives. Thus, one of the strongest arguments for the market parallels Winston Churchill's case for democracy: It doesn't work very well, but it does work better than the alternatives that have been tried from time to time.

## The Alternative of Price Controls: Some Problems

Consider what happens if the government tries to keep a price down by setting a price ceiling. Specifically, suppose it sets the price at $P_1$, below the equilibrium at $E$ in Figure 4-9. The result is a shortage, $AB$. Eager buyers have trouble finding the good. Thus, when the United States had a ceiling on gasoline prices in 1979, drivers had to wait in long lines at gas stations. Obviously, they wasted time — not to speak of the gasoline they wasted while waiting in line. Until recently, most goods and services produced in the nations of Eastern Europe and the former Soviet Union were subject to price ceilings imposed by the planning authorities. The result was chronic shortages of many commodities, and shoppers waiting patiently in long lines, even though they couldn't be sure that the available supplies would last until they reached the front of the line.

Moreover, ***price controls*** tend to create illegal ***black markets*** where goods are sold at prices higher than the regulated legal ones. As a result, the shortages in the regular distribution channels become even more severe, as producers divert supplies to the black market where they can get a higher price. And the queues in the regular stores may become even longer, as ordinary buyers are joined by speculators who don't want the price-controlled good for their own use, but instead want to make a profit by buying it at the low controlled price and reselling it at the higher black-market price. When black markets exist, many buyers may end up paying even more for the goods than they would in a free, uncontrolled, market. Black marketeers charge higher prices to compensate for the risks they take, and because they have to use informal, inefficient marketing arrangements.

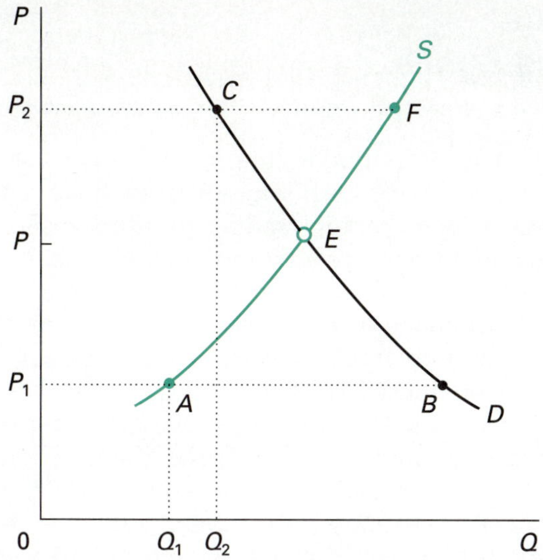


**FIGURE 4-9 Price-setting by the government.**
If the government sets a price ceiling at $P_1$ to keep the price below the equilibrium at *E*, the result is a shortage, *AB*. Observe that the consumers end up with less: the quantity supplied at *A* is less than at equilibrium *E*.

On the other hand, if the government sets a price floor at $P_2$, the result is a surplus. The government can keep the price at $P_2$ if it is willing to buy the surplus, *CF*. Again, the public ends up with less—at *C*—than it would get at equilibrium *E*. Thus, when the government sets the price, consumers get a smaller quantity, *whether the price is set above or below its equilibrium.*

A *black market* is one in which sales take place at a price above the legal maximum.

Price controls can create other problems. For example, in its desire to prevent labour unrest in the mid-1980s, the Polish government kept bread fixed at a low price—so low that is was less than the price of wheat that went into making the bread. Farmers found that it was cheaper to feed their livestock bread rather than grain. This represented a waste of the resources that had been used to make wheat into bread.

## The Market Mechanism: Limitations and Problems

Although the market has impressive strengths, it is also the target of substantial criticisms:

1. While the market provides a high degree of freedom for participants in the economy, *it may give the weak and the helpless little more than the freedom to starve*. In a market, producers do not respond solely to the needs or the eagerness of consumers to have products. Rather, they respond to those desires of consumers that are backed up with cash. Thus, under a system of *laissez-faire*, the pets of the rich may have better meals and better health care than the children of the poor.

2. Markets *simply won't work* in some areas. Where there is a military threat, individuals cannot provide their own defence. An individual who buys a rifle has no hope of standing against a foreign power. Organized military forces, financed by the government, are needed. The police and the judicial system are other services that can only be provided by the government. No matter how well the market works in general, people can't be permitted to "buy" a judge.

3. In a laissez-faire system, *prices are not always the result of impersonal market forces*. In many markets, one or more participants have the power to influence price. *The monopolist or oligopolist may restrict production in order to keep the price high*, as we shall see in detail in later chapters.

4. Activities by private consumers or producers may have undesirable *side effects*. Nobody owns the air or the rivers. Consequently, in the absence of government restraints, manufacturers use them freely as garbage dumps, harming those downwind or downstream. The market provides no incentive to limit such negative side effects.

5. An unregulated system of private enterprise may be *quite unstable*, with periods of inflationary boom giving way to sharp recessions. Economic instability was a particularly severe problem in the early 1930s, when the economies of many countries collapsed into a deep depression. Another recent example of market instability is the market for office space (see Box 4-3).

6. In a laissez-faire system, businesses may do an excellent job of satisfying consumer wants as expressed in the marketplace. But should the businesses be given high marks, if they have *created the wants in the first place* by advertising? In the words of John Kenneth Galbraith, "It involves an exercise of imagination to suppose that the taste

## APPLICATIONS AND ILLUSTRATIONS BOX 4-3

### Supply and Demand in Action: The Market for Big-City Office Space

In the late 1980s, buoyant demand and limited supply combined to make Tokyo the most expensive city in the world in which to rent an office. In 1988, office space in downtown Tokyo rented for an average of \$1750 per $m^2$ per year. For a space 4 m × 3 m, that meant an annual rental of \$21,000. Not surprisingly, many junior executives found themselves cramped in offices that were little bigger than closets.

New York was far behind, with an annual rental of "only" \$450. That was cheaper than London (\$1550), Paris (\$700), or Hong Kong (\$650). Hong Kong is often classified as a less developed area. How can offices be so expensive? One reason is the short supply of land: Hong Kong has 5.5 million people crowded in an area about 52 $km^2$. Another reason is the booming economy. Hong Kong is one of the best places to do business in all of East Asia, and firms are willing to pay the high rents.

These high prices for office space stimulated a substantial increase in supply. Even though downtown land is inherently limited, the amount of office space can still be augmented by constructing taller buildings. Another possibility is to develop new office districts in areas some distance from the existing downtown.

One of the most succesful office developers in the 1970s and 1980s was Toronto-based Olympia & York, controlled by the brothers Paul and Albert Reichmann. Olympia & York owned many of the large office buildings in downtown Toronto, and had also become one of the largest suppliers of office space in New York City. By the end of the 1980s, the Reichmanns were one of the richest families in the world, and were engaged in a huge but risky development of a new building complex (the Canary Wharf project) in the lucrative London market.

As the 1990s began, the increasing supply of office space was beginning to have an effect on the market, leading to more vacancies and a trend toward lower rental rates. An increased supply was not the only explanation: Advances in communications and data processing technology were making it possible for businesses to cut costs by making do with fewer administrative personnel, decreasing the demand for office space. Then, when the 1990/92 worldwide recession struck, the effect of these long-term trends was dramatically reinforced: The bottom fell out of the market.

A number of developers, especially those that had borrowed heavily to finance their projects, went bankrupt. Olympia & York lost control of most of their buildings, as creditors moved in to demand repayment; by late 1992, most of O & Y's holdings were once again in the Toronto market. Other developers, and the banks and trust companies that had financed them, suffered heavy losses as well. (The most famous case was Royal Trustco, who avoided bankruptcy only by being taken over by the Royal Bank of Canada.)

In one sense, the forces of supply and demand did what they are supposed to do. When office space was scarce, its price rose, and more was constructed; when the supply/demand balance changed, the price dropped sharply, and new construction came to a halt. But the cost of these fluctuations was high, to the developers who went bankrupt (and their employees), and to the institutions that had lent them money. We are left with the question: Is it really necessary to have this degree of instability and disruption in order for the market mechanism to do its job?

so expressed originates with the consumer."[2] In this case, the producer is sovereign, not the consumer. According to Galbraith, the consumer is a puppet, manipulated by producers with the aid of the advertising industry's bag of tricks. Many of the wants that producers create and then satisfy are trivial: for example, the demands for automobile chrome and junk food.

Without arguing the merits of each and every product, defenders of the market system make a countercase, based in part on the question: "Compared with what?" If market demands are dismissed, who then is to decide which products are "meritorious" and which are not? Government officials? Should not people be permitted the freedom to make their own mistakes? And why should we assume that created wants are without merit? After all, we are not born with a taste for art or good music. Our taste for good music is created when we listen to it. Galbraith certainly wouldn't suggest that symphony orchestras are without merit simply because they satisfy the desire for good music that they have created. But who then is to decide which "created" wants are socially desirable?

If these criticisms of the market are taken far enough, they can be made into a case for replacing the market with an alternative system. Traditionally, Marxist economists have laid particular emphasis on points 1, 5, and 6 in their argument that the market should be replaced with central planning and government direction of the economy.

However, these criticisms are also often made by those who seek to reform, rather than replace, the market system. The recent economic history of Western Europe, North America, and many other parts of the globe has been written to a significant extent by such reformers. If the market does not provide a living for the weak and the helpless, then its outcome should be modified by private and public assistance programs. If monopoly firms have excessive market power, they should be broken up or their market power should be restrained by the government. If an unregulated market means that only American television programs would be shown in Canada, the government should regulate the television industry to protect Canadian culture. Where there are undesirable side effects, such as pollution, they should be limited by taxation or control programs. In defence, justice, the police, and other areas where the market won't work or works very poorly, the government should assume responsibility for the provision of services.

Although the market is a vital mechanism, it has sufficient weaknesses to provide the government with a major economic role. This role will be the subject of the next chapter.

[2] John Kenneth Galbraith, "Economics as a System of Belief," *American Economic Review*, May 1970, p. 474. See also Galbraith, *The New Industrial State* (Boston: Houghton Mifflin, 1967).

## KEY POINTS

1. Every economy has limited resources and involves specialization and exchange. In every economy, a mechanism is needed to answer three fundamental questions:
   (a) *What* will be produced?
   (b) *How* will it be produced?
   (c) *For whom* will it be produced?

2. There are two principal mechanisms for answering these questions:
   (a) The market, where individuals are free to make their own contracts and transactions.
   (b) The government, which can use taxation, spending, regulation, and government-owned enterprises to influence *what*, *how*, and *for whom*.

   In the real world, all countries have mixed economies that rely on both market and government action. However, the mixture differs among countries. Canada and other Western countries place a relatively heavy reliance on the market. In countries such as China and North Korea, the government has a much more pervasive influence. In the former Soviet Union and Eastern Europe, government planning was much more important than markets until the early 1990s.

3. *Prices* play a key role in markets, providing information and incentives to buyers and sellers.

4. Markets vary substantially, with some being dominated by one or a few producers, while others have many producers and consumers. A market

is *perfectly competitive* if there are many buyers and many sellers, with no single buyer or seller having any influence over the price.

5. In a perfectly competitive market, equilibrium price and quantity are established by the intersection of the demand and supply curves.

6. In drawing both the demand and supply curves, the *ceteris paribus* assumption is made — that "other things" do not change. Everything that can affect the quantity demanded or supplied—with the sole exception of price — is held constant when a demand or supply curve is constructed.

7. If any of these "other things"—such as consumer incomes or the prices of other goods — do change, the demand or supply curve will shift.

8. *What* the economy produces is determined primarily in the market for goods and services in the upper box of Figure 4-8. On the other hand, *how* and *for whom* are determined primarily in the factor markets (the lower box). However, there are numerous interactions among markets. The answer to each of the three questions depends on what happens in both the upper and lower boxes.

9. There is a substantial case to be made for the market system, because it encourages firms to produce what people demand, and because it encourages the careful use of scarce goods and resources. Nevertheless, the market also has significant weaknesses, which provide the government with an important economic role.

## KEY TERMS

**what? how? for whom?**
**market**
**central planning**
**capitalist economy**
**free enterprise**
**mixed economy**
**prices as information**
**prices as incentives**
**monopoly**
**oligopoly**
**perfect competition**
**price taker**
**imperfect competition**
**market power**
**industry**
**firm**
**plant**
**demand**
**supply**
**market equilibrium**
**surplus (excess supply)**
**shortage (excess demand)**
**ceteris paribus**
**demand shifter**
**inferior good**
**normal (superior) good**
**substitutes**
**complements (complementary goods)**
**supply shifter**
**joint products**
**product markets**
**factor markets**
**price control**
**black market**

## PROBLEMS

4-1. Figure 4-6 illustrates the effect of a freeze in Brazil on the coffee market. How might the resulting change in the price of coffee affect the tea market? Explain with the help of a diagram showing the demand for and supply of tea.

4-2. The relatively high incomes of doctors give students an incentive to study medicine. Other than the expected income and costs of training, what are the important things that affect career decisions?

4-3. It is often said that "the market has no ethics. It is impersonal." But individual participants in the market do have ethical values, and these values may be backed up with social pressures. Suppose that in a certain society, it is considered not quite proper to be associated with a distillery. With the help of demand and supply diagrams, explain how this view will affect:
(a) The demand and/or supply of labour in the alcohol industry.
(b) The willingness of people to invest their funds in the alcohol industry, and the profitability of that industry.

4-4. Suppose that social sanctions are backed up by law, and that people caught selling marijuana are given stiff jail sentences. How will this affect the demand for and supply of marijuana? The price of marijuana? The quantity sold? The incomes of those selling marijuana?

*4-5. In distinguishing between substitutes and complements, the text listed a number of simple cases. Tea and coffee are substitutes, while cars and gasoline are complements. However, it is worth looking more closely at one example that may not seem quite so simple: heating oil and insulation. How would you correct or rebut the following erroneous argument:

> Heating oil and insulation are complements, not substitutes, because they are used together. In Winnipeg, Manitoba, people use a lot of heating oil and a lot of insulation. In Miami, Florida, people don't use much of either.

Try to answer this question without looking at the following hints. But, if you have difficulty, consider these hints:

(a) Think about the market for heating oil and insulation in a single place, say, Winnipeg. When the price of heating oil goes up in Winnipeg, do you think that this causes the demand curve for insulation to shift to the right or to the left? Does this make insulation a complement or substitute for heating oil, according to the definitions in the text?

(b) Are natural gas and oil substitutes or complements? Suppose the erroneous statement given above had mentioned heating oil and natural gas, rather than heating oil and insulation.

(c) If we accept the erroneous statement shown above, can't we argue in a similar manner that there are no such things as substitutes? For example, wouldn't we also accept the following incorrect conclusion: "In the Niagara Region, more apples and more cherries are sold than in the Northwest Territories. Therefore, apples and cherries are used together. They are complements, not substitutes." Do you see that this statement is incorrect, because it departs from the standard assumption that "other things remain unchanged?" In identifying complements and substitutes, we must not switch from one location and population (Northwest Territories) to another (Southern Ontario); we must look at a single set of people, such as the Winnipeg example in part (a). Do you see now why economists emphasize the assumption that "other things remain unchanged" (*ceteris paribus*)?

CHAPTER

# 5 THE ECONOMIC ROLE OF THE GOVERNMENT

*In answering that question [on the role of the State] it would be necessary to enter into a large consideration of what the Government can do for the benefit of those subject to it, and that is a very wide question, on which people may differ.*

*John Stuart Mill,* in evidence before the Select Committee on the Income and Property Tax, 1852

The defects and limitations of the market system, outlined at the end of Chapter 4, provide a reason for the government to play an important role in the economy. In the words of Adam Smith, there are economic functions " . . . which, though they may be in the highest degree advantageous to a great society, are, however, of such a nature, that the profit could never repay the expence to any individual, or small group of individuals"; consequently, these functions must be undertaken by the government.

In Chapter 4, we described briefly how the government affects the economy in four principal ways: by *spending*, *taxation*, *regulation*, and by running *public enterprises*. For example, when the government *spends* for roads or for ships for the navy, then production is affected: More roads and ships are built. The primary function of *taxation* is to raise revenue for the government; taxes are an unpleasant necessity. But taxes may also be used for secondary purposes. For example, if the government wants to discourage the production of some goods, it can put a tax on them. (This will raise their price and lead consumers to buy less.) The government also influences economic behaviour through direct *regulation*. Regulations regarding seat belts and other safety equipment have affected the design of automobiles; safety requirements affect the way in which coal is mined; and government regulations limit the amount of pollution that manufacturers can discharge into the air and water. Finally, the government indirectly affects many sectors of the economy through the activities of *public enterprises*. For example, because the CBC has a policy of favouring Canadian programming, more Canadians have jobs in symphony orchestras or in the television industry, and TV viewers spend less of their time watching foreign programs.

Figure 5-1 provides a simplifed illustration of the way spending and taxation by government fits into the circular flow of income illustrated earlier in Figure 3-3. Arrows 1 and 2 are the same as in that earlier diagram: Arrow 1 represents payments by households for the goods and services they buy in the marketplace from the business firms that supply them, while arrow 2 represents payments by firms for the factor services (of labour, capital, etc.) provided by the households. Arrows 3 and 4 are the taxes that government collects from households and firms in order to finance its activities; government spending (arrows 5 and 6) includes payments to firms and households who provide goods or services to the government, as well as other payments such as transfers to raise the incomes of poor families or to subsidize business firms in depressed regions. In an economy that relies primarily on the private market, the flows represented by arrows 1 and 2 are large relative to those in arrows 3 to 6; in an economy such as that in the former Soviet Union where the government dominated economic life, the opposite is true.

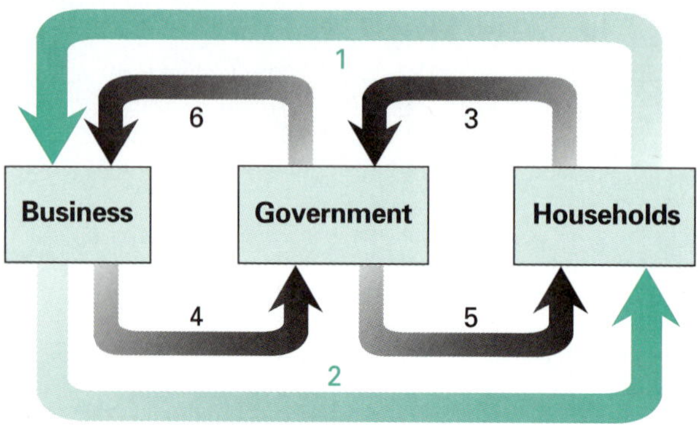


**FIGURE 5-1 The circular flow in an economy with government.**

This figure shows the modification that must be made in earlier circular flow diagrams (Figures 3-3 and 4-8) when government is added. Arrow 1 represents payments by households for consumer goods and services; arrow 2 represents payments by firms for factor services (labour, capital, etc.). Arrows 3 and 4 are tax payments by households and firms, respectively, to the government; and arrows 5 and 6 are payments by government to firms and households for goods or services supplied, or as income transfers.

In contrast with the private market, where people have an option of buying or not, government activities generally involve compulsion. Taxes must be paid; people are not allowed to opt out of the system when the time rolls around for paying income taxes. Similarly, government regulations involve compulsion; car manufacturers must install safety equipment. And compulsion sometimes exists even in a government spending program. Young people must go to school (although their parents do have the option of choosing a private school rather than one run by the government).

Later sections of this chapter will consider how the government can use spending, taxation, regulation, and public enterprise to improve the outcome of the private market. As a preliminary, it is necessary to look at some facts showing how the government's role has expanded, and what the government is currently doing.

## THE GROWTH OF GOVERNMENT EXPENDITURES

During the nineteenth and early twentieth centuries, government expenditures covered little more than the expenses of the army and police, a few public works, and the salaries of judges, legislators, and a small body of government officials. Except for wartime periods when spending shot upward to pay for munitions, weapons, and personnel, government spending was small. As late as 1928, all levels of government (federal, provincial, and local) together spent less than $800 million a year. Of this total, about two-thirds was spent by provincial and local governments. Highway maintenance and education were typical government programs. This does not mean, however, that a rigid policy of laissez-faire was followed. Even during the nineteenth century, the Canadian government participated in some important sectors of the economy, notably railroad building.

With the Great Depression of the 1930s, there came a major increase in government activity. Distress and unemployment were widespread, and it was increasingly hard to believe that the workings of the private market would lead to the best of all possible worlds. Public sector spending increased rapidly as all levels of government tried to alleviate the burden on the unemployed and to create new jobs for them in the public sector. Then, as Canada became heavily involved in World War II, huge federal government spending was required to pay for military equipment and for the salaries of military personnel.

When the war ended in 1945, the nation demobilized and government spending fell by about 30%. But the decline was only temporary. Over the past three decades, spending at all levels of government has increased rapidly, to total no less than $340 billion by 1991 (Figure 5-2).

### Government Expenditures in Perspective

Clearly, government spending has become very large. It is hard for the average citizen, accustomed to dealing with a family budget measured in hundreds or thousands of dollars, to comprehend government budgets measured in billions of dollars. A billion dollars may be more meaningful if it is reduced to a personal level: A billion dollars represents about $40 for every man, woman, and child in Canada. Thus, with total annual budgets amounting to $340 billion, our federal, provincial, and local governments spent more than $12,500 per Canadian in 1991. The magnitude of a billion dollars may be illustrated in another way. When the government borrows $1 billion at an interest rate of 10% per annum, its interest payments amount to more than $270,000 *per day*.

But the expenditures shown in Figure 5-2 can give a misleading impression of the size of the government. While the government is spending more and more, so are private individuals and businesses. For both the government and the private sectors, these rising expenditures reflect two major trends: More and more goods and services are being bought, and at higher and higher prices. We can see government expenditures in better perspective by examining them, not in dollar terms (as in Figure 5-2), but rather as a percentage of total spending in Canada.[1]

When we do this in Figure 5-3 on page 78, the increase in government expenditures does not look quite as dramatic. Following the wartime peak of about 50% of total Canadian spending, government spending fell to less than 25% in the mid-1940s, and the percentage then rose only slowly until the mid-1960s. However, since then it has again risen at a rapid pace and, by the early 1990s, total government spending had surpassed the wartime level of more than 50% of total spending.

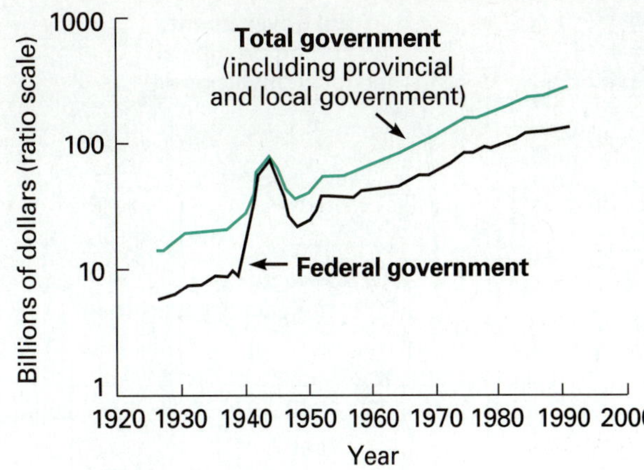


**FIGURE 5-2 Government expenditures, 1926–1991.**

The most rapid rate of increase in government spending came during 1940–1945, as the federal government had to spend enormous sums to pay for the war. In the last two decades, government spending has again increased rapidly; most of this increase has been accounted for by non-defence expenditures at all levels of government (federal, provincial, and local).

*Source*: Statistics Canada, *CANSIM Databank*. Reproduced by permission of the Minister of Supply and Services Canada.

## Government Purchases versus Transfers

A further complication in measuring the size of the government arises because of the two major categories of government expenditures: (1) *purchases of goods and services*, and (2) *transfer payments*.

Government purchases of goods include items such as telephones, computers, and army trucks. The government purchases services when it hires schoolteachers, police officers, and employees for government departments. When the government purchases such goods and services, *it makes a direct claim on the productive capacity of the nation.* For example, when it spends $1000 for a computer terminal, then plastic, wiring, and labour are used to manufacture the terminal. Similarly, the purchase of services involves a claim on productive resources. The police officer hired by the government must spend time on the beat, and thus becomes unavailable for work in the private sector.

Government ***transfer payments***, on the other hand, are payments for which the recipient does not provide any good or service in return. Social assistance payments to low-income families are examples of transfer payments, as are Old Age Security (OAS) and Unemployment Insurance benefits.

In contrast with government purchases, transfer payments represent no direct claim by the government on the productive capacity of the nation. For example, when the government pays OAS benefits to retired people, there is no reallocation of the nation's product away from the private sector toward the government sector. Unlike the computer manufacturer that produces a terminal and ships it to the government to get the payment of $1000, the OAS benefit recipient does not use up productive resources to provide the government with a good or a service in return for the benefit. This does not mean, of course, that the Old Age Security program is unimportant. When the government collects taxes[2] to finance it

[1] The measure of total spending—gross domestic product (GDP)—will be explained in Chapter 6.

[2] Payments into social insurance funds such as the Canada Pension Plan or Unemployment Insurance are sometimes called *contributions*, on the grounds that individuals acquire a right to pensions and other benefits as a reward for their payments. But it is also correct to label these contributions as taxes, since they are involuntary payments that must be made to the government. (Furthermore, while benefits sometimes bear some relation to the "contributions" that an individual has made, they are not closely tied to previous "contributions.")

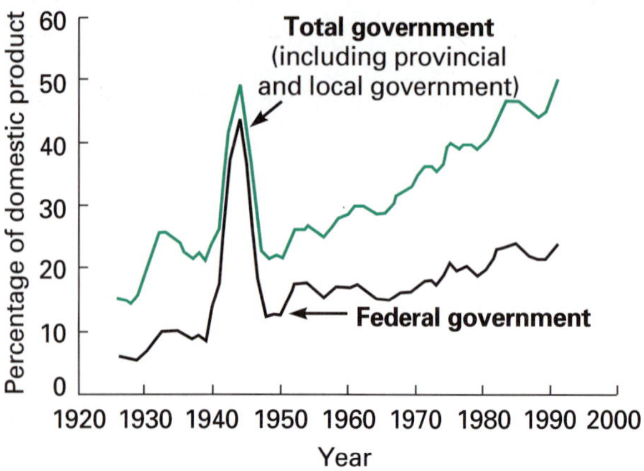


**FIGURE 5-3 Total government expenditures (including transfers).**

If we look at what the government takes for itself plus what it takes to redistribute in the form of transfers, then the government has laid claim to a growing share of total output and spending in Canada.

*Source*: Statistics Canada, *CANSIM Databank*. Reproduced by permission of the Minister of Supply and Services Canada.

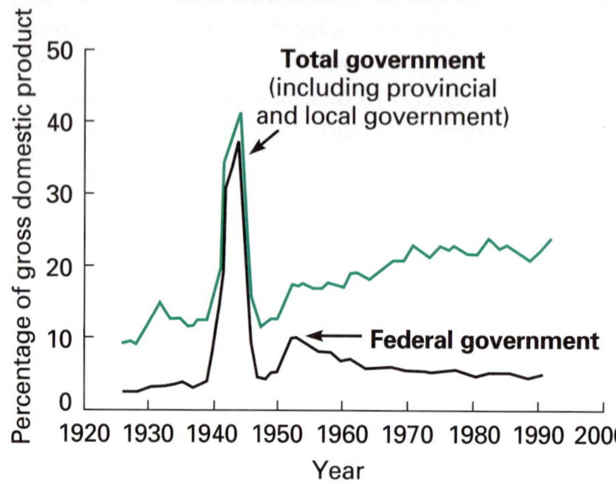


**FIGURE 5-4 Government purchases of goods and services.**

However, as a percentage of total spending, government purchases of goods and services have changed much more slowly over the past two decades

*Source*: Statistics Canada, *CANSIM Databank*. Reproduced by permission of the Minister of Supply and Services Canada.

and pays benefits to retirees, the pattern of consumer spending is affected. Retirees have more disposable income, and those of working age who pay taxes, have less. As a consequence, producers find themselves faced with greater demands for the things that older, retired people want, and with smaller demands for the products desired by the working population. Therefore, although the system of government transfer payments affects the amount of the nation's product that various individuals can purchase, it does not redirect the economy toward production for the government.

A *transfer payment* is a payment by the government to an individual, for which the individual does not provide a good or service in return.

Figure 5-3 showed total government expenditures, including transfers. Another way of measuring the size of the government is to look only at government purchases of goods and services; that is, expenditures excluding transfers, as shown in Figure 5-4. These are the expenditures that make a direct claim on the productive resources of the economy. As a share of total Canadian spending, government purchases of goods and services stayed relatively constant between the early 1950s and the mid-1960s. Even though the percentage has risen in the last 20 years, by the early 1990s it had risen to only about 24% — a bit more than half its wartime peak.

We can thus get two somewhat different impressions of the government's size, compared with the size of the economy. If we look only at purchases of goods and services, then the percentage of national product going to the government has been rising fairly slowly over the past two decades. If, on the other hand, we include transfers, the government's percentage has been increasing much more rapidly. Thus, the principal reason for the government's increasing share of the economy is not that it is directly claiming more and more of the nation's output for itself. Instead, the increasing share is mostly due to the claiming of more revenue by the government to be redistributed in the form of transfer payments such as Old Age Security benefits and social welfare assistance.

While the government is a major participant in the Canadian economy, the governments in some European countries assume an even larger role. In a country such as Sweden, taxes have to be very high to pay for the cradle-to-grave welfare system. But, in other countries, the role of the government is smaller, and tax collections are a smaller percentage of income. In spite of its rapid achievement of a standard of living similar to Western Europe's, Japan has remained a low-tax country, collecting only about half as large a share in taxes as do the Western European countries. It is also the case that the U.S. government collects a significantly smaller share of total income as taxes than does the Canadian government.

# THE BUDGETS OF THE CANADIAN GOVERNMENTS

## Federal Government Expenditures

Details on federal government expenditures in Canada, and on the taxes that finance these expenditures, are provided in panel (a) of Table 5-1. This table includes both purchases of goods and services and transfer payments to persons as well as to other levels of government. In Canada's federal system, the share of the federal government in total government spending on goods and services is comparatively small. Thus, expenditures on current goods and services in Table 5-1 are a relatively small portion of the expenditures shown (around one-fifth of the total). Included in this share is defence spending, as well as the cost of maintaining the federal civil service in Ottawa and elsewhere in Canada.

"Social services" is now the single largest expenditure item, accounting for almost 30% of the federal budget. This item includes Old Age Security and Guaranteed Income Supplement payments to retired people, family allowances[3], and Unemployment Insurance benefits.

The federal government also transfers a large share of its revenue to provincial and local governments: Item (8) includes "general purpose transfers" as well as transfers specifically intended to help cover provincial costs for health care, education, and social welfare.

By far the fastest-growing expenditure category in recent years has been "debt charges," that is, interest on the public debt. In 1991, it was the second largest item on the expenditure side, at over $40 billion, close to one-third of federal government revenue. The

[3] Beginning in 1993, the earlier system of universal family allowances was replaced by a child tax benefit that goes only to those taxpayers with relatively low incomes.

**TABLE 5-1 Federal Government Expenditure and Revenue Fiscal Year Ending March 31, 1991**

| (a) **Expenditure** | **Billions of Dollars** | **Percentage** |
|---|---|---|
| 1. General Services | 6.9 | 4 |
| 2. Protection of Persons and Property | 14.1 | 9 |
| 3. Transportation and Communication | 3.5 | 2 |
| 4. Health | — | — |
| 5. Social Services | 42.8 | 28 |
| 6. Education | 1.6 | 1 |
| 7. Resource Conservation & Industrial Development | 5.1 | 3 |
| 8. Transfers to other levels of government | 26.7 | 17 |
| 9. Debt Charges | 41.0 | 26 |
| 10. Other Expenditure | 13.3 | 9 |
| Total | 155.0 | |
| (b) **Revenue** | **Billions of Dollars** | **Percentage** |
| 1. Personal Income Tax | 60.3 | 48 |
| 2. Corporation Income Tax | 12.4 | 10 |
| 3. Non-Resident Income Tax | 1.5 | 1 |
| 4. General Sales Tax | 16.2 | 13 |
| 5. Excise Duties and Special Taxes | 12.6 | 10 |
| 6. Unemployment Insurance Contributions | 12.7 | 10 |
| 7. Return on Investment | 6.3 | 5 |
| 8. Miscellaneous Non-tax Revenue | 13.3 | 4 |
| Total | 126.5 | |

*Source:* Compiled by the author from Canadian Tax Foundation, *The National Finances 1991.*

main reason for this rapid growth is that the size of the debt itself has grown rapidly. In 1975, the federal debt was less than $40 billion; at the end of 1991, it was just about $340 billion. (We will discuss the public debt in more detail in Chapter 10.)

## Provincial and Local Government Expenditures

As can be seen from Figure 5-3, the share of total public expenditure accounted for by provincial and local governments is about as large as the federal government's share, thus reflecting Canada's relatively decentralized system of government. (In the United States, federal government spending is closer to two-thirds of total public sector spending.) Panel (a) in Table 5-2 gives a breakdown of provincial/local expenditure. The largest expenditure items at this level of government are the costs of education (20%) and health care (23%). These costs have been growing rapidly in the past several decades. Spending on social services other than education and health account for a smaller share in the provincial/local budget than in the federal budget. While provincial and local governments pay the cost of social assistance to families or individuals with low income, the expenditures on such welfare programs in 1991 was not nearly as high as the federal government's expenditures on programs such as family allowances, Old Age Security and Unemployment Insurance.

## Government Receipts

Details on the revenue derived from taxation at the federal and provincial/local levels are shown in panel (b) of Tables 5-1 and 5-2.

The federal and provincial ***income taxes*** on individuals yield the largest share of tax revenue at both levels of government: 48% of total federal tax revenue and 22% for provincial/local governments. Collection of the federal and provincial income taxes has been largely centralized, so that (except in Quebec) both are computed on the basis of the same income tax return prepared by the taxpayer at the end of April,

**TABLE 5-2** Consolidated Provincial/Local Government Revenue and Expenditure Fiscal Year Ended Nearest to March 1, 1991

| (a) **Expenditure** | **Billions of Dollars** | **Percentage** |
|---|---|---|
| 1. General Services | 11.1 | 6 |
| 2. Protection of Persons and Property | 9.3 | 5 |
| 3. Transportation and Communication | 11.6 | 7 |
| 4. Health | 40.1 | 23 |
| 5. Social Services | 23.9 | 13 |
| 6. Education | 35.8 | 20 |
| 7. Resource Conservation & Industrial Development | 7.3 | 4 |
| 8. Debt Charges | 26.1 | 11 |
| 9. Other Expenditure | 17.5 | 10 |
| Total | 176.7 | |

| (b) **Revenue** | **Billions of Dollars** | **Percentage** |
|---|---|---|
| 1. Personal Income Tax | 37.3 | 22 |
| 2. Corporation Income Tax | 6.9 | 4 |
| 3. Non-Resident Income Tax | — | — |
| 4. General Sales Tax | 19.1 | 11 |
| 5. Other Consumption Taxes | 8.7 | 5 |
| 6. Health and Social Insurance Levies | 9.4 | 5 |
| 7. Other Tax Revenue | 30.2 | 17 |
| 8. Natural Resource Revenue | 6.0 | 3 |
| 9. Return on Investment | 13.4 | 8 |
| 10. Miscellaneous Non-tax Revenue | 15.1 | 9 |
| 11. Total transfer from the federal government and government enterprises | 26.7 | 15 |
| Total | 172.8 | |

*Source:* Compiled by the authors from Canadian Tax Foundation, *The National Finances 1991.*

and the actual taxes are paid to the federal government which then remits the provinces' shares to the provincial treasuries. In all provinces except Quebec, a person's provincial income tax liability is computed as a percentage of his or her federal income tax, but the percentage varies: In 1991, it ranged from a low of 44% in the Northwest Territories to a high of 62% in Newfoundland.[4] For the same taxable income, the percentage paid as income tax therefore varies from province to province.

In Table 5-3, column 2, we have computed the 1992 federal and provincial income tax payable for a taxpayer living in Ontario where the provincial tax was about 54.5% of the federal tax. The ***average tax rate***, shown in column 3, is simply the total tax divided by income. Observe that the income tax is a ***progressive tax***: the average percentage tax increases as taxable income increases.

Note also the concept of the ***marginal tax rate*** shown in the last column; this is the percentage tax payable on *additional* income. For example, in the tax bracket with income of less than $29,600, the marginal tax rate is 27%. Within this bracket, if income rises by $100 (from $25,000 to $25,100, say), an extra $27 must be paid in taxes. The marginal tax rate becomes higher as taxable income rises: It is the higher marginal tax rate that pulls up the *average* tax rate as income rises.

If a tax takes a larger percentage of income as income rises, the tax is *progressive.*

If a tax takes a smaller percentage of income as income rises, the tax is *regressive.*

If a tax takes a constant percentage of income, the tax is *proportional.*

[4] In Quebec, the provincial income tax is computed directly from the individual's taxable income, and the tax is collected directly by the province.

Various kinds of *sales and excise taxes* are levied by both the provincial and federal governments. The broadly based Goods and Services Tax (GST), and the provincial sales taxes, are the most important ones. Both the GST and the provincial sales taxes are levied as a uniform percentage of the value of most goods and services, with specific exceptions. (For example, food is exempted from both the GST and provincial sales taxes.) In addition, there are various federal and provincial excise taxes on specific commodities (such as tobacco, beer and liquor, cosmetics, gasoline, and fuel oil). The federal government also collects customs duties on goods imported into Canada. While the customs duties are imposed partly to raise revenue, they also have the function of protecting Canadian producers from foreign competition by making imported goods more expensive.

The GST and other federal sales and excise taxes together represent the second most important source of tax revenue for the federal government, and sales taxes are second in importance (next to the personal income tax) for provincial governments as well. Local governments raise almost nine-tenths of their tax revenue from *property taxes*, that is, taxes imposed on the ownership of land and houses. (Property taxes are included in "other tax revenue" in Table 5-2, panel (b).)

The *corporate income tax* is an important source of revenue for both the provincial and federal governments. Like the personal income tax, the total corporation income tax is collected by the federal government, which then remits the provinces' shares to the provincial treasuries.[5] The basic corporation income tax schedule has only two rates for a given type of corporation. For example, for small Canadian-controlled corporations in the manufacturing sector, it is about 20%, while for a large corporation it is

[5] There are two exceptions to this procedure: Quebec and Ontario, where the tax is collected directly by the provincial governments.

**TABLE 5-3 Federal and Provincial Income Tax, Ontario Residents, 1992†**

| (1) Taxable Income | (2) Income Tax | (3) Income Tax as Percent of Income | (4) Marginal Tax Rate |
|---|---|---|---|
| $ 25,000 | $ 4,741 | 19% | 27% |
| 40,000 | 10,286 | 26% | 41% |
| 60,000 | 18,689 | 31% | 47% |
| 100,000 | 38,270 | 38% | 50% |
| 200,000 | 88,042 | 44% | 50% |

†We have assumed that the taxpayer has a non-refundable tax credit of $1,268.

*Source:* Compiled from Revenue Canada, *General Tax Guide for Residents of Ontario,* 1992.

around 45% (the rates vary somewhat from province to province). Business income (or "net income") of corporations is computed by deducting all business expenses from total revenues; in other words, the tax is levied on corporate profits.

Although it remains important, the corporation income tax was a less significant revenue source in the early 1990s than it had been in previous years, reflecting substantial reductions in the tax rates. On the other hand, various kinds of *social insurance contributions* have increased in importance, both at the federal and provincial levels. For the provinces, health insurance premiums or payroll taxes to finance health insurance are important. For the federal government, the most signficant item by far is Unemployment Insurance contributions, which in 1991 accounted for as much as 10% of total revenue.

With expenditures of $155 billion and tax revenues of $126.5 billion, the federal government ran a deficit of some 28.5 billion in 1990/91. By historical and international standards, this deficit, and the deficits throughout the 1980s, were very large, and the question of what to do about them has become a central one in the Canadian debate about economic policy in the early 1990s, not only at the federal but also at the provincial level.

In the early 1980s and in 1990/91, the large deficits could in part be explained by the recessions that the economy was going through: In recessionary times, government revenues from various kinds of taxes tend to fall, and spending on programs such as Unemployment Insurance and social assistance rises. But relatively large deficits were incurred in the middle and late 1980s as well, even though the economy was quite prosperous in those years. (As Box 5-1 explains, the problem of large deficits has not been unique to Canada: They have been large in the United States as well.)

If a government's revenues exceed its expenditures, it has a budget *surplus*.

If a government's expenditures exceed its revenues, it has a budget *deficit*.

If a government's revenues are approximately equal to its expenditures, its budget is *balanced*.

## Intergovernmental Transfers

The total expenditures of provincial and local governments in recent decades have been substantially larger than the amounts of *tax* revenue collected by these governments. To make up for the shortfall, they have had to rely on financial support from higher levels of government.

Local governments, whose expenditures have been growing rapidly and whose only substantial source of tax revenue is the property tax, have been receiving large transfers from the provincial governments. The provincial governments, in turn, have also needed large amounts of revenue, not only to pay for the transfers to the local governments, but also to finance the rapidly growing cost of health care, post-secondary education, and social welfare. (Under the Constitution, and formerly under the British North America Act, programs in these areas are the responsibility of the provincial governments.)

Not surprisingly, the subject of ***intergovernmental transfers*** has been controversial in recent years. As the federal government has struggled to reduce its deficit, it has cut back on its transfers to the provinces. As a result, the provinces have had to restrain their spending in sectors such as health and post-secondary education, and raise taxes; reduced federal/provincial transfers also help explain the rapidly growing deficits in some provincial budgets. Provincial governments have also responded by cutting back their own transfers to local governments, forcing them to hold the line on spending and to raise taxes as well. (For more detail on federal/provincial transfers, see Box 5-1.)

# GOVERNMENT REGULATION

The billions of dollars that governments spend or collect in taxes have a substantial effect on the types of goods produced and on who gets those goods. But the size of budgets cannot be taken as the sole measure of the government's economic impact. Business behaviour is significantly influenced also by various regulatory progams, even though the costs of administering these programs show up as comparatively small items in the government's budget.

For example, regulations imposed by the government of Ontario have forced the International Nickel Corporation (INCO) to install complicated antipollution equipment in order to reduce the emissions of sulphur dioxide from its plant in Sudbury, Ontario. The cost of the equipment, which will be borne by INCO, will be much higher than the government's cost of administering the antipollution program.

Government measures to limit various abuses of private business have a long history in Canada. In 1889, a section was put into the Criminal Code pro-

## TOOLS AND TECHNIQUES BOX 5-1

## Federal Transfers to the Provinces

### Established Programs Financing

Established Programs Financing (EPF) transfers are the largest among the three major federal/provincial transfer programs, amounting to over $20.8 billion in 1992/93. EPF was put in place in 1977 in lieu of the then existing transfer programs in the areas of health care and post-secondary education. In part, EPF was a response to federal concern over the lack of control over expenditures under these transfer programs. In part, too, as the name implies, there was a sense that these programs were now "established" and that a different federal role in financing them was appropriate.

Prior to 1986, per capita entitlements were escalated annually according to growth in per capita GNP. Beginning in 1986, this escalator was reduced by two percentage points annually. Since 1990/91, the per capita entitlement has been frozen at its 1989/90 level. As of 1995/96, entitlements are slated to grow again, then at the rate of growth of per capita GNP less 3%.

In calculating the total EPF transfers, the federal government includes both its direct cash payments to the provinces and a portion of the income tax revenue it collects and passes on to the provinces.

The provinces themselves have long claimed that the value of the tax transfer is

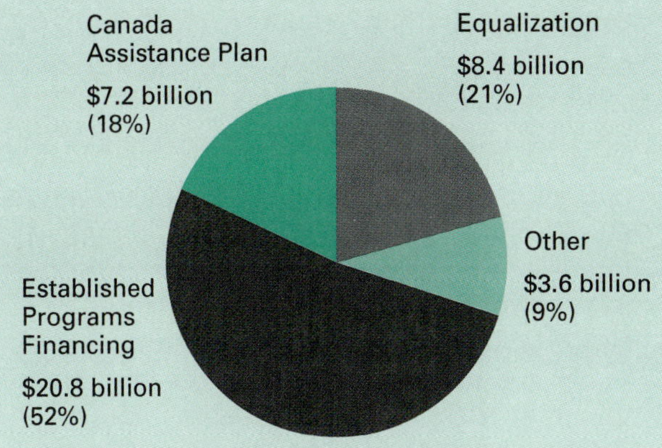


**(a) Total Federal Transfers to Provinces, 1992/93**

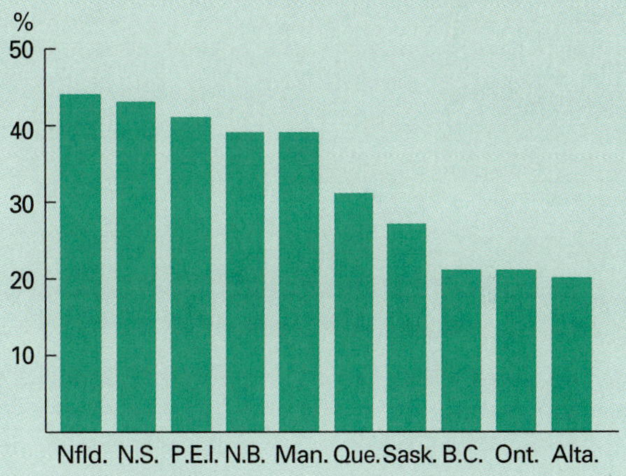


**(b) Major federal transfers as a share of provincial revenues, 1992/93**

**Federal transfers to the provinces.**

Panel (a) shows total federal transfers to the provinces for 1992/93. The largest single transfer is through the Established Programs Financing (EPF) program, amounting to 52% of the total. The total EPF transfer—cash and tax—amounted to $20.8 billion. Fiscal equalization amounted to 21% of the total, or $8.4 billion. The Canada Assistance Plan (CAP) amounted to 18% of the total, or $7.2 billion.

Panel (b) shows major federal transfers as a share of provincial revenues by province. For 1992/93, major federal transfers ranged from 44% of provincial revenues in Newfoundland to 20% in Alberta. Federal transfers are particularly important in those provinces that receive equalization payments, especially in the four Atlantic provinces.

*Source*: *Federal Transfers to the Provinces*, Department of Finance, Ottawa, July 1992; "Federal-Provincial Programs: The Need for Change," Budget Paper D, 1992 Budget, Government of Ontario, 1992; *The Equalization Program*, mimeo, Federal-Provincial Fiscal Relations Division, Department of Finance, Ottawa, November 1992; "Federal Transfers to the Provinces: Quebec's Point of View," Appendix E in *1991–1992 Budget Speech and Additional Information*, Government of Quebec, May 1991.

**BOX 5-1 continued**

not a transfer at all; that the erosion in the direct cash transfer signifies a diminished and rapidly falling federal commitment to funding programs in health care and post-secondary education.

## The Fiscal Equalization Program

The fiscal equalization program provides unconditional revenue transfers to the so-called have-not provinces, designed to raise their individual fiscal capacities up to the equalization standard. Fiscal capacity is a measure of a province's potential to generate revenues on a per capita basis from a standardized set of revenue sources including income taxes, sales taxes, natural resource royalties, and the like. Where a province's fiscal capacity is below the average for the so-called representative five provinces — Quebec, Ontario, Manitoba, Saskatchewan, and British Columbia—the difference is made up through an unconditional revenue transfer from the federal government.

Since 1982, the principle of revenue equalization has been enshrined in the Constitution. Section 36(2) of the Constitution Act, 1982 states that:

> Parliament and the government of Canada are committed to the principle of making equalization payments to ensure that provincial governments have sufficient revenues to provide reasonably comparable levels of public services at reasonably comparable levels of taxation.

In various forms, however, the fiscal equalization program has been in existence since 1957. The traditional have-not provinces — those with positive entitlements under the program — are the four Atlantic provinces (Newfoundland, Prince Edward Island, Nova Scotia, and New Brunswick), Quebec, Manitoba, and Saskatchewan. In the past, however, Alberta has also been a recipient under the equalization program.

## The Canada Assistance Plan

Prior to 1990/91, the Canada Assistance Plan (CAP) was the only remaining program in which the federal and provincial governments paid an equal share of the total costs. Under CAP, the federal government provided matching grants to the provinces in respect of eligible expenditures in the areas of social assistance and social services. Eligible expenditures included those directed at the disabled, single mothers, children, the aged, and the unemployed as well as child care, homemaker, and rehabilitation services, to name a few. Provinces are solely responsible for program administration.

As part of the federal government's expenditure control program instituted in 1990/91, growth in transfers under CAP to each of the "have" provinces—Ontario, Alberta, and British Columbia—was restricted to a maximum of 5% annually. This growth ceiling is to remain in effect until 1995/96. The province of Ontario has estimated the three-year shortfall in transfers to the affected provinces since 1990/91 to be in excess of $4 billion, 85% of which is borne by Ontario alone.

viding sanctions against attempts by business to limit competition in order to raise prices and profits in an industry. This section was the predecessor of the present Competition Act, which outlaws agreements between firms not to undercut each others' prices.

There are many other forms of government ***regulation***. For example, the Department of Health and Welfare tests the effectiveness and safety of drugs before they are permitted into the market. Government regulation is especially detailed in financial markets: Canada's chartered banks are supervised and controlled by the Bank of Canada. In those provinces with privately owned telephone companies, rates are regulated by the provincial government. Radio and television communications are regulated by the Canadian Radio-television and Telecommunications Commission (CRTC). The Canadian Transport Commission regulates the railroad and airline industries, while provincial Highway Transport Boards are responsible for supervising and controlling the trucking industry. The regulatory activities of the National Energy Board were at the forefront in the conflict between the federal government and the Western provinces over energy policy in the 1970s and early 1980s. Another area of rapidly growing regulation has been agriculture, where federal and provincial agencies have been created to control and supervise the marketing of a wide variety of farm products ranging from wheat to eggs, dairy products, and even asparagus.

The role of government regulation over the economy grew at a rapid pace in the 1960s and 1970s. In the 1970s, there was particular emphasis on regulation affecting the environment, health and safety, transportation, product standards, business licensing, and land use planning.

## Problems with Government Regulation

In many areas, regulation is relatively uncontroversial. For example, few people complain about a government agency that certifies the airworthiness of aircraft. Similarly, there is widespread support for government regulation to keep unsafe drugs off the market. For each of these cases, regulation was established to deal with a problem area where the free market had been tried and found wanting.

However, by the late 1970s, many observers began to feel that in some areas, regulation was becoming very cumbersome or too restrictive. Business executives were complaining over long delays in obtaining regulatory approval for major projects; such delays, they said, can add substantially to the cost of projects. There were suggestions that the standards used to evaluate the safety of drugs may be too restrictive. For example, when saccharin was temporarily banned after experiments showed that massive doses of the chemical appeared to increase the risk of cancer in laboratory animals, critics pointed out that more lives might be lost from problems caused by being overweight (as people could no longer use saccharin instead of sugar to keep their weight down) than from an increased incidence of cancer. Provincial marketing boards for agricultural products have had their policies questioned with increasing frequency. True, unregulated markets for agricultural products or transportation may have various disadvantages; for example, they might lead to large fluctuations in the prices of foodstuffs. But regulation may also have disadvantages: It might cause waste and higher consumer prices, and be unfair to individual producers.

As a result of these criticisms, the 1980s saw a trend toward reduction of the extent of regulation in various sectors, both in Canada and the United States. While regulation in agricultural markets was largely left intact, major steps were taken toward deregulation in the Canadian airline, rail, and trucking industries. (By the early 1990s, there was even concern that deregulation in the airline industry had gone too far, as both of Canada's major airlines were experiencing large financial losses.) But although Canada was, by and large, reasonably happy to follow the U.S. trend toward deregulation in the transport sector, it was less happy with the reduced emphasis on *environmental* regulation south of the border. For example, in spite of considerable Canadian pressure, it was not until the early 1990s that there was a significant U.S. commitment to reduce the amount of acid rain pollution from American power plants.

What is needed is a sense of balance. The private market mechanism has substantial defects. But government agencies also have defects; they are not run by superhumans capable of solving all our problems. In some cases, such as protection of the environment, we should give them more effective regulatory power. But in other cases, such as air transportation or some types of farm products, it may be better to live with the defects of the market. Trying to cure these defects through regulation may be more costly than the defects themselves.

Regulation in the public interest is made particularly difficult because of the political clout of producers. When regulations are being developed, the affected industry makes its views known forcefully. But the views of consumers and taxpayers are diffuse and often remain underrepresented.

The predominance of producer influence is not simply the result of a conspiracy of wealth. Rather, it is an intrinsic feature of a highly specialized economy. Each of us has a major, narrow, special interest as a producer; and each of us has a minor interest in a wide range of industries whose goods we consume. We are much more likely to react when our particular industry is affected by government policy; we are much less likely to express our diffused interest as consumers. Narrow producer interests are expressed not only by business, but also by labour. For example, some of the loudest early criticism of airline deregulation came from representatives for unions of flight attendants and employees of the Canadian Transport Commission. Unions concentrate their attention on events in their particular industry, even though the union members are also consumers using a wide range of products. We repeat: This prevalence of producer influence is primarily a result of modern technology and a high degree of specialization; it is not primarily a result of our particular system. It exists in a wide variety of politico-economic systems, including those of the United States, Britain, France, Germany, Japan, and the former Soviet Union.

# PUBLIC ENTERPRISE

In addition to the influence Canadian governments exert over the economy through their regulatory activities, they also participate directly in many markets through government-owned firms. Petro-Canada, the CBC, and Hydro-Québec are all examples of ***Crown corporations***. Most Crown corporations are similar to private business firms in the sense that they derive most of their revenue from selling various goods or services to the public. The economic significance of such government enterprises is much greater in Canada than in the United States. For example, it has been estimated that Crown corporations accounted for about 15% of all capital investment in Canada in the early 1980s; the corresponding figure for the United States was less than 5%.

> *Crown corporations* are government-owned firms that derive most of their revenues from selling goods or services to the public, sometimes in direct competition with privately owned firms in the same market.

Crown corporations exist in a wide variety of markets. Many of them are *natural monopolies*, where economies of scale are substantial so that the market can support no more than one firm large enough to exploit these economies of scale. (Natural monopoly is explained in more detail in the companion volume to this book, *Microeconomics*.) In the United States, most firms in naturally monopolistic markets are privately owned but heavily regulated by the government; in Canada, they are often government-owned instead — for example, corporations producing electric power or telephone companies in the Prairie provinces. Crown corporations also exist in more competitive markets — for example, in transport and communication where government-owned corporations such as Canadian National, Via Rail, and CBC operate in direct competition with privately owned firms.

Part of the function of the government-owned companies is to serve various submarkets that private companies are reluctant to serve — rail service to small, remote communities; television transmissions to the Arctic; or radio programs featuring classical music, for example. In other cases, they undertake tasks that may be potentially profitable in the long run but require very large initial investments and involve such a high degree of risk that private firms are unwilling to invest. An example of such a "pioneer enterprise" is Atomic Energy of Canada Limited, which developed the CANDU nuclear reactor.

Not all ventures into new technology are financial successes. For example, Canadair Ltd. of Montreal, which until 1986 was a federal Crown corporation, was subsidized to the tune of several *billion* dollars by the Canadian taxpayers when it developed the technologically advanced Challenger executive jet in the early 1980s. Although the Challenger has subsequently done relatively well in international markets, the government was able to recover only a small fraction of the money that had been invested in developing the plane, when it sold Canadair to private interests.

In many provinces, there are government-owned development corporations that provide financial support for industrial development and, in many cases, governments also create Crown corporations by taking over firms that otherwise would close down. Thus, the B.C. government owns and operates a newsprint mill at Ocean Falls; Nova Scotia owns a steel mill in Sydney; and a federal Crown corporation is responsible for the operation of Cape Breton coal mines. Often, government "bailouts" of failing private firms are undertaken to protect communities in which the firm provides a large share of total employment.

In recent years, there has been considerable debate over possible reforms that might improve the efficiency of government firms. The debate has focused on two main issues: accountability and privatization.

## Accountability

While most Crown corporations cover a large portion of their costs using revenue they earn from the sale of goods and services, they usually don't cover them all. As the owner, the government is often called on to pay subsidies for certain tasks the corporations undertake, to provide guarantees for repayment of money they borrow, or simply to cover operating deficits of the firms. This is not surprising. Most Crown corporations are established because governments want to use them to do things that are not privately profitable (such as providing air and rail service to distant communities) and that require a subsidy. But once it is clear that a Crown corporation is not necessarily expected to cover *all* its costs, the question arises: Where does one draw the line? If the corporation's managers are given a blank cheque, they are likely to spend too much. The managers must be *accountable* to someone and, since it is the government that owns the firm, their accountability must ultimately be to the politicians who make the decisions about government spending. Thus, the reform proposals in this area have focused on ways of strengthening the political control over Crown corporations by providing more precise definitions of the objectives that they are expected to serve and by providing the politicians with better information about current and future spending plans.

### Privatization

In some cases, the original reason for establishing a public enterprise may disappear over time. For example, an unprofitable firm that has been taken over by a provincial government in order to preserve jobs may become profitable again, or a new technology developed by a Crown corporation may become ready for commercial application. In such cases, one possible strategy is to *privatize* the public enterprise —that is, to turn it over to private ownership.

At the federal level, a program for reducing the scope of government enterprise through privatization was an important part of the platform of the 1979/80 Conservative government under Joe Clark; the proposal to privatize Petro-Canada gave rise to considerable controversy. The privatization policy was revived when the Mulroney government came to power in the mid-1980s. A number of Crown corporations were sold, including Canadair and de Havilland, another government-owned aircraft manufacturer, and by the early 1990s, privatization of both Petro-Canada and Air Canada was well underway.

To some extent, the arguments for ***privatization*** are ideological. They are generally supported by private firms that object to competition from government-subsidized Crown corporations. But there is also another argument based on the idea that managers of private firms have stronger incentives to perform efficiently than managers of public enterprises. The reason is that if managers of private firms perform inefficiently, this is quickly reflected in a reduction in the value of the firms' shares. To prevent this, the firms' owners (shareholders) will put pressure on the managers to perform better or will even replace the management. On the other hand, if managers of publicly owned firms perform inefficiently, the incentive to improve performance is less strong—for two reasons. First, the managers may be able to claim that they are losing money because the government is forcing them to continue various unprofitable activities, not because they are inefficient. Second, since shares of publicly owned firms are not traded in the market, the taxpayers (who are the ones that ultimately will carry the burden of an inefficient performance) may be only very imperfectly aware of the firms' performance.

The evidence on the relative efficiency of managers in public and private firms is mixed. Some studies have shown that private firms operating in a heavily regulated market are no more efficient than public firms in the same market. On the other hand, evidence suggests that private firms providing electricity and water to municipalities in the United States are able to produce these services at a significantly lower cost than government-owned ones.

## THE ECONOMIC ROLE OF THE GOVERNMENT: What Should the Government Do?

With budgets of governments and Crown corporations reaching billions of dollars and with an extensive list of government regulations, the Canadian economy is clearly a substantial distance away from a pure market system of laissez-faire. What principles and objectives guide the government when it intervenes?

The government intervenes in the economy for many reasons; it is hard to summarize them all. But we will look at five of the main reasons.

## 1. The Government Provides What the Private Market Can't

Consider defence expenditures. For obvious political reasons, defence cannot be left to the private market. As countries like Somalia and Yugoslavia in the 1990s illustrate, when a country's political system functions so badly that competing armies are organized, the country is close to disintegration. But there is also a compelling economic reason that defence is a responsibility of the government.

The difference between defence and an average good is the following. If I buy food at the store, I get to eat it; if I buy a movie ticket, I get to see the film; if I buy a car, I get to drive it. In contrast, if I want a larger, better equipped army, my offer to purchase a rifle for the army will not add in any measurable way to my own security. My neighbour and the average person in New Brunswick or Manitoba will benefit as much from the extra rifle as I do. In other words, the benefit from defence expenditures goes broadly to all citizens; it does not go specifically to the individual who pays. If defence is to be provided, it must be financed by the government, which collects taxes to ensure that everyone contributes.

Such goods—where the benefit goes to the public regardless of who pays — are sometimes known as *public goods*.

## 2. Externalities

An ***externality*** is a side effect — good or bad — of production or consumption. For example, when individuals are immunized against an infectious disease, they receive a substantial benefit: They are assured that they won't get the disease. But there is an *external benefit* as well, because others gain too: They are assured that the inoculated individuals will not catch the disease and pass it along to them. Similarly, there is an external benefit when people have their houses painted: The neighbourhood becomes more attractive.

An *external cost* occurs when a factory pollutes the air. The cost is borne by those who breathe the polluted air.

> An *externality* is a side effect of production or consumption. Persons or businesses other than the producer or consumer are affected.
>
> An externality may be either positive (for example, vaccinations) or negative (for example, pollution).

Because of the effects on others, the government may wish to encourage activities that create external benefits, and to discourage those with external costs. It can do so with the use of any of its four major tools: expenditures, public enterprise, regulation, or taxation. The government spends money for public health programs for the immunization of the young. In order to reduce pollution, it may pass regulations on the types of automobiles that can be built. And taxes on gasoline or on pollution-producing factories might likewise be used to discourage pollution.

The existence of an externality does not in itself make a compelling case for government action; the government should not be concerned with insignificant externalities or other trivial matters. Thus, private incentives are generally enough to ensure that homes will be painted; the government does not usually intervene. However, there is growing concern over more serious externalities: While little was done about pollution two decades ago, major efforts are now directed toward cleaning up the air and water and preventing further environmental deterioration.

## 3. Merit Goods

Government intervention may also be based on the paternalistic view that there are cases in which people are not the best judges of what is good for them. According to this view, the government should encourage the consumption of ***merit goods***—those that are deemed particularly desirable—and discourage the consumption of harmful products. People's inability to pick the "right" goods may be the result of short-sightedness, ignorance, addiction, or manipulation by producers. (Recall the brief discussion in Chapter 4 of Galbraith's views on created wants.)

In some cases, the government attempts merely to correct ignorance in areas where the public may have difficulty determining (or facing?) the facts. The requirement of a health warning on cigarette packages is an example. But, in other instances, the government goes further: to outright prohibition, as in the case of heroin and other hard drugs.

The view that "the government knows best" is generally greeted with scepticism; the government intervenes relatively sparingly to tell adults what they should or should not consume. (Children are, however, another matter; they are not allowed to reject the merit good, education.) However, substantial government direction does occur in welfare programs, presumably on the ground that those who get themselves into financial difficulties may not be able to make wise consumption decisions. Thus, part of the assistance to the poor consists of subsidized day-care centres and housing programs rather than outright ***unconditional grants*** of money. In this way, the government attempts to direct consumption toward basic necessities such as housing and care for the children.

## 4. Helping the Poor

The market provides the goods and services desired by those with the money to buy them, but it provides little for the poor. In order to help the impoverished and move toward a more humane society, programs have been established to provide assistance for old people, the handicapped, and the needy in general.

With few exceptions, Canadians agree that the government must be responsible for providing the poor with a decent living standard. However, there continues to be a good deal of controversy over the issue of whether the current system does a good job of meeting this responsibility. Part of the problem is that there is a large number of agencies and programs that affect the well-being of the poor; indeed, it is perhaps inaccurate to speak of a welfare "system" at all. The result may be a lack of consistency. Some of the money being spent may go to people who are not really poor while some who are poverty stricken may "fall between the cracks" and get little or no help. Another difficulty lies in how to reconcile conflicting objectives. How can help be given to the needy without weakening the incentive to work? How can assistance be guaranteed to abandoned mothers without weakening the incentives of fathers to stay with their families? How can we provide affordable housing for low-income families without creating ghettos of the poor? There are no easy answers to such questions.

## 5. The Government and Economic Stability

Finally, if we go back to the beginning of the upswing in government activity—to the Great Depression of the 1930s—we find that the primary motivation was not to affect the kinds of products made in the economy nor specifically to aid the poor. Rather, the aim was to increase the quantity of production. With unemployment rates exceeding 15% of the labour force year after year, the problem was to produce more — more production of almost anything would help put people back to work. Since the dark days of the 1930s, a major responsibility of the government has been to promote a high level of employment and stability in the economy.

# TAXATION

> The art of taxation consists of plucking the goose so as to obtain the largest amount of feathers with the least possible amount of hissing.
>
> Jean Baptiste Colbert, Seventeenth-century French statesman

The major objective of taxation is to raise revenues—to obtain feathers—without too much hissing. But other objectives are also important in the design of a tax system.

## 1. Neutrality . . .

In many ways, the market system works admirably. Adam Smith's "invisible hand" provides the consuming public with a vast flow of goods and services. As a starting point, therefore, a tax system should be designed to be neutral. That is, it should disturb market forces as little as possible, unless there is a compelling reason to the contrary.

For the sake of illustration, consider a far-fetched example. Suppose that blue cars were taxed at 10% and green cars not at all. This tax would clearly not be neutral regarding blue and green cars. People would have an incentive to buy green cars; blue cars would practically disappear from the market. A tax that introduces such a distortion would make no sense.

While this illustration is silly, real taxes do introduce distortions. For example, several centuries ago, houses in parts of Europe were taxed according to the number of windows. As a result, houses were built with fewer windows. To a lesser degree, the current property tax introduces a perverse incentive. If you have your house painted and your roof repaired, the government's evaluation of your house (the assessed value) may be raised and your taxes increased as a consequence. Therefore, property taxes encourage you to let your property deteriorate.

The problem is that every tax provides an incentive to do something to avoid it. So long as taxes must be collected, complete ***tax neutrality*** is impossible. The objective of the tax system must therefore be more modest: to *aim* toward neutrality. As a starting point in the design of a tax system, the disturbance to the market that comes from taxation should be minimized.

## 2. . . . and Nonneutrality: Meeting Social Objectives by Tax Incentives

There is, however, an important modification that must be made to the neutrality principle. In some cases, it may be desirable to disturb the private market.

For example, the government might tax polluting activities, so that firms will do less polluting. The market is disturbed, but in a desirable way. Another example is the tax on cigarettes, which, in addition to its prime objective of raising revenue for the government, also discourages cigarette consumption.

Taxation and regulation can be used to correct the failures of the private market. But the two approaches are quite different in one respect. Regulation aims at *overriding* the market mechanism, forbidding or limiting specific behaviour on the part of business. Taxation aims at *using* the market mechanism, but making it work better. When there are externalities, such as pollution, the signals of the market are incomplete; businesses or individuals who pollute the air do not have to pay the cost. Taxation of externalities can improve the outcome of the market by making the signals facing businesses and individuals more complete: Taxation makes polluters pay a penalty and gives them an incentive to reduce pollution.

## 3. Simplicity

To anyone who has wasted several spring weekends sweating over an income tax form, simplicity of the tax system is devoutly desired. Of course, we live in a complex world and the tax code must to some degree reflect this complexity. Even so, it is difficult to avoid the impression that the Canadian tax code is more complicated than is necessary. In part, this is because simplification of the code would involve the abolition of various special rules that have been legislated over the years in order to provide tax relief for certain particular types of income or for particular ways of spending or investing it. When simplifying changes are proposed, there will be vocal opposition from those taxpayers or firms who will lose from the changes. An example of this problem was provided in the mid-1960s, when a comprehensive set of revisions of Canada's tax laws were recommended by the Carter Commission on Taxation.[6] If all of the commission's proposals had been adopted, the structure of the Canadian tax system would have been greatly simplified with a much more uniform tax treatment of different sorts of income. As it turned out, however, many of the special rules in the existing tax laws were in fact retained and, while some of the commission's recommendations for change were accepted by the government, they were only partially implemented.

## 4. Equity

Taxation represents coercion; taxes are collected by force if necessary. Therefore, it is important that taxes both be fair and give the appearance of being fair. There are, however, two different principles for judging fairness.

### The Benefit Principle

This principle recognizes that the purpose of taxation is to pay for government services. Therefore, let those who gain the most from government services pay the most. If this principle is adopted, then a question arises: Why not simply set prices for government services that people can voluntarily pay if they want the services? In other words, why not charge a price for a government service, just as Via Rail charges for railway tickets?

This approach may work in some cases — for example, for a toll road from which drivers can be excluded if they do not pay. But it will not work for public goods that benefit people even if they do not pay; for example, defence, disease control programs, or air traffic control. Everyone will enjoy them, but no one will want to pay for them. It is the function of the government to determine whether such programs are worthwhile. Once the decision is made to go ahead, people must be required to support the program through taxes. (The benefit principle is discussed further in *Microeconomics*, the companion volume to this book.)

### Ability to Pay

If the government sets taxes according to the benefit principle, it does not redistribute income. People are simply taxed in proportion to their individual benefits from government programs. But while it might make sense to apply the benefit principle of taxation to the financing of programs to provide public goods or merit goods (such as education and health services), it cannot very well be applied to government programs to help the poor. The purpose of these programs is to transfer resources from those who are relatively well off — that is, whose *ability to pay* is greater — to those who have lower income and wealth, and therefore are less able to pay.

If the only taxes were a progressive income tax and an inheritance tax, and if at the same time the

[6] *The Royal Commission on Taxation Report* (Ottawa: Queen's Printer, 1966). The commission derived its popular name from its chairman, K.L. Carter.

government provided assistance to those at the bottom of the economic ladder, it would substantially redistribute income from the rich to the poor. But the world is not so simple. There are different levels of government and each one levies several different kinds of taxes. When all the taxes are taken together, it is not so clear that government is taking a substantially larger percentage of income from the rich than from the poor, as we shall see in the next section.

## THE BURDEN OF TAXES: Who Ultimately Pays?

It is difficult to determine who bears the burden of many of our taxes. For example, consider the relatively simple case of the Canada Pension Plan contribution. (As we noted in footnote 2, even though it is called a "contribution" it is essentially equivalent to a tax.) Part of this tax is deducted from the take-home pay of the worker. In 1991, it was deducted at the rate of 2.3% of the worker's gross income, subject to a maximum contribution of $632.50. This maximum was reached at an income of $27,500. Therefore, the same $632.50 was paid by employees with an income of $30,000 or, say, a $60,000 income. Thus, this tax is regressive: The employee earning $30,000 per year pays twice as large a percentage of gross income as the employee earning $60,000 per year.

The burden in this case is simple to see. However, it is not so clear for the other portion of this tax which was levied on the *employer* (also 2.3% of gross income). Does that tax come out of the employer's profits? Or is it passed on to the consumer in the form of higher prices? Or, possibly, this half may also fall on the worker: If employers did not have to pay part of the workers' Canada Pension Plan contributions, they might be willing to pay a higher wage.

As another example, consider the corporation income tax. It is sometimes maintained that this tax is a relatively painless way of raising government revenue because it is levied on corporate profits and not on the incomes of individuals. However, this argument is suspect for at least two reasons. First, corporations' profits influence the individual incomes of shareholders, so that a profits tax does directly affect the income of some individuals. Second, a higher rate of corporation income tax may be "passed on" in the form of higher prices, so that the tax is, in effect, "paid" by the buyers of the corporations' products. When we recognize this, we cannot even tell whether the corporation income tax is ultimately progressive or regressive!

As these examples show, the question of tax burden—of who ultimately pays—is complicated, even when we are looking at only a single particular tax. Needless to say, estimating the burden — or *incidence* — of *all* Canadian taxes, federal, provincial, and local, is even more difficult. Nevertheless, the problem of the incidence of the tax system as a whole has been studied by a number of economists, each using a somewhat different method and different assumptions. Figure 5-5 illustrates a set of incidence estimates by Professor John Whalley of the University of Western Ontario; the data refer to the early 1970s. The solid black curve in the middle refers to his "central case"; it implies that the system was progressive, since total taxes paid as a fraction

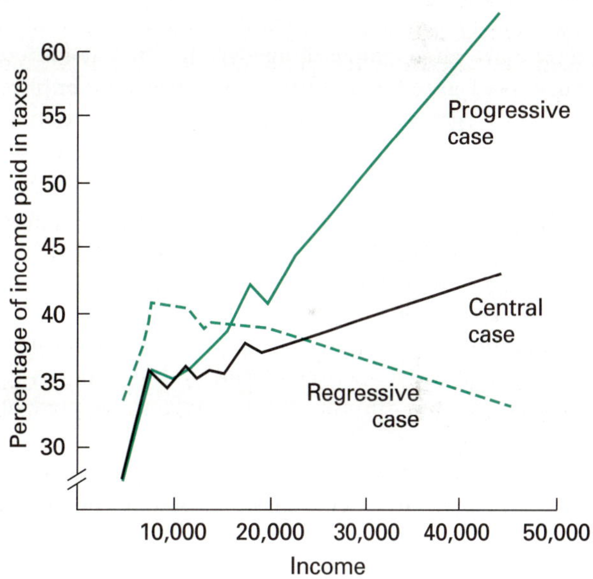


**FIGURE 5-5 Estimates of the overall incidence of Canadian taxes.**

Many estimates of the overall incidence of Canadian taxes suggest that the system is neither highly progressive (except in the lowest income brackets) nor highly regressive, as illustrated by the broken colour curve. However, with different assumptions concerning the burden of taxes on the income of those who own capital (who earn profits of interest), the estimated incidence pattern may become quite different, as shown by the solid colour and solid black curves.

*Source*: John Whalley, "Regression or progression: the taxing question of incidence analysis", *Canadian Journal of Economics*, November 1984, Table 5 and Table 6.

of income rises from 27% for the lowest income group to 43% as it reaches the highest income group. What is somewhat surprising, though, is that the curve is relatively flat in the intermediate range. When most of us think of taxes, we think first of the income tax with its definitely progressive rate structure. But as the estimates by Whalley and others have shown, a large part of the progressive effect of the personal income tax is offset by other taxes (such as sales and excise taxes and social security contributions) that are regressive.[7]

The incidence estimates of Whalley and others have to be very carefully interpreted. As Whalley notes, they all depend on both the precise definition of income, and on several somewhat arbitrary assumptions concerning the incidence of the burden of particular taxes (such as social security contributions or the corporation income tax). By changing these assumptions, one can produce a significantly different picture of the overall pattern of tax incidence. As an example, consider the two coloured curves in Figure 5-5. The broken coloured line implies a highly regressive distribution of the tax burden. It results from assuming that the burden of taxes on business profits and interest income is "shifted forward" to consumers in the form of higher prices (rather than resulting in lower income of the owners of capital). The solid coloured line, in contrast, shows a more progressive incidence pattern; it results from taking into account not just taxes this year, but also taxes in future years — in particular, how taxes will reduce income on the future return on present savings.

While this discussion illustrates that the estimates of total tax incidence must be taken with more than a grain of salt, most of those who have worked on the incidence problem agree on one thing: The degree of progressivity in the overall tax system is considerably smaller than one would be led to believe if one simply looked at the structure of personal income tax rates. This is true not only because many other types of taxes are regressive, but also because of a variety of "loopholes," some of which provide particularly attractive opportunities for rich people to reduce their taxes.

[7] Earlier work by W. Irwin Gillespie indicated a much less progressive tax system than implied by Whalley's estimates. As Whalley points out, however, the difference is largely due to the fact that Gillespie measures taxes as a proportion of income *before government transfers*. Since such transfers constitute a relatively large proportion of the income of people in the lower income classes, this substantially raises the estimate of taxes as a proportion of income in these classes.

# TAX LOOPHOLES

Loopholes are provisions of the law that permit the reduction of taxes. Thus, those who use ***tax loopholes*** are acting perfectly legally to *avoid* taxes and should be sharply distinguished from those who act illegally to *evade* taxes, perhaps by padding their deductions or understating their income. The term loophole clearly implies that the tax provision is unfair and, as there can be strong disagreement over just what is fair, there is likewise some disagreement over just what constitutes a loophole. However, here are some of the items that are often put on the list.

## 1. Capital Gains

When an asset is sold for more than it cost, the seller has made a ***capital gain***. For example, if you buy stock in MacMillan Bloedel for $1000 and the value of the stock later rises to $1500, you have made a capital gain of $500. Under current rules, capital gains are taxed more lightly than other kinds of income. For most individuals, capital gains escape income tax altogether, in part because gains resulting from the sale of a "principal residence" are excluded, and second, because only capital gains in excess of $100,000 (over a person's lifetime) are taxed. Moreover, those with capital gains in excess of $100,000 only have to include three-quarters of their actual gains in taxable income. Clearly, these rules are of substantial benefit to taxpayers who receive large portions of their income as capital gains, such as those who sell large blocks of common stock.

## 2. Imputed Income from Owner-Occupied Housing

The Canadian tax system favours homeowners, for the following reason. For people who have a substantial amount invested as equity in their own homes, out-of-pocket housing costs (that is, costs of maintenance, property taxes, and mortgage payments) are lower than the amount of rent paid by people who live in rental housing of a comparable standard. The difference represents a return on the homeowner's equity. While most other income from capital (such as interest on bonds) is taxed, the implicit ***return on homeowner's equity*** is not. The benefits of this loophole are greater for people with high incomes — and, thus, high marginal tax rates — and expensive homes. (In some countries, including the United States, homeowners also are allowed to deduct mortgage interest from taxable income. This is a second big tax advantage of home ownership. Mortgage interest has never been deductible in Canada, although the Conservative government of Joe Clark was planning legislation to introduce such a provision at the time the Liberals returned to power in 1980.)

### 3. Preferences to Some Corporations

For small business corporations (those with less than $200,000 of taxable income) the rate of federal corporation income tax is substantially lower than the rate for large corporations. Corporations engaged in manufacturing and processing in Canada are treated more favourably than other firms for tax purposes: Their federal income tax rate is some five percentage points lower than for other firms. Manufacturing firms also benefit from special rules that allow them to reduce their taxable income by writing off the cost of new capital equipment in a relatively short time. (This is called "accelerated depreciation.") In addition, many of them have been protected against competition from abroad by tariffs on imported foreign goods. Corporations investing in new productive facilities in so-called "slow growth areas" and in the Atlantic provinces receive an ***investment tax credit*** in the range of 15% to 30% of the cost of the investment.

Special tax law provisions have also created loopholes of varying size in specific industries. For example, during the 1970s and 1980s, resource-based industries benefited from special deductions and tax rules that reduced both their corporate income tax liabilities, and the personal income tax of those who owned their shares. The income tax laws also contain various provisions to reduce the tax burden on Canadian farmers.

## TAX REFORM IN THE 1980s

In the late 1980s, there was increasing dissatisfaction with the way in which the proliferation of special rules and loopholes had increased the complexity of the Canadian tax system, and made it less effective in redistributing income from the rich to the poor.

Even though the Carter Commission had recommended drastic changes to the tax system, there had been little in the way of major reform during the 1960s and 1970s. (An important exception was a move in the mid-1970s to *index* the tax system—that is, to make the system less sensitive to the distortionary impact of inflation; we will discuss tax indexing further in Chapter 16.) Partly as a result of tax reductions and tax reform in the United States in the early 1980s, interest in ***tax reform*** picked up in Canada as well at that time.

While there were many different reform proposals, most participants in the debate gradually came to agree on three elements that should be part of an effective tax reform package.

### 1. The Tax Base Should Be Broadened

One proposal was that the tax base should be broadened; that is, many existing deductions and loopholes that reduce the taxes of particular individuals or groups should be reduced or eliminated. Not only would this simplify the tax structure, it would also make the tax system fairer. Under the existing system, people with the same income often end up paying very different amounts of tax depending on the deductions and exemptions they are allowed.

By ***broadening the tax base***, more revenue could be collected at existing tax rates. This leads to the second type of reform proposal.

### 2. There Should Be a Reduction in Income Tax Rates

In the 1980s, there was increasing evidence from various countries that high marginal income tax rates might do considerable damage to a country's economic performance by reducing individuals' willingness to work and save, and by causing a great deal of energy and resources to be wasted in the search for ways to avoid taxes. In a number of countries, including Britain and the United States (Box 5-2), marginal tax rates were decreased considerably.

The proposals for reducing tax rates often went together with suggestions to simplify the tax structure by reducing the number of tax brackets in the income tax schedule. A particularly simple proposal was for a *flat tax*, which would have a single tax rate (say, 20%) applied to all income over and above some basic exemption.

### 3. Deductions Should Be Replaced by Tax Credits

Before 1988, the income tax law allowed taxpayers in particular categories (such as those with dependants, those who were over age 65, or those who were disabled) to deduct certain amounts when calculating their taxable income, thereby reducing the tax they had to pay. A problem with such deductions is that their value to the taxpayer — that is, the amount by which they reduce the tax payable — depends on the taxpayer's marginal tax rate. For example, the 1987 deduction of roughly $2600 for an elderly person led to a tax saving of $1300 for a person with an income of, say, $60,000, whose combined marginal rate of federal and provincial income tax was 50%. On the other hand, for a retired person with an income of only $20,000 and a combined marginal rate of 30%, the tax reduction would be only $780.

This problem can be overcome by replacing ***tax deductions*** with provisions for ***tax credits***. For example, instead of allowing taxpayers over age 65 to deduct $2600 when calculating taxable income, one might simply allow them to deduct a fixed sum from their tax liability.

A *deduction* (or *exemption*) reduces the tax payable by the amount of the deduction multiplied by the taxpayer's marginal tax rate. A *tax credit* reduces the tax payable by the amount of the credit — that is, by the same dollar amount for every taxpayer who can claim it.

## The 1988 Tax Reforms

Discussions of a set of tax reforms that would incorporate these three elements took place throughout the 1980s. In 1987, the federal government issued a White Paper outlining specific suggestions for changing both the personal and corporation income tax, as well as the federal "manufacturers sales tax" which existed at that time. After extensive consultation and some modifications, the reform proposals were implemented in stages, between 1989 and 1991.

The reforms reflected all three of the elements discussed above. The tax bases for the personal and corporation income taxes were broadened by the elimination of a number of loopholes. For example, an earlier rule that had exempted the first $1000 of interest and dividend income from personal income tax was abolished, and the rules governing "tax shelter investments" (such as Canadian films and hobby farms) were tightened. The effective rate of tax on capital gains (above the $100,000 exemption) was increased. With respect to the corporation income tax, the preferences given to firms in the manufacturing and resource sectors were reduced. At the same time, the rates of federal personal and corporation income taxes were generally reduced, and the structure of tax rates was simplified. For example, the number of tax brackets in the personal income tax schedule was reduced from ten to just three. The highest marginal rate of federal personal income tax was reduced by five percentage points; for a taxpayer living in a province where the provincial income tax is 50% of the federal tax, the combined federal/provincial marginal rate fell from 51% to 43.5%. Finally, a number of existing deductions and exemptions in the personal income tax law were converted to tax credits. They included the "basic personal exemption," the "married exemption," and the exemptions for dependent children and for persons over age 65.

Introduction and implementation of the *Goods and Services Tax* (GST) in 1990/91 represented the second stage of the reform package. Again, there was a substantial broadening of the tax base: The federal manufacturers sales tax, which the GST replaced, had covered only manufactured goods comprising about one-third of all goods and services, while only certain specific categories (notably food) were exempted from the GST. In contrast to the manufacturers sales tax, which essentially was collected as a "single-stage" tax as a percentage of the value of the manufacturers' sales, the GST is a multi-stage tax where the amount that a firm pays is calculated as a percentage of the value of its sales *minus* the GST that the firm has paid on its purchases of inputs from other firms. This means that in effect, a firm pays tax on the basis of the value of its output less the cost of the inputs that it has bought from other firms; that is, on the basis of the *value it has added* to these inputs. A tax of this kind is sometimes referred to as a *value added tax* (*VAT*). VATs typically account for a large share of government tax revenues in European countries, where they are levied at rates of 20% or more.

Since a sales tax tends to be regressive, an increased reliance on sales tax revenue by the federal government would, by itself, tend to make the tax system as a whole less progressive. To offset this tendency, the reform provided for the introduction of a relatively large sales tax credit (in the personal income tax) that compensates the poor for the burden of increased sales taxes.

The credit is *refundable*; that is, the full amount is available only to individuals with income below a specific threshold level. For people with higher income, the credit is gradually reduced until it disappears altogether at a higher income level.

The 1988 reform package has been criticized by some observers for not going far enough in making the tax system more efficient and fair. Nevertheless, most economists agree that it has taken us a considerable distance in the right direction: The new system is simpler than the old, and the substitution of tax credits for many earlier exemptions and deductions has reduced the share of the total tax burden born by the poor.

## APPLICATIONS AND ILLUSTRATIONS BOX 5-2

## The Legacy of Reaganomics

*Government is not the solution to our problems.*
*Government is the problem.*

*Ronald Reagan*

In the 1980 presidential campaign in the United States, the basic election promise of the Republican candidate Ronald Reagan was that if elected, he would fundamentally change the economic strategy of his Democratic predecessor Jimmy Carter. He stated two goals. First, he was going to restore fiscal responsibility by eliminating, or at least sharply reducing, the federal government deficit. His second promise was a reflection of his strongly held view that government in the United States had gone far beyond its appropriate role of providing protection from external enemies, and providing domestic law and order. One of his objectives, said Reagan, was to "get the government off the backs of the people." By loosening the heavy hand of government, the administration hoped to invigorate the private enterprise economy, and to unleash a strong economic expansion.

When he took office in January 1981, these objectives were translated into an economic program which was quickly given the label "Reaganomics." It included the following strategic components:

1. Increase defence expenditures.
2. Restrain, and where possible reduce domestic (nondefence) spending by the federal government.
3. Restrain the growth of government regulation.
4. Cut tax rates.

Reagan and his advisers were convinced that this strategy, and especially the tax cuts and reductions in regulation, would produce an unprecedented rate of economic growth. Such a strong expansion would help increase revenues, since people must pay more in taxes when their incomes rise. Cuts in domestic programs would also help to lower government deficits. In the early budget projections made in 1981, the administration forecast a balanced budget by the end of President Reagan's first term in 1984.

Reality turned out very differently. In fiscal 1979, Jimmy Carter's last year in office, the federal deficit was estimated at less than $30 billion. During Reagan's first four years, the deficits were $74 billion, $79 billion, $126 billion, and $202 billion. What went wrong with the early predictions? Several factors can be cited.

1. The economy's response to lower tax rates and reduced regulation was much less vigorous than the Reagan administration had hoped for. Although the economy grew at healthy rates during most of the 1980s, the increased growth rates were not nearly enough to compensate for the effects of lower tax rates.
2. Domestic spending was a great deal more difficult to cut than expected. In particular, interest on the debt was much higher than the projections made in 1981.

The federal deficits in the United States continued to be large during the second Reagan administration. Nevertheless, the simple precepts of Reaganomics remained popular. One of the reasons Vice-President George Bush beat the Democratic candidate Michael Dukakis in the 1988 election was that he promised to continue Reagan's commitment to no major tax increases. ("Read my lips: No new taxes.")

The ideology of Reaganomics may indirectly have contributed to the difficulty of con-

**BOX 5-2 continued**

trolling the federal deficit in Canada as well. The Mulroney government probably had reason to believe that the popularity of Reagan's low-tax policies reflected the attitudes of many Canadians as well, and therefore may have considered it politically risky to raise taxes; expenditure cuts are difficult and painful at the best of times. Moreover, many business people argued strongly that since we were in the process of negotiating a free trade deal with the United States, we could even less afford to raise taxes in Canada, since higher taxes here would make it harder for Canadian firms to compete in the North American market.

For the Clinton administration in the United States, and the new Canadian government that took power in late 1993, deficit control remains one of the most important and troublesome legacies of the Reaganomics of the 1980s.

## Why Can't We Get Rid of All the Loopholes?

While the 1988 reforms went some distance toward reducing the size of various loopholes in the tax system, there were only a few that were eliminated altogether. Why is it so difficult to get rid of the loopholes and create a simple and fair tax system once and for all? There are several possible reasons.

First, there will always be disagreement over precisely what is fair. For example, most economists would probably agree that fairness would require some taxation of imputed income from owner-occupied housing, but that feeling is unlikely to be shared by the majority of the population who own homes. Indeed, many Canadians agreed with Joe Clark's proposals to give even *more* tax relief to homeowners by permitting deduction of mortgage interest from taxable income.

A second complication is the political problem. Clearly, those who benefit from loopholes have an incentive to lobby for their continuation. Moreover, reform is complicated by the fact that fairness is only one of the major objectives in a tax system. Most of the loopholes were put in expressly to promote national goals that the proponents considered important. For example, the investment tax credit was introduced to stimulate capital investment in Canada. It was made larger in the Atlantic provinces and in certain other areas with high unemployment in order to create more industrial capacity and job opportunities there. The favourable tax treatment of capital gains has been justified as an incentive for entrepreneurs to take risks. Accelerated depreciation, lower corporation tax rates, and tariff protection favouring the manufacturing industry are defended on the grounds that they will create a more diversified economy in Canada and reduce our traditional dependence on resource-based industries. (The pros and cons of such tariff protection are discussed in the companion volume to this book, *Microeconomics*.)

Therefore, many of the activities that the loopholes encourage contribute to long-standing Canadian goals such as industrialization, regional equalization, and so on. But some of the arguments for special tax treatment are more convincing than others. Furthermore, the question should be asked: Is the tax system the best way to promote diverse national goals?

Unfortunately, there is no all-purpose answer to this question. Many economists favour the use of taxes to achieve some goals—to discourage pollution, say. But few believe in using the tax system to favour the manufacturing industry through a whole host of preferential tax rules. In taxation, as in so many areas of economics, the policy maker is left with the problem of balancing conflicting national goals.

## KEY POINTS

1. The defects and limitations of the market provide the government with an important economic role. The government affects the economy through expenditures, taxation, and regulation.

2. In dollar terms, government spending has skyrocketed since 1926. However, as a percentage of national product, the growth of government spending has been much slower.

3. Of the federal expenditures, transfer payments have risen much more rapidly than expenditures for goods and services. Provincial government spending has been rising especially fast in the areas of health care and education.

4. Personal income taxes, sales and excise taxes, and corporation income taxes are the main sources of revenue for the federal and provincial governments. For local governments, property taxes are the most important. Provincial governments also benefit from revenue sharing by the federal government and local governments receive large transfers from provincial governments.

5. Since the early 1980s, the federal government has had substantial budget deficits, leading to rapidly rising levels of debt; the interest payments on the debt, in turn, have contributed to the deficit. In recent years, large deficits have also been incurred by several provincial govenments.

6. Government regulatory agencies are active in many areas, regulating many activities of private firms in order to protect the public against monopolies, and from business practices such as the sale of unsafe products or destruction of the environment.

7. Federal and provincial governments operate a large number of Crown corporations. There are many reasons for establishing government-owned businesses. In markets that are natural monopolies, government ownership may be a better alternative than a regulated monopoly under private ownership, or government ownership may be the best way to meet a social objective such as the provision of television programming in remote areas. Sometimes, government takes over private firms as a way of protecting jobs in particular communities.

8. The primary reasons for government intervention in the economy are to:
   (a) Provide public goods that cannot be supplied by the market because individuals have no incentive to buy them; individuals get the benefits regardless of who buys.
   (b) Deal with externalities, such as pollution.
   (c) Encourage the consumption of merit goods, and discourage or prohibit harmful products.
   (d) Help the poor.
   (e) Help stabilize the economy.

9. A number of objectives are important in the design of a tax system:
   (a) In general, neutrality is a desirable objective.
   (b) In some cases, however, the government should alter market signals by taxation. For example, a tax can be used to discourage pollution.
   (c) Taxes should be reasonably simple and easily understood.
   (d) Taxes should be fair. There are two ways of judging fairness: the benefit principle and the ability to pay principle.

10. The burden or incidence of taxes (that is, who ultimately pays the taxes) is hard to determine. But the rich don't bear as heavy a burden as the personal income tax rates suggest.

11. A major step toward simplifying the tax system and closing loopholes was taken in the two-stage tax reform of 1988–1991. The first stage involved broadening the base for the personal and corporation income taxes while reducing the tax rates for most taxpayers. In the personal income tax, a number of existing deductions were converted to tax credits. In the second stage of the reform, the broadly based GST replaced the existing manufacturers sales tax. A refundable sales tax credit reduces the burden of the sales tax on low-income families and individuals.

## KEY TERMS

**regulation**
**purchases of goods and services**
**transfer payment**
**personal income tax**
**corporate income tax**
**marginal tax rate**
**average tax rate**
**progressive tax**
**regressive tax**
**proportional tax**
**budget deficit (surplus)**
**Crown corporation**
**privatization**
**intergovernmental transfers**
**government regulation**
**unconditional grant**
**externality**
**public goods**
**tax neutrality**
**merit good**
**tax incidence**
**tax loophole**
**investment tax credit**
**capital gain**
**return on homeowner's equity**
**broadening the tax base**
**tax credits**
**tax deductions**
**tax reform**

## PROBLEMS

5-1. "That government governs best which governs least." Do you agree? Why or why not? Does the government perform more functions than it should? If so, what activities would you like it to reduce or stop altogether? Are there any additional functions that the government should undertake? If so, which ones? How should they be paid for?

5-2. "Provincial and local governments are closer to the people than the federal government. Therefore, they should be given some of the functions of the federal government." Are there federal functions that might be turned over to the provinces and local governments? Do you think they should be turned over? Why or why not? Are there functions that the federal government can do much better than the provinces or local governments? If so, which ones?

5-3. The government engages in research. For example, the government has agricultural experimental stations; it also undertakes defence-related research. Why do you think the government engages in these two types of research while leaving most other research to private business? Does the government have any major advantages in undertaking research? Any major disadvantages?

5-4. Consider two views of the tax system:

(a) "The government promotes social goals, such as health care research and the arts, through direct payments. It also promotes health care research and the arts by encouraging private giving. This is done by making gifts deductible from taxable income. Tax deductions may be an even more effective way of supporting health care research, the arts, and other desirable causes than direct government grants. Therefore, such deductions do not constitute 'loopholes.' Rather, they represent an efficient way of achieving important social goals."

(b) "The income tax is a mess. Homeowners get a tax break, but renters do not. The rich are able to escape taxes by making gifts to universities, the arts, and to charities. The only way to get equity into the system is to eliminate all deductions and make all income subject to tax."

Which of these arguments is stronger? Why?

5-5. Consider the following income tax function

$$T = \bar{T} + tY$$

where $Y$ denotes the individual's income and $T$ denotes the amount of income tax he or she must pay (or receive as a transfer if negative). $\bar{T}$ and $t$ are tax variables: $t$ is constant and denotes the marginal tax rate ($0 < t < 1$), and $\bar{T}$ is a constant dollar figure that can be less than, greater than, or equal to zero.

Using the definitions of progressive, proportional, and regressive taxes in the text, show how the above tax can be any of these depending on the value of $\bar{T}$.

# PART 2

# FOUNDATIONS OF MICROECONOMIC ANALYSIS: THE COMPETITIVE MODEL

The five chapters of Part 1 have set the stage for the study of economics, providing analytical and institutional background and outlining the major objectives of high employment, price stability, growth, efficiency, and an equitable distribution of income.

The questions of what policies should be used to achieve the first three objectives are studied in the *Macroeconomics* volume that forms a companion to this book. In this volume, we focus on the problems of *efficiency* and *equity* in the way we use our economy's limited resources. Specifically, the rest of the book provides answers to the central microeconomic questions introduced in Chapter 4: What is produced? How is it produced? For whom is it produced?

In Part 2, we describe how resources are allocated in a system of competitive markets. In Chapters 7 to 10, the curtain goes up on the two main sets of characters in microeconomics: consumers who demand products, and producers who supply them. First, however, we begin the study of microeconomics by discussing, in Chapter 6, a characteristic of demand and supply curves that plays a key role in many applications, namely, their *elasticity*—that is, the responsiveness of the quantities supplied or demanded to a change in price. In Chapter 7, we go behind the demand curve and study the way consumers choose among goods. It is the discussion here that provides the theoretical underpinning for our later interpretation of the demand curve as measuring the *marginal benefit* of a good to consumers, an interpretation that is critical to our later analysis of efficient resource allocation in a system of competitive markets.

The next three chapters focus on the firm, with Chapter 8 providing institutional background on the various ways in which the firm may be organized and raise capital for its operation, while Chapter 9 contains a discussion of the determinants of the firm's cost of production in the short and long runs. Chapter 10 then gives the interpretation of the competitive supply curve as a measure of the *marginal cost* of supplying one more unit in the market. In Chapter 11, finally, we explain that it is the equalization of marginal cost of production and marginal benefit of consumption that, under certain conditions, makes a system of competitive markets an efficient device for allocating resources.

CHAPTER

6

# APPLICATIONS OF DEMAND AND SUPPLY: THE CONCEPT OF ELASTICITY

*We might as reasonably dispute whether it is the upper or the under blade of a pair of scissors that cuts a piece of paper, as whether the value is governed by utility [demand] or cost of production [supply].*

*Alfred Marshall,* Principles of Economics

Suppose that you are the manager of the Northlands Coliseum, the home of the Edmonton Oilers. You have been selling tickets for \$15 each but, for reasons you cannot understand, recent games have not been sellouts and you are losing money. The owner who hired you may be a millionaire, but he has large expenses and wants something done to stop the losses. Specifically, he suggests that you raise the price of tickets to \$20. This suggestion bothers you, particularly when it leaks out to the newspapers. Not only do sportswriters denounce the "greed" of the owner, but they also argue that higher prices will backfire, causing fans to stay away in droves. As a consequence, total revenue from ticket sales will fall—or so say the sportswriters.

Who is right — the owner or the sportswriters? You cannot be sure. The answer depends on what happens to ticket sales when prices rise. If many people do stay away, your revenues will indeed fall. On the other hand, if people keep coming regardless of the higher price, your revenues will rise.

Thus, to answer the question, you must consider how responsive your sales are to a change in price. That is, you must consider the *price elasticity* of the demand for tickets.

This chapter will:

- explain the concept of price elasticity of demand
- show how total revenue depends on price elasticity
- explain the similar concept of price elasticity of supply
- show how elasticities are important for answering a wide variety of questions, such as:
  - — Who bears the burden of a sales tax: the buyer or the seller?
  - —What happens to government revenues when a tax is increased?
  - —What are the effects of rent control?
- explain a number of other elasticity concepts, such as income elasticity.

In the appendix to this chapter, finally, we make use of several elasticity concepts to analyse a number of problems and policies in Canadian agriculture.

## THE PRICE ELASTICITY OF DEMAND

The ***price elasticity of demand*** — sometimes known, more simply, as the *elasticity of demand*—measures how strongly buyers respond to a change in price. Specifically, the price elasticity of demand, $\varepsilon_d$, is defined:

$$\textbf{Price elasticity of demand, } \varepsilon_d = \frac{\textbf{percentage change in quantity demanded}}{\textbf{percentage change in price}} \qquad \textbf{(6-1)}$$

## Examples

Some price increases cause a sharp reduction in purchases; others have little effect. For example, when the price of cars increases by 1%, car buyers respond strongly; they reduce their purchases by about 2%. Thus, the price elasticity of demand for cars can be calculated:

$$\varepsilon_d = \frac{-2\%}{1\%} = -2$$

On the other hand, when the price of gasoline goes up by 1%, buyers respond much more weakly. Most drivers stay on the road, and their purchases of gasoline fall only a little—about 0.2% during the first few months. (Over a period of years, they respond somewhat more strongly, since they gradually replace their cars with more fuel-efficient models.) Thus, the short-run price elasticity of demand for gasoline can be calculated:

$$\varepsilon_d = \frac{-0.2\%}{1\%} = -0.2$$

## Dropping the Minus Sign

Buyers of cars thus respond more strongly to a change in price than do buyers of gasoline. To avoid confusion when comparing elasticities, economists sometimes drop the negative sign, and report only the *absolute value* of elasticity. When they do this, they can state unambiguously that the elasticity of demand for cars (2.0) is higher than the elasticity of demand for gasoline (0.2). Note how awkward it is to make a comparison when the negative signs are retained: Is −2.0 higher or lower than −0.2?

For simplicity, and to avoid confusion, we will drop the minus signs in the elasticity measurements below. There is not much cost in doing this. Price elasticities of demand are always negative; when the price changes, the quantity demanded moves in the opposite direction. Thus, the elasticity formula (6-1) always gives a negative number. We should remember that the price elasticity of demand is negative, whether the minus sign is reported or not.

## Elastic and Inelastic Demand

Demand curves may be divided into three categories, depending on the absolute value of the elasticity:

If $|\varepsilon_d| < 1$, the demand is ***inelastic***. The percentage change in quantity demanded is less than the percentage change in price.

If $|\varepsilon_d| = 1$, the demand curve has ***unitary*** elasticity. The percentage change in quantity demanded equals the percentage change in price.

If $|\varepsilon_d| > 1$, the demand curve is ***elastic***. The percentage change in quantity demanded is greater than the percentage change in price.

The two vertical lines | | mean absolute value; that is, the negative sign is dropped.

Note that elasticity is defined in terms of *percentage* changes, not changes in the number of units. If we used simply the number of units, our calculation would be arbitrarily affected by the unit chosen. For example, the change from \$2 to \$4 is two units, if prices are measured in dollars. But measured in cents, the same change from \$2 to \$4 is 200 units. Similarly, the change in quantity would depend on whether we were measuring in bushels or tonnes. By using percentages, we avoid such problems. A change from \$2 to \$4 is the same percentage change, whether we measure in dollars or cents.

## The Beginning-point Problem

However, an annoying problem remains. A change from \$2 to \$4 can be considered either 100% (if we start from \$2 and double it to \$4) or 50% (if we begin at \$4 and cut it in half to \$2). This means that if we calculate elasticity in a simple way, our results depend on which point we start from. For example, consider demand between points *A* and *B* in Figure 6-1, where:

| | Quantity | Price |
|---|---|---|
| *A* | 40 | \$4 |
| *B* | 60 | \$2 |

If we begin at point *A* and move to *B*, quantity increases by 50% (from 40 to 60) while price falls by 50% (from \$4 to \$2). This gives the following calculation:

$$\varepsilon_d = \frac{\textbf{percentage change in } Q}{\textbf{percentage change in } P} = \frac{50\%}{50\%} = 1$$

However, if we begin at *B*, we calculate the decrease in quantity at 33.3% (from 60 to 40), while price increases by 100% (from \$2 to \$4). This gives:

$$\varepsilon_d = \frac{33.3\%}{100\%} = 0.333$$

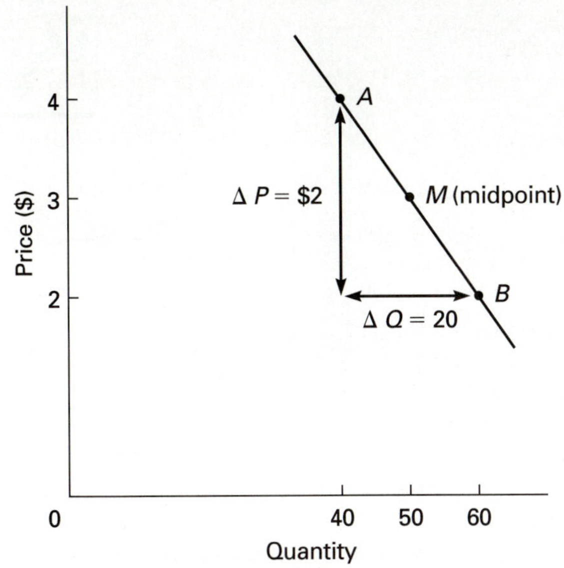


**FIGURE 6-1 Elasticity of demand: The midpoint calculation.**

Suppose we want to calculate the elasticity of the demand curve between *A* and *B*. If we start from *A* and use this as the basis for calculation, we find an elasticity of −1.00. Alternatively, if we start from *B*, we calculate an elasticity of −0.33.

Our measurement of elasticity should not depend on the starting point. This problem can be solved by avoiding either end and using the middle point *M* instead. This gives an elasticity of 0.6, as calculated in the text. (The Greek letter Δ means "change in.")

This is unsatisfactory; the measure of elasticity between *A* and *B* should not depend on the starting point.

## Two Solutions

Economists have two ways to deal with this problem:

1. The most straightforward way is to avoid either end of the demand curve, and use the average or middle point instead. In the ***midpoint formula*** for elasticity, we use the *average* quantity and *average* price:

$$\varepsilon_d = \frac{\textbf{change in } Q\textbf{, as \% of the average of the two quantities}}{\textbf{change in } P\textbf{, as \% of the average of the two prices}}$$

For the section of the demand curve between *A* and *B* in Figure 6-1, the change in quantity = 20 and the average quantity = 50 (that is, [40 + 60]/2); thus, the numerator is 40% (that is, [20/50] × 100%). The change in price = \$2 and the average price = \$3 (that is, [\$4 + \$2]/2); thus, the denominator is 66.7% (that is, [\$2/\$3] × 100%). Applying the midpoint formula, we get:

$$\varepsilon_d = \frac{\mathbf{40\%}}{\mathbf{66.7\%}} = \mathbf{0.60}$$

2. An alternative that provides a good approximation is to look at short segments of the demand curve, in which case the starting point becomes unimportant. The percentage difference between \$2.00 and \$2.01 is about the same, regardless of which price is used as the base.[1]

To see why the concept of elasticity is important, consider two examples — one from agriculture and one from manufacturing.

## The Elasticity of Demand: What Happens to Total Revenue?

There isn't a farmer in the country who complains when he has a good crop. But the more thoughtful ones may be concerned if all the other farmers in North America have a good crop, too. The reason is simple: When a bumper crop is thrown on the market, the price falls, and that can hurt farmers more than they gain from the increase in quantity. Paradoxically, farmers may receive less revenue from a large crop than a small one. While each individual farmer has an incentive to "make hay while the sun shines," farmers as a whole may be worse off if the crop is large.

This possibility is illustrated in the left panel of Figure 6-2. In this hypothetical example, the initial position is *A*. Farmers sell 40 million bushels at a price of \$4. This gives them total revenue of \$160 million — that is, the price of \$4 times the quantity of 40 million. This total revenue is illustrated by the size of the rectangle below and to the left of point *A*. The base of this rectangle measures quantity *Q*, while the height measures price *P*. Thus, the area of the rectan-

[1] Students who have taken calculus will recognize that this method can be taken to the limit, where the length approaches zero. When this is done, elasticity can be measured at a point on the demand curve. One reason that economists use calculus is to avoid irksome difficulties such as the beginning-point problem.

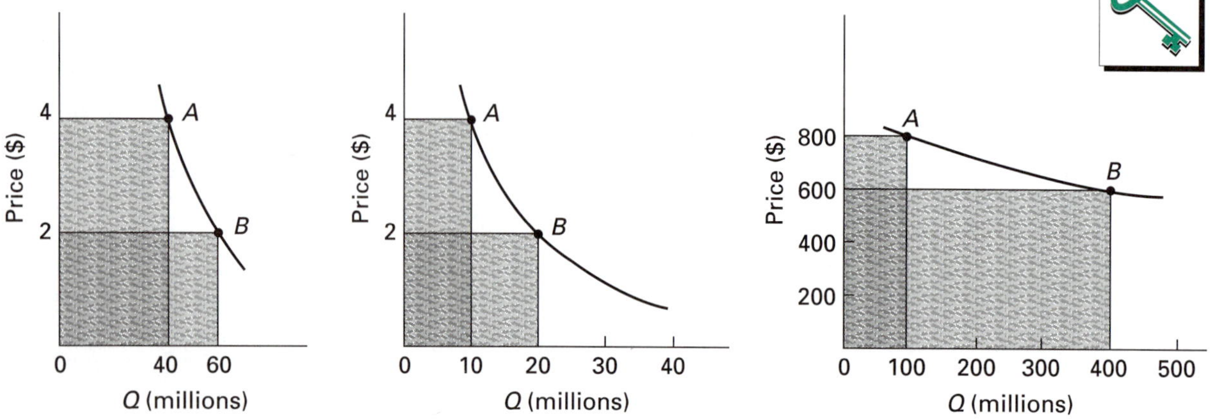


**FIGURE 6-2 Elasticity of demand and total revenue.**
The elasticity of demand falls into three categories, depending on what happens to the total revenue of sellers. If a fall in price causes a fall in total revenue, demand is inelastic (left panel). If a fall in price causes a rise in total revenue, quantity is responding strongly; the demand is elastic (right panel). If the increase in quantity is barely sufficient to compensate for the lower price, total revenue is constant, and elasticity of demand is 1 (centre panel).

gle—its base $Q$ times its height $P$—is a measure of the total revenue, $P \times Q$.

> ***Total revenue* is the $P \times Q$ rectangle below and to the left of a point on the demand curve.**

Now, suppose that, with a bumper crop of 60 million bushels, the price collapses all the way to \$2. The new total revenue is the $P \times Q$ rectangle below and to the left of point $B$: \$2 × 60 million = \$120 million. In this illustration, the total revenue of farmers falls from \$160 million to \$120 million when they produce more. The increase in quantity is too small to compensate farmers for the lower price.

In this case, demand is inelastic—that is, the absolute value of the elasticity is less than 1. (This is the same demand as in Figure 6-1. As already noted, its elasticity is 0.6 in the range between $A$ and $B$).

The second example is taken from the early history of the automobile. At the beginning of the twentieth century, the automobile was a plaything of the rich. Henry Ford determined to change this. He mass-produced his Model T and cut prices, gambling that the increase in sales would more than compensate for the lower price. He was right. As he cut prices, his revenues soared.

This case is illustrated in the right panel of Figure 6-2. Buyers are very responsive to a change in price. A reduction in price causes the quantity to increase by a much larger percentage, with the result that the total revenue rectangle ($P \times Q$) becomes larger. Demand is elastic—that is, the absolute value of elasticity is more than 1.

The centre panel of Figure 6-2 shows the intermediate, borderline case where the increase in the quantity demanded just balances the fall in price. Whenever the price falls, the quantity increases by the same percentage. This is just enough to leave total revenue constant. In this case, elasticity is 1.

In each case, as consumers move down along the demand curve, two conflicting forces are working on total revenue:

1. The increase in quantity works to increase revenue.
2. The fall in price works to depress revenue.

If demand is elastic, the percentage increase in quantity is greater than the percentage fall in price. Thus, the increase in quantity more than compensates for the fall in price, and total revenue increases.

If demand is inelastic, the percentage increase in quantity is less than the percentage fall in price. The fall in price overwhelms the effect of the increasing quantity, and total revenue falls.

If demand has an elasticity of 1, quantity and price change by the same percentage. They just offset one another; total revenue does not change when price changes.

Elasticity, then, helps to explain the Northlands Coliseum puzzle with which the chapter opened. The owner assumed that the demand was inelastic, and that a rise in price would increase revenues. The sportswriters were arguing the opposite — that demand was elastic, and a price increase would reduce revenues.

The effects of a price change on total revenues are summarized in Table 6-1.

## Elasticity and Slope

In Figure 6-2, the flattest demand curve (in the right panel) is the most elastic, and the steepest demand curve (in the left panel) was the least elastic. This raises a question: Can we judge elasticity by the flatness of the curve? Is "high elasticity" just another way of saying "low slope"?

The answer is no. The slope of a curve is not a good measure of elasticity. The reason is that the slope of a curve is measured by the *absolute* change in price divided by the *absolute* change in quantity. In contrast, *percentage* changes are used to measure elasticity.

Two specific examples in Figure 6-3 demonstrate why slope and elasticity are not the same. Panel (a) shows a demand curve with a constant total revenue. As already noted, this curve has a constant elasticity of 1 throughout its range. But it does not have a constant slope; it becomes flatter as quantity increases.

The second example is a straight-line demand: Figure 6-3(b). It has a constant slope, but its elasticity changes, becoming lower as we move down along it. The calculations in Table 6-2 show that elasticity is 2 in the range between $A$ and $B$, while elasticity is only 0.5 in the range between $B$ and $C$.[2] Thus, constant slope does not mean constant elasticity, nor does constant elasticity mean constant slope.

All is not lost, however. There is one generalization we can make about slope and elasticity. If we compare two demand curves *that pass through the same point*, then the flatter one is more elastic. For example, point $A$ is in exactly the same position in the first two panels of Figure 6-3. In each case, $P$ = \$5 and $Q$ = 10. At this point, the demand curve in panel (b) is flatter than the demand curve in panel (a), and it also has a higher elasticity. Finally, panel (c) of Figure 6-3 shows two extreme cases:

1. If demand is vertical, quantity is completely unresponsive to a change in price. No matter what happens to price, the change in quantity is zero. Thus, the numerator in the elasticity formula is zero and elasticity is, therefore, zero.
2. The other extreme is a horizontal demand. In this case, price does not change. Thus, the denominator of the elasticity formula is zero, and elasticity is infinite. This horizontal demand is spoken of as being ***infinitely elastic*** or ***perfectly elastic***.

## WHAT DETERMINES ELASTICITY OF DEMAND?

Why is the demand for some products highly elastic, while the demand for others is inelastic?

### 1. Substitutability

Items that have good substitutes generally have a more elastic demand than those that do not. For

[2] If you have trouble remembering that elasticity falls as we move downward to the right along a straight-line demand, here's a tip. As we move to the right and $Q$ becomes larger, any specific increase in $Q$ represents a smaller and smaller percentage increase. Thus, the elasticity gets smaller and smaller.

**TABLE 6-1 Elasticity and Total Revenue (when price falls)**

| If | Then | Therefore | Therefore, Total Revenue *TR* |
|---|---|---|---|
| $\varepsilon_d > 1$ | % change in $Q$ > % change in $P$ | Rise in *TR* due to rise in $Q$ > fall in *TR* due to fall in $P$ | Rises |
| $\varepsilon_d = 1$ | % change in $Q$ = % change in $P$ | Rise in *TR* due to rise in $Q$ = fall in *TR* due to fall in $P$ | Doesn't change |
| $\varepsilon_d < 1$ | % change in $Q$ < % change in $P$ | Rise in *TR* due to rise in $Q$ < fall in *TR* due to fall in $P$ | Falls |

example, sugar has reasonably close substitutes, such as corn syrup or honey. In contrast, salt does not have such good substitutes. The elasticity of demand for sugar is higher than for salt. In particular, manufacturers of soft drinks shift to corn syrup and away from sugar when the price of sugar rises.

Because of the importance of substitutes, the elasticity of demand is lower for a product if we define it broadly than if we define it narrowly. For example, the elasticity of demand for Chevrolet cars is high, because Fords, Chryslers, and Hondas are very good substitutes. However, the demand for all *cars* as a group is much lower, because there is no close substitute for the automobile. Similarly, the demand for beef is much more elastic than the demand for all food (Table 6-3). Chicken and pork are reasonably good substitutes for beef, but there is no substitute for food as a whole.

## 2. Necessities versus Luxuries

Essentials such as food generally have an inelastic demand because purchasers feel they can scarcely do without. Note the problem faced by farmers. They produce something—food—that is essential for survival. But the elasticity of demand for such essentials is generally low, and farmers can accordingly be penalized with lower revenues when they produce a bumper crop.

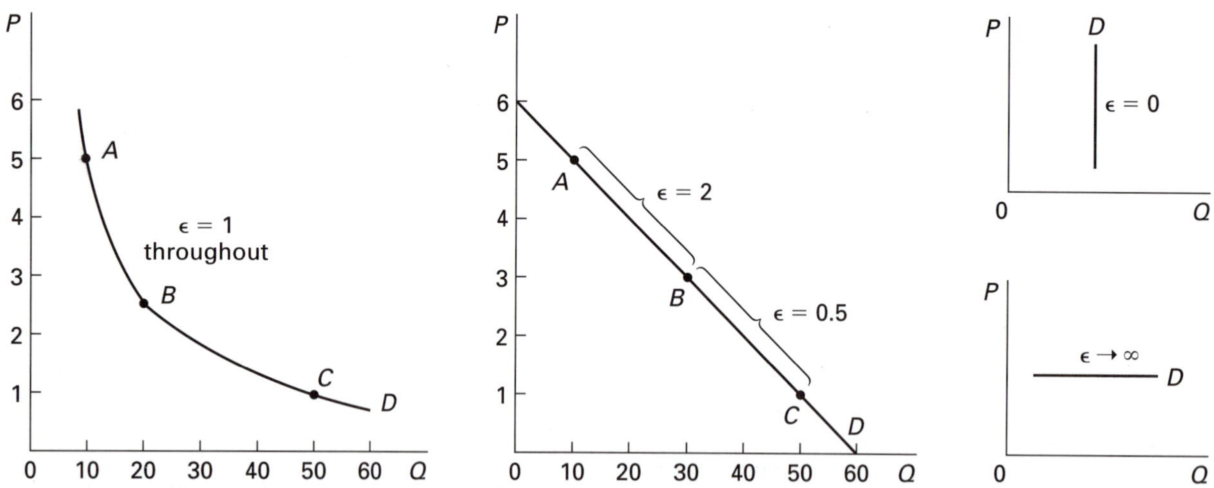


**(a) Constant elasticity of 1.** **(b) Constant slope.** **(c) Special cases.**

**FIGURE 6-3 Elasticity and slope are not the same.**
The curve on the left has a constant elasticity of 1 throughout. But it consistently gets flatter as we move to the right. The straight-line demand in panel (b) has a changing elasticity, in spite of its constant slope. Two special cases are shown in panel (c): a vertical demand curve, with an elasticity of zero; and a horizontal demand curve, with an infinite elasticity.

**TABLE 6-2 Calculating Elasticity along a Straight Line†**

| Figure 6-3(b) Point: | (1) $Q$ | (2) Change in $Q$ ($\Delta Q$) | (3) Average $Q$: $\frac{Q_1 + Q_2}{2}$ | (4) Percentage Change in $Q$ (2) ÷ (3) × 100% | (5) $P$ | (6) Change in $P$ ($\Delta P$) | (7) Average $P$: $\frac{P_1 + P_2}{2}$ | (8) Percentage Change in $P$ (6) ÷ (7) × 100% | (9) Elasticity (4) ÷ (8) |
|---|---|---|---|---|---|---|---|---|---|
| A | 10 | | | | 5 | | | | |
| | | 20 | 20 | 100% | | 2 | 4 | 50% | 2 |
| B | 30 | | | | 3 | | | | |
| | | 20 | 40 | 50% | | 2 | 2 | 100% | 0.5 |
| C | 50 | | | | 1 | | | | |

† In order to avoid the beginning-point problem, this table uses the midpoint or average approach. Observe that changes in quantity are calculated as a percentage of the average quantity (columns 3 and 4), and changes in price are similarly calculated as a percentage of the average price (columns 7 and 8).

**TABLE 6-3 Estimated Price Elasticities of Demand**

Elasticity very low (below 0.5)
- Salt
- Coffee
- Gasoline (in the short run)
- All food (taken as a single good)

Elasticity low (0.5 to 0.8)
- Gasoline (in the long run)
- Cigarettes

Elasticity about 1
- Beef
- Housing
- China and tableware

Elasticity high (1.2 to 2.0)
- Furniture
- Electricity

Elasticity very high (above 2.0)
- Millinery
- Foreign travel

*Source:* A number of studies, including H.S. Houthakker and Lester D. Taylor, *Consumer Demand in the United States* (Cambridge, Mass.: Harvard University Press, 1966).

Luxuries generally have a more elastic demand. For example, luxuries such as foreign vacations have an elastic demand because purchasers can stop buying them if their prices rise. When the value of the Canadian dollar soared in terms of other currencies (such as the British pound) in the mid-1980s, travel to Europe became cheap and many Canadians took vacations in England.

### 3. Percentage of Income

Big items in a budget generally have a more elastic demand than small items. To cite an extreme example, the demand for houses is more elastic than the demand for toothpicks. Purchasers may spend a week trying to negotiate a price reduction of 1% on a new house. But they won't even notice a 20% drop in the price of toothpicks. Thus, for small items, consumers are insensitive to price.

### 4. Time

The elasticity of demand generally increases with time. One example has already been cited near the beginning of the chapter. If the price of gasoline rises, there is very little immediate effect on the quantity that people buy. The typical car may be driven less, but not much less; most drivers are not going to stay off the road just to save gasoline. It takes some time for drivers to switch to smaller cars and longer yet for the auto companies to design and build more fuel-efficient models. But when they do, the public's purchases of gasoline are further reduced. Thus, quantity responds more in the long run than in the short.

However, there can be exceptions to this general rule, particularly for durable goods such as cars. Suppose the price of cars rises. In this case, the quantity demanded may fall sharply and quickly. The reason is that most drivers can keep their cars longer; they can stay out of the market for a while when the price rises. However, as time passes, the old cars wear out, and drivers feel compelled to buy replacements. Thus, the demand for cars is less elastic over a period of one or two years than it is over a very short period of a month or two.

## THE PRICE ELASTICITY OF SUPPLY

Just as elasticity of demand describes the responsiveness of buyers to a change in price, so elasticity of supply describes the responsiveness of sellers. The ***price elasticity of supply***, $\varepsilon_S$, is defined:

$$\varepsilon_S = \frac{\textbf{percentage change in quantity supplied}}{\textbf{percentage change in price}} \quad \textbf{(6-2)}$$

Supply is elastic if producers respond strongly to price changes, or inelastic if they respond relatively weakly. Specifically:

If $\varepsilon_S < 1$, the supply curve is inelastic. The percentage change in quantity supplied is less than the percentage change in price.

If $\varepsilon_S = 1$, the supply curve has unitary elasticity. The percentage change in quantity supplied equals the percentage change in price.

If $\varepsilon_S > 1$, the supply curve is elastic. The percentage change in quantity supplied is greater than the percentage change in price.

In a diagram showing a supply curve, there is a simple way to determine if supply is elastic or inelastic. If supply has an elasticity of 1, quantity increases by the same percentage or fraction as does price. Thus, the supply curve traces out a *straight line from the origin*, as illustrated in Figure 6-4(b). (Note that the slope does not have to be 45°; any straight line from the origin has an elasticity of 1.) If supply is steeper than a straight line through the origin, then quantity changes by a smaller percentage than price; supply is inelastic, panel (a). On the other hand, if supply is flatter than a line through the origin, it is elastic, panel (c). Thus, to tell if supply is elastic, we

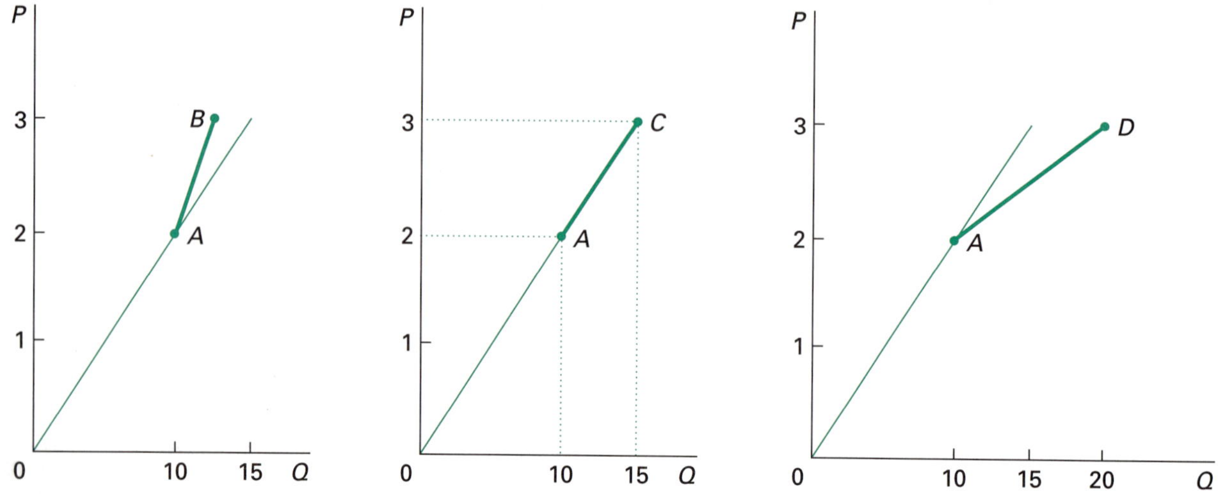


(a) $\epsilon_S < 1$ (b) $\epsilon_S = 1$ (c) $\epsilon_S > 1$

**FIGURE 6-4 Elasticity of supply.**
In the centre panel, a supply curve with an elasticity of 1 is a straight line going through the origin. An increase of 50% in price causes the same 50% increase in the quantity supplied. If the response of quantity is stronger, elasticity is greater than 1 (right panel). If the response is weaker, elasticity is less than 1 (left panel).

can use a simple test: Draw a straight line through the origin to the supply curve. Is the supply curve flatter than this straight line? If so, it is elastic.

## WHAT DETERMINES ELASTICITY OF SUPPLY?

The main determinants of elasticity of supply are:

### 1. Time

When the price of a good increases, producers may want to sell a lot more, but they may have to expand their capacity to do so. This may take time. Quantity thus may respond more strongly and elasticity, accordingly, may be higher as time passes.

This idea was emphasized almost a century ago by Alfred Marshall, Cambridge University's great economist and teacher. Marshall distinguished three time periods:

- The momentary or immediate effect, before producers have had a chance to respond at all
- The short-run effect, when firms can increase output, using their existing plant and equipment
- The long-run effect, after existing firms have been able to add new capacity, and new firms have been able to enter.

Suppose demand for a perishable commodity like fresh fish suddenly rises from $D_1$ to $D_2$ in Figure 6-5(a). On the first day, the quantity supplied is not influenced at all by price. Whatever has been caught ($Q_1$) is put on the market, regardless of price. The immediate supply $S$ is completely inelastic, and the shift in demand causes a sharp rise in price to $P_2$.

In the days that follow, the higher price induces fishing boat captains to increase their crews, and to fish somewhat longer hours. The quantity of fish caught and offered for sale increases. Thus, supply becomes more elastic in panel (b), and price settles down somewhat to $P_3$. But this is not the long-run equilibrium. As more time passes, new boats can be built, and even more fish caught. Thus, in the long run, supply is even more elastic, as shown in panel (c). The result is a further moderation of price, to $P_4$.

### 2. Substitutes or Complements in Production?

Does an item have a close substitute in production? That is, can the labour, land, and equipment used to

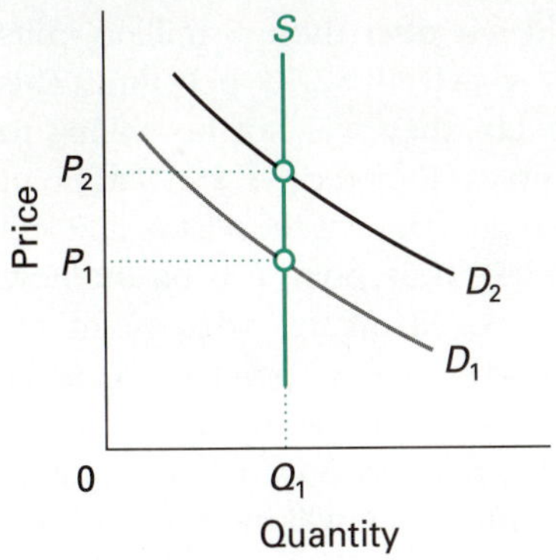


**(a) Immediate effect.**

On the first day, supply is completely inelastic. Thus, the shift in demand from $D_1$ to $D_2$ results in a very large price increase, to $P_2$.

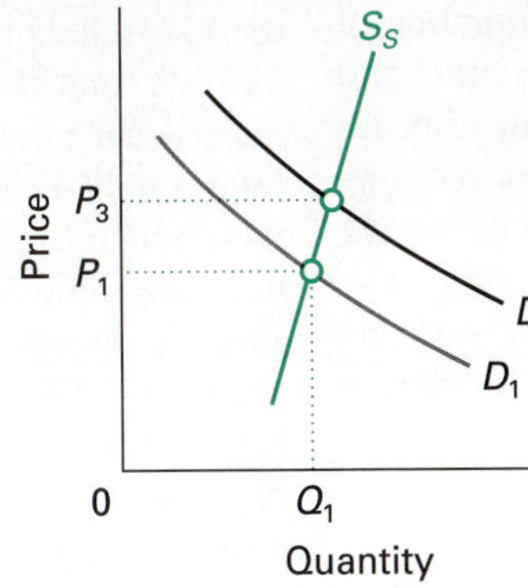


**(b) Short-run effect.**

Supply now has some elasticity, since the catch of fish can be increased by hiring larger crews and using existing boats more heavily. Thus the price rise is moderated to $P_3$.

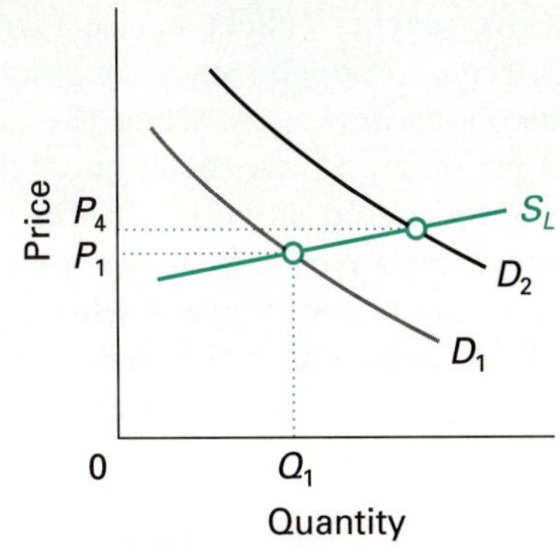


**(c) Long-run effect.**

Supply now has even greater elasticity, since there is now time for new boats to be built. As a result, more fish are sold and the price settles down further to $P_4$.

**FIGURE 6-5 How the elasticity of supply changes over time.**

produce it be readily switched into the production of another good? If so, quantity will generally respond strongly to price, and the elasticity of supply will be high. Thus, the elasticity of supply is greater for an individual grain — such as rye — than for all grains taken together. The reason is that, in the face of a fall in the price of rye, a farmer is able to reduce the quantity grown by shifting production into a substitute grain like wheat or barley. This ability of producers to respond to a change in price works to make the supply of rye elastic.

On the other hand, if the price of all grain falls, a farmer will have more difficulty in shifting out of grain production because there are no close substitute activities. It would be very expensive to move into a less closely related activity, such as dairy farming, because of the high costs of new capital equipment. Because farmers are less able to respond, the elasticity of supply is smaller for all grains as a group than it is for a single grain. In short, products like rye with a close substitute in production have a more elastic supply than goods without a close substitute in production.

In contrast to substitutes—such as rye and wheat —other goods may be complements in production, or *joint products*. When you produce one, you get the other—for example, beef and hides. Most of the value of a steer is in the meat, and relatively little in the hide. Therefore, the decision to butcher a steer is influenced strongly by the price beef, but very little by the price of hides. Once the steer has been butchered, the relatively unimportant hide will be sold regardless of the price. In other words, the supply of hides is inelastic because hides are a relatively unimportant joint product.

### 3. The Feasibility and Cost of Storage

Goods that rot quickly must be put on the market regardless of price; their elasticity of supply is low. In Marshall's day, when refrigeration was inadequate, it was not feasible to store fish from day to day. This made his example particularly striking. Today, with better and cheaper refrigeration, the elasticity of fish supply is not zero even for a single day. In the face of a collapse in price, suppliers have the option of withdrawing some of their catch and putting the extra fish on ice for a day or two.

## SIGNIFICANCE OF ELASTICITY

A number of examples will illustrate just how much the concept of elasticity can enrich demand-and-supply analysis.

## Incidence of a Tax: Who Pays?

Governments collect excise taxes on a number of specific products, such as gasoline, cigarettes, and alcoholic beverages. When the government imposes a tax of, say, \$1, we might guess that the tax will simply be passed along to the buyer, who will pay \$1 more. However, this is not generally the case. The question of ***incidence*** — who actually pays — is one of the more interesting and important tax questions for governments, whether at the federal, provincial, or local level.

The *incidence of a tax* is the division of the burden. Who actually pays the tax, the buyer or the seller?

An *excise tax* is a tax on a specific product, such as gasoline or cigarettes.

To shed light on this question, consider the supply and demand for a good shown in Figure 6-6(a). The initial equilibrium before the tax is at $E_1$, with 6 million units sold at a price of \$2. Suppose now that the government imposes a tax of \$1 per unit, which it collects from sellers. Who bears the burden of this tax?

The effect of the tax is to shift the supply curve upward by the full \$1, from $S_1$ to $S_2$. To see why, consider any point on the supply curve — say, 8 million units. Point $A$ on the supply curve $S_1$ shows that before the tax, sellers would not offer these 8 million units for sale unless they received \$2.50 per unit. This means that after the tax, they will not be willing to offer 8 million units unless they receive \$3.50 at point $B$—enough to pay the government the \$1 tax and still have the same \$2.50 left. Thus, point $B$ is on the new, after-tax supply curve $S_2$. No matter what point we consider on $S_1$, the corresponding point on $S_2$ is \$1 higher. Thus, the entire supply curve shifts upward by the amount of the tax. But this does not necessarily mean that the equilibrium price will increase by \$1.

On the contrary, observe what happens when the \$1 tax is imposed in Figure 6-6(a). The upward shift of the supply curve causes the equilibrium to move from $E_1$ to $E_2$. The price that consumers pay goes up 25¢, from \$2.00 to \$2.25. Thus, consumers bear only 25¢ of the burden of the tax. Sellers bear the remaining 75¢. It is true that their selling price rises by 25¢, from \$2.00 to \$2.25. But \$1 of this total must go to the government, so sellers get only \$1.25 after tax or 75¢ less than the \$2.00 they originally got in the no-tax situation at $E_1$. The brace brackets along the vertical axis illustrate how the \$1 tax is split up into the 25¢ burden on buyers and the 75¢ burden on sellers.

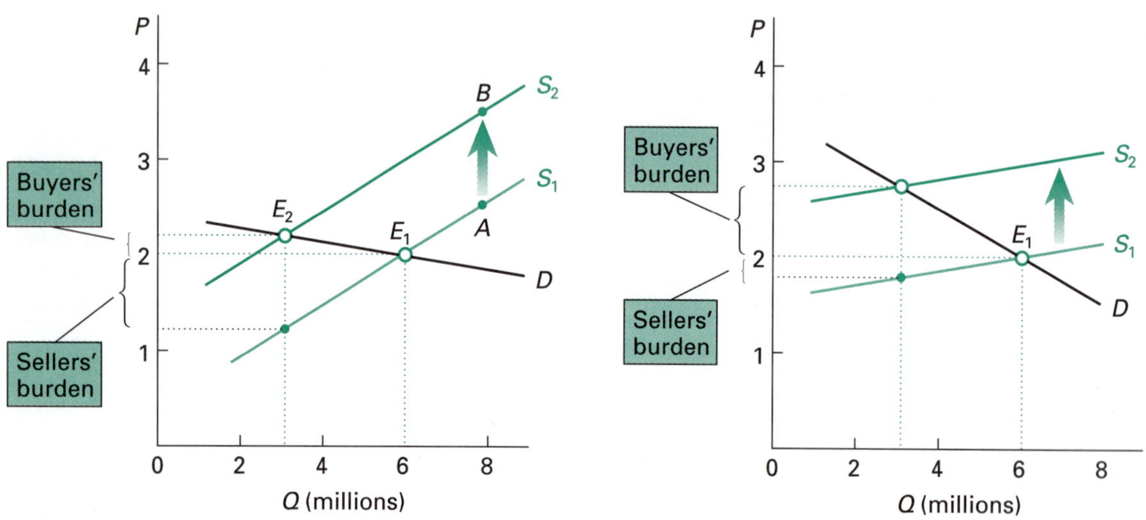


**(a) Sellers bear most of the burden.**

**(b) Buyers bear most of the burden.**

**FIGURE 6-6 Elasticity and the incidence of a tax.**
If the demand curve is more elastic than the supply curve, then sellers bear more of the tax burden than buyers, as shown in the left panel. But if the supply curve is more elastic, buyers will be stuck with the greater burden— as illustrated in the right panel.

The reason that buyers bear a smaller share of the burden in this case is that they are more responsive to changes in price than are sellers. Demand is more elastic than supply. However, in panel (b) the reverse is true. Here, sellers are more responsive to a change in price; supply is more elastic than demand. As a result, sellers bear the lighter burden; most of the tax is *shifted forward* to the buyer.

These conclusions can best be understood if we think of two groups in a market, one buying, the other selling. Suppose one group—it doesn't matter which—takes the view: "We aren't all that keen to stay in the market. If the price moves against us, we can back away. In responding to price changes, we're flexible, sensitive, *elastic*." Suppose the other group feels: "We have no choice; we must stay in the market. Even if price moves against us, we can't back away. We're inflexible, unresponsive, *inelastic*." It is no surprise that this second group will bear most of the burden of a tax and, in other situations as well, will be in the more vulnerable position.

## Elasticity and Tax Revenue

Not only does elasticity determine who bears the burden of a tax; it also affects the amount of revenue the government collects.

If the government of Quebec puts an excise tax on gasoline sold in the province, most Quebec drivers have little choice but to pay. Their only alternative is to drive less. But consider specifically the drivers who live in Hull which is situated on the Quebec-Ontario border, just across from the city of Ottawa on the Ontario side of the Ottawa River. Unless Ontario also introduces a gasoline tax, Hull motorists do have an alternative: They can avoid the higher Quebec tax by driving across the river and filling up in Ottawa. The elasticity of demand for gasoline in the province of Quebec as a whole may be low but, for the city of Hull, it is high because gasoline bought in Ottawa is a close substitute for gas bought in Quebec.

Figure 6-7 shows why this is important. The first panel illustrates what happens in a place like Mon-

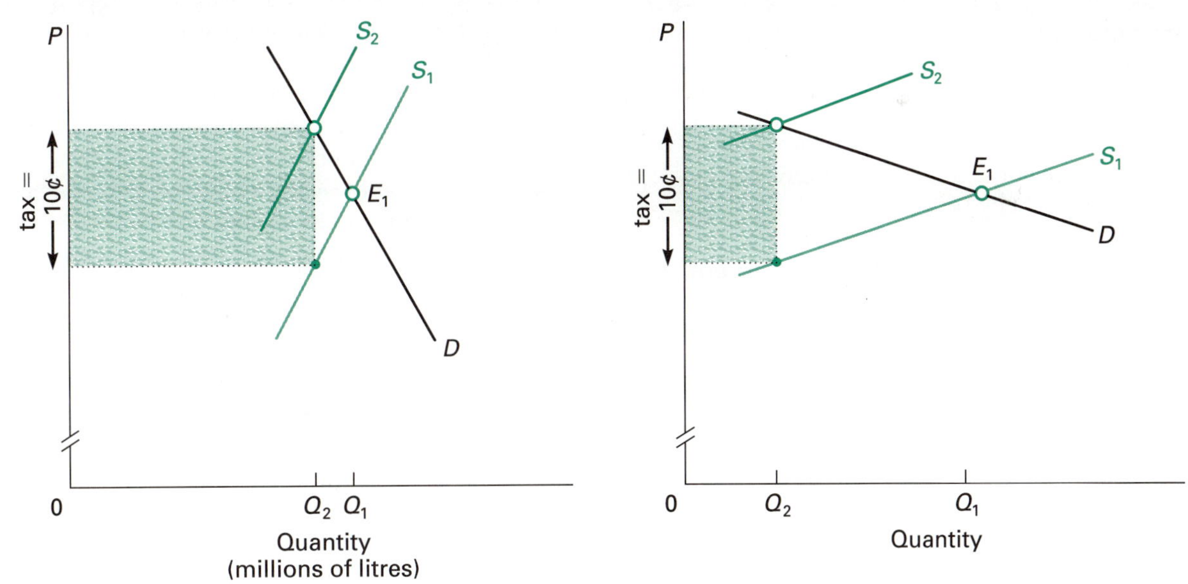


**(a) Low elasticity, high tax revenues.** **(b) High elasticity, low tax revenues.**

**FIGURE 6-7 Tax collections depend on elasticities.**
For a city such as Montreal, say, elasticities of demand and supply of gasoline are low, as in the left panel. A tax therefore causes a relatively small change in quantity. For a city like Hull just across the river from another province, elasticities of demand and supply are much larger, as in the right panel. If the Quebec government increases its gasoline tax, the quantities sold in Hull may fall sharply, and tax revenues collected in Hull will be small.

treal, far from the Ontario border, when the Quebec government imposes a tax of, say, 10¢ a litre. Both demand and supply are shown as quite inelastic. In the face of the tax, quantity falls only a little, and government revenues collected from motorists in Montreal are high. (Revenues are equal to the shaded area, which is the quantity sold $Q_2$ times the tax of 10¢.)

However, in a place like the city of Hull, the quantity sold may decrease sharply when the government imposes a tax, as illustrated in panel (b). Not only is the demand for gas in Hull quite elastic because drivers can buy gas on the Ontario side, but supply elasticity is also high because sellers can close down their stations in Hull and set up operations just across the river in Ottawa. As a result, tax revenues collected in Hull may be quite small, as illustrated by the small shaded area in Figure 6-7(b).

(In fact, when the Quebec government did raise the provincial tax on gasoline several years ago, gas station operators in Hull managed to get the government to agree to apply a lower tax rate in Hull than in the rest of Quebec: Even if they didn't know the definition of demand elasticity, the operators knew that they would lose a large amount of sales if they passed on the tax increase to their customers, since drivers had the option of filling up on the other side of the river.)

In summary, the effects of a tax depend on elasticity in two ways:

1. The *incidence* of a tax depends on the relative elasticities of demand and supply. Those with the lower elasticity bear the larger burden. If supply is less elastic than demand, sellers bear most of the tax. If demand is less elastic than supply, buyers bear most of the burden.
2. The *revenues* from a tax depend on the elasticities of demand and supply. If both elasticities are high, quantity will fall sharply when the tax is imposed, and this will depress revenues. The lower the elasticities of demand and supply, the smaller will be the decline in quantity, and the greater the revenue.

Consequently, when governments tax individual products, they generally pick items with low elasticities of demand, such as cigarettes and alcoholic beverages. (Low elasticities are only one reason to pick cigarettes and alcohol. Legislators generally face less political opposition when they raise such "sin taxes.")

Elasticities are also the key to understanding the effects of many other policies. Consider, for example, the effects of rent control laws.

## Rent Control

A number of cities—such as Paris, Vienna, New York, and Toronto—have extensive experience with rent controls. Controls are popular with tenants, who want affordable housing. But, like many other quick fixes, their long-term effects can be unpleasant. To understand why, we call on the distinction between the inelastic short-run supply and the much more elastic long-run supply.

Figure 6-8(a) illustrates what happens when rent control is imposed. The maximum rent that owners can legally charge is set at $R_1$, below the equilibrium rent $R_E$. In the short run, the number of apartments is approximately fixed, as shown by short-run supply $S_S$. At the low controlled rent $R_1$, there is a shortage of $AB$ units, and it is difficult to find an apartment. When a renter moves out, there is a scramble to get the vacant apartment. This basic effect of rent control — that apartments become hard to find — is important.

However, even greater shortages develop as time passes. Rent controls reduce the construction of new apartment buildings, because they reduce the rental income that owners can hope to receive. Furthermore, owners of rent-controlled buildings in cities such as New York have sometimes simply let them deteriorate since they couldn't hope to recoup the cost of repairs by charging higher rents; in some cases, landlords have even abandoned their buildings. The results have been devastating in some areas. As Swedish economist Assar Lindbeck has concluded: "Next to bombing, rent control seems in many cases to be the most efficient technique so far known for destroying cities."[3]

The gradual decline in the quantity of apartments is illustrated by the move from $B$ to $F$, $G$, and finally to point $H$ on the long-run supply curve $S_L$. This curve shows the ultimate effect on quantity (at $H$) after apartment owners have adjusted completely to the new level of rents ($R_1$).

In the short run, most tenants benefit from the controls. They pay a lower price, and they get almost the same amount of housing at $B$ as at the free-market equilibrium $E$. Over the long run, however, it is doubtful that renters benefit on average. While they still pay a lower price, they have less housing at $H$ than at $E$. It is exceedingly difficult for newcomers to find a place to live.

---

[3] Assar Lindbeck, *The Political Economy of the New Left* (New York: Harper and Row, 1971), p. 39.

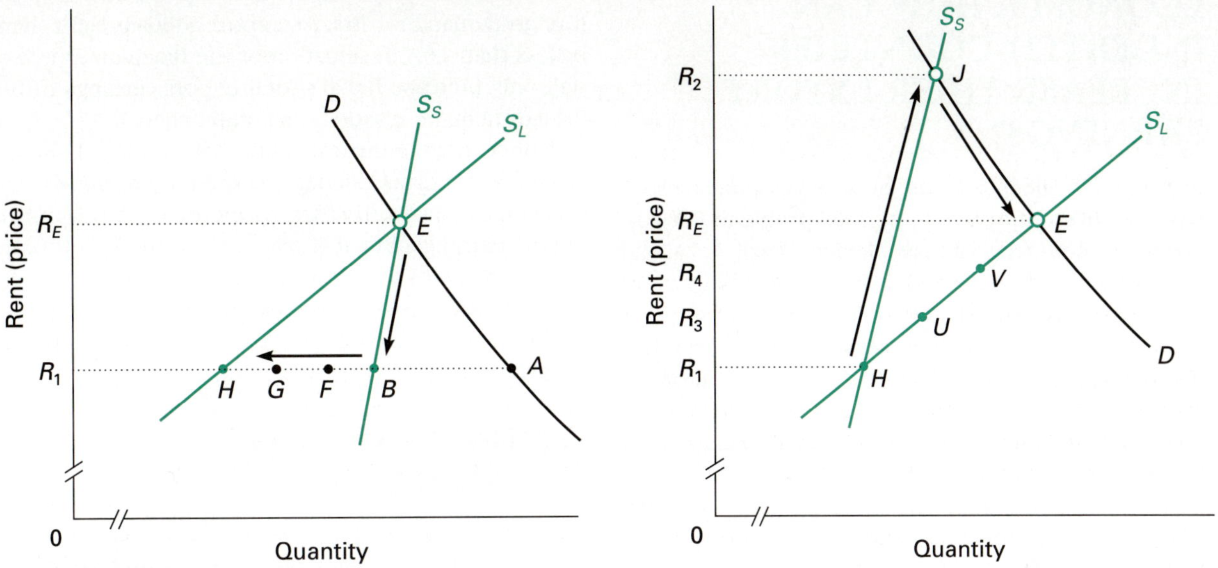


**(a) Imposition of rent control.** **(b) Getting rid of rent control.**

**FIGURE 6-8 Effects of rent control.**
Panel (a) shows the effects of rent control. In the short run, there is a shortage of *AB*, and apartments are hard to find. As time passes, new construction declines and old buildings are abandoned. The shortage becomes more severe, eventually increasing to distance *AH*, with point *H* being on the long-run supply curve. Panel (b) shows what happens if rent controls are suddenly eliminated. Rents shoot up to $R_2$. It is only as new buildings are constructed that the rents subside to the long-run equilibrium *E*. (This figure builds on the distinction between short-run and long-run supply shown earlier in Figure 6-5.)

Once the problems are recognized, it may already be too late to eliminate rent controls without severe pain. Just as the major gains to tenants come in the first few years of rent control, so the major penalties to tenants come in the first few years of decontrol, for reasons shown in Figure 6-8(b). Once point *H* has been reached, the stock of housing has been reduced. There is a new short-run supply curve ($S_2$), reflecting the new, smaller stock of housing. If rent control is suddenly ended, even a sizeable increase in price will not cause much increase in the number of apartments in the short run. That is, the short-run supply is inelastic because new buildings cannot be constructed quickly. Thus, a sudden abolition of controls can lead to a very sharp jump in rents. In fact, rents can jump all the way up to $R_2$ (point *J*), far above the initial free-market rent of $R_E$. Any politician supporting decontrol may have to face a group of enraged tenant voters. It is only as time passes, and new buildings are constructed, that rents move gradually back down from *J* toward the long-run equilibrium at *E*.

One way to avoid the worst of the adjustment problem is to remove controls gradually. By slowly increasing permissible rents, the jump up to *J* can be avoided. If the rent ceiling is gradually increased from $R_1$ to $R_E$, the stock of housing will have time to increase. For example, if the rent ceiling is raised first to $R_3$, the stock of housing will gradually adjust to point *U* on the long-run supply curve. Then the ceiling can be raised to $R_4$, causing an increase in the housing stock to *V*. Finally, if the ceiling is raised to $R_E$, the housing stock will adjust to its long-run equilibrium at *E*. Controls can then be abolished without an upward jump in rents. A number of economists have suggested that rent controls be phased out in this gradual manner.[4]

[4] For example, Anthony Downs, *Rental Housing in the 1980s* (Washington: The Brookings Institution, 1983), p. 9. Downs recommends that the phasing out of controls be combined with rent subsidies for the poor.

## LIVING IN A GLOBAL ECONOMY: HOW CAN INDEBTED COUNTRIES INCREASE THEIR EXPORT EARNINGS?

In the early 1980s, a number of developing nations were confronted by a very serious problem. For several years, countries such as Mexico, Brazil, Peru, and the Philippines had been spending substantially more on imports than they had earned by exporting goods and services to other countries. Part of the problem was the increase that had occurred in world oil prices in the 1970s and early 1980s. Because their demand for oil was inelastic, when its U.S.-dollar price rose in the world market, they were not able to reduce their oil consumption by very much. As a result, the total number of dollars they spent on importing oil increased.

To cover the difference between their import spending and export earnings, these countries had been borrowing heavily in the world capital market. But in the early 1980s, there was a crisis: The banks, governments, and other institutions that had been lending money to them now refused to lend additional amounts. Instead, they insisted on repayment of past loans. Because they had been borrowing in international currencies such as U.S. dollars, the debtor nations now needed to increase their exports in order to earn more dollars in the world market. How could they do this?

One answer was that governments could encourage exports by devaluing their domestic currencies; that is, by increasing the price of foreign currencies in terms of domestic money. For example, if the Brazilian government were to raise the price of an American dollar in terms of Brazilian cruzeiros by 20%, a Brazilian exporters could reduce the dollar price of the goods they were selling in the world market by 20%, and still earn as many cruzeiros per unit of exports as before. By lowering the U.S.-dollar price of their export goods, Brazilian exporters would be more competitive in the world markets, and Brazil's export earnings (measured in U.S. dollars) would increase.

Or would they? True, the lower dollar prices offered by Brazilian exporters would increase their sales. But each unit of exports would also bring in a smaller number of dollars. How do we know whether the total number of dollars earned by exporters would rise or fall?

Once more, the answer involves an elasticity. Specifically, we need to know: Is the price elasticity of foreign demand for Brazil's export goods greater than or less than 1? A devaluation of the Brazilian cruzeiro will only increase Brazil's total export earnings if the foreign demand elasticity is greater than 1.

Notice that if the elasticity is less than 1, Brazil would face a cruel dilemma. If the creditors insist on repayment, Brazil *must* try to increase its U.S.-dollar export earnings. But if it tries to do this by offering its export goods at lower prices in the world market, its total earnings will not rise: Brazil will simply not be able to increase its export earnings by a devaluation.

## OTHER ELASTICITY MEASURES

Prices play a strategic role in the market system, providing signals and incentives to buyers and sellers. In microeconomics, one of the central questions is how buyers respond to a change in price. The strength of their response is, of course, exactly what the price elasticity of demands is designed to measure. However, buyers also respond to other influences, such as income. To measure the strength of this response, economists also use an elasticity concept.

### Income Elasticity of Demand

Just as price elasticity measures how the quantity demanded responds to price changes, so ***income elasticity*** measures how the quantity demanded responds to income changes. Formally,

$$\textbf{Income elasticity of demand} = \frac{\textbf{percentage change in quantity demanded}}{\textbf{percentage change in income}} \qquad \textbf{(6-3)}$$

Notice how similar this is to the definition of price elasticity presented earlier (Equation (6-1)).

The North American auto market provides an example of a high income elasticity of demand. Various estimates place this elasticity between 2.5 and 3. In other words, there is an increase of 2.5% to 3% in the quantity of new cars purchased in response to a 1% increase in income. On the other hand, the income elasticity of gasoline is about 1 and of tobacco is considerably less (about 0.5). Thus, the demand for tobacco is "income inelastic"; when income rises, tobacco purchases rise by a smaller percentage. Recall that income is a "demand shifter"; when income rises, the demand curve generally shifts to the right. Income elasticity of demand measures the magnitude of that shift. In the case of automobiles, the shift is more important than in the case of tobacco. For a small category of goods — *inferior* goods — an increase in income shifts the demand curve to the *left*. Purchases decline as income rises. In such cases, the income elasticity of demand is negative.

For a *normal* good, the income elasticity of demand is positive. An increase in income causes an increase in the quantity demanded.

## Cross Elasticity of Demand

The quantity of a good demanded depends not only on its own price, but also on the prices of other goods. For example, the demand for cars depends on the price of gasoline. The strength of this effect is measured by the ***cross elasticity of demand*** (also sometimes known as the *cross-price elasticity* of demand). Formally,

$$\text{Cross elasticity of demand for } X \text{ with respect to the price of } Y = \frac{\text{percentage change in quantity of } X \text{ demanded}}{\text{percentage change in the price of } Y} \qquad \text{(6-4)}$$

As in the case of income elasticity, it is important to report the sign of the cross elasticity. If it is positive, an increase in the price of *Y* causes an *increase* in the quantity of *X* demanded, and the goods are ***substitutes***. For example, beef and pork are substitutes: A 1% increase in the price of pork causes the quantity of beef demanded to increase by about 0.3%. That is, it causes the demand curve for beef to shift to the right by 0.3%. A 1% increase in the price of butter causes the quantity of margarine demanded to increase by about 0.8%. Thus, butter and margarine are even closer substitutes than beef and pork.

On the other hand, if cross elasticity is negative, an increase in the price of *Y* causes a *decrease* in the quantity of *X* demanded. The goods are ***complements***. When you buy one, you also tend to buy the other. Thus, for example, cars and gasoline are complements. When the price of cars (*Y*) increases, people buy fewer cars and drive less. The demand for gasoline (*X*) is reduced; that is, it shifts to the left. Cross elasticity in Equation (6-4) is negative, and measures the magnitude of this shift.

To sum up: The sign of the income elasticity determines whether goods are normal goods (+) or inferior goods (−). The sign of the cross elasticity determines whether goods are substitutes (+) or complements (−). In each case, the numerical value of the elasticity measures the strength of the effect. Finally, when the simple term "elasticity" is used, it means price elasticity.

## KEY POINTS

1. Price elasticity of demand measures the responsiveness of quantity demanded to price; the more responsive, the more elastic. Similarly, elasticity of supply measures the responsiveness of quantity supplied to price.
2. The price elasticities of demand and supply are calculated using percentage changes in price and quantity, not absolute changes.
3. Over a segment of a demand curve, percentage calculations are different depending on which end is chosen as the starting point. Elasticity should not depend on this arbitrary choice. To avoid this problem, calculations are based on the midpoint or average of the two ends.
4. Price elasticity of demand determines what happens to total revenue as price changes. If demand is elastic, a fall in price will raise revenues ($P \times Q$). If demand is inelastic, a fall in price will lower revenues. Finally, if demand has an elasticity of 1, total revenue will not be affected by a change in price.
5. The slope (flatness) of a demand or supply curve is not a measure of its elasticity. Nevertheless, if two curves pass through the same point, the flatter curve is the more elastic.
6. Price elasticity of demand depends on a number of characteristics. Specifically, elasticity of demand tends to be high:

(a) if the good is a luxury rather than a necessity
(b) if the good is a big-ticket item rather than a small percentage of the consumers' total expenditures
(c) if the good has close substitutes
(d) if the time period is long.

7. Price elasticity of supply tends to be high:
(a) if the time period is long
(b) if the good has close substitutes in production; that is, if the productive factors can easily be switched to other products
(c) if the good can be easily stored.

8. The incidence of a tax depends on the relative elasticities of demand and supply. Those on the side with the higher elasticity are willing to back away from the market; they can't be stuck with much of the burden. Those on the side with the lower elasticity bear the larger burden. If supply is less elastic than demand, sellers bear most of the tax. If demand is less elastic than supply, buyers bear most of the burden.

9. The revenues from a tax depend on the elasticities of demand and supply. If both elasticities are high, quantity will fall sharply when the tax is imposed, and this will depress revenues. The lower the elasticities of demand and supply, the smaller will be the decline in quantity, and the greater the revenue.

10. Because elasticities of supply are higher in the long run than in the short, most of the adverse effects of rent controls come only with the passage of time. The number of apartments gradually declines if rents are kept artificially low.

11. Just as price elasticity of demand measures the responsiveness of the quantity demanded to a change in price, so the income elasticity of demand measures the responsiveness of the quantity demanded to a change in income.

12. Elasticities can be just as important in international trade as in the domestic economy. If the elasticity of demand for a developing country's export goods is less than 1, the country will not be able to earn more foreign currency (such as U.S. dollars) by offering its goods at lower U.S.-dollar prices in the world market.

## KEY TERMS

**price elasticity of demand**
**inelastic demand**
**unitary elasticity**
**elastic demand**
**midpoint formula**
**total revenue as a $P \times Q$ rectangle**
**perfectly (infinitely) elastic demand**
**price elasticity of supply**
**incidence of an excise tax**
**income elasticity of demand**
**cross elasticity of demand**
**substitutes**
**complements**

## PROBLEMS

6-1. Several years ago, a *New York Times* editorial stated that a 50% increase in the price of gasoline would lower its consumption by an estimated 10%. Does this imply anything about the elasticity of supply? Of demand? If so, what?

6-2. Fill in the blanks. In the figure at right:
Curve with greatest elasticity is ______________
Next greatest elasticity is ______________
Next greatest is ______________
Lowest elasticity is ______________
Unit elasticity is ______________

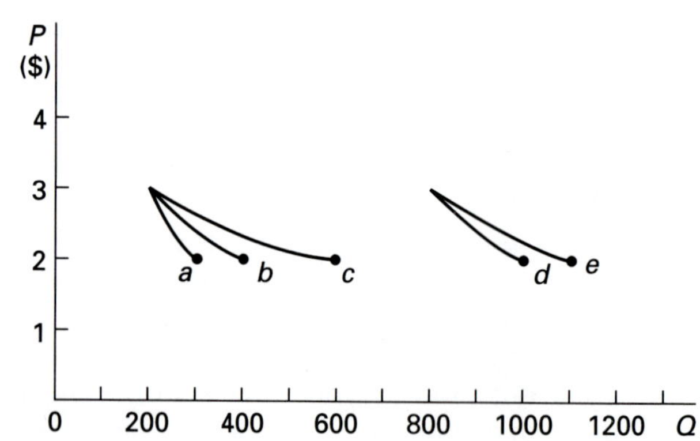

6-3. (a) Why don't we define elasticity much more simply, as just the slope of a curve; that is, elasticity = (the change in *Q*)/(the change in *P*)? (Hint: Plot exactly the same demand curve as in Figure 6-1 but change the scale in which you measure price. Specifically, measure price in quarters, not in dollars, so that the heights of *A* and *B* are now four times as great. What happens to the slope of *D*?)

(b) "Slope is a poor measure because it depends on the arbitrary scale in which *P* (or *Q*) is measured." Is this statement true or false? Explain why.

6-4. Using the midpoint formula, calculate the elasticity of the section *AB* in the demand curve shown below. Do the same for the section *CE*. Consider the following statement: "Since *AB* and *CE* have the same slope but different elasticity, this shows once again that slope does not necessarily reflect elasticity." Is this true or false?

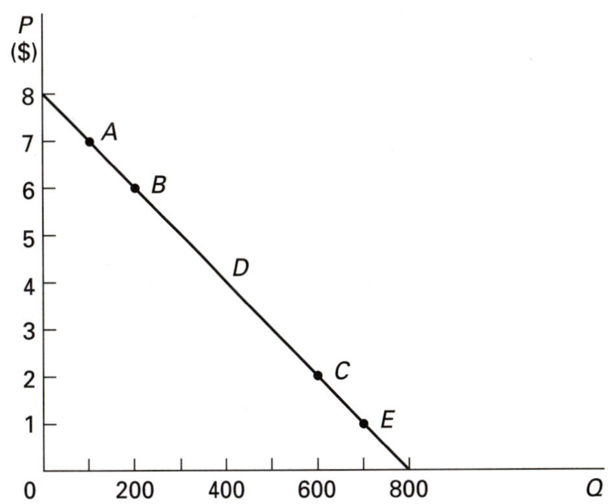


6-5. (a) If the Brazilian government raises the price of foreign currencies (such as U.S. dollars) in terms of Brazilian cruzeiros, it will influence the cruzeiro price of imported goods. Would this change help the Brazilian government raise the U.S. dollars it needs to repay its international loans?

(b) In the text we stated that if the elasticity of foreign demand for Brazilian export goods was less than 1, Brazil could not increase its total dollar earnings from exports by offering its goods at lower U.S.-dollar prices. Can you think of some other way Brazil could increase its total export earnings in this case?

6-6. "Heating oil for homes has a greater elasticity in the long run than in the short." Do you agree? Explain.

6-7. Would you expect the income elasticity of food to be higher or lower than that of restaurant meals? Explain.

# APPENDIX 6-A

## APPLYING ELASTICITY: WHAT ARE THE SPECIAL PROBLEMS OF AGRICULTURE?

The two decades between World War I and World War II were times of distress for Canadian agriculture. Farm prices and land values fell sharply and bankruptcies were common. In response, the government greatly expanded its policies of assistance to farmers. Over the decades that followed, these policies have been modified and extended, and new ones added. Today, Canadian governments are deeply involved in agriculture through a wide range of policies designed to raise farm incomes.

One of the most important of these is the policy of supporting the price that the farmer receives for a number of commodities. Since the 1930s, the federal and provincial governments have intervened in the market to support the prices of many farm products. In the early 1990s, various kinds of government support programs existed in the markets for wheat, barley, oats, eggs, dairy products, cattle, hogs, sheep, and turkeys, and in other markets as well. In the simplest kind of program, the government announces a support price, and stands ready to buy at that price. When market prices are weak, and farmers cannot get a higher price by selling on the private market, they can sell instead to the government at the support price. (For example, in the late 1950s, and again in the mid-1970s, the government had to buy large amounts of eggs and skim milk powder because it was offering relatively high support prices for these products.)[5]

Why does the government offer price guarantees to farmers, but not to other producers? One reason is that agriculture has historically suffered from two special problems. Agricultural prices have been *unstable*, fluctuating up and down from year to year; and they have shown a tendency to *fall*, compared to the price of other goods. To understand each of these problems, we first ask: "What would happen to agricultural prices if there were no government intervention in these markets?" As we shall see, the concept of elasticity is very important in providing an answer.

### Year-to-Year Price Instability

In Figure 6-9, we show the problems that arise because agricultural demand and supply are inelastic in the short run. Demand for farm products is relatively inelastic because people must satisfy their appetite for food no matter what happens to price. Supply is also inelastic in the short run for several reasons. In some cases the product is perishable; in other cases, the crop is already planted and it is too late for farmers to respond much to a change in price.

As an example, suppose Figure 6-9 represents the Ontario market for a perishable product like tomatoes. In a normal year with demand $D$ and supply $S_1$, equilibrium is at $E_1$ with price $P_1$. But with a bumper crop, the resulting supply curve shifts to $S_2$. Because the product is perishable and expensive to transport, the whole crop has to be quickly sold in the Ontario market, no matter what the price. As a result, equilibrium shifts to $E_2$, and the price falls all the way to $P_2$. In this example, a bumper crop cuts price by a third! Worse yet for Ontario's tomato farmers: The inelasticity of demand has meant that their income has been reduced (from the rectangle enclosed below and to the left of $E_1$ to the smaller rectangle below and to the left of $E_2$). Similarly, you can confirm that a poor

[5] In recent years, the government has tried to avoid large direct purchases of farm products; instead, it has used different and more complicated methods for supporting farm prices. We will discuss some of these alternative methods in Chapter 11.

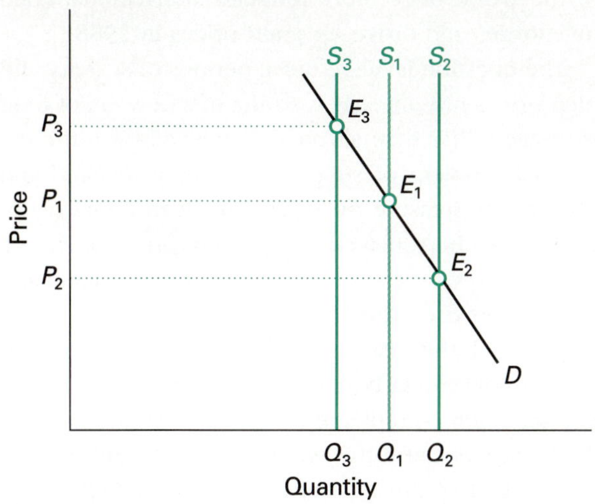


**FIGURE 6-9 Short-run instability of farm price and income.**

In a normal year, inelastic demand $D$ and supply $S_1$ result in equilibrium at $E_1$. However, if there is a bumper crop and $Q_2$ is put on the market, equilibrium is at $E_2$ and price falls from $P_1$ to $P_2$. Because demand is inelastic, farm income is lower at $E_2$ than at the normal equilibrium $E_1$. But if there is a poor crop $Q_3$, equilibrium is at $E_3$ and farm income is higher than normal.

crop that results in equilibrium at $E_3$ will raise farmers' income. In short, because both demand and supply are inelastic, relatively small variations in crop yield result in large price fluctuations. Moreover, the better the crop, the lower farm income may be as a result.

If we consider a product that can be relatively easily transported all over the world (such as wheat or soy beans), we can let Figure 6-9 represent the whole world market for the product.[6] For example, $D$ may represent the (relatively inelastic) world demand for wheat, and $S_1$ the world supply from all producing countries. A large wheat crop in one or more of the world's wheat-growing areas will shift the world supply curve to the right ($S_2$); because world demand is inelastic, the result is a large decline in the world price of wheat. (This is the case that concerned the thoughtful farmer in the introduction to this chapter.) On the other hand, a poor harvest in an important wheat-growing nation (such as Russia, for example) may send the world price of wheat skyrocketing, as happened in 1973 and 1974, and again in 1988.

## Long-run Downward Trend in Price

The second farm problem is best understood by considering our economic history. If we go back far enough, farming was our largest activity, with the majority of the population working on the soil. With old-fashioned techniques of agricultural production, an individual family could do little more than produce enough for itself.

However, with improvements in agricultural methods and technology, productivity increased. A typical farm family could produce more and more food: enough for two families, then three, then four, and so on. As that happened, the number of people required on the farm to produce food fell to a smaller and smaller fraction of the population. This decline has had effects that have reached far beyond agriculture. In fact, one of the essential requirements for North America's industrial development has been the ability of farmers to produce more food than they consume. Without this capability, the labour force necessary for a developing industry would never have been released from the task of grubbing a bare living out of the soil. It was no accident that the industrial revolution in Britain in the eighteenth century was preceded by a revolution in agricultural productivity. And that agricultural revolution has continued at a rapid pace: A typical Canadian or American farm family today supplies food for itself and over 20 non-farm families as well.

However, this huge increase in agricultural productivity has been a mixed blessing for the farmers who have achieved it. Once again, elasticity is the key to understanding why. In panel (a) of Figure 6-10, $E_1$ represents the initial equilibrium in an earlier period, at the intersection of long-run supply $S_1$ and demand $D_1$; demand is relatively inelastic because food is a neces-

[6] If a good can be easily transported, its price will not fluctuate very much in response to variations in the local crop of a province or even a country. For example, a large corn crop in Canada need not lead to low corn prices here: If the price in Canada falls even slightly below the world price, Canadian farmers will start selling their corn in foreign markets instead. By doing so, they will prevent the Canadian price from falling below the world price. However, the world price of goods such as grains may fluctuate substantially in response to variations in the total worldwide crop.

sity. Over many decades, $D$ has been shifting to the right from $D_1$ to $D_2$ because of (1) the increase in the total food-consuming population and (2) the rising income of that population. However, the effects of rising income have been fairly modest. Although consumers purchase more of almost everything as their incomes rise, their expenditures on food rise less rapidly than their expenditures on many other goods. With rising income, people may double their expenditures on clothes and triple their expenditures on vacations, but they increase their food consumption by only a small amount. After all, how much more can anyone eat? That is, *the income elasticity of demand for food is low*; food purchases respond weakly to an increase in income.

On the other hand, over these same decades there has been an even greater shift in supply (from $S_1$ to $S_2$ in panel (a) of Figure 6-10) because of rapid improvements in farm productivity. With supply shifting to the right more rapidly than demand, price has fallen to a new equilibrium at $E_2$. However, as price falls, farmers — and, even more important, their children — leave the farm to pursue more highly paid careers in the city. Because they do, the proportion of the population on the farm falls. This outflow of people from the farm also means that there is a less rapid increase in farm output than would otherwise occur. In other words, agricultural supply $S_2$ shifts less rapidly to the right. In turn, this means a less severe price reduction.

This, in a nutshell, is the history of North American agriculture: Because productivity has outrun demand, the proportion of the population on the farm has fallen. By becoming more and more productive, farmers are doing a great service to the public in terms of providing large quantities of food at a very low price. But their very success has meant that farmers are producing themselves — or their neighbours — out of jobs.

## Will the Future Bring Food Scarcity?

Prices in North American agriculture would be even more depressed were it not for our large exports of food products to other parts of the world. These exports became particularly important in the early 1970s as a result of crop failures in the Soviet Union and elsewhere. And drought conditions in many parts of the world once more reduced international grain inventories and drove up grain prices in 1988.

The question is: Were these periods of scarcity and high prices just an early warning of a new era of food shortage rather than surplus? Specifically, will the traditional problem of supply outrunning demand and downward pressure on price shown in panel (a) of Figure 6-10 be replaced by the new problem shown in panel (b) where supply shifts less than demand and food prices rise rather than fall?

Some of the reasons put forward for expecting food supply to lag behind demand are not very convincing — for example, the claim that we are facing a food crisis because the world is running out of land. In fact, studies indicate quite the contrary: Only about half of the world's arable land is now being used, and much of the unused acreage has good agricultural potential. Moreover, recent advances in technology have allowed us to increase output by expanding our use of other inputs — like fertilizer — rather than land. If this trend continues, our future requirements for additional land may not be as great as is often supposed.

However, there are other reasons that food supply may lag behind demand that are not so easy to dismiss. For example, there is the continuing question of how much damage is being done to the environment by the heavy use of fertilizers and pesticides. Moreover, in some parts of the world (including the southwest United States) there is a problem of the depletion of ground water because so much has been drawn off for irrigation purposes. The deforestation of many areas — particularly in the developing world — has interfered with a steady supply of water and made soil erosion worse. It has also contributed to the greenhouse effect that appears to be causing a gradual warming of the world's climate. Trees help reduce the greenhouse effect by transforming carbon dioxide into oxygen; with fewer trees, there is faster accumulation of carbon dioxide in the Earth's atmosphere. The greenhouse effect, in turn, may lead to an increasing frequency of droughts in many parts of the world, with less food production as a consequence.

To decide whether the future situation will be the one shown in panel (a) or panel (b) of Figure 6-10 requires projecting not only world food supply but also demand. This projection requires an answer to the difficult question: Will the rapid population

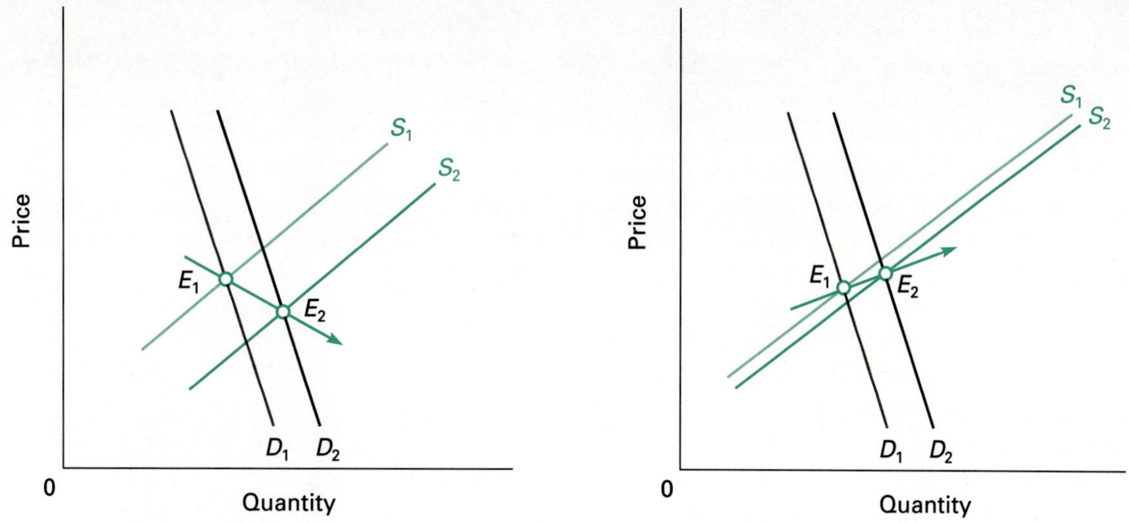


**(a) Will the traditional problem of agriculture continue or ...**

**... (b) will the situation change?**

**FIGURE 6-10 The long-run trend in agriculture.**
The classic problem of agriculture in panel (a) has been that supply has shifted to the right more rapidly than demand. Hence, price has fallen. This situation may repeat itself in the future or it may, as some people predict, change to the situation shown in panel (b). There, shifts in supply do not keep pace with shifts in demand and price rises.

increase in the developing countries continue, or will these countries begin to show the lower birthrate patterns observed in the industrialized parts of the world?

In the late 1980s, it was impossible to predict whether, in the next century, we will face a continued surplus in agriculture or a severe world scarcity. All we can say for sure is that in the 1980s, the major agricultural problem facing governments both in North America and Europe was not food scarcity. Quite the contrary: The problem was what to do about large surpluses.

# CHAPTER 7 DEMAND AND UTILITY

*When you have nothing else to wear*
*but cloth of gold and satins rare,*
*for cloth of gold you cease to care*
*Gilbert and Sullivan,* The Gondoliers

In the *Wealth of Nations*, Adam Smith posed the famous *paradox of value*. He observed that water is one of the most useful commodities in the world; we would die without it. Yet its price is low. In contrast, diamonds are quite unnecessary; people can easily live without them. Yet their price is high. Is the economic world upside down?

This chapter will provide an answer to Adam Smith's puzzle. It will also explain:

- how the overall market demand curve for a product — such as movie tickets or shoes — can be derived from the demands of individual consumers
- how demand depends on the satisfaction or utility that a product provides
- how consumers can make the best choice among the many products offered for sale
- how consumers are concerned not only with the monetary cost of products, but also with the time they spend to buy or use products.

## MARKET DEMAND AS THE SUM OF INDIVIDUAL DEMANDS

Behind the ***market demand*** for a good or service lie the demands of individual consumers. Of course, not all people are alike. Some are rich; others poor. Some love the movies; others find them a bore. But in spite of different tastes, their ***individual demands*** can be added to find the market demand. Figure 7-1 shows how. To keep things simple, two individuals represent the millions of consumers in the economy. Ann Johnson's demand, panel (a), shows how many movie tickets she is willing and able to buy per month at various prices. Note that Bill Kelly's demand, panel (b), is quite different; he won't go at all if the price rises above $10. At any given price, the quantities demanded by each consumer are added horizontally to find the corresponding point on the market demand in panel (c). For example, at a price of $6, Ann demands 7 movie tickets, while Bill demands 6. Thus, the total number of tickets demanded at $6 is the sum: 6 + 7 = 13. Of course, in a community with thousands of people, thousands of individual demand curves would have to be added horizontally to get the market demand curve.

Observe that individual demand curves are labelled with a small *d* in Figure 7-1, to distinguish them from the market demand with a capital *D*.

## DIMINISHING MARGINAL UTILITY

Why do the individual demand curves slope downward? Why would Ann and Bill go to the movies more often at a lower price?

One way of answering this question was already suggested earlier in Chapter 4. When the price of a good falls, it becomes cheaper compared to other items. Consumers therefore *switch* away from the other items, and buy more of the lower-priced item

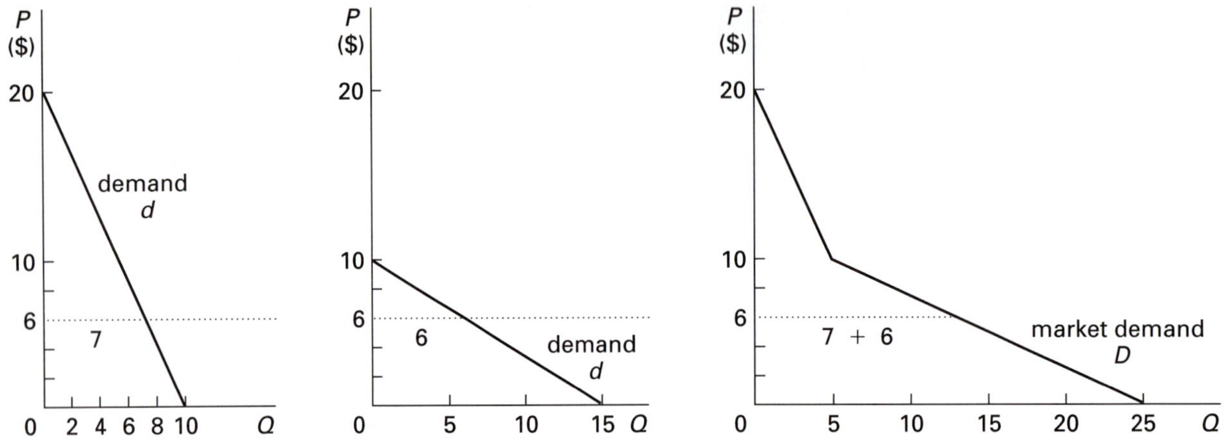


**(a) Ann Johnson's demand.** **(b) Bill Kelly's demand.** **(c) Market demand.**

**FIGURE 7-1 Adding individual demand curves to get market demand.**
To find the quantity at each price, horizontally add the quantities demanded by all individual consumers. For example, at a price of $6, add the 7 units demanded by Ann Johnson to the 6 demanded by Bill Kelly, to get the 13 units demanded in total.

instead. For example, when the price of chicken falls, people eat more chicken and less beef and fish.

But even though this answer makes intuitive sense, it is not really a good basis for a *theory* of demand: It doesn't tell us *why* people buy more of a good that has become cheaper. Thus, economists have been trying to look more deeply at the way people make choices in the marketplace. In doing so, they have considered how a person's well-being—or ***utility***—would depend on the quantities of various goods and services they consume. Over a century ago, English economist William Stanley Jevons suggested looking at an individual's total food consumption as the sum of ten equal parts:

> If his food be reduced by the last part, he will suffer but little; if a second tenth part be deficient, he will feel the want distinctly; the subtraction of the third part will be decidedly injurious; with every subsequent subtraction . . . his sufferings will be more serious until he will be on the verge of starvation.[1]

Not quite so lyrical as the quotation that opened the chapter, with Gilbert and Sullivan's cloth of gold and satins rare! But Jevons hit upon an important idea. The less food people have, the more highly they value it. Or, to restate the same point, the more they have, the less highly they value another unit. The benefit—in terms of satisfaction or utility—provided by each additional unit becomes smaller and smaller. The principle put forward by Jevons is thus referred to as the ***law of diminishing marginal utility***.

The *marginal utility* of a good or service is the increase in satisfaction that an individual receives from consuming one additional unit of that good or service. The *law of diminishing marginal utility* states that the marginal utility of a good or service will decline as more units of that good or service are consumed.

Unfortunately, we must be careful with this "law." There can be exceptions. A second ski lesson, for example, may provide more utility than the first—fewer bruises and more fun. But, as more and more lessons are purchased, marginal utility eventually must fall. The 100th lesson during the season will provide less satisfaction than the 99th.

The term *marginal* is worth emphasizing because it plays such a central role in many areas of economics. Marginal utility is the *extra* or *added* utility from consuming one more unit.

[1] William Stanley Jevons, *Theory of Political Economy* (1871).

Suppose we had some way of actually measuring the satisfaction or utility that people get from consuming a good, such as pizza. (In reality, of course, we cannot directly measure utility. But as we will see shortly, there is a way around that problem.) If we could do this, we could illustrate the idea of diminishing marginal utility in a diagram, such as Figure 7-2 and the accompanying Table 7-1. The dark bars or "stairsteps" in panel (a) show how total utility increases as more is consumed. For example, when consumption increases from 2 to 3 pizzas per week, total utility increases from 18 to 23 units or "utils." ("Util" is a term sometimes used to denote an imaginary "unit of utility.") Thus, the marginal utility of the third pizza is the upward step of 5, from 18 to 23 utils. These marginal utility stairsteps in panel (a) are reproduced as the marginal utility bars in panel (b). The stairsteps become smaller as the number of pizzas increases in panel (a); this means diminishing marginal utility in panel (b).

As long as each additional pizza provides some marginal utility, total utility increases. There are, however, situations where a consumer has too much of a product—so much so that an additional unit provides no benefit and is a nuisance instead. In that case (unit 6 in Figure 7-2), the marginal utility is negative, panel (b), and this causes total utility to start downward, panel (a).

**TABLE 7-1 Total and Marginal Utility**

| (1) Quantity: Pizzas per week | (2) Total Utility (units) | (3) Marginal Utility (increase in total utility) (units) |
|---|---|---|
| 1 | 10 | 10 |
| 2 | 18 | 8 |
| 3 | 23 | 5 |
| 4 | 24 | 1 |
| 5 | 24 | 0 |
| 6 | 23 | −1 |

## MARGINAL BENEFIT AND THE CONSUMER'S EQUILIBRIUM

Since there is no way of directly measuring an individual's satisfaction or utility, we cannot directly observe how marginal utility diminishes as more units

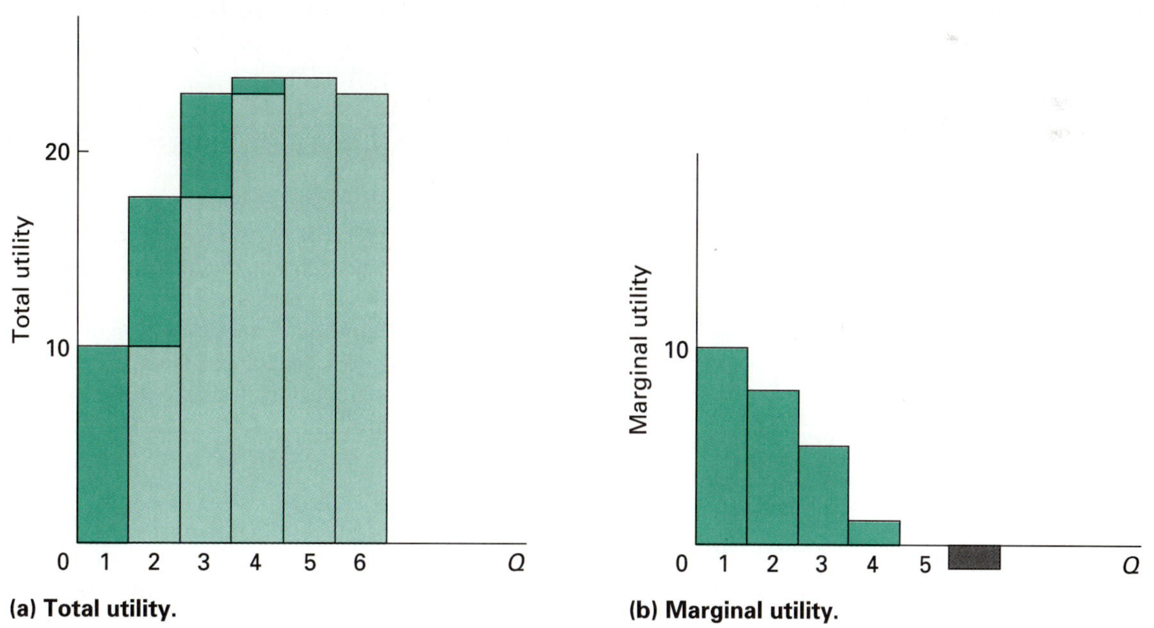


**FIGURE 7-2 Total and marginal utility.**
This figure illustrates the numbers shown in the table. Marginal utility represents the increase in total utility when one more unit is consumed. Thus, the marginal utility blocks in panel (b) are the same as the dark stairsteps in panel (a) that show how total utility increases.

of a good are consumed. But there is something else that we *can* observe (at least in principle): How much people would be *willing to pay* in order to get an extra unit. This concept is sometimes referred to as the ***marginal benefit*** of a good or service.

The *marginal benefit* is the maximum amount of money that a person is willing to pay for having an additional unit of a good or service, per unit of time.

How would you expect the marginal benefit of additional units to change, as more and more units of a good are consumed? The answer: It would decrease, for essentially the same reason that the marginal utility of a good decreases as more units are consumed. As an example, in Figure 7-3, we have shown Ann Johnson's marginal benefit for movies. Her marginal benefit of seeing a fourth movie is less than for the third one. She is willing to pay only $6 to see the fourth movie, reflecting the fact that she gets less utility or enjoyment from it. Thus, we have the principle of ***diminishing marginal benefit***: The marginal benefit of a good or service will become smaller and smaller as more units are consumed.[2]

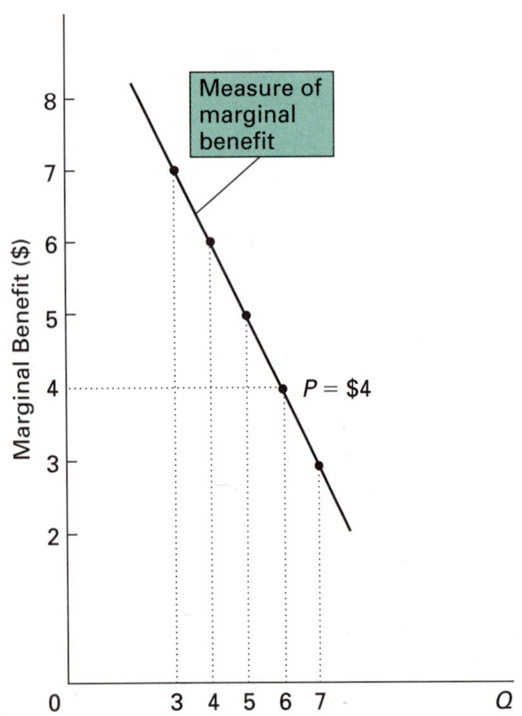


**FIGURE 7-3 Diminishing marginal benefit.**
As the individual consumes more and more units of a good, her marginal benefit—willingness to pay for an additional unit—becomes smaller.

As you may now realize, a marginal benefit schedule such as that in Figure 7-3 is closely related to the individual's demand curve. To see this, consider how the consumer in Figure 7-3 decides how many units to buy if the market price is $4 per unit as shown. Consider first the third unit. It will obivously be bought: The marginal benefit schedule tells us that the consumer would be *willing* to pay as much as $7 to consume this unit. Since she *can* buy it for only $4, she clearly is better off if she *does* buy it. Since the fourth and fifth units are also valued above their price of $4, the consumer will also buy them. The sixth will be the last one purchased because the $4 benefit it provides is just equal to its $4 price.

When the consumer buys four units, she is picking the best point—the point that yields the *maximum utility*—given her total budget and the price of the good. Economists refer to this point as the consumer's *equilibrium*.

**A consumer reaches equilibrium—that is, reaches the point of maximum utility, given her budget—by buying additional units of a good until the marginal benefit it provides falls to the level of its price; that is, until: MB = *P***

It is easy to confirm that the consumer should not go beyond this point to purchase more. For example, it would be a mistake to purchase the seventh unit because the $4 price of that unit exceeds the $3 benefit from it. Similarly, if the market price falls to $2, the consumer buys 8 units. That is, the consumer buys additional units until the marginal benefit has once again fallen to equal the price. Thus, whenever the consumer is in equilibrium—that is, has reached the point of maximum utility—the *market price of the good equals the marginal benefit of the last unit purchased*.

But it is now easy to see why a fall in the price of a good induces the consumer to buy more of it—that is, why demand curves slope downward to the right.

[2] Obviously, the principle of diminishing marginal benefit is closely related to Jevons's idea of diminishing marginal utility: If we measure "utils" in terms of money, they are the same thing. However, for some purposes, money may not be a good yardstick for measuring utility. The reason is that the utility obtained from a dollar may change.

Suppose, for example, that the price of going to a movie in Figure 7-3 falls from $4 to $2, and consider the seventh unit (which the consumer does *not* buy if the market price is $4). According to the marginal benefit schedule, the consumer is *willing* to pay as much as $3 for the seventh unit (and $2 for the eighth unit). Therefore, the consumer is clearly better off buying these units. She will buy more movies until the marginal benefit has fallen to the new (lower) market price.

A marginal benefit curve for a good shows which units a consumer will buy (those for which the marginal benefit — the consumer's willingness to pay — exceeds the market price), or not buy (those for which the marginal benefit is less than the market price). As noted above, therefore, the marginal benefit curve is closely related to the consumer's demand curve for the good. (Recall again what a demand curve shows: The quantity that the consumer will buy at different market prices.) Indeed, in many practical applications, they are treated as if they were the same, and we will do so throughout most of this book. However, the two curves are not *exactly* identical: A demand curve is, strictly speaking, only an approximation to the marginal benefit curve, and *vice versa*. Nevertheless, in most cases the approximation is very close, so that we can use them interchangeably.

## CONSUMER'S SURPLUS

Let us return now to Ann Johnson's demand for movie tickets. At a price of $4, Ann is willing to buy 6 tickets. But she is *barely* willing to buy the sixth ticket; it is barely worth its price of $4.

However, consider one of the earlier units, say the third. The demand curve tells us that she *would* have bought this unit even if the market price had been as high as $7. But if we interpret the demand curve as a marginal benefit curve, this tells us that the marginal benefit of the third unit is as high as $7. Thus on this unit, she reaps a *surplus*: Since she would have been willing to pay as much as $7 for it, but only had to pay the market price of $4, the surplus is $3. Similarly, there are surpluses on all units to the left of the sixth unit—large surpluses on the first few units, and a much smaller surplus of only $1 on the fifth unit. The total surplus— referred to as the ***consumer surplus*** — is equal to the triangular shaded area in Figure 7-4.

*Consumer surplus* for a particular unit consumed is the difference between the maximum amount the consumer *would be willing* to pay for that unit, and the amount *actually* paid in the market. The consumer surplus on all units the consumer buys is the total net benefit (measured in dollars) that a consumer gets from being able to purchase each unit of the good at the market price.

Geometrically, consumer surplus can be approximately measured by the area under the demand curve and above the price, the shaded area in Figure 7-4.

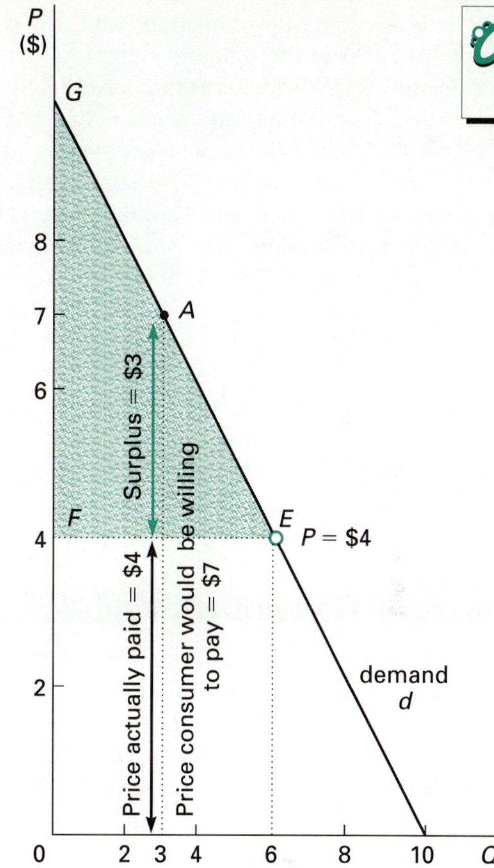


**FIGURE 7-4 The demand curve and consumer surplus.**

The consumer would have been willing to pay as much as $7 for the third unit, at point *A*. But its price is only $4. Therefore, the consumer gains a surplus of $3 on this unit. The total surplus on all units purchased is measured by the triangular shaded area *EFG*.

For the same reason that the demand curve is only an approximation to the marginal benefit curve, the geometric measure of consumer surplus also is not an exact measure of consumer surplus. In most cases, however, it is a close approximation[3], and we will often make use of it in the following chapters.

The consumer surplus idea was first introduced by the famous British economist and teacher Alfred Marshall (1842–1924). It illustrates how people can gain from purchases of movie tickets—or hamburgers, or cars, or a host of other products. Suppliers may gain, too; the production of films may be very profitable, and may provide high incomes to actors and technical workers. Thus, when one group (consumers) gain, this does *not* mean that some other group (producers) must lose. The marketplace is not a "zero sum game," in which one group loses what another gains. Instead, both consumers and producers can gain through specialization and exchange that add to the general prosperity.

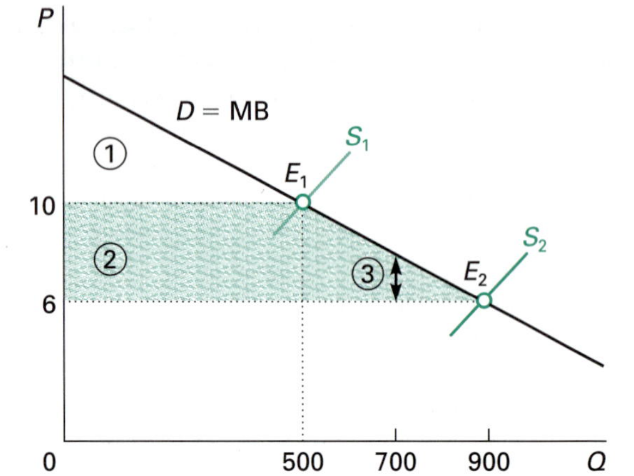


**FIGURE 7-5 An increase in consumer surplus.** When the price falls, consumers are better off. In this diagram, they pay \$4 less for each of the first 500 units, for a total gain of \$2000 (area 2). They also gain additional consumer surplus (area 3) on the additional 400 units bought when the price falls from \$10 (at $E_1$) to \$6 (at $E_2$).

## Changes in Consumer Surplus

When the price of a good falls, consumers are clearly better off. The increase in consumer surplus is a measure of how much. In Figure 7-5, initial equilibrium between supply and market demand is at point $E_1$, with consumers buying 500 units at a price of \$10. Consumers enjoy an initial surplus equal to the triangular area 1. Now suppose the equilibrium moves to $E_2$ as a result of a rightward shift in the supply curve. The price drops from \$10 to \$6, with consumers now buying 900 units. Now their consumer surplus is the larger triangle made up of areas 1 + 2 + 3, for a net gain of areas 2 + 3.

In more detail, the increase in consumer surplus can be looked on the following way. Consumers save \$4 per unit on each of the first 500 units, or a total gain of \$2000 as shown by area 2. But they also reap a surplus on the additional 400 units that they now buy at the lower price. For example, the surplus on the 700th unit is illustrated by the black arrow that measures the difference between the \$8 the consumer would have been willing to pay for that unit and the \$6 price actually paid. The gain from all 400 additional units is, therefore, equal to area 3. Thus, when the price falls from \$10 to \$6, the total gain to consumers is equal to areas 2 + 3. If price *increases*, consumers *lose* this amount.

**If the market price falls, the gain to consumers is shown by the horizontal area (areas 2 + 3 in Figure 7-5) between the old and new price and to the left of the demand curve. This is the increase in consumer surplus. If price increases, consumers lose this amount.**

# THE PARADOX OF VALUE

The distinction between *marginal* benefit and *total* benefit, or utility, helps to solve the puzzle posed by Adam Smith in the *Wealth of Nations*. How can diamonds, which are quite unnecessary, carry so high a price, when the price of water is so low?

[3] To see why it is an approximation, consider, for example, the third unit. According to Figure 7-4, the consumer is willing to pay \$7 for that unit. But \$7 is *the maximum amount she is willing to pay for the third unit if she can buy all three units for no more than \$7 each.* If we make her pay more than \$7 each for the first two units, she probably would *not* be willing to pay as much as \$7 for the third unit: She would then have less money left to spend on other things, and therefore would probably be less keen to buy a third unit of this good. But this reasoning applies to the other units as well, so that the area under the demand curve and above the price in Figure 7-4 is a little bit of an overestimate of the total consumer surplus on all units together.

A very useful discussion, showing how close the approximation is likely to be, may be found in Robert D. Willig, "Consumer surplus without apology," *American Economic Review*, September 1976, pp. 589–97.

To explain this paradox—often referred to as the ***paradox of value*** — we must consider both demand and supply. The price of water is low because it is so plentiful; a huge quantity can be supplied at a very low price. Because it is cheap, people consume a large quantity, using it even in ways in which it provides very little satisfaction, such as washing the car or watering the lawn. Thus, its low price means a low marginal benefit for the last unit bought by consumers, illustrated by the distance *BE* in Figure 7-6(a).

On the other hand, diamonds sell at a high price because they are very scarce and costly to produce; they can be supplied only at a high price. Consequently, they are bought only by the most eager people; the only buyers are people whose marginal benefit is high enough to justify the high price. Thus, the high price of diamonds means that, *at the margin*—where we look at only the last unit consumed—diamonds are more valuable than water.

However, this is only part of the story. The total benefit of water includes not only the benefit of the last glass we use, but of every glass. The ones that keep us from dying of thirst have a very high benefit indeed. In fact, the marginal benefit of one of those first units of water, say *A*, is so high that we don't have enough room at the top of the diagram to show it. In other words, the total benefit from water—the shaded area in panel (a)—is so large that there isn't room to show it in full. Compare this to the relatively small total benefit from diamonds—the shaded area in panel (b). Thus, we conclude that, overall, water is much more valuable than diamonds, even though its price is lower; that is, even though its value at the margin is less. The paradox of value is resolved.

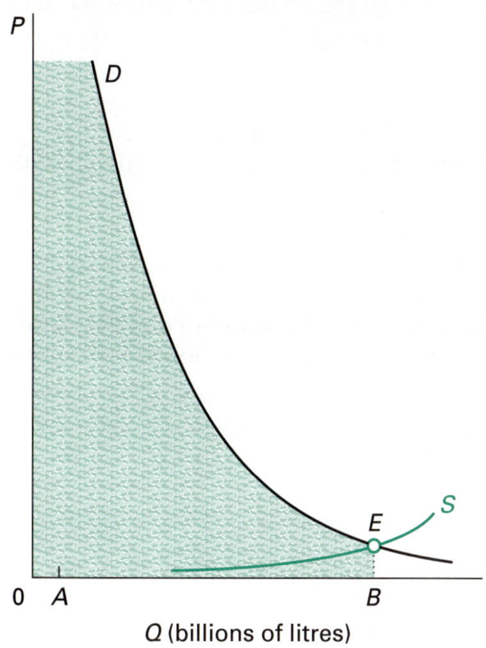


**(a) Water.**

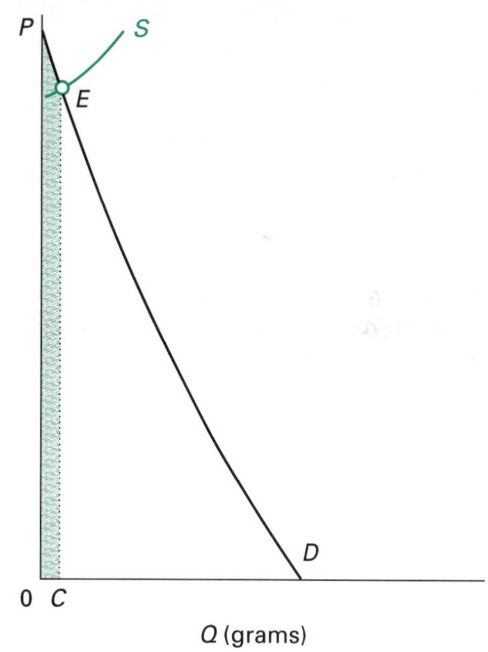


**(b) Diamonds.**

**FIGURE 7-6 The paradox of value.**
Market prices are determined by demand and supply. Because of the plentiful supply of water, its price is low. Even though the first few units provide enormous benefit (at *A*), consumers also use it in less important ways—for example, to wash the car. Its marginal benefit is low, as shown by the distance *BE*, even though the total benefit is very large indeed. For diamonds the story is the opposite—a high marginal benefit, but a much smaller total benefit.

## THE CONSUMER'S EQUILIBRIUM: ANOTHER LOOK

An alternative way to illustrate how consumers choose what quantity of a good to buy, is to use the concept of ***indifference curves***. To illustrate this concept, suppose for simplicity that we are looking at a consumer who values only two goods: food, and another good which for the moment we simply call *x*. In Figure 7-7, we measure units of food consumed per month along the horizontal axis, and units of *x* on the vertical axis. Thus, any point in the diagram represents a combination of food and *x* that the consumer might be enjoying. For example, at point *A* he consumes 5 units of food and 5 units of good *x* per month. At this stage, we consider purely hypothetical combinations of food and *x*, without worrying about how much each good costs, or whether the consumer's income is high enough for him to afford it.

To draw an indifference curve through point *A*, we ask the consumer the following hypothetical question: What is the *smallest* number of additional units of *x* that you would accept in exchange for giving up one unit of food, and still consider yourself as well off as before? Let's say the answer is: "One unit of *x*." Assuming the consumer is telling us the truth, we may conclude that he is *indifferent* between the combinations (5 food, 5 *x*) and (4 food, 6 *x*). That is, if we had an index representing the consumer's utility at different combinations of food and *x*, *the value of the utility index would be the same* at points *A* and *B*.

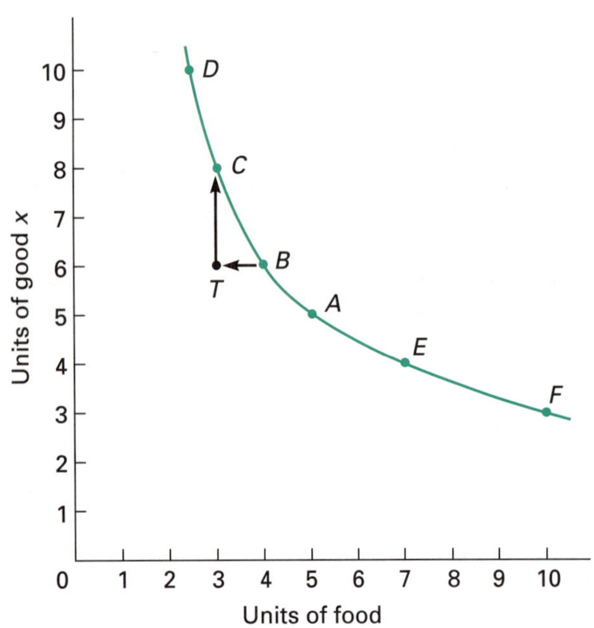


**FIGURE 7-7 An indifference curve.**

An indifference curve joins all points where the individual has the same level of utility or satisfaction. The individual is "indifferent" among the various points on an indifference curve.

On an *indifference curve*, each point represents the same level of satisfaction or utility. An individual is indifferent among the various points on the indifference curve.

Now let's continue the experiment, asking the individual under what conditions he would be willing to give up one more unit of food. Based on the answer, we plot point *C*. Proceeding the same way, we find point *D*, and so on. To derive *E* and *F*, we start at *A* and move in the opposite direction, asking the consumer how many additional units of food he would have to receive in order to compensate for the loss of one unit of *x*.

Note that, as we have drawn the indifference curve, when the individual moves upward and to the left, he asks for larger and larger amounts of *x* to compensate for a further loss of one unit of food. The reason is that as the individual moves up along the indifference curve, the consumption basket includes less and less food and more and more *x*. When we reach points where the consumption basket only includes a small amount of food, he will only be willing to go even hungrier—to give up yet another unit of scarce food — if he is compensated by a large amount of *x* (of which he already has a lot). Because the individual is increasingly reluctant to give up food as he has less and less, the indifference curve generally has the "bowed" shape shown.

(Although indifference curves usually are bowed, this need not always be the case. For example, a two-car family might be indifferent among the choices of (*A*) two Chevrolets, no Ford; (*B*) one Chevrolet, one Ford; or (*C*) no Chevrolets, two Fords. Then, with Chevrolets on one axis and Fords on the other, the indifference curve joining points *A*, *B*, and *C* is a straight line. The reason is that this particular family considers the two cars to be *perfect substitutes* for each other.)

## THE MARGINAL RATE OF SUBSTITUTION: THE SLOPE OF THE INDIFFERENCE CURVE

In moving from $B$ to $C$ in Figure 7-7, notice that the slope of the indifference curve is approximately 2. (Technically, it is $-2$, but we ignore the negative sign.) The slope has an important economic meaning. It is the amount of $x$ ($TC = 2$) that is required to compensate for the loss of one unit of food ($BT = 1$)—that is, it is the ***marginal rate of substitution of x for food***.

> The *marginal rate of substitution* (MRS) of $x$ for food is the amount of $x$ required to compensate for the loss of one unit of food, while leaving the consumer equally well off.
>
> Geometrically, it is the slope of the indifference curve (with the negative sign ignored).

When an indifference curve has the shape shown in Figure 7-7—that is, when its slope decreases as we move down along the curve—this is referred to as the principle of ***diminishing marginal rate of substitution***. As we will see shortly, this principle is closely related to the idea of diminishing marginal utility discussed previously.

## MARGINAL UTILITY AND THE MARGINAL RATE OF SUBSTITUTION

If we let $x$ in the preceding discussion stand for some specific good—say, clothing—an indifference curve such as the one shown in Figure 7-7 shows various combinations of food and clothing that leave the consumer equally well off. Thus the marginal rate of substitution of clothing for food as we go from point $B$ to point $C$, say, shows how many units of clothing it takes to compensate the consumer for the loss of one unit of food.

Earlier in this chapter, we introduced the concept of the consumer's marginal utility of a good. It turns out that it is possible to relate the concept of the marginal rate of substitution between two goods—such as clothing and food—to their marginal utilities.

Recall from the earlier discussion that the marginal utility of a good was the increase in the consumer's utility as we add one more unit of that good to his hypothetical consumption basket. Equivalently, it can be thought of as the *loss* in utility as we *take away* one unit of that good from the consumption basket. Thus starting at point $B$ in Figure 7-7, $MU_{food}$ measures the loss in the consumer's utility when we reduce the amount of food by one unit. Similarly, the marginal utility of clothing can be used to measure the increase or decrease in the consumer's utility as we add or subtract a unit of clothing from his consumption basket. For example, the increase in utility as we add one unit of clothing is $MU_{clothing}$.

Now consider again a move from $B$ to $C$ in Figure 7-7. Reducing the number of units of food from 4 units to 3 units reduces the consumer's utility by $MU_{food}$. On the other hand, as we give him additional units of clothing, his utility is increased: Each additional unit of clothing increases his utility by $MU_{clothing}$. But by the definition of the marginal rate of substitution, if we give him MRS units, the increase in his utility is exactly the same as the decrease in utility he suffered when we took one unit of food away. That is:

$$\mathbf{MU_{food} = MRS \times MU_{clothing}}$$

Dividing both sides by $MU_{clothing}$, we get:

$$\mathbf{MRS = \frac{MU_{food}}{MU_{clothing}}}$$

In other words, the slope of the indifference curve—the marginal rate of substitution—is closely related to the concept of marginal utility that we discussed earlier. Specifically, the marginal rate of substitution is just the ratio of the marginal utility of food to the marginal utility of clothing in this case.

### Diminishing Marginal Rate of Substitution and Diminishing Marginal Utility

As we move down and to the right along the indifference curve in Figure 7-7, we are considering consumption baskets with more and more food, but less and less clothing. According to the principle of diminishing marginal utility, this will cause the marginal utility of food to fall and the marginal utility of clothing to rise. That is, the ratio ($MU_{food}/MU_{clothing}$), which as we have just seen is the same as the marginal rate of substitution of clothing for food, will fall. Thus we see that the principle of diminishing marginal rate of substitution is, in fact, just the principle of diminishing marginal utility in disguise.

## WILLINGNESS TO PAY AND THE MARGINAL RATE OF SUBSTITUTION

In the preceding example, an indifference curve such as the one in Figure 7-7 was used to illustrate the consumer's preferences by looking at different combinations of two specific goods such as food and clothing. However, if we want to relate the indifference curve concept to an individual's demand curve for a single good, we must consider how the individual chooses between this good and all other goods.

At first glance, this would appear to be something much more difficult to illustrate in a diagram: After all, in a two-dimensional diagram, we can only show two goods. Fortunately, however, there is a way out. Specifically, we can let "the other good" (good $x$, measured along the vertical axis) represent *money that the consumer can spend on all other goods*. If we assume that the prices of all these other goods remain constant, we can then construct indifference curves between a good such as food, on the one hand, and $x$, money left to spend on other goods, on the other hand. Although we won't know precisely how the consumer will reduce her purchases of other goods if the amount of $x$ is reduced by some specific amount, it should still be possible to find the least amount of additional food she must be given in order to be as well off as before. In other words, we can find combinations of food and $x$ among which the consumer is indifferent — that is, we can construct indifference curves involving food and $x$.

Thus, points such as $A$ and $B$ on a given indifference curve like the one labelled $u_2$ in Figure 7-8 represent equal-utility combinations of food on the one hand, and money to spend on other goods on the other: The consumer is indifferent between the consumption baskets $A$ and $B$ because they correspond to the same level of utility.

As before, the slope of the indifference curve represents the marginal rate of substitution of $x$ for food. For example, at point $A$ the slope of the indifference curve labelled $u_2$ in Figure 7-8 is approximately 20: The marginal rate of substitution of money for food is \$20. Equivalently, *the consumer's willingness to pay* for the last unit of food is \$20: Since the consumer would have to be given \$20 in order to give up that unit of food, her (maximum) willingness to pay to get it in the first place must be \$20. As we move down and to the right along the indifference curve, its slope diminishes. That is, the marginal rate of substitution of money for food falls. But this is the same as saying that the consumer's willingness to pay — or equivalently, her *marginal benefit* — for additional units of food becomes smaller and smaller as additional units are consumed. Thus, when we let $x$ along the vertical axis represent "money to spend on other things," the principle of diminishing marginal rate of substitution turns out to be the same as the principle of diminishing marginal benefit that we discussed earlier.

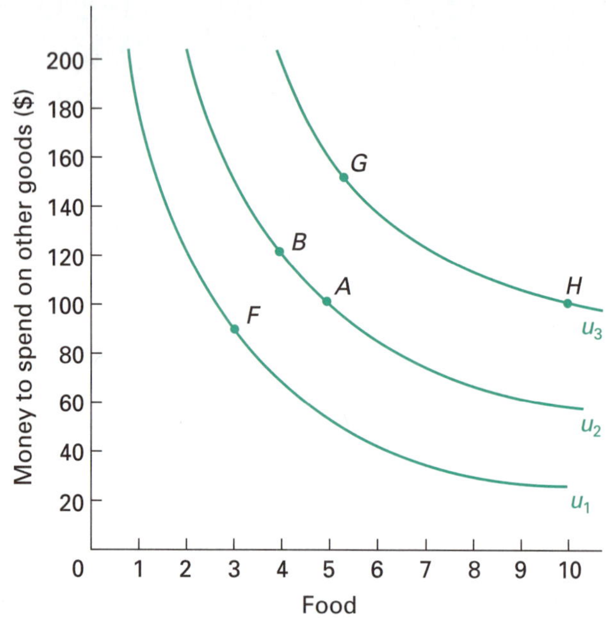


**FIGURE 7-8 An indifference map.**
An individual has a whole set of indifference curves, each curve representing a different level of utility. Thus $u_2$ represents a higher level of utility than $u_1$, and $u_3$ a still higher level.

Starting with a given point such as $A$ in Figure 7-8, we again construct the indifference curve that goes through $A$ by finding other combinations of food and $x$ that yield the same level of utility as $A$. However, instead of starting at point $A$, the consumer might have started at another point, such as $F$ or $G$; there is an indifference curve that passes through each of these points as well. In other words, by starting at different points, we can construct a whole collection of indifference curves. Together, they form an ***indifference map*** such as in Figure 7-8.

While all points on a single indifference curve represent the same level of utility or satisfaction, points on another indifference curve represent a different level of satisfaction. Observe that at point $G$, the consumer has more food *and* more $x$ than at $B$. Thus, the individual prefers $G$ to $B$. Because other points on $u_3$—such as $H$—are equivalent to $G$, they must also be preferred to $F$ and to every other point on $u_2$ (such as point $A$). Therefore, indifference curve $u_3$ represents a higher level of satisfaction or utility than does $u_2$. The farther away the indifference curve is from the origin (up and to the right), the greater the level of satisfaction.

Incidentally, an indifference map such as Figure 7-8 illustrates how three variables can be shown in a diagram with only two dimensions. The three variables are the quantity of food, the amount of money to spend on other things, *and the individual's utility*. We can visualize this system of indifference curves as mapping out a utility hill, with each curve representing a contour line showing points with equal utility, just as a geographer's contour line shows points of equal height above sea level. Moving from the origin up and to the right, the consumer goes up the utility hill to higher and higher levels of satisfaction.[4]

An important property of indifference curves is that they cannot cross. That is, if one point on indifference curve A, say, lies below and to the left of a point on another indifference curve B, then there can be *no* point on A that is both above and to the right of any point on B (see Box 7-1).

[4] One advantage of the indifference-curve approach, as compared to the marginal utility approach, is that we don't have to measure how high up any given point on the map is. All we need to know is how various combinations are ranked. That is, we need to know that $G$ is above $F$; we don't need to know how much above. Thus, the indifference curve does not require the idea of measurable marginal utility.

## TOOLS AND TECHNIQUES — BOX 7-1

### Why Indifference Curves Cannot Cross

To show why indifference curves cannot cross, we require one basic assumption: that the consumer's utility is higher if she has more of both goods. To show why two indifference curves can't cross, we use this assumption and the definition of an indifference curve and show that if they *did* cross, contrary to the hypothesis, we run into a contradiction. Specifically we will show that if two curves cross (such as those labelled A and B in the figure), they can't be true indifference curves.

Comparing points 1 and 2, the consumer's utility must be higher at point 2 since it involves more consumption of both goods. Therefore, using the definition of an indifference curve, the consumer's utility at *any* point on curve A must be higher than the utility at *any* point on curve B. In particular, therefore, it would mean that utility would be higher at point 4 (which is on curve A) than at point 3 (on curve B). But that can't be true, because at point 3, the consumer has more of both goods. Since a similar argument can be used for any two curves that cross, we have established that if two curves *do* cross, they can't both be indifference curves.

(As an exercise, try to use a similar argument to explain why a geographer's contour lines can't cross, either.)

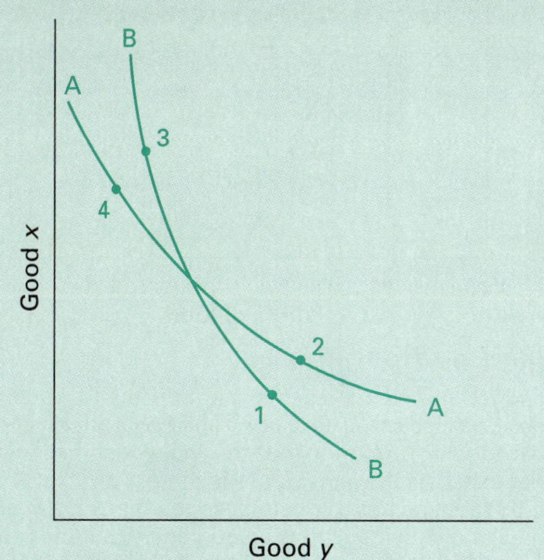


**Why indifference curves can't cross.**

## THE BUDGET LIMITATION

As we have seen, the indifference map reflects the individual's *desires* or *preferences*; the individual prefers $G$ to $F$ in Figure 7-8 and is indifferent between $H$ and $G$. However, the individual's behaviour depends not only on *wants*, but also on *ability* to buy.

What the individual is able to buy depends on two things: money income and the price of food. If the individual's income is \$100, while the price of food is \$20 per unit, the various options open to the individual are illustrated by the ***budget line*** *KL* in Figure 7-9.

> The *budget line*—sometimes called an *income line* or *price line*—shows the various combinations of goods that can be purchased by an individual with a given money income and facing a given set of prices.

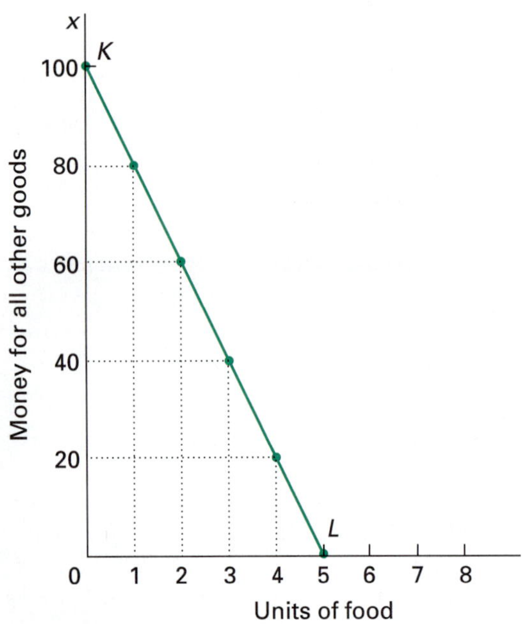


**FIGURE 7-9 The budget line.**

The budget line *KL* represents the individual's limited income. Each point on this line represents a combination of food and good *x* that the individual can buy, and that exhausts the individual's income.

The budget line has a constant slope. At any point on the line, if the individual buys an additional unit of food, the cost of \$20; that is, the individual will have 20 fewer units of good *x* (dollars to spend on other goods and services).

Now consider first point $K$ in Figure 7-9. At point $K$, the individual spends nothing on food, so that the entire \$100 can be used to buy other things. At the other extreme, if the individual were to spend the whole income of \$100 on food at \$20 per unit, 5 units could be bought, as shown by point $L$.

As long as the market price of food is constant, the budget line will necessarily be a *straight* line between $K$ and $L$—that is, it will have a constant slope. To see this, note that if you start at point $K$, the first unit of food will cost you \$20. That is, if you move to the right from 0 units to 1 unit of food, you have to move 20 units down along the vertical axis. But this is also true for the second, third, . . . units of food: Moving one unit to the right, you will always have to move 20 units down. Thus, the slope of the budget line is constant. Specifically, its slope can most easily be found as:

**The slope of the budget line between $K$ and $L$ is:**

$$\frac{\textbf{vertical distance } 0K}{\textbf{horizontal distance } 0L} = \frac{100}{5} = 20$$

Since the vertical distance $0K$ reflects the consumer's total income, and the horizontal distance is the number of units of food that can be bought if all of this income is spent on food, the slope of the budget line must reflect the price per unit of food.

## THE CONSUMER'S EQUILIBRIUM

Faced with the budget limit $KL$, which combination of $x$ and food will the individual choose? As before, we look for the answer by appealing to the idea of utility maximization. That is, we ask: Which one, among all possible combinations of $x$ and food along the budget line $KL$ that the individual can buy, will give her the highest possible utility?

To see the answer, recall that every point on a *given* indifference curve corresponds to the same level of utility, and furthermore, that indifference curves further up and to the right in the diagram correspond to higher and higher levels of utility.

The consumer's best choice, therefore, is to find that point along the budget line that enables her to reach the highest possible indifference curve. In Figure 7-10, that point is $E$, where the indifference curve $u_3$ just touches the budget line. Note that every other point on the budget line lies to the left and below $u_3$. Point *E*, therefore, gives the consumer the highest possible utility, given that she can't exceed her budget. Any other affordable purchase, like *M*, is less attractive because it leaves the individual on a lower indifference curve—$u_2$ rather than $u_3$.

A consumer maximizes satisfaction or utility by moving along the budget line to the highest attainable indifference curve. This is achieved at a *point of tangency* such as *E* in Figure 7-10.

A point of tangency, of course, is a point where the slope of the indifference curve is equal to the slope of the budget line. But as we saw earlier, the slope of an indifference curve such as $u_3$ at point *E* equals the consumer's marginal rate of substitution of money for food. That is, it reflects the ratio of the marginal utility of food to the marginal utility of a dollar spent on any other good. Since the slopes of the indifference curve and the budget line are the same at *E*, this ratio must equal $P_{food}$, the slope of the budget line. Thus at point *E*:

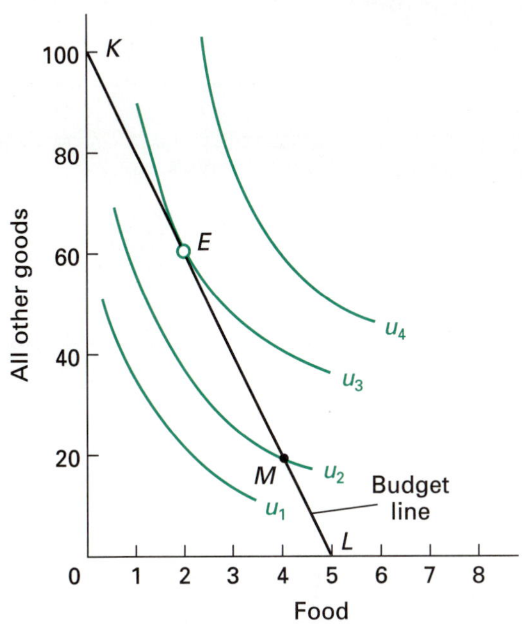


**FIGURE 7-10 The consumer's equilibrium.**
To achieve equilibrium with the highest level of satisfaction, the individual moves along the budget line to the point *E* of tangency with the highest achievable indifference curve.

$$\frac{\mathbf{MU_{food}}}{\mathbf{MU\ of\ a\ \$\ spent\ on\ other\ goods}} = P_{food}$$

If we rearrange terms, we can also write this as:

$$\frac{\mathbf{MU_{food}}}{P_{food}} = \mathbf{MU\ of\ a\ \$\ spent\ on\ other\ goods}$$

As we saw before, the marginal rate of substitution of money for food at point *E* can also be interpreted as the marginal benefit (the consumer's willingness to pay) for the last unit of food. Figure 7-10, therefore, confirms our earlier rule: In equilibrium, the consumer increases the consumption of a good (such as food in this example) until the marginal benefit of the last unit equals the market price.

In Box 7-2, we give an example that shows that in equilibrium, the ratio of the marginal utility of the last unit of a good to its price must be the same for *every* good the consumer buys.

In conclusion, we re-emphasize that the budget line and the indifference map are independent of one another. The indifference map shows the individual's preferences; in defining the indifference map, no attention is paid to what the individual can actually afford. What the individual can afford is shown by the budget line. When the indifference map and the budget line are brought together, the choice of the consumer is determined.

## The Consumer's Equilibrium When Income Changes

Suppose now the consumer in Figure 7-10 has an increase in income; specifically suppose her income rises by 20%.

Clearly, this means that the budget line will shift up and out: With a higher income, she can now buy combinations of *x* and food that she could not afford before. In fact, we can be more specific. As long as the price of food stays constant, it is clear that the new budget line will be parallel to the old one: Since the price of food hasn't changed, the budget line must have the same slope as before. With a 20% increase in income (to 120), the new budget line will therefore be a straight line between the points *K′* (at 120 along the vertical axis) and *L′* (at 6 units of food along the horizontal axis) in Figure 7-11.

As before, the consumer will maximize utility by finding that point along the budget line that enables her to reach the highest possible indifference curve,

## TOOLS AND TECHNIQUES — BOX 7-2

## How the Consumer Chooses Among Many Goods

Consider the example in the table below, where the consumer has an income of \$10 and is choosing between hamburgers priced at \$2 and paperback mystery novels priced at \$4. At these prices, what purchases does the consumer rank most highly? The highest-ranking choice is the item that gives the most for the money—that is, the highest marginal utility (MU) or satisfaction per dollar. This is the first hamburger, which provides 12 "utils" for a price of \$2, or 6 utils per dollar. The second hamburger gives the second highest utility per dollar, namely 5 utils per dollar. (This is the number of utils, 10, divided by the price of \$2.) Hamburger #3 and mystery #1 are tied for third place; they each provide 4 utils per dollar. Next comes hamburger #4, tied with mystery #2.

These rankings are summarized in part B of the table. The consumer goes as far down this list as income allows. This is to line 3, where the total expenditure of \$10 exhausts the income of \$10. The best choice the consumer can make is this: Buy 3 hamburgers and 1 mystery.

Note that, when the consumer is making the best, utility-maximizing choice, the MU/*P* ratio is the same for the last unit of both goods (4 utils per dollar). In general, where the consumer is faced with many goods, the consumer makes the best choice by following the optimal purchase rule:

$$\frac{MU_1}{P_1} = \frac{MU_2}{P_2} = \frac{MU_3}{P_3} = \text{MU of last \$1 spent on any other good} \qquad (7\text{-}2)$$

**($MU_1$ is the marginal utility of the first good, $P_1$ is the price of the first good, and so on.)**

In other words, maximum attainable satisfaction requires that the marginal utility of the last dollar spent on good #1 be the same as the marginal utility of the last dollar spent on every other good.

**Maximizing Utility (consumer with income of \$10)**

A. Calculating Marginal Utility per Dollar

| | **Hamburgers (price *P* = \$2)** | | **Mystery Novels (price = \$4)** | |
|---|---|---|---|---|
| **Unit #** | **Marginal Utility (MU) (utils)** | **Marginal Utility per dollar (MU/*P*)** | **Marginal Utility (utils)** | **Marginal Utility per dollar (MU/*P*)** |
| 1 | 12 | 6 | 16 | 4 ← |
| 2 | 10 | 5 | 12 | 3 |
| 3 | 8 | 4 ← | 8 | 2 |
| 4 | 6 | 3 | 4 | 1 |

B. Rank of Purchases

| **Rank of Hamburgers (H) and Mystery Novels (M)** | **Cumulative Expenditure** |
|---|---|
| 1. Hamburger #1, at 6 utils per dollar | 1H @ \$2 = \$2 |
| 2. H #2, at 5 utils per dollar | 2H @ \$2 = \$4 |
| 3. H #3 and Mystery #1, tied at 4 utils per dollar | 3H @ \$2 + 1M @ \$4 = \$10 |
| 4. H #4 and M #2, tied at 3 utils per dollar | 4H @ \$2 + 2M @ \$4 = \$16 |

The consumer buys 3 hamburgers and 1 mystery novel, using the total income of \$10 and equating the MU/*P* ratio of hamburgers and novels.

**BOX 7-2 continued**

To see why, suppose that the consumer makes a mistake, and stops somewhere else in the table. Suppose that the individual erroneously decides to buy 1 hamburger and 2 mysteries with the income of \$10. Observe that the optimal purchase rule (Equation (7-2)) is violated. The MU/*P* ratio for the second mystery is only 3; the second mystery provides only 3 utils per dollar. But the hamburger provides 6 utils per dollar. Because hamburgers provide more utility per dollar, the consumer can make a better choice by switching away from mysteries, and buying more hamburgers instead. Specifically, the best decision is to buy one fewer mystery, and use the \$4 to buy two more hamburgers instead. Observe that, when this is done, the consumer gains 18 utils from the additional hamburgers (that is, 10 utils for the second plus 8 utils for the third), while giving up only 12 utils when the second book is forgone.

Thus, when expenditures are rearranged to satisfy Equation (7-2), there is a net gain of 6 units of utility (18 for the two additional hamburgers minus 12 for the book forgone). Once Equation (7-2) is met — with 3 hamburgers and 1 book—the consumer is picking the best package of goods; no improvement can be made by a further rearrangement of purchases. (Try it. Within the budget constraint of \$10, the consumer cannot pick any combination that yields more utility than the 3 hamburgers and 1 book.)

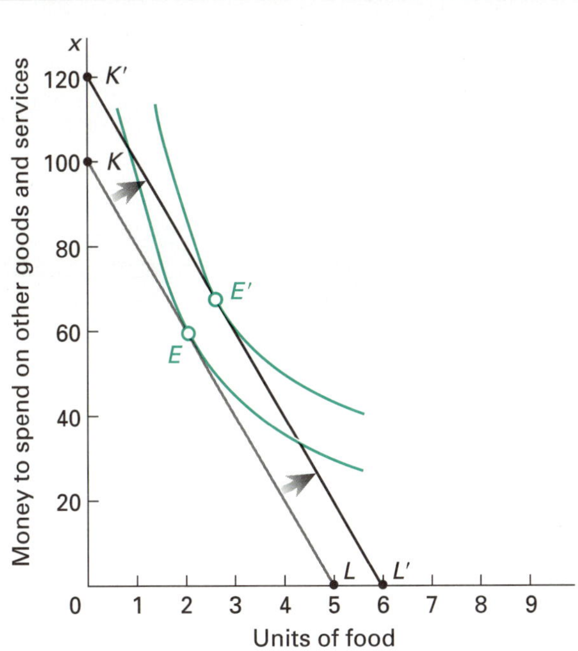


**FIGURE 7-11 The consumer's response to an increase in income.**

If prices stay unchanged and the consumer's income increases by 20%, the budget line will shift. The new budget line will intersect both axes 20% further away from the origin than the old one (that is, at 120 units of *x* (*K*′) and 6 units of food (*L*′). Its slope is the same as before: At any point, the consumer has to give up \$20 to acquire another unit of food.

at point *E*′ in Figure 7-11. Note that at *E*′, the consumer has increased both her purchases of food *and* of other goods. Thus, both are normal goods. (Recall the definition of a normal good from Chapter 4.) If food, for example, was an inferior good, the new equilibrium would lie further up along *K*′*L*′, at a quantity of food less than at *E* on the original budget line.

## An Application: Cash Assistance vs. Aid in Kind

In Figure 7-12, we use the indifference-curve approach to illustrate what may happen when the government comes to the assistance of poor people by providing them with specific goods or services.

Suppose initially that the budget line for a family with low income (\$16,000 per year) is given by *AB*, and that the family chooses point *E*; at this point, the family spends \$4000 on housing, consuming only 2 units. Suppose now the government decides to help this family by providing it with 4 units of housing free of charge. More precisely, the government provides the family with a *voucher* worth \$8000, which can only be used toward paying rent on an apartment. (If the family chooses an apartment that costs more than \$8000 per year, it has to make up the difference out of its own resources; if the rent is less than \$8000, the government keeps the difference.)

At first glance, it might look as if the family had simply received an increase in income of \$8000. In

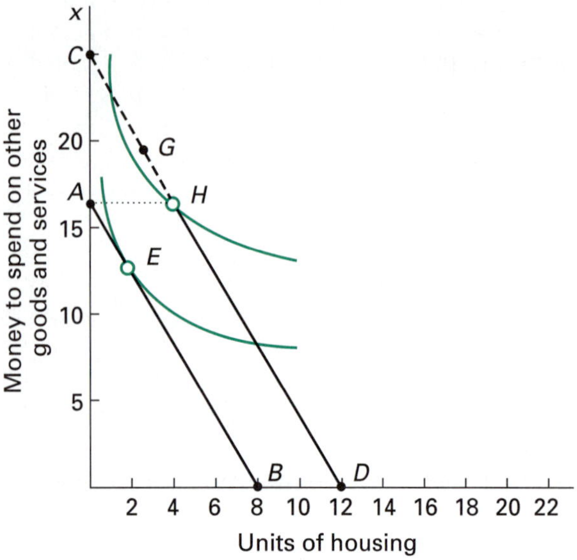


**FIGURE 7-12 Government provision of housing.**
The horizontal axis measures the number of units of housing services the family consumes. When the family's budget line is *AB*, its equilibrium is at *E* where 2 units are consumed, at a cost of \$4000 per year (each "unit of housing" costs \$2000 per year).

If the government provides a subsidy of up to \$8000 per year (4 units of housing) *that can only be used to purchase housing*, the family's equilibrium is at point *H*. At this point, the cost of the family's housing is exactly equal to the government subsidy. The family cannot reach a point such as *G*, because the government subsidy can only be used to pay for housing, not for other goods and services.

other words, it looks like its budget line has shifted to *CD* in Figure 7-12. But has it?

The answer: Not quite. To see this, note that the family will only get the full grant of \$8000 if it pays at least \$8000 in rent—that is, buys at least 4 units of housing. If it buys less housing, the income available to buy other goods and services is still only \$16,000.

In Figure 7-12, this means that effectively, the family's budget line is *HD*, not *CD*. The segment *CH* is not attainable: No matter how little housing the family buys, the maximum amount of money it will have available to spend on other things is no more than \$16,000.

As Figure 7-12 shows, the point on *HD* that gives the family the highest level of utility is *H*, where the family consumes housing services that cost exactly the amount that the government provides as a rent subsidy: The family spends none of its own money on housing. Note also another interesting thing. If the family had received an *untied cash grant*—that is, a

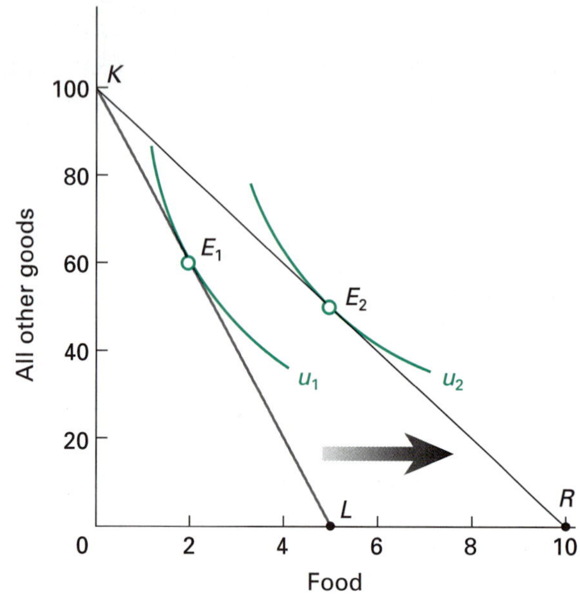


**(a) Using indifference curves.**

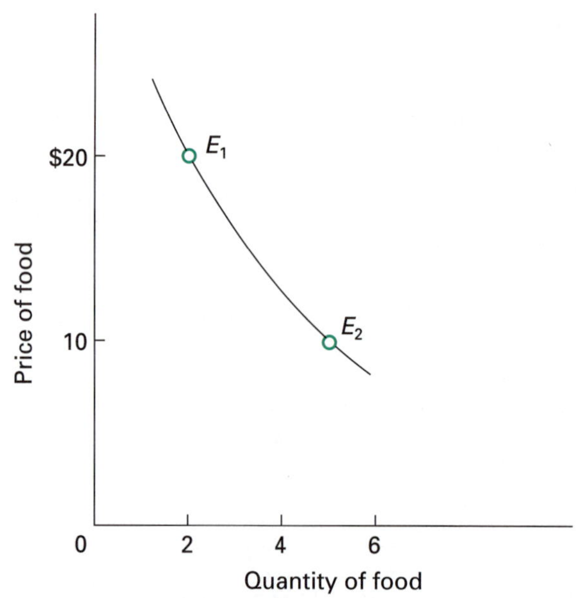


**(b) The corresponding demand curve for food.**

**FIGURE 7-13 The effect of a fall in the price of food.**
As the price of food falls from \$20 to \$10, the budget line rotates counterclockwise from *KL* to *KR*. As a result, the quantity purchased increases from 2 to 5 units. In panel (b), exactly this same information about price and quantity is shown; again the consumer moves from point $E_1$ to $E_2$. In panel (b) these points define the consumer's demand curve.

grant that could be used to buy not just housing services, but other things as well — it would have been able to reach a higher level of utility (for example, *G* in Figure 7-12), even though it wouldn't cost the government any more.

## DERIVING A DEMAND CURVE FROM AN INDIFFERENCE MAP

The most important application of the indifference curve-budget line analysis is to show how an individual consumer reacts to a change in the price of a commodity (food, in this example). In other words, it can be used to better understand individual demand curves.[5]

When food was originally priced at \$20 per unit, we have seen that the budget line was *KL* and the equilibrium was $E_1$ (Figure 7-13(a)). Now suppose that the price of food falls to \$10. Because the price has changed, the slope of the budget line changes. Specifically, the budget line rotates from *KL* to *KR*. If all \$100 is spent on food, the consumer can now buy 10 units at point *R*. That is, the slope of the budget line is only half of what it was before: The amount of money that has to be given up per unit of food is only half of what it was before.

Faced with the new budget line *KR*, the consumer again searches for his or her highest achievable indifference curve, finding it at the point of tangency $E_2$.

These two points of equilibrium, $E_1$ and $E_2$, can be used to derive two points on the demand curve of the individual. Observe how the two points on the demand curve in panel (b) of Figure 7-13 correspond to the two points on the indifference curves in panel (a). At $E_1$, 2 units are bought at a price of \$20 per unit; at $E_2$, 5 units are bought at \$10. Thus, the individual's demand curve can be derived from his or her indifference map plus the budget line, which rotates as the price of the good changes.

[5] Originally, the use of indifference curves in deriving individual demand curves was based on a desire to avoid having to rely on the concept of marginal utility. Since we have no way of independently measuring marginal utility, it was argued that there was no way of independently verifying whether or not the law of diminishing marginal utility was in fact true. In contrast, the principle of diminishing marginal rate of substitution could, at least in principle, be independently verified: By simply asking people (and assuming they gave truthful answers), we could find combinations of goods and services among which they were indifferent.

More importantly, the technique of indifference curve analysis has proved useful in other areas of microeconomics. As we will see later, similar techniques can be used in studying production (Chapter 9), and in demonstrating the efficiency of perfect competition (Chapter 11).

## The Results of a Price Change: Substitution and Income Effects

When the price of food falls, *ceteris paribus*, the household buys more of it, for two reasons. First, food becomes cheaper compared to other goods. Consequently, the consumer *switches* from other goods to food. This is called the ***substitution effect***. Second, when the price of food falls, the purchasing power of the consumer's money income increases. This allows the consumer to buy more of everything — including food. This increase in food purchases is called the ***income effect***.

This distinction is illustrated in Figure 7-14, which shows how the increase in food purchases from $Q_1$

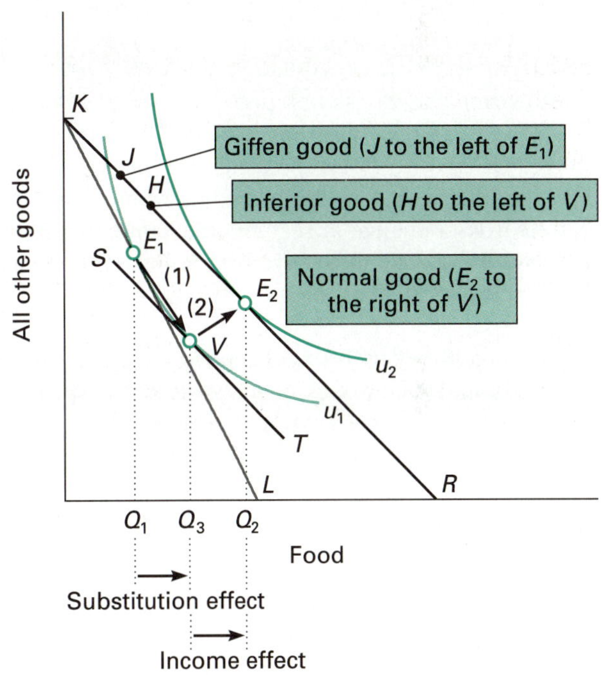


**FIGURE 7-14 The substitution and income effects of a price reduction.**

With the fall in the price of food, there is a move from equilibrium $E_1$ to $E_2$, which can be decomposed into two parts:

The move from $E_1$ to *V* illustrates the substitution effect by holding real income constant. (*V* is on the same indifference curve as $E_1$.)

The move from *V* to $E_2$ shows the income effect by holding relative prices constant. (The slopes at *V* and $E_2$ are the same.)

Note: Both effects are measured along the *Q* axis. $Q_1Q_3$ is the substitution effect, and $Q_3Q_2$ the income effect.

to $Q_2$ can be broken down into substitution and income effects. To look at the effects of substitution alone, we keep the consumer on the original indifference curve $u_1$. This means that ***real income*** is held constant. At the same time, we allow the slope of the price line to change to reflect the lower price of food. Thus, we find a new price line *ST* parallel to *KR*— thus reflecting the new price — but tangent to the original indifference curve $u_1$ at point *V*. The *substitution effect* is the quantity change $Q_1Q_3$ associated with the move from $E_1$ to *V*.

A consumer's *real income* remains constant whenever the consumer remains on the same indifference curve.

The *substitution effect* is the change in the quantity purchased that would occur as a result of a change only in relative prices, with real income held constant. In Figure 7-14, it is the distance from $Q_1$ to $Q_3$.

However, the consumer does not actually move from $E_1$ to *V*, but rather from $E_1$ to $E_2$. The rest of the move — from *V* to $E_2$ — represents the *income effect*. Observe that a shift in the price line from *ST* to *KR* results from a change in real income alone; that is, it involves no change in relative prices, since the slope of *ST* and *KR* are the same.

The *income effect* is the change in the quantity purchased that would occur as a result of a change only in real income. In Figure 7-14, it is the distance from $Q_3$ to $Q_2$.

When the price of food falls, the shape of the indifference curve guarantees that the substitution effect will lead an individual to buy more food and less of other goods; that is, arrow (1) points down and to the right in Figure 7-14.

However, the sign of the income effect is not certain. For the vast majority of goods — the *normal goods* — the income effect will lead an individual to buy more of the good; $E_2$ is to the right of *V* in Figure 7-14. But, as explained in Chapter 4, for *inferior goods*, the income effect is different; an increase in income alone *reduces* the quantity purchased. In this case, an indifference curve touches budget line *KR* at a point, such as *H*, to the left of *V*. (To illustrate this possibility, erase $u_2$ and draw in this other indifference curve, ensuring that it is tangent to *KR* at *H*.)

Economists have been fascinated with the logical possibility that the income effect might not only be negative, but also be sufficiently strong to more than offset the substitution effect. In this case, an indifference curve would be tangent to *KR* at a point, such as *J*, to the left of $E_1$. Then the reduction in the price of the good would lead to a move from $E_1$ to *J* and a reduction in the purchase of that good. Such an outcome is extremely rare, if it happens at all. One example has been attributed to Victorian economist Giffen, involving the purchase of potatoes in a very poor economy. In such a special case, a fall in the price of the basic staple — potatoes — might so increase people's real income and their purchases of meat and other expensive foods that they would buy fewer potatoes. Notice that such a peculiar good — a so-called ***Giffen good*** — would have a strange demand curve. It would slope downward and *to the left*.

# EXTENSIONS OF DEMAND THEORY

Time is Money.

Ben Franklin

In deciding whether to buy a product, the consumer considers the utility that the product will yield and its cost. Cost is a broad concept, covering more than just the purchase price. Other costs include:

- *transactions costs*. These are the costs, in addition to the purchase price, incurred when buying the good.
- the *costs of using* a product. For example, once a car has been purchased, there will be continuing costs in the form of gasoline, insurance, etc.

## Transactions Costs

To illustrate ***transactions costs***, suppose that, after studying the profit prospects of Hiram Walker & Sons, Ltd., you buy 100 shares of Hiram Walker stock from a "discount" broker. In addition to the cost of the stock itself, you incur two transactions costs:

1. The commission charged by the broker. Discount brokers provide one and only one service: buying or selling stocks. For this, they charge a fee or commission. Because they do not give advice or provide information on companies, the transaction also involves a second cost.
2. Search cost, also called information cost. This is the cost of collecting information needed to make an

informed decision. This cost includes not only the time you spend in your study of Hiram Walker, but also any out-of-pocket expenses you may incur. For example, you may subscribe to publications that provide information on corporations.

You may decide to go to a full-service broker, who will charge more than a discount broker but will offer information and advice on which stocks to buy. In this case, the commission covers not only the cost of actually executing the transaction, but some of the search costs, too.

*Search cost* or *information cost* is the time and money spent in collecting the information necessary to make a decision to buy or sell.

It's not just stockbrokers who are in the information business. Real estate agents also provide information to both buyers and sellers. They give buyers information about houses that are available. They provide sellers with advice on pricing of a home, and information on who the buyers are.

If you're selling a house, should you go to a real estate agent—to whom you will have to pay a commission if the house is sold—or should you place an ad in the paper and try to sell the house on your own? You usually do better by going to an agent; agents are in the business of making contacts with potential buyers. Specialization in marketing may be just as important as specialization in other skills, such as law or medicine.

Nevertheless, you should beware. Whenever you deal with people who provide information or advice, it's important to ask: Is the information or advice really in your interest, or are the agents being influenced—consciously or subconsciously—by quite different interests of their own? For example, is the real estate agent suggesting that you set a low price on your home, to make it easy to sell? Will the doctor, who advises you to have an operation, actually do the operation and receive a fee? (Getting a "second opinion" is generally wise. Even in cases where there is no conflict of interest, a second opinion can provide additional information.) Doesn't the stockbroker have an interest in getting you to buy, in order to earn commissions?

## How Do Search Costs Influence Market Price?

The greater the information of consumers and the more willing they are to bear search costs by seeking alternative sellers, the less dealers will be able to charge higher prices than their competitors do. Thus, search reduces not only the average price the public pays, but also the variation in prices. Moreover, the percentage variation in price will be less for large-ticket items such as cars—where it pays the public to search intensively — than for small-ticket items where it's not worth the trouble. Thus, a grocer may be able to raise the price of salt by 10% without anyone noticing. But a car dealer who tries to charge 10% more than the competition will soon be out of business.

Search efforts provide several benefits. Individuals who search generally purchase products that better satisfy their requirements. Moreover, the benefits go beyond the individual. The more information the public has, the less likely it is that a poor product will survive in the marketplace. In addition, high-priced firms are under pressure to cut prices in order to retain their customers; prices, therefore, tend to be lower. Of course, if all these things happen, it becomes less necessary for an individual to incur large search costs. There will be less risk of being overcharged, or ending up with a shoddy product. Thus, paradoxically, the more searching the public does, the less any individual buyer needs to search.

## Time Costs in Consumption

Time represents a major part of search costs — for example, the time a consumer spends shopping around at various car dealers. Time can be important not only in searching for products, but also in using them.

Examples abound. One reason car buyers are concerned about reliability is that they don't want to waste a lot of time driving the car back and forth to the dealer for repairs. Time may also be an important consideration in other purchases. For example, a train ticket between Toronto and Winnipeg costs only about half as much as an airline ticket. But most people don't take the train because it takes more time. Moreover, people with high incomes—whose time is valuable — incur higher costs in travelling by train. The less affluent may take a train or bus. The rich fly.

Time cost helps to explain consumption patterns, not only within Canada but also among countries. In North America we buy costly home appliances: They save valuable time. In poorer countries, the laundry is more likely to be done by hand.

## KEY POINTS

1. The market demand is the sum of the individual demands.
2. As a consumer consumes more of a product, its marginal benefit eventually declines.
3. The downward-sloping demand curve reflects declining marginal benefit.
4. The height of the demand curve gives a monetary measure of the marginal benefit of the good to the buyer. When you see a demand curve, you should visualize the vertical marginal benefit arrows beneath it.
5. The total benefit derived from a product—such as water—exceeds the total amount ($P \times Q$) that consumers spend for it. The excess of benefit over the price paid is *consumer surplus*. Consumer surplus is measured by the triangle below the demand curve and above the price.
6. When price falls, consumer surplus increases by the horizontal area to the left of the demand curve and between the old and the new price.
7. Water provides much more total benefit than diamonds. However, water has a much lower price and, therefore, the consumer continues to purchase additional units until its marginal benefit is low. Water is used not only in high priority uses, such as drinking, but also in lower priority uses, such as watering the lawn.
8. An indifference curve shows various combinations of the quantities consumed of two goods that give the consumer the same level of utility. The slope of an indifference curve, referred to as the marginal rate of substitution between the two goods, reflects the ratio of their marginal utilities.
9. If both goods are subject to the law of diminishing marginal utility, the slope of the indifference curve will become smaller and smaller (in absolute value) as the consumer moves toward combinations further down and to the right along an indifference curve. That is, the indifference curve reflects the diminishing marginal rate of substitution of one good for the other.
10. Indifference curves lying further up and to the right on an indifference map correspond to higher levels of utility than those closer to the origin. Like the contour lines on a geographer's map, indifference curves cannot cross.
11. A budget line shows the various combinations of two goods that the consumer can afford to buy, given his or her limited income. To maximize utility, the consumer selects that combination of quantities on the budget line that enables him or her to reach an indifference curve that is tangent to (just touches) the budget line.
12. The change in the quantity consumed of a good when its price changes can be separated into a substitution effect and an income effect. Because of the principle of diminishing marginal rate of substitution, the substitution effect of a price decrease is always positive. The income effect of a price decrease is positive for a normal good, negative for an inferior good.

## KEY TERMS

**market demand**
**individual demand**
**utility**
**law of diminishing marginal utility**
**marginal utility**
**marginal benefit**
**diminishing marginal benefit**
**consumer surplus**
**paradox of value**
**indifference curve**
**marginal rate of substitution**
**diminishing marginal rate of substitution**
**indifference map**
**budget line**
**point of tangency**
**substitution effect**
**income effect**
**real income**
**Giffen good**
**transaction cost**

## PROBLEMS

7-1. Suppose each of three individuals has unit elasticity of demand for a particular good. Without drawing any diagrams, can you guess what the elasticity of the total market demand for this good will be? Now draw diagrams showing each of the individual demands, and how the market demand is constructed. How does the slope of market demand compare with the slope of the individual demands? Is market demand, therefore, more elastic? Explain why or why not.

7-2. Using your own example, explain why marginal utility must eventually fall. Can you think of anything for which your marginal utility rises over a range?

7-3. Redo the table in Box 7-2, on the assumption that the price of mystery novels is \$2, not \$4. With an income of \$10, how many hamburgers and mysteries will the consumer buy? What happens to this individual's demand for mysteries as the price falls from \$4 to \$2? Next, suppose that the consumer's income rises to \$12, while the price of mysteries and hamburgers each remain at \$2. What will this individual buy now?

7-4. What does the budget line look like if the price per unit of the good on the horizontal axis falls when more is purchased?

7-5. Consider an individual whose indifference curves between dental services and all other goods exhibit diminishing marginal rate of substitution everywhere. The government considers dental services a merit good and wishes to induce individuals to go to the dentist more often than they do now, in the absence of any government dental program. Two policies, which would cost the government exactly the same amount of money, have been suggested:

POLICY A: The government will rebate to the individual 50% of all dentists' bills, thus lowering the relative (and absolute) price of dental care by half.

POLICY B: Assume the cost of Policy A to the government is \$R for this individual. Policy B consists of the government simply giving the individual a lump-sum payment of \$R to spend as he or she wishes. That is, the price of a unit of dental services is not changed, but the individual's income is increased by the amount of the lump-sum payment.

For the questions below, plot all other goods (a composite good) on the vertical axis and let its price be \$1. Measure units of dental services on the horizontal axis and let their price (before Policy A) be $P$.

(a) Demonstrate that a utility-maximizing individual will prefer Policy B.

(b) Demonstrate that a government whose objective is to maximize individuals' consumption of dental services will prefer Policy A.

7-6. Consider a club that serves seven-course dinners to members only. An individual's annual demand for club dinners is given by

$$P = 25 - 0.1D$$

where $P$ denotes the price per dinner and D denotes the number of meals the individual eats at the club per year.

What is the maximum this individual would pay as a membership fee for the right to dine at the club for \$5 per meal? Support your analysis with a diagram.

7-7. "People with preferences that exhibit a diminishing marginal rate of substitution always prefer commodity bundles they cannot afford to those they can." Assess the veracity of this statement.

7-8. Gasoline is a normal good. Show the substitution and income effects of a price increase.

CHAPTER 8

# BUSINESS ORGANIZATION AND FINANCE

*Business is a game — the greatest game in the world if you know how to play it.*

*Thomas J. Watson, Sr.,* of IBM

The demand for a consumer good depends on the choices of millions of single individuals and families. The supply side is more complex. Some goods are supplied by single individuals — for example, the wheat produced by an individual farmer. But most production is carried on by groups of people working within business corporations. Some corporations are quite small — for example, the local firm selling heating oil to homeowners. Others are much larger and more complex: huge corporations such as Canadian Pacific Ltd., Alcan Aluminum, or Molson Breweries.

This chapter will:

- outline the main types of business organization
- summarize the objectives that businesses pursue
- explain how a business gets the funds to finance expansion
- explain the motivations of the buyers and sellers of stocks and bonds, and some of the reasons that stock prices fluctuate
- explain the distinction between accounting cost and opportunity cost.

This chapter provides background for the next five chapters, which will explain the decisions that firms face as they produce and sell their products.

## BUSINESS ORGANIZATIONS

There are three types of business organization: the ***sole proprietorship***, the ***partnership***, and the ***corporation***. The sole proprietorship and the partnership are the most common forms of very small business, although even a one-person business may be a corporation. At the other end of the spectrum, large businesses are almost exclusively corporations, although there are some exceptions. For example, large law firms are partnerships.

### Sole Proprietorships and Partnerships: Their Advantages and Disadvantages

A sole proprietorship is the easiest form of business to establish; there is little fuss or bother. If I decide to make pottery in my basement or design computer software in a spare bedroom, I may do so. I can begin tomorrow, without going through legal and organizational hassles. A sole proprietorship has advantages for someone who wants to experiment with a new line of work — a fact that may explain why so many sole proprietorships go out of business so quickly.

The sole proprietorship is flexible and uncomplicated. The proprietor buys the materials needed, hires any help that is necessary and can be afforded, and undertakes to pay the bills. The profits of the business belong to the owner, to be shared by no one — except the government, which collects its share in the form of personal income taxes paid by the owner.

However, the sole proprietorship has disadvantages. Most obviously, there are limits to how much one individual can manage. Consider a typical small enterprise, the gasoline station. In this sort of business, a single owner has problems. While help can be hired to operate the pumps, there are advantages in having someone around who is "in charge." Yet one individual would find it a crushing burden to try to be present during the long hours that the gas station is open. The obvious solution is to take on a partner, who will be jointly responsible.

Some partnerships are made up of just two people; others include dozens of partners. In a typical partnership, each partner agrees to provide some fraction of the work and some of the financing. In return, each partner receives an agreed share of the profits or suffers an agreed share of the losses. Again, the partnership is easily established; a simple oral agreement will do.

Both the sole proprietorship and the partnership are simple and flexible forms of business organization. If they are well run and profitable, they will expand. The owners/partners will want to hire more workers, and raise more funds to finance the purchase of more capital— that is, larger facilities, more inventory, and more machinery and equipment.

But here a problem may arise. While partnerships and sole proprietorships may be flexible and efficient as a way to run relatively small businesses, they have major limitations when the business becomes larger.

Some amount of expansion can be *self-financed.* The owner or owners can contribute additional funds from their personal assets, or the profits generated by the business itself can be ploughed back to purchase new buildings or equipment. But for a more rapid expansion, the business will have to borrow from the outside. It may mortgage property, or borrow from suppliers, banks, or other financial institutions. It is here that difficulties are likely to arise.

Part of the problem is that it may be risky for a sole proprietor, for example, to finance expansion by borrowing. If a proprietorship runs into difficulty, the owner can lose more than his or her original investment. Personal assets may be lost in order to pay the *creditors*—that is, those to whom the business owes money. In short, a proprietor has ***unlimited liability*** for all the debts of the business.

One way of dealing with this problem is to bring in new owners to help with the financing— that is, to take on new partners. In doing so, a carrot, in the form of a share of the profits, can be dangled in front of potential investors. But with the carrot comes a stick. With a partnership, there is a particular form of risk: *Each partner is liable for the obligations undertaken by the other partner or partners*, and each partner runs the risk of being left "holding the bag" if the other partners are unable to meet their shares of the obligations of the partnership. Thus, in gaining a right to a share of the profits, a prospective new partner also undertakes unlimited liability for the debts of the business. Consequently, outside investors will be reluctant to share in the partnership unless they have carefully investigated it and have developed an exceptionally high degree of confidence in the partners. This may make it very hard for a partnership to get the financing needed for expansion.

Sole proprietorships and partnerships may also have problems with the *continuity* of the business, and this may create hardships for the firm's employees and others (such as suppliers) who depend on it for making a living. For example, when a sole proprietor dies, the business may too—unless an heir takes over the shop or farm and continues to run it. Continuity is an even more awkward problem in a partnership. When a partner dies, the original partnership automatically ends, and a new partnership must be formed. A new partnership agreement is likewise necessary whenever a new partner is admitted. This is not surprising: After all, each of the partners will be liable for the acts of the new partner.

## The Corporation

> ***Corporation***, *n.* An ingenious device for obtaining individual profit without individual responsibility.
>
> Ambrose Bierce, *The Devil's Dictionary*

The major advantage of the corporate form of organization is that it *limits the liability* of its owners: All they can lose is their initial investment. When new investors buy ***shares*** of the ***common stock*** of a business, they thereby acquire partial ownership of the business without facing the danger of unlimited liability. If the business goes bankrupt and is unable to pay its debts, the owners lose the purchase price of their shares, but not their homes or other personal property. By reducing the risks of investors, the corporate form of business makes it feasible to tap a wide pool of investment funds. Thus, the corporation is the form of business most suited to rapid growth with the use of outside funds.

> Each *share of common stock* represents a fraction of the *ownership* (that is, a fraction of the *equity*) of a corporation.

Because of the limited liability, a corporation's creditors cannot lay claim to the personal property of the owners if the corporation fails—although they can claim the assets of the corporation itself.

Corporations must inform those with whom they do business of this limited liability; they do so by tacking to their corporate title the designation "Ltd." or "Limited." ("Inc." or "Incorporated" is used in the United States.) The French and Spanish use an even more colourful warning: Corporations' titles are followed by the letters S.A. — for *Société Anonyme*, or *Sociedad Anonima* (anonymous society).

When the corporate form of business was first used in Britain some centuries ago, corporation charters were awarded only rarely, by special grants of the King and Parliament. Several of these corporations played a major role in strengthening the economic connections between Britain and the colonies, operating under the protection of British military power. They included the famous East India Company and the Hudson's Bay Company, which was originally formed in 1670 to participate in the profitable but risky fur trade between Europe and North America.

During the nineteenth century, however, a major revolution occurred in business and legal thinking, and the modern corporation emerged. General incorporation laws were passed, granting to anyone the right to form a corporation. The formation of a corporation is generally a straightforward and uncomplicated legal procedure, although there are a few important exceptions— such as banking, where government regulation is important. In addition to limited liability, the corporation offers the advantage of continuity. In law, the corporation is a fictitious "legal person." When one of the shareholders dies, the corporation survives; the shares of the deceased are inherited by his or her heirs, without the corporation's organization being disturbed. The heirs need not be concerned about accepting the shares, since they are not liable for the corporation's debts. Furthermore, the corporation survives even if some of the shareholders want to get out of the business. These shareholders can sell their shares to anyone willing to buy; there is no need to reorganize the company.

## Corporation Taxes

The profits of a proprietorship or a partnership are taxed as the personal income of the proprietor or partners. When a corporation is established, taxation becomes more complicated.

Even though a corporation is owned by its shareholders, the income earned by the corporation is not considered to be part of the shareholders' taxable income until it is actually paid out to them in the form of *dividends* (or until the shareholder sells the stock at a profit, in which case the profit must be shown as a capital gain). Most corporations will pay out only a part of their income as dividends and will keep the rest in the business as retained earnings (which may be used to pay off the corporation's debt, finance expansion of the business, or be invested in financial assets to earn interest).

All earnings of a corporation, whether paid out as dividends or retained in the business are, of course, subject to the corporation income tax. For a wealthy person who would pay a high rate of personal income tax, the tax law may nevertheless make it profitable to incorporate his or her business. While the combined rate of federal/provincial corporation income tax was between 41% and 46% in most provinces in 1993, the owner might be able to take advantage of the lower rate of roughly 18%–23% applicable to small corporations. As long as the owner keeps dividends low and ploughs most of the earnings back into the business, the amount of tax paid will be considerably lower than it would have been if the same business had been run as a proprietorship or partnership.

## Double Taxation and the Dividend Tax Credit

While there are possible tax advantages of this kind for small corporations (and wealthy shareholders with high personal tax rates), for large corporations that pay out most of their income as dividends, the situation is quite different. In fact, there is ***double taxation*** of the owners' income from the corporation: First, it is subject to the corporation income tax (which is levied at higher rates for large corporations) and, second, the dividends paid out become subject to tax as personal income of the owners.

Under earlier Canadian tax law, this double taxation led to a very high effective tax rate on dividend income, and created a strong incentive for large corporations to retain most of their earnings, in order to avoid the second round of taxation. Under present tax rules, however, the problem of double taxation has been substantially reduced, if not entirely eliminated, by means of a ***dividend tax credit***. While the detailed provisions in the law are complex, the essential idea is simple. The total amount of personal income tax payable by a recipient of dividend income from a Canadian corporation is reduced by a credit that is intended to roughly represent the recipient's share of the income tax already paid by the corporation. The result is that the total tax paid on corporate income paid out as dividends is similar to what it would have been if it had been treated as personal income of the shareholder in the first place — that is, before payment of corporation income tax.

Eliminating the double taxation of dividend income clearly has reduced the incentive for corporations to keep most of their profits as retained earnings. However, the change in the capital gains taxation introduced in 1985 worked in the other direction. Shareholders in corporations that retain most of their earnings will usually experience a capital gain, as the value of the corporation's shares increases to reflect the reinvested profits. But under the 1985 tax rules, much of such capital gains are non-taxable even if the shareholder "realizes" his or her capital gain by selling the shares.

In summary, the three types of business organization are compared in Table 8-1.

## HOW A CORPORATION FINANCES EXPANSION

Like single proprietorships and partnerships, corporations employ labour and other factors of production such as capital to produce the goods and services that are sold in the market. A corporation can obtain the funds it needs to finance its capital stock in the same way as a proprietorship or partnership; that is, by borrowing from banks or ploughing profits back into the business. But a large corporation also has other options. It can issue common stock, bonds, or other securities.

### Common Stock

When it sells additional shares of common stock, the corporation takes on new part-owners, since each share represents a fraction of the ownership of the corporation. As a part-owner, the purchaser of common stock not only receives a share of any dividends paid by the corporation, but also gets the right to vote for the corporation's directors who, in turn, choose the corporate officers and set the corporation's policies.

### Bonds

Rather than take on new owners by issuing additional common stock, the corporation may raise funds by selling bonds. A bond represents debt of the corporation; it is an I.O.U. that the corporation is obliged to repay,

**TABLE 8-1 Types of Business Organization**

| Type of Firm | Advantages | Disadvantages |
|---|---|---|
| Individual Proprietorship | 1. Easy to establish<br>2. Simple organization; owner makes the decisions<br>3. Earnings taxed only once, as personal income of owner | 1. Unlimited liability; owner's personal assets are at risk<br>2. Limited ability to raise funds for expansion<br>3. Business generally terminates with death of owner (although it may be taken over by an heir) |
| Partnership | 1. Permits management responsibilities to be shared by several owners<br>2. Earnings taxed only as personal income of partners | 1. Unlimited liability; owners' personal assets are at risk<br>2. More complicated than individual proprietorship; danger of conflict among partners<br>3. Less able than corporations to raise funds<br>4. Business must be terminated or reorganized with death of any partner |
| Corporation | 1. Limited liability for owners<br>2. Company is not terminated with death of owners<br>3. Much larger, more complex organizations are possible than with other two types<br>4. Corporations are generally more able to raise funds for expansion | 1. Tax treatment more complicated since profits are subject to corporate income tax and must also be included in shareholders' taxable income<br>2. Management can be complicated; managers may pay little attention to interests of stockholders |

whether it is making profits or not. If the corporation doesn't pay, it can be sued by the bondholder.

A bond is a long-term form of debt, which does not fall due for repayment until 10, 15, or more years from the time it was initially sold (issued) by the corporation. Bonds usually come in large denominations —for example, $100,000. The original buyer normally pays the corporation a sum equal to the face value of the bond; in effect, the original buyer is lending $100,000 to the corporation. In return for the $100,000, the corporation is committed to make two sets of payments to the bondholder:

1. Interest payments that must be made periodically — normally semi-annually— during the life of the bond. If the interest rate is, say, 10% per annum on a bond with a $100,000 face value, the interest payment will be $5000 (that is, 5%) every 6 months.
2. A payment of the $100,000 ***face value***, or ***principal***, when the date of maturity arrives. That is, the corporation must repay the amount of the loan at maturity.

Since a bond commits the corporation to make the payments of interest and principal, it provides the purchaser an assured, steady income— provided the corporation avoids bankruptcy. Common stock, on the other hand, involves a substantial risk. During periods of difficulty, the corporation may reduce or eliminate the dividend, and the market price of the stock may plummet. But, while bonds provide more safety than stocks, they offer less excitement. Unlike the owner of common stock, the bondholder cannot look forward to rising dividends if the company hits the jackpot. The bondholder will get no more than the interest and principal specified in the bond contract. Generally, bonds are safe; but they are also dull.

Bonds are not the only type of debt that a corporation can issue. It also may issue *notes*, which are similar to bonds, except that they have only a few years to maturity. *Commercial paper* is even shorter term, being normally issued for just a few months.

Some investors desire an income-earning security "between stocks and bonds," that is, one that will provide more safety than common stock, while still offering a larger potential return than bonds if the company does well. These investors may choose *convertible bonds* (or *debentures*) or *preferred stock*.

## Convertible Bonds

Convertible bonds are like ordinary bonds, with one additional feature. Prior to a given date, they may be exchanged for common stock in some fixed ratio— for example, one bond for ten shares of common stock. If the outlook for the corporation becomes favourable, the holder of convertible bonds may exchange them for common stock, and thus own shares of the growing corporation. If, on the other hand, the company fails to prosper, convertible bonds may be held to maturity, when the bondholder will receive repayment of the principal.

Because the holder has the option of converting, the interest rate on convertible bonds is normally less than the rate on regular bonds, often substantially less. Therefore, if you are thinking about buying convertible bonds, you have to weigh two conflicting considerations. The interest payments that you receive will be low. But you will have the option to convert into common stock, an option that may become valuable in the event the business is successful.

## Preferred Stock

Preferred stock, like common stock, represents ownership, and not debt. The corporation is legally obligated to make interest payments to bondholders, but it is not legally required to pay dividends to preferred or common shareholders. Preferred shareholders, however, have a claim on profits that precedes— or is "preferred" to— the claim of the common shareholder. The preferred shareholder has a right to receive specific dividends (for example, $2 per share) before the common shareholder can be paid any dividend at all. But, on the other hand, the preferred shareholder does not have the possibility of large gains open to the common shareholder. While the common shareholder may hope for rising dividends if the corporation prospers, the preferred shareholder will at most receive the specified dividend.

As a general rule, all types of securities— common stock, preferred stock, and bonds— may be resold by the original purchasers.

# FINANCIAL MARKETS

Buildings, inventories, machinery and equipment, and so on, is the capital that businesses use, along with labour, to produce goods and services for the market. Issuing common stock or bonds, or borrowing from financial institutions, represent different methods that businesses can use to raise the funds to acquire this capital. The interest paid on bonds and other forms of debt is part of the businesses' cost of using capital; the dividends and capital gains that accrue to shareholders, and the interest that asset-owning households are paid on bonds or on the deposits they hold in financial institutions, represent the income they earn by supplying capital funds to the business sector. (Recall how we illustrated these transactions in the circular-flow diagrams in Chapters 3, 4, and 5, for example.)

Financial institutions and financial markets (such as the markets for stocks and bonds) perform two very important functions in the economy. On the one hand, they help determine which firms will expand —that is, in which firms and industries the economy's capital will be employed. On the other hand, financial markets also help produce the kinds of financial assets (stocks, bonds, deposits in banks and trust companies, etc.) that best correspond to the objectives of those who hold those assets—that is, those who supply the capital resources that are used by the business sector.

In some ways, the markets for financial assets such as stocks and bonds are similar to the markets for wheat and shoes, or automobiles. For example, an increase in the demand for General Motors stock will tend to bid its price up, just as an increase in the demand for shoes will tend to bid their price up.

Nevertheless, in one very important way, the market for stocks and bonds is quite different from the market for shoes or cars. When you wish to buy a pair of shoes or a car, you can examine the available merchandise and make a reasonably good judgement as to its quality. But when you buy a common stock, you are, in effect, buying a future prospect— something that is clearly intangible and about which it may be very difficult to reach an informed and balanced judgement. Similarly, when you buy a bond, you are buying a set of promises made by the bond issuer to pay interest and principal on schedule.

Because average investors can have such difficulty in evaluating the prospects of a corporation, there is a strong case for regulations that require the disclosure of information by firms issuing securities. Such regulations are enforced by provincial securities commissions. Before offering securities to the public, companies are required to issue a *prospectus*, which is a formal statement of the current position and the future prospects of the corporation. In addition, of course, if a firm is a public corporation, investors also have access to the accounts and financial reports that such corporations have to make available to their shareholders and others. The basic principles of business accounting are briefly described later in this chapter.

## Buyers of Securities: Who Are Canada's Capitalists?

The funds that business firms raise in the financial markets are supplied by those who buy and hold shares, bonds, and other securities. Indirectly, the owners of these assets (and those who own nonfinancial assets such as houses or equity in unincorporated businesses) are the suppliers of the economy's capital services. Who are the capitalists in the Canadian economy?

The answer to this question is complicated. One reason is that the shares of many corporations are owned, in whole or in part, by other corporations. ***Holding companies*** (such as Power Corporation of Montreal, or Bell Canada Enterprises) are companies whose assets consist of shares (or sometimes bonds) in other corporations. Thus, to find the individuals and families who are the ultimate owners of much of the economy's capital, one sometimes has to follow a paper trail through a complex network of interlocking corporations and holding companies who own each others' shares. Another complication is that many companies in Canada are foreign-owned. Often, they are subsidiaries of U.S. firms, meaning that most or all of their shares are owned by the U.S. parent company.

Of those shares that are not held by other corporations, or owned by foreign residents, a substantial portion are held by numerous small investors, who might have bought shares in individual corporations whose prospects they liked, or in ***mutual funds*** whose managers assemble a portfolio of shares from individual corporations and then in turn sell shares in these portfolios to individual investors.

But in Canada, there are two other groups of investors that play a very important role in the economy: A small group of wealthy families who own or control a number of Canada's largest companies; and large *institutional* investors, primarily pension funds and insurance companies.

The relative importance of these groups is greater in Canada than in the United States where most corporations are "widely held." (In widely held corporations, no single owner has a block of shares large enough to control the election of corporate directors and the firm's major business decisions.) It has been established that roughly 70% of Canada's largest corporations have a "controlling shareholder" that holds more than 20% of the voting power in corporate elections.[1]

[1] Kathryn Montgomery and David Leighton, "The Unseen Revolution," *Business Quarterly*, Autumn 1993, pp. 43–48.

When the controlling interest in a corporation is held by an individual or a family, its directors and managers will in effect be appointed by the controlling shareholder. However, for widely held corporations, it is not clear who effectively controls them. As explained in Box 8-1, many people have argued that in this situtation, real control may end up with a self-perpetuating group of managers who may not necessarily act in the interests of the shareholders.

## APPLICATIONS AND ILLUSTRATIONS BOX 8-1

### Who Controls the Corporation?

If a company's stock is spread among a large number of shareholders, it may, in practice, be run by a group of insiders made up of the directors and senior management. Many shareholders do not go to the annual shareholders' meeting; it is not worth the time and effort to show up.

The separation of ownership and control of corporations was pointed out as early as 1932 by A.A. Berle and Gardner C. Means in their book *The Modern Corporation and Private Property.* Berle and Means found that the stockholding of the 200 largest U.S. corporations was very diffuse. For 88 of them, no single family or group of business associates owned as much as 10% of the stock. A later study indicated that, by 1963, ownership was spread even more thinly. What was true of 88 of the 200 largest corporations in the earlier period was by then true of 169. Thus, the separation between ownership and control apparently was becoming wider, increasing the chance that the interest of executives will be given greater weight than the interests of the shareholder-owners.

Where control is effectively in the hands of management rather than the owners, the question arises as to what difference this makes. There is an obvious community of interest between management and shareholders: Both groups want a corporation that is profitable. Management is obviously interested in the success of the corporation, since their jobs may be lost if the corporation goes under.

But, while similar, the interests of management and shareholders are not identical. Recent research has emphasized the general problem of *principals* (in this case, shareholders) who employ *agents* (corporate executives) to act on their behalf. The agents may pursue their own goals instead. They may, for example, hire incompetent friends or relatives. Or, they may be more interested in the preservation of their own jobs than in profits.

This does not mean, however, that the management is free to do anything it pleases. If things go badly, a group of dissident shareholders may ask other shareholders to give them their *proxies*—that is, the right to vote on their behalf at the annual meeting. If the dissident group gets enough proxies, it can vote the management out. Furthermore, if the company is badly run, the price of its stock is likely to be depressed. An outsider may then buy the company by offering shareholders a higher price, hoping to reap a big gain by installing new, more vigorous management. There has been a rash of such takeovers or buyouts in recent years.

Note that it is not just corporations that are run by "agents" whose interests may differ from the "principals." The same is likely to be the case in any big organization, including government. Presidents and prime ministers, who act as agents for the voting public, may pursue their own agendas rather than the public interest—whatever that may be.

Why not avoid such "agent" problems by having smaller organizations in which "principals" can manage and protect their own interests directly? The answer is, big organizations may be efficient, enjoying economies of scale. A small corporation with a few hundred employees may be easy to manage, but it cannot produce low-cost cars.

The case where controlling ownership is by institutional investors, such as pension funds or mutual insurance companies, is of particular interest. The returns to these funds benefit the workers who belong to the pension plan, or the owners of the life insurance policies whose value and premium costs depend on the insurance companies' fortunes.

Thus, the managers of these institutions have an obligation to get the best possible return on their investment. In order to accomplish this, some institutional investors have begun to exercise their voting power to elect at least some of the corporations' directors, and take a more active interest in the way "their" corporations are managed.

## The Objectives of Buyers of Securities

In spite of disclosure requirements, purchasers of securities face an uncertain future. Because of the risks that they face, they do not simply choose the bond that has the highest interest rate; the likelihood that the company will actually repay is also important. Indeed, purchasers of securities have three objectives to balance: return, risk, and liquidity.

***Return*** is the annual yield, measured as a percentage of the cost of the security. For example, if a bond is purchased for $10,000 and it pays interest of $1200 per year, then it yields 12%.

***Risk*** is the chance that something will go wrong. For example, the company may go bankrupt and the bondholder may lose both interest and principal. There are various ways in which risk can be reduced: by buying bonds rather than stocks; by buying "blue chip" securities of large, stable corporations, and by *diversification*—that is, holding the stocks of a number of companies in different industries.

Finally, ***liquidity*** reflects the ability of the owner to sell an asset on short notice, with little cost and bother. A passbook account in a trust company is highly liquid. Unless the trust company has run into financial difficulty, the account may be withdrawn at any time for its full dollar value. (Thus, in addition to handling paperwork and evaluating borrowers' creditworthiness, trust companies and other financial intermediaries provide their depositors with liquidity.) At the other end of the spectrum, real estate or paintings are very illiquid. If you have to sell your home on short notice, you may have to accept a price that is much lower than you could get with a more lengthy selling effort.

While investors look for a combination of high return, low risk, and high liquidity, they do not all weigh the three objectives equally. Some — particularly those with steady incomes who are saving for the distant future — do not consider liquidity important, while others (perhaps those with children about to enter university) want to keep liquid investments on which they can draw in the near future. Different investors may have quite different attitudes toward risk.

## The Objectives of Issuers of Securities

A private company raising funds also has three objectives to balance: to obtain funds in such a way as to achieve a high *return* for the corporation's shareholders; to avoid *risk*; and to assure the *availability* of money when it is needed.

A corporation balances risk and return when it chooses whether to issue stocks or bonds. In contrast with the view from the buyer's side, the view of the corporation selling securities is that *bonds* have a *higher* risk than common stock. If the corporation sells bonds, interest payments must be made no matter how badly the company may be doing. Thus, a large outstanding debt can put a corporation in a precarious position. If business slackens, it may be unable to meet large payments for interest and principal, and may as a result be driven into bankruptcy. There is no such risk with common stock, since the company can cut dividends in the event of a downturn in business.

While it is safer for a corporation to issue stock, there is a disadvantage. Additional stock involves taking on new part-owners. If the company does well, the rising profits go partially to the new shareholders; the original shareholders must share their bonanza. In contrast, consider what happens if bonds are issued — that is, if the ***leverage*** of the corporation is increased. After the required payment of interest on the bonds, any large profits go only to the original shareholders. Thus, the more highly leveraged a corporation is, the greater is the uncertainty for its owners. Their potential gain is large, but so is their potential loss, including the possibility of bankruptcy. As a group, shareholders and corporate managers tend to be optimistic. They consequently may try to maximize their expected gains by a high degree of leverage. Furthermore, limited liability provides an incentive for leverage. If things go well, shareholders can earn many times their original investment. But if things go poorly, they can lose their original investment only once. Thus, a company may be highly leveraged in order to keep the potential gains in the hands of a few shareholders, while much of the risk is borne by bondholders and other creditors. Even though a company takes risk into account when it issues stocks or bonds, it has a temptation to discount the importance of risk, since someone else will suffer much of the possible loss.

If corporate managers were free to leverage to their hearts' content, the economy might be wildly unstable. When businesses go bankrupt, their employees may be thrown out of work, and other businesses to whom they owe money may also go bankrupt. Fortunately, however, there are limits to leverage. As leverage increases, the rising risks to bondholders make them cautious. They become increasingly reluctant to buy that company's bonds unless the bonds yield a very high return. If leverage becomes great enough, the company may find it impossible to sell bonds or to borrow from banks or others. Leverage is limited by the caution of lenders.

The final objective of corporations issuing securities is to assure the availability of money when it is needed. As a general rule, it is not advisable to finance a new factory with short-term borrowing. It is unwise to have to keep repaying a short-term debt and borrowing money again each year to finance a factory over, say, a 20-year lifetime. In some of those years, funds may be unavailable to borrowers, or may be available only at a very high interest rate. New factories, therefore, should be financed by long-term borrowing, or by the issue of additional stock, or by retained profits.

In order to ensure the availability of money for unpredictable requirements that can arise, a corporation may arrange a ***line of credit*** at a bank. A line of credit is a commitment by a bank to lend up to a specified limit at the request of the company. Similarly, builders may get commitments from trust companies to provide mortgage money in the future. Such commitments allow builders to make firm plans for construction.

## The Bond Market

Because security buyers balance risk and return, risky securities generally must have higher yields, or nobody will buy them. This shows up in bond market yields: Riskier bonds will yield a ***risk premium*** making their returns higher than safer bonds.

A *risk premium* is the difference between the yields on two grades of bonds because of differences in their risk.

While the most important reason for differences in bond yields is difference in risk, other influences are at work as well. There are very large quantities of Canadian government bonds outstanding, and the market for these bonds is very active, with relatively small selling costs. (The gap is small between the "bid" price, at which bond dealers are ready to buy, and the "offer" price, at which they are ready to sell.) Thus, government bonds provide a liquidity advantage; less loss results if the buyer has to turn around quickly and sell them. Federal government bonds, therefore, have low yields for two reasons: Because they are highly liquid, and because they carry little or no risk. (In an extreme situation, the federal government has the constitutional right to print money to pay interest and principal on its bonds.)

A notable feature in the bond market was the sharp upward movement of all interest rates between 1965 and 1981. An important reason for this was the acceleration of inflation during that period. When inflation is high, bondholders recognize that interest and principal will be repaid in the future when money is less valuable than at present. They therefore hesitate to purchase bonds unless interest rates are high enough to compensate for the declining value of money. Since 1981, the rate of inflation has declined substantially, and interest rates have receded: By the early 1990s, they were lower than they had been for decades.

## The Stock Market

Stocks of major corporations already held by the public are usually bought and sold on the stock exchanges, such as those in Toronto, Montreal, and Vancouver. Stockbrokers throughout the country maintain close contact with the exchanges, buying and selling stocks on behalf of their customers.

A *broker* acts as a representative of a buyer or seller, offering to buy or sell on behalf of clients.

Prices fluctuate on the stock exchanges in response to changes in demand and supply. Stock purchasers are interested in such things as the current and expected future profits of the corporation. Thus, stock prices may rise rapidly during periods of prosperity, when profit prospects appear good.

In the 1920s, the desire to "get rich quick" in the stock market became a national mania. With stocks rising, many investors learned that individuals, too, could use leverage to increase their potential gains; they borrowed large sums to buy stocks in the expectation that their prices would rise. Then came the Great Crash of 1929.[2] As Figure 8-1 shows, by 1932 stock prices had fallen to a fraction of their 1929 values. Many investors were wiped out, especially investors who had borrowed heavily to speculate in the stock market during the 1929 boom.

Another major upswing in stock averages occurred in the 1950s and 1960s, when the Canadian economy had the longest continuous expansion on record. Common stocks promised a share in the nation's prosperity. And they were widely looked on as a hedge against inflation. After all, stocks represent ownership of corporations and, in a period of inflation, the dollar value of a corporation's plant and equipment should rise with the general increase in prices. This comforting viewpoint was plausible, but it was not borne out by unfolding events. From the late 1960s to 1977, stock prices rose very little even though inflationary pressures accelerated. During most of the 1970s, stock market participants came to the view that inflation was very unhealthy for the economy, and signs of accelerating inflation were generally followed by declines in stock prices.

Between 1977 and 1981, Canadian stock prices rose rapidly. The popular Toronto Stock Exchange

[2] For some of the drama of the collapse, see John Kenneth Galbraith, *The Great Crash, 1929* (Boston: Houghton Mifflin, 1961) or Frederick Lewis Allen, *The Lords of Creation* (New York: Harper, 1935), Ch. 13.

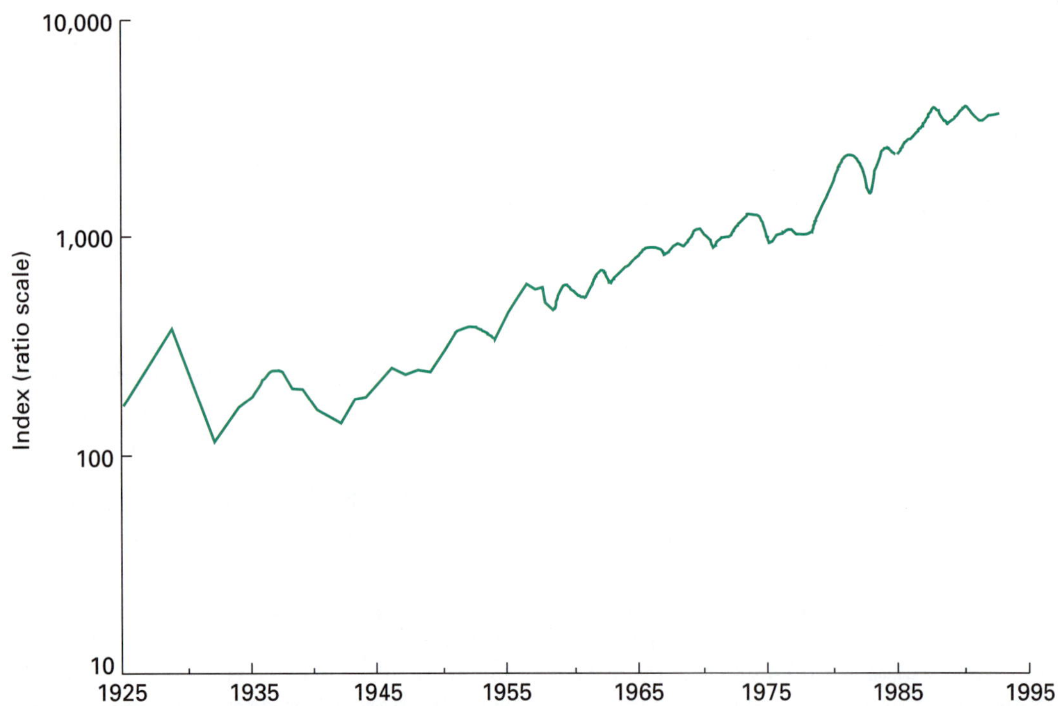


**FIGURE 8-1 Canadian stock prices, 1925–1992.**
The biggest swing in stock prices, in percentage terms, took place during the "bull market" of the 1920s, and the collapsing "bear market" of 1929–1932. In the 25 years following World War II, stock prices rose about fivefold. During most of the 1970s, they remained relatively stable, but then they rose substantially again between 1977 and 1981. Following a sharp decline during the 1981/82 recession, they rose rapidly again until the "mini-crash" in late 1987. The subsequent recovery was slow, and it was not until 1993 that the market reached its pre-1987 high.

*Source:* Constructed by authors from data in the *CANSIM Databank* and F.H. Leacy, M.C. Urquhart, and K.A.H. Buckley, eds., *Historical Statistics of Canada*, 2nd ed. (Ottawa: Statistics Canada, 1982). Reproduced by permission of the Minister of Supply and Services Canada.

stock price index (the TSE 300 Composite Index) more than doubled during this period. In part, this was explained by the dramatic rise in the share values of Canada's energy resource companies in response to the increase in world oil prices in 1979/80. While stock prices fell sharply during the 1981/82 recession, as Figure 8-1 shows they rose steadily once again from 1982 to 1987. One reason for this increase was the strong expansion following the recession. Another was that inflation appeared to be under much better control than during the 1970s. Stock prices in the United States also rose substantially during this period. This was not unusual: Canadian and U.S. stock markets often move along broadly similar trends.

The increase in share prices in the North American markets was especially rapid in 1987: Between January and August, the TSE 300 increased by almost 20%. By the fall, this strong increase had made many investors nervous: They were wondering how long the uptrend would continue, and whether it would not be a good idea to "get out of the market" (sell their shares) before prices started falling. In mid-October, many investors started selling. On October 19, "Black Monday," an almost panicky wave of selling swept over both the New York and Toronto markets. At the close on Tuesday, the TSE had plunged by 17%. In New York, the Dow Jones index fell by 23% in a single day. This was a sharper fall than had occurred in any one day in 1929. Over $500 *billion* in stock values evaporated. But the underlying economy in North America was much stronger than it had been in 1929. A healthy rate of growth continued through 1989, in contrast to the economic collapse that followed the stock market crash of 1929.

With a growing economy, stock prices also rose again, and by late 1989, they had come close to their pre-crash high. However, when another deep recession occurred from 1990–1992 and corporate profits plummeted, the TSE index fell by a large amount. Finally, when the economy began to recover from the recession, corporate profits revived and in August 1993, the index did surpass its previous record high, which had been established before the 1987 crash.

With these large fluctuations, many investors who have had their savings in the stock market have been through a rough time indeed. The experience of the 1980s once again reminded investors of an important lesson: While the stock market may be a great place to get rich when times are good, it is also a place where large amounts can be quickly lost.

# BUSINESS ACCOUNTING: THE BALANCE SHEET AND THE INCOME STATEMENT

As we noted earlier, an individual investor or financial institution who is thinking of investing in a firm by buying the shares or bonds that the firm issues, will be interested in having as much information as possible about the firm's past performance and future prospects. For existing firms, the basic source of this kind of information is the accounts and financial reports that they issue on a regular basis. An accurate and informative set of accounts is also an indispensable tool for the firm's managers, as a basis for decisions about investments, marketing, and measures to reduce the costs of production and administration. In addition, businesses are required to keep accounts for tax purposes.

There are two basic types of business accounts:

1. The ***balance sheet***, which gives a picture of the company's financial status at a point in time; for example, at the close of business on December 31 of last year.
2. The ***income statement*** — also called the ***profit-and-loss statement*** — which summarizes the company's transactions over a period of time, such as a year.

The income statement records the flow of payments into and out of a company over a period of time. It is like a record of the amount of water that has flowed into and out of Lake Huron during a year. The balance sheet, on the other hand, measures the situation at a specific point in time. It is like a measure of the stock of water in Lake Huron today at noon.

## The Balance Sheet

The balance sheet shows (1) the ***assets*** that a company owns, (2) the ***liabilities*** that it owes, and (3) the company's ***net worth*** — that is, the value of the ***ownership*** (or ***equity***) of the shareholders. Assets must be exactly equal to the total of liabilities plus ownership. To use a simple illustration: If you have a car worth $7000 (an asset), on which you still owe $4000 to the bank (your debt or liability), then $3000 is the value of your ownership in the car. The same fundamental equation also holds for a corporation:

*Assets* = *liabilities* (what is owed) + *net worth* (the value of ownership).

The *net worth* of a corporation — the amount the shareholders own—is equal to the assets minus the liabilities of the corporation.

Assets are listed on the left side of the balance sheet, while liabilities and net worth are listed on the right. Because of the fundamental equation, the two sides must add to the same total. The balance sheet must balance.

As an example, consider Table 8-2, which shows the balance sheet of Northern Telecommunications Ltd., of Toronto, a producer of telephone switchboard systems and other equipment.

## The Left-Hand, Asset Side

Northern Telecom has sizeable assets in the form of cash (bank accounts), marketable short-term securities issued by other corporations or the government, and accounts receivable—for example, the value of communications systems that have already been delivered to customers but not yet paid for. It has sizeable inventories of materials and parts, and of terminals and office equipment ready for sale. It also has major assets in the form of land, plant (buildings), and equipment.

## The Right-Hand Side, Showing Liabilities and Net Worth

Northern Telecom has a number of short-term liabilities: amounts that the company has not yet paid for the copper, plastics, and other material it has bought from suppliers (accounts payable); wages and salaries not yet paid for work already performed (accrued liabilities); and other short-term debt. In addition, at the end of 1991, Northern Telecom had an outstanding long-term debt of $1.16 billion. (If debt matures within one year, it is short term; in more than one year, long term.)

At the end of 1991, Northern Telecom's total assets were $9.53 billion, and its liabilities were $5.86 billion. The net worth—the ownership of all shareholders — was therefore $3.67 billion. Of this, about one-fourth ($1.025 billion) had been paid in by shareholders purchasing shares from the company. The rest ($2.65 billion) represented retained earnings; that is, profits made over the years that had been ploughed back into the business.[3]

[3] "Retained earnings" may sound like a pool of funds that the corporation has readily available. However, this is generally not the case. Most retained earnings are not held in the form of cash; most are used to buy equipment or other items.

Suppose that, in the first year of its operation, a corporation earns $1000, and retains it all. (It pays no dividend.) The $1000 may be used to buy a new machine. Then, as a result, the following changes occur in the balance sheet:

Change in:

| Assets: | | Net worth: | |
|---|---|---|---|
| Machinery | +$1000 | Retained earnings | +$1000 |

The retained earnings have not been held in the form of idle cash; they have been put to work to buy machinery. The machinery shows up on the asset side. When the retained earnings are included in net worth, the balance sheet balances.

**TABLE 8-2 Northern Telecom Balance Sheet, December 31, 1991 (Simplified; millions of dollars)**

| Assets | | | Liabilities and Net Worth | | |
|---|---|---|---|---|---|
| 1. Current assets | | $3,779 | 6. Current liabilities | | $3,607 |
| (a) Cash & short term | $ 183 | | (a) Notes payable | $ 629 | |
| (b) Accounts receivable | 2,521 | | (b) Accounts payable and accrued and other current liabilities | 2,978 | |
| (c) Inventories | 848 | | 7. Long-term debt | | 1,161 |
| (d) Other current assets | 227 | | (a) To subsidiary companies | 276 | |
| 2. Plant and equipment | | 1,987 | (b) To others | 1,170 | |
| 3. Investments in subsidiary companies | | 182 | (c) Less: amount included in current liabilities | (285) | |
| 4. Other assets | | 3,586 | 8. Other liabilities* | | 1,095 |
| 5. Total assets (Items 1 + 2 + 3 + 4) | | $9,534 | 9. Total liabilities | | $5,863 |
| | | | 10. Net worth (5 − 8) | | $3,671 |
| | | | (a) Common stock | $1,025 | |
| | | | (b) Retained earnings | 2,646 | |
| | | | 11. Total liabilities and net worth (9 + 10) | | $9,534 |

*Source:* Northern Telecommunications Ltd., *Annual Report 1991.*
*Includes preferred shares.

At the end of 1991, there were about 246 million shares of Northern Telecom common stock outstanding. Each share represented an equity, or ***book value***, of around $14.90—that is, $3.67 billion in net worth divided by 246 million shares.

The *book value* of a stock is its net worth per share. It is calculated by dividing the total net worth of the company by the number of shares outstanding.

If you are thinking of buying common stock of a company, its book value is one of the things that should interest you. If it has a high book value, you will be buying ownership of a lot of assets. However, don't get carried away by a high book value. If the assets happen to be machinery and equipment that can be used only to produce buggy whips or other items for which there is no demand, the high book value may not be worth very much; the assets may not earn much income in the future. On the other hand, the stock of a profitable corporation like Northern Telecom may sell for substantially more than its book value. During 1991, Northern Telecom stock sold in the range between $30 and $52.

## The Income Statement

While the balance sheet shows the assets, liabilities, and net worth of a corporation at a point in time, the income statement shows what has happened *during a period of time* — for example, during a calendar year. A simplified version of Northern Telecom's income statement for the year 1991 is shown in Table 8-3.

During that year, the company had $8.18 billion in revenues from the sale and servicing of telephone equipment, as well as $102 million of investment income. Costs of $7.35 billion must be subtracted from revenues to calculate before-tax profit of $710 million. Corporation income taxes were $195 million, leaving an after-tax profit of $515 million, or $2.09 per share. Of this after-tax profit, $97 million was paid in dividends to shareholders, and $418 million was retained by the company. Observe that the retained earnings in Table 8-2 are substantially greater than those shown in Table 8-3. The reason is this: The income statement in the latter shows the retained earnings during only one year, 1991. In contrast, the balance sheet in Table 8-2 shows all retained earnings accumulated over the entire lifetime of the company.

Most of Northern Telecom's costs are reasonably straightforward. The company pays wages to its workforce, buys materials from outside suppliers, and spends large sums on research and development. These costs are included in items 3(a) and 3(c) in Table 8-3. However, one cost item, ***depreciation*** (line 3(b)), needs to be explained. Depreciation is a way of spreading out the costs of plant and equipment used by a firm.

## Depreciation

Consider the specific example of a machine acquired by Northern Telecom during 1991 for use on its production line. This machine did not wear out during 1991; it will continue to be used in coming years. Therefore, in calculating the cost of production in 1991, it would be misleading to count the full purchase price of the machine. Instead, only a fraction is

**TABLE 8-3 Northern Telecom Income Statement for the Year 1991 (Simplified; millions of dollars)**

| | | |
|---|---|---|
| 1. Sales revenue | | $8,183 |
| 2. Investment income* | | 102 |
| 3. Less: Costs of operations | | 7,354 |
| (a) Research and development costs | $ 948 | |
| (b) Depreciation | 485 | |
| (c) Wages, salaries, and other operating costs | 5,921 | |
| 4. Less: Interest costs | | 221 |
| 5. Earnings (profit) before taxes (1 + 2 − 3 − 4) | | 710 |
| 6. Less: Corporation income taxes | | 195 |
| 7. Net earnings (net profit) (5 − 6) | | 515 |
| (a) Dividends | 97 | |
| (b) Retained earnings | 418 | |

*Source:* Northern Telecommunications Ltd., *Annual Report 1991.*
*Includes earnings on equity in associated companies.

counted as a cost during 1991, with other fractions being allocated to future years while the machine is still in use.

The most straightforward way to allocate the cost of a machine is to estimate its expected life, and then spread the cost evenly over the lifetime. For example, if a $10,000 machine were expected to last five years, then depreciation would be $2000 in each of these years.

Depreciation accounting is not an exact science. Not only does the useful lifetime of a machine depend on physical wear and tear, but it also depends on obsolescence, which cannot be accurately forecast. Even if a machine could be permanently maintained in brand-new condition, it would eventually become obsolete; that is, its useful life would end as new and more efficient machines became available.

However, an even greater complication arises because of the tax laws. Note that depreciation is a cost that is subtracted before taxable income is calculated (Table 8-3). As a result, firms have an incentive to take their depreciation as soon as the law permits. The more depreciation they take, the lower is their taxable income, and therefore the lower is their tax. If the government speeds up—or *accelerates*—the rate at which firms are allowed to depreciate plant and equipment, it can encourage them to invest and expand.

> *Depreciation* is an element of cost. It is either (1) an estimate of the decline in the value of plant or equipment during the year, because of wear and obsolescence; or (2) the amount that tax laws allow business to count as a cost of using plant or equipment during the year.

## ACCOUNTING COST VS. OPPORTUNITY COST

Although economists often make use of the information provided in firms' income statements, the concept of cost (and of profits) used by economists is not quite the same as that of accountants. From the viewpoint of an economist, the basic principle in defining cost is that *resources have alternative uses*. We have already encountered this principle — the principle of ***opportunity cost***—when we discussed the production possibilities curve in Chapter 2. Thus in Figure 2-2, page 35, the opportunity cost, from the point of view of society, of producing more clothing was that it forced us to make do with less food. (In the simple two-good economy considered in the example, production of additional clothing could only be accomplished by transferring some productive resources from the food industry.) Similarly, we can argue that from the viewpoint of the owner of a firm, the true cost of using a productive resource in the firm is the value or return that the resource could get in its best alternative use. This cost need not be identical to the explicit out-of-pocket costs recorded in conventional accounts.

To see the distinction, consider an example. Suppose you have a friend who operates a store, and she asks you to study her business. The breakdown of her accounting costs in column (a) of Table 8-4 suggests that she has a good thing going. With revenue of $500,000 and costs of $420,000, she is earning an accounting profit of $80,000.

However, you dig more deeply. You discover that she could earn a $50,000 salary by accepting a job from an insurance company. This is an ***implicit cost***

**TABLE 8-4 Measurement of Costs and Profits (thousands of dollars)**

| (a) By accountants | | |
|---|---|---|
| Total revenue | | $500 |
| Costs (out-of-pocket) | | |
| Labour | $ 40 | |
| Materials | 350 | |
| Rent | 30 | |
| Total costs | 420 | 420 |
| Accounting profit | | $ 80 |

| (b) By economists | | |
|---|---|---|
| Total revenue | | $500 |
| Explicit (out-of-pocket) costs | | |
| Labour | $ 40 | |
| Materials | 350 | |
| Rent | 30 | |
| Implicit costs (income forgone) | | |
| Owner's salary | 50 | |
| Normal profit | 20 | |
| Total costs | 490 | 490 |
| Economic (above-normal) profit | | $ 10 |

(or ***imputed cost***) because it is not paid out-of-pocket. But we must include it, as we have done in column (b), or we would not have an adequate picture of the true economic costs in operating this business — that is, the cost of all the resources used, including her own time. And we would not be able to judge whether she is doing as well in this business as she could in another activity, namely, working for the insurance company.

In Table 8-4, opportunity costs include *both* the explicit out-of-pocket costs and the implicit costs. The explicit out-of-pocket costs are opportunity costs; for example, the $30,000 in rent is the going price for using the store. If your friend does not use the store, some other retailer will. Similarly, $40,000 is the going price for labour; it represents what the employees could earn in alternative jobs. The implicit cost of $50,000, representing the salary that she has to forgo in order to run her store, is also an opportunity cost.

Opportunity cost indicates *how much an input must be paid to keep it in its present use*. For example, your friend must earn $50,000—her opportunity cost — or she will have an incentive to shift out of her present activity into the higher-return insurance business. (Incidentally, your friend may have strong non-monetary preferences for running her own store, such as the freedom to be her own boss. In such circumstances, she might be willing to stay in retailing even if she didn't cover her full $50,000 opportunity cost. Although such non-monetary motives may be important, we ignore them in the simplified story presented here.)

You also discover that your friend has other opportunity costs that must be included in column (b). For example, she has some of her own funds tied up in this business. What would be her best alternative use of these funds? She indicates that if she did not have to use her own savings in the business, she would invest them in a retirement savings plan, in which she would expect them to yield an annual return of $20,000. This $20,000 represents the *opportunity cost of the capital* she has tied up in the business. A corporation or other kind of firm would usually have to earn an accounting profit at least equal to the owners' opportunity cost of capital in order to stay in business. For this reason, economists refer to this return as ***normal profit***.

We emphasize that whenever we draw a cost curve in later chapters, *we include not only explicit out-of-pocket accounting costs, but also implicit costs, such as normal profit.*

Therefore, in our example, costs are the full $490,000 shown in column (b) of Table 8-4. This broad definition means that costs tell us how much all the resources employed by the firm could be earning elsewhere. Since her $500,000 of revenues exceed this $490,000 cost, she has earned ***above-normal profit*** or ***economic profit*** of $10,000. To an economist, the word "profit" means above-normal profit unless otherwise stated. It is the $10,000 above-normal profit that allows you to judge that your friend does indeed have a good thing going. Her business not only provides her an appropriate $50,000 income for her own time and an appropriate return for the capital she has invested, but also provides an additional $10,000. If the existing firms in an industry are making such above-normal profits, there is an incentive for other entrepreneurs to move into this business, to get in on a good thing — as we shall see in detail in Chapter 10.

Now suppose that salaries in other jobs increase. Specifically, suppose the insurance company increases its offer to your friend from $50,000 to $65,000. When column (b) is accordingly recalculated, the $10,000 of above-normal profit becomes an economic loss of $5000. Even though your friend still earns an income from her business, she is no longer able to earn as much as in her best alternative activity. As long as she views this alternative line of work as equally interesting, she has an incentive to move.

Thus, *economic profit* (or loss) *provides a signal, indicating whether resources are being attracted to* (or repelled from) *an activity*.

## KEY POINTS

1. There are three forms of business organization: the sole proprietorship, the partnership, and the corporation.
2. Sole proprietorships and partnerships are simple and flexible. On the other hand, corporations also have advantages: (a) limited liability; (b) automatic continuity, even if one or more of the owners should die; and (c) better access to funds for financing growth.

3. A corporation can obtain financing by issuing (selling) common stock. All three types of businesses may raise funds by borrowing. Large corporations, however, find it easier than sole proprietorships or partnerships to borrow. They may do so by issuing bonds, notes, or commercial paper.
4. The purchaser of securities balances three important objectives: high return, low risk, and high liquidity.
5. A company that issues new securities also tries to find the best balance among three objectives: (1) to keep the return of the corporation's shareholders as high as possible, (2) to avoid risk, and (3) to assure the availability of money when needed.
6. In general, bonds are less risky than common stocks for buyers of securities. However, it is more risky for corporations to issue bonds or other debt than it is to issue new stock, since interest on the debt is a legal obligation. If the corporation doesn't pay interest, it may be forced into bankruptcy. However, the corporation can cut dividends on its stock.
7. When corporations increase their debts, they thereby increase their leverage; that is, they increase their ratio of debt to net worth. While this raises their potential gain, it also increases their risk of bankruptcy, since they must make interest and principal payments no matter how bad business is.
8. Because stocks and bonds represent claims on future profits or interest payments, the evaluation of the issuer's prospects are extremely important for anyone buying a security. To help protect the purchaser, provincial securities commissions require corporations to make relevant information available to the public.
9. By cost, economists mean "opportunity" cost. Thus, economists include not only the explicit accounting costs, but also implicit costs, such as the normal profit on capital invested in the enterprise.
10. After all such opportunity costs have been covered, any remaining economic profit (that is, above-normal profit) provides an indication of how much more resources are earning in this activity than in the next best alternative. If present firms are making such a profit, resources are attracted into this industry. On the other hand, if present firms are not covering their opportunity costs — that is, if they are suffering an economic loss—then resources are encouraged to move out.

## KEY TERMS

**sole proprietorship**
**partnership**
**unlimited/limited liability**
**corporation**
**common stock/shares**
**equity (ownership)**
**double taxation of dividends**
**dividend tax credit**
**principal (or face value) of a bond**
**holding company**
**mutual funds**
**yield (or return)**
**risk**
**liquidity**
**leverage**
**line of credit**
**risk premium**
**balance sheet**
**income statement (profit-and-loss statement)**
**assets**
**liabilities**
**net worth**
**book value**
**depreciation**
**implicit (imputed) cost**
**opportunity cost**
**normal profit**
**above-normal (economic) profit**

## PROBLEMS

8-1. Even though many corporations are large, a corporation may be very small, with only one owner. For example, a small building contractor may set up a corporation. Can you explain why?

8-2. Suppose you are an investment adviser, and a 50-year-old person comes to you for advice on how to invest $100,000 for retirement. What advice would you give? What advice would you give to a young couple who want to temporarily invest $20,000 that they expect to use for a down payment on a home two years from now?

8-3. If a corporation increases its leverage, what are the advantages and/or disadvantages for:

(a) the owner of a share of the corporation's stock;

(b) the owner of a $100,000 bond of the corporation?

8-4. Suppose you own shares in a mining company that is planning to raise additional funds in order to finance production in a new mine in a remote area of Northern Ontario. In your opinion, the new mine is going to be much more profitable than most people believe.

(a) How would you like to see the company raise its additional funds: (i) by issuing 20-year bonds? (ii) by selling preferred shares? (iii) by issuing additional common stock? Explain your answer.

(b) How would your answer change if you thought the new mine was going to be much *less* profitable than most people believed?

8-5. "Fairness requires that interest income received by individuals should be taxed at the same rate as dividend income. Moreover, fairness also requires that the profits of corporations should be taxed at roughly the same rate as the income of individuals." Do you agree or disagree? Explain your reasoning.

8-6. In Table 8-4, the accounting cost for labour in column (a) is the same as the economic cost in column (b). Suppose now that your friend misjudges the labour market and pays workers $500 per week when she could get them for $350. What is the "economic cost" of a worker in this case?

8-7. Suppose a farmer in Saskatchewan provides a statement of his cost to his income tax accountant. Are there any opportunity costs that he is likely to omit? Explain.

CHAPTER

# 9 THE COSTS OF PRODUCTION

*For which of you, desiring to build a tower, does not first sit down and count the cost. . .?*

*Luke 14:28, RSV*

Businesses make profits by selling at a price that exceeds cost. In the pursuit of profits, business executives thus have two major concerns: (1) What price can they get? (2) How do they keep costs down while still maintaining or improving quality?

The following chapters (10 to 13) will show how price depends on the type of market in which a business operates. Does the business have many competitors or does it have the market to itself? But first, we investigate the costs of production in this chapter.

## THE SHORT RUN AND THE LONG

Like consumers, business firms have choices to make. One of the most important has to do with the way in which goods are produced: What *combination of inputs* will a firm use in the productive process? For example, will an automobile manufacturer be able to produce most cheaply by using a highly automated assembly line, with a great deal of equipment and only a few workers? Will the wheat farmer use a lot of fertilizer on each hectare, or produce the wheat using more land and less fertilizer?

However, the freedom of action of a business is severely limited in the short run. For example, the way in which Inco Ltd. of Sudbury produces nickel this year is largely determined by decisions already made in the past. Inco already has in place the mine shafts, smelters, and transport equipment that it will use in this year's production; it is too late now to order new machines or open up new mines. In the short run, its decisions are limited: How many tonnes of nickel will it produce, and how many workers will it employ to produce it? Over the longer run, of course, Inco has much more freedom. If it is making decisions on what it will be doing five or ten years from now, it will have time to expand its capital by opening up new mines or factories and by buying new equipment. Or it can reduce its capital stock by deciding not to replace obsolete plant or equipment.

Thus, economists make a distinction between the ***short run*** and the ***long run***. In the short run, one or more inputs are fixed. For example, Inco has only a fixed quantity of ore deposits and mining equipment, and a farmer has only a fixed quantity of land. In the long run, a firm can pick from a full menu of choices. It can choose to produce in a ***capital-intensive*** manner—with many machines and few workers — or in a ***labour-intensive*** manner — with many workers and few machines.

The *short run* is the period when one or more inputs are fixed.

The *long run* is the period when the firm is able to change the quantities of all inputs, including capital and land.

The short run is not defined as any specific number of weeks, months, or years. Instead, it is the time period when plant, equipment, or some other input is fixed, *whatever* that period might be. In some industries, the short run may last many years. For example, it takes a decade or more to design and construct a large nuclear power plant. In other industries, the short run may be just a matter of days. For example, a student entrepreneur can buy a word processor quickly, and thus acquire the capital equipment to set up business typing term papers. Furthermore, the short run may be briefer for an expanding firm than for a contracting firm. An expanding firm may be able to acquire new equipment quickly, while a contracting firm may be able to reduce its capital stock only slowly. There may be no market in which it can sell its used machinery, and its capital stock may take years to wear out.

## COSTS IN THE SHORT RUN

In the short run, output can be raised by increasing the quantities of variable inputs, such as labour, raw materials, and parts and supplies bought from other businesses. Because some inputs (plant and equipment) are fixed in the short run, while others are variable, a firm's ***total costs*** may be divided into two components: (1) ***fixed costs*** and (2) ***variable costs***.

### 1. Fixed Costs or Overhead Costs

Fixed costs (FC) are the costs that do not change as output changes. They are incurred even if no output is produced at all. For example, even if no output is produced, the firm will still have to pay interest on the funds it has borrowed to buy equipment or to construct buildings. Factories and equipment will depreciate even if they stand unused. And firms will still have to buy insurance against fire and other risks.

Table 9-1 shows the short-run costs of a hypothetical manufacturer of shoes. Note that fixed costs (column 2) remain constant at $35, regardless of the quantity of output *q* (column 1).

### 2. Variable Costs

On the other hand, variable costs (VC) do increase as output increases, since the firm uses more variable inputs, such as labour, raw materials, and electricity.

> *Fixed costs* (FC) are those costs that do not change as output changes.
>
> *Variable costs* (VC) are those costs that *do* change as output changes.
>
> *Total costs* (TC) are the sum of fixed costs and variable costs: TC = FC + VC.

## Marginal Cost

One of the decisions that businesses face is: "Should we expand our production?" In this decision, a key role is played by ***marginal cost*** (MC)—that is, the *additional* cost as output increases by one unit.

> *Marginal cost* (MC) is the increase in total cost when one additional unit is produced.

Marginal cost is calculated in column 5 of Table 9-1. For example, as the firm's output increases from 6 to 7 units, its total cost in column 4 increases from $190 to $245, or by $55. Thus, the marginal cost of the seventh pair of shoes is $55. Similarly, the marginal cost of the sixth unit is calculated as $190 − $150 or $40.[1]

[1] Sometimes a firm makes decisions in batches, rather than one unit at a time. For example, a small pharmaceutical firm might want to decide whether to increase production by 1000 bottles of aspirin from, say, 200,000 bottles to 201,000. If the additional costs are $200, then the marginal cost over this range is 20 cents per bottle —that is, $200/1000.

**TABLE 9-1 Short-run Costs of a Hypothetical Firm Producing Shoes**

| (1) Quantity produced (pairs) *q* | (2) Fixed cost FC | (3) Variable cost VC | (4) Total cost TC = FC + VC = (2) + (3) | (5) Marginal cost MC = change in total cost | (6) Average total cost ATC = TC ÷ *q* = (4) ÷ (1) | (7) Average fixed cost AFC = FC ÷ *q* = (2) ÷ (1) | (8) Average variable cost AVC = VC ÷ *q* = (3) ÷ (1) |
|---|---|---|---|---|---|---|---|
| 0 | $35 | 0 | $ 35 | | — | — | — |
| | | | | $ 59 − $ 35 = $24 | | | |
| 1 | 35 | $ 24 | 59 | | $59 | $35 | $24 |
| | | | | 75 − 59 = 16 | | | |
| 2 | 35 | 40 | 75 | | 37.50 | 17.50 | 20 |
| | | | | 95 − 75 = 20 | | | |
| 3 | 35 | 60 | 95 | | 31.67 | 11.67 | 20 |
| | | | | 120 − 95 = 25 | | | |
| 4 | 35 | 85 | 120 | | 30 | 8.75 | 21.25 |
| | | | | 150 − 120 = 30 | | | |
| 5 | 35 | 115 | 150 | | 30 | 7 | 23 |
| | | | | 190 − 150 = 40 | | | |
| 6 | 35 | 155 | 190 | | 31.67 | 5.83 | 25.83 |
| | | | | 245 − 190 = 55 | | | |
| 7 | 35 | 210 | 245 | | 35 | 5 | 30 |

## Average Total Cost

The firm may also be interested in its cost *per unit* of output. At an output of 5 units, the per-unit cost or ***average total cost*** (ATC) is simply the $150 in total costs divided by the 5 units, or $30 per unit. Similarly, average total cost can be calculated at any other output by dividing total cost by the number of units. This is done in column 6 of Table 9-1.

> *Average total cost* (ATC), also known as *average cost* (AC), is total cost divided by the number of units produced.

We have already seen that total cost can be broken down into fixed cost and variable cost. Similarly, average cost can be broken down into its two components:

**Average cost = average fixed cost + average variable cost**

Average fixed cost (AFC) is fixed cost divided by output. In the example in Table 9-1, fixed cost is $35. Thus, at an output of 5 units, the firm's average fixed cost in column 7 is $35/5 or $7. Similarly, *average variable cost* (AVC) is variable cost divided by output. At an output of 5 units, the firm's variable cost is $115. Therefore, its average variable cost (column 8) is $115/5 or $23.

> *Average fixed cost* (AFC) is fixed cost divided by output.
>
> *Average variable cost* (AVC) is variable cost divided by output.

**ATC = AFC + AVC**

The various costs in Table 9-1 are reproduced in Figure 9-1. In panel (a), the short black arrow shows fixed cost; this cost remains constant at $35 regardless of output. To this fixed cost, we add the variable cost to get the total cost. For example, at an output

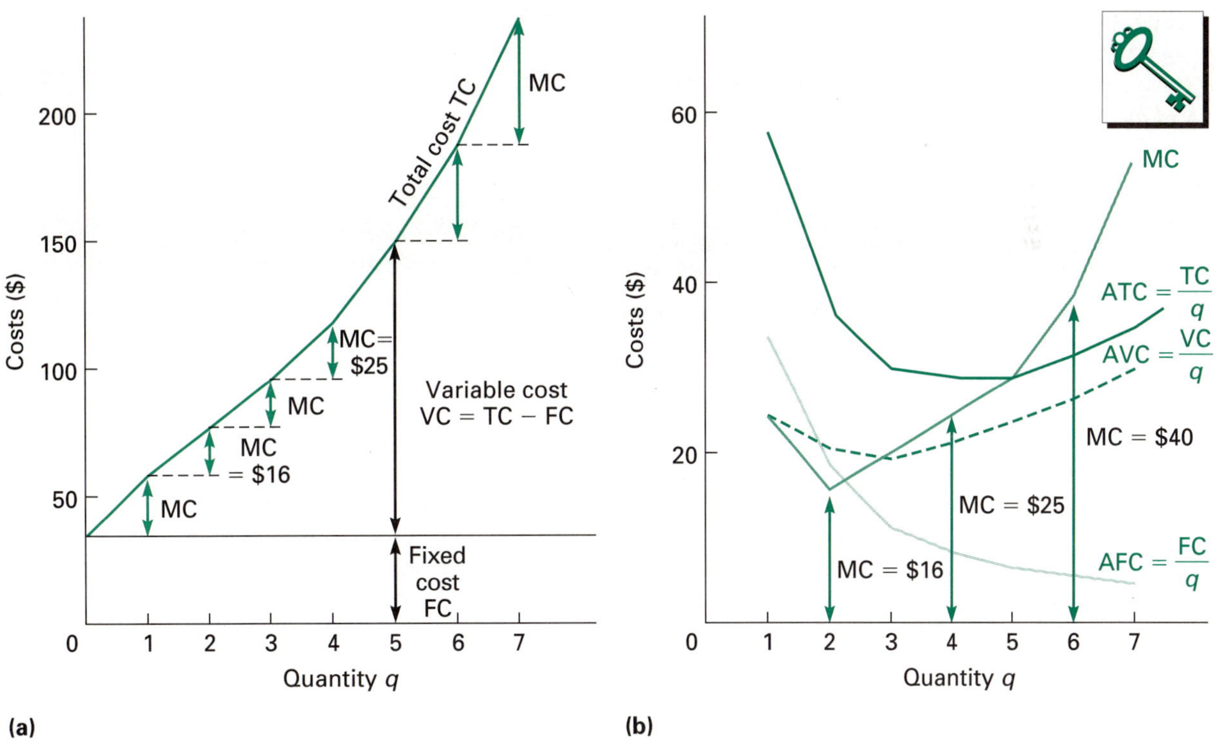


**FIGURE 9-1 Short-run costs.**
This figure illustrates the short-run costs of the firm in Table 9-1. In panel (a), total cost is the sum of fixed cost and variable cost. Marginal cost indicates how much total cost is increasing, and is shown by the set of coloured arrows in panel (a) or in panel (b). In panel (b), average total cost is the total cost divided by the number of units produced.

of 5 units, variable cost is $115, as shown by the long black arrow. The important concept of marginal cost MC is illustrated with the coloured arrows; MC shows how total cost increases as each successive unit of production is added.

Panel (b) illustrates average costs. Its vertical scale is stretched out, compared to panel (a), in order to make it easier to read. Note that average total cost falls at first, and then eventually rises. Average variable cost also traces out a U shape. In contrast, average fixed cost (AFC) falls continuously as output increases. It must: After all, fixed cost — $35, in this case — is being spread out over more and more units as output increases.

Note that panel (a) shows total cost and its components, while panel (b) shows the various average cost curves. Marginal cost, which will play a key role in future chapters, is shown in both panels. For example, the marginal cost of the second unit is $16; that's how much total cost increases in panel (a) when the second unit is produced. In panel (b), the marginal cost curve is constructed by extracting the MC arrows from panel (a), and graphing them. (The MC arrows are longer in panel (b), since the vertical axis is stretched out.)

## THE RELATIONSHIP BETWEEN AVERAGE AND MARGINAL COSTS

In Figure 9-1(b), observe that, whenever marginal cost is below the average total cost curve, the ATC is falling. This *must* be so; the low marginal cost drags down the average. When the marginal cost is above the average cost, it pulls the average up; the average cost curve rises. Finally, when the marginal cost equals the average cost — as it does for the fifth unit — then marginal cost has a neutral effect. It neither pulls the average up nor drags it down. Average cost is flat; it has reached its lowest point. Thus, *the marginal cost curve cuts through the lowest point on the average total cost curve*. (The same is true of average variable cost: MC cuts through its lowest point, too.)

This relationship between average and marginal is a general one; it applies to more than cost curves. For example, if you have an average grade of 80 on your first two chemistry exams, a lower grade of 65 on your third exam will drag your average down to 75 (that is, 80 + 80 + 65, divided by 3). On the other hand, if you come through with a high grade of 95 on that third, "marginal" exam, you will pull your average up. Finally, if your third exam grade is 80, this will leave your average score unchanged at 80. Box 9-1 shows how the relationship between marginal and average also holds in baseball.

## THE SHORT-RUN PRODUCTION FUNCTION

Costs of production depend on two things: (1) the amount of inputs used in the productive process, and (2) the prices of these inputs.

The first of these points — the relationship between the quantity of inputs and the amount of output — is summed up in the ***production function***. Specifically, the production function shows how the quantity of output changes as the quantities of inputs are changed. In the long-run production function, the quantities of *all* inputs can be changed. However, in the short run, some factors — such as plant and equipment — are fixed in quantity. Thus, the short-run production function shows how output changes as the quantities of labour and other variable inputs change, while the quantities of other factors — such as plant and equipment — are fixed.

The *production function* shows how the quantity of output changes as the quantities of inputs change. In the production function, both output and inputs are measured in physical units (rather than dollars).

The *short-run production function* shows how output changes as the quantities of labour and other variable inputs change, while the quantities of other inputs — plant, equipment, and land — are fixed.

### Total, Average, and Marginal Product

The first three columns of Table 9-2 provide a simple, hypothetical example of a short-run production function for a bicycle factory that has only one variable factor of production, labour. The first column shows the number of units of labour; the second column shows the fixed quantity of capital input; and the third column shows the amount of output associated with each quantity of labour input. For example, if the firm employs 3 workers (column 1), its *total product* (TP) is 18 bicycles per week (column 3). To emphasize that total product is being measured in physical terms rather than dollars, it is sometimes called total *physical* product (TPP).

## APPLICATIONS AND ILLUSTRATIONS BOX 9-1

## Why a Firm's Costs Are Like a Baseball Player's Average

Late in the 1980 season, Kansas City's George Brett had the best chance to hit the magic .400 (40 hits in each 100 times at bat) since Ted Williams of the Boston Red Sox did it with .406 in 1941. The numbers below show Brett's batting performance during one week in September. In the first three games against Chicago and Detroit, he batted a disappointing .250 (one hit in each four times at bat). Since this marginal performance (shown in colour in the figure) was below his average in the .380s, it pulled his average down. But in the next three games, his fortunes improved: He batted .500 or better. Since this marginal performance was above his average, it pulled his average up.

Did Brett go on to hit .400? Although the last three games shown here started him off on a hitting streak that carried him over .400 for a week in late September, he couldn't maintain the pace. He finished the season with .390.

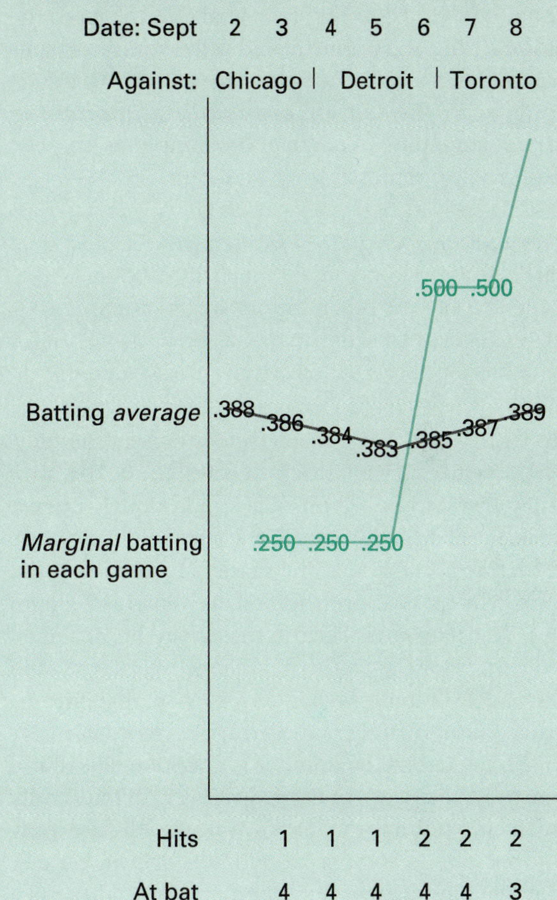


From the total product, we can calculate ***marginal product*** (MP) and ***average product*** (AP). The marginal product of labour is shown in column 4; it is the *change* in output as one more unit of labour is added. For example, when the labour input increases from 3 to 4 units, output increases from 18 to 21 bicycles. The MP of the fourth unit of labour is, therefore, 3 bicycles. Average product is shown in column 5; it is the total product divided by the number of units of labour input.

The *marginal product* (MP) of an input is the increase in the quantity of output when one more unit of the input is added, with the amount of other inputs held constant.

Figure 9-2 displays the numbers in the first five columns of Table 9-2 graphically. In panel (b), we again see that when a marginal measure is above the average, the average is rising; when the marginal is below the average, the average is falling; when the marginal equals the average, the average is flat. However, there is one notable difference between Figure 9-2(b) and Figure 9-1(b). The average cost curve of Figure 9-1(b) traced out a U shape; the average product (AP) curve in Figure 9-2(b) is an *inverted* U. Thus, the AP curve is flat at its *top*, not at its bottom; the MP curve cuts through the peak of the average product curve when 3 workers are employed. The earlier conclusion can, therefore, be sharpened up: A marginal curve cuts through either the lowest *or* the highest point of an average curve.

## The Law of Diminishing Returns

Observe in Figure 9-2(b) that although the marginal product of the second worker is above the first, the addition of the third, fourth, and fifth workers results in smaller and smaller additions to output. This is in keeping with the ***law of eventually diminishing returns***, sometimes known more simply as the law of diminishing returns.

> The *law of eventually diminishing returns*: If more units of one input (such as labour) are added while all other inputs (such as capital) are held constant, the marginal product of the variable input (labour) must eventually decline.

To explain this law, consider more closely the bicycle firm with a given stock of capital. As the firm initially hires more labour, each additional worker increases the firm's output by a substantial amount. Indeed, it is possible that the marginal product of the second worker is above the first, as shown in Figure 9-2(b). The reason is that the plant may be designed for several workers, so that a single worker would waste a lot of time walking from one machine to another. But ultimately, as the firm hires more workers and its fixed capital equipment is operated closer and closer to capacity, an additional worker will add only a small amount to the firm's output. All the new employee can do is work on odd jobs or wait for one of the machines to be free. In other words, there is a decrease in the marginal product of labour. One can envision a situation where there are so many workers that some get in the way and actually hamper production. In this case, the marginal product would be negative, as shown when the eighth worker is added in Figure 9-2(b).

The law of diminishing returns is easily confirmed in agriculture. As more workers are added to a constant amount of land — say, 100 hectares — the marginal product of labour *must* eventually fall. If it did not, then the entire world could be fed from this single farm — or, for that matter, from your back garden.

In Part 4 of this book, we shall see that the law of diminishing returns is a key to explaining wages and other income payments. For now, it is important because it explains why marginal costs must ultimately rise.

# MARGINAL PRODUCT AND MARGINAL COST

At the beginning of the previous section on the short-run production function, we noted that costs of production depend on two things: (1) the amount of inputs used in the productive process and (2) the prices of these inputs. Having dealt with the production function, we find it a short step to bring the prices of inputs into the calculations in order to find costs. In the last column of Table 9-2, marginal cost is calculated on the assumption that the cost of hiring a worker is $300 per week.

Note that the first worker has a marginal product of 5 bicycles. Since it costs $300 per week to hire that worker (shown in column 6), the marginal cost of those 5 bicycles is $60 each. Similarly, the marginal cost of bicycles is $100 when the fourth worker is added — that is, the $300 of the worker divided by the 3 additional bicycles produced.

Thus, we establish a significant relationship between marginal product and marginal cost. Because the marginal product eventually must decrease, short-run marginal cost must eventually increase.

## The U-Shaped Average Cost Curve

We can now explain in detail why the short-run average cost curve of the typical firm is U-shaped. It slopes downward at the beginning because fixed costs are being spread over more units; fixed costs per unit of output decline rapidly, as illustrated earlier in Figure 9-1(b). However, as output increases, marginal cost must eventually rise. Indeed, if output is increased to the point where machines and other equipment are being fully utilized, marginal cost will rise very high, and will certainly exceed average cost. As a result, average cost will increase. To sum up: The spreading out of fixed costs works toward an initial reduction in average costs. But, as output increases further, rising marginal costs eventually take over and pull the average cost curve upward, giving it a U shape.

# COSTS IN THE LONG RUN

Although the quantity of capital is fixed in the short run, it can be changed in the long run. In the long run, there are no fixed costs; all costs can vary. The firm has to decide not only how much labour it will use; it also has to decide on the amount of plant and equipment.

**TABLE 9-2 Short-run Production Function of a Hypothetical Firm Making Bicycles**

| Units of Labour L (1) | Units of Capital K (2) | Total Product TP (3) | Marginal Product of Labour MP (4) = Δ (3) | Average Product of Labour AP (5) = (3) ÷ (1) | Wage per Worker *W* (6) | Marginal Cost MC (7) = (6) ÷ (4) |
|---|---|---|---|---|---|---|
| 0 | 1 | 0 | | — | — | — |
| | | | 5 | | | |
| 1 | 1 | 5 | | 5 | $300 | $ 60 |
| | | | 7 | | | |
| 2 | 1 | 12 | | 6 | 300 | 42.86 |
| | | | 6 | | | |
| 3 | 1 | 18 | | 6 | 300 | 50 |
| | | | 3 | | | |
| 4 | 1 | 21 | | 5.25 | 300 | 100 |
| | | | 2 | | | |
| 5 | 1 | 23 | | 4.6 | 300 | 150 |
| | | | 1 | | | |
| 6 | 1 | 24 | | 4 | 300 | 300 |
| | | | 0 | | | |
| 7 | 1 | 24 | | 3.43 | 300 | — |
| | | | −1 | | | |
| 8 | 1 | 23 | | 2.88 | 300 | — |

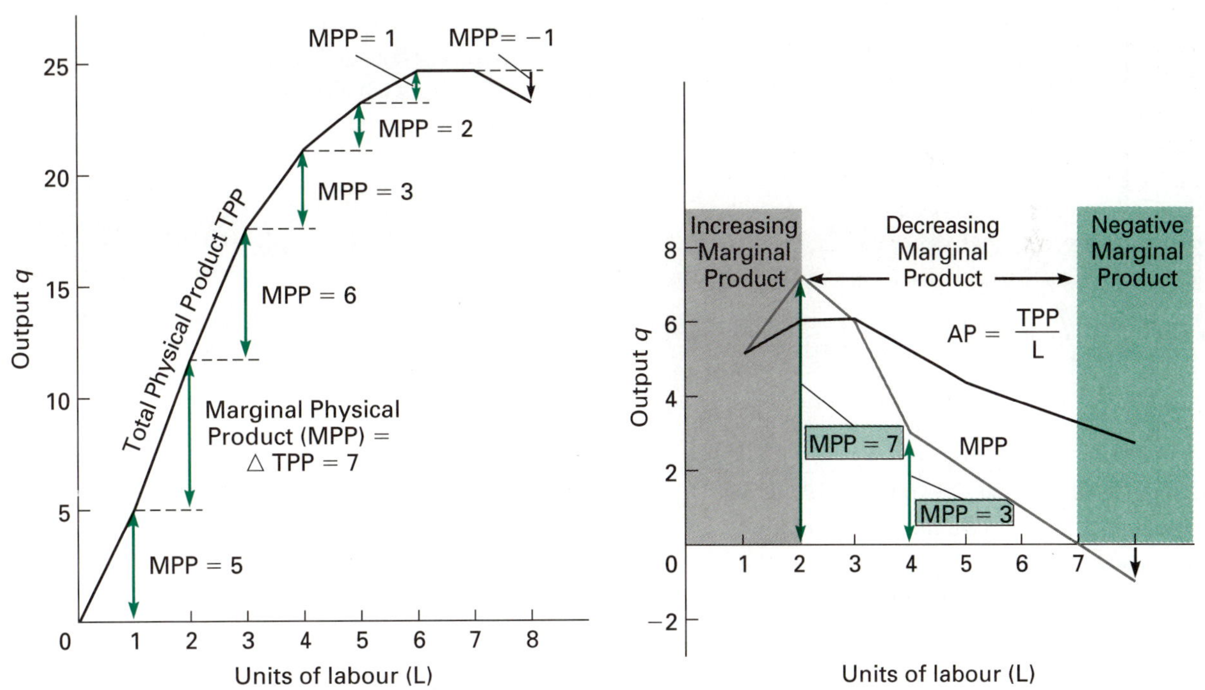


(a) (b)

**FIGURE 9-2 Total and marginal product curves.** In panel (a), marginal product measures how much total product changes when one more unit of labour is used. Panel (b) illustrates the average and marginal product of labour of the hypothetical firm shown in Table 9-2.

Consider, for example, a small bicycle company that has been producing a low output of 100 units per week. Suppose that this firm now wants to expand from 100 units to a larger output, say, 140 per week. It could do so by hiring more labour while continuing to use its present small stock of capital. But if it does this, it will face diminishing returns to the additional labour; as a consequence, average cost will rise.

An alternative way to expand output is to *both* hire more labour, *and* increase the amount of capital by installing more machinery and equipment. By using more capital, the firm increases its fixed costs. But because a larger amount of machinery and equipment makes each worker more productive, fewer workers will be needed to produce a given amount of output. This is illustrated in Figure 9-3. When the firm only has a small amount of capital (say, 2 units), the short-run production function is given by the curve labelled $TPP_1$. With this amount of capital equipment, as many as 80 workers are necessary to produce an output of 140 units (point *A*). When the firm's capital is increased (to 6 units, say), the short-run production function shifts up to $TPP_2$. As a result, it is now possible to produce 140 units with a smaller number of workers (at point *B* on $TPP_2$, the number of workers employed is only 30). The smaller number of workers means that the *variable* cost of producing this amount of output is smaller. Thus, expanding the amount of capital equipment involves trading an increase in fixed costs for a reduction in variable costs.

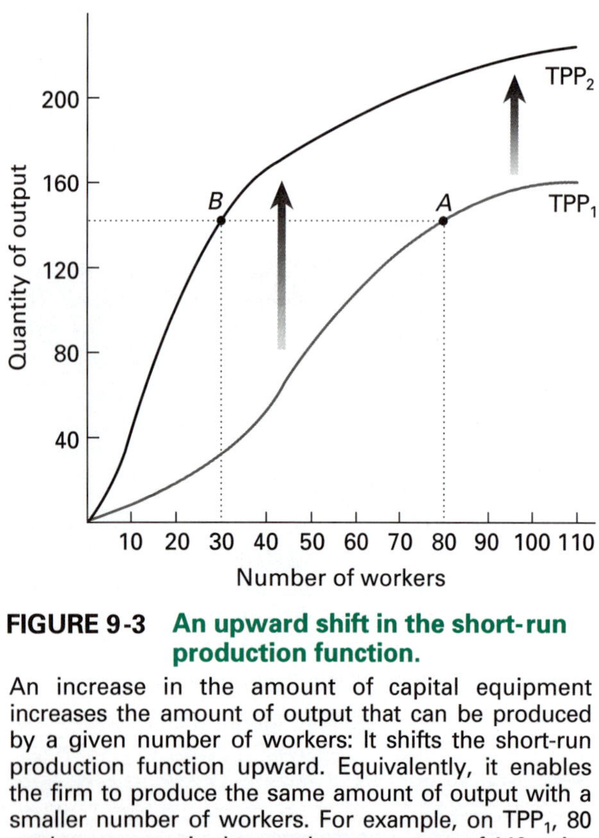


**FIGURE 9-3 An upward shift in the short-run production function.**

An increase in the amount of capital equipment increases the amount of output that can be produced by a given number of workers: It shifts the short-run production function upward. Equivalently, it enables the firm to produce the same amount of output with a smaller number of workers. For example, on $TPP_1$, 80 workers are required to produce an output of 140 units. On $TPP_2$, with a larger amount of capital, only 30 workers are needed to produce 140 units.

An alternative way to illustrate the idea that different combinations of capital and labour can be used to produce a given amount of output is shown in Figure 9-4. Point *A* is the initial position where the firm has a small amount of capital (2 units) only. As Figure 9-3 showed, in order to produce 140 units per week with this small capital stock, the firm has to employ 80 workers. At point *B*, on the other hand, the firm uses a large amount of capital (6 units); because this makes each worker more productive, an output level of 140 units per week can now be reached with only 30 workers.

Points *A* and *B* are not, of course, the only combinations of capital and labour that can be used to produce 140 units. By finding other combinations, we can construct a continuous curve such as the one labelled $q_1$ in Figure 9-4. Because each point on a curve of this kind shows a combination of inputs that yield the *same* output, it is referred to as an ***equal-output curve*** or an ***isoquant***.

On an *isoquant* (equal-output curve), each point represents a possible combination of inputs that the firm can choose to produce a given quantity of output.

The isoquant labelled $q_1$ in Figure 9-4 corresponds to a given output of 140 units per week. If we want to produce a larger amount (say, 200 units per week), we must obviously use more of one or both inputs. Therefore, all points on an isoquant corresponding to an output of more than 140 units must lie above and to the right of the $q_1$ isoquant; the isoquant labelled $q_2$, corresponding to an output of 200 units per week is an example. By picking different quantities of output, we can generate a whole family of isoquants.

As you have probably noticed already, isoquants are similar to the indifference curves (or equal-utility curves) introduced in Chapter 7. Just as the indifference map in Figure 7-8 showed a whole family of

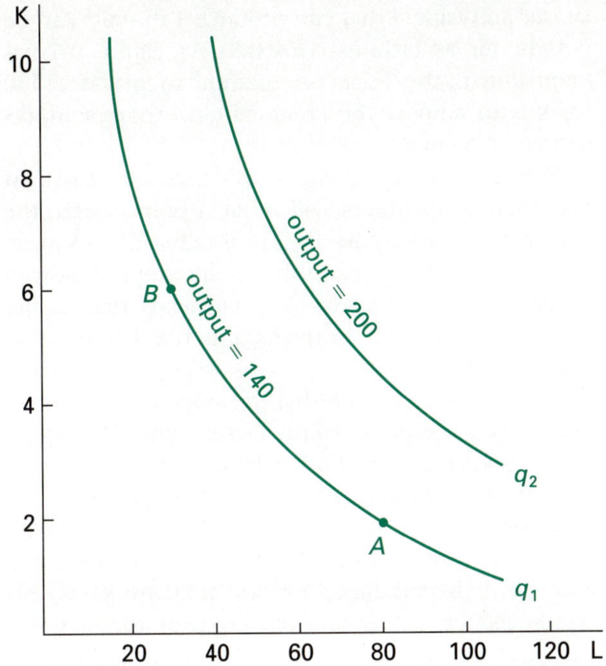


**FIGURE 9-4 Isoquants (equal-output curves).**
An isoquant shows different combinations of productive factors (capital and labour) that can be used to produce a given amount of output. At point *A*, 140 units of output are produced using 2 units of capital and 80 workers; alternatively, the same output can be produced using 6 units of capital and only 30 workers (point *B*).

Isoquants corresponding to larger amounts of output lie out further in the diagram. For example, the combinations of capital and labour needed to produce 200 units of output are shown by $q_2$, which is above and to the right of $q_1$.

indifference curves, each representing a higher level of utility as the household moved up and to the right from the origin, so the production function provides a whole set of equal-output curves that also form a hill. As the firm moves up and to the right, using more inputs, it reaches higher output levels.

In one respect, however, the equal-output curves of the producer contain more information than the indifference curves of the consumer: Each equal-output curve represents a *specific quantity* of output. For example, the two curves in Figure 9-4 correspond to output levels of 140 and 200 units respectively. On the other hand, all we know about indifference curves is whether they represent "higher" or "lower" levels of satisfaction. We don't know how many "units of utility" they represent.

## Finding the Least-cost Combination of Inputs

To find the least costly combination of inputs to produce a given quantity of output, the information in the isoquant diagram must be supplemented with information about input prices. If we know how much it costs to use one unit of labour, or one unit of capital services, we can calculate the total cost of purchasing the combination of inputs corresponding to any point in Figure 9-4. In particular, we can find the total cost of producing at any point on the isoquant $q_1$. The problem of finding the minimum cost of producing 140 units of output is therefore equivalent to the problem of finding the least-cost combination of inputs along this isoquant.

Diagrammatically, we can show the least-cost choice of inputs with the help of an ***iso-cost line*** (also referred to as an ***equal cost curve***). For example, suppose the cost of one unit of labour is \$1500 per month, while the monthly cost of using a machine is \$15,000. (This cost is calculated taking into account both the cost of financing the machine over its useful lifetime, and the cost of operating and maintaining it.) Since the cost of one worker is \$1500 per month, the total cost of employing 100 workers is \$150,000. But \$150,000 is also the cost of using 10 machines. Thus points *C* and *D* in Figure 9-5 represent the same total cost. Moreover, any point on a straight line joining *C* and *D* also represents a combination of labour and capital that together cost \$150,000. (For example, the cost of 50 workers and 5 machines at point *E* is also \$150,000 [(50 × \$1500) + (5 × \$15,000) = \$150,000].)

If we begin at a point such as *G* with a smaller number of workers, we get a new iso-cost line such as *FG* in Figure 9-5, representing combinations of labour and capital that can be bought for another, lower, total amount. (For example, the total cost of any combination along the iso-cost line *FG* is \$100,000.) However, as long as the prices of capital and labour remain unchanged, every iso-cost line will have the same slope. In Figure 9-5, the slope of both iso-cost lines is 0.1: The \$1500 that is saved when the firm employs one less worker would be enough to pay for 1/10 of one machine. Note that the slope directly reflects the prices of capital and labour services. Specifically, the slope of 0.1 in this example is

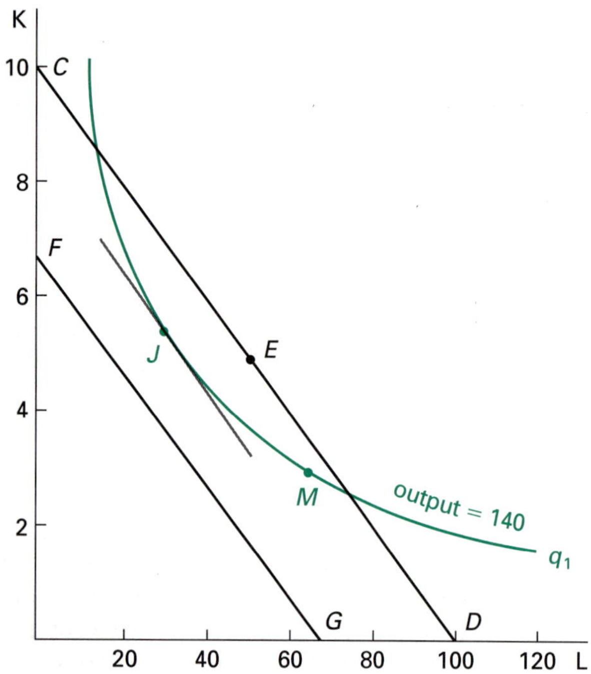


**FIGURE 9-5 Finding the least-cost combination of inputs.**

An iso-cost line shows different combinations of capital and labour services that can be bought for a given total cost. For example, when each worker is paid $1500 per month, and each machine costs $15,000 per month to use, each point on line *DC* (for example, point *E*) represents a total cost of $150,000.

Point *J* is the least-cost combination of capital and labour that can be used to produce an output of 140 units. Any other combination on the isoquant for an output of 140 lies above and to the right of the iso-cost line through point *J*.

just the ratio of the prices of labour and capital services: $1500/$15,000.

The isoquant $q_1$ in Figure 9-5 shows the various combinations of capital and labour that could be used to produce 140 units of output. It is immediately clear that it is possible to produce 140 units (the amount of output that can be produced by any combination of labour and capital on the isoquant $q_1$) at a lower cost than $150,000. For example, 140 units can be produced by a combination such as 67 units of labour and 3 units of capital (point *M* in Figure 9-5), which would cost only $145,500 ([67 × $1500] + [3 × $15,000]), and therefore is on a lower iso-cost line than the one corresponding to $150,000. On the other hand, it is not possible to produce 140 units at a cost of $100,000: None of the combinations of labour and capital that can produce 140 units can be bought for as little as $100,000. As Figure 9-5 has been drawn, the least-cost method to produce 140 units is to employ the combination of factor inputs shown at point *J*.

You can see from Figure 9-5 that the least-cost combination of inputs will be at a point where the lowest possible iso-cost line just touches the isoquant. As long as the isoquants have the smooth bowed shape shown in Figure 9-5, this means that at the least-cost point, the isoquant and the iso-cost line *have the same slope*.

We have already seen that the slope of the iso-cost line reflects the prices of the factor inputs. The slope of the isoquant, on the other hand, can be related to the *marginal products* of labour and capital. To see this, consider two points such as *N* and *O* in Figure 9-6. As we move from *N* to *O*, we decrease the amount of labour input by one unit. By itself, this would reduce the amount of output by the marginal

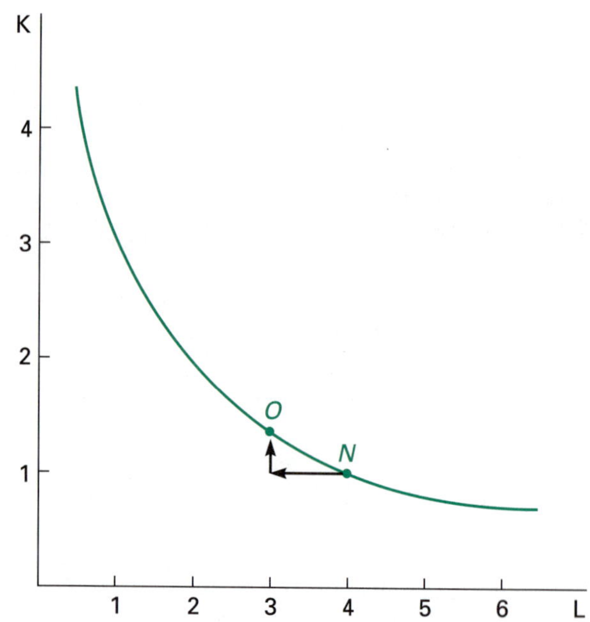


**FIGURE 9-6 The slope of the isoquant.**

Starting at point *N*, the loss of output if we reduce the amount of labour by one unit is just the marginal product of labour. To get back to the isoquant (at point *O*), the quantity of capital has to be increased by an amount that depends on the marginal product of capital. The slope of the isoquant equals the ratio of the marginal products $MP_L/MP_K$.

product of this labour unit. (By definition, the marginal product of the last unit of labour is the amount of extra output that it adds when it is hired; this has to be the same as the amount of output that is lost when it is withdrawn.) How many units of extra capital input do we need in order to get back to the original level of output (that is, to get back to the isoquant)? The answer depends on the marginal product of capital. For example, if the marginal product of labour is 10 and the marginal product of a machine is 40, we need approximately 0.25 additional units of capital services to compensate for the loss of one unit of labour. More generally, the slope of an isoquant at any combination of labour and capital inputs is:

$$\textbf{slope of isoquant} = \frac{\textbf{marginal product of labour}}{\textbf{marginal product of capital}}$$

(Note how similar this is to the discussion in Chapter 7. There, we saw that the slope of an indifference curve—the consumer's marginal rate of substitution, MRS—was equal to the ratio of the marginal utilities of the two goods. By analogy, the ratio of the marginal products of the two factors along an isoquant is sometimes referred to as the ***marginal rate of technical substitution***.)

In the earlier discussion, we saw that the slope of iso-cost lines such as those in Figure 9-5 is equal to the ratio of the prices of labour and capital. Suppose we denote the price of labour services by $w$, and the price of capital services by $r$. We then have the following conclusion: At the least-cost combination of inputs (where the slopes of the iso-cost line and the isoquant are the same), the ratio of the factor prices, $w/r$ is the same as the ratio of the marginal products, $MP_L/MP_K$.

**At the least-cost combination of labour and capital, the ratio of the marginal products of labour and capital equals the ratio of their prices:**

$$\frac{MP_L}{MP_K} = \frac{w}{r}$$

In the appendix to this chapter, we explain how this important result helps us understand how firms change their production techniques when factor prices change; it is also a result that will be important in the analysis of the markets for productive factors in later chapters.

## The Envelope Curve and the Best Combination of Inputs

The average total cost (ATC) curve in Figure 9-1(b) is a *short-run* curve: It is derived on the assumption that the amount of capital (and the amount of fixed cost associated with using this capital) is given and fixed. However, in the long run, the amount of capital can be varied. In general, the long-run average cost (LAC) curve (the curve that shows the minimum average cost of production for different amounts of output when capital as well as labour is allowed to vary) will look different from the short-run average cost (SAC) curves corresponding to fixed amounts of capital.

To see the relationship between LAC and SAC curves, let's look at a firm whose capital stock starts out at $K_0$ units (Figure 9-7). In the short run, the amount of capital is fixed: Whatever the amount of output the firm wants to produce, it can only use $K_0$ units of capital; the only way to increase output, say, is to increase the amount of labour, the variable factor.

Now consider three different levels of output, say 50, 100, and 150 units. The isoquants showing the various amounts of labour and capital that can be used to produce these amounts are also shown in Figure 9-7. If we know the per-unit prices of capital and labour services (so that we know the slope of the iso-cost lines in the figure), we can find the *hypothetical* least-cost combinations for producing 50, 100, and 150 units of output respectively. These points, which are shown as *A*, *B*, and *C* in the figure, provide information about long-run average cost. For example, if the iso-cost line going through point *A* represents a total cost of \$600, the height of the LAC curve at 50 units of output is \$12 (\$600/50 = \$12).

In the short run, however, points such as *A* and *C* in Figure 9-7 cannot be reached by the firm: In the short run, the amount of capital services is fixed at $K_0$ units. Thus in the short run, if the firm wants to produce 50 units, it will have to move to point *A′*, and similarly if it wants to produce 150 units, it will have to move to point *C′*. But the average cost of producing 150 units at point *C′* is clearly higher than what the firm could achieve if it were able to produce at point *C*. (The grey iso-cost line going through point *C′* represents a higher total cost than the iso-cost line going through point *C*.) Similarly, the average cost of producing 50 units using the combination of inputs shown at point $A'$ is higher than with the combination at point $A$. Thus at output levels of 50 or 150 units, for example, the short-run average cost curve $SAC_1$ lies above the long-run average cost curve, as shown in Figure 9-8. At an output level of 100 units, however, the $SAC_1$ and LAC are the same. Why? Because, as point $B$ in Figure 9-7 shows, the least-cost combination of capital and labour to produce 100 units happens to have precisely $K_0$ units of capital, the amount of capital that the firm has to begin with.

Notice also that for different amounts of the fixed factor, we get a different SAC curve. For example, if the firm starts out with $K_1$ units of capital, its short-run average cost curve is $SAC_2$ in Figure 9-8. And notice that with $K_1$ units of capital, the height of the $SAC_2$ curve is the same as that of the LAC curve at an output level of 150 units, since the least-cost combination of inputs to produce 150 units (point $C$ in Figure 9-7) has $K_1$ units of capital. A curve such as the LAC curve in Figure 9-8 is sometimes called an *envelope curve* because it encloses all the short-run SAC curves from below (see Figure 9-9). (While it does seem quite easy to draw this curve, the economist who introduced the idea had difficulty, as explained in Box 9-2.)

The envelope curve thus provides the answer to a key question facing the producer: In the long run, what is the lowest-cost combination of labour and capital inputs? The best quantity of capital depends on the desired quantity of output. For example, if the firm wants to produce output $q_4$, it picks the quantity of capital that corresponds to $SAC_4$, and hires the quantity of labour needed to produce at point $J$.

We emphasize that LAC shows the *lowest* average cost at which each output (such as $q_3$ or $q_4$) can be produced in the long run, when producers have the opportunity to adjust their quantity of capital. Points in the grey area below LAC cannot be achieved with present technology and with present factor prices. Points in the coloured area above LAC could be chosen. But a technically efficient firm rejects any such point in favour of a lower-cost point on LAC — although it may temporarily produce in the coloured area in the short run before it has a chance to adjust its capital stock.

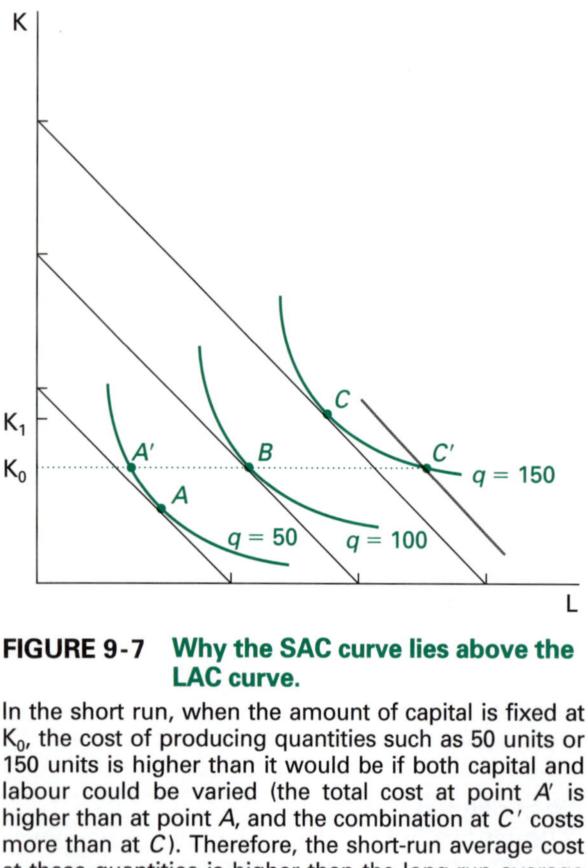


**FIGURE 9-7 Why the SAC curve lies above the LAC curve.**

In the short run, when the amount of capital is fixed at $K_0$, the cost of producing quantities such as 50 units or 150 units is higher than it would be if both capital and labour could be varied (the total cost at point $A'$ is higher than at point $A$, and the combination at $C'$ costs more than at $C$). Therefore, the short-run average cost at these quantities is higher than the long-run average cost. Only at an output of 100 units are the short-run and long-run average costs the same.

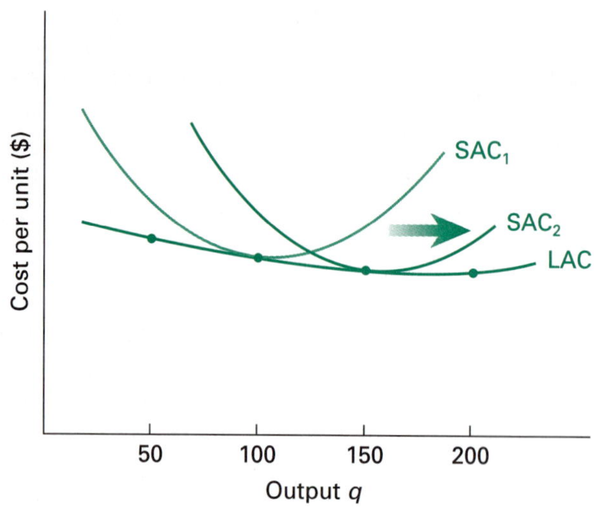


**FIGURE 9-8 Shifts in the SAC curve.**

When the amount of capital is increased, the short-run average cost curve shifts to the right. For example, the curve $SAC_2$ corresponds to the amount of capital $K_1$ in Figure 9-7, and is further to the right than $SAC_1$, which has $K_0$ units of capital.

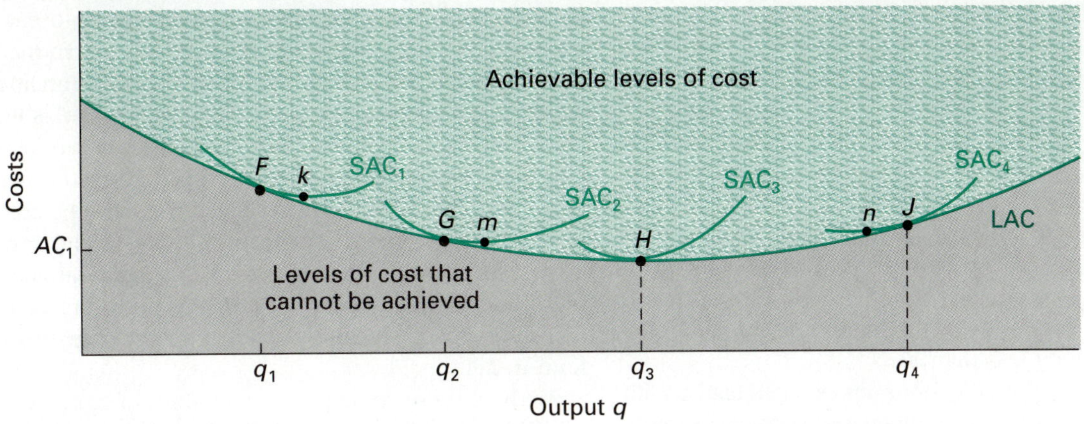


**FIGURE 9-9 The long-run envelope cost curve.**
The SAC curves are the short-run average cost curves that apply if the capital stock is fixed at various levels, 1, 2, 3, etc. LAC is the long-run average cost curve that encloses all of them from below. The envelope curve is useful when the firm is planning for the long run, when it is free to select any quantity of capital. For example, to produce $q_3$, it would select capital stock 3, thus operating on $SAC_3$ at point *H* and keeping its average cost down to the lowest possible level—that is, the height of *H*. Similarly, to produce $q_4$, it would select capital stock 4, thus operating on $SAC_4$ at point *J* and keeping its cost down to the lowest possible level for that output.

## TOOLS AND TECHNIQUES — BOX 9-2

### If You Have Had Trouble Drawing Curves in Economics, You Are Not Alone

The discerning reader will notice in Figure 9-9 that LAC touches the lowest short-run curve ($SAC_3$) at its minimum point. But it doesn't touch any other SAC curve at its minimum. For example, it touches $SAC_1$ slightly to the left of its minimum point *k*.

This is such a subtle problem that it was missed by Jacob Viner, the Canadian economist who first developed the idea of the "envelope" curve. He asked his draftsman to draw an envelope curve to pass through the minimum point on each SAC curve. His draftsman knew that this couldn't be done, and said so. Viner insisted. The draftsman thereupon presented him with a long-run curve that went through the minimum points on each SAC. But it clearly wasn't an envelope curve. (To confirm this, sketch a curve through the minimum points, such as *k*, *m*, and *n*, and you will see that it is not the envelope curve LAC at all.) Viner permitted the erroneous diagram to appear in his article, complaining that his obstinate draftsman "saw some mathematical objection . . . which I could not succeed in understanding."*

There was a sequel. In the 1930s, Viner was unimpressed with Keynes's new theory of unemployment and income. On his arrival in North America, Keynes was asked to name the world's greatest living economist. He reportedly replied that modesty prevented him from naming the greatest, but the second greatest was surely Viner's draftsman.

*Jacob Viner, "Cost Curves and Supply Curves," 1931, reprinted in George J. Stigler and Kenneth E. Boulding, *Readings in Price Theory* (Homewood, Ill.: Richard D. Irwin, 1952), p. 214.

## ECONOMIES OF SCALE

Observe that, to the left of $H$ in Figure 9-9, long-run average cost falls as output increases. The question arises: How can that be? How can the cost per unit fall when output is increased from, say, 100 units to 200?

The answer lies in ***economies of scale***. Recall from Chapter 3 that economies of scale exist if an $x\%$ increase in the quantity of *all* inputs results in an increase of more than $x\%$ in the quantity of output. Equivalently, economies of scale exist if it is possible to increase output by $x\%$ by increasing the quantities of all inputs by less than $x\%$.

The way in which economies of scale lead to falling average costs may be illustrated with an example. Suppose that a firm faces fixed input prices. That is, it won't bid up the wage rate, regardless of how many workers it hires; nor will it bid up the price of steel or machinery, no matter how much it buys. Then, an increase of (say) 100% in the quantity of all inputs raises total costs by the same 100%. (Twice as many inputs are used, and prices remain constant.) But, with economies of scale, output rises by more than 100%. Equivalently, if there are economies of scale, we can increase output by 100% by increasing the quantities of inputs by *less* than 100%. Either way, we reach the same conclusion: With total costs rising more slowly than output, average cost per unit falls. That is: *If input prices are constant, economies of scale mean falling long-run average costs.*[2]

In Figure 9-8, economies of scale and falling average cost imply that the minimum total cost of producing 100 units (corresponding to the iso-cost line through point $B$ in Figure 9-7), say, is less than twice as large as the total cost of producing 50 units. Thus with economies of scale, the outward parallel shift of the iso-cost line as we move from point $A$ to point $B$ in Figure 9-7 is less than proportional to the increase in output. For example, the intercepts of the iso-cost line through $B$ along either the capital or labour axis are less than twice as far out from the origin as the intercepts of the iso-cost line through $A$, and the distance between the origin and point $B$ is less than twice that between the origin and point $A$.

In turn, another question arises: Why should economies of scale exist? There are several reasons. Greater output may make greater specialization possible, and workers may become adept at specialized tasks—like the workers in Adam Smith's pin factory (Chapter 3). It also means that more highly specialized machinery can be used in assembly-line operations. Furthermore, with a greater output, a firm may be better able to use its talent. If a production-line supervisor is able to direct 20 workers but is in charge of only 10, output and the number of workers employed can be doubled without requiring another supervisor. Similarly, the firm's executives may be able to handle more work and responsibility; as the firm grows and output increases, new managers are initially not required. Therefore, there is less management cost for each unit of output and average costs tend to fall.

With all these reasons for economies of scale, why are there ever ***diseconomies of scale***, where LAC turns up (as it does at output $q_3$ in Figure 9-9)? The supervisor example provides a clue. Suppose output and employment, which have already doubled, now increase by another five times. In addition to the original supervisor, five new ones must now be hired. So far, it seems that average cost need not change, since there has been the same proportionate increase in both output and costs. But another person may now be required just to coordinate activities among the six supervisors. Thus, as a company grows, new tiers of management may have to be created. Eventually, a point is reached where management becomes too costly and unwieldy, and decision making becomes too cumbersome and slow. There are just too many people between the vice-president who makes the final production decisions and the workers on the line who carry them out. Consequently, average costs increase. Thus, it is not only the short-run cost curve that is U-shaped. So is the long-run cost curve. (But the long-run curve is much wider and more gently sloping!)

There are *diseconomies of scale* if an $x\%$ increase in the quantity of *all* inputs causes the quantity of output to increase by less than $x\%$. (For example, if all inputs increase by 100%, output increases by less than 100%.)

There are *constant returns to scale* if an $x\%$ increase in the quantity of all inputs causes the quantity of output to increase by the same $x\%$.

The point where decision making becomes unwieldy generally occurs much earlier in agriculture than in industry. Consequently, point $H$, where LAC begins to rise, is encountered at a relatively small output. One reason is that on a relatively small farm, the

[2] However, if a firm bids up the price of inputs, its average cost may rise even though there are economies of scale.

owner-operator has the opportunity and incentive to make crucial decisions with great speed. When the sun shines, the farmer makes hay. When crops are ripe, the farmer drops secondary activities, and works very hard to harvest the crops. On the other hand, if the farm were part of a huge company, the crop could be lost by the time decision making worked its way through several echelons of management.

## The Range of Constant Returns and Minimum Efficient Scale

While diseconomies of scale and higher average costs set in at an early stage in agriculture, they come at a much larger output in most manufacturing firms. This is one of the reasons for the existence and continued growth of large corporations like IBM and Canadian General Electric.

It is also possible that there may be constant returns to scale and a horizontal long-run cost curve over a considerable range, as illustrated in Figure 9-10. In this case, firms with quite different sizes may have similar costs and compete on a relatively even footing. For example, in the North American auto industry, GM is much larger than Ford which, in turn, is much larger than Chrysler. But their costs of producing a car are not greatly different. (Actually, the three firms are organized differently, with General Motors producing more of its own parts and the other two buying a much larger fraction of their parts from outside suppliers. As a consequence, the relative costs of the three companies shifted as conditions changed in the market for parts. GM used to have a significant cost advantage. But the advantage shifted to Ford in the 1980s, when parts produced in-house became more expensive than parts bought from outside.)

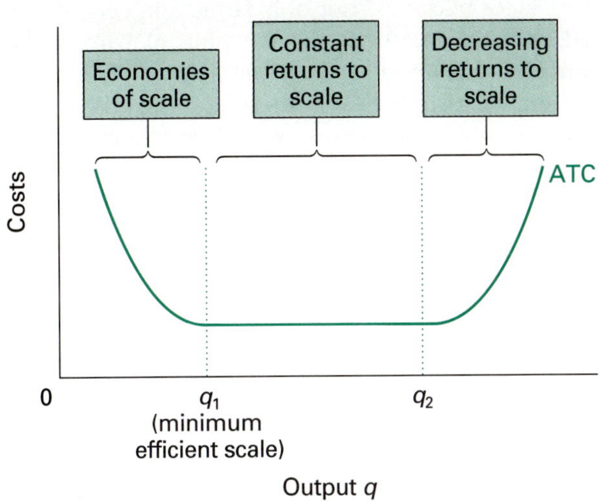


**FIGURE 9-10 Minimum efficient scale.**
For some firms, the envelope curve flattens out, and there are constant returns over a range—illustrated here as the range from $q_1$ to $q_2$. Output $q_1$ represents the *minimum efficient scale.*

If returns to scale are constant over a wide range, as illustrated in Figure 9-10, companies are in a good position to compete once they have reached the ***minimum efficient scale*** at which long-run average cost levels out. But they can have a very tough time if they remain stuck far to the left. For example, even though Ford and Chrysler are in a relatively good position to compete with GM, American Motors was too small. It suffered a string of losses before it was taken over by Chrysler in 1987.

The *minimum efficient scale* is the output or scale at which average total costs reach their minimum.

There are some industries in which even a huge corporation may not have exhausted all the advantages of size. The large commercial airplane industry is one example: Boeing of Seattle, Washington, could produce aircraft more cheaply if it produced twice as many. In such an industry, there is a strong tendency for small competitors to be driven out. In the whole world, there are only three major producers of large passenger aircraft—Boeing, McDonnell Douglas, and Airbus of Europe. Indeed, it is quite possible that Boeing would be the only survivor in the absence of two factors aiding its competitors: (1) product differentiation (aircraft are somewhat different, and airlines have different needs) and (2) government subsidies, particularly to Airbus. (Product differentiation also explains the existence of a number of smaller firms that produce planes for specialized markets such as executive jet aircraft, water bombers to fight forest fires, and so on. Canada's two major aircraft manufacturers—de Havilland and Canadair—have survived in the marketplace by producing these types of specialty aircraft. However, de Havilland was taken over by Boeing in 1988.)

Finally, it is important to recognize that in the phrase "minimum efficient scale," the term "efficient" is used in a very specific way, *applying to costs only*. The minimum efficient scale is the output at which unit costs reach a minimum. But this is not necessarily the most efficient output in terms of the overall operation of the economy. Perhaps Boeing could produce planes more cheaply if it doubled its output. But, if it did so, our economy would not become more efficient. We would be producing more planes than the airlines could put to good use. To study the overall efficiency of the economy, we will have to look beyond the cost side to consider demand, too.

## Economies of Scale and Diminishing Returns

It is possible for a firm to enjoy "economies of scale" and *also* face the "law of diminishing returns." Since economies of scale mean falling costs and diminishing returns mean rising costs, we might well wonder: How is this possible?

The answer is that the law of diminishing returns is a short-run concept that applies if only one input (labour) changes, while economies of scale is a long-run concept that applies when *all* factors are variable.

Figure 9-11 illustrates how the same firm can face both economies of scale and diminishing returns. *In the short run*, as more labour is applied to the given capital stock, marginal costs rise, as shown by arrow *f* along the short-run marginal cost curve $SMC_1$. These rising costs are a reflection of diminishing returns.

**FIGURE 9-11 How a firm can face both economies of scale and diminishing returns.**

This firm faces diminishing returns, as shown by arrow *f*. Its marginal cost curve $SMC_1$ rises in the short run, as long as its capital stock is fixed at level 1. For this firm, there are also economies of scale, as shown by arrow *e*; its long-run average cost LAC falls as it is able to increase its use of *all* factors.

However, as capital increases *in the long run*, costs fall as the firm moves down along LAC (arrow *e*). These are economies of scale.

## LIVING IN A GLOBAL ECONOMY: THE QUEST FOR LOWER COSTS

In this chapter, we have considered some of the important decisions a firm must make in its search for lower costs. For example, how much capital should it acquire in the long run?

But so far, input prices have been taken as given. Another way in which a firm can reduce its costs is by searching for cheaper sources for its inputs. Thus, a firm's purchasing department may play a very important role, looking for low-cost suppliers of machinery, materials, and other inputs.

One way to obtain low-cost inputs is to move to the place where they are located. Thus, in the eighteenth and nineteenth centuries, farmers were drawn to the low-cost land in the Canadian West. In the late nineteenth and early twentieth centuries, the North American steel industry concentrated in Pennsylvania, with its low-cost, plentiful coal. A few decades later, many textile firms migrated to the southern parts of the United States, attracted by low wages.

The search for lower-cost inputs can cross national boundaries. Thus, the low-cost land of the Prairie provinces beckoned not only farmers in central Canada, but also the tired and the poor of Europe. The search for low-cost oil drew the major oil companies to the Middle East, Venezuela, and Nigeria. As the richest sources of iron ore around Lake Superior were exhausted, steel producers turned to new, cheaper sources of supply in eastern Canada and Venezuela. Now, in the search for low wage rates, manufacturers of cars and car parts have been moving some of their production from Michigan and Ontario to Korea and Mexico.

Such moves have created controversy. Corporations have been criticized for their willingness to move production abroad, since it means a loss of Canadian jobs. Nevertheless, a strong case can be made that the international search for lower costs is on balance beneficial to Canada. It adds to the overall efficiency of the world economy — as will be explained in detail in Chapter 19. Most obviously, consumers gain when they can buy inexpensive goods produced with low-cost foreign inputs.

Furthermore, while adjustments can be very painful, they can leave even the initial losers in an improved situation. For example, the province of Quebec has in recent years lost large numbers of jobs in its traditional labour-intensive industries, such as shoes, textiles, and furniture because production has moved to other countries where wages are lower. Yet, in recent years, the Montreal region has been able to replace some of these lost jobs with other, higher-paying ones in pharmaceutical research, financial services, and other expanding industries.

## KEY POINTS

1. In the long run, there are no fixed costs; the producer can choose any combination of capital and labour.
2. In the short run, however, the stock of capital cannot be changed; capital costs represent a *fixed* or *overhead* cost.
3. Total costs = fixed costs + variable costs.
4. Marginal cost = the change in total cost when one more unit is produced. The marginal cost curve cuts through the lowest point on the average cost curve.
5. The production function shows how the quantity of output changes as the quantities of inputs change. The *short-run* production function shows how output changes as the quantities of labour and other variable inputs change, while the quantities of other inputs — plant, equipment, and land — are fixed.
6. The law of eventually diminishing returns states that as more and more of one factor (for example, labour) is employed while all other factors remain constant, the marginal product of that factor (labour) must eventually decline.
7. Marginal costs depend on marginal product. The law of eventually diminishing returns means that marginal cost must eventually rise.
8. An isoquant shows different combinations of the quantities of two factors, such as capital and labour, that the firm can use to produce a specific quantity of output. In the long run, when all factors are variable, the firm can pick the lowest-cost combination of fixed factors (such as capital) and variable factors (such as labour) to produce a given quantity of output.
9. The marginal rate of technical substitution between two factors is the slope of the isoquant at a given point. The slope of the isoquant reflects the ratio of the marginal products of the factors.
10. An iso-cost line shows the various combinations of the factors that can be bought for a given total cost. The slope of an iso-cost line reflects the ratio of the prices of the factors. The firm minimizes the total cost of producing a given amount of output by moving to a point on the isoquant where it just touches (is tangent to) an iso-cost line.
11. The long-run average cost curve is the envelope of the short-run average cost curves, and shows the minimum average cost of producing any given amount of output when firms are able to combine the fixed and variable factors so as to produce each level of output as cheaply as possible.
12. Economies of scale exist when an $x$% increase in all inputs causes output to rise by more than $x$%. There are diseconomies of scale when an $x$% increase in all inputs causes output to rise by less than $x$%.
13. Even when there are economies of scale, a firm, nevertheless, may face diminishing returns. Economies of scale mean that average cost falls in the long run, when *all* factors of production are increased in the same proportion. Diminishing returns mean that marginal cost rises in the short run when only *one* factor of production is increased.

## KEY TERMS

**short run**
**long run**
**capital-intensive vs. labour-intensive production**
**fixed cost**
**variable cost**
**total cost**
**marginal cost**
**average cost**
**production function**
**marginal product of labour**
**average product of labour**
**law of diminishing returns**
**equal-output curve**
**isoquant**
**iso-cost line**
**equal-cost line**
**marginal rate of technical substitution**
**economies of scale**
**constant returns to scale**
**diseconomies of scale**
**minimum efficient scale**

## PROBLEMS

9-1. Suppose that the firm in Table 9-1 had fixed costs of $500 rather than $35, while variable costs remained the same. Recalculate Table 9-1.
   (a) Do higher fixed costs change marginal costs? Why or why not?
   (b) Does the output at which average cost reaches a minimum increase, decrease, or remain the same? Why?

9-2. For each of the following, explain whether you agree or disagree, and why:
   (a) Whenever MC is rising, average total cost must be rising.
   (b) Whenever MC is rising, average variable cost must be rising.
   (c) Whenever MC is above average total cost, average total cost must be rising.
   (d) Whenever MC is above average variable cost, average variable cost must be rising.
   (e) Whenever MC is above average fixed cost, average fixed cost must be rising.
   (f) Whenever ATC is above MC, MC must be rising.

9-3. (This problem is for those who have studied Appendix 9-A.)
   (a) If the price of capital is $30 per unit and the price of labour is $20 per unit, the least-cost way of producing 24 units of output is to use 3 units of labour and 2 units of capital. How much more is the cost incurred by the firm that instead uses 6 units of labour and 1.5 units of capital to produce the same level of output? Illustrate this information in an isoquant/iso-cost diagram similar to Figure 9-12.
   (b) If, instead, the price of capital is $20 per unit and the price of labour is $30 per unit, how much less is the firm's cost if it uses 2 units of labour and 3 units of capital rather than 3 units of labour and 2 units of capital? Illustrate this on a diagram also.

9-4. Use isoquant/iso-cost analysis to derive the shape of the TC curve and the corresponding SAC curve in the presence of (a) diseconomies of scale, (b) constant returns to scale, and (c) economies of scale.

9-5. Consider a set of isoquants of the shape shown in Figure 9-4. When drawn this way, labour and capital are somewhat imperfect substitutes in the production of the good in question. That is, as more and more labour is used in the production process, successively fewer units of capital can be released while maintaining the same level of output. For example, combinations of labour and capital to produce 1000 cars per day might be {K, L} = {1, 1000}, {10, 100}, {25, 40}, {50, 20}, {100, 10}, or {1000, 1}, etc. (Draw these combinations on graph paper to verify the shape of this single isoquant.)
   (a) Suppose now that the technology were such that capital and labour were perfect substitutes in production. For example, suppose that 1000 cars per day could be produced using 4 robots (capital) or 50 labourers, or any linear combination of these such as 2 robots and 25 labourers, or 1 robot and 75 labourers. Draw a set of isoquants for this technology.
   (b) Suppose now that labour and capital are not substitutes at all in production. That is, they must be used in fixed proportions such as one carpenter to one hammer. Adding a hammer adds nothing to output unless

another carpenter is hired, or hiring an additional carpenter but no hammer adds nothing to production—they must be hired in pairs to increase production. Draw a set of isoquants for this technology.

(c) Now consider three factories all determined to produce 1000 cars per day. Factory A's technology is that described in the beginning of the question. Factory B's is that described in part (a) above, and Factory C's technology is that described in part (b). If you were a union member working in the automobile industry attempting to increase your wages conditional on retaining your job, which factory bests suits your objectives? Explain.

9-6. Consider the following table, which represents a firm's long-run production function. Units of capital are measured vertically, units of labour are measured horizontally, and the output per period from each combination of labour and capital is shown in the unshaded boxes.

(a) Does the above technology exhibit increasing, decreasing, or constant returns to scale? Explain.

(b) Does this technology accord with the law of eventually diminishing returns? Explain.

(c) If this firm is committed to producing 48 units per period,

(i) What is the least costly combination of inputs when input prices are \$4 and \$6, respectively, for labour and capital?

(ii) What is the least costly combination of inputs when input prices are \$7 and \$6, respectively, for labour and capital? (Note the impact of this wage increase on the demands for both inputs.)

| | | | L | A | B | O | U | R | | | |
|---|---|---|---|---|---|---|---|---|---|---|---|
| | | 1 | 2 | 3 | 4 | 5 | 6 | 7 | 8 | 9 | 10 |
| | 1 | 2 | 4 | 6 | 8 | 10 | 12 | 14 | 16 | 18 | 20 |
| C | 2 | 4 | 8 | 12 | 16 | 20 | 24 | 28 | 32 | 36 | 40 |
| A | 3 | 6 | 12 | 18 | 24 | 30 | 36 | 42 | 48 | 54 | 60 |
| P | 4 | 8 | 16 | 24 | 32 | 40 | 48 | 56 | 64 | 72 | 80 |
| I | 5 | 10 | 20 | 30 | 40 | 50 | 60 | 70 | 80 | 90 | 100 |
| T | 6 | 12 | 24 | 36 | 48 | 60 | 72 | 84 | 96 | 108 | 120 |
| A | 7 | 14 | 28 | 42 | 56 | 70 | 84 | 98 | 112 | 126 | 140 |
| L | 8 | 16 | 32 | 48 | 64 | 80 | 96 | 112 | 128 | 144 | 160 |
| | 9 | 18 | 36 | 54 | 72 | 90 | 108 | 126 | 144 | 162 | 180 |
| | 10 | 20 | 40 | 60 | 80 | 100 | 120 | 140 | 160 | 180 | 200 |

# APPENDIX 9-A

## THE EFFECT OF A CHANGE IN THE PRICE OF INPUTS

When the prices of productive factors change, it is generally efficient for firms to change the combination in which the factors are used to produce given levels of output. To see this, consider Figure 9-12. Suppose first that the price of capital services is $30 per unit, and the price of labour is $20 per unit. With these prices, any iso-cost line in Figure 9-12 will have a slope of 2/3; the iso-cost lines labelled $c_2$, $c_4$, and $c_5$ in the figure have all been drawn with this slope.

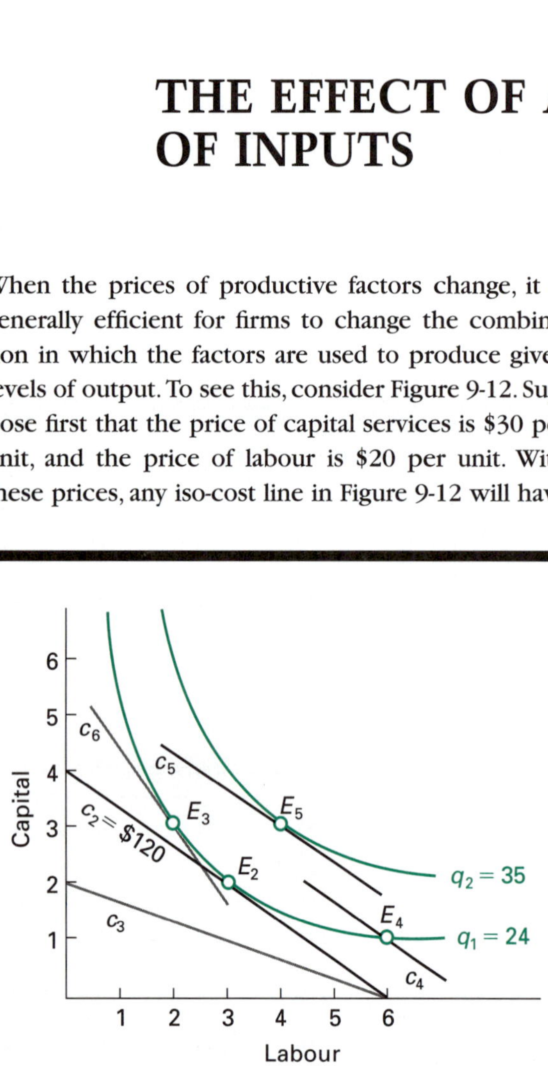


**FIGURE 9-12 The effect of a change in factor prices.**

When the price of capital is $30 per unit, and the price of labour is $20, the minimum-cost combinations for producing 24 and 35 units are at $E_2$ and $E_5$, respectively. If capital becomes cheaper relative to labour, the iso-cost lines will become steeper (for example, $c_6$ in the figure). This will make it efficient for the firm to use more capital and less labour to produce a given amount of output. For example, to produce 24 units, the firm will move to $E_3$ from $E_2$.

The two isoquants shown in the diagram correspond to output levels of 24 and 35 units, respectively. With the initial factor prices, the lowest-cost combination to produce 24 units of output is at $E_2$, using 2 units of capital and 3 units of labour; to produce 35 units, the lowest-cost combination is at $E_5$.

As discussed in the text, the slope of the iso-cost lines will change when the prices of the factors change. For example, if the price of capital rises from $30 to $60 while the price of labour is unchanged, you can confirm that flatter line $c_3$ is now the new $120 equal-cost line. You can visualize the whole family of new equal-cost lines parallel to it. Thus, an equal-cost line for the firm is similar to a budget line for the consumer, whose slope depends on the relative price of the items being purchased.

Now suppose that capital has become *less* (rather than more) expensive relative to labour, and the equal-cost lines, therefore, have become steeper. Specifically, suppose the new set of equal-cost lines is $c_6$ and the family of lines parallel to it. To produce 24 units of output, the firm no longer uses input combination $E_2$. Instead, it shifts to $E_3$, the point of tangency with one of its new equal-cost lines. This type of shift up and to the left will also occur along $q_2$ and all the other equal-output lines. Thus, the firm moves up and to the left, substituting an input that has become relatively less expensive (capital) for the one that has become relatively more expensive (labour).

CHAPTER

# 10 SUPPLY IN A PERFECTLY COMPETITIVE MARKET

*Business is never so healthy as when, like a chicken, it must do a certain amount of scratching for what it gets.*

*Henry Ford*

If markets are perfectly competitive — with many buyers and many sellers — Adam Smith's invisible hand will be at work. In the pursuit of private profit, firms will generally serve the interests of society. Chapter 11 will explain how. In the present chapter, we set the stage by addressing a question faced by a perfectly competitive firm: How much should it produce?

## PERFECT COMPETITION AS A LIMITING CASE

When answering the question of whether a market is perfectly competitive, economists focus on an important factor: To what extent can an individual firm in the market control the price of what it sells?

In practice, firms vary considerably in their ability to control price. A huge corporation such as Boeing can have substantial control over the price of its product. Other firms, such as the local gas station, have very little control. It is true that a station may be in a particularly strategic location and, as a result, may be able to charge a few cents more than its competition. But it cannot charge 10¢ more per litre without losing its customers.

Perfect competition may be looked on as a limiting case where individual producers and buyers have *no control at all* over price. Economists identify a number of characteristics of perfect competition:

1. There are a *large number of buyers* and a *large number of sellers*.
2. Each buyer and each seller is a ***price taker***; none has any control over price.
3. The product is *standardized* or *homogeneous*. No firm has an advantage in terms of design, quality of product, or location at which the product is sold.
4. Each buyer and each seller has *perfect information* about prices and products. There are no ignorant buyers who might go to a higher-priced firm, giving that firm some freedom to charge high prices.
5. There is ***freedom of entry and exit***. Firms face not only the actual competition of many producers of the same product. They also face competition from new producers who will enter the market if the price rises. If the price falls, firms are free to leave the industry.

Historically, farm products have provided the classic examples of perfect competition. There are many producers and many buyers of wheat; no single producer or consumer has any control over price; each grade of wheat is a standardized product; daily and hourly price quotations are available to buyers and sellers; and it is relatively easy for farmers to start or stop producing wheat.

It is true that, in recent decades, price supports and other government programs mean that the prices and quantities of many crops are no longer set by impersonal market forces. In this chapter, we will ignore this complication, and study what happens in the absence of government intervention.

It is also true, of course, that all the characteristics of perfect competition are unlikely to be fully met in the real world. For example, some farmers pay little attention to price quotations. But as long as many farmers do watch prices, the quantity supplied may respond to price in a way very close to that suggested by the theory of perfect competition.

Perfect competition may be looked on as a limiting case. Some markets are very close to the perfectly competitive ideal. Others — such as the market for cars or aircraft — are quite different; individual producers of cars or aircraft do have an ability to set the price of their output.

## Perfect Competition: Demand as Seen by an Individual Producer

Chapter 7 showed how the market demand curve can be derived by a horizontal summing of the demands of individual buyers. This idea is repeated in Figure 10-1. The demands of the various flour mills that purchase wheat are shown on the left. These individual demand curves slope downward; when the price falls, each miller wants to buy more. When these demands are added horizontally, they give the market demand shown in the centre panel.

There is, however, another type of individual demand curve — the demand curve as seen by the individual seller. This is shown at the right. In a perfectly competitive market, the price is set by the impersonal forces of demand and supply. Once price has been set at, say, $4 per bushel, the individual farmer can sell any quantity at that price — whether 100 bushels or 10,000. The farmer has no need to cut the price in order to sell more; no matter how much the individual farmer dumps on the market, it will be a mere drop in the bucket, and will not depress the price. Nor can an individual farmer push up the price by withholding wheat. If the farmer tries to get a higher price — $4.10, for example — there will be no takers; buyers will turn to the many other farmers willing to sell at the going price of $4. As a result, the demand curve as seen by the individual producer is horizontal, as illustrated in Figure 10-1.

Thus, in a perfectly competitive market:

> **The demand of an individual *buyer* slopes downward to the right.**
>
> **The demand facing an individual *seller* is horizontal.**

## Marginal Revenue

The demand facing an individual seller is horizontal. Because the price is given for the perfect competitor, each additional unit sold will increase the firm's total

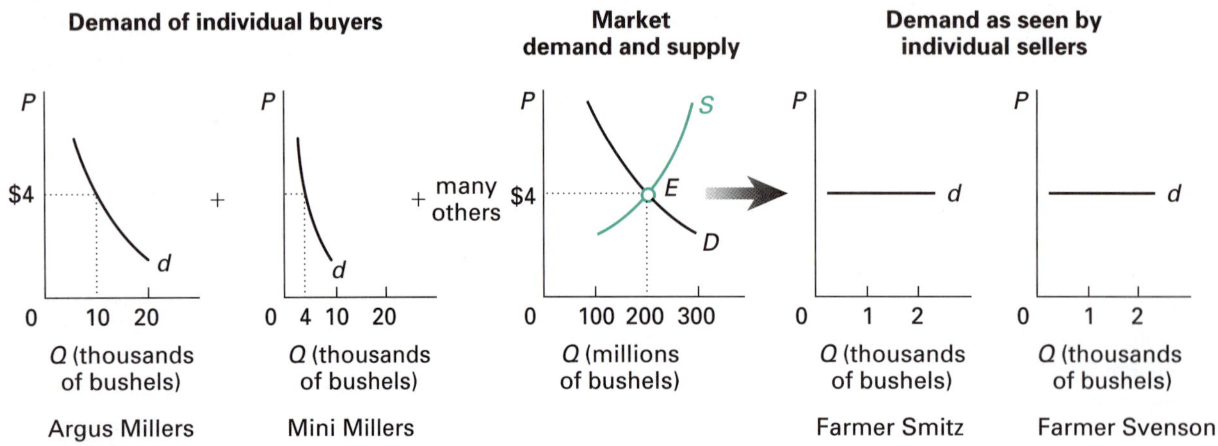


**FIGURE 10-1 Demand curves of individual buyers and sellers.**
As the price increases, each individual buyer will be less eager, and will reduce the quantity demanded. Thus, the demand curves of individual buyers slope downward to the right, as illustrated on the left. In contrast, the demand curve that the individual seller faces is perfectly horizontal in a competitive market, as shown on the right. The individual seller cannot charge a higher price without losing all sales, and there is no need to cut price below the market price in order to sell more.

revenue by an amount equal to the price. Consider, for example, a perfectly competitive firm that faces a price of $40. If it sells one unit, it will have revenues of $40; if it sells two units, it will have revenues of $80. Each time it sells one more unit, its total revenue will rise by $40. Its ***marginal revenue*** is, therefore, equal to the $40 price.

*Marginal revenue* (MR) is the increase in total revenue when one more unit is sold.

For the perfectly competitive firm, the marginal revenue curve is the same as the demand curve that it faces. Both demand and marginal revenue trace out the same horizontal line, with the height being equal to the price of the good established in the marketplace.

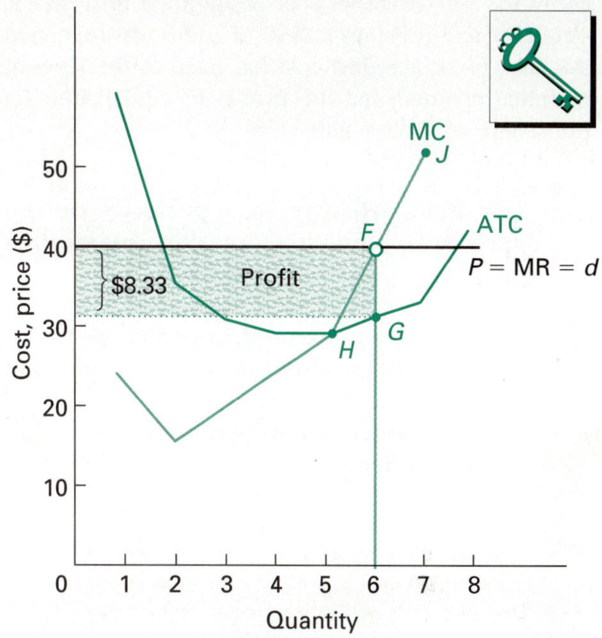


**FIGURE 10-2 Profit maximization for a perfectly competitive firm.**
The firm maximizes profits by choosing output where $P$ = MC. When the price is $40, this is at an output of 6 units. Profits are illustrated by the shaded colour area, which equals the $8.33 profit per unit times the 6 units produced. Note: This show the same firm as Table 10-1.

## PROFIT MAXIMIZATION: MARGINAL REVENUE = MARGINAL COST

To determine how much a firm will produce in order to maximize profits, we must know both marginal revenue and marginal cost.

Figure 10-2 illustrates a perfectly competitive firm facing a price and marginal revenue of $40, as illustrated by the horizontal line $P$ = MR = $d$. The best output for this firm is 6 units, at $F$, where marginal cost MC equals marginal revenue MR. A decision to produce a greater output, say, 7, would be a mistake, since the $55 marginal cost of producing that seventh unit exceeds the $40 of additional revenue that it brings in. On the other hand, if the the firm is pro-

**TABLE 10-1 Profit Maximization by a Hypothetical Shoe Firm Facing a Price of $40**

| (1) Quantity of output *q* | (2) Total cost TC | (3) Marginal cost MC | (4) Average total cost ATC (4) = (2) ÷ (1) | (5) Total revenue TR | (6) Marginal revenue MR = Average revenue AR = Price *P* | (7) Profit or loss (7) = (5) − (2) |
|---|---|---|---|---|---|---|
| 0 | 35 | | — | 0 | | −35 |
| | | 24 | | | 40 | |
| 1 | 59 | | 59 | 40 | | −19 |
| | | 16 | | | 40 | |
| 2 | 75 | | 37.50 | 80 | | 5 |
| | | 20 | | | 40 | |
| 3 | 95 | | 31.67 | 120 | | 25 |
| | | 25 | | | 40 | |
| 4 | 120 | | 30 | 160 | | 40 |
| | | 30 | | | 40 | |
| 5 | 150 | | 30 | 200 | | 50 |
| | | 40 | | | 40 | |
| 6 | 190 | | 31.67 | 240 | | 50 ← |
| | | 55 | | | 40 | |
| 7 | 245 | | 35 | 280 | | 35 |
| | | 85 | | | 40 | |
| 8 | 330 | | 41.25 | 320 | | −10 |

ducing less, say, 4 units, expansion will be in its interest. Why? The marginal cost of adding a fifth unit is only $30, and it brings in $40 of additional revenues. But, at 6 units, marginal cost has risen to the level of marginal revenue, and the firm is in equilibrium. Its profits are at a maximum.

> **Any firm, whether in a perfectly or imperfectly competitive market, maximizes profits by producing where:**
>
> **MC = MR**
>
> **The decision to expand, contract, or maintain current production depends on what is happening *at the margin*.**
>
> **For a perfectly competitive firm,**
>
> **MR = Price *P***
>
> **Therefore, a perfectly competitive firm maximizes profits where:**
>
> **MC = MR = *P***

This can be confirmed in Table 10-1. Columns 2, 3, and 4 list the firm's costs. (This is the same hypothetical shoe firm whose costs were first shown in Table 9-1.) Column 5 shows how the firm's total revenue increases by $40 each time output is expanded by 1 unit, giving the constant marginal revenue of $40 in column 6. Profits are calculated in the last column as total revenue minus total cost. The firm's maximum profit is $50, and this is realized at an output of 6 units. The arrow on the right marks this as the output the firm will produce. (Profit is also $50 when 5 units are produced. In cases like this, economists assume that the firm produces the larger number.) Note that at this profit-maximizing output of 6, marginal cost in column 3 is equal to the marginal revenue of $40 in column 6. This confirms our conclusion that the firm maximizes profit where its marginal cost is equal to marginal revenue.

If the firm is producing more than the equilibrium quantity, the excess of marginal cost over marginal revenue will drag profits down. For example, if the firm adds a seventh unit, marginal cost is $55 while marginal revenue is only $40. The difference of $15 is reflected in profits, which go down by the same $15, from $50 to $35.

In Figure 10-2, total profits are shown by the shaded colour area. This profit area of $50 is equal to the number of units (6) times the per-unit profit of $8.33. This per-unit profit can be found by subtracting the average total cost ($31.67, in column 4, Table 10-1) from the average revenue ($40, in column 6).

## Another View of Profit Maximization: Total Revenue and Total Cost

Graphing a firm's marginal revenue and marginal cost curves in Figure 10-2 is not the only way we can illustrate how it maximizes its profit. We can alternatively graph its total revenue and total cost curves, as in Figure 10-3. Specifically, we first plot the firm's total

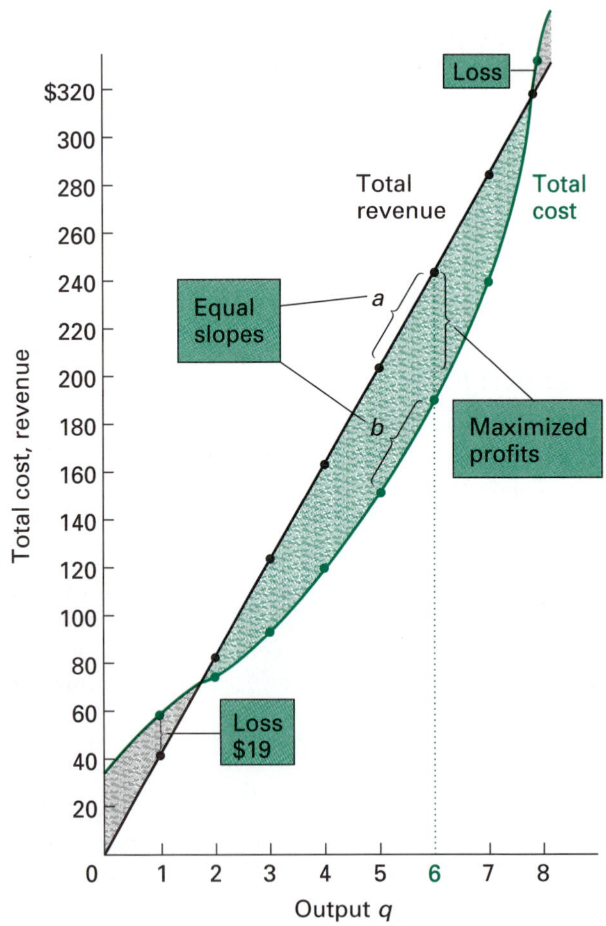


**FIGURE 10-3 Another view of profit maximization.** When the price of the firm's output is constant, the relationship between output and total revenue is a straight line: An additional unit of output always increases total revenue by the same amount. In the range where marginal cost is rising, the slope of the total *cost* curve becomes steeper and steeper.

The firm's total revenue is maximized at the output level where the vertical distance between total revenue and total cost is largest. At that point, the slope of the total cost curve must be the same as the slope of the total revenue curve.

cost curve (in colour), taken from Table 10-1. Next, the firm's total revenue is plotted as the straight line from the origin. Since the firm faces a given price of $40, total revenue is $40 when one unit is sold, $80 when two are sold, $120 when three are sold, and so on. Note that the slope of this line, for a firm in a competitive market, by definition, is the firm's marginal revenue; marginal revenue, in turn, is the same as price.

Initially, if the firm produces only 1 unit of output, it operates at a loss of $19. Its total cost of $59 exceeds its total revenue of $40. However, as it increases output, it moves upward to the right out of the grey loss area into the profit range, where total revenue has risen above total cost. Finally, at 8 units or more of output, total cost rises above total revenue, and the firm again operates at a loss.

Where in the range between 2 and 7 units of output does the firm maximize profits? The answer is at 6 units, the output where its profit (the vertical distance between the total revenue and total cost curves) is greatest.[1]

When profit is maximized—at the sixth unit—the *slopes* of the total revenue and total cost curves are the same. Specifically, the slope of segment *a* equals the slope of segment *b*. We have already seen that the slope of the total revenue line is marginal revenue. Likewise, the slope of the total cost curve measures marginal cost.[2]

Thus, when the firm picks its maximum profit, it is picking the place where the total revenue and the total cost curves have the same slope. In doing so, it is equating MR and MC—just as it did when it maximized profits in Figure 10-2.

## SHORT-RUN SUPPLY OF A PERFECTLY COMPETITIVE FIRM

The firm facing a $40 price responds by producing 6 units. What does it do if the price rises to $55?

To answer this question, visualize the horizontal price line shifting up to a new price of $55 in Figure 10-2. This new price line once again represents marginal revenue. The firm will respond by increasing its production to 7 units, moving to point *J* where MC again equals MR. Alternatively, suppose that the price falls to $30. Output will now be cut back to 5 units at *H*, where MC once again equals MR.

Notice that, in showing how much output the firm will supply at various prices, we are defining the firm's supply curve. As price rises, the firm follows its marginal cost curve upward; as price falls, it follows its marginal cost curve downward. Thus, *the MC curve defines the supply curve of the individual firm* —subject to one important qualification.

### The Shutdown Point

The qualification is that the firm might produce nothing at all. If it does produce, MC does indeed determine the quantity supplied. However, if the price falls low enough, the firm will shut down. The next important question therefore is: How far can the price fall before the firm closes down and stops producing altogether?

This question is addressed in Figure 10-4 and corresponding Table 10-2, which show the problem that the firm faces as the price declines. By the time that price has fallen to $30, the firm finds that its profits have disappeared. It picks the best point, at *H*, where its MC equals the MR of $30. But at this point, the price is no higher than average total cost; profits have fallen to zero. The best the firm can do is break even.

> The *break-even point* is the lowest point on the average total cost curve. When the price is at this height, the firm makes zero economic profits.

The ***break-even point*** can also be illustrated in a diagram such as Figure 10-3 where we showed total cost and total revenue on the vertical axis. The total revenue curve shown in that figure was drawn for a market price of $40 per unit, and is repeated as "TR ($P = 40$)" in Figure 10-5. With a lower market price, the total revenue curve will be less steep, but it will still be a straight line through the origin. Thus, to illustrate falling market price, you just rotate the straight-line total revenue function around the origin, giving it a smaller slope. It is easy to see that as you consider lower and lower prices, the maximum amount of profit the firm can earn—that is, the maximum vertical distance between the total revenue and total cost curves — becomes smaller and smaller. The break-even point occurs when the total revenue

---

[1] Again, profits are the same at 5 units, and we again follow the convention, assuming that the larger output is sold. We also assume that the firm can't produce a fraction of a unit; for example, it can't produce $5^1/_2$ units.

[2] Readers familiar with calculus will see why it is a valuable tool in economics. Marginal cost is simply the first derivative (slope) of the total cost curve.

curve has rotated so far that it just touches the total cost curve at a single point (point *A* in Figure 10-5). This point is the break-even point: It represents the only output level for which the firm does not make a loss, since it is the only quantity at which total revenue is large enough to cover total cost.

It might seem that this is the lowest price at which the firm would be willing to produce. Any lower price will result in losses. However, in the short run, the firm *cannot escape losses by shutting down*. The reason is that it has fixed costs; it has expenses even if it produces nothing. The difficult question then becomes: How can the firm minimize losses? By shutting down or by continuing to produce?

Suppose that the price falls to $25. MC equals MR at *L* in Figure 10-4, at an output of 4 units. This is the best point to produce—if the firm produces anything at all. Should it do so?

The answer is yes. If it produces 4 units, its total costs will be $120 (Table 10-2); its total revenues $100; and it will accordingly suffer a loss of $20. But this loss is less than the fixed cost of $35, which will be the amount it will lose if it shuts down. If it shuts down, it will have nothing to sell, and its revenues will be zero.

There is another way of looking at the firm's decision to produce 4 units. If it does so, it will have to pay out $85 in variable costs. Total revenues of $100 exceed these variable costs. The $100 in revenues will more than justify the decision to produce. The $15 by which revenues exceed variable costs will reduce losses; the $15 can be used to pay part of the fixed costs. Losses will be only $20 when 4 units are produced, compared to the $35 that the firm will suffer if it shuts down.

Thus, as long as the firm is at least covering its variable costs, it continues to produce. That remains true as long as the price is above the ***shutdown point***, *K*, which is the minimum point on the average variable cost curve. If the price reaches this level—$20—then the loss reaches $35, as calculated in the last column of Table 10-2 and illustrated by the grey rectangle in Figure 10-4. At this point, the loss from producing those units is $35 ($11.67 × 3), the same as the $35 loss in fixed costs that the firm suffers if it shuts down. The firm is indifferent as to whether it shuts down or continues to produce. At any lower price, it would shut down; its losses from producing would exceed the $35 fixed costs.

The *shutdown point* is the minimum point on the average variable cost curve, where the MC curve cuts the AVC curve. If the price is below this point, the firm produces nothing.

(For an example of a case where the shutdown principle was ignored for political reasons, see Box 10-1.)

Thus, the firm's supply curve corresponds to its MC curve, *provided that* the price is above the minimum point on the AVC.

A firm's *short-run supply curve* is that part of its marginal cost curve MC that lies above its average variable cost curve AVC.

This is a key point in this chapter:

**A perfectly competitive firm's supply curve reflects marginal cost. The height of the supply curve at a given quantity of output is equal to the firm's marginal cost at that quantity.**

## THE SHORT-RUN MARKET SUPPLY CURVE

Chapter 7 showed how the market demand curve *D* is the horizontal sum of the demand curves *d* of individual consumers. Similarly, the ***short-run market supply curve*** *S* can be drawn by horizontally summing the short-run supply curves *s* of the individual producers. (As before, lower cases represent the individual participants, and capital letters represent the whole market demand or supply.)

This horizontal summation is illustrated in Figure 10-6, where two firms are taken as representative of the many, many producers in a competitive market. The dashed horizontal section at the bottom of each individual supply curve is at the shutdown price; the firm would be unwilling to supply anything at a lower price.

## SUPPLY IN THE LONG RUN

In the long run, cost and supply conditions are different from those of the short run in several ways:

1. In the long run, there are no fixed costs. All costs are variable. For example, costs for equipment—in the form of depreciation and maintenance costs—are fixed in the short run. But, as equipment wears out, a decision has to be made whether or not to replace it. At this point, the firm has a choice; equipment costs are variable.

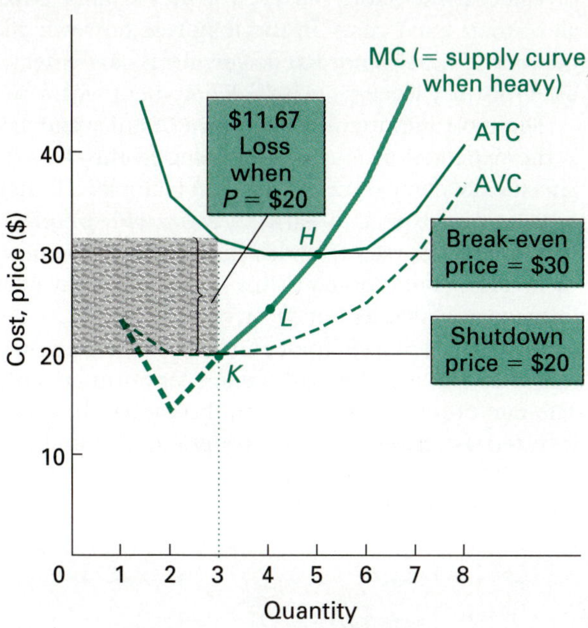


**FIGURE 10-4 Producing at a loss.**

If the price is below $30, the firm suffers a loss. The firm minimizes this loss by producing where $P$ = MC, so long as price is at or above the $20 which will cover average variable cost. If the price is even lower, the firm cannot cover its AVC, and will shut down.

Thus, the MC curve represents the short-run supply curve of the individual firm, provided that the price is at or above the minimum point on the AVC curve. The short-run supply is thus the heavy, solid portion of the MC curve above the point where it intersects the AVC curve.

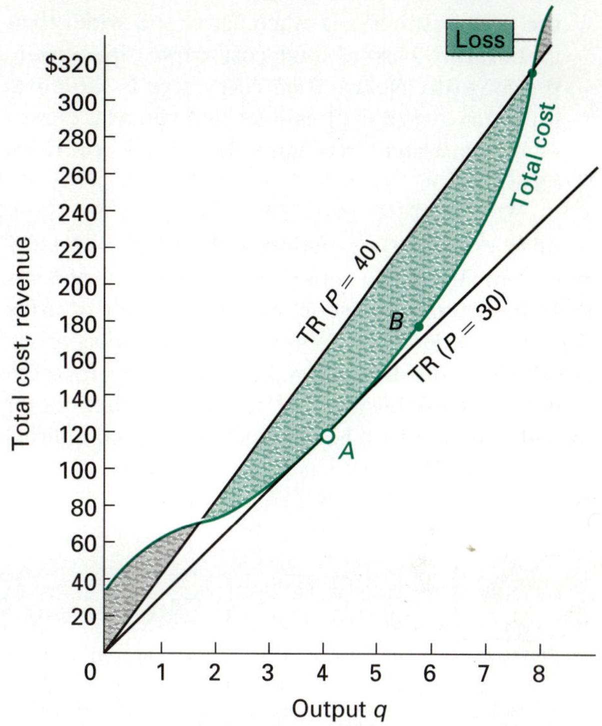


**FIGURE 10-5 The break-even point: Another view.**

When the price of the firm's output falls, the slope of the total revenue curve becomes less steep. Consequently, the firm's maximum profit (the vertical distance between the total revenue curve and the total cost curve) becomes smaller. When price has fallen to the break-even level ($P$ = 30), the total revenue curve just touches the total cost curve (point $A$).

**TABLE 10-2 Minimizing Loss as Price Falls**

| (1) | (2) | (3) | (4) | (5) | (6) | (7) | (8) | (9) | (10) | (11) | (12) | (13) |
|---|---|---|---|---|---|---|---|---|---|---|---|---|
| | | | | | | | **Best output (shown by arrow) if:** | | | | | |
| | | | | | | | **Price = $30 = MR** | | **Price = $25 = MR** | | **Price = $20 = MR** | |
| **Quantity** $q$ | **Fixed cost FC** | **Variable cost VC** | **Total cost TC** | **Marginal cost MC** | **Average total cost ATC** | **Average variable cost AVC** | **Total revenue TR** | **Profit (+) or loss (−) TR − TC** | **Total revenue TR** | **Profit (+) or loss (−) TR − TC** | **Total revenue TR** | **Profit (+) or loss (−) TR − TC** |
| 1 | 35 | 24 | 59 | 24 | 59 | 24 | 30 | −29 | 25 | −34 | 20 | −39 |
| 2 | 35 | 40 | 75 | 16 | 37.50 | 20 | 60 | −15 | 50 | −25 | 40 | −35 |
| 3 | 35 | 60 | 95 | **20** | 31.67 | 20 | 90 | −5 | 75 | −20 | 60 | −35 ← |
| 4 | 35 | 85 | 120 | **25** | 30 | 21 | 120 | 0 | 100 | −20 ← | 80 | −40 |
| 5 | 35 | 115 | 150 | **30** | 30 | 23 | 150 | 0 ← | 125 | −25 | 100 | −50 |
| 6 | 35 | 155 | 190 | 40 | 31.67 | 26 | 180 | −10 | 150 | −40 | 120 | −70 |

2. Because the firm can change the quantity of plant and equipment in the long run, the long-run average total cost curve is much flatter and wider than a short-run average total cost curve. Specifically, the long-run average total cost curve is the envelope curve of all the possible short-run ATC curves — as illustrated in Figure 9-9 in the previous chapter.

Another difference between short-run and long-run supply has to do with the entry and exit of firms in an industry. In the short run, the number of firms supplying an industry's output can be taken as given. On the one hand, it may take a long time for new firms to get established and to start production; on the other hand, as we have already seen, existing firms with established production facilities may continue to produce in the short run even if they cannot cover all of their fixed costs. In the long run, however, the number of firms is not fixed: New firms may enter, or old firms may leave, as existing equipment wears out.

The most important determinant of entry and exit is the expected profitability of being in the industry. Specifically, entry of new firms will take place if their owners can expect to earn an ***economic profit*** — that is, a higher rate of return than they could expect by investing in other industries, or by buying financial instruments such as bonds or bank deposits. As discussed in Chapter 8, the return on financial instruments constitutes the firm owners' opportunity cost: The rate of return they earn on the capital they have invested as shareholders or proprietors must be at

## APPLICATIONS AND ILLUSTRATIONS BOX 10-1
## Ignoring the Shutdown Principle: The Case of Sysco

When a firm's revenues cannot cover its variable costs in the short run, loss-minimizing behaviour dictates that it shut down immediately. If it incurs short-run losses but earns revenues sufficient to cover its variable costs, it should make the long-run decision to shut down as soon as it can. Such behaviour in either circumstance accords not only with the self-interest of firm owners, but also with the public interest. Avoiding losses promotes the well-being of the owners: Economic losses signal that the value of the inputs used to produce the good or service exceeds the value to society of the output. Closure avoids excessive losses by the firm and the waste of scarce resources by society. Whereas firms, unfettered by government regulations, will generally heed the economic signal that losses send, governments often ignore them — to the detriment of society. The case of steel-making in Cape Breton, Nova Scotia, provides an illustration.

On 13 October 1967, Dominion Steel and Coal Corporation announced its intention to shut its steel mill in Sydney, Nova Scotia, because of the losses the company had incurred in that and previous years. At the time, that plant was employing more than 4000 workers and the industry had already been the beneficiary of $250 million in subsidies. One week later, the government of Nova Scotia, wanting to preserve jobs in this chronically depressed area, bought the corporation for $25 million, thus creating the Sydney Steel Corporation (Sysco). The government's intention was to run the company only until another buyer could be found.

Dominion Steel and Coal Corporation's prognosis for the viability of the plant was correct, as the plant continued to suffer losses. Indeed, it was pointed out shortly after the government took over the firm—and regularly thereafter— that Sysco's losses were such that it would cost the people of Nova Scotia less to pay the workers their salaries to stay at home rather than to actually produce steel. (Thus, even if wages had been treated as a fixed cost, not a variable cost, loss minimization would have required that Sysco be shut down.)

In the late 1980s, the government determined that the firm could only be made profitable if it were modernized, which would require transforming its blast furnace opera-

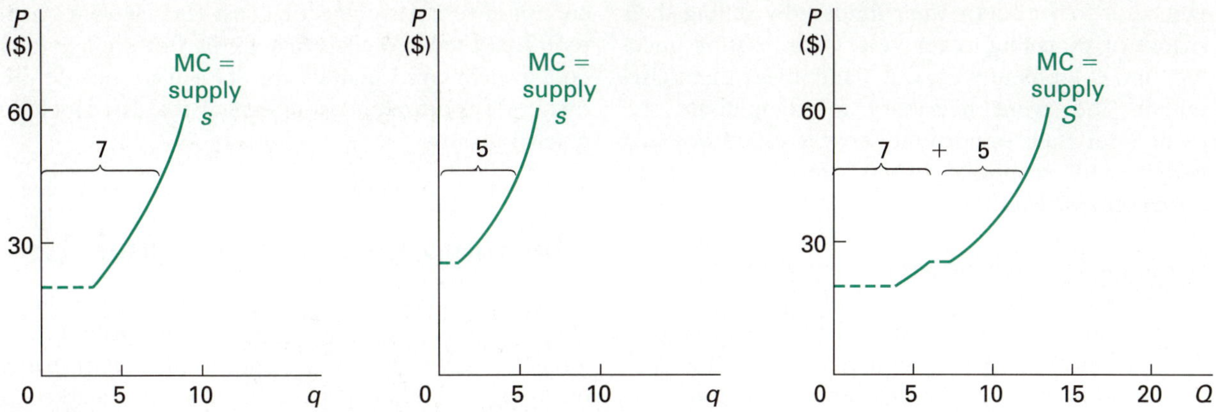


(a) Firm A's supply. (b) Firm B's supply. (c) Market supply.

**FIGURE 10-6 Adding individual supply curves to get short-run market supply.**
By adding horizontally the amounts that each firm is willing to produce at a given price, we can find the corresponding point on the short-run market supply curve. For simplicity, this figure shows only two firms, which are representative of the many firms in a perfectly competitive market.

**BOX 10-1 continued**

tion into an electric arc furnace operation capable of producing heat-hardened rails. The conversion process began in 1988 at a cost of some $280 million.

Sysco incurred a loss of $214 million in the 1988/89 fiscal year. Of this, $105 million involved writing off now outdated equipment and severance pay for workers who would no longer be needed, and another $109 million consisted of interest payments on its debt load, and other depreciation and operating losses. Still, the minister of industry was confident that modernization would cause the plant to be profitable so that it might attract a private sector buyer. A "bright future" was just around the corner.

Nevertheless, the plant incurred losses of $30 million in 1989/90 and $62 million in 1990/91. In 1991, the provincial government took over Sysco's accumulated debt of $785 million. By 1991, employment had been reduced to 370 mill workers and 230 positions in support services and management.

Nor did the situation improve. By 1992, Sysco was losing about $1 million per week. Since 1967, it had already absorbed $2 billion in direct and indirect subsidies, and its debt was again rising, this time on the order of $140 million to the provincial government and an additional $25 million to banks. Moreover, its prospects for orders were not good — because of its heavy subsidization, the American government had set a 103% countervailing duty on its output. Although it did receive rail orders from abroad, critics pointed out that Sysco was selling them for less than what they cost to produce.

From a weekly loss of $1 million in the early 1990s, Sysco's loss had fallen to $600,000 per week by 1993, due largely to modernization and more layoffs. Critics then, as they had in 1967 and throughout the intervening 26 years of government ownership, demanded that the plant be sold for whatever price it could fetch, or simply be shut down. Consistently, however, the government announced that any sale be conditional on the buyer keeping the plant in Cape Breton subject to employment guarantees. Thus, for 26 years — and counting — the economic signal sent by Sysco's losses has fallen on deaf political ears.

least as high as this opportunity cost, otherwise they will want to withdraw their funds — by selling their shares, or by failing to reinvest when existing buildings and equipment wear out—and invest them elsewhere. The profit necessary to compensate the owners for their opportunity cost is called ***normal profit***, and economic profits are referred to as ***above-normal*** profits.

*Economic profits* or *above-normal* profits are profits in excess of the firm owners' opportunity cost of capital. In order for owners to keep their funds invested in an industry, the firms in the industry must earn at least *normal profits*; that is, a rate of profit sufficient to compensate the owners for the opportunity cost of their capital.

In the long run, when firms in an industry earn above-normal profits—that is, positive economic profits — there is a tendency for new firms to enter the industry. Conversely, when firms earn below-normal profits — negative economic profits — they will gradually leave the industry as their buildings and equipment wear out.

We emphasize again that these are long-run tendencies. For example, firms with below-normal profits will continue to produce in the short run as long as price is above the shutdown point, even though they are not covering average total cost. (Recall from Chapter 9 that the fixed costs that are part of average total cost in economic analysis are defined to include the owners' opportunity cost of capital; that is, to include normal profits.)

## The Importance of Entry and Exit

Figure 10-7 illustrates how the entry of new firms affects supply. Initially, with 300 similar firms in the industry, each supplying 10 units at price $P_1$ in panel (a), there are 3000 units supplied to the market in panel (b). Indeed, at any price such as $P_1$, the quantity supplied to the market is found by horizontally multiplying the supply $s$ of the individual firm in panel (a) by 300. In other words, to derive the industry's supply curve $S_{300}$, we repeat the procedure already shown in Figure 10-6; we horizontally sum the supply curves of all the individual firms.

If 100 similar new firms enter, increasing the number to 400, then 4000 units are supplied at price $P_1$; the supply curve shifts from $S_{300}$ to $S_{400}$. On the other hand, if 100 firms leave, the supply curve shifts to the left, from $S_{300}$ to $S_{200}$.

Entry and exit are the keys to understanding the long-run equilibrium of a competitive industry. They

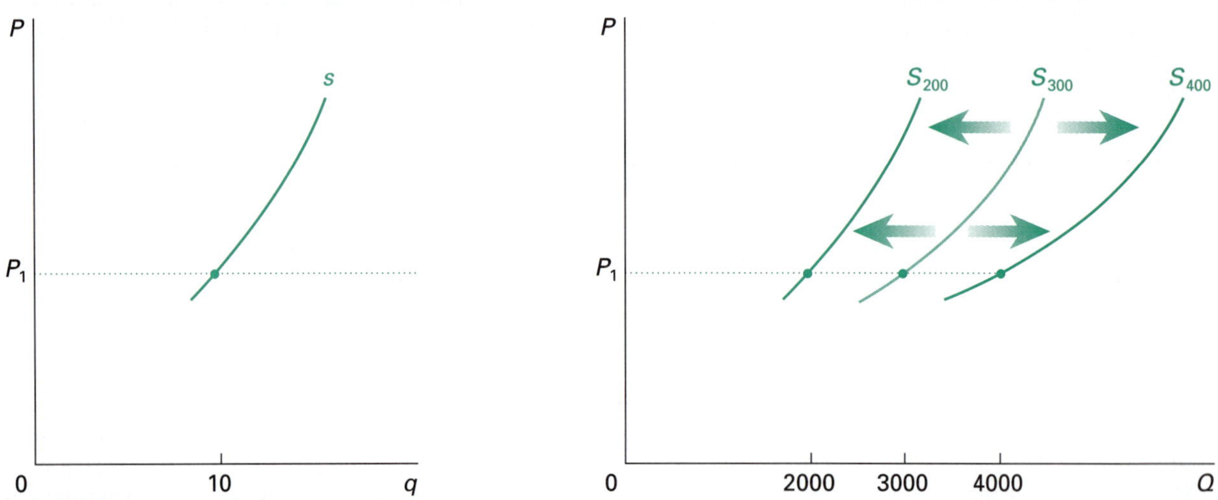


**(a) Supply by an individual firm.** **(b) Supply by all firms in the industry.**

**FIGURE 10-7 Supply curve shifts as new firms enter or old firms leave.**
If 100 new firms enter, the industry's supply curve shifts rightward, from $S_{300}$ to $S_{400}$. If 100 firms leave the industry, the supply curve shifts leftward, from $S_{300}$ to $S_{200}$.

ensure that, in the long run, firms in a perfectly competitive industry make normal profits, but no more. In brief, the reason is this: When price is sufficiently high to create above-normal profits, new firms enter. As a result, the quantity offered for sale increases. The price is consequently bid down, thus working to eliminate above-normal profits. Alternatively, if price is too low to provide normal profits, firms leave. This reduces the quantity supplied. The price as a result is bid up until firms are earning normal profits.

To explain this in detail, we distinguish two possibilities.

## Case 1: Perfectly Elastic Long-run Supply

In the first case, every input is uniform or ***homogeneous***. All land is identical, all entrepreneurs are equally skilful, all workers have the same talents, and so on. In addition, the industry is not very large in the economy. As a result, the industry does not bid up the prices of its inputs when it expands; expansion of the industry causes no change in input prices. In brief, new entrants can obtain the same quality of inputs as existing firms, and inputs are available at stable prices. In these circumstances, *the long-run supply curve will be horizontal.*

Figure 10-8 illustrates why. Panel (a) shows an individual firm; panel (b) shows the demand and supply for the whole industry. In this example, there initially are 1000 identical firms. For each, the short-run supply curve *s* coincides with the short-run marginal cost curve SMC. For the market as a whole, the short-run supply curve is found by adding 1000 such individual supply curves horizontally. This gives the short-run market supply curve $S_{1000}$ in panel (b).

Initially, the industry is in equilibrium at $E_1$ in panel (b). For some time, price has been stable at $P_1$ and output stable at 5000 units. Each of the 1000 firms produces an output of 5 units, as shown in panel (a). Each of these firms is making only a normal profit, producing at *H*, which is the lowest point on its short-run average total cost curve SAC and also the lowest point on its long-run average total cost curve LAC.

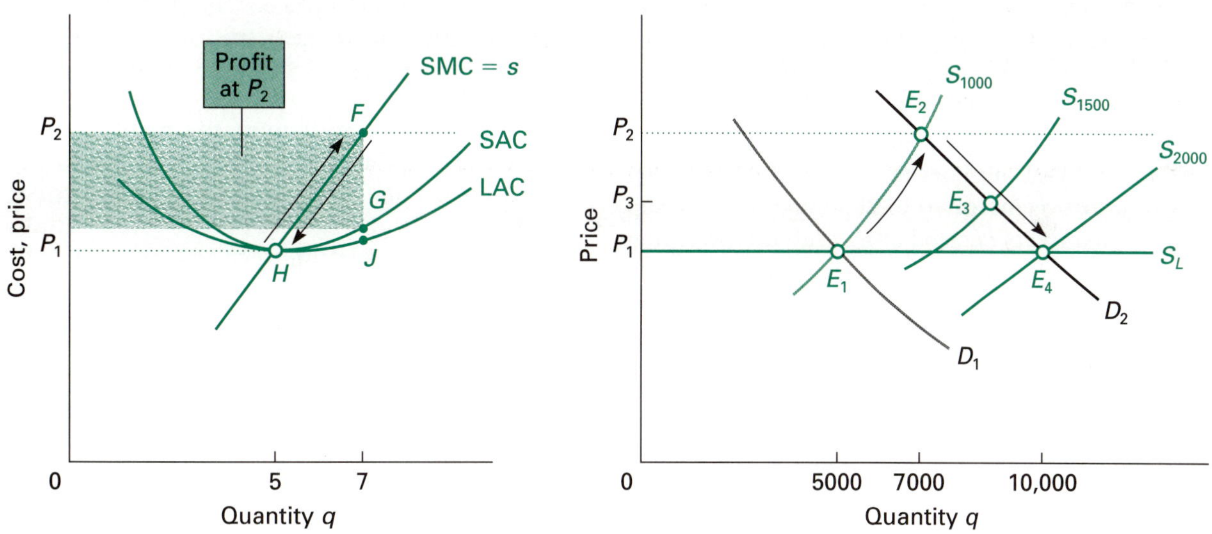


**(a) Firm.** **(b) Industry.**

**FIGURE 10-8 Long-run adjustment to an increase in demand.**

In this diagram, both the firm and the industry are initially in equilibrium at price $P_1$. The firm in panel (a) is at *H*, producing 5 units. The industry is in equilibrium at $E_1$, with 5000 units sold. There are 1000 firms like the one in the left panel.

Now suppose that demand increases from $D_1$ to $D_2$ in the right panel. In the short run, the price rises to $P_2$, and firms make profits shown by the shaded area in panel (a). New firms enter, shifting supply to the right in panel (b). The price falls. In the long run, the price drops all the way back to $P_1$ at new equilibrium $E_4$. The individual firm in panel (a) moves back to *H*; it no longer makes profits, and there is no further incentive for new firms to enter. Therefore, $E_4$ is a long-run equilibrium for the industry, and *H* is the corresponding equilibrium for the firm.

At $H$, the individual firm breaks even; $P_1$ is just sufficient to cover the firm's average cost. Because existing firms are earning no above-normal (economic) profit, there is no incentive for new firms to enter. $H$ is a long-run equilibrium for the firm (panel (a)), and $E_1$ is the corresponding long-run equilibrium for the industry (panel (b)).

Now consider what happens if demand increases to $D_2$. In the short run, before the amount of capital and the number of firms can change, the higher demand causes a rise in price to $P_2$, with the industry moving up the short-run supply curve $S_{1000}$ to new equilibrium $E_2$ (panel (b)). In the face of the higher price, each firm in the left panel moves up its short-run supply curve to $F$, where it makes a short-run profit equal to the coloured area. That is, it makes a profit of $FG$ on each of the 7 units it produces. This is above-normal profit, since normal profit is included in calculating the average cost curve.

This profit attracts new entrants, who want to "get in on a good thing." As new firms come in, the short-run supply curve of the industry shifts to the right (panel (b)). By the time the number of firms has increased to 1500, the short-run supply curve is $S_{1500}$, and the equilibrium has moved to $E_3$. But the resulting price $P_3$ is still high enough to provide above-normal profits, and new firms continue to enter.

The process of entry will continue until price falls to $P_1$ and above-normal profit is eliminated. In panel (b), observe that this does not happen until the number of firms has increased to 2000, and the new supply $S_{2000}$ intersects demand at $E_4$. With the price now back to $P_1$, each firm in panel (a) has reacted by moving back down its supply curve from point $F$ to zero-profit point $H$. At the new long-run equilibrium $E_4$ (panel (b)), 10,000 units are sold, with each of the 2000 firms producing 5 units.

We can now construct the ***long-run market supply curve*** $S_L$ in panel (b) by joining points of long-run equilibrium such as $E_1$ and $E_4$. Unlike short-run supply curves $S_{1000}$, $S_{1500}$, and $S_{2000}$—each of which is drawn on the assumption of a specific number of firms—supply curve $S_L$ applies to the long run when there is time for the number of firms to change. Observe that this long-run supply curve $S_L$ is horizontal or *perfectly elastic*; in the long run, price doesn't rise at all as a result of an increase in demand. The reason is that the higher demand can be satisfied by new firms entering the industry, producing at the same cost as the existing firms. They can do so because they have access to inputs of the same quality, at stable prices.[3]

## Efficient Scale in the Long Run

Whenever the market is in long-run equilibrium at a point on $S_L$, (panel (b), Figure 10-8), the individual firm produces at $H$ (panel (a)), which is not only the lowest point on the short-run average cost curve SAC, but also the lowest point on the long-run average cost curve LAC. That is, the firm has the appropriate amount of plant and equipment to produce at its ***efficient scale***. Why is that? Why won't a firm expand, increasing its plant and equipment when demand increases?

Suppose the firm in panel (a) has already decided to expand in an attempt to hold on to a market of 7 units. By adding additional plant and equipment, it can reduce its average cost for those 7 units from $G$ (on SAC) to $J$, a point on its long-run average cost curve LAC. But observe that point $J$ is above $P_1$, the price at which new competitors can enter the market and sell the product. In the face of such competition, the firm will suffer losses if it stays at $J$. It therefore cuts back; as plant and equipment becomes obsolete or worn out, it is not replaced. The firm moves back to its most efficient size at $H$, the lowest point on its long-run average cost curve.

> **In long-run equilibrium, the firm produces at the efficient scale—that is, at the lowest point on its long-run average cost curve. The firm's average cost is the lowest attainable with existing technology and with existing input prices.**

There is one qualification. In some industries, there may be no single most efficient size; the LAC curve may be horizontal over a range when it reaches its minimum. In such circumstances, a firm may indeed expand and stay at a larger size when demand increases. Where the LAC curves of individual firms

[3] As we saw above, the short-run competitive market supply curve can be derived by horizontally summing the individual firms' short-run marginal cost curve (remember, an individual firm's short-run supply curve is its short-run marginal cost curve). Is it possible to derive the long-run market supply curve in an analogous way? The answer: No, because in the long run, change in the quantity supplied to the market depends primarily on entry of new firms, not on changes in the quantity supplied by existing firms. Thus, even though it is technically possible to derive the long-run marginal cost curve (LMC) for a firm with a U-shaped long-run average cost curve, we have not done so, since the long-run market supply curve does not depend on the firms' LMC curves.

are horizontal, firms of various sizes can coexist, and we cannot tell how many firms there will be in long-run equilibrium.

## A Fall in Demand

A similar argument applies if demand declines from $D_1$ to $D_3$ in Figure 10-9. The industry in panel (b) moves to a new short-run equilibrium $E_5$, with price depressed to $P_4$. In response to the lower price, each individual firm in panel (a) moves down its short-run supply curve from $H$ to $K$. Each firm suffers losses because the price is now less than average cost. As their old equipment wears out, firms decide not to replace it; they prefer to leave the industry altogether. As a consequence, the supply curve in panel (b) shifts to the left. This continues until the industry reaches a new equilibrium at $E_6$, with only 600 firms. Price has gone back up to $P_1$, and each individual firm in panel (a) has responded by moving back up to $H$. At this point, the firm no longer suffers a loss, and therefore there is no further incentive for firms to leave. Again we see that the long-run industry supply $S_L$, defined by joining the long-run equilibrium points such as $E_1$ and $E_6$, is horizontal.

# Case 2: A Rising Long-run Supply Curve

A horizontal long-run supply curve is a special case. Even in the long run, the supply curves of many industries slope upward to the right. This happens if costs rise as new firms enter, either because these firms bid up the prices of inputs or because they have to use inputs of lower quality. For example, new wheat growers may find that the highest quality land is already being used by existing producers; the only land still available may be less productive.

Such a case is illustrated in Figure 10-10. As before, an increase in demand from $D_1$ to $D_2$ in the right panel causes a move to a new short-run equilibrium at $E_2$. At high price $P_2$, profits of existing firms encourage new entrants. As in case 1, the new entrants increase supply and this brings the price down from $P_2$ — but in this case, not all the way down to $P_1$. Instead, price falls only to $P_3$. At that point, a new firm producing on the best land that's left — relatively poor land on which costs of production are relatively high — is just able to cover its costs. There is no further incentive for firms to enter. Thus, the long-run

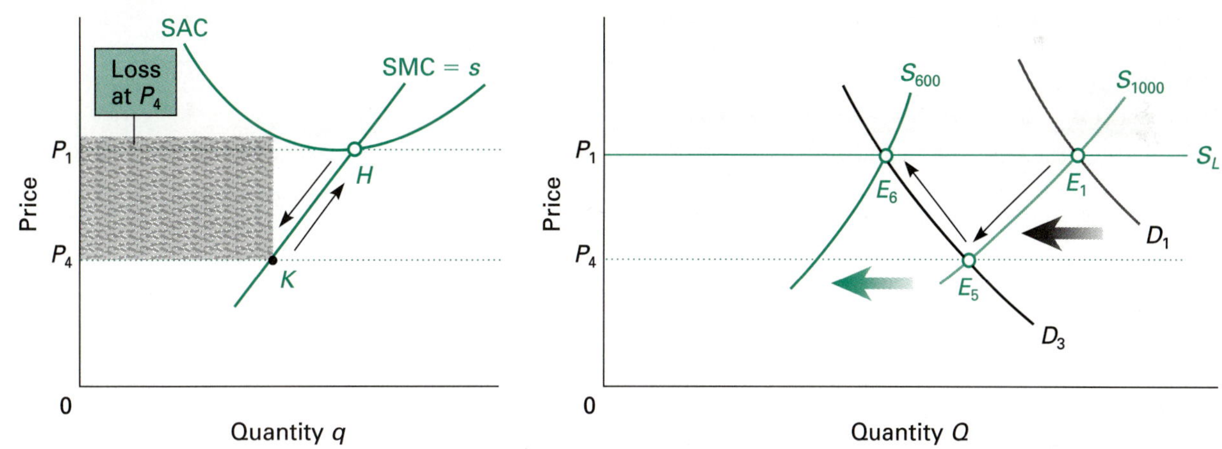


**(a) An individual firm.** **(b) The industry.**

**FIGURE 10-9 Long-run adjustment to a decrease in demand.**
In this diagram, the initial equilibrium is the same as in Figure 10-8. Now, however, demand decreases from $D_1$ to $D_3$ in panel (b). In the short run, the price falls to $P_4$, and each firm in panel (a) suffers a loss because the price is too low to cover its average cost. Some firms leave the industry, shifting the supply curve to the left in panel (b). The price recovers. In the long run, the price moves all the way back to $P_1$, at the new long-run equilibrium $E_6$. Each of the remaining firms moves back to $H$ in panel (a), and no longer suffers losses. Consequently, there is no further pressure for firms to leave.

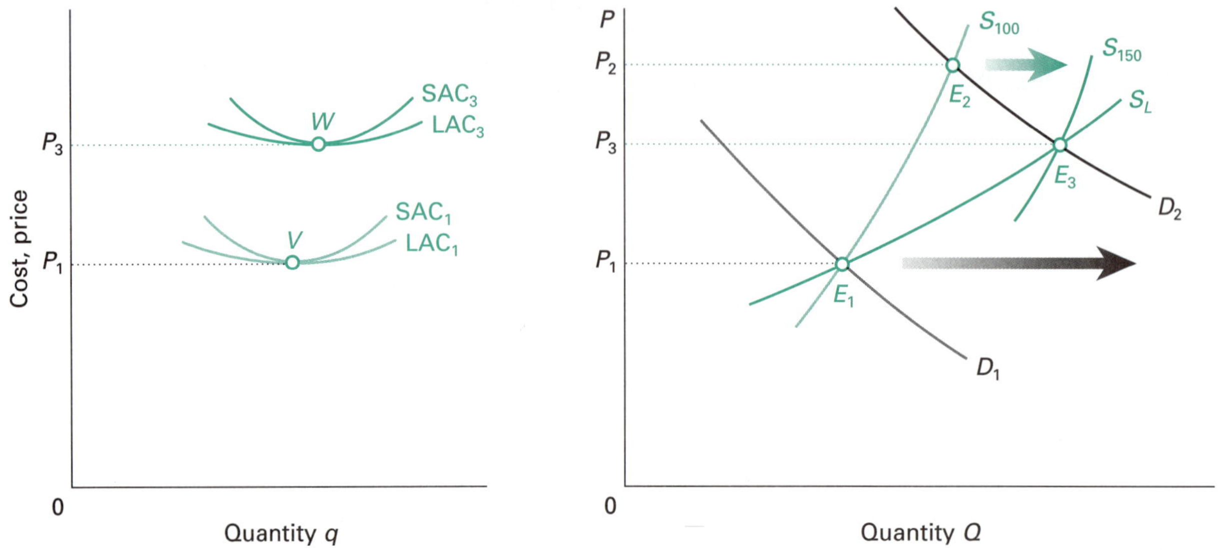


**(a) Firm.** **(b) Industry.**

**FIGURE 10-10 Long-run adjustment to an increase in demand when the supply curve is rising.** In this diagram, factors of production are not uniform in quality; some land is more suitable than other land for growing wheat. When demand increases from $D_1$ to $D_2$ in panel (b), the price rises to $P_2$ in the short run. The profits of existing farms attract new entrants. As the number of farms increases from 100 to 150, the short-run industry supply moves from $S_{100}$ to $S_{150}$. As a result, price declines from $P_2$ to $P_3$. However, it does not fall all the way back down to $P_1$ because the new entrants must use land that is less suitable for growing wheat. In the long run, the competition for the best land will bid its rent upwards, causing the cost curves of the initial firms in panel (a) to shift upward as profits are transformed into payments to land and other specialized factors of production.

supply curve $S_L$, constructed by joining long-run equilibrium points such as $E_1$ and $E_3$, slopes upward. It is more elastic than the short-run supply curves $S_{100}$ and $S_{150}$, but not perfectly elastic.

As the price of wheat increases and wheat farming is extended to less productive land, the costs of the original farmers will rise, as illustrated by the upward movement of the long-run cost curve from LAC$_1$ to LAC$_3$ in panel (a) of Figure 10-10. The reason is that their land will become more valuable. Rents on this original land will be bid up. New farmers are willing to pay a higher rent to get this land since their alternative is to move to less productive land. When this land is sold, it will go for a higher price; the land will be more valuable because of the rise in the price of wheat.

Competition in the market for land will push the average costs of the original wheat farms all the way up to the point where they again equal the price, at $W$ in panel (a). The reason is straightforward. If the average cost of a farm remained below price $P_3$, the farmer using this land would reap an above-normal profit. Other farmers would be eager to get such land, and competition would bid up its rent or selling price until such above-normal profits disappeared. Thus, competition for the most desirable land will mean that short-run profits will disappear as rents or prices of land increase; profits will be transformed into higher payments for land.

Note that we must be careful when interpreting a cost curve such as LAC$_3$ in Figure 10-10(a). At $W$, the firm is producing at its minimum average cost. But this does not mean that a fall in price would drive this farm out of the wheat industry. On the contrary, there is a cushion in this farm's costs. If the price of wheat falls, rents on this land will fall; costs will follow prices back down to point $V$ if demand shifts back to $D_1$ in panel (b).

## THE REALLOCATION OF RESOURCES: THE ROLE OF PROFITS

The discussion in the preceding paragraphs again points to an important feature of a market-based, capitalist economy. In such an economy, profits and losses provide both a *signal* and an *incentive* to business that the economy's resources should be reallocated. Profits are obviously important to individual businesses. They are also important because they promote economic efficiency. Specifically, profits encourage entrepreneurs to redeploy resources in response to changes in consumers' demand.

For example, when consumers demand more of a product, they bid up the price. The resulting short-run profits (Figure 10-8) encourage entrepreneurs to enter the industry, increasing output in response to consumers' demand.

Similarly, if demand for a product falls, price declines and businesses suffer short-term losses. The losses drive some producers out of the industry. In response to the decline in demand, less is produced. Some of the labour and capital in this industry are shifted elsewhere in the economy, where demand is stronger and where the resources can be put to better use. Again, as demand changes, prices and profits respond, providing a powerful incentive for firms to produce the goods and services that the public wants.

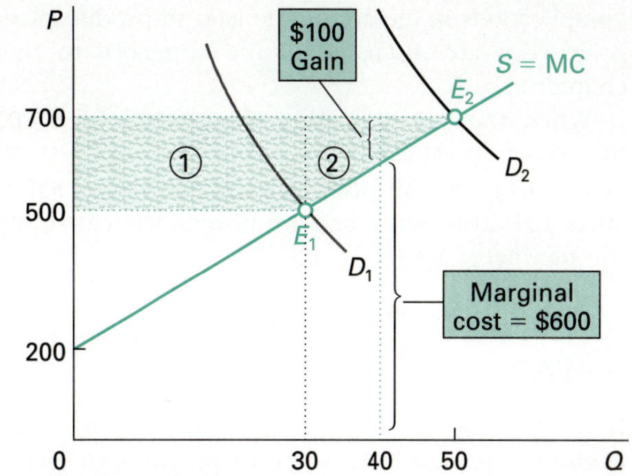


**FIGURE 10-11 The gain to producers when price rises.**

When the price rises from $500 to $700, producers gain. On each of the initial 30 units, they gain $200, as shown by area 1. On additional units produced, they gain the difference between the price and the marginal cost. For example, on the fortieth unit, the price is $700, while the marginal cost is $600. Thus, producers gain $100 on that unit. The gain on all such additional units is area 2, giving a total gain to producers of areas 1 + 2 when the price increases from $500 to $700.

## THE GAINS TO PRODUCERS FROM A HIGHER PRICE

When the price of a product rises, producers benefit. Figure 10-11 illustrates how much they gain when the price rises from $500 to $700.

At the lower price, firms produce at $E_1$ on their supply curve. Thirty units are sold. When the price increases to $700, output goes up to 50 units, at $E_2$.

For each of the initial 30 units, producers get an additional $200 when the price rises. This provides a gain of $200 × 30 = $6000, as illustrated by area 1.

There is also a gain on the additional 20 units. Consider one of these, say, unit 40. The marginal cost of that unit is measured by the height of the supply curve $S$—in this case, $600. (Recall that the supply curve is derived from the marginal cost curves of the producing firms, as explained in Figures 10-4 and 10-6.) Because the marginal cost of unit 40 is $600, while it fetches a price of $700, the producer gains $100 on that unit. Similar gains are made because price exceeds the marginal cost of other units as output increases from 30 to 50, giving a gain of triangular area 2. Thus, producers gain by areas 1 + 2 when price increases from $500 to $700.

Such gains go to somebody on the production side, but the recipients may be quite different in the short and the long run. In the short run, firms already in the industry capture the gain in the form of profits. In the long run, new firms enter and bid up the price of land or other specialized factors of production. Specialized factors of production may include labour with a particular skill. For example, as demand increases and the price of auto repairs goes up, service stations find that they must pay higher wages to attract and keep skilled mechanics.

Note that in the case where the supply curve is horizontal (case 1, above), the price of the product does not rise in the long run, and there is therefore no long-run gain to producers when demand increases. There are no specialized factors of production; inputs of equal quality are ready to enter the industry at stable prices. The competition from new entrants prevents any rise in the prices of inputs already being used by the industry. (Some additional complications in measuring the gain to producers as price rises are discussed in the appendix to this chapter.)

When the price increases from \$500 to \$700, the gain to producers is measured by areas 1 + 2, Figure 10-11. If the price falls from \$700 to \$500, areas 1 + 2 likewise measure how much worse off the producers are.

## REPRISE: THE BURDEN OF A TAX

It is now possible to investigate the effects of an excise tax in detail. Figure 10-12 provides an elaboration of the idea presented earlier in Figure 6-6. Once again, the brackets on the vertical axis illustrate how the burden of a \$1 tax is divided. In the example in Figure 10-12, the buyer pays 60¢ more, and the producer gets 40¢ less.

However, the total burden on buyers and sellers depends not only on the change in the price that each faces; it also depends on the number of units bought and sold.

In Figure 10-12, the number of units decreases from 5000 to 3000 as a result of the tax. The total burden on buyers is areas 1 + 2 — that is, the decrease in consumer surplus when the price that they pay increases. The price to producers goes down, and this inflicts a burden on them equal to areas 3 + 4.

Observe that the total burden to buyers and sellers together — areas 1 + 2 + 3 + 4 — exceeds the amount that the government collects in taxes. By collecting \$1 in tax on each of the 3000 units sold, the government gets revenues of \$3000 — that is, areas 1 + 3.

The \$3000 that goes out of the pockets of the buyers and sellers and into the government's treasury is known as the ***primary burden*** of the tax. The additionai burden on buyers and sellers — namely areas 2 + 4—is the ***excess burden*** of the tax. It does not "go" to anybody. It is a net loss in economic efficiency as a result of the tax, which results when buyers cut back their purchases by 2000 units. In the absence of a tax, consumers would have enjoyed area 2, and producers area 4.

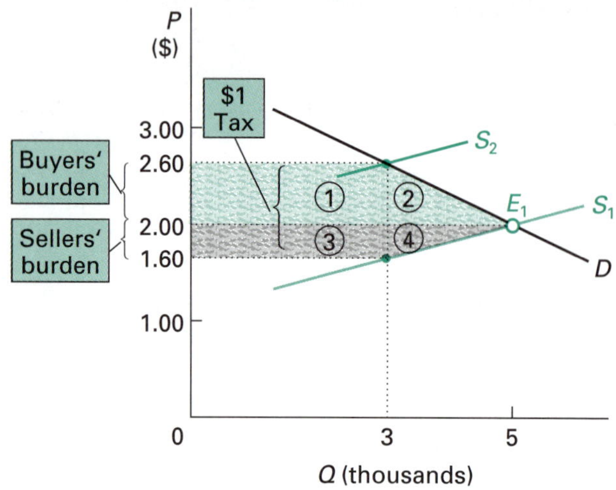


**FIGURE 10-12 The excess burden of a tax.**
Except in an extreme case where either the demand or surplus curve is horizontal, a tax will fall partly on consumers and partly on producers. In this example, the price increases from \$2 to \$2.60 when the \$1 tax is imposed, and the reduction in consumer surplus is therefore equal to areas 1 + 2. The price received by producers, net of tax, falls from \$2 to \$1.60. As a result, producers are worse off by areas 3 + 4. Thus, consumers and producers together are worse off by areas 1 + 2 + 3 + 4. The government's tax collections amount only to areas 1 + 3—that is, the tax of \$1 times the 3000 units sold. Thus, the losses to buyers and sellers together exceed the amount of tax collection by areas 2 + 4. Areas 2 + 4 are accordingly the excess burden of the tax; they represent a net loss to society.

The *primary burden* of a tax is the amount paid by the taxpayers to the government.

The *excess burden* of a tax is the loss in economic efficiency that results when people change their behaviour in response to the tax.

## KEY POINTS

1. An individual producer in a perfectly competitive market has no control over price. Hence, the demand curve facing each individual producer is perfectly elastic.
2. In a perfectly competitive market, a firm's marginal revenue MR = price *P*.

3. A firm maximizes profits by picking the output where MC = MR.
4. The short-run supply of a perfectly competitive firm is the portion of its marginal cost curve MC that lies above its average variable cost curve AVC.
5. If existing firms are making an above-normal profit, new firms will be attracted into that industry.
6. An industry's long-run supply is more elastic than its short-run supply. One important reason is that in response to a higher price, new firms enter. As a result, industry output increases.
7. If new firms can enter an industry without bidding up the prices of inputs, long-run supply is completely elastic. But if input prices are bid up as new firms enter, long-run supply is not completely elastic; it slopes upward.
8. A price increase provides a gain to producers equal to the area to the left of the supply curve, and between the old and the new price (areas 1 + 2 in Figure 10-11).
9. When the equilibrium quantity bought and sold in a market decreases as a result of a tax, the total burden borne by buyers and sellers together is greater than the amount of revenue the government collects. The difference is the excess burden of the tax.

## KEY TERMS

**price taker**
**freedom of entry and exit**
**marginal revenue**
**profit maximization where MR = MC**
**break-even point**
**shutdown point**
**economic profit**
**normal profit**
**above-normal profit**
**short-run market supply curve**
**long-run market supply curve**
**efficient scale**
**homogeneous inputs**
**primary burden of a tax**
**excess burden of a tax**

## PROBLEMS

10-1. Consider a perfectly competitive firm in the short run. Suppose marginal cost MC is $50, while marginal revenue MR is $90. Should the firm expand production? What happens to profit if it produces one more unit?

10-2. (a) Recalculate Table 10-1 and find the profit-maximizing output if the firm's price is $55. What is the profit at this output?
(b) Recalculate Table 10-1 and find the profit-maximizing output if the firm's price is $50. What happens to output as the price increases from $40 to $50? Why?

10-3. Suppose the fixed costs of the firm in Table 10-2 were $70 rather than $35.
(a) Recalculate the table.
(b) What happens to ATC? To MC? To the output of the firm? To profit?
(c) Does the output at which ATC reaches a minimum increase, decrease, or remain the same? Why?
(d) Calculate average variable cost AVC. Does the output at which AVC reaches a minimum increase, decrease, or remain the same? Why?
(e) If your answers were different for (c) and (d), explain why.
(f) At what price will this firm shut down? How does this compare with the shutdown price in Figure 10-4?

10-4. (a) Consider a firm operating at the lowest point on its SAC and LAC curves, for example, point *H* in Figure 10-8(a). Does its short-run supply extend below this point? If so, how far? Why?

(b) Suppose price falls below this point. Explain how the firm, with the benefit of hindsight, would view its original decision to enter this industry. What would its output be in the short run, and in the long run? What does this suggest about the relative elasticities of short-run supply and long-run supply?

10-5. Use a figure like Figure 10-12 to illustrate the gain to (a) consumers and (b) producers' associated with moving from a situation in which $P >$ MC to one where $P =$ MC in a perfectly competitive market. Relate the relative sizes of the gain in consumers surplus and the gain to producers to the concepts of demand and supply elasticity.

10-6. A firm (in the short run) is currently producing at a level of output that minimizes average total cost at $10 per unit. The price it can sell its output for in a competitive market is $8. What would you, a consultant, advise this firm to do? A diagram must be used to support your analysis.

10-7. Explain why economists include normal profit as a "cost." If above-normal profit exists, what does this tell us?

# APPENDIX 10-A

## USING THE SUPPLY CURVE TO MEASURE PRODUCER GAINS: SOME COMPLICATIONS

As we have seen in Figure 10-10, the long-run supply curve may slope upward because of different qualities of factors of production, such as different qualities of land used to grow wheat. In this case, a rise in the price of the product results in a gain for producers, measured in Figure 10-11 by the area to the left of the supply curve, and between the old and the new price, that is, areas 1 + 2. However, other forces may also affect the slope of the long-run supply curve, and these other forces may make this area to the left of the supply curve an imperfect measure of producer gain. In this appendix, we consider several examples.

### Case 1

First, the long-run supply curve may slope upward even if all factors of production have stable prices and their quality is uniform. For example, the supply of trucking services may slope upward even if the factors of production (drivers, trucks, etc.) are of uniform quality. The reason is that as more and more trucks are operated, the roads become congested. Trucks move more slowly and, as a consequence, the costs of the trucking companies rise. In turn, this makes the supply curve of trucking services slope upward.

In this case, an increase in the demand for trucking may cause an increase in the long-run equilibrium price, without any gain for producers—in particular, without any benefit to any factor of production in the trucking industry. The higher price may simply be dissipated in the higher costs resulting from road congestion.

### Case 2

It is even possible for the long-run supply curve to slope *downward* if all factors of production are of uniform quality. Consider the case of a metal-fabricating industry made up of a number of competitive firms located in a small city near Montreal. As the industry grows, the costs facing each firm may fall. This may occur, for example, because the Hamilton supplier who is shipping unprocessed steel to this industry is now delivering much more. There are economies of scale in shipping, and the resulting cost savings may be passed along to the firms buying steel.

### Case 3

Finally, there may be a combination of forces at work. For example, the long-run supply curve of the metal-fabricating industry may be horizontal because two sets of forces are balanced: As this industry expands, the fall in the price of unprocessed steel may be just offset by the rise in rents on land it uses.

In this case, an increase in output will be associated with a gain to producers. Specifically, the owners of land gain—even though the supply curve is horizontal and therefore provides no indication whatsoever of any gain for producers from expansion of this industry.

To sum up: Case 1 shows that the area to the left of the supply curve may exaggerate the gain for producers in an expanding industry; it may suggest a gain where none exists. On the other hand, case 3 illustrates how the area to the left of the supply curve may understate the gain to producers. In that instance, there was a gain, but it couldn't be shown to the left of the supply curve because the supply curve was horizontal.

Because of such complications, the supply curve can be used only as a rough first approximation in measuring producer gains, even in the long run.

CHAPTER 11

# PERFECT COMPETITION AND ECONOMIC EFFICIENCY

*Under perfect competition, the business dodoes, dinosaurs and great ground sloths are in for a bad time — as they should be.*

*R.H. Bork and W.S. Bowman, Jr.*

In Chapter 7, we examined how consumers in a perfectly competitive market respond to the price they face. In Chapter 10, we studied how producers on the other side of such a market respond. In this chapter, these two sides are brought together in order to *describe* how a perfectly competitive market operates. This will then be used to *evaluate* its performance from the point of view of society as a whole. Does a perfectly competitive market force producers to be efficient, as the quote above suggests? And how well does it deliver the goods and services the public wants?

This chapter shows that, if two important assumptions are satisfied, a perfectly competitive market does provide an efficient result: Neither too much nor too little output is produced. Future chapters will illustrate why other market structures typically do not result in allocative efficiency. For example, we shall see in the next chapter that monopoly is not efficient: Too little output is produced.

## Two Important Assumptions

Thus far, we have made no distinction between the private benefit a good provides to those who buy it, and the benefit it provides to society as a whole—its ***social benefit***. Often the two are the same. For example, when someone buys beefsteak, the only benefit that goes to society is the benefit received by that individual. There is no additional benefit to anyone else. However, private and social benefit don't always coincide in this way. For example, if your neighbours hire a gardener, they receive a benefit; but there is an additional benefit that goes to you and others as the neighbourhood becomes more pleasant to look at.

But, for now, we will ignore this complication. It is assumed that the purchaser is the only one who benefits from the good; that is, the benefit received by the purchaser represents the total benefit to society. Thus:

> ***Assumption 1.*** **Social benefit is the same as the private benefit of the purchaser. More precisely, the marginal benefit of a good to society as a whole—which we shall call $MB_S$—is the same as MB, its marginal benefit to those who buy it. Either can be measured by the price paid for a unit of the good.**
>
> $$MB_S = MB \text{ to consumers} \qquad (11\text{-}1)$$

Note that, even though we measure the marginal benefit of a good in terms of money, we can also think of it as the value of this good *relative to the value of other goods and services the consumer could have bought instead*. (Recall the discussion in Chapter 7 where we looked at the consumer's decision as to how many units of a good to buy, as a decision between "units of this good" and "money left over to spend on other goods.")

We make a similar assumption about ***social cost*** (compared with private cost):

***Assumption 2.*** **The cost of a good to society is the same as the private cost incurred by producers of this good. More precisely, the marginal cost of a good to society as a whole—which we shall call $MC_S$—is the same as MC, its marginal cost to producers. When producers sell the good in a competitive market, either can be measured by the price they receive per unit.**

$$MC_S = \text{MC to producers} \qquad (11\text{-}2)$$

Again, although the marginal cost of a good is measured in terms of money, we may also think of it as an opportunity cost in the form of other goods and services that society gives up by using resources to produce this good. The marginal cost to producers reflects the cost of the productive resources they have to buy in order to produce a unit of this good, and the assumption implies that the cost of these resources is a good measure of the value of the goods and services they could produce if they were employed in some other industry.

Just as the assumption of Equation (11-1) requires that the only one who benefits from a good is the one who buys it, the assumption of Equation (11-2) also will be true only if the total cost of producing a good is borne by the supplier. Usually, this is the case. For example, the cost to society of producing wheat, say, is just the cost of the seed, fertilizer, fuel, etc., that farmers pay, and the opportunity cost of the resources they provide themselves (such as their own land, labour, and capital). However, there are again exceptions. The cost to society of paper may be not only the private cost incurred by the firms producing it, but also the cost to those people living downstream who suffer if these firms dump polluting wastes into the river.

Exceptions to these two assumptions are important and will be the focus of attention in Chapters 21, 22, and 23. But until then, we will limit ourselves to describing perfectly competitive markets in the large number of cases where these two assumptions are valid.

## HOW A PERFECTLY COMPETITIVE MARKET WORKS

Figures 11-1 and 11-2 illustrate the decisions of many consumers and many producers in a perfectly com-

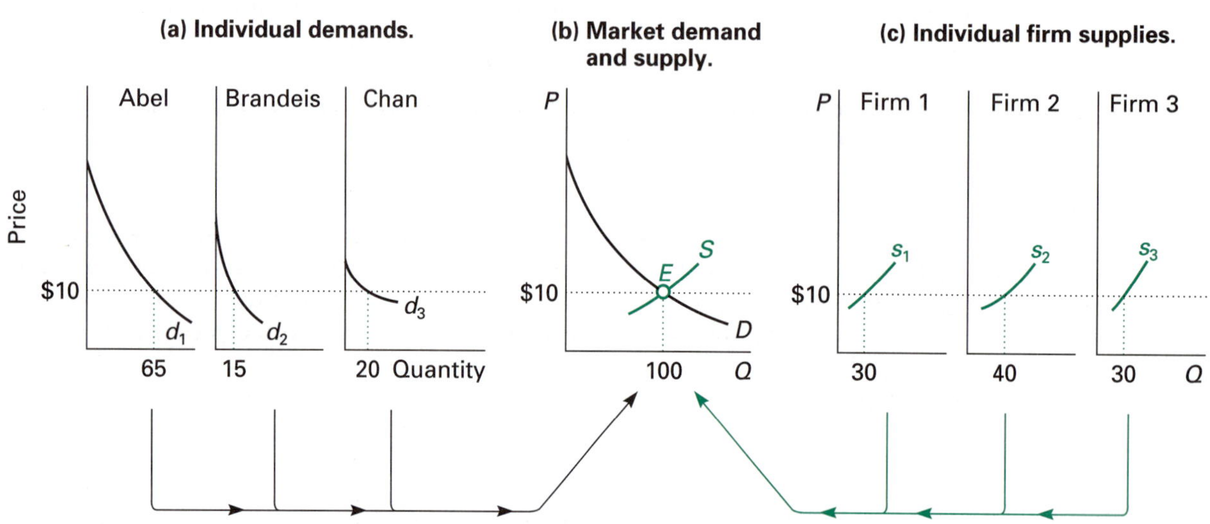


**FIGURE 11-1 Individual consumers and producers in a perfectly competitive market.** In panel (b), market demand $D$ is the sum of the individual demands in panel (a), while market supply $S$ is the sum of the supplies of individual firms in panel (c). The perfectly competitive solution, where $S$ and $D$ intersect, is at a price of $10 and an output of 100 units. The colour perpendiculars in panel (a) show how each consumer continues to purchase until marginal benefit MB equals the $10 price, while the colour perpendiculars in panel (c) show how much each firm produces to the point where its marginal cost MC is equal to this $10 price. Since each consumer's MB is equal, therefore, to each producer's MC, any change in production or consump-tion would result in an efficiency loss.

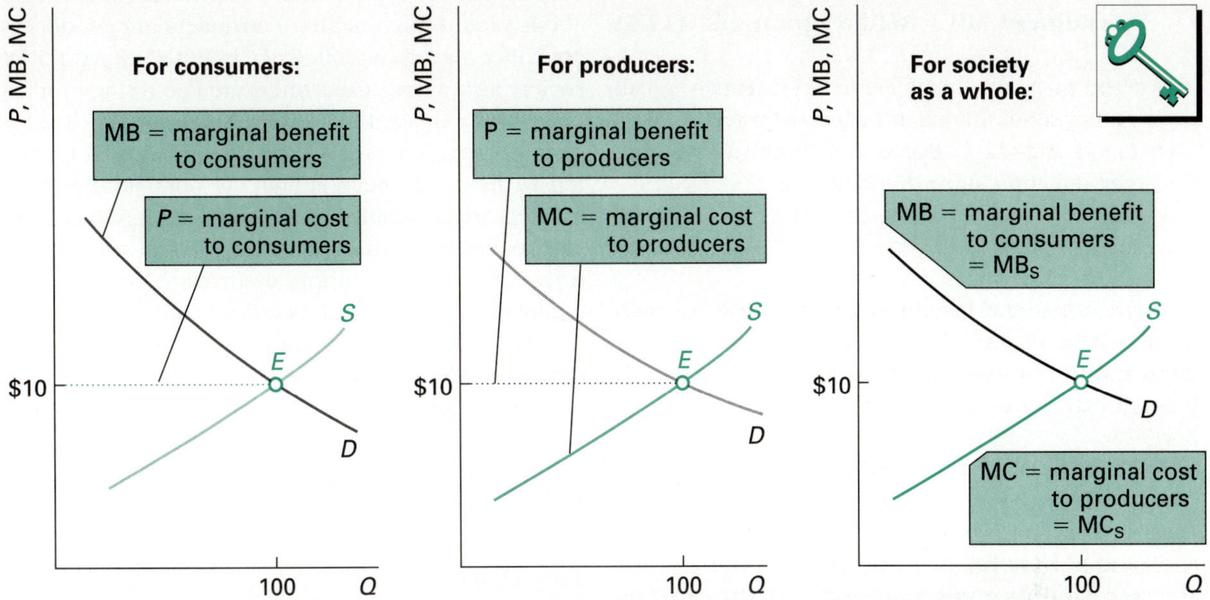


**(a)** If consumers purchase until *their* marginal benefit is equal to *their* marginal cost, that is, if

consumers' MB = *P*...

**(b)** and firms produce until *their* marginal benefit is equal to *their* marginal cost, that is, if

*P* = MC to producers ...

**(c)** then the consumers' marginal benefit MB will be equated to the producers' marginal cost MC; that is,

MB = MC

**FIGURE 11-2** **The competitive market: The equalization of marginal benefit and marginal cost leads to an efficient output.**

This is an elaboration of panel (b) in Figure 11-1.

petitive market. In the middle panel of Figure 11-1, note that supply and demand are equal at an equilibrium output of 100 units and a $10 price. At this equilibrium, the quantity purchased by each consumer is shown in panel (a) on the left, while the quantity sold by each producer is shown in panel (c) on the right. (As always, we use only a few consumers and producers to represent the very large number of participants in this market.)

In Figure 11-1, the centre panel showing *S* and *D* is so important that it is reproduced in Figure 11-2. In panel (a) of Figure 11-2 we show what's happening to consumers, as originally described in Figure 7-3. The demand curve tells us that, faced with a price of $10, consumers will purchase 100 units. That is, consumers facing a $10 price move to point *E* on the demand curve. Let's interpret that decision in more detail. As long as consumers are purchasing less than 100 units, their marginal benefit (given by the height of the demand curve) will be greater then their marginal cost of another unit (given by the $10 price *P*). Hence, it will be in their interest to buy another unit, and to continue to do so up to point *E* where their marginal benefit MB becomes equal to their marginal cost *P*.

$$\textbf{For consumers: MB} = P \qquad \textbf{(11-3)}$$

Panel (b) of Figure 11-2 shows what's happening to producers, as originally described in Figure 10-2. Producing firms make the decision that is best for *them* by continuing to produce and sell this good until *their* marginal benefit equals their marginal cost. In perfect competition, the marginal benefit that they get from selling one more unit is the price *P*. Therefore, they produce 100 units.

$$\textbf{For producers: } P = \textbf{MC} \qquad \textbf{(11-4)}$$

From these two equations, it follows that

$$\textbf{consumers' MB} = \textbf{MC to producers} \quad \textbf{(11-5)}$$

as we see in panel (c) of Figure 11-2. Finally, recall the two key assumptions introduced earlier in Equations (11-1) and (11-2). Because of these two assumptions, the equation above becomes:

$$\mathbf{MB_S = MC_S} \quad \textbf{(11-6)}$$

That is, the marginal benefit to society equals the marginal cost to society. This is the condition that provides an efficient outcome for society as a whole, as we will confirm in the next section.

**The efficient outcome for society is where $\mathbf{MB_S = MC_S}$.**
**This occurs in perfect competition, if social benefits are the same as benefits to consumers and social costs are the same as costs to producers.**

To sum up so far: Under perfect competition, with consumers making their best decision by equating their marginal benefit and marginal cost in panel (a) of Figure 11-2, and producers making *their* best decision by equating their marginal benefit and marginal cost in panel (b), the result in panel (c) is an efficient output for society as a whole. Notice that this comes about even though neither consumers nor producers are concerned about efficiency from the viewpoint of society as a whole. Consumers are just trying to maximize utility (make themselves as well off as possible), given the market prices they face. Producers are trying to make as much money as possible. Provided markets are competitive and the prices to which consumers and producers react are allowed to adjust in response to excess supply or demand, the resulting equilibrium is nevertheless efficient in this sense.

This is such an important conclusion in economics that we emphasize it in Box 11-1 and now illustrate it with two examples.

## DEMONSTRATING WHY PERFECT COMPETITION IS EFFICIENT

It has just been shown that if the assumptions in Equations (11-1) and (11-2) hold, perfect competition equates the marginal benefit to society $MB_S$ and the marginal cost to society $MC_S$. We will now demonstrate that when $MB_S = MC_S$, the outcome is efficient.

In Figure 11-3 we reproduce the market supply and demand curves from panel (c) of Figure 11-2.

### TOOLS AND TECHNIQUES — BOX 11-1
### Conditions that Result in an Efficient Solution

Since MB and MC represent marginal private benefits and costs, and $MB_S$ and $MC_S$ represent marginal social benefits and costs, then:

If social and private benefits are the same,

$$MB_S = MB \quad (11\text{-}1)$$

and if consumers in a perfectly competitive market act in their own self-interest by purchasing up to the point where their marginal benefit equals price

$$MB = P \quad (11\text{-}3)$$

and if producers in a perfectly competitive market act in their own self-interest by producing up to the point where their marginal cost equals price,

$$P = MC \quad (11\text{-}4)$$

and if private and social costs are the same,

$$MC = MC_S \quad (11\text{-}2)$$

then Adam Smith's "invisible hand" works; the pursuit of private interest by both consumers and producers yields a result that is in the interest of society as a whole

$$MB_S = MC_S \quad (11\text{-}6)$$

That is, there is an efficient solution.

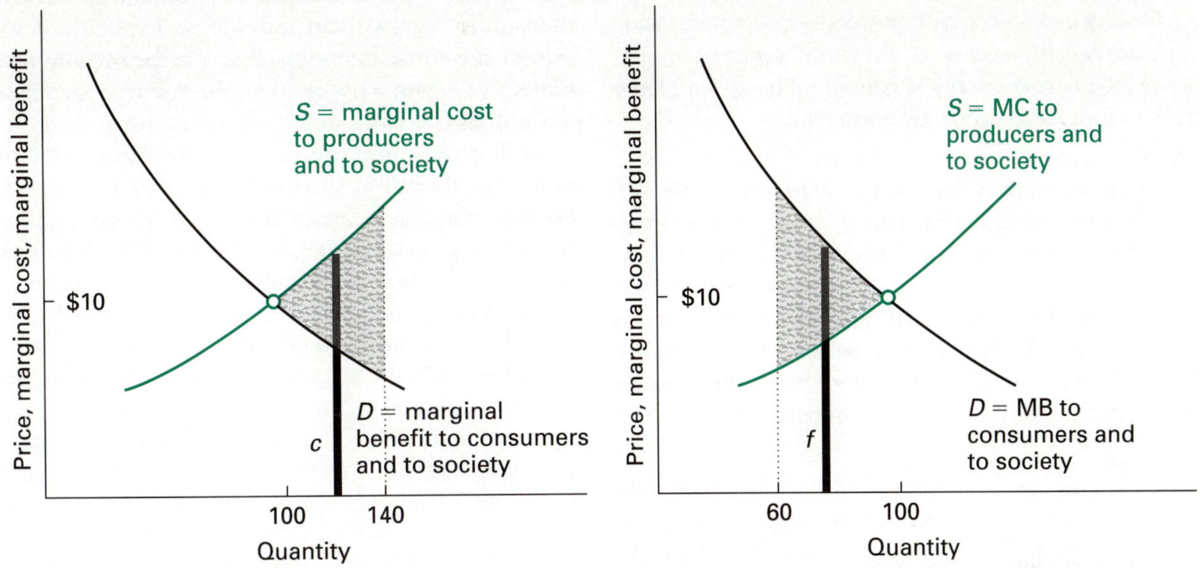


**(a) Too much.** Output is 140, which is greater than the perfectly competitive equilibrium of 100 where marginal benefit to society is equal to marginal cost to society. On each of these 40 additional units there is an efficiency loss because marginal cost (the height of the supply curve) exceeds marginal benefit (the height of the demand curve). The total efficiency loss from all such units of excess output is the shaded triangle.

**(b) Too little.** Output is restricted to only 60 units, less than the perfectly competitive level of 100. On each of these 40 units forgone, marginal benefit (the height of the demand curve) would have exceeded marginal cost (the height of the supply curve). There is therefore an efficiency loss because these potentially beneficial units are not produced. This loss is shown as the shaded triangle.

**FIGURE 11-3 Inefficient quantities of output.**

Now suppose output is expanded beyond the perfectly competitive quantity of 100 units where marginal benefit to society equals marginal cost to society. Specifically, in panel (a) of Figure 11-3, suppose the quantity is 140 units. This outcome is inefficient, as we can see by considering any one of the additional units of output beyond 100—unit *c*, for example. The benefit it provides to society is shown by the black bar, the height of the demand curve. However, its cost is even greater, as shown by both this black bar and the grey bar above it—that is, the height of the supply curve. Thus, the marginal cost of this unit exceeds the benefit it provides; there is a net loss to society shown by the grey bar. The sum of all similar losses on all the excess units of output in the range between 100 and 140 is shown by the black triangle. This is the efficiency loss from producing too much. This idea is important. Even though something such as food may be inherently very good — and, indeed, essential to life itself— it is possible to produce too much of it.

On the other hand, suppose that for some reason output is less than 100 units—say, the 60 units shown in panel (b). This outcome is also inefficient; to see why, consider one of the units that is no longer produced, say *f*. Its cost would have been the black bar under the supply curve, and its benefit the black bar plus the grey bar under the demand curve. Thus, the net benefit to society of producing it would have been the grey bar—that is, the amount by which benefits to consumers exceed costs of production. Or, to put the same point another way, society incurs the loss of this grey bar because this potentially beneficial unit is not produced. The sum of all such losses through the range of restricted output from 100 down to 60 is the black triangle. This is the efficiency loss from producing too little. An example is the rent control program described earlier in Chapter 6, which leads to a reduced output of housing units and, therefore, an efficiency loss.

Thus, the perfectly competitive output of 100 units is the efficient output, where marginal benefit and marginal cost to society are equal. There is an efficiency loss if either more or less is produced.

This idea of an ***efficiency loss***—sometimes called a ***deadweight loss*** — is a central concept in the study of microeconomics; you should master Figure 11-3 before proceeding. In particular:

> **An efficiency loss—or deadweight loss—occurs whenever there is a move away from the output where the marginal benefit to society is equal to the marginal cost to society. Such an efficiency loss from producing too much or too little can be shown graphically by triangle-shaped areas, such as those in Figure 11-3.**

Finally, as an alternative demonstration of why ***allocative efficiency*** occurs at the perfectly competitive output—where marginal benefit and cost to society are equal— return to Figure 11-1, where we first illustrated the perfectly competitive market. Suppose you are an all-powerful bureaucrat or czar and think you can do better than this perfectly competitive solution. Specifically, suppose that you arbitrarily order that, instead of the equilibrium quantity of 100 units, 40 more units are to be produced. Try as you like, you cannot avoid a social loss on those additional units. On the one hand, they must cost more than \$10 to produce. Regardless of the firms you select to produce them in panel (c), those firms will have to move to the right, up their supply curves to a higher marginal cost. At the same time, those additional units will be consumed by individuals in panel (a) who value them at less than \$10. No matter who gets to consume these units, those individuals will move to the right, down their demand curves to a lower marginal benefit. Because the cost of each additional unit is greater than \$10, and the benefit it provides is less than \$10, there is a net social loss— that is, an efficiency loss. You thought you could do better. In fact, you did worse.

## COMPETITION AND EFFICIENCY: THE TWO-GOOD CASE

As an alternative to using demand and supply curves to show that perfect competition leads to an efficient amount of output, we can also use the indifference curve concept that was introduced in Chapter 7, and the production possibilities curve (PPC) from Chapter 2. Because we are limited to two-dimensional diagrams, however, we can only do so explicitly if we look at a simple economy that produces only two goods; we again choose our old friends, food and clothing as the two goods.

To illustrate how the prices of food and clothing guide the allocation of resources, suppose first that we start out at a point such as *A* on the production possibilities curve in Figure 11-4. The PPC has been drawn so that its slope at point *A* is 1/2. That is, when the economy produces 13 units of food and 10 units of clothing, the opportunity cost of an additional unit of clothing is only 1/2 unit of food. Equivalently, the productive resources that are used to produce the last unit of food at point *A* could have been used instead to produce as much as two units of clothing. (Recall from Chapter 2 the reason why the PPC has the

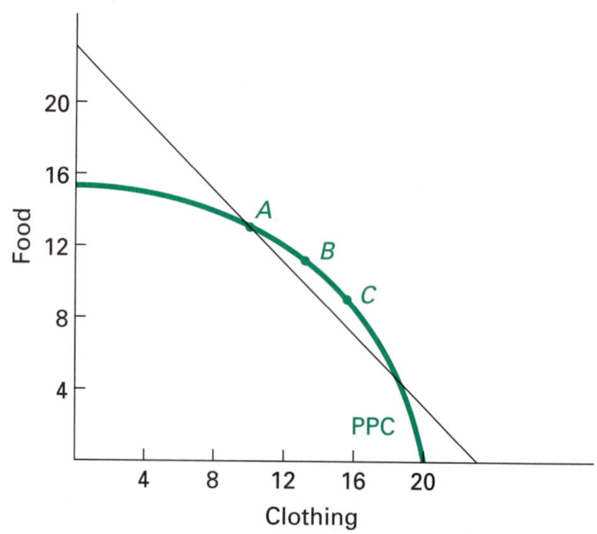


**FIGURE 11-4 Prices and marginal costs in equilibrium: Another view.**

If the prices for one unit of food and one unit of clothing are both \$10, point *A* cannot be a long-run equilibrium point on the production possibilities curve PPC. The slope of the PPC at *A* is 1/2, telling us that the resources needed to produce the last unit of food could be used instead to produce two units of clothing. But if the prices of food and clothing are the same, two units of clothing would give twice as much revenue as one unit of food. Therefore, resources would be transferred from the food to the clothing industry, and the economy would move toward point *B*.

bowed shape shown in Figure 11-4, becoming flatter as we move upward along it, producing more and more food and less and less clothing: As more and more food is produced, the food industry is forced to utilize even those productive resources that are best suited to produce clothing, not food. Thus, the opportunity cost of producing more food becomes higher and higher.)

Now suppose that the firms in the food and clothing industries sell their products in competitive markets, and suppose initially that the prices of both food and clothing are each $10 per unit. Thus the total revenue of the firms in the food industry is $130, while those in the clothing industry receive $100.

## Producers' Response

As we know from circular-flow diagrams such as Figure 3-3 or 4-8, the revenues of the firms in the economy get passed on as incomes to households, as wages, interest, or profits of lenders and shareholders, land rent to farmers, and so on. The households then use these incomes to buy the food and clothing that the firms produce, as the process continues in a never-ending circle.

In the indifference curve diagrams in Chapter 7, we represented the households' budget limitation by a budget line showing different combinations of goods that consumers could buy out of their total income, at given prices. The position of the budget line was determined by the households' total income, and its slope reflected the price of the good on the horizontal axis, relative to the prices of other goods. In Figure 11-4, we have drawn such a budget line *for all households together*. Since the households' total income is equal to the total revenue that firms earn from the production of food and clothing at point *A*, the line must go through this point. (Because every dollar the firms earn goes back as income to households, the households' total income will be high enough to buy what the firms produce.) Moreover, the slope of the budget line equals (negative) 1, since both goods cost $10 per unit.

Point *A*, however, cannot be a long-run equilibrium when the prices of food and clothing both are $10 per unit. Recall again that the slope of the PPC at point *A* is 1/2, meaning that the resources needed to produce one unit of food could be used instead to produce *two* units of clothing. But if the firms pay the same prices for the labour and other resources they use in production, this must mean that at point *A*, *the firms in the food industry are making losses, and those in the clothing industry are making (above-normal) profits*. Through the process of entry and exit, resources will then be transferred out of the food industry and into the clothing industry, moving the economy to a point such as *B* or *C*. In fact, if the prices of one unit of food and one unit of clothing remain equal, resources will continue to be reallocated to the clothing industry until the slope of the PPC equals (negative) 1, which occurs at point *C*. At that point, the opportunity cost of the last unit of food is exactly one unit of clothing: The resources that could be saved by producing one less unit of food could produce no more than one additional unit of clothing. Thus moving these resources from the food to the clothing industry (or vice versa) would yield no net profit since the prices of food and clothing are the same.

Note that a budget line through point *C* with a slope of (negative) 1 would be tangent to the PPC. It would, therefore, correspond to the highest total income that the economy can generate when the prices of food and clothing are $10 each. Thus, the competitive economy in this example would be efficient in the sense that it would lead to the highest possible household income, at the given prices of food and clothing.

## Market Equilibrium

In Figure 11-5, we put this theory of competitive producer behaviour together with our earlier theory of consumer behaviour, in which we described consumer preferences with a set of indifference curves. In a perfectly competitive economy in which every producer and every consumer takes prices as given, equilibrium is at *E* in Figure 11-5. On the one hand, as firms reallocate resources in response to profits or losses, the economy moves toward a point such as *E*, at which the income line is tangent to the PPC—that is, the point where the total income of the economy is maximized, given the prices of food and clothing. At the same time, consumers maximize their utility by also selecting point *E*—because this is the point of tangency between their highest attainable indifference curve $u_2$ and the income line *L*. Thus, the community as a whole achieves an efficient solution, because at *E* it is producing the combination of food and clothing that lifts it to its highest attainable level of utility $u_2$. Given the community's ability to produce, as shown by its PPC, there is no way it can reach a higher level of satisfaction than $u_2$. For example, it's not possible to reach $u_3$.

This, then, is our alternative illustration of the proposition established in Figure 11-2: A competitive economy leads to an efficient solution.[1]

It should be emphasized again that this efficient solution results from producers on the one hand and consumers on the other responding independently to the competitive market prices reflected in the slope of the income line $L$.[2] This, in turn, raises the final question: Why does the competitive market generate the relative prices shown by the slope of the income line $L$ through point $E$ in Figure 11-5? To answer this question, suppose that initially the relative prices are different; specifically, suppose that they are shown by line $L_1$ in Figure 11-6. (The flatter slope of $L_1$ reflects a lower relative price of clothing.) Facing these relative prices, producers maximize their income by producing at $A$, the point of tangency between the PPC and income line $L_1$. But consumers try to consume at

[1] According to this analysis, there seems to be a unique efficient solution at $E$. Later in this chapter, however, we will see that in general, the efficient allocation of resources in an economy is *not* unique. For each income distribution there may be a different efficient solution.

This puzzle is resolved by noting that in Figure 11-5 we have drawn a set of indifference curves for the *community as a whole*, rather than for an individual household. There are problems in defining such a community indifference system; there is no simple way of "adding up" the preferences of all the individuals in the nation. To illustrate, consider the simple extreme case of a two-person economy. If I have all the income, my preferences are the ones that count; if you have all the income, it is your preferences that count. In other words, a community's preferences depend on who has the income. This means that there is no unique community indifference system; the community's indifference map can change every time there is a change in the distribution of income. Nor, as a consequence, is there any unique efficient equilibrium; the equilibrium depends on how the nation's income is distributed.

[2] To illustrate what can go wrong if producers do not act as perfect competitors, suppose that the producers of clothing form a monopoly and restrict the supply of clothing. In other words, the economy moves to the left of $E$ in Figure 11-5 and it is no longer possible to reach indifference curve $u_2$. Consequently, the nation's utility is less than a maximum, that is, less than $u_2$.

## ECONOMICS IN HISTORY — BOX 11-2

### Pareto and the Elimination of Deadweight Loss

A bit of extra effort and imagination can increase our understanding of the important idea of efficiency.

A change that will make at least one individual better off without hurting anyone else is called a *Pareto-improvement*, after Italian economist Vilfredo Pareto (1848–1923), who originated the idea. If we have made all such Pareto-improvements, we arrive at a *Pareto-optimum*. This is exactly what economists mean by an efficient solution. It means that all deadweight losses have been eliminated—that is, all possible Pareto-improvements have been made. It is no longer possible to make any individual better off without making somebody else worse off.

The idea of a Pareto-improvement can be illustrated by referring back to Figure 11-1. Suppose that initially Brandeis gets one less unit than we have shown there (namely, 14 units), while Chan gets one more (21 units). A Pareto-improvement is now possible because we can make Chan better off without hurting anyone else—that is, without hurting Brandeis, the only other person involved. Here's how. Let Chan sell that one unit to Brandeis for $10. Chan benefits from this transaction: Because he values his twentieth unit at $10, he values his twenty-first unit—the one he is giving up—at less than $10; so he benefits when he receives $10 for it. At the same time, Brandeis has not been hurt because he values the unit he receives—his fifteenth—at exactly the same $10 that he pays for it.

This Pareto-improvement is possible because initially all producers and consumers did not value their last unit equally. But, with this transaction, we have reached the perfectly competitive solution in Figure 11-1, where all consumers and producers do value their last unit equally, at $10. That is, the marginal benefit MB for every consumer is now equal to the MB for every other consumer, and is also equal to the marginal cost MC for every producer. Consequently, any further Pareto-improvement is impossible. Therefore, this perfectly competitive solution is Pareto-optimal, that is, efficient.

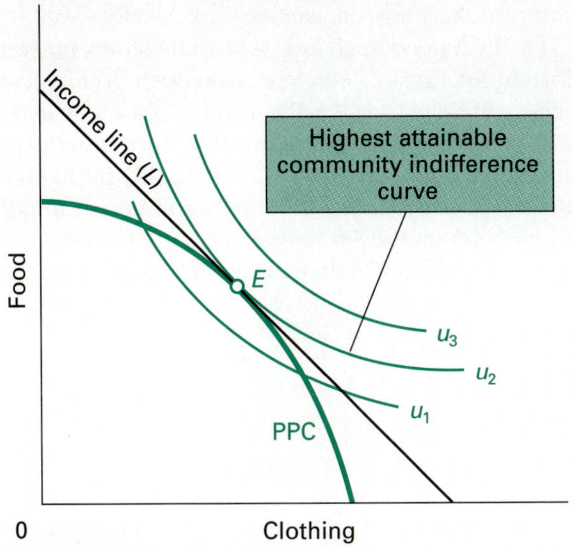


**FIGURE 11-5 The competitive equilibrium.**
The competitive equilibrium occurs at *E*. Producers pick the point where the PPC is tangent to the highest attainable income line. Consumers pick the point where the income line is tangent to the highest attainable indifference curve. At this point, *E*, the production possibilities curve and the indifference curve are tangent. The maximum level of utility $u_2$ is achieved, given the productive capacity of the economy as shown by the PPC.

*B*, the point of tangency between income line $L_1$ and indifference curve $u_3$. However, they are, in fact, unable to reach point *B*, since the economy is incapable of producing this combination of food and clothing. (*B* is outside the PPC.) As a consequence, markets are out of equilibrium. The quantity $C_B$ of clothing demanded by consumers exceeds the quantity $C_A$ supplied by producers; the price of clothing consequently rises. At the same time, the quantity $F_B$ of food demanded is less than the quantity $F_A$ supplied; the price of food falls. As the relative prices of food and clothing change, the slope of the income line changes. Specifically, the income line rotates from $L_1$ toward *L*. In response, producers move from *A* toward *E*, while consumers move from *B* toward *E*. This movement continues until the income line actually becomes *L* and producers and consumers have moved all the way to *E*. It is only then that demand and supply are brought into equilibrium. Thus, the equilibrium prices are indeed those reflected in line *L*.

A further discussion of efficiency is provided in Box 11-2, opposite.

# EFFICIENCY IN THE SHORT RUN AND IN THE LONG RUN

In Chapter 6, we distinguished between the short-run supply curve and the long-run supply curve. When we say, in this chapter, that an equilibrium where the demand curve intersects the competitive supply curve is efficient, are we talking about the short-run or long-run supply curve?

The answer is: Both. In the short run, the number of firms in the industry, and the buildings and capital equipment of each firm, are fixed. The only question, from either the firms' or society's point of view, is: Are we using the right amount of variable factors, and producing the efficient amount of output, given these fixed factors? If the assumptions earlier in the chapter are valid, the answer is yes, provided we produce the quantity where the short-run industry supply curve intersects the demand curve. Thus in the short run, a

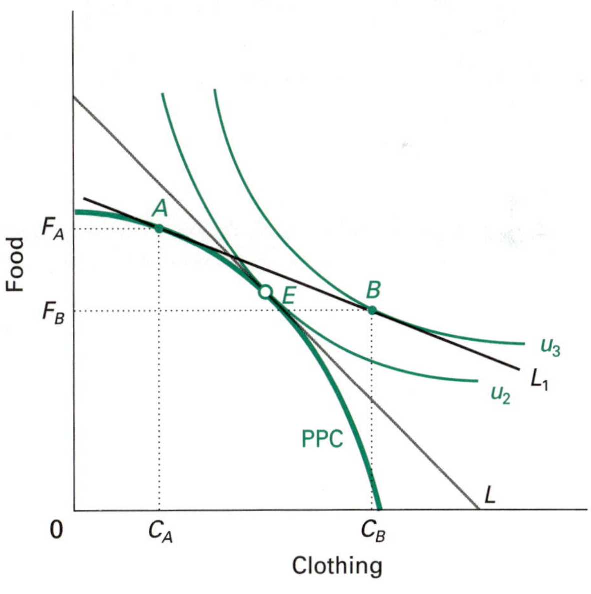


**FIGURE 11-6 How markets adjust from an initial point of disequilibrium.**
If the relative price of clothing is originally below its equilibrium—that is, if prices are those reflected in $L_1$ rather than *L*—producers will want to produce at *A* and consumers will want to consume at *B*. As a result, there will be a shortage of clothing equal to $C_B - C_A$ and a surplus of food equal to $F_A - F_B$. Consequently, the price of clothing will rise and the price of food will fall until these prices reach their equilibrium values, reflected in the slope of the income line *L*.

point such as $E_2$ in Figure 10-8(b) is efficient, if the market demand curve is at $D_2$.

However, point $E_2$ is not an efficient long-run equilibrium. In Figure 11-7, at a price of $P_1$, existing firms such as A with short-run average cost curve $SAC_A$ and B with short-run average cost curve $SAC_B$ are earning economic profits. Thus, a new firm could enter the market and make a profit as well. That is, the benefit to society of the additional units of output it could produce (the marginal social benefit, measured by value of the additional units at the market price) would be higher than than the cost of producing these units (the marginal social cost). In the long run, a competitive equilibrium is not efficient unless all economic profits have been eliminated.

But as we saw in Chapter 10, with free entry, economic profits will gradually be eliminated. New firms of efficient scale ($SAC_B$ in Figure 11-7) will enter; as a result, firms that are not of efficient scale ($SAC_A$) will either be eliminated, or have to expand until they become efficient. With more firms in the market, output will increase and price will fall. In the long-run competitive equilibrium, all surviving firms will be of efficient scale and produce at a point such as *C*; the equilibrium price will be $P^*$. Since $SAC_B$ represents the most efficient plant size, point *C* is the minimum point on the long-run average cost curve as well.

Finally, a point such as *C* is also the short-run equilibrium for firms of efficient scale, with average cost curves like $SAC_B$, when the market price equals $P^*$. When the market price is equal to the value at the minimum point on the SAC curve, the profit-maximizing quantity (where $P$ = MC) will be at the minimum point on the SAC curve, since the marginal cost curve cuts the SAC curve at the minimum point.

## LIVING IN A GLOBAL ECONOMY: FREER ENTRY INTO THE LONDON FINANCIAL MARKET

Several years ago, the British government decided to relax regulations in the financial markets. In the "Big Bang" of 1986, it abruptly swept many regulations aside, including barriers restricting foreign firms operating in London. Many banks and other financial institutions from New York, Tokyo, and the world's other

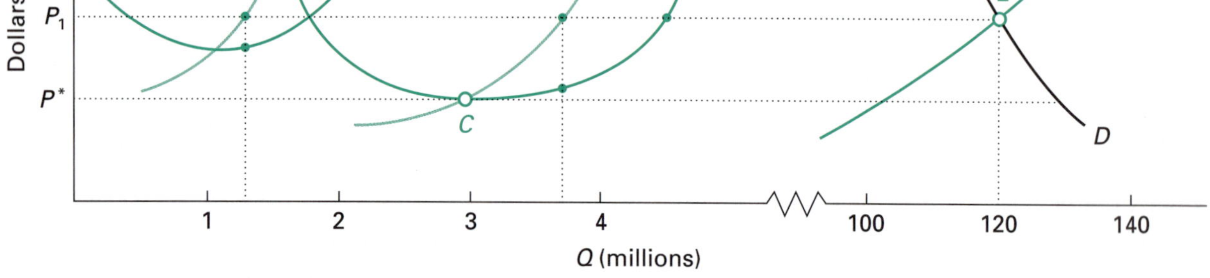


**FIGURE 11-7 Efficiency in the short run and in the long run.**
In the short run, a point such as *E* is efficient, even though some firms are earning economic profits: As long as each firm is producing where price equals short-run marginal cost, society is making the best possible use of the existing productive capacity. Equivalently, society's variable factors are allocated efficiently.

In the long run, an equilibrium is efficient only if all economic profits are eliminated. That is, each firm must have productive equipment that puts it on the lowest possible short-run average cost curve (the lowest point on the long-run average cost curve), and produce the amount corresponding to the minimum point on this curve (point *C*). Note that when the price of output is $P^*$, point *C* is also firm B's short-run equilibrium: $MC_B$ cuts $SAC_B$ at its minimum point.

financial centres seized the opportunity. The resulting intense competition quickly drove down the fees for financial services, such as buying or selling stocks or bonds. Although this industry may still not precisely follow the perfectly competitive model, opening up the entry of new firms has made it far more competitive and efficient.

In terms of Figure 11-3(b), the pre-1986 supply was well to the left of *S* because of government regulations that restricted foreign firms. Price was high, and there was an inefficiently low quantity of services provided. When regulations were relaxed and the output of foreign firms consequently increased, the supply curve shifted to the right toward *S*. Prices fell and quantity increased toward the efficient amount where *S* equals *D*.

## OTHER TYPES OF EFFICIENCY

Thus far we have shown only how a perfectly competitive market can provide *allocative* efficiency. How does this market measure up in terms of ***technological*** and ***dynamic*** efficiency?

### Technological, or Technical, Efficiency

Technological, or technical, efficiency means avoiding outright waste. Thus, a restaurant is technically inefficient if it produces a standard meal using the same amount of capital, but twice as much labour as other restaurants. A construction firm is technically inefficient if it destroys its machinery because it fails to keep it oiled. In brief, technical inefficiency exists if there is poor management and unnecessarily high costs. To illustrate, in panel (a) of Figure 11-8, technical inefficiency raises the firm's average cost curve up to $AC_2$, compared with the average cost curve $AC_1$ of a technically efficient firm.

Perfect competition works toward technical efficiency as well as allocative efficiency. If a firm is inefficient and is therefore producing at a high-cost point, such as *F*, it won't be able to survive in competition with technically efficient firms that produce with average costs at *G*. Thus, there is a tendency for inefficient firms to go the way of the dinosaurs — to become extinct, by being driven out of business by their existing competitors or by new firms with lower costs. (Note how perfect competition puts pressure on firms to produce at the lowest point on their average cost curves. We also saw this in our earlier example in Figure 9-9, where the firms that survive in the long run produce at the lowest point *H*.)

In contrast to the firm in perfect competition, a monopoly firm may be protected from the pressures of competition. If it has a stranglehold on a market—because of a patent, for example—it can survive even if management is sloppy; it doesn't have to worry about facing new competitors. But even though

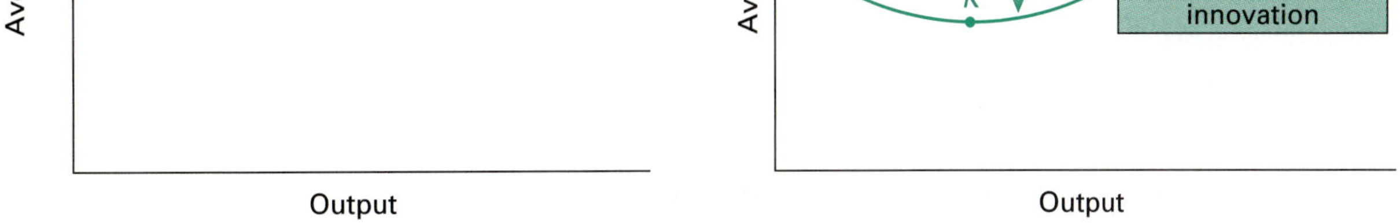


**(a)** Perfect competition results in technological efficiency because it forces inefficient firms operating on $AC_2$ (at a point such as *F*) down to $AC_1$ to a point such as *G*.

**(b)** In this case an innovation shifts the average cost curve down. Perfectly competitive firms at a point such as *G* are now forced down to a "new technology" point such as *K* or are driven out of business.

**FIGURE 11-8 How perfect competition promotes technical and dynamic efficiency.**

monopoly does not have to achieve technical efficiency, it still has an incentive to do so; greater technical efficiency means greater profits. Therefore, in later chapters we will generally show monopoly firms producing on their technically efficient average cost curves.

## Dynamic Efficiency

Dynamic efficiency exists when changes are occurring at the best rate—for example, when new technology is being developed and adopted at the best rate. While a competitive market gets high marks for promoting allocative efficiency and technical efficiency, its superiority is less clear in terms of dynamic efficiency.

In some ways, perfect competition does indeed promote dynamic efficiency. Suppose, for example, that a new process or new invention has been discovered that reduces costs. This shifts the average cost curve down as shown in panel (b) of Figure 11-8. Firms that do not lower their costs by adapting to this new technology will be left producing at a point such as *G*, at a disadvantage in competing with firms using the new technology and producing at a point such as *K*. Thus, firms that ignore new technology and are consequently unable to compete will also go the way of the dinosaurs. We conclude that by forcing firms to *adopt* new technology, perfect competition promotes dynamic efficiency.

However, let's go one step further and ask the question: What sort of market does the best job of *creating* new technology in the first place? There is considerable debate over this question, with many contending that, in this respect, perfect competition is not necessarily best. It is easier for a large, monopolistic firm to finance the research necessary for many innovations. Furthermore, a large firm has more incentive to engage in research, since it may have a large enough share of the total market to reap many of the gains. In contrast, no individual farmer has much incentive to try to develop a new strain of wheat; most of the gains would go to other farmers. (It is this lack of incentive for individual farmers that has led the government into supporting agricultural research.)

In conclusion, the competitive market scores high in two of the three aspects of efficiency including allocative efficiency—which will be our focus in the next few chapters.

## REPRISE: HOW THE COMPETITIVE MARKET DETERMINES WHO WILL PRODUCE AND WHO WILL CONSUME

Figure 11-9 shows how a competitive market answers two key questions: Who will produce a good, and who will consume it?

Panel (a) shows how demand and supply determine the equilibrium quantity and $15 price. Panel (b) illustrates how the $15 price acts as a barrier that determines who will consume this good. Thus, price

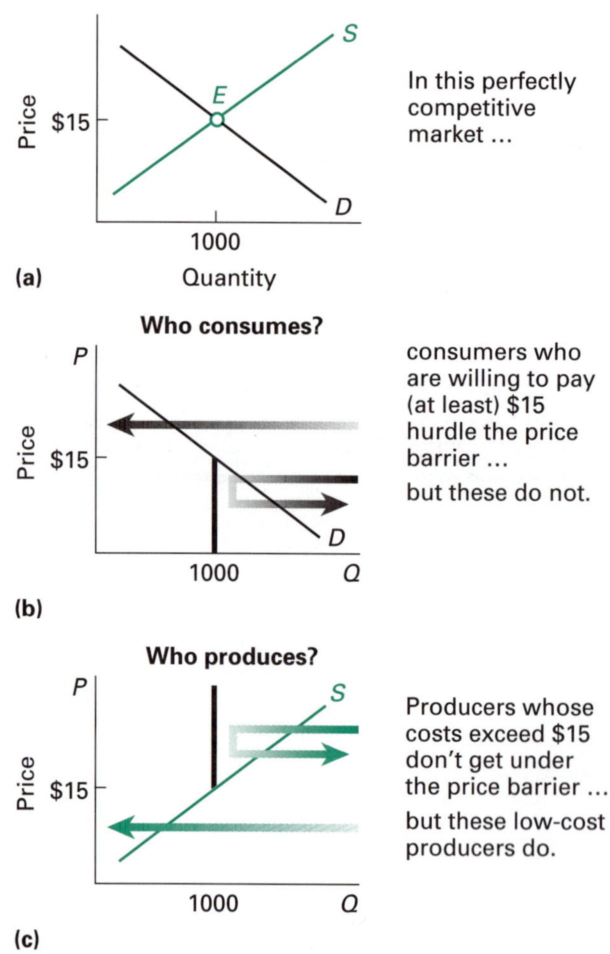


**FIGURE 11-9 Price as a barrier that screens buyers and sellers in a competitive market.**

acts as a ***rationing device***. Those who value the good at $15 a unit or more will buy it; those who place less value on it, won't buy it. In panel (c), this same price also acts as a barrier, blocking out all high-cost producers who are unable to sell it for $15. Thus, a perfectly competitive price screens out unenthusiastic buyers and high-cost sellers; both groups are excluded from the market because of one simple criterion — they are unwilling or unable to meet the market price. Thus, the answer of a perfectly competitive market to the question: "Which firms will produce a good?" is "Those that can do so least expensively." Its answer to the question: "Which individuals will get to consume the good?" is "Those who place the highest dollar value on it."

## PREVIEW: PROBLEMS WITH THE COMPETITIVE MARKET

So far, this analysis has painted a rosy picture of how well perfectly competitive markets work. The examples of inefficient outcomes occurred when the government intervened to overrule the workings of a competitive market. When the government czar dictated output, too much was produced. When the government set a rent ceiling, too little housing was produced. Indeed, up to this point, the analysis has had a strong laissez-faire message: The government should leave the market alone, its wonders to perform.

However, this gives a distorted view of the Canadian economy. In particular, our conclusion that a perfectly competitive market is efficient depends on the four basic conditions listed in Table 11-1, and they are often violated. Table 11-1 shows how they may be violated, and lists the chapters that deal with each case. When these conditions are violated, a laissez-faire economy will operate inefficiently. Government intervention may make the economy work more efficiently, not less. Furthermore, *even when all four conditions are met*, the outcome will not necessarily be quite as good as this chapter has so far suggested, as we shall now see.

## RESERVATIONS ABOUT THE PERFECTLY COMPETITIVE OUTCOME

### 1. It Depends on the Distribution of Income

Let's return again to Figure 11-1. Looking at the individual demand curves in panel (a), suppose that Abel has a higher income than Brandeis and this is the reason why he has greater demand for this good. (Remember, demand depends both on desire for the product and ability to pay. With his higher income, Abel has a greater ability to pay.) Figure 11-10 is almost identical to Figure 11-1, with only the one change shown in panel (a): The incomes of Abel and Brandeis are reversed. Brandeis now has the high income and hence high demand, while Abel has the low income and low demand, as shown by the first two individual demand curves in this diagram. Since nothing else need change,[3] the rest of Figure 11-10 is the same as before. In this diagram, just as in Figure 11-1, a perfectly competitive market yields an efficient

[3] With the switch in incomes, market price need not be exactly the same $10 as in Figure 11-1, but this is an unimportant detail that does not affect the argument.

**TABLE 11-1** **How the Four Basic Conditions that Lead to Efficiency Can Be Violated**

| | Condition | Will be violated if: | Considered in Chapter(s): |
|---|---|---|---|
| (11-1) | $MB_S = MB$ | There are benefits to others than purchasers; for example, neighbours enjoy a well-kept garden | 23 |
| (11-2) | $MC = MC_S$ | There is pollution or other costs not borne by producers | 21, 22 |
| (11-3) | $MB = P$ | A single buyer has some influence over price. This may occur if there are only a few buyers | 16 |
| (11-4) | $P = MC$ | A single seller has some influence over price. This may occur if there are only a few sellers | 12, 13 |

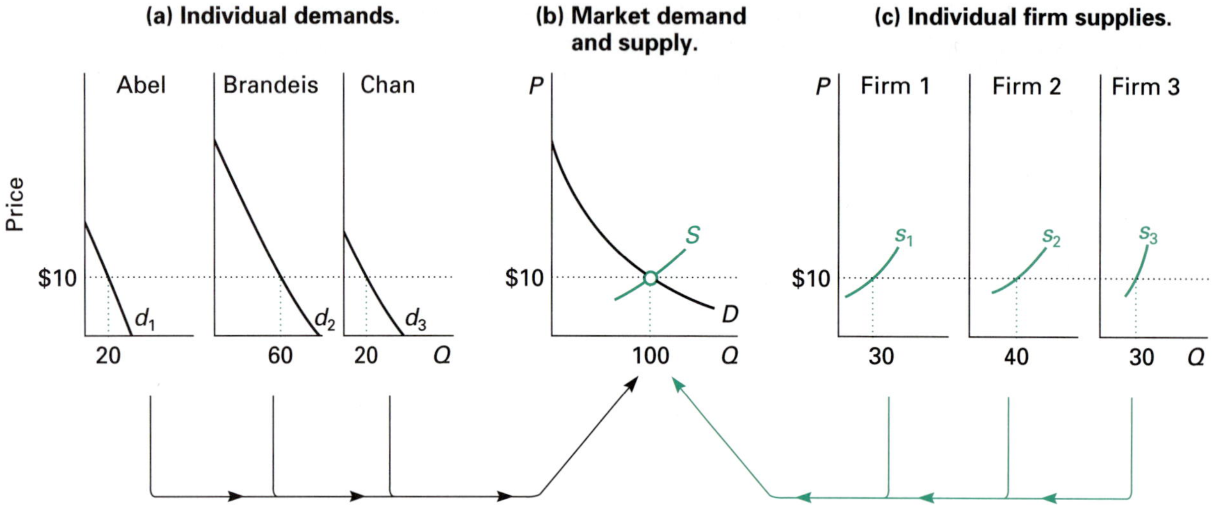


**FIGURE 11-10 Another efficient, perfectly competitive solution.**
This figure is similar to Figure 11-1, except that Brandeis now has a greater income and demand than Abel, and consequently consumes the greater quantity (60 units). This diagram also shows a perfectly competitive solution just like the one in Figure 11-1. Both solutions are efficient, but which is better? An economist can't judge, because in the move from Figure 11-1 to this figure it is impossible to compare Brandeis's utility gain with Abel's utility loss.

solution. However, it is a quite different solution. There is no way that economists can be certain which of the two solutions is better. All we can say is that both are efficient.

Abel and Brandeis, of course, will each have a clear opinion on which is better: Abel prefers Figure 11-1, where he gets most of this good (65 units), while Brandeis will prefer Figure 11-10, where he gets the lion's share. However, from the point of view of society as a whole, there is no way to judge. True, if it were possible to meter the heads of these two individuals and conclude that, in moving from Figure 11-1 to Figure 11-10, Brandeis's gain in satisfaction or utility exceeds Abel's loss, one might judge the pattern in Figure 11-10 superior. But this cannot be done, since *there is no way of comparing the utility or satisfaction one person gets from a good with the utility or satisfaction someone else gets from it.*

To sum up: A perfectly competitive economy does not, in general, have a single, ***unique***, equilibrium. For each possible ***distribution of income***, there is a different perfectly competitive solution. Each of these solutions is efficient, but it is not possible to demonstrate that one is better than the rest. The question of how income should be distributed is one that economists alone cannot answer, although Chapter 18 will shed more light on it.

## 2. The Moral Hazard and Adverse Selection Problems

Insurance is a valuable service that is bought and sold. Even if the market for insurance were perfectly competitive—and often it is not—a problem of ***moral hazard*** would remain. Buyers' behaviour may change once they acquire insurance. For example, once they get fire and theft insurance, they may no longer be so careful to lock their doors or take fire precautions. Consequently, more buildings may burn down, and this is a loss to society. Similarly, when drivers get insurance, they may become careless.

In both cases, the result will be higher insurance premiums, as there is an increased risk that a loss will occur. A second form of moral hazard may arise once a loss has occurred: If the cost of rebuilding your house, or repairing your car will be paid by an insurance company, you have an incentive to ask for the most thorough job possible, and the highest quality that money can buy. In contrast, you have little or no incentive to look at the cost. The result is that the average cost per claim tends to be high, again raising the cost of insurance.

Even here, however, competitive markets may work in a rough-and-ready way to limit losses. For example, in the typical auto insurance policy, drivers still have two reasons for being careful. First, any ***deductible*** clause means that to some degree they are risking their own money. For example, drivers with a $200 deductible run a risk because they have to pay the first $200 of damages. (A ***co-payment***, under which the insured pays a percentage of the cost of repairs, also gives the insured at least some incentive to hold down the cost of repairs.) Second, drivers know that their insurance rates will rise if they have accidents.

Some of the clearest cases of inefficiency occur when the government offers insurance. For example, suppose the government offers storm insurance without tying the premiums closely to risks. As a result, people have an incentive to build cottages too close to the ocean. Inefficiency results because the government provides coverage for mistakes that otherwise would not have been made.

> *Moral hazard* is present (1) when people who are insured become less careful in protecting themselves against risk, and (2) when the average cost of a claim is high because when the insurance company pays, the insured have no incentive to look for inexpensive providers of insured services (for example, in having a damaged car repaired).

Another problem that sometimes arises in insurance markets is that of ***adverse selection***. This problem occurs in cases when different individuals face different risks of loss. If the insurers can't tell which individuals are at high risk — of disability and death, for example — they will have to charge everyone a premium that reflects the *average* risk and claims cost. From the viewpoint of those at low risk, however (for example, people with healthy lifestyles and no family history of serious illness), the premium may then appear excessively high. (Since everyone is paying the same premium, the insurer must earn more in premium revenue from the low-risk groups than it pays out in claims to these groups: It needs this surplus because for the high-risk groups, the insurer has to pay out more in claims than it receives as premiums from these groups.) But if the low-risk groups find the premiums too high, they may drop out of the market. (That is, they may choose to go without insurance.) If they do, the insurer will be left with only high-risk clients. As a result, premiums will have to go even higher.

One way to overcome the adverse selection problem is for insurers to make systematic efforts to find out who the high-risk people are. By doing so, they can offer coverage at lower premium cost to those who are *not* at high risk. However, those at high risk will see their premiums rise; or they may be denied coverage altogether. This, once again, raises an equity issue: Is it fair that people whose risk of serious illness or death is high because of an inherited problem, for example, should have to pay higher premiums for life insurance or health insurance? Most of us would say no: Health insurance, for example, should be available to everyone on the same terms. (This is one of the reasons that most countries provide health insurance coverage for their citizens through government plans that cover everyone on the same terms.)

## 3. Buyers or Sellers May Be Misled By Price Signals

The basic features of perfectly competitive markets have now been outlined. However, there are a number of additional complications. For example, a market price acts as a signal to which both consumers and producers react. What happens if they get the wrong message?

To illustrate this problem, consider the hog cycle, a specific case where producers misread the price signal. Recall from Figure 6-9 in Appendix 6-A how a small shift in the supply of an agricultural product—perhaps because of crop failure or disease in a herd —will result in a substantial change in price. It can now be shown that this instability may be made worse if there is a time lag between the decision to produce an agricultural good and its eventual delivery to the market. There are many examples of this sort of delay: Wheat must be planted in the fall or spring for harvest in the summer, and the decision to breed cattle is made several years before the beef is eventually sold.

In such situations, an initial disturbance may set off a ***cycle of price fluctuations***, with price high one year, low the next, high the next, and so on. To illustrate, suppose that, because of some initial disturbance, hogs become very scarce; perhaps disease kills a large number. As a result, the price is unusually high. Seeing this high price, farmers are induced to expand hog production. When these hogs come to market at a later date, the result will be an oversupply, and the price will fall. In turn, this depressed price will induce farmers to switch out of hogs, and this shift will create a scarcity in the next period that will lead once again to an abnormally high price. Thus, the cycle continues because producers misread the market price signals and erroneously use today's price in making their production decisions. Even though this market is perfectly competitive, it follows a cyclical pattern and, therefore, does not work well—a point confirmed in the next section.

# SPECULATION AND PRICE INSTABILITY

A cycle of fluctuating prices may be broken in several ways. First, after perhaps two or three sharp changes in price, more and more farmers may recognize what is happening and accordingly stop making the erroneous assumption that today's price provides a good prediction of tomorrow's price. As they do, the price cycle is moderated. The second way that price fluctuations may be reduced is if others in the economy — *speculators* — recognize what is happening and take action.

## Speculation as a Stabilizing Influence

The public often views speculators as gamblers whose profits or losses have little or no effect on the general well-being. However, the actions of speculators may benefit the economy as a whole, as we will now show. Then, the following section will demonstrate how speculation may damage the economy.

To illustrate how ***speculation*** works, suppose that the price in a hog cycle was high last year and is accordingly low this year. Now a number of people realize: "This has happened before. This is that hog cycle again. Because price is low this year a lot of farmers will be getting out of hogs. Next year pork will be scarce and the price will go way up again. Let's buy some of this year's cheap pork, refrigerate it, and sell it next year."

> *Speculation* is the purchase of an item in the hope of making a profit from a rise in its price, or the sale of an item in the expectation that its price will fall.

From the viewpoint of society as a whole, is such stabilizing speculation beneficial? The answer is, yes. To see why, consider what happens when speculators buy pork this year when its price is low, and then sell it next year when its price is high.

For the speculator, this venture will be profitable — if the costs of storage, etc., are not too high — because it puts into practice the advice any stockbroker will give: Buy low and sell high. The remarkable thing is that this action not only benefits those who undertake it, but also society as a whole because it moderates the price cycle. Why? The speculators' purchase of pork when it is cheap creates an additional demand that prevents its price from falling quite so far. And when the speculators sell pork later at a high price, this creates an additional supply that prevents the price from rising quite so far. Thus, the cycle is moderated by speculation.

Panel (a) of Figure 11-11 shows the demand curve for pork this year. In the absence of speculation, initial equilibrium is at $E_1$, with low price $P_1$ because of high output $Q_1$. Panel (b) shows next year with the same demand curve but with lower production $Q_2$. In the absence of speculation, equilibrium is at $E_2$ and the price is a high $P_2$.

Now suppose that speculators enter the market. This year in panel (a), they buy $Q_1Q_1'$ units when the price is low, store them, and sell them next year when the price is high. This year their purchases reduce the available supply from $Q_1$ to $Q_1'$. Therefore, price is raised from $P_1$ to $P_1'$. Next year, their sales increase the supply from $Q_2$ to $Q_2'$. This lowers the price from $P_2$ to $P_2'$. Note that the cyclical swing in price may be almost eliminated: In Figure 11-11, speculation changes price in the two years to $P_1'$ and $P_2'$ and there is very little difference between the two. The only reason that there is a difference at all is that speculators have to earn a return to cover their storage and interest costs—and to compensate them for the risk they run if they guess wrong, and the price in the second year falls instead of rises.

The speculation in Figure 11-11 not only provides an adequate return for speculators; it is also beneficial for society as a whole. True, reduced consumption this year takes away benefits from the public now, as shown by the grey area in panel (a) of Figure 11-11. To confirm this loss, note that since typical unit $j$ is no longer consumed, the marginal benefit to consumers shown by the heavy black bar is eliminated. The total loss, because all such benefits are eliminated in the range $Q_1'Q_1$, is the total grey area. However, this year's loss to consumers in panel (a) will be more than offset by an even greater increase in benefit to consumers next year in panel (b) (the coloured area).

The reason for this difference is that in this year of plenty when there is a glut, the public is losing units that it doesn't value highly because its appetite is already reasonably satisfied. But next year when there is a scarcity, a "relatively hungry" public will be getting back these units when they do have a high value. The difference between the grey and coloured

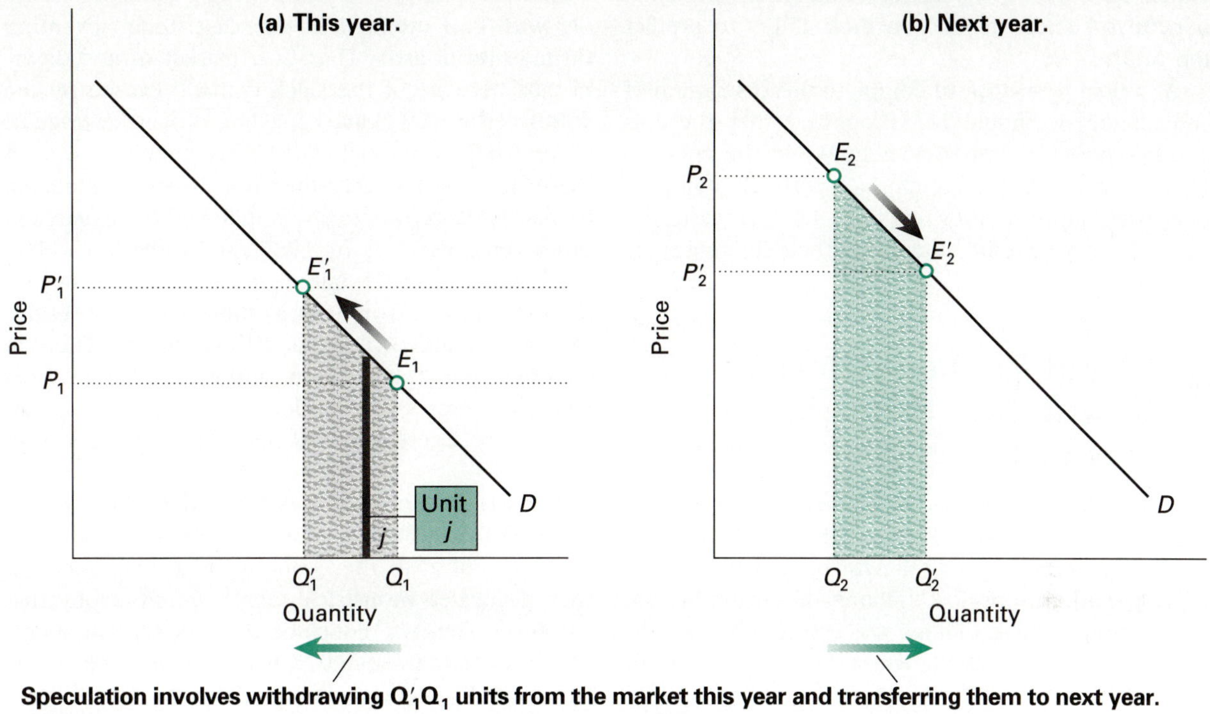


**FIGURE 11-11 How speculation may have the beneficial effect of stabilizing price.** Without speculation, equilibrium this year is at $E_1$ and next year at $E_2$. Successful speculation reduces the available supply on the market this year from $Q_1$ to $Q_1'$ and transfers it to next year, thus increasing the supply then by this same amount, from $Q_2$ to $Q_2'$. This raises the price this year and lowers it next year until the two are almost equal. The beneficial effect of speculation is the difference between the coloured area of gain from increased consumption next year and the smaller grey area of loss from decreased consumption this year.

areas, therefore, indicates the net benefit to society from this speculation.

In short, when speculators succeed in making a profit by "buying low and selling high," they reduce the fluctuation in price. They also reduce the fluctuation in the quantity consumed: Without speculation, different quantities — $Q_1$ and $Q_2$ — would be consumed each year; with speculation, roughly the same quantities are consumed—$Q_1'$ and $Q_2'$. By ironing out the fluctuation in quantities—that is, by moving some of this good from a year of glut to a year of scarcity —speculation provides a benefit to society.

Moreover, this conclusion— that there is a benefit from eliminating a price cycle— means that there is a loss from having a price cycle in the first place. A pattern of stable prices would be better for society. This then leads us to our second major reservation about a perfectly competitive market: It may lead to unstable prices if there is a failure in the timing and signalling mechanism. If this unstable price pattern is not ironed out by speculators, the public loses.

## Speculation as a Destabilizing Influence

So far, speculators emerge as heroes, but only because it has been assumed that they can predict the future correctly. However, they may guess wrong and, if they do, their actions can result in a loss both to themselves and to society. For example, suppose they purchase and store pork this year on the expectation that there will be a greater shortage and higher price next year, and they are wrong; there is a glut and lower prices instead. In this case, speculators lose because the pork they hold falls in price. Moreover, society as a whole also loses, because speculators move some of today's supply into next year's period of plenty, when pork is valued even less. Thus, both the individual success of speculators *and* their potential benefit to society depend on their ability to predict the future.

As a final postscript to complete this discussion of speculation, it should be recognized that there is another possible cost to society. While the speculators described so far operate in a perfectly competitive way, suppose they do not. In this case the outcome may be quite different as the following story illustrates.

## The Hunt Brothers: Down at Heel, with Less than a Billion Dollars Left

H.L. Hunt believed he had a "genius gene" which he passed on to his sons. He died in 1954 before he could find out how wrong he was. Bunker and several of H.L.'s other sons lost billions of dollars in the 1980s. One of these billions was lost in silver speculation. A great deal can be learned from this story of personal disaster.

To set the stage, note that on rare occasions, speculators may try to ***corner a market***, that is, buy enough of the good to become the dominant holder, and thus acquire the power to set a higher price. To see why this sort of anti-competitive speculation is quite different from perfectly competitive speculation, note that the perfectly competitive speculators who buy today to sell next year are *hoping* for a future shortage and higher price. On the other hand, the speculator who tries to corner a market may be trying to *create* a future shortage and higher price: If he can succeed in becoming the dominant holder, he can then create a future shortage by, say, cutting his sales in half. In this case, there is an efficiency loss; society loses because of the artificially created shortage.

Even if the speculator doesn't succeed in cornering the market, heavy purchases or sales may be damaging for society because of the price swings that result. In the example provided by Bunker Hunt and his brothers, their heavy purchases of silver contributed to the rise in its price from less than $10 an ounce in 1979 to a record level of more than $50 in January 1980. By that time, the Hunt group held an estimated *one-sixth* of the Western world's stock of silver. Improbable though it might seem — and although the Hunts still had a long way to go — it appeared they might be trying to corner the world market in silver. (One investigator was not so sure; he wondered if they were just playing a game of monopoly with real money.) In any case, their adventure turned into disaster. The silver market turned down, in part because of the slack demand caused by the 1980 recession. A wave of selling drove the price of silver back down below $10 an ounce; it was in this price collapse that the Hunts lost an estimated $1 billion. Moreover, this was followed by disasters in other ventures. Thus, by 1987, the brothers who had been worth over $5 billion in 1982 were down to their last billion. Worse yet, as Bunker Hunt observed, "A billion bucks isn't what it used to be." Then, in October 1988, Bunker Hunt and one of his brothers filed for protection under U.S. bankruptcy law, surely the largest personal filing in North American history.

In assessing the damages from their silver speculation, no one pretended that such price gyrations were beneficial to the economy as a whole; indeed, they dislocated industries, such as photography, that use silver. Thus, we conclude that this type of speculation is costly to society, *whether or not* the speculator actually succeeds in cornering the market.

# GOVERNMENT AGRICULTURAL PRICE SUPPORTS

One of the arguments for agricultural price supports is that the government thereby acts like the stabilizing speculators in Figure 11-11, preventing the severe fluctuations in price that would otherwise occur. The problem of price instability is particularly serious in agriculture partly because producers may misread price signals—as we saw in our earlier example of a pork cycle. In addition, prices may be unstable because agricultural goods are sold in perfectly competitive markets where supply and demand are relatively inelastic and supply may shift dramatically because of changes in the weather. For example, without government intervention, the prices of wheat and other grains could rise by 50% in a year of drought and fall by 50% in a year of glut. This does not happen elsewhere in the economy: The prices of cars or clothing simply do not gyrate in this way.

Moderating such fluctuations in price through a government price support program can have the same favourable effect as the successful, perfectly competitive speculation in Figure 11-11. For example, suppose that the government commits itself to maintaining price at a support level of $P_1'$ in panel (a) of Figure 11-11. In a bumper crop year, it buys up quantity $Q_1'Q_1$, thus keeping price up to the $P_1'$ support level. Then, in the poor crop year in panel (b) when there is a shortage, the government sells the accumulated stock, thus keeping price down. In short, the government moderates price fluctuations just as stabilizing speculators might, by moving goods from a period of plenty in panel (a) to a period of crop failure in panel (b). As a consequence, the nation realizes an efficiency gain.

From the viewpoint of the producers, an undesirable side effect of price stabilization is that it may, paradoxically, lead to less stable farm *income*. Total farm income depends both on the prices of agricultural products and on the quantities produced. If there is no price stabilization, prices will tend to be high in years when the quantity produced is low (for example, because of bad weather or floods). On the other hand, in good years with bumper crops, prices will tend to be low. As a result of the tendency for prices and quantities to move in opposite directions, income fluctuations may be *less* severe when prices are *not* stabilized.

However, in reality, farmers tend to be enthusiastic supporters of agricultural price support programs. The reason is that such programs usually do not just aim at *stabilizing* prices. In addition, such programs often have the effect of *raising the average price* that farmers receive. This has two consequences.

First, there is a transfer of income to farmers who get the higher price, from either consumers who may end up paying more for products such as milk and eggs, or taxpayers who pay subsidies that raise the price received by farmers to a level above the market price.

Second, however, agricultural support programs that raise average farm prices are also likely to lead to efficiency losses. Even though they may stabilize prices and production, they may stabilize them at the wrong level. For this reason, the amounts produced may be either too large or too small, relative to the efficient amount that would be produced in a stable competitive market. In either case, there is an efficiency loss. (Further details on the effects of different types of farm support programs are provided in Appendix 11-A.)

But if farm support programs lead to efficiency losses, how does one defend the idea of farm price guarantees designed to raise farm income? One argument is that it will help cure farm poverty. But a program of price guarantees that subsidizes the *production of farm products*, such as eggs, rather than a program that subsidizes the *income of poor farmers*, is a very ineffective method of curing poverty. The reason is that a price guarantee subsidizes the wealthy high-volume farmer much more than the poor low-volume farmer. This raises the question: Wouldn't it be better to subsidize the poor farmers directly, simply because they are poor, rather than subsidize *all* farmers according to how many eggs (or other farm products) they produce?

## KEY POINTS

1. For society as a whole, the output where marginal social cost is equal to marginal social benefit provides allocative efficiency.
2. If social costs are the same as private costs and social benefits the same as private benefits, a perfectly competitive market results in an efficient output. In these circumstances, perfect competition eliminates deadweight loss; it allocates resources efficiently.
3. Perfect competition also encourages technological efficiency by putting pressure on firms to operate on their lowest possible average cost curves.
4. Perfectly competitive firms need not be the best at introducing innovations. Large firms have more financial strength and more incentive to develop new products, and thus may be better at promoting dynamic efficiency. However, perfectly competitive firms do have a strong incentive to adopt innovations, once they exist.
5. For each distribution of income, there is a different perfectly competitive result. Economics cannot tell us clearly which one is best.
6. One problem with a perfectly competitive market is that its price signals may be misread, and price may fluctuate as a result. An example is the hog cycle that occurs if producers erroneously assume that price this year is a good indication of what price will be next year.
7. Speculation may be beneficial in a perfectly competitive market if it reduces price fluctuations. Competitive speculators, if successful in buying

low and selling high, will tend to stabilize price. The actions of unsuccessful speculators will not stabilize price, nor will they be beneficial to society.

8. By stabilizing prices and production in agricultural markets, government agricultural support programs may benefit the nation. But when they have the effect of raising average prices received by farmers, they are more difficult to justify. By leading to inefficiencies, they may become a very costly way of curing farm poverty.

## KEY TERMS

**social (versus private) benefit**
**social (versus private) cost**
**allocative efficiency**
**efficiency loss (deadweight loss)**
**technological or technical efficiency**
**dynamic efficiency**
**price as a rationing device**
**non-uniqueness of competitive equilibrium**
**distribution of income and competitive equilibrium**
**moral hazard**
**deductible co-payment**
**adverse selection**
**speculation**
**cycle of price fluctuations**
**stabilizing versus destabilizing speculation**
**cornering a market**

## PROBLEMS

11-1. Critically assess the following statement in the context of the assumptions of Equations (11-1) and (11-2) made at the beginning of this chapter. "A perfectly competitive price that all buyers and sellers take as given is the key link in orchestrating production and consumption in an efficient way." Do you agree? If so, illustrate. If not, explain why not.

11-2. Apply the analysis of this chapter to show in a diagram the efficiency loss resulting from rent controls that inhibit the price of rental accommodation from rising to its equilibrium level. Who are the gainers and who are the losers?

11-3. Apply the analysis of this chapter to show in a diagram how a tax (such as a congestion toll on a highway) may be used to induce an efficient level of output given an initial situation where $MC_S > MC$.

*11-4. Adapt Figure 11-5 to illustrate the effects of (a) an income tax imposed on the owners of society's resources and (b) a sales tax imposed on clothing. (In both cases, you may assume that the revenues from the tax are given back to the households as transfers.)

11-5. What moral hazards, if any, can arise in:
(a) fire insurance?
(b) storm insurance?
(c) health insurance?
(d) life insurance?

Are there any cases where insurance would reduce the chance of an unfavourable outcome?

# APPENDIX 11-A

## FORMS OF FARM ASSISTANCE

Before World War II, family incomes in farming were generally below the average for the economy as a whole. Farmers were especially hard hit during the Depression of the 1930s: Cash income of Canadian farmers fell by some 60% from 1928 to 1932, while wages in manufacturing fell by less than 45% over a comparable period. However, by the 1980s, even though many farmers were still poor, average farm incomes had caught up and were roughly the same as incomes elsewhere.

Part of the reason for the improvement in farm income was a wide variety of government assistance programs. Most important were programs aimed directly at raising farm prices.

## Support Prices and Deficiency Payments

In the absence of any government action, equilibrium in the market for milk is shown at $E_1$ in each of the panels of Figure 11-12. Income of dairy farmers is equal to the rectangle below and to the left of $E_1$ — that is, price $P_1$ times quantity $Q_1$. The two panels illustrate two different ways the government may raise the price the farmer receives.

### (a) Price Supports

In panel (a) the government supports the price of milk at a higher level $P_2$. Farmers respond to this price incentive by moving up their supply curve from $E_1$ to $E_2$. At the same time, consumers are discouraged by this higher price and move back up their demand curve from $E_1$ to $E_3$. Thus, at this higher price there is now an oversupply equal to $E_3E_2$, which must be purchased by the government at a cost to the taxpayer equal to the entire shaded area; this taxpayer cost is the number of litres the government must buy up — the base of the rectangle — times the price it must pay for each litre — the height of the rectangle. However, this government program has increased farm income from the original rectangle below and to the left of $E_1$ to the larger rectangle below and to the left of $E_2$; that is, farmers now receive price $P_2$ on the $Q_2$ litres they sell.

### (b) Deficiency Payments

This alternative policy, shown in panel (b), is of equal benefit to the farmer. In this case, the government again guarantees the same price $P_2$ to farmers, who again respond in the same way by moving up their supply curve from $E_1$ to $E_2$ and thus, as before, produce $Q_2$. However, in this case the government makes no attempt to maintain the market price at $P_2$ by buying up the surplus. Instead, it lets the market price "find its own level." Because $Q_2$ is coming into the market, price falls to $P_4$. (Point $E_4$ on the demand curve tells us that large quantity $Q_2$ will be purchased only at low price $P_4$.)

Dairy farmers are guaranteed $P_2$ per litre by the government, but they are getting only $P_4$ from the market. The government, therefore, must put up the difference; in other words, it must pay a subsidy $P_2P_4$ to farmers for each litre of milk they sell. Multiplying this by $Q_2$, the number of litres sold, yields the entire shaded area — the total subsidy paid by the government to farmers.

### How Do Policies (a) and (b) Compare?

Note that each of these policies involves an efficiency loss because the government is inducing farmers to produce $Q_2$, which is more than the efficient, perfectly competitive quantity $Q_1$. (We re-emphasize: Here we are considering policies that *permanently* increase the price received by farmers, not policies

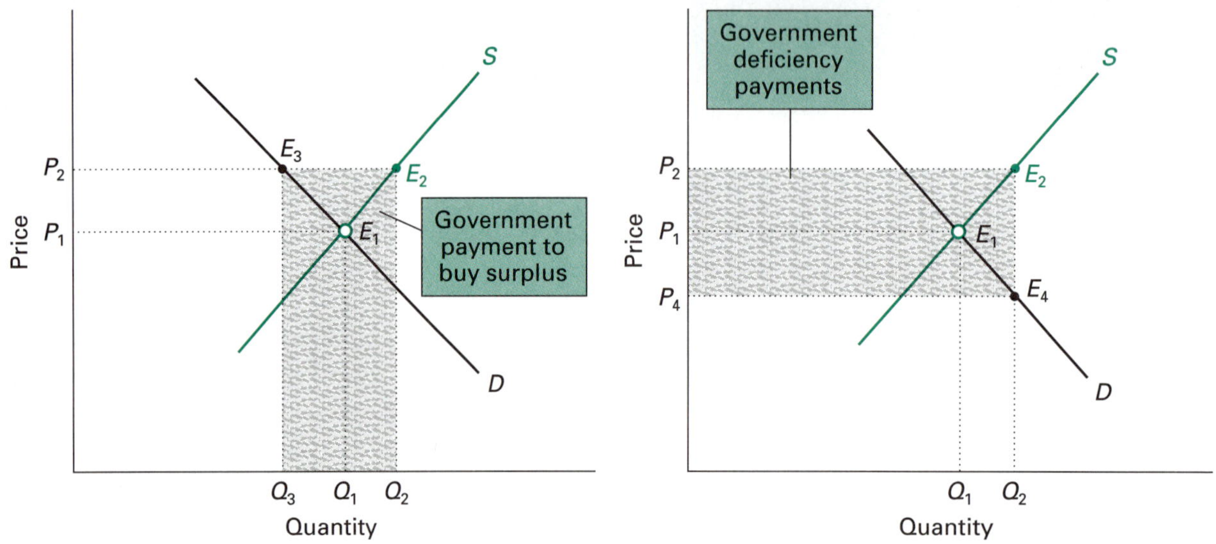


**(a) Price support at $P_2$.** The government must buy the surplus production.

**(b) Deficiency payment.** The government pays farmers $P_2P_4$ for each litre sold.

**FIGURE 11-12 Alternative farm assistance programs.**

Under either program (a) or (b), the government guarantees the farmers will receive $P_2$ per litre. They consequently move up their supply curve from equilibrium $E_1$ to $E_2$.

*In panel (a),* the government provides a *price support* by fixing the market price at $P_2$. Consumers move up their demand curve from $E_1$ to $E_3$. The difference in the amount produced at $E_2$ and consumed at $E_3$ must be purchased by the government, at a cost shown by the entire shaded area.

*In panel (b),* the government still guarantees farmers price $P_2$, but makes no attempt to keep up the price paid by consumers. As a consequence, this price falls to $P_4$, the highest price consumers will pay if they are to buythe large quantity $Q_2$ that is produced. Since farmers have been guaranteed a price $P_2$ and are receiving only $P_4$ from buyers, the government pays them the difference, that is, a *deficiency payment* of $P_2P_4$ on each litre. Since farmers are producing $Q_2$ litres, the total payment they receive from the government is the entire shaded area. Thus, in either panel (a) or (b), the large unshaded rectangle is what consumers pay when they buy the milk, while the shaded rectangle is the cost to taxpayers. In either case, the taxpaying/consuming public pays the same total amount for milk—that is, the entire area below and to the left of $E_2$.

that smooth out fluctuating prices.) As a consequence, there is triangular efficiency loss $E_1E_2E_4$ in panel (b). Note that this is the same sort of loss that was first illustrated in Figure 11-3(a) on page 207. The efficiency loss in panel (a) is likely to be even greater: The quantity $Q_3Q_2$ that the public doesn't get may be simply thrown away.

Which policy do farmers prefer? The answer is that they generally favour the price support policy in panel (a). They view it as providing a fair price for their milk whereas they sometimes regard the deficiency payment in panel (b) as a subsidy from the public purse. In fact, the two policies benefit farmers equally: Under either scheme their income increases from the area below and to the left of $E_1$ to the area below and to the left of $E_2$. Moreover, under either scheme, the large area below and to the left of $E_2$ also represents the total cost of milk to the public. This includes both the shaded rectangle that the public pays in taxes for the government support program, and the unshaded rectangle that consumers pay when they buy milk. (Specifically, consumers pay the unshaded area below and to the left of $E_3$ in panel (a), and the unshaded area below and to the left of $E_4$ in panel (b).) In short, under either program, farmers receive the same amount for their milk while the taxpaying/consuming public pays the same amount for milk.

There is, however, one good reason for the public to prefer the deficiency payment policy: It gets more milk—$Q_2$ in panel (b) rather than the $Q_3$ in panel (a). Public preference for this policy clearly holds as long as the surplus farm produce bought by the government is not needed to build up adequate buffer stocks, or simply cannot be stored, so that it will either spoil or have to be sold at give-away prices.

Because of the problem of unwanted surpluses that occurs under the policy in panel (a), many Canadian farm support programs now rely principally on deficiency payments (panel (b)). However, the method in panel (a) is still used for products such as eggs and milk. To avoid overproduction leading to unwanted surpluses, the marketing boards administering these programs have put strict limits on the amounts that each producer is allowed to produce. (A farmer is not allowed to produce more eggs or milk than is specified in the *quota* issued to him by the marketing board.) By controlling the total amounts produced, the government tries to limit total output to $Q_3$ in panel (a), the amount that consumers want to buy at the support price.

But sometimes, the marketing boards miscalculate, and a surplus emerges. This can place the government in an embarrassing position. For example, in 1975 Canadian industrial buyers had to pay the support price of 38 cents/lb. for powdered milk. At the same time, the government was selling surplus powdered milk to foreign buyers for 6 cents/lb. And in the middle of the 1970s, between 20 and 30 million eggs, many of which had been stored so long they were rotten, simply had to be thrown away. To the consumers who were paying good money for eggs in the supermarket, this seemed an absurd situation.

Other countries with price supports of the type shown in panel (a) have had similar difficulties. Faced with the prospect that an accumulated butter surplus would otherwise spoil, the European Common Market sold it to the Russians for roughly one-quarter the support price its own citizens were paying.

Programs of price supports and deficiency payments are at least as extensive in American agriculture as they are in Canada. For products such as cotton, rice, and wheat, the U.S. government has not only fixed the market price, but has also given farmers deficiency payments on top of this price (that is, it has paid a production subsidy on top of the support price). As farmers have responded to the higher prices, the government has been forced to buy up increasing surpluses. The cost of these purchases to the public treasury grew especially rapidly in the 1980s. The reason was that the target price—that is, the inducement to farmers to produce—had been set to increase automatically each year with inflation, at a rate that turned out to be unrealistically high and that, therefore, induced an unexpectedly large supply.

By the early 1990s, the high cost of these policies in Europe and Japan as well as in Canada and the United States, had produced considerable support for policy reforms aimed at reducing the degree of protection of the agricultural sector in many countries. Proposals along these lines figured prominently in the negotiations about international trade rules in the so-called Uruguay Round of the General Agreement on Tariffs and Trade (GATT). One purpose of these negotiations was to increase the possibilities for countries who are relatively efficient producers of certain types of food products (such as Canada and Argentina in wheat, for example) to export their products to countries with less efficient agricultural sectors, without having to compete against heavily subsidized exports of surplus food from the United States and the EC, or with heavily subsidized domestic producers in the importing countries. However, although even the EC countries (whose agricultural sectors were among the most heavily subidized in the world) were offering to cut their subsidies by as much as 30%, the United States was holding out for an agreement with even deeper subsidy cuts. The EC countries were unwilling to go further, in part because of intense political pressure from their farm lobby groups. As a result, by mid-1993 negotiations had come to a standstill, and it was not clear whether, in the end, there would be any agreement at all to reduce subsidies.

## PROBLEM

11-6. If you are working for the government, and your only concern is to minimize the money the government has to pay to farmers, would you prefer the program in panel (a) or panel (b) of Figure 11-12:

(a) if the demand curve passing through $E_1$ is very elastic?

(b) if demand is very inelastic?

PART 3

# THE MARKET MECHANISM: SOME PROBLEMS

The message from Part 2 has generally been an optimistic one. Under certain conditions, the market mechanism will produce allocative efficiency: The economy will produce the right combination of outputs, using the right combination of inputs.

We should remember the qualifying clause, however: "Under certain conditions." In reality, these conditions (that marginal social and marginal private benefits be the same, and that marginal private and marginal social costs be the same) may *not* be fulfilled. One reason, referred to in Chapter 5, is *externalities*—side effects of production and consumption. The way externalities may lead to inefficient allocation is studied in Part 5, in Chapters 21–23.

In Part 3, we focus on another reason that may introduce a divergence between marginal private and social benefit: *market structure*.

- Markets may be *perfectly competitive*, with individual producers and sellers being unable to influence market price. If so (and if there are no externalities), Adam Smith's invisible hand will be at work. In the pursuit of profit, firms will generally serve the interests of society, providing an efficient outcome.
- On the other hand, markets may be *imperfectly competitive*, with individual producers having the power to influence price. If so, there will be a difference between marginal social benefit and marginal private benefit to the firm, and Adam Smith's invisible hand will fail. In the pursuit of profit, a firm will generally produce less than the efficient, socially desirable amount.

The latter result is most easily established in the case of a *monopoly* where there is only a single seller in the market (Chapter 12); in this case, the seller can reduce sales and set a high price without fear of competition. However, it is not only monopoly that may lead to an inefficient outcome. A more common market form is where markets are dominated by a small number of sellers, or where there is substantial product differentiation. These market forms, referred to as *oligopoly* and *monopolistically competitive* markets, also may sometimes lead to inefficient outcomes (Chapter 13).

In Chapter 14, some of the ways that government intervenes to regulate businesses are examined. Through its *competition policy*, the government discourages monopolization of industry and forbids price-setting conspiracies among oligopolists. (However, other types of government regulation have reduced competition and efficiency in some industries, by restricting the entry of new firms.)

CHAPTER

# 12 MONOPOLY

*The monopolists, by keeping the market constantly understocked . . . sell their commodities much above the natural price.*

*Adam Smith,* Wealth of Nations

At one end of the market spectrum, there is perfect competition, with many sellers. At the other end, there is *monopoly*, with only one seller. (The Greek word *monos* means "single" and *polein* means "to sell.") Chapter 11 showed that, under certain conditions, perfect competition is efficient. This chapter will demonstrate that monopoly is not. A case, therefore, can be made for government intervention in the marketplace. In what way should the government intervene? This question is discussed later in the chapter. But, to begin, we consider the conditions that lead to monopoly.

## WHAT CAUSES MONOPOLY?

There are four major reasons why there may be only one firm selling a good:

1. *Monopoly may be based on control over an input or technique*. A firm may control something essential that no other firm can acquire. One example is the ownership of a necessary resource; for example, Alcoa's control over bauxite supplies allowed it to monopolize the sale of aluminum before World War II. Another example is the ownership of a ***patent***. For example, under Canadian law, a pharmaceutical firm that develops a new drug is granted the exclusive right to produce and sell it for a period of 20 years. (Patents are designed to encourage expenditure on research by allowing inventors to reap a substantial reward.) When an existing firm owns an essential patent or has exclusive control over a resource, new firms might like to enter the industry, but they cannot; the industry remains monopolized.
2. ***Legal monopoly***. It is sometimes illegal for more than one company to sell a good or service. For example, in the 1970s, a private trucking firm was sometimes given the exclusive right to service a particular community. Similarly, before 1984, it was illegal for a private company to set up in competition with Canada Post in the delivery of letters. (Since 1984, private couriers *are* allowed to deliver letters, but the law forces them to charge much higher rates than Canada Post.)
3. *Monopoly resulting from mergers*. If permitted by law, several producers may merge into a single firm in order to charge a higher price and increase their profits. However, once these firms have merged to create a monopoly, it may not be easy to maintain. New firms may be attracted by the high price.
4. *Natural monopoly*. A natural monopoly exists when economies of scale are so important that one firm can produce the total output of the industry at lower cost than could two or more firms. An example is the local telephone service. It obviously costs less to string one set of telephone wires instead of two down a street.

The prevalence of monopoly depends partly on how narrowly a market is defined. When the jumbo jet was first introduced, Boeing had a temporary monopoly; other companies had not yet developed their jumbos to compete with the 747. However,

Boeing did not have a monopoly in the broader market for airliners, since it still had to compete with McDonnell Douglas and other firms in the sale of smaller aircraft. As another illustration, the local gas company has a monopoly in providing natural gas, but not in the broader market of heating homes where it must compete with firms supplying oil and electricity. Similarly, in some cities, Bell Canada has a monopoly in local, conventional telephone services. However, in the market for long-distance service, it has to compete with Unitel and other firms. It also faces competition in the market for cellular phone service in many places. Indeed, in the very broadest sense, every producer competes with every other producer for the consumer's dollar. If you buy a new TV, you may help to pay for it by turning down your thermostat and thus reducing your gas bill. Therefore, in a very broad sense, the gas company is in competition even with the producer of TVs.

However, if markets are defined in a reasonably limited way, significant areas of monopoly exist — in local water service, local gas service, and local electrical service, to name a few. Note that these kinds of services must be *produced* locally: A resident of Winnipeg can't very well have his home hooked up to the natural gas distribution system in Regina if he is unhappy with the service of the local gas distributor. Thus, competition from distant sellers is effectively eliminated, and it makes sense to define the market in this relatively narrow way.

Nonetheless, the importance of monopoly should not be overstated. ***Oligopoly*** —where the industry is dominated by a few sellers—is much more important in the Canadian and North American economy. Some of our largest industries are oligopolies, including automobiles, heavy construction equipment, pulp and paper, large electrical appliances, and steel.

Although oligopoly occurs more frequently than monopoly, it is appropriate to consider monopoly first, because monopoly is logically at the other extreme to perfect competition. When this study of monopoly is complete, the stage will be set for a study in Chapter 13 of the oligopoly markets in between.

## NATURAL MONOPOLY: WHEN ECONOMIES OF SCALE LEAD TO A SINGLE FIRM

The cost conditions that lead to natural monopoly are shown in panel (b) of Figure 12-1, and are contrasted with cost conditions that do not in panel (a). The two products are assumed to have identical demand curves in order to highlight the difference in their costs — the central issue in explaining natural monopoly.

In the industry shown in panel (a), a typical firm's minimum efficient scale — that is, the output where its long-run average cost curve AC reaches a minimum—is at only 10 units of output. Since this is only a very small portion of the total market, total demand cannot be satisfied by one firm operating at its minimum cost. Instead, the least costly way of servicing this market is to have many small firms producing just 10 units each. If a firm tries to produce at higher volume, say 20 units, it will incur a relatively high cost that will leave it unable to compete with smaller, lower-cost firms. With many small firms surviving, the result is perfect competition.

In panel (b), AC reaches the same minimum value of $100, but only when a much larger volume of output is produced. Unlike the AC curve in panel (a), which reaches a minimum and turns up at a very small volume, AC in panel (b) continues downward. The minimum efficient scale doesn't occur until about 1000 units of output. Thus, the least expensive way of servicing the market is with one firm. This industry is a ***natural monopoly***.

> *Natural monopoly* occurs when the average cost of a single firm falls over such an extended range of output that one firm can produce the total quantity sold at a lower average cost than could two or more firms.

Why might costs continue to fall through much or all of the range needed to satisfy total market demand? The answer may be: high fixed cost, that is, high overhead. Local electric, telephone, water, and gas services are all natural monopolies, because the fixed cost in running electric or telephone wires, or in laying water or gas pipes, is very high relative to variable cost. To illustrate what happens when fixed costs dominate, set fixed cost in Table 9-1 at $1000, rather than just $35, and recalculate average cost. Note how AC continues to fall as this $1000 of fixed overhead is spread over a larger and larger number of units of output.

To verify that the cost curve in panel (b) in Figure 12-1 leads naturally to a monopoly, suppose that initially a few firms are each producing 100 units at point *F*. This low volume results in a high average cost of $200 for each firm. An aggressive firm will

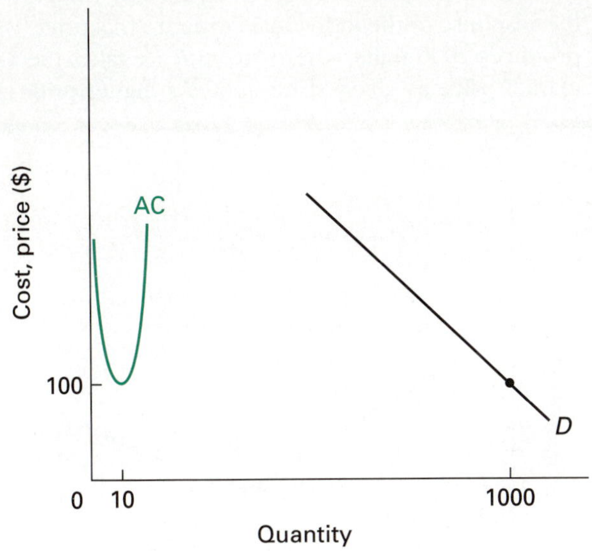


**(a) Perfect competition.**
Long-run AC of a typical firm reaches a minimum and turns up at a relatively low output. To satisfy market demand at the lowest possible cost, there must be many firms, each producing a small quantity.

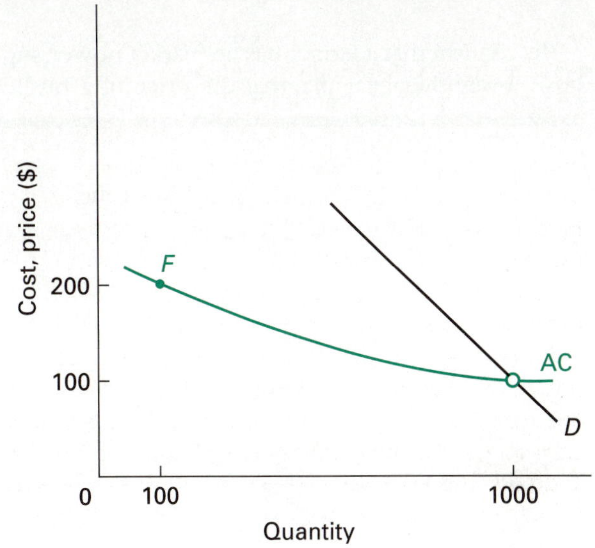


**(b) Natural monopoly.**
Long-run AC continues to fall through a wide range of output, reaching a minimum about where it cuts *D*, or beyond. This demand can be satisfied at lowest cost by a single firm.

**FIGURE 12-1** **How cost conditions can lead to natural monopoly.**

discover that by increasing its output, it can lower its cost, and hence offer its product at a lower price than its competitors. Thus, it can squeeze them out of business. In such a case of natural monopoly, competition tends to drive all firms but one out of the market. Small firms, with their relatively high costs, simply cannot compete with the single large firm operating at lower average cost.

Consumers obviously benefit from the low price during the period of competition when the industry is being "shaken down" and the number of firms reduced. However, this favourable situation for the consumer is likely to disappear once the successful firm has eliminated all its competitors and has emerged as a monopoly. It now has to worry little about the entry of new competitors. With its high volume—and therefore low cost—the monopoly can greet any new entrants with whatever price cutting is necessary to drive them into bankruptcy. With little fear of present or future competition, the monopoly is then free to raise its price. As a result, consumers of this product are at the mercy of the monopolist, except insofar as they are prepared to cut back their purchases in the face of a higher price—or insofar as the government regulates price. The question is: If the monopoly is free of regulation, how high will it set its price? But before we answer this, we need to make one more distinction between perfect competition and monopoly.

## THE DIFFERENCE IN THE DEMAND FACING A PERFECT COMPETITOR AND A MONOPOLIST

A perfectly competitive firm must take the market price as given. For example, an individual cattle rancher never thinks of asking $5 per hundredweight more for his beef, because he knows he won't get it; and he never offers to sell his meat for $5 less, since he can sell all of it for the going market price. The cattle farmer has no ***market power***: As an individual producer among many, he is unable, by reducing the quantity he supplies, to have any noticeable influence on price.

The *market power* of a firm is its ability to influence its price, and thereby its profit.

To confirm that a farmer has no market power, suppose, as another example, that the price of a bushel of wheat is \$4, as determined by market supply and demand in panel (b) of Figure 12-2. Panel (a) shows the response of the individual farmer to this price. He produces 2000 units, where MC = *P*. He takes the \$4 market price as given. If he quotes a higher price—

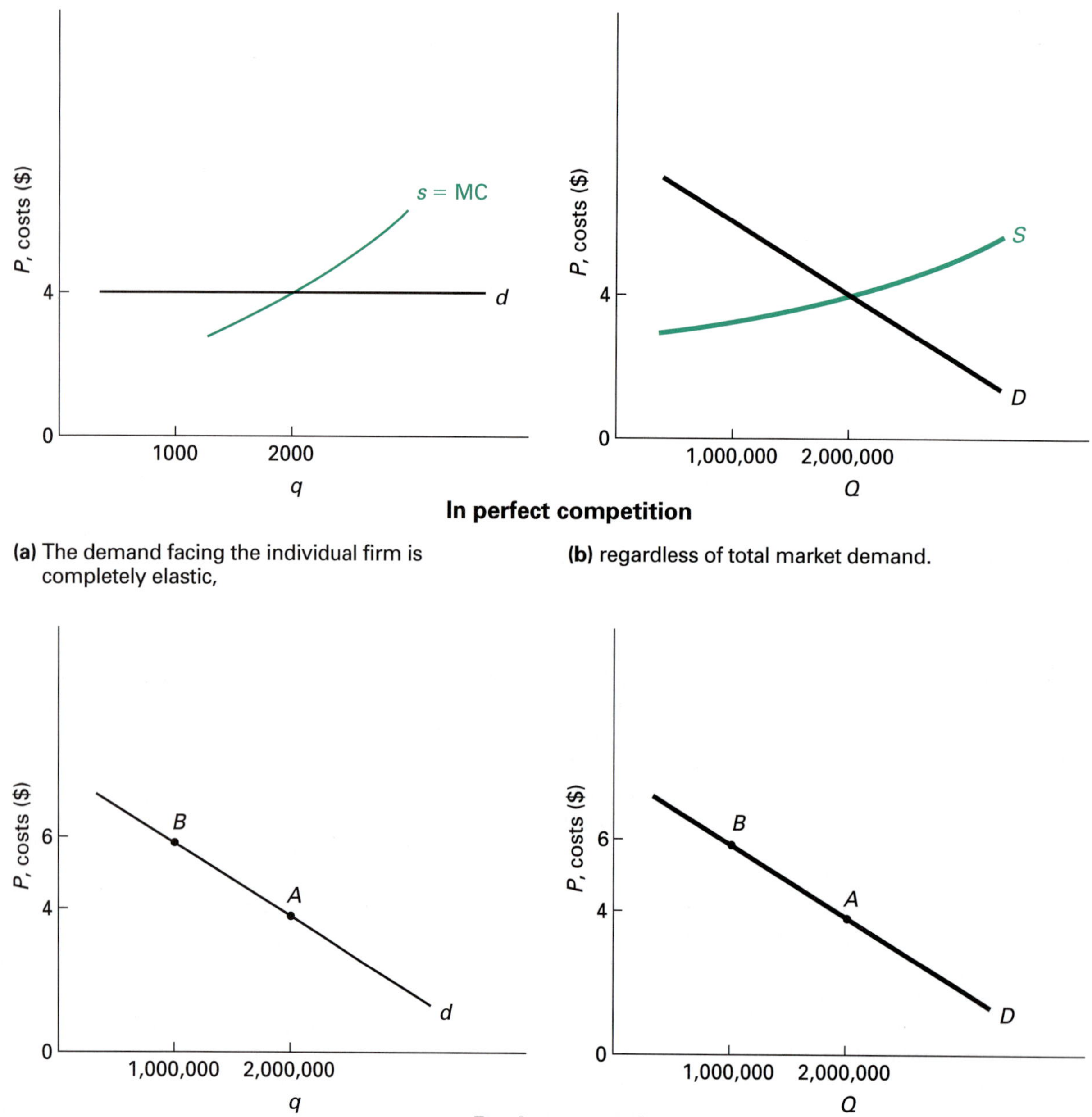


**(a)** The demand facing the individual firm is completely elastic,

**(b)** regardless of total market demand.

**(c)** The demand facing the solitary firm is the same as

**(d)** the total market demand.

**FIGURE 12-2 The difference in the demand facing the monopolist and the perfect competitor.** On the left, the demand facing an individual firm is marked with a small *d*. Market demand is shown on the right with a heavy line, and is marked with a capital *D*.

say \$4.20—the completely elastic demand indicates that he won't be able to sell any units. He can't make the higher price stick. Alternatively, if he tries to raise market price by reducing his output and making this good scarce, that won't work either. Specifically, suppose he cuts his output in half, from 2000 to 1000 units. This will reduce market supply in panel (b), shifting *S* to the left, but by such a trivial amount—only 1000 units — that this action won't even be noticed in the market. If you try to draw the new supply curve, you will find that you are essentially just drawing a line over the old supply *S*. The market price, as determined in panel (b), will, therefore, remain the same. The farmer has tried to raise the price, but this attempt to exercise market power has failed miserably. As an individual seller, he has no influence whatsoever over price.

The situation facing a monopoly is quite different, as shown in panels (c) and (d). In panel (d), total market demand is exactly the same as in the competitive case above. The only difference is that this market demand is now satisfied by a single monopoly firm. In other words, *the demand facing the individual firm in panel (c) is exactly the same as the total market demand in panel (d)*.

As a result, the monopoly can indeed affect price. To confirm this, suppose that it is initially selling at a \$4 price. Because it is the only seller, this firm alone is supplying all the 2 million units sold, shown at point *A* in both panel (c) and panel (d). Now suppose the monopoly raises the price to \$6. Because it is the only seller, it can make this price stick, although sales will fall from 2 million to 1 million units.

In short, the monopoly firm has market demand within its grasp. It can move along the market demand curve from a point such as *A* to *B*, selecting the one that suits it best. On the other hand, the perfect competitor has no control over market price; instead, the individual firm faces its own completely elastic demand curve, and all it can do is select the quantity to sell. While the monopolist can raise the price, the perfect competitor must take price as given. The monopolist is a ***price maker***; the perfect competitor is a ***price taker***.

## WHAT PRICE DOES THE MONOPOLIST SELECT?

As we saw in Chapter 10, any firm — whether a monopolist or perfect competitor—maximizes profit by selecting the output where its *marginal cost MC equals its marginal revenue MR* (see page 185). In that earlier chapter we also saw that marginal revenue for the perfectly competitive firm is the given market price at which it sells. In our present example, marginal revenue for the perfectly competitive firm in panel (a) of Figure 12-2 is the \$4 selling price; no matter how many units the firm sells, its revenue will increase by \$4 if it sells one more. In other words, its marginal revenue schedule is identical to its completely elastic demand curve. However, for the monopolist, *marginal revenue is not equal to the selling price*, and the marginal revenue curve is different from the demand curve.

### What Is the Marginal Revenue of a Monopolist?

Suppose the monopoly firm in Figure 12-3 moves from *B* to *C* along its demand curve. At *B* it was selling 1 unit at \$50, but now at *C* it is selling 2 units at a price of \$45 each. In other words, at *C* its average revenue AR is \$45. What is its marginal revenue for that second unit? What additional revenue does it receive because it is selling 2 units rather than 1? To calculate the answer, note that the monopoly's total revenue from selling 1 unit was \$50; but when it sells 2, its total revenue is \$90. Thus, its revenue has risen by \$40; this is its marginal revenue from the sale of the second unit. Note that the firm's marginal revenue of \$40 is less than the \$45 price. This point is worth emphasizing:

> **For a monopolist, marginal revenue MR is less than price *P*.**

Table 12-1 shows the monopolist's marginal revenue at each output. Total revenue is given in column 3, while column 4 shows how this total revenue changes for each successive unit sold. This marginal revenue schedule MR is graphed in Figure 12-3. Note how the monopoly's marginal revenue curve lies below its demand curve.

The demand and marginal revenue curves now become the stepping stones needed to answer the following question: How high does a profit-maximizing monopoly set its price?

### Monopoly Output and Price

Like any other firm, the monopoly maximizes profit by equating marginal cost MC with marginal revenue MR. An illustration is provided in panel (a) of Figure 12-4, where the monopolist's *D* and MR curves, similar to those in the preceding diagram, and its MC and AC curves are drawn in. The monopoly selects output

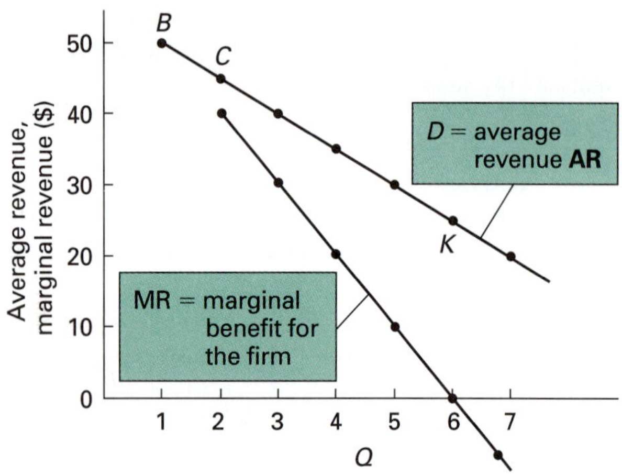


**FIGURE 12-3 Why a monopolist's demand (AR) and marginal revenue (MR) differ.**

Numbers are drawn from Table 12-1. At point *B*, the monopoly sells 1 unit for \$50. At point *C*, it sells 2 units for \$45 each, for a total revenue of \$90. The sale of the second unit increases its total revenue by \$90 − \$50 = \$40, which is its marginal revenue. Another way to calculate this is to note that the monopoly receives a \$45 price on the sale of the second unit from which it must deduct the \$5 "loss" on the first unit because it is getting only \$45 for it rather than the original \$50.

**TABLE 12-1 How Marginal Revenue for a Monopolist Is Derived from Demand (Average Revenue) Information**

| Demand | | | |
|---|---|---|---|
| (1) Quantity (*Q*) | (2) Price *P* (average revenue) | (3) Total revenue (*P* × *Q*) | (4) Marginal revenue (MR) |
| 1 | \$50 | \$ 50 | |
| | | | (90 − 50) = \$40 |
| 2 | 45 | 90 | |
| | | | (120 − 90) = 30 |
| 3 | 40 | 120 | |
| | | | (140 − 120) = 20 |
| 4 | 35 | 140 | |
| | | | (150 − 140) = 10 |
| 5 | 30 | 150 | |
| | | | (150 − 150) = 0 |
| 6 | 25 | 150 | |
| | | | (140 − 150) = −10 |
| 7 | 20 | 140 | |

$Q_1$ where MC and MR intersect. This is the output that maximizes its profit. If the firm selects any other output—whether greater or smaller—its profit will be less. For example, the firm would make a mistake not to produce unit $Q_2$, since that unit adds more to its revenues (at *W*) than it adds to its cost (at *T*).

> **A monopolist—like a perfect competitor—maximizes profit by selecting output where:**
>
> **Marginal cost MC = marginal revenue MR**
>
> **However, for the monopolist—unlike the perfect competitor—MR is less than price.**

With its output thus determined at $Q_1$, what price does the firm then charge? In other words, what is the maximum price the monopoly can charge and still sell quantity $Q_1$? The answer is given by the demand curve, which indicates at point *E* that the firm can charge a price as high as $P_1$ and still sell those $Q_1$ units. This choice by the monopolist of output $Q_1$ and price $P_1$ is often referred to as its selection of the ***profit-maximizing point*** (*E*) on its demand curve.

A monopoly, like any other firm, must address another important question: Should it be in business at all? For the firm shown in this diagram, the answer is yes. In selling $Q_1$ units, it makes an above-normal or monopoly profit of *EV* on each unit. This is the difference between the price it gets for selling each unit—the height of *E* on the demand curve—and its average cost of producing each unit, that is, the height of *V* on the AC curve. The monopoly will remain in business as long as it can cover its costs, including a normal profit—that is, as long as its selling price *E* is at least as high as its average cost *V*. (Recall from Chapter 9 that the average cost curve includes normal profit.) However, if the demand curve lies below the average cost curve throughout its entire range, it is not possible for the monopoly to cover its costs, and it will leave this business in the long run.

If distance *EV* is the firm's profit per unit, what is its total profit? The answer is the large shaded area in panel (b)—that is, the per-unit profit *EV* times $P_1E$, the number of units sold. This area is shaded in colour to represent above-normal profit, in contrast to losses, which will appear later in grey.

These two panels show in two equivalent ways how the monopoly firm maximizes profit: In panel (a), it equates MC and MR. Alternatively, in panel (b), it arrives at the same output $Q_1$ by selecting the point *E* on its demand curve that maximizes the shaded profit area. That is, it selects the point *E* that creates a larger profit rectangle than would be created by selecting any other point on its demand curve, such as *F*.

We shall use these two approaches interchangeably. For now, we concentrate on the MC = MR approach in panel (a). However, we will later use the approach in panel (b) because it clearly shows the profits that the firm is attempting to maximize. Moreover, panel (b) demonstrates both conditions that a firm must satisfy: It ensures (1) that the condition that MC = MR is met and (2) that the firm is operating at a profit—or, more precisely, that the firm is not operating at a loss that would drive it out of business in the long run.

## Monopoly Profit: An Alternative View

In Chapter 10, we used a diagram (Figure 10-3) showing *total* cost and *total* revenue to illustrate how a firm in a perfectly competitive market would choose what quantity to produce in order to maximize profits. A similar diagram can also be used to show how a monopolist selects the profit-maximizing combination of quantity and price on the demand curve for its product.

As before, the curve TC shows how the total cost of production changes with the quantity produced. Recall again that the intercept of the TC curve on the vertical axis shows the firm's fixed costs (*F* in Figure 12-5). Marginal cost (the increase in total cost as one more unit is produced) is represented by the slope of the total cost curve. Similarly, the slope of the total revenue curve TR shows marginal revenue, the increase in total revenue as one more unit is sold.

For the perfectly competitive firm, marginal revenue is constant and equal to the market price. (No matter how many units it sells, the addition to total revenue by selling one more unit is just the market price.) But when marginal revenue is constant, the slope of the TR curve must be constant. Thus, for a perfectly competitive firm, the TR curve is a straight

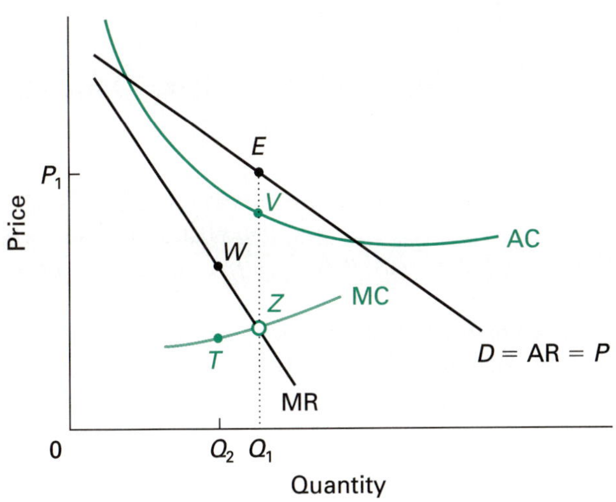


**(a) The firm examines marginal revenue and marginal cost, and equates the two.** Profit is maximized at output $Q_1$, where MR = MC. If output is less, at $Q_2$, the firm can increase its profit by producing one more unit, since the additional cost of this unit is only *T*, while it provides a marginal revenue of *W*. Thus, the firm produces this additional unit—and continues for the same reason to expand output so long as MR lies above MC; in other words, up to output $Q_1$, where MR and MC are equal. Similarly, if the monopoly is producing an output greater than $Q_1$, it will contract. Only at $Q_1$, where MC = MR, is there no incentive to expand or contract.

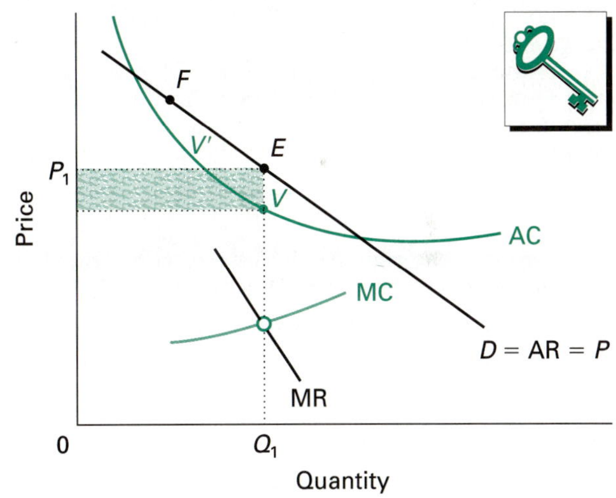


**(b) The firm examines average revenue and average cost, and maximizes the coloured profit area.** At *E*, the firm earns the profit shown by the coloured area, because it is producing $P_1E$ units at a profit of *EV* on each. (Since average revenue is *E*, and average cost is *V*, average profit is *EV*.) The firm selects the point *E* on its demand curve that maximizes this coloured profit area. Selection of any other point, such as *F*, leads to a smaller profit area.

**FIGURE 12-4** **Two equivalent views of the profit-maximizing equilibrium of a monopoly.**

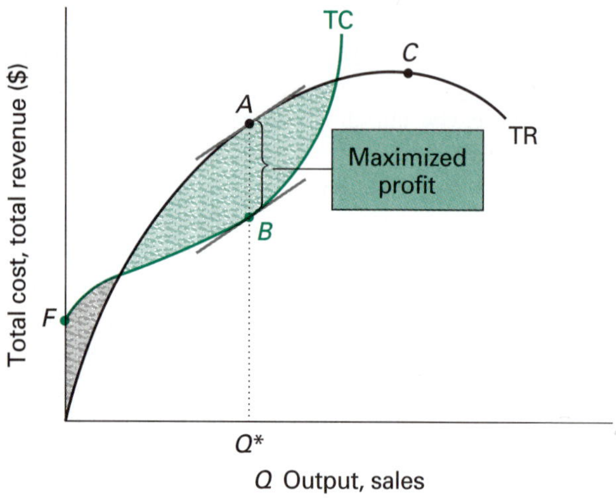


**FIGURE 12-5 A monopolist's profit-maximizing output: An alternative view.**

For a monopolist, the relationship between output and total revenue is not a straight line. Instead, it is a line with diminishing slope: The increase in total revenue (marginal revenue) becomes smaller and smaller as we move up along the TR curve. At point *C*, marginal revenue is zero: From that point on, increased output *reduces* total revenue.

The monopolist's profit is maximized at *Q**, where the vertical distance *AB* between the total revenue and total cost curves is largest. At that point, the slopes of the two curves must be equal.

line through the origin (such as the total revenue line in Figure 10-3).

As we have just seen, however, for a monopolist, marginal revenue is *not* constant. Instead, it falls as more and more units are sold. Thus the slope of the total revenue curve becomes smaller and smaller as additional units are produced and sold.

In Figure 12-5, the profit-maximizing quantity is where the vertical distance between the TR and TC curves is as large as possible; this is the quantity where the "profit rectangle" shown in Figure 12-4 is maximized. But a moment's reflection should convince you that at this profit-maximizing quantity, *the slopes of the TR and TC curves must be the same.* Thus, Figure 12-5 just confirms what we already knew: The monopolist's profits are maximized at the quantity where marginal cost equals marginal revenue.

The two ways a monopolist maximizes profit are also illustrated by the firm shown in Table 12-2. In columns 4 and 5 it maximizes profit by selecting the output of 4 units where MR = MC. In column 7, it selects exactly that same output by maximizing its profit directly.

## Profit Maximization for a Monopolist: Two Remaining Clarifications

### A Monopolist Produces Where Demand is Elastic.

Although a monopoly can quote the price at which it will sell, it still does not have complete freedom in the marketplace. It can only sell what consumers will buy; in other words, *it is only free to select a point on its demand curve.*

But whatever point a monopolist does select, it is certain that it will be on the *elastic* portion of its demand curve. Why is this so?

**TABLE 12-2 Two Methods of Profit Maximization for the Monopolist**

| Demand | | | | | | |
|---|---|---|---|---|---|---|
| (1) Quantity Q from Table 12-1 | (2) Price P from Table 12-1 | (3) Total Cost TC | (4) Marginal Cost MC | (5) Marginal Revenue MR [col(4) in Table 12-1] | (6) Total Revenue TR (1) × (2) [col(3) in Table 12-1] | (7) Profit = TR − TC (6) − (3) |
| 1 | $50 | $ 60 | | | $50 | 50 − 60 = $−10 |
| | | | (70 − 60) = $10 | $40 | | |
| 2 | 45 | 70 | | | 90 | 90 − 70 = 20 |
| | | | (85 − 70) = 15 | 30 | | |
| 3 | 40 | 85 | | | 120 | 120 − 85 = 35 |
| | | | (105 − 85) = 20 ⟷ | 20 | | |
| 4 | 35 | 105 | | | 140 | 140 − 105 = 35 ← |
| | | | (130 − 105) = 25 | 10 | | |
| 5 | 30 | 130 | | | 150 | 150 − 130 = 20 |
| | | | (160 − 130) = 30 | 0 | | |
| 6 | 25 | 160 | | | 150 | 150 − 160 = −10 |
| | | | (195 − 160) = 35 | −10 | | |
| 7 | 20 | 195 | | | 140 | 140 − 195 = −55 |

In Figure 12-4 the firm's equilibrium is where MR = MC; since its MC is positive, its MR must also be positive. This means that its total revenue TR must increase as its price falls and output increases; that is, its demand must be elastic (Figure 6-2 or Table 6-1).

Table 12-2 provides a simple illustration. The monopoly will select between 0 and 5 units of output, where its demand is elastic. (As its output increases and price falls, its total revenue increases.) It won't sell, say, 7 units of output, because the seventh would reduce its total revenue from $150 to $140. It makes no sense at all to sell that seventh unit when it costs something to produce, but does not increase the firm's revenue.

We can also use Figure 12-5 to confirm this conclusion. As long as marginal cost is positive, the TC curve will always have a positive slope. Therefore, the profit-maximizing quantity must always be somewhere on the upward-sloping portion of the TR curve — that is, at a quantity where demand is elastic so that increasing the amount sold leads to higher total revenue.

### A Monopolist Does Not Have a Supply Curve.

Although there is a demand curve in Figure 12-4, there is no supply curve. How is this to be explained? Recall that a supply curve shows the quantity that will be supplied at various given prices by a large number of sellers—with none having influence over price. But the monopoly firm considered here does have influence over price; it does not take price as given. Instead, it *sets* price. Therefore, there is no supply curve. The first two rows of Table 12-3 compare the "many-sellers" case of perfect competition where there is a supply curve, with the "single-seller" case of monopoly where there is not.

Of course, on the other side of the market, a similar complication can arise. For your future reference, the third row of this table shows the "single-buyer" case of monopsony, where, as expected, there is no demand curve. The reason is that a demand curve exists only if there is a large number of buyers—with none having any influence over price. But a monopsony is only one buyer who sets price. For example, the only manufacturing firm in a small town will be a monopsonist in the labour market; it will be able to set the wage rate it will pay. In such cases, there is no demand curve.

Now that the description of how a monopolist will maximize its profit is complete, it is appropriate to consider how efficient that decision will be from the point of view of society as a whole.

## IS MONOPOLY EFFICIENT?

> No one can argue that a monopolist is impelled by "an invisible hand" to serve the public interest.
>
> R.H. Tawney

How well do monopoly firms perform in the three categories of efficiency: technological efficiency, dynamic efficiency, and allocative efficiency?

A monopoly may be *technologically inefficient*; the firm may not be operating on its lowest possible cost curve. Because it has no competition, a monopoly may be careless in its cost controls, and resources may be wasted as a consequence. In drawing our diagrams, we have been ignoring this kind of inefficiency. However, in doing so we should not forget: Technological inefficiency in monopoly industries may impose a cost on society.

The relationship between monopoly and *dynamic efficiency* is less clear. As noted in the previous chapter, large, profitable monopolistic firms may have a greater financial capacity to engage in research and development than smaller, perfectly competitive firms. This research and development may lead to

**TABLE 12-3** Types of Markets

| Type | Characteristic | Is there a supply curve? | Is there a demand curve? | How is price determined? |
|---|---|---|---|---|
| Perfect competition | Many buyers and sellers, with no single market participant affecting price | Yes | Yes | By intersection of demand and supply curves |
| Monopoly | One seller, many buyers | No | Yes | By seller, facing market demand |
| Monopsony | One buyer, many sellers | Yes | No | By buyer, facing market demand |
| More complex cases | Few buyers, few sellers | No | No | In complex manner |

new techniques of production that will lower the firm's cost curves.

The prospect of gaining a monopoly position may also act as a powerful *incentive* for research and development. For example, Bombardier Ltd. had an incentive to develop the snowmobile, because it provided the firm with a temporary monopoly in the market for snowmobiles. But the development of new or improved products is a source of growth and improved living standards in society. Thus, allowing firms to reap at least some of the profits they can earn by having a monopoly position in the market for the new product they have developed may be dynamically efficient, by stimulating more innovation. This argument, in fact, provides the rationale for the patent and copyright laws that exist in Canada and other countries. Under these laws, the government creates and enforces a time-limited legal monopoly for firms or individuals who have developed a new product (such as a better drug to control high blood pressure, or an improved computer program for word processing): The registered owner of the patent or copyright is the only firm that can legally sell this drug or program, until the patent or copyright expires.

Finally, consider the central concept of efficiency studied by economists: *allocative efficiency*—or just "efficiency," for short. As we saw in the previous chapter, a good is being produced efficiently if its marginal social cost is equal to its marginal social benefit. To simplify our task, we continue the assumptions of the last chapter, that the marginal social cost $MC_S$ = MC to the producer, and that the marginal social benefit $MB_S$ = MB to consumers. The MB to consumers—and, therefore, to society as a whole—is measured by the height of the demand curve *D* in Figure 12-6. The marginal cost to society is MC, the marginal cost of this good to the only firm producing it. Since society's marginal cost intersects society's marginal benefit at *R*, the efficient quantity of output is $Q_1$.

However, this is not the output that the monopoly produces. Instead, as we have seen, it produces the smaller and, therefore, inefficient output $Q_2$, where MC = MR. The reason that it produces too little is that the firm equates marginal cost MC not with the marginal benefit *to society* (the height of the demand curve) but instead with MR, the marginal benefit *to the firm* itself. Thus, Adam Smith's invisible hand fails. The pursuit of benefit by an individual firm does not result in the best output for society.

The ***efficiency loss*** (also referred to as ***welfare loss***) that results because monopoly produces too little ($Q_2$ rather than $Q_1$) appears as the coloured triangle-like area. Note its similarity to the triangle in Figure 11-3(b), which also showed the efficiency loss from too little output.

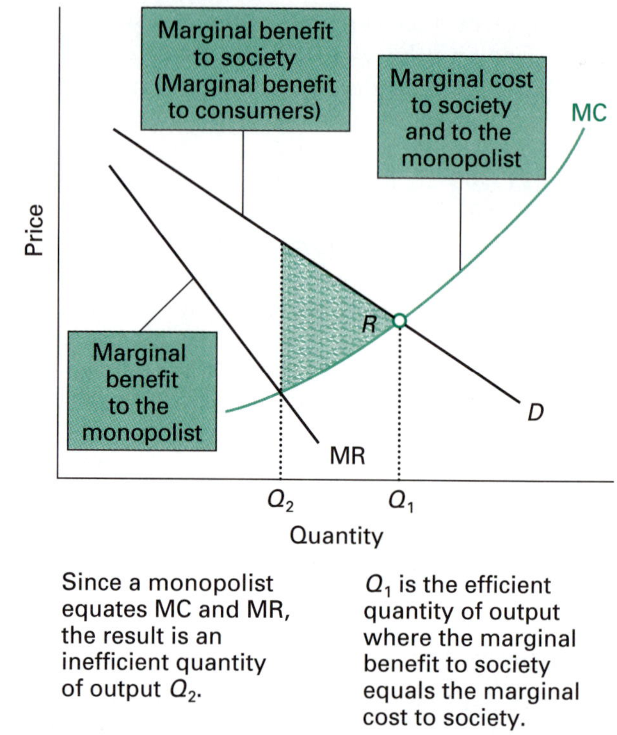


**FIGURE 12-6 Monopoly results in allocative inefficiency. The invisible hand goes astray.**

Monopoly results in output $Q_2$, which is less than the efficient output $Q_1$. Each of the units of reduced output between $Q_1$ and $Q_2$ would offer a higher marginal benefit to society (shown by the height of the demand curve *D*) than its marginal cost to society. It would therefore be beneficial to produce these units, and the efficiency loss from monopoly occurs because these potentially beneficial units are not produced. This loss is shown by the coloured triangle-like area.

## Monopoly Resulting from Mergers

As a specific example of how monopoly can reduce efficiency, consider what happens if a group of perfectly competitive firms merge to form a monopoly.

Figure 12-7(a) illustrates a perfectly competitive industry with output $Q_1$. Chapter 11 showed in detail

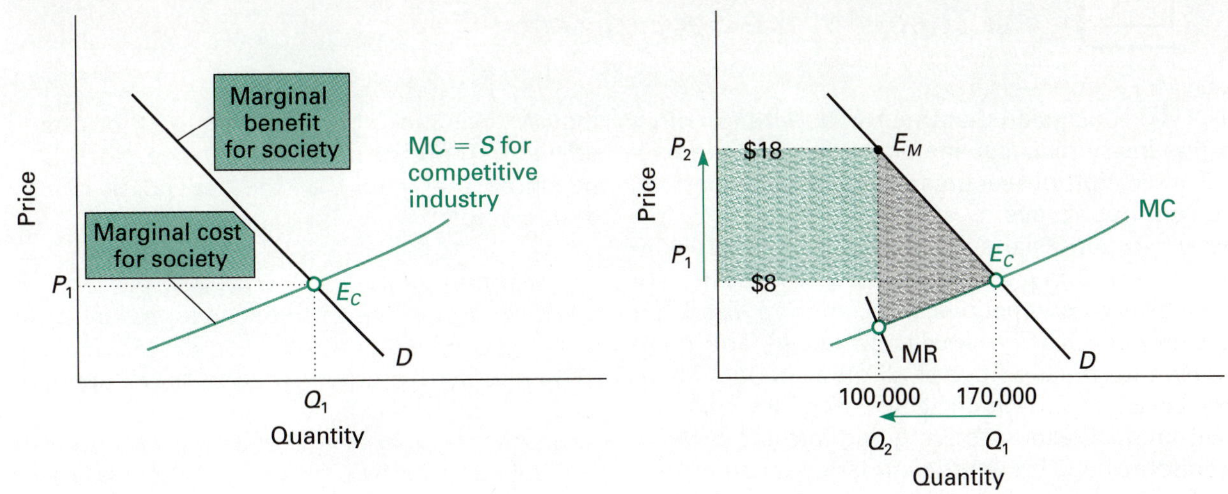


**(a) Perfect competition,** with industry supply *S* reflecting the supplies of many individual firms.

**(b) When a monopoly is formed,** equilibrium output is no longer where MC intersects *D* but rather where MC intersects MR. Consequently, the monopoly selects point $E_M$ on its demand curve, where output is less and price is higher than under perfect competition at $E_C$.

**FIGURE 12-7** **When a perfectly competitive industry (panel a), is monopolized (panel b), the result is an efficiency loss (grey area) and a transfer of income (coloured area).**

why this perfectly competitive output is efficient: At output $Q_1$, supply—reflecting marginal costs to firms and to society—is equal to demand, reflecting marginal benefits to consumers and to society.

Now suppose in panel (b) that these small firms merge in order to form a monopoly and raise price. Further suppose that the merger leaves costs and demand unchanged; in other words, the cost and demand curves for the monopoly in panel (b) are exactly the same as the supply (cost) and demand curves that existed under perfect competition in panel (a). What price and quantity does the monopoly select in order to maximize its profits?

It follows the monopolist's strategy, calculating its marginal revenue curve MR from its demand curve *D*. It then reduces output from $Q_1$ to $Q_2$, where MC = MR, and raises price from $P_1$ to $P_2$. In other words, it selects point $E_M$ on the demand curve. The reduction in output from $Q_1$ to $Q_2$ means that too little is being produced, creating the triangular grey efficiency loss in panel (b).

The monopolist's policy of restricting output is designed to make the good scarce so that its price can be raised. For producers who form a monopoly, it is this ability to raise price that provides them with an opportunity for profit that wasn't available to them when they were perfect competitors.

## THE TRANSFER EFFECT OF MONOPOLY

If only efficiency is considered, then the clear judgement is that society is harmed if a perfectly competitive industry is monopolized (Figure 12-7). While this conclusion is generally correct, it's not absolutely airtight, for two reasons. One is described in Box 12-1. The other arises because of the ***transfer effects*** associated with monopoly.

Consider what happens when a perfectly competitive industry is monopolized. Consumers suffer while the monopolized producers benefit. In Figure 12-7(b), the price that consumers pay and producers receive rises by \$10. With 100,000 units still being purchased, there is a transfer from consumers to producers equal to the \$1 million coloured rectangle (100,000 units times \$10 a unit).

## TOOLS AND TECHNIQUES BOX 12-1
## The Theory of the Second Best

The conclusion that the monopolization of an industry results in inefficiency—that is, a misallocation of resources—is generally correct, but not always.

To understand why, consider industry *X* in an economy where all other industries are perfectly competitive. If *X* is monopolized, not enough of *X*'s output is produced, and there is too much output of all other goods. There is allocative inefficiency: Too few of the nation's resources are going into the production of *X*. This is the standard conclusion.

But, now suppose that all other industries are themselves monopolized, but *X* is perfectly competitive. In this case, there will be too little output of all the other goods; in other words, there will be too much *X*. What happens if industry *X* is now monopolized? This will reduce its output, moving it in the right direction by bringing it back closer into line with the other industries. Thus, the allocation of the nation's resources may actually be improved.

This is known as the ***problem of the second best***. The first-best economy is one in which all industries behave in a competitive way. If one industry is then monopolized, the economy becomes less efficient. However, in a second-best world — one in which some industries are already monopolized — it is unclear whether monopoly in yet another industry will make the economy more or less efficient. There is no simple answer to this question; the theory of the second best is quite complex.

> The *theory of the second best* is the theory of how to get the best results in remaining markets when one or more markets have monopoly or other imperfections about which nothing can be done.

(An example of a second-best situation involving traffic congestion is discussed in Appendix 12-B.)

A second-best argument is sometimes made in support of government policies to monopolize an agricultural industry—that is, raise price by restricting output. Since the rest of the economy is pervaded by monopoly, so the argument goes, monopolizing agriculture may improve the nation's resource allocation. By and large, economists remain unimpressed with this argument and continue to recommend that we aim at the "first-best" solution by reducing monopoly influence wherever it may be found. Hence, the theory of the second best is introduced here, not as a reason for encouraging monopoly in any specific sector, but rather as a warning that the economic world is seldom as simple as we might hope.

This coloured area cancels out in dollar terms; the monopolized producers gain the $1 million while consumers lose it. However, it may not cancel out in terms of satisfaction. That is, the gain in satisfaction to producers who receive this extra $1 million may conceivably be greater than the reduction in satisfaction to consumers who lose it. For example, suppose that the item is something like the grapes from which champagne is made; the farmers who produce the grapes get together to set up a marketing association that raises the price. The consumers of champagne are so wealthy they hardly notice the increase in price. However, if the farmers who produce the grapes have low incomes, they may get very great satisfaction from the additional $1 million they receive. In this case, most people would conclude that the act of transferring income can provide a net benefit. Moreover, it is conceivable that such a benefit might offset the grey efficiency loss that arises because output declines from $Q_1$ to $Q_2$. In this case, one could argue that the monopolization of the industry would be desirable.

While this argument is logically correct, it is also somewhat strained; we have picked a very special case. Normally, a transfer from consumers to the owners of a monopoly would be judged inequitable, with consumers losing more satisfaction than the wealthier monopoly owners would gain. In this case, the transfer would add a further reason — along with inefficiency — to support the conclusion that the monopolization of the industry results in a net loss to society.[1]

Note that this problem of whether the $1 million is of equal benefit to buyers and sellers arises in evaluating almost every economic policy, whether it is controlling monopoly price, limiting pollution, or opening trade with foreign countries. Most policies result in a change in some market price and, hence, a transfer of income between buyers and sellers. Thus, any normative conclusion on whether the policy is desirable or not requires a reasonable working assumption of how people compare in their valuation of income.[2] Anyone unprepared to make such an assumption is restricted to positive economics — to an analysis of economic events, policies, and institutions, without any judgement on whether or not they have been beneficial to the community as a whole.

## Agricultural Marketing Boards

In most industries, agreements among competing producers to get together in order to create a monopoly are outlawed by competition laws in Canada and the United States, whether the monopoly results from a merger or from agreements between independent firms to fix prices. (We will discuss these laws in some detail in Chapter 14.) In other industries, however, Canada's federal and provincial governments have acted in the opposite direction. A competitive industry has been provided with a ***marketing board*** — that is, a government-sanctioned marketing association that can quote a price for all the firms, and thus allows these competitive firms to act like a monopoly. Specifically, by quoting a higher price, the agency can move these firms up their market demand curve — something they cannot do by acting individually.

In panel (a) of Figure 12-8, point $E_1$ is the equilibrium in a competitive industry before any attempt is made to create a monopoly. The market price is $80, with 1000 units being sold. At the same time, the situation of one of the 100 individual firms in the industry is shown in panel (b). The firm is in equilibrium at $F_1$, producing 10 units and just covering its costs. (Note that panel (a) essentially repeats the argument developed for the industry in Figure 12-7, while panel (b) details what happens to an individual firm.)

When a marketing association is formed, all producers speak with one voice and quote a higher price. Suppose the price the association decides[3] on is $140, well above the competitive $80 level. The industry consequently moves up its demand curve in panel (a) from $E_1$ to $E_2$. To make this higher price stick, the association must, like any monopolist, reduce sales from 1000 units to 600. This cut implies that the individual firm in panel (b) must decrease its output from 10 to a quota of 6. Therefore, the firm moves from $F_1$ to $F_2$. Despite the fact that its output has been reduced, its increased price now allows it to earn the economic profit shown as the coloured area.

The monopolization of this industry has had the expected results. Producers benefit from their new-found profit, while consumers lose because of increased price. On balance, there is an overall efficiency loss shown by the grey area in panel (a).

When they are not supervised by government, there are strong pressures for producer associations to come apart. While it is in the collective interest of all firms to restrict their output in order to raise price to $140, at this high price it is in the interest of the individual firm to *expand* output. In fact, at the $140 price, the firm in panel (b) has an incentive to produce, not at $F_2$, but at $B$ where MC intersects the given price. The problem, then, for an industry association is how to compel each individual firm to operate in the collective interest at $F_2$, rather than attempt to pursue its own interest at $B$. This discipline is essential: If some firms start to produce more than their quota, more than 600 units will come onto the market, and price will fall. Moreover, getting existing firms to stick to their quotas is not the only problem: The entry of new firms, attracted by the coloured above-normal profits, would also drive price down.

The problems of enforcing quota limitations on production and restricting entry would make it diffi-

[1] Any full evaluation of monopoly involves examining several other issues as well. For example, if firms hire lawyers to help them establish or strengthen a monopoly position, it's reasonable to argue that, from society's point of view, these legal resources are being wasted. See Anne Krueger, "The Political Economy of the Rent-Seeking Society," *American Economic Review*, June 1974, pp. 291–303; and Richard Posner, "The Social Costs of Monopoly and Regulation," *Journal of Political Economy*, August 1975, pp. 807–28.

[2] The same issue arises in macroeconomics. During any period in which the nation's per capita income increases, most Canadians benefit, but a few are hurt. Any judgement that such an income increase has been of benefit to the nation overall involves a reasonable assumption about how people compare in their valuation of income.

[3] In reality, marketing boards must negotiate with consumer representatives and government officials before setting the market price. We disregard this complication in the following, however.

cult for private marketing associations to monopolize their industries, even if it were legal for them to do so. However, many agricultural marketing boards can do so more easily, since they have been given government authority to fix prices and impose quota limits on the output that each producer is allowed to market. (A marketing board can be established by a majority vote of all producers of a particular commodity in a province. Once the majority have voted for a marketing board, all producers must join, even those who voted against the board.) Thus, through the marketing boards, some producers in agriculture are able to do what marketing associations in other industries cannot legally accomplish: They get a measure of control over prices and output in their industry.

Government-sanctioned marketing boards have become very common in Canada. A study prepared for the Canadian Consumer Research Council[4] listed 95 provincial marketing boards in 1974; the commodities that they covered ranged from eggs, milk, cheese, and hogs, to apples, asparagus, blueberries, and mushrooms. While most marketing boards are provincial in scope, federal legislation has helped the provincial boards coordinate their activities in several markets, thereby creating, in effect, a set of nationwide marketing agencies.

Since production controls may lead to substantial increases in price to the Canadian public and to an efficiency loss such the grey area in Figure 12-8(a), why does the government allow the formation of marketing boards with the power to fix prices and control output? In support of marketing boards, farmers point to the special problems facing agriculture, discussed in Chapter 6. Supply and demand forces would lead to highly unstable prices and incomes in the markets for many farm products if there were no government policy to support farm prices. Since the support policies we discussed in the appendix to Chapter 11 tend to become very expensive for the government, relying on marketing boards may appear as an attractive alternative. The boards can stabilize prices at a level that is satisfactory to producers; and since production is controlled, the government does not have to buy up large quantities of farm products to support the price. However, the effect of the boards on consumers, of course, is quite a different matter.

[4] The study is quoted in Christopher Green, *Canadian Industrial Organization and Policy* (Toronto: McGraw-Hill Ryerson, 1980), pp. 286–87.

Although producers argue that consumers, too, benefit from more stable prices, critics argue that this gain is more than offset by the consumers' loss from higher prices on average. In the critics' view, the reason government-created marketing board monopolies are tolerated, is that they transfer real income to a group that many consider especially deserving, namely farmers.

## GOVERNMENT POLICIES TO CONTROL MONOPOLY

Other than in agriculture, government policies generally aim to protect the public from the effects of monopoly. In formulating such policies, the government should begin with the question: "Is the industry in question a natural monopoly or not?" Suppose it is not; suppose the monopoly is the result of mergers of efficient, competitive firms. In this case, we've just seen that there is a strong argument for preventing monopolization. To achieve this objective, competition laws have been passed. They will be considered in Chapter 14.

The balance of this chapter will concentrate on the other case, where the industry is a natural monopoly. Because of economies of scale, the average cost curve AC for a firm keeps falling over a wide range of output, as illustrated in Figure 12-9. The least expensive way for market demand to be satisfied is by one large producer. Breaking the monopoly up into a number of smaller firms would raise costs. There is no need for more than one set of electrical wires running down a street; nor for more than one set of gas lines. Graphically, breaking up the natural monopoly in Figure 12-9 into a number of small firms, each with output $Q_3$, would raise average cost to $C$; the benefits from economies of scale would be lost. In the case shown here, everyone would lose. The monopoly would lose its monopoly profit. Moreover, consumers would also be damaged: Even if the new, perhaps highly competitive firms were to earn no economic profit, they would still have to sell at a high price $P_3$ just to cover their high costs, and that price would be higher than the price $P_1$ that consumers were paying before the monopoly was broken up.

Thus, breaking up a natural monopoly is no solution at all. Indeed, breaking the firm up is a move in the wrong direction because this raises costs. A more promising policy is to get the firm to expand from $E_1$ down its demand curve to the efficient point $E_2$, where the marginal benefit to consumers (and to

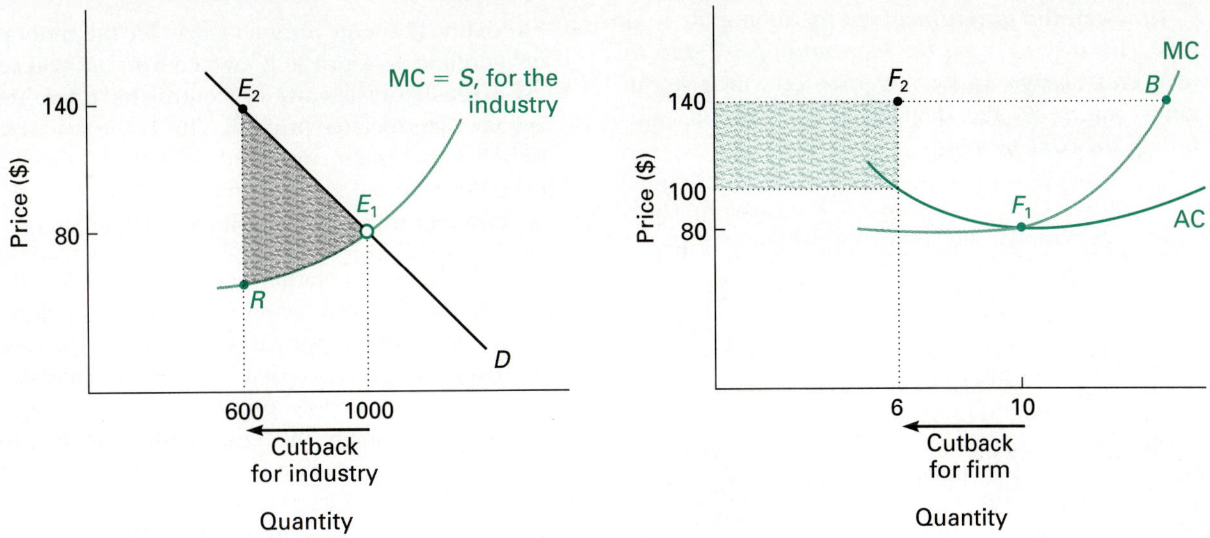


**(a) The industry.** **(b) A firm.**

**FIGURE 12-8 Effect of a producers' association or government marketing board on an industry and on an individual firm.**

Panel (a) illustrates a competitive industry. Market equilibrium is at $E_1$ where $D = S$. When this industry is monopolized by a producers' association or government marketing board, equilibrium moves from $E_1$ to $E_2$. The association raises price from \$80 to \$140, and this reduces industry sales from 1000 units to 600.

In turn, the sales of the individual firm in panel (b) must be reduced from 10 units to a quota of 6. This means that the firm moves from $F_1$ to $F_2$ where it makes the \$240 profit shown by the coloured area: On each of its 6 units, it earns a \$40 profit. Although this reduction in output has generated profits, each firm facing the given \$140 price would like to *increase* its output, by moving from $F_2$ to $B$, where MC = price. However, such additional output would drive market price down; the industry in panel (a) would slide down its demand curve from $E_2$ toward $E_1$, with the individual firm in panel (b) moving from $F_2$ to the non-profit point $F_1$.

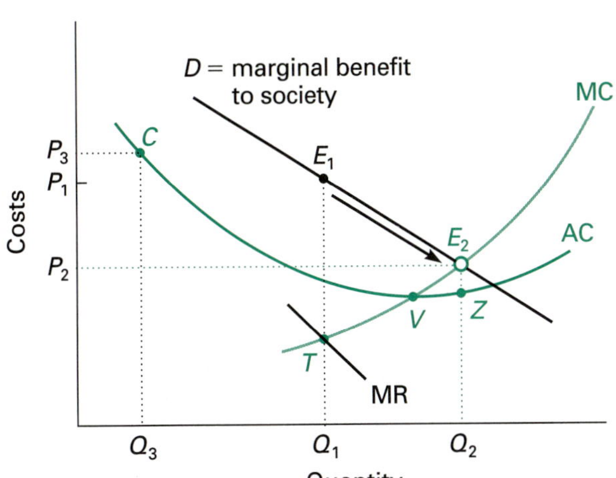


**FIGURE 12-9 Natural monopoly: Regulating price rather than breaking up the firm.**

Without price regulation, the monopoly produces at $E_1$, where MR = MC. If the government sets a maximum price of $P_2$, the firm is pushed down its demand curve to point $E_2$. Its output increases from $Q_1$ to the efficient $Q_2$ where the marginal benefit to society $D$ is equal to MC. The efficiency gain is the elimination of the original "triangle" of monopoly inefficiency $E_1E_2T$.

society) is equal to the marginal cost to the firm (and to society).

How can the government get the monopoly to do this? The answer is: *Set the maximum price that the firm can charge at $P_2$*, the price at which its MC curve intersects the demand curve. This is called ***marginal cost pricing***.

*Marginal cost pricing* is setting price at the level where MC intersects the demand curve.

Since the monopoly is now prohibited from raising price, it is forced to act like a perfectly competitive firm, taking price $P_2$ as given. Like the perfectly competitive firm, it will produce at point $E_2$, where its MC curve rises to the level of its given price $P_2$. Because $E_2$ is the efficient output where MC intersects demand, this policy has eliminated the original efficiency loss due to monopoly. (That original efficiency loss was triangle $E_1E_2T$, because the monopoly chose equilibrium $E_1$ rather than the efficient equilibrium $E_2$.)

Note that, in forcing the move to the efficient point $E_2$, the government has *not* broken up this natural monopoly. It has simply *removed the monopoly's market power*—that is, the power of the monopoly to set a high price. In practice, there are two ways the government can do this:

1. It may take over and operate the monopolized activity, setting the price of its output at $P_2$. Provision of utilities such as water and electricity by city governments is an example of this type of solution.
2. Alternatively, the government may let the monopoly continue as a privately owned firm but will set up a regulatory agency to control its price; the agency then dictates price $P_2$. This is the way telephone services are provided in most of Canada. (The Prairie provinces are an exception: There the government owns the telephone companies.)

Consider how well marginal cost pricing solves the monopoly abuse of producing too little at too high a price. The monopoly is forced to reduce its price, and consequently it sells more; that is, its output increases. In addition, its monopoly profit has been reduced. Since the firm initially maximized profit at $E_1$, any other point on the demand curve, such as $E_2$, will result in less profit. However, its profit has not necessarily been eliminated; in Figure 12-9, a per-unit profit of $E_2Z$ remains.

Unfortunately, dealing with monopoly is often not so easy in practice. Although marginal cost pricing still allows a profit in the example shown in Figure 12-9, in other circumstances it may lead to a loss. For example, if the AC curve in Figure 12-9 passes above $E_2$ rather than below it, then there would be a loss, rather than a profit, at $E_2$. In such cases, marginal cost pricing at $E_2$ is not a satisfactory policy, since it would drive the firm out of business. Such a monopoly requires some other form of price regulation. This difficult case is dealt with in Box 12-2.

## TOOLS AND TECHNIQUES — BOX 12-2
## Unfortunately, Dealing with Natural Monopoly Is Often Not So Simple

In Figure 12-9, average cost reached a minimum and turned up at point *V* before it reached the demand curve; that is, it turned up to the left of the demand curve. The figure below presents an even clearer case of natural monopoly, where the average cost curve AC continues to fall until after it has crossed the demand curve. In this instance, the regulation of monopoly price presents special problems.

To see why, suppose the government tries to apply the policy of marginal cost pricing that worked so well in Figure 12-9. In panel (a) of the figure here, it again tries to drive the monopoly firm down its demand curve from its original profit-maximizing equilibrium $E_1$ to the efficient point $E_2$, where marginal cost intersects demand. As before, suppose it attempts to do so by regulating price at $P_2$. This policy will not work because the price $P_2$ is not high enough to cover average cost at *G*. The firm's per-unit loss is $GE_2$, and its total loss is the grey area. Eventually, the firm will be driven out of business—a worse outcome than at the original $E_1$. In this case, marginal cost pricing is a failure.

A different approach is required. In order to improve on the free-market outcome at $E_1$, the government has three main options.

**BOX 12-2 continued**

## 1. Average Cost Pricing

The lowest price the government can set without eventually forcing the firm out of business is $P_3$, which will result in a new equilibrium at $E_3$. Here price is barely high enough to cover average cost; the firm just breaks even. This policy is called ***average cost pricing***. Once again, the regulatory agency takes away the monopoly's power to select a point on its demand curve; the agency makes the decision on the appropriate point and makes it stick by regulating price.

> *Average cost pricing* is setting price at the level where AC intersects the demand curve.

In theory, break-even price $P_3$ should be easy for the regulatory agency to find. If the firm is earning an (above-normal) profit—as it would, for example, at $E_1$—price is too high; so lower it. If the firm is operating at a loss, at a point such as $E_2$, price is too low; so raise it. This simple rule of thumb will bring the regulators to $P_3$, the price that just covers costs, including a fair return on the capital the owners have invested. In practice, however, $P_3$ is very difficult to determine, largely because of problems in defining or measuring (1) a fair percentage return to capital and (2) the amount of capital invested.

Finally, the effect on efficiency of average cost pricing is shown in panel (b) of the figure. If it were possible to move the monopoly all the way down its demand curve from $E_1$ to $E_2$, the result would be the now familiar triangular efficiency gain shown as areas 4 + 5. However, average cost pricing allows us to move this firm only part way, from $E_1$ to $E_3$. Therefore, the gain is limited to area 4.

We conclude that since this policy of average cost pricing increases monopoly output from $Q_1$ to $Q_3$, it results in a gain in allocative efficiency. (Remember that, unless we state otherwise, the word "efficiency" means "allocative efficiency.")

Unfortunately, however, this policy, and any of the others discussed in this box or in Figure 12-9, may lead to a loss in technical efficiency—that is, the firm may not operate on its lowest possible cost curve. After all, why should the firm in the figure here strive hard to lower its costs, when a reduction in costs will cause the regulatory agency to correspondingly lower price? Why shouldn't the firm's executives be allowed generous expense accounts, since such costs are simply passed on to consumers in the form of higher prices? No matter what the firm does, it isn't allowed to make an above-normal profit; so why should it tightly control its costs? (At best, the firm can earn an above-normal profit only temporarily, between the date it reduces its costs and the date the regulatory agency reduces the price.) Consequently, price regulation will increase overall efficiency only if the increase in allocative efficiency outweighs any loss in technical efficiency.

## 2. Government Subsidy plus Marginal Cost Pricing

Another option is to force the firm all the way down its demand curve from $E_1$ to efficient point $E_2$ by marginal cost pricing, while at the same time paying the firm whatever lump-sum subsidy is necessary to cover its loss. In other words, a regulated price of $P_2$ drives the firm down its demand curve to point $E_2$ (thus capturing the entire possible efficiency gain 4 + 5), while a subsidy equal to the grey area in panel (a) keeps the firm in business.

Although this policy may be attractive in theory, it raises such serious problems in practice that it is seldom used. It is difficult for the public to understand why a government committed to controlling the market power of monopoly should end up subsidizing it. The point that the government is also regulating price — and thus eliminating the profit of the monopoly—is difficult to explain to the public. Moreover, the policy of taking money out of the monopolist's pocket with one hand (the regulated price) while putting it back with the other (the subsidy) may strike the public as being inconsistent, even though it is not. In addition, the general problem in price regulation reappears here. As long as the government is committed to subsidizing

**BOX 12-2 continued**

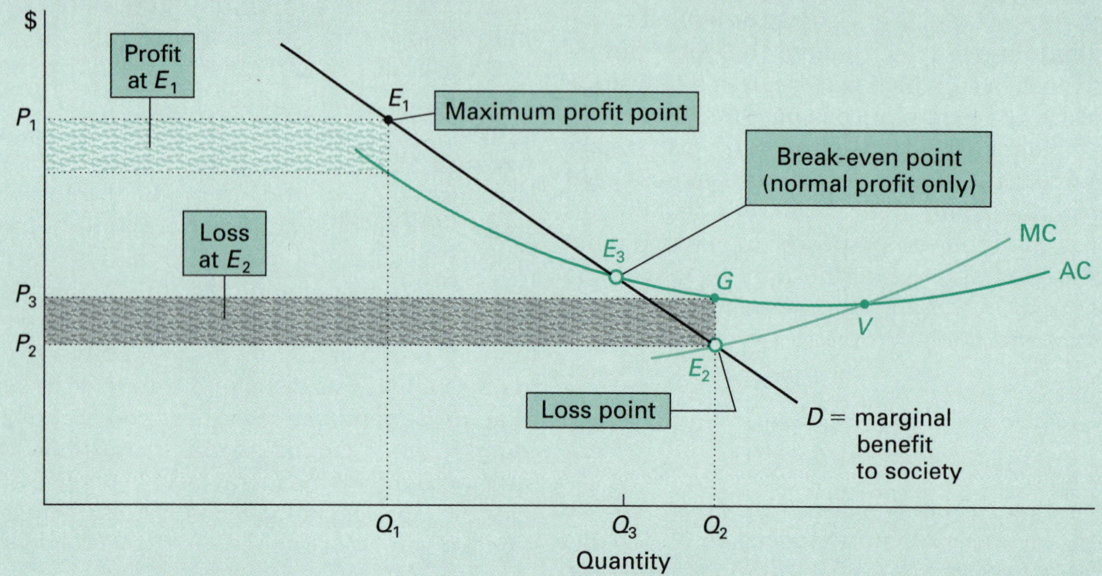


**(a) Average cost pricing.** An unrestricted monopoly would maximize profit by selecting point $E_1$ on its demand curve. (The profit it would earn is shown by the coloured area.) Average cost pricing involves driving the monopoly down its demand curve to $E_3$, by setting a price ceiling at $P_3$. At this point the firm just breaks even, earning only the normal profit necessary to keep it in business. Marginal cost pricing—that is, setting price at $P_2$ in order to drive the monopoly further down its demand curve to $E_2$—is not feasible, because price $P_2$ is below average cost. Thus, the firm would incur the loss shown by the grey area, and eventually go out of business.

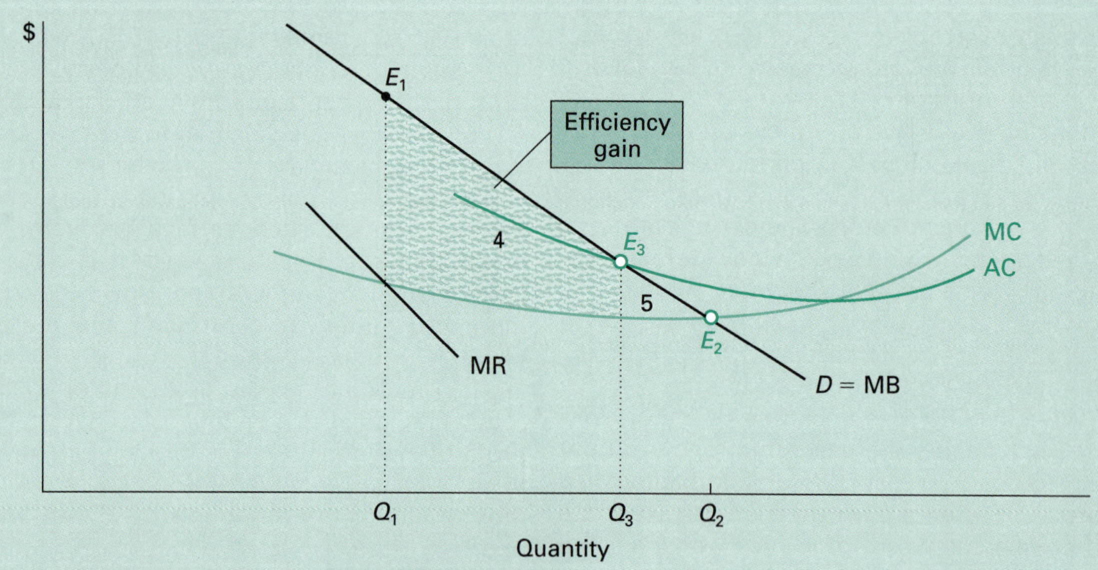


**(b) Efficiency gains that are achieved (4) and those that are not (5).** If it were feasible to drive the monopoly firm all the way down its demand curve from $E_1$ to $E_2$, then there would be an efficiency gain of areas 4 + 5. But since the firm can be driven down only to $E_3$, the efficiency gain is limited to area 4.

**Regulating monopoly: The difficult case.**

**BOX 12-2 continued**

the costs of a monopolist, how can those costs be controlled? A firm may be very successful in holding costs down as long as it has to meet the test of the marketplace where failure means bankruptcy, but it may be far less successful in controlling its costs if it knows it will receive a subsidy for any loss it incurs.

### 3. Government Ownership

The political problems in granting a subsidy are less severe if the government owns the monopoly, which it can then operate at efficient point $E_2$, charging the public $P_2$. Again, taxpayers must subsidize the loss that results. Government-owned mass transit systems are often cited as examples; government subsidies often cover a large portion of the costs of the typical large urban public transportation system.

Finally, we re-emphasize that the same problem arises here as with the other policies discussed in this box: As long as the firm's management receives whatever subsidy is necessary to cover its costs, it has inadequate incentive to keep costs down. There is a good reason why this may become a serious problem in a public enterprise. Even in a private enterprise, the owners (shareholders) may have problems in controlling a management that is inefficient or pursuing its own interests at the expense of the owners' interests. However, in a public enterprise this is even more difficult because of the layers of government bureaucracy separating the managers of the enterprise from its owners—in this case, the taxpayers. (Problems of a bureaucracy are examined further in Chapter 23.)

Finally, the example in Figure 12-9 presents a puzzle: A government price ceiling *increases* efficiency here but, in other circumstances, a government price ceiling — such as the ceiling on rents described in Chapter 6 — *reduces* efficiency. How is this possible? The answer: The ceiling on rents moved an industry away from an efficient, perfectly competitive equilibrium. On the other hand, the price ceiling in Figure 12-9 moves an inefficient monopoly at $E_1$ toward an efficient equilibrium at $E_2$.

Clearly, government intervention can be a powerful tool, since it can move a market away from its free-market equilibrium. While this can be damaging if the free market is initially competitive, it can be beneficial if the free market is initially monopolized. For this reason, economists oppose price regulation in some circumstances but favour it in others.

## THE SPECIAL CASE OF DISCRIMINATING MONOPOLY: LETTING A MONOPOLIST ACT LIKE A MONOPOLIST— IN SPADES

The argument so far is that a monopolist should not be allowed the freedom to set a high price. However, this general rule has an interesting exception that can be illustrated in the special case of the only dentist in a small town.

In panel (a) of Figure 12-10, the "broken" demand curve *D* shows the total demand for the dentist's services from all patients in the community. The diagram also shows her average costs, which, as always, include her opportunity costs — the income she could earn elsewhere.

If she must quote the same price for her services to all patients, she will not stay in this community: The average cost curve AC is always above the demand curve *D*, regardless of what price she picks. Consequently, there is no single price she can select that will cover her costs. The best she can do is to select a point such as *E* on the demand curve, setting her fee at $P_1$ and selling quantity $Q_1^T$. However, she still suffers a loss. Specifically, her total loss, compared with what she could earn elsewhere, is area 1; that is, $Q_1^T$ units sold at a loss of $CP_1$ on each.

If this were the end of the story, this community would lose its dentist. Her departure would mean a substantial loss to the people in the town: They would lose all the consumer surplus they could have had on her services. (A moment's reflection will convince you that the consumer surplus you can have from the services of a dentist may be very large

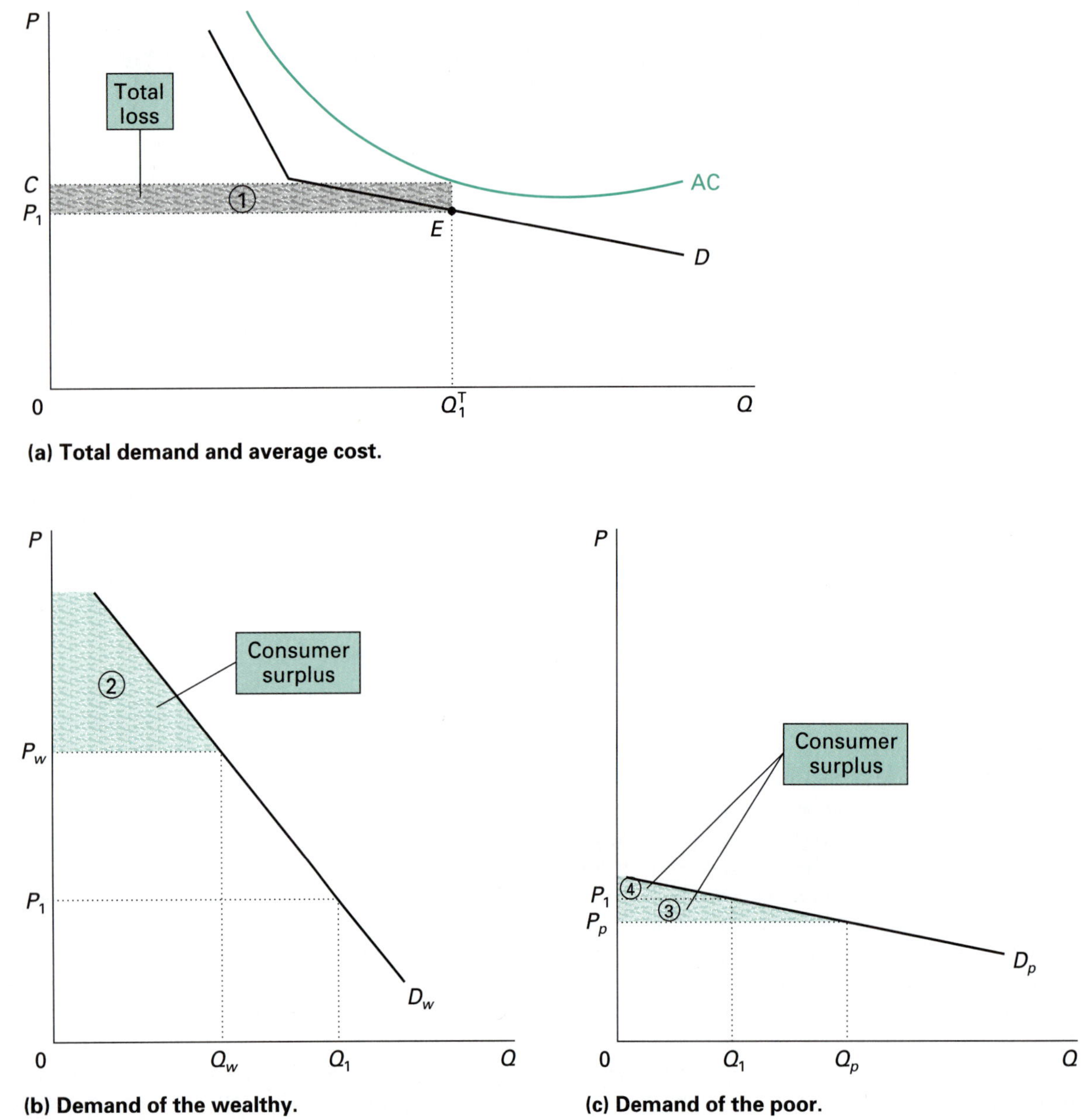


**FIGURE 12-10 When discriminating monopoly may be justified.**

If the dentist can charge only one price, she will leave town, because the total demand *D* (panel (a)), always lies below AC. Any point such as *E* that she might select on *D* would thus leave her operating at a loss, shown by the grey area 1.

On the other hand, she will stay if she is allowed to earn a profit by discriminating—charging a higher fee, $P_w$, to the wealthy (panel (b)), and a lower fee, $P_p$, to the poor (panel (c)). On her $Q_w$ of services sold to the wealthy, she increases her income to area ($Q_w \times P_w$), which is larger than her revenue from that group at $P_1$ and quantity $Q_1$ (panel (b)). Likewise, her revenue from her low-income patients, area $Q_p \times P_p$ in panel (c), is larger than what she would earn from that group at the price $P_1$. Thus, her average revenue from both groups may now be high enough to cover her average cost.

At the same time, her patients benefit because they keep their dentist. The low-income patients in panel (c) will enjoy a consumer surplus of areas 3 + 4, and the wealthy patients in panel (b) one of area 2.

indeed. When you have a bad toothache, the amount that you would be *willing* to pay for treatment is likely to be very large, much higher than the price you actually have to pay!)

But isn't there some other way she could be allowed to charge for her services so that she could earn a higher income and be convinced to stay after all? The answer is yes. Indeed, she can charge more in a way that will not only increase her earnings, but leave a net benefit to the community as well. Here's how: she can act as a ***discriminating monopolist***, selling her services at a higher price to some patients than to others.

Specifically, suppose the total demand shown in panel (a) of Figure 12-10 is made up of the demand of the wealthy (shown in panel (b)) and those with low incomes (shown in panel (c)). Suppose the dentist decides to charge a different price to each group. At the initial price $P_1$, the demand of the wealthy patients is inelastic. Thus, she could earn a larger revenue from them by charging them a higher price. In contrast, the demand of her low-income patients is *elastic* at the original price $P_1$; if they are charged a *lower* price, the total amount they spend on dental care will increase. Thus, by charging different prices and selling fewer services to the wealthy and more services to those with low incomes, the dentist can earn a higher total revenue from *both* groups. For example, if she charges $P_w$ to the wealthy in panel (b), her total revenue is $(P_w \times Q_w)$, which is higher than $(P_1 \times Q_1)$, the amount that she earned from this group at the initial price $P_1$; similarly, at $P_p$ she increases her earnings from those with low incomes, as panel (c) shows.

With higher earnings from both groups, her *average* revenue may now be high enough to cover her average cost; as a result, she may stay in town. And note that both the wealthy and the low-income patients benefit as a result. The consumer surplus enjoyed by the poor (areas 3 + 4 in panel (c)) is larger than it would have been at price $P_1$, and the wealthy still enjoy a consumer surplus (area 2 in panel (b)) that they would have lost if she had not stayed in the town. The conclusion: Price discrimination is justified in this case because it benefits everyone concerned.

However, even in cases when price discrimination is *desirable*, it may not be *possible*. To make different prices stick, the discriminating monopolist must be able to divide the market, preventing individuals who can buy at the low price from turning around and selling to those who are charged the higher price. In our example, the dentist is able to divide the market: A poor patient who is able to buy a root-canal job at a bargain price obviously cannot turn around and sell it to a rich friend. On the other hand, a bus company may not be able to divide its adult market, charging some customers $10 and others $20. The reason is that those who are able to buy cheap $10 tickets may sell them to the others for a price like $15 that benefits both groups. (However, the bus company *can* divide its market between adults and children, since an adult can't buy a cheap ticket from a child and use it on a bus. The company may also give a discount to senior citizens, since they are also relatively easy to identify, and those who are not over 65 usually don't want to pretend that they are.)

Finally, it should be re-emphasized that price discrimination by the monopolist in Figure 12-10 is desirable because *D* does not overlap AC, and the dentist would leave otherwise. However, price discrimination cannot be similarly justified in the normal case of monopoly where *D* does overlap AC and the monopolist can, therefore, at least cover costs by quoting a single price. (Appendix 12-A discusses an even more extreme case of discriminating monopoly.)

## LIVING IN A GLOBAL ECONOMY: THE WORLD'S LARGEST FIRM

Nippon Telegraph and Telephone (NTT) is the dominant firm in Japanese communications. It is also the world's largest firm. By 1988, the total value of its outstanding stock was over $295 billion—more than the total value of the eight largest U.S. companies. In a world in which many North American companies would be happy to see their stock selling for, say 20 times earnings, NTT was selling for 250 times earnings. (Non-comparable accounting practices explain some of this large difference.)

Until 1985, NTT had a complete monopoly over Japanese internal telecommunications. Although it now faces several competing firms, they have a difficult task ahead, since NTT is giving every evidence of being a very tough competitor. Its huge size gives it economies of scale, and its ability to offer a very wide range of telephone services and equipment—ranging from data networks to handset telephones—gives it ***economies of scope***.

*Economies of scope* occur when the addition of a new product reduces the cost of existing products.

For example, when NTT develops a new kind of telephone, there is no additional cost of transporting this to market, since it can be shipped in the same trucks as the existing phones. Thus, the average cost of transporting each kind of phone is reduced.

An important area where new technology is creating opportunities for exploiting economies of scope is telecommunications. Industry analysts foresee a future "electronic superhighway," based on fibre optic technology, that will combine cable television and telephone services, as well as provide home shopping and movies-on-demand, through a single network. A series of large "interactive media deals" in the United States in the early 1990s was a sign that these opportunities are being taken very seriously. In the largest of these deals, Bell Atlantic, a regional U.S. phone company, agreed to buy Telecommunications Inc., the largest U.S. cable operator, in a transaction potentially worth $30 billion.

## KEY POINTS

1. Monopoly means that there is a single seller. This situation may occur when a firm controls something essential to the production or sale of a good—such as a patent, resource, or government licence. Or it may occur if a number of firms merge.

2. Another important reason for monopoly is that a firm's costs may fall over such a wide range of output that total market demand can be most inexpensively satisfied by a single firm. This is a natural monopoly. Even if there are initially many firms in such an industry, they will tend to be eliminated by competition, with the single large firm that emerges able to undercut any present or future competitors.

3. A monopoly can do something a perfectly competitive firm cannot: Because it faces a demand curve that slopes downward to the right, it can quote the price at which it will sell.

4. Whereas marginal revenue MR for a perfect competitor is the same as price, MR for a monopoly is less than price; that is, a monopoly's MR curve lies below its demand curve. The demand curve represents the marginal benefit of the good to consumers and to society. The lower MR represents the marginal benefit to the monopolistic firm.

5. A monopolist maximizes profit by equating MC with MR, not with price. As a consequence, monopoly results in an inefficiently low output. It also results in a transfer of income from consumers to the monopolist.

6. In some agricultural markets, government legislation has encouraged the formulation of monopolylike marketing boards. Although producers argue that the boards benefit both producers and consumers by stabilizing prices, critics argue that the boards have transfer and efficiency effects similar to those of other monopolies.

7. If the firm is not a natural monopoly — but instead is, say, the result of a merger — a strong case can be made for breaking it up. In Canada, we have competition laws that prevent such a monopoly from being formed in the first place. These laws will be described in Chapter 14.

8. If the firm is a natural monopoly, breaking it up would raise costs. A preferred government policy is to set the maximum price the monopolist can charge. Facing this given price, the monopolist is forced into the price taking role of the perfect competitor and, consequently, increases output to a more efficient quantity.

9. A case can sometimes be made for allowing a monopoly to price-discriminate, that is, to charge a higher price to one group than to another. One example is a dentist in a small town who charges a higher price to her wealthy patients. Such discriminatory pricing may be justified if the good or service cannot otherwise be produced.

## KEY TERMS

**patent**
**legal monopoly**
**oligopoly**
**natural monopoly**
**market power**
**merger**
**price maker**
**price taker**
**profit-maximizing point on demend curve**
**efficiency (welfare) loss from monopoly**
**transfer effect of monopoly**
**marketing board**
**marginal cost pricing**
**discriminating monopoly**
**economies of scope**

## PROBLEMS

12-1. Consider an industry in which the discovery and development of advanced machinery and technology mean that, as time passes, average costs for a firm tend to drift lower and lower; that is, through time the average cost for an individual firm moves from $AC_1$ to $AC_2$ in the accompanying diagram. What do you think would happen in such an industry? Explain why. From the point of view of society as a whole, does the falling cost involve any advantages? Any disadvantages? In your view, how do these compare?

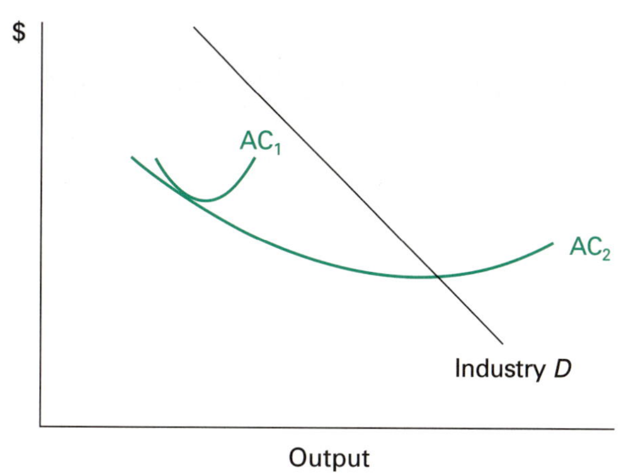


12-2. (a) If the firm with $AC_2$ in the above diagram is not regulated, would you expect that all the monopoly profits would go to the firm's owners? If not, who else do you think might eventually capture a share of these profits?

(b) Draw in the marginal cost curve that corresponds to $AC_2$. Show the best level at which to set regulated price. Explain why it is best.

12-3. "Marginal revenue for a monopolist equals the marginal benefit of its product to society." Do you agree or not? Explain.

12-4. The diagram on page 252 shows the demand and the costs the government faces in providing a public utility service (say, electricity) in a certain city.

(a) If the government is interested only in maximizing the utility's profit — or minimizing its loss—show the price it will set and how much it will produce and sell. Also show its profit or loss.

(b) Is this output the best from the viewpoint of allocative efficiency? If so, explain why. If not, show what the efficient output is and explain why. What price does the firm set to achieve the efficient output, and what is its profit or loss at that output?

(c) Suppose that this public utility is allowed to set discriminatory prices. It decides to charge the public a higher rate for its initial purchases while, for any additional purchases, it continues to charge the rate it set in part (b). Could the public utility sell an efficient output and still make profits by following a policy of price discrimination?

(d) Do you see now why public utilities are sometimes allowed to set discriminatory rates?

(e) In the section "The Special Case of Discriminating Monopoly," it was observed that for successful discrimination, a firm must be able to segregate its market and prevent resale among buyers. The dentist has no great problem in segregating her market. How about the public utility selling electricity?

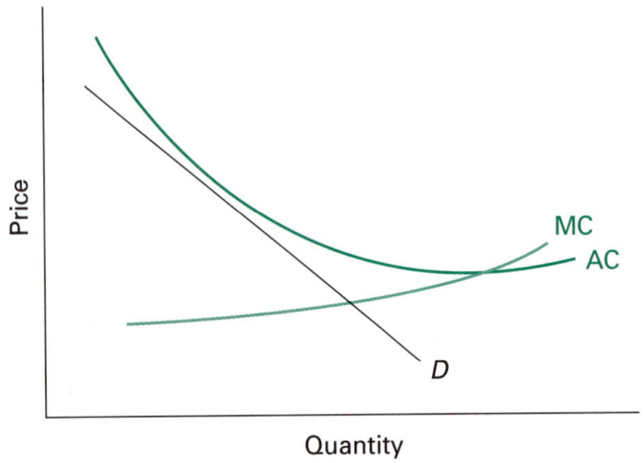


12-5. Consider a profit-maximizing monopoly with U-shaped cost curves. The government now levies a 50% tax on this firm's profits. Explain fully the impact of this tax on the amount the monopolist produces and the price it charges for its product.

12-6. Evaluate the following policy recommendation: "The sole objective in regulating monopoly price is to eliminate excess profits. And this is easy to do. Just examine the firm's current operations, calculate its average cost (including normal profit), and set price at this level."

12-7. Show the profit that the firm in Figure 12-8(b) would capture if it could get away with producing at point *B*. Is this an equilibrium if all firms try to do the same? Explain.

12-8. The British Columbia Milk Marketing Board sells milk at a price more than 10% above the free-market level. The board has also made it illegal to sell reconstituted milk, that is, powdered milk mixed with water and fresh milk. The reason given for this action is to protect the consumer from an inferior product. Yet, in tests, consumers cannot distinguish this milk from fresh milk, and it would cost far less. Is the marketing board protecting consumers or some other group?

# APPENDIX 12-A

## THE PARADOXICAL CASE OF THE PERFECTLY DISCRIMINATING MONOPOLIST

In the example in the text where price discrimination enables the small-town dentist to cover her fixed costs and stay in town, both sides gain from the price discrimination. The dentist gains because she is able to cover her fixed costs (and perhaps earn some above-normal profit as well), and the families in town gain as well because they get at least *some* consumer surplus: Some of the dentist's services are sold to families that would be willing to pay more for them than they are actually charged. (In Figure 12-10, rich families gain a surplus of area 2 and poor families gain areas 3 + 4.)

In the example in the text, the dentist-monopolist charges only two different prices, one to the families she considers rich, and a lower price to those she judges to be poor. However, not all rich families are equally rich, nor are all poor families equally poor. Moreover, people's willingness to pay for a good or service may be influenced not only by income, but by other factors as well. We may ask, therefore, whether a price-discriminating monopoly firm couldn't increase its profits even more by charging more than two different prices.

In general, the answer is yes, provided the monopolist has some way of knowing individuals' willingness to pay (and still assuming that individual buyers cannot resell the good or service to others). To see this, let's look at a simple hypothetical example of an entrepreneur who is thinking of bringing cable television to a small town, and suppose that the entrepreneur in fact does know the maximum monthly amount that each household is willing to pay for cable service. This information is summarized in the market demand curve for cable television in Figure 12-11. The intercept on the vertical axis shows that the household that is most eager to subscribe has a willingness to pay of $1000 per month. On the other hand, some families are not prepared to pay anything for cable service: The demand curve intersects the horizontal axis. Suppose also that once the town's cable system is in place, the marginal cost of allowing additional families to use it, is zero.

In this situation, if the monopoly firm is allowed to price-discriminate, it will make maximum profits by charging each household a price that equals the family's maximum willingness to pay. Because the marginal cost of allowing an additional family to receive the service is zero, it is in the monopolist's interest to extend service to any household that is willing to pay any amount at all, no matter how small. This case, where each buyer is charged his or her maximum willingness to pay, is referred to as ***a perfectly discriminating monopoly***. Note that under perfect price discrimination, no buyer enjoys any consumer surplus: Since consumer surplus is equal to the *maximum* amount that the buyer would be willing to pay, less the *actual* amount he or she has to pay, there can be no consumer surplus when each buyer is actually charged the maximum they are willing to pay.

A *perfectly discriminating monopolist* charges each buyer an amount equal to his or her maximum willingness to pay. Under perfectly discriminating monopoly, there is no consumer surplus.

(A special feature of the cable television example is that each buyer purchases only one unit. (No

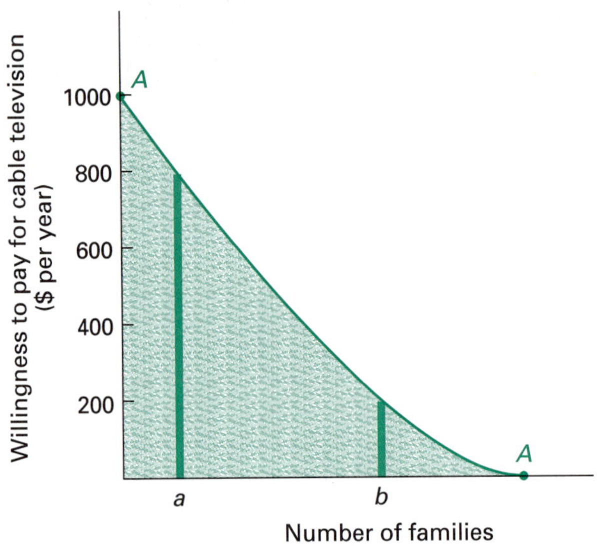


**FIGURE 12-11 A perfectly discriminating monopolist.**

The curve *AA* shows the maximum amount that each family is willing to pay for cable service. For example, a family far to the left in the diagram (bar *a*) is willing to pay as much as $800 per year; in contrast, family *b* toward the right end of the diagram is only willing to pay $200 per year.

If the cable company can charge each family the maximum amount that it is willing to pay, its total revenue will be the whole coloured area under *AA*. In this case, there would be no consumer surplus.

Assuming that the marginal cost of providing service to an additional family is zero, it would be in the monopolist's interest to supply it to each family that is willing to pay anything at all for it. This is also the efficient solution: With a perfectly discriminating monopolist, there is no efficiency loss.

household will want to buy more than one subscription to the same cable service!) When we consider goods and services for which individual buyers purchase more than one unit, perfect price discrimination is more complicated. However, if the monopolist knows each individual buyer's demand schedule, it can still be accomplished. In that case, the monopolist gets the maximum profit from each individual buyer by offering a deal under which the buyer's cost per unit depends on the number of units bought. For example, if an individual's maximum willingness to pay were $12, $8, $5, and $3 for the first, second, third, and fourth units, respectively, and the monopolist's marginal cost were $4 per unit, the monopolist would get the maximum profit by offering this buyer a package deal of three units for just under $25. The buyer would also be willing to buy two units for $20 or four units for $28, say. However, with a marginal cost of $4 per unit, either of these packages would yield the monopolist less profit than a package of three for $25.)

An interesting thing to note about a perfectly discriminating monopoly is that the quantity produced by the monopolist will be approximately the same as that which would be produced if the firm were forced to practice marginal cost pricing. The reason is that for a perfectly discriminating monopolist, the marginal revenue from selling an additional unit is just the price at which that unit is sold: The monopolist does not have to reduce the price on all units sold in order to sell additional units. Thus, we can think of a perfectly discriminating monopolist as selling additional units at successively lower prices, until it reaches the unit for which price equals marginal cost.

But if the firm produces and sells every unit for which price is greater than or equal to marginal cost, *there is no allocative efficiency loss.*

From the viewpoint of consumers, perfectly discriminating monopoly is the worst possible market form: It eliminates all consumer surplus. But from the viewpoint of the monopoly firm, it is the *best* possible market form: It gives more monopoly profit than any other. Thus, in comparison with a perfectly competitive market, or a monopolist that is forced to practice marginal cost pricing, perfectly discriminating monopoly implies a large transfer effect from buyer to seller. Paradoxically, however, it does not lead to any efficiency loss. Thus we see, once again, that in order to assess the significance of monopoly (or any other market form), it is not enough to look at efficiency effects; transfer effects must be taken into account as well.

Although the case of perfectly discriminating monopoly is interesting from a theoretical point of view, its practical significance should not be exaggerated. In reality, firms have no way of knowing the maximum willingness to pay of individual buyers; moreover, for most goods and services it is difficult and costly to prevent resale. Thus in the real world, no firm comes close to being a perfectly discriminating monopolist.

# APPENDIX 12-B

## PUBLIC TRANSIT PRICING

In the discussion of regulated monopoly, we showed that, in principle, allocative efficiency would require that the firm should be forced to set its price at marginal cost. However, as explained in Box 12-1 on the theory of second best, this conclusion may have to be modified if the price that the monopolist charges has an influence in markets which themselves are not competitive, or are distorted in some fashion.

As an example of this situation, consider a public transit system, usually operated by an agency of a municipal government. It could set fares for its subway, bus, streetcar, or light rail transit rides equal to marginal cost. Ostensibly, this would appear to be efficient pricing but, if it did so, it would likely be missing out on an opportunity to enhance social welfare.

A usual problem in cities is traffic congestion. When automobile drivers enter a roadway, they may consider the cost of their trips in terms of gasoline, time, and other operating costs, but they do not take into account the extra time (congestion) cost they impose on other drivers. That is, there is a divergence of private and social costs. This divergence is illustrated in the diagram below drawn for rush-hour conditions.[5]

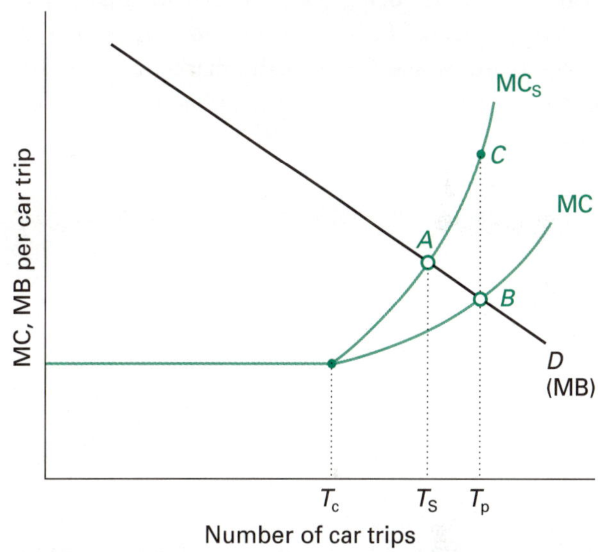


**FIGURE 12-12**

Here, there is no extra congestion cost if $T_c$ or fewer trips are being made. As more drivers enter roadways, however, the marginal congestion cost mounts, shown by the vertical distance between private marginal cost (MC) and social marginal cost ($MC_S$). The socially optimal number of trips is $T_S$ where the marginal benefit to society of a trip (MB) given by the demand curve is just equal to $MC_S$. However, drivers taking into account only the private costs they incur will make $T_p$ trips, where their marginal benefit is equal to their marginal cost. The result is too many trips being made and a welfare loss shown by triangle *ABC*.

A usual solution when too many resources are being devoted to a good or service is to tax it, thus increasing its cost to consumers and thus reducing consumption. In this case, the optimal per-unit tax is given by the distance *AC*. If it were possible to charge this tax, a "first" best allocation would result and public transit authorities would maximize welfare by pricing fares at marginal cost.

However, this direct solution may be neither feasible nor desirable. The social problem here is that traffic is moving too slowly because of congestion. The required per-unit tax would usually be collected as a toll, but having to stop at a tollbooth to pay it

[5] This divergence between the private and social cost is an example of an *externality*; this concept will be further discussed in Chapters 21 to 23.

would slow traffic down even more. Instead of curing the problem, this solution may exacerbate it.

Given road congestion that cannot be dealt with directly by optimal pricing, there is a role for second-best pricing of public transit, a substitute for travel by car. Instead of pricing public transit rides at marginal cost—thus achieving efficiency, *but only in this market*—the transit authority could price (subsidize) fares below marginal cost. This would cause a welfare loss in the market for public transit, but it would also cause the demand curve for trips by car to shift to the left because the two are substitutes. As too many car trips were being made originally, this policy would decrease the welfare loss in that market. As long as the welfare gain in the market for car trips exceeds the welfare loss in the public transit market, a net social gain would result.

The second-best price for public transit is that which causes the marginal welfare gain in the market for car trips to be just equal to the marginal social loss in the public transit market. It is "second" best because society is doing as well as it can given that the "first"-best solution is not feasible.

How low can the second-best fare be? Conceivably, it could be negative, where it is worthwhile to pay people to take public transit instead of driving their cars. Usually, however, public transit fares are only partially subsidized. An exception was Calgary in the mid-1980s where public transit users were not charged for rides in the downtown core. This was efficient because of the severe congestion problem there.

CHAPTER 13

# MARKETS BETWEEN MONOPOLY AND PERFECT COMPETITION

*People of the same trade seldom meet together, even for merriment and diversion, but the conversation ends in a conspiracy against the public, or in some contrivance to raise prices.*

*Adam Smith,* Wealth of Nations

Monopoly represents the clearest form of market power; the monopoly firm is alone in the marketplace and has the power to choose its selling price. But even though there are some markets that are controlled by a single monopoly firm, most of the giants in Canadian business are not monopolists. Air Canada competes with Canadian Airlines and several regional carriers in the market for domestic air travel; and Canadian National competes with CPR in railroad transport. In the market for telecommunications equipment, Northern Telecom faces competition from international firms such as the American IT&T, Western Electric, and Sweden's L.M. Erickson; General Motors of Canada has to contend with Ford, Chrysler, Toyota, Hyundai, Volkswagen, and others. In the market for petroleum products, Imperial Oil has to compete with Shell and other foreign-owned companies — as well as with Canadian-owned Petrocan. *Oligopoly* — where a market is dominated by a *few* sellers — is more significant in the Canadian economy than outright monopoly.

This chapter describes several kinds of markets which, like oligopoly, lie in the middle ground between the extremes of monopoly on the one hand, and perfect competition on the other:

1. *Monopolistic competition*: This occurs when a firm has many competitors, but is nonetheless still able to exercise some small influence over its price because it is selling a differentiated product. Monopolistic competition is common in retailing and some service sectors.
2. In contrast, *oligopoly* is a market that is dominated by a few sellers, each with considerable influence over price. A special case of oligopoly to which we will pay particular attention below is *duopoly*, a market with only two sellers.

The first line of Table 13-1 sets out the basic characteristics of a perfectly competitive market. This chapter will explain lines B, C, and D, showing how each of the other market forms is similar or different. Monopolistic competition is the same as perfect competition in some respects: It has a large number of firms and easy entry. However, it is different because of its non-standardized product and the consequent power of each firm to exercise some influence over its price. Oligopoly and duopoly are different from perfect competition in all of the four features shown in Table 13-1.

This chapter begins with the market closest to perfect competition — *monopolistic competition* — and then moves to a discussion of markets with fewer sellers.

## MONOPOLISTIC COMPETITION

The ***product differentiation*** that gives rise to ***monopolistic competition*** in some industries may be based on consumers' perception of quality differences among the goods or services offered by differ-

**TABLE 13-1 Types of Market Structure**

| Type of Market | (1) Number of firms | (2) Type of Product | (3) Entry | (4) Influence over Price | Examples |
|---|---|---|---|---|---|
| A Perfect Competition | Many small firms | Standardized | Easy | None (price taker) | Some agricultural products |
| B Monopolistic Competition | Many small firms | Differentiated | Easy | A little | Some retail trade and services |
| C Oligopoly | A few firms | Usually differentiated (though it may be standardized) | Difficult | Some (price searcher) | Autos, computers (for a standardized product: steel) |
| D Duopoly | Two | Usually differentiated | Difficult | Some (price searcher) | Long-distance air travel in Canada |
| E Monopoly | One | — | Difficult or impossible | Substantial (price maker, unless government regulated) | Local telephone service |

ent sellers, or simply on people's taste for variety. In any case, the result is that the sellers have *some* ability to control the price of what they sell: In contrast to a seller in a perfectly competitive market, a monopolistically competitive firm will not lose *all* its sales if it raises its price relative to its competitors. You can think of many examples: restaurants; auto repair shops and gas stations; interior decorators and hair stylists; firms that produce handicraft items for gift shops and others. Because there are many sellers, each one only has a fairly limited ability to raise price. For example, a hair stylist in a large city has many competitors. But even so, she still retains some influence over her price. If she raises it by a small amount — perhaps by 25¢ or 50¢ — she won't lose much business; few of her customers will be willing to switch to someone with a different style. But she is limited in her ability to raise price. If she tries to raise it by several dollars, many of her customers will go elsewhere.

Even if products are physically identical, they may still be differentiated in other respects. For example, tubes of Crest toothpaste are sold in stores in different *locations*. Although the products are physically the same, the closer store's toothpaste is "better" because it is more convenient. As a result, the consumer will be willing to pay a few cents more for it. Thus, location gives each store some control over its price; it can charge a few cents more and not lose all its customers. Similarly, a gasoline station with a particularly convenient location can charge more. However, it doesn't have much control over price. If it charges a much higher price, buyers will bypass it to go to one of its less expensive, though less convenient, competitors.

When we discussed the case of perfectly competitive markets in Chapter 10, we illustrated the firms' lack of control over the price of their product by noting that the demand curve facing an individual seller was perfectly horizontal. A firm in a competitive market can sell as much as it wants at the common market price, but if it were to demand even a small amount more than its competitors, it would lose all its sales. In contrast, a firm in a monopolistically competitive industry will not lose all its sales if it raises price: Because it sells a differentiated product, there will still be some buyers that prefer this firm's goods or services over those of its competitors. Therefore, such a firm does not face a perfectly horizontal demand curve. Instead, its demand curve slopes downward to the right, just like a monopolist's.

However, in contrast to a monopoly, a monopolistically competitive industry has many sellers that offer close substitutes for the goods or services of any individual seller. As we saw in Chapter 6, a good or service with close substitutes will have a relatively elastic demand curve. Thus, even though the sellers offer a differentiated product, the demand curve facing each individual producer tends to be quite elastic, with relatively little slope, as illustrated by the demand curves drawn in Figure 13-1.

What explains the large number of sellers in a typical monopolistically competitive industry? The answer is that, by definition, *there are no significant*

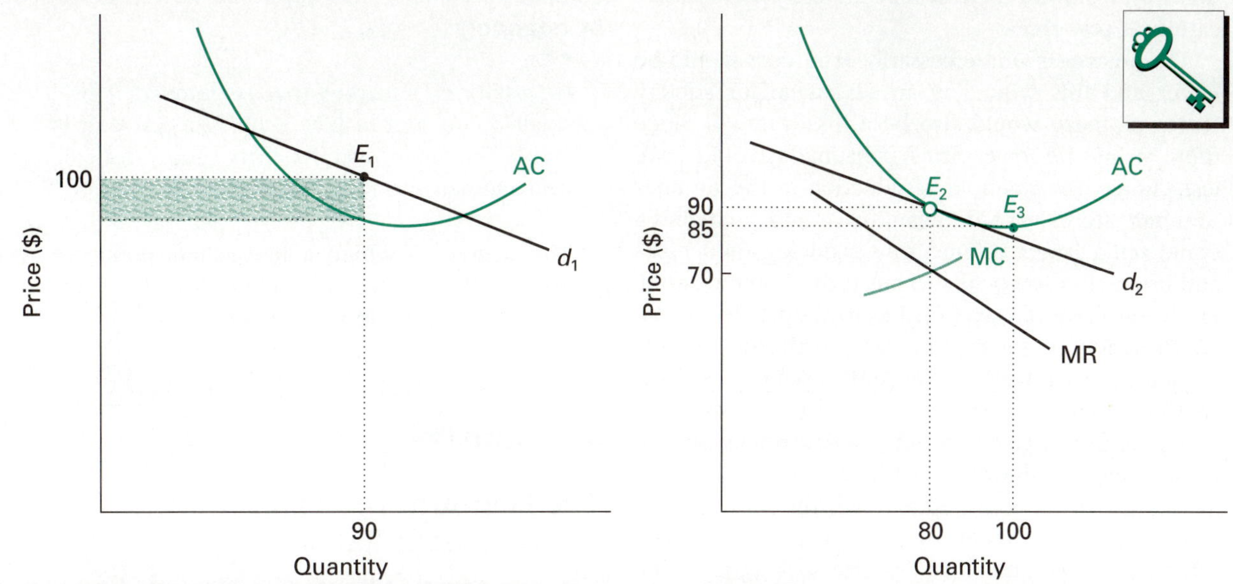


**(a) In the short run.** The firm faces a sloping demand $d_1$ because its product is differentiated. Short-run equilibrium is at $E_1$ with the above-normal profit shown in the coloured area. This attracts new firms into the industry, shifting this firm's *d* to the left until a new equilibrium is reached at $E_2$ in panel (b).

**(b) In the long run.** This is a long-run equilibrium because above-normal profits have been eliminated by the entry of new firms. (Note: In these two panels, AC is the same. The only thing that changes is demand, which shifts to the left from $d_1$ to $d_2$ as a result of the new entrants.)

**FIGURE 13-1 Equilibrium for a typical firm in monopolistic competition.**

*barriers to entry* in such industries. For example, it's relatively easy to get into small-scale retailing; it is not necessary to have a vast pool of funds to buy or rent a single drugstore. Similarly, it is easy to start a small neighbourhood restaurant, or set up an arts and crafts studio to produce tourist souvenirs.

Because entry of new firms is easy, *firms in monopolistically competitive industries cannot, in the long run, earn above-normal profits*. Where existing firms *are* making above-normal profits in the short run, new entrants come in, eliminating these excess profits, as illustrated in Figure 13-1. Initially, the typical firm shown in panel (a) is operating at $E_1$ and earning a profit shown by the coloured area. But, as new competitors enter and capture some of its sales, it gets a smaller share of the total market, and the demand curve facing the firm, therefore, shifts to the left. This process continues until its demand becomes *tangent* to the average cost curve, as shown in panel (b). Faced with this new demand curve, the best the firm can now do is to select the point of tangency $E_2$ where it earns no excess profit. Any other point on the demand curve would leave it operating at a loss. Thus, just as free entry eliminates above-normal profits for the typical firm in perfect competition, so free entry also eliminates such profits for the firm in monopolistic competition. (Contrast this with the case of a monopoly. As long as there is no entry, the monopoly firm's individual demand curve remains identical with the market demand curve, and it can go on earning above-normal profit.)

In terms of efficiency, how does monopolistic competition rate? At first glance, panel (b) of Figure 13-1 suggests that monopolistic competition is inefficient: At the firm's output of 80 units, MC ($70) is less than price ($90), so this is apparently an inefficient quantity of output. Put another way, it is often claimed that there is ***excess capacity***, with too many firms in the industry, each producing too few units. Consumer demand could be satisfied at lower cost if there were fewer firms, each producing more — that is, if the typical firm in panel (b) were to move from $E_2$ to $E_3$ by increasing its output from 80 to 100 units, thus lowering its average cost to the minimum of $85. If the industry were changed in this way, wouldn't the result be a more efficient allocation of resources?

The answer is: not necessarily. True, cost would be lower, and this would be an advantage for society. However, there would also be a disadvantage. Since there would be fewer firms, consumers would have less choice. For example, a reduction in the number of retail stores would mean that those remaining could sell a larger volume, thus reducing their costs and prices. But it would also mean that some customers would have to travel further to shop. Perhaps the convenience of local stores is worth the slightly higher price we have to pay. And as people living in small communities are well aware, the advantage of shopping in a large city is not just that prices may be lower. Equally important is the greater variety and availability of "specialty items" that the monopolistically competitive retail industry in large cities can offer. Thus, it is difficult to criticize strongly the inefficiencies — if any — that arise from monopolistic competition.

In conclusion, monopolistic competition is sufficiently similar to perfect competition — in terms of large numbers, free entry, and a reasonably high level of efficiency — that economists do not recommend government regulation of firms in this market, particularly when regulation itself can introduce inefficiencies.

However, public policy problems can arise in the case of oligopoly, where firms are larger and fewer, and thus typically have greater influence over price.

## OLIGOPOLY

While the large number of small retail stores that exist in a sizeable metropolitan area may be monopolistic competitors, if there are only three stores that operate alone in a small, isolated village, they are oligopolists. Similarly, the three North American auto companies are oligopolists; each has some influence over price, and also knows that any price change it makes will be noticed by the others, who may well react. For example, if GM cuts its price, Ford and Chrysler may follow suit. True, with increased competition from foreign makes, the North American car market has become more competitive. But it is still an oligopoly: For example, if Honda of Japan is thinking of reducing the prices of its new models in Canada, it certainly keeps an eye on Ford and General Motors who might decide to give discounts on *their* models in response. In other words, before deciding on its price, each firm must take into account the possible reactions of its competitors. This is the important new issue raised by ***oligopoly***.

> *Oligopoly* is a market that is dominated by a small number of sellers. Each firm has considerable influence over its price, and must take into account the reaction of the others.

The degree to which a few sellers dominate an industry — that is, the concentration of the industry — can be measured in several ways.

## Measuring the Concentration of an Industry

### The Four-firm and Eight-firm Concentration Ratios

These are shown in Figure 13-2. The ***four-firm concentration ratio*** measures the percentage of an industry's output produced by its four largest firms, while the eight-firm ratio measures the percentage of output produced by its eight largest firms. Figure 13-2 shows that the tobacco products, transportation equipment (which includes motor vehicles), and petroleum and coal products industries are dominated to a considerable degree by the largest few firms. But also notice that there are many industries that are not, such as the furniture, clothing, and construction industries. Moreover, the figure shows the relative importance of the four or eight largest firms in sales *by domestic producers*; the degree of concentration in *total* sales in the Canadian market is much smaller in many industries where imports account for a large share of sales.

### The Herfindahl-Hirschman Index

This is a somewhat more complicated way of measuring the concentration of an industry. To understand it, first consider a monopoly — an industry with the maximum possible degree of concentration. One firm produces 100% of the industry's output. To calculate the ***Herfindahl-Hirschman Index*** (HHI), this percentage is squared:

> **$(100)^2$ = 10,000, the largest value the index can take**

Formally, the Herfindahl-Hirschman Index is constructed by squaring the percentage market share of

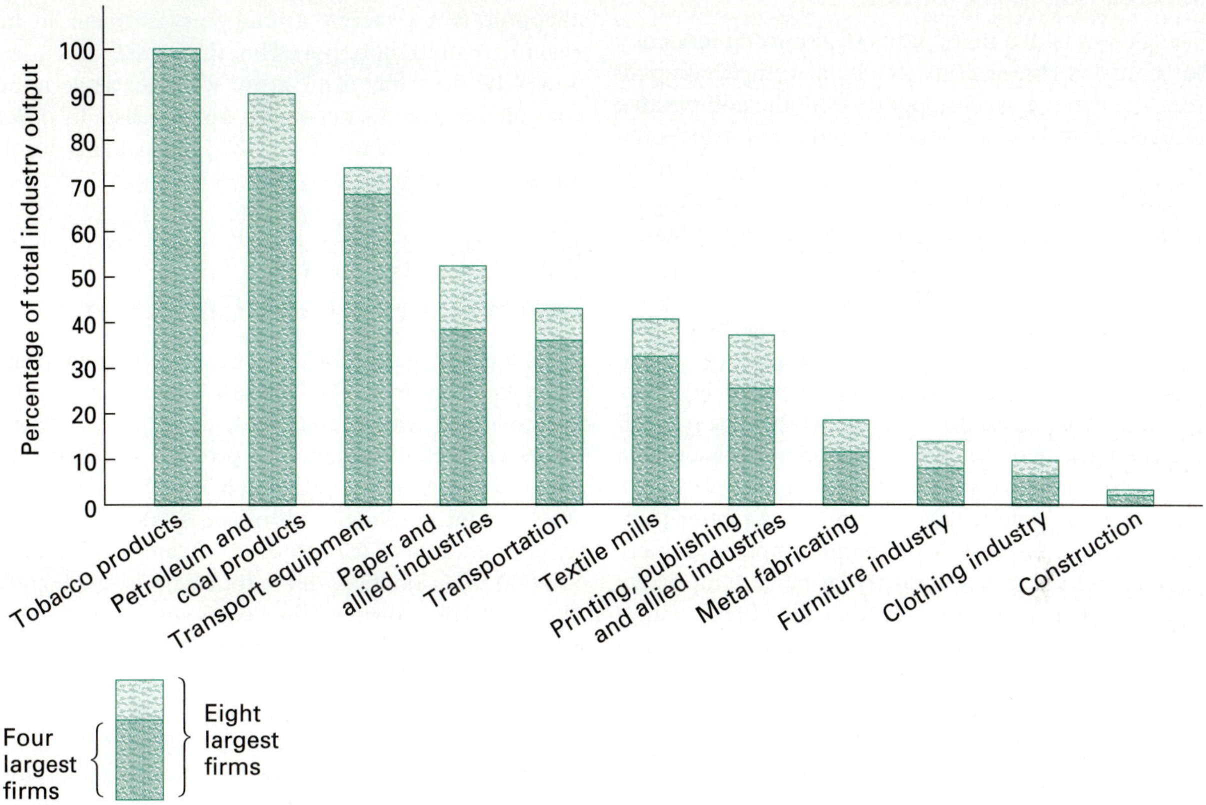


**FIGURE 13-2** **Concentration ratios showing the importance of the "big four" and "big eight" in selected industries, 1988 (shares of output sold by domestic firms).**

*Source*: Statistics Canada, *Annual Report of the Minister of Industry, Science and Technology under the Corporations and Labour Unions Returns Act (CALURA), Part 1, Corporations, 1988* (Ottawa: Minister of Supply and Services Canada, 1991). Reprinted by permission of the Minister of Supply and Services Canada.

each firm, and then adding up these numbers. To illustrate further, consider a nearly monopolized industry. One firm produces 90% of the output, while the only other firm produces 10%. In this case, the HHI becomes

$$90^2 + 10^2 = 8200$$

still a very high value. Notice that the value of the HHI falls as the number of firms in the industry increases.

Next, suppose that there are again two firms in the industry, but the first one no longer dominates. Instead, they both produce the same amount; their market share is 50% each. Again squaring percentage shares, the HHI becomes

$$50^2 + 50^2 = 5000$$

Thus, the HHI falls as the market shares of the firms become more equal.

Finally, note that, in a perfectly competitive market with 100 firms, each making 1% of total sales, the HHI would be much smaller:

$$1^2 + 1^2 + 1^2 + \ldots \text{ to 100 terms} = 100$$

The HHI does a good job of taking into account the number of firms in an industry, and the degree of equality in their market shares. These are two characteristics that are important in any evaluation of the concentration of an industry. Moreover, because this index is based on the shares of all firms, it is superior to the four-firm (or eight-firm) concentration ratio, which takes into account only the four (or eight) largest firms.

## Has Concentration Been Increasing or Decreasing Over Time?

The answer is that there has been no strong tendency for Canada's largest firms to eliminate their competitors and emerge as monopolists from the competitive struggle. (Studies of American industrial concentration have shown that this holds true in the United States as well.) In the past decade, the overall competitiveness in the North American economy may, if anything, have been getting somewhat *greater* because of the rise of new industries, such as microcomputers with many small, highly competitive firms, and because of the increasing importance of service industries, where firms are generally small. In addition, reductions in transport costs and other barriers to international trade, as well as the growing economic strength of countries such as Japan and South Korea, has exposed Canadian manufacturing to greater competition from imports. For example, import competition has made the auto industry far more competitive than the high concentration ratio for transportation equipment in Figure 13-2 suggests. (However, in some cases, the government has limited this competition by introducing barriers to international trade, such as the limits on the imports of Japanese cars.) Failure to take imports into account limits the validity of any measure of concentration based on domestic output.

Thus, neither Canada nor the United States is becoming an increasingly monopolized economy; oligopoly is not merely a temporary stop on an inevitable road to monopoly. This, then, raises the question: Why do a few firms grow so large, while none goes all the way to become a monopolist? In other words, why are there typically several firms in an industry rather than just one?

# Natural Oligopoly: The Importance of Cost Conditions

Costs are one reason for there being only a few firms in an industry. In many industries, there are economies of scale with average cost declining as output increases. A plant designed to produce 100,000 cars per year can operate at a much lower average cost than a plant designed to produce 10,000. But costs do not continue to fall forever. If a plant is producing 500,000 units, doubling its output won't significantly reduce its costs further. When costs cease to fall, there is no longer this cost incentive for firms to continue to grow into a monopoly position.

The result is ***natural oligopoly***. Panel (b) of Figure 13-3 illustrates how this market form falls somewhere between the extremes of perfect competition and natural monopoly. Note that average cost for an

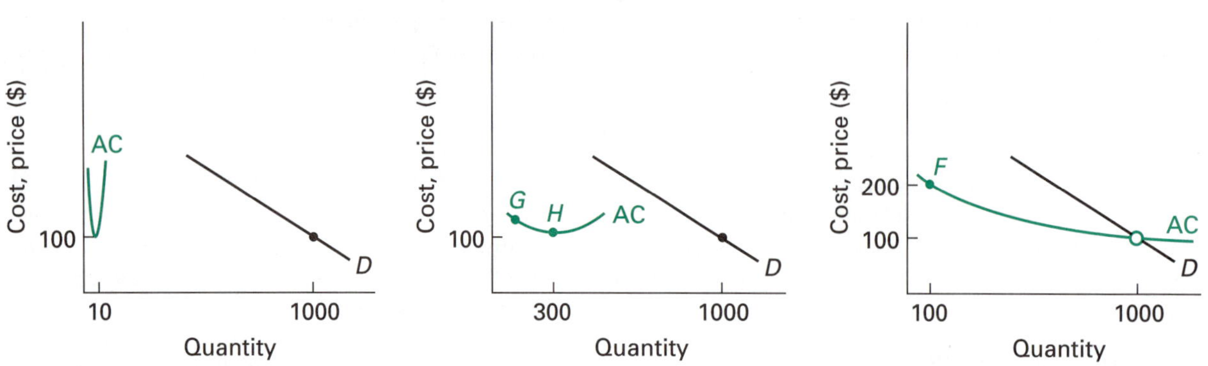


**(a) Perfect competition.** Long-run AC curve turns up at relatively low level of output.

**(b) Natural oligopoly.** Intermediate case: Long-run AC reaches its minimum at a sizeable fraction of the total market. Several large firms will be able to get at or close to minimum cost, but small firms will have high average costs at *G*, say, and will find it difficult to compete.

**(c) Natural monopoly.** Long-run AC curve continues to fall, not reaching a minimum until about where it cuts *D*, or beyond.

**FIGURE 13-3 Natural oligopoly compared with perfect competition and natural monopoly.**

individual firm continues to fall over a considerable range, up to an output of 300 units. (Compare this to perfect competition in panel (a), where costs stop falling at an output of 10 units.) If existing firms in panel (b) are producing less than 300 units, they have an incentive to expand. However, at an output of 300 units—still far short of satisfying total market demand of 1000 units—costs stop falling. At this point, existing firms no longer reap a cost advantage by expanding further.

*Natural oligopoly* occurs when the average costs of individual firms fall over a large enough range so that a few firms can produce the total quantity sold at the lowest average cost.

However, it is not just cost conditions that account for the persistence of oligopoly. Oligopoly represents a balance of forces that encourage concentration and those that work against it.

## Other Influences in Oligopoly Markets

One of the strongest forces working toward larger and larger corporations is the *incentive* such firms have to acquire market power. The larger a firm becomes by internal growth or by buying its competitors — or by driving them out of business — the greater its power to set price. For this reason, a firm in natural oligopoly, with no further opportunities to cut costs by expanding, may nonetheless still seek to expand in order to push competitors out of the market and thus acquire more power to raise price.

On the other side, the government provides a countervailing force that deters the expansion of firms and discourages the monopolization of an industry. Specifically, the government has passed *competition laws* — formerly referred to as *anti-combines laws* — as a countervailing force. Competition laws prohibit such practices as *predatory pricing*—that is, attempts by large firms to drive a smaller competitor out of business by temporarily charging very low prices. By prohibiting this, the law tries to protect the small competitors of large firms, in order to protect consumers against the higher price that large firms might charge if they were to become like monopolists.

Another factor that also works to protect the consumer against monopoly is the threat of competition from imported goods. Even if a large firm establishes a monopolylike position in the *Canadian* market, it still may face competition from foreign firms, so that it cannot raise its price above the price of comparable imported goods.

The product differentiation that exists in many oligopolistic markets also discourages monopolization. A car is not just a car; there are many kinds—it's a differentiated product. For many years, American Motors was very successful in the production of a very special kind of vehicle — a four-wheel-drive Jeep. The profits it obtained by its strength in producing this highly differentiated product kept the firm in business for a long time, and thus prevented the broader auto industry from becoming even more concentrated. Likewise, product differentiation is important in many other oligopolistic (and monopolistically competitive) industries. Sears Ltd. sells Kenmore brand washing machines that are similar but not identical to the Whirlpool or Maytag brands. Beer brewed by Labatt is not the same as that produced by Molson (though some people can't tell the difference). However, the product differentiation that is so important in many oligopolistic markets may not be significant in others. In the basic steel industry, for example, one company's product is much the same as another's.

Thus, oligopoly is often a stable market form because government competition policy and product differentiation prevent large firms from driving out their rivals. But what prevents oligopoly from drifting in the other direction toward more competition, with a large number of new firms entering the market? The answer is that there are often substantial ***barriers to entry*** for new firms.

## BARRIERS TO ENTRY

The economies of scale that make an industry a natural oligopoly also act as an important barrier to the entry of new firms. For example, in the natural oligopoly shown in Figure 13-3(b), there are three large firms, each operating at *H* at a high 300-unit volume of output. Each has far lower costs of $100 per unit than a new smaller firm producing 100 units of output, with costs at $130 a unit (point *G*). Because of this difference in costs, it will be easy for existing high-volume producers to undercut the price of a new entrant that is starting up at low volume and higher costs. For this reason, new firms may have to enter the industry on a grand scale. It is important for them to have the financial resources — the "deep pockets" — necessary to set up a productive facility large enough to move them quickly into the high-volume, low-cost range of production. Therefore, new competition in oligopolistic markets often comes not just from struggling new firms but also from giants in other industries. For example, Xerox was faced with new competition when IBM, Kodak, and several Japanese firms entered the market for office copiers.

There are other barriers to entry. For example, it is often very difficult for a new firm to compete with existing firms that produce "name-brand" products that have been widely advertised and accepted by the public in the past.[1] For example, anyone thinking of producing a new type of tire must recognize that one problem in entering such an industry will be overcoming the acceptance by the public of such brand names as Goodyear or Motomaster.

New producers of items such as breakfast foods, soft drinks, or cosmetics may also encounter difficulty in getting their products into the stores and before the view of the public. Stores tend to provide more favourable treatment for well-known products that they know will sell, and established brands may provide retailers with incentives to keep new competitors out. A new entrant may be caught in a vicious circle: It can't sell unless stores give it shelf space; but stores won't give it shelf space until it can prove it can sell. (See Box 13-1.) A similar problem faces new manufacturers of microcomputers. How do they get their products into the stores when most stores can comfortably stock no more than eight or ten models? One option is to sell through their own stores, as Tandy (Radio Shack) does. However, Tandy was already in the retail business, selling CB radios and other electronics before it developed its computers. Setting up a new retail chain can be very expensive and this presents a barrier to small entrants.

Government may also create legal barriers to entry. Until recently, government regulations severely restricted entry into the airline business, thereby creating a stable oligopoly for the existing firms.

While it is true that oligopoly is often a stable form of market structure, this point should not be overstated. In the rapidly changing North American economy, there are many exceptions. On the one hand, some industries are becoming less concentrated. For example, new "mini-mills" are providing competition to established steel producers, as technological changes have reduced the importance of economies of scale in steel; there is a similar trend in the beer-brewing industry. On the other hand, some other industries have drifted toward a more concentrated form of oligopoly.

[1] In "Industrial Economics: An Overview," *Economic Journal*, September 1988, p. 669, MIT's R. Schmalensee cites evidence that the more heavily an industry advertises, the more difficult it is for new firms to enter. This article has been drawn on heavily, because it provides a useful summary of much recent research on the topics covered in this chapter and the next.

## THE OLIGOPOLIST AS A PRICE SEARCHER

Prices are determined quite differently in perfect competition, monopoly, and oligopoly. In perfect competition, price is determined by the impersonal forces of demand and supply. Firms are *price takers*; the individual firm has no influence over price. In monopoly, the firm is a *price maker*. It is able to choose the price at which it will sell, by selecting a point on the market demand curve. In oligopoly, the firm is a ***price searcher***. Although it has some influence over price, it can't set a price in the simple way that a monopolist can. Instead, in its pricing decisions it faces a major complication: How will its competitors react? If it reduces price, will they follow? Will its action set off a price war? Where might this lead? In an oligopoly, the firms are mutually interdependent; each is sensitive to the actions of the others.

The world of oligopoly can resemble a chess game, with move and countermove. And, like a chess game, the outcome may be unpredictable. Often, the search by oligopolists for an equilibrium price can be quite complex. Oligopoly is one of the most challenging areas of economic theory, since it can't be analysed using simple models like those used to describe perfect competition or monopoly.

For this reason, it is not possible here to do more than emphasize a few highlights. The next section describes oligopolists who recognize their common interest in raising prices, and enter into a ***collusive agreement*** to act as though they were a monopoly. This is followed by a description of oligopolists who abandon this common interest in order to pursue their individual interests. As a result, the collusive arrangement comes apart.

### Collusion

In Canada and the United States, an agreement to fix prices is against the law. To see why, let's look at the economic effects of a ***cartel***, the most formal type of collusion.

> A *cartel* is a formal agreement among firms to set price and share the market.

## APPLICATIONS AND ILLUSTRATIONS BOX 13-1

### Competition for Shelf Space

Shelf space has been described as "the most vigorously contested real estate in Canada" and represents both a barrier to entry and a weapon of non-price competition.

First, many retailers demand payment before they will place a new product on their shelves. For example, Certalan Inc. of Montreal was the manufacturer of Pressdent, Canada's first pump toothpaste. In 1982, it had to pay $20,000 in listing fees just to get one major grocery chain to carry the product. The now-defunct Millie's Chips in Nova Scotia also faced such demands, although not from all retailers. These flat fees can range up to $100,000, and they amounted to 2% of all sales in 1980. Instead of listing fees, firms may pay up to 50% of their sales revenues to a retailer for putting their product on the shelves. For products already established in stores, producers may pay as much as $50,000 to have their product placed on end-of-aisle shelves, apparently premium sites. Other payment schemes may involve volume discounts, buyback offers, cooperative advertising, and special rebates. Those who pay these fees describe them as kickbacks amounting to coercion. By whatever name, they represent barriers to entry.

Most manufacturers, however, are willing to pay these fees and realize that any shelf space they occupy cannot be occupied by their competitors. Standard strategies involve product proliferation, both by size and type. Thus softdrink manufacturers produce ordinary, diet, with-caffeine, without-caffeine, in-glass-bottles, in-cans, and in-plastic-bottles varieties in assorted flavours and sizes. Detergent conglomerates behave similarly.

Indeed, cynics claim the great Coke "mistake" of the 1980s was not really a mistake but rather a carefully crafted strategy to win more space. Coca Cola announced that it would no longer produce what to then had been ordinary Coke, but would replace it with *New Coke*. Whether the consumer protest this move evoked was real or manufactured is debatable but, in any case, the company apparently relented and paired its new product with the old one, now going by the moniker *Coke Classic*. In the end, Coke's shelf space expanded.

A strategy used by some firms to gain shelf space is to create their own, thus making it more feasible for retailers to accept the new product. An example of this is L'Eggs pantyhose. Each pair was packaged in a plastic egg which fit into a stand-alone display case delivered with the first order. As retailers did not have to use existing shelf space to house the product, they were more willing to carry it.

Another method of achieving shelf space is to drive a competitor out. CBS television's *60 Minutes* news magazine reported the case of Royal Crown Cola in the United States, whose main competitors were Coca Cola and Pepsi Cola. In an attempt to drive Royal Crown from the market, Coke signed exclusive sales agreements with retailers, covering 26 weeks. The essence of the contract was that for the weeks in question, no other bottler would be allowed to sell their product for less than Coke. Next, Pepsi also signed contracts covering another 26 weeks. Given the number of weeks in any year, Royal Crown Cola could never be the lowest-priced cola in these stores.

As a simple example, consider a hypothetical market in which there are three similar firms. Suppose that, while maintaining their separate corporate identities with their own plants and sales forces, they get together to agree on a common price. In their collective interest, what is the best price? The answer: the price that a monopolist would pick — that is, the price that maximizes their combined profits. This price is determined in Figure 13-4 as follows. The three arrows in panel (a) show how the marginal cost

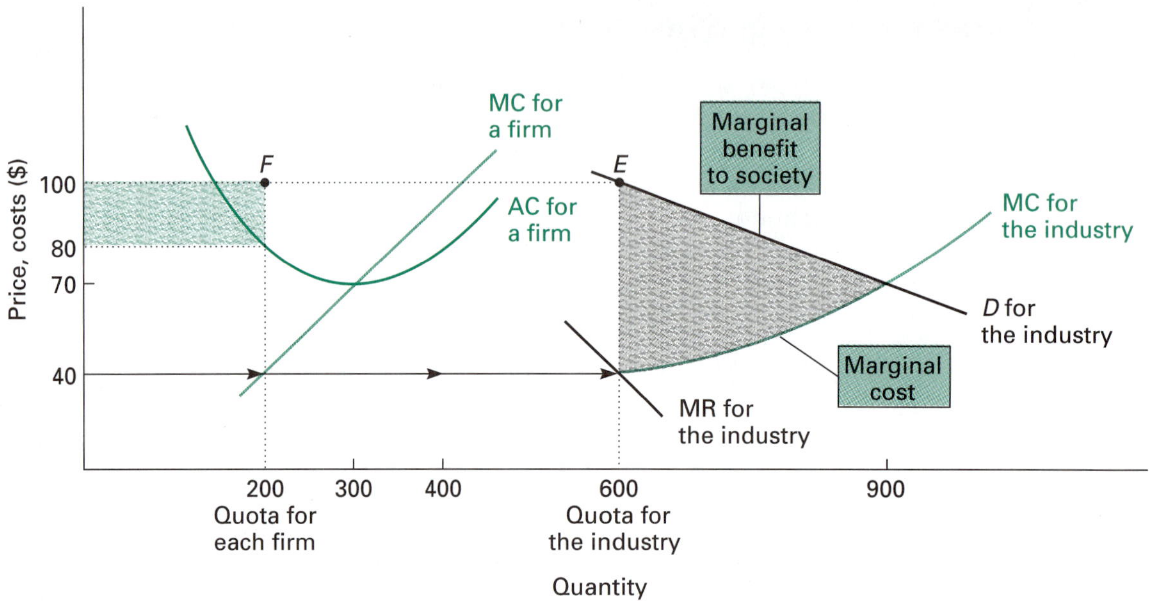


**(a) Picture of one of the three firms.** **(b) Picture of the industry.**

**FIGURE 13-4 Collusion by three oligopolists.**
In panel (b), MC for the industry is shown as the horizontal sum of the MC curves for the three individual firms on the left, and MR for the industry is calculated from the industry's demand *D*. The maximization of industry profit requires that output be 600 units, where the industry's MC = MR, and that price be $100. Each of the three firms is therefore allowed a quota of 200 units in panel (a), where it earns the coloured profit area. However, this arrangement may come apart if individual firms facing the $100 price cannot resist the temptation to cheat by selling more than their 200-unit quota. (Each firm can sell an additional unit for $100, while its cost of producing it is only $40.)

curves of the three individual firms are added horizontally to create MC, the marginal cost curve of the industry in panel (b). The highest profit for the industry is earned at an output of 600 units, where the industry's MC curve cuts its marginal revenue curve MR. (MR may be calculated from the demand curve for the industry, just as it was for the monopoly in Chapter 12.) Point *E* on the demand curve shows that the profit-maximizing output of 600 units can be sold at $100.

Thus, the collusive oligopoly can maximize profits by behaving as if it were a monopoly. However, it faces a problem that the monopolist doesn't have to worry about: How is the restricted production of 600 units to be divided among the three firms? The simplest solution is to set a quota of 200 units for each, as shown in panel (a). Each firm sells at point *F*, where it makes a profit of $4000, illustrated by the coloured area. That is, it sells 200 units at a profit of $20 each, the difference between the selling price of $100 and the average cost of $80.

While this collusive arrangement benefits the three firms, it is harmful to the economy as a whole. Just as in the case of monopoly, too little is produced, as shown in panel (b). For an efficient allocation of resources, output should not be 600 units. Instead it should be 900, where the marginal cost to society equals the marginal benefit to society—that is, where the industry's marginal cost curve intersects the demand curve. The efficiency loss from collusion, like monopoly, results in too little output as shown by the grey triangle-like area in Figure 13-4. In a cartel, Adam Smith's "invisible hand" fails, as Smith himself recognized in the quotation at the beginning of this chapter.

There are several ways that participants in a cartel can agree to limit sales, in addition to the equal division just described. For example, in the 1950s, an agreement between General Electric and Westinghouse effectively limited Westinghouse to a small share of the market for light bulbs. (Westinghouse agreed to pay General Electric a royalty for the right to produce GE's improved light bulb, providing Westinghouse confined itself to selling only a limited quantity of bulbs.) Another way to divide the market is to use historical market shares — or, even more simply, geographical areas. For example, two European firms agreed in the 1920s to carve up the market for explosives. Dynamit was allowed exclusive rights in certain continental European markets, in exchange for leaving British Empire markets to Nobel, a firm established by the Swedish industrialist who later donated the funds from which the annual Nobel prizes are awarded.

## The Breakdown of Collusion: The Incentive to Cheat

Market-sharing arrangements tend to be unstable, whether the firms have agreed on equal shares or not. Each firm in the cartel has an incentive to cheat by producing more than its allotted share. (While this is "cheating" as viewed by the other members of the cartel, it may still be in the public interest: More production moves the industry to a larger, more efficient output.)

To see why firms cheat, note in panel (a) of Figure 13-4 that an individual firm producing 200 units of output could produce another unit at a marginal cost of only $40. If it could sell this unit for the going price of $100 by stealing away a sale from one of its competitors, the firm's profit would increase by $60. Thus, it has an incentive to step up sales efforts or give secret price rebates in order to win customers. Even if a firm grants a 30%, 40%, or even 50% rebate on the selling price of $100, it will still receive more from this sale than its marginal cost. (Notice how similar this is to the case of monopolization of a competitive industry discussed in Chapter 12.)

Thus, the cartel's problem is this: The members have a collective interest in restricting sales in order to keep the price up. However, each member has an individual interest in selling more than its allotted share. If individual interests come to dominate, with firms producing beyond their quotas, industry output in panel (b) will increase beyond 600 units, and there will be a move down the demand curve from *E* to a lower price. In other words, a struggle by firms to increase their market share may destroy the cartel. Because of the strength of the individual interest, cartels have often collapsed after short and stormy histories.

When a cartel breaks down, the struggle over markets may become intense. This is particularly true if the cost advantages of large-scale production have been increasing as a result of technological change. In this case, a natural oligopoly may be evolving into a natural monopoly. In the absence of government intervention, only one firm will ultimately survive. The question is, which one? Each firm wants to be the victor; each has an incentive to try to gain an advantage over its rivals by expanding rapidly to gain the lower costs from large-scale production. Excess production is likely, with firms pushing frantically for sales. The result may be ***cut-throat competition*** — that is, sales at a price below cost in order to drive rivals out of business. During ***price wars***, the prize sometimes goes to the firm with the "deepest pockets" (the largest financial resources), which enable it to sustain heavy short-term losses while it is cutting the throats of its rivals.

# WHERE CARTELS ARE ILLEGAL, HOW DO OLIGOPOLISTS DETERMINE PRICE?

As the story of ***OPEC*** (in Appendix 13-B) illustrates, oligopolists can try to avoid price wars by forming a cartel and agreeing on price and market shares. For the OPEC countries, their efforts to do so have been a story of failure as much as success. But, for oligopolistic firms within Canada and many other countries, there is an additional problem: Such collusion is illegal. Producers may not even be able to *discuss* prices with their competitors without risking a jail sentence. How, then, do oligopolists reduce the pressure of price competition? How do they avoid price wars and arrive at a reasonably profitable price?

There is a large number of possible answers to this question; indeed, this is what makes the study of oligopoly more complicated and challenging than perfect competition or monopoly. One possible explanation is based on the idea that each firm faces a "kinked demand curve." Although this concept has been criticized for being an oversimplified and in some respects incomplete approach to explaining oligopoly firms' behaviour, it provides important insights into how each oligopolist must take the others' responses into account.

## The Kinked Demand Curve

The best way to understand this idea is to put yourself in the position of one of the three large oligopolists in an industry. Suppose that, in assessing how your competitors will react if you change your price, you expect the worst. Then:

1. If you cut your price, competing firms will take this as a challenge. They will not want you to take customers away from them and, therefore, they will meet your price cut with a price cut of their own. As a result, you cannot hope to capture a larger share of the market by cutting your price.
2. On the other hand, if you raise price, your competitors consider this a golden opportunity. By keeping their own selling price stable, they will be able to capture a share of your sales.

In short, your competitors behave in a nonsymmetric way: If you drop your price they will follow you but, if you raise your price, they will not.

Figure 13-5 shows how this behaviour leads to a kinked demand curve and to price stability. Panel (a) illustrates an industry with three firms of similar size. Each initially has one-third of total sales, with point $E_1$ showing your initial price and sales. If you change price and if your competitors were to follow, you

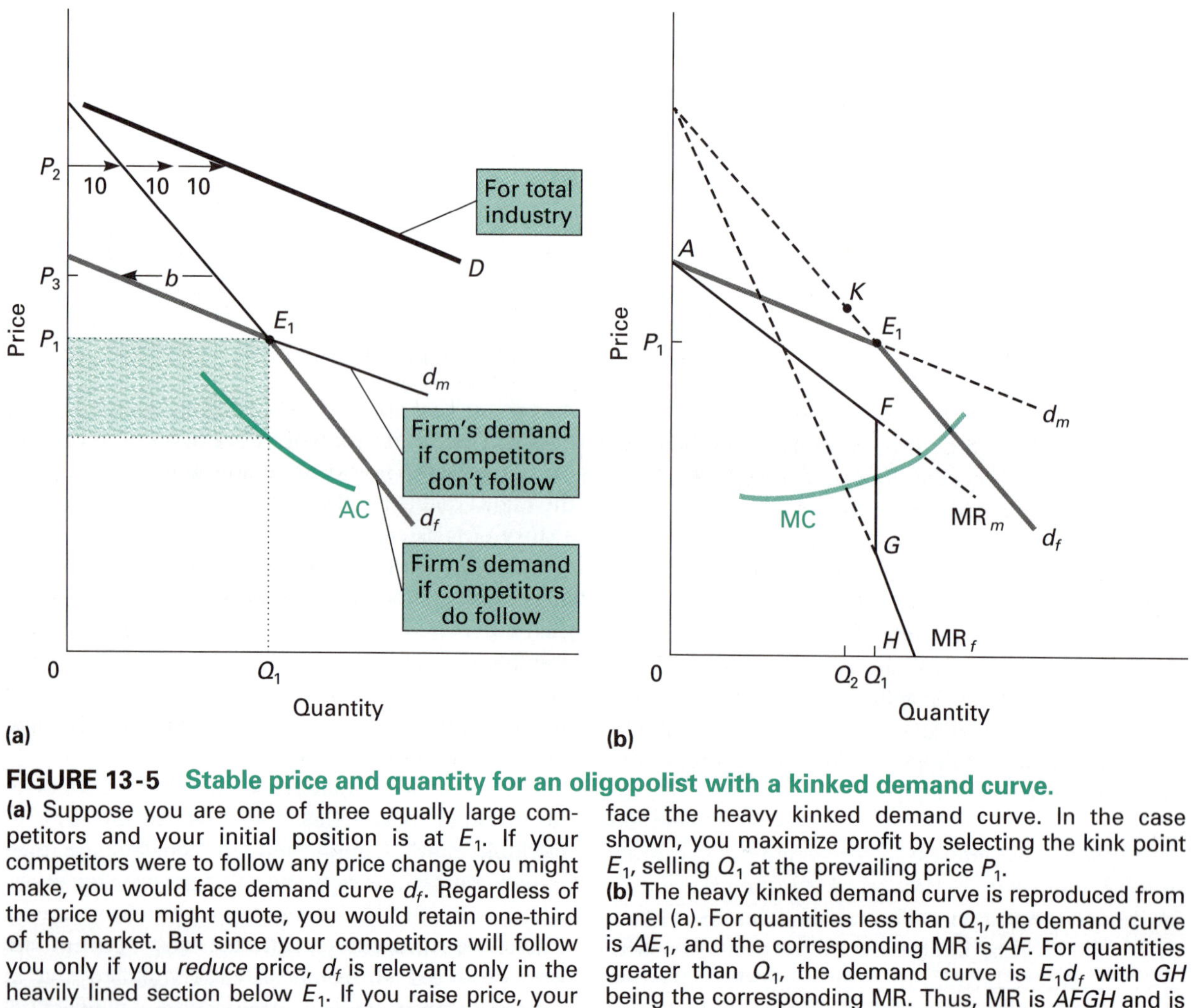


**FIGURE 13-5 Stable price and quantity for an oligopolist with a kinked demand curve.**

**(a)** Suppose you are one of three equally large competitors and your initial position is at $E_1$. If your competitors were to follow any price change you might make, you would face demand curve $d_f$. Regardless of the price you might quote, you would retain one-third of the market. But since your competitors will follow you only if you *reduce* price, $d_f$ is relevant only in the heavily lined section below $E_1$. If you raise price, your competitors will *not* follow and thus will cut into your market share, as shown by arrow *b*. Therefore, above $E_1$ you will face demand curve $d_m$. In short, if your competitors follow your price down but not up, you face the heavy kinked demand curve. In the case shown, you maximize profit by selecting the kink point $E_1$, selling $Q_1$ at the prevailing price $P_1$.

**(b)** The heavy kinked demand curve is reproduced from panel (a). For quantities less than $Q_1$, the demand curve is $AE_1$, and the corresponding MR is *AF*. For quantities greater than $Q_1$, the demand curve is $E_1d_f$ with *GH* being the corresponding MR. Thus, MR is *AFGH* and is intersected by MC at quantity $Q_1$, with the firm accordingly charging price $P_1$. Moreover, the firm's quantity and price won't change, even if marginal cost rises all the way up to *F*, or falls all the way down to *G*.

would retain your present one-third of the market. Thus, you would move along the relatively steep demand curve $d_f$. (At any price, say $P_2$, the quantity you would sell on $d_f$ would be one-third of the total industry demand $D$.)

However, $d_f$ is relevant only if you quote a price *below* the existing price at $E_1$. If you quote a price above this — say $P_3$ — your competitors will not follow. Instead, they will stand pat. Because you will now be quoting a higher price than they are, you will lose part of your market to them, as shown by arrow *b*.

Therefore, if you drop your price below $E_1$, you face demand $d_f$, while if you raise your price above $E_1$, you face demand $d_m$. In other words, the behaviour of your competitors presents you with the ***kinked demand curve*** shown by the heavy lines.

The *kinked demand curve* shown by the heavy grey lines in Figure 13-5 is the demand the oligopolistic firm faces if its competitors follow its price down but not up.

Faced with this demand curve, how do you maximize profit? The likely answer: Select point $E_1$, where the kink occurs. Thus, you sell $Q_1$ at the prevailing market price $P_1$; this maximizes your coloured profit area. By experimenting, you can see that the coloured profit area shrinks if you move either to the left or right of $Q_1$.

Panel (b) confirms that $Q_1$ is the profit-maximizing point. This diagram shows the firm's marginal cost curve MC, and its kinked demand curve reproduced from panel (a). What is MR when the demand curve is kinked? If you start at point *A* and move down the demand curve from *A* to $E_1$, your corresponding marginal revenue curve is *AF*. But once you get to the kink $E_1$, you move down the demand curve $d_f$, with the corresponding marginal revenue curve now being $MR_f$. Thus, the marginal revenue curve is the solid line traced by *AF*, followed by a sharp drop to *G* and then *GH*. This marginal revenue curve intersects MC at $Q_1$, the profit-maximizing output already identified in panel (a). It is now clear why output and price are stable. If marginal cost MC shifts anywhere up to *F*, or shifts anywhere down to *G*, MC and MR will still intersect in the range *FG*. Output will remain at $Q_1$ and price at $P_1$, even though there has been a large change in costs.

The idea of a kinked demand curve was first developed in the 1930s. It has had continuing appeal as a way of explaining why oligopoly prices are stable and, in particular, why they often remain firm during recessions when demand declines. There are, nevertheless, important exceptions. For example, during the severe recessions of 1982 and 1990–1992, auto manufacturers offered rebates — in effect, price reductions — in order to increase their lagging sales. Perhaps this was because they were no longer strong oligopolists. Because of intense competition from imported cars, the big three no longer dominated the market so completely.

The theory of the kinked demand curve is controversial. In the first place, it can be criticized for being an incomplete theory, as previously noted. While it may explain price stability, it does not explain how price is established in the first place. For example, in Figure 13-5, price remains at $P_1$ because it started out at $P_1$ and that is where the kink occurs. But how did price get to be $P_1$ in the first place? It has no explanation, like the "smile without the cat" in Alice in Wonderland. A second difficulty with the kinked demand curve is that in reality, prices are not nearly as rigid as the theory suggests. As already noted, automobile prices have occasionally fallen. And they have frequently risen. Over the years, the prices of large, mainframe computers have been cut many times, even though a few producers dominate the market. Thus, the theory of the kinked demand curve explains too much; it explains something (price stability) that frequently does not exist.

The most important criticism of the kinked-demand-curve approach, however, is that it depends crucially on an assumption that is to some extent arbitrary, and that may not be true in reality: that the oligopoly firm *knows* how its competitors will react if it changes its price. (They will follow its price up but not down.) But in reality, the firm cannot be certain that this will happen. Instead, it has the difficult task of *trying to predict its rivals' reactions*. Moreover, this task can't be avoided. If the firm can't make at least an educated guess on how its competitors will react, it doesn't know what sort of demand and marginal revenue curves it faces and, consequently, will not be able to maximize its profits.

## OLIGOPOLY: THE INSIGHTS OF GAME THEORY

To make the theory of oligopoly more complete and realistic, we must consider the question how an oligopoly firm guesses what its rivals will do if it lowers its price. Notice how this question brings us back to the chess game analogy. Before deciding on its "move" (whether or not to lower its price), the oligopolist has to guess what moves its opponents are going to make in response. In making this guess, however, the firm must take into account what its opponents, in turn, will expect its own countermove to be, and so on.

The idea that the decision-making problems faced by oligopolists are similar to those of players in games such as chess or poker is the basis for an important branch of economic analysis called ***game theory***, which originated with the work of mathematician John von Neumann and economist Oskar Morgenstern. Their 1944 book *Theory of Games and Economic Behavior* remains a classic in the field. Although many of the applications of game theory have been used in economics, game theoretic ideas have also been used in other areas such as military strategy, and the analysis of political decision making.

The simplest kind of application of game theory to oligopoly behaviour is in the case of an industry with only two firms; as noted in the introduction, this special case is sometimes referred to as ***duopoly***. The game theoretic analysis of duopoly can best be introduced by a non-economic example that is easy to understand: the case of the ***prisoner's dilemma***.

## The Prisoner's Dilemma

Two thieves, Blake and Reid, have been caught robbing a bank, a crime they have committed many times before. In two separate and isolated jail cells, they are each given a choice: "Each of you can be jailed for two years for the job you were caught doing last night. But, if one of you confesses to the whole series of robberies, your sentence will be reduced to one year, with your accomplice being put away for eight years. He is being offered the same deal and the same incentive to confess on you. If you both confess, you both get 5 years. You each have an hour to decide."

In terms of game theory, the choices facing each thief are set out in the ***payoff matrix*** of all possible outcomes in Table 13-2. Each outcome for Reid is shown in colour, and each outcome for Blake is shown in black. It is evident that the best collective outcome for both is not to confess (cell I). But each is under great pressure to confess. For example, Reid can see an advantage in confessing no matter what Blake may do. If Blake doesn't confess, then the outcome will be in the top half of this matrix (that is, in cell I or II). In this case Reid's confession would move the outcome from cell I to cell II, thus reducing his sentence from two years to one. On the other hand, if Blake does confess—and the outcome is, therefore, in the lower half of this table—then Reid's confession would move the outcome from cell III to cell IV, reducing his sentence from eight years to five. Thus, Reid is likely to confess. And Blake, facing exactly the same choice, is also likely to confess. If both confess, the outcome is in cell IV; both serve five years instead of the two they would have served if they had both held out.

An exception may occur if they have foreseen this problem and have a prearranged agreement not to confess. But this is not enough. Each must trust the other to hold to that agreement regardless of pressure. Thus, a key consideration influencing the strategy of each is information, or lack of it, about how the other will ultimately behave (as opposed to just promise) under this sort of duress.

## Duopoly Pricing

A similar dilemma may face two firms, Blackstone and Redpath, when selecting their price. The payoff matrix shown in Table 13-3 is, in fact, exactly the same as the payoff matrix in Table 13-2, except that it shows the dollar losses facing two competing duopoly firms in a short-run recession in which there is no hope of either firm making a profit. All that either can do is minimize its loss.

**TABLE 13-2 Payoff Matrix in Prisoner's Dilemma**

| | | Reid's choices | |
|---|---|---|---|
| | | don't confess | confess |
| Blake's choices | don't confess | I<br>2 years<br>2 years | II<br>1 year<br>8 years |
| | confess | III<br>8 years<br>1 year | IV<br>5 years<br>5 years |

**TABLE 13-3 Hypothetical Payoff Matrix in Duopoly Pricing**

| | | Redpath's choices | |
|---|---|---|---|
| | | **$12 price** | **$10 price** |
| Blackstone's choices | $12 price | I<br>$2 million loss<br>$2 million loss | II<br>$1 million loss<br>$8 million loss |
| | $10 price | III<br>$8 million loss<br>$1 million loss | IV<br>$5 million loss<br>$5 million loss |

Cell I shows the $2 million loss that each will suffer if they both hold price at the higher $12 level. Cell IV shows the much greater $5 million loss that each will suffer if they both cut their price to $10. The other two cells show the incentive each firm has to cut its price— exactly the same sort of incentive that the two prisoners had to confess. This illustrates how, in a duopoly market just as in the oligopoly market studied earlier, it is in the firms' collective interest to collude by holding up price, but it is in the individual interest of each firm to cut price.

If this "game" is to be played only once, and the two firms do not have an agreement to quote a $12 price (or, even if they do, they can't trust each other), then it is very likely that they will engage in price competition; the equilibrium will be cell IV for exactly the same reason as it was for the two prisoners who didn't trust each other.[2]

## A Complication: Repeated Games

Although the game theoretic analysis of the duopoly is interesting, the implicit assumption that the game is played *only once* is unrealistic. Suppose instead that this "game" is to be repeated. This is typically the case in business; firms set their price, but they can then change it in the "next play of the game."

In this case, there is still some incentive to cut price and, as a consequence, the equilibrium may continue to be in cell IV. However, there is now an increased chance of a collusive, high-price outcome in cell I. Each firm may now use a "stand-pat" strategy of setting its price at $12, and only cutting it if the other firm does. True, Blackstone risks taking a greater loss in the first period when it is vulnerable to price-cutting by Redpath. But offsetting this risk is the possible high reward if Redpath also follows this "stand-pat" strategy and the higher price, therefore, does "stick"; in this case the outcome will be to their mutual advantage, in cell I rather than IV. But why should competitor Redpath also stand pat? The answer is for precisely the same reason that Blackstone does; the numbers in Table 13-3 and, hence, the incentives are exactly the same for both firms.

This analysis suggests that several issues are important to the duopolist trying to figure out a pricing strategy:

1. Is the decision a "game" that takes place once and for all, or does it recur?
2. How much can each firm trust the other — or, more broadly, how much information does each firm have about the other? This is important even in a recurring game. For example, if you know your competitor can't be trusted and will be cutting price immediately, you should also start off by cutting your price and thus avoid the first-period loss that you will otherwise face.
3. In a repeated game, how long is each time period? For example, how long does it take for your competitor to realize that you are cheating by cutting your price to $10 in violation of an (unspoken) understanding to hold it at $12? The more rapidly your competitor can detect your cheating and respond by also cutting price, the less incentive you have to cheat. On the other hand, if you can escape detection completely, you have a much stronger incentive to cheat because your competitor won't realize and, therefore, won't retaliate. To prevent detection, or at least delay it, oligopolists may be secretive about their price reductions.
4. Once your competitor has detected your cheating, how long does it take to retaliate? If you are cut-

[2] As will be further discussed in Appendix 13-A, cell IV represents *Nash equilibrium*. In such an equilibrium, each firm has made its best choice on the assumption that the other firm sticks to its existing strategy.

ting price, then your competitor may retaliate immediately with a similar price cut. On the other hand, if you are competing in some other way (by increased advertising, for example) your competitor cannot retaliate immediately; it takes time to launch an advertising campaign. (Advertising and other forms of non-price competition will be discussed below.)

5. How difficult is it to reach an outcome based on an implicit understanding of the competing firms' interest in the first place? Bear in mind that a collusive outcome, such as the one shown in cell I of Table 13-3, may be in the collective interests of the two firms, but not in the interests of society. It is for this reason that there is competition legislation that outlaws overt collusion and any flow of information between firms that would make "tacit collusion" easier—as we shall see in the next chapter.

In summary, game theory sheds additional light on some of the points encountered earlier in this chapter, such as the critical question of how competitors may react to a change in a firm's price. It also draws attention to the possible advantages that firms can gain by developing methods of indirect communication, leading them to implicit agreements to act in a way that is in their common interest, even when overt agreements are illegal. In some industries, this may be accomplished by tacit recognition of a particular firm as being the ***price leader***. By unspoken agreement, the price leader is given the responsibility to initiate price changes: If and when the price leader changes its price, other firms will follow. (Conversely, other firms will *not* change their prices unless the leader does.)

## Price Leadership

To illustrate price leadership, suppose that you are the price leader in the sense that you are confident that if you change your price, your competitors will follow. Then the demand curve you face is no longer kinked. Instead, in Figure 13-5(b) it is the line $d_f$ throughout its entire length because your competitors will follow any price change you may make, either down or up. Moreover, your marginal revenue curve will be the corresponding $MR_f$, also throughout its entire length. In these circumstances, you will reduce output to $Q_2$, where MC = $MR_f$, and lead the industry up to a new, higher price at $K$—provided you are correct and the other firms do indeed follow your lead.

If your leadership is assured, the result may approach that of a cartel. As leader, you will select the price at point $K$ at the output where MC = $MR_f$, and your profits are thus maximized. Moreover, this price should be approximately the one that will maximize profits for the industry as a whole; this is why the other firms may be willing to accept your leadership. The outcome at $K$ is the same monopolylike solution that would result from collusion. Therefore, although collusion does not formally exist, the result may be similar: Firms arrive at the profit-maximizing price, not by illegally agreeing on it beforehand, but simply by following the leader.

However, price leadership may not always be effective in preventing price competition. Because there is no formal agreement, others may not follow your leadership after all; the problem of "cheating" may be substantial. The leader may find others shaving prices — or providing rebates — in order to increase their market shares. For example, in the Canadian cement industry, Canada Cement Ltd. held as much as 80% of the market at the end of World War II, and acted as the undisputed price leader in this industry. But, because it was the price leader, it did not compete aggressively by reducing prices when other firms expanded their market shares. Therefore, in a ten-year span after the war, its market share fell to less than 50%. Thus, all the advantages in an industry need not go to the giant. Smaller firms may have a major advantage: They may be able to compete aggressively without provoking competitive responses from the giant.

In practice, it may be quite difficult to identify any clear pattern of price leadership. There may be no firm that acts consistently as leader; first one company may take the initiative in changing prices, then another. General Motors does not always announce its new model prices first; the initiative is sometimes exercised by Ford. Furthermore, price leadership may be quite tentative. One firm may announce a price increase to see if others follow. If they don't, the price change may be rescinded. This sort of "trial and error" pricing may just be a way for the firm to test whether or not it can, in fact, act as a price leader.

Firms in an oligopolistic industry may sometimes also end up quoting the same price even though there is no price leadership. For example, many Canadian oligopolies face competition from imports. This may make it easier for firms to guess at the price that other firms will set and, hence, quote the same price. All of them are likely to set a price below—but not too far below — the price of imports. In such an industry, the Canadian price of the good will rise when the foreign price increases, or when the cost of imports is raised by other factors such as a fall in the international value of the Canadian dollar or an increase in the customs duty charged by the government on imports of the good.

Finally, even when oligopolists follow a pattern of price leadership, we cannot be certain that they are exerting monopoly power. If costs have generally risen by 10%, say, an oligopolist may raise price by about 10% in the expectation that others will follow. Price leadership has apparently occurred; yet the firms may merely be responding to rising costs, rather than exploiting monopoly power at the expense of the public.

## Focal-point Pricing

Harvard's Thomas Schelling gives the following non-economic example to illustrate how independent firms may end up quoting the same price even though there is no price leadership, nor any collusion, nor even any pre-existing price:

> You are to meet someone in New York City. You have not been instructed where to meet; you have no prior understanding with the person on where to meet; and you cannot communicate with each other. You are simply told that you will have to guess where to meet and he is being told the same thing and that you will just have to try to make your guesses coincide. You are told the date but not the hour of this meeting; the two of you must guess the exact minute of the date for the meeting. At what time will you appear at the chosen meeting place?[3]

Of the thousands of possible choices, Schelling discovered that most people selected high noon at the information booth at Grand Central Station. Both are "focal points" because they provide the best guess of what the other person will do. So, too, with price: A retailer who wants to guess the price that competitors will charge for a new product in the range of say, $11.20 to $12.40, may well select the focal point $11.98. This price is based on the familiar tradition of "charging $12 but making it seem like $11." Thus, without any communication whatsoever between firms, this focal point of $11.98 may become the industry price.

[3] Thomas C. Schelling, *The Strategy of Conflict* (Cambridge, Mass.: Harvard University Press, 1960), p. 56.

## Cost-plus Pricing

Under ***cost-plus pricing***, a firm determines its price by adding a specified mark-up of, say, 20% to its average cost. Economists have been uncomfortable with this idea because it raises two nagging questions: (1) Why does the firm pick 20% rather than some other figure? (2) Since average cost AC changes with output, how does the firm know its average cost without first knowing its output? In practice, firms may solve this problem by arbitrarily specifying a target output of, say, 85% of capacity; then their average cost is determined by the height of the AC curve at this specified output level. Finally, by adding on their fixed percentage mark-up, they arrive at a price.

This approach presumes that a firm pricing this way will be able to sell roughly its target quantity, using the target mark-up. However, if it is under pressure from price-cutting competitors, it may have little hope of doing so. To prevent its sales from falling, it may have to reduce its mark-up. Although such a firm may view itself as engaged in fixed-mark-up (cost-plus) pricing, it may, in fact, not be doing this. Instead, it may only start with cost-plus as a rule of thumb, and then may adjust its price in response to market pressures like any other profit-maximizing firm. Its mark-up may not be a fixed percentage at all.

# NON-PRICE COMPETITION

Price is not the only dimension in which oligopolistic firms compete; they also compete in other ways, such as better service, research and development, or advertising. These kinds of ***non-price competition*** are often preferred to price competition because there is less risk of starting a price war in which all participants lose. Indeed, firms often compete vigorously in these non-price dimensions; there is little evidence that they collude to reduce these expenditures.

## Advertising

The firm that advertises has a simple objective: to make people want more of its product. That does not mean, however, that more advertising is better. Since advertising must be paid for, it also shifts the cost curve up. At some point, the firm will find that enough advertising is enough; any more advertising would involve a further cost that can no longer be justified by increased sales.

In an oligopoly, an important goal of advertising is to capture the competitor's market. Thus, for example, the primary objective of Molson's advertising is to take sales away from Labatt and other brewing companies. General Motors advertises to take new car sales away from Ford and the Japanese.

Advertising also increases the total market demand for the product. A monopoly firm will sometimes advertise, not to take sales away from competitors (since it has none) but instead to increase the demand for its product. For example, local cable television companies advertise the various services they offer even though each has a local monopoly. Some associations of perfect competitors also advertise to increase total market demand, even though no single producer would find it profitable to do so. For example, milk producers' associations advertise to draw attention to the invigorating properties of milk, and the Ontario Egg Marketing Board advertises to encourage people to eat more eggs.

While monopolists or perfect competitors may occasionally advertise, the most heavily advertised products lie in the battleground in between—that is, in monopolistic competition and, even more important, in oligopoly. For example, a firm such as Toyota may benefit from advertising because it increases the total demand for automobiles—but even more important, because it takes sales away from its rivals.

Is advertising beneficial from the point of view of society as a whole? This is a controversial question. On behalf of their industry, advertising agencies make the following points:

1. Advertising helps the consumer to make better decisions. It informs the public of new products and of improvements in old ones. By informing consumers of what is available, it reduces search costs. For example, advertising may tell consumers where the bargains are, so they can save time and effort in shopping.
2. Advertising helps new producers to compete. By informing the public of a new product, it helps the producer to expand sales and may thereby lower costs.
3. Advertising supports the communications industry. Radio and TV are financed by advertising revenues. If we didn't pay for our entertainment this way, we would have to pay for it in some other way. Even the mundane classified ads play a significant role in the support of newspapers.
4. Advertising results in higher-quality products. The goodwill built up from past advertising of a brand name may be an asset of great value for a firm—an asset it will be careful not to damage by turning out a shoddy product.

On the other side, critics respond:

1. Most advertising represents a waste. The heaviest advertising takes place in oligopolistic markets where firm A's major motive is to steal customers from firm B, and B advertises to protect itself from losing sales to A. After advertising, A and B may share the market in roughly the same way as before. Little has changed, except that costs have gone up. Consumers pay more for this product merely because it is advertised. Even if firms recognize the waste, they can't opt out, because they would lose market share to competitors.
2. Where advertising is not a self-cancelling waste, it can be pernicious, creating frivolous wants, distorting tastes, and increasing the materialism of an already materialistic society. Advertising of products such as liquor and cigarettes has drawn especially sharp criticism, and regulations have been passed to limit it, particularly in radio and television. (Canadian cigarette manufacturers have, in fact, voluntarily agreed among themselves to stop all radio and TV advertising of cigarettes, partly to avert this type of criticism.)
3. Advertising that sells products to some people may be offensive to the vast majority. We cannot listen to radio or TV without being bombarded with tasteless ads.
4. Advertising may lead to distorted news coverage. It may be difficult for a newspaper to provide a balanced treatment of a labour dispute if it is getting a great deal of advertising revenue from the firms involved, but none from the labour union. (However, if a lot of workers buy the paper, the pressures may even out.)

Since it is difficult to compare these conflicting claims, our conclusion is that the statement that advertising involves "all loss" is too extreme, and so is the statement that advertising involves "no loss whatsoever."

## Other Non-price Ways in Which Firms Compete

A firm can hire a larger sales staff in order to beat the bushes for customers. As Box 13-1 explained, oligopolists also use a variety of strategies to get retailers to display their products more prominently than the competitions'. Oligopoly firms may also spend more on research, development, or design to improve the quality or attractiveness of their products. The typical oligopoly firm, such as an auto or appliance company, is locked in a struggle to match not only its competitors' price, but also their advertising, sales force, service, and improvements in design and quality. Little wonder that the world of the oligopolist seems more competitive than that of the farmer, who may operate in a "perfectly competitive" market but who never even thinks of a neighbour as a competitor. But remember: According to the economist's definition, farming is the more competitive industry, because a single farmer has no influence whatsoever over price (unless, of course, farmers are members of a legally sanctioned cartel, such as a marketing board).

## DON'T JUST COUNT NUMBERS: THE CONCEPT OF CONTESTABLE MARKETS

When one observes a market in which there is only a single firm, there is a natural tendency to conclude that it is a monopoly, with all the problems that this raises, including high price and restricted output.

However, even though a firm is technically a monopoly—in the sense that it is a single seller—it may not be able to behave like one by raising its price and restricting its output. In this case, the difficult policy problems of monopoly may not arise.

For example, consider a route that only one airline is now flying. It may appear that this airline has monopoly power. But, in fact, it may not if it is operating in a ***contestable market***. In such a case, any attempt by the airline to exercise monopoly power by raising its price will result in a profit that will attract another airline into flying this route; that is, another airline will "contest" this market. This *potential* competition forces the airline to behave like a competitor even though it is a single seller. The moral is this. In analysing any market—and in particular, in analysing what appears to be a monopoly—don't just count the number of actual sellers. Emphasis must also be placed on freedom of entry—that is, on the potential new sellers. How contestable is the market?

Airline routes have been cited as examples of contestable markets, provided there are no problems in acquiring landing rights, etc., and an airline can, therefore, easily shift planes in and out of routes. Note that for entry to be free, exit must also be free. Just as entry into a nightclub isn't free if you know you have to pay to get out, entry into an industry isn't free if a firm knows it faces losses if it has to leave.

Another example of a contestable market might be a small town with only two or three contractors building houses. If they can restrict entry of new competitors in some way—for example, by getting special zoning restrictions or acquiring all the available land—an oligopoly model with long-run profits may be the best way to describe their behaviour. But if they can't restrict entry and local carpenters can start to build houses, there may be enough potential competition to keep the two or three existing firms from raising their prices in an attempt to earn above-normal profits. Similarly, the only carpenter in a village may not be able to charge high prices because this will simply cause somebody else to take up carpentry. In contrast, people can't simply "take up" dentistry; they must go to dental school and be licensed. Thus, the dentist has more market power than the carpenter. Once again, we see the importance of ease of entry. It is not only existing competition, but also potential competition that matters.

## KEY POINTS

1. Monopolistic competition occurs when there are many small firms with differentiated products and no barriers to entry — such as patents or economies of large-scale production. Because each firm is selling a differentiated product, it has some small control over price; it faces a slightly sloping demand curve rather than the completely flat demand facing a perfect competitor. Because of free entry, above-normal profits disappear in the long run.
2. Price could be reduced below the level that occurs in monopolistic competition, but only at the cost of providing consumers with less choice. Therefore, little case can be made for government regulation.
3. When an industry is dominated by only a few firms, and there are barriers to the entry of new competitors, the result is oligopoly. In an oligopoly, there is an incentive for firms to collude so that they can act like a monopolist in raising price and restricting output. Such monopolylike behaviour would lead to an inefficient allocation of resources. One deterrent to such collusive behaviour is the difficulty of establishing and

enforcing the production quotas or market sharing that is typically required to maintain a high price. Even more important are the legal prohibitions against collusion.

4. Competition laws prohibit Canadian firms from engaging in overt collusion. Nevertheless, there are forms of tacit collusion—such as price leadership—that are difficult to prosecute but may allow oligopolists to exercise some degree of monopolylike power.
5. Oligopolists often prefer to compete in ways other than cutting price. They may try to capture sales from rivals by extensive advertising campaigns or by expenditures on research to develop better products.
6. Duopoly is a market in which there are two sellers. Game theory is one method of analysing the pricing policy of duopolists—or, by extension, the policy of several oligopolists. It highlights a basic issue that arises when there are only two, or a very few, large firms: Before a firm changes its price, it should take into account how its competitors may react.
7. In analysing any market, counting the number of competitors is not enough. One must also examine the freedom of entry; is the market "contestable"? If it is, even a single producer may have little monopoly power.

## KEY TERMS

**product differentiation**
**monopolistic competition**
**excess capacity in monopolistic competition**
**oligopoly**
**four-firm concentration ratio**
**Herfindahl-Hirschman Index**
**natural oligopoly**
**barriers to entry**
**price searcher**
**collusive agreement**
**cartel**
**cut-throat competition**
**price war**
**Organization of Petroleum Exporting Countries (OPEC)**
**kinked demand curve**
**game theory**
**duopoly**
**prisoner's dilemma**
**payoff matrix**
**price leader**
**focal-point pricing**
**cost-plus pricing**
**non-price competition**
**contestable market**

## PROBLEMS

13-1. If there are only four large firms in your industry, explain why collusion would be in your economic interest as a producer. Explain how consumers of your product would be affected. Describe the problems involved in arranging a collusive agreement and making it stick. Would the agreement be legal?

13-2. (a) What will be the value of the four-firm concentration ratio in the following industries? What will be the Herfindahl-Hirschman Index?
(i) a monopoly (ii) an industry in which there are three equal-sized firms (iii) an industry with three firms, one with 50% of the market, and two with 25% each.
(b) In your view, does the four-firm concentration ratio or the Herfindahl-Hirschman Index do a better job of describing the degree of industry concentration? Explain your answer, using as an illustration your calculations in part (a).

13-3. Canadian governments derive large amounts of revenue from excise taxes on alcoholic beverages and tobacco; they also pay most of the cost of providing health care to Canadians. With this (and other factors) in mind, argue the case for and against a ban on advertising of liquor, beer, and tobacco products.

In 1972, when Canadian tobacco manufacturers agreed among themselves to stop radio and TV advertising, their decision was widely applauded as a sign of increasing social responsibility in the industry. Can you think of some reason (other than a sense of social responsibility) that the firms agreed to put this restriction on themselves?

13-4. At one time, American lawyers who cut their fees below the level allowed by their state bar association could be disbarred. How would you evaluate this regulation from an economic point of view? If you were a lawyer, how would you view it?

13-5. In trying to get Blake and Reid (Table 13-2) to confess, should the police try to get each to think that the other (a) has confessed, or (b) has not confessed? Why?

13-6. Use your imagination to construct a payoff matrix illustrating the game that would result in a duopoly if each firm has two possible strategies: (i) continue as is or (ii) market a new product it has just discovered that takes a much longer time to wear out.

13-7. The table below shows the situation faced by Blackstone and Redpath, the two firms in Table 13-3, in a later year of prosperity. Each figure now represents profit rather than loss. Explain the conditions under which they might jointly maximize profit. Explain why they might engage in price competition.

**Profit Matrix in Duopoly**

| | | **Redpath** | |
|---|---|---|---|
| | | **$14 price** | **$11 price** |
| Blackstone | $14 price | I<br>$10 million<br>$8 million | II<br>$14 million<br>$2 million |
| | $11 price | III<br>$3 million<br>$11 million | IV<br>$4 million<br>$3 million |

# APPENDIX 13-A

## GAME THEORY: The Concept of Nash Equilibrium

### Nash Equilibria and Dominated Strategies

The simple duopoly problem with a payoff matrix like Table 13-3 in the text can be used to illustrate certain concepts and principles that game theorists have used in analysing more complex decision-making situations. Specifically, in trying to explain why, in a once-and-for-all game, the two firms are not likely to stick with a $12 price (cell I in the matrix), even though this is the strategy that minimizes their joint loss, game theorists make two observations.

1. For either firm, the alternative of setting a $12 price is a *dominated strategy*. That is, it is a strategy that yields the firm a larger loss (lower profit) than setting a price of $10, *no matter what strategy the other firm chooses*. (For example, Blackstone will do better with a price of $10 whether Redpath chooses a $10 *or* a $12 price. If Redpath chooses $12, Blackstone reduces its loss by $1 million (from $2 million in cell I to $1 million in cell III) by choosing a price of $10 rather than $12; if Redpath chooses $10, Blackstone reduces its loss by $3 million (compare cells II and IV) by choosing $10.) Assuming firms are reluctant to choose a dominated strategy, neither firm will choose a $12 price.
2. Cell IV is the only one that represents a *Nash equilibrium*, in which both players have selected their best strategy *given the strategy of the other player*. If both players choose a price of $10, neither has an incentive to raise the price to $12 on its own, because doing so would increase its loss from $5 million to $8 million if the other firm stays put. None of the other cells represent a Nash equilibrium. For example, starting from cell I, either firm would reduce its loss by $1 million by lowering its price to $10 if the other firm didn't choose to lower its price as well.

### Nash Equilibrium in a Cournot Duopoly Game

The concept of Nash equilibrium can be used to find a solution to a version of a simple duopoly game first studied by French economist Augustin Cournot in 1838.

To make matters simple, suppose we have a duopoly market in which each of two firms has access to a very rich natural resource from which each supplies a good to the market at zero marginal cost. Suppose the market demand curve for the good is linear, like the curve labelled *DD* in Figure 13-6.

If the firms could get together to form a monopoly, they would together supply a quantity such as 600 in Figure 13-6, at which their joint total revenue (of 1200) was at a maximum. (When total revenue is maximized, marginal revenue equals zero; since we are assuming that marginal cost for either firm is zero, their joint profits are maximized where marginal revenue equals zero as well.)

At the point where their joint total revenue is maximized, supplying additional units to the market would reduce total revenue. For example, if the joint monopoly were to supply 100 additional units, it would gain additional revenue equal to coloured area

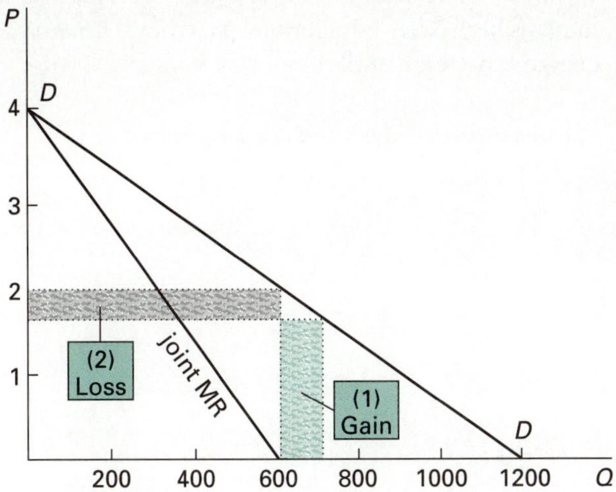


**FIGURE 13-6 Duopoloy: The monopoly solution.** If the duopolists manage to act together so as to maximize their *joint* profits, the amount produced would be 600. At that amount, their total revenue (and therefore, since production costs are zero, their joint profit) is largest. (Because area 2 is slightly larger than area 1, it does not pay to increase sales by 100 units.)

1 on these units. However, this additional revenue would be more than offset by the loss that the firms would jointly incur because they would have to reduce the price on the original 600 units; this loss is equivalent to grey area 2, which is slightly larger than area 1.

Suppose now that instead of acting as a monopoly, the firms begin to compete with each other. Specifically, let's assume that each firm decides what quantity to put on the market, *taking the quantity supplied by the other firm as given*. In making its decision, each firm is assumed to look only at the effect that its actions will have on its own revenue; it pays no attention to the revenue earned by the other firm.

It is now easy to see that in this duopoly game, the equilibrium will occur at a larger quantity and a lower price than in the joint monopoly solution. Suppose we start from the monopoly quantity (600 units), and that initially, each firm supplies one-half of that quantity. To either firm, it now appears possible to increase revenue by increasing the quantity it puts on the market, *as long as it takes the quantity supplied by the other firm as given*. For example, if firm 1 increases its supply by 100 units, it gains area 1 by selling these units. However, the loss it expects to suffer because the market price falls is only *half* of area 2; the other half of the loss will be borne by the other firm.

The Nash equilibrium in this simple game will occur at a quantity of 800 in Figure 13-7. At this point, the gain that either firm could realize by selling an additional unit is precisely counterbalanced by the loss that it suffers on *its own* original sales. For any smaller quantity (say, 750 units), it would pay either firm to increase its own supply. (For example, coloured area 1′, the additional revenue that one of the firms could get by selling an additional 50 units, is slightly larger than one-half of grey area 2′ in the figure.) More generally, equilibrium will occur at the point where the expected marginal revenue *to each individual firm* is zero. At this point, neither firm will have an incentive to change the quantity it supplies, given the other firm's quantity.

In our analysis of a monopoly firm in Chapter 12, we saw that the firm's profit maximization problem could be solved by either finding the optimum quan-

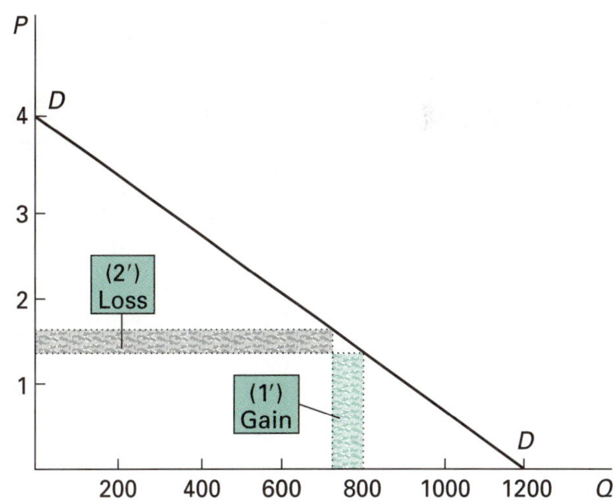


**FIGURE 13-7 Duopoloy: The Cournot solution.** If both duopolists take the amount supplied by the other as given, the equilibrium solution will be a total production of 800 units. When each firm produces 400 units, the additional revenue that it would earn by selling an additional unit would be just offset by the loss it would incur on *its own* existing sales.

tity, or the optimum price: Either one tells us the profit-maximizing point on the market demand curve. When we look at a duopoly game, however, it makes a difference whether we assume that the firms choose quantity (as in the Cournot analysis), or price. Surprisingly, in a simple duopoly game of price setting where each firm decides on its price, taking the *price* of the other firm as given,[4] we get a different (and implausible) Nash equilibrium: that both firms will charge a price of zero!

[4] Sometimes referred to as a *Bertrand* duopoly problem.

## PROBLEM

13-8. In discussing Figure 13-7, we assumed that each firm supplied the same amount. Explain what would happen if both firms together supplied 800 units, but one firm supplied 200 units and the other supplied 600 units.

# APPENDIX 13-B

## THE OPEC STORY OF COLLUSION AND CHEATING

The most conspicuous collusive arrangement of recent decades has been the Organization of Petroleum Exporting Countries (OPEC), a loose but initially effective price-fixing association of many of the major oil exporters, including a number of Middle Eastern nations, Indonesia, Nigeria, and Venezuela. The prime objective of OPEC was to raise the price of oil and, in less than a decade—between 1973 and 1982—the price rose from $3 a barrel to above $30, as shown in Figure 13-8. The result was far and away the greatest peacetime transfer of wealth among nations in history, as the OPEC countries became wealthy at the expense of oil-importing countries. Why was OPEC this successful in the 1970s? And why was it far less successful in the 1980s, when the price of oil fell, at one point dropping below $10?

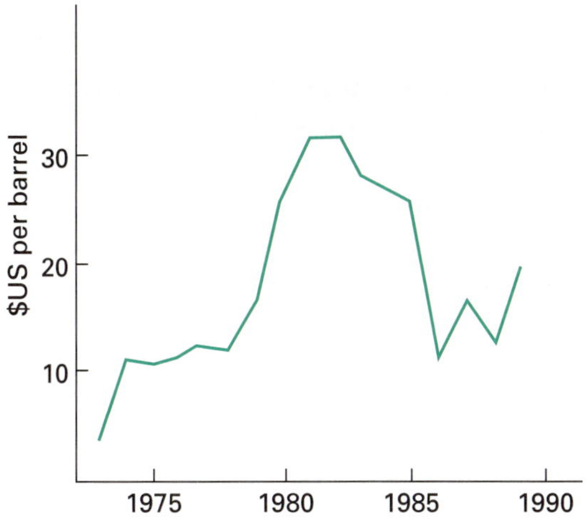


**FIGURE 13-8 Oil price on world markets.**
There have been two periods of very rapid increases in the price of oil—1973 to 1974 and 1979 to 1980. By the early 1980s, the U.S.-dollar price of oil had started to decline, and in 1986 the price on average was below $12; for a brief time, it even dipped below $10.

*Source*: Compiled from data in IMF, *International Financial Statistics*, various issues.

### The 1970s When Everything Went Right for OPEC

OPEC's early success was surprising because, during the 1970s, it did not enforce the formal production quotas on its members that a cartel typically requires to maintain a high price. Instead, its success in raising and maintaining price was due to a number of very favourable special conditions.

1. During the 1970s, Canada, the United States, and a number of other oil-importing countries imposed controls that kept their domestic prices below the high world price that OPEC was setting. Thus, North American consumers were saved from having to pay the full OPEC price. But, precisely because they didn't have to pay this high price, they did not cut back their purchases as much as they would have otherwise. In other words, energy policies in North America and elsewhere made the demand for OPEC oil less elastic—that is, less sensitive to an increase in the world price. This meant that as OPEC raised its price, it did not suffer a big loss in sales.
2. At the same time, the demand for OPEC oil by all countries was expanding — that is, the demand curve facing OPEC was shifting to the right. A dramatic example occurred during the Iranian revolution in 1979, when oil users made large purchases to increase their inventories in order to

insure themselves against a future disruption in supply.

3. Because demand was inelastic and shifting to the right, OPEC was under very little pressure to enforce production quotas during the 1970s. Nevertheless, for non-economic reasons, the Arab countries put an embargo on sales to the United States and other countries supporting Israel in the 1973 Yom Kippur War. As a result, OPEC's oil exports fell by about 25%. This helped make OPEC's 1973 price increase stick.
4. As the dominant supplier in OPEC, Saudi Arabia was prepared to maintain the high price by taking special actions.

## The Key Role of the Saudis

Whenever it appeared that a substantial oversupply was developing on the world oil market, Saudi Arabia would reduce its own production. Thus, the Saudis acted as a "residual supplier," satisfying only the demand that was left unsatisfied by other OPEC suppliers. This Saudi limitation of supply kept the price from falling.

Thus, during the 1970s, OPEC had one of the characteristics of a cartel: It set price. But it was not a cartel in the sense of enforcing formal production quotas to limit the sales of each member country. Instead, there were several factors that kept price up by keeping production from exceeding demand. Moreover, even when this did happen, the Saudis stood ready to eliminate the excess production by cutting back on their own output. For this reason, some experts downplay OPEC in the 1970s as a traditional cartel, and instead emphasize the leadership role played by the Saudis.

## Falling Price in the 1980s: The Attempt to Enforce Production Quotas

Because of the high price of oil during the 1970s, it was not surprising that, by the early 1980s, new sources of supply had developed in Mexico, the North Sea, and elsewhere. Thus, OPEC was satisfying a smaller proportion of world demand at a time when world demand itself was declining because of (i) a severe recession, and (ii) a change in policies in the United States, Canada, and other importing nations that gradually allowed their domestic prices to rise to the world level, thus giving consumers a strong incentive to reduce oil purchases. With demand falling short of production, OPEC finally moved to restrict its output by enforcing production quotas on its members.

Initially, this attempt was not very successful, with a number of OPEC members cheating by selling more than their quotas. Thus, Saudi Arabia, as the residual producer, was forced to make more and more cuts in its own output. Eventually, by 1986, the Saudis had cut their production back to less than 2 million barrels per day, even though their capacity was about 10 million. At this point, the Saudis decided that it was better to sell more, even though this would break the price. Moreover, they wanted to show other OPEC producers how costly it would be if these other producers did not abide by their quotas. When the Saudis turned up their production and increased their sales, the price fell to about $10 a barrel in 1986 (Figure 13-8).

The lesson was apparently not lost on other OPEC producers. Subsequent attempts by OPEC to enforce production quotas, while far from completely successful, were at least successful enough in the 1986–1988 period to keep the price of oil well above $10, though still far below the $34 price that had once been reached.

This leaves four major questions outstanding for the future: (1) How successful will OPEC be in enforcing production quotas? (2) How substantial will the supplies of non-OPEC producers be — supplies that reduce OPEC's dominant role in the world oil market and hence reduce OPEC's ability to hold price up? (3) Will OPEC be able to draw non-OPEC producers — such as those in the North Sea and Mexico — into its output and price-fixing decisions? (4) Will world demand for oil increase enough to absorb the oil production of OPEC and non-OPEC nations? If this happens, then OPEC will no longer have to restrict its supply in order to keep price up; a cartel will no longer be necessary.

In short, by the beginning of the 1990s, OPEC had become a classic example illustrating the three difficult problems a cartel faces. It needs to (i) set a production quota for each member; (ii) ensure that each member abides by its quota; and (iii) prevent outside producers from expanding production and undercutting the cartel's price.

# APPENDIX 13-C

## A MARKET WITH ELEMENTS OF BOTH COMPETITION AND MONOPOLY

One of the markets in the broad range between monopoly and perfect competition is the market in Figure 13-9 with elements of both. There are many small firms acting as perfect competitors by taking price as given and one large firm acting like a monopolist by determining price.

In panel (a), $D$ represents total market demand, while $S$ represents the marginal cost and hence the supply of the small producers who act as perfectly competitive "price takers." If they were the only firms, this industry would be perfectly competitive with equilibrium at $E_0$ and price $P_0$.

But they are not the only firms. In this industry there is also the very large firm shown in panel (b) that can produce a huge quantity at a relatively low price as shown by its MC curve. It is large enough that it *can* influence price. What price should it quote?

It can't select a price at $P_0$ or above, because at this price all market demand is already satisfied by the existing firms. So this raises the important question: What is the demand for the large firm's output? The answer is: demand curve $d$ in panel (b); that is, the market demand $D$ in panel (a) that is left unsatisfied by the small firms. For example, at price $P_2$, note the difference between $D$ and $S$ indicated in panel (a); this is the market demand $D$ that is not satisfied by $S$, the supply of the small firms. This is the large firm's demand and therefore is reproduced in panel (b). The section at price $P_1$ is derived in the same way. The collection of all such sections defines the large firm's demand curve $d$.

Since it faces a sloping demand $d$, the large firm can—just like a monopoly—select the best point on that curve, which is at $R$, where its MC equals its MR. Consequently, it will quote price $P_1$ and sell quantity

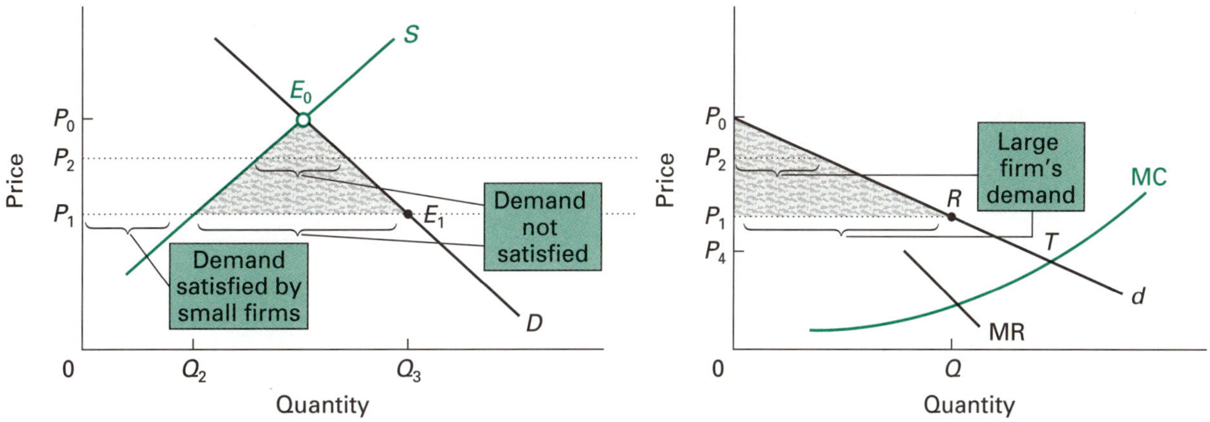


**(a) View of the total market.** **(b) View of the large, low-cost firm.**

**FIGURE 13-9** **A market with elements of both competition and monopoly.**

$Q$. The resulting equilibrium for the industry is shown in panel (a) at $E_1$. The large producer has set price at $P_1$, and the small firms — as price takers — respond according to their supply curve $S$ by producing the quantity $Q_2$ indicated in panel (a). This, along with the output of the new firm indicated in panel (b), just satisfies total market demand $D$.

Note how this analysis blends elements of competition and monopoly. On the one hand, there is a large number of small firms taking market price as given; they represent the competitive element. At the same time, there is also a large firm, which, although technically not a monopoly, nonetheless in one important respect acts like one: Rather than take market price as given, it sets price by selecting the profit-maximizing point on its sloping demand curve. But, in another respect, this large firm is not like a monopoly: Demand $d$ that it faces depends not only on how much consumers want to buy, but also on how much its competitors sell. Thus, like a monopoly, it must keep its eye on the consumer; but, unlike a monopoly, it must also keep an eye on its competitors. And, if you refer to it as a monopoly, you will be quickly corrected, since it is not the only seller; in fact, it is severely restricted in its actions by competing firms. (Consider how much higher it could raise the price if its competitors did not exist and it could operate on total market demand $D$ rather than just its own $d$.)

One example of this type of market might be the international oil market discussed in Appendix 13-B, if all OPEC members except Saudi Arabia were completely to ignore their production quotas. In this situation, Saudi Arabia would be the large residual producer, satisfying the demand left unsatisfied by the other OPEC countries. As the dominant producer, it would determine the price, while the other OPEC members would take that price as given and produce like perfect competitors without being restricted by their quotas.

Of course, this model does not perfectly describe the real world of OPEC. While other OPEC members sometimes do ignore their quotas, at other times they abide by them (more or less). If they all abide by them, then the outcome would be a collusive cartel. The real world of OPEC seems to fall somewhere between these two models, with the willingness of OPEC members to abide by their quotas determining which model is more relevant.

One final observation on Figure 13-9: One might expect that if a large, dominant firm with monopoly power enters an industry, price would rise. But this isn't necessarily so, if that dominant firm has low costs. To see why, note that if the large producer is *not* in the industry, then the price in Figure 13-9(a) is $P_0$. But when that producer does come into the industry, the price falls to $P_1$. In this case, the entry of a firm with monopoly influence into a perfectly competitive industry lowers, rather than raises, price. The reason is that the large, low-cost firm adds greatly to the quantity that the industry can supply at a low price. (Note in our example how the MC curve for the large firm in panel (b) indicates that its costs remain low over a wide range of output, in comparison with the costs of the small firms, as reflected in the $S$ curve in panel (a).) This introduces a theme that will be of great importance in the next chapter: Before judging against an increase in the monopolization of an industry, one must consider how costs are affected.

# CHAPTER 14 GOVERNMENT REGULATION OF BUSINESS

*Government . . . promotes our happiness . . . by restraining our vices.*

*Thomas Paine,* Common Sense

One of the principal ways the government influences the economy is by regulations on private business. For example, the government enforces rules that limit the exercise of market power by large firms. Government regulation has been used to promote safety and health in our workplaces, highways, and the environment.

The growth in government regulation was especially rapid, both in Canada and the United States, during the 1960s and 1970s. In this chapter and in Chapter 22, we discuss questions such as: What forms of regulation developed during this period? How successful was it in accomplishing what it was designed to do?

During the 1980s, there was a trend toward less regulation in many countries. In the United States, the airline industry was deregulated as early as 1980. In Canada, the trend toward deregulation started a little later but, by the end of the 1980s, a considerable amount of simplification and reduction of regulation occurred in several sectors. Will the trend toward deregulation continue in other sectors in the 1990s?

Government regulation of business falls into four major categories:

1. Laws to prevent firms from reducing competition by such acts as collusion, or driving competitors out of business through means such as cut-throat pricing.
2. Regulatory controls over an industry's price and conditions of entry. Within this broad category, two quite different kinds of regulation should be distinguished:
   (a) Regulation of natural monopoly in sectors such as production of electric power or telephone services. Since this form of regulation has already been studied in Chapter 12 we will concentrate here on type (b).
   (b) Regulation of naturally more competitive industries such as trucking or dairy farming.
3. Environmental regulation designed to protect the quality of resources such as our air and water. Included in this category are limits on the amounts of air and water pollutants that firms may emit; the requirements for environmental impact studies of large industrial projects; and rules that specify maximum emission levels from cars and trucks.
4. Other types of quality-of-life regulation; for example, standards to protect the health, safety, and working conditions of Canadians. This type of regulation grew rapidly in the 1970s and 1980s.

Environmental and quality-of-life regulation (categories 3 and 4) will be examined in Chapters 22 and 23. Here we look at the first two categories, beginning with government regulations to safeguard competition, sometimes referred to as Canada's ***competition policy***.

The most important element of our competition policy is the ***Competition Act***, the legislation that outlaws various strategies business firms could use to lessen competition in an industry, and that specifies the penalties for breaking the rules. The legislation in the Competition Act is sometimes referred to as *anti-trust law* or *anti-combines law*. (Historically, much of the early North American legislation in this field was passed to help fight the power of the industrial "trusts" or "combines" that were formed as groups of large firms banded together to monopolize various industries in the nineteenth and early twentieth centuries. "Anti-trust" is the term used in the United States; in Canada, the predecessor to the Competition Act was the Combines Investigation Act.)

Before studying the law itself, we look at the difficult economic questions that must be considered in developing a sensible competition policy.

## I. COMPETITION POLICY: SOME PROBLEMS

The task of developing policies to deal with the market power of monopolists and oligopolists is not an easy one. One difficult problem is how to effectively prevent large firms in an oligopolistic industry from entering into agreements or understandings that reduce price competition: How does the government know when such agreements exist? Another problem has to do with the role of large firms in the economy. In an industry with only a few large firms, each firm is likely to have substantial market power. If the industry had a larger number of small firms, it would probably be more competitive: Individual firms would be more likely to behave as price takers. But even though competition generally promotes efficiency, there are many industries in which small firms simply cannot produce as efficiently as large firms. Therefore, it is not certain that preventing firms from acquiring a large share of the market will improve the performance of the economy. In business, big isn't necessarily bad.

We now look at these problems in more detail.

### What Constitutes Collusion?

In order to protect the consuming public, the Competition Act prohibits ***collusive agreements*** (or "conspiracies") by oligopolists to raise prices. But proving that collusion has taken place in a particular instance is easier said than done. There may be exceptional cases, of course, where collusion is easy to establish (see Box 14-1). For example, competitors may have formal meetings with the specific intention

**APPLICATIONS AND ILLUSTRATIONS** **BOX 14-1**

**Long Distance: The Next Best Thing to Being There**

A price-fixing agreement does not necessarily require extensive negotiations; sometimes a simple phone call will do. A report in *Time* magazine (7 March 1983) describes an apparent attempt by American Airlines' Robert Crandall to strike a price-fixing deal in a call to Braniff Airline chairman Howard Putnam. This excerpt — which Putnam taped without telling Crandall — picks up a discussion of how difficult it was for the two airlines to make a profit, when they were both flying the same routes and cutting prices.

Crandall: . . . there's no reason I can see, all right, to put both [our] companies out of business.

Putnam: But if you're going to overlay a route of American's on top of . . . every route that Braniff has—I can't just sit here and allow you to bury us without giving our best effort.

Crandall: Oh, sure, but Eastern and Delta do the same thing in Atlanta and have for years.

Putnam: Do you have a suggestion for me?

Crandall: Yes, I have a suggestion for you. Raise your [expletive] fares 20%. I'll raise mine the next morning.

Putnam: Robert, we. . . .

Crandall: You'll make more money and I will too.

Putnam: We can't talk about pricing.

Crandall: Oh [expletive] Howard. We can talk about any [expletive] thing we want to talk about.

In this case, no price fixing actually occurred because Putnam didn't take the bait. However, if he had, this tape could have put them both in jail.

of fixing a common price and splitting up the market. If this can be proved, they can be fined—or perhaps even sent to jail — for their efforts. But consider a more complex case, such as a group of building contractors who have an understanding that they will inform each other when they are bidding on major construction projects, and who take turns submitting the lowest bid. Such collusion may be difficult to prove: After all, each firm may submit a different bid. Or consider the case where oligopolists with a common interest end up setting the same price without even so much as a wink or a nod because all firms follow a price leader. Certainly we cannot make it illegal to quote the current market price. If a firm is only "meeting the (price) competition," how can it be condemned? After all, doesn't a perfectly competitive producer (like the wheat farmer) sell at the going market price? Similar prices do not prove collusion.

A further complication is that collusion among firms in an industry isn't always a bad thing. For example, those who are critical of cigarette advertising would argue that the 1971 agreement among Canadian tobacco companies to stop advertising on radio and TV was a good thing. (Similarly, the current ban on advertising of hard liquor in the electronic media originated in a voluntary agreement among distillers to stop such advertising.) Or, as another example, if U.S. auto manufacturers were allowed to "collude" by sharing their research, they might develop pollution-control and safety equipment more quickly and cheaply. However, because they are afraid that any form of collusion is going to attract the attention of the regulators, they have been reluctant to get together in their research. (As we will see shortly, the present Canadian competition legislation tries to deal with this problem by specifying various types of beneficial cooperation that firms *can* engage in without running afoul of the law.)

Thus, proving collusion and deciding how vigorously it should be fought are difficult issues that complicate the tasks of framing the rules of competition policy and of enforcing those rules once they have been set. Even more difficult problems arise when we consider the other major way in which competition in an industry may be reduced: There may be a reduction in the number of firms in the industry as some firms are driven out or are taken over by others. Although competition may be reduced as the remaining large firms begin to dominate the market, allowing large firms to emerge may be advantageous for other reasons.

## Are There Advantages to Large Size?

In a number of industries, there are ***advantages to large size***, for several reasons:

1. *Large firms can better afford research and development.* Because of their very large sales, big firms may be able to finance large research and development (R&D) projects that could not be undertaken by small firms. These expenditures benefit not only the firms that are thereby able to develop the profitable new products, but also society as a whole, which benefits as these new products become available. In his classic defence of large firms, Joseph Schumpeter wrote:

   > As soon as we go into details and inquire into the individual items in which progress was most conspicuous, the trail leads not to the doors of those firms that work under conditions of comparatively free competition but precisely to the doors of the large concerns—which, as in the case of agricultural machinery, also account for much of the progress in the competitive sector—and a shocking suspicion dawns upon us that big business may have had more to do with creating that standard of life than keeping it down.[1]

   Although large firms with their heavy R&D expenditures are often the source of innovation, their role should not be exaggerated. Many innovations come not from firms that are already large, but from firms that are small and seeking to become large. For example, the snowmobile was originally developed by Montreal-based Bombardier, then a relatively small company. And the personal computer was introduced by upstart Apple, not by the giants of the computer industry.

2. *Large firms can capture economies of scale.* In many industries, economies of scale can be realized only by very large firms. As we have already noted, in any decision whether to use competition law to try to prevent a firm from becoming a monopoly in an industry, a crucial question arises: Is the industry a natural monopoly based on economies of large-scale production? If the answer is yes, then preventing the firm from becoming a monopoly would also prevent production from taking place at minimum average costs. A better

[1] Joseph Schumpeter, *Capitalism, Socialism, and Democracy*, 3rd ed. (New York: Harper, 1942), p. 82.

solution may be to allow the monopoly to form, but to regulate the monopolist's price. On the other hand, if the industry is not a natural monopoly, it is appropriate to use competition law to prevent a single firm from becoming a monopolist.

In earlier Canadian competition law, there were no explicit references to economies of scale as a reason for allowing a firm to dominate the market for a particular good. However, during the debate in the early 1980s that led to the present Competition Act, the Economic Council of Canada put forward proposals under which a large firm would be allowed to increase its market share (by taking over one of its smaller rivals) if its increased size would make possible "substantially" reduced costs of production. On the other hand, if average cost would not be "substantially" reduced, a takeover would not be allowed if it would cause a single firm to dominate the market. This compromise between the views that "monopoly is bad" and "big is better" is reflected in the Competition Act.

Finally, there is another factor that must be carefully considered in deciding to what extent a single firm should be allowed to dominate a Canadian industry: the ***intensity of foreign competition***. In markets where there is substantial competition between foreign and domestic firms, there should be far less objection if a few very large firms come to dominate output and sales of the Canadian industry. There are two reasons:

1. A Canadian firm may simply be unable to compete with imports unless it is large enough to capture economies of scale. (Sometimes this argument applies even in markets as big as the United States. With the increasing competition of auto imports from Japan and Europe in the 1980s, no one was talking about the earlier proposals to increase competition in the U.S. auto market by breaking up General Motors into a number of smaller firms.)
2. Because of competition from imports, the market power of large Canadian firms is reduced: They are not as free to raise prices as they would be without import competition.

Reductions in tariffs and other artificial barriers to international trade, as well as falling costs of transportation and communication, have increased trade and intensified foreign competition in most Canadian industries in recent decades. Although trade barriers have been reduced in many countries, the most important developments from a Canadian point of view have been the moves toward almost completely free trade throughout North America, as a result of the Canada/United States Free Trade Agreement, which came into effect in 1990, and its extension to Mexico through NAFTA, the North American Free Trade Agreement. When these agreements become fully implemented, the relevant question for Canadian competition policy will no longer be whether a firm has a dominant position in the Canadian industry. Instead, it will become: Is this firm large enough to exercise monopoly power in the entire *North American* market?[2]

## What Is Unfair Competition?

In many cases, it is difficult to tell whether a firm that is taking a growing market share in an industry is deliberately trying to create a monopoly for itself, or whether it is just growing because it is more efficient than other firms. However, the *method* by which it is increasing its market share may give an indication. For example, a firm that already has a large market share may try to increase it by actions that are systematically designed to drive its smaller competitors out of the industry. This raises a general question: How aggressively should a big firm be allowed to compete with smaller ones? Sometimes the large firm doesn't compete aggressively— but instead provides a high-price umbrella under which its small, less efficient competitors can survive. (Some U.S. observers believe that General Motors during the 1960s priced cars high enough to protect Chrysler, fearing that a Chrysler bankruptcy would lead the government to try to break up GM.) On the other hand, the large firm sometimes does compete aggressively, by ***cut-throat competition*** designed to force its small competitors out of business. If successful, this puts it in a monopoly position, in which it can then turn around and raise price.

*Cut-throat competition* (sometimes called *predatory pricing*) is pricing below costs in order to drive competitors out of business.

The classic Canadian case of cut-throat competition was the Eddy Match Company, which succeeded in driving several potential competitors out of the

[2] By mid-1993, the United States had not yet ratified NAFTA, although Canada and Mexico had done so. The Canada/United States FTA and NAFTA will be further discussed in Chapter 20.

market for wooden matches between 1928 and 1949. In each case, Eddy Match subsequently bought up the company it had driven bankrupt. In 1951, however, Eddy was convicted of violating the anti-combines legislation through its predatory pricing practices.

It is very difficult to draw a line between fair competition and unfair, cut-throat competition. One might think, for example, that a fair price to charge might be one that just covers the firm's costs (including a normal profit). But it's not that easy. One reason is that a firm typically produces many products, and it's not clear how some costs (in particular, overhead) should be allocated among them. Furthermore, pricing below costs may not always reflect cut-throat competition aimed at eliminating competitors. In the early 1980s, both GM and Ford suffered large losses (that is, they priced below average costs). But they weren't trying to "cut Chrysler's throat." Rather, they were frantically trying to hold their shares of the North American market in the face of stiff Japanese competition. Because of such real-world complexities, it is very difficult even to define — let alone control — "unfair" competition.

## The Difficult Problem of Mergers

Another way in which a big firm may become even bigger is through a *merger* or *takeover* of another firm. How to deal with mergers is perhaps the most difficult issue of all in competition policy.

The nature of the problem is most clearly seen in the case of a ***horizontal merger*** involving the union of two firms which previously competed with one another. On the one hand, it is obviously anti-competitive: The new firm will now have the market share of both the original ones. On the other hand, the merger or takeover may make it possible for the firm to take advantage of previously unexploited economies of scale. For example, production may now be concentrated in one plant. Or it may be possible to achieve cost reductions in marketing, management, and research and development.

A ***vertical merger*** — in which company A merges with its supplier B — need not greatly reduce competition, as long as neither A nor B have very large shares of the market. But sometimes, vertical mergers may indirectly reduce competition. Thus, between 1945 and 1960, a group of Canadian cardboard box manufacturers (who had already been convicted for a price-fixing agreement before World War II) proceeded to merge vertically with container board firms that supplied them with cardboard. Thus, the cardboard box producers were able to consolidate their hold on the market for boxes: By supplying cardboard only to firms inside the group, they made entry of new firms difficult, and were able to get together in a new scheme to raise prices without much fear of competition. (In 1966, they were again convicted of price fixing.)

The third type of merger is a ***conglomerate merger*** where a firm joins another in a completely different activity. Whether such mergers adversely affect competition — and, if so, by how much — is a controversial issue. A conglomerate merger may invigorate a weak company in an industry by providing it with new capital and more aggressive management. In such cases, competition can be enhanced. But a merger may help an already strong company to increase its dominance of an industry. The issue of conglomerate mergers has become increasingly important in both Canada and the United States during the last two decades, and we discuss it in some detail in the appendix to this chapter.

A *horizontal merger* involves a union of firms in the same competing activity.

A *vertical merger* involves a union of a firm and its supplier.

A *conglomerate merger* involves a union of firms in unrelated activities.

# CANADA'S COMPETITION LAW: A SUMMARY

As early as 1899, a House of Commons committee was appointed to investigate monopolistic activities in a number of Canadian industries. Following the committee's report, provisions that outlawed various practices to limit competition were put into Canada's Criminal Code. Over the years, these provisions have been changed and extended; in 1910, they were put into a separate Combines Investigation Act. However, until fairly recently, the 1899 provisions still made up the core of Canada's competition laws.

By the 1970s, there was growing dissatisfaction with the anti-combines legislation. True, in a number of cases the government had been successful in prosecuting firms that had engaged in anti-competitive behaviour (such as Eddy Match in the early 1950s, and the cardboard producers in the 1960s). But the government had also lost on a number of occasions. A particularly notable case involved the New Brunswick industrialist, K.C. Irving, who had obtained a monopoly in the market for English-language newspapers in that province by buying up all five of the existing papers. After an appeal to the Supreme Court of Canada, Irving was acquitted on a "monopoly and merger" charge. In order to win a conviction under the Combines Investigation Act, the government had to show not only that these takeovers had created a monopoly, but also that the monopoly had been operated "to the detriment or against the interests of the public." Moreover, the "monopoly and merger" provision, and indeed most of the Combines Investigation Act, was part of Canada's criminal law. Under criminal law, the defendant is always presumed innocent, and the government can win a case only if it can prove "beyond a reasonable doubt" that a defendant is guilty. But, to prove "beyond a reasonable doubt" that a particular monopoly is against the public interest is not easy, in general.

Thus, many economists and lawyers argued that both the presumption of the defendant's innocence and the restrictive definitions of the law made it very difficult for the government to prevent large firms from establishing and maintaining a monopoly position: In their view, new, less restrictive, rules were needed. At the same time, others argued that the rules should not make it *too easy* for the government to win a conviction. For example, in industries subject to stiff international competition, a policy that made it possible for the government to prevent any firm from achieving a dominant position in the Canadian market might make it impossible for Canadian firms to become big enough to compete effectively in the world market.

Following studies by the Economic Council of Canada and others, the government introduced proposals for a new Competition Act as early as 1971. The Competition Act became highly controversial right from the beginning, and the actual process of reform turned out to be very slow. Some changes to the Combines Investigation Act were made in 1976, but the most important reforms (including changing the name of the act) were not passed until 1986.

In response to the criticisms of the old legislation, the 1986 Competition Act removed some of the most restrictive provisions that reduced the effectiveness of the old act, and large parts of the competition legislation were moved from criminal to civil law, making it easier for the government to win convictions. A major thrust of the new legislation was the recognition that, in industries where goods and services flow freely across the border, international trade is an important way to ensure that the Canadian domestic market will remain competitive. Moreover, in determining whether to allow a reorganization of a Canadian industry (for example, through a major takeover), the authorities should take into account whether or not this reorganization would result in efficiency gains that would improve Canada's international trade performance.

## 1. Collusive Agreements

Section 32 of the Competition Act prohibits agreements or conspiracies to fix prices, or to limit output in order to raise prices. It provides for both fines and imprisonment of the persons responsible for the conspiracy or agreement. In 1988, the government won a case against several printing firms that were found guilty of having colluded to "rig" their bids on contracts to supply business forms to government agencies in Nova Scotia and Saskatchewan; the Saskatchewan case resulted in a fine of $1.6 million, the largest ever in the history of Canadian competition law.

Contrary to most other provisions in the Competition Act, section 32 still remains part of criminal law, so that the Crown has to prove "beyond a reasonable doubt" that a conspiracy or an explicit agreement exists among the participating firms—a difficult task because competing firms may very well quote similar prices without an explicit agreement (for example, in an industry with a price leader). Moreover, as in the old Combines Investigation Act, section 32 only prohibits conspiracies or agreements under which firms "unduly" limit production, or in which price fixing by a group of firms "unduly" lessens competition in the market. Canadian courts have long struggled with the question of what "unduly" means but, by and large, they have interpreted it narrowly, making it difficult for the government to prosecute price fixing: In order for the government to be sure of winning a case, the price-fixing agreement has to be a flagrant one and involve virtually all firms in an industry.

As noted above, while firms may sometimes try to collude in order to reduce competition, they may at other times engage in cooperation that *benefits* the public interest. One of the innovations in the 1986 reforms was to specify a list of types of cooperation that are explicitly permitted, and therefore will not be interpreted by the courts as being anti-competitive. The list includes activities such as cooperation in research and development, collaborative efforts to define product standards and to protect the environment, and agreements to limit the extent of advertising and promotion.

## 2. Mergers and Abuse of Dominant Position

One of the most controversial parts of the old Combines Investigation Act was section 33, which dealt with "monopoly and merger." Section 33 specified that, in certain circumstances, it was a criminal offence for a firm to try to create a monopoly position for itself, through a takeover of competing firms, or by trying to drive its competitors out of business through cut-throat competition, or by other means. But again, the government had to prove "beyond a reasonable doubt" that the monopoly had been, or would be, operated "to the detriment or against the interests of the public" in order to win a conviction. Therefore, successful prosecutions were rare: A takeover, for example, can always be theoretically justified by citing "expected" cost reductions as a result of the increased opportunities to exploit economies of scale.

In the 1986 reforms, the old monopoly and merger provisions were abolished and replaced by two new sets of provisions dealing with mergers and "abuse of dominant position" respectively. Neither is part of Canada's court-enforced criminal law. Instead, enforcement is the responsibility of the ***Bureau of Competition Policy***, who may refer particular cases to a new *Competition Tribunal*, a quasi-judicial body composed of both judges and non-judicial experts (such as economists). The relevant section in the Competition Act gives a list of examples of anti-competitive acts that are illegal. It includes practices such as "selling articles at a price lower than the acquisition cost for the purpose of disciplining or eliminating a competitor"; or "use of fighting brands introduced selectively on a temporary basis to discipline or eliminate a competitor."

With respect to mergers, the new Competition Act introduces a requirement that when the firms involved have sufficiently large assets or sales, they must get prior approval from the Director of the Bureau of Competition Policy before the merger can take place. At the request of the Director, the Competition Tribunal may issue an order preventing the merger if it finds that the merger would substantially reduce competition in the market. Section 65 in the act suggests certain factors that the tribunal may take into account in deciding whether a merger will, in fact, reduce competition substantially. These include the extent of foreign competition; whether one of the firms would be likely to go out of business if the merger does not go ahead; and whether or not there are close substitutes in the market for the products supplied by the firms involved in the merger. The act also recognizes that the disadvantage of reduced competition must be weighed against any increase in efficiency (for example, due to increased economies of scale).

A particularly interesting test case that may arise in the mid-1990s will be if the negotiations between Air Canada and Canadian Airlines result in an application to merge the two. By 1993, the recession (and the fierce competition between the two companies) had brought PWA, the owner of Canadian Airlines, close to bankruptcy, and Air Canada was trying to take it over. However, PWA was resisting the merger, and was seeking an alliance with one of the largest U.S. carriers, American Airlines, instead. Ironically, one of the obstacles to a deal between Canadian Airlines and American Airlines was the fact that Air Canada and Canadian Airlines had earlier been allowed to operate a joint computer reservation system. In trying to block the deal (and increase the chances that its own takeover bid would succeed), Air Canada went to court to try to force Canadian Airlines to stay with this reservation system, rather than switch to the one operated by American Airlines.

## 3. Price Discrimination

The Competition Act (like U.S. anti-trust law) has a section that outlaws certain forms of *price discrimination*. (As we saw in Chapter 12, price discrimination occurs when a seller charges different prices to different buyers.)

In the U.S. law against price discrimination (the Robinson-Patman Act) the objective appears to have been to protect smaller buyers — such as individual retail stores — against larger competitors, such as chain stores. Specifically, U.S. law makes it illegal, with certain exceptions, for manufacturing firms to sell their goods to chain stores at substantially lower prices than they charge smaller retailers. One can argue that restriction on this type of price discrimination is desirable, because it makes it easier for many small firms to survive in retailing, and, therefore, it promotes competition. But one can also argue that because the law allows small and inefficient retail firms to survive, the average costs of distribution will be higher.

On the other hand, under Canadian competition law, price discrimination is illegal only if it involves different prices for buyers who buy goods of like quality *and quantity*. Specifically, therefore, it is generally legal in Canada for a producer to charge lower prices to buyers (such as chain stores) that purchase a large quantity. Thus, in contrast to U.S. legislation, Canada's competition law has not hindered the development of efficient large-scale firms in the retailing industry.

## 4. Other Provisions

***Resale price maintenance:*** In Canada, it is against the law for a manufacturer to fix the price at which retailers sell their goods to the public. Even though a manufacturing firm may "suggest" a list price (a price at which the firm would like to see its product sold in stores), it cannot force retailers to maintain that price, nor can it refuse to supply retailers who offer to sell the product to the public at a lower price.

The effect of these provisions has been to stimulate price competition in the retail sector by allowing the development of discount outlets (such as Consumers Distributing).

*Misleading advertising and tied selling:* The Competition Act also has certain minor provisions prohibiting *misleading advertising* and some cases of ***tied selling***. Tied selling, sometimes also called *full-line forcing*, means that a firm with one particularly appealing product forces retailers who want to carry that product to also carry the firm's full line of related products. A good example of this is the practice that some oil companies have used in the past: They have forced the service stations that distributed their brand of gasoline to also carry the company's full line of automotive products, such as tires and batteries. Another example is a policy that Bell Canada used to follow: Before the anti-combines authorities forced it to abandon the practice in 1980, Bell required all subscribers to its telephone services to use only equipment supplied by its subsidiary Northern Telecom.

## Final Observations: How to Achieve Workable Competition

When Canada's anti-combines legislation and U.S. antitrust laws were introduced in the late nineteenth century, support for these laws was strong. There was much public resentment of the growing U.S. business giants and their predatory methods, and of the anticompetitive cartels that were formed in Canada by domestic firms protected by the government's high-tariff policy against competition from imports. But, since the days of the "robber barons," there have been relatively few black and white situations. The history of Canada's competition legislation is largely the story of difficult grey areas.

Over the years, it gradually became clear that Canada cannot simply try to preserve competition by ensuring that there are many small firms competing with each other in every industry. Economies of large-scale production and the small Canadian market necessarily mean that, in many industries, there is room for, at most, only a few firms of efficient size. This is one of the reasons the existing competition law is written in such a flexible, qualified way.

In the face of the need to balance the complex considerations of market power and the need to achieve economies of scale in the limited Canadian market, it may be too much to hope for a simple solution. Perfect competition is the perfect answer only in textbooks. In the real world, we must settle for "***workable competition***," where we gain many of the advantages of large-scale business, but curb the more flagrant abuses. One analyst has compared competition legislation with traffic laws. Going 85 kilometres an hour in an 80-kilometre zone represents no calamity. But the police are there to catch the speeder who goes 100. The fact that we might get caught makes most of us drive a little more carefully. Similarly, the competition cases that have been won by the government remind business executives that there are stiff fines (and adverse publicity) awaiting the flagrant offender; they are likely to be more careful as a result.

# II. REGULATION OF PRICE AND ENTRY

> . . . [In the U.S. airline industry] it appears that the prime obstacle to efficiency has been regulation itself and the most creative thing a regulator can do is remove his or her body from the market entryway.
>
> Alfred Kahn, former chairman of the U.S. Civil Aeronautics Board

In Chapter 12, we examined in detail the strong case that can be made for government regulation of a natural monopoly, such as the local telephone company. (Regulation forced the firm to act more like a perfect competitor facing a given market price.) Here we discuss a policy that is much more difficult to justify:

government regulation of a naturally more competitive industry, such as trucking or agriculture. As will become evident, regulation in this case typically allows firms to act in a *less* competitive way. For example, regulation may reduce competition by blocking the entry of potential new firms. Therefore, it is no surprise that this form of ***price and entry regulation*** is often welcomed by the firms that are already in the industry. (A preview of some of the problems that arise is given in Box 14-2.)

## A Case History: Regulation of Rail and Truck Transport

Trucking is a good example of an industry that, if left on its own, would be relatively competitive: Entry is easy, and scale economies are fairly insignificant. Yet the trucking industry has been extensively regulated in all Canadian provinces except Alberta, with government controls being imposed on both entry and pricing.

Regulation of the for-hire trucking industry in Canada had its beginnings in the 1930s during the Great Depression. In part, it came about as an indirect result of another type of regulation that had its origins much earlier: Regulation of rail transport.

It was almost inevitable that the Canadian government should become heavily involved both in supporting and regulating the railroads during the 1800s: Because of the enormous expense of building the railroad network necessary to serve the expanding economy (particularly the wheat-based economy of the Prairies), the railroad companies needed both direct financial support and assurance that they would be able to earn a reasonable return on their investment. To get this assurance, they pressured the government to grant them local monopolies on rail service between particular areas or communities. In some respects, rail transport has the characteristics of a local monopoly: It would clearly not be efficient for several competing firms to each build their own railroad track between two communities. Thus, it made sense for the government to encourage the development of rail transport by agreeing to grant local monopoly rights between specific communities. But having done so, the government had to make sure that the companies did not abuse this monopoly position by overcharging railroad users. Therefore, the government generally maintained control over the freight rates that the companies could charge, and also regulated other aspects of the railroads' activities, such as frequency of service.

A particularly important motive for railway regulation in Canada has always been to ensure that low-cost and reasonably efficient service would not be restricted to large cities and to the more densely populated parts of Canada: Smaller localities and remote areas, it has been argued, deserve good rail service too. But service to small communities in thinly populated areas can only be provided at a high average cost. (The heavy fixed costs of this industry — track, locomotives, and other equipment — must be spread over a small traffic volume.) As a solution to this dilemma, the regulatory authorities allowed a certain amount of ***cross-subsidization***, that is, allowed the railroads to recoup their losses on the unprofitable low-volume traffic to small cities by letting them

### APPLICATIONS AND ILLUSTRATIONS BOX 14-2

### The Parable of the Parking Lots

Producers have a natural interest to narrow the market and raise the price.

Adam Smith, *Wealth of Nations*

Henry Manne, professor of law at the University of Miami, tells a simple parable to illustrate the problems of government regulation which protects existing firms by blocking the entry of new firms.*

Once upon a time in a city not far away, thousands of people would crowd into the local football stadium on a Saturday afternoon. The problem of parking was initially solved by a number of big commercial park-

* Henry Manne, "The Parable of the Parking Lots," *Public Interest* no. 23 (Spring 1971), pp. 10–15. Abbreviated with the author's permission.

**BOX 14-2 continued**

ing lots whose owners formed the Association of Professional Parking Lot Employers (APPLE). But, as time passed and crowds grew, every plumber, lawyer, and schoolteacher who owned a house in the neighborhood went into the parking business on Saturday afternoon, and cars appeared in every driveway and on most lawns. Members of APPLE viewed the entry of these "amateurs" into their business with no great enthusiasm, especially since some were charging a lower fee. Stories began to circulate about their fly-by-night methods, and the dents they had put in two cars (although, on investigation, it was discovered that denting was an equally serious problem in the commercial lots).

At a meeting of all members of APPLE, emotions and applause ran high as one speaker after another pointed out—in some cases, in a very statesmanlike way — that parking should be viewed, not as a business, but as a profession governed by professional standards. In particular, cut-throat price competiton with amateurs should be regarded as unethical. The one concrete proposal, quickly adopted, was that APPLE members should contribute $1 per parking spot "to improve their public image, and put their case before the proper authorities."

No accounting was ever made of this money, but it must have been spent wisely, since within a few months the city council passed an ordinance to regulate industry price and to require that anyone parking cars must be licensed. However, it turned out to be difficult for an independent house owner to get a licence; it required passing a special driving test to be "professionally administered" by APPLE, a $27,000 investment in parking facilities, and $500,000 in liability insurance. Since every commercial lot found its costs consequently increasing by 20%, the city council approved a 20% increase in parking fees. (Within a year, APPLE had requested that the city council guarantee the liability insurance, so that people would have no fear of parking in commercial lots. One argument put forward by an APPLE spokesman was that this idea was similar in its intent to recent congressional legislation setting up an insurance scheme for stockbrokers.)

On the next football afternoon, a funny thing happened on the way to the stadium. Since police were out in large numbers to enforce the ordinance, driveways and lawns were empty and long lines of cars were backed up waiting to get into each commercial lot. The snarl was even worse after the game. Some people simply gave up waiting for their cars and had to return to retrieve them next day. (There was even a rumour that one car was never found.) In response, APPLE decided to go ahead with a "statistical-logistic study of the whole socioeconomic situation" by two computer science professors at the local university. Their report cited the archaic methods of the industry and pointed out that what each firm needed was fewer quill pens and more time on a computer.

As the parking lots began to computerize their operations it became quite clear that in the face of these rising costs, a further increase in parking fees was required. The increase was quickly approved by city councillors relieved that, in the modernization of the industry, they had finally found a solution. But, unfortunately, it was no solution after all. The problem, it turned out, was not so much deciding which car should be moved where, as actually moving it—and that continued to be done by attendants who had become surly and uncooperative because of the pressure they were facing.

Relief, however, did appear in two forms. First, many people got fed up with the hassle and started watching the game on TV. Second, small boys who lived in the houses closest to the stadium went into the car wash business on Saturday afternoon. They charged $5, but it was worth the price, since they guaranteed a top-quality job. (In fact, they guaranteed that they would spend at least two hours on it.) And they always had as many cars as they could handle, even on rainy days—in fact, especially on rainy days.

charge rates well above average cost on the profitable high-volume routes.

> *Cross-subsidization* by a firm or a public agency means that the firm or agency uses revenues generated in profitable lines of activity to offset losses in other less profitable lines.

Cross-subsidization has played a particularly important role in the system of grain transport from the Prairie provinces. Until the mid-1980s, prairie farmers paid very low rates for the transport of grain to the seaports at Vancouver, Churchill, and the Lakehead, from which much of the grain is exported. The so-called statutory rates that the railroads were allowed to charge on such grain shipments were originally set in an 1897 agreement between the CPR and the Canadian government (the Crow's Nest Pass Agreement), and subsequently became part of the Canadian Railway Act. Despite numerous attempts by the railroads to have the rates renegotiated, they remained unchanged over the years, with the result that by the mid-1980s, the railroads could cover only a fraction of the *variable* costs of shipping this grain. (They covered the rest of their costs by charging higher rates on more profitable routes.)

During the early part of the 1900s, when railway transport constituted the only really practical method of shipping, the system of regulation and cross-subsidization was relatively easy to maintain. However, during the 1920s and 1930s the railroads began facing increasingly intense competition from commercial trucking, in particular, on high-volume, short-haul shipments of high-value commodities. (Few truckers were interested in serving the transport needs of sparsely populated areas, even though trucking would have been an efficient alternative to railroad freight in such areas; the truckers could not compete because the government regulators had forced the railways to maintain low rates on these routes.)

Thus, a serious problem developed: Competition from trucking on the profitable high-volume routes tended to squeeze out the railroads' profits on these routes, and thus reduced their ability to cross-subsidize their less profitable activities. The railroads, therefore, began to lobby intensively for extending the system of regulation to the trucking industry as well. Truckers' representatives also supported the proposals for regulation of their own industry: Because of the Depression, competition among truckers had intensified, and many new firms were entering the trucking business. With support from both the railroads and the trucking industry, several provinces introduced trucking regulation.

From the 1930s, regulation of the trucking industry became more widespread and increasingly detailed. All provinces except Alberta developed controls over entry into both intraprovincial and interprovincial trucking, and granted trucking licences subject to a wide variety of restrictions. Thus, a licence might specify what kinds of goods the firm may ship, what routes it may follow, and whether or not the firm is allowed to unload or pick up goods on the way. The frequency of service to different communities may also be specified, just as in the federal regulation of railroads. And several provinces regulated trucking *rates* within their borders. Moreover, in all the provinces, the trucking industry established "tariff bureaus" to provide advice and information to trucking firms on various matters, including the rates charged by other firms. This tended to lessen competition, because it made it easier for all firms to quote the same price. (It can be argued that such "cartelizing" activity by tariff bureaus is in violation of the Competition Act. But the government couldn't prosecute the truckers because the act does not apply to regulated industries.)

## The Effects of Trucking Regulation

There is no doubt that the provincial regulation of trucking had very extensive effects on the transport industry in Canada. It also was a costly process: Apart from the substantial costs of paying for the personnel and other expenditures of the regulatory agencies themselves (costs that have been borne by the provincial taxpayers), there also have been heavy costs incurred by the trucking firms in dealing with the agencies. In a study done for the Economic Council of Canada, Norman Bonsor of Lakehead University estimated that the firms' costs of preparing and presenting applications for licence extensions, responding to other firms' applications for new licences, and so on, amounted to at least $40 million annually. Those costs have been borne either by the firms themselves or by their customers in the form of higher prices.

But more important than these direct costs were the indirect effects of regulation on the cost and efficiency of firms in the industry. In another study for the Economic Council, James McRae and David Prescott found that the highest trucking rates were in

Ontario, Quebec, and British Columbia. In Alberta where there was no regulation, rates were considerably lower. But, in spite of the higher rates, profits of trucking firms in Ontario, Quebec, and B.C. were no higher than in Alberta. Therefore, McRae and Prescott conclude, regulation in Ontario, Quebec, and B.C. resulted in inefficiency—that is, higher costs of trucking. (As an example of this inefficiency, regulation made it difficult for firms to reduce either the number of kilometres that their trucks have to run empty or the amount of idle truck time.)

## Regulation in Other Canadian Industries

The trucking industry is not the only example of a ***regulated industry*** in Canada. For example, the airline industry has been subject to federal controls that until recently included regulation of both entry and fares. Local governments control entry in the taxi business in most municipalities. The oil and gas industry became more and more extensively regulated in the 1970s and 1980s, and entry into the broadcasting and telecommunications industry is federally controlled by the Canadian Radio-television and Telecommunications Commission (CRTC). The growth of regulation has been especially rapid in agriculture, where provincial marketing boards now control both the output and prices of a large variety of agricultural products.

Another area where regulation has been extensive is in government licensing and certification requirements for specific occupations: Legislation in various provinces sets standards of practice and entry qualifications for a wide variety of occupational groups, ranging from doctors, lawyers, and architects to interior decorators, music teachers, and timber scalers. (As an example of the trend in this direction, the Economic Council cites the instance of Quebec where, during a two-year period in the mid-1970s, no less than 23 occupational groups applied for status as "professional corporations" under the province's regulatory legislation.)

The motives for regulating these various industries have been different. In the case of the airline industry (and also in trucking) there was fear that unregulated firms would provide inadequate service to areas of low population density, or would engage in unfettered competition that could lead to destructive price wars and periodic disruption of the industry. In the case of agriculture, one reason was the belief that, without it, prices of farm products would be highly unstable. In the broadcasting field, one of the main motives for regulation has been the fear that unregulated firms would not produce an adequate supply of distinctively Canadian programming and news reporting. In the occupations and professions that have been regulated, the argument has been that the public needs to be protected against fraudulent or harmful practices. (Some forms of occupational or professional licensing (for example, in medicine) are more justified than others such as interior decoration: If doctors aren't licensed—and anyone can enter the profession—patients who can't tell which "doctors" are competent and which are not may, literally, make life-and-death choices.)

Although regulation may have helped to solve the problems cited above, it also created a whole set of new problems: Regulation raises prices because it raises costs — or because it provides firms with monopoly power (as in the case of profitable trucking firms that held the exclusive licence to specific routes).

Because price and entry regulation introduces the possibility of monopoly profits and reduces the competitive pressure on inefficient producers, it is generally supported by the majority of producers already in the regulated industry. In some cases, regulation raises the possibility that the industry may become like a private price-fixing cartel — except that, because it is regulated by the government, it is exempt from the penalties of the competition law. (Some economists argue that many agricultural marketing boards in Canada resemble private cartels.) Similarly, occupational regulation has been strongly supported by those already in the regulated professions, not only because it protects the public, but also because it has sometimes given the professional associations the opportunity to legally reduce price competition by restricting entry and enforcing uniform fee schedules. Thus, for the public, the result has been not just higher quality service, but also higher prices.

# DEREGULATION IN THE 1980s

While regulation grew rapidly in the 1960s and early 1970s, by the late 1970s many people were becoming disillusioned with some of the results. It seemed that regulation had been shifting more and more toward restriction of competition, with a resulting increase in prices and loss of economic efficiency.

By the mid-1980s, the move toward ***deregulation*** was in full swing, especially in the transport sector.

The Crow's Nest Pass subsidy was greatly reduced in order to release funds for improvement of the railroad track. By the late 1980s, rate setting by the railroads had been substantially deregulated. In 1985, an agreement was struck between federal and provincial transport ministers to move toward less restrictive regulation of trucking rates and of the entry of new firms into the industry, and in 1988, the "Freedom To Move" policy, under which the only requirement for entering the trucking business is a test to show that you can drive one, came into effect.

Another area in which dramatic deregulation took place was financial services. Many earlier restrictions that had prevented competition between chartered banks and trust companies were abolished, and banks were now allowed to enter the brokerage business; within a few years, four of Canada's largest banks had bought investment dealerships. In the early 1990s, banks have even begun pushing for the right to start selling insurance, something they still cannot do under existing restrictions. Other areas that were deregulated included natural gas and long-distance telephone service, where competition had become intense by the early 1990s.

Perhaps the most dramatic example of deregulation and restructuring, however, came in the airline industry, which had become more or less completely deregulated by 1990. (Deregulation was also accompanied by another important development: the privatization of Air Canada, which until it was privatized had been a Crown corporation.)

Deregulation of the Canadian airline industry came some ten years later than it did in the United States. The American experience, therefore, provided a fair amount of evidence of what to expect from deregulation in Canada. (See Box 14-3.)

In some respects, the effects in Canada were similar to what they had been in the United States. On average, passengers paid less for air travel, mostly because many more people were using discount fares. The efficiency of airline operations increased, with fewer planes flying half-empty. Service to smaller cities was maintained, as small regional airlines expanded their operations, or new ones entered the market.

But in one respect, there was also an important difference between the Canadian and U.S. experiences. Because the U.S. market is so large, there is room for a number of major airlines of minimum efficient size, as well as for smaller independent ones serving local markets. In the smaller Canadian market, that does not appear to be true. As discussed earlier, by the early 1990s, only two major airlines still survived, Air Canada and Canadian Airlines. Moreover, between them they had acquired 11 medium-sized regional airlines, with the result that almost all air travel on scheduled routes was provided by these two firms. Even so, both of them were in a very shaky financial state, with mounting losses and large debt burdens. (In fact, PWA, the parent corporation of Canadian Airlines, became unable to meet its debt payments and had to negotiate new arrangements with its creditors.) To some observers, it was beginning to look as if the Canadian airline industry was a natural monopoly, and there were calls for a return to a regulated environment.

However, supporters of deregulation argued that there was another way of overcoming Canada's market size problem: negotiating an "open-skies" treaty with the United States, under which airlines in either country would be allowed to transport passengers between cities in the other country. (Although deregulation in both the United States and Canada has meant that any domestic carrier is allowed to compete on any domestic route, foreign carriers do not yet have this right.) While this would mean increased

## APPLICATIONS AND ILLUSTRATIONS — BOX 14-3
### Airline Deregulation in the United States

In the United States, the airline industry was substantially deregulated as early as 1978, when Congress passed the Airline Deregulation Act. Following deregulation, major changes immediately began to occur.

1. Increased competition made more discount fares available to the public. In 1976, 15% of travellers flew on discount fares, but by 1987 this figure had increased to 90%. The price of discount fares also fell.

**BOX 14-3 continued**

In response to the greater availability and lower price of discount fares, airline travel increased greatly—by a full 40% in the first year of deregulation alone. The U.S. Council of Economic Advisors estimated that deregulation provided the travelling public with more than $11 billion per year of benefits in the form of more flying at lower prices.

2. Increased competition and freedom from regulation also made the airlines more efficient; this was why they were able to offer bargain fares. They were now free to more efficiently allocate their aircraft between routes. For example, the major airlines no longer had to fly their big jets almost empty out of the small cities they had previously been forced to service. In many cases, they dropped these routes.

3. This didn't mean the end of service to these cities, since new airlines usually moved in to take up the slack. Because they used smaller aircraft, they could offer more frequent service. Thus, even the public in small cities who had been predicted to be the big losers, enjoyed the benefit of more frequent flights (though admittedly, in smaller planes). Moreover, once they got to big-city connecting points they became the big-city passengers who won hands down, since these passengers received the greatest cut in discount fares and also, due to heavier airline travel, enjoyed more frequent service on large aircraft.

4. This restructuring of the industry, along with the freer entry of new firms, led predictably to an increased number of airlines; between 1978 and 1987, 200 new firms entered the industry. But when the industry shakeup came in the late 1980s and early 1990s, it was dramatic. By 1987, as a result of bankruptcies and mergers, there were fewer than 80 airline companies. When the recession struck in 1990/91, air travel was hard hit, and several large and well-established firms disappeared, including Eastern, Pan American, and TWA.

5. The fear that smaller commuter airlines wouldn't be able to compete with the giants turned out to be unfounded. True, their costs per passenger mile were higher, but only because they were flying shorter routes; if the giants came in to compete on these routes, their costs rose to the same level.

6. With increased travel, the skies and airports became more congested with increased delays, and the government was slow to take action to reduce this problem. Suggested solutions included peak-load pricing, under which airports would charge higher landing fees in rush hours as an incentive for private planes and other small aircraft to fly at less congested times, or allocating landing slots to airlines and allowing them to buy or rent such slots from each other. This would allow a market price to develop for the right to land at a certain time. This price would not only allocate the slots to the "highest value" flights, but would also give the airport authorities a way to evaluate how much another runway would be worth to the flying public.

7. As airlines were flying more flights over big cities, the resulting congestion led to more near-misses and concerns over safety. It became clear that while other forms of regulation were being relaxed, safety regulation should *not* be. In any case, there was no evidence that the airlines were becoming less safe, even though they faced increasing competition and greater congestion. Indeed, it was possible to argue that airline deregulation had made the total travel by the American public *safer*; an estimated 800 lives were saved per year because, as deregulation brought lower fares, Americans travelled more by air (where there are only 0.3 deaths per billion passenger miles) and less in autos, which are about 100 times as dangerous.

competition for Canadian Airlines and Air Canada in the Canadian market, it would also mean that they could realize economies of scale by expanding their operations in the U.S. market, and the Canadian public would gain the benefits of a more competitive market for air travel.

## CONCLUDING OBSERVATIONS: Shifts in Economic Decision Making

Federal and provincial officials and politicians are faced with a wide array of pressures from individuals and groups seeking the help of government in improving their economic condition, or in reducing the detrimental side effects of business decisions. It is not surprising that they are often tempted to respond to these pressures by passing a new law or setting up a regulatory agency. Although this response does not involve spending a large amount of the taxpayers' money, the public still pays in hidden ways—for example, through higher prices for cars because of pollution controls, or higher transportation costs because of regulatory inefficiency.

The increase in regulation in the 1960s and 1970s resulted in a substantial shift in decision making away from the economic marketplace: Business decisions previously taken by firms in the marketplace were becoming increasingly influenced by regulatory agencies, the federal and provincial governments, and the courts.

But, as the public became more aware of these ***hidden costs of regulation***, the process of increasing regulation gradually came to a halt in the 1980s. Instead of new regulatory initiatives that would further reduce the scope of marketplace decision making, there was reform of Canada's competition law: This reform can be interpreted as an attempt at *increasing* the use of the market mechanism in allocating resources, by making markets more competitive. And, in some areas such as transportation and financial services, there was a substantial *reduction* in the influence of regulation.

Because various interest groups will continue to plead their causes, the pressure for more regulation will always remain to some extent. Nevertheless, the days of rapid regulatory growth appear to be over, and a more balanced approach toward regulation seems to be firmly established in both the United States and Canada.

In many areas, the reduction in regulation may well succeed in making the economy work more efficiently. At the same time, if we continue to move gradually back toward more market-based decision making in the 1990s, it becomes important to recognize that there are some areas, such as pollution and safety, where substantial control must continue to be exercised by the government. While recognizing this, economists raise still another question: Can government control in these areas be achieved less expensively and more effectively by *modifying* the market mechanism rather than *replacing* it by detailed bureaucratic decision making? Answering this question is one of our major objectives in Chapter 22.

## KEY POINTS

1. Federal and provincial governments regulate business in several ways: (a) through competition law, which is designed to keep markets competitive by limiting the amount of market power that a firm or a group of firms can accumulate; (b) through regulatory agencies, which control price and conditions of entry into certain industries—including both natural monopolies (such as local phone companies or railroads) and more naturally competitive industries, such as trucking, or milk and egg production.
2. Competition policy raises difficult questions. For example, when is price cutting unfair or "predatory"? How do you know when firms are colluding? How effective is import competition in limiting market power of Canadian oligopolists?
3. The Competition Act strengthens competition in the Canadian economy because violations can lead to fines, jail terms, and damaging adverse publicity. The main sections of the act deal with price fixing and other forms of collusion to

reduce competition, and merger and "abuse of dominant position"; other important sections deal with price discrimination, resale price maintenance, and misleading advertising and tied selling.

4. Competition policy in Canada was substantially strengthened by reforms in the 1970s and 1980s. The reforms included removal of many provisions from criminal law (thereby making it easier for the government to obtain convictions), and explicit recognition that the disadvantage of having only one or a few firms in an industry has to be weighed against the cost advantages of large-scale production. It was also recognized that the intensity of foreign competition is an important determinant of the extent of competition in oligopolistic Canadian industries.
5. Although government regulation may be appropriate for dealing with natural monopolies, its usefulness in industries that are naturally more competitive, such as trucking or agriculture, is less clear. Many economists have charged that government regulation in such industries has increasingly become a legal way of limiting competition and raising the market price.
6. Growing regulation and a larger economic role for the government meant that, in the 1960s and 1970s, economic decision making in Canada was gradually shifted from the marketplace to the political arena or the courts.
7. In the 1980s, a trend emerged toward deregulation and more emphasis on making the market mechanism work more efficiently. By the end of the 1980s, regulation had become much less restrictive, if not abolished, in sectors such as trucking, domestic air transport, financial services, and long-distance telecommunications.

## KEY TERMS

**competition policy**
**Competition Act**
**collusive agreements**
**advantages to large size**
**intensity of foreign competition**
**cut-throat competition or predatory pricing**
**horizontal merger**
**vertical merger**
**conglomerate merger**
**Bureau of Competition Policy**
**resale price maintenance**
**tied selling**
**workable competition**
**price and entry regulation**
**cross-subsidization**
**regulated industries**
**deregulation**
**hidden costs of regulation**

## PROBLEMS

14-1. Which of the following agreements between firms in an industry do you judge desirable? Undesirable? Explain your reasoning.
- (a) an agreement to reduce output by 10% to end a glut on the market
- (b) an agreement to quote the same price
- (c) an agreement by the CN and CP railroads to lay the same width of track.

14-2. Assume that wheat producers in the Canadian West are price takers on the world wheat market. The West ships wheat to eastern Canada where the world price prevails. Producers in the West must pay the associated transportation costs.

Construct a diagram similar to Figure 10-12 showing the supply of and demand for Western wheat in eastern Canada, treating transportation costs as part of the cost of supply. In the diagram, illustrate the changes in consumers' and producers' surpluses that would result from subsidization of transportation costs. In addition, indicate the area that represents the amount paid in transportation subsidies. (Hint: In answering this question, note that the subsidy will make the equilibrium quantity *larger* than the efficient quantity.) In this context, do you think that regulated freight rates, such as the former Crow Rate, constitute "good" policy?

14-3. To understand cross-subsidization better, consider a simplified example in which there are two individuals: A lives in a large city, B in a small one. Initially, in an unregulated situation, A gets airline service at price $P_1$, while B gets none. Draw the demand curves for both individuals. Show how it may be possible to get a collective benefit (an increase in the combined consumer surplus of both individuals taken together) by the following policy of cross-subsidization: A is forced to pay a price above $P_1$ (and has consumer surplus reduced) in order to allow B for the first time to have airline service (and thereby enjoy a consumer surplus).

14-4. In the 1986 Competition Act, it is stipulated that agreements between firms to restrict advertising, or to define uniform product standards, should not be considered examples of anti-competitive collusion. Argue both the case for and against allowing these types of agreements.

14-5. It was noted in the text that before 1980, Bell Canada would only allow its customers to use telephone equipment supplied by its subsidiary Northern Telecom.

(a) Assuming there was no technical reason for this requirement, why do you think Bell tried to impose it? (Hint: Remember that as a natural monopoly, the rates Bell can charge for telephone services are regulated.)

(b) Explain how you think the ruling that forced Bell to abolish this requirement affected competition and the users of telephone services.

(c) Can you think of other possible ways (other than forcing Bell to abandon the practice) that the regulatory authorities could have dealt with the problem?

# APPENDIX 14-A

## MERGERS, TAKEOVERS, AND LEVERAGED BUY-OUTS

In this appendix we discuss an issue that was only briefly touched upon in the text, but one that has become increasingly important in recent years: The issue of conglomerate mergers, that is, mergers of firms in unrelated activities. While the possible anticompetitive effects of horizontal and vertical mergers are fairly obvious, it is not so clear that conglomerate mergers and takeovers adversely affect the national interest. We discuss the pros and cons of mergers and takeovers from the points of view of both the acquiring firm and the "target" firm. We also consider various strategies that can be used when there is a "takeover battle," or when it takes the form of a "leveraged buy-out"; these types of mergers became common in the 1980s.

### Mergers: The Interests of the Acquiring Firm

What are the incentives for one firm to acquire another? In the main text, we focused on one possible incentive: the desire to acquire a bigger market share. But this is not the only reason for mergers and takeovers. In particular, it does not explain conglomerate mergers or takeovers where the firms that are merged are in different industries.

Sometimes, mergers may be motivated by tax considerations. For example, it may pay for a profitable company—firm A—to take over a company—firm B—that has been suffering losses: Firm A may then use the past accumulated losses of B to reduce its taxable income and thus reduce its tax liability. Another example of takeovers induced by tax considerations was the spate of takeovers of foreign-owned firms in the oil and gas industry by Canadian companies (such as Dome Petroleum) in the early 1980s. Under the National Energy Program introduced by the Liberal government in 1979, foreign-owned firms were discriminated against in that they had to pay higher taxes and were not eligible for subsidies that Canadian companies could claim. Thus, energy assets in Canada were worth more if they were owned by Canadians than if they were foreign-owned, and there was an incentive for Canadian-owned firms to acquire the assets of foreign-owned firms. (In general, however, tax advantages play a much smaller role in explaining mergers or takeovers in Canada than in the United States. The reason is that in Canada, the system of dividend tax credits, explained in Chapter 8, has effectively eliminated the double taxation of dividend income. In the United States, dividend income is still subject to double taxation: Before it becomes after-tax income of the shareholder, it has been subject to both the corporation income tax and the personal income tax of the shareholder. Therefore, profitable firms in the United States have more incentive than profitable Canadian firms to use their profits in other ways than paying them out as dividends, and using them to take over other firms is one alternative.)

In the case of a horizontal merger, such as the purchase by one steel company of another, the new higher-volume company may be able to achieve economies of scale simply because its output of steel has increased. In the case of any kind of merger, the acquisition of another business may be a challenging way for a firm to use underutilized management talent. That is, expanding the firm may be a way of achieving economies of scale in management. There may also be economies of scale in R&D. To illustrate, Saab-Scania, a Swedish conglomerate, produces aircraft, trucks, and automobiles, thereby reducing the design and engineering costs of each. Another incentive for a merger is to diversify by expanding into a new business. For example, if a firm is producing ski equipment with profits in the winter, its management may be interested in acquiring a tennis equipment company to provide profits in the summer.

Another factor that plays a role in making a corporation interested in a takeover is the price of the "target firm's" shares. From the viewpoint of the acquiring firm, an attractive target is a firm whose shares are priced low relative to the value of its assets and profit potential. For example, firm A's shares may be priced low in the stock market because it has weak management. If firm B is a well-managed firm with an abundance of talented executives, a takeover will be an attractive strategy: If B takes over A, it can ease out the existing managers of A and install its own managers instead. With better management, the profits of A are likely to rise, and the prices of its shares will rise as well. The market price of the shares of the *acquiring* firm may also play a role in some cases. For example, the price of shares in well-managed company B may be high relative to the value of its fixed assets, or in relation to its actual earnings, simply because the market recognizes the superior competence of its managers. This makes a takeover look like an attractive strategy from the viewpoint of B's managers and shareholders: It can pay for the shares of target firm A by issuing a relatively small amount of its own high-priced shares. Thus, share prices in the stock market may play a role in indicating which firms may be involved in takeovers, either as acquiring firms or as targets.

## Mergers: The Interests of the Target Firm

Shareholders of a firm may welcome a takeover bid by another firm, since they are typically offered more than the current market price of their stock. Thus, one game in the stock market is to try to identify and buy the stock of potential target companies before they actually receive takeover bids.

While the *shareholders* of a target firm may welcome a takeover bid, a quite different view may be taken by its *management*—the president, vice-presidents, etc., who run the company. Why would managers object? After all, they are frequently also large shareholders, and this gives them an incentive to welcome a takeover. However, *in their role as managers* they often oppose a takeover because the corporate reorganization that follows may place their jobs in jeopardy. In order to protect managers in the event of a merger, they are sometimes offered a "golden parachute" contract—that is, the right to a large financial settlement if they decide to "bail out" of the merged firm, or if they are fired.

If the management of a target firm agrees, the takeover is a "friendly" one, and there may be little fanfare in the press. The highly publicized struggles occur when the takeover is contested, because management decides to resist the acquiring firm, which is then called a "shark" or a "black knight."

Dramatic takeover struggles have been common in the United States for several years. In the mid-1980s, they became more frequent in Canada as well. A spectacular example was the battle that occurred in the summer of 1985 when Unicorp of Toronto took over Union Gas of Chatham, Ontario. It was a classic struggle, with Union's management trying desperately, but ultimately unsuccessfully, to stave off the takeover. (The resistance operation was code-named "Project Doug Harvey," in honour of a former Montreal Canadien defenceman.)

## White Knights, Greenmail, and Other Forms of Shark Repellent

The Unicorp/Union Gas example can be used to illustrate some of the strategies the management of a target firm may use to resist an unfriendly takeover:

1. The target firm may use various legal manoeuvres to block the takeover. In the Unicorp/Union Gas fracas, Union Gas tried to invoke a regulation that no shareholder could hold more than 20% of the shares of a regulated utility, such as a distributor of natural gas. (The attempt failed on a technicality: Formally, Unicorp took over not Union Gas but Union Enterprises, a holding company with 100% ownership of Union Gas and some allied companies. The government ruled that the ownership restriction did not apply to such a holding company.)
2. When a target firm realizes its stock is being accumulated by a "shark," the target firm may buy back this stock by offering the shark a premium price

for it, that is, a price above its current market value. Because some view this payoff in the face of a threat as a legal form of blackmail, it is called "greenmail."

Who bears the cost of this greenmail? The answer is: the other shareholders who don't get paid off; they are left with a company of diminished value because money has been wasted in this payoff. Thus, the payment of greenmail is a way for top executives to save their jobs by using small shareholders' money to pay off big shareholders (the sharks). Sometimes smaller shareholders become so infuriated that they sue the executives for making this payment. An interesting variant of the greenmail strategy was considered by Union Gas: It was proposed that the firm's employee pension fund would buy back the Union Gas shares that Unicorp had already acquired. In such a case, it would be the employees in the pension plan who would pay the greenmail.

3. Another way of dealing with a shark is the Pac-Man strategy of eating it before it eats you. In the Unicorp/Union Gas battle, it was in fact suggested that Union Gas might turn around and take over Unicorp, paying for the purchase with an issue of Union Gas shares. However, nothing came of this, so Union tried a fourth form of resistance:

4. Find a "white knight," a friendly company with compatible goals and substantial resources that is invited to take over the target company in order to prevent it from falling into unfriendly hands. In the Union Gas case, Redpath Industries was initially considered for the role of white knight; the president of Union Gas, former Ontario Treasurer Darcy McKeough, was also the chairman of Redpath. When this did not work out, Union tried a fifth strategy:

5. Take a poison pill: That is, the target firm takes some action that makes it less attractive to the shark. To make itself a less attractive target, Union Gas bought control of a third corporation, Burns Foods Ltd. of Calgary, paying for the purchase with an issue of $125 million in Union Gas voting preferred shares. As a result of this increase in the number of outstanding voting shares in Union Gas, Unicorp had to buy a larger number of shares than before in order to get voting control of Union Gas. When the takeover was finally accomplished in spite of Union's resistance, Unicorp found itself the unwilling owner of Burns Foods as well.

## Leveraged Buy-outs (LBOs) and Break-up Artists

Leveraged buy-outs occur when an acquiring firm or group of firms borrows heavily to buy the stock of a target firm, such as the giant U.S. firm R.J.R. Nabisco. That particular deal (in 1988/89) was of interest not only because it was by far the largest takeover in history, but also because the bidding was opened by a group led by some of the managers of R.J.R. Nabisco, including its Canadian-born president Ross Johnson.

Johnson argued that he was just getting shareholders a higher price for their shares; and, in fact, the shares almost doubled in price before the bidding was over. But critics charged that the deal was designed to provide Johnson with enormous personal gain. Had his bid succeeded, Johnson's own multi-million-dollar stake in the new company would have immediately increased by about ten times, with a *further tenfold increase* possible over the next five years. Johnson was also criticized for "attacking the company from the inside, using insider information." This raised a problem of increasing interest to economists — namely, a principal/agent problem with "asymmetric information," since the agent (Johnson) had more information than the principals (the shareholders).

In many LBOs, the new owners are referred to as break-up artists. One of the prime examples is Canada's Robert Campeau who borrowed heavily in 1988 to buy up several very large U.S. companies from which he then sold off major parts. Break-up artists have no choice: They have to sell off many of the acquired firms' assets piece by piece in order to reduce their staggering debt. Such "borrowing to break up a company" may often be profitable, but it is highly risky since most of the firm's earnings initially have to go into paying interest on the large debt load. If sales fall in a recession or interest rates rise, earnings may no longer be sufficient to cover these interest payments, as happened to Campeau's companies in 1989.

## Conclusions on Mergers: Winners, Losers, and the Interest of Society as a Whole

Recent evidence suggests that the big benefits from a takeover go to the target firm's shareholders who receive a higher price for their stock. Benefits also go to the lawyers and investment bankers who provide advice. These benefits might reflect an efficiency gain for society if there were no losers.

But, in reality, there are losers. One is typically the government; since an additional slice of the target firm's earnings now has to go as interest on heavy new debts, it never shows up as corporate profits that can be taxed. Original bondholders in the target firm frequently lose also because a takeover leaves them with bonds in a more heavily indebted and, therefore, risky company. (When the first takeover bid for R.J.R. Nabisco was announced, the value of the company's bonds fell by 20%.)

Employees of the target company who are fired in the corporate reorganization also lose as their human capital (expertise in the firm's operations) disappears. A new management without ties to employees or communities will find it easier to fire loyal employees of long standing. This may be one of the reasons that a new management can get higher earnings out of the firm's assets. But this does not happen without a cost.

Overall, these losses probably offset only some of the gains in a typical takeover. On balance, there are likely to be net remaining gains which reflect an increase in efficiency resulting from the more effective organization of assets. Moreover, efficiency may increase not only in the firms that are actually taken over but also in many firms that are not taken over but have been forced to reorganize to improve their performance in the face of just a *threatened* takeover.

While the judgement so far is favourable for many takeovers, several concerns remain.

1. To avoid becoming takeover targets, are managers becoming so preoccupied with increasing the earnings on their assets in the short run, that they damage their long-run earnings?
2. Are acquiring firms trying to capture monopoly positions by taking over rivals? The proposed merger between Air Canada and Canadian Airlines in the early 1990s has certainly raised this concern. But while some takeovers make firms larger, break-up artists are splitting up other firms into smaller pieces.
3. During the height of the "takeover binge" in the late 1980s, another concern was: Are takeovers being financed by too much debt? Because LBOs make the corporate sector more highly leveraged, it was argued, they might make it more vulnerable to bankruptcies in the next recession. In turn, might this not spill over, damaging financial institutions that have been supplying funds, and thus increase the likelihood of a financial crisis?

In some respects, the recession of 1990–1992 suggested that these concerns were justified: Part of the reason there were so many layoffs, and the recovery after the recession was so slow, was that there were so many highly indebted firms that had to reduce their payroll and lay off workers in order to survive; there were also quite a few job losses because of bankruptcies.

But, even though a number of financial institutions suffered severe losses, and some (like the well-established Royal Trustco) even went under, there was no general financial crisis. Moreover, the financial institutions that suffered the most severe losses were not necessarily those that had been most involved in financing LBOs, but instead those that had large loans in the commercial real estate sector which experienced a catastrophic downturn during the recession.

# PART 4 FACTOR MARKETS AND INCOME DISTRIBUTION

In Part 4, the central topic will be *income distribution: For whom* is the nation's output produced? We shall be asking questions such as: What determines the income that labour receives in the form of wages (Chapter 15)? What are the role and the effects of trade unions in the labour market (Chapter 16)? What determines the interest and profit of owners of capital and the rental income of landowners (Chapter 17)? How unequal are incomes in Canada, and to what extent do government taxes and transfer payments change the nation's distribution of income (Chapter 18)?

To answer such questions, we shall be turning our attention from the markets for goods and services to the markets for labour, capital, and other factors of production. It will be no great surprise to find that factor markets are much like product markets. Sometimes they operate efficiently; sometimes they do not. Therefore, some of Part 4 will represent applications of the tools developed in Parts 2 and 3 to a challenging new set of problems.

Before proceeding, we re-emphasize one of the important messages from the preceding chapters. Almost any government policy, from regulating a monopoly to imposing a tariff, will change a market price. When a price changes, there are two effects: an *efficiency* effect and a *transfer* from one group to another. (For example, a price rise hurts buyers and benefits sellers; thus, it causes a transfer from buyers to sellers.)

In the analysis of product markets in Parts 2 and 3, the focus was on efficiency. But we have seen that a policy that increases efficiency cannot be judged on this ground alone; its transfer effects must also be recognized. When we shift our major focus to income distribution in Part 4, a similar conclusion is reached: Any policy designed to transfer income cannot be judged only according to this criterion; its effect on efficiency must also be examined carefully. This conclusion is important for such issues as minimum wage legislation to improve the incomes of low-paid workers, labour laws designed to improve the bargaining position and real wages of workers, or subsidies to higher education as a device to raise the incomes of those who otherwise couldn't afford to go to university.

CHAPTER

# 15 WAGES IN A PERFECTLY COMPETITIVE ECONOMY

*In a thriving town the people who have great (capital) to employ, frequently cannot get the number of workmen they want, and therefore bid against one another in order to get as many as they can which raises the wages of labour, and lowers the profits of (capital).*

*Adam Smith,* Wealth of Nations

The wage rate is the price of labour, and the market for labour is somewhat similar to the market for a good, such as wheat or machinery. Of course, these two markets are far from being completely the same. Labour is not just a commodity; labour involves people, and this makes a big difference. For example, if manufacturers wish to abuse their machines, that is pretty much their own business; the cost will come when the machines wear out quickly, and no case can be made for government intervention. Not so in the labour market. If an employer abuses workers by putting them in jobs where there are major health hazards, or risks of injury, government intervention to set standards is justified. As another example, some business executives have peculiar quirks about their products. In the early days of the automobile, Henry Ford's attitude was, "You can have any colour of car you want — so long as it is black." No question of public policy arose; Ford paid for his views with lost sales when competitors were willing to give buyers their choice of colours. In contrast, personal quirks in the market for labour can be pernicious. If an employer just doesn't like women or native Canadians, the government may reasonably intervene to enforce anti-discrimination laws. Machines have no rights, but workers do.

Although the labour market is different in these respects from other markets, still it may be analysed in much the same way. In this chapter, we ask:

- What affects labour demand?
- What affects labour supply?
- When is a free labour market efficient, and when is it not? (An economy cannot be efficient overall, unless it has both efficient product markets — as explained in Chapter 11 — and efficient markets for labour and other factors.)
- Can the government intervene in the labour market to transfer income to labour, just as it sometimes intervenes in a product market to transfer income from one group to another?
- When the government does intervene, what effect does its intervention have on efficiency?

## A PERFECTLY COMPETITIVE LABOUR MARKET

This chapter deals with a perfectly competitive market for labour in *a specific industry*. Such a labour market has characteristics similar to a perfectly competitive market for a product:

1. There are so many buyers of labour service (employers) and sellers (workers) that none has any market power to influence the wage rate.
2. Labour is standardized. All workers are equally skilful and equally productive in the industry being studied.

3. Workers are mobile. They are not prevented from moving from one job to another.

Since labour markets are typically more complicated than this, each of these simplifying assumptions will eventually be relaxed. The next chapter relaxes the first assumption, that nobody has the market power to influence the wage rate. What happens when workers form a labour union in order to acquire market power and raise wages? Or when employers have market power, and are, therefore, able to keep wages down? Chapter 17 relaxes the second and most unrealistic assumption — that all workers are equally productive. What happens to wage patterns when some workers are better educated or more skilful than others? Finally, the last section of the present chapter relaxes the third assumption that labour is mobile. What happens when employers prevent minorities from taking certain jobs, and limit them instead to low-productivity, low-income jobs?

However, the initial task in this chapter is to describe a perfectly competitive market, in which all three assumptions do hold. To do so, first consider the question: What determines the demand for labour? Although the main focus of this chapter is on the labour market in a specific industry (such as bicycles), let's first set the stage by examining the labour demand by a single firm — an individual producer of bicycles.

# THE DEMAND FOR LABOUR

In Canada and the United States, ***real wage rates per hour*** are now more than five times as high as they were in 1900. They have increased because of rising labour productivity.

The *real wage rate* is the nominal (or dollar) wage rate adjusted for inflation. The statement that the real wage is five times as high now as in 1900 means that the hourly wage will now buy five times as many goods and services as in 1900.

To describe the concept of labour productivity more precisely and examine its central role in determining the demand for labour, let's return again to the hypothetical firm in Chapter 9 which produces shoes, with a given stock of plant and machinery.

## The Value of the Marginal Product of Labour

The first two columns in Table 15-1 repeat information from Table 9-2, p. 168; they show how this firm can increase its physical output (column 2) by hiring more labour (column 1). Column 3 shows the *marginal product* — that is, the *increase* in total product

**TABLE 15-1** **Marginal Physical Product, Marginal Revenue Product, and Value of the Marginal Product of Labour†**

| (1) Number of workers | (2) Total physical product | (3) Marginal physical product, MPP (change in column 2 because one more worker is hired) | (4) Price per unit of product | (5) Marginal revenue product, MRP (also VMP, the value of the marginal product, if output sold in perfect competition) (5) = (3) × (4) |
|---|---|---|---|---|
| 0 | 0 | | | |
| | | 5 | $20 | $100 |
| 1 | 5 | | | |
| | | 7 | $20 | $140 |
| 2 | 12 | | | |
| | | 6 | $20 | $120 |
| 3 | 18 | | | |
| | | 3 | $20 | $ 60 |
| 4 | 21 | | | |
| | | 2 | $20 | $ 40 |
| 5 | 23 | | | |

In this hypothetical example, marginal physical product falls, provided that more than two workers are hired (column 3). Thus, beyond the second worker there are diminishing returns to labour.

†Shown for a hypothetical firm with a given capital stock and selling in a competitive market at a constant price.

— as each additional worker is hired. For example, hiring the second worker increases output from 5 to 12 units in column 2. To emphasize that marginal product is measured in physical units—for example, pairs of shoes—economists often refer to this concept as ***marginal physical product*** (MPP). Thus, the marginal physical product of that second worker is 7 units, shown in column 3.

> The *marginal physical product* (MPP) of labour is the additional number of units of output a firm can produce because it has one more unit of labour.

However, in order to decide on the best number of workers to hire, the firm is not primarily interested in the marginal physical product. Instead, it is interested in how its total *revenue* (measured in terms of money rather than in physical units) increases as it hires each additional worker. This concept is called its ***marginal revenue product*** (MRP).

> The *marginal revenue product* (MRP) of labour is the amount the firm's revenue increases because it has one more unit of labour.

The marginal revenue product for the firm in Table 15-1 is calculated in the last column, on the assumption that this firm is selling its output in a perfectly competitive market in which it cannot influence price. Specifically, the price of its output remains $20 per unit in column 4 no matter how many units it sells. In this case, the additional revenue from hiring the second worker is $140—that is, the 7 additional units that the second worker produces times the $20 price of each unit. Observe that, in this example, each marginal revenue product in the last column is the marginal physical product in column 3 times the $20 price—that is, it is the ***value of the marginal product*** (VMP).

> *Value of the marginal product* (VMP) = marginal physical product × product price. If the firm's output is sold in a perfectly competitive market, VMP = marginal revenue product.

As long as perfect competition exists in the product market with product price being constant—as assumed here—the firm's marginal revenue product is the same as the value of its marginal product. However, if the product is sold in an imperfect market, with the prices in column 4 consequently changing rather than being constant, then MRP and VMP are not the same. (An example is given in problem 15-3.)

How many units of labour will the firm hire? To answer this question, first take the marginal revenue product figures in the last column of Table 15-1 and graph them as the heavy line in Figure 15-1. If the daily wage paid to each worker is the $60 shown by the coloured line, this firm will stop hiring when it has employed four workers. (The fifth won't be hired because that worker would provide only $40 of additional revenue but would be paid a wage of $60.) Note that, in deciding how much labour to hire, the firm uses a familiar guideline. It hires labour up to the point where its marginal benefit (the marginal revenue product of labour) is equal to its marginal cost (the wage rate).

**In a perfectly competitive labour market, the profit-maximizing firm hires labour to the point where the marginal revenue**

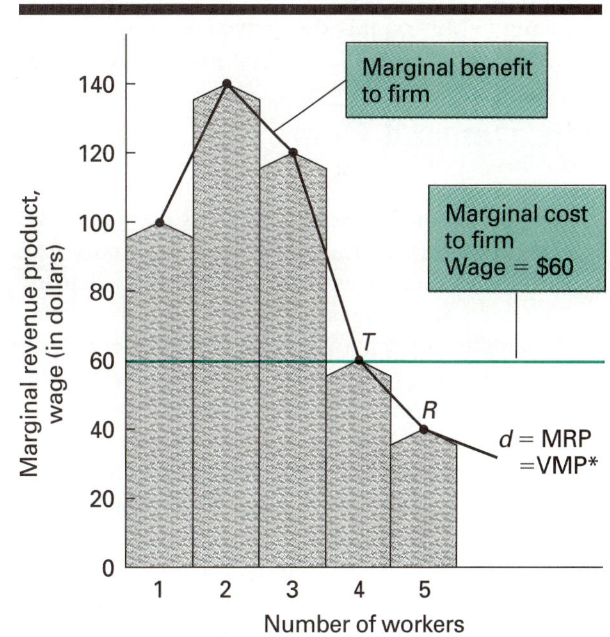


**FIGURE 15-1 A firm's demand for labour is the marginal revenue product of labour (MRP in column 5 of Table 15-1).**

The points on the MRP curve represent points on the firm's demand curve. For example, point *T* on the MRP curve is also on the demand curve, because at a wage rate of $60 the firm hires four workers.

*If product also sold in perfect competition

**product (MRP) of labour equals the wage rate (*W*), that is, where**

**MRP = *W*** (15-1)

As we have seen, MRP = VMP when the firm sells its output in a perfectly competitive market, as assumed here. In this case, the preceding conclusion and Equation (15-1) can be restated:

**If its labour market and output market are perfectly competitive, the profit-maximizing firm will hire labour to the point where the value of the marginal product (VMP) equals the wage rate (*W*), that is, where**

**VMP = *W*** (15-2)

What is true of labour is also true of any other factor.

**If all factor and output markets are perfectly competitive, the profit-maximizing firm hires each factor of production to the point where the value of its marginal product (VMP) equals the price (or wage) of the factor.** (15-3)

## The Demand Curve for Labour

The next question is: What is the firm's ***demand curve for labour?*** The answer is, its marginal revenue product curve. To see why, note that point *T* on the firm's MRP curve is also a point on its demand curve (since, at a \$60 wage, the firm hires four workers). Similarly, any other point on this MRP curve, say *R*, is also a point on the firm's demand curve. (At a \$40 wage, the firm would hire five workers.) With each point on the MRP curve representing a point on the labour demand curve, the two curves coincide. Accordingly, the MRP curve in Figure 15-1 is labelled the demand curve for labour *d*. Notice that, as before, the height of the demand curve measures the benefit — and hence the maximum willingness to pay — to the employer, of the particular unit of labour.

**A set of vertical bars, such as those shown in Figure 15-1, can be visualized as being enclosed beneath the demand curve for labour. Each bar shows the marginal benefit to the firm that hires another worker —that is, the marginal revenue product.**

In the short run, if labour is the only variable factor of production, the hiring rules of Equations (15-1) and (15-2) are equivalent to the profit-maximizing *production* decisions for competitive firms and monopolists discussed in Chapters 10 and 12. To see this, note that hiring an additional worker is the same thing as increasing production by MPP units of output. The marginal cost of producing these extra units is just *W*, the cost of hiring this worker. What is the marginal revenue? The answer: For a competitive firm, it is the price of the product *P*, times MPP—or VMP. For a monopolist (or, more generally, for any firm that faces a downward-sloping demand curve for its output), it is the additional revenue that results from selling the extra units — that is, MRP. (Thus Equation (15-1), but not Equation (15-2), provides the right hiring and production rules for a monopolist; for a competitive firm, either one gives the correct rule.)

On reflection, the equivalence between the profit-maximizing rules for hiring and for production should not come as a surprise. Whether we think of the firm as deciding how much output to produce (which, in the short run, determines how much labour it will have to hire), or how many workers to hire (which, in the short run, determines the amount of output) shouldn't make any difference: We should get the same answer in either case.

Finally, you should now work through problem 15-1 to see how the firm's income is divided between the wages it pays to labour and the amount it has left over to pay interest, profit, and rent to other factors of production. This will be a useful introduction to our discussion later in this chapter of how income is divided.

## What Causes a Shift in the Demand for Labour?

Another way of asking this question is: What causes a shift in the marginal revenue product schedule in column 5 of Table 15-1? There are two possible answers. First, labour may become more productive, that is, the marginal physical product of labour in column 3 may increase. Second, there may be a change in the price of the firm's output in column 4. For example, if this price rises from \$20 to \$30, all the marginal revenue product figures in column 5 will correspondingly rise, causing the demand for labour to shift upward to $d_2$ in Figure 15-2. Examples of such a shift in demand include the increased demand for carpenters resulting from an increase in the demand for — and price of — houses, and the increased demand for farm labour following an increase in the price of wheat. Both these examples illustrate the

***derived demand*** for labour. Labour is demanded, not for its own sake directly, but for the goods and services it produces.

> *Derived demand* exists when a good or service is demanded because of its usefulness in producing some other good or service. Thus, there is a derived demand for labour to produce cars and for land to grow wheat.

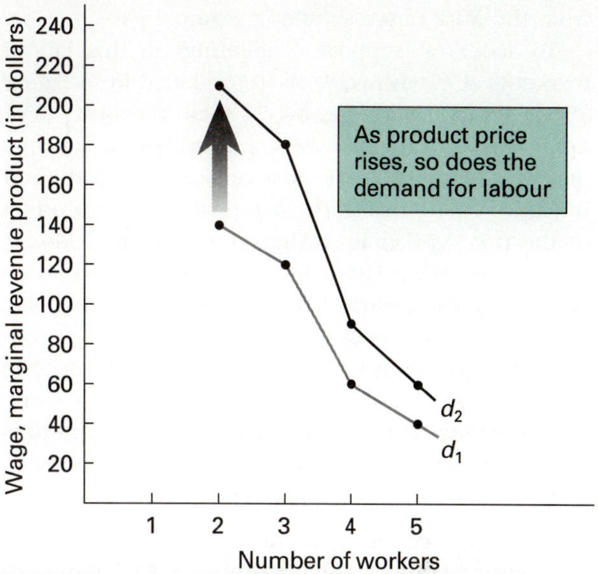


**FIGURE 15-2 The firm's derived demand for labour**

$d_1$ is the marginal revenue product of labour when product price is \$20. (It is calculated in column 5 of Table 15-1 and has already appeared as *d* in Figure 15-1.) $d_2$ is the marginal revenue product of labour if product price rises to \$30. (This is a recalculation of column 5 in Table 15-1, with \$30 replacing \$20 in column 4.)

## The Labour Market for an Industry

Now let us turn from the demand for labour by a firm (*d*) to the demand for labour by an industry (*D*). In a perfectly competitive economy, the industry's demand for labour is the horizontal sum of the demands by the individual firms in somewhat the same way that the market demand for a good (Figure 7-1) is the sum of the demands of individual consumers.[1] Such an industry demand curve for labour *D* is shown in Figure 15-3, along with the industry supply curve of labour *S*, which will be described later. Together, *S* and *D* determine *W*, the wage rate for the industry.

# THE DEMAND FOR LABOUR AND THE DIVISION OF INCOME

A major topic in the rest of this book is how the nation's income is divided or "distributed." The marginal revenue product of labour curve (the demand for labour) can throw light on this issue. Specifically,

**FIGURE 15-3 Determination of an industry's wage rate.**

In a perfectly competitive labour market, the wage rate *W* is determined by the intersection of the demand and supply curves for labour.

[1] In interpreting the industry demand curve, it is important to remember that the individual firms' demand curves have been drawn on the assumption that the price of the industry's output does not change as the firms hire more workers. Therefore, if we construct the industry demand curve by horizontally adding the demands of the individual firms, what we get is an industry demand curve that shows how many workers would be hired at different wage rates *provided that the price of the industry's output did not change*.

But when we consider the industry as a whole, it is not particularly realistic to assume that the price of its output will stay constant when the amount of employment changes. For example, if all firms were to increase their hiring in response to a fall in wages, the resulting increase in industry output would tend to reduce the price of this output. This price decrease, in turn, would shift the individual firms' labour demand curves to the left. Consequently, the amount of industry employment in the new equilibrium would be less than we would predict by just adding up the individual firms' demand for labour at the lower wage, but at the initial (higher) price of output.

the income going to labour and the income going to other factors of production in an industry can be read from the MRP curve shown in Figure 15-4.

To see how, suppose equilibrium in this labour market is at $E$, with wage $W$ (reproduced from Figure 15-3). What is the industry's total revenue?[2] The employment of the first worker increases the revenue of the industry by $a$, the first vertical bar on the left in Figure 15-4—that is, the marginal revenue product of the first worker is $a$. The second worker adds $b$, and so on to the last worker, who adds $j$. The total revenue of the industry is the sum of all these bars —that is, shaded areas 1 + 2.

What part of this total revenue goes to labour? The answer is area 2, since wage $W$ is paid to the $N$ workers employed. Thus, if the labour market is competitive, the industry's revenue is distributed as follows:

> **Labour receives income equal to the wage rate times the number of workers employed. This labour income is the rectangle below and to the left of the equilibrium point on the demand curve for labour.**

After labour is paid the amount given by area 2, area 1 remains. This is what is left for other factors of production: interest and profit to capital, rent to land, and so on. Thus:

> **After labour is paid, all other factors of production together receive the triangular area enclosed above and to the left of the equilibrium point on the demand curve for labour.**

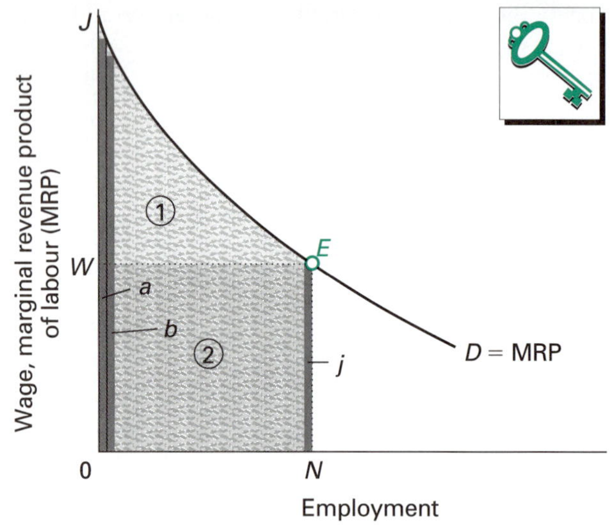


**FIGURE 15-4 An industry's demand curve for labour and the distribution of income.**

Total income earned by all factors of production is areas 1 + 2. Of this, area 2 is paid to labour and area 1 goes to other factors of production.

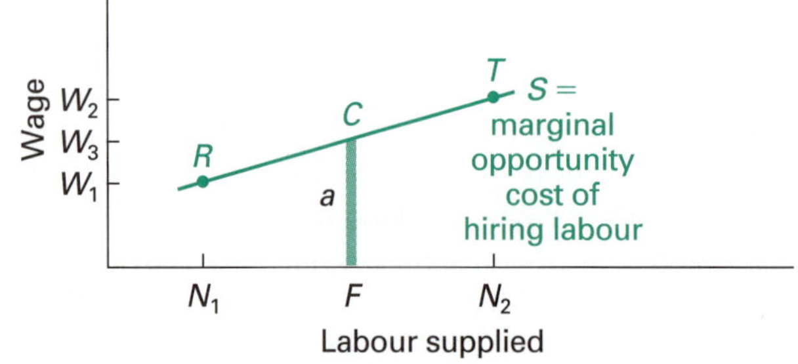


**FIGURE 15-5 Supply of labour for the furniture industry.**

The upward-sloping supply curve for labour shows how an increase in the wage paid by the furniture industry increases the number of workers seeking jobs there. Moreover, in a perfectly competitive economy, the height of the supply curve at any point like $C$ reflects the opportunity cost of hiring another worker $F$ in the furniture industry—that is, the value of the worker's marginal product in the previous job in the textile industry. Thus, the supply curve for labour reflects the opportunity cost of hiring one more worker, just as the supply curve for a product reflects the cost of producing one more unit of output.

## AN INDUSTRY'S SUPPLY OF LABOUR IN A PERFECTLY COMPETITIVE ECONOMY

The labour supply for an industry, first shown in Figure 15-3, is examined in more detail in Figure 15-5. As the wage rate rises from $W_1$ to $W_2$, the labour supplied to this industry increases from $N_1$ to $N_2$; workers

[2] More precisely, what is the industry's value added—that is, the value of the industry's output after deducting the costs of all its inputs purchased from other industries (like the cost of steel to the auto industry)? Throughout this analysis, we define the total revenue of an industry in this value-added sense.

are drawn in from other industries by this increasingly attractive wage rate. As a specific example, the labour supply curve for this industry—say, the furniture industry—tells us that when the wage rate rises to $W_3$, worker $F$ is drawn into this industry.

In order to persuade this worker to move, the wage rate $W_3$ must be high enough to cover the individual's ***transfer price***. Specifically, the wage must be high enough to compensate the worker for:

1. the wage paid in the industry from which the worker is moving, say, the textile industry
2. moving costs, both financial and psychological
3. differences in the pleasantness of working conditions in the furniture industry, compared to the textile industry.

Item 2 may be substantial. For example, workers who moved their families from the Maritimes to Alberta in the 1970s when that province's oil and gas industry was booming, and then back again as oil prices fell in the mid-1980s, might agree with the quip that "three moves is as bad as a fire." On the other hand, moving costs may be zero for the worker who is moving from a textile factory to take a job at a furniture factory next door. Item 3 may be either positive or negative: If the new job in furniture is not as pleasant as the old job in textiles, a higher wage will be needed to induce the worker to move. If, on the other hand, the new job in furniture is more pleasant, the worker may be willing to come for a lower wage than in the old textile job.

Items 2 and 3 should be taken into account, and will be later in Box 15-1. However, for the moment, we consider only the first item, which is usually the most important. The wage in the textile industry the worker is leaving was also the value of the worker's marginal product there. (Remember from Equation (15-2) that in the perfectly competitive economy we are studying, the wage in any industry is equal to the value of the worker's marginal product there.) Thus, the height of the coloured bar at $F$ represents the value of this worker's output in the alternative activity of producing textiles. This is what society loses when this worker leaves the textile industry — the *opportunity cost* of having this worker in the furniture industry. Therefore, as long as moving costs and differences in working conditions are ignored:

> **The height of an industry's supply curve for labour will, in a perfectly competitive economy, measure the opportunity cost to society of having another worker hired in this industry.**

This leads us to the appropriate way to view a supply curve for labour:

> **A labour supply curve for any industry A should be visualized with a whole set of bars beneath it, with each representing the value of the marginal product of that worker in alternative industry B. Thus, each bar represents the opportunity cost of employing labour in industry A.**

This chapter and the next concentrate on the supply of labour facing an individual industry, with the supply of labour for the economy as a whole being dealt with in the appendix to this chapter. However, note in passing that when the economywide supply of labour is examined, the question is no longer "As the wage rate rises, how many workers will be attracted in from other industries?" since there are no "other industries." Instead, other questions come to the fore, such as "If the wage rate rises, will workers sacrifice some leisure to work more? Will a higher wage induce people to enter the labour force? Will it encourage more people to immigrate?"

## THE INVISIBLE HAND IN A PERFECTLY COMPETITIVE ECONOMY

In Chapter 11, we saw that under certain conditions, the quantity of a good or service produced in a perfectly competitive industry governed by the forces of supply and demand was the *economically efficient* quantity. A quantity that was either larger or smaller than that corresponding to the equilibrium between the supply and demand would imply an efficiency loss. We may now ask whether a similar conclusion holds in a perfectly competitive labour market. Does Adam Smith's invisible hand work in factor markets as it did in product markets? In a perfectly competitive economy, will market prices result in an ***efficient allocation of labour***?

Panel (a) in Figure 15-6 (page 319) illustrates the labour market for an industry in a perfectly competitive economy. The quantity of employment is $N_1$ and the wage is $W_1$. This is efficient because it satisfies our criterion: The marginal benefit to society of any activity—in this case, hiring labour in this industry—must be equal to its marginal cost to society. The two are equal in panel (a) because demand reflects the marginal benefit of labour (that is, the value of its marginal product in this industry) while supply reflects labour's marginal cost (that is, the value of its marginal product elsewhere). The efficiency of this result is perhaps most clearly seen by showing in panels (b) and (c) that any other solution is inefficient.

For example, consider the industry in panel (b) where, for some reason, employment is greater than $N_1$. Specifically, suppose it is $N_2$. Let $f$ represent one of the units of "excess employment." The benefit from employing this worker here is the value of this worker's marginal product (which hereafter will be abbreviated to "marginal productivity"). This is shown graphically as the empty bar under the labour demand curve. However, the cost of employing this worker is this worker's marginal productivity in an alternative activity, shown by the height of the supply curve, that is, the empty bar plus the black bar above it. The difference is the black bar, which is the efficiency loss to society because this worker is in this industry rather than in a higher-productivity job elsewhere. The total efficiency loss to society for all such excess workers in the range $N_1N_2$ is the grey triangle.

On the other hand, at employment $N_3$ in panel (c), there are too few workers in this industry. To confirm, consider one worker $g$ who might be employed here, but is not. The cost of employing this worker here is the worker's marginal product in an alternative activity, shown by the empty bar under the supply curve. However, the benefit from employing this worker here is this individual's marginal product in this industry, shown by the empty bar plus the black bar under the demand curve. The difference is the black bar, which represents this worker's greater marginal product here than elsewhere; this is lost because this individual is not employed here. Finally, the sum of all such losses over the range $N_3N_1$ is the grey triangle, which shows the total efficiency loss to society. In brief, this loss occurs because workers are *not* hired in this industry even though they would be more productive here than elsewhere.

To sum up: There is an efficiency loss if employment in this industry is greater or less than the perfectly competitive quantity $N_1$ in panel (a). (Further detail on this point is provided in Box 15-1.) Thus, this analysis confirms the clear analogy between the labour market, where perfect competition generates

## TOOLS AND TECHNIQUES — BOX 15-1

### Does an Invisible Hand Bring Efficiency to the Labour Market?

The earlier analysis of the product market in Figure 11-2 is now extended to a factor market in the figure below. If all individual employers and employees make decisions that are in their own self-interest, the result will be efficient as long as perfect competition prevails throughout the economy. In panel (a), employers in this industry maximize their profit by hiring labour up to the point where their marginal benefit from doing so (the marginal productivity of labour in this industry) is equal to their marginal cost of hiring labour —that is, the wage they have to pay. In panel (b), workers pursue their self-interest by offering their labour services up to the point where their marginal benefit (the wage they can earn here) is equal to their marginal cost of offering their services — that is, the wage they could earn elsewhere (their opportunity cost). The result in panel (c) is an efficient one for society, made possible because of the key role played by a competitive wage rate. It is the employers' reaction to this wage in panel (a) and the workers' reaction to this same wage in panel (b) that ensure in panel (c) that the marginal productivity of labour will be the same in this industry and elsewhere. Therefore, the nation's output cannot be increased by shifting labour into this industry or out of it. In short, as long as no single individual or firm on either side of the market can influence $W$, it is the key in orchestrating the actions of employers and employees in an efficient way.

In the figure below, it has been assumed that the height of the supply curve for labour reflects the marginal productivity of labour in other industries; that is, it reflects only item 1 on page 315. But what about items 2 and 3,

**BOX 15-1 continued**

which also determine the height of the supply curve; namely, the costs of moving and the pleasantness of the jobs? Do they upset the conclusion that a competitive market is efficient? The answer is no, because if a worker has to relocate in another city in order to get a new job, resources must be used in moving the worker's furniture and other possessions. From the point of view of society, it is not efficient for the worker to move unless that individual's marginal productivity (and wage) in the new industry is higher by an amount sufficient to cover the costs of the move. But it must be—otherwise the worker won't move. Accordingly, the operation of the market leads to an efficient result.

Likewise, item 3 does not cause inefficiency. Suppose that the new job is more attractive and, therefore, the worker moves even though his or her wage and marginal productivity are somewhat less here than elsewhere. Since this worker is producing less here, this seems to be an undesirable move. But that is not so. For economic welfare, we should count more than the goods and services produced. It is also important for people to enjoy their jobs. If the pleasantness of the new job at least compensates for the worker's lower wage, no loss of efficiency occurs. And this will be the case: The pleasantness of the new job must compensate for the lower wage—otherwise the worker won't move.

Finally, for some individuals, the alternative forgone when taking a job in a particular industry is not a job elsewhere, but giving up income from self-employment such as being a freelance copy editor, or the value (to themselves and their families) of work they do at home. Again, however, there is no reason why self-employment and household work should not be regarded as social benefits as well as private. As long as the social and private values of these activities are the same, therefore, the supply curve of labour does represent the marginal opportunity cost to society, and a competitive labour market leads to an efficient solution.

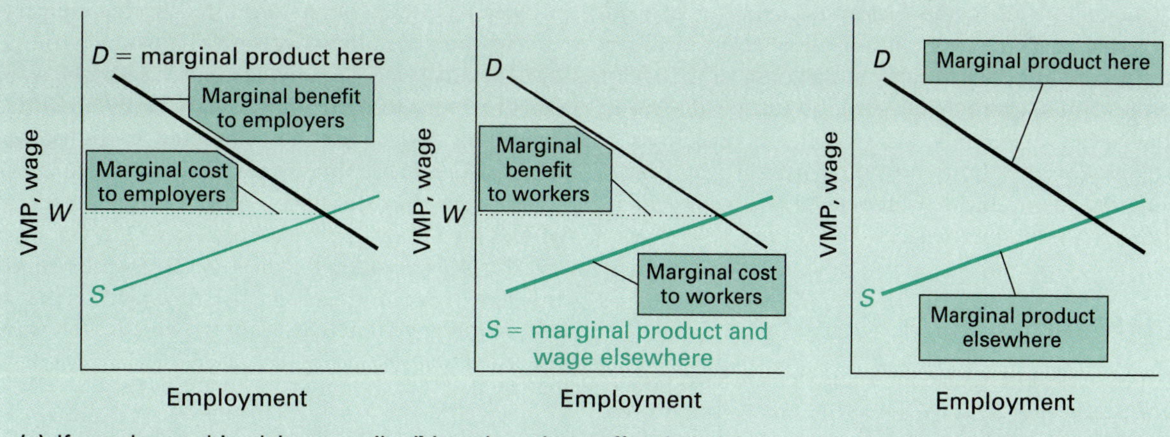


**(a)** If employers hire labour until *their* marginal benefit equals their marginal cost,...

**(b)** and workers offer their labour until *their* marginal benefit equals their marginal cost,...

**(c)** then the marginal benefit to society (marginal product here) will be equated to the marginal cost to society (marginal product elsewhere) and the resulting outcome will be efficient.

**How the pursuit of private benefit in a perfectly competitive economy results in the efficient employment of labour. (Compare with Figure 11-2.)**

an efficient level of employment in each industry, and the product market in Chapter 11, where perfect competition generates efficient output.

## SOME COMPLICATIONS

As always, we can make no claim that perfect competition necessarily results in the best of all possible worlds. It satisfies only one of society's important objectives: *the elimination of deadweight inefficiency*. However, it does not address the question: How fair is the resulting distribution of income between labour and other factors of production? This important and difficult question is left to Chapter 18.

Moreover, in practice there may be a number of departures from the very simple perfectly competitive model described here. For example, there may be external spillover costs or benefits. Externalities may arise in a labour market just as in a product market. To illustrate, the public in a large city may receive an external benefit when musicians are hired for the local symphony orchestra, because musicians may make an indirect contribution to the cultural life of the community merely by living there — in addition, of course, to the direct benefit they provide whenever they play in a concert. This external benefit will mean that a free, perfectly competitive market will result in "too little hiring of musicians"—just as external benefits lead to too little production of a good. (External costs and benefits — which result in differences between private and social cost, or between private and social benefit— will be further discussed in Chapters 21 to 23.)

Now consider how the labour market may depart from the competitive outcome if the government imposes a minimum wage.

## THE MINIMUM WAGE

Workers in most Canadian industries are covered by ***minimum wage laws*** which stipulate the lowest hourly wages that employers are allowed to pay. For example, in those industries covered by the federal Canada Labour Code, employers had to pay experienced workers at least $4.00 per hour in 1992. Other industries are covered by provincial minimum wage laws. In 1992, provincial minimum wages were generally higher than the federal minimum. For example, in Quebec the basic minimum rate was $5.55 per hour, and in the Northwest Territories it was as high as $6.50.

The purpose of the federal and provincial minimum wages has been to raise labour income and thus reduce the poverty problem. But what effect has the minimum wage legislation had? To analyse this question, consider two cases: (1) the effects on an industry if it is the only one covered by the minimum wage and (2) the effects if the *entire economy* is covered by the minimum wage. (At present, the Canadian economy is somewhere between these two polar cases, but moving closer over time toward case 2.) To keep matters simple, we disregard the difference between the federal and provincial minimum wage rates, and the different rates that apply to certain kinds of workers, and suppose that there is only a single rate which applies in all jurisdictions.

### Case 1: Only One Industry Is Covered by the Minimum Wage

This case can be described in panel (c) of Figure 15-6. Suppose that there is initially a perfectly competitive, free-market wage of $W_1$, where supply equals demand for labour. Then, the government imposes a minimum wage $W_3$, above $W_1$. Because of the higher wage, employers hire fewer workers. Equilibrium moves back up the demand curve from $E_1$ to $E_3$, with the number of workers employed falling from $N_1$ to $N_3$. As a result, there is the grey efficiency loss because too few workers are hired in this industry.

Why then does the government introduce this policy? The answer is: to provide a fairer, equitable wage, and thus help to solve the poverty problem. In fact, this policy indeed can be expected to redistribute income. As a first approximation, the winners are the $N_3$ workers who still have a job in this industry and who enjoy a wage increase from $W_1$ to $W_3$. The losers are the $N_3N_1$ workers who lose their jobs in this industry or are not hired in the first place. They are left in lower-productivity jobs paying lower wages elsewhere.

### Case 2: All Industries Are Covered by the Minimum Wage

The result in this case is the same in many respects. The winners are those who retain their jobs, while the losers are those who do not. However, there is now one important difference. Those who lose their jobs do not get jobs elsewhere. Since the whole economy is covered, there are no other jobs for them to get. Because they become unemployed, they lose far

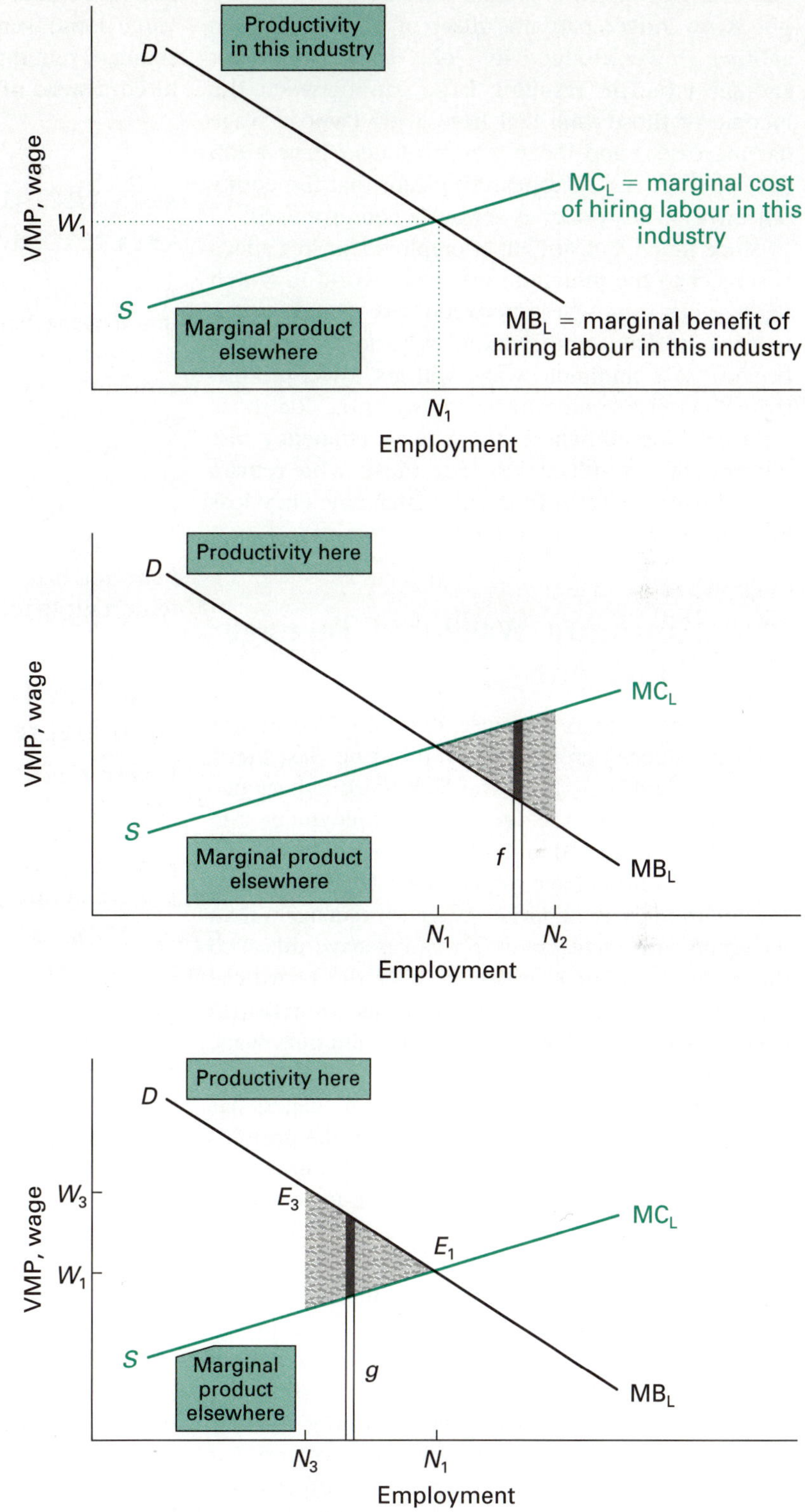


**(a)** At the perfectly competitive amount of employment $N_1$, there is an efficient number of workers in this industry—because $D$ (the marginal benefit of hiring another worker) is just equal to $S$ (the marginal cost of hiring another worker).

**(b)** $N_2$ is inefficient. There are too many workers in this industry—individuals like $f$ who produce less here (the hollow bar) than they could elsewhere (hollow bar plus solid bar).

**(c)** $N_3$ is also inefficient. There are too few workers in this industry. Employment should be increased by hiring workers like $g$, who would produce more here (the hollow bar plus the solid bar) than they do elsewhere (the hollow bar).

**FIGURE 15-6 Why the labour market is efficient in a perfectly competitive economy.**

more than in case 1. Moreover, the overall efficiency loss to the economy is greater because their lost output is no longer partially offset by their output in another, lower-productivity job. They don't get another job. The resulting large gap between the income of those who still have a job (whose wage has increased) and those who no longer have a job (whose wage has disappeared) means that the equity objective of this policy is seriously compromised.

Since much, but not all, of employment in Canada is subject to the minimum wage, the world in which we live lies somewhere between case 1 and case 2: It is likely that some workers who lose their jobs because of a minimum wage will get lower-productivity jobs elsewhere, but some will not. For those who get jobs elsewhere, there is an efficiency loss because they produce less. For those who remain unemployed, there is an even greater efficiency loss because they produce nothing.

## The Minimum Wage and Teenage Unemployment

Who are the workers who lose their jobs? The answer often is: minority groups who tend to be "last hired, first fired" and teenagers who lack work experience and skills. Because the teenage unemployment rate usually is more than double the rate for adults, a number of economists have argued for a "two-tiered system," with a lower minimum wage for teenagers than for adults. In Canada, most provinces have followed this suggestion. For example, in 1992 the provincial minimum wage for employees under age 18 in British Columbia was $5.00, while the adult minimum wage was $5.50.

However, such special treatment for teenagers has been opposed by some labour unions on the grounds that employers might lay off adults with families to support in order to hire teenagers at a lower wage. While such proposals increase efficiency because fewer teenagers are left unemployed, they reduce efficiency because more adults are left unemployed. Moreover, the proposals have been criticized for not being fair. If teenagers are given special treatment because of their lack of experience, why shouldn't groups facing other disadvantages also be given special treatment to encourage their employment? For example, why not also give special treatment — a lower minimum wage — to workers who are near retirement, who may have lost some of their mental or physical sharpness? With a two-tiered system giving special treatment only to teenagers, people near retirement face a double problem. They have to convince employers not only that they are worth the standard minimum wage but also that they should be hired instead of lower-wage teenagers.

## Has the Minimum Wage Been Overrated?

In one respect the answer is: no. Traditionally, the minimum wage has been more effective than the standard analysis suggests, because of its "ripple effect" in raising the wage not only of the unskilled, but also of more skilled workers who are above the minimum. The reason is primarily that unions representing skilled workers have bargained hard to maintain a gap between the two wage levels.

On the other hand, there are several reasons for believing that the minimum wage may have been less important than is often supposed.

### 1. It May Have Less Effect on Efficiency than Figure 15-6(c) Suggests.

It is true that in perfect competition, the minimum wage does lead to the efficiency loss shown in that diagram. However, in the imperfectly competitive labour markets described in the next chapter, it may lead to an efficiency gain.

### 2. There are Fewer Clear Winners and Clear Losers than the Standard Analysis Implies.

Often it is difficult to distinguish between the winners who get the minimum wage jobs and the losers who do not. The reason is that there is a high turnover rate in minimum wage jobs. Therefore, workers share these jobs to some extent. Thus, many individuals are both part-time winners (when they have one of the minimum wage jobs) and part-time losers (when they do not). This means that the concern about clear losers who end up without any jobs at all is sometimes exaggerated. It also means that there are fewer clear winners. Moreover, even for a "winner" who still has a job and has got a wage increase, part of this increase may be an illusion if employers who have to pay the higher wage cover this additional cost by cutting back on other benefits to labour, such as on-the-job training.

### 3. The Minimum Wage Has Had a Disappointing Equity Effect.

Many of the individuals whose income is raised by the minimum wage are not from poor families. For example, some are teenagers from well-to-do families. Insofar as the minimum wage has raised the income of the non-poor as well as the poor, it has not been very effective in making incomes more equal.

## DISCRIMINATION IN THE LABOUR MARKET: AN INTRODUCTION

In our discussion of the minimum wage, we noted that minorities in the labour market, such as female workers, often bear a relatively heavy burden of any unemployment because they are among the first to be laid off. Worse yet: They may have trouble even before this, in just getting a job in the first place. We shall now show how they may be the victims of ***discriminatory hiring*** by employers. In this analysis we will use labour demand and supply curves to identify some of the economic effects. However, it must be recognized that discrimination also has social, moral, and political effects, which cannot be dealt with in such a simple framework.

What happens if employers favour one group for the better positions and offer only inferior jobs to women or minorities, such as native Canadians, even when these workers have skill and training equal to that of other workers?

To set the stage, the left side of panel (a) of Figure 15-7 shows the situation in an economy in which there is no discrimination. Notice that we are now describing the labour market for the economy *as a whole*, rather than for a single industry; discrimination is an economywide problem. Thus, the demand curve $D$ includes the demands of *all* hiring firms in the economy. As a first approximation, we assume that the number of workers in the economy as a whole is given, with the supply curve of labour consequently being vertical.

In the labour market shown on the left side of panel (a) in Figure 15-7, wage $W$ is paid to $N$ workers — $N_M$ men and $N_W$ women. No distinction is made between them; that is, in hiring workers, employers do not discriminate by gender.

What happens if discrimination is introduced into this market? Specifically, consider the extreme case where employers no longer hire women to do the same jobs as men in the main labour market but hire them instead only for low-productivity, dead-end jobs.

In this extreme case, there is a ***dual labour market***. The two quite separate labour markets are shown on both sides of panel (a) in Figure 15-7. On the left side, showing the main labour market for men only, supply shifts from $S$ to $S_M$. The wage rate consequently rises from $W$ to $W_M$. In the labour market for women on the right, demand for labour $D$ is low, reflecting the fact that the only jobs available are low-productivity tasks. Supply in this market is $S_W$. The wage rate is $W_W$, substantially less than the wage $W$ that women received before discrimination.

The effects of such discrimination on each group and on the overall efficiency of the economy may be summarized:

1. *Female workers lose.* Because their wage rate is depressed from $W$ to $W_W$, their total wage income falls from area 3 on the left side of Figure 15-7(a) to area 6 on the right side. (They may also suffer higher unemployment, which does not show up in this diagram.)
2. *Male workers gain.* Because their wage rate rises from $W$ to $W_M$, their total wage income rises by area 1 on the left side of panel (a)—that is, it increases from area 4 to areas 4 + 1.
3. *Owners of other factors of production lose.* Specifically, the income earned by capital and other non-labour factors of production in the main labour market decreases by areas 1 + 2. (According to Figure 15-7, their income before discrimination was areas 7 + 1 + 2; but afterwards it is only area 7, plus area 5, which they now receive from the female labour market.) Assuming areas 2 and 5 roughly cancel, there is a net loss of area 1, which is a transfer from other factors to the male workers who receive this wage increase. This suggests that discrimination is not in the interest of employers because it depresses their profits (included in area 7). In other words, employers have an economic incentive *not* to discriminate; this incentive acts as a market pressure that tends to reduce discrimination. Another way to view this point is to note that there is a profit opportunity for employers who do not discriminate in hiring: They can increase their profit by hiring women at the low prevailing wage for women and putting them in high-productivity jobs. The more employers do this, the more the separate female market shrinks and the greater the upward pressure on women's wages; in other words, the greater the extent to

which the male-female wage differential is reduced by market pressure.

Yet, despite this market pressure, discrimination continues. One reason is that economics is not a controlling influence over long-standing prejudices of employers. A second explanation is that employers may simply be responding to discriminatory pressure from their customers. A car dealership may not hire a female salesperson if its customers are prejudiced against buying from women. The problem is still prejudice, but it may be prejudice in society beyond the hiring firm.

4. *There may be little effect on families with male wage earners.* Because some non-labour factors of production (such as capital and land) are owned by families that include male wage earners, there may be little effect on all such families taken together. It is true that male wage earners gain area 1; but this is, in part, a transfer from other factors owned by such families. In addition, many families with male wage earners also include one or more female workers, so that the effect on family income of higher wages for men are partly offset by the lower earnings of women.
5. *There is an efficiency loss.* When we turn from the transfer effects to the efficiency effects shown in panel (b) of this diagram, we see that the total product of the economy falls. Because female workers are forced out of the main labour market, the value of output falls by the dark shaded area on the left side of Figure 15-7(b).[3] This is only partially offset by the new coloured output produced in the segregated market on the right side. The difference is the reduced total output of the economy, that is, the efficiency loss that results from discrimination.
6. *This efficiency loss is borne primarily by single women and families with no male wage earner.* Because there may be little net effect on all families with male wage earners taken together, single working women or families headed by a working woman suffer most, and perhaps all, of the efficiency loss from discrimination. To confirm this, notice that the reduction in female income from area 3 to area 6 in panel (a) is essentially the same as the efficiency loss (the difference between the dark shaded area and the coloured area in panel (b)).

Empirical studies on the extent and consequences of labour market discrimination in Canada have focused on the problem of discrimination against women, and the debate over legislative proposals to reduce discrimination has centred on this problem as well. (In the United States, the problem of discrimination against blacks has historically been more important.) In the next section, we briefly consider the recent Canadian debate on the issue of legislation to reduce discrimination.

## Discrimination Against Women and Minorities: The Equal Pay Debate

Government legislation to reduce discrimination in the labour market exists in all Canadian provinces as well as at the federal level. When anti-discrimination laws were first passed in the 1950s, the basic principle was that employers had to provide "***equal pay for equal work***." However, in practice this wording created a problem: How do you define "equal work"? The early legislation took a restrictive view of what constituted "equal work": Even very small differences in the jobs that employees performed were considered sufficient to allow the employer to pay different wages. Furthermore, the legislation usually applied only to employees working for the same firm in a single geographic location.

Because of its restricted applicability, the early legislation came under increasing criticism. The principle of "equal pay for equal work" may have been effective in *some* cases. As a simple example, it may have forced hospitals to pay the same wages to male and female nurses. But empirical studies have shown that discrimination in pay against women who perform "equal work" in this restricted sense only amounts to a small proportion of the overall earnings gap between men and women. This early legislation did not deal with a more important reason for the overall earnings gap: differences in pay between men and women who perform *different* jobs. To see the problem, suppose the government succeeds in getting men and women paid exactly the same salary of, say, \$30,000 a year in nursing. Further suppose that the government also succeeds in getting both men and women paid exactly the same salary of, say, \$36,000 a year as electricians. Then isn't there still a

[3] You can visualize this area as being made up of a whole set of vertical bars, each representing the productivity that is lost when a woman is forced out of this market and there is one less worker employed here.

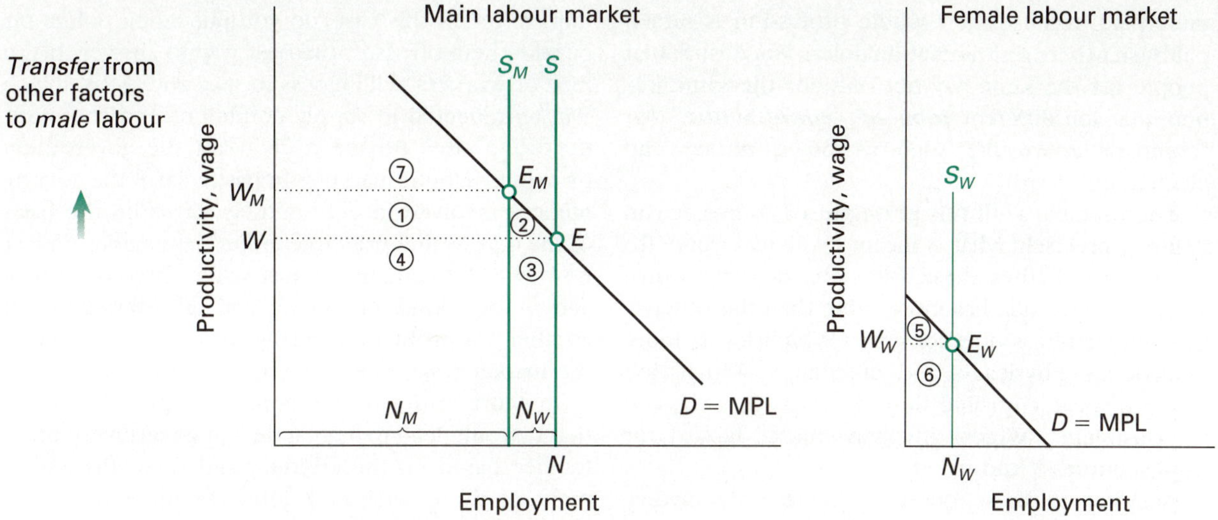


**(a) How discrimination affects wages and incomes.**
In a market *without discrimination*, equilibrium is at $E$ on the left side of panel (a). The wage received by all workers is $W$ with $N_M$ men and $N_W$ women employed. *With discrimination*, women are forced into the female market on the right, where equilibrium is $E_W$. Thus women's wage rates fall from $W$ to $W_W$ and the wage income of female workers falls from area 3 to area 6. Meanwhile, the forced departure of women from the main labour market on the left reduced labour supply there from $N$ to $N_M$, thus raising wages of men from $W$ to $W_M$, and raising the wage income of male workers by area 1 (that is, from area 4 to areas 4 + 1).

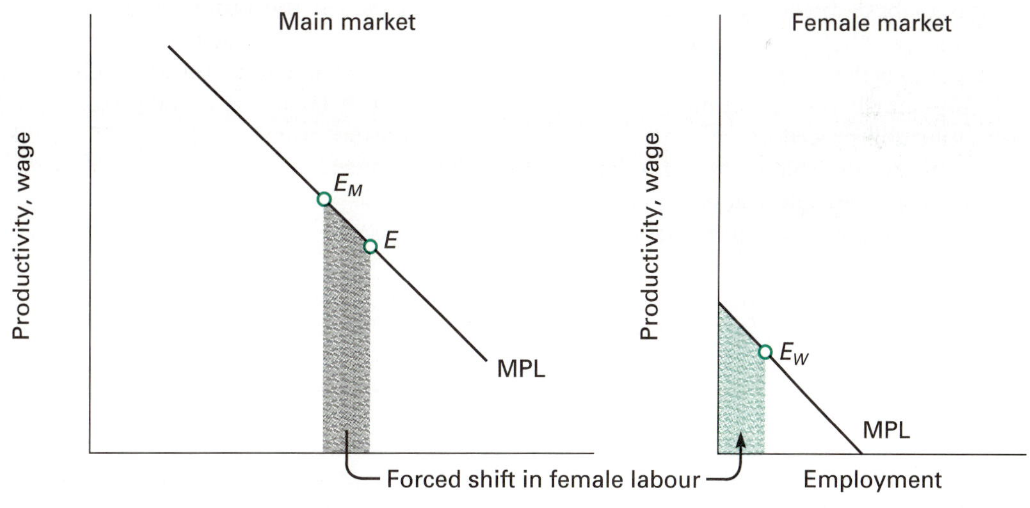


**(b) The efficiency effects of discrimination.**
As a result of the forced departure of female labour from this main labour market, there is lost output of the dark area under the marginal productivity curve. This is more than… the output (coloured area) produced by labour when it is hired in this low-productivity female market. The efficiency loss is the difference in these two areas—the reduced output of female labour because it is shifted from high- to low-productivity jobs.

**FIGURE 15-7** **An introduction to the economics of labour-market discrimination.**

problem? After all, most nurses are women while most electricians are men. Aren't women being underpaid because their whole profession is underpaid? Isn't there discrimination unless you ensure that people get the same pay not only for the same job, but *also* for different ***jobs of "equal value"*** (or "comparable worth") such as being nurses and electricians?

The problem with this principle, of course, lies in defining precisely what is meant by "equal value." To determine whether these two jobs do have equal value—or that one has more value than the other—one must address questions like: Which job is more demanding physically and mentally? Which job requires greater qualifications, knowledge, skill, and responsibility? Which involves more hazard or unpleasantness? And so on.

Answers to these questions necessarily involve some arbitrariness. Nevertheless, a number of attempts have been made by job evaluation analysts to construct scoring systems that would make it possible to systematically compare different jobs. Studies based on such comparisons have generally found that on average, women are paid less (perhaps as much as 20% less) for jobs with similar point scores. Many observers have interpreted these findings as conclusive evidence of gender discrimination, and many provinces have broadened their anti-discrimination legislation so that it can be applied in cases where different jobs have been found to be "of equal value" or "substantially similar" on the basis of some type of job evaluation procedure.

But there are still many who believe that the "equal-value" principle will prove difficult to apply in practice. The critics ask questions like: How can one possibly evaluate or trade off the greater risks required in washing windows in a skyscraper with the greater academic qualifications required in nursing? A job that 10% of the population views as pleasant may be viewed by others as downright unpleasant. In this case, do you put rating points on, or take them off? Isn't the best way to answer this to look at workers' willingness to take such jobs, which will be reflected in supply conditions and, therefore, the wage rate? Do we really want the government overriding labour markets? In particular, if the government is involved in determining wages on the basis of the equal-value principle rather than market forces, how will the economy adjust when there is a shortage of one kind of labour and an oversupply of another—a problem normally solved by a change in the market wage rate?

In short, critics of the equal-value principle argue that it would lead to a great deal of government interference based on the arbitrary and subjective judgement of those who rank jobs. On the other hand, proponents argue that continuing to rely on the market would allow discrimination to continue, and that's unacceptable.

The controversy over the problem of equal pay is reflected in the 1985 report of the MacDonald Commission.[4] On the one hand, the report concludes that there is a case for stronger legislation to reduce discrimination, given the evidence of substantial pay differentials between men and women in comparable jobs. On the other hand, the possible harmful side effects of more stringent equal pay legislation are discussed at length and, although the commission comes out in favour of existing federal and provincial policies to promote equal pay for work "of equal value," it does not recommend any new legislative initiatives.

[4] *Report of the Royal Commission on the Economic Union and Development Prospects for Canada*, Vol. II, Ch. 15. Much of the discussion in the preceding paragraphs is based on the extensive analysis of the equal pay issue in that chapter.

## KEY POINTS

1. In a perfectly competitive labour market, a firm will hire workers until the marginal revenue product (MRP) of labour equals the wage rate. Thus, the demand for labour reflects MRP. If output markets are also perfectly competitive, MRP equals the value of the marginal product (VMP). Therefore, the demand for labour also reflects VMP.
2. Demand for labour in an industry, say textiles, may shift because of an increase in the price of textiles. Thus, the demand for labour is "derived" from the demand for textiles. Labour demand may also shift because labour becomes more productive.
3. The supply of labour for an industry reflects the opportunity cost of hiring more workers, which is their marginal productivity elsewhere (that is, the value of their marginal product in other industries). The supply of labour also depends on other factors, such as the pleasantness of the job and costs of moving.

4. Adam Smith's invisible hand works to allocate labour in the most efficient way in a perfectly competitive economy. If all market participants (employers and employees) pursue their individual economic gain, the result is an efficient solution for society as a whole.
5. If labour markets are perfectly competitive, the introduction of a minimum wage above the existing wage level will result in an efficiency loss. It will benefit workers who retain their jobs but hurt workers who become unemployed.
6. However, if labour markets are not perfectly competitive, then a minimum wage may result in an efficiency gain, rather than loss, as the next chapter will demonstrate.
7. Discrimination by employers in hiring female workers will result in an efficiency loss that is borne primarily by women who get segregated into low-wage and low-productivity jobs.
8. To reduce gender discrimination by employers, federal and provincial laws guarantee "equal pay for equal work." It is more difficult to identify and deal with discrimination when men and women hold different jobs. One suggested solution is to require employers to pay women the same as men in jobs "of equal value." Implementing such a policy involves a number of practical problems. However, anti-discrimination legislation at the federal and provincial levels has been moving toward adoption of the principle of "equal pay for work of equal value."

## KEY TERMS

**real wage rate**
**marginal physical product of labour**
**marginal revenue product of labour**
**value of marginal product of labour**
**demand curve for labour**
**derived demand**
**transfer price**
**efficient allocation of labour**
**minimum wage laws**
**discrimination in hiring**
**dual labour market**
**equal pay for equal work**
**jobs of equal value**

## PROBLEMS

15-1. In Figure 15-1, we concluded that at a $60 wage, the firm hires four workers.

(a) What, then, is its total revenue? (Use the data in Table 15-1.) What is its total wage bill? How much of its total revenue remains after its wages have been paid; that is, how much does the firm have left over for interest, rent, and profit for its other factors of production?

(b) In Figure 15-1, show the areas that represent: (i) the firm's total revenue; (ii) the part of this revenue that it pays to labour; and (iii) the part that is left for other factors of production.

15-2. The curve in Figure 15-1 showing the firm's marginal revenue product is drawn on the assumption of a given $20 price for the firm's output. But now suppose that, because of decreased consumer demand for this output, its price falls to $10. Show graphically what happens to the firm's MRP curve. What happens to its demand for labour curve? Does the firm change its employment? If so, by how much? Is this a further illustration of how "producers dance to the consumers' tune"?

15-3. In this chapter, perfectly competitive labour and product markets have been assumed. To see why imperfect competition in product markets is important, return to Table 15-1, but now make the assumption that the firm has influence over its price. Specifically, assume that the figures reading down column 4 are $24, $23, $22, $21, and $20. Now, MRP in column 5 does not equal the value of the marginal product

(VMP). Confirm this by calculating MRP and VMP.

15-4. Would a minimum wage be more likely to raise the total income of labour if the elasticity of demand for labour is low rather than high? Explain why or why not.

15-5. In a number of provinces, payroll taxes are used to fund health care programs. Such taxes are levied as a percentage of firms' wage bills. At the level of an industry, use a figure such as Figure 15-3 to illustrate the distribution of the burden of such a tax (as in Figure 10-12). Separate this into the distribution of the primary burden and the excess burden.

# APPENDIX 15-A

## THE ECONOMYWIDE SUPPLY OF LABOUR

As a first rough approximation, the supply of labour for the economy as a whole—rather than just for one industry — is sometimes viewed as a vertical line, reflecting the given labour force in the whole economy. Because it is vertical, the quantity of labour that will be supplied is independent of the wage rate. However, there are two reasons the supply curve may not be completely vertical after all. That is, there are two reasons the total amount of labour supplied may change if the wage changes.

(a) The *labour force participation rate* may change; that is, there may be a change in the proportion of the population in the labour market.

(b) There may be a change in the average *number of hours worked* by the existing labour force.

While a wage increase is likely to change the quantity of labour supplied, it is not clear whether it will increase it or decrease it. This is because a wage increase exerts two conflicting pressures:

1. The *substitution effect*. Since the reward for work (the wage rate) has increased relative to the reward from leisure, people have an incentive to substitute, working more and taking less leisure.
2. The *income effect*. This effect works in the opposite direction. A higher wage means higher income and thus allows workers to acquire more of everything they want: not only more goods, but also more leisure. In acquiring more leisure, they work less.

Which of these two conflicting effects dominates? We cannot be sure. As Figure 15-8 is drawn, the two are exactly balanced at wage $W_3$, where the quantity of labour supplied is at a maximum. However, if the initial wage is lower than this, the substitution effect dominates. As the wage rate rises from, say, $W_1$ to $W_2$, people increase the amount they work from $Q_1$ to $Q_2$. On the other hand, at a wage above $W_3$, the income effect dominates. Workers now have reached a high enough wage that they can say: "Let's use any further increase not only to buy more goods, but also to buy more leisure." In other words, an increase in the wage rate induces them to work less. Specifically, if the

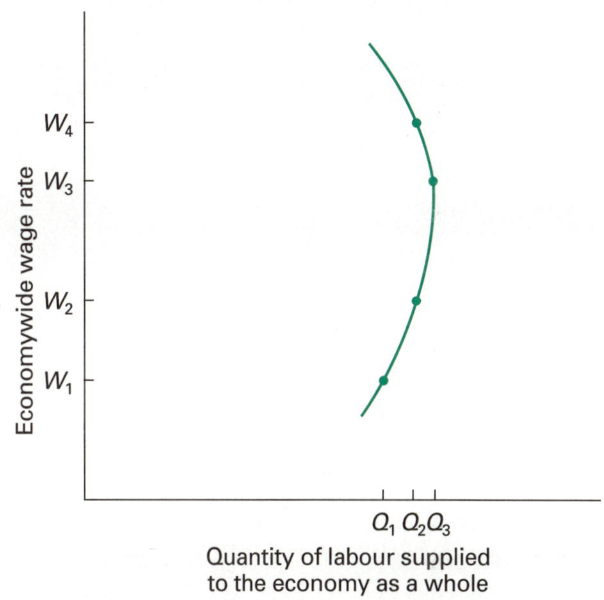


**FIGURE 15-8 The supply of labour in the economy as a whole, rather than just in a single industry.**

At low wage $W_1$, an increase in the wage to $W_2$ results in an increase in the quantity of labour supplied from $Q_1$ to $Q_2$. However, at some higher wage rate ($W_3$) workers achieve a high enough income level that they can afford to take part of any further increase in income in the form of leisure. Accordingly, they work less; the labour supply curve is backward bending.

wage rate rises from $W_3$ to $W_4$, they reduce the quantity of labour they supply. In this range, the labour supply curve is described as "backward bending."

Note that the income and substitution effects discussed here are very similar to those illustrated in Figure 7-14 in Chapter 7. In more advanced treatments, the labour supply decision is often analysed using an indifference curve diagram with the consumer's leisure (non-work) on one axis, and income from work on the other.

CHAPTER

# 16 WAGES IN IMPERFECTLY COMPETITIVE LABOUR MARKETS

*Trade unionism is not socialism. It is the capitalism of the proletariat.*

*George Bernard Shaw*

Like Rodney Dangerfield, baseball players sometimes "don't get no respect." Ted Turner, owner of the Atlanta Braves, has been quoted as saying "I don't understand why grown men play this game anyhow. They ought to be lawyers or garbage men. Games should be left for kids." By 1993, players could laugh about these comments all the way to the bank. It was no longer unusual for a star to get over $5 million a year. Twenty years before, things were different. Players got only a small fraction of their present-day salaries. This chapter will show why.

More generally, the objective of this chapter is to describe departures from perfect competition in labour markets. Specifically, it covers:

- imperfect competition on the supply side of the labour market, when unions acquire the market power to bargain for a higher wage
- imperfect competition on the demand side, when employers acquire the market power to keep wages down
- imperfect competition on both sides of the market, in the special circumstances of bilateral monopoly
- the effect of strikes, and measures to prevent or resolve them
- a review of why wage differences exist.

When market power exists on both sides of the market, the result is ***bilateral (two-way) monopoly***. This is the situation that we wish eventually to study in this chapter. However, in order to work up to this complicated subject, we first address two preliminary questions: What happens if there is market power only on the supply side of the labour market? And what happens if there is market power only on the demand side? First, we will examine unions. Although one of their major functions is to exercise market power to increase wages, they have other significant roles as well.

## LABOUR UNIONS: THE BENEFITS OF COLLECTIVE ACTION

It is sometimes said that a perfectly competitive labour market "has no memory, and no future." In such a market, people are hired or fired simply on the basis of what they can do *today*. However, in the real world, people work not only for the wage they receive today, but also in order to ensure a secure job for the future. In other words, people have a ***stake*** in their jobs. An important role of the union is to protect the stake of the workers, to give them a collective voice not only in the setting of wages but also, more generally, in the conditions of employment.[1] With the backing of unions, workers are protected from arbitrary dismissal or changes in the "rules of the game" by management. Because of these assurances, workers are able to commit themselves to an occupation more completely than they could in a timeless, impersonal, perfectly competitive market.

[1] This chapter and, in particular, this discussion of labour's voice, draws heavily on Richard B. Freeman and James L. Medoff, *What do unions do?* (New York: Basic Books, 1984).

## Collective Bargaining

When workers express their voice by getting together in a union, to engage in ***collective bargaining***, they overcome three disadvantages of "standing alone": (1) a single worker may have difficulty even getting management to listen, let alone negotiate to remove a grievance; (2) management may retaliate personally against an individual who is complaining; and (3) even if an individual were to succeed in negotiating a change, it is unlikely to be worth the effort. Most of the benefits would go to other workers. In this sense, the resolution of a labour grievance is a "public good"; *all workers benefit, regardless of who negotiates it.* Negotiations are, therefore, undertaken collectively—by a union.

> *Collective bargaining* is any negotiation between a union and management over wages, fringe benefits, hiring policies, job security, or working conditions.

In addition to raising wages by negotiating higher pay rates, unions may attempt to raise wages indirectly, by negotiating other terms of employment. For example, unions may:

1. Collectively attempt to negotiate a shorter work week and early retirement. Such changes reduce the supply of labour, and thus put upward pressure on wages.
2. Negotiate with employers to hire only union members, and then limit union membership by imposing barriers to entry, such as high initiation fees or long periods of apprenticeship. This approach also restricts the supply of labour, and thus raises wage rates.

In such negotiations, a union may, of course, have other objectives besides just raising wages. For example, a shorter work week may be desired for its own sake, and apprenticeship may be a way of screening bumbling amateurs out of dangerous occupations. Not surprisingly, motives are sometimes mixed. The charge has been made that organized medicine—the Canadian Medical Association or the American Medical Association—have acted like unions. For example, the AMA has in the past used its power to limit the number of medical schools and the number of students admitted to these schools. While the stated reason for this tough policy was to improve the quality of medical service, it also restricted the supply of graduating doctors and thus increased the incomes of the members of the AMA. In Canada, organized medicine has recently been campaigning against legislation allowing midwives to assist women who want to have their babies at home. The doctors say they consider home births too risky. But sceptics have suggested that the campaign can also be seen as a way to protect the incomes of hospital-based obstetricians.

Another negotiating objective of unions is to establish clear rules on the conditions under which workers can be laid off or discharged. This is particularly important for older workers who would have difficulty finding other jobs. Accordingly, unions work hard to establish ***seniority rules*** to protect those who have been on the job longest, and who have the most to lose if they are discharged.

> *Seniority rules* give preference to those who have been longest on the job. Individuals with seniority are typically the last to be discharged or laid off, and the first to be rehired.

Without seniority rules, older workers might be in a vulnerable situation. Over the years, their productivity may have declined. In the absence of seniority rules they might be the *first* to be laid off. Thus, union-negotiated rules can be viewed as a way of reducing older workers' vulnerability.

In addition to seniority rules, unions attempt to provide job security in a number of other ways. For example, in the 1980s, the Canadian Auto Workers union worked hard to get the Canadian government to negotiate with the Japanese government for a limit on the number of cars that Japan exports to Canada, and to get the Japanese to invest in production facilities in Canada. In the 1990s, many unions campaigned actively against the North American Free Trade Agreement (NAFTA), fearing that it would cause many companies to close their plants in Canada and transfer production to Mexico where wages are much lower.

While unions in the past have focused their attention on wages, job security, and conditions on the shop floor, an important question is whether unions in the future will seek broader areas of influence, such as a voice in the nation's boardrooms. Germany has experimented with ***co-determination***: Labour and management have an equal number of seats on the board of directors, with the owners making the decision in the event of a tie. In the United States, Douglas Fraser, then president of the United Auto Workers, in 1980 became the first union leader to get a seat on the board of a major U.S. corporation—Chrysler. This was not so much the result of a change in any underlying philosophy of management-labour relations as it was an act of desperation to save a near-bankrupt company: The UAW got a seat on Chrysler's board in exchange for deferring several hundred million dollars in wages and benefits. More recently, a number of Canadian unions have essentially taken over plants or companies that were scheduled to be closed or threatened by bankruptcy, in order to save their members' jobs. A well publicized example is Algoma Steel in Sault Ste. Marie, Ontario.

Before examining the detailed economic effects of unions, we first briefly review the long struggle to establish unions in Canada and the United States.

## LABOUR UNIONS: THEIR HISTORICAL DEVELOPMENT

The beginning of the North American union movement dates back to an era when a relatively powerless labour force lived in poverty, or near to it. In the last third of the nineteenth century, the Knights of Labour emerged, hoping to become the one great organization that might speak for all labour in both Canada and the United States. Like the labour movement in England and a number of other European countries, the organization sought to make labour a unified force for radical political change.

The importance of the Knights of Labour as a political force came to an end in the 1880s, partly as a result of the bloody Haymarket Riot in Chicago in 1886, for which the Knights were given responsibility. In Canada, the role as the nation's leading labour organization was taken over by the Trades and Labour Congress of Canada (TLC), founded in 1886. It became affiliated with the American Federation of Labor (AFL) and its objectives and methods closely resembled those of the AFL.

The AFL, following the philosophy of its leader Samuel Gompers, concentrated on the bread-and-butter issues of improving wages and working conditions, rather than on pursuing a political class struggle. When asked what labour wanted, Gompers had a simple answer: "More."

Although the Canadian labour movement continued for many years to follow the bread-and-butter approach of the AFL and TLC, its approach gradually changed. Unions in Canada began to take a more active political role, starting with the association formed between labour groups and the Co-operative Commonwealth Federation (CCF) in Saskatchewan in the 1930s, and continuing at the present time through the links between organized labour and the New Democratic Party (the NDP, which succeeded the CCF). But labour still remains uncommitted on many political issues, and workers do not always vote along traditional party lines. This contrasts with the pattern in England and some other European countries, where the labour movement has been a leading political force represented by one of the most powerful political parties.

Following an early rapid increase in membership before and during World War I, the history of Canadian unions can be divided into three distinct phases: (1) a period of stagnating membership during the 1920s and 1930s; (2) rapid growth for the next decade and a half; (3) a period of fluctuating membership since the 1950s (Figure 16-1).

### The Period Before World War II

Until the 1940s, unions in Canada generally developed in a hostile climate. On the one hand, business

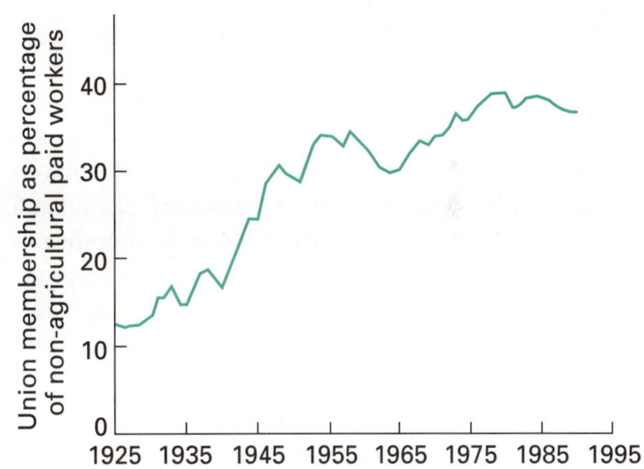


**FIGURE 16-1 Major trends in Canadian union membership (relative to total employment).**

Canadian union membership remained low until the beginning of World War II. During the 1940s and early 1950s it rose rapidly. A second period of substantial growth in union membership occurred between 1965 and 1980. However, since that time, it has declined somewhat.

*Source*: From Series E175-177 in F.H. Leacy, M.C. Urquhart, and K.A.H. Buckley, eds., *Historical Statistics of Canada*, 2nd ed. (Ottawa: Statistics Canada, 1982), and table 6.8 in *Canada Year Book, 1992* (Ottawa: Supply and Services Canada).

executives strongly resisted any attempts to unionize their firms, and would frequently retaliate against pro-union workers by firing them and then blacklisting them with other potential employers. They would also sometimes use so-called ***yellow-dog contracts***:

A *yellow-dog contract* required a worker to sign a commitment not to join a union in order to get a job.

An important early question was how the courts would treat labour-management disputes. In particular, in the light of the 1892 amendments to the Criminal Code making it an offence to enter a conspiracy in restraint of trade, would the courts interpret unions as criminal conspiracies? Judgements either for or against unions seemed possible. On the one hand, a union could be viewed as a restraint on trade, since it is a combination of workers seeking to raise wages, just as a collusive monopoly is a combination of sellers seeking to raise price. On the other hand, an argument could be made for excluding unions on the grounds that "labour is not an article of commerce." By and large, the courts' judgements during this early period did not favour labour.

There were several other reasons why union growth was thwarted during the 1920s and early 1930s. The TLC in Canada (like the AFL in the United States) lost ground because it remained committed to the early principle of ***craft unions***, that is, unions representing workers with a common skill. Craft unions did not appeal to the increasing number of unskilled workers in mass production industries, such as steel and autos. These workers felt that they would be more effectively represented by ***industrial unions*** comprising all workers within a given industry.

A *craft union*, such as a plumbers' or carpenters' union, represents a group of workers having a common skill, regardless of the industry in which they are working.

An *industrial union*, such as the Canadian Auto Workers, draws on all workers in an industry or group of industries, regardless of the workers' specific skills.

Moreover, there was growth in employer resistance to unionism. Employers introduced paternalistic schemes providing labour with relatively generous benefits in an attempt to demonstrate that workers would do better outside a union than in. And, as a result of growing court hostility toward unions, employers were allowed to use injunctions (court orders) to prevent unions from picketing, striking, or pursuing almost any other activity judged threatening to business.

## The Period of Union Growth During and After World War II

In the latter half of the 1930s, union membership grew quickly in the United States. (This was facilitated by several new U.S. laws that improved the climate for unions. In the 1932 Norris-La Guardia Act, yellow-dog contracts were outlawed, and the 1935 Wagner Act firmly declared that workers had the legal right to form unions; it also prohibited employers from certain unfair labour practices, such as firing and blacklisting pro-union workers.)

In contrast, Canadian union membership grew very slowly during the 1930s: Canadian labour legislation remained relatively unchanged during the Depression. It was not until the beginning of World War II that Canadian labour law began to be reformed. In 1939, the Criminal Code was amended so that it became illegal for an employer to dismiss an employee for being a member of a union and later, during the war, the government explicitly recognized the right of workers to organize.

An important landmark in Canadian labour law came at the end of 1945, following a long strike by workers of the Ford Motor Company of Canada over the issue of union security. The strike was ended when an arbitration decision was given by Mr. Justice Ivan Rand of Canada's Supreme Court. In his decision, Mr. Justice Rand spelled out a series of rules that have since become known as the ***Rand Formula***. Specifically, the Rand Formula made it compulsory for all Ford workers to contribute to the union (through a dues check-off system administered by the company), whether or not they belonged to the union. It also required that a government-supervised vote by all employees had to be held before there could be a strike, and specified penalties for illegal strikes during the term of a collective agreement. The Rand Formula set an important precedent on the question of the rights of unions, and various versions of the formula have been used in a large number of collective agreements; in Ontario, it has been incorporated into the province's labour laws.

Apart from the legislative changes strengthening the position of unions, the rapid growth of union membership in Canada and in the United States during the 1940s and early 1950s was also facilitated by the trend toward industrial unions in large sectors, such as the steel and automotive industries. In 1936, several U.S. union leaders, led by John L. Lewis, started this drive by splitting away from the AFL (which continued to concentrate on craft unions) and forming the Congress of Industrial Organizations (the CIO) which was committed instead to industrial unionism.

In Canada, a similar split in the labour movement took place three years later when the TLC (which was affiliated with the AFL) expelled the Canadian branches of the American CIO unions; in 1940, these Canadian branch unions formed the Canadian Congress of Labour (CCL)—the Canadian counterpart of the CIO. While the craft-based TLC and the industrial-based CCL operated as separate organizations until the mid-1950s, the advantages of labour unity gradually made them move closer together and, in 1956, they joined forces in a merger which created the ***Canadian Labour Congress (CLC)***. (In the United States, a merger creating the AFL-CIO had taken place a year earlier.) The CLC now includes most of Canada's large labour unions.

## The Changing Pattern of Unionism Since the 1960s

Following a period of stagnation in the late 1950s and early 1960s, union membership as a percentage of the labour force again grew during the late 1960s and the 1970s, before stabilizing again in the 1980s. The increase in union membership in this period, however, was of a very different kind from the increase that took place in the 1940s and 1950s. In recent decades, the *composition* of Canada's labour unions has changed considerably. Rapid growth has occurred in the ***national unions***, that is, independent Canadian unions. By contrast, membership in the more traditional ***international unions*** (sometimes also called *continental unions*), which are affiliated with American unions, has declined. Part of this decline has occurred because some Canadian affiliates of U.S. unions have broken away to form independent Canadian unions. The most important example of this was in 1986 when a majority of the more than 100,000 members of the Canadian branch of the United Auto Workers voted to go it alone and form the Canadian Auto Workers union (CAW), with Bob White as their leader.

A *national union* is an independent Canadian union with no formal affiliation to unions outside of Canada. An *international union* is a union that is affiliated with a foreign (usually American) union.

Growth in union membership has been particularly fast in the public sector. Since ***public sector unions*** are national unions, this trend is another explanation for the increasing dominance of national unions in Canada in recent years.

An important factor contributing to increasing unionization among government employees was the passage in 1966/67 of the ***Public Service Staff Relations Act***, which gave federal civil servants the right to collective bargaining and the right to strike. Following this legislation, membership in the *Public Service Alliance of Canada* (PSAC) rose steadily, and the majority of federal government employees now belong to the PSAC. Unions representing provincial government employees have also become important as have organizations such as the *Canadian Union of Public Employees* (CUPE, whose members work for public sector institutions such as municipal governments, hospitals, and provincially owned hydro companies) and the *Canadian Union of Postal Workers* (CUPW), which represents the inside postal employees. (The problems raised by public sector labour relations will be further discussed later in this chapter.)

Turning to the relatively slow growth of union membership *outside* the public sector, there are several explanations. First, during the 1960s and 1970s, there was a decrease in the proportion of workers employed in heavy industry (where union membership generally is high) and an increase in the share of employment in the private service sector (where unions traditionally have been less strong). Second, the share in the labour force of women, part-time workers, and young people has been increasing. For various reasons, it may be more difficult to attract workers in these groups to the union movement. Unlike the previous generation of workers, they do not remember the 1930s, when the labour force felt desperately powerless and had to look to the union for protection. Moreover, recent events have made many younger workers less enthusiastic about unions: the corruption and violence in the American union movement, and a number of unpopular strikes in the public sector (such as strikes by postal workers, school teachers, public transit workers, air traffic controllers, and garbage collectors).

The public's negative attitude toward the union movement has been even more evident in the United States than in Canada. American labour legislation after World War II has been amended in ways that make it more difficult for a union to control the labour force in a company. Thus, the 1947 Taft-Hartley Act prohibits strikes due to conflicts between unions over whose members will do specific jobs. It also forbids the "check-off" of union dues unless workers agree to it in writing.

But the most controversial provision of the Taft-Hartley Act is contained in its famous section 14(b). This recognizes state ***right-to-work laws*** based on the principle of an ***open shop***: They forbid compulsory unionism, and thus make the ***closed shop*** and the ***union shop*** illegal. About 20 U.S. states—mostly in the South—have passed such laws. Union leaders considered section 14(b) to be overtly anti-union, and they have worked hard for its repeal.

A *closed shop* means that a firm can hire only workers who are already union members.

A *union shop* permits the hiring of non-union members, but requires those who are not yet members to join the union within a specified period (such as 30 days).

A *right-to-work law* outlaws the closed shop and the union shop in favour of the *open shop* (in which there is no requirement to join a union).

In Canada, existing labour legislation does not attempt to restrict union practices in this way. On the contrary, under the Rand Formula discussed above, one of the provisions is a compulsory check-off system under which all workers are required to contribute financially to the union, and contracts negotiated under the Rand Formula provide for a form of union shop; closed shop contracts are also legal in Canada.

The stronger position of the labour movement in Canada than in the United States is also reflected in the proportion of workers that are unionized. While union membership in Canada has hovered between 30% and 40% of the labour force in the 1980s and early 1990s, in the United States the proportion has declined substantially, falling below one-fifth by the mid-1980s. (Box 16-1 discusses some of the problems the American union movement has been facing in recent decades.)

## LABOUR UNIONS: THE EXERCISE OF MARKET POWER

Since unions are important actors in the process that determines wages and working conditions in many industries, they must be included in any realistic analysis of the labour market. Statistical studies indicate that unions have succeeded in their major task of raising wages. Canadian union members typically earn some 10% to 30% more than non-union workers in comparable activities. However, it has been suggested that some of this higher wage can be explained by the fact that union workers are different; for example, unionized firms are able to hire more productive workers who could be earning a higher wage whether they were in a union or not. This means that, for workers with the same productivity and other characteristics, a union might be able to raise wages by an average of perhaps 15%.[2]

In this section we consider the effects of a union that exercises its market power to raise the wage rate of its members. We also examine what happens when a union bargains to ensure employment for its members.

### The Economic Effects When a Union Negotiates Higher Wages: A First Approximation

We begin by assuming a perfectly competitive labour market, with equilibrium at $E_1$ in Figure 16-2. Employers have no market power and take the wage rate as given. Workers have no market power and also take the wage rate as given.

Now suppose that this industry is unionized—that is, the workers who supply labour form a monopoly (a union) that raises the wage rate from $W_1$ to $W_2$. The enforcement of this higher wage requires "union discipline"; members must not be allowed to offer their labour services for less than $W_2$. Faced with this wage, employers react by moving up their demand curve

[2] See Wayne Simpson, "The Impact of Unions on the Structure of Canadian Wages: An Empirical Analysis with Micro Data," *Canadian Journal of Economics*, vol. 18, 1985, pp. 164–81, and Glenn M. Macdonald, "The Size and Structure of Union-Nonunion Wage Differentials in Canadian Industry," *Canadian Journal of Economics*, vol. 16, 1983, pp. 480–85. For evidence from the United States, see H.G. Lewis, *Union Relative-Wage Effects: a Survey* (Chicago: University of Chicago Press, 1986), Ch. 9; and G. Chowdhury and S. Nickell, "Hourly Earnings in the United States," *Journal of Labor Economics*, January 1985, p. 62.

from $E_1$ to $E_2$. Because the union has raised wages, employment is reduced from $N_1$ to $N_2$.

*Efficiency effect.* There is the standard deadweight efficiency loss shown by the grey triangle. This loss occurs because employment has been reduced from its perfectly competitive, efficient amount at $N_1$ to $N_2$, and displaced workers have had to move to industries where their productivity is lower. (This is the efficiency loss from too little employment described in detail in Figure 15-6(c).)

*Transfer effects.* Capital and other non-labour factors of production lose areas 3 + 4. (You can see this by using the explanation of either Figure 15-4 or 15-7 in the previous chapter. At the initial equilibrium $E_1$, they earned areas 6 + 3 + 4. After the union is formed and equilibrium moves to $E_2$, they earn only area 6, for a net loss of 3 + 4.) Of this loss, 3 is a transfer to the $N_2$ workers who retain their jobs in this industry and enjoy a wage increase of $W_1W_2$. This is the reason they formed a union: to acquire area 3 of income that the owners of capital and other factors of production would otherwise receive. However, while these $N_2$ workers in the industry gain, there is a loss to the $N_2N_1$ workers who would like to work in this industry but who must instead take lower-productivity, lower-wage jobs elsewhere.

In conclusion, we emphasize two important points:

1. In judging that inefficiency results from the unionization of an industry—and from the other labour market changes we examine — we must make assumptions similar to those we made in analysing product markets. For example, we assume that perfectly competitive conditions exist elsewhere in the economy. Moreover, we also keep in mind that, although we can make the statement that the move from $E_1$ to $E_2$ in Figure 16-2 is inefficient, we cannot make the stronger statement that this move has an adverse overall effect, without making some assumption about how the winners and the losers compare in their evaluation of income. Remember: Efficiency is desirable, but it's not the whole story.

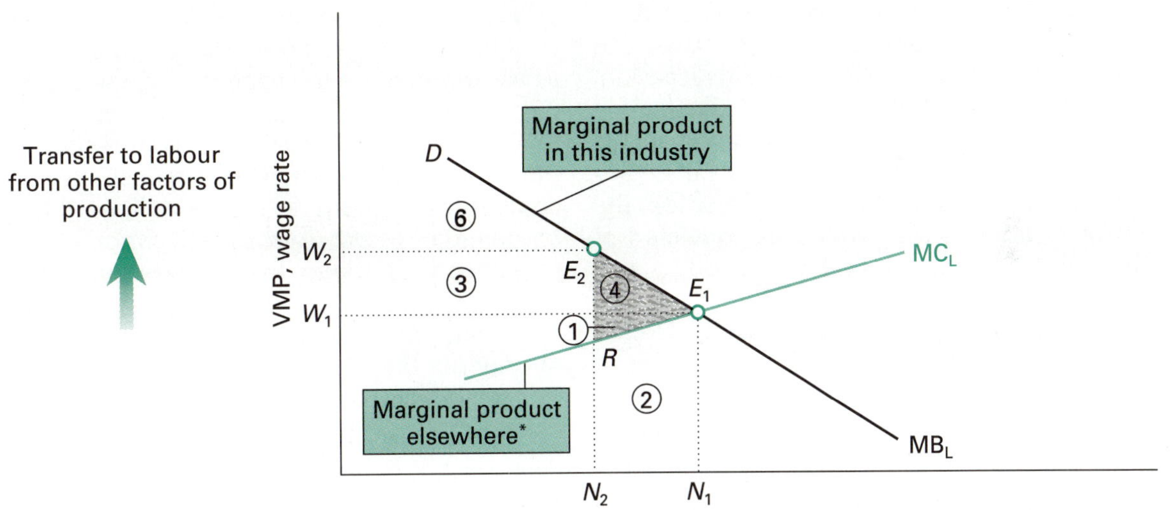


**FIGURE 16-2 The effects of unionizing an industry in a previously competitive labour market.** When a union is formed and raises the wage rate from $W_1$ to $W_2$, equilibrium moves from the perfectly competitive point $E_1$ to $E_2$; that is, employers respond by reducing employment from $N_1$ to $N_2$. The result is the efficiency loss shown by areas 4 + 1. This reflects the fact that $N_2N_1$ workers don't have jobs in this industry where their productivity would be high, as shown by the height of the demand curve *D*; instead they have to take jobs elsewhere with lower productivity, given by the height of the marginal-cost-for-labour curve.* The grey triangular wedge between these two curves is the nation's lost productivity—its efficiency loss.

*If there is a monopoly— in this case a union— then this curve ceases to be a supply curve. (Remember: a monopoly has no supply curve.)

2. Figure 16-2 illustrates once again the similarity of the markets for labour and goods. Specifically, note how the monopolization of a labour market in Figure 16-2 is similar to the monopolization of a product market in Figure 12-6, except, of course, that we are now talking about the wage and employment of labour rather than the price and quantity of a product.[3]

## Job Security

Job security may become the prime objective of a union if employment is shrinking — for example, because of reduced demand for the product, the introduction of labour-saving machines, or the growth of imports. There are three principal ways that a union may try to prevent the loss of jobs. First, it may

[3] There is an important reason we cannot analyse monopoly in a labour market in exactly the same way as we analyse monopoly in a product market. In a product market, a monopoly firm will take into account any loss of sales (reduction in output) that results from its high price. However, in a labour market, it is not clear how fully a union will take into account any reduced employment that results from its high wage. This may be particularly true if the industry is growing and if the high wage does not displace any of the current union members, but instead reduces only the number of new workers coming into the industry. This difficulty prevents us from applying the standard analysis of monopoly to determine precisely how high the union will raise the wage rate.

### APPLICATIONS AND ILLUSTRATIONS — BOX 16-1

### Problems in the American Union Movement

Part of the negative public attitude toward the union movement in the United States stems from a number of well-publicized instances of violence and corruption in major American unions. In the late 1960s, an unsuccessful challenger for the leadership of the United Mine Workers (UMW) was murdered in his sleep, along with his family, after he threatened to expose irregularities in the union; the former leader of the UMW was convicted of arranging the murder, and sentenced to several life terms in jail. In the Teamsters, the largest and most powerful union in the United States, four recent presidents have been in trouble with the law. Three spent time in jail, and charges against the fourth were dropped because he was dying. In 1988, the U.S. government announced that it was taking legal action against the union's leaders because of their ties to organized crime.

A combination of factors increased the pressure on American unions in the 1980s. In August 1981, in response to an illegal strike by air traffic controllers, President Reagan fired the striking workers. In a number of industries, unions have been unable to prevent a decline in real wages. In the airline industry, deregulation has meant a much more competitive environment. To survive, the airline companies have put pressure on employees to accept lower wages. In the construction industry, some unions were forced to accept lower real wages during the severe recession of 1981/82. In autos and steel, the unions made substantial wage concessions in the early 1980s because of intense foreign competition. A number of unions found their bargaining power weakened when firms threatened to move to the less unionized southern states or abroad.

Management opposition to unions became stronger in the 1980s. Some firms threatened to declare bankruptcy in order to escape from existing labour contracts and pay workers less. As an example of how embattled and defensive the unions had become, some of the members of the United Food and Commercial Workers International Union took a 25% cut in hourly wages while others lost their jobs altogether and were replaced by non-union workers at a 50% lower wage. Economic pressures forced a number of unions to accept such two-tiered wage contracts under which new workers could be hired at substantially lower wages than those paid to old workers.

seek protection from import competition by asking the government to impose tariffs or quotas on imports. Second, it may negotiate a reduction in the number of hours in a standard work week; if all workers work fewer hours, no worker need be laid off. (Moreover, if the union is able to negotiate a sufficient increase in the hourly wage rate, its members may not suffer any income reduction; they may work less for the same pay.)

The third way that a strong union may deal with falling employment is to use its bargaining strength to negotiate a ***featherbedding*** agreement. One example was the case of the railroad firemen who had their jobs guaranteed even after coal-burning locomotives were replaced by diesels, which had no fire.

*Featherbedding* is the employment of labour in superfluous jobs.

What is the effect of such superfluous work? The answer is that it generally keeps employment in that industry higher than in a perfectly competitive labour market.[4] Specifically, it keeps the number of jobs at $N_2$ in Figure 15-6(b) rather than allowing it to decrease to the competitive number $N_1$. Moreover, it leads to an efficiency loss which often exceeds the grey triangle shown in that earlier diagram. The reason is that this triangular efficiency loss is based on the assumption that employers use the extra workers they hire as productively as possible. However, many featherbedding contracts require that employers not only hire more workers, but also assign them to tasks with low or even zero productivity. This makes the efficiency loss greater.

Is this criticism of featherbedding too severe? Because it protects workers who might otherwise have difficulty in getting another job, isn't it a way of introducing compassion into the economic system? The answer is yes, but it is a bad way to do it. Far better to ease labour's shift into other jobs than to have society carry an overhead of unproductive employment into the future. One compromise way of negotiating the end to a featherbedding contract is for the company to guarantee that all those individuals now holding jobs will continue to be employed, but they will not be replaced. Although this may be a costly solution, it at least guarantees that the problem will disappear as the present workforce reaches retirement age. This is far superior to a featherbedding contract, where the inefficiency doesn't disappear when people in non-productive jobs retire, because they continue to be replaced. (More on the relation between efficiency and compassion is provided in Box 16-2.)

## HOW UNIONS INCREASE EFFICIENCY: THE OTHER SIDE OF THE COIN

In our analysis so far, we have seen how a union may reduce efficiency by negotiating an increase in wages that reduces employment. But this is only part of the story. A union may also have *favourable* effects on efficiency.

1. Unions can set up grievance procedures; this may improve the morale of the workforce and improve communication between workers and management. This may lead to better decision making.
2. By providing workers with a collective voice, a union makes it possible for them to improve their working conditions rather than quitting.[5] Because unions reduce "quit-rates" and labour turnover, there is less disruption in the workplace.
3. If the labour market is not initially perfectly competitive because market power is held by *employers* on the other side of the market, then, as we shall now show, the formation of a union may be a counterbalance that increases efficiency.

[4] This is not always the case, however. Featherbedding was a contributing factor in the death of some newspapers in the United Kingdom. In particular, some union contracts required that newspapers receiving typeset copy from advertisers had to reset this copy in "bogus" type which was not actually used. Featherbedding, therefore, may have resulted in fewer newspaper jobs even though it may have kept up the number of typesetting jobs.

[5] The fact that unions exist may even lead to an improvement in working conditions in firms that are *not* unionized. These firms may fear that if they don't improve their working conditions, their workers may form a union. The existence of a union may also benefit non-union workers *in the same firm*. Many firms that sign a contract with a union for higher wages pass on the same increase to their non-union labour force. However, the conclusion that unions raise non-union wages is still a subject of debate because, in another respect, unions exert downward pressure on non-union wages: The higher union wage reduces employment in union jobs; this, in turn, increases the number of workers looking for non-union jobs and, consequently, tends to lower wages there.

## APPLICATIONS AND ILLUSTRATIONS BOX 16-2

### The Conflicting Objectives of Compassion and Efficiency

Two centuries ago, at the beginning of the industrial revolution in Britain, labour-saving machinery was introduced into the textile industry. Displaced workers in those days had much bleaker prospects than today: It was harder to find another job. Without a job, a worker's family faced severe malnutrition or worse. Consequently, there were riots in which workers (the Luddites) broke into the factories, destroying the new labour-saving machines. While recognizing their plight, we might ask: Suppose they had succeeded? Suppose labour-saving machinery had been banned, and their primitive handcrafting jobs guaranteed? If they and their heirs had been successful in thwarting technological change, wouldn't our situation today be very much like theirs two centuries ago? And, if so, what progress would we have made against the problem that concerned them most: poverty?

Although labour-saving machinery may create transitional unemployment, it creates far better jobs in the long run. When bulldozers are introduced, whole armies of workers with shovels lose their jobs. But, in the long run, this is highly beneficial both for society and, in most cases, for the workers who initially lose their jobs. This is not only true of the ditchdiggers who get high-productivity and high-paying jobs driving the bulldozers. It is also true of other ditchdiggers who get high-productivity jobs in new, growing industries, such as electronics, aircraft, and so on. These jobs exist because the introduction of bulldozers and other machines increases our ability to produce and, therefore, raises our income and purchasing power. This, in turn, means that we can afford to buy products that did not exist before.

In brief, society benefits because the labour force is engaged in more productive activities than ditchdigging. Because machines now perform many routine jobs, we produce more. The resulting increase in our income allows us to afford more compassion—that is, we are able to insure people against the extremes of poverty that had to be faced in earlier, less productive eras. The point is a simple one. In protecting people against severe economic adversity, it is important not to use methods that thwart progress by locking in inefficiency.

## MONOPSONY: MARKET POWER ON THE EMPLOYERS' SIDE OF THE LABOUR MARKET

Employers typically quote the wage rate they will pay. In doing so, they frequently do not act like perfect competitors who take a market wage as given. Instead, they exercise a degree of market power. In particular, any firm that employs a large fraction of a local labour force will have an influence over the wage rate.

To analyse this situation, we initially assume exactly the same perfectly competitive market that we began with in the previous diagram, with equilibrium at $E_1$ reproduced in Figure 16-3. This time, instead of introducing monopoly (a single seller, in the form of a union) we introduce ***monopsony***—a single buyer, that is, a single employer of labour. What happens if this single employer quotes a lower wage rate, while workers on the other side of the market act as perfect competitors, taking this wage rate as given? Specifically, suppose that the employer quotes a wage $W_2$ below the perfectly competitive wage $W_1$. In response to wage $W_2$, some workers leave this now unattractive industry for other jobs. In other words, they move down their supply curve from $E_1$ to a new equilibrium at $E_2$. The result is the grey triangular efficiency loss, because employment at $N_2$ is less than the perfectly competitive amount at $N_1$. (Details on this move from equilibrium $E_1$ to $E_2$ are given in Box 16-3.)

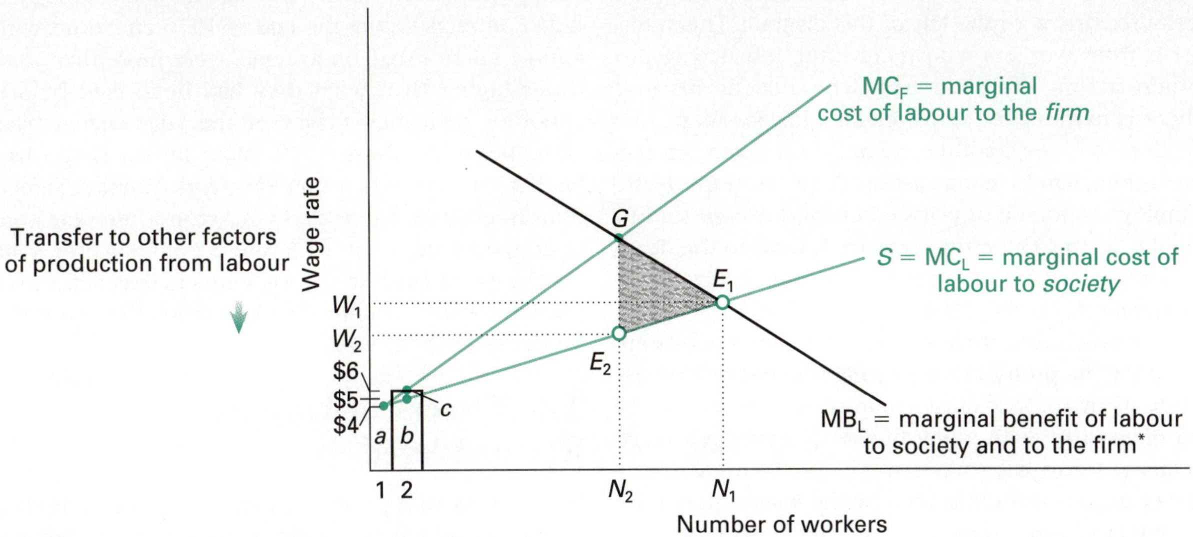


**FIGURE 16-3 Effects when a perfectly competitive labour market is monopsonized.**
When a monopsony is formed, equilibrium moves from the perfectly competitive point $E_1$ to $E_2$.* (Because the monopsonist quotes lower wage $W_2$, fewer workers offer their labour services and employment falls from $N_1$ to $N_2$.) As first explained in Figure 15-6(c), there is the efficiency loss shown by the grey triangle because too few workers are employed in this industry. The lower wage also results in a transfer from labour to other factors of production, as indicated by the coloured arrow on the left.

*If monopsony exists, then $MB_L$ ceases to be a demand curve. (A monopsonist has no demand curve for essentially the same reason that a monopolist has no supply curve.)

## TOOLS AND TECHNIQUES — BOX 16-3

## How Far Does a Monopsonist Try to Reduce the Wage Rate?

To choose the wage rate that will maximize its profits, the monopsony firm first calculates its marginal cost of hiring labour $MC_F$ from the supply of labour *S*. This calculation is illustrated in the lower left-hand corner of Figure 16-3: From the *S* curve we see that the firm must pay $4 an hour at point *a* to hire one worker, and $5 an hour at point *b* to hire two. However, the firm's marginal cost $MC_F$ of hiring the second worker is not $5, but is instead $6: the $5 × 2 = $10 it costs to hire the two workers less the $4 it cost to hire one. Thus, $MC_F$, the marginal cost of labour to the monopsony firm, lies above the supply curve of labour *S*.

To maximize profit, this firm hires labour to the point *G* where its marginal cost of hiring labour $MC_F$ is equal to the marginal benefit it receives from hiring labour. With its desired employment thus being $N_2$, what's the lowest wage it can quote? The answer is $W_2$, which is the point on the *S* curve above $N_2$. At this wage rate, the supply curve *S* indicates that just exactly the desired number of workers ($N_2$) will offer their services to this firm.

Finally, Figure 16-3 provides another view of why an efficiency loss (the grey triangular area) arises from an employment level of $N_2$: The private firm equates the marginal benefit of labour $MB_L$ not to *society's* marginal cost $MC_L$, but instead to its *own* marginal cost $MC_F$. Since the marginal benefit and cost of labour to society are not equated, the solution is not an efficient one.

At the same time, the reduction in the wage paid by the employer results in the transfer shown by the coloured arrow to the left of this diagram. This transfer is from workers who receive the lower wage, to other factors of production who benefit because there is more of the firm's income left for them.

Here we see another example of Adam Smith's "invisible hand" gone astray. The monopsonistic employer's pursuit of private benefit does *not* lead to public benefit. Quite the contrary. It leads to the deadweight efficiency loss shown by the grey triangle in Figure 16-3.

In reality, there are few cases in which monopsony occurs in its pure form with only *one* buyer. There is more likely to be a small group of employers, that is, an *oligopsony* with a few buyers. In quoting a wage rate, each firm has some latitude but, to a greater or lesser degree, it is influenced by the wages quoted by competing firms. On the one hand, competition among these firms may leave each with very little influence over the wage it can quote. In this case, the wage may be close to the competitive level $W_1$. On the other hand, if the few oligopsonists collude, perhaps in some covert way, they may together lower the wage rate well below $W_1$ toward the level $W_2$ that a monopsonist would choose.

Although monopsony rarely occurs in its pure form, with only one buyer, there has been one notable example: the monopsony power that the owners of baseball clubs used to have in buying the services of their players.

## Monopsony and Baseball Salaries

Before 1976, each team in major league baseball was, in effect, a monopsonist with respect to the players on the team: Under the "reserve clause" that was in effect then, a player was not allowed to offer his services to another team except with the consent of his own team. Thus, if a player was not happy with the salary that his team offered, his only option was to retire from the game.

Many players realized that, as monopsony buyers, their clubs were able to pay them a much lower salary than they would have had to pay if they had to compete with other teams who also wanted the player's services (they would pay a salary such as $W_2$ rather than $W_1$ in Figure 16-3). Consequently, the players pushed hard for the right to become "free agents" in certain circumstances, and in 1976, the rules were finally changed to allow this. For a number of players who were able to take advantage of the free-agency rule, it quickly became clear how much the earlier reserve clause had been costing them. For example, six players who became free agents and had signed new contracts before the end of 1976 ended up with annual salaries that, on average, were more than *four times* higher than what they had been paid before. (Another early beneficiary of the rule change was Dave Winfield whose 1979 salary in San Diego had been $350,000. When the New York Yankees signed him in 1980 as a free agent, he won a ten-year contract worth between $1.5 and $2 million per year. Twelve years later, at age 41, Winfield was still a star, playing for the Toronto Blue Jays when they won the World Series in 1992.)

## The Effects of Unions Reconsidered

We are now in a position to show why our criticism of unions, which was valid if markets were initially competitive, is not necessarily justified if there is monopsony power on the other side of the market.

Figure 16-4 shows how a union that pushes up wages can actually raise, rather than lower, economic efficiency. This will occur, for example, if there has been a monopsony firm hiring labour, and this firm has lowered the wage rate from the competitive level $W$ to $W_1$. At this lower wage, fewer workers have been offering their labour services to this industry. Therefore, because of monopsony in this labour market, employment has been reduced from $N$ to $N_1$ — that is, equilibrium has moved from $E$ to $E_1$ — with a consequent efficiency loss of areas 1 + 2. If a union is now formed and raises the wage rate from $W_1$ to $W_2$ — moving the equilibrium from $E_1$ to $E_2$ — the efficiency loss is reduced from areas 1 + 2 to just area 2. In other words, the formation of this union results in an efficiency gain of area 1. Of course, the union also benefits union members by recapturing some of the income previously lost to the monopsonist.

Thus, the following case can be made for unions. When workers form a union in a labour market dominated by a monopsonistic employer quoting a take-it-or-leave-it wage like $W_1$, they send a representative to the bargaining table who can counter by presenting the same sort of take-it-or-leave-it offer to management: "If you do not accept our wage claim, then we will strike your firm, withdrawing all workers from the job and closing down your operations." Thus, the union allows workers to speak from a position of strength, and the wage will then be negotiated between union and management. Typically, it will lie somewhere between the initial "take-it-or-leave-it" offers of the two parties, that is, somewhere between management's take-it-or-leave-it offer of $W_1$ in Figure 16-4, and labour's take-it-or-leave-it demand of, say, $W_3$. Only in this way can labour exercise what John Kenneth Galbraith calls ***countervailing power*** to prevent the wage from being lowered all the way to management's target level of $W_1$. Moreover, if labour is able, through such bargaining, to raise its wage from $W_1$ to, say, $W_2$, it will be promoting not only its own interest, but also the increase of overall economic efficiency.[6] Furthermore, union practices such as picketing are a means of increasing the union's countervailing power by making it more difficult for the employer to hire strike breakers.

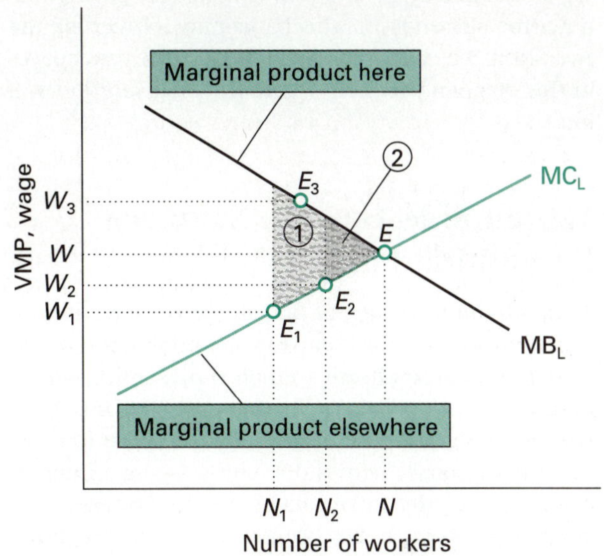


**FIGURE 16-4 How inefficiency may be reduced if a union raises wages in a monopsonized labour market.**

Before the union, the monopsonist set the wage rate at $W_1$; with equilibrium at $E_1$, there was an efficiency loss of 1 + 2. When the union is formed, it raises the wage to $W_2$. Equilibrium moves from $E_1$ to $E_2$, some employment is restored, and the efficiency loss is reduced to area 2. Consequently, the increased wage improves efficiency by area 1. It also transfers income from the monopsonist to labour. But if the union pushes the wage up past the competitive wage $W$—for example, toward $W_3$—equilibrium will be shifted away from $E$ toward $E_3$, and efficiency will be reduced once again.

## A Complication

Such is the case for unions. However, it does not justify every exercise of market power. If a union gets very strong and pushes the wage up beyond $W$ toward $W_3$, equilibrium will shift away from $E$ toward $E_3$ and efficiency will once again be reduced.

Thus, the typical policy problem in the labour market is not that one side has market power and the other does not but, rather, that the relative power of the two may be unbalanced. If the government is pursuing the objective of making labour markets more efficient, it should be careful if it is reducing the bargaining power of one group and not the other. True, if it is reducing the market power of the group already in the stronger position, it will be increasing efficiency. But if it is reducing the market power of the group already in the *weaker* position, it will be reducing efficiency.

This discussion also allows us to sharpen up our earlier conclusion about a minimum wage. If a minimum wage raises the wage rate in Figure 16-4 from an existing very low level like $W_1$ toward the competitive level $W$, employment and efficiency in this labour market are increased rather than decreased. On the other hand, if the minimum wage is set at a higher level and, therefore, raises the wage rate *away from* $W$ and toward $W_3$, employment and efficiency are reduced. Therefore, a useful guideline for a minimum wage is to set it near the competitive wage level in most industries. (This guideline is difficult to put into practice, however, because competitive wage rates are difficult to estimate and are different among industries. Furthermore, the government may be paying little attention to the objective of efficiency if it is concentrating on the redistribution of income instead.)

## BILATERAL MONOPOLY: RELATIVE BARGAINING POWER

When both sides have market power as in Figure 16-4, they push in opposite directions. While the

[6] This is another example of the *theory of the second best*, first encountered in Box 12-1. If there is only a single firm in a small town, it will be able to exercise monopsony influence over the wage rate. The economist's "first-best" efficient solution—with perfect competition on both sides of the market—is simply not possible, no matter how desirable it might be. Instead, we must look for a second-best solution. This may involve workers forming a union in order to influence price and thus counterbalance the power that the monopsonist already enjoys on the other side of the market. In his *American Capitalism: The Concept of Countervailing Power* (Boston: Houghton Mifflin Company, 1952) John Kenneth Galbraith favoured strong unions as a way of balancing employers' power.

employer tries to keep the wage rate down close to $W_1$, the union tries to push it up close to $W_3$. The outcome depends on the bargaining power of the two sides. We cannot tell by looking at the two curves in this diagram precisely where the final solution will be.

## Which Side Has the Stronger Bargaining Position?

To see the importance of bargaining power, suppose that there is only one company in a mining town, and that it faces an ineffective union representing only a minority of the workers. In this case, the company will be in a good position to keep the wage low. On the other hand, if there is one union facing a number of employers, the union may have the stronger bargaining position. It has sometimes been suggested that this used to be the situation in the auto industry — although Ford and GM could scarcely be considered weak bargaining adversaries.

If the Canadian Auto Workers judges that its negotiations with the industry are not proceeding in a satisfactory way, it typically threatens to pull its workers out on strike in one of the auto companies, say, Ford. If it does so, Ford workers on strike will get income support from a union strike fund drawn from contributions by workers in all the auto companies. But the company being struck (Ford) does not get the same sort of support from the other companies in the industry. True, Ford may get moral support from the other firms, but they still go on selling cars and cutting into Ford's market. And therein lies Ford's problem. If it is shut down by a strike and unable to produce cars, it will find that its share of the market is being eroded and that its profits are falling. In fact, a strong union may have the power to drive a company bankrupt — and sometimes this does happen, although not by design.

Workers rightly regard driving a firm out of business as "overkill," since this would destroy their jobs. Consequently, a union is unlikely to pick as its target one of the financially weak companies in an industry. If a firm is already close to bankruptcy, a strike threat may be very ineffective. It may be met only by the resigned observation: "If we agree to your wage demand, we go bankrupt. If we don't and you strike, we go bankrupt. There is nothing we can do." The negotiations may end there. Consequently, the union will select as its target a company that is reasonably sound financially — one that is both able to afford a sizeable wage increase and can be hurt a great deal by a strike without being driven bankrupt.

## STRIKES

The bargaining position of either side can also depend on its ability to outlast the other in a long strike. For example, the credibility of a strike threat by a union depends in part on the size of its strike fund. If this has been depleted by earlier strikes, the union is in a weak position. The company can play a strong hand, making a low offer near $W_1$ and sticking close to it, with the knowledge that the union cannot afford to strike. Another influence that may weaken a union's bargaining position is the existence of widespread unemployment in the economy, which makes workers very uncertain about the alternative jobs they can get, and thus makes them less willing to strike.

On the other hand, a company will be in a weak bargaining position if *it* cannot afford a strike. This may be the case for several reasons:

1. A strike may be very costly to a capital-intensive firm that must face high overhead costs whether or not the strike occurs. An example is an airline with a fleet of very expensive aircraft that would be left idle on the runway.
2. A construction company that has to pay heavy penalties for delay in completing a project may be forced to capitulate to a strike threat by the union. As the city of Montreal discovered in 1967, and Vancouver in 1985, a city that is playing host to a major international event, such as the Olympic Games or an international exhibition (such as Vancouver's Expo 86), is in a particularly vulnerable position in this respect.
3. A strike may cost a firm a lot in terms of lost sales. This may be particularly important in a period of prosperity when the firm has high sales. It may also be important for a firm producing a perishable good or service. Such a firm may be in a weak bargaining position because sales and profits lost during a strike may be lost forever. ("Perishable" is used broadly, applying not only to physically perishable goods, such as fruit, but also to goods that go out of date, such as yesterday's newspaper.)

Of course, firms producing goods that are not perishable are in a much stronger position — especially if these firms have accumulated large inventories and can consequently keep selling right through a strike.

It is no accident that before critical wage negotiations, companies try to build up inventories, just as unions try to build up strike funds.

It is also no surprise that a strike becomes less likely if both sides have been financially weakened by a long and costly strike during the previous contract negotiation.

## The Cost of a Strike

Strikes are costly to both sides: to labour in the form of lost wages, to management in the form of lost sales and profits. To illustrate this, suppose that, in the absence of a strike, the wage is *W* in Figure 16-5, with employment *N*. Then a strike that reduces employment to zero involves a temporary cost in terms of lost output valued at areas 1 + 2. Labour loses income 1—that is, its wage *W* times employment *N*—while the income lost by other factors is the remaining area 2. (Note, however, that both of these losses will eventually disappear if and when labour and other factors get employment elsewhere.)

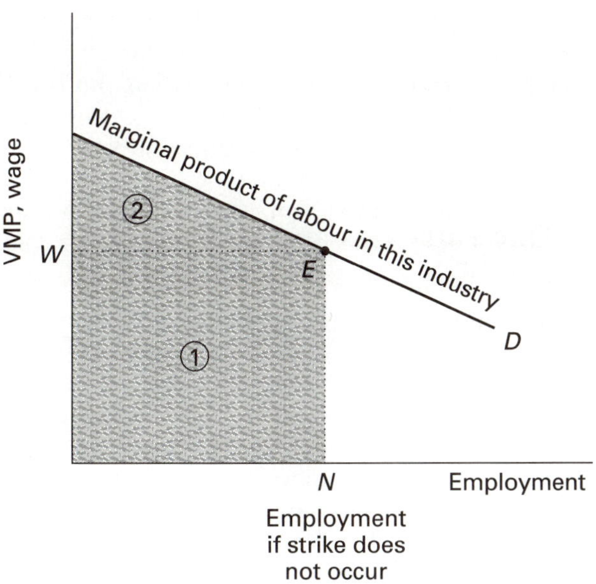


**FIGURE 16-5 Short-run cost of a strike to labour and other factors of production.**

Without a strike, the value of total output in this industry is areas 1 + 2, as first noted in Figure 15-4. Labour earns area 1, and other factors of production earn 2. But if a strike does occur, both these income areas are lost. (The cost may be less if some of the production lost during a strike can be made up after the strike is settled; or if, in anticipation of the strike, the firm is able to increase its output and inventories.)

Since both parties face a substantial loss in the event of a strike, it is often assumed that when a strike does occur, it is the result of an error in judgement by at least one of the conflicting parties. However, this need not be the case, as we will now show.

## Labour-Management Negotiations to Avoid Strikes

Case (a) in Figure 16-6 illustrates the overwhelming majority of situations: Labour and management should be able to find a wage to agree on and thus avoid a strike. The range of wages management is willing to pay (arrow M) and the range of wages labour is willing to take (arrow L) overlap through the shaded range $W_1W_2$. Any wage rate in this positive, shaded "contract zone" is acceptable to both parties. (Remember: The term "wage rate" means total compensation to labour, including fringe benefits and improvements in working conditions.)

The actual negotiations may begin with labour demanding $W_4$ and management offering $W_3$. To the public, it appears that they are far apart and there is little hope of an agreement. However, as the negotiations proceed, both sides compromise—trading off one claim against another. Often, neither party will officially concede anything; this may be viewed as a sign of weakness. Instead, each simply remains silent on a claim made by the other and this "trade" is thereafter mutually recognized. Thus, management "moves up" its arrow M and labour "moves down" its arrow L, until they reach a point of agreement at, say, $W_5$. In settling on this, management's negotiating team claims success; labour has been negotiated all the way down from its original demand of $W_4$. The union is also able to claim success; it has negotiated management all the way up from its original offer of $W_3$.

Most labour negotiations follow this sort of pattern and result in an agreement; a strike is avoided, and there are no stories in the newspapers. The highly publicized cases are those where a strike *does* occur. How does this happen? One answer is shown in panel (b) where L and M do not overlap. There is *no* wage acceptable to both parties, regardless of the negotiating skill they may display. This case will be considered in a moment, but first it is important to explain why a strike may occur even in panel (a) where there *is* a mutually acceptable range of wage rates. Several reasons have been cited.

## 1. Inept Negotiating

One or both of the parties may engage in poor bargaining strategy. For example, suppose that management's initial offer is far below $W_3$ — in fact, so low that it is viewed by labour as an insult. The anger that results may sour the negotiations enough to cause an unnecessary strike. An alternative bargaining error by management may be to make an initial offer that is too generous. Specifically, suppose management initially offers $W_1$, and states that this is its final, best possible offer (which it is; note that $W_1$ is right at the top of arrow M). The problem is that the union leaders may not believe it. They may view it as a standard opening offer and attempt to negotiate it up. When this attempt fails, a strike occurs because wage $W_1$ cannot be accepted by the union. It will look foolish to its members if it has gone through weeks or months of negotiations and has been unable to budge the company. Management seems to have dictated the wage from the beginning, and all that the union has done is to make concessions. Why do the workers need such a union? Thus, although management has been very generous in offering $W_1$, it has inadvertently caused a strike because it has not "played the negotiating game." It has not followed the cardinal rule of "giving the other side a ladder to climb down."

More generally, the problem of inept negotiating has been described by Lloyd Reynolds of Yale University as follows.

> Negotiators may stake out firm positions from which it is later difficult to retreat, may misread the signals from the other side, or may be unable to surmount the tactical difficulties of graceful concession.

While economic forces set the background and help to define the limits $W_1W_2$ within which the negotiated wage will fall, collective bargaining has some of the characteristics of a poker game: The wage negotiated is very much the product of the bargaining skills of the participants. Without minimal skills, there may be no bargain at all.

## 2. Irrationality

To illustrate, a strike may occur if labour is irrational and holds out for a wage of $W_4$ even though it knows that management can't pay more than $W_1$.

## 3. Lack of Information

Even though the negotiators are expert and rational, a strike may still occur because of "***asymmetric information***" — that is, one side knows something the other does not. For example, even though management knows that its best offer is $W_1$, labour may not know this, since it has far less information about how profitable the firm may be. If labour holds out for $W_4$, a strike occurs. Such a strike can also be viewed as a way that one side (or both) acquires information. In this case, when management doesn't accept $W_4$ and the strike continues, labour gains the information that the firm is not as profitable as it seemed to be and, therefore, cannot afford to pay this wage after all.

## 4. Either Side May Want a Strike to Establish Its Credibility.

When one side threatens a strike in future negotiations, the other side will know it is not bluffing if a strike did occur the last time around. Credibility is very important for each side because it may make it possible to get satisfactory settlements in the future simply by threatening to strike (or to let a strike happen), rather than by actually striking. This explains why strikes are less likely if a strike has occurred in the previous contract negotiation. In this case, each side knows that the other is not bluffing, and is prepared to strike (or accept a strike). Each side may also be financially drained from the earlier strike.

## 5. One Party Has an Extraneous Objective.

For example, a company may want a strike as a means of weakening or destroying workers' support for their union. Alternatively, the union may want a strike in the belief that it will improve labour solidarity and morale.

All the above are possible reasons for a strike even though a contract zone does exist, as in panel (a) of Figure 16-6. This then leaves the final reason for a strike.

## 6. A Positive Contract Zone Does Not Exist.

This possibility is illustrated with case (b) in Figure 16-6. Here a strike cannot be avoided, because the positions (arrows) of the two parties do not overlap. On the eve of the strike, there is no wage that is acceptable to both. Each party would rather have a strike than agree to the other side's last offer.

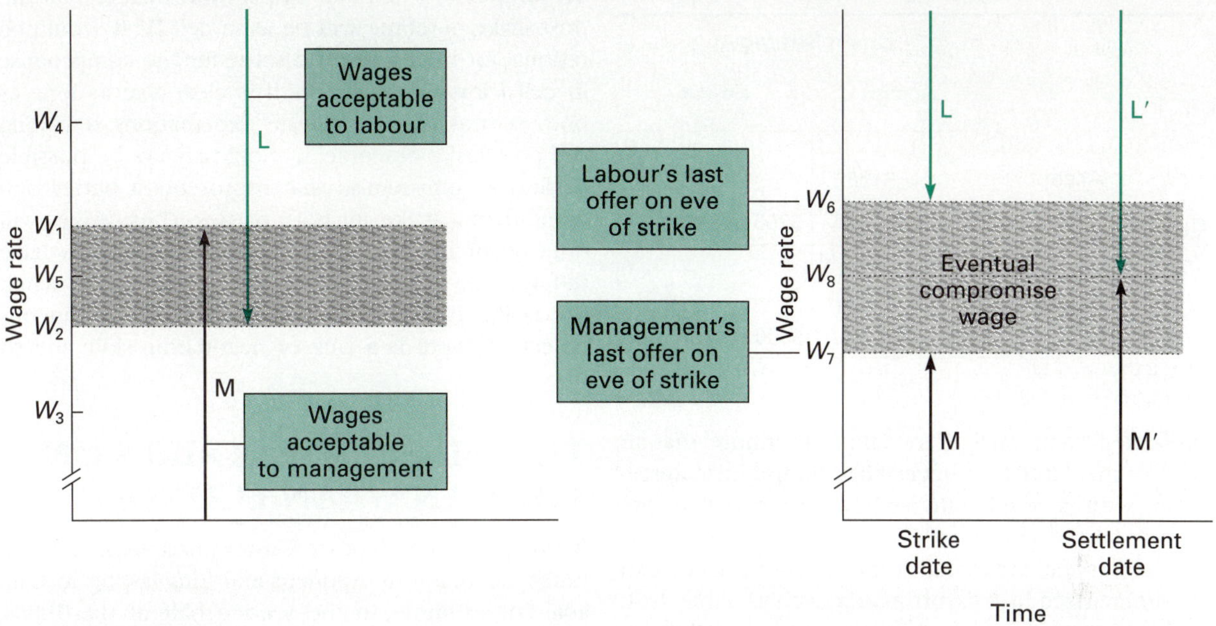


**Case (a): Strike can be avoided (but it may not be).**

**Case (b): Strike cannot be avoided.**

**FIGURE 16-6 Some of the reasons why strikes occur.**
On the eve of the strike (case (b)), management has two choices: settle for $W_6$, or have a strike with an eventual compromise wage like $W_8$. Thus, lowering the eventual wage is the benefit for management from allowing the strike to take place. The question for management is how this compares with the profit lost because of the strike.

Labour's two choices on the eve of the strike are: settle for $W_7$, or have a strike with eventual wage $W_8$. An increased wage is therefore a benefit for labour from allowing the strike to take place. The question for the union is how this compares to the wages lost because of the strike.

However, the longer the strike goes on, the farther the two parties move to the right in this diagram, and the more likely it is that each side will modify its previous strong position — that is, the more likely it is that the two arrows L′ and M′ will approach each other. Workers on the picket lines increasingly feel the financial pinch of lost wages. Similarly, management sees its losses mount. Both recognize that the other does, in fact, mean business. Thus, L′ and M′ eventually meet and the strike is settled, at a compromise wage, such as $W_8$. But, precisely because $W_8$ is a compromise wage, it is more attractive for each side than its opponent's last offer before the strike. Thus, achieving a more attractive wage is an incentive for each side to accept a strike rather than to capitulate to the other on the eve of the strike. (Sometimes, one side "loses a strike," and is forced to settle at or very near the pre-strike offer of the other. In this case, it has made a mistake by not settling earlier.)

## Wage Bargaining and Game Theory

If a strike does occur in a case when there *does* exist a positive contract zone (case (a) in Figure 16-6), both sides are worse off than they would be if an agreement had been reached to settle for a wage somewhere in the contract zone between $W_1$ and $W_2$. Thus in one sense, when a strike occurs, it can be thought of as an outcome that is analogous to what happens in a game like that illustrated by the "prisoner's dilemma" which we discussed in Chapter 13. For example, in the case of the duopoly pricing problem described on pages 270–272, both firms would be better off if they both chose the high price. However, if neither trusts the other, both are likely to choose the lower price, with the result that both are worse off.

To illustrate the similarity between a strike and the prisoner's dilemma, suppose that, in the course of a wage negotiation, management and labour have both

**TABLE 16-1 Payoff Matrix in a Wage Bargaining Game**

| | | Union Strategy | |
|---|---|---|---|
| | | **Accept** | **Reject** |
| Company Strategy | Accept | I: $18/hr.; $1 billion | II: $22/hr.; $200 million |
| | Reject | III: $15/hr.; $1.3 billion | IV: $17/hr.; $600 million |

presented their "final offers" and furthermore, that an outside mediator has suggested a compromise agreement with a wage rate somewhere between the union's and management's offers.

The possible outcomes of the bargaining game can be summarized in a payoff matrix such as Table 16-1. Both sides may accept the compromise (cell I), in which case the wage will be $18/hour and the firm's profits will be $1 billion. Alternatively, the compromise may be rejected. If the union rejects the compromise, management may choose to accept the union's final offer; the outcome then is cell II, with a wage of $22/hour and profits of $200 million. Similarly, cell III shows what happens if management rejects the compromise, and the union accepts the company's final offer. Finally, none of the offers may be accepted, in which case there is a strike. If a strike occurs, there will be a period when workers get no wages, and the company earns no profits. Thus, for example, if the post-strike wage is $17 (that is, just below the compromise wage in cell I), the firm's profits are likely to be lower (profits are $600 million in cell IV, as opposed to $1 billion in cell I).

But even though the payoff matrix in Table 16-1 looks similar to the one used to illustrate the duopoly pricing game in Chapter 13, the two games are, in fact, very different. In particular, the duopoly pricing game (and other games such as the prisoner's dilemma) are examples of games in which the players do not communicate with each other but instead decide independently on what strategies to pursue. Union-management bargaining, on the other hand, is a game in which there *is* communication: The parties get together to negotiate an outcome that is mutually profitable. Thus, while it makes sense to expect the duopolists in Chapter 13 to end up with the low-price, low-profit outcome, it does not make sense to expect the parties to end up with the "strike" outcome in cell IV in Table 16-1 if both believe that the post-strike outcome will be as in cell IV: It would be rational for both parties to settle for the compromise in cell I instead. Moreover, it is clear that as long as both parties have the same expectations regarding the post-strike outcome, it should always be possible to find a compromise that represents a better outcome than a strike, for both parties. Thus, strikes will only occur in cases such as when the parties have different expectations about what will happen when the strike is over; one party has some extraneous objective; there is a lack of negotiating skill; and so on.

## THE IMPACT OF STRIKES ON THE CANADIAN ECONOMY

In comparison with other Western nations, labour disputes are relatively frequent and long-lasting in Canada. For example, in the second half of the 1980s, Canadian workers on average lost more than three times as many working days to strikes as U.S. workers. In relation to the total labour market, however, the number of workers affected by strikes remains small: As a percentage of total time worked, time lost in strikes in recent years has never been more than about one-third of 1% and has averaged less than half that amount. Thus, the average Canadian worker spends less than half a day a year on strike; time lost to industrial disputes has usually been less than time lost due to industrial accidents and illness.[7]

Nevertheless, strikes may be more costly to the economy than these figures suggest. They may result not only in lost output in the industries where the strikes occur but may also inflict ***spillover costs*** on other industries.

### Spillover Costs of a Strike

To illustrate, suppose that when the tire industry is on strike the value of the lost output and income *in that industry* is shown as area 3 in panel (a) of Figure 16-7; this is similar to areas 1 + 2 together in Figure

[7] Wildcat strikes—sudden walkouts by small groups of workers—are relatively uncommon in Canada. However, they are more frequent in some other countries like Britain, where they have contributed to the decline of several important industries. Such strikes can be more disruptive than a full-scale strike that follows a breakdown in union-management contract negotiations. Wildcat strikes may be the result of unions that are too weak to prevent their members from taking actions that harm the workers in the industry as a whole.

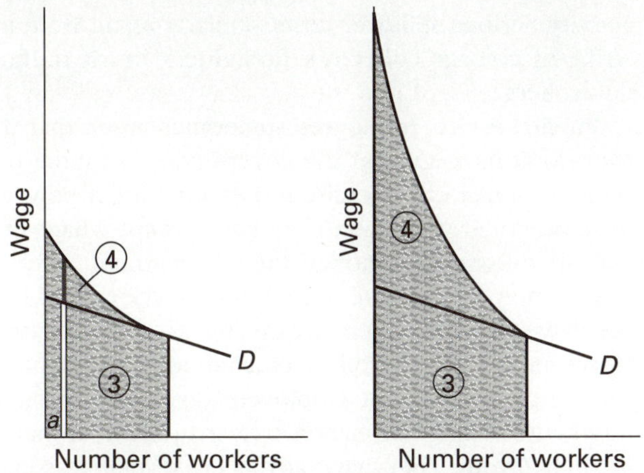


**(a)** When a strike occurs in tire production, area 3 shows the internal cost to the industry—the value of the lost output of tires. Area 4 shows the additional external cost to the public and, in particular, to the auto industry where production is dislocated because tire supplies have dried up. More specifically, the fact that worker *"a"* becomes unemployed means that there is a loss of this individual's output of tires, as shown by the empty bar. However, there is a further cost shown by the dark bar, because of the dislocation in the auto industry, where car production is delayed because of the shortage of tires.

**(b)** If the shortage of tires becomes so severe that auto companies have to lay off workers, area 4 of spillover cost from the strike may be more severe than area 3 of internal cost to the tire industry.

**FIGURE 16-7** **Spillover cost of a strike.**

16-5. But the loss may not end here: As tire supplies are depleted, auto production may be delayed or dislocated. This disruption involves a cost to the auto industry and inconvenience to the car-buying public. Since these are costs that are not incurred by any firm or individual in the tire industry, they are external, spillover costs of the strike and are shown as area 4. In short, if a strike occurs in the industry, it will involve both internal cost 3 to the industry plus external cost 4 elsewhere in the economy.

In panel (b) we see that the situation could be worse. If one or more auto companies are eventually forced to shut down, the value of the lost output in the auto industry and the inconvenience to the public —shown as area 4—may exceed the value of the lost output in the tire industry, shown as area 3.

Other illustrations abound. When mine workers go on an extended strike, the external cost of a coal shortage to electric power stations and their customers may exceed the costs to owners and labour in the mines. In a 1978 strike by engineers and deck officers on the Great Lakes freighters, lost income of the shipping companies represented only a small part of the cost of the strike. Far more important were the losses to Prairie farmers and the mining and steel companies, as wheat exports were halted and iron ore could no longer be shipped on the St. Lawrence Seaway.

Thus, the general public often has a stake in a strike decision in a specific industry. But the public *is not represented* in the negotiations that lead to a strike. Its attitude is often: "While labour and management in this industry are fighting over how area 3 is to be divided, we are losing area 4. Something is very wrong. True, strikes may play a role in resolving disputes by forcing the two sides to compromise. But isn't there some far less damaging way of doing this?"

## Last-resort Procedures to Prevent Strikes

In cases where major negotiations are deadlocked, the federal or provincial government may appoint an impartial outsider (often a judge) to study the situation and suggest a compromise settlement. This is called ***mediation*** or ***conciliation*** — of the conflict. Although mediators cannot make binding recommendations on how the conflicts will be settled, they may be very helpful in resolving disputes for several reasons: A mediator may be able to (1) discover a solution that the two contending parties have overlooked; (2) find out who is bluffing and who is not, thus reducing the risk of a strike because one side has miscalculated the true position of the other; (3) provide a means of saving face for parties that are otherwise locked into highly publicized positions from which there is no graceful retreat. For example, a union can go back to its members and say: "We didn't capitulate to the bosses. We accepted the recommendation of an impartial third party." Thus, the two sides may be able to achieve a settlement because they are able to shift the responsibility (blame) onto the mediator.

A more forceful technique to resolve a dispute is ***arbitration*** with a binding decision by an impartial third party. Conventional arbitration has been criticized because it often leads arbitrators to "split-the-difference," in an attempt to appear impartial. Thus, critics charge, an arbitrator may be less concerned with the objective facts than with finding a decision that both parties will accept and that will thus strengthen the arbitrator's reputation. Another criticism is that knowledge by the two conflicting parties that arbitration can be used can have "chilling" effects on the negotiations leading up to it. Each party becomes reluctant to make any prior concession, since any such concession would automatically reduce its award when the arbitrator eventually "splits the difference."

One solution is ***final-offer arbitration***, under which the arbitrator is forced to accept, without compromise, the final offer of one of the parties. This provides a strong incentive for each party to come up with a reasonable final offer; the more reasonable, the more likely it is to be accepted by the arbitrator. There is some evidence to suggest that in these situations, labour's final offer is accepted at least as often as management's; but there is a smaller average increase in wages than under conventional arbitration. One explanation is that risk-averse unions don't gamble, but make a very reasonable final offer.

Conciliation and arbitration are examples of measures to make it easier for the parties to reach a solution that is better than a strike *for both sides*. Because unions and management usually recognize that it is in their interest to work cooperatively in trying to avoid a strike, arbitration is often used after a voluntary agreement by both sides to abide by the arbitrator's decision. Another, much more drastic, approach is sometimes suggested: ***compulsory arbitration***, whereby the government *forces* both parties to submit their dispute to an arbitrator, who then decides on a binding settlement. Although this seems like a simple solution, it has caused bitterness in countries that have relied extensively on it.

## Disputes Involving Public Service Employees

The most damaging strikes are usually those with large external or spillover costs. These costs — illustrated in panel (b) of Figure 16-7 — tend to be particularly large in the public sector. When transit workers go on strike, area 3 of lost income of these workers and the transit authority is typically far less than area 4 — the spillover cost of tying up the city's economic activity. Serious spillover costs similarly result from a strike of garbage collectors, firefighters, or air traffic controllers.

Public service employees sometimes argue that if they don't have a union, the government as a monopsony employer can exercise too much market power in setting their wage rate. They must accept whatever "take-it-or-leave-it" contract the government offers. Accordingly, as we have seen, public service employees have recently been organizing at a rapid rate. However, critics of public sector unions have argued that, once government employees do form a strong union, the balance of market power tips too strongly in their favour. They have advanced several reasons for this view:

1. Because public servants — such as the police or transit workers — provide essential services, their threat of a strike becomes a very potent weapon. Whereas a strike in the private sector puts pressure on employers to settle because of the income they will lose, a strike in the public sector (in the post office, for example) puts pressure on the employers (the government) because of the votes it may lose from an irate public suffering from the suspension of an essential service.
2. A government may find it easier than a private employer to raise the funds necessary to pay a higher wage. For example, the government may increase taxes, or borrow. Another way to avoid a strike may be to provide a generous increase in pensions, a relatively painless measure because it commits a future — rather than the present — government to pay employees when they retire. Thus, it has appeal to politicians whose major concern is to win the next election.
3. In private industry a strike may drive a firm out of business. Thus, strikers run the risk that their jobs may disappear; this prospect acts as a restraint on labour demands. But there is far less restraint of this kind in the public service. True, a strike may cost the government an election. But this is a serious problem only for the government officials who are voted out of their jobs. It is a far smaller threat to public service workers whose jobs are likely to exist no matter who wins the next election. This puts a public sector union in a strong bargaining position.
4. Public employees and their dependants may become a significant percentage of the voting pop-

ulation. This weakens the resistance of elected officials to their demands.

As noted earlier, Canada's federal and provincial laws allow most government employees to strike. But some (such as hospital workers in some provinces) do not have this right. Moreover, in some countries, including the United States, strikes of public sector workers are generally illegal. But even when such strikes *are* illegal, workers sometimes resort to them. (Workers may also strike in disguised ways, such as reporting in sick or all resigning at the same time.) The question has, therefore, been raised, in Canada and elsewhere, whether all public sector workers *should* have the right to strike.

Many observers have argued that they shouldn't: If garbage collectors go on strike, pollution may threaten public health. If firefighters or the police go on strike, people may die in fires or be victimized by criminals. In the face of such strike threats, a government may feel almost forced to meet labour demands. Surely no group of individuals should hold this sort of power over a country's elected government.

Unfortunately, however, the problem is not quite that simple. If workers are not allowed to strike, they may reasonably demand some other mechanism for achieving a fair wage and for negotiating with the employer about working conditions. One approach used by the federal government to deal with the wage issue has been to provide civil servants with salaries equal to those in comparable private sector jobs. But this provides neither a simple nor a complete solution. One difficulty is the problem of defining what is meant by a "comparable" private sector job. And what downward adjustment, if any, should be made to government salaries because of attractive pensions and greater job security?

## WAGE DIFFERENCES: WHY DO THEY EXIST?

In answering this question, we shall draw together and expand on some of the points made in the last two chapters.

1. First, there may be ***dynamic differentials*** in wage rates. For example, if there is a large increase in the demand for construction workers in Alberta, their wages will rise above wages earned elsewhere; a dynamic differential is created. Eventually, this higher Alberta wage will attract workers from other parts of the country, and the Alberta wage will settle back toward the wage level elsewhere; the dynamic differential declines. Such differentials are only temporary; the speed with which they disappear depends on the mobility of the labour force.

   A *dynamic wage differential* arises because of changing demand or supply conditions in the labour market. It declines over time as labour moves out of jobs with relatively low wages and into those that pay a relatively high wage.

2. Some of the wage differential in Alberta may not disappear over time. For example, wages may remain higher in northern Alberta to compensate for some disadvantage of working there, such as the colder climate. Similar ***compensating wage differentials*** may arise in jobs offering less security or less pleasant working conditions.

   *Compensating wage differentials* result if labour views some jobs as less attractive than others. Employers have to pay a higher wage to fill the unattractive jobs.

   For example, jobs with high stress generally pay higher wages, and repetitive, boring jobs may also pay higher wages. On the other hand, some unpleasant jobs do not carry the higher wage one would expect. Instead, they have a higher turnover rate. This suggests that there may be a pool of available workers who take jobs without realizing they are unpleasant. When they do realize it, they quit.

3. Some wage differences reflect *monopsony or monopoly power*. Thus, workers in a small town facing a monopsony employer may receive a low wage. On the other hand, workers who are exercising market power through a union tend to get higher wages. A particularly high wage may be received by workers who are not only able to exercise market power in their own labour market through a strong union, but who are also employed by a firm with monopoly influence over *its* product market. In the late 1980s, for example, workers at INCO of Sudbury were able to earn a high income not only because of the strength of their union, but also because they worked for a company that was able to earn oligopoly profits in the world market for nickel. In short, this union was able to negotiate wage increases out of INCO's oligopoly profits.

4. The more *capital a firm has per worker*, the more likely it is that workers will be able to negotiate higher wages. For example, the more huge jets an airline has sitting idle at great cost, the more willing it may be to concede a few cents on a labour contract.

The two preceding points provide some explanation of why workers often get a higher wage simply because of the industry they are in. For example, wages are much higher in the chemical industry than in the textile industry. Moreover, this seems to hold true, regardless of the job. Janitors and highly skilled machine operators both earn more if they are in the chemical industry than if they are in textiles.

5. *Barriers to entry*—another departure from perfect competition—may result in wage differentials. For example, long apprenticeship requirements that keep new entrants out of a labour market may keep wages up. Discrimination can depress the wages and salaries of ethnic minorities and women.

6. Some companies use a strategy of paying a higher wage in order to *have their choice of the most productive workers*. If they succeed, their costs may not be higher. However, workers who get a job there do receive a higher income.

7. Finally, wage differences exist because people have different *talents, education, and training*. This is a major topic in the next chapter.

## KEY POINTS

1. Labour markets are often imperfect. Workers form unions to exercise monopoly power on the supply side of the market. On the other side of the market, employers may exercise monopsony power. Examples include a government that hires public service employees and a private firm that is the only major employer in a small town.
2. Unions provide labour with a collective voice. In collective bargaining, unions promote the interests of their workers by pressing for such improvements as (a) better working conditions; (b) seniority rules to protect long-time workers; and (c) higher wages.
3. If a union is formed in a perfectly competitive labour market without externalities and uses its market power to raise the wage rate, then there is an overall efficiency loss. The reason is that some workers are not hired in this industry even though they would be more productive here than elsewhere. Moreover, by raising the wage rate, the union transfers income to labour from other factors of production. On the other side of the market, if employers acquire monopsony power and lower the wage below its perfectly competitive level, there will be the same sort of efficiency loss. But while the efficiency effects of monopoly and monopsony will be similar, their transfer effects will be in opposite directions. When a monopsonist lowers wages, the transfer is *from* labour to other factors of production.
4. If a labour market is already monopsonized by a single employer, it no longer necessarily follows that efficiency will be reduced if a union is formed to raise the wage rate. In fact, if the union's market power is used only to offset the market power of the employer, efficiency can be *increased*.
5. A union may increase efficiency in other ways, too. By providing workers with a collective voice, it may improve their performance and reduce costly turnover of the labour force. A union may increase productivity by improving morale and communication between labour and management. On the other hand, a union may negotiate featherbedding rules, which reduce efficiency.
6. Bilateral monopoly occurs when market power exists on both sides of the labour market: Unions with monopoly power bargain with employers with monopsony power. The wage that results will fall between the high wage an unopposed union would seek and the low wage an unopposed monopsonist would offer. But, within these limits, it is difficult to predict where the wage rate will be set. It will be heavily influenced by the bargaining power of each side. For exam-

ple, a large union strike fund will increase the union's bargaining power, while a large inventory of finished goods will increase the bargaining power of management. Bargaining is also affected by the negotiating expertise of labour and management. An incompetent negotiator who won't provide the other side with a face-saving compromise may prevent an agreement from being reached.

7. Membership in public sector unions has grown rapidly in recent years. Such unions may have a strong bargaining position, particularly if their members provide an essential service. To avoid a strike, a government employer may be willing to tax or borrow to meet a wage claim that would drive a private employer out of business. An important policy issue is whether public sector employees should have the right to strike.

## KEY TERMS

**bilateral monopoly**
**collective bargaining**
**seniority rules**
**co-determination**
**yellow-dog contract**
**craft union**
**industrial union**
**Rand Formula**
**Canadian Labour Congress (CLC)**
**national union**
**international (continental) union**
**public sector unions**
**Public Service Staff Relations Act**
**right-to-work law**
**open shop**
**closed shop**
**union shop**
**featherbedding**
**monopsony**
**countervailing power**
**asymmetric information**
**spillover costs of a strike**
**mediation (conciliation)**
**arbitration**
**final-offer arbitration**
**compulsory arbitration**
**dynamic wage differentials**
**compensating wage differentialss**

## PROBLEMS

16-1. "Monopsony in the labour market may have exactly the same effect on efficiency as a union." Is this possible? Explain. Would the transfer effects be the same in the two cases?

16-2. In Figure 16-4, suppose that the initial wage rate in a unionized labour market is at $W_3$. If employers form a bargaining association and successfully negotiate a lower wage rate, show how efficiency is affected. Consider two cases: What happens if the association negotiates the wage down to $W_2$? Down to $W_1$?

16-3. Using a diagram similar to Figure 16-4, illustrate the effects of minimum wage legislation in a monopsonized labour market.

16-4. (a) Why might a union agree to a two-tiered contract, with a lower wage for new workers, provided the old, higher wage continues for existing workers?

(b) If the lower wage for new workers is equal to the perfectly competitive wage, what will be the effect on efficiency? Why?

(c) Explain how a two-tiered wage may affect the job security of present high-wage workers.

16-5. Use a diagram to show how the theory of the second best applies to labour forming a union in a market that is already monopsonized.

16-6. Consider a single firm with a demand function for labour given by

$$L_d = 10{,}000 - 2W$$

per week, where $W$ denotes the weekly wage. And, consider a union with a weekly supply of labour function to this firm, given by

$$L_s = 3W$$

(a) If the union behaves as a *monopolist* in the provision of labour services while the firm behaves *competitively*, what will be the wage and the level of employment in this market? Show your calculations and indicate your answers on a properly drawn diagram.

(b) If the union behaves *competitively* while the firm behaves as a *monopsonist* in the hiring of labour services, what will be the wage and the level of employment in this market? Show your calculations and indicate your answers on the same diagram as in (a).

(c) If a *bilateral monopoly* were to exist in this labour market, your answers to (a) and (b) would likely determine each side's initial bargaining position in labour negotiations. If it were to prevail, which one would involve the lesser welfare loss to society? Support your answer by calculating the welfare loss attributable to both the union's and the firm's initial bargaining position.

CHAPTER

# 17 OTHER INCOMES

*Buy land. They ain't making any more of the stuff.*
*Will Rogers*

As the economy expanded toward its cyclical peak in 1989, unemployment fell and wages rose: There was a substantial increase in total *labour income*. But, in the late 1980s, there was an even faster increase in the other components of total Canadian income. As business expanded, the *return to capital* rose. Then, as the economy went into a deep recession between 1990 and 1992, production stagnated and unemployment rose. Total labour income declined. The return to capital fell dramatically as interest rates came down and corporate profits plummeted. Because of the recession, world prices of important Canadian export commodities such as metals and forest products also declined, reducing the rents on many natural resources (such as mineral deposits and forest land).

In this chapter, we discuss the factors that determine non-labour incomes. Even though labour income — wages and salaries — account for nearly three-quarters of total income, these other forms of income play a very important part in the economy.

To begin, consider the income to capital, which comes in several forms. First, *interest income* is received by those who provide ***debt capital***; that is, those who lend money to businesses— or to others —to finance the purchase of machinery or the construction of new buildings. (One way to lend a firm money is to buy its bonds. Another way is to lend money to a bank or other financial intermediary which, in turn, lends it out to the firm.) Second, *profits* are earned by those who own ***equity capital***; that is, those who own small businesses outright or who own shares of a corporation's stock. Although the individual who buys stocks and bonds may view them quite differently, in this chapter we emphasize their similarity. Both represent a way in which people can contribute to the expansion of the nation's capital stock and receive income in return.

Income is earned not only on ***physical capital***, such as machinery and buildings, but also on ***human capital***. An example is the human capital you are now accumulating in the form of an education. Your expenditure of time and money today will increase your productivity in the future and hence increase your income. Thus, an investment in human capital is like an investment in a machine or some other form of physical capital: It is an expenditure today that is expected to pay off in the future.

## INTEREST: THE RETURN TO DEBT CAPITAL

To start with, let's suppose that firms finance investment only by borrowing. Borrowing takes place in the *market for loanable funds*, where lenders who supply funds come together with borrowers who demand funds. Like a competitive commodity market, a perfectly competitive market for loans can be studied with supply and demand curves.

### Investment and the Demand for Investable Funds

Figure 17-1 shows the demand curve for loans by firms seeking the funds to finance investment projects—for example, funds to acquire new machinery or to construct new apartment buildings. (Households who take up loans to buy cars or major appli-

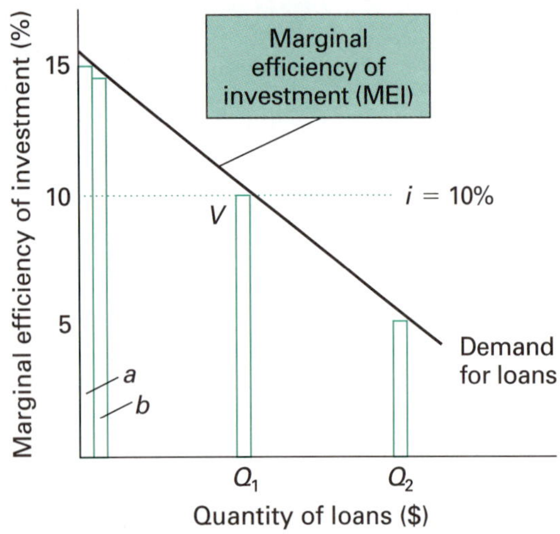


**FIGURE 17-1 The marginal efficiency of investment and the demand for loans.**

Investment opportunities are ranked in order, starting with those yielding the highest return on the left. The resulting MEI schedule is also the demand for loans. For example, if the interest rate is 10%, firms will demand $Q_1$ of loans. They keep borrowing to point *V*, where the marginal benefit of borrowing (the MEI schedule) is equal to the marginal cost of borrowing (the interest rate).

ances also participate in this market, but in this simple introduction we avoid this complication.) Just as the demand for labour depends on the productivity of labour, so does the demand for loans to buy machinery depend on how productive that machinery will be. Specifically, it depends on the ***rate of return*** (expressed as a percentage return on the funds invested) that is expected from the investment. Investing in a particular project will only be profitable if the project's rate of return is higher than the interest rate the firm has to pay on the funds it borrows to finance it. (This rate is sometimes referred to as the firm's *cost of capital.*) Thus, the amount that will be invested will depend on the rate of interest.

Because the demand curve for loans depends on the profitability of investment projects, we refer to it in Figure 17-1 as the ***marginal efficiency of investment*** (MEI) curve. The MEI curve reflects the potential investment projects that can be undertaken, in descending order of profitability. Suppose bar *a* on the far left of Figure 17-1 represents the investment in machinery with the highest return (MEI) of 15%. For example, consider a machine that costs \$100,000 and lasts only one year. If this machine generates enough sales to cover labour, materials, etc., and leave \$115,000 in addition, it provides a rate of return of 15%. Specifically, this \$115,000 repays the firm for its initial \$100,000 investment and provides a \$15,000 return—that is, a 15% return—on this investment.

The next most attractive investment is *b*, which yields a 14.5% return; and so on. The result is the marginal efficiency of investment curve (MEI). This curve also represents the demand for investment loans. For example, if the interest rate is 10%, $Q_1$ of loans will be demanded. Firms will wish to invest in all the high-return opportunities to the left of *V*, but none to the right where the return has fallen below the 10% cost of borrowing money.

Recall from Chapter 15 that firms hire labour services to the point where the marginal revenue product of labour is equal to the price of labour (the wage rate). Similarly, Figure 17-1 shows how firms acquire capital to the point where the marginal efficiency of investment equals the price of capital services (the interest rate).

## Roundabout Production, with Interest as the Reward for Waiting

Investment is often described as ***roundabout*** or ***indirect production***. Rather than using resources today to produce consumer goods directly, society produces an even greater amount of consumer goods *indirectly* by a roundabout method: First, resources are used to produce capital goods, and then this capital is used—together with labour and land—to produce consumer goods.

The greater quantity of consumer goods that is eventually produced in this way is the incentive for undertaking roundabout production. However, roundabout production is not possible unless some people are prepared to defer their consumption today; that is, people must be willing to save. This is necessary in order to release the resources that would otherwise go into producing consumer goods, and allow these resources to produce capital goods instead. For their decision to defer consumption—to wait before enjoying their income — savers receive an interest return. Thus, the interest rate can be viewed as a *reward to savers for waiting*, just as the wage rate is a reward to labour for its time and effort.

To illustrate how consumers decide how much to save out of current income—that is, how much consumption to defer—let's consider the case of a self-employed couple who are planning to retire in 20 years. In Figure 17-2, we measure the couple's consumption in an average pre-retirement year along the horizontal axis; along the vertical axis, we measure their expected annual average consumption in the post-retirement years.

One *possible* choice that the couple could make would be to consume their entire income in each pre-retirement year. If they did that, however, they would find themselves with no accumulated assets at the time of retirement. That is, they would find themselves at a point such as *A* in Figure 17-2: With zero retirement assets, they would not be able to finance *any* post-retirement consumption. (In reality, of course, people without retirement assets will get some funds from government programs such as Old Age Security, social assistance, and so on. For simplicity, we disregard such programs here.) Clearly, this would not be a *wise* choice.

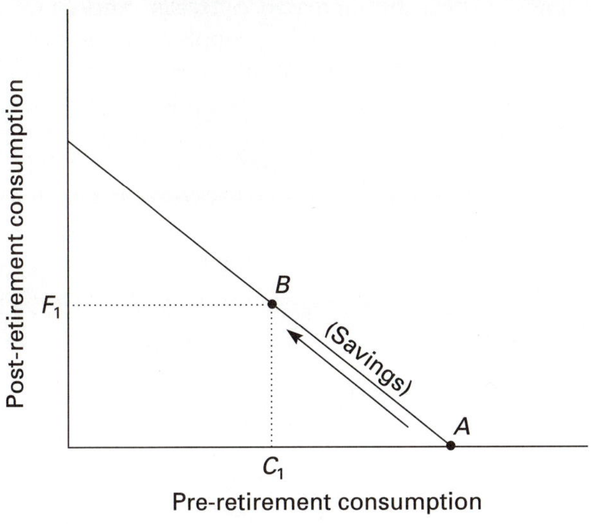


**FIGURE 17-2 The choice between pre-retirement and post-retirement consumption.**

If a family consumes all its income (doesn't save anything) during the years before retirement, it will have no assets out of which to finance consumption after retirement (point *A*). By reducing its consumption in the pre-retirement years (that is, by saving), the family can increase its ability to consume in the post-retirement years. For example, by reducing its pre-retirement consumption from *A* to $C_1$, the family expects to be able to consume an amount of $F_1$ each year after retirement (point *B*).

The slope of the line *AB* depends on the return the family can earn on the assets it saves; that is, on the rate of interest.

Suppose instead that the couple decides to save a portion of their income during each pre-retirement year. By doing so, they would accumulate some assets, which they could then use to finance consumption during retirement. That is, by reducing their pre-retirement consumption (moving to the left in Figure 17-2), they could afford a higher level of post-retirement consumption, moving upward in the figure to a point such as *B*.

Most individuals and families do, of course, save for retirement in some way. The most common method is by belonging to a pension plan at work (where the savings consist of a combination of employer and employee contributions, which otherwise would be part of the worker's take-home pay). Many families also save for retirement by paying off the mortgage on the home they own. This effectively increases their post-retirement income since it reduces the amount they must spend on housing. Finally, many individuals save by voluntarily putting money into Registered Retirement Savings Plans (RRSPs); subject to certain limitations, such savings are tax deductible.

What determines the slope of the line we have drawn between *A* and *B*? The answer: The *rate of interest* (rate of return) that the couple earn on their savings. There are two reasons for this. First, the higher the rate of interest, the faster will be the rate of growth in the value of the assets the couple accumulates through its annual savings, and thus the larger will be the total value of the assets that they will have available at the time of retirement. Second, a higher rate of interest means that the couple can afford a larger level of consumption in their post-retirement years, for a given asset value. For example, many pension plans stipulate that the assets in an employee's pension fund at retirement will be used to purchase an ***annuity*** (from a life insurance company, say) which pays a fixed sum per month as long as the employee (and/or his or her spouse) is alive. The monthly payments under such annuities are larger the higher the rate of interest.

Thus a line such as the one through points *A* and *B* in Figure 17-2 is analogous to the budget lines (first discussed in Chapter 7) that describe the choices that are open to consumers. In this example, they show the combinations of pre-retirement and post-retirement consumption that can be reached by a consumer with a given pre-retirement income.

In general, we would expect the couple in our example to take into account both the utility they expect to enjoy from post-retirement consumption, as well as the reduction they would suffer in utility if they were to reduce their pre-retirement consumption, when they decide how much to save. If we assume, as in Chapter 7, that consumers choose among the alternatives available to them by finding the one yielding the highest level of utility, the best combination in Figure 17-3 will be where the budget line just touches that indifference curve which corresponds to the highest attainable utility level. At this point, the slope of the indifference curve (the *marginal rate of substitution of future consumption for present consumption*) equals the slope of the budget line, and therefore, indirectly, reflects the rate of interest.

We can derive the *supply curve for savings* by seeing how the consumer's choice between present and future consumption changes when the interest rate changes. Consider, for example, the two budget lines in Figure 17-3. $C_0F_1$ with the lesser slope (disregarding the minus sign) corresponds to a lower rate of interest, while $C_0F_2$ corresponds to a higher interest rate. Since $C_0$ represents the consumer's current income, savings is the difference between $C_0$ and the amount of current consumption the consumer chooses. At the lower interest rate (say, $i_0$ in Figure 17-4), savings is distance $C_0C_1$; at the higher rate of interest (say, $i_1$) corresponding to the budget line $C_0F_2$, savings is $C_0C_2$. Thus, measuring savings along the horizontal axis in Figure 17-4, we get points *G* and *H* on the supply curve of savings.

Notice that a relatively high rate of interest (such as $i_1$) can be interpreted to mean that *future consumption has become relatively cheap*: A given amount of savings buys a larger amount of future consumption. But that is the same as saying that the opportunity cost of present consumption has become higher: An additional unit of present consumption means sacrificing a larger amount of *future* consumption when interest rates are high. A supply curve such as *S* reflects this rising opportunity cost. For example, to induce consumers to sacrifice enough present consumption so as to yield savings in the amount of $S_1$, a rate of interest of $i_0$% is sufficient. However, to induce consumers to save $S_2$—that is, to reduce their current consumption by enough to increase savings from $S_1$ to $S_2$—the opportunity cost of present consumption must be increased by raising the interest rate from $i_0$ to $i_1$. Thus, a rising supply curve of savings reflects the rising opportunity cost of sacrificing larger amounts of present consumption.

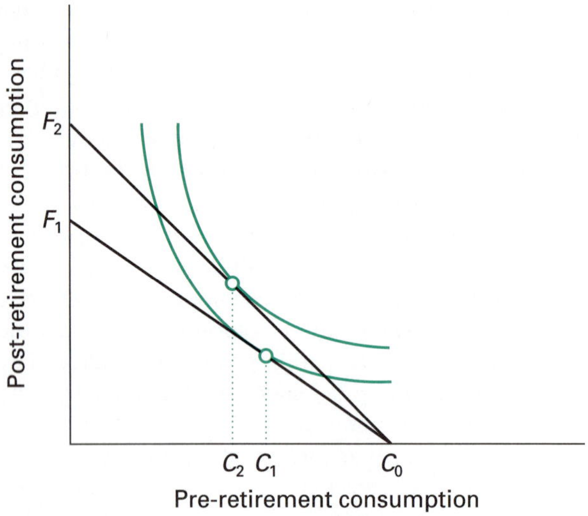


**FIGURE 17-3 The choice between present and future consumption.**
When the rate of interest is low (line $C_0F_1$), the family's utility-maximizing rate of savings is $C_0C_1$. At a higher rate of interest, a given amount of savings results in a larger amount of post-retirement consumption ($C_0F_2$ is steeper than $C_0F_1$). The family now saves the amount $C_0C_2$.

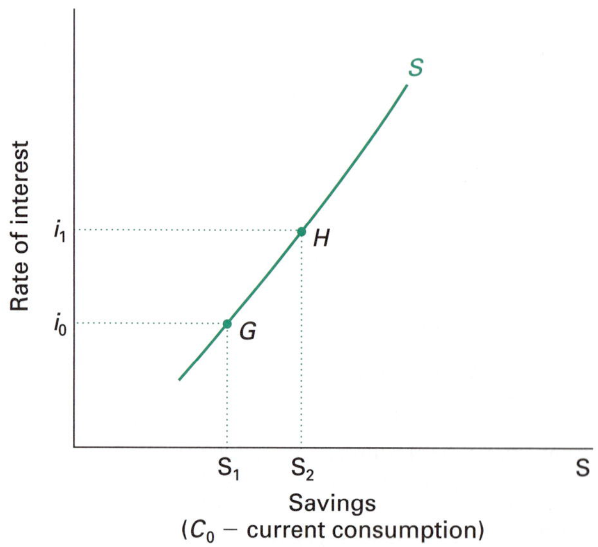


**FIGURE 17-4 Savings and the rate of interest.**
In this figure, $i_0$ and $i_1$ are the rates of interest underlying the curves $C_0F_1$ and $C_0F_2$, respectively, in Figure 17-3. $S_1$ and $S_2$ are the same as $C_0C_1$ and $C_0C_2$, respectively.

In Figure 17-5, the demand for investment (MEI) is reproduced from Figure 17-1, and the supply of funds by lenders is reproduced from Figure 17-4. In a perfectly competitive capital market, equilibrium is at *E*, where demand and supply intersect. In this example, the equilibrium rate of interest is 6%.

It is important to emphasize that this 6% interest rate reflects the height of the demand curve at *E*. In other words, *the marginal efficiency of investment is 6%*. We can take $1 worth of goods today and invest it to produce $1.06 of goods next year. In short, by investing in capital, we can convert present goods into a larger amount of future goods.

**Through investment, present goods can be *exchanged for* a larger amount of future goods. Thus, present goods are *worth more* than future goods, with the interest rate telling us how much more.**

## Risk and Other Influences on the Interest Rate

Although there is only one interest rate shown in Figure 17-5, in fact, there are many rates of interest. A very large and financially sound corporation will be able to borrow funds at a low interest rate, since lenders view this loan as relatively risk-free. But a company in shaky financial condition will have to pay a higher interest rate to compensate lenders for the greater risk that the loan will not be repaid. Thus, the interest rate shown in Figure 17-5 may be viewed as the ***base rate of interest*** that applies to a risk-free loan; as such, it is the best simple measure of the marginal efficiency of investment. Even though we continue to concentrate on this base rate, we should keep in mind that in reality there is a whole array of interest rates on loans of varying degrees of risk. Moreover, as will be discussed below, some of the return to capital comes in the form of dividends and capital gains on funds that individuals have invested in the stock market. *On average*, the return to such funds is higher than the returns on safer assets such as bonds. To a large extent, this reflects the much greater risk that is incurred when savings are held in this form.

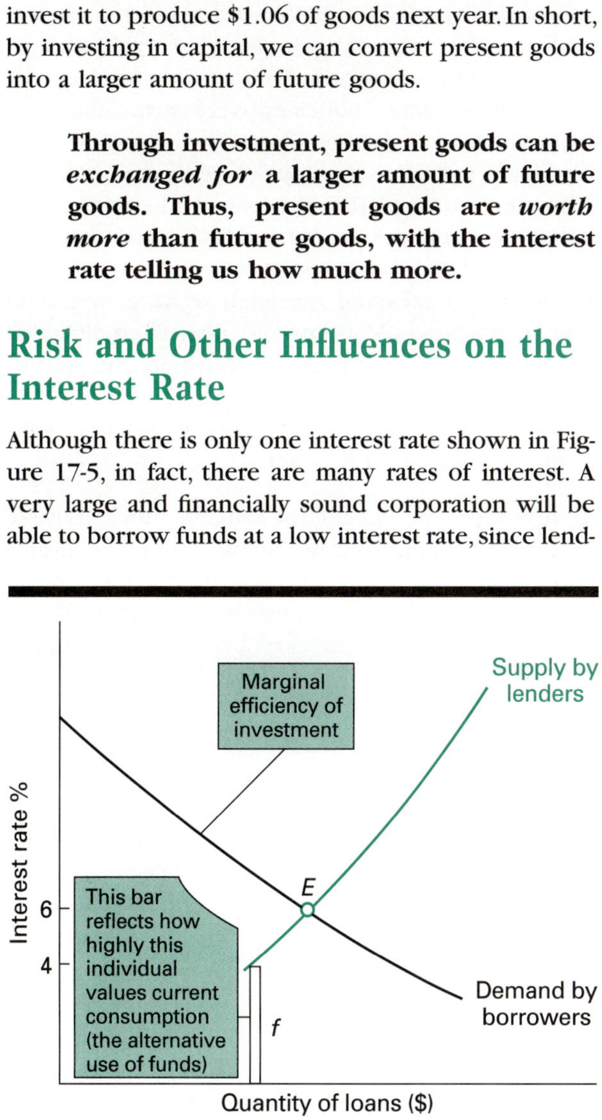


**FIGURE 17-5 The market for loans.**
The demand for loans is reproduced from Figure 17-1. It reflects the marginal efficiency of investment. The supply of loans depends on how highly lenders value money in its alternative use—current consumption. The equilibrium is at *E* with a 6% interest rate.

Interest rates also reflect the *expectation of inflation.* (This macroeconomic issue is dealt with in Chapter 16 in the *Macroeconomics* volume that forms a companion to this book. For simplicity, in this microeconomic analysis we describe a non-inflationary world.) In addition, interest rates today depend on the *length of term of the loans* and the *expectation of future changes in interest rates.* For example, suppose short-term interest rates today are low, but are expected to rise starting from next year because of an increase in the demand for loans by business. In this case, lenders will not be willing to make long-term loans (for, say, five or ten years) unless the interest rates they receive on these loans are considerably higher than today's short-term rates. Therefore, the expectation of a *future* change in interest rates will change the relationship between short-term and long-term interest rates *today.*

As we have seen in earlier chapters, an important question in product or labour markets is: What happens if the government intervenes to impose some restriction? This is also an important question in the capital market—that is, in the market for loans.

## Effects of an Interest Rate Ceiling

Figure 17-6 shows what happens in a perfectly competitive capital market when the government imposes a ceiling on the interest rate that can be charged by banks. Original equilibrium before the imposition of a ceiling is shown at *E*, with the interest rate at $i_1$. When the government sets a ceiling below this rate, say at $i_2$, the market no longer clears. There

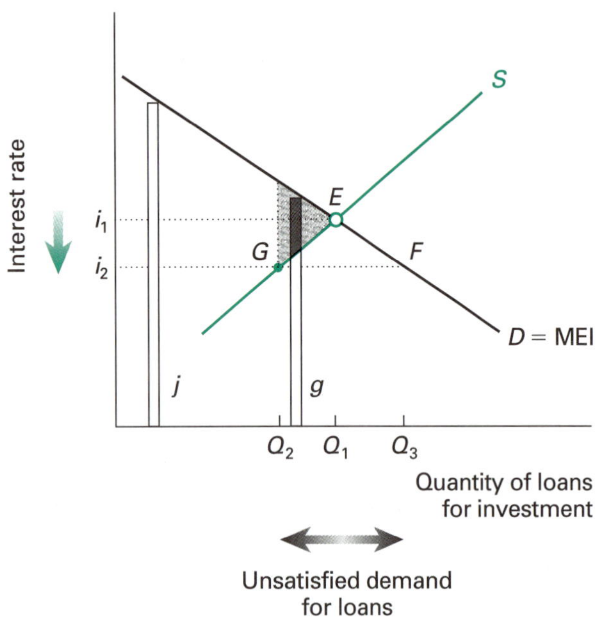


**FIGURE 17-6 Effects of an interest rate ceiling.** Before the interest rate ceiling, equilibrium in this competitive capital market is at $E$, with $Q_1$ of investment funds loaned out at interest rate $i_1$. When a ceiling of $i_2$ is imposed, borrowers are attracted by the lower rate and seek $Q_3$ loans; that is, borrowers try to move down their demand curve from $E$ to $F$. However, only $Q_2$ of loans are available because lenders, discouraged by the reduced interest return, move down their supply curve from $E$ to $G$. Thus, equilibrium shifts from $E$ to $G$, loans are reduced from $Q_1$ to $Q_2$, and there is $Q_2Q_3$ unsatisfied demand for loans. There is an efficiency loss because economically justified investment projects such as $g$ in the range $Q_2Q_1$ are "knocked out"—they cannot be undertaken because of lack of funds. This is a loss because the cost of project $g$ would have been only the hollow bar under the supply curve (the cost to the lender of having to reduce consumption), while the benefit of project $g$ would have been the hollow bar plus the solid bar under the demand curve (that is, the return on this investment). Thus, the net loss because this particular project is cancelled is the solid bar. The efficiency loss from all such cancelled projects in the relevant range $Q_2Q_1$ is the grey triangle.

The arrow on the left shows the transfer from lenders to those borrowers lucky enough to get the bargain funds.

is a shortage of funds of *GF*. Unsatisfied borrowers cannot find loans.

One of the arguments in favour of an interest rate ceiling is that it will reduce the burden of interest payments that must be paid by relatively poor individuals and small firms. The lower interest rate does result in a transfer from lenders to borrowers—*but only to those borrowers lucky enough to get loans.* (This transfer is shown by the wide arrow on the left.) However, there is no guarantee that this redistribution will "help the poor" since they are the ones who are most likely to be turned down when seeking a loan. If you had \$100,000 to lend out and there were many people who wanted to borrow it from you, would you lend it to the wealthy or to the poor? Thus, it is often the rich who get the bargain loans to finance their big homes and business ventures. (In the early 1990s, some politicians were advocating controls on the interest rates charged by banks and other financial institutions on unpaid credit card balances. However, one argument that was made *against* this proposal was that it would not help those with low incomes: If financial institutions were forced to reduce these rates, the argument went, people with low incomes would simply be denied credit cards, forcing them to raise funds in other, more expensive ways, or go without credit altogether.)

Moreover, an interest rate ceiling has two unfavourable effects on efficiency.

1. It reduces the quantity of loanable funds available for investment from the initial, perfectly competitive amount $Q_1$ to the smaller quantity $Q_2$. As expected, the result is a now-familiar grey triangle, showing the efficiency loss because there are too few investment funds available. This is detailed in the caption to Figure 17-6.
2. Not only is there an efficiency loss because the quantity of investment funds is reduced; *in addition*, there may be a loss because the wrong borrowers may get the funds. Because the interest rate ceiling makes the demand for loans $Q_3$ greater than the supply $Q_2$, the limited supply must be ***rationed*** in some way. Whatever rationing method lenders may use, there will be a second efficiency loss unless the $Q_2$ of available funds is rationed out to exactly the right set of borrowers—that is, those borrowers such as $j$ to the left of $Q_2$, who have the investment projects with the highest productivity (MEI). In other words, the projects that are knocked out must be the low-productivity ones such as $g$ in the range $Q_2Q_1$. But suppose this isn't the case. Suppose, for example, that high-productivity project $j$ on the left is the one that is knocked out, not $g$. (The promoter of $g$ may have been able to borrow by being more persuasive to a lender who is rationing loans.)

There is now a second efficiency loss, because an even more productive investment (*j* rather than *g*) is knocked out. (Moreover, as illustrated in problem 17-1(b), this rationing inefficiency may be even worse, since there are now borrowers with even less productive projects in the range $Q_1Q_3$ who now, for the first time, apply for loans, and it's possible some may get them. If they do, higher productivity investments will lose out. Why do these borrowers apply, when they didn't originally? The answer is that the artificially lower interest rate has made their projects profitable for the first time.)

This second source of inefficiency — above and beyond the grey triangle in Figure 17-6—may be summarized as follows. In an unrestricted, perfectly competitive capital market, the interest rate is a price that allocates funds to the most productive investment projects. When the government intervenes to set an interest rate ceiling, some other allocating device must be used, and there is then a risk that the wrong set of projects will get the funds.

We emphasize that this is just another illustration of the general problem that applies to *any* form of price-fixing, such as our earlier example of rent control. Not only does rent control result in fewer apartments for rent but, in addition, the "wrong" people may get the apartments. For example, a retired couple may continue to hang on to a choice Toronto apartment even though they now spend nine months a year in Florida and would give up the apartment if they had to pay the higher free-market rent.

Returning to the interest rate ceiling, we once again conclude: If we wish to transfer income from the rich to the poor, changing a market price like the interest rate may be an unwise way to do it. In the first place, an interest rate ceiling may be an ineffective form of transfer because it may not move income from the rich to the poor at all. Instead, it may benefit the rich who get the scarce loans, and hurt the poor who don't. Moreover, an interest rate ceiling may have damaging effects on efficiency. Isn't it better for the government to do any transferring directly, by taxing the rich and subsidizing the poor? The answer is yes, *provided* the government can do so without incurring large efficiency losses of a different sort — an issue to be discussed in Chapter 24.

## NORMAL PROFIT: A RETURN TO EQUITY CAPITAL

Thus far, we have assumed that all investment projects are financed by borrowing. Now let's broaden our analysis to include "equity finance" — that is, funds a firm raises by selling its stock (or by retaining some of its earnings). When a firm sells its stock, those who buy it obtain a share of the ownership and future profits of the firm.

In Chapters 9 and 10, we drew a distinction between two kinds of profit. First, ***normal profit*** reflects opportunity cost — the return necessary to induce and hold funds in one activity rather than another. Second, ***above-normal profit*** is any additional return beyond this. We defer discussion of above-normal profit to a later section; for now we concentrate on normal profit.

For those who provide equity funds, what is their normal profit? That is, what is the opportunity cost of these funds? The answer is: the return the funds could earn in their best alternative use. An alternative to buying stock is to buy interest-bearing securities. Thus, normal profit can be viewed as the base rate of interest plus an appropriate premium for risk—a risk that may be substantial because the entire amount that is put into the ownership of a firm may be wiped out. (Profit is sometimes described as a reward for risk taking. However, it is more than this, since it must also include a base rate of return needed to attract funds away from interest-bearing alternatives.)

Figure 17-5 can now be recast in the more general form shown in Figure 17-7, which represents the total market for investment funds. Now *D* includes the total demand by business for investment funds, whether these funds are raised by borrowing or by the sale of stock; and *S* is the corresponding supply. The resulting equilibrium *Q* is the quantity of both debt and equity funds provided by savers to those who invest.

## THE ROLE OF FACTOR PRICES

We have examined the pricing of two factors of production — labour and capital. We now pause to consider how factor prices influence both the individual firm's decisions on using these factors and their allocation across the economy as a whole.

### How Factor Prices Influence Decisions by Individual Firms

In its decision making, a firm must address several issues. On the one hand, it must decide on how much labour and how much capital equipment it will use. At the same time, it must decide which goods to produce and how much of each. To illustrate, suppose

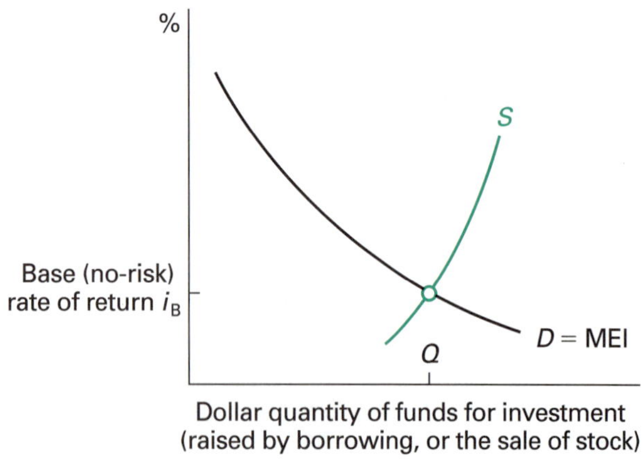


**FIGURE 17-7 The market for investment funds (a generalization of Figure 17-5).**
Whereas Figure 17-5 showed only borrowing, this diagram shows two ways that business may raise funds: by borrowing or by equity finance (the sale of stock). *D* is the demand for funds—in either debt or equity form—to finance new investment, while *S* is the corresponding supply of funds. In equilibrium, the base rate of return, in the absence of risk, would be $i_B$. However, in a risky world, the return any specific business must actually pay for the funds it raises will be $i_B$ plus an appropriate amount to compensate the lender for risk.

the wage rate rises. The firm responds by using less labour and more capital; that is, it ***substitutes*** capital for labour because labour has become more expensive. Moreover, because of the higher wage, the firm may also reduce the output of its final products, especially those requiring a great deal of labour.

As a further example of how factor and product decisions are interrelated, suppose there is an increase in the price of one of the firm's products. In response, the firm will increase its output of this good by hiring more factors of production and/or by shifting production away from one of its other outputs. In short, the firm's decisions on what to produce and the amount of factors to employ are not separate decisions. Instead, they are all *elements of one overall decision*.

### How Factor Prices Influence the Allocation of Scarce Resources Throughout the Economy

Just as price acts as the screening mechanism for deciding who will consume a good and who will not (Figure 11-9), so a factor price acts as a screening device to determine how a scarce resource will be used. For example, the wage rate acts as a screen to determine the particular activities in which society's scarce labour will be employed. In a competitive, fully employed economy, the wage rate rises as productivity increases. This conveys a clear message to those producers who can no longer afford the higher wage. The message is: Society can no longer afford to have its scarce labour employed in your activity. There are now too many other, more productive pursuits. This may seem harsh, but it is the sign of economic progress. Think back, for a moment, to all the things that labour used to do, but no longer does. At our current high wage rates, it doesn't pay to hire workers to hoe field corn anymore, as in the "good old days." Household servants have almost vanished.

Similarly, we have seen how the interest rate is a market price that acts as a screen to determine in which particular projects investment will take place. When that screening device is replaced by another—such as the rationing that occurs when an interest rate ceiling is imposed — investment funds are unlikely to go to the most productive projects.

## THE RETURN TO HUMAN CAPITAL

Income is earned not only by investment in machinery and other physical capital, but also by investment in *human capital*—the acquisition of skills, training, and education.[1]

Our investment in human capital is very large, probably exceeding the nation's investment in physical capital, such as machinery. Improving the machinery in our heads is more important than improving the machinery in our factories!

In many essential respects, an investment in human capital is similar to an investment in physical capital: Current consumption is reduced in the expectation

[1] For a sample of early work in this field, see G.S. Becker, *Human Capital: A Theoretical and Empirical Analysis, with Special Reference to Education*, 2nd ed. (New York: National Bureau of Economic Research, 1975), and Jacob Mincer, *Schooling, Experience and Earnings* (New York: National Bureau of Economic Research, 1974). For a survey of more recent research on the value of an education, see R.J. Willis, "Wage Determinants: A Survey and Reinterpretation of Human Capital Earnings Functions," in O.C. Ashenfelter and R. Layard, eds., *Handbook of Labor Economics* (Amsterdam: North Holland Press, 1985). An early Canadian work on human capital is Bruce Wilkinson's *Studies in the Economics of Education* (Ottawa: Department of Labour, 1965).

of higher future income and consumption. For example, students give up the income they could make if they were not busy studying; they live frugally in the hope that the education will pay off in higher income after graduation. Similarly, apprentices may be willing to work for abnormally low wages if they are receiving training that is likely to lead to a better job.

By recognizing the importance of human capital, we recognize that everyone in the labour force is not equally productive; we are relaxing our earlier assumption that all workers are similar. In fact, the quality of labour depends on the amount of education, skill, and experience that various individuals have acquired. Some have a lot of human capital, others very little. Frequently, their incomes reflect this. This means that when we say that three-quarters of Canadian national income is paid in the form of wages and salaries, we should recognize that this includes not only a basic payment for the time and effort of unskilled labour, but also a return on the human capital that skilled workers have acquired.

Who pays for the investment in human capital? In the case of education, much of the investment is undertaken by the individuals who spend their time studying instead of earning an income. However, governments also invest: Federal, provincial, and local governments all help to finance education. One justification for these expenditures is that it is only fair to provide educational opportunity for all. Another is that education provides not only a benefit to those who acquire it, but spillover benefits to others in society as well. For example, if a highly educated doctor discovers a new vaccine, it may not only increase the discoverer's own income, but will also benefit the public, which now has protection from a disease. In the face of such spillover benefits, the unaided free market may not provide enough investment in human capital, so the government also contributes.

On-the-job apprenticeship or training in industry also represents an investment in human capital. There are several ways the initial cost of this investment may be covered. For example, workers may accept a low wage during the apprenticeship period when their productivity is still low. However, as noted earlier, the possibility of using this arrangement is limited by the minimum wage laws. Alternatively, employers may pay apprentices a standard wage and thereby bear the initial costs of this investment. But this option raises a serious problem for employers, since they are investing in an asset—in the form of skill or training— that they do not own. Workers are not slaves, and they can always quit and go to work elsewhere, taking the training with them. (Of course, the ease with which they can do so depends on how specific their expertise is to the company that trained them.) This is another reason why there may be underinvestment in human capital: Employers may not invest as heavily in training programs as they would if workers would guarantee to stay on the job and thus allow employers to "get their money back."

## The Return on Human Capital: What Is a University Education Worth?

Suppose we wish to calculate a percentage rate of return on a human investment such as a university degree. This can be done in much the same way as we would calculate a percentage rate of return on a physical investment such as machinery: The initial costs are compared with the eventual payoff, in the form of a higher income. Figure 17-8 shows a hypothetical income pattern for those with a university degree and those with only a high-school education.

What is the cost of a university education? First, there is the income forgone during the actual period of study. This cost can be visualized as a set of arrows such as *a*, one for each year spent at university. But that's not the only sacrifice students make. Even after their education is complete, their average incomes at first are below the incomes of people without a degree who have four years of experience and seniority instead. This cost to university students is the set of arrows such as *b*. However, this income disadvantage of university graduates disappears fairly quickly. By point *F* in their late twenties they have caught up. Arrow *c* shows that by their late thirties they have gone well ahead—and they stay ahead.

Thus, the costs and benefits of a university education can be summed up as follows:

1. The *costs* include both (a) the income forgone during university and the later "catch-up period," shown as the grey area in Figure 17-8, and (b) a set of costs not shown in this diagram, including tuition and any higher costs of living in university residence than elsewhere.
2. The *benefits* are in the form of a higher income later, as shown by the coloured area.

By comparing these initial costs and eventual benefits, we can calculate a percentage return on a university education (an investment in human capital) in much the same way as we earlier estimated the percentage return on physical capital, such as machinery.

However, such calculations raise problems. For example, is it reasonable to claim that the higher income of graduates—shown by the coloured area in Figure 17-8—is all due to their university education? The answer is no. One reason for their higher earnings is that they are, on average, more talented and hardworking; they aren't dropouts. Thus, even without a university education, they would still earn more, on average. Accordingly, one task is to sort out how much of their higher income should be attributed to their education, and how much to their greater talent and perseverance. A second difficulty is that the *private* rate of return to the individual acquiring an education is not the same as the *social* rate of return to the nation as a whole. (For adjustments in the private rate necessary to derive the social rate, see Box 17-1.)

American studies that have attempted to take this complication into account found private returns to an undergraduate degree of 8%–10%, with social returns probably being somewhat lower. Because the costs of post-secondary education are more heavily subsidized in Canada, the gap between the social and private returns is probably wider in Canada than in the United States.

Thus, we see that education is indeed an investment; costs incurred in acquiring an education today do yield a return in terms of higher income in the future. This is particularly true of a high-school education, which traditionally has had a higher return than a university education. Moreover, a high-school education is a relatively good investment in another sense: It yields returns that are favourable relative to returns to physical capital. Thus, if you wish, you could view your high-school education purely and simply as an investment; it needs no further justification.

While a university education may also be viewed as an investment, part of its justification may also lie in its other benefits in the form of "consumption" gains. For example, a university education provides many individuals with a greater appreciation of history and literature. One might also consider the psychological benefits that well-educated people receive because they have more interesting and challenging jobs. To illustrate: Even if the income were the same, it would be more interesting and pleasant to design a bridge than to pour the cement. Then, too, jobs may come with what the British call "perks" (perquisites). For example, expense-paid business trips are often

## TOOLS AND TECHNIQUES — BOX 17-1
## Why Private and Social Returns on Education Differ

To estimate the social return to investment in higher education, the estimated private rate of return should ideally be adjusted as follows:

1. Adjust it upward to take account of any external benefits, such as the spillover benefit from the education of the doctor who discovers a new vaccine.
2. Adjust it downward to take account of government subsidies to higher education. These are costs of the investment to society but not to the private individuals being educated. Because private individuals do not take these costs into account, they are not included in the calculation of private rates of return.

There are other reasons why private and social rates of return may differ. Employers pay university graduates more, not only because education has made them more productive but also because it has given them a "credential." In other words, education acts as a *screening device* that tells employers which individuals have the capacity and diligence to learn. Because it gives graduates the best jobs, it provides them with a private return in the form of a higher income. But what benefit to society overall is provided by such a mechanism that gives the best jobs to one group rather than another? The traditional answer has been: Very little. However, it may be argued that there is some social benefit to screening because it tends to match up the more talented people with the best jobs. If there were no university screening mechanism, it would take longer for these jobs and people to "find" each other, with some output and income being lost during this period.

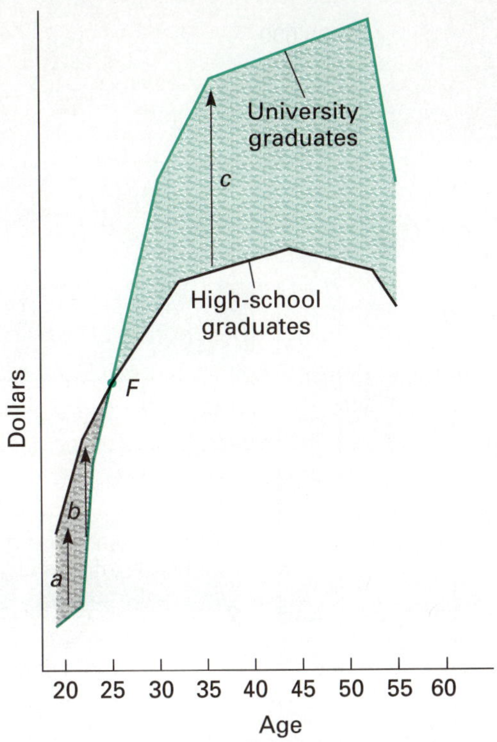


**FIGURE 17-8 Typical lifetime profiles of income, with and without a university education.**

Hypothetical earnings over the life cycle for high-school graduates and university graduates.

fun. On the other hand, those at the top often work hard, under great pressure.

## The Complex Nature of Wages and Salaries

In the preceding section, we have seen some of the reasons an individual's wage or salary may reflect far more than just a basic wage rate. For example, an individual's income may be higher because of education. Or, it may be higher because of some specific talent or ability: Steffi Graf was born with a great natural ability to hit a tennis ball; others are born with a special talent for solving mathematical problems.

Figure 17-9 illustrates this idea. An initial point of reference is provided on the left by the base income of $22,000 earned by an unskilled labourer with no special talent or training. The remaining three individuals work as consultants for a large firm. Individual A is educated up to an MBA and has five years' experience. He earns $55,000; this is what he could earn in an alternative occupation. (This includes the $22,000 base wage plus a $33,000 return on his education and experience.) In other words, $55,000 is his income and also his opportunity cost. Individual B has exactly the same education and experience as A, and the same $55,000 opportunity cost. However, her income is another $23,000 higher because she has a special flair for solving the problems encountered by this firm. Finally, individual C has exactly the same education, experience, and opportunity cost as A and B. But he has an even more incisive mind in dealing with this firm's problems. His income consequently is a hefty $135,000.

Three components of income can be distinguished:

1. The $22,000 base income for unskilled work.
2. The additional $33,000 of income that these consultants could earn in other jobs because of their education and experience.

The first two components represent opportunity cost. The last one does not:

3. Additional returns to those with special talents. This third item falls under the economists' broad definition of ***rent***.

Economists use the term *rent* in a broad sense, to identify the return to any factor of production in excess of its opportunity cost.

Thus, rent is the gap between what a factor *is* earning and what it *could* earn elsewhere. Expressed this way, we see that there are two reasons that an individual's income might include a very large rent component: (1) The income he or she *is* earning may be very high and (2) what he or she *could* earn elsewhere is low. We continue to focus on the first reason here, while the second is considered in Box 17-2.

## RENT

What do Mario Lemieux, Luciano Pavarotti, and a hectare of Southern Ontario farmland have in common? The answer to this question is: They all are like business executive C in Figure 17-9; they all earn an economic *rent* because of their superior quality. Pavarotti has an exceptional voice. Lemieux plays outstanding hockey. A hectare of good Southern Ontario land yields unusually large quantities of corn.

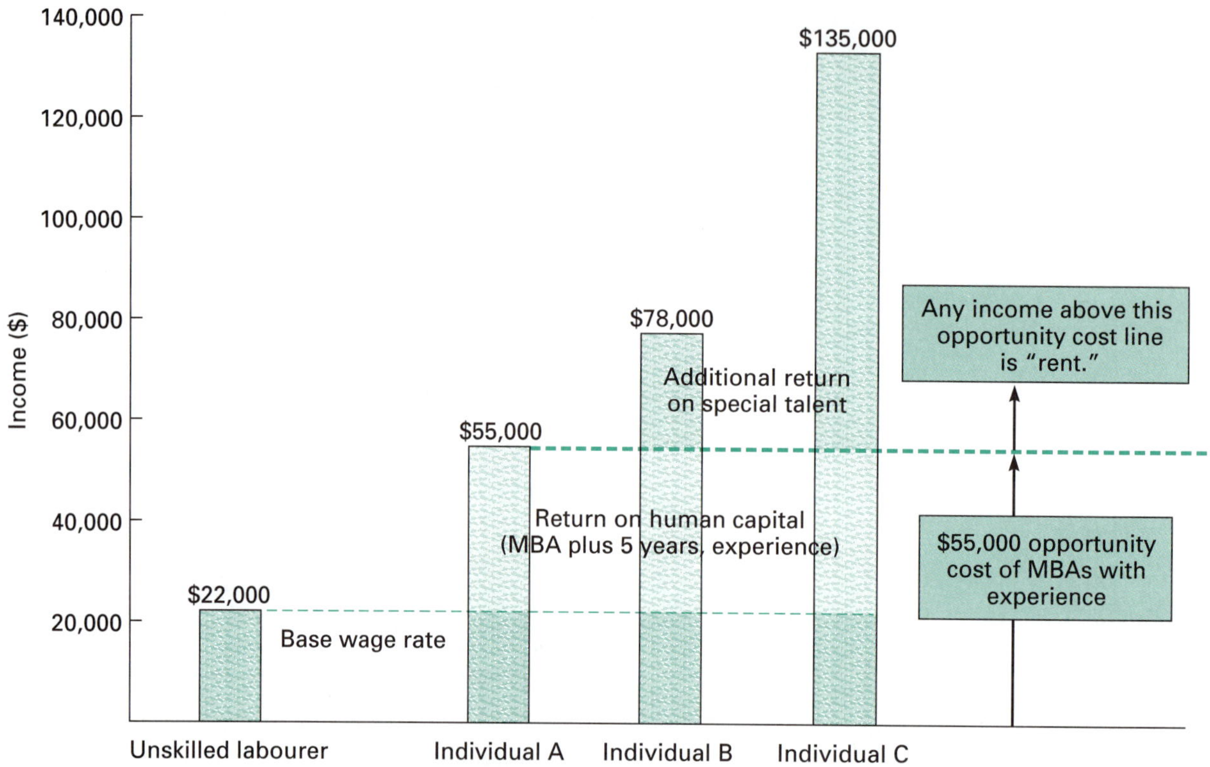


**FIGURE 17-9 Dividing income into its components.**
Individuals A, B, and C have the same qualifications—an MBA plus five years' experience—and the same $55,000 opportunity cost, shown by the dashed coloured line. Any surplus income above this is rent. Thus, A earns no rent, B earns $23,000 rent, and C—with the greatest natural talent for the job—earns $80,000 rent.

## TOOLS AND TECHNIQUES BOX 17-2
## Rent and Opportunity Cost

Recall that rent is defined as the difference between what a factor is earning and what it could earn elsewhere (its opportunity cost). The three business executives in Figure 17-9 had the same $55,000 opportunity cost but different incomes, so they had different rents. Here, we consider individuals who have the same income but different opportunity costs. Differences in rent occur in this case as well, as we shall now show.

In Figure 1, panel (a), we show a labour market in which all individuals have the same salary *Y*. But their opportunity costs vary. Thus, individuals *a* and *b* have the two different opportunity costs shown by the two hollow bars. Therefore, their rents will vary.

To show this in detail, first consider individual *a*. She has barely been attracted into this industry by income *Y*, since this is what she can earn elsewhere (her opportunity cost). Because there is no difference between her income and her opportunity cost, she earns no rent.

**BOX 17-2 continued**

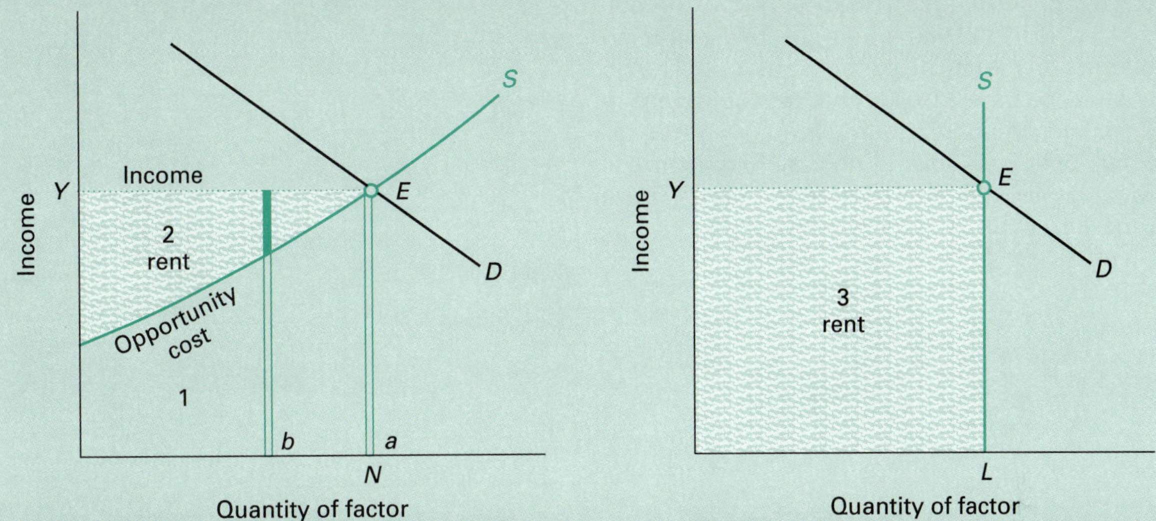


**(a)** All individuals in this panel earn the same income *Y*, but they have different opportunity costs, as given by the height of the curve *S*. The difference between their income and opportunity cost is rent. For individual *b*, this is the dark coloured bar, while for individual *a*, it is zero. For all individuals, it is the entire shaded area.

**(b)** None of the plots of land in this panel has any other use. All plots have zero opportunity cost, and their supply is completely inelastic. Therefore, their entire income 3 is rent.

**FIGURE 1** **Rent of a factor of production that (a) has an alternative use (such as labour), and (b) one that does not (such as some types of land).**

The situation for individual *b* is different. His opportunity cost (potential income elsewhere) is shown by the lower hollow bar. The difference between this and his actual income *Y* is the coloured bar; this is his rent. Visualizing similar coloured bars representing the rents of other workers, we conclude that the rent earned by all *N* workers in this industry is the coloured triangle 2.

To sum up this example: The *N* workers, all earning salary *Y*, have a total salary income of areas 1 + 2. Of this, area 1 is their opportunity cost, while area 2 is their rent.

The income of any other factor of production can similarly be divided into opportunity cost and rent components. In particular, we are interested in the land shown in panel (b), which has a completely inelastic supply because it can't be used for anything but agriculture. In other words, quantity *L* will be supplied no matter what its price may be. Because this land can't earn anything in any other use (its opportunity cost is zero) all its income 3 is rent.

Finally, we can recap our discussion of rent with the simple example shown in Figure 2, which illustrates how an individual can earn rent because (1) he's very good at what he's doing (the issue addressed in the main text) or (2) he's very bad at anything else (the issue addressed in this box). Washington is a better basketball player than team-mate McTavish, and his higher income reflects this. If they had the same opportunity costs — that is, the same ability to earn income elsewhere — Washington would have a higher rent. But

**BOX 17-2 continued**

they don't have the same opportunity costs. Whereas Washington could play pro football instead for $100,000 a year, McTavish has no talent other than basketball. His opportunity cost is the bare $15,000 that he could earn in unskilled manual labour. Because his opportunity cost is so low, almost all his income is rent; indeed, for this reason he earns more rent than even Washington.

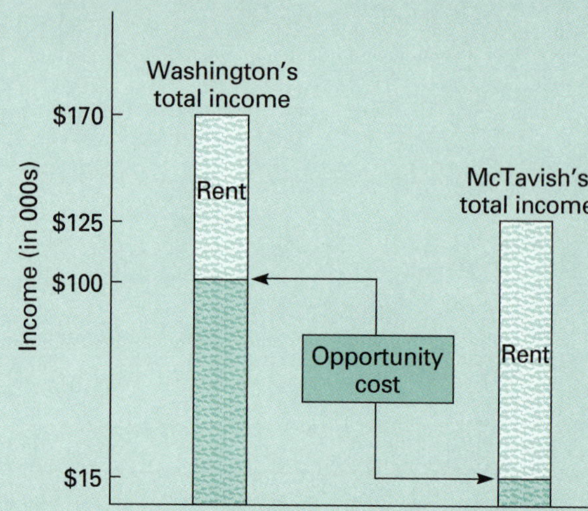


**FIGURE 2 Why rent depends both on (1) how productive a factor is in its present use, and (2) how unproductive it is in any other use.**

Washington has more basketball talent and earns a higher salary. If the opportunity costs of the players were the same, Washington would earn the higher rent. But their opportunity costs are not the same. In fact, McTavish's is so much lower that rent makes up a larger part of his income than it does Washington's.

## Rent on Agricultural Land, Based on Differences in Quality

> All economic analyses begin with the cultivation of the earth. . . . To the economist, . . . the green plain is a sort of burial place of hidden treasure, where all the forethought and industry of man are set at naught by the caprice of the power which hid the treasure. . . . Thus is Man mocked by earth his stepmother, and never knows as he tugs at her closed hand whether it contains diamonds or flints, good red wheat or a few clayey and blighted cabbages.
>
> George Bernard Shaw

Figure 17-10 shows three plots of land with no alternative use but to grow a crop. In other words, their opportunity cost is zero. It therefore follows, from the preceding definition, that any income they earn is rent. In this special case, economists' and the public's definition of rent coincide: It is the income earned by land.

Relatively poor land C has such low productivity that with a $3 price of wheat, it has just been brought into cultivation. The value of the wheat it produces is barely sufficient to cover the costs of fertilizer, machinery, the farmer's time, and other inputs. Therefore, it earns no rent. Land B is more fertile soil that grows enough wheat per hectare to pay for other

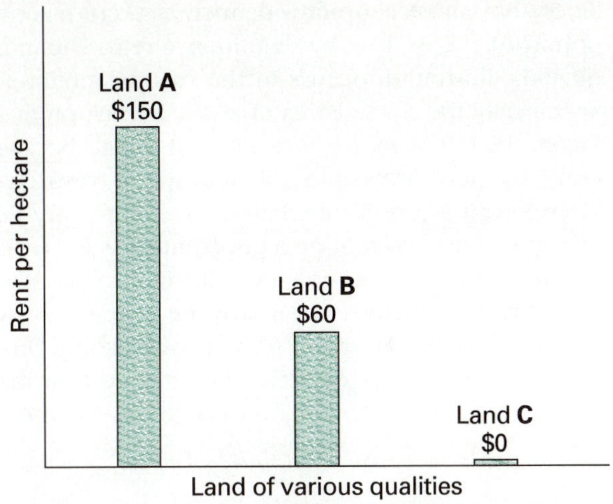


**FIGURE 17-10** **Rent based on differences in quality of land (based on wheat price of $3 per bushel).**

Marginal land C, which is just barely fertile enough to cultivate, earns no rent. High-productivity land A earns the highest rent.

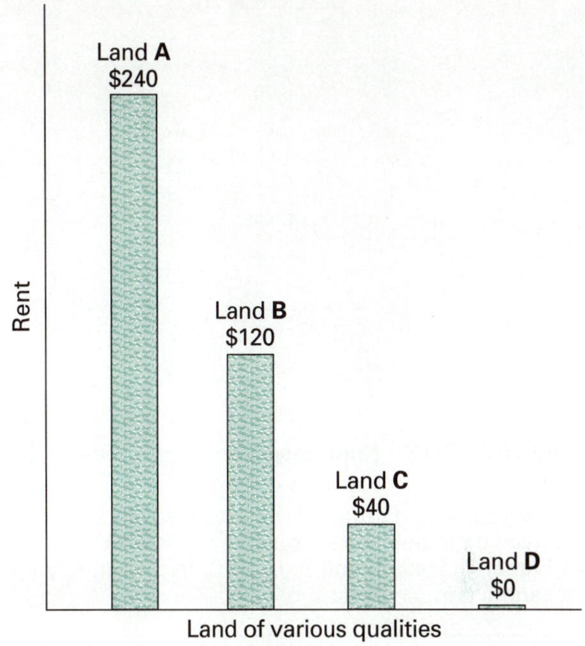


**FIGURE 17-11** **How rents increase when the price of wheat increases.**

This figure is the same as Figure 17-10 except that the price of wheat has risen from $3 to $4 per bushel. Because of this increased price, all existing plots of land earn greater income—that is, greater rent. Moreover, less productive plot *D* is brought into cultivation for the first time.

inputs and leave $60 per hectare; that is, its rent is $60 per hectare. Land A is even more productive and earns a rent of $150.

Of course, the rent on these plots of land depends on the price of wheat. Suppose that, because of crop failures elsewhere in the world, the price of wheat rises from the initial $3 a bushel (in Figure 17-10) to $4. The result is shown in Figure 17-11. Land C, which previously earned no rent, now does. And the rents earned by plots A and B increase. Land D is now the marginal land, just brought into cultivation and earning zero rent.

## Another Example of Rent: The Income from Mineral Deposits

A mineral deposit may also earn an economic rent. To confirm this statement, reinterpret Figures 17-10 and 17-11 as follows. Mineral deposit A is a rich vein of ore, easy to reach. Mineral deposit B is also a rich vein of ore, but difficult to reach and extract. Deposit C is of poorer quality and so difficult to reach that initially in Figure 17-10 it is barely being mined. In Figure 17-11 we see how an increase in the price of ore increases the rent earned on each of these deposits and induces the mining of low-yield deposit D for the first time.

## Rent on Land Because of Its Location

Land may yield economic rent not only because of its fertility but also because of its location. To illustrate, land A in Figure 17-12 is in the prime business district of a city and can be used in a highly productive way. A business might wish to locate there for a variety of reasons: It might want to be close to suppliers and competitors so that it can easily keep up with new developments and innovations in the industry. Or, it might wish to have access to the large labour pool that exists in this area of high-density population. Or,

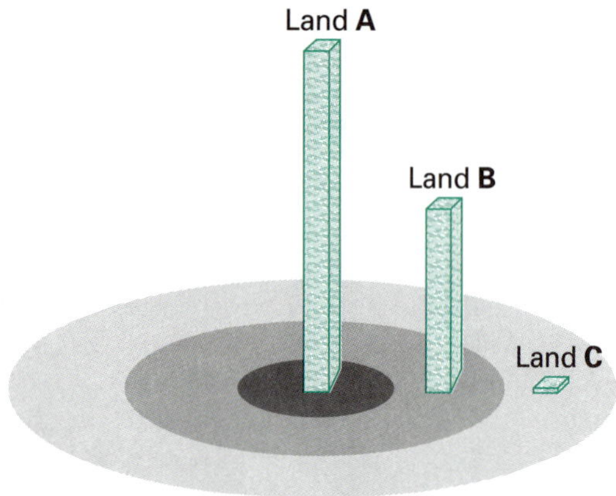


**FIGURE 17-12 Rent based on differences in the location of land.**

Compare with Figure 17-10. Because of its greater convenience and lower transport costs, land A earns a higher rent than land B. Land C, in a relatively poor location, earns no rent.

it might wish to be close to the population centre in order to reduce the cost of transporting its product to market.

For all these reasons, land A earns a rent. Land B is less attractive since it is not in this prime district, and it earns a smaller rent. Finally, land C earns no rent because it is even farther away and, therefore, involves even higher costs of inconvenience and transportation.

These blocks in Figure 17-12, just like the bars in the previous diagram, give us a picture of how rents compare. Because the selling price of land depends on the rent it can earn—as we shall soon see in more detail— these blocks also give us a picture of how land *prices* over an urban area will compare.

Finally, note that although the heights of the blocks have been drawn to reflect rents and land values, they may also provide some rough indication of where the tallest buildings will be constructed. Office space becomes more and more expensive to construct as a building gets higher and higher. Consequently, if land is cheap, you buy more land and build sideways. But if land is expensive enough, you conserve it by building up. Thus, buildings tend to be tallest in the prime, most expensive locations.

## Above-normal Profit as a Rent

Since above-normal profit is defined as a return above opportunity cost, it is, by definition, a rent. The most obvious illustration occurs in the case of monopoly. Specifically, the shaded area of above-normal profit in Figure 12-4 is a ***monopoly rent***. It exists because entry by new firms into the industry is restricted. Therefore, it is a rent on whatever restricts entry. For example, it may be rent on a government licence that is granted to one firm (or a few) that blocks out other potential competitors. Or, it may be rent on a patented product that other firms cannot copy. Or, if there are economies of scale, the existing firm may earn a rent since no other firm can afford to enter.

# HOW RENTS ARE CAPITALIZED

If land plots A and B in Figure 17-12 are put up for sale, we would expect A to sell for a higher price; it will be more valuable because of the higher rent it can earn. This is generally true: Higher rents result in higher land values. But can't we be more precise about how the value of land is determined?

If you had the money and you were interested in buying land B in Figure 17-10, how much would you be willing to pay for it? Bear in mind that, as an alternative, you can always purchase bonds (or stocks) instead and earn a rate of return of, say, 6%. Because the rent of land B is \$60 per year, you should be willing to pay about \$1000 for it. This gives you the same 6% rate of return on your land (a \$60 return on \$1000) as on the alternative of buying bonds. Moreover, the competition of other potential buyers who feel the same way will ensure that the price of land B will settle at about \$1000—as long as the rent on B is expected to remain at \$60 per year.

However, when the rent on land B doubles in Figure 17-11 to \$120, potential buyers will be attracted by this higher income it can earn, and will begin to bid up the price of this land. This process will continue until the price of this land roughly doubles to \$2000, where its rate of return will again be the same 6% as before — that is, a \$120 return on \$2000. To describe this process, we say that an increase in rent is ***capitalized*** in the value of the land.

In practice, there are many complications. In particular, the price of land will be affected not only by present rents but by expected *future* rents too. If a single year's rent increases by 20%, the price of land may increase by more than 20% if people expect rents to continue rising.[2]

The fact that land prices reflect rents leads us to be sceptical of government programs to raise farm income by raising the price of commodities. One major effect of such programs may be to cause higher rents (a shift from Figure 17-10 to 17-11) and consequently a higher value for farmland. Thus, the benefit tends to go to the owners of farmland when the programs are introduced. By and large, it does not go to those who want to farm by renting land. And, if new farmers purchase the land, they will be passing their eventual income increase from farming over to those who sell the land at a high price. Paradoxically, the higher price of farm products may make farming *less* attractive for newcomers: They now have a greater problem of raising the money necessary to purchase the higher-priced farmland. Thus, government price supports designed to "help out the small farmer" may, in fact, keep those of limited means out of farming altogether.

As we saw in Chapter 12, some farm programs involve marketing boards that drive up prices of farm products by using a system of production quotas that limit the supply of the products. (Such programs exist in milk and egg production, for example.) The price increases brought about by these programs will also give rise to rent—but, in this case, it is a rent earned by the quota owners. If these quotas can be bought and sold, the rent becomes capitalized into the value of a production quota. Thus, the benefit goes to those who are originally given production quotas by the government; new farmers will have to buy production quotas from the original quota owners if they want to enter the business.[3]

Moreover, serious problems arise even for those who do raise the necessary funds to buy land or production quotas by borrowing heavily on a big mortgage. They will be able to earn a living—and make those big mortgage payments—only if the government marketing boards continue to keep up price. So these farmers of *necessity* become strong supporters of the marketing board programs: Without these programs, farm prices would fall and the farmers would no longer be able to make their mortgage payments. In short, when government price-support programs are introduced, they benefit those who initially own the land or those who get the original production quotas. But if these initial owners sell the land or the quotas, they are "out-of-reach": For example, if they have retired to Florida on the proceeds of their sales, they cannot be damaged if the farm support program is then reversed. Instead, the damage all falls on the *new* owners.

Other economic rents—besides those on land or production quotas—may also be capitalized. Like other cities, Vancouver limits the number of taxis: A driver must have a licence to operate a cab. Because this requirement makes taxis scarce in Vancouver, the fares collected by each taxi are greater. But this higher income (rent) becomes capitalized in the value of the taxi licence. In the late 1980s, a Vancouver taxi licence was worth somewhere around three to four times as much as the cost of a new taxi. Thus, someone who wants to own and operate a cab in Vancouver faces the same problem as someone who wants to start producing a crop that is regulated by a marketing board. He may be able to do reasonably well once he gets into the business, but how does he raise the money to get started in the first place?

Finally, taxi licences raise this issue: Rather than let the licence owners benefit from the policy of restricting the number of cabs, would it not have been better for Vancouver to have *auctioned off* the rights to operate cabs for only one or two years at a time? Then the city would have been able to collect the rents. Moreover, individual drivers could now enter the industry far more easily. They would have to buy the right to operate a cab for one or two years, rather than the far more expensive right to operate it permanently (the cost they now incur when they buy the licence).

## Taxing Rent

Rent has always been a natural target for taxation. About a century ago, Henry George built a powerful single-tax movement on the idea that nothing should be taxed but land rents. (His book *Progress and Pov-*

[2] Further detail on how an income flow (such as rent or interest) is capitalized in the value of an asset (such as land or a bond) is given in Box 12-1 in the *Macroeconomics* volume that forms a companion to this text. The "capitalization of an income flow" is just another way of saying "the calculation of the present value of an income flow."

[3] Why does the rent get capitalized into the value of farmland in one case, and into the value of quota in the other? The answer is simple: In the first case, you can get access to the rent by buying land (since the government allows anybody to produce as much as they like). But with supply management in a marketing board system, land without quota does not give you access to the rent; only quota does.

*erty* sold millions of copies, and he almost won an election as mayor of New York.) Why, asked George, shouldn't we tax land rents, since they represent a pure windfall? Owners obviously don't produce the land, nor do they work for their rental incomes. Instead, they just hold the land and become wealthy from "unearned increments" as the population increases and rents rise. George argued that the land rents belong to the public as a whole, and should be taxed away from the owners and used for public purposes.

George's case was based not only on equity but also on efficiency. A levy on land rents is one of the few taxes that need not distort resource allocation. Even if half the rent on land is taxed away, it will still remain in cultivation. What else can the owner do with it? And because the quantity of land in use is not affected, there is no reason to expect an efficiency loss. (Compare this with a tax on any other factor of production. For example, a tax on wages can affect the incentive to work and might thus affect the amount of work done.)

However, George's proposal to tax land rent raises two serious difficulties— in addition to the obvious problem that, as a single tax, it would not raise nearly enough money to cover today's large government expenditures. First, if present owners paid the current high price when they bought their land, rents are not a windfall to them at all but just a reasonable return on their large initial expenditure. (Why tax those who bought land and not those who bought stocks or bonds instead?) The only windfall is to the previous owners who sold the land for a high price. But they may now be living in Bermuda, beyond the reach of the taxing authority. Second, in practice it may be impossible to separate the rent on land from the return on buildings. If you tax a landlord's income, you will be taxing *both*. But the return on buildings —or on any other improvements on the land—is not a return on the land itself. Instead, it is a return to *capital*, and it cannot be taxed without causing distortion and inefficiency. For example, a tax on the returns from apartments will reduce the quantity of apartments in the market, and thus cause an efficiency loss.

## KEY POINTS

1. Those who provide the nation's capital stock receive income in several forms. For example, those who own businesses receive profits. Those who lend money to businesses to purchase plant or equipment receive interest.
2. In a perfectly competitive capital market, the interest rate is determined by the demand and supply of loanable funds. Demand reflects how productive these funds will be when they are invested (the marginal efficiency of investment). Supply reflects how highly savers value money in its alternative use—current consumption.
3. Because capital is productive, present goods can be exchanged for even more future goods. Therefore, present goods are worth more than future goods. The interest rate indicates how much more.
4. The interest rate also acts as a screening device that allocates funds to investment projects with the highest productivity. A government ceiling that lowers the interest rate below its perfectly competitive level results in two kinds of efficiency loss: (1) It reduces the total funds available for investment and (2) it may result in funds being allocated to the wrong set of projects. It also results in a transfer from lenders to those borrowers who are able to get loans. This doesn't necessarily benefit poor individuals or small businesses, because they may be the potential borrowers who do *not* get loans; banks prefer to lend to wealthy individuals and large businesses.
5. Income is earned not only on machinery and other forms of physical capital, but also on human capital — that is, on skills, training, and education. The individuals who own the human capital are not the only ones who bear the initial cost of the investment. Governments also invest by subsidizing education, and businesses invest by subsidizing training programs.
6. Economists define rent as the return to any factor of production above its opportunity cost. Those with superior talents in any occupation, whether

it be business or basketball, earn a rent.

7. Land also earns a rent—except for plots that are not cultivated or have just barely been brought into cultivation. The most fertile plots earn the largest rent. If the price of farm products increases, rents on all cultivated plots of land rise and new plots are brought into cultivation.

8. Rent is also earned on land because of its location. Mineral deposits similarly earn rent, with the richest, most accessible deposits earning the highest rents. Above-normal profits earned by a firm are also a form of rent. In the case of monopoly, these rents are typically due to something—such as a patent or a government licence—that blocks entry by potential competitors.

9. The higher the rent earned by an asset such as a plot of land, the higher its value; thus, rents are "capitalized." This, in turn, has important implications for any agricultural supply management policy that creates rent on production quotas. Although such a policy obviously benefits those who get the quotas, it won't necessarily increase the income of those who subsequently have to buy quotas to get into farming. Quite the contrary: It tends to discourage new entrants by increasing the initial cost of buying a quota.

## KEY TERMS

**debt and equity capital**
**physical and human capital**
**rate of return**
**marginal efficiency of investment (MEI)**
**roundabout (indirect) production**
**annuity**
**base (risk-free) rate of interest**
**rationing of funds (with an interest rate ceiling)**
**normal and above-normal profit**
**substitution between factors of production**
**monopoly rent**
**capitalization of rent**

## PROBLEMS

17-1. (a) Using a three-panel diagram such as Figure 11-9, show how the interest rate acts as a monitoring device to determine which investments will be undertaken and which will not.

(b) Just as the return to projects *j* and *g* are shown in Figure 17-6, show the return to project *h*, in the range $Q_1Q_3$ to the right. Now suppose that *g* is knocked out by the interest rate ceiling at $i_2$. Is it also possible, as banks ration funds, for project *j* to lose out to *h*? How could this happen? If it does happen, what is the efficiency loss? What is the other efficiency loss?

(c) Use a diagram such as Figure 17-6 to show how rent controls result in an efficiency loss even without any "rationing errors" and in a further efficiency loss if rationing errors do occur.

17-2. Suppose that all the agricultural land within 100 kilometres of Toronto is equally fertile. Suppose, also, that all corn must be sold in Toronto and that the cost of transporting it there depends only on distance. What pattern of land rent would you expect over this area?

17-3. Why might a firm pay a very high salary to attract an executive from a competing firm? Illustrate your discussion with a diagram.

17-4. If expectations change, with borrowers and lenders expecting that interest rates will fall in the future, what is likely to happen to the interest rate that a firm has to pay in order to sell long-term bonds today?

17-5. "In a world in which labour is free to switch jobs, there will be inadequate investment in human capital in the form of job training." Do you agree? Explain why or why not. How might our minimum wage laws be changed to reduce this problem?

17-6. The public's idea of rent does not coincide with the economist's definition. How are the two concepts different? Give an example of (a) a return that an economist considers rent, but the public does not; (b) a return that the public considers rent, but the economist does not; and (c) a return that both consider rent.

17-7. The number of doctors is limited because anyone practising medicine must have a licence. Are rents generated in this case? To whom do they go? Is the objective of licensing to affect doctors' income, or is there some other reason?

17-8. Which, if any, of the following statements is true? If one is false, correct it. "An increase in the price of oil brings previously uneconomic sources of oil into production. It does not affect the rent on existing oil fields."

17-9. Suppose Vancouver imposed its taxi restriction by allowing only a restricted set of *individuals* to drive cabs. Would rents be generated in this case? If so, who would earn these rents?

CHAPTER

# 18 INCOME INEQUALITY

*"I had a better year than he did."*

*Baseball great Babe Ruth, when told that he made more money than the President of the United States.*

In 1991, the average wage in Canadian manufacturing was about $15 an hour. Based on a 40-hour work week for 50 weeks, this wage would produce an annual income of about $30,000. In the same year, Raghib Ismail, a 21-year old football player in his third year at Notre Dame University in Indiana, signed a four-year contract with the Toronto Argonauts and its owner Bruce McNall. The contract guaranteed him over $20 *million* over the next four years (with prospects of another $10 million of potential earnings from "related sources"). On a list of the most highly paid professional athletes in 1991, the first hockey player was Wayne Gretzky. Although he only appeared as number 40 on the list, his estimated earnings were $3.5 million a year *from his salary alone*; if his income from endorsing products (ranging from rental cars to jeans) is added, the figure becomes much higher.

All this raises a question: Should a football player earn that much more than the Prime Minister of Canada? Should a successful pop musician earn many times more than a highly skilled violinist in a symphony orchestra?

Looking at the distribution of income in Canada, we can find many cases of large differentials between people who all appear to work equally hard, and to be good at their jobs. In this chapter we will look at the Canadian income distribution to see whether such examples are the exception or the rule. How unequal are Canadian incomes? Is inequality increasing or decreasing?

Our second task will be to address the question: What is a *fair* distribution of income? Is it the income distribution that results from the free play of market forces? Or, is it an equal income for all? Or, is it some compromise between the two?

To begin, we review why income differences arise in the first place. Why do some people earn so much more than others?

## REVIEW: WHY DO INCOMES DIFFER?

In earlier chapters, we have seen how market forces result in quite different incomes for different people. For example, the high income of a surgeon is in part a return to *human capital*; it provides compensation for the years of forgone income and hard study in medical school. It may also be partly a *rent* on greater-than-average *innate talent*. Of course, other individuals have gifts of quite a different sort; star athletes and entertainers also earn very large rents.

Income differences also arise because of wealth. Those who own stocks, bonds, and other forms of property receive income from them. There are even greater differences in wealth than in income. Data from 1984 show that one-quarter of Canadian families and individuals had net wealth of less than $5000. At the other extreme, 5% of all individuals and families had wealth over $300,000. The average net wealth among the 25% with the least wealth (taking into account the fact that some in this group had *negative* net wealth, i.e., had more debts than assets) was just about zero. In contrast, the 5% with the most net wealth owned some 38% of total wealth.

*Family background* explains some income differences. Canada may be a land of opportunity where someone from a poor, low-status family can achieve prominence and success. However, coming from the "right family" does help, especially if parents provide not only a silver spoon but also practical advice and inspiration. And working women or members of minority groups may have a lower income because of *discrimination*.

In addition, income differences may arise because of the exercise of *market power*. People who find themselves in a monopoly position may be able to profit handsomely in terms of increased income.

There are also income differences because some people work at more dangerous or unpleasant jobs. Thus, the construction worker in a dangerous job may receive a *compensating wage differential*, that is, a higher wage to compensate for the risks faced. At the other extreme, artists may accept a lower income, in order to pursue a career that they find particularly pleasant.

Income differences also may arise because some people *work harder* than others. For example, a specific doctor's income may be lower because of a personal decision to sacrifice income for leisure; an example is the doctor with a clinic at a ski resort who goes skiing in the morning and sets broken bones in the afternoon. On the other hand, many doctors work very long hours, and this helps to explain their high incomes.

Some income differences may be the result of differences in *health* or just plain *luck*. An example is the talented hockey player who is injured in the eye by a high stick and must give up hockey and the large income that may go with it. But, just as bad luck can lower income, good luck can raise it. Being "the right person at the right time" is sometimes a way of earning a windfall income. In the 1950s, Ingemar Johansson, a burly young Swede, was working as a road construction labourer, following some minor trouble with the law. Someone suggested that he try boxing. Within a few years, he had become heavyweight champion of the world, and wealthy enough to retire in luxury.

Of all the causes of income differences, which is most important? It is difficult to give an unambiguous answer, but *human capital* appears to be a strong candidate. Statistics Canada data show that in comparison with low-income groups, families and individuals in high-income groups derive a much higher proportion of their income from wages and salaries. In a U.S. study, Jacob Mincer found that differences in human capital explained roughly 60% of differences in American incomes.[1]

## HOW MUCH INCOME INEQUALITY IS THERE?

> It's the rich whot gets the gryvy,
> It's the poor whot gets the blime.
>
> English ballad, World War II.

Are wide differences in individual incomes the exception or the rule? When we look at the income of all Canadians, how much inequality is there?

Table 18-1 shows the distribution of Canadian incomes. However, these figures were calculated before taking into account government policies that tend to raise the relative income of the poor, such as Unemployment Insurance, Old Age Security, and taxes. Excluding these policies, the poor are very poor indeed: The lowest-income fifth of the population receive less than 3% of the nation's income. At the other extreme, the highest-income fifth of the population receive almost 43% of the nation's income.

This unequal distribution is illustrated with a ***Lorenz curve***. The first step in drawing such a curve is to rearrange the data in panel (a) of Table 18-1 to obtain the ***cumulative income distribution*** in the third column of panel (b). For example, in the second row, the poorest 40% of the population earn 13.7% of the nation's income. (To get this figure, we add the first two numbers in panel (a).) This point, labelled *J*, is then plotted in Figure 18-1, along with other points that are similarly calculated. The result is the Lorenz curve of Canadian income.

To get some feel for how much inequality this curve represents, we ask: What would this Lorenz curve look like if all families received exactly the same income? In that case, we would observe point *F* instead of point *J*: The "lowest" 40% of the population would receive 40% of the income. And instead of point *K* we would observe point *G* (60% of the population would receive 60% of the income). When

[1] Jacob Mincer, "Education, Experience, Earnings and Employment," in F. Thomas Juster, ed., *Education, Income and Human Behavior* (New York: McGraw-Hill, 1975), p. 73.

**TABLE 18-1 Income Distribution of Canadian Families in 1990 (before taxes and transfers)**

| (a) INCOME DISTRIBUTION | | (b) CUMULATIVE INCOME DISTRIBUTION | | | |
|---|---|---|---|---|---|
| **Population** | **Share of Total Income** | **Population** | **Share of Total Income** | | **Point in Fig. 18-1** |
| Low 20% | gets 2.7% | First 20% | gets | 2.7% | *H* |
| Second 20% | gets 11.0 | First 40% | gets 2.7 + 11.0 | 13.7 | *J* |
| Third 20% | gets 18.0 | First 60% | gets 13.7 + 18.0 | 31.7 | *K* |
| Fourth 20% | gets 25.5 | First 80% | gets 31.7 + 25.5 | 57.2 | *L* |
| High 20% | gets 42.8 | Total | gets 57.2 + 42.8 | 100.0 | *M* |

*Source:* Statistics Canada, *Income After-Tax, Distributions by Size in Canada 1990*, p. 24.

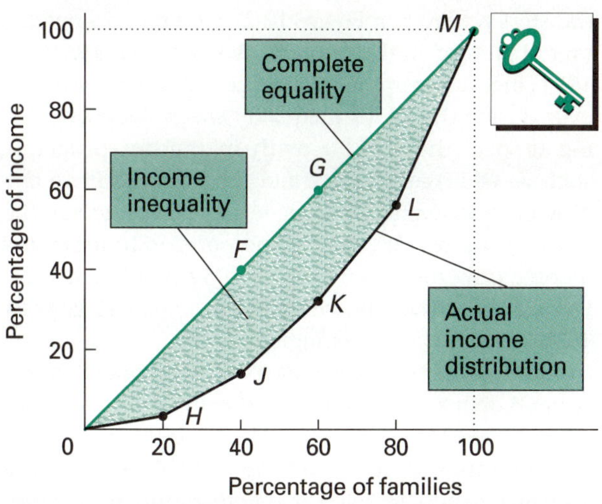


**FIGURE 18-1 Lorenz curve showing before-tax-and-transfer income distribution in Canada.**

If every family had exactly the same income, the Canadian income distribution would follow the 45° "complete equality" line. The actual income distribution is shown by the curve that lies below this—with the coloured slice between the two showing the amount of income inequality.

*Source*: Statistics Canada, *Income After-Tax, Distributions by Size in Canada 1990*, p. 24.

we join all points like *F* and *G*, the result is the "complete equality" line 0*FGM*; that is, the 45° straight line from the origin. Thus, income inequality is shown by the amount of bow in the Lorenz curve; that is, by the size of the colour slice between the curve and the 45° line.

In fact, *inequality is not as serious a problem as this diagram suggests*. One reason: Even if each family were earning exactly the same *lifetime* income, the Lorenz curve would still not coincide with the 45° line. We would still observe some "inequality slice." The reason is that during any single year, we would observe some young families starting out with a low income and some middle-aged families in their earning prime with a high income. Inequality exists in that year for these families, even though they have exactly the same lifetime income pattern.

Nonetheless, even when such influences are taken fully into account, a substantial degree of inequality exists. Society's response is to reduce this inequality by government taxation that concentrates more heavily on the rich, and government expenditure programs such as Old Age Security, Unemployment Insurance, and social assistance payments that raise the relative income of the poor.

## HOW MUCH INEQUALITY DOES THE GOVERNMENT NOW ELIMINATE?

The degree to which government taxes and transfer payments reduce inequality in the nation's income distribution is shown in Figure 18-2. The shaded area is exactly the same as in Figure 18-1. However, here it is broken down into a light grey area that shows how much the government reduces inequality, and a colour area that shows how much still remains.

Whereas curve *a* is a reproduction of the before-taxes-and-transfers curve graphed in Figure 18-1, curve *b* shows the major shift toward equality that occurs as a result of government ***cash transfer programs***, including social assistance, Old Age Security, and Unemployment Insurance. (Government programs that shift this curve are discussed in more detail in Chapter 24.) Curve *c* shows the further shift that results from the effect of taxation. Together, transfers and taxes eliminate approximately one-fourth of total inequality.[2] In addition, however, the remaining inequality is reduced by ***transfers in kind***: Because government programs provide the same standards of health care and education to rich and poor alike, and subsidize the housing costs of low-income Canadians, total real income is more equal than after-tax money income. When all programs are considered, the overall picture is one of a government that is making substantial transfers of income to the poor, in the process eliminating more than a quarter of the nation's income inequality. Claims that the government is not very effective in changing the nation's income distribution have frequently been based on calculations that do not take into account all of these programs, in particular, in-kind transfers.

One surprise in this diagram is that taxation, often supposed to be a great income redistributor, is relatively ineffective in reducing income inequality. Certainly taxes are a large enough item in our income to make a big difference. But they do not change the nation's income distribution as much as one might expect because, on balance, they are not highly progressive. While it is true, as noted in Chapter 5, that *income* taxes are progressive—that is, the rates rise as incomes rise — other taxes are regressive. Moreover, loopholes (such as the partial exemption of capital gains from income taxation) ease the burden of taxes on the wealthy.

On the other hand, the more explicit transfer programs, such as Unemployment Insurance, Old Age Security, and other forms of cash transfer seem, when taken together, to be more effective. However, we must be cautious about this conclusion. It is quite true that the payments they provide to the poor *directly* reduce inequality— that is, shift the Lorenz curve up from *a* to *b*. But *indirectly* they *increase* inequality (make the Lorenz curve *a* lower than it would otherwise be) because of their side effects. For example, the income guarantee provided by programs such as Unemployment Insurance makes unemployed people less desperate to get a job quickly, because they can at least survive without one. Moreover, for some couples the incentive to stay together may be reduced by an income guarantee that ensures that they can get welfare if they separate. When a couple breaks up, one medium-income family may become two poor families.

These effects reduce the per-family earned income at the low end of the scale and give Lorenz curve *a* a bigger bow than it would otherwise have. In short, income-support programs have two conflicting effects on income inequality. Indirectly they make it worse by giving the "before-transfers" curve *a* a bigger bow. But directly they make it better, by shifting the Lorenz curve up from *a* to the "after-transfers" curve *b*.

How has income inequality changed over time? If we look at the inequality of income after government transfers (curve *b* in Figure 18-2), we find a somewhat mixed picture. In the two decades between 1951 and 1971, inequality appeared to actually *increase*. However, during the 1970s inequality was reduced, reflecting in part the rapid growth in transfer programs, such as Old Age Security and the increase in Unemployment Insurance benefit levels. Nevertheless, the share of the poorest 20% of the population in pre-tax income only rose from 4.4% in 1951 to 4.7% in 1981. During the 1980s, however, it rose substantially. By 1990, it had reached as high as 6.4%.

Although an increase by two percentage points (from 4.4% in 1951 to 6.4% some 40 years later) may appear like slow progress, it should be kept in mind that the numbers represent the relative shares out of a growing income. Even if the *share* of the poorest 20% were to remain constant, this would not mean that the *real income* in this group had stayed constant. Instead, it would mean that the real income of the poorest 20% had been rising at about the same rate as the average income in the population as a whole. Thus, during the 1960s and 1970s, large numbers of people were moving out of poverty, even though inequality did not change by much. By the same token, the increase in the share of the poorest 20% during the 1980s has not meant a large reduction in the percentage of the population living in poverty. Because of the deep recession in 1981/82 and the persistently high unemployment rates during the recovery, there was even an *increase* in the percentage in poverty during the mid-1980s, and by 1990 (when a severe recession was beginning once again), the percentage was not much lower than at the beginning of the 1980s.

[2] Perhaps more than this. Remember that if we were to achieve complete equality of *lifetime* incomes, the Lorenz curve would still have a bow below the 45° line, because in any specific year the middle-aged would have a higher income than the young.

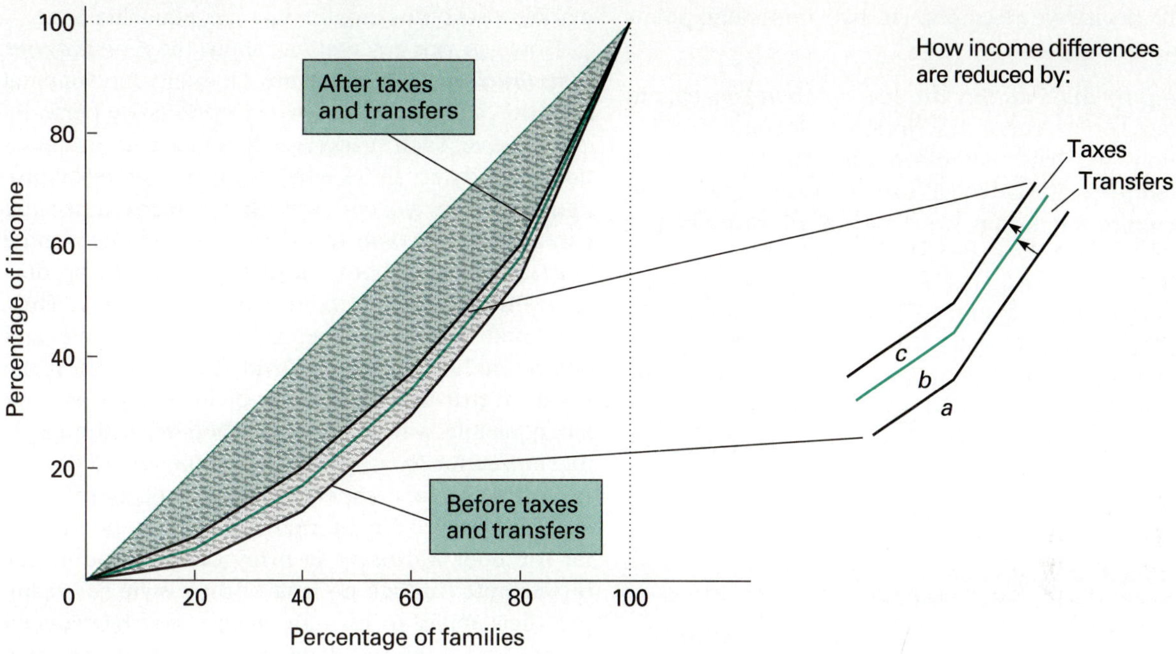


**FIGURE 18-2** **How government taxes and transfers reduce income inequality.**
The reduction in income equality resulting from taxes and transfers by all levels of government in 1990 was somewhere between one-fifth to one-fourth. Taxes, which shifted the curve from *b* to *c*, were a relatively unimportant form of equalization compared to government transfer programs, which reduced inequality from curve *a* to curve *b*.

*Source*: Based on Statistics Canada, *Income After-Tax, Distributions by Size in Canada 1990*, p. 24.

The increase in the percentage of people in poverty in the mid-1980s was even more pronounced in the United States than in Canada. Between the early 1970s and early 1980s, the percentage of the U.S. population that was classified as poor rose by as much as one-third. Part of the explanation was of course the severe recession in the early 1980s. But another reason was the retrenchment in some U.S. social welfare programs that took place during the Reagan administrations of 1980–1988. For example, there were changes in the eligibility rules for welfare, which resulted in a smaller number of people receiving assistance.

Now let's turn from the question "What *is* the income distribution?" to "What *should* the income distribution be?" In deriving policies that affect the distribution of income, what should we set as a target? Is there such a thing as a "fair" or "equitable" distribution?

## WHAT IS AN EQUITABLE INCOME DISTRIBUTION?

See how the fates their gifts allot,
For A is happy—B is not.
Yet B is worthy, I dare say,
Of more prosperity than A.

If I were fortune—which I'm not—
B should enjoy A's happy lot,
And A should die in miserie—
That is, assuming I am B.

Gilbert and Sullivan, *The Mikado*

A search for an equitable or just distribution of income for society will lead us into treacherous intellectual terrain, from which some of the world's noted philosophers have been unable to escape with reputations intact. Although we cannot expect to arrive at any definitive answer in this elementary treatment, we can at least identify some of the important issues.

To begin, we re-emphasize two important points made in Chapter 1.

1. *Equity and equality are two different concepts.* In our Lorenz curve description of income distribution, we have addressed only the question of ***equality***: How equal *are* incomes? This is an empirical question. We can answer it by looking at the facts — by examining how much each Canadian family earns. On the other hand, the question of ***equity*** is not what incomes are, but rather what they *should be*. What income distribution is fair and just? This is an ethical issue on which people are not unanimous. Some believe that equity is equality—that it is fair for everyone to receive the same income. On the other hand, many believe that equity is not equality—for example, the individual who works harder or more effectively should be paid more.

   *Equal* means "of the same size." *Equitable* means "fair." The two are not necessarily the same.

2. We emphasize again that government policy cannot be designed just to achieve equity — that is, a fair division of the nation's income pie. Instead, it must also take into account other, often conflicting goals such as efficiency — increasing the size of that pie. However, to sharpen our idea of equity, suppose for now that this is our only concern. *On grounds of equity alone*, what is the best distribution of income?

   Of the many possible answers, consider three: first, the distribution that results from the free play of the economic marketplace; second, a completely equal distribution of income; and third, some compromise between the two.

## Is the Free Market's Distribution of Income Equitable?

> Whatever is, is right.
>
> Alexander Pope, *Essay on Man*

In economics, few would agree that whatever is, is necessarily right. *The free market does not do a satisfactory job of distributing income*. Consider a monopolist who makes a fortune by successfully cornering the world's supply of a good, selling some at a very high price, and letting the unsold balance rot. In such cases it is very difficult to argue that the free market distributes income in a fair, equitable way.

However, our reservations about the ***free-market distribution of income*** are far more fundamental than this, and apply even when markets are perfectly competitive. Such markets will, under certain conditions (no externalities, etc.) allocate factors of production in an *efficient* way that will maximize the nation's total income. In the process, they determine a set of prices of both goods and factors of production — the wages of labour, rents on land, etc. Thus, they both maximize the nation's income pie and determine how it will be divided. But we can make no claim that they necessarily divide the pie up in a fair, equitable way. Remember: The size of the pie is maximized for *those who have the income to pay for it*. Output in a competitive market economy may include luxuries for the rich and too few necessities for the poor. Moreover, in many cases the poor may be destitute through no fault of their own. For example, their ability to earn an income may be reduced because of health problems or disability; or they may have become impoverished by having to pay the cost of expensive health services not covered by insurance. Even the strongest supporters of the free market, while championing its efficiencies, will still vote for aid for those who are destitute. In almost all countries, there is widespread public support for government programs to protect those who need expensive medical care. To repeat: The case in favour of a system of free, competitive markets with little government intervention is based on the expectation that such a system would lead to efficiency, not that it would lead to equity.

Perhaps the best illustration is this: In a perfectly competitive economy, rents on land efficiently direct the nation's scarce land into its most productive uses; if rents are forced below the competitive level, land may be used in wasteful ways. However, the payment of these rents to those who own the land does not necessarily give us a fair distribution of income. We can see this point by considering an extreme example of land that has been inherited by the idle rich. Why should they earn an income many times that of the able and hardworking people whom they hire to manage and work this land?

## Equality as a Target

The idea that we should aim for complete equality has an immediate appeal. (See Box 18-1.) Since every-

## ECONOMICS IN HISTORY BOX 18-1
### Rawls on Equality

Harvard philosophy professor John Rawls has argued that income equality is a desirable goal — except in special circumstances. His analysis starts in a promising way. A consensus on the fair distribution of income is difficult to achieve because everyone has a special axe to grind. Those with high incomes favour a system in which inequality is allowed, because it lets them keep their higher income. Those with low incomes are likely to advocate equality because it will improve their position. Rawls, therefore, suggests that, to get an objective view, people must be *removed from their present situation* and placed in an *original position* where they decide what the distribution of income should be, without knowing the specific place *they themselves* will eventually take in this distribution. What income distribution will they choose?

Here are the essentials of Rawls's argument. The typical person in the original position will think something like this: "Whatever income distribution is chosen, with my luck, chances are that I'll end up at the bottom. So I'll vote for the income distribution that will leave me, the lowest one on the totem pole, as well off as possible." Since everyone is similarly situated in the original position, Rawls argues that all will reason in the same way. He concludes that a consensus will develop in favour of an equal distribution of income — unless there is an unequal distribution that leaves *everyone* better off. This is what Rawls calls the ***difference principle.***[1]

While Rawls's approach will generally lead to equality, there are circumstances in which it will not. To illustrate, we use two extreme examples, but the argument applies in less extreme cases as well. For the first example, suppose people in the original position choose between the two income distributions shown in Table A. Option *A* represents complete equality, with everyone's annual income at $5000. Now suppose it is possible to move to option *B*, where everyone's income is $10,000 except for the last individual, whose income is $5100. (Suppose that this move is possible because there was previously a very high tax aimed at equalizing income. When the tax is removed, people respond by working more.) Because everyone benefits, Rawlsian logic leads to a move from *A* to *B* — a move *away from equality.*[2] Most people would agree with such a move. So far, Rawls's theory is not controversial. In the circumstances shown in Table A, Rawls, like almost everyone else, would allow inequality.

Table B illustrates the second, more likely situation, with options *A* and *C*. As before, the move away from equality (in this case, from *A* to *C*) benefits almost everyone by $5000. But now we recognize that any such substantial change is likely to leave at least one person worse off. (Note in the last column how the income of the last individual is reduced by $100.) In this case, Rawls argues that peo-

**TABLE A When Rawls's Theory Leads to Inequality: An Example**

| | Income of all individuals (but one) | Income of last individual |
|---|---|---|
| Option *A* (equality) | $ 5,000 | $5,000 |
| Option *B* (inequality) | $10,000 | $5,100* |

*Option *B* chosen because everyone is better off.

[1] In his *Theory of Justice* (Cambridge, Mass.: Harvard University Press, 1971), p. 63, Rawls was concerned with more than income: "All social values—liberty and opportunity, income and wealth, and the bases of self-respect—are to be distributed equally unless an unequal distribution of any, or all, of these values is to everyone's advantage." While we consider the lowest-income individual in our examples, Rawls's focus is on a typical individual in the lowest-income group. But this does not seriously affect his conclusion or our evaluation of it.

[2] Envy is not taken into account: It is assumed that nobody's happiness is reduced by the knowledge that someone else has become richer.

**BOX 18-1 continued**

**TABLE B When Rawls's Theory Leads to Equality: An Example**

| | Income of all individuals (but one) | Income of last individual |
|---|---|---|
| Option *A* (equality) | $ 5,000 | $5,000* |
| Option *C* (inequality) | $10,000 | $4,900 |

*Option *A* chosen because a move to *C* would damage the last individual

ple in an original position would choose option *A*. With their concern about ending up at the bottom of the totem pole, they would focus on the figures in the last column and prefer *A* with its $5000 income to *C* with its $4900 income. Thus, according to Rawls, people would choose equality.

It is here, when he puts forward a strong argument in favour of equality, that Rawls's theory is open to criticism. Ask yourself: If you were in Rawls's original position, without knowledge of where you would eventually end up, which option would you choose? Would you join the consensus Rawls expects in favour of option *A*? Most people would find *C* difficult to resist. The minuscule risk of being $100 worse off seems trivial in comparison with the near certainty of being $5000 better off. This seems to be a risk well worth taking. Indeed, those who would select Rawls's option *A* are those who would *avoid risk at almost any cost*. How in the world would you find anyone so risk averse? (Observe that the risk you would be taking in choosing income distribution *C* rather than *A* would be the same as your risk at the race track or the stock exchange if you were to bet $100 for a chance to win $5000, with odds *in your favour* of 25 million to 1. Why those odds? There are 25 million people in Canada. In moving from option *A* to *C*, they would all "win" $5000—except for the one who would lose $100. (With such odds, who in the world would turn down such a bet?)

(Try an experiment to see the difficulty with Rawls's argument. Change the number in the bottom left corner of Table B to $100,000. Rawls's argument still leads to the choice of equality (option *A*). Would this be your choice? If so, would you choose option *A* or *C* if the number were even higher, say $1 million? Or $1 billion? Won't you eventually come around to option *C* and give up voting in a Rawlsian way?)

Because people in an original position would not necessarily vote for equality option *A* over *C*, Rawls does not make a convincing case for equality. The difficulty is that his argument is based on the assumption that people's only concern is with what is happening in the last column in the two tables—that is, with that last, poorest individual. Specifically, the choice is based on *maximizing* the *minimum* income; hence, this is often referred to as the ***maximin*** criterion. But why should we completely ignore the vast majority and be totally preoccupied with that last individual?

In a later reconsideration of the maximin criterion,[3] Rawls concluded that although he

[3] See John Rawls, "Some Reasons for the Maximin Criterion," *American Economic Review*, May 1974, pp. 141–46.

Advocates of income equality were immediately attracted to Rawls's theory because it seemed to provide a firmer foundation for equality than the traditional argument. According to the earlier argument, equality is a desirable goal because it would maximize the total utility of all individuals in society. However, this conclusion follows only if it can be assumed that all individuals have the same capacity to enjoy income. (If this assumption does not hold, we can improve the outcome by moving away from complete equality, by transferring some income away from those who are less able to enjoy it to those who are more able to enjoy it.) Unfortunately, there is no way we can confirm or deny the assumption that people enjoy income equally. Remember, there is no way to meter people's heads to compare the satisfaction they get from $1 of income. Therefore, this traditional argument does not provide convincing support for income equality. Nor, as we have seen in this box, does Rawls's theory. Like the older theory, it has a weak link, in this case the assumption that the only concern is for the lowest person on the totem pole. Moreover, many of those who believe in equality became less enthusiastic about Rawls's theory when they discovered that it allows for a very substantial degree of inequality—as we have seen in Table A and as Rawls himself has re-emphasized. (Rawls, "Some Reasons for the Maximin Criterion," p. 145.)

**BOX 18-1 continued**

still viewed it as attractive, "a deeper investigation . . . may show that some other conception of justice is more reasonable. In any case, the idea that economists may find most useful . . . is that of the original position. This perspective . . . may prove illuminating for economic theory."

one has certain other rights, such as the right to vote and equality before the law, why should each of us not have equality in our access to the marketplace—the right of equal economic reward? In other words, since everyone has an equal vote to cast in elections, why shouldn't everyone have equal dollar "votes" to spend in the marketplace? The answer is that in practice, it would be prohibitively costly to give everyone this right: An equal division of the pie would greatly shrink its size.

However, even if this cost did not exist, there would still be fundamental philosophical problems. For example, the right to an equal economic reward would come into conflict with the right of equality before the law — in particular, the principle that those who break the law should be punished for their crimes. Those who have to pay fines should *not* be left with an equal number of economic votes.

Moreover, there are practical problems. For example, how is equality to be defined? One way is to define it, most simply, as "equal money incomes." But this answer is not satisfactory, because not everyone works the same number of hours. Those who decide on shorter working hours are taking some of their potential income in the form of leisure, rather than cash. Therefore, income should be defined more broadly to include both income taken in the form of cash and "income" taken in the form of leisure. Fairness requires that an individual who takes a lot of income in one form—leisure—should get less in the other form — cash. Similarly, those whose work is dangerous should be paid higher money wages to compensate them for the risk. According to this approach, the *overall* economic position (rather than just money income) should be equalized.

Unfortunately, this broader approach raises as many problems as it solves. If the overall position of individuals is to be equalized, those who have unpleasant jobs should be paid high enough wages to compensate them, and those whose jobs are fun should accordingly be paid less. But how do we handle the following problem. Some people find a particular job—such as teaching—extremely rewarding, while others find it a bore. Should the first group be paid less than the second, in order to make them equal? Quite apart from the practical problem of determining how much each teacher likes the job—in a situation in which they would all have an incentive to lie — this broad approach would lead to an unsatisfactory result: People would be paid for hating their jobs. Since those who love teaching generally make the best teachers, this would mean that the best teachers would be paid the least. Surely this would not be fair.

Worse yet, bored, dissatisfied teachers often don't work so hard; they take "leisure on the job." Would it be fair to pay them a premium salary, when those taking a lot of leisure at home would receive low pay?

Therefore, we conclude that considerations of *equity alone* have not led us to complete equality as a meaningful objective. We are sceptical of this objective, just as we were sceptical earlier of the free-market determination of income. How about some compromise between the two?

## A Compromise Between the Free Market and Complete Equality

It is easy to conclude that both the free-market and complete-equality approaches involve serious problems. What is far more difficult is to say where in the broad range in between we should aim. We will not be able to answer that question. But here are some suggestions for you to consider as you grapple with it (and you must, as a voter).

### Make It a Fair Race, . . .

Suppose we think of participating in the economy as being in a race in which each runner's income is determined by his or her finish. The egalitarian view that "justice is income equality" implies that the government should equalize all rewards at the end of the race: Give everyone a bronze medal — no golds, and no booby prizes. As the Dodo in *Alice in Wonderland* put it, "Everybody has won, and all must have prizes."

An alternative view is that the responsibility of the government is only to ensure that the race is *fair*. Fairness in this sense could be taken to require several things:

1. Everyone should race under the same rules: No one should cheat. Most Canadians were delighted when Ben Johnson's success as a sprinter brought him fame and fortune in 1986 and 1987. But when performance-enhancing steroids were found in his system at the 1988 Olympics, few sympathized with his plight as sponsors cancelled the lucrative endorsement contracts they had earlier negotiated with him. Similarly, most Canadians see nothing wrong when some people earn high incomes through hard work because they have saved in the past to accumulate investments or because they have acquired large amounts of human capital through long years of study. But when we see others winning large "prizes" through corruption or misuse of public office, by cheating on their income taxes, or by violating rules on the use of inside information in the stock market, our sense of fairness is offended.
2. Fairness also requires that the government should make every effort to eliminate *dis*advantages that some people suffer through no fault of their own. No one should start with a 50-metre handicap because of being a woman, or a native Canadian, or the child of parents who are not influential.

In this view, everyone participating in the economic race has a right, namely the right to ***equality of opportunity***. But there should not be ***equality of reward***. That is, everyone should have the right to an equal *start*—but not to an equal *finish*.

While the idea of equal opportunity is appealing, it too is difficult to define. Buried in any definition of a fair race is a judgement on *which advantages and disadvantages are unfair and should be removed, and which should not*. Advantages of race, gender, and ethnic background clearly should be removed. But what should we do about advantages arising from differences in natural ability? Should an individual in the economic race be penalized for natural business talent so that all may have an equal start? Does it make any more sense to do this than to penalize a marathon runner for strong legs? If we were to embark on such a penalty or handicap system, we would end up in the world of Box 18-2, where Kurt Vonnegut's Handicapper General weighs down naturally talented ballerinas with bags of birdshot. In such a world, nobody would come close to breaking the four-minute mile; the economy would fall far short of its potential.

### . . . but Modify the Rewards.

It is quite possible to have a fair race, yet still have a bad system of rewards. For example, suppose the winner were to be given a million dollars, and the loser were to be thrown, Roman style, to the lions. Believing in a fair economic race does not prevent us from modifying its rewards—in other words, using taxes and transfer payments to reduce the income differences that result.

To the authors, this idea of a fair race and a modified system of rewards that reduces but does not eliminate income inequality seems to be an appealing principle. But again, the idea is not as simple as it sounds. Is not an individual's economic life less like a standard race than like a relay race? Moreover, a relay race with no beginning or end? The race you run depends on the start you get, in terms of your whole background, including your family wealth. A first reaction is that it should not be like this. To keep the race fair, everyone should be started off equally, without any advantage of inherited wealth. Should we, therefore, tax away all inheritances and, for the same reason, gifts?

This is a difficult proposal to defend, even on equity grounds. Consider two men with equal incomes. One spends it all. The other wishes to save in order to pass wealth on to his children. Is it fair to impose a tax that prohibits him from doing so? Is not charity a virtue? What can one say of a society that prevents gifts to family or friends?

## Conclusions: Can We Pin Down the Idea of Equity?

Unfortunately, the answer is no. The only conclusions we have been able to reach are both negative. Equity is not complete equality of income, nor is it the income distribution that the free market generates. We are left somewhere in between. We conclude that in terms of equity considerations alone, we should move from a free-market distribution some distance, but not the whole way, toward equalizing incomes.

To further complicate matters, any such move tends to involve an efficiency cost in terms of a

## APPLICATIONS AND ILLUSTRATIONS BOX 18-2

### Kurt Vonnegut on Why Only Horses and Golfers Should Be Handicapped*

The year was 2081, and everybody was finally equal. They weren't only equal before God and the law. They were equal every which way. Nobody was smarter than anybody else. Nobody was better looking than anybody else. Nobody was stronger or quicker than anybody else. All this equality was due to the 211th, 212th, and 213th Amendments to the Constitution, and to the unceasing vigilance of agents of the United States Handicapper General . . .

George [Bergeron, whose] intelligence was way above normal, had a little mental handicap radio in his ear. He was required by law to wear it at all times. It was tuned to a government transmitter. Every twenty seconds or so, the transmitter would send out some sharp noise to keep people like George from taking unfair advantage of their brains. . . .

On the television screen were ballerinas. . . . They weren't really very good—no better than anybody else would have been anyway. They were burdened with sashweights and bags of birdshot and their faces were masked, so that no one, seeing a free and graceful gesture or a pretty face, would feel like something the cat drug in. George was toying with the vague notion that maybe dancers shouldn't be handicapped. But he didn't get very far with it before another noise in his ear radio scattered his thoughts. . . .

George began to think glimmeringly about his abnormal son who was now in jail, about Harrison, but a twenty-one-gun salute in his head stopped that. "Boy," said Hazel, "that was a doozy, wasn't it?" It was such a doozy that George was white and trembling, and tears stood on the rims of his red eyes. Two of the eight ballerinas had collapsed to the studio floor, were holding their temples. . . .

The television program was suddenly interrupted for a news bulletin. It wasn't clear at first as to what the bulletin was about, since the announcer, like all announcers, had a serious speech impediment. For about half a minute, and in a state of high excitement, the announcer tried to say, "Ladies and gentlemen—"

He finally gave up, handed the bulletin to a ballerina to read. . . . "That's all right — " Hazel said of the announcer, "he tried. That's the big thing. He tried to the best he could with what God gave him. He should get a nice raise for trying so hard."

"Ladies and gentlemen—" said the ballerina, . . . "Harrison Bergeron, age fourteen . . . has just escaped from jail, where he was held on suspicion of plotting to overthrow the government. He is a genius and an athlete, is under-handicapped, and should be regarded as extremely dangerous."

A police photograph of Harrison Bergeron was flashed on the screen. . . . Harrison's appearance was Halloween and hardware. Nobody had ever born heavier handicaps. . . . Instead of a little ear radio for a mental handicap, he wore a tremendous pair of earphones, and spectacles with thick wavy lenses. The spectacles were intended to make him not only half blind, but to give him whanging headaches besides.

Scrap metal was hung all over him. Ordinarily, there was a certain symmetry, a military neatness to the handicaps issued to strong people, but Harrison looked like a walking junkyard.

---

* Abridgment of "Harrison Bergeron" from *Welcome to the Monkey House* by Kurt Vonnegut Jr., Copyright © 1961 by Kurt Vonnegut, Jr. Originally published in *Fantasy and Science Fiction.* Reprinted by permission of *Delacorte Press/Seymour Lawrence.*

shrinking national pie. The reason—to be examined in detail in Chapter 24—is that guaranteeing people an income tends to reduce their incentive to work, and they produce less. Because of this efficiency cost, it is desirable to stop short of the degree of equality that would be chosen if equity were the sole objective.

In practice, we have already introduced tax and expenditure policies that have moved us some distance toward equalizing incomes, as Figure 18-2 has illustrated. It is possible that we have not yet moved far enough; it is also possible that we have moved too far. The question of how the nation's income should be distributed is likely to remain an issue of continuing debate. However, it is important that the dispute about how the total income pie should be divided does not become so heated and exhausting that the total size of that pie is substantially reduced. To return to our earlier analogy: If all participants had spent their energies in a squabble about how the race should be run and how the rewards should be divided, no one would have broken the four-minute mile.

## KEY POINTS

1. Large differences exist in the incomes of Canadians. Some have high incomes because of their human capital, wealth, native talent, family background, market power, or just plain luck. Others have low incomes because they enjoy none of these advantages or because of some other factor; for example, they may suffer from discrimination.
2. If we examine the Canadian income distribution before government taxes and transfers are taken into account, we observe a great deal of inequality. The poorest 20% receive only 2.7% of the nation's income, while the highest 20% get nearly 43%.
3. About a quarter of this inequality is eliminated by government transfer expenditures that are concentrated heavily on the poor, and by progressive taxes that draw heavily from the rich. However, our tax system overall is not as progressive as the income tax alone, and taxes do much less equalizing than government transfer payments.
4. The most effective government expenditure in equalizing income is transfers such as Old Age Security, social assistance, and Unemployment Insurance. But other government expenditures, both in cash and in kind, also play a role.
5. Equality is a question of fact: How equal *are* incomes? On the other hand, equity is a matter of judgement: What pattern of incomes is fair? A strong case can be made that neither a completely equal distribution of incomes nor the unequal free-market distribution is equitable. A desirable target seems to lie somewhere in between.
6. While it is very difficult to be more precise than this, some rough guidelines have been suggested. For example, the "economic race" should be kept as fair as possible. In other words, everyone should have an equal opportunity. The government should ensure that no one starts at a disadvantage because of race or gender. However, the appealing principle of equality of opportunity conflicts with the equally appealing principle that parents should be able to help their children.
7. Equal opportunity need not result in equal reward. Even if everyone could be given an equal start, there is no reason to expect that all will finish in a tie. Some will get greater rewards than others. The second responsibility of the government is to modify rewards—that is, to reduce income inequality by taxes and transfer payments.
8. Finally, even if we could determine an equitable income distribution, it does not follow that the government should continue to redistribute income up to this point. The reason is that the act of redistributing income—changing the division of the national pie—affects the incentive to work and hence the level of efficiency (the size of that pie). Therefore, a compromise should be selected between the conflicting objectives of equity and efficiency.

## KEY TERMS

**cumulative income distribution**
**Lorenz curve**
**cash transfers**
**transfers in kind**
**difference between equity and equality**
**free market distribution of income**
***Rawls's difference principle**
***maximin**
**equality of opportunity**
**equality of reward**

* For those who have studied Box 18-1.

## PROBLEMS

18-1. Explain how the marketplace generates a rent (in the form of high income) for those with high reputation, just as for those with great skill.

18-2. Explain why you agree or disagree with the following statement: "Free-market prices of factors of production help to maximize the total national income pie and also divide it in an equitable way."

18-3. (This question is based on Box 18-1.) Is the following statement true or false? If true, explain it. If false, correct it: Rawls's maximin principle is to *maximize* the *minimum* possible income. However, this is the preference only of people who are unwilling to risk any of their income in the hope of acquiring more. Many people are not like this, including all those individuals who bet a small part of their income at the races or Monte Carlo in the hope of winning more.

18-4. In Canada, not only is the distribution of income across individuals quite uneven, it is also uneven across regions. Does your region exhibit above or below average income? What reasons can you offer for this? What federal policies may have an effect on this?

18-5. Is it possible that the degree of competition in the labour market would be one explanation for the distribution of income? For example, suppose the labour market in a particular region became perfectly competitive instead of a monopsony. What would be the effect on the distribution of income?

# PART 5 MICROECONOMIC ISSUES OF OUR TIME

Part 5 will extend the analysis of product and factor markets in Parts 2–4 to consider a number of issues that are of critical importance to the efficiency and equity of the Canadian economy.

The first two chapters deal with *international trade*. Chapter 19 describes how countries benefit from such trade, through specialization and increased competition. Chapter 20 discusses international trade *policy* and describes some of the ways in which governments intervene in the international marketplace by imposing barriers to trade. However, in recent years, some trade barriers have been coming down. The most important recent initiative in this direction, from a Canadian point of view, of course, is the 1988 Free Trade Agreement between Canada and the United States; we also discuss the extension of this agreement to include Mexico under the North American Free Trade Agreement (NAFTA).

As noted in earlier chapters, one reason that competitive markets may fail to allocate resources efficiently is externalities—side effects in production and consumption. Chapters 21–23 address the externalities issue in several different contexts.

In Chapter 21, we consider a question of particular importance to Canada: What constitutes an efficient pattern of exploitation of our *natural resources*? The chapter shows the problem that arises in the case of *common property resources*—that is, resources that are not owned by any individual or firm, but can be used by anyone. In particular, it shows how the utilization of a common property resource may give rise to a divergence between marginal social cost and marginal private cost; that is, give rise to an externality. In Chapter 22, the problems of pollution and *environmental protection* are addressed, and we explain how pollution externalities can also be interpreted as another form of the common property problem.

In Chapter 23, we consider the case of *positive* externalities, in particular, the extreme case of *public goods*; the role of the government in the areas of health and safety legislation is also discussed. Finally, Chapter 24 reviews the main social programs to reduce poverty and create a more equal distribution of income that exist in Canada, and considers the efficiency-equity conflicts that may arise in the design of such programs. Our discussion pays particular attention to a much-debated proposal designed to reduce this conflict: the Negative Income Tax (NIT).

# CHAPTER 19

# WHAT ARE THE GAINS FROM INTERNATIONAL TRADE?

*Instructed ships shall sail to quick commerce*
*By which remotest regions are allied*
*Which makes one city of the universe*
*Where some may gain and all may be supplied.*

*John Dryden (1632–1700)*

Economic gains come from specialization. One of the reasons for the high material standard of living in Canada is our high degree of ***specialization***. Pulp and paper are produced near the great forests of Northern Ontario, Quebec, and British Columbia; wheat is produced in the Western provinces; petrochemicals, cars, and car parts are manufactured in Southern Ontario. By such specialization we are able to increase our total output of goods and services.

Just as specialization within Canada increases output and efficiency, so too does specialization among Canada and other countries. There are three basic reasons. The first one is new, while the last two have already been noted in Chapter 3:

- increased competition
- economies of scale
- comparative advantage

Each of these will be described in turn, with comparative advantage left to the end, so that this traditional benefit from trade can be examined in more detail.

In the great debate on trade policy—free trade vs. protection — the gains from trade discussed in this chapter represent the case *for* free trade. The arguments for tariffs or other trade restrictions will be discussed in the next chapter.

Before describing the gains from trade, we begin with a brief description of the pattern of Canada's international trade. Which countries are our most important trading partners? What do we sell to them and what do we buy from them?

## WITH WHOM DO WE TRADE? WHAT DO WE TRADE?

The answers are provided in Table 19-1. From the first column, it is evident that Canada's most important trading partner is the United States. Of course, this is no surprise, since distance and transport costs — natural deterrents to trade — are at a minimum in our trade with the United States. (Many Americans don't realize the importance of their trade with Canada. The reason is that U.S. purchases from Canada include raw materials (base metals) and manufactured goods (telecommunications equipment) that are not as familiar to the U.S. public as the consumer goods (watches, cars, and radios) that Americans buy from Europe and Japan.) Japan is also a key trading partner of ours, as are the large countries in the European Community (EC) and Latin America.

The position of the United States as Canada's leading trading partner has, of course, been strengthened by the Canada/United States Free Trade Agreement (FTA) that came into effect on 1 January 1989. Under this agreement, all tariffs and most other restrictions on trade between the two countries are gradually being eliminated over a ten-year period. The negotiation of the North American Free Trade Agreement (NAFTA) in 1992/93 means that the trend toward fewer trade restrictions has been broadened to include Mexico, so that our trade with that country (which in the early 1990s was quite small) is likely to expand substantially as well.

The right-hand side of Table 19-1 indicates that we trade a wide variety of goods. Our exports to other countries include such diverse items as grain from the Prairies and mining equipment from London, Ontario. And our imports include computers and other equipment essential to Canadian industry as well as consumer goods, such as tropical foodstuffs, shirts, and shoes. For a nation on wheels, cars and trucks account for an important part of our trade: Our purchases of cars and car parts made up more than 20% of our total imports. (Of course, we also have large *exports* of transportation equipment, including both car and car parts; in 1990 these exports were even larger than our imports in this category.)

## BENEFITS FROM TRADE: MARKETS BECOME MORE COMPETITIVE

Consider the monopoly firm illustrated in Figure 19-1. Initially, without international trade, this firm has the Canadian market all to itself in panel (a). If it is not subject to government regulation, it will be able to set a monopoly price. In panel (b), we see what happens when trade is opened up. The potential demand facing the Canadian producer is much larger, as shown by the total world demand curve. Therefore, the firm is now able to go after foreign markets as well as the domestic Canadian market. But it is no longer able to take the domestic market for granted, since it faces ***increased competition*** here from foreign producers. Thus, foreign trade can transform a natural monopoly in the domestic market in panel (a) into a natural oligopoly in the world market in panel (b). In the process, this firm's monopoly control of the Canadian market is broken, and its ability to exercise market power (charge a high price) is reduced. As shown earlier, a lower, more competitive price results in an improved allocation of resources, with a corresponding efficiency gain.

On the other hand, if the industry is originally a natural oligopoly, international trade can make it substantially more competitive. To illustrate, consider the Canadian firm in Figure 19-2 that, before trade, has about one-third of the domestic market. After trade is opened up in panel (b), this firm will have a much smaller fraction of the market, because the market is now the whole world. Again, increased competition will tend to keep price down, with Canadian consumers benefiting. Furthermore, they gain in other ways as well, if the domestic producer is forced to compete in non-price aspects, such as quality or design. Thus, the North American auto industry has been pressured into producing smaller cars as a result of competition, first from European firms in the late 1950s and, more recently, from Japanese and South Korean auto makers.

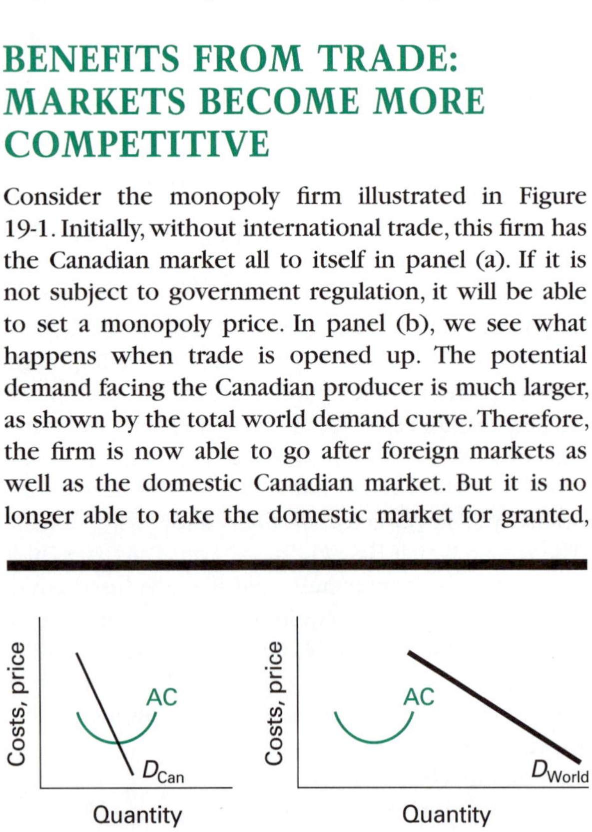


**(a) Without trade** (like Figure 13-3(c)). Without trade, home market demand can support only one low-cost producer. The result: a natural monopoly.

**(b) With trade** (like Figure 13-3(b)). With trade, market demand is greater, but the number of producers is also greater, because it now includes both Canadian and foreign firms. The result: a natural oligopoly.

**FIGURE 19-1 How international trade breaks down monopoly power.**

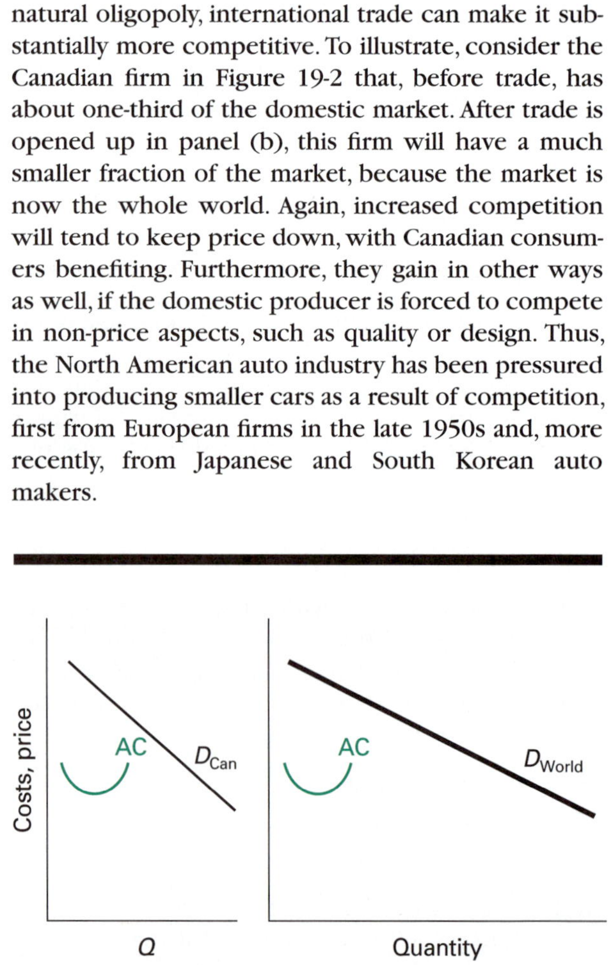


**(a) Without trade** (like Figure 13-3(b)). Without trade, the Canadian market can support only about three producers.

**(b) With trade** (closer to Figure 13-3(a)). With trade, market demand is greater, but the number of producers is also greater since it now includes both Canadian and foreign firms.

**FIGURE 19-2 How international trade makes an oligopoly more competitive.**

**TABLE 19-1 Merchandise Trade Patterns of Canada in 1990 (in billions of dollars)**

**With Whom Do We Trade?**

| Exports: 1990 Canadian Sales to: | |
|---|---|
| U.S.A. | 110.4 |
| U.K. | 3.5 |
| Other EC | 8.5 |
| Japan | 7.7 |
| Other OECD | 3.5 |
| All other countries | 12.9 |
| TOTAL | 146.5 |

| Imports: 1990 Canadian Purchases from: | |
|---|---|
| U.S.A. | 92.9 |
| U.K. | 4.9 |
| Other EC | 10.0 |
| Japan | 8.2 |
| Other OECD | 5.0 |
| All other countries | 14.6 |
| TOTAL | 135.6 |

**What Do We Trade?**

| Exports: 1990 Canadian Sales of: | |
|---|---|
| Farm and fish products | 13.3 |
| Forest products | 20.9 |
| Energy materials (of which crude petroleum and natural gas: 9.3) | 14.7 |
| Other metals and minerals | 19.1 |
| Chemicals and fertilizers | 7.2 |
| Manufactured goods (of which motor vehicles and parts: 33.9) | 68.5 |
| Other exports | 2.8 |
| TOTAL | 146.5 |

| Imports: 1990 Canadian Purchases of: | |
|---|---|
| Food | 9.1 |
| Energy materials | 8.2 |
| Industrial materials | 24.5 |
| Construction materials | 2.5 |
| Motor vehicles and parts | 30.6 |
| Other transportation equipment and parts | 4.8 |
| Producer's equipment | 37.9 |
| Other manufactured consumer goods | 15.9 |
| Other imports | 2.1 |
| TOTAL | 135.6 |

*Source: Bank of Canada Review,* December 1991.

# BENEFITS FROM TRADE: ECONOMIES OF SCALE

In the face of ***economies of scale*** (falling average cost as output expands), there are two additional potential gains from trade.

## New Products Become Available

Specifically, international trade may make it profitable to produce goods that otherwise would not be produced at all. Panel (a) in Figure 19-3 illustrates such a product. Demand is too low in the domestic economy to allow this good to be profitably produced. But when the foreign market becomes available, demand becomes large enough to cover average costs (the rightward shift in *D* makes it now overlap AC) and the item is introduced. An outstanding example is Toronto-based Northern Telecom. Toward the end of the 1970s, Northern Telecom began to invest heavily in developing digital switching technology for use in office communications networks and by phone companies. (This technology is especially useful when communications systems are used both for voice

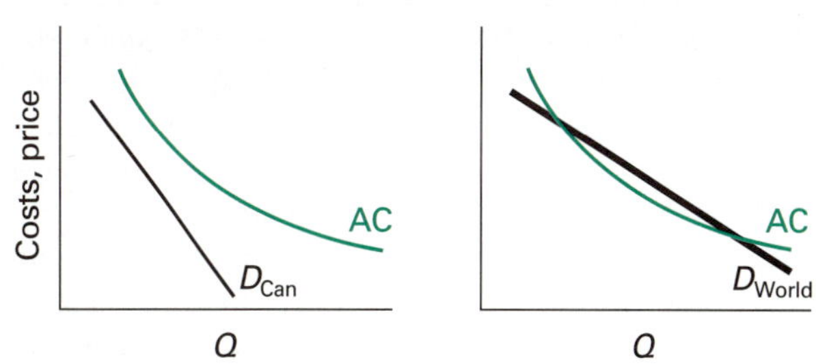


**(a) Without trade** — Without trade this good will not be produced,

**(b) Same good, with trade** — but with trade, it will be produced.

**FIGURE 19-3 How international trade may create new products.**

The AC curves in these two figures are identical. But because of trade, the demand curve in panel (b) is much farther to the right.

communications and transfer of data between computers.) By the mid-1980s, Northern Telecom had become a world leader in this field. Most of its sales were outside Canada: Foreign sales outpaced domestic sales by a wide margin. If Northern Telecom had not been able to count on foreign sales, there would have been little prospect of recouping the enormous research and development costs for the new technology; most probably, this would have meant that the lead would have gone to an American firm, such as AT&T, which has a much larger domestic market.

### Existing Goods Can Be Produced More Efficiently

Where there are economies of scale, trade can lead to more efficient production. For example, with the elimination of tariff barriers within the European Community (EC), a manufacturer in any member country can sell freely to buyers in all member countries. This has allowed European producers to manufacture goods, such as household appliances, in much larger volume. In industries with economies of scale, this larger volume has meant lower cost, which in turn has made it possible for these products to be sold at a lower price. Thus, this increase in efficiency from economies of scale is beneficial to buyers, not only in the countries where these goods are produced, but also in the other European countries where they can be purchased tariff-free. The potential economies-of-scale gains provided one of the most important arguments in favour of the Canada/United States FTA, as well as NAFTA. Since the Canadian market is relatively small, firms in many Canadian manufacturing industries have difficulty achieving the low costs of large-scale production if they are limited to the domestic market. True, some Canadian manufacturing firms may not be able to survive under free trade. But for those that *are* able to successfully compete in the entire North American market, achieving economies of scale will no longer be a problem.

## GAINS FROM TRADE: COMPARATIVE ADVANTAGE

Even if the above reasons for trade did not exist, there would still be the strong traditional argument that remains valid in any case: the benefit from ***comparative advantage***.

The basic idea has already been introduced in Chapter 3. Even though the lawyer cited there may be more skilful (that is, may have an ***absolute advantage***) in both law and gardening, she does not do both. Thus, absolute advantage does not determine what she does. Instead, she concentrates on law, the activity in which she has a comparative advantage, and buys the services of a gardener. By specializing in this way, she can acquire more gardening services than if she were to take the time to do it herself. It is *comparative* advantage that determines what she does.

Internationally, the idea is exactly the same: Even though Canada may be better—that is, have an absolute advantage—in producing both snowmobiles and radios, it may be in our interest to concentrate on snowmobiles and other products in which we have a comparative advantage, and leave radios to other countries. By specializing in snowmobiles, we may be able to acquire more radios through trade than we could produce ourselves.

The idea of comparative advantage was developed in the early nineteenth century by David Ricardo, an English economist, financier, and member of the British Parliament. In his simplified illustration of this idea, Ricardo assumed that markets were perfectly competitive, that there were no transport costs, that all production costs were constant, and that the only input was labour. He also assumed that there were only two countries (we shall call them Canada and Britain) producing two goods (we shall call them food and clothing).

### Absolute Advantage

As a preliminary, Table 19-2 shows the case where each country has an *absolute advantage* in the production of one good. In the first column, we see that a clothing worker in Britain can outproduce a worker in Canada (4 to 3), so by definition Britain has an absolute advantage in clothing. Similarly, in the second column we see that Canada has an absolute advantage in food, since a Canadian worker can outproduce a British worker (2 to 1). The most efficient allocation of resources is to have Canada specialize in food and Britain in clothing as the calculations at the bottom of Table 19-2 confirm.

So far, it seems that each country specializes in the good in which it has an absolute advantage. But this is not always so. We shall now show that the key to specialization is *comparative* advantage rather than absolute advantage.

**TABLE 19-2 Illustration of Absolute Advantage**

**Hypothetical Output per Worker in Britain and Canada**

| | Clothing | Food |
|---|---|---|
| Canada | 3 units | 2 units |
| Britain | 4 units | 1 unit |

In the first column, Britain has an absolute advantage in clothing production because a worker can produce 4 units compared with only 3 in Canada. In the second column, Canada has an absolute advantage in food, because a worker here can produce 2 units, compared with only 1 in Britain. Both countries together can produce more total output when Canada specializes in food and Britain specializes in clothing.

To confirm, suppose specialization has not occurred; in other words, suppose that each country is initially producing both goods. Now suppose that they begin to specialize—Canada in food, Britain in clothing. Therefore, a worker in Canada is switched out of clothing and into food production. At the same time, a worker in Britain is switched in the opposite direction (out of food and into clothing). As a result of these two switches:

| | Clothing output changes by | Food output changes by |
|---|---|---|
| In Canada | −3 | +2 |
| In Britain | +4 | −1 |
| Therefore, net world output changes by | +1 | +1 |

**TABLE 19-3 Illustration of Comparative Advantage**

**Hypothetical Output per Worker in Britain and Canada**

| | Clothing | Food |
|---|---|---|
| Canada | 6 units | 3 units |
| Britain | 4 units | 1 unit |

In the bottom row, one British worker can produce either 4 units of clothing or 1 unit of food. Thus, the opportunity cost of 1 unit of food in Britain is 4 units of clothing. In the row above, we see that a Canadian worker can produce either 6 units of clothing or 3 of food. The opportunity cost of food in Canada is therefore 6/3 = 2 units of clothing. (Notice how we calculate this opportunity cost by taking the ratio of the figures in the Canadian row, just as we calculated the British cost (4/1) from the figures in the British row.) Since the opportunity cost of food in Canada is less than in Britain, Canada has a comparative advantage in food and specializes in this good.

To confirm that this specialization will increase total world output, again suppose that each country is initially producing both goods. Now suppose they begin to specialize: Canada switches one worker out of clothing and into food, and Britain switches two workers out of food and into clothing. Then:

| | Clothing output changes by | Food output changes by |
|---|---|---|
| In Canada | −6 | +3 |
| In Britain | +8 | −2 |
| Therefore, net world output changes by | +2 | +1 |

## Comparative Advantage

Table 19-3 illustrates the more difficult case where one country, Canada (like the lawyer in Box 3-2), has an absolute advantage in the production of both goods: A Canadian worker outproduces a British worker in both clothing (6 to 4) and food (3 to 1). Nonetheless, Canada—like the lawyer of Chapter 3—will not try to satisfy its requirements by producing both goods itself. Instead, it will specialize in one and buy the other from Britain, as we shall now explain.

Our first step is to calculate the ***opportunity cost*** of food in each country. First, in Britain: The second row of Table 19-3 tells us that a British worker who is now producing 1 unit of food could, instead, be producing 4 units of clothing. In other words, in Britain *the opportunity cost of 1 unit of food is 4 units of clothing.* Since prices tend to reflect costs, we would expect these two goods to exchange in Britain for the same 1:4 ratio. That is, in the absence of international trade, 1 unit of food will exchange in Britain for 4 units of clothing. The minimum price that food producers will be willing to accept for a unit of food must be 4 times as high as the price of a unit of clothing, since a unit of food costs 4 times as much to produce. Moreover, at this price of food, domestic consumers will adjust their purchases of food and clothing until the maximum amount they are willing to pay for the last unit of food is 4 times as high as the price of clothing.

On the other hand, what is the opportunity cost of food in Canada? The first row of Table 19-3 tells us that a Canadian worker who is producing 3 units of food could instead be producing 6 units of clothing. In other words, in Canada the opportunity cost of a unit of food is 6/3 = 2 units of clothing. Consequently, we would expect the two goods to exchange in Canada at this 1:2 ratio. That is, before trade, 1 unit of food will exchange in Canada for 2 units of clothing.

Since the opportunity cost of food in Canada is less (2 units of clothing versus 4 in Britain), we say that Canada has a comparative advantage in food. By definition:

A country's *comparative advantage* is the good that it can produce relatively cheaply; that is, at lower opportunity cost than its trading partner.

A similar set of calculations, again using the figures in Table 19-3, shows that in clothing, Britain has a lower opportunity cost and hence a comparative advantage.[1] Notice that in this simple two-country, two-good example if Canada has a comparative advantage in one good (food), Britain *must* have a comparative advantage in the other (clothing).

## Gains from Trade

Both countries will benefit if they specialize in their product of comparative advantage and trade for the other — at any price ratio between the 1:2 price ratio that would prevail in an isolated Canada and the 1:4 in Britain. Suppose this price ratio — often called the "terms of trade" — is 1:3; that is, 1 unit of food exchanges internationally for 3 units of clothing. The determination of this price ratio depends not only on the cost conditions that we have been describing, but also on demand in these two countries. For example, the more strongly Britons demand food — the Canadian export good — the higher the price of food will be.

But a price of food that is only 3 times as high as the price of clothing is less than the minimum amount British food producers are willing to accept. Therefore, Britain stops producing food and specializes in clothing. Similarly, Canadian clothing producers will stop production: Canada specializes in food instead.

Let's now show how Canada benefits by specializing in its product of comparative advantage, food, and by trading to satisfy its clothing needs. Specifically, for each Canadian worker taken out of clothing production, Canada loses 6 units of clothing. However, that worker instead now produces 3 units of food, which can then be traded (at the 1:3 international price ratio) for 9 units of clothing — for a clear gain of 3 units of clothing.

[1] In Britain the opportunity cost of clothing is 1/4 of a unit of food; that is, 1/4 of a unit of food must be given up to acquire 1 unit of clothing. Similarly, in Canada the opportunity cost of clothing is 3/6 or 1/2 of a unit of food. With its lower opportunity cost of clothing, Britain has a comparative advantage in clothing.

Similarly, Britain also gains by specializing in its product of comparative advantage — clothing — and trading it for food. In switching a worker from food to clothing production, Britain loses 1 unit of food. But that worker produces 4 units of clothing instead, and this output can be traded (at the 1:3 international price ratio) for 4/3 or 1⅓ units of food — for a gain of 1/3 units of food.

To sum up this example, there are ***gains from trade*** for both countries. Canada benefits by specializing in food (its comparative advantage) and trading for clothing. At the same time Britain benefits by specializing in clothing (its comparative advantage) and trading for food. The reason that there are gains from trade is that the cost ratios in the two rows of Table 19-3 (namely 6/3 and 4/1) are different. If these ratios (that is, opportunity costs) were the same, there would be no comparative advantage and no gain from trade.

Comparative advantage thus leads to gains from trade. But why does comparative advantage exist? Why does Canada have a comparative advantage in food? One important reason is our large endowment of highly productive land, especially in the Prairies. Similarly, the reason that Saudi Arabia specializes in oil is its huge endowment of this resource. On the other hand, a country like India, with its huge pool of unskilled labour, tends to have a comparative advantage in activities that require a great deal of labour. Comparative advantage depends not only on such resource endowments, but also on skills and technology. For example, our highly developed technology gives us a comparative advantage in producing items such as telecommunications equipment.

### Diagrammatic Illustration

The gain to Canada from trade may be illustrated in another way. Figure 19-4 shows the Canadian production possibilities curve (PPC), derived from the Canadian figures in the first row of Table 19-3, assuming that there are 20 million workers in Canada. For example, if they all work at producing clothing, each of the 20 million workers will produce 6 units for a total of 120 million units of clothing, as shown at point *A*. Or, if they all work at producing food (3 units each), they will produce 60 million units of food and no clothing at point *C*. Finally, if half the workers produce food and half clothing, then the 10 million workers in clothing will produce 60 units (6 units each) while the other 10 million workers in food will produce 30 units at point *B*. In this simple Ricardian

## APPLICATIONS AND ILLUSTRATIONS — BOX 19-1

### Wages and Trade

Using Tables 19-2 and 19-3, will wages be higher in Canada or Britain?

The answer is: In Canada, because labour is more productive here. (Remember, in Table 19-3 Canada has an absolute advantage in the production of both goods.) Because they can *produce* more goods, Canadian workers can be *paid* "more goods," that is, a higher real wage. Moreover, Canadians will have a higher real income whether or not the two countries trade. What trade and specialization make possible is an increase in real income in both countries.

This conclusion will hold even when we consider two countries such as Canada and Mexico where wage rates are very different. The prospective gains to Canada from increasing trade with Mexico are further discussed in the next chapter.

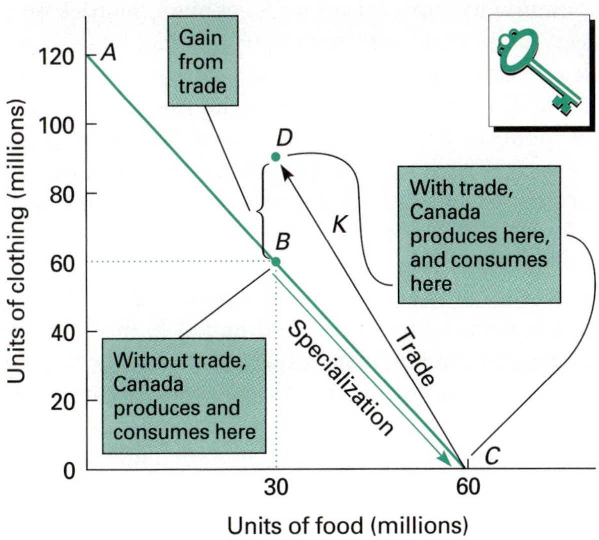


**FIGURE 19-4 Gains from trade.**

Canada's production possibilities curve *AC* is derived from the first row in Table 19-3, on the assumption that there are 20 million workers in Canada. Suppose that, without trade, Canada produces and consumes at point *B*. When trade is opened, Canada can (1) *specialize* in food, by shifting production from *B* to *C*, and (2) *trade* 30 units of food for 90 units of clothing at the prevailing 1:3 international price ratio. Thus, Canada can move from *C* to *D*. The Canadian gain from trade is the increase in clothing consumption from the original 60 units at point *B* to the 90 units at point *D*.

example, the constant figures in the first row of Table 19-3 ensure that the production possibilities curve AC is a straight line. The opportunity cost of food in Canada remains constant as we move down this curve: No matter how much food we may be producing, we must give up 2 units of clothing in order to produce 1 more unit of food.

Before trade, Canada will produce and consume at a point on the production possibilities curve, such as *B*. With trade, Canada can benefit by the following two steps.

1. *Specialize*. Shift production from *B* to *C*, as shown by the coloured arrow. That is, produce 30 million more units of food by giving up 60 million units of clothing. Thus, Canada concentrates on food, the good in which it has a comparative advantage.
2. *Trade*. Trade these 30 million additional units of food at the 1:3 international price ratio for 90 million units of clothing. This second step is shown by the black arrow.

As a result of this specialization and trade, Canada's consumption can rise from point *B* to point *D*. In other words, there are 30 million more units of clothing available for consumption; this is Canada's *real income gain*, or efficiency gain from trade.

In panel (a) of Figure 19-5, we show that such a gain from trade exists even when opportunity costs are not constant; that is, in the more usual case when the production possibilities curve is not a straight line. This diagram also shows that, although trade induces a country to specialize, it will often not specialize completely: Canada moves from *B* to *C*, but not all the way to complete specialization at *F*. And one frequently observes this pattern: A country not only specializes in and exports its product of comparative advantage—in this case, food—it also produces other goods as well; in this example, it produces *some* clothing at point *C*. (For details on why such a country will not specialize completely, see the caption to this diagram.)[2]

## Trade and Technological Change: Their Similarities

Panel (a) of Figure 19-5 has shown how trade allows a country to consume at a point, such as *D*, that is, beyond its production possibilities curve (PPC). True, *production* is always limited by a country's PPC, but consumption can be greater because of the gain from trade. In other words, international trade is the way for countries to break out of their production limitation and reach a point of consumption beyond it.

In panel (b) we see that ***technological change*** has the same effect of allowing us to move from point *B* to a higher point of consumption *D*. But it does so by shifting the production possibilities curve outward.

Trade and technological change are also alike in another significant respect. Though they generally provide a benefit to the nation as a whole, they do not necessarily benefit *every* group within the nation. Thus, there are often groups that object vehemently to trade or to technological change. For example, during the first period of rapid technological change in the textile industry about two centuries ago, workers feared that the new machinery being introduced would eliminate their jobs. (Some workers did indeed lose their jobs, even though machinery has ultimately made possible jobs with much higher productivity and pay.) This fear of job loss led some workers at that time to throw their wooden shoes — in French, *sabots* — into the machinery; hence, the word "sabotage" was coined. Similarly, international trade may displace textile workers, if production is shifted from textiles — where some markets have been lost to imports — to newsprint or transport equipment, where we have a comparative advantage and export. Once again, those who are harmed may strongly object. In this case, they need not throw their shoes into the machinery; restrictions on imports are the way to seek protection. Note that trade restrictions and sabotage are similar in one respect: Both prevent a general improvement in the standard of living in order to protect a specific group.

The temporary unemployment that follows either trade or technological change is a problem, but one that can easily be exaggerated. Historically, workers displaced by technological change have usually been fairly quickly absorbed elsewhere, as have workers displaced by imports. For example, this was true in Europe, when the Common Market (the European Community) opened up trade among countries on a very large scale, and temporary unemployment was less than expected. And even though many jobs in traditional North American industries were lost as imports from Japan and other Southeast Asian countries grew rapidly after World War II, this was accomplished without any secular increase in unemployment. Between the late 1970s and the early 1990s, however, unemployment in North America rose substantially in comparison to earlier periods. While many factors have contributed to this increase in unemployment, many observers blamed it at least in part on import competition. The fear of increased unemployment has also been a key factor in the Canadian debate over the issue of free trade with the United States and Mexico.

While there are striking similarities between trade and technological change, there is an important difference. Technological change is permanent: Once the production possibilities curve shifts outward in panel (b) of Figure 19-5, it doesn't shift back. In contrast, a trade gain is not necessarily permanent. If trade is sharply reduced — for example, because of the imposition of high tariffs—then most of the gains from trade are lost. That is, the country in panel (a) moves from *D* back toward point *B*.

## International Trade and Exchange Rates

One reason that international trade is different from domestic trade is that different countries use differ-

[2] Figure 19-5(a) can also be used to show how demand also influences specialization and trade. (In this elementary treatment we have emphasized the other side of the coin: the importance of costs, as reflected in the production possibilities curve. But demand is important, too.) Suppose there is an increase in both countries in the demand for food; as a consequence its price rises. Therefore, less food is needed to buy a given quantity of clothing. In other words, the trade arrow becomes steeper. Consequently, it is no longer tangent to the production possibilities curve at point *C*, but instead at a point to the right, say *G*. *G* is, therefore, the best production point for this country. (The reason the point of tangency is best is given in the caption to Figure 19-5(a).) Thus, this country specializes even more, by moving from *B* not just to *C*, but to *G*. (And, of course, from point *G*, it trades up and to the left along its new, steeper trade arrow.) To sum up: In response to increased demand, this country's production pattern changes; by producing even more food, it specializes to an even greater degree than before.

ent kinds of money. Thus international trade involves not only exchanges of goods and services, but also exchanges of different currencies. For example, when a Canadian importer buys a shipment of electronic calculators, say, from a seller in the United States, the importer first has to go to the ***foreign exchange market*** to buy American dollars in exchange for Canadian dollars, since an American seller typically will want to be paid in U.S. dollars, not Canadian dollars. The Canadian-dollar cost of importing the calculators, therefore, depends in part on the ***exchange rate*** between the Canadian dollar and the U.S. dollar. For example, if each U.S. dollar costs Cdn.$1.25, the cost of a shipment of calculators for which the American seller charges U.S.$20,000 will be Cdn.$25,000. On the other hand, if each U.S. dollar only costs Cdn.$1.10, the Canadian-dollar cost will only be Cdn.$22,000. Similarly, the exchange rate between the Canadian dollar and the American dollar is important for Canadian exporters. For example, a Canadian firm that can sell plywood in the American market at a price of U.S.$8 per sheet will receive Cdn.$10 per sheet if the exchange rate is Cdn.$1.25 per U.S. dollar; if the exchange rate is Cdn.$1.10 = U.S.$1, the exporter will only receive Cdn.$8.80 per sheet.

A *foreign exchange rate* is the price of one currency (say, the U.S. dollar) in terms of another (say, the Canadian dollar). A *foreign exchange*

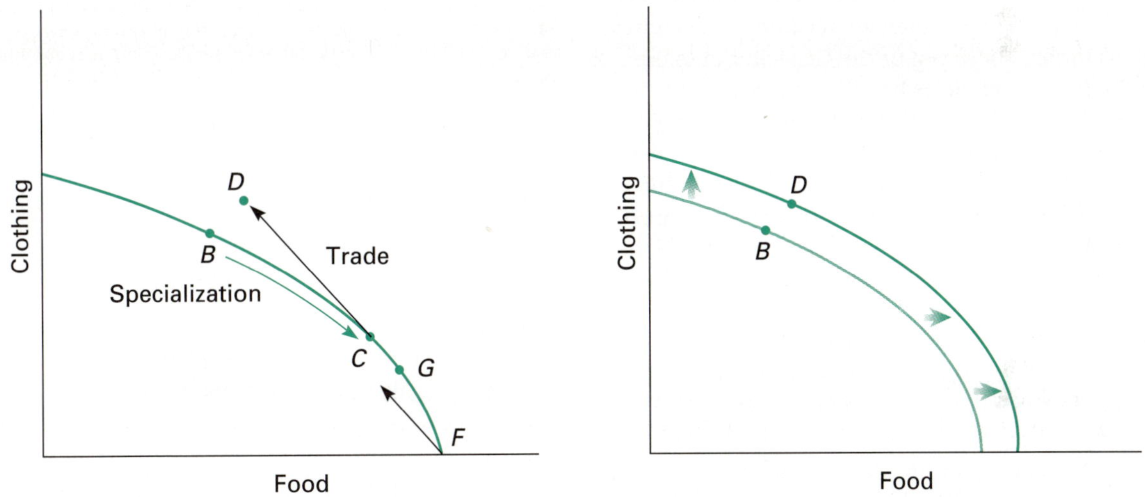


**(a) International trade.** Specialization and trade allow us to increase our consumption from *B* to *D*. Note that the production possibilities curve does not shift. We just move to a different point *C* on this curve as we specialize in the production of food. Then, by exporting food and importing clothing, we reach consumption point *D* beyond the production possibilities curve. (Why don't we specialize completely, by moving from *B* not just to *C*, but all the way to *F*? The answer is that we would then be trading along the arrow at *F*, and this doesn't allow us to reach the high consumption point *D* that is achievable by specializing in *C* and trading along the higher arrow. For exactly the same reason that *F* is inferior to *C*, *any* other point on the production possibilities curve is also inferior to *C*. Therefore tangency point *C* is best.)

**(b) Technological change.** Technological change shifts the production possibilities curve outward, so that production and consumption may be increased from *B* to *D*. (Similar to Figure 2-4.)

**FIGURE 19-5** **Both trade and technological change allow us to increase consumption.**

*market* is the market where different currencies are exchanged.

Exchange rates are studied in more detail in Chapters 14 and 19 in the *Macroeconomics* volume, which forms a companion to this book. As discussed there, in the long run there is a tendency for exchange rates to adjust so as to bring about equilibrium in a country's international transactions: When the exchange rates have reached such an equilibrium, producers of goods for which the country does have a comparative advantage will be able to compete successfully in world markets, and employment in these industries will grow. However, the process of exchange rate adjustment is sometimes slow, and in the short run, incomplete adjustments may sometimes contribute to a country's unemployment problem. For example, in the period 1981–1985, the value of the American dollar had become very high in relation to currencies such as the Japanese yen or the German Deutschmark (that is, these currencies had become relatively cheap in terms of U.S. dollars). But this was also a period when imports into the United States rose substantially, and many American jobs were lost in industries that were unable to compete with imports. Similarly, many observers blamed at least part of the high unemployment in Canada during the recession in the early 1990s on the high value of the Canadian dollar during the years 1989–1991: The high dollar made it difficult for Canadian industries to compete with imports, and reduced profitability in our export industries. Conversely, the decline in the value of the Canadian dollar in 1992 meant that imports became more costly (as importers had to pay more for each U.S. dollar), and increased profitability in our export industries. As Canadian firms faced reduced competition from imports and better export markets, the employment situation gradually improved.

# GAINS FROM TRADE: ILLUSTRATION USING DEMAND AND SUPPLY

While in many respects the analysis above is the best way to illustrate the gains from trade, it is oversimplified in one way: It is a "two-good model" that lumps all Canadian exports into a single food category and all imports into a single clothing category. In contrast, the supply and demand analysis that will now be developed can be used to examine an individual export and an individual import.

## Efficiency Gain on a Typical Export: Wheat

Figure 19-6 shows the Canadian demand and supply curves for wheat. Without trade, equilibrium in the domestic market is at point $A$, where the nation's supply and demand intersect. Thus, $Q_A$ is produced at price $P_A$. At the same time, the price in the rest of the world (expressed in Canadian dollars) is at the higher level $P$, reflecting the higher costs of producing wheat in foreign countries.

When trade is opened, Canadian producers discover that they can sell abroad at this higher price $P$, and they begin to do so. Moreover, since they can sell at $P$ abroad, they will be unwilling to sell at any lower price in the home market. Thus, the domestic price rises to the world level $P$.[3]

[3] More realistically, the Canadian price rises to the foreign price less transportation costs. However, to keep this illustration simple, we assume that transport costs and other similar complications do not exist.

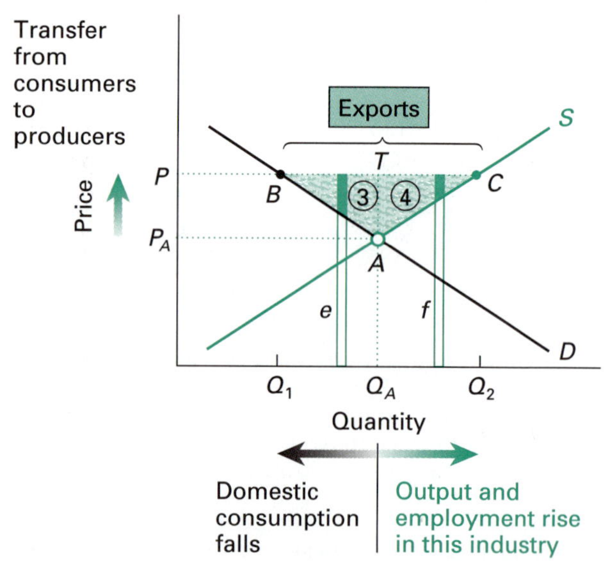


**FIGURE 19-6 Detailed effects of the export of an individual good—wheat.**

With trade, price increases from $P_A$ to $P$ with $Q_1Q_2$ exported. In part, these exports come from reduced consumption ($Q_1Q_A$); the net gain on these units is area 3. The other part of these exports comes from increased production ($Q_AQ_2$); the net gain on these units is area 4. Thus, the total efficiency gain from exporting is the entire coloured area. There is a transfer effect as well, shown by the coloured arrow on the left: Because price has risen, producers gain at consumers' expense.

Canadian producers, earning this more attractive price, expand their output. Specifically, they move up their supply curve from $A$ to $C$, increasing their output from $Q_A$ to $Q_2$. But, of course, consumers view this higher price quite differently. They move up their demand curve from $A$ to $B$, thus reducing their consumption from $Q_A$ to $Q_1$. In short, $Q_2$ is now produced and $Q_1$ is consumed, with the difference ($Q_1Q_2$) being exported. Thus, these Canadian exports come partly from increased production and partly from reduced domestic consumption.

To understand these two effects in detail, first consider one of the units of reduced consumption $Q_1Q_A$, say unit $e$. The consumers' benefit from this lost unit of consumption is shown as the hollow bar under the demand curve. (Recall that demand reflects marginal benefit.) But the gain from exporting this unit is the export price $P$ that is received for it, as shown by the hollow bar plus the solid bar above. Hence, the net gain from exporting it, rather than consuming it, is the solid bar. The sum of all such solid bars throughout the relevant range $Q_1Q_A$ is the coloured triangle 3. This is the gain from switching goods from consumption to a more highly valued use, namely, export.

Next, consider one of the units of increased production for export $Q_AQ_2$, say unit $f$. The cost of producing it is the hollow bar under the supply curve. (Recall that supply reflects marginal cost.) But the benefit from producing it is the export price $P$ received for it, which is the hollow bar plus the solid bar. Therefore, the net gain from producing it for export is the solid bar. The sum of all such solid bars through the relevant range $Q_AQ_2$ is represented by the coloured triangle 4. This is the efficiency gain from expanding production for export.

The total gain from exporting is shown as the sum of both these effects; in other words, the total coloured area in Figure 19-6. In simple terms, this gain indicates that wheat can be sold to foreigners for more than it costs to produce it, or more than is lost by switching it away from domestic consumption.

Of course, this coloured area will represent an efficiency *loss* if producers are *not* allowed to export. It demonstrates that interference in a competitive world market may be damaging, in the same way that we have seen that interference in a competitive home market may be damaging.

## Efficiency Gain on a Typical Import: Woollens

A parallel analysis illustrates the gain from importing a specific item. Figure 19-7 shows the Canadian supply and demand curves for an import-competing product such as woollens. Without trade, equilibrium in the domestic market is at point $A$, with price $P_A$ and quantity $Q_A$ produced and consumed. At the same time, the price in the rest of the world (expressed in Canadian dollars) is at the lower level $P$, reflecting the lower costs of production there.

When trade is opened, Canadian consumers can buy imported woollens at this lower price $P$. Since they will be unwilling to buy from Canadian producers at higher price $P_A$, the domestic price will fall to the world level $P$. At this lower price, Canadian consumers increase their purchases; they move down their demand curve from $A$ to $J$, increasing their consumption from $Q_A$ to $Q_6$. At the same time, domestic producers respond to lower price $P$ by moving down their supply curve from $A$ to $H$, thus reducing their output from $Q_A$ to $Q_5$. In short, $Q_5$ is now produced

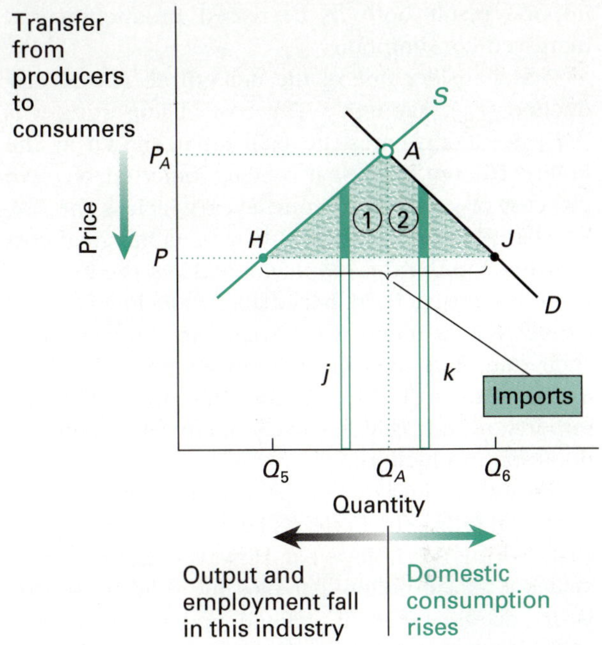


**FIGURE 19-7 Detailed effects of the import of an individual good—woollens.**

With trade, price decreases from $P_A$ to $P$, with $HJ$ imported. This reduces domestic production by $Q_AQ_5$; the net gain on these units is area 1. Imports also result in increased consumption of $Q_AQ_6$; the net gain on these units is area 2. Thus, the total efficiency gain from importing this good is the entire coloured area. There is also a transfer effect, shown by the coloured arrow on the left: Because price has fallen, consumers gain at producers' expense.

in Canada while $Q_6$ is consumed; the difference ($Q_5Q_6$) is the amount imported. Thus, Canadian imports result both in decreased production and increased consumption.

First, consider one of the units of decreased production $Q_AQ_5$, say unit *j*. The cost of importing it is the price *P* that must be paid for it, shown as the hollow bar. But because it is being imported, we save the cost of producing it ourselves, which is the hollow bar plus the solid bar—that is, its marginal cost as defined under the supply curve. Thus, the net gain from importing it, rather than producing it more expensively at home, is the solid bar. The sum of all such solid bars over the relevant range $Q_5Q_A$ is coloured triangle 1. This is the gain from allowing imports to displace relatively inefficient, high-cost domestic production.

Finally, consider one of the units of increased consumption $Q_AQ_6$, say unit *k*. Its cost is the import price *P* shown by the hollow bar. However, the consumer values it as the hollow bar plus the solid bar—that is, its marginal benefit defined under the demand curve. Therefore, the net benefit from this unit of increased consumption is the solid bar, and the sum of all such benefits is the coloured triangle 2. This is the efficiency gain from allowing consumption to expand in response to a bargain international price.

The total efficiency gain on both accounts is the whole coloured area in Figure 19-7. In simplest terms, this area shows that we can benefit by buying a low-cost import because it allows us to cut back our own inefficient, high-cost production; it also allows us to increase our consumption of a bargain-priced good.

## WINNERS AND LOSERS FROM INTERNATIONAL TRADE

While trade leads to an overall gain in efficiency, it is important to emphasize again that not all groups benefit. For example, in Figure 19-6, trade brings an increase in the price of wheat. As a result, wheat farmers gain while consumers lose. This transfer is shown by the coloured arrow to the left of the diagram. On the other hand, the import in Figure 19-7 results in the opposite sort of transfer. Because it lowers price, consumers benefit while producers lose.

These benefits and losses to each group as a result of imports are shown more precisely in the alternative analysis set out in Figure 19-8. Each panel in this diagram reproduces the Canadian supply and demand curves for woollens from Figure 19-7. The gain to the

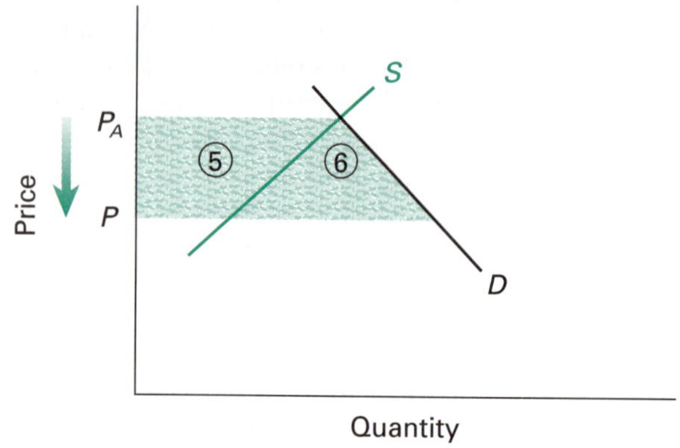


**(a)** As price falls because of imports, consumers gain,

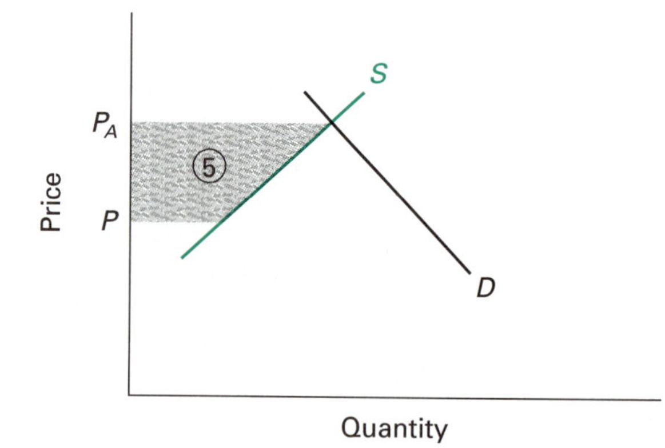


**(b)** but producers lose.

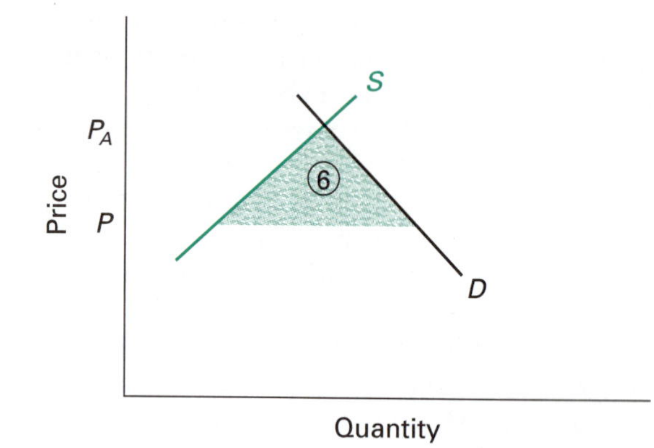


**(c)** Overall result: area 5 is transferred from producers to consumers, and there is a net gain of area 6.

**FIGURE 19-8 Detailed effects of an import of woollens. (An alternative to Figure 19-7.)**

nation's consumers from a lower price is shown by the coloured area in panel (a) enclosed to the left of the demand curve. At the same time, producers receive a lower price, and lose sales to imports. As a result, producer surplus is reduced by the grey area in panel (b) enclosed to the left of the supply curve.[4] Because this area 5 also appears as a coloured gain in panel (a), it is a ***transfer*** from the producers who lose it in panel (b) to the consumers who receive it in panel (a). At the same time, area 6 in panel (a) is a coloured gain not offset by a grey loss. This net gain of area 6 is reproduced in panel (c). This is, of course, exactly the same coloured ***efficiency gain*** that appeared in the preceding diagram.[5] Finally, in any such analysis, it's important to repeat an earlier warning: In concluding that there will be an efficiency gain, we have assumed that the consumers' valuation of a $1 increase in income is roughly the same as the producers' valuation of a $1 reduction in income — or, at least, that they are sufficiently similar so that our conclusions are not upset.

As a current example of how imports affect various groups in Canada, consider our imports of textiles from the Far East. The effect on Canadian textile producers is clear. They are damaged because these imports depress the domestic price of textiles and reduce their sales. At the same time, it is clear to Canadian consumers that they benefit from a lower textile price. What is not always clear, however, is the net effect on the nation as a whole. This analysis suggests that the overall effect is favourable, since the gain to consumers is greater than the loss to producers.

Finally, note that while output and employment fall in the typical import-competing industry shown in Figure 19-7, they rise in the export industries as shown in Figure 19-6. When both these effects are taken into account, there is no reason to expect either a large increase or decrease in employment as a result of trade — although unemployment may rise during the adjustment period. We emphasize: The principal point of international trade — like technological change — is *not* to increase employment; it is to increase real income. A more efficient economy will be better able to generate high-income jobs in the future.

## FOREIGN INVESTMENT IN CANADA: IMPORTING CAPITAL SERVICES

In the discussion so far, we have shown the gains to the economy from trade in goods. In reality, of course, there is also a large amount of trade in services. A typical example is tourism. For example, many Canadians enjoy vacations in Florida or the Caribbean. When Canadian tourists pay foreigners for travel and hotel services, these services represent Canadian imports. Conversely, when American or Japanese tourists visit Canada, we export services to Japan and the United States.

A country may also export or import the services of productive factors such as labour and capital. For example, Turkey exports labour services to Germany and other European countries when Turkish workers accept jobs there as temporary "guest workers."

In the Canadian case, an especially important item is imports of capital services. Historically, a substantial proportion of the funds that have been invested in Canada's resource industries or manufacturing have been supplied by foreign savers. (In recent years, most of the foreign capital coming in has come from the United States; during the late nineteenth and early twentieth century, most of it came from Britain.)

Foreign funds are invested in Canada in two ways. First, ***direct investment*** occurs when foreigners establish or expand firms that they control, or when they buy control of an existing Canadian enterprise. Second, ***portfolio investment*** takes place when foreigners buy stocks, bonds, or other financial instruments issued by Canadian-controlled corporations, or by the Canadian federal or provincial governments.

The net flows of both types of foreign investment in Canada has fluctuated widely over the years. Relative to GDP, the largest total inflow occurred before World War I. During the Great Depression in the 1930s and during World War II, normal international capital movement essentially came to a halt. However, since World War II, Canada has again had large inflows of foreign capital: As Figure 19-9 shows, the net inflow was especially large (as a percentage of GDP) during most of the 1950s and early 1960s. Since the mid-1970s, capital flows have fluctuated substantially. However, while the net inflow of *all* types of

[4] For a review of the basic idea of how consumer surplus changes as price changes, see Figure 7-5. For a similar review of producer surplus — a concept we will also now be frequently using — see Figure 10-11.

[5] The method of Figure 19-8 can also be used to explain Figure 19-6 more fully. Specifically, as price rises in Figure 19-6:
(a) Consumer surplus falls by $PBAP_A$.
(b) Producer surplus rises by $PCAP_A$.
(c) Thus, the net effects are a transfer of $PBAP_A$ from consumers to producers, and an efficiency gain of *ABC*.

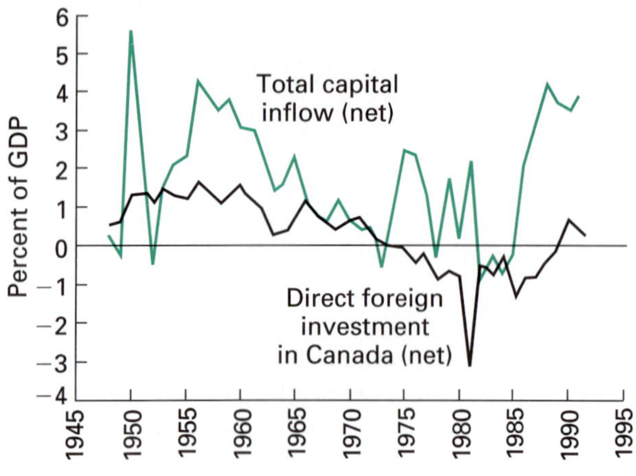


**FIGURE 19-9 Net foreign capital inflows into Canada, 1948–1991 (percent of GDP).**

During the 1950s and early 1960s, Canada received large net capital inflows, including substantial amounts of direct foreign investment. In the late 1980s and early 1990s, capital inflows became large once again; during this period, a large share represented foreign borrowing by the federal and provincial governments.

*Source*: Compiled from K. Buckley and M. Urquhart, eds., *Historical Statistics of Canada*, 1st ed. (Toronto and Cambridge: Cambridge University Press and Macmillan of Canada, 1965) and *Bank of Canada Review*.

foreign investment has been very large in some years (especially since 1986), the net inflow of *direct* investment has been much smaller than in the 1950s and 1960s. Since the mid-1970s, net foreign direct investment has, in fact, been negative in most years — that is, Canadian direct investment in foreign countries (or takeovers of firms in Canada that were previously foreign-controlled) has been larger than foreign direct investment in Canada.

Why is so much investment in Canada financed by foreign savers? Is it (1) because Canadians are unwilling to save as much as people in other countries? or (2) because our economy has so many attractive investment opportunities?

While savings (as a percentage of income) is lower in Canada than in some countries — most notably Japan — during most of the 1970s and 1980s it was higher than in many other countries, in particular, the United States. This suggests we must look to the second explanation: Canada attracts foreign savings because its market and natural resources offer investment opportunities with a good return. Historically, domestic savings has not been sufficient to satisfy the large investment demand in Canada.

Just as a nation may get a positive net gain from importing goods for which it has a comparative disadvantage, it may also realize a net gain through importing capital services. To see this, we use a diagram illustrating the market for investment funds, similar to Figure 17-7 in Chapter 17, where we plot the quantity of funds along the horizontal axis, and the rate of return (the price of capital services) on the vertical axis. In Figure 19-10, $S_d$ represents the supply of domestic savings in Canada, while $S_t$ is the total supply of savings, including the foreign capital. ($S_f$ is the supply of foreign capital to Canada; thus, $S_t$ is found by horizontally adding $S_f$ to $S_d$.) In the absence

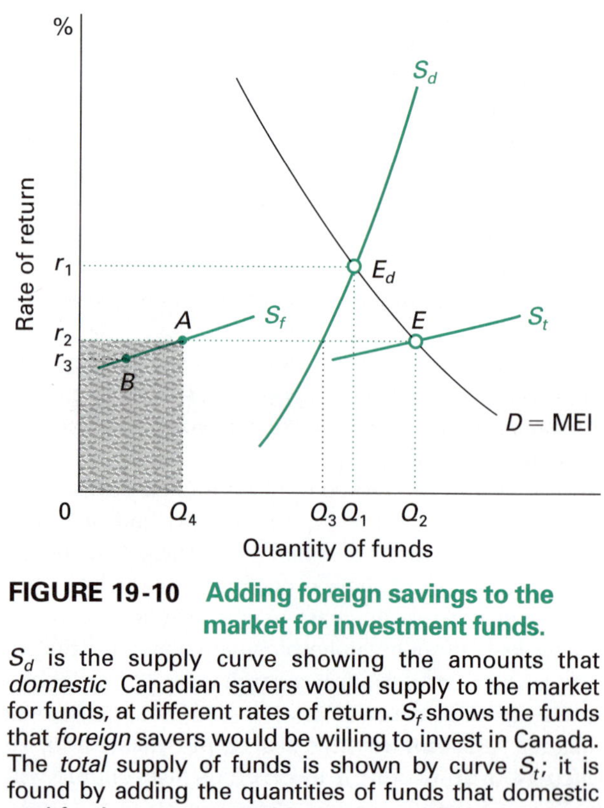


**FIGURE 19-10 Adding foreign savings to the market for investment funds.**

$S_d$ is the supply curve showing the amounts that *domestic* Canadian savers would supply to the market for funds, at different rates of return. $S_f$ shows the funds that *foreign* savers would be willing to invest in Canada. The *total* supply of funds is shown by curve $S_t$; it is found by adding the quantities of funds that domestic *and* foreign savers would supply at different rates of return.

Without foreign capital, equilibrium would be at $E_d$, the intersection of the demand curve for funds with the domestic supply curve. When foreign capital does come in, equilibrium occurs at $E$. At the equilibrium rate of return $r_2$, we can see from the $S_f$ curve that foreign savers would supply the amount $Q_4$; this amount must be the same as $Q_3Q_2$.

of foreign investment, equilibrium between supply and demand for investment funds would occur at $E_d$. But, of course, foreign capital *does* come into Canada, attracted by the relatively high rate of return here. With foreign funds coming in—and with the supply of savings accordingly being $S_t$ rather than just $S_d$—equilibrium occurs at $E$ rather than $E_d$. Thus, the inflow of foreign funds reduces the rate of return to investment in Canada from $r_1$ to $r_2$ and increases the amount of investment in Canada from $Q_1$ to $Q_2$. However, the quantity of investment in Canada that is financed *by Canadians* is reduced somewhat, from $Q_1$ to $Q_3$, with the balance $Q_3Q_2$ (which equals quantity $0Q_4$) now being supplied by foreigners.

The world as a whole benefits from the flow of foreign capital into Canada, since the rate of return is higher here than elsewhere; world savings is being used more efficiently than it would be if it were confined to lower-return investments outside Canada. But this does not *necessarily* mean that Canadians benefit. True, output is greater in Canada because investment is greater. But a lot of the benefit of this investment goes to foreigners. Specifically, foreigners earn a rate of return $r_2$ on their investment in Canada—that is, an income equal to the shaded grey rectangle in Figure 19-10.

To analyse whether or not Canadians on balance benefit, consider Figure 19-11. First, the inflow of foreign savings means that Canadians save $Q_3Q_1$ less; that is, their consumption increases by $Q_3Q_1$. But recall from Figure 17-5 that for any given amount of saving, the height of the Canadian supply curve $S$ reflects the value of an additional unit of current consumption. Therefore, the value that Canadians place on $Q_3Q_1$ additional units of consumption is areas 2 + 4 under the curve $S_d$.

However, on this $Q_3Q_1$ of investment in Canada, income 4 must be paid to foreigners. (They are earning return $r_2$ on these funds.) Therefore, the net benefit to Canadians is area 2 — the benefit Canadians receive because foreigners undertake some of the investing in Canada, thus allowing Canadians to use these funds for higher-valued consumption.

Second, the inflow of foreign savings into Canada not only takes the place of Canadian savings, it also results in an increase ($Q_2Q_1$) in total investment in Canada, resulting in additional output equal to areas 3 + 5. (The return on the last unit of investment at $Q_2$ is $r_2$; the return on the preceding units is given by the height of the MEI curve.) Of this, area 5 is paid to foreign investors, leaving a net gain to Canada of area 3. This is the net benefit to Canada of using foreign funds whose productivity exceeds their cost.

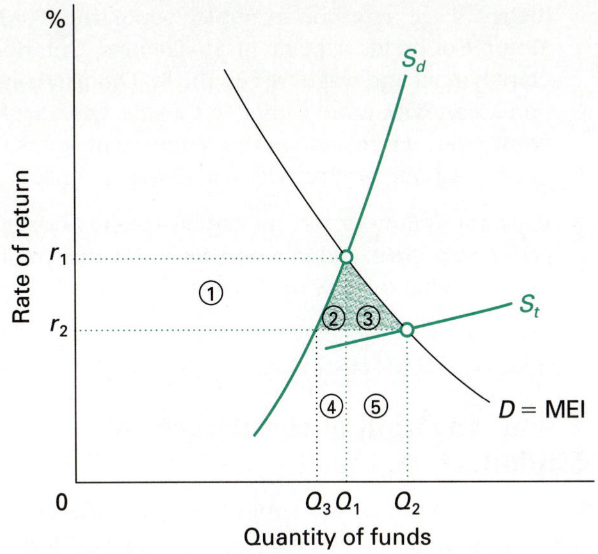


**FIGURE 19-11 The effects of foreign investment in Canada.**

The demand curve and the domestic and total supply curves for funds are reproduced from Figure 19-10. When $Q_3Q_2$ of foreign investment comes in, driving the equilibrium rate of return down from $r_1$ (the equilibrium rate without foreign capital) to $r_2$, there are two effects. First, total investment increases by $Q_1Q_2$; the return on this extra investment equals areas 3 + 5. Second, Canadian savers increase current consumption, since their savings fall by $Q_3Q_1$; the value of this extra consumption is areas 2 + 4. However, since areas 4 + 5 (which are equal to the grey shaded area in Figure 19-10), are paid as a return to the foreign investors, the net gain to Canada is only areas 2 + 3. (Area 1 represents a transfer from Canadian savers to owners of other Canadian factors of production.)

Thus, economic analysis suggests that capital imports result in overall efficiency gains to Canada of areas 2 + 3—gains that are similar to the gains from the imports of goods, as may be seen by comparing Figure 19-11 to Figure 19-8. However, we saw earlier that while imports of goods provide an overall gain, they affect various groups differently — benefiting some and hurting others. The same is true of capital imports. Specifically:

1. Canadian savers (owners of capital) lose, because the rate of return on investment in Canada is depressed from $r_1$ to $r_2$. (The return to Canadian capitalists is reduced by foreign competition.)

2. Canadian labour benefits because more capital in Canada means more demand for labour and a higher wage rate; for example, when the Ford Motor Co. builds a plant in St. Thomas, Ontario, employment and wages rise in the St. Thomas/London area. (With more capital in Canada, Canadians work with more and better equipment; consequently, labour productivity—and wages—rise.)

Thus, the inflow of foreign capital results both in an ***efficiency gain***, and in a transfer of income from Canadian capital owners to Canadian labour.[6]

## Some Complications

### 1. The Taxation of the Return to Capital

Foreign-owned firms are subject to the same basic rate of corporation income tax as domestic firms: about 40% of profits in most provinces. Moreover, most interest and dividends paid to foreigners are subject to a Canadian ***withholding tax*** of 15%. Thus, a fraction of the earnings of foreign capital does not go to foreigners at all; rather, it ends up in the Canadian treasury. Therefore, areas 2 + 3 in Figure 19-11 may understate the Canadian gain from capital inflows. (It is interesting to note that this tax benefit to Canada is a loss to foreign countries. Specifically, when foreign firms invest in Canada rather than at home—in the United States, say—there is a transfer of income from the treasury in Washington to Ottawa. The profits of U.S.-owned firms operating in Canada are taxed by Ottawa; if the profits were earned in the United States instead, they would be taxed by Washington to the benefit of American taxpayers.)

### 2. Can We Reduce the Cost of Foreign Capital?

As we will see in our discussion of international trade policy in Chapter 20, one logically valid argument in favour of a tariff or other import restriction is that, by reducing imports, it may reduce the price we have to pay for them—that is, the price foreign firms get when they supply imports to us. A similar argument applies to the ***cost of foreign capital***: If we reduce our imports of capital, this may reduce the net returns we have to pay foreigners to induce them to supply capital to us. In short, we may acquire capital less expensively, and we will benefit from this, just as we would from less expensive imports of goods. (If, for example, capital imports were reduced from *A* to *B* in Figure 19-10, the net return we would have to offer to get this amount of foreign capital would be reduced from $r_2$ to $r_3$.)

However, while this argument is logically valid, its significance in practice depends on the answer to an empirical question: Does the supply curve of foreign capital slope upward? If the supply curve is horizontal, rather than upward sloping, a reduction in the amount of foreign capital will not reduce its cost: The cost will remain at $r_2$ no matter how much capital we import. Some Canadian economists believe that the supply curve of foreign capital facing Canada is virtually horizontal; others believe that is has a significant upward slope.

In the 1970s and early 1980s, the inflow of direct foreign investment into Canada was, in fact, reduced by the restrictions and screening requirements imposed by the federal government's Foreign Investment Review Agency (FIRA) and by some of the provisions of the National Energy Program that were intended to limit the extent of foreign ownership in Canada's oil and gas sector. (For a discussion of why the government may want to follow such policies, see Appendix 19-A.) However, while these policies probably reduced the amount of foreign investment, they may not have reduced the net cost to Canada of attracting foreign capital. Instead, they may have raised it: Foreign investors may have become unwilling to invest in Canada unless they could expect a *higher* return to compensate for the risk of investing in a country whose policies were seen as hostile and costly to investors. (In the mid-1980s, FIRA was disbanded and replaced by Investment Canada, which has eased many restrictions on foreign investment. Furthermore, the Canada/United States Free Trade Agreement has provided American investors with assurance that such restrictions will not be re-imposed. This has made them much less concerned about the political risks of investing in Canada.)

---

[6] In our discussion of the gains and losses from capital flows, we have ignored an important complication: A capital inflow this year affects not only the return on Canadian-owned capital, but also on foreign-owned capital invested in the past. This complication (which does not upset our conclusions) is taken into account in G.D.A. MacDougall, "The Benefits and Costs of Private Investment from Abroad: A Theoretic Approach," *Economic Record*, March 1960; reprinted in Richard E. Caves and Harry G. Johnson, eds., *Readings in International Economics* (Homewood, Ill.: Richard D. Irwin, 1968), pp. 172–94.

## KEY POINTS

1. In this chapter, a strong case has been made for international trade; the next chapter will deal with the case for tariffs and other restraints on trade.
2. There are three major sources of benefit from trade: (a) greater competition, (b) economies of scale, and (c) comparative advantage.
3. When trade is opened, countries specialize in certain products, increasing their output of these goods. If there are economies of scale, costs fall as a result of this increase in output.
4. Even if costs do not fall with rising output, trade will be beneficial if countries specialize in the goods in which they have a comparative advantage, that is, in those products in which they are relatively most efficient. We saw this not only in the Ricardian case where cost is constant, but also even in cases, such as the one shown in Figure 19-6, where cost (the supply curve) rises as output increases.
5. Because trade lowers the domestic prices of goods we import and raises the prices of goods we export, it hurts some while benefiting others. Consumers of imports benefit, while consumers of exported goods are harmed. To some degree, but not completely, these are the same people, so this transfer partly cancels out. In addition, producers of exports benefit, while producers of import-competing goods are hurt. This provides an incentive for firms that produce both to specialize by increasing their production of exports and decreasing their production of import-competing goods.
6. International trade is similar in many respects to technological change. Both increase real income by allowing a nation to consume more: Trade allows a country to consume beyond its production possibilities curve, while technological change shifts the production possibilities curve out. Trade and technological change can cause the same sort of short-run unemployment until workers who have lost their jobs shift to new, more productive employment.
7. A large share of the total supply of investment in the Canadian economy is provided by foreign savers. Basic economic analysis indicates that there is a triangular efficiency gain (areas 2 + 3 in Figure 19-11) from such investment, similar to the efficiency gains from international trade.

## KEY TERMS

**specialization**
**increased competition**
**economies of scale**
**comparative advantage**
**absolute advantage**
**opportunity cost**
**gain from trade**
**trade compared to technological change**
**foreign exchange market**
**exchange rate**
**exports: efficiency and transfer effects**
**imports: efficiency and transfer effects**
**direct foreign investment**
**foreign portfolio investment**
**efficiency gain from foreign investment**
**withholding tax**
**cost of foreign capital**

## PROBLEMS

19-1. Suppose that there are economies of scale in the production of both $X$ and $Y$. If Britain specializes in one and Canada in the other, is it possible for both countries to benefit? Explain your answer. Does this answer still hold if the cost curves for each good are identical in the two countries? (Hint: Review the discussion of economies of scale in Chapter 3.)

19-2. Explain the efficiency gains or losses in Canada if each province were to impose high barriers against its imports from the other provinces.

19-3. Return to Table 19-2, where costs are constant. (a) Change the upper left number 3 to 5. Does Britain now have an absolute advantage in either good? A comparative advantage in either?

Draw a diagram such as Figure 19-4 to show the potential Canadian gain from trade, again assuming that there are 20 million workers in Canada and the international price ratio is 3:1. (b) Now change that same upper left number to 8. Which country now has a comparative advantage in food? In clothing? Are there potential gains from trade? Why or why not?

19-4. In moving from *B* to *D*, the country in Figure 19-4 consumes more clothing, but not more food. Therefore, it takes all its gains from specialization and trade in increased clothing. Now suppose that it decides to consume less clothing, that is, it stops trading at point *K*, with its trade arrow now being only *CK*, rather than *CD*. Will all the gains from specialization and trade be in clothing? In food? Or in some combination of the two? Graphically show exactly what the gains will be.

19-5. Canada may be modelled as a small open economy (SOE) — we take world prices for traded goods as given. If the world price for oil ($P_w$) is below the price that would prevail in the absence of trade, $P_a$, illustrate the efficiency gain associated with free trade in oil. Assuming that exports of oil are prohibited, illustrate the efficiency loss resulting from pricing oil below the world price. (Note that this would require a subsidy on imported oil.)

19-6. Use Figure 19-10 (instead of Figure 19-11) to illustrate the transfer and efficiency effects of restricting the free flow of foreign investment into Canada.

19-7. Canada's domestic demand and supply functions, respectively, for some commodity per period are given by

$$Q_d = 1100 - 100P$$

and

$$Q_s = 100P - 100$$

(a) In the absence of trade, what is the equilibrium domestic price of this commodity, and what is the quantity produced and consumed in Canada?

Now suppose that Canada has a comparative advantage in the production of this good relative to the rest of world. As a small open economy, Canadians can purchase or sell as much of this commodity as they like for the world price of $9 per unit.

If Canada were to be transformed from a no-trade to a free-trade state in the purchase and sale of this commodity,

(b) Of Canadian producers and consumers, which group would gain? What is their welfare gain?
(c) Of Canadian producers and consumers, which group would lose? What is their welfare loss?
(d) How many units of this commodity will be exported or imported per period?
(e) What is the value of this export or import per period?

19-8. Canada's domestic demand and supply functions, respectively, for some commodity per period are given by

$$Q_d = 20{,}000 - 100P$$

and

$$Q_s = 200P - 1000$$

(a) In the absence of trade, what is the equilibrium domestic price of this commodity, and what is the quantity produced and consumed in Canada?

Now suppose that Canada has a comparative disadvantage in the production of this good relative to the rest of world. As a small open economy, Canadians can purchase or sell as much of this commodity as they like for the world price of $40 per unit.

If Canada were to be transformed from a no-trade to a free-trade state in the purchase and sale of this commodity:

(b) Of Canadian producers and consumers, which group would gain? What is their welfare gain?
(c) Of Canadian producers and consumers, which group would lose? What is their welfare loss?
(d) How many units of this commodity will be exported or imported per period?
(e) What is the value of this export or import per period?

# APPENDIX 19-A

## THE ISSUE OF FOREIGN OWNERSHIP AND CONTROL

The conclusion in the main text that capital imports yield net benefits is far from universally accepted. Many of the objections are based on concerns about the potential political consequences of international investment. Before we address some of these concerns, we set the stage by considering several preliminary matters. First, we return to the distinction between direct and portfolio investment. Then we look at the volume of foreign investment in Canada, and the objectives of those engaged in direct investment.

### Direct vs. Portfolio Investment

Not all international investment is considered equally objectionable by those who are uneasy about its implications for our political independence.

Most critics express greatest concern over direct investment. After all, when foreigners (mostly Americans) own and control businesses in Canada, it is they who make the principal business decisions, not Canadians. On the other hand, no such overt control exists with portfolio investment, and as a result this type of investment is generally considered less objectionable.

However, foreign portfolio investment may cause a different kind of problem. A country that has borrowed large amounts abroad is subject to constraints on its economic policy: It has to make sure it can repay interest and principal. Thus, as we discuss in Chapter 19 in the *Macroeconomics* volume, a number of the heavily indebted developing nations in Latin America and elsewhere have been forced by the International Monetary Fund to adopt harsh economic measures, involving reduced government spending and tighter monetary policies, as a condition for obtaining the additional loans they needed to pay the interest and principal on their *old* loans.

Indeed, countries that have large inflows of portfolio investment often have problems that do not arise in the case of direct foreign investment. If the borrowed funds are used to finance current consumption or cover a government deficit, the borrowings do not pay off in terms of higher domestic output in the future. Yet the interest and principal payments must still be met. In contrast, the dividend payments to foreign capitalists that are made on direct foreign investments can be financed out of the returns generated by the foreign investments themselves. If the investments do not generate a return, the foreign investors themselves bear the consequence: If there are no profits, they get nothing back from their investments.

### Foreign Control in the Canadian Economy

What is the extent of foreign control in the Canadian economy? As Table 19-4 shows, it is substantial, although it varies greatly among economic sectors. Manufacturing has the highest degree of foreign ownership, with over 45% of the assets in that sector owned by foreign-controlled firms. Manufacturing industries such as tobacco products and rubber products are almost entirely foreign-controlled, and foreign firms account for 70%–75% of the assets in the large chemical (C3) and transportation equipment industries (C4, which includes the Canadian subsidiaries of the giant U.S. car manufacturers). Foreign ownership is also substantial in the energy sector: Oil and gas extraction and petroleum refining are included in categories B1 (mineral fuels) and C5 (petroleum and coal products) both of which have large shares of foreign control. But foreign ownership

**TABLE 19-4 Foreign-controlled Firms' Share in Total Corporate Assets: Selected Industries, 1987 (Percent)**

| Industry | Percentage held by foreign-controlled firms | |
|---|---|---|
| | Sector | Averages |
| A. Agriculture, forestry, and fishing | | 3 |
| B. Mining | | 31 |
| 1. Mineral fuels | 37 | |
| 2. Metal mining | 18 | |
| C. Manufacturing | | 46 |
| 1. Tobacco products | 100 | |
| 2. Rubber products | 89 | |
| 3. Chemicals and chemical products | 72 | |
| 4. Transport equipment | 75 | |
| 5. Petroleum and coal products | 68 | |
| 6. Paper and allied industries | 22 | |
| 7. Food products | 37 | |
| 8. Primary metal manufacturing | 19 | |
| 9. Furniture industries | 14 | |
| D. Construction | | 6 |
| E. Public utilities | | 0.6 |
| F. Wholesale trade | | 31 |
| G. Retail trade | | 13 |
| H. Services | | 13 |
| Average for all sectors (non-financial industries) | 25 | |

*Source: Annual Report of the Minister of Industry Science and Technology Canada under the Corporations and Labour Unions Returns Act, 1987* (Ottawa: Statistics Canada and Minister of Supply and Services, 1990), Part 1, *Corporations*. Reproduced by permission of the Minister of Supply and Services Canada.

in the energy sector has been falling: In the late 1970s, for example, foreigners controlled 60%–70% of the assets in energy firms.

Other manufacturing industries (such as iron and steel, included in C8, or furniture making) have relatively small shares of foreign ownership, and in sectors such as retail trade and services, foreign control is relatively limited.

## Why Do They Come?

In some cases, foreign direct investment occurs when a group of foreign capitalists get together and start a new firm (or take over an existing one) in Canada. The International Nickel Corporation (INCO) in Sudbury, Ontario, is an example of this form of foreign investment. But a much more common form of direct investment is when a multinational corporation builds a plant in Canada, or takes over ownership of a Canadian firm.

Why do firms find it worthwhile to establish subsidiaries and branch plants in foreign countries? In large part, they do so to gain the advantages of large organizations:

1. A firm with many plants and large output may have lower costs because research and development expenses can be spread over a larger volume of output. The advantages of size may be achieved by a foreign firm both by increasing its domestic production, and by acquiring foreign subsidiaries which can use the technology the firm has developed at home.
2. Similarly, there may be economies in advertising and marketing. This is particularly important in the U.S.-Canadian case: Most Canadians live close to the border, speak the same language as Americans, and are exposed to U.S. advertising. Because Canadians hear of Kodak film, for example, Kodak has a valuable advantage in selling in the Canadian market.
3. There may also be economies in using management resources. For example, the present U.S. management may also be able to manage a Canadian subsidiary with relatively little additional effort. For a new firm trying to compete with the multinational, however, the cost of acquiring specialized management skills may be much higher.

In an important early study of foreign investment in Canada, Richard Caves of Harvard University found that these three factors have been important explanations for foreign ownership of Canadian industry. In particular, the evidence suggested that industries with large research and development and marketing expenditures tend to have a large degree of foreign control. He also found that in industries marked by multiplant firms (such as automobiles), foreign multinationals tend to dominate the Canadian market.[7]

[7] Richard E. Caves, "Causes of Direct Investment: Foreign Firms' Shares in Canadian and United Kingdom Manufacturing Industries," *Review of Economics and Statistics*, August 1974, pp. 279–93.

4. Firms may reduce their risks by owning their own sources of supply, rather than buying these supplies on the open market. Thus, producers of metal products may own mines, and newspapers may own the forests used to produce pulp and paper. For this reason, U.S. firms may acquire Canadian mines or other resources.
5. Finally, foreign firms have set up subsidiaries in Canada because of the Canadian tariff. In the automobile industry, for example, one reason for U.S. firms to come to Canada originally was to produce inside the Canadian tariff wall. (It was less expensive to produce in Canada than to produce in the United States and export to Canada, paying the required tariff.)

As the Canada/United States Free Trade Agreement is implemented over the next few years, this reason for American firms to invest in Canada will gradually disappear. However, it will remain an incentive for firms from other countries. For example, the upsurge in investment by Japanese and Korean car manufacturers in North America in the 1980s was in large part to ensure that they could continue selling their cars in that market even if Canada or the United States were to restrict imports of cars from outside of North America.

## CONSEQUENCES OF FOREIGN OWNERSHIP AND CONTROL

Even though the growth of multinational corporations and of foreign ownership may represent an economically efficient pattern of production, many economists and politicians in Canada are concerned, for other reasons, about foreign investment and, particularly, direct investment. In many cases, the concern is based on considerations of political sovereignty. Moreover, some observers fear that an excessive foreign influence will retard the growth of a distinctly Canadian culture.

With respect to the question of political sovereignty, the problem of ***extraterritoriality*** has long been a sore point in U.S.-Canadian relations. Extraterritoriality refers to an application of U.S. laws and regulations to foreign subsidiaries of U.S. firms, even though these subsidiaries are operating outside the United States. An example is the U.S. Trading With the Enemies Act. Under this act, firms require approval by the U.S. government to export goods to certain communist countries, notably North Korea, North Vietnam, and Cuba. Because the act has also applied to foreign subsidiaries of U.S. firms, several deals involving exports from subsidiaries in Canada to these countries have been blocked in the past by lack of approval from the U.S. government. Another example of the extraterritoriality principle is the application of U.S. anti-trust law to Canadian subsidiaries of U.S. firms.

The economic consequences to Canada of extraterritoriality have probably not been very great. But from the viewpoint of asserting Canadian political independence, extraterritoriality is a major aggravation.

Because of the desire to encourage a distinctly Canadian culture, special rules have been introduced to limit the extent of foreign involvement in our communications industry (radio, television, and the publishing of magazines and other periodicals). These rules cover not only foreign investment of firms in these industries, but also the content being communicated. Thus, an extensive set of rules specify the amount of Canadian programming that radio and television stations must offer. The issue of Canadian culture gave rise to some hard bargaining during the 1988 negotiation of the Canada/United States Free Trade Agreement. In the end, the Americans recognized how sensitive this issue is in Canada, and agreed to a number of protective provisions for cultural industries.

CHAPTER

# 20 INTERNATIONAL TRADE: POLICY DEBATES

*Protectionism is the institutionalization of economic failure.*
*Former British Prime Minister Edward Heath*

Japanese barriers against rice imports have been so severe that the price to Japanese consumers has recently been more than *six times* the world price. In Europe, import restrictions and agricultural price supports were so high that when the Europeans came to sell their butter surplus on the world market in 1987, the best they could do was to sell it to the Soviet Union at a discount of *93% below its European cost.* While Canada and the United States have been calling for an end to such practices, they still have protectionist policies themselves. In a world moving toward a global economy in which many governments are committed to a policy of freer trade—at least on paper—how could such trade-distorting policies have survived? Given the potential gains from trade described in the last chapter, why does virtually every nation still restrict its imports with barriers such as tariffs (taxes imposed on imported goods as they enter a country) or quotas (limits on the number of units that can be imported)?

It is true that, since the 1930s, we have made great progress in reducing tariffs. Much of the progress has come as a result of *multilateral* negotiations, where countries get together to reach agreement on tariff reductions and other trade matters. In the Kennedy Round and Tokyo Round of trade negotiations in the 1960s and 1970s, most of the non-communist industrial nations of the world agreed to cut their tariffs by more than half, and additional cuts are now mandated in the recently concluded Uruguay Round. For Canada, further important reductions in trade barriers have occurred as a result of bilateral agreements with the United States. Specifically, the 1965 Auto Pact has allowed manufacturers meeting certain conditions to move cars duty-free from Canada into the United States, or into Canada from the United States (or, for that matter, from Mexico or any other country). And the 1989 Canada/U.S. Free Trade Agreement (FTA), with its far wider coverage of almost all industries, is now eliminating tariffs and many other barriers to trade between the two countries. Moreover, in 1992, the two countries negotiated NAFTA, the North American Free Trade Agreement—a modified extension of the Canada/U.S. FTA that will cut barriers to our trade with Mexico as well. Assuming U.S. ratification, which is far from guaranteed, NAFTA will come into effect on 1 January 1994, and may eventually be extended to other countries in the Western hemisphere, and perhaps beyond.

Negotiating tariff reductions has been a long and arduous process. Moreover, as tariffs have been reduced, they have often been replaced by non-tariff barriers (NTBs) such as quotas.

In this chapter we will see why ***tariffs***, ***quotas***, and other trade restrictions have not disappeared. Two basic reasons are: (1) They may have been introduced for non-economic motives such as the desire to protect a defence industry, or a cultural industry judged necessary to maintain national identity. (2) A country may restrict imports for special economic reasons, some of which are fallacious, but some of which may contain a kernel of truth.

## NON-ECONOMIC EXPLANATIONS OF TRADE BARRIERS

### An Industry May Be Essential for National Defence

Two centuries ago, Adam Smith argued that we should be willing to protect the important goal of national defence even if such protection involves an economic cost — that is, even if foreign countries have a comparative advantage in producing military supplies. The basic argument is simple. A country doesn't want to be dependent on a foreign supply for defence equipment that can be cut off in wartime or in some crisis when it is needed most.

By 1993, following the collapse of the Soviet Union, this argument had lost some of its practical force. However, it does remain valid so long as nations, for whatever reasons, maintain a defence capability.

### A Canadian Cultural Industry Should Be Protected to Maintain Our National Identity

It can be argued that at least some (though certainly not all) of the movies, books, and TV programs that Canadians consume should be produced in Canada. But without protection or some other form of subsidy, such an industry may not exist: Economies of scale (due to high editorial and other overhead costs) mean that the per-unit cost for a low-volume Canadian magazine may be substantially more than for a high-volume U.S. magazine — even one with a special Canadian edition run off with a few selected inserts on Canada. In short, higher costs in the much smaller market make it impossible for Canadian producers of culture to compete.

### People Vote for Their Present Jobs

Increased international trade means that some jobs are lost in import-competing industries. Although new jobs are created in export industries, people are more concerned about the present import-competing jobs they may lose than the possibility of new export-based jobs. (Who knows for sure who will actually get these new export jobs?) Therefore, workers who don't want to take risks vote against increased trade and in favour of the trade restrictions that protect their current jobs.

However, even if we look only at imports, Figure 19-8 indicated that the losses to producers from increased imports are more than offset by gains to consumers. Why then can't a politician sell the idea of allowing imports in more freely?

The answer is that individuals tend to think and vote as producers, not as consumers. The reason is that the large benefit from, say, lower-priced imported shirts is spread widely among millions of consumers, with each benefiting by such a small amount that nobody is likely to switch votes on this account. On the producers' side, however, things are different. Here, fewer individuals are affected by increased shirt imports, but the effect on these individuals — whether in management or labour—is much greater, and may be enough not only to determine how they vote, but also to induce them to invest heavily in lobbying efforts. Therefore, the producers' interest in protection is heard by politicians while the free-trade interests of consumers frequently are not. (See Box 20-1.)

Thus it is no surprise that 200 years after Adam Smith, protection still lives on. In fact, we would have even more severe trade restrictions except for the fact that export industries have a strong interest in international trade, and put pressure on governments to remove barriers to this trade.

## ECONOMIC ARGUMENTS FOR PROTECTION

Some of the economic arguments for protection are fallacious, while others contain an element of truth. First, the fallacious arguments:

### 1. "Buy Canadian Because It Keeps Our Money at Home."

For example, if I buy a calculator from Taiwan, I get the calculator, and the Taiwanese get the dollars. But if I buy a calculator made in Canada instead, I get the calculator, and the dollars stay here.

This argument fails to recognize why the Taiwanese export to us. They don't do so merely for the joy of earning and holding Canadian dollars. Like you or me, they earn money to buy things. To a large extent, they use dollars to buy such things as newsprint from us. In other words, when we import calculators it is newsprint that we ultimately give up, not dollars. Alternatively, if we buy calculators at home, we also give up goods such as newsprint (because resources

## ECONOMICS IN HISTORY — BOX 20-1

### What Happens if the Consumer Is Forgotten: Bastiat's Negative Railway

The absurdity of ignoring the interests of the consumer has never been more eloquently stated than by the French economist Frédéric Bastiat (1801–1850):*

> It has been proposed that the railway from Paris to Madrid should have a break at Bordeaux, for if goods and passengers are forced to stop at that town, profits will accrue to bargemen, pedlars, commissionaires, hotel-keepers, etc. But if Bordeaux has a right to profit by a gap in the line of railway, and if such profit is considered in the public interest, then Angoulême, Poitiers, Tours, Orléans, nay, more, all the intermediate places, Ruffec, Châtellerault, etc., should also demand gaps, as being for the general interest. For the more these breaks in the line are multiplied, the greater will be the increase of consignments, commissions, transhipments, etc., along the whole extent of the railway. In this way, we shall succeed in having a line of railway composed of successive gaps, which we may call a Negative Railway.

* Abridged from Frédéric Bastiat, *Economic Sophisms* (Edinburgh: Oliver and Boyd, Ltd., 1873), pp. 80–81.

producing those will have to be diverted to producing calculators.) Which way of acquiring calculators —from the Taiwanese or ourselves—will cost us less newsprint? The answer was given in Chapter 19: Calculators will cost us less — in terms of other goods forgone — if we buy them from Taiwan, provided, of course, that Taiwan has a comparative advantage in producing calculators.[1]

This illustrates an important principle. Whenever you encounter what seems to be a superficially correct theoretical argument for protecting a Canadian industry, ask yourself: Does it apply to all imports? If it does — including bananas that could be produced in Canada, but in greenhouses at far too high a cost —then it implies that Canada should end all its trade, and there is a logical fallacy in it somewhere.

## 2. "We Can't Compete with Cheap Foreign Labour."

Why is labour more expensive in Canada than in most countries like, say, South Korea? The answer is that wages are higher in Canada because labour is more productive; it can produce more goods. Consequently it can be "paid more goods," that is, its real wage is higher. (See Box 19-1.) When we take into account both our higher wages *and* our higher productivity, we find that we can compete internationally in some goods, but not others. While we cannot compete with cheap labour in countries like South Korea in products in which they have a comparative advantage, we *can* compete in products of our comparative advantage, where our higher labour productivity more than offsets our higher wage. These are the products on which we should be concentrating. (For more on the argument that we will be unable to compete with foreign producers, see Box 20-2.)

In the recent NAFTA debate, many opponents have focused on the Mexican advantage of cheap labour without adequately recognizing Mexico's problem of lower productivity. This problem involves not only lower Mexican productivity on the factory floor that may be dramatically improved in some cases, but not others, by multinationals bringing in their highly efficient methods. There are also other Mexican productivity problems that will be more difficult and take longer to cure such as inadequate roads and telephone systems, and other deficiencies in industrial infrastructure. Even longer-term productivity problems will require improved Mexican education and, in some cases, work attitudes. Thus, the question is

[1] As we saw in Chapter 3, for a country that is importing capital, imports of goods and services may be substantially greater than exports. In this case, the argument in this section is no longer so clear-cut; there may be a lag of months or years between our imports and foreign purchases of our goods. Nevertheless, our main point is still valid. The ultimate purpose of our trading partners in selling goods to Canada is to acquire the Canadian dollars to buy goods from us.

## APPLICATIONS AND ILLUSTRATIONS BOX 20-2
### The Petition of the Candlemakers

Sometimes the argument that we can't compete with cheap foreign labour appears in the slightly different form: "We can't compete with cheap foreign products." This idea has never been more effectively criticized than by Frédéric Bastiat over a hundred years ago. Here is his satirical description of an appeal by French candlemakers to the government to protect them from the free sunlight that was supposedly ruining their business:*

> We are subjected to the intolerable competition of a foreign rival, who enjoys, it would seem, such superior facilities for the production of light, that he is enabled to inundate our national market at so exceedingly reduced a price, that, the moment he makes his appearance, he draws off all custom from us; and thus an important branch of French industry, with all its innumerable ramifications, is suddenly reduced to a state of complete stagnation. This rival is not other than the sun.
>
> Our petition is, that it would please your honourable body to pass a law whereby shall be directed the shutting up of all windows, dormers, skylights, shutters, curtains, in a word, all openings, holes, chinks, and fissures through which the light of the sun is used to penetrate into our dwellings, to the prejudice of the profitable manufactures which we flatter ourselves we have been enabled to bestow upon the country; which country cannot, therefore, without ingratitude, leave us now to struggle unprotected through so unequal a contest. . . .
>
> Does it not argue the greatest inconsistency to check as you do the importation of coal, iron, cheese, and goods of foreign manufacture, merely because . . . their price approaches zero, while at the same time you freely admit, and without limitation, the light of the sun, whose price is during the whole day at zero?

* Abridged from Frédéric Bastiat, *Economic Sophisms*, pp. 56–60.

how the extended process of improving Mexican productivity will compare to the Mexican wage increases that are generated in response.

## 3. "Tariffs Should Be Tailored to Equalize Costs at Home and Abroad."

This apparently plausible "scientific tariff" recommendation misses the whole point of international trade: Gains from trade are based on cost differences between countries; we import bananas or radios precisely because they can be produced more cheaply abroad than at home. Eliminate cost differences and you eliminate the incentive to trade; thus to the degree that we were successful in the essentially impossible task of equalizing costs, all we would do is strangle trade, losing all the gains from it that we now enjoy. This is another "bananas" recommendation that would result in expensive Canadian greenhouse production behind a high enough tariff to equalize costs with imports from the Caribbean.

Here are the arguments for protection that contain at least some element of truth.

## 4. "If We Buy Steel from Hamilton rather than from Tokyo, Employment Will Rise in Hamilton rather than in Tokyo."

This statement may be true, particularly if there is large-scale unemployment in Hamilton. Why, then, does it not provide a very strong case for restricting trade, ranking in importance with the efficiency argument for free trade in the previous chapter? Why don't we use import restrictions to raise and maintain Canadian employment? There are two problems with this suggestion.

(a) If we protect an industry's employment by import restrictions, how can its price be kept from rising rapidly? If the government becomes committed to providing an industry with whatever trade barrier it needs to protect its employment from imports, what is to prevent it from raising its price and perhaps even increasing its profits by relaxing its quality standards?

To illustrate: By 1979, the Big Three were already losing auto sales to imports. In 1981, the U.S. and Canadian governments pressured the Japanese into imposing "voluntary" limits on the number of cars they exported to North America. Consequently, they concentrated on high-priced models, on which per-unit profit margins were higher. Thus this policy was ultimately damaging to the Big Three because it drove the Japanese auto makers upmarket so that now, with their Lexus, Infinity, and Acura models they pose the greatest threat to the Europeans in the world market for luxury cars.

In the short term, however, this policy did benefit North American producers because, by creating an artificial scarcity of Japanese cars, it reduced competition and allowed the Big Three to increase sales and raise price. (U.S. estimates in the early 1980s indicated that import restrictions raised the average auto price by more than $900.) While this was damaging to Canadian and U.S. car buyers, it generated profits for the Big Three which, in turn, allowed them to pay their executives large bonuses and their labour force increased wages. (However, wage increases were substantially smaller than they had been in earlier years, when competition from foreign cars was still weak.) This raised the question: Why should other workers earning far lower wages be asked to subsidize auto workers and auto executives by paying higher prices for cars? By the mid-1980s the pressure on the Japanese to limit their auto exports was being reduced. But by then we had taught the Japanese how restricting their exports to North America would allow them to raise their selling price and hence profit — far above the essentially zero level they were earning in the more competitive Japanese domestic market. So for some time they continued informally to restrict their exports — thus charging us a higher price — with their explanation being that they did not want to trigger further North American protection against them. In short, we had taught them how to cartelize their sales in North America (that is, reduce quantity to increase price) in a way that North American producers could not, without risking a jail sentence.

(b) If we protect our employment by a "***beggar-my-neighbour***" policy of import restraints, won't our trading partners solve their problem by retaliating and reducing their imports from us?

In periods of worldwide recession, all countries are tempted to engage in such a beggar-my-neighbour policy. But if all countries attempt to solve unemployment this way, or if a few do and the rest retaliate, the result will be a general disruption of trade. Rather than falling, worldwide unemployment may rise, as it did in the 1930s when such policies made the worldwide depression worse.

If there is large-scale domestic unemployment, the cure should be sought in domestic monetary and fiscal policies (discussed in the *Macroeconomics* volume that forms a companion to this book), not in mutually destructive trade restrictions.

## 5. "Restricting Trade Will Diversify a Nation's Economy."

This is true. Just as trade leads a country to specialize, restricting trade leads to the opposite: ***diversification***. Isn't it a good thing for a country to diversify—to avoid putting all its eggs in one basket?

The answer is, perhaps. But for countries, like individuals, the risks from ***specialization*** are often more than offset by the gains. (The risk of a future oversupply of lawyers or doctors does not prevent individuals from taking up these specialized careers. They expect that their gains will outweigh the risks they run.)

Developed countries like Canada already have diversified economies that weaken the case for using protection to increase diversification further. True, Canada has large exports of primary products, such as wheat, lumber, and natural gas, but we export a wide enough range of these goods to avoid being highly sensitive to fluctuations in the world price of any single one. Furthermore, even though our primary exports are large, our exports of a wide range of manufactured goods are even larger (Table 19-1).

According to studies of trade liberalization such as that of Harris and Cox cited below, the Canadian economy would still remain diversified, even with completely free trade. These studies suggest that we would not give up the production of a whole category of goods (such as industrial products) to concentrate on another (such as agricultural products). Indeed, it would be unlikely that we would completely give up even one industry (say, sporting goods) in order to specialize in another (say, electrical machinery). Instead, the evidence suggests that trade leads to specialization in certain *kinds* of sporting goods, and certain *kinds* of electrical machinery. For industrial countries, expanded trade has generally not resulted in a narrow range of products.

## 6. "Restricting Imports May Reduce the Price We Have to Pay for Them."

If Canada imposes a tariff on, say, coffee, Canadians will buy less on the international market. As a result, the world demand for coffee decreases—that is, the demand curve shifts to the left — and the price of coffee falls. Thus, by restricting this import, Canada would be able to acquire coffee at a more favourable price.[2] This is sometimes referred to as *improving our terms of trade*, that is, reducing the price of what we buy compared to the price of what we sell.

This argument has little or no practical relevance for a small country like Canada, because our demand for coffee or any other good we import represents such a small fraction of world demand. For example, even if the Canadian government were to prohibit almost all imports of coffee (a frightening thought to many of us), world demand for coffee would drop by less than one-half of 1%, with an imperceptible impact on the world price of coffee and Canada's terms of trade.

## 7. "Restricting Trade Will Make Us Less Dependent on Foreign Supplies."

This argument also has little practical relevance for Canada. If our supply of a good from one or a few countries is cut off, we can get it from other suppliers. Even in the high-profile case of oil — an important commodity with world supply coming from a small number of often politically unstable countries—Canada would have far less problem than the United States, Europe, or Japan because we are much more self-sufficient in energy.

## 8. "We Need to Protect Our Infant Industries."

This argument is that a country may not be able to compete with other nations in an industry with economies of scale until this industry is well established and operating at high volume and low cost. This may be true even in an industry where the country will eventually have a comparative advantage and be able to produce very cheaply. This raises a question: Shouldn't such an industry be protected from being wiped out by tough foreign competition during the delicate period of its infancy?

Although this argument is logically valid, it raises two practical questions: (1) How do you know that the only advantage of foreign countries is that their industry is already established? For example, if a country is thinking of protecting an infant watch industry, how does it know that the only advantage of the Swiss and Japanese is that their industry is already established? Maybe they enjoy some basic advantage in watchmaking. If so, a watchmaking industry established elsewhere may never be able to compete. (2) When does an infant subsidy become an old-age pension? Industries that receive protection as infants seldom seem to grow up, but instead become permanently dependent on their tariffs. One reason is that, once established, these industries employ many people who vote; thus, protection continues to go to them, rather than to the real infants who have not yet hired a large enough labour force to give them voting clout.[3]

## 9. "Protection Can Be Used to Engineer a Comparative Advantage."

The traditional example of comparative advantage begins with differences in costs. In the example in Chapter 19, Canada was simply assumed to have a comparative advantage in food, and Britain in clothing. Critics point out that, while some differences in costs depend on gifts of nature such as the wheat-growing capacity of the Canadian Prairies or the oil-rich lands of the Middle East, comparative advantage can often be created or "engineered." For example, a

[2] Although Canada as a nation pays a lower price to, say, Brazil, the price paid by individual Canadian coffee buyers rises — because they must pay not only Brazil for the coffee, but also the Canadian government for the tariff it collects. (It is in response to this higher price they are paying that individual Canadian buyers reduce their coffee purchases.)

[3] A third practical question is this: If such an industry will eventually be a profitable one, why shouldn't its owners cover any initial losses out of their future profits? One possible answer is that capital markets do not work "perfectly" to supply firms like this with the funds necessary to get them through the initial period of losses.

country can encourage the accumulation of capital and thus acquire a comparative advantage in an industry that requires plentiful capital. Alternatively, a country may develop a comparative advantage in a high-tech industry by providing it with protection that will allow it to attract and retain the engineers and scientists who will provide it with a comparative advantage that will allow it to compete in the future.

Note that this argument is a variation on the infant industry theme. In either case, protection is viewed by its proponents as a way to develop new industries with a comparative advantage in the future. Thus, this argument raises the same sort of critical questions as the infant industry argument. How do you know whether your policy will succeed, or whether it will create an industry requiring permanent protection? Why not subsidize the industry in some other—generally more efficient—way; in the high-tech example, by subsidizing the research and education of scientists? Moreover, this high-tech argument raises a further question: Since, unlike a traditional infant, this industry does not start with a comparative advantage, why should one go to all the trouble of creating it? Two possible answers are: This industry may generate positive externalities that benefit other industries or the public; or it may earn above-normal profit. These cases are examined in the next two sections.

## 10. "Industries with Positive Externalities Should Be Protected."

High-tech firms often provide benefits not only to their own employees and shareholders, but also to the public at large. As an example of such a positive externality, consider the U.S. firm, American Telephone and Telegraph (AT&T). Its Bell Labs developed the transistor, but only a small part of the benefits went to AT&T employees and shareholders. The general public also has benefited greatly because transistors have improved the quality of computers, audio equipment, automobiles, and even inexpensive watches. Since a free market will result in "too little" output from high-tech industries with positive externalities, protection should be used—so the argument goes—to encourage them. (This is similar to the argument that, even in a closed economy, activities with positive externalities should be encouraged with a subsidy.)

However, the existence of positive externalities does not necessarily make a compelling case for protection of high-tech industries. In a rapidly changing industry, protection can have unforeseen consequences. For example, in 1986, the United States pressured Japan into raising the prices and limiting the exports of its computer chips sold in the United States. This encouraged U.S. production of chips. But, by raising costs and creating shortages of chips, it weakened the competitive position of the U.S. computer industry that uses chips.

Furthermore, a country that protects high-tech industries may find that this triggers retaliation by other countries. Thus, if it wants to encourage the chip industry, this should be done with a domestic policy that will not trigger retaliation, will not raise the price of chips, and therefore will not discourage the computer industry. Examples of such policies include not only government assistance for the education and training of technicians or engineers, but possibly also the relaxation of competition laws to permit firms to engage in joint research, design, and development. (In September 1993, the U.S. government allowed auto manufacturers there to participate in the joint research and development of a much more fuel-efficient car.)

## 11. "The Existence of Imperfect Competition May Justify Protection."

To illustrate: If there is a monopoly firm in country A earning monopoly rents (above-normal profits) in servicing the markets of A and B, then could not country B have achieved a long-term income gain (based on acquiring these monopoly rents) by attracting that firm in the first place by offering it generous protection? The answer logically is yes, as it is in a host of other special imperfect market conditions. But it is difficult to use such special cases to justify a policy of protection since this would open the door for firms seeking protection to try to establish that these special, justifying conditions exist, even if they do not.

More important, this argument for protection, like the others described in this section, assumes no retaliation by trading partners; and in the world in which we live, that cannot be presumed.

## Free Trade vs. Protection: A Summary

This discussion shows that an issue should not be judged by counting up the number of arguments for and against. There are only a few arguments *for* free trade, but they are very impressive, such as the real income gains from comparative advantage and economies of scale.

On the other hand, there is a whole battery of arguments for protection. Some are downright illogical—for example, the argument that tariffs should be tailored to equalize costs between countries. Those that do make some sense — like the infant industry argument or the use of protection to stimulate high-tech industries — lose their attraction if other countries retaliate by protecting their industries, too. In this case, the world economy becomes less efficient as it is split up into small national markets. All countries collectively lose, and any individual country is likely to lose as well. Free trade still remains the appropriate target.

Free trade means the elimination of not only tariffs, but also a whole set of other trade restrictions known as ***non-tariff barriers*** (NTBs).

## NON-TARIFF BARRIERS (NTBs)

Here are a few of the most important.

### Quotas

One of the standard *non-tariff barriers* is a quota that limits the quantity of a good that can be imported. Under certain conditions, a quota may be equivalent to a tariff (as shown in the appendix to this chapter). For example, the quotas on textiles and apparel imposed by some highly developed countries have been as restrictive as a tariff of 50% or more. This has been particularly damaging to the less developed countries that have a comparative advantage in these products. According to some experts, this damage more than offsets the benefits these countries receive from the special low tariff rates that a number of highly developed countries apply to imports from them.

### Health or Quality Standards

Countries may impose NTBs in the form of stiff quality or health standards that may be difficult for imports to satisfy. If such standards lead to an improvement in the nation's health, they may be justified even though they have the unfortunate side effect of restricting trade. On the other hand, if they have little effect on the nation's health, they may be just a way of reducing imports. For example, the Japanese at one time prevented the import of Perrier (a natural sparkling mineral water from France) by requiring that it be boiled.

It is often difficult to determine whether a health standard has been imposed to protect health or to protect domestic industries. For example, in an "international food fight" in 1989, the Europeans banned imports of U.S. beef that had been fed growth hormones on the ground that this was a health hazard. The U.S. government argued that the meat was safe, and that the Europeans were using health regulations as a pretext to protect their own beef industry. In cases like this, it is not easy to sort out how much of the health concern is valid and how much is an excuse for protection. As shown below, the same is true of environmental standards.

### Bureaucracy and Red Tape

A country may impose other NTBs, such as complex and costly customs procedures, to discourage or delay imports. For example, to discourage imports of Japanese video cassette recorders in 1982, the French required all imported VCRs to be cleared through the tiny customs office at Poitiers, an inland town far from any main port—ironically, the same small town used about 150 years ago by Frédéric Bastiat (Box 20-1) to illustrate how ridiculous protection could become.

## CANADIAN TARIFFS, 1870–1990

In the history of the Canadian tariff (Figure 20-1) two trends stand out: a dramatic increase from the late 1870s until 1890, and a gradual fall since—except for the period of the Great Depression of the 1930s when the Canadian government raised tariffs in an attempt to protect domestic employment. (But beware: Figure 20-1 describes only tariffs and not the NTBs that have become increasingly important.)

### The National Policy

Beginning in 1854, British North America and the United States participated in a limited free trade agreement, which was abrogated by the United States in 1866. Following Confederation in 1867, Canada maintained low tariffs in the hope of reviving the free trade agreement. However, U.S. tariffs remained, and in the late 1870s, Sir John A. Macdonald announced the National Policy of high tariffs, which at that time was seen as a method of nation-building: By making imports more expensive, the policy would induce

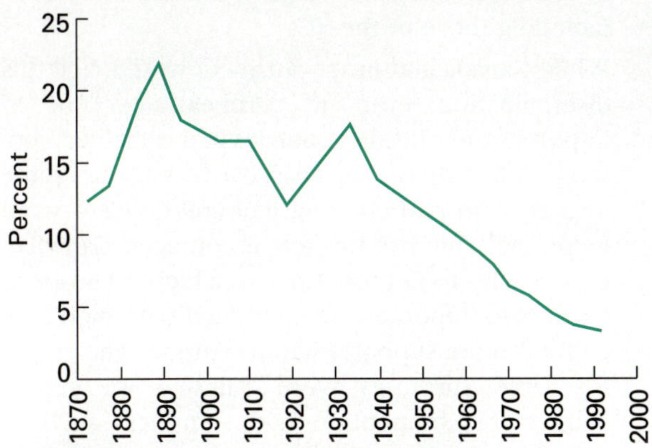


**FIGURE 20-1 Average Canadian tariff rates.** Canada has had high tariffs sometimes and low tariffs at other times. But since the mid-1930s, the trend has been down, so that now our tariffs average less than 5%. Increasingly, the focus is on how non-tariff barriers restrict trade.

*Source*: Compiled by authors from data in F.H. Leacy, M.C. Urquhart, and K.A.H. Buckley, eds., *Historical Statistics of Canada*, 2nd ed. (Ottawa: Statistics Canada, 1982); *Bank of Canada Review*, June 1992; and *The National Finances* (various issues).

Canadian consumers to buy more goods from industrial firms in Canada, whose growth would be stimulated; the reduction in north-south trade between Canada and the United States would stimulate east-west trade between the Canadian provinces (which was also encouraged by the Canadian Pacific Railway that was to be built in the 1880s.) But the policy of high tariff protection was regionally divisive then, as it has remained since. It meant higher prices not only for people in Ontario and Quebec, where industry was growing in response to the tariff, but also for consumers in the West and the Maritime provinces where there was little industrial growth. They viewed the tariff as benefiting Ontario and Quebec at their expense.

During the decades before the Great Depression, Canadian tariffs gradually fell from the high levels of the late nineteenth century. As we noted above, however, tariffs were raised substantially in the 1930s on imports from countries outside of the Commonwealth. (Under the system of Commonwealth Preference introduced at that time, Commonwealth countries imposed lower tariffs on imports from each other.)

Since the 1930s, the trend in Canadian tariff protection has again been downwards. A reduction in average tariffs took place in 1935, through a ***bilateral*** (two-way) agreement between Canada and the United States in which both countries agreed to cut tariffs on imports from the other. After World War II, there was a shift away from bilateral negotiations, and from ***plurilateral*** tariff negotiations, such as Commonwealth Preference, involving several countries. Instead, countries turned to ***multilateral*** negotiations in which the large number of nations belonging to the ***General Agreement on Tariffs and Trade*** (GATT) agreed to cut their tariffs against each other.

> *Multilateral* trade negotiations involve tariff reductions by all participating countries. *Plurilateral* negotiations involve several countries. *Trilateral* negotiations include three countries, *bilateral* involve two. *Unilateral* action is taken by one country alone.

## MULTILATERAL NEGOTIATIONS: THE GENERAL AGREEMENT ON TARIFFS AND TRADE (GATT)

Since 1947 when Canada and 22 other nations signed the GATT, it has been the major forum in which all participating countries have negotiated lower trade barriers. In the 1967 ***Kennedy Round***, tariffs were cut on average by about one-third, and in the subsequent ***Tokyo Round***, by another third. Moreover, tariffs on civilian aircraft were eliminated.

Following this, there was a period in which the world drifted slowly back toward more protectionism. To forestall this, the ***Uruguay Round*** of negotiations began in 1986 with the objective of reducing not only tariffs, but also NTBs. After seven years of grinding negotiations, agreement was finally reached in 1993. (See Box 20-5.)

## A PLURILATERAL AGREEMENT: THE EUROPEAN COMMUNITY (EC)

An important move away from multilateralism was the plurilateral agreement reached in Europe in the late 1950s, with the formation of the ***European Community*** (EC), which includes Germany, France,

Italy, Holland, Belgium, and Luxembourg (later joined by Britain and more recently by Spain and several other countries). Its provisions are similar to that of any *customs union*, that is, tariff-free trade among all participating nations and a common tariff against goods from outsiders. But, as a *common market*, its provisions go far beyond this to include other measures of economic coordination such as a common policy of agricultural price supports. The eventual objective has been to create a large barrier-free market like the United States, in which goods, services, people, and capital could move without restriction.

One of the reasons for the formation of the EC was that the member countries wanted to make it impossible for France and Germany to go to war again; thus, they eventually wanted to move some distance toward political union. They also had a strong economic motive: to gain the benefits of freer trade among themselves. Since formation of the EC, its member countries have made substantial economic progress, although it is difficult to assess how much has been due to the formation of the EC, and how much has been due to other causes. It is also difficult to assess how the EC has affected outside countries like Canada. On the one hand, by inducing more rapid European growth, it has made Europe a better potential customer for Canadian exports. However, the formation of the EC has raised two problems for an "outsider" like Canada:

1. Whereas before the EC, Canadian and German firms producing machinery faced the same tariff barriers in selling in the French market, Canadian firms now still face this tariff but competing German firms do not. Thus, the EC creates ***discrimination*** against Canada and provides *preference* to the Germans in the French market. More broadly, the EC discriminates against all outside countries like Canada, and provides preference for all EC countries like Germany in all other EC markets like France.[4] The only way Canada can eliminate the discrimination it faces is by participating in multilateral negotiations that eliminate all tariffs, including those of the EC.
2. While Canada and other outsiders would face this discrimination even if European barriers to imports from outside countries had remained constant, in fact these European barriers against some imports — in particular, agricultural goods — were increased. This has further discouraged Canadian export sales to Europe. Moreover, higher European barriers to imports were combined with high agricultural price supports within Europe. The resulting large surpluses were dumped on export markets in competition with suppliers such as Canada, Australia, and the United States. (An example cited earlier was the EC sale of butter to the Soviet Union for a 93% discount below its European cost, with the European taxpayer making up the difference.) Such heavily subsidized European exports have reduced Canadian export sales to Third World countries. Moreover, the United States attempted to retain its markets in Third World countries by matching the export subsidies paid by the EC. In the resulting subsidy war between the United States and the EC, it was virtually impossible for relatively small countries like Canada and Australia to compete, because their treasuries simply could not afford it. It is little wonder that agricultural disputes between the United States and Europe became a major block in completing the Uruguay Round.

## A BILATERAL AGREEMENT: THE CANADA/U.S. FREE TRADE AGREEMENT (FTA)

Faced with stiff competition in the international marketplace, the majority of Canadian manufacturers did an about-face during the 1980s; their traditional opposition to a ***Canada/United States Free Trade Agreement*** turned to support. This was the result of a number of concerns: How could Canadian producers, supplying a widely dispersed home market of less than 25 million people, expect to compete internationally with producers in the United States, Japan, or Europe, with their tariff-free home markets of more than 100 million people? How could Canadian producers, who depend on the U.S. market for about 70% of their export sales, maintain their access to that market in the face of growing U.S. protectionism?

In 1988, largely in response to the fear by Canadian exporters of facing increasing barriers at the U.S. bor-

[4] While the Germans benefit from this preference — and their resulting increase in exports to partner countries like France — they may benefit or lose on their new imports from partner countries. They benefit if their partners are the lowest-cost world source; in this case, their increased purchases from partners result in "trade creation." However, Germany may lose if, in giving its partners preferential duty-free access to its market, Germans switch their import purchases from the lowest-cost world source of supply, which is outside the EC, to a higher-cost source within the EC. This is the case of "trade diversion" and its cost is defined by the higher price paid for imports.

It is theoretically possible for this cost to exceed the benefits a country gets from participating in the EC, or in any free trade agreement.

der, the Canadian government negotiated a free trade agreement with the United States designed not only to prevent serious damage to our existing access to the U.S. market, but also to improve that access. The FTA came into effect in January 1989 following a tumultuous election dominated by that issue in late 1988.

This bilateral agreement will eliminate tariffs and many (but not all) of the other trade barriers between the two countries by 1998. Because the bilateral trade of Canada and the United States is so large, the FTA is expected to provide substantial benefits from comparative advantage, economies of scale, and increased competition in the production of goods.

In addition, the FTA will provide a special benefit to Canada. At present, many Canadian industrial exports pay a U.S. tariff at the border which goes to the U.S. treasury. With the elimination of this tariff, Canadian exporters will no longer pay this "tax" to Washington.[5]

In addition to liberalizing trade in goods, the FTA provides for broad liberalization in services; for example, architects are now able to move freely and sell their services in either country. The Canada/U.S. agreement also puts pressure on other countries to support multilateral free trade because it creates discrimination against outsiders trying to export into the FTA (just as the EC has created discrimination against Canadian firms trying to export into Europe). The only way outsiders can reduce this discrimination is by pressing for multilateral tariff reductions by all countries beyond those already achieved in the Uruguay Round. (While the creation of a free trade agreement increases the incentive for outsiders to push for multilateral trade liberalization, it is not at all clear that it affects the incentives for insiders in the same way, since such an agreement already gives them some of the gains from multilateral liberalization. A free trade agreement also gives each member country preference in its partner's market — an advantage it may resist losing in a multilateral negotiation. On the other hand, a free trade agreement will make producers in any member country like Canada much stronger international competitors by subjecting them to more intense competition from partner countries like the United States; since this will make them far better prepared to "take on the world," it will reduce their fear and political resistance to multilateral free trade.)

## How is the FTA Working Out?

Most of the concerns voiced when the FTA was being debated have not been realized, such as the fears about how it would damage our sovereignty,[6] cultural industries, or health care and other social programs. (The dominant risk for culture or social programs has become the fiscal cutbacks as the federal and provincial governments try to limit debt growth.) However, there was one concern in the FTA debate that appears to have been justified.

## The Adjustment as Canadian Industry Rationalizes

The FTA has triggered a ***rationalization*** of Canadian production as Canadian firms have been moving toward greater specialization, producing each item at higher volume for both the Canadian and U.S. markets and therefore, because of economies of scale, at lower cost. In doing so, Canadian producers have been responding to both a carrot and a stick. The carrot has been freer access to the large U.S. market. The stick has been the removal of the Canadian tariff, which has left many Canadian firms unable to compete with less expensive imports unless they have been prepared to rationalize and thus reduce their costs. The reductions in Canadian costs (that is, increases in productivity) should allow Canadian producers to reduce their prices and eventually increase their wages. (Indeed, inexpensive imports may force them to reduce their prices.) It is because of both

[5] Since removal of the U.S. tariff would allow Canadians to retain tariffs previously paid to the U.S. treasury, why wouldn't removal of the *Canadian* tariff allow *Americans* to retain tariffs previously paid to the *Canadian* treasury? The reason is that because of the relative size of the two economies, North American prices of industrial goods are typically determined in the United States rather than Canada. Thus, Canadian importers must take the U.S. price as given and they must raise the price of imports as they come into Canada by the amount of the Canadian tariff. Accordingly, the Canadian tariff that is collected by Ottawa is ultimately paid not by U.S. exporters, but by Canadian consumers who pay a higher price. Thus, any change in the Canadian tariff won't affect Americans at all — only groups within Canada.

[6] The FTA — like the Uruguay Round or, for that matter, any military agreement — does have some effect on our freedom and independence. Specifically, we give up some freedom to restrict our imports, in exchange for negotiating greater freedom to export by limiting the freedom of the United States to restrict its imports from us. Moreover, there is a special sense in which more secure (though not guaranteed) access to the U.S. market under the FTA may increase Canada's freedom and independence. Prior to the FTA, the U.S. was freer to take unilateral protectionist action against Canadian exports. In response, the Canadian government was continuously appealing for relief to the U.S. government — often at times when the two countries had unresolved disputes on which Canada was under pressure to make equivalent concessions.

these lower prices and increased wages that Canadian real income should rise.[7]

Following the rationalization of Canadian industry, manufacturers in Ontario and Quebec should face no substantial locational disadvantages in competing with the United States in a variety of products.[8] The existing Canadian industrial corridor between Windsor and Quebec City is a reasonably good location to produce highly processed goods for North American distribution once barriers to trade have been removed. This corridor is at the northern edge of the largest market in North America—that is, the market enclosed in the Chicago/Boston/Baltimore triangle. In this respect, Toronto is a considerably better location than the "out-of-the-way" Minneapolis-St. Paul area (which, despite its location, has been able to attract and retain considerable industry in free trade competition with other U.S. cities).

## Trade Liberalization and Jobs

While the long-term prospect for Canada in the FTA is favourable, there is a short-term cost. In the FTA rationalization now taking place there will be jobs lost and jobs gained. Thus, specific groups of workers are facing ***adjustment costs*** because they have to acquire new skills and, in some cases, move to new communities. It is important that the cost that falls on these individuals should be shared by the majority who benefit from the change in policy. Moreover, the assistance provided to these individuals should be in a form that helps the economy to adjust (such as retraining or relocation subsidies) rather than in a form that *discourages* adjustment (such as disguised forms of protection that continue to prop up an inefficient industry).

It is important to keep the cost of Canadian adjustment to free trade in perspective by recognizing that it has been grafted onto other adjustments that have been generating substantial job losses:

- The introduction of the FTA has coincided with an extended worldwide recession that has reduced demand in Canada, the United States, and many other important Canadian trading partners.
- In highly developed countries worldwide, there has been a continuing long-term reduction in the percentage of total jobs that are in manufacturing, as increases in productivity (most obviously, due to the introduction of robotics) have displaced labour. This has recently been compounded by large companies like IBM, Phillips, and Northern Telecom that have been downsizing in a highly publicized way as small companies have quietly been established and grown.
- Canadians have been switching jobs as a result of domestic technological change, such as the introduction of computers and word processors; because of increased demand for some products and declining demand for others; and as a result of increased competition from imports from countries like Japan in high-tech products, like South Korea in autos, and like India and other less developed countries in textiles; and as a result of fluctuations in the Canadian dollar that have changed the price of Canadian goods on the world market. Such pressures have meant that roughly 20% of Canadian workers have traditionally been voluntarily or involuntarily separated from their jobs in a normal year (a surprisingly large number that indicates that, despite its flaws, the Canadian labour market works well). Compared to these other pressures, those generated by the FTA should be less intense; for one reason, the predictable, phased-out tariff reductions under the FTA of at most 1% or 2% a year are unlikely to have as much effect on Canada's competitive position as the greater percentage fluctuations that typically take place in the value of the Canadian dollar. (For more on the Canadian dollar and macroeconomic pressures on Canada's trading industries, see Box 20-3.)

There has been a tendency — not only by opponents but also by some of the supporters of the FTA—to focus on its immediate impact on jobs without adequately recognizing that, like technological change, free trade is not designed to cure short-term

[7] Some calculations suggest a real income gain to Canadians as low as 1%–2% of GDP. Others, most notably those by Richard Harris of Simon Fraser University and David Cox of Queen's University, point to real income gains to Canadians as high as 9% of Canadian GDP. The Harris-Cox estimates are described in Richard G. Harris, "Summary of a Project on the General Equilibrium Evolution of Canadian Trade Policy," Ch. 8 in John Whalley, ed., *Canada-United States Free Trade*, Collected Research Studies of the Royal Commission on the Economic Union and Development Prospects for Canada, vol. 11 (Toronto: University of Toronto Press, 1985), pp. 157–77. This estimate by Harris and Cox is consistent with an estimate published in 1967 by R.J. Wonnacott and P. Wonnacott, in *Free Trade Between the United States and Canada: The Potential Economic Effects* (Cambridge, Mass.: Harvard University Press).

[8] There are obviously many complications, such as taxation, that could affect this broad picture. In addition, Canadian wages may be higher or lower than those in the United States, depending on the regions in each country being compared, and the value of the exchange rate.

## TOOLS AND TECHNIQUES — BOX 20-3
## How Macroeconomic Pressure and Fighting Inflation Made Canadian Adjustment to the Canada/U.S. FTA More Difficult

In the initial years in which the Canadian economy was adjusting to the FTA, the Bank of Canada was engaged in an anti-inflation monetary policy that put pressure on all Canadian industry by raising interest rates. Moreover, these higher rates attracted foreign capital and thus raised the value of the Canadian dollar, making it more difficult for Canadian firms to compete internationally. This threw the major burden of this macroeconomic adjustment to fight inflation onto Canada's trade-related (export and import-competing) industries at precisely the time that they were under pressure to adjust to increased U.S. competition under the FTA. The good news is that inflation has now—at least temporarily—been driven below 2% and interest rates (which reflect inflation, among other things) have accordingly fallen, bringing down the value of the Canadian dollar and making it easier for Canadian trade-related industries to compete internationally.

unemployment (which is better left to monetary and fiscal policy). Rather, it is designed to improve Canadian productivity and real income and thereby increase the ability of the Canadian economy to create high-income jobs in the future. In evaluating technological change (to take two obvious examples, replacing workers on shovels with bulldozers or introducing word processors and computers into an office) it makes no sense to count jobs lost. By increasing Canadian productivity and income — and hence demand — such technological changes will indirectly create better jobs in the future — although these are now impossible to identify. Moreover, we have little choice; if we want to remain competitive, we must be continuously accepting — and initiating — technological change. So too with trade. We have little choice but to participate in a world of expanding trade. And it makes no sense to count high-visibility jobs lost from trade liberalization when the higher-productivity jobs created by this policy are often so difficult to identify.

However, there is one big difference between trade liberalization and technological change. While both indirectly create jobs that are difficult to identify, trade liberalization — unlike technological change — also directly creates jobs that are far easier to identify, namely, jobs in expanding export activities due to improved access to foreign markets.

# The Effect of the FTA on Canadian Trade Performance

One would expect that removing trade barriers between Canada and the United States would lead to an increase in Canadian imports from the United States of products facing reduced Canadian barriers (but less effect on products that were not liberalized by the FTA because, for example, they were already moving duty-free). One would also expect the same effect in the other direction: an increase in Canadian exports in products where the FTA has reduced U.S. barriers.

In the first four years of the FTA (1989–1992) the value of Canadian imports from the United States rose in the liberalized category by 28% and in the non-liberalized category by less than 1%. There has been no sign of the import flood that many feared; the 28% increase over these four years is less than 7% a year.

On the export side, in a reversal of pre-FTA trends, Canadian exports to the United States in these same four years increased by 33% in sectors liberalized by the FTA, and by 9% in sectors not liberalized. Thus exports have been one of the success stories in a period of recession. But not all exports—just exports to the United States that were liberalized by the FTA. While there are other factors that may make these results either more or less encouraging, recognition of the two potentially strongest influences — the value of the Canadian dollar, and growth in income in the two countries — does not change the overall conclusion: In the sectors where the FTA has liberalized trade, Canadian export performance in the United States has been somewhat stronger than U.S. export performance in Canada. These figures suggest that in terms of overall net job creation, the Canadian recession would have been worse without the FTA. Because the industries that have been successful under free trade tend not to be as labour-intensive as the unsuccessful ones, it cannot be concluded yet that jobs created or maintained by the expanding export industries have compensated for the losses in import-competing sectors. However, it is known that the sectors expanding under free trade pay their employees, on average, higher wages than those hurt by the agreement.[9]

Even if the FTA were to have reduced the net job loss in Canada from the recession, this could only be viewed as a special bonus. The main point of the FTA remains the longer-term benefit from inducing Canadian industry to rationalize to service broader international markets and thus increase Canadian productivity and income, and keep the economy competitive. But the FTA does raise a short-run problem: Whether or not it has increased total job opportunities in Canada, it has added another layer to the job switching that has been taking place in Canada in response to other influences such as technological change, shifts in demand, and increasing imports from the Far East.

## Unfinished Business: The FTA Improves, But Doesn't Guarantee, Access into the U.S. Market

One of the provisions of the FTA is a new dispute-settlement mechanism to reduce the risk that either country will take politically motivated actions against imports from the other. However, this goes only a limited distance toward guaranteeing free trade, since it only ensures a fair *application* by each country of its existing trade laws, and it is far from clear that these U.S. (and similar Canadian) laws are themselves fair. To illustrate, the United States can take action — that is, impose "trade remedies" — against imports from Canada that are damaging a U.S. industry in two circumstances:

1. The United States can impose a ***countervailing*** duty if a Canadian export to the United States has been receiving government subsidies.
2. The United States can impose an ***anti-dumping*** duty on a Canadian export that is being dumped in the United States — that is, an export that is being sold at a lower price in the United States than in Canada or is being sold in the United States at "less than fair value." While this sounds reasonable enough in theory, in practice it is not, and one need not be a trade expert to see why. Less than fair value is defined as less than cost plus a markup. But in a recession many Canadian firms are temporarily operating at a loss — that is, are producing at less than cost — and therefore at less than fair value. Thus they automatically become potential targets for U.S. anti-dumping duties on their exports. A U.S. study has concluded that, in a recent year, most firms *in the United States* would have been targets for such U.S. action had they been on foreign soil and exporting into the United States.

It is important to keep these U.S. trade remedies in perspective. Such U.S. trade actions have occurred in only a few sectors, and in many instances the dispute-settlement panels set up in the FTA have resolved the problem by judging in Canada's favour. In the 1992 judgement of Gordon Ritchie, former deputy Canadian trade negotiator of the FTA and long-time critic of U.S. trade remedies, Canada has won the panel decisions it should have won, and lost the ones it should have lost (that is, cases in which the U.S. complaint against Canadian subsidization or dumping was justified). But the problem remains that even if an overtly protectionist U.S. interest is eventually thwarted by a panel decision, its initiation of expensive legal action can be a form of potential harassment that adds to the risk facing Canadian firms exporting to the United States.

---

[9] The above estimates of the FTA's effects have been drawn or calculated from Daniel Schwanen, "What Has Happened Under Free Trade?" (Toronto: C.D. Howe Institute, Commentary #52), September 1993. These estimates exclude oil and autos: the latter is an important sector that was liberalized by the FTA in its formal provisions but little in its actual operation which had already been almost completely liberalized. (Including autos and oil further increases the Canadian export surplus, as does the expression of all changes in absolute, rather than percentage terms.)

Finally, during this period there was no similar increase in the Canadian export surplus in our trade with the rest of the world; indeed our exports declined by 2% while our imports increased by 14%.

The question is: Do we negotiate reform of these trade remedy laws by establishing a code to define which subsidies will be allowed and which will not? How can we come up with a reasonable definition of when dumping is occurring and when it is not? Perhaps, as some studies have suggested, we should even replace anti-dumping laws with the domestic competition laws of the two countries.

## A TRILATERAL NEGOTIATION: THE NORTH AMERICAN FREE TRADE AGREEMENT (NAFTA)

When the Canada/U.S. FTA came into effect, the Mexicans were impressed by its provisions and approached the United States, seeking to negotiate a similar agreement. The question for Canada was: Should we let the United States and Mexico go ahead on their own and negotiate a bilateral free trade agreement, thus leaving the United States with two bilateral free trade agreements, one with Canada and one with Mexico? Or should we participate, thus transforming our bilateral agreement with the United States into NAFTA, a trilateral agreement including Mexico?

### Should Canada Have Participated in Negotiating NAFTA?

A major problem with participating was that Canada was already heavily involved in adjusting to its own free trade with the United States. Why take on a further competitive challenge with another country — Mexico — so soon? However, the Canadian decision could not be delayed. The U.S.-Mexican bus was about to leave. Should Canada get on or off? The Canadian decision was to participate in the negotiations, thus creating the ***North American Free Trade Agreement***.

NAFTA will:

- provide Canadian exporters with improved duty-free access to the Mexican market with its high growth potential;
- provide Canadian consumers with the benefits of duty-free imports from Mexico;
- provide Canadian industry with the low-cost Mexican inputs necessary to keep it competitive. In this respect, Mexico will do for Canada and the United States what Portugal and Spain have done for the European Community.

However, the inexpensive Mexican goods that will be so beneficial for the Canadian consumer and the industries that use them will put pressure on competing Canadian firms that produce these same items; this is the problem of taking on more competition while still adjusting to the FTA with the United States. Nonetheless, for two reasons, increased Mexican competition in the Canadian market is likely to be less intense than popularly imagined: First, Canada's imports from Mexico have been relatively small; in 1989, they were only 2% of our imports from the United States. Second, in many items Canadian barriers to Mexican goods are already so low, there's little left to be removed in NAFTA. On the other hand, Mexico will be removing far more substantial barriers against Canadian goods. Hence, there is little reason to be pessimistic about Canada's export/import potential.

To illustrate the low remaining Canadian barriers, Mexican goods have already been coming into Canada with reduced tariffs designed to assist developing countries. Moreover, in the most important import sector — autos and parts — over 90% of imports from Mexico have been coming into Canada completely free of duty under the Canada/U.S. Auto Pact. Because Canadian firms have already had to compete in this way with inexpensive imports from Mexico (and other less developed countries enjoying similar benefits), it is not clear that the competition Canadian industry will have to face with NAFTA will greatly exceed the competition it would have had to face in any case without NAFTA.

In addition, Canada also had a strong defensive motive to participate in NAFTA, just as it has had in the Tokyo, Kennedy, and Uruguay Rounds of the GATT: to avoid the costs of being an outsider to any free trade agreement that includes its important trading partners — in this case the United States, its most important trading partner by a wide margin. To illustrate the costs of being excluded from NAFTA and allowing the United States and Mexico to negotiate their own bilateral free trade agreement, Canadian exporters would not only fail to get the better, duty-free access to the Mexican market that NAFTA would provide. Instead, they would get worse access to Mexico because they would face discrimination there in competing against the United States, since U.S. firms would get duty-free access to that market while Canadian firms would not. Moreover, Canadian firms would face stiffer competition from U.S. and perhaps Mexican firms where it counts far more — in the critical U.S. market — because (i) U.S. firms would get a cost advantage because they would get duty-free inputs from Mexico while Canadian firms would not; and (ii) in negotiating its bilateral free trade agreement with the United States, Mexico might be able to acquire better access to the U.S. market than Canada was able to negotiate in its free trade agreement with the United States. (A possible example has occurred in bidding on U.S. government purchases, where the Americans have now been willing to liberalize their trade more in NAFTA than they did in the earlier Canada/U.S. FTA.)

Another defensive reason for Canada to participate in NAFTA has been to ensure that this agreement sets the appropriate precedent for any further trade liberalization in the Western hemisphere: Such liberalization should be in the form of an expanding free trade agreement in which each country will see free trade in every direction as it looks out over all other participating countries. If Canada had not participated, the result would have been a hub-and-spoke system in which the United States as the hub would have had a bilateral free trade agreement with one spoke (Canada), another bilateral free trade agreement with a second spoke (Mexico), and perhaps eventually spoke bilaterals with other partners as well. (See Figure 20-2.) This would have given the United States an advantage at the expense of its partners, because it would have become the only location from which firms would have been able to trade freely in all directions. (Firms in other participating countries would have faced free trade with the United States, but a maze of barriers to trade with other participating countries.)

In short, if Canada had failed to participate, and had thus blocked the development of a full hemispheric free trade agreement, it would have opened

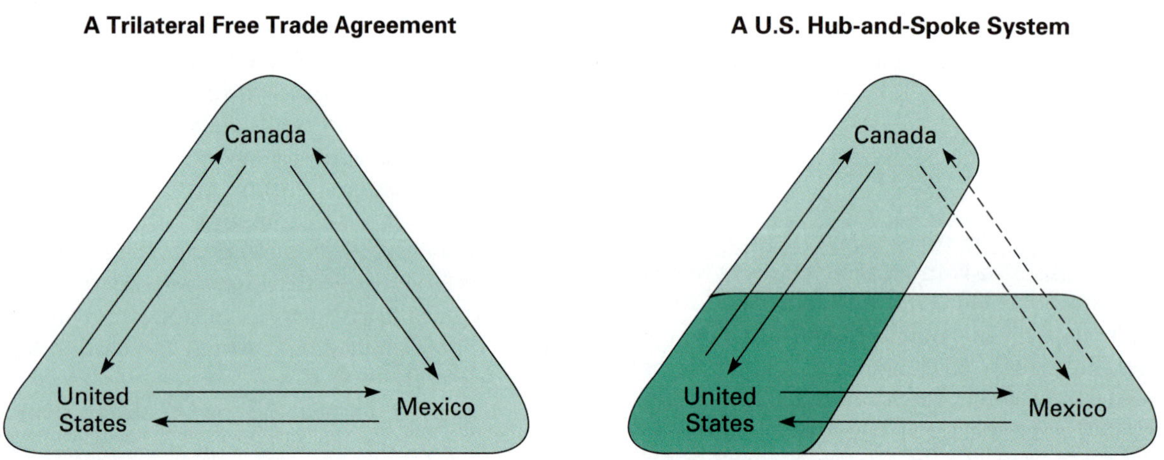


**(a)** In NAFTA, a trilateral free trade agreement, all three countries trade freely with each other. As each country looks out over this trading system, it sees free trade in all directions.

**(b)** In this system, the U.S. hub would have two bilateral agreements, one with Canada and one with Mexico. All trade with the United States in this system would be free (solid arrows); but trade between Canada and Mexico (dashed arrows) would still face barriers. As the United States looked out over such a system, it would see free trade in all directions. But each of its partners would see trade only with the United States, and discriminatory barriers in all other directions—a problem that would become worse were the United States to add additional bilateral spoke agreements with other countries.

**FIGURE 20-2** **A trilateral free trade agreement or a U.S.-centred hub-and-spoke system?**

the way for the United States, already the wealthiest and most dominant country, to increase its dominance at the expense of Canada and relatively poor countries in Latin America, which would all have had to face serious discrimination in competing throughout the Western hemisphere.

## NAFTA: Fortress North America?

One of NAFTA's major strengths is that, in liberalizing trade and investment within North America — with the increased efficiency and real income that this offers — it does not, on balance, appear to raise trade barriers significantly against outside countries. This relatively favourable treatment of outsiders is important in keeping NAFTA consistent with further multilateral liberalization in the GATT. In particular, NAFTA members do not increase their tariffs against outsiders' products as, for example, the British had to in agriculture when they joined the European Community. Moreover, NAFTA is open-ended to new applicants in the Western hemisphere, and perhaps beyond — subject to approval by existing members.

There is, however, one respect in which NAFTA does damage outsiders: its more demanding ***rules of origin***, certainly in textiles and clothing, probably in autos, and possibly in footwear.

## NAFTA's Changes in Rules of Origin

As a free trade agreement, NAFTA has rules of origin to ensure that a certain amount of North American transformation or content is included in any product shipped across any of its internal borders, for example, across the U.S.-Canadian border. But because NAFTA has made rules of origin more demanding, trade with outsiders like Japan has been restricted; for example, NAFTA's increase in the North American content that Honda must put in its cars produced in Canada for sale in the United States is likely to reduce Honda's import of parts from Japan. Thus raising content requirements is a policy that can be used to protect North American producers — in this case, of auto parts — against foreign competition. However, it is a particularly insidious form of protection that may be increasingly used in the future, because it is generally not understood by the public and raises conflicts not only with outside countries, but also among free trade partners. A publicized example was the recent dispute between the Canadian and U.S. governments over whether or not Honda in Canada was satisfying content requirements on its cars exported to the United States, as set out in the Canada/U.S. FTA.

To reduce such future disputes, NAFTA does make rules of origin much clearer than in the Canada/U.S. FTA. This is the favourable side, at least in part offsetting the unfavourable increases in content requirement.

It is interesting to note that all rules of origin could be eliminated in a customs union in which all countries would have the same tariff against outsiders. (In that case, there would be no problem of "trade deflection," as explained, along with other issues raised by rules of origin, in Box 20-4.)

## NAFTA and Computer Trade

The brightest side of NAFTA is that it essentially establishes a customs union in one industry — computers — since all participants move to the same common external tariff, zero, for many items. This makes rules of origin no longer necessary. Moreover, this has been done in a way to mute traditional Canadian objections to a customs union, that is, the large country — the United States — would set the common external tariff, and it could be raised in a protective way. The reason that these objections do not arise in NAFTA's computer agreement is that the common external tariff is very low and any member country can unilaterally cut this tariff even further in the Uruguay Round. Note also the benefit to outsiders who now face a lower tariff in exporting computer products to North America — a benefit which, at least in part, offsets their cost from NAFTA's more restrictive rules of origin.

## TRADE AND THE ENVIRONMENT IN NAFTA

NAFTA now includes two side agreements or parallel accords in which each country agrees to allow its two partners to impose penalties on it if it fails to enforce its own labour laws (for example, on child labour or minimum wage) or its own environmental laws. Note the compromise here: Each of the three countries, including the United States, which insisted on these accords, judged that giving its trading partners influence over its setting of its own domestic laws would have been an unacceptable encroachment on its sovereignty. But each was prepared to accept pressure from its partners if it failed to *enforce* its own laws.

## TOOLS AND TECHNIQUES — BOX 20-4
## Rules of Origin: The Preferred Form of Future Protection?

Any free trade agreement, such as NAFTA, in which partner countries have different tariffs against outsiders, has to have rules of origin to prevent *trade deflection.* An example of such deflection would occur if a German firm that wanted to export cars to Mexico were able to avoid a high Mexican tariff by shipping these cars first into the low-tariff United States and thence duty-free into Mexico (under NAFTA). Such deflection is prevented by NAFTA's rules of origin requiring that any product shipped across the Mexican-U.S. border — or any other duty-free border within NAFTA—must first be physically transformed or have a certain percentage of its content produced within NAFTA. For example, the German auto exporter could satisfy NAFTA's content requirement by shipping parts (rather than cars) to the United States and then having them assembled there—along with some U.S., Canadian, or Mexican parts — prior to their final shipment into Mexico.

The problem is that as rules of origin are made more demanding, they not only become more and more protective against outsiders but they raise other problems as well: (1) they become increasingly difficult to monitor in a fair and non-arbitrary manner in a world in which a typical multinational can scarcely identify what has been produced where; and (2) they protect the member country with the large market not only from outsiders, but also *from its free trade partners.* A German firm that wishes to produce in North America in order to sell in the large U.S. market will prefer a U.S. location where it won't have to ship across any internal NAFTA border (and therefore won't have to satisfy any rules of origin). Better to locate there than in Mexico or Canada where it will have to satisfy these restrictive rules. Thus, the more demanding the rules of origin, the more advantage the United States gets at its partners' expense and the greater the potential conflict between free trade partners — a most unfortunate characteristic of a policy that seems to be developing into the preferred form of future protection.

Moreover, this compromise addresses most (though not all) of the environmental concerns, since such concerns have been concentrated on Mexico — and the major problem there has been lax enforcement rather than inadequate domestic laws. Thus the three countries have been able to ensure a higher level of environmental discipline in North America. (They have also established a fund to clean up the Mexican-U.S. border, but it isn't yet clear how it will be financed.)

However, there is a potential problem with these side agreements. The way discipline can be imposed on a member country if it fails to comply in enforcing its own domestic laws is through penalties in the form of trade sanctions, that is, tariffs on its exports.[10] Thus the concern has been that two new trade remedies may be created — similar to the anti-dumping and countervailing remedies that have sometimes been used by U.S. protective interests to damage Canadian exports to the United States, even under the Canada/U.S. FTA. How could the negotiators prevent this, that is, prevent protectionist industries from capturing the environmental accord, and using it not to improve the environment, but instead to restrict trade?

The negotiators were successful in limiting the potential protective damage from both the labour and environmental accords in two ways:

1. Any investigation or punitive action against a NAFTA country allegedly failing to enforce its domestic labour or environmental laws can only be triggered by *both* its NAFTA partners. Thus, the United States alone cannot unilaterally take action against Mexico or Canada, and consequently, U.S. firms with protectionist objectives will be severely limited in their ability to use labour or environmental issues to harass imports from Canada or Mexico.

[10] As noted below, Canada is subject to sanctions, but of a different kind than Mexico and the United States.

Thus there has been a big unforeseen benefit of Canadian participation in NAFTA (in addition to the clearly foreseen benefit described above of keeping NAFTA trilateralized and free of hub-and-spoke distortions). If there were only two countries in this negotiation — i.e., the United States and Mexico — then protective labour or environmental action against one country would have had to be triggered by its one and only partner. However, with three countries involved, it has been possible to require that two countries do this triggering, and the protective potential of the environmental and labour agreements has thereby been greatly reduced. One might speculate on another benefit from Canadian participation in NAFTA. Would it be possible to reduce countervailing and anti-dumping harassment — by, say, the United States against Canada—by requiring that any such action also be triggered by both its NAFTA partners, that is, in our example, by both Mexico and the United States, rather than by the United States alone?

2. Canada will not be subject to trade sanctions. Instead, if it fails to comply, the Canadian government will have to pay a fine of U.S.$20 million initially, increasing with the growth in trade.[11] Thus there will still be pressure on firms in Canada to abide by Canadian environmental laws. However, this pressure will be exercised by the Canadian government; it will not directly distort trade.

In conclusion, while it has been important for Canada to participate in trilateralizing the negotiation of *free trade* in North America, it has also been important for Canada to be *excluded* from the potentially *protective* dimension of that negotiation, that is, trade sanctions to enforce the parallel accords.

## MULTILATERAL LIBERALIZATION: THE SUCCESS OF THE URUGUAY ROUND

Following the ratification of NAFTA in November, 1993, in a stormy debate in the U.S. Congress, U.S. negotiators turned their efforts to resolving their disputes with the Europeans, for example, on agricultural trade. The result: Within a month the two parties reached an agreement, which was then transformed into a multilateral GATT accord — in effect, the successful completion of the Uruguay Round. Like any other trade agreement, this was far from perfect and full of compromises (see Box 20-5). Nonetheless, it made 1993 a vintage year for trade liberalization.

## IMPORTS FROM THE EMERGING LESS DEVELOPED COUNTRIES

While the Canada/U.S. FTA, NAFTA, and the Uruguay Round have dominated the debate on trade policy in Canada over the last decade, there was another important development in North American trade: the rapid growth of imports from a number of newly industrialized countries (NICs). Where most of the pressure of foreign competition had earlier come from Japan, by the mid-1980s countries such as Taiwan and South Korea had also emerged as serious competitors. In industries where wages made up a large proportion of total production costs, Canadian firms were finding it particularly difficult to compete with producers in low-wage countries.

The export performance of the NICs has been impressive. Between 1965 and 1976, some increased their exports almost ten times. This is why countries like Taiwan, Hong Kong, and South Korea have been able to lift themselves out of the abject poverty that still grips many other countries that remain underdeveloped. But the growth of imports from these countries has raised a demand for protection by competing industries in the highly developed countries.

While the problem facing competing Canadian industries should be recognized, it is far from clear that we should provide them with the protection they seek. Before making any such decision, we should ask the same questions that have arisen in the debate on liberalizing trade with Mexico: Wouldn't it be better for us to concentrate less on the low-wage industries in Canada that produce cheap clothing, cheap shoes, and the other low-technology products that less developed countries can sell to us? Shouldn't we instead be concentrating on higher-wage, higher-technology products (including perhaps more expensive, specialized lines of clothing and shoes)? Allowing less developed countries (LDCs) to sell to us not only provides us with bargain goods; it may also be the most effective way we can assist them to

[11] This collective ability of trading partners to take legal action against a country judged in violation of its agreements is, in the view of some experts, somewhat similar to the system used in the European Community. If these fines were to be frequently paid, this could become a real problem. But it is hard to see how it might come to this, since the Canadian government could instead take prior action to enforce its own environmental laws. In a situation likely to be highly publicized, it would be facing pressure not only from its trading partners, but also from environmental groups and Canadian taxpayers.

## APPLICATIONS AND ILLUSTRATIONS BOX 20-5

### The 1993 GATT Agreement

On many fronts, this agreement represents a major advance. For example:

1. In many sectors tariffs are reduced, and in some products the major industrial nations have agreed to eliminate tariffs completely. These products include pharmaceuticals, construction equipment, paper, steel and medical equipment. This worldwide liberalization is beneficial not only because of the trade it creates, but also because it reduces the distorting trade-diverting effects of otherwise beneficial plurilateral, trilateral, or bilateral free trade agreements. NAFTA provides an example: The more that worldwide tariffs fall—including U.S. tariffs — the less discrimination the Japanese will face in the U.S. market in competition with Mexico, and fewer U.S. import purchases will be diverted from Japan to Mexico.
2. Trade in services, as well as goods, has been liberalized. Markets will be opened in accounting and legal services and software, and there will be some limited liberalization in financial services.
3. MFA (Multifibre Agreement) quotas by the developed countries on imports of clothing and textiles from the less developed countries will be phased out over ten years.
4. A multilateral Trading Organization is created that will have more authority than the existing GATT secretariat that it will replace. A stronger and faster mechanism is established to deal with dumping and subsidy disputes.
5. In the contentious area of agriculture, the subsidization of exports will be reduced. This will provide a major benefit to Canadian grain farmers, since competition in subsidizing exports between the United States and the EC had been driving down international prices in a trade war in which small exporting countries like Canada had been financially unable to compete.
6. The Japanese will lift their ban on rice imports. Stiff Canadian quotas on imports of dairy products and chicken will be replaced by equivalent tariffs, which will then be phased out. Thus Canadian marketing boards will eventually lose their protection. However, there were two remarkable features of this Canadian "liberalization." First, the equivalent tariffs that replaced the Canadian quotas were in the triple-digit range, running up to 350% on butter. This indicated the severity of the quotas and how damaging they had been to Canadian consumers. (To put these tariffs in perspective, there had been an earlier heated debate in Canada leading to an exemption of Canadian food products from a GST of only 7%.) Second, the Canadian government cited as a "victory for Canada" its ability to impose these tariffs, and viewed as a threat the possibility that the United States might, by invoking the Canada–U.S. FTA, be able to have these tariffs phased out more quickly. There has arguably been no better example of the upside-down economic world created by politicians focusing on the interests of producers but not consumers.[1]
7. Citing special problems (noted early in this chapter) that cultural industries face in competing with high-volume, low-cost imports, the French blocked a U.S. attempt to open markets in these products, just as Canadians had blocked a similar attempt by the United States in the negotiation of the Canada–U.S. FTA.

---

[1] In 1993, there was a special reason why politicians put heavy weight on the interests of producers: Dairy producers are relatively heavily concentrated in Quebec and the political separation of that province had again become an issue.

overcome poverty. Moreover, it may also be the method that is most effective politically. When LDCs receive grants from Canada or other countries, controversy often arises over the distribution of the grant money between different population groups within the LDCs, and LDC governments may resent it when the Canadian authorities intervene to control the use of the funds. People in the LDCs may instead prefer a chance to solve their own problems, by being given greater opportunities to produce and sell in our markets. One such important opportunity will be provided by the recent GATT agreement phasing out quotas against their clothing and textile exports.

Finally, there is another reason to reduce our trade barriers against imports from these countries. The creation of the Canada/U.S. FTA and NAFTA has left them, as outsiders, facing discrimination in North America. Thus, the final objective in Canadian trade policy should not be North American free trade but instead multilateral free trade in which such discrimination disappears, and all countries collectively enjoy maximum benefits from trade liberalization.

## KEY POINTS

1. Trade restrictions, such as tariffs or quotas, result in an efficiency loss. (The gains from trade, discussed in Chapter 19, are eroded as trade is reduced.)
2. Trade restrictions on a good also transfer income from consumers to producers. One reason countries have trade restrictions is that producers generally have more political power than consumers.
3. While many statements on the long list of economic arguments for protection are fallacious, some have a degree of economic merit. A less developed country, now exporting only a natural resource, may protect a domestic industry in order to diversify its economy, thus reducing its economic risks. An even stronger case can be made if the industry in question is a "promising infant," that is, an industry of comparative advantage if only it can be firmly established. (The problem is, however, that such infant support frequently becomes an old-age pension.)
4. A risk of foreign retaliation arises when we impose a tariff, for example, in an attempt to cure a Canadian unemployment problem. Since such a tariff would simply shift our unemployment problem onto our trading partners, their likely reaction would be to impose their own tariffs, thus shifting the unemployment problem back onto us — in particular, onto our export industries.
5. Under Sir John A. Macdonald's National Policy introduced in the late 1870s, Canada imposed relatively high tariffs in order to encourage domestic manufacturing. During the twentieth century, and especially since World War II, the tariffs imposed by Canada and other countries have been falling.
6. However, as tariffs have been reduced, a number of countries have made frequent use of nontariff barriers in order to respond to domestic pressures for protection against foreign competition. NTBs have increasingly come to be the focus of negotiations in the GATT, and are now central issues in the Uruguay Round.
7. In the 1980s, the debate on Canadian trade policy was focused on the negotiation of a free trade agreement with the United States, which came into effect on 1 January 1989. The agreement provides for the elimination of tariffs on bilateral U.S.-Canadian trade, and a reduction in some NTBs. While the long-run gain from this agreement in increasing Canadian productivity and income will be accompanied by short-term pain in import-competing industries, that pain is being reduced by increased exports where the FTA has provided more open access to the U.S. market.
8. The problem with NAFTA is that Canadian industry will have to respond to increased competition from Mexico at a time when it has not yet fully adjusted to the far more substantial competition from the United States under the Canada/U.S. FTA. However, there have been a number of benefits from Canadian participation

in NAFTA, such as acquiring benefits from free trade with another potentially important partner, and preventing the United States from leading hemispheric trade liberalization into a damaging hub-and-spoke pattern.

9. Canada's participation in NAFTA has also made the environmental and labour accords less vulnerable to capture by protectionist interests.

10. Recently, imports from the less developed countries have been growing as industries in these countries have become more competitive with North American producers. The increased availability of low-cost imports has benefited North American consumers. Some of the more successful LDCs have now become newly industrialized countries (NICs), with rapidly growing exports that have reduced the poverty problems in the NICs.

## KEY TERMS

**tariff**
**quota**
**tailored tariff**
**beggar-my-neighbour policy**
**diversification versus specialization**
**infant industry protection**
**terms of trade improvement**
**non-tariff barriers (NTBs)**
**multilateral negotiations**
**plurilateral negotiations**
**bilateral negotiations**
**unilateral action**
**General Agreement on Tariffs and Trade (GATT)**
**Kennedy Round**
**Tokyo Round**
**Uruguay Round**
**European Community (EC)**
**discrimination**
**Canada/United States Free Trade Agreement**
**rationalization**
**tariff escalation**
**adjustment costs**
**countervailing duties**
**anti-dumping duties**
**North American Free Trade Agreement (NAFTA)**
**rules of origin**
**trade deflection**
**hub-and-spoke trading systems**

## PROBLEMS

20-1. "The higher the tariff on an import, the more revenue the government collects." Is this statement true or not? Explain.

20-2. (a) Using a diagram such as Figure 19-8, show the effect of a "prohibitive" Canadian tariff that completely eliminates our import of a good.
(b) Using a similar diagram, explain the effects of a foreign tariff that prevents us from exporting a good.
(c) What are the effects if we prohibit our exports of this good? Why, then, might our government impose such a restriction?

20-3. "Transport costs are like tariffs. Both deter trade. If either were reduced, countries would reap increased benefits from trade. Raising tariffs is much the same as going back to shipping goods in old, expensive clipper ships." Do you agree? Why or why not? (Hint: Don't forget that the government collects revenues from tariffs.)

20-4. Illustrate the effects of an export tax in terms of changes in consumers' and producers' surpluses and revenues to government. In what circumstances might a country choose to levy export taxes?

20-5. Why might a country voluntarily restrict its exports? Illustrate this using a diagram.

20-6. Canada's annual domestic demand and supply functions, respectively, for snowmobiles are given by

$$Q_d = 37{,}000 - 2P$$

and

$$Q_s = P - 1000$$

Assume that all snowmobiles are identical, that domestic and world markets are competitive, that Canada is a small open economy, and that the world price of snowmobiles is $6000.

(a) If Canada imposes no tariff on foreign-made snowmobiles, how many snowmobiles will Canadian consumers purchase each year?
(b) Of this number, how many will be produced domestically?
(c) What is the value of snowmobiles imported into Canada?

If Canada now levied a $4000-per-unit tariff on foreign-made snowmobiles,

(d) How many snowmobiles would Canadians now purchase annually and how many of these would be imported?
(e) What would be the value of this import (and by how much would this tariff make foreign producers worse off)?
(f) Of Canadian producers and consumers, who loses because of this tariff and by how much?
(g) Who in Canada gains because of this tariff? By how much?
(h) Does the levying of this tariff cause a net welfare gain or loss in Canada? Of what magnitude?

# APPENDIX 20-A

## THE EFFECTS OF A TARIFF OR QUOTA THAT REDUCES IMPORTS

### Effects of a Tariff

Typically, a Canadian tariff will not end our import of a good (as in problem 20-2(a)), but will only reduce it. In Figure 20-3, we consider this case.

In panel (a), point *A* is the "no-trade" equilibrium while *J* is the free trade equilibrium, with imports *HJ*. Now suppose that we impose a tariff *t* that reduces but does not eliminate this trade. In this case we would (correctly) expect an equilibrium somewhere between *A* and *J*, at a point such as *K*. Thus, tariff *t* raises price from the free trade level $P_w$ to $P_t$, shifts equilibrium from *J* to *K*, and reduces our imports from the free trade level *HJ* to *RK*.

The effects on all parties concerned are shown in panels (b), (c), and (d). As the Canadian price rises from $P_w$ to $P_t$, consumer surplus is reduced by the grey area enclosed to the left of the demand curve in panel (b), while producers benefit from an increase in producer surplus (the coloured area 3 enclosed to the left of the supply curve in panel (c)). But now there is another effect, not encountered before, that is shown as area 4. This is the benefit to Canadian taxpayers because the government is now collecting tariff revenue. (A tariff *t*, equal to *RF*, is collected on each of the *RK* units imported—for a total revenue of area 4.)

Since the two coloured benefits in panel (c) also appear as grey losses in panel (b), they are transfers. Specifically, area 4 is the transfer from consumers (who pay more) to the government (which collects the duty), while area 3 is a transfer from consumers to producers. But some of the grey loss in panel (b) is not cancelled out by coloured gains in panel (c). This balance is the net efficiency loss to society, shown as the two grey triangles in panel (d).[12] We conclude that a tariff results in these efficiency losses and a transfer from consumers to producers. Moreover, when a tariff only reduces (rather than eliminates) an import, there is another transfer as well—from consumers to taxpayers.

### Effects of a Quota

Trade may be restricted by a tariff or by a non-tariff barrier (NTB), such as a quota. Such a restriction limits the number of units of a good that can be imported, and has many effects similar to a tariff. For example, in Figure 20-3(a), we saw that a tariff *t* raised price in the Canadian market from $P_w$ to $P_t$, and thus reduced imports from *HJ* to *RK*. An equivalent, even more direct way of reducing imports by the same amount would be simply to ban any imports in excess of *RK*; in other words, impose a quota limit of *RK*. If we do this, the new equilibrium will again be at the same point *K*, just as it was with the tariff.

Therefore, a quota of *RK* is sometimes referred to as the "quota equivalent of tariff *t*." It leads to the same inefficiency in resource allocation as tariff *t*.

[12] These two efficiency effects are marked 1 and 2 because they correspond to the two triangular efficiency effects first encountered in Figure 19-7. (Of course, colours are reversed because in that earlier diagram, trade was being opened so there were efficiency gains, whereas in this diagram trade is being restricted so there are efficiency losses. As an exercise, you should be able to confirm that triangle 1 in Figure 20-3(d) is the efficiency loss that results because inexpensive imports have been replaced by higher-cost domestic production, while triangle 2 is the efficiency loss that results because consumers have been prevented from purchasing this good at the lowest possible price.)

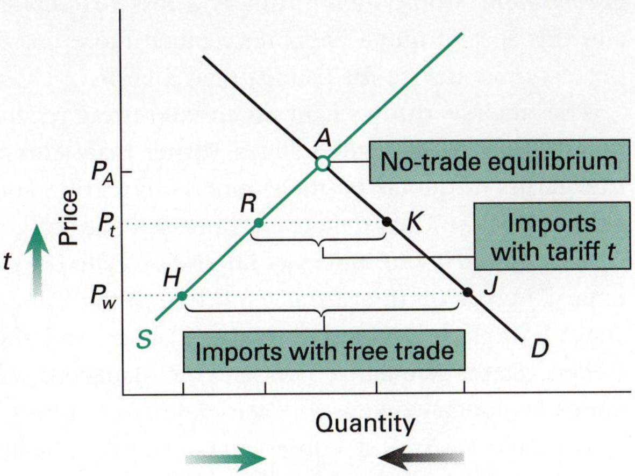


**(a)** Under free trade, the Canadian domestic price is the same as the world price $P_w$; equilibrium is at $J$, with imports of $HJ$. With tariff $t$, the Canadian domestic price rises from $P_w$ to $P_t$; equilibrium is at $K$, with imports of $RK$.

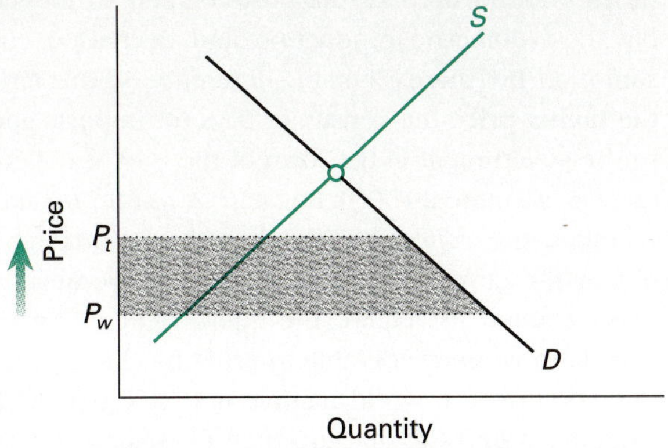


**(b)** Because price rises, consumers lose.

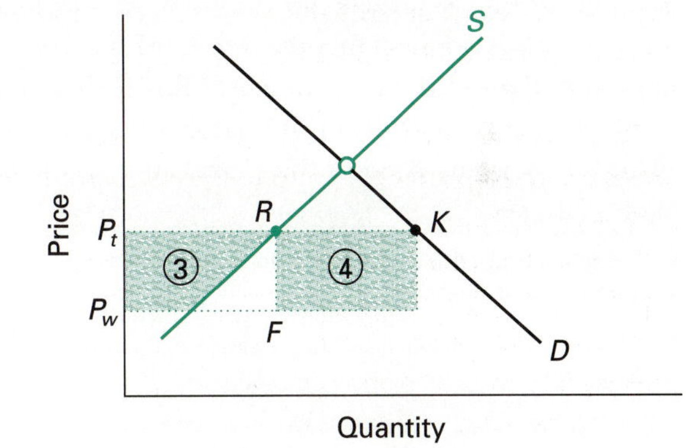


**(c)** But producers gain area 3 and the treasury gains area 4. As a result there is a transfer 3 from consumers to producers, and a transfer 4 from consumers to the treasury.

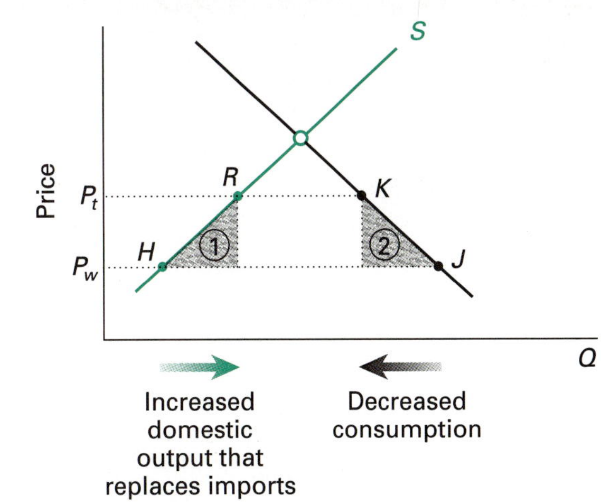


**(d)** There are also efficiency losses of areas 1 + 2.

**FIGURE 20-3 Effects of a tariff.**

The domestic Canadian supply is $S$. Under free trade, there is (by assumption) a completely elastic world supply at price $P_w$. Therefore, the total supply on the Canadian market—from both domestic and foreign sources—is $SHJ$. This intersects Canadian demand $D$ at point $J$, the free trade equilibrium involving imports of $HJ$. But when tariff $t$ is imposed, the world supply shifts up by this same amount $t$. (Foreign suppliers now require their original $P_w$ plus an amount $t$ to compensate them for the tariff they must pay at the Canadian border.) With this upward shift in foreign supply, the total supply on the Canadian market—from both domestic and foreign sources—becomes $SRK$. This intersects Canadian demand $D$ at point $K$, which is the new equilibrium under the tariff. Note that price has increased from $P_w$ to $P_t$, by the amount of the tariff. Imports have decreased from $HJ$ to $RK$ and Canadian consumption has decreased by the black arrow below the baseline. At the same time, Canadian output has increased by the coloured arrow; hence, employment in this industry has increased.

Specifically, by making the good scarce, the quota raises price in the Canadian market, and so induces high-cost domestic production and decreased consumption. But there is one big difference. With a tariff, the higher price the consumer pays for imports goes to the government in the form of the duty it collects (area 4 in Figure 20-3(c)). But *with a quota, no such revenues are collected.* Therefore, this amount goes not to the government but instead to whomever is lucky enough to acquire the quota right to import (that is, to whomever is able to profit by (1) acquiring this good on the world market at cost $P_w$, then (2) shipping it into Canada, and then (3) selling it there at price $P_t$). If these rights, or import licences, are granted by the Canadian government to Canadian importers, this windfall income 4 goes to the importers rather than to the government.[13] But, if the quota rights somehow end up in the hands of the foreign firms that sell this good in the Canadian market, *this income goes to them rather than to the Canadian government.* Consequently, this is a loss to Canada, and this sort of quota becomes a much more costly protectionist device for Canada than a tariff.

This analysis throws light on an interesting recent policy issue in the United States. Rather than administer tariffs or quotas on their imports of textiles and colour TVs, the United States has pressed hard to get certain countries to agree to impose so-called "voluntary" quotas on their firms exporting to the United States. (We have already seen that Canada and the United States similarly pressed the Japanese to impose voluntary quotas on their exports of autos to North America.) As a consequence, the Americans have lost income 4 to these foreign firms exporting to them (as well, of course, as efficiency losses 1 and 2 that follow from any form of protection). Why then do Americans pressure foreign countries to impose these quotas? Why don't they impose their own import restrictions instead? One reason is that, if they were to impose trade restrictions themselves, then according to the GATT (General Agreement on Tariffs and Trade), they would be subject to retaliation by the foreign country.

[13] One solution to ensure against this loss would be for the Canadian government to auction off these quota rights. Since the total revenue raised by the government from this sale would be roughly area 4, such a quota would have effects similar to those of the tariff in Figure 20-3.

CHAPTER 21

# NATURAL RESOURCES: ARE WE USING THEM AT THE RIGHT RATE?

*The . . . economy of the future might be called the "spaceman economy," in which the earth has become a single space ship, without unlimited reservoirs of anything.*

*Kenneth Boulding*

At about the time the price of oil began its dramatic rise in the early 1970s, a group of researchers at the Massachusetts Institute of Technology (MIT) developed a computer model to analyse the long-run outlook for natural resources. They came to an alarming conclusion:

> If the present growth trends in world population, industrialization, pollution, food production, and resource depletion continue unchanged, the limits to growth on this planet will be reached sometime within the next one hundred years. The most probable result will be a rather sudden and uncontrollable decline in both population and industrial capacity.[1]

Because of their grim predictions, the MIT group quickly became known as the "doomsday" theorists. Their analysis dramatized the fact that, even in a world of modern technology, humankind must carefully manage its natural resources if we want our standard of living to remain high, let alone continue to rise.

In one sense, the role of natural resources in the economy is similar to that of capital. Plentiful supplies of natural resources raise the productivity of human labour just like machinery and other capital equipment does, and thereby contribute to our high standard of living. Like privately owned capital, privately owned resources yield income to their owners, in the form of rents on land and other resources, as explained in Chapter 17.

However, natural resources also have certain characteristics that set them apart from capital, and which suggest that they are much more important in the economy than we would be led to believe if we just looked, for example, at the share of resource rents in national income. In particular, unlike capital which can always be recreated if it wears out or is destroyed, certain natural resources cannot be reproduced if they disappear. Some resources are inherently nonrenewable: oil, or ores such as copper or iron. But even resources that are renewable under normal circumstances, such as fish, game, or fertile agricultural land, may disappear altogether or lose their productivity if they are not properly managed. And certain types of resources such as air and water are fundamental to human existence: We can not live without adequate supplies of both.

In spite of the dangers that loom if we don't manage our resources properly, however, many economists felt that in some ways, the doomsday scenario painted by the MIT researchers was overly pessimistic. It is, of course, true that if all present trends continue indefinitely, we — or our descendants — will indeed face doom sooner or later. However, it is not necessary to have a complicated computer model to show this. There are many simple illustrations that will do. For example, if we project from a period in which the fruit-fly population is growing, in a relatively few years the Earth will be buried kilometres

[1] Donella H. Meadows, et al., *The Limits to Growth* (New York: Universe Books, 1972), p. 30.

deep in fruit flies. Any such projection provides an illustration, not of good economics or biology but of the mathematical magic of mechanically compounding a rate of growth.[2]

It is far more challenging and relevant to ask: Why will the population of fruit flies eventually stop growing at a constant rate? What major changes in our present economic and social system will take place to alter existing trends and prevent a future doomsday? One important answer is: If a resource comes to be in critically short supply, its price will rise. This, in turn, will have a number of consequences that will be studied in this chapter. For example, it will encourage conservation and stimulate the development of substitutes. To illustrate, an increase in the price of base metals will speed up the development of plastic and ceramic substitutes. Thus, the projection of present trends is unlikely to be nearly as useful in telling us what will happen in the future as in telling us which resources will become scarce. Where will conservation have to occur? Where will consumption have to be reduced and substitutes be developed?

This chapter will also address a number of other, related questions:

- What is the most efficient rate at which to use resources?
- Under what circumstances might the free market permit a too rapid use of resources?
- If resources are being used too rapidly, is there anything the government can do? Specifically, how can the government assist the market forces that can help us to conserve?

For Canada, these issues are clearly more important than for most other countries, because so much of our economic activity depends on natural resources. Mining, fishing, and production of timber, wood pulp, and newsprint are all examples of important Canadian industries that make extensive use of natural resources. Another resource that will become more and more important in the future is fresh water. In the U.S. Midwest, there are fears of increasingly frequent drought conditions, and groundwater levels have been falling as more water has been withdrawn for irrigating farm fields. One solution that has been proposed is for the United States to import water from Canada through large-scale diversions from the Great Lakes, or even through a canal system all the way from Hudson Bay. In Canada, these proposals have been highly controversial: During the debate over the Canada/United States Free Trade Agreement in the late 1980s, Canadian environmentalists sought assurances that the agreement would not automatically allow the United States unlimited access to Canadian water resources.

[2] To confirm the magic of compound growth, consider this: We will give you a million dollars, if you will give us just 1 cent today, 2 cents tomorrow, 4 cents the next day, and so on, for just 1 month.

## CHARACTERISTICS OF NATURAL RESOURCES: WHERE ARE CONSERVATION PROBLEMS MOST LIKELY TO ARISE?

Some raw materials are much more likely than others to cause future problems on a global scale. What characteristics should we consider, if we are trying to anticipate problems?

### 1. What is the Supply/Demand Relationship?

The oil problem came to the fore in the early 1970s because the balance between supply and demand was upset. Demand was rising with the worldwide economic boom. The growth in oil discoveries was tapering off, raising doubts that the long-run supply would be adequate to permit the continuation of past patterns of heavy use. Furthermore, supply was temporarily disrupted by export restrictions imposed by a number of oil-exporting nations.

While oil was a good example of a resource where supply fell short of demand (at least during part of the 1970s), there are other natural resources that are so plentiful that it is hard to imagine such a problem arising. For example, computer chips are made of silicon, which comes from sand. We don't need to worry about a shortage of silicon. Conservation is not a problem for sand as it could be for oil.

### 2. How Substantial are the Costs of Adjustment: Are Users Heavily Dependent on the Resource?

Oil frequently dominated the headlines in the past two decades because users have become so dependent on it; it is difficult to do without. If the supply of gasoline to gas stations is interrupted, there may be long lines at the pumps that have received gasoline — as there were in the United States in 1979. The problem affects us in a direct and obvious way.

On the other hand, we can imagine raw materials running out and hardly anyone would notice or care. Consider, for example, a rare clay used to make a pigment for artists' paints. If it runs out, artists may have trouble reproducing exactly that hue, but few people will notice or care.

### 3. When the Resource is Used, Does It Disappear?

Oil has another characteristic: when it is used, it is burned up; the resulting gases dissipate into the atmosphere. In contrast, when iron ore or copper is used, its scrap can be recycled. Thus, we don't have to worry about running out of copper or steel in the same way as we do about oil.

The next two questions are very important, and a substantial part of this chapter will be devoted to analysing them.

### 4. Is the Resource Renewable or Non-renewable?

Even if the units of a resource that we use are destroyed, nature may restore them. For example, fish are used up when they are eaten. However, new fish hatch and grow. Fish are thus a ***renewable*** resource. So are trees. In contrast, oil, copper, and iron ore are ***non-renewable*** resources. There is only a finite amount in the ground; no more is being created. If we use these resources at a constant rate, then sooner or later the resources in the ground will be completely depleted. The need for conservation, therefore, can arise more clearly in the case of a non-renewable resource such as oil than for a renewable resource such as fish.

### 5. Is the Resource Common Property or Privately Owned?

Even if a resource is renewable, it may have to be conserved. For example, too many fish may be caught and a species thereby endangered. The problem is that nobody owns the oceans, rivers, and lakes, nor the fish that swim there. Fish are thus a ***common-property*** resource. As we will explain, the result is that each individual fishing-boat captain pays little attention to conservation. As individuals, they have inadequate incentive to reduce their catch, even if the result would be more fish for all in the future.

Timber is also a renewable resource, but, unlike fish, it is often ***privately owned***. Owners cutting trees do have an incentive to conserve and to plant new trees. They will benefit in the future because they will own the extra trees that they plant or leave standing.

This chapter begins with a detailed demonstration of why a free market does a far less satisfactory job of conserving a common-property resource such as fish than a privately owned resource such as timber. This will be followed by an analysis of the conservation of a non-renewable resource such as base metals. Finally, attention is directed to oil, a non-renewable resource that has raised a wide range of special conservation issues.

## THE DIFFICULTY IN CONSERVING A COMMON-PROPERTY RESOURCE: FISH

The problem of overfishing is illustrated in Figure 21-1. *D* is the market demand for fish. The height of this curve, as usual, reflects the marginal benefit of these fish to the consuming public. In deciding how many fish to catch — that is, how intensively to fish — a fishing-boat captain will only take into account the marginal cost that he himself has to bear: the cost of hiring a crew, running and maintaining his boat, mending nets, and so on. Thus the competitive supply curve labelled *S* in Figure 21-1 (the lower of the two coloured curves, above the hollow coloured arrow on the left) is based on these costs. Because they are borne by the private agents or firms who actually make the decisions about how much to produce or supply, these costs are referred to as *private costs*.

However, *S* does *not* take into account an important additional cost (corresponding to the height of the solid coloured arrow on the left in the diagram). Specifically, it does not take into account the possibility that the more we fish today, the smaller is the amount of fish that will be available for those who fish in the future. The reason is that from the viewpoint of each individual fishing-boat captain, the cost of reduced stocks of fish in the future will largely be borne by others — other fishing crews and those who consume fish. Or, looking at the matter another way, the amount of fish caught by an individual fishing crew today will have a negligible impact on the amount of fish that *this same crew* will be able to catch in the future. Therefore, the reduction in the future stock that occurs when fish are caught by the crew today is not a private cost that is taken into account by the crew. Instead, it is largely an ***external cost*** — a cost imposed on others; the external cost is

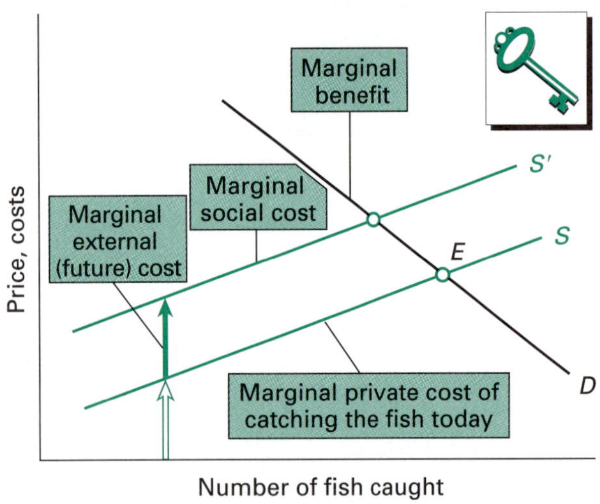


**FIGURE 21-1 Market for a common-property resource: fish.**

$S'$, the marginal social cost of fishing today, includes the hollow arrow on the left representing marginal private cost, including labour, mending nets, etc., plus the solid arrow above it representing external cost because there will be fewer fish available in the future. Those who fish take into account only their marginal private cost and ignore the external future cost. Therefore, their supply curve is $S$ and the equilibrium is at $E$, where $S = D$.

the vertical distance between the $S$ and $S'$ curves in Figure 21-1 (the solid coloured arrow on the left).

*Private* or *internal* costs are those costs incurred by those who actually produce or consume a good. *External* costs—also known as *spillover* costs—are costs borne by others.

Later on, we will demonstrate a very important conclusion about any economic activity (such as fishing in this example) where there is a significant external cost. For such activities, *an unregulated competitive market does not yield an efficient outcome* as the caption to Figure 21-3 explains. Specifically, the amount of output produced in a perfectly competitive market will be larger than the amount that would be efficient from society's point of view. Before we show this, however, we must first look at another question: How should the economically efficient amount of production from a non-renewable resource be determined?

## THE MAXIMUM SUSTAINABLE YIELD OF A RENEWABLE RESOURCE

The statement "the more we fish today, the less there will be to catch in the future" is sometimes true, but sometimes not. To make it more precise, first note that, in certain circumstances, fishing today may have a disastrous effect on future catches; in other cases, it may have little or no effect at all. As an example of a disaster, suppose the fish population is so reduced in number that it can barely survive. Reducing that population further by fishing today may, like shooting carrier pigeons, extinguish the species and reduce *all* future catches to zero.

At the other extreme, the fish population may initially be so large that it cannot grow further. There are no further natural food sources to sustain it and, for every fish that is hatched, another must die. In this case, fishing today will have little effect on the fish population and, therefore, on future catches. If we don't prevent the fish population from growing by catching some, it will be prevented from growing by lack of food.

These two cases, and the many other possibilities, are illustrated in Figure 21-2. This diagram shows how the *growth* in a fish population on the vertical axis depends on the *size* of the population on the horizontal axis. Point $D$ indicates that the maximum size of the population is 10 million fish. This is the point at which there are so many fish that their population cannot increase further: For each new fish, an existing one will die. If there is no fishing, the fish population will grow toward this number, but not beyond. To confirm this, note that at any point to the left of $D$, such as $K$, the fish population will grow (by the height of $K$). As a result, the population will be greater in the next period, causing a movement to the right, which will continue as long as the curve lies above the axis. But once $D$ is reached, there is no further increase in the number of fish.

There is no reason why a hungry human race should be particularly interested in this "no fishing" solution. There is little satisfaction in knowing that the sea is as full of fish as it can possibly get. Instead, consider a point such as $C$ that does involve fishing. Here the fish population is $X_c$ = 2 million, and is increasing by $Y_c$ = 1⅓ million fish per year. At this point, we can take out the natural increase of 1⅓ million fish year after year without reducing the 2 million population. Hence, this curve is known as the ***sustainable yield*** curve.

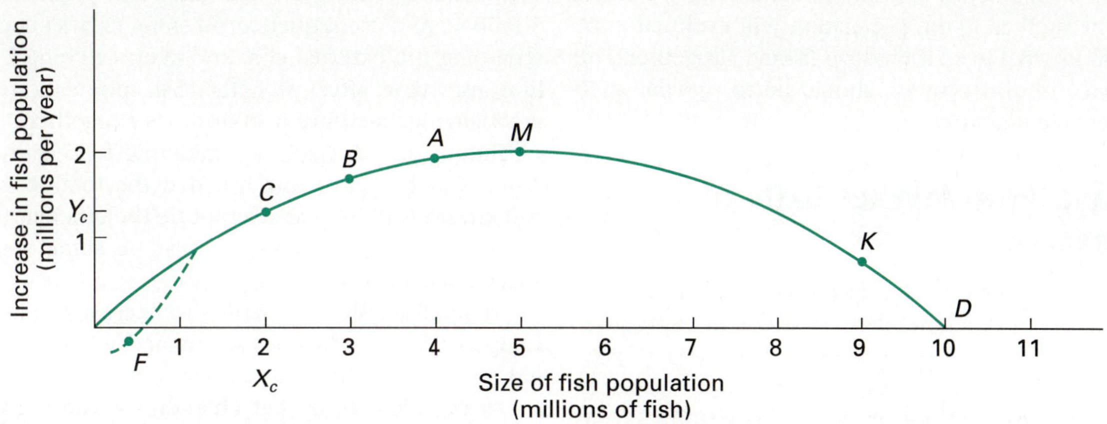


**FIGURE 21-2 Sustainable yield curve.**
At point *C*, the population of fish on the horizontal axis is 2 million, and will increase by 1.33 million per year, measured on the vertical axis. Therefore, 1.33 million is the sustainable yield; it is the number of fish that can be caught each year and still leave the population constant at 2 million. As we move to the right along this curve it rises at first: The larger the fish population, the greater its natural increase. However, this increase reaches a maximum at *M*, where a fish population of 5 million generates a "maximum sustainable yield" of 2 million, the largest number that can be caught per year and still leave the fish population intact. To the right of *M*, the sustainable yield curve falls as the ocean becomes increasingly crowded with fish.

*Sustainable yield* is the amount of a renewable resource (such as fish) that can be harvested while still leaving next season's population constant.

The highest point *M* on this sustainable yield curve is the ***maximum sustainable yield***. This is the maximum number of fish (in this case, 2 million) that can be caught on a continuing basis without depleting the parent stock. To harvest fish at this maximum rate requires a parent population of 5 million, measured along the horizontal axis. A reasonable conservation objective is to prevent the resource from falling below this quantity of 5 million.

Now consider the situation long ago, before large-scale commercial fishing. This is illustrated by a point such as *K*, with the ocean almost as full of fish as it could get. As human population and our demands on the seas increased, the fish population was reduced by heavy commercial fishing; there was a move to the left in this diagram. However, as long as the fish population still remained above 5 million (that is, to the right of the maximum sustainable yield at *M*), there was no conservation problem. As we harvested more, the fish population fell, but it became more able to regenerate itself. That is, the natural increase — as shown by the height of the curve — became greater as we moved from *K* toward *M*. It is not until point *M*, where the fish population is only 5 million, that we encounter the conservation problem. If at this point we continue to harvest more than the natural increase, we will continue to reduce the fish population. But now, with each such decline, the fish population becomes less able to regenerate itself; that is, each movement to the left leads to a lower point on the yield curve, closer to the point where the fish population can barely survive. If we do not limit catches, we may risk extinguishing a whole species, just as we extinguished the carrier pigeon.

Exterminating a species is not just a theoretical possibility. This almost happened with herring in 1969 as a result of the development of larger, more efficient fishing boats. Moreover, the introduction of sonar for chasing down whales has meant that some types of whale would face extinction if there were no controls over whaling.

To understand fully the dangers of overfishing, suppose the yield curve is the dashed curve on the left in Figure 21-2. In this case, heavy fishing may do irreversible damage to the species. This will occur, for example, if we have fished the population down to one-quarter of a million fish and are consequently at point *F*. There are still some fish, but they cannot find other fish to spawn. There is no longer a natural increase. Instead, there is a natural decrease in population: *F* lies below the horizontal axis. If we reach a point such as *F*, the population will eventually die out on its own even if we stop fishing altogether. The first rule of conservation should be to prevent such irreversible disasters.

## Why a Free Market Fails to Conserve

Now let's return to the explanation of how overfishing arises because fish is a common-property resource.

Suppose the competitive supply curve—the supply curve based on private, internal costs only—is as shown by the curve *S* in Figure 21-3. With this supply curve, the equilibrium in the market for fish will be at point *E* where the amount of fish caught each year is 3 million.

But an annual catch of 3 million per year is not sustainable. Returning to Figure 21-2, we see that the *maximum* sustainable yield is no more than 2 million, which occurs when the initial fish population is 5 million. As a consequence, if fishing crews keep disregarding the external cost and keep catching 3 million fish year after year, the fish population will gradually decline until it disappears altogether.[3]

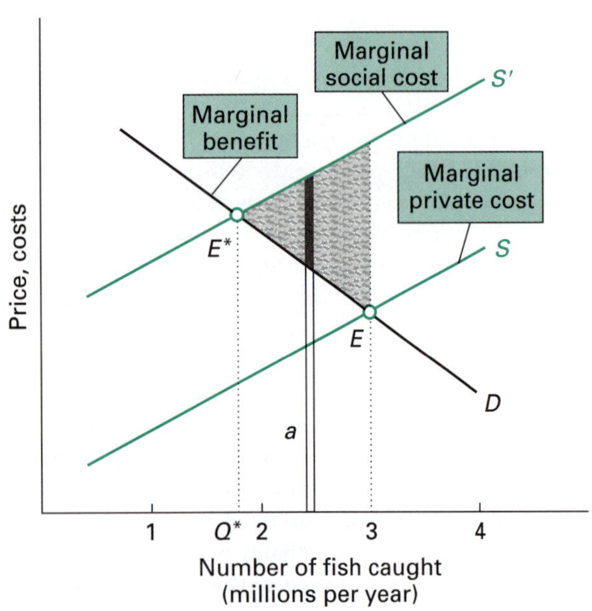


**FIGURE 21-3 The efficiency loss from overfishing.**

When the external cost is not taken into account, equilibrium will be at *E*, with 3 million fish being caught each season. However, because the efficient equilibrium is at *E** where marginal social cost equals marginal benefit, there is an efficiency loss given by the grey triangle.

Thus an annual catch of 3 million fish is clearly too much: Catching so many fish that the total stock of fish gradually disappears cannot be the efficient thing to do. The efficient amount must be some smaller, sustainable, quantity.

To find the efficient quantity to harvest, recall from Chapter 11 that efficiency is attained when the marginal social benefit of an activity equals its marginal social cost. Just as in that chapter, we can continue to measure the marginal social benefit by the consumers' willingness to pay for fish—that is, by the height of the demand curve. However, the problem in the case of fishing is that the competitive supply curve no longer represents the marginal social cost. As we noted in Figure 21-1 earlier, the competitive supply curve *S* in this case only reflects the marginal *private* cost — the actual costs faced by individual fishing boats. To find the marginal *social* cost, we must add the external cost—the costs borne by future members of society who will be worse off when today's overfishing results in tomorrow's depleted stocks.

**Marginal social cost is the sum of (1) marginal private cost, and (2) marginal external cost.**

Adding the marginal external cost to the marginal private cost produces the marginal social cost curve *S*′ in Figure 21-3. Thus, the efficient quantity of fishing is at point *E** in the figure (at an annual quantity *Q** of a little less than 2 million fish per year). The efficiency loss from overfishing that occurs in the perfectly competitive equilibrium at point *E* is shown as the grey triangle. To confirm, consider *a*, one of the "excess" fish caught. The hollow bar under the demand curve is the marginal benefit of catching *a*, while its marginal cost—including the external cost of reduced future catches—is this same bar plus the black bar above it. Thus, the net loss from catching this fish is the black bar, and the sum of the losses on all the other "excess" fish caught over the range *Q** to 3 million is the grey triangle. In short, this triangle

[3] More realistically, when the fish population becomes sufficiently small, the private cost of fishing will begin to rise, causing fishermen to leave the industry.

shows the efficiency loss from overfishing because conservation concerns about the future fish population are ignored.

As we have drawn Figure 21-3, the socially efficient amount of fish to catch is close to, but not exactly the same as, the maximum sustainable yield of 2 million fish in Figure 21-2. This is no coincidence: In the long run, the economically efficient "harvest" from a renewable resource such as fish or timber is likely to be approximately the same as the maximum sustainable yield. However, the two concepts are not identical. The exact relationship between them is complicated; the appendix to this chapter contains a brief discussion of this issue.

## Measures to Induce Appropriate Conservation of a Common-property Resource

Three approaches may be used to provide better conservation of a common-property resource. That is, there are three ways to reduce the catch in Figure 21-3 from the inefficient overfishing quantity 3 million to the efficient quantity $Q^*$ and thus eliminate the triangular efficiency loss. We will illustrate these three approaches by considering the problem of conserving the fish population in offshore fisheries such as those off the coast of British Columbia or the Atlantic provinces. To simplify matters, we will disregard a difficulty that arises in offshore fisheries because of the fact that fish swim: Even if we try to conserve by reducing the catches that *Canadian* fishing crews are allowed to land, won't the fish just be caught by foreign fishing crews operating off our coastlines? (We briefly consider this problem in Box 21-1.)

### 1. Place Limits on the Catch.

The government may encourage conservation directly by restricting the amount of fish each boat is allowed to land. Or, it may shorten the fishing season, allowing fishing during only certain periods of the year. In other cases, more peculiar non-price restraints have been imposed, such as setting a maximum size of the boats that fishing crews are allowed to use.

While this sort of limitation on equipment may indirectly reduce the size of the catch, it is far from clear by how much. To rephrase this point in terms of Figure 21-3, there is no way of pinpointing whether the catch is changed from 3 million to more or less than the desired target $Q^*$. This is important because a restriction that is too severe may be worse than no restriction at all. Moreover, even if the government restriction on equipment *were* to reduce the catch to exactly the desired target $Q^*$, it would be an expensive way of doing it. The reason is that labour would be wasted because each crew would be able to use only a relatively small boat; therefore, more people would be engaged in fishing. The same problem arises if each fishing boat is limited in the amount of fish it can land: Too much labour or too many boats are expended in the effort.

The problem with this first approach to conservation is that it does not use the market mechanism. We now turn to two alternative approaches that do.

### 2. Impose a Tax or a Fishing Fee.

The government could deal with the externality by using a tax. Specifically, it could impose a tax equal to the external cost: Tax those who catch fish today according to the damage they do to future catches. In other words, tax them or charge them a fishing fee equal to the marginal external cost shown by the vertical distance between the $S$ and $S'$ curves in Figure 21-3. This will raise their supply curve from $S$ to $S'$, thereby "internalizing the externality." That is, this tax will force decision makers to take into account the external as well as the internal costs of their actions. Accordingly, it will result in an efficient catch $Q^*$, where $D$ intersects the new supply curve $S'$.

There is, of course, a problem that arises whenever the government tries to use a tax to internalize an external cost. Specifically, how do we know the correct tax *rate*? Can the external cost of fishing—in this case, the cost associated with the reduction in future catches—be estimated accurately?

### 3. Create Property Rights.

To avoid the problem of having to estimate the external cost, there may be a simpler way of achieving efficiency. In certain circumstances, a common-property resource may be transformed into private property. For example, a large common pasture may be divided into 50 smaller fields, with one given to each of the families that previously used the commons. Once these fields have been fenced, each family will have an incentive not to overgraze its particular field.

It is not so easy to create ***property rights*** in the case of fish. However, in some cases it may be possible. For example, where fish are drawn from a number of small inland lakes, the fishing rights to each

## TOOLS AND TECHNIQUES BOX 21-1
## Managing an Offshore Fishery: Two Problems

The difficulties and pitfalls that beset the authorities when they try to manage a renewable resource, such as an ocean fishery, are well illustrated by the Canadian experience with the management of the fisheries off the coasts of British Columbia and the Atlantic provinces. Here we focus on two principal issues. First, which of the three conservation policies discussed in the text (on page 443) have, in fact, been used and how effective have they been? Second, fish that swim in an ocean may be caught not only by Canadians but also by foreign fishing crews. What measures can we use to protect the fish population in this situation?

### 1. Methods of Regulation

At present, several different methods are used to control fishing of different species, such as Pacific salmon, cod, herring, and shellfish such as lobster and scallops. In some cases, the government has restricted the number of fishermen allowed to enter the fleet while, in other cases, it has limited the number of days that fishing is allowed. Also, there have been controls on the type of gear that fishing crews may use. At various times, there have been controls on the number of boats that could be used or on the tonnage of each boat.

According to a study by the Economic Council of Canada, the results of these conservation policies had not been entirely satisfactory. On the positive side, the authorities had usually succeeded in preventing gross overfishing of most species. But their control methods had not been very precise and, from time to time, there has been overharvesting; in the early 1990s, the Newfoundland cod fishery had to be closed down. Another serious problem was that the regulatory methods used had raised the cost of harvesting. For example, the reduction in the legal number of days for fishing induced fishermen to get large boats and expensive fish-finding equipment. If the fishing season had been longer, it would have been possible to land the same total catch with much less expensive equipment. The Economic Council estimated that the extra costs due to the inefficient harvesting methods might run as high as $750 million to $1 billion a year for Canada's ocean fisheries.

The alternative regulation methods proposed by the council as a way of overcoming these problems were similar to those discussed in the text. Specifically, the council proposed a combination of (1) a "landing tax" on the value of the tonnage brought to shore by fishermen and (2) a system of transferable "stinted landing rights" that would give each fisherman the right to harvest a fixed maximum tonnage each season. Because the government would be able to control the landing rights, it could set a relatively low landing tax without risking problems with overharvesting. One advantage of a low landing tax is that it reduces the opposition of existing fishermen to the regulatory change. Because the landing rights would be transferable, they would not inhibit rationalization in the fishing industry: Efficient fishermen with large catches would be able to buy additional rights from others who wanted to reduce their fishing effort or perhaps leave the industry altogether.

### 2. International Complications

There are several areas where Canadian boats are fishing in competition with foreigners. One is the Georges Bank fishing ground located southwest of Nova Scotia, off the coast of Massachusetts. Up until the mid-1970s, most of the fish in the area was caught by long-distance trawlers from the Soviet Union and Eastern Europe. In 1977, however, both the United States and Canada followed

**BOX 21-1 continued**

the example of many other countries and extended their territorial waters as far as 200 miles offshore so that most foreigners were banned from fishing in the area. But there was a problem: If both Canada and the United States simply define anything within 200 miles of their coastlines as part of their territorial waters, there will be areas in the ocean that fall in the territorial waters of both countries. This problem arises in several places: off British Columbia in the Strait of Juan de Fuca; in the Beaufort Sea (where the Yukon adjoins Alaska); and, in particular, in a sector off the east coast that includes Georges Bank.

Up until 1985, the issue of overlapping claims had not been resolved in any of these areas, and both Canadian and U.S. fishing crews fished Georges Bank. Who was responsible for regulating the fishery so as to prevent overfishing? The answer: Canadian crews were regulated by the Canadian government, while U.S. crews were subject to U.S. regulations. According to the Canadian fishermen, American regulations were much less strict than those imposed on Canadians. As a result, Canadians lost in two ways. First, they got a smaller share of the total catch in each year. Second, they would suffer in future years because the large catches of the U.S. fishermen would deplete the fish population.

Although the boundary issue was resolved through a 1985 arbitration ruling by the International Court of Justice in the Hague, an important problem still remained: Since fish populations migrate across Georges Bank, overfishing on one side of the boundary could hurt catches on both sides. A dramatic example of this problem occurred in 1992 in the fishing grounds east of Newfoundland. The mainstay of this fishery, and of much of the fish processing industry in Newfoundland, was northern cod, which was caught by both Canadian boats, and by European boats fishing outside the 200-mile limit. Although both sides had been complaining that the other side was overfishing and that the stocks of cod appeared to be diminishing, both sides were reluctant to cut back on allowable catches; Canadian fishermen also charged that some European boats were exceeding their quotas. In 1992, the minister of fisheries, John Crosbie, was forced to take an extremely painful step: The northern cod fishery was simply closed down, throwing large numbers of fishermen and processing workers into unemployment.

separate lake might be granted or sold to an individual, who would then have an incentive to limit the fishing in that lake. (In Box 21-1, we discuss some suggestions on how to introduce different kinds of property rights in an ocean fishery.)

To see how property rights result in desirable conservation, consider the case of timber, much of which is, in fact, held by private owners.

## A PRIVATELY OWNED RESOURCE: TIMBER

The market for timber is illustrated in Figure 21-4, with curve *S* representing the supply curve. Consider a single unit of output, *b*. The height of the supply curve *S* shows the price required to induce the owner to cut and sell that unit today. This price, sometimes known as the ***reservation price***, covers two costs:

1. The direct cost of harvesting the timber — the wages of lumberjacks, the cost of hauling, etc., shown by the hollow coloured arrow — plus
2. The cost to the owner because less timber will be left to cut in the future. This is shown by the solid coloured arrow.

The *reservation price* of a privately owned resource includes both the cost of harvesting or extracting the resource today and the amount necessary to compensate the owner for the reduction in the resource available in the future. In other words, it is the height of supply curve *S* in Figure 21-4.

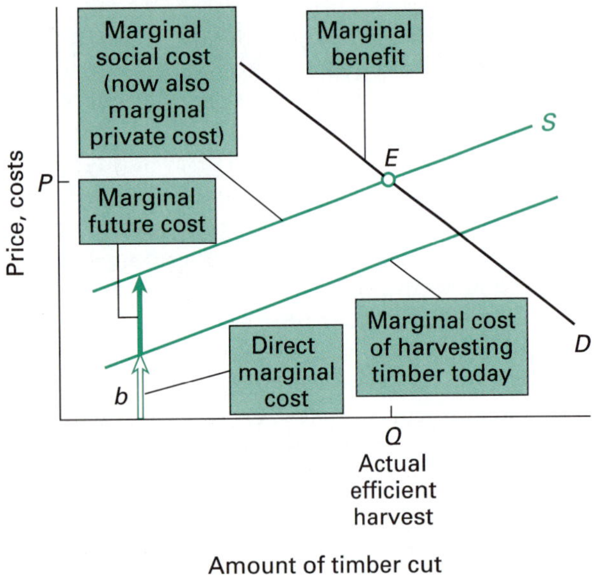


**FIGURE 21-4 Market for a privately owned natural resource: timber.**

This is the same as the earlier example in Figure 21-1 except that the resource is now privately owned. In assessing what their harvesting today costs them, the private owners do include the solid coloured arrow of future cost. Thus, their supply is *S*, and equilibrium is at *E*, with an efficient harvest *Q*.

Observe that Figure 21-4 is very similar to Figure 21-1 or Figure 21-3. In each diagram, there are two curves that slope upward to the right. The lower curve represents the direct cost of production—the harvesting cost of cutting the trees or catching the fish. Moreover, in each diagram the vertical distance between the two curves is a reflection of the conservation problem. It measures the cost of having fewer trees or fish available to harvest in the future.

However, there is one big difference between the two diagrams. In the case of a common-property resource, such as fish in Figure 21-3, producers take into account only the direct costs. Therefore, their supply curve is the lower curve, and the result is a socially inefficient output. Future costs are ignored and there is inadequate conservation. In contrast, timber owners in Figure 21-4 do conserve. They do take into account the solid coloured arrow that measures the cost of having fewer trees in the future. This is an internal cost to the owners. Therefore, their supply curve is the upper curve. Thus, for a privately owned resource such as timber, equilibrium is at *E* and output is the socially efficient quantity. There is adequate conservation. (In Box 21-2, we give two examples of how problems may arise when the exploitation of a resource which itself may be privately owned has detrimental side effects on an important common-property resource: the natural environment.)

## Rent and the Reservation Price

At an equilibrium such as *E* in the market for a privately owned resource, the price that producers receive is higher than the out-of-pocket cost of harvesting the resource, because the equilibrium price includes the owner's opportunity cost of harvesting the resource today rather than saving it for tomorrow. For an individual resource owner, the difference between the total revenue and the total cost of harvesting represents a return on the ownership of the resource. As we saw in Chapter 17, economists conventionally distinguish between such returns and the return on man-made capital; the return on a natural resource is called *rent* while the return on capital is classified as interest or "normal profit." Thus, the owner's reservation price referred to above can also be interpreted as the sum of the cost of harvesting, and the per-unit resource rent.

In the case where the producer who harvests the resource also is the owner, the rent represents an opportunity cost, rather than an explicit out-of-pocket cost. (If you don't remember the distinction, look again at the example of the person operating a store on pp. 158–59 in Chapter 8.) However, many resources are harvested by firms that don't own the resources themselves. In this case, they will have to pay explicit rents to the owners in order to be allowed access to the resources; as before, these rents have to be high enough to compensate the owner for the opportunity cost of harvesting part of the resource today rather than saving it for tomorrow.

By raising the private marginal cost of production, and thus raising the competitive supply curve, the explicit resource rents or opportunity costs serve the purpose of reducing the equilibrium quantity produced each year, so that more is conserved for the future. In the case of a common-property resource, there is no private owner to whom rent has to be paid, or who takes into account the opportunity cost of harvesting the resource today. As a result, the problem of overuse in the short run, and inadequate conservation, will arise, unless harvesting is regulated in some other way.

The question *how large* the resource rent should be in order for the efficient amount of conservation to occur, is complicated. It is briefly discussed in the appendix to this chapter. As explained there, one of the factors that influences rents is the real (inflation-adjusted) rate of interest. As you will see, the rate of interest also plays an important part in the somewhat different type of conservation problem we discuss in the next section.

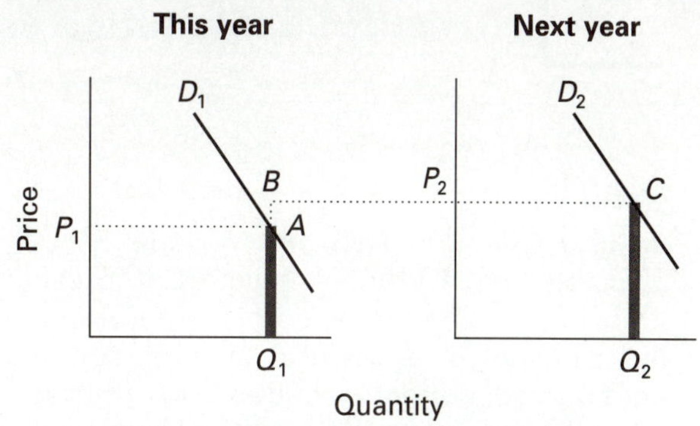


**FIGURE 21-5 Efficient pricing pattern for a non-renewable resource over two years.**
Efficient pricing requires that the gap *AB* between prices in the two years be equal to the interest rate. Efficiency also requires that the amount of the resource used up ($Q_1 + Q_2$) be equal to the total quantity available.

# CONSERVATION OF NON-RENEWABLE RESOURCES[4]

Timber and fish are examples of renewable resources. In this section, we turn to the conservation problem that arises when we are dealing with non-renewable resources. As a highly simplified example, suppose there is a limited quantity of a metal that will be completely replaced in two years by a cheaper plastic substitute of equal quality. Conservation requires that we do not use up all of this metal this year but, instead, use it up over the next two years in the most efficient way. (Because cheaper plastic will then become available, there is no need to save any metal beyond this date.)

In a perfectly competitive market, what will be the quantity used up this year and next year?

## How the Market Conserves the Resource

The equilibrium price and quantity in the two years is shown in Figure 21-5. The resource prices $P_1$ and $P_2$ in the two years will be determined so that the following two conditions are met:

1. The quantities used in the two years will add up to the total available quantity $Q$, that is, $Q_1 + Q_2 = Q$. In other words, the holders of the resource will sell it off in the two years, because it will be worth less thereafter, once the cheaper substitute becomes available.
2. Price $P_2$ will be higher than $P_1$ by a gap $AB$ equal to the interest rate. Thus, if the interest rate is 8%, $P_2$ should be 8% higher than $P_1$.

Why wouldn't there be the same price of, say, $100 per unit in the two years? The answer is: In this case, holders of the resource would want to sell it all in the first year, earn interest of 8% on the $100 proceeds, and thus have $108 in the second year. This is better than holding it until the second year and selling it for $100 then. Note that the incentive for selling it all in the first year is the interest rate. With resource holders trying to sell it all in the first year, the supply in the second year dries up, and price rises then. A new equilibrium is reached when the second-year price rises above the first-year price by the amount of the interest rate. Then and only then will the "interest rate incentive" to sell it all in the first year disappear, and supplies become available to satisfy the demand in both years.

It should be emphasized that, because price is lower this year, the quantity $Q_1$ that the owners can sell now is greater than the $Q_2$ they can sell next year. (Assume, in Figure 21-5, that "other things are equal," that is, $D_1$ is the same as $D_2$.)

(In the above discussion, we have implicitly made the assumption that there is no cost of extracting and

[4] Note to instructors: This section on non-renewable resources is slightly more demanding. However, it can be skipped without loss of continuity. It is based on the principles first worked out in L.C. Gray, "Rent Under the Assumption of Exhaustibility," *Quarterly Journal of Economics*, vol. 28, 1914, pp. 466–89, and in Harold Hotelling's classic article that inspired the study of natural resource economics a half century ago: "Economics of Exhaustible Resources," *Journal of Political Economy*, April 1929, pp. 137–75. For a summary of some of the research that these articles have stimulated, see S. Devarajan and A.C. Fisher, "Hotelling's 'Economics of Exhaustible Resources': Fifty Years Later," *Journal of Economic Literature*, March 1981, pp. 65–73.

## APPLICATIONS AND ILLUSTRATIONS BOX 21-2

## Resource Exploitation and the Environment: Two Cases

### 1. The Northern Spotted Owl vs. Logging

In 1991, the U.S. Fish and Wildlife Service proposed that 4.7 million hectares of forest in Washington, Oregon, and northern California be designated as critical habitat for the endangered northern spotted owl, thus terminating most logging on this land. Opponents claimed that the proposal would result in the loss of more than 20,000 jobs and U.S.$340 million in wages. State legislators and officials complained that their tax revenues would fall by $166 million, that social service spending would increase, and that increased crime, child abuse, alcoholism, and suicide would ensue. In July 1993, President Clinton moved on the proposal, but tied it to $1.2 billion of economic aid to the area. A month later, the wildlife service also moved to protect the marbled murrelet, which nests in the same forests as the northern spotted owl.

### 2. Green vs. Copper: Tatshenshini vs. Windy Craggy

In June 1993, the Government of British Columbia announced that it was setting aside land in the north-westernmost corner of the province for the Tatshenshini-Alsek World Wilderness Reserve which, when combined with neighbouring national parks and reserves in B.C., the Yukon, and Alaska would create an 8.5-million hectare wilderness park. Unfortunately, the land sits on an $8.5 billion gold and copper deposit, including the Windy Craggy mine project. The Windy Craggy deposit is reputed to be the largest undeveloped copper deposit in North America, itself valued between $110 and $620 million. Over the past ten years, $48 million had been spent exploring the site.

Environmentalists argue that the area is one of the few remaining grizzly bear strongholds and that it is the habitat of both the rare glacier bear and the Dall sheep. Preservation is also required to sustain the Tatshenshini-Alsek for salmon. They also point out that copper mining in the area would only be profitable if the price of copper were to more than double from its current level.

The B.C. government determined that the wilderness park and mining could not coexist. In their opinion, no technology exists to assure that acid drainage from mine tailings would not leak into the river in the event of an earthquake.

Proponents of mining in the area point out the value of the deposit, the 500 permanent jobs Windy Craggy alone would create, and that this mine would only occupy 11,000 hectares including roads, the open-pit mine, and community structures. They also argue that there are 20,000 grizzly bears in northern B.C., but very few in the Tatshenshini area. In six seasons of exploring, no more than eight grizzlies were seen in any one year. Furthermore, they point out that Dall sheep live in the Yukon, not in the wilderness surrounding the Windy Craggy site. Concerning the salmon thought to be threatened, the revenue to Alaska fisheries from salmon caught in the Alsek River was $200,000 in 1992. They compare this to the $130 million in revenues earned from statewide salmon fishing that year. Also, they argue that a recent geological report states that the Windy Craggy area is stable, and that, in any case, earthquake-resistant building technologies exist.

The B.C. government, however, has made its decision and plans to nominate Tatshenshini-Alsek as a United Nations heritage site. The government also plans to negotiate compensation packages for the holders of 20 mineral claims in the area. Still, Royal Oak Mines, which owns a controlling interest in Windy Craggy, is not giving up. They plan discussions with the Champagne-Aishihik people who have a land claim pending in the area. The hope of the Champagne-Aishihik is that a way can be found to accommodate both mining and fishing.

marketing the resource. In reality, of course, there are such costs. When they are taken into account, the price per unit of the resource will not generally be increasing by the same percentage as the rate of interest. Instead, the *rent* per unit—that is, the price less the per-unit cost of extraction and marketing—will be increasing at this rate.)

## Dynamic Efficiency in a Perfectly Competitive Market for a Resource

The price pattern above—low this year, higher next—results in the efficient allocation of this resource over time, with the resource being used in both years but more heavily this year than next. While this is too complicated to prove in an introductory book, it can be intuitively confirmed by noting that, from society's point of view, it is better for more of the resource to be used this year than next. An example of this is an iron ore resource that can be used to produce steel for capital equipment and will allow us to be more productive next year. Thus, we can produce more by putting some of this resource to productive use right away than by holding it and not using it until next year. And the lower price this year does indeed result in a greater amount $Q_1$ of this resource being used this year than next ($Q_2$).

To sum up the message of Figure 21-5: Conservation doesn't mean to stop using any of the resource at all. This solution would be the same as not having any of the resource. There is no point in holding a valuable resource until its value disappears because it has been replaced by a substitute. Instead, conservation means using a resource in the efficient pattern over time. This is what occurs under perfect competition in Figure 21-5. Other things equal, some of the resource is used this year and some the next, with more used this year. This is efficient because of the productivity of the resource in capital investment. This is an example of how perfect competition results in ***dynamic efficiency***.

> *Dynamic efficiency* occurs when an economic activity (such as the use of a resource) takes place at the best rate, that is, the best pattern over time (as in Figure 21-5).

The key to the efficient pattern of prices is the interest rate. This is not surprising since the interest rate is a measure of how much more society can produce by using a resource this year rather than the next (a point that we already discussed in some detail in Chapter 17).

Again, it should be emphasized that no claim can be made that the efficient price pattern in Figure 21-5 will necessarily prevail. In fact, it may not. For example, if the supply of this resource is controlled by a small number of producers, they may, like any other oligopolists, use their market power to set prices above the perfectly competitive levels $P_1$ and $P_2$. True, higher prices will mean that some of this resource will not be used up by the end of year 2, when it will be displaced by substitutes. However, the oligopolists may still have maximized profits because of the increased price on the amount that they actually do sell. This is just an extension of our conclusion in Chapter 13 that it may be profitable for colluding oligopolists to raise price, even though they sell less as a consequence.

## Why the Real World Is More Complicated

In Figure 21-5, it was assumed that the resource will be completely replaced by a substitute in two years. Figure 21-6 extends this analysis to the case where the resource is replaced after a longer period—specifically, after year 4. This does not necessarily mean that a substitute eliminates all demand in succeeding years. In fact, there is still a demand for the metal in year 5, namely, $D_5$. However, this demand lies below $P_5$; the inexpensive substitute has pushed the demand curve for this metal below the price line $P'$, so none is used thereafter.

## Market Prices that Promote Conservation and Other Forms of Adjustment

As time passes and the resource becomes more and more scarce, its price rises. This triggers several kinds of market adjustments.

### 1. Substitution in Consumption and Production

As resource prices rise, people are encouraged to use less. For example, as the price of oil increases, people turn down their thermostats. Likewise, as copper has become more scarce and expensive, construction firms producing houses or factories have replaced copper pipe with plastic pipe. This is illustrated in Figure 21-6, where price rises in year 2 while other things remain constant ($D_2$ is identical to $D_1$). The higher price pushes users of this resource in year 2 up their demand curve to the left. Thus, this resource is conserved; the smaller amount $Q_2$ is used, rather than $Q_1$.

### 2. Intensified Search for the Resource

As the price of a resource rises, there is an incentive to find more of it by increased search. True, for a non-renewable resource in finite supply this cannot be a solution forever; someday there will be no more left to find. But, for many such resources, that day is far in the future. Indeed, for many resources, we are now discovering reserves at least as fast as we are using them. An example cited by MIT's Morris Adelman is oil, often regarded as a resource in critical supply, with North American oil fields on the wane. In 1945, there were 20 billion barrels of reserves in the United States (excluding Alaska). In the next four decades, 100 billion were used and 100 billion discovered, so that in the late 1980s reserves were still 20 billion. Reserves were being found about as fast as they were being used.

While this pattern may not continue in North America, it is expected that it will continue in many other less mature oil-producing countries, where for decades more oil has been found than used. And the higher the price of oil, the more intense this search will be. When more of the resource is discovered, Figure 21-6 shows how the "crisis" of short supply and high price is relieved. With more $Q$ now available to distribute over time, the whole price staircase $PP'$ will shift down. In response to the price reduction, the quantity used each year will be increased.

### 3. Discovery and Development of Substitutes

To illustrate: The discovery of optical fibres made of glass has displaced copper in communications systems. This could not have been predicted 20 years ago, since almost nothing was known of fibre optics then. Even though we can't precisely predict future technology, we can expect that copper will be further displaced in the future by more innovations.

With the reduced demand for the resource, a given amount $Q$ will "go further" in Figure 21-6, and the crisis of short supply will again be relieved; the price staircase will shift down. The same is true if demand is lower than expected because of a reduced rate of population growth.

## OIL: A RESOURCE WITH VERY SPECIAL PROBLEMS

Any discussion of scarce natural resources would be incomplete without some reference to the resource problem that has been an important issue in public policy over the last two decades: oil. Recall that the world price of oil rose from less than $3 a barrel in 1973 to more than U.S.$30 in 1982. (However, in the mid-1980s, oil prices fell substantially; by the early 1990s they were back to around $15 per barrel.)

In one sense, the huge price increase in the late 1970s and early 1980s may have been a good thing: It put pressure on energy users around the world to conserve a non-renewable resource. But the main reason the world oil price rose was not a desire to bring about conservation: Instead, the high price was brought about by OPEC, a cartel of many of the world's oil-exporting nations, for the purpose of increasing their revenues from oil exports. And OPEC's gain was other countries' loss: Those countries that have large net imports of oil and other forms of energy were clearly hurt. The effects on a country like Canada were less clear-cut. On the one hand, we were hurt by the higher prices that we had to pay for the oil we imported into eastern Canada; but, on the other hand, we gained from the higher prices we received on our *exports* of oil and natural gas from the western provinces. (Because natural gas is a close substitute for oil, its price tends to move with the price of oil.) Since Canada's energy exports (in the form of oil, natural gas, and electricity) have typically exceeded its energy imports, Canada as a whole enjoyed a modest net benefit from rising energy prices.

But even though Canada's wealth of energy resources helped protect us from the consequences of the world oil price increase, the developments in the international oil market in the 1970s forced the government to confront several difficult questions. In particular:

1. Should it try to protect all Canadian energy users by preventing energy prices in Canada from rising to world levels, or would it be better to take a hands-off attitude, allowing the price to rise?
2. Should it allow producers of oil, gas, and electricity to cash in on rising world energy prices by raising their exports of Canadian energy resources?

With respect to the pricing question, the government initially chose to keep Canadian energy prices

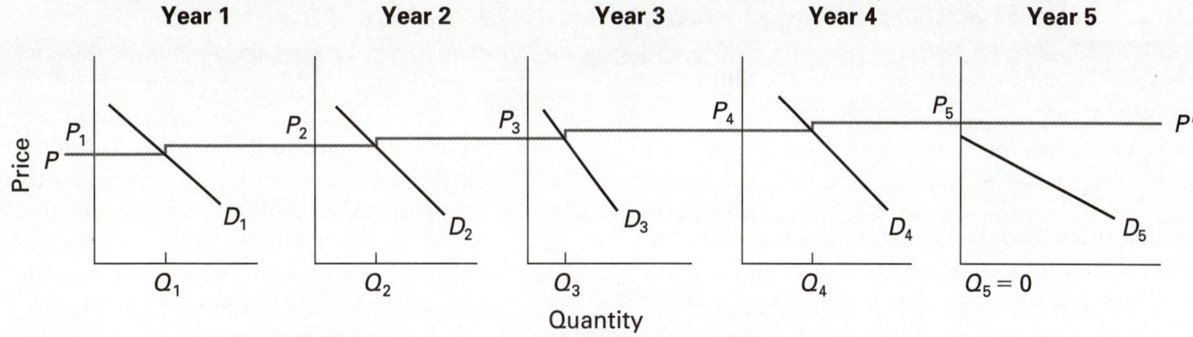


**FIGURE 21-6 Efficient pricing pattern for a non-renewable resource over a longer period.** This figure extends Figure 21-5. Determining the efficient, perfectly competitive pattern of price and resource use over time may be viewed as fitting a "price staircase" $PP'$ to the demand curves, with the restriction that $Q_1 + Q_2 + Q_3 \ldots$ be equal to the total fixed available quantity of the resource. As before, the height of each step in this staircase is the interest rate.

below the world level. To protect Canadian energy users, it froze the Canadian oil price at $3.80 a barrel (far below the world price of more than $10 a barrel). During the latter part of the 1970s, the government gradually allowed the domestic price to rise, but not enough to keep up with the increase in world prices: Thus, the Canadian price remained substantially below the world price throughout the last half of the decade.

The Progressive Conservative government under Joe Clark that was elected in 1979 tried to change the low-price policy. However, the Conservatives were defeated after less than a year in office, and in the ***National Energy Program*** (NEP) introduced by the Liberal government in 1980, the consumer price of oil was again set well below the world price. It was not until the mid-1980s that the Canadian domestic price essentially reached the world price.

The problem of oil and gas pricing in Canada is complicated because of a number of factors, including the fact that many of the firms producing oil and gas in Canada are foreign-owned, and that our oil and gas deposits are concentrated primarily in the western provinces. Because of these factors, distributional effects play a very important role in the debate over Canadian energy policy. One of the main arguments against a high-price strategy was that it would imply a redistribution of real income from Canadian energy users to foreign-owned oil companies and from the relatively poor Atlantic provinces to resource-rich Alberta. These distributional issues are briefly discussed in Box 21-3. Here we concentrate on the aggregative efficiency effects of the pricing policy.

A policy that keeps the domestic price of oil—or any other internationally traded commodity—below the world price leads to an efficiency loss. The reasons are illustrated in Figure 21-7.

## Implications of Keeping the Domestic Canadian Price Below the World Price

Without government intervention, the domestic price would be the same as the world price, $P_w$. At this price, the quantity demanded in Canada would be $P_wC$, of which $P_wB$ would be produced in Canada. The balance $BC$ would be imported. Now consider the effect of government controls that kept the Canadian price below $P_w$, at $P_1$.

Consumers responded to the lower price $P_1$ by moving down their demand curve from $C$ to $F$; thus consumption increased by arrow 1. In addition, the lower price induced domestic producers to move down their supply curve from $B$ to $A$; Canadian oil production decreased by arrow 2. With consumption expanded and production contracted, the difference between the two—that is, imports—increased from $BC$ to $AF$.

This increase in imports was one of the most important effects of this policy of holding down the domestic price of oil. However, there were other effects as well:

## TOOLS AND TECHNIQUES BOX 21-3

### The International Income Transfer as the World Price of Oil Increased: OPEC as a "Conserving Monopolist"?

> What we are witnessing in . . . oil and raw material prices is virtually the same as what is going on between trade unions and employers' associations on the national level. It is a struggle for the distribution and use of the national product, a struggle for the world product.
>
> Helmut Schmidt, then Minister of Finance of the Federal Republic of Germany

So far in this book we have considered several kinds of changes in the economy that may cause income transfers within Canada. For example, if a marketing board restricts supply and drives up the price in a previously competitive agricultural industry, there is a transfer from Canadian consumers to Canadian farmers. Or, if the provincial government raises the excise tax on beer, there is a transfer from Canadian beer drinkers to taxpayers. While these transfers represent losses to some Canadians (beer drinkers or consumers of farm products), these losses are in large measure offset by the gains of others (farmers, provincial taxpayers).

As Canada and other countries allowed domestic oil prices to gradually rise toward world prices following the huge OPEC-induced increase in the world oil price in the 1970s, there was a large transfer of real income from energy users in those countries. Who were the gainers? In countries that were more or less self-sufficient in energy, the gainers were domestic energy producers. But, for countries such as Japan and some European nations who depend on imports for a large part of their energy needs, the transfers from energy users were not offset by gains to domestic producers. Instead, many of the gains from a higher oil price went to foreign producers — in particular, producers in the OPEC nations. From the viewpoint of the citizens in an importing nation like Japan, such transfers were a dead loss.

What about the Canadian case? Because Canada is largely self-sufficient in energy, increases in energy prices in Canada mostly result in a transfer from Canadian energy users to firms that produce energy from Canadian resources. But there is a catch: Many of these firms are not owned by Canadians, but instead by foreigners. From the viewpoint of the well-being of Canadians, therefore, the transfers are to some extent a dead loss: A substantial part of any increase in energy prices is transferred from Canadians to foreign owners of the multinational oil companies that operate in Canada.

In reality, the issue is more complicated because governments collect taxes and royalties from the energy sector. Thus, while higher energy prices in Canada during the 1970s meant higher profits for foreign-owned oil companies, some of these profits were taxed away, and thus went to Canadian taxpayers. However, here we have yet another complication. Because much of the taxation of energy resources has been under the jurisdiction of the province in which the oil and gas is extracted, much of the transfer went from energy users all over Canada to taxpayers in the western provinces where most of our oil and gas resources are located.

1. Because the domestic price was kept below the world price, Canadian oil consumers benefited. (The "oil price shock" was not as severe for them as it would otherwise have been.) At the same time, Canadian producers were hurt because the price they received ($P_1$) was not as high as it would have otherwise been. Thus, this policy benefited consumers at the expense of producers. However, even though the Canadian oil price didn't rise as high as the world price, it neverthe-

less rose very substantially relative to the early 1970s; in comparison with the early 1970s, there had already been a large transfer in the opposite direction, from consumers to producers. Thus, the policy of keeping the domestic price from rising as rapidly as the world price was judged to be a "fair" or equitable one because it prevented this transfer from consumers to producers from becoming even bigger. As we show in Box 21-3, the issue of transfers was particularly sensitive because many of the producing firms were foreign-owned.

2. Canadian oil consumers were not encouraged to conserve. Instead their oil consumption was higher, as shown by arrow 1. The result, as detailed in the caption to the diagram, was an efficiency loss of grey triangle *CJF*—reflecting the fact that imported oil was costing more (the world price $P_w$) than the benefit consumers were getting from it (the height of the demand curve *CF*).
3. The reduction in domestic oil production shown by arrow 2 resulted in another efficiency loss—grey triangle *HBA*, also described in detail in the caption to this diagram. The reason for this efficiency loss is that we were importing oil at high cost $P_w$ rather than producing it domestically at the lower cost shown by the height of the supply curve *AB*.
4. It was very expensive for the government to make such a simple price control system work. Importers had to pay $P_w$ to buy oil on the world market. In forcing them to sell it at the lower price $P_1$, the government had to pay them the difference—that is, a subsidy of $P_w P_1 = AH$ per barrel. Thus, the total subsidy that the government had to pay on the *AF* barrels imported was $AH \times AF$ = area *HAFJ*.

To reduce problems 3 and 4, the government's National Energy Program actually used a more complex system than the one described so far. Instead of fixing a single domestic price for oil, the government specified a number of prices, falling into three basic categories:

(a) The relatively high price paid for "new oil"—that is, oil from newly drilled wells.

(b) A lower price $P_1$ that producers could charge for "old oil," that is, oil from wells already in production.

(c) A "blended price" that domestic *buyers* had to pay.

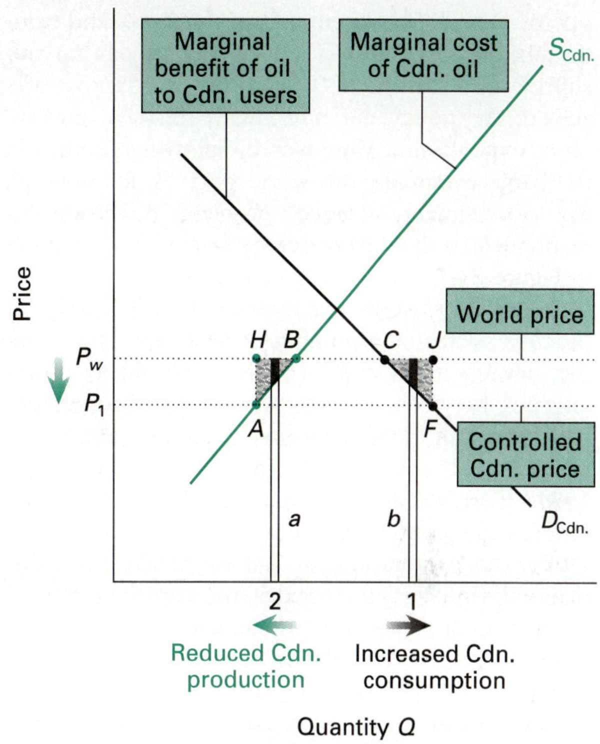


**FIGURE 21-7 The effects of keeping the domestic Canadian price of oil ($P_1$) below the world price ($P_w$).** The first effect was increased domestic consumption equal to arrow 1 that had to be satisfied by increased imports. The result was an efficiency loss because each of these barrels, such as *b*, cost more to import (the height of the hollow bar plus the solid black bar) than the benefit it provided to consumers (the hollow bar). Therefore, there was a loss on this barrel equal to the solid black bar. Adding up the similar losses on all the other barrels over the relevant range *CJ* of increased consumption yielded the triangular efficiency loss *CJF*. At the same time, keeping the domestic price below $P_w$ at $P_1$ also resulted in arrow 2 of reduced domestic oil production; this also had to be covered by increased imports. The result was an efficiency loss because each of these barrels, such as *a*, cost more to import (the height of the hollow bar plus the solid black bar) than it would have cost if it had been produced domestically instead (the height of the hollow bar). The result was a loss on this barrel equal to the solid black bar. Adding up the similar losses on all the other barrels over the relevant range *HB* of decreased Canadian production yields the triangular efficiency loss *HBA*.

This blended price was lower than the high producer price for new oil, but not as low as the producer price for old oil; the difference between the blended price and this producer price was due to a tax that the government collected on the domestic sale of old oil. The revenue from this tax—and from the tax on oil exports—was enough to pay for the subsidy on oil imports. Thus, problem 4 above was solved; the policy did not involve massive government expenditure. Moreover, by allowing producers to charge essentially the world price $P_w$ for new oil, the government avoided problem 3. Producers responded to this high price by operating at point *B* in Figure 21-7.

In theory, it was an ingenious solution. However, in practice it created a number of problems. For example, because there was no way of physically distinguishing between old and new oil, illegal operators were given an incentive to use complex transactions to disguise the source of old oil. Toward the mid-1980s, there was less and less enthusiasm for the system of price controls in the energy sector. By the late 1980s, the control system had essentially been dismantled. (In the United States, the earlier system of controls over oil and gas pricing had also been abandoned, consistent with the Reagan administration's general philosophy of deregulation.)

The decision to abandon the price control system was made easier, of course, by the fact that in the late 1980s, world oil prices had come down substantially from their peak in the early 1980s. For this reason, some of the optimistic projections of an increase in Canadian oil production under world pricing had to be revised. A number of energy megaprojects were cancelled, and for a long time, the future of the large Hibernia field off the coast of Newfoundland looked uncertain. (However, in the early 1990s, the federal government reaffirmed its commitment to support the development of Hibernia.)

## Oil Pricing, Conservation, and Energy Security

In the discussion of oil pricing so far, we have focused on the issues of efficiency and transfers between consumers and producers. Looking at efficiency alone, the discussion has pointed to the conclusion that the best policy is to simply allow the domestic Canadian price to follow the world price. By adopting this policy, we would have eliminated the efficiency losses (illustrated by triangles *CJF* and *HBA* in Figure 21-7) that arose when Canada had to increase oil imports to make up for any shortfall in domestic production.

However, another important issue in Canadian energy policy is the problem of potential instability in the world oil market. In particular, the volatile political situation in the Middle East, which supplies a large portion of the oil traded in the international market, may suddenly be disrupted. How should we take this problem of instability into account in formulating Canadian energy policy?

Surprisingly, the answer is that when we allow for the instability problem, the best strategy may be to set the Canadian domestic price even *higher* than the world price. The logic is this: A sudden disruption in world oil supplies may involve very high costs to Canada, especially if oil-using industries are forced to cut back production or if we run out of oil for home heating. (Any disruption of supplies of imported oil to Canada would affect the United States as well, so there is little possibility that we could import American oil in a crisis.) The risk of having to bear the costs of emergency measures can be viewed as an additional cost of depending on oil imports, rather than being self-sufficient. This risk-related cost should be added to the world price $P_w$ that we have to pay for oil in order to arrive at its true cost. According to this argument, efficiency requires that domestic Canadian price should fully reflect this cost and therefore should be above $P_w$. (Efficiency requires that the domestic price faced by consumers and producers provides a clear message of *all* the costs of a good.) Therefore, oil should be taxed to raise its price *above* $P_w$. The case for raising the domestic price above the world price applies even more strongly in the United States, since it is more dependent than Canada on imported oil.

In recent years, another argument for raising the consumer price of oil has been made with increasing frequency: When oil is burned, it contributes to air pollution and the greenhouse effect. This issue will be studied in the next chapter.

## KEY POINTS

1. In extracting common-property resources, such as fish, that are publicly owned, fishing crews do not take into account how this year's harvest will affect future harvests. The result is an efficiency loss: Too much is harvested today.
2. In an attempt to solve this problem by reducing the current catch of fish, the government may impose various restrictions, such as requiring fishing licences or setting off-season limits on fishing.
3. Another way to reduce the harvest to an efficient level is to establish property rights. Once the resource becomes privately owned, its supply will reflect not only the current cost of harvesting it, but also the amount necessary to compensate the owner for the adverse effect of present harvests on future resource supplies.
4. Special problems arise when a resource is non-renewable. If current rates of consumption continue, such a resource must someday be exhausted. This simple observation has led to a number of "doomsday studies" that predict the collapse of our economic system. However, one problem with many of these studies is that they take inadequate account of price adjustments: As such resources become scarcer, their prices rise; this encourages conservation and stimulates the search for substitutes.
5. The policy of keeping the domestic Canadian oil price below the world price led to two kinds of efficiency loss: (1) It reduced conservation efforts by oil users and (2) it discouraged production by domestic producers. It also resulted in a large transfer from the oil companies to oil users, and from the Western provinces to the rest of the country.

## KEY TERMS

**common-property resource**
**privately owned resource**
**external cost**
**sustainable yield curve**
**maximum sustainable yield**
**creation of property rights**
**reservation price**
**dynamic efficiency**
**renewable resource**
**non-renewable resource**
**induced innovation**
**National Energy Program**

## PROBLEMS

21-1. Suppose 50 boats are fishing in an ocean area. Would there be any reason for the government to allow the boat owners to sign an agreement restricting the amount each catches? Is it possible that restricting the catch, which began as a conservation measure, may become a means of exercising market power? Explain. Can you think of any other examples of people who become conservationists because it is a way of providing themselves with more market power? If those who already have their ski chalets in British Columbia become conservationists and prevent new ski runs and chalets from being built, what would this do to the value of their chalets?

21-2. Using Figure 21-6, explain how conservation measures may be taken too far. Specifically, explain why it would be inefficient to cut back consumption one unit below $Q_1$ in year 1 in order to conserve that unit for use in year 5. Also explain what happens to the price staircase in Figure 21-6 if (a) existing deposits of the resource turn out to be less plentiful than expected; (b) there is an unexpected increase in demand for this resource.

21-3. The problem of efficient timing in harvesting timber is illustrated in the diagram below. For example, point *A* indicates that if we wait 15 years before harvesting again, a hectare will yield 10 units of timber. Which point represents a forest in which there is no longer any timber growth? Would you cut timber every 15, 30, or 66 years? Explain. (Assume that cutting and replanting costs are negligible.)

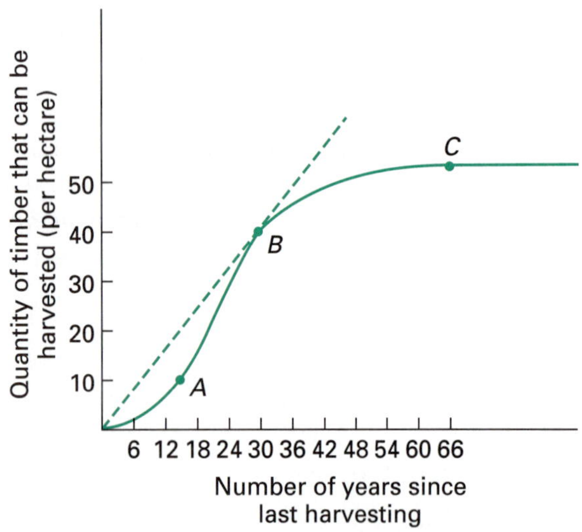


21-4. In 1865, doomsday forecasters predicted that economic growth couldn't continue far into the future because the world would run out of coal, the prime source of energy at that time.

(a) If you had lived then, how would you have evaluated this claim?

(b) Knowing what you do now about energy reserves and the way coal has been replaced as an energy source, what would you say about any attempt to use this 1865 argument to apply restrictions on North American coal production today?

21-5. (a) Did holding the Canadian oil price down in the 1970s increase or decrease the international transfer from Canada to oil-exporting countries? In your answer, explain the effect of holding the price down on domestic production and consumption and, therefore, the effect on Canadian oil imports.

(b) Explain why you agree or disagree with the statement: "To reduce a domestic transfer (from domestic users to domestic producers) the Canadian government followed a policy that made the international transfer worse."

# APPENDIX 21-A

## SUSTAINABLE YIELD AND THE EFFICIENT RATE OF HARVESTING OF A RENEWABLE RESOURCE

In the text, we showed that for a common-property renewable resource, an unregulated perfectly competitive market would lead to an inefficient rate of harvesting over time. Because individual producers (such as fishing-boat captains in our example) would fail to take into account the effect of the current harvest on the future availability of the resource, there would initally be overharvesting: The end result might even be that the resource disappeared altogether, as almost happened with the prairie buffalo. We also showed that for a privately owned renewable resource, the problem of overharvesting tends to disappear. The reason is that when a resource is privately owned, the opportunity cost of having less of the resource in the future is an internal cost to the resource owner. For a common-property resource, the opportunity cost, from the viewpoint of those who harvest the resource, is an external cost that they do not take into account.

In this appendix, we consider the question: How high is this opportunity cost? That is, how high is the level of *resource rent* that should be included as part of the producers' marginal cost in order to reduce overharvesting and bring about a socially efficient rate of resource exploitation instead?

To consider this question, let's look first at the case of a privately owned resource such as timber. Specifically, consider a company that owns a large tract of forest land. The sustainable yield from the forest depends on how long the trees are allowed to grow before they are cut. The average amount of wood in the forest's standing trees also depends on this. Therefore, forest scientists can establish a sustainable yield curve for a tract of land, such as Figure 21-8. Figure 21-8 is similar to Figure 21-2 in the text. Along the vertical axis, we measure the quantity of timber (in cubic metres) harvested every year, while along the horizontal axis, we measure the average stock of timber (again measured in cubic metres of wood) on the land.

To simplify matters, we first assume that the present and future prices of wood are expected to remain constant, and also that the cost per cubic metre of harvesting wood is constant, regardless of the amount being harvested and regardless of the age at which the trees are cut. With these assumptions, it is possible to show that in most cases, the firm's best policy is to manage its forest in such a way as to move toward a point on the sustainable yield curve. (The only exception would be in cases where the land was so unproductive that the best policy would be to cut all the wood at once and then abandon the land, or convert it into some other use.)

Let's now consider the question which point on the sustainable yield curve the company will aim for. Suppose we begin at a point such as *A* in Figure 21-8, somewhat to the left of the point of maximum sustainable yield (MSY). Would it pay the company to move to a point closer to the maximum, such as *B*?

To raise the sustainable yield from point *A*, the company has to follow a strategy of letting the trees grow for a little bit longer before they are cut. In deciding whether it pays to do this, the company has to first look at how much extra wood it gets by letting the trees grow longer. Second, however, it must also take into account that by cutting the trees later, it will forgo the interest it could have earned by cutting the trees earlier and investing the money in the capital market. For example, suppose that between their twenty-ninth and thirtieth year, the amount of wood in the average tree increases by 4%. If the real (inflation-corrected) rate of interest is 5%, it is therefore better to cut the tree at age 29 and invest the money, than to leave the tree in the forest for another year. Conversely, if the amount of wood on average grows by 7%, say, between the twentieth and twenty-first year, cutting the trees at age 20 is too early. (At what age *should* the tree be cut? The answer: At the age when the amount of wood grows at approximately the same percentage rate as the rate of interest in the economy.)

Returning to Figure 21-8, moving from point *A* to point *B* will only pay if the increase in the sustainable yield that can be obtained by following a strategy of delaying the harvest is large enough to offset the interest forgone by doing so. As we get closer and closer to the point of maximum sustainable yield, the increased yield becomes smaller and smaller. Taking the interest rate effect into account means that it doesn't pay to go *all* the way to the point of maximum sustainable yield; the most profitable point on the sustainable yield curve must lie somewhat to the left of the maximum. Moreover, the higher the rate of interest, the further to the left is the best point, since with a higher rate of interest the trees will be harvested earlier, which moves us to the left in the diagram, reducing the sustainable yield.

If the market for wood is perfectly competitive, the point on the sustainable yield curve that is the most profitable one for the company will also represent the point that is efficient from the viewpoint of society. At this point, trees are left in the forest until the return on letting them grow for another year is the same as the rate of interest in the economy. That is, the marginal return on "investing" in trees (leaving them a little longer in the forest) is the same as the marginal efficiency of investment elsewhere in the economy.

Now suppose all forests in the economy are efficiently managed in this way. This means that the amount of wood supplied to the market is the same, constant, amount every year. Suppose the amount is at $Q_1$ in Figure 21-9. When this is the quantity supplied, the demand curve $D_A$ for wood tells us that the equilibrium price will be $P_1$. Given this equilibrium price, we can now find the equilibrium resource rent per unit of wood harvested: It is simply the amount that must be added to the marginal cost of harvesting to raise the market price to $P_1$—that is, the price that must prevail in the market to limit the quantity demanded to the same (socially efficient) quantity that is supplied every year to the market.

What happens if the demand curve for wood shifts out? Suppose in particular that a change in tastes shifts the demand curve in Figure 21-9 from its original position $D_A$ to $D_B$, and it is expected to remain in this new position forever. If the quantity supplied to the market each year remains at $Q_1$, the price will rise to $P_2$, and the resource rent would increase to $(P_2 - \text{MC})$. And this is, in fact, the new equilibrium. Even though the net revenue that a forest owner can get by selling wood today has increased, so has the opportunity cost of reduced sales in the future, since the price is expected to remain high tomorrow as well. Therefore, as long as the amount of forest land and the rate of interest in the economy do not change, a shift in the demand curve won't affect the efficient rate of output. However, the resource rent per unit of wood has to increase in order to keep the quantity demanded equal to the quantity supplied, as before.

In the case of a common-property resource such as fish, the socially efficient amount to harvest is not the same as what is privately profitable. Therefore, as we saw in the text, the government has to use other methods to limit the harvest to the efficient amount. (For example, it could charge producers a tax per unit supplied to the market.) Nevertheless, the principles that should be used to determine the efficient rate of harvesting are the same as those we have just discussed, and if the government uses a tax to limit the amount harvested, such a tax serves exactly the same function as the resource rent in the case of a privately owned resource.

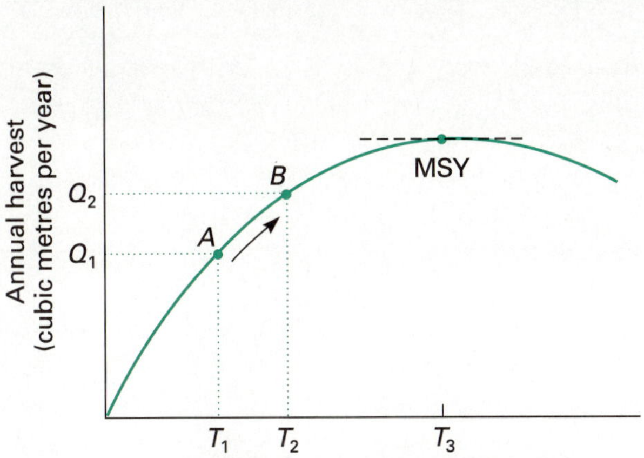


**FIGURE 21-8 Finding the optimum sustainable yield: timber.**

If the amount of timber in the forest is $T_1$, $Q_1$ cubic metres ($m^3$) of wood can be harvested year after year; if the stock is $T_2$, the annual sustainable harvest is $Q_2$. (The maximum sustainable yield, MSY, occurs at an even higher stock, $T_3$.)

Although the annual revenue from selling wood is higher at point *B*, point *A* may be more profitable. The reason is that in moving from point *A* to point *B*, the firm must temporarily reduce its harvest in order to allow the stock of timber to build up to $T_2$. If the rate of interest that can be earned on the revenue from harvesting $Q_1$ today is high enough, the increase in the size of the future harvest may not be enough to compensate.

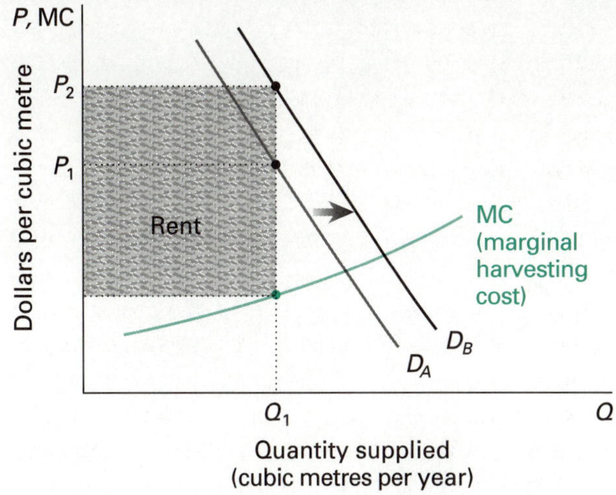


**FIGURE 21-9 Rent on an efficiently managed renewable resource.**

If the demand curve for wood is $D_A$, and $Q_1$ is the efficient rate of sustainable harvesting, the equilibrium resource rent is just the difference between $P_1$, the price at which the quantity demanded equals $Q_1$, and the marginal cost of harvesting MC.

If there is an outward shift in the demand curve to $D_B$, the equilibrium price increases to $P_2$, and the amount of rent increases. However, as long as the rate of interest is the same as before, the efficient annual harvest remains the same, at $Q_1$.

CHAPTER

# 22 THE ECONOMICS OF PROTECTING THE ENVIRONMENT

*The difference between inefficient and efficient . . . policies to control pollution can mean scores, perhaps hundreds, of billions of dollars released for other useful purposes over the next several decades.*

*Allen V. Kneese and Charles L. Schultze*

Like the ancient mariner, a captain sails the high seas, searching for a spot to dump a barge-full of garbage. Meanwhile, past dumping of chemicals has made Times Beach, Missouri, a ghost town. Its inhabitants have left, its houses are boarded up, and the wind whistles through its empty streets. In Bhopal, India, a leak in a Union Carbide plant released toxic gases that killed almost 3000 people. In the hot, dry summer of 1988, Prairie grain farmers and people sweltering in the cities of Southern Ontario were wondering: Is this an early warning of damage the human race may be doing to the atmosphere? And in the early 1990s, parents were warned that children shouldn't be playing out of doors in the middle of the day. Damage to the ozone layer meant that potentially dangerous levels of ultraviolet radiation were reaching the Earth's surface.

True, some of these problems are not new; for decades the air in large cities has been polluted. However, environmental threats have now become more serious. One reason has been the development of more than four million synthetic chemicals. Many are very useful, such as the modern herbicides and fertilizers that contribute to agricultural productivity. The problem is that some of their side effects are not benevolent. For example, the chemical that leaked at Bhopal was used to produce an insecticide that becomes relatively harmless to humans a few days after it is sprayed on crops. But, when accidentally released at the wrong time, it is lethal. In the Great Lakes region, scientists have identified nearly a thousand different chemicals that enter the lakes from factories, chemical waste dumps, sewage plants, and farm fields. Even very small amounts of highly toxic chemicals, such as PCBs and dioxins, are enough to gradually cause high concentrations in birds, fish, and humans—and these are chemicals that never break down naturally. Warns Pollution Probe, an environmental lobby group based in Toronto: "Unless governments really come to grips with the problem soon, the water from Lake Ontario will be undrinkable in ten years."

To deal with such problems, various laws have been passed and regulatory bodies set up to protect our environment by reducing the pollution of our water, soil, and air. The fundamental questions we consider in this chapter are: How can economic analysis help explain why deterioration of the environment has become such an important problem in today's world? How can economic principles help us in designing more efficient policies for environmental protection?

## MEASURES TO CONTROL POLLUTION

Both the federal and the provincial governments have responded to the pollution problem by passing legislation to protect the environment. The most important federal statutes are the Canadian Water Act, the Clean Air Act, and the Environmental Contaminants

Act.[1] However, because constitutional authority for legislation over the environment mainly rests with the provinces, enforcement of these federal statutes also requires separate provincial legislation, and all provinces have their own anti-pollution laws. Most of the time, federal and provincial officials cooperate in enforcing anti-pollution laws; but, occasionally, the job is made more difficult by disagreements between the two levels of government about the question of who has jurisdiction over a particular area of environmental regulation.

One of the most important roles of federal legislation has been to take the lead in setting acceptable *standards* for the quality of our air and water. The federal government also provides a nationwide system for monitoring pollution, by measuring the concentrations of pollutants in the air and water. Federal tax laws also encourage investment in anti-pollution equipment by private firms: It allows the firms to reduce their corporate tax liability by letting them depreciate the cost of such investments over a short period.

Another role of the government's environmental legislation is to limit the pollution discharged by *products*. This legislation covers such pollutants as emissions from cars and trucks, radiation from television sets and alarm clocks with illuminated dials, and chlorofluorocarbons (CFCs) that damage the Earth's ozone layer.

While pollution continues to be an enormous problem, government environmental regulation and the large investments in anti-pollution equipment nevertheless have had considerable success: There has been substantial progress in cleaning up the environment. Today, the air in Canada's cities is less befouled by lead, carbon monoxide, and other noxious gases than it was in the early 1970s. In the Great Lakes, commercial fishing is once again allowed in areas where it was previously prohibited, and the beaches of Lake Erie, once closed to swimming because of the polluted water, have now been opened again.

However, the environmental laws are to be judged not only by such instances where the environment has improved, but also by a number of instances where the environment has not improved — where the sole "success" has been to keep the environment from getting worse. It is important to recognize that pollution will be a continuing problem, because we will never be able to eliminate it completely. Even if we were to bring industry to a standstill by closing down every plant that did any polluting whatsoever, pollutants from millions of country barnyards and city streets would still wash into our streams. Since it is not possible to *eliminate* pollution, the practical questions are:

> **How far should pollution be cut back? What costs should we be willing to bear?**

## POLLUTION: THE EXPENSIVE JOB OF CONTROL

No matter how an environmental clean-up is initially financed, the public eventually bears the burden in one of the following ways:

1. Taxpayers bear not only the cost of subsidizing waste disposal plants and pollution control equipment, but also the cost of operating the agencies that monitor the environment and enforce the clean-up regulations.
2. Business firms face costs in complying with the regulations, such as the costs of installing pollution controls or using cleaner, more expensive fuel. Eventually, these costs are passed on to the firms' wage earners or shareholders, or on to the public, which may have to pay a higher price for the firms' products.
3. Alternatively, to the degree that firms cover their costs of reducing pollution by investing less in capital equipment, our growth of productivity and output is reduced. In this case, the opportunity cost of controlling pollution is slower growth. Thus, the public pays in the future.
4. The most highly publicized cost occurs when jobs are lost because pollution control standards force a plant to close down.

In the choice between creating jobs and protecting the environment, job creation often wins, especially in depressed areas. In November 1985, the government of Nova Scotia faced the decision of whether to resume local production of coke for its steel mill in Sydney, or to permanently close the coke ovens and import the coke from elsewhere. Federal officials recommended closing. Earlier studies (when the coke ovens were operating) had found elevated levels of carcinogenic chemicals in the air in Sydney, and death rates from cancer and lung diseases were significantly higher among people living downwind from the plant than among those living upwind, or elsewhere in Canada. Nevertheless, the government

[1] Other federal statutes also deal with environmental issues. The Ocean Dumping Control Act, the Northern Inland Water Act, the Arctic Waters Pollution Protection Act, and parts of the Fisheries Act are important examples.

decided to re-open the ovens: To keep them closed would have meant a loss of jobs both at Sydney Steel and in the Cape Breton coal fields (where the coal for the local coke production is mined).

In one way or another, the cost of controlling pollution touches us all. It is a large tab—no one really knows how large. It has been estimated that properly cleaning up just one of the leaking chemical dumps in the Niagara Falls area might cost as much as $300 million. With respect to air pollution, American government officials have estimated that the substantial reduction in air pollution that is scheduled to take place by the end of the century could cost more than $20 *billion* per year. Will there be an even greater cost in the future if collective measures are required to repair and protect the outer atmosphere and to arrest the "greenhouse effect" that scientists believe is causing a gradual warming of the Earth's temperature?

Because it is so costly to control pollution, we should use the least expensive methods. Unfortunately, governments often have not used these methods in the past: One of the major criticisms of past pollution-control policies is that they have been far too expensive.[2] This chapter will explain why, and outline a better approach. (A worse policy, but one that is sometimes recommended, is described in Box 22-1.) But first, we consider why government intervention is necessary in the first place. Why does the private market fail? Why can't we count on Adam Smith's "invisible hand" to limit pollution?

[2] For a thorough discussion of the U.S. experience with pollution controls, see T.H. Tietenberg, "Uncommon Sense: the Program to Reform Pollution Control Policy," in L.W. Weiss and M.W. Klass, eds., *Regulatory Reform: What Actually Happened* (Boston: Little, Brown, 1986), pp. 286–89.

## POLLUTION: AN EXTERNAL COST

The reason that private markets can't be relied upon to control pollution is that, from the viewpoint of private firms, pollution is an ***external cost***. (Recall from Chapter 21 that ***internal costs*** are those incurred by those who actually produce or consume a good, whereas external, "spillover," costs are costs borne by someone else.) Because of this external cost, private and social costs differ. To understand why, consider a pulp and paper factory located on a river. The costs of paper to society include not only the internal, private costs faced by the pulp and paper firm—such as the costs of labour and raw materials—but also the cost to those who live downstream and must put up with the wastes that the firm releases into the river. While the pulp and paper firm has to pay for its internal costs, any cost downstream is external to its operation, since this cost is borne by others.

Consider a simple illustration. Suppose that each unit of a product is treated with an ounce of a fluid that is then released as waste into a river. Suppose also that each of these ounces of fluid then imposes a constant damage to those downstream. Then each

### APPLICATIONS AND ILLUSTRATIONS — BOX 22-1

### Why Not Control Pollution by Ending Economic Growth?

Industrial growth generally means more industrial waste. Therefore, why not deal with the pollution problem by stopping industrial growth? The answer is that it would be a very inefficient policy. Stopping growth would only stop the increase in pollution. It would not reduce existing pollution. Thus, as a way of reducing pollution, a no-growth policy would be inferior to our present policies, which have allowed us to reduce some kinds of pollution even though the economy has been growing. To have achieved such a reduction in pollution simply by limiting GDP would have required not zero growth, but instead a reduction in GDP.

Thus, as a way of reducing pollution, limiting output would be extraordinarily expensive, yet ineffective. It is like killing a rat by burning your house down. Even if you cure the problem, the side effects are appalling. Better by far to find a cure specifically designed to deal with the problem. If the problem is a rat, get a trap. If the problem is pollution, find a policy that directly reduces it.

unit of output imposes a constant external pollution cost, shown as the short, coloured arrow in Figure 22-1. When it is added to the internal cost borne by producers (the black arrow MC), the result is the tall hollow arrow $MC_S$, the marginal cost of this good to society. $MC_S$ is a constant height above MC because of our assumption of a constant external cost for each unit of output.

External costs cause a misallocation of resources, even if markets are perfectly competitive. Figure 22-2 shows why. MC and $MC_S$ are reproduced from Figure 22-1, and demand $D$ represents this good's marginal benefit—both private and social. $S_1$ shows what firms are willing to supply. This curve measures internal private costs—the only costs that the firms making supply decisions have to face. With demand $D$ and supply $S_1$, the perfectly competitive equilibrium is $E_1$.

For society, $E_1$ is not an efficient outcome because it equalizes marginal social benefit and marginal *private* cost only. An efficient solution requires that marginal social benefit be equal to marginal ***social cost*** $MC_S$. This occurs at $E_2$, at the smaller output $Q_2$. Thus, in a perfectly competitive market, firms produce too much of a polluting good—$Q_1$, rather than the efficient amount $Q_2$. It is efficient to cut back production of this good and use the resources to produce something else instead.

To confirm that $Q_1$ is an inefficient output, note that the benefit from the last unit produced is the hollow bar under the demand curve. However, its cost is even greater, since it includes both its private cost (this same bar) and its external cost shown by the black bar. Hence, this black bar represents the net loss in producing this last unit $Q_1$. Since there is a similar loss in the production of each of the other "excess" units between $Q_2$ and $Q_1$, the total efficiency loss is measured by the grey triangle.

## POLLUTION AND PROPERTY RIGHTS

The conclusion from Figure 22-2 — that in an unregulated industry with polluting firms, competitive markets will not lead to the efficient amount of output—is similar to the conclusion from Figure 21-1 in the previous chapter. In that figure, we showed the efficiency loss that results from the overharvesting that occurs when private firms exploit a common property resource. Just as in Figure 22-2, the efficiency loss in Figure 21-1 exists because there is a

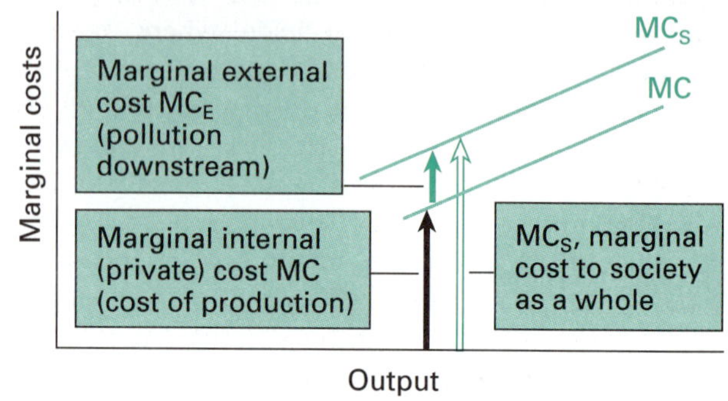


**FIGURE 22-1 With pollution, private and social costs differ.**

The marginal cost to society of a good, shown by the tall arrow $MC_S$ includes both the marginal internal cost MC to the producing firm and the marginal external cost $MC_E$ not borne by the producing firm.

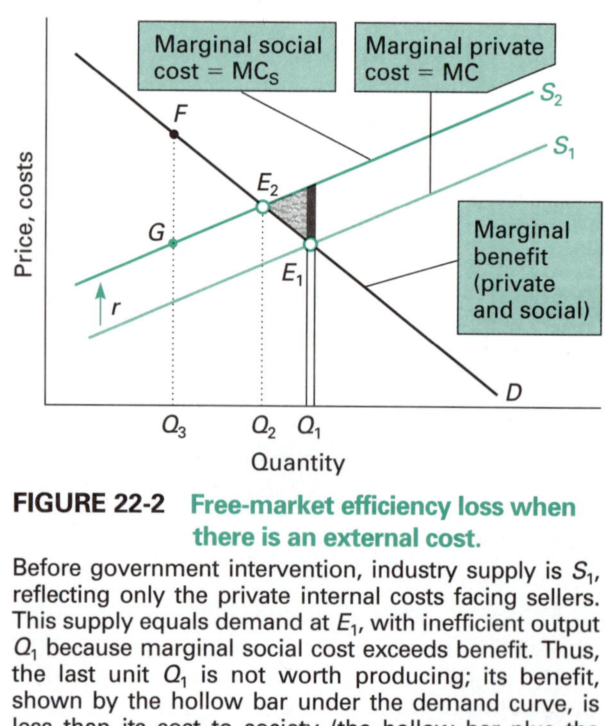


**FIGURE 22-2 Free-market efficiency loss when there is an external cost.**

Before government intervention, industry supply is $S_1$, reflecting only the private internal costs facing sellers. This supply equals demand at $E_1$, with inefficient output $Q_1$ because marginal social cost exceeds benefit. Thus, the last unit $Q_1$ is not worth producing; its benefit, shown by the hollow bar under the demand curve, is less than its cost to society (the hollow bar plus the black bar under the $S_2$ curve). The efficiency loss is the sum of all such bars—that is, the grey triangle.

If the government imposes a tax $r$, producers are forced to face both the internal and external costs, so that their supply curve shifts up from $S_1$ to $S_2$. $D$ and $S_2$ now yield an equilibrium at $E_2$, with output $Q_2$. This is efficient because marginal social cost and benefit are equal.

difference between private and social cost. In the case of a common property resource, the difference arises because the harvesting firm does not take into account the external cost of harvesting the resource now (that is, the opportunity cost consisting of the reduction in the amount of the resource that will be available in the future).

As pointed out in a famous 1960 article by University of Chicago economist Ronald Coase, the problem of ***pollution*** can also be interpreted ***as a common-property problem*** in disguise. If we think of clean air and clean water as important natural resources, we can think of air and water pollution as activities that use up some of these resources. Although the polluting firms do not "harvest" air and water for sale, the clean air and clean water they destroy when they pollute can be thought of as inputs that they use when they produce their products. Because they don't pay for these inputs, their private costs don't reflect the total social cost of production; the external cost of pollution can be thought of as the cost of having less clean air and water for the rest of society.

In an earlier era, when North America's population was small and industrial activity was limited, pollution was not a significant problem: Nature provided such an abundance of clean air and water in relation to the pollution generated by the economy that there was little reason to make any effort to control it. Air and water could safely be treated as resources in unlimited supply. That is, there was no harm in treating them as common-property resources that everyone was free to use as much of as they liked. Although some degree of pollution existed, the abundance of clean air and water meant that it did not have to be considered a significant external cost. In other words, there was no significant difference between the marginal private cost (MC) and the marginal social cost ($MC_S$) such as in Figure 22-2.

However, as population and industrial activity grew, so did pollution. As it did, clean air and water could no longer be treated as resources in unlimited supply. They became scarce goods, with a significant economic value. Consequently, pollution — that is, reduction in the supplies of clean air and water — became costly. The external cost in Figure 22-2 could no longer be neglected: Allowing consumers and firms to use clean air and water as common property has become harmful. (The diagram in Box 22-2 p. 469 illustrates the historical development of the pollution problem.)

In Chapter 21, we saw that if a resource is privately owned, such as timber, the problem of overharvesting was much less likely to exist than in the case of a common-property resource. The reason was that, unlike users of a common-property resource, each individual owner of a privately owned resource does have an incentive to take into account the opportunity cost of having a smaller quantity of the resource tomorrow if more is used today. The problem with a common-property resource is that there is something valuable *over which there are no individual property rights*. It is property held "in common," by all members of society. But, paradoxically, because the resource "belongs to all, it belongs to no one." As long as it is not privately owned by individuals or firms, there can't be a market for it: A common-property resource such as clean drinking water, for example, can't be bought and sold. If no one owns it and charges for its use, it will be used in wasteful ways. For example, the water will be used to carry off pollutants and the river will become a public sewer.

## Property Rights in the Environment?

If the problem of pollution arises because consumers and firms treat the environment like a common-property resource that no one owns, could we not overcome the problem by creating ***private property rights*** in the environment? For example, why not reduce water pollution by providing those living downstream with the property right to clean water? Suppose, for example, that they can sue or charge any polluting firm an amount that compensates them for any damage they incur. Specifically, suppose in Figure 22-2 that those living downstream can charge firms *r* per unit of pollution that these firms emit. Polluting firms are now in the same position as they would be if the government imposed a tax of *r* per unit of output in this industry; the only difference is that they would pay this "tax" to the residents downstream, not to the government. In either case, they have the same incentive to reduce their output from $Q_1$ to $Q_2$, where inefficiency has been eliminated. It seems as though proper assignment of property rights over the water might be one way to deal with the pollution problem.

In his 1960 article, Coase put this argument forward, and went one step further. He argued that, strictly from the point of view of economic efficiency, it does not matter *who* holds the property rights. In our example, it does not matter whether those downstream have the property rights and are compensated $r$ per unit by the upstream polluting firms, or if the upstream firms have the property rights. True, if the upstream firms have the rights, they are free to dump waste into the river. However, those living downstream will be willing to pay them $r$ for each unit that the pollution is reduced. Therefore, the upstream firms will find it profitable to cut back their pollution.[3]

Thus, according to Coase, if the pollution problem arises because there are no property rights, and therefore no market, for the resources such as clean air and water that make up the environment, the solution is to create such property rights. By doing so, you create markets that make it possible for Adam Smith's invisible hand to work to reduce or eliminate inefficiency. Some other form of government intervention is not necessary. All the government needs to do is to establish a market and then let it work.

## The Problem of Transactions Costs

The fundamental insight in Coase's article is that when well-defined property rights exist, it is possible for the parties that are affected by a problem such as pollution—the polluter and those who are hurt by it—to get together and make a deal *that makes both parties better off*. For example, if property rights to the water in a river are held by the downstream residents, they will only allow the firms upstream to pollute the river if the deal they can strike with the firms gives them enough money to make them better off than they would be if they didn't allow the firms to pollute. The firms, on the other hand, will only agree to the deal if it makes *them* better off; that is, if paying for the right to create a certain amount of pollution is cheaper than trying to produce with no pollution. Similarly, if the polluting firms own the property rights to the water, the downstream residents will only pay the firms to reduce pollution to the extent they are better off by doing so (rather than continuing to suffer from unrestricted pollution), and the firms will only agree to the deal if the cost of reducing pollution is less than what they receive for doing it.

However, as a practical solution to the pollution problem, the simple suggestion to "create property rights and let the market work" has one fatal flaw: For many types of pollution, the costs of organizing such deals—the ***transactions costs***—are much too high. For example, how do a thousand residents on a river and the hundreds of polluting firms upstream organize themselves to make and receive payments? To illustrate, suppose the property rights to the water are owned by the polluting upstream firms. How do downstream residents get together to pay these firms to reduce their pollution? Specifically, how do the downstream residents keep some of their members from becoming "free riders," that is, people who are happy to have a payment made — and their pollution thereby reduced — but who won't contribute themselves?[4]

Another problem is: How do downstream residents know which firms are polluting the river and which are not? Moreover, if the downstream residents do reach an agreement with the polluting firms, how do they know that these firms do indeed reduce their pollution? Even attempting to solve these problems may involve substantial transactions costs.

Thus, even though the concept of property rights is helpful in principle, a workable policy of pollution control requires us to pay attention to the practical issues of administrative simplicity and enforcement cost as well.

# CONTROLLING POLLUTION: THE SIMPLE CASE

Because of transactions costs, creating property rights is not always a practical method of controlling pollution and protecting the environment. Other methods must be used instead.

Just as in the case of a common-property resource discussed in the last chapter, a relatively simple way

[3] Those living downstream will be willing to pay this $r$ per unit because this is what pollution costs them; $r$ is, therefore, what they would be willing to pay to get rid of a unit. Moreover, since the polluting firms receive a payment of $r$ per unit for reducing pollution, they will cut back to $Q_2$—for the same reason that they cut back that far in the face of the government's $r$ per-unit tax. (It doesn't matter whether firms are paid $r$ per unit for cutting back, or are taxed $r$ per unit if they do not cut back. In either case they have the same incentive to cut back.)

[4] These problems may be far less serious if the property rights are held, not by the upstream firms but by the downstream residents, and if the payment (fine) to be paid to them by the upstream firms is set by the courts. Polluting firms would then respond to this fine just as they did to the tax in Figure 22-2. In fact, this policy is effectively the same as the pollution tax in that earlier diagram—except in one important respect: The residents downstream, rather than the government, receive the payment from the polluting firms.

for the government to increase efficiency in a case such as that depicted in Figure 22-2 is to levy a per-unit tax $r$ on producers, equal to the marginal external cost (the black bar). Such a tax imposes a cost on producers equal to the cost to others of their pollution. Once again, the tax ***internalizes the externality***: The producer is forced to face the external cost just like the internal cost. As a result of the tax, the supply curve shifts up from $S_1$ to $S_2$; to confirm, recall that supply reflects marginal cost, and this has risen by the amount of the tax that must be paid. The new equilibrium is at $E_2$, where demand and new supply $S_2$ intersect. The new output of $Q_2$ is efficient because marginal benefit equals marginal social cost. Finally, the efficiency gain from this tax policy is the grey triangle, the original efficiency loss that has now been eliminated. In brief, as a result of this tax, society gets a benefit that the market would otherwise not deliver — cleaner water.

Another way of controlling the output of polluting firms is sometimes suggested: Simply set physical limits on the amount of output they are allowed to produce.

However, such limits may or may not help to solve the problem; in fact, if the limit is set at the wrong quantity, it may even be worse than doing nothing at all. For example, suppose output is limited to $Q_3$ in Figure 22-2. As an exercise, you can show that too little will be produced, and there will be a loss to society of triangle $FE_2G$. Since this loss exceeds the original loss, the cure in this case is worse than the original problem. Rather than imposing an arbitrary limit on output, if the cost of pollution can be estimated, a better approach is to impose a tax equal to this cost. Then the correct degree of pressure will be applied to the market to push it back from the initial output $Q_1$ to the efficient $Q_2$.

Of course, if the government sets exactly the right output limit (at $Q_2$ in Figure 22-2), this policy can yield the same efficiency improvement as a tax equal to the external cost. However, it is easy to see that in order to set the output limit at the correct, efficient level, the government needs to know not only the external cost, but also the position of the marginal private cost curve. Thus, one advantage with a tax rather than a physical output limit is that the tax solution requires less information. As you will see later, the issue of finding a method of environmental protection that does not put unrealistic demands on the government's ability to collect information is a very important one.

## CONTROLLING POLLUTION: A MORE COMPLEX CASE

Although a policy of taxing the output of polluting industries can reduce the damage that these industries do to the environment, in many cases it may not be the most practical or least costly method of doing so. For one thing, if the problem is to reduce pollution in a particular airspace — say, over Toronto — or any particular body of water, such as Lake Erie, the problem is not just a single polluting industry, as shown in Figure 22-2, but many. Since different industries generate different amounts of pollution per unit of output, this means that the government has to estimate the "right" tax rates for many industries, not just one. Second, and more importantly, pollution and output are not locked together in the fixed way assumed in Figure 22-2, in which each additional unit of output generates a constant amount of pollution. In the more typical case, the amount of pollution may vary. A good may be produced with a large amount of pollution if wastes are dumped without restriction into the water or air. However, if wastes are treated, or if cleaner fuels are used, there will be less pollution.

Consider a firm that begins to treat its wastes, or uses cleaner but more expensive fuels. This firm reduces pollution, but at a cost. This cost of reducing pollution for all firms in a locality is shown in Figure 22-3 as the curve MCR. ("R" stands for reducing pollution.) It is drawn by first graphing point $Q_1$, the amount of pollution that will occur if it is not restricted in any way. As pollution is cut back, firms move to the *left* up the MCR curve. At first, clean-up costs are low as the easy battles are won; the least expensive ways of reducing pollution are used first. For example, pollution unit $Q_2$ can be eliminated at the low cost shown by the short bar. However, the more pollution is reduced, the higher becomes the cost of further clean-up; that is, the MCR curve becomes higher and higher as firms move to the left in this diagram.

Until the last few decades, there were few restrictions on pollution. Therefore, firms generally dumped pollutants rather than going to the expense of treating them. The result was heavy pollution at $Q_1$. Some of our lakes and rivers became open sewers.

To prevent this, suppose the government wishes to reduce pollution dramatically. Specifically, suppose it wants to cut pollution in half — from $Q_1$ to $Q_3$. Consider three policies that might be used.

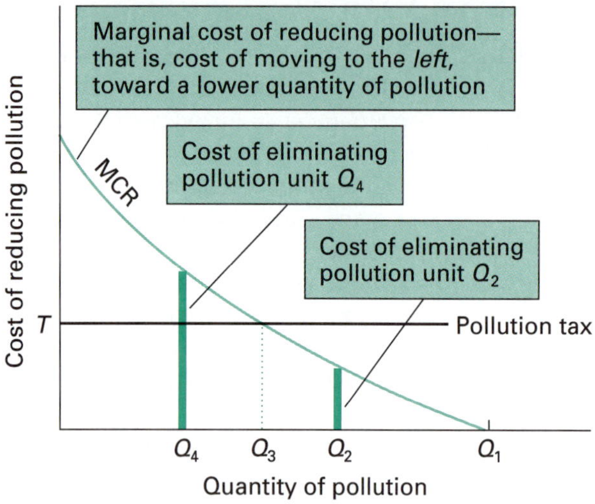


**FIGURE 22-3 The cost of reducing pollution and the effect of a tax.**

If no controls are imposed, the amount of pollution would be $Q_1$. Moving back to the left along MCR, we see the cost of reducing pollution by one more unit—for example, by installing pollution-control equipment. Thus, if pollution has been restricted all the way back to $Q_4$, any further reduction would be at the very high cost shown by the tall bar.

If pollution tax $T$ is imposed, firms voluntarily reduce pollution from $Q_1$ to $Q_3$. Firms to the right of $Q_3$ will stop polluting, because this costs less (for example, the short bar at $Q_2$) than the cost of paying the tax $T$. But firms to the left of $Q_3$ continue to pollute and pay the tax $T$, because this costs less than reducing pollution (the tall bar).

## Option 1. A Pollution Tax

Assume that the government levies an ***effluent fee*** —that is, a tax on each unit of pollution discharged into the environment.

An *effluent fee* is a charge for each unit of a particular kind of pollution (for example, each tonne of sulphur dioxide) that a firm discharges.

Specifically, in Figure 22-3, suppose that tax $T$ is charged for each unit of pollution. Then, firms eliminate pollution in the right-hand tail of the MCR curve, where it costs less to stop polluting (for example, the short bar) than to continue to pollute and pay the tax $T$. However, pollution is reduced only to $Q_3$, where the tax line intersects MCR. To the left of this point, the costs of reducing pollution (the tall bar) are higher than the tax $T$. Thus, in this range, firms pay the tax and continue to pollute.

## Option 2. Command-and-Control: A Physical Limit on the Pollution by Each Firm

Why go to all the trouble of setting the pollution tax in Figure 22-3 when pollution could be cut by the same amount to $Q_3$ by a simple, direct control—specifically, by requiring every firm to cut its emissions by half? The answer is that although this approach would achieve the same reduction in pollution, it would involve heavier clean-up costs.

The reason is that firms *do not all face the same costs in reducing pollution*. With a tax, pollution is cut back by firms that can do so at the lowest cost —that is, by firms to the right of $Q_3$. Firms to the left of $Q_3$ continue to pollute. However, if all firms are required to cut their pollution in half, firms to the left of $Q_3$ must now also participate— at the high cost illustrated by the tall bar.

Therefore, the advantage of a pollution tax is that it "lets the market work." With firms reacting to the tax, pollution is reduced by those firms that can do so in the least expensive way. Thus, society devotes fewer real resources to the clean-up task. The savings can be substantial. Recent estimates suggest that a pollution tax could cost society 70% to 80% less than a policy requiring all firms to reduce pollution by the same fraction.

While economists have long recognized that pollution taxes are more efficient than direct regulation (except for radioactive wastes and other materials that are so toxic that they must be banned outright), North American governments have found it politically difficult to introduce such taxes. As a result, economists and environmental officials have recently been considering a third compromise solution that allows the government to set physical limits on pollution, but also "lets the market work," and hence avoids unnecessarily large clean-up costs.

## Option 3. Physical Limits on Pollution with Trade Allowed in Emissions Permits

Under this third option, the authorities set a specific limit on the amount of pollution that each firm is permitted. For example, in Figure 22-3, each firm is given permits to pollute just half as much as in the past. So far, this is just like option 2. But now a twist is added to let the market work: If a firm to the right of $Q_3$ eliminates all its pollution—rather than just half—it ends up with an "***emissions permit***" which it can use at another location or sell to a firm to the left of $Q_3$. It can be shown that if the firms in Figure 22-3 are perfectly competitive, these permits will sell for price $T$. Therefore, firms have exactly the same incentive $T$ to clean up as under option 1, and the result is exactly the same pattern of low-cost clean-up. Specifically, firms to the right of $Q_3$ gain by selling their permits for $T$ and cleaning up pollution at the low cost shown by the short bar. Firms to the left of $Q_3$ find it cheaper to buy permits costing $T$ and continue to pollute, than to clean up at the high cost shown by the tall bar.[5] Thus, pollution is reduced by those firms to the right of $Q_3$ who can do so at the lowest cost. Therefore, 1 and 3 are equally low-cost options, and are superior to option 2. It is only under option 2, which requires all firms to reduce pollution by a fixed amount, that clean-up involves higher costs, because some of it must be undertaken by firms to the left of $Q_3$. The general principle is this:

> **Pollution can be reduced at lower cost if the government enlists the power of the market. It can change incentives by imposing a tax, or introducing marketable emissions permits and then letting private firms respond. The firms are the ones that know best what their costs are, and thus are best able to select the response that will minimize those costs.**

This, then, is our basic conclusion: Because the command-and-control option 2 does not use the market, it is more costly than the tax option 1 or the emissions-trading option 3 that do use the market. But, in comparing options 1 and 3, which is preferable?

## How Does Option 1 (Effluent Fees) Compare to Option 3 (Emissions Trading)?

These two options differ in several respects.

1. Any error or uncertainty in setting a tax may result in too much pollution. This is particularly true in a period of inflation when a \$1 effluent fee becomes less and less of a deterrent. If such a tax is to remain fully effective, it must be adjusted upward with inflation. However, with emissions trading, inflation raises no such problem; the government can achieve the appropriate reduction in pollution by limiting the number of emissions permits.
2. Businesses prefer emissions trading because it is likely to cost less. With a tax, as in option 1, existing firms lose: Either they have to pay the tax (to the extent that they continue to pollute), or they have to incur the costs necessary to reduce pollution. But with marketable permits under option 3, existing firms need not lose. For example, suppose the government issues free permits to existing firms. In that case, a firm that is able to reduce its own pollution at a relatively low cost may actually gain. Instead of continuing to pollute up to the amount permitted by its allocation of permits, it may be better off reducing its own pollution and selling some of its permits to other firms less able to reduce their pollution. And those firms that continued to pollute would only have to pay for permits if they chose to pollute *more* than allowed by the permits they were given by the government (rather than pay a tax on *all* of their pollution, as in option 1).

However, while the polluting firms clearly prefer this policy of free permits, such a policy is likely to be unpopular with the general public. Why should businesses that have polluted in the past be granted valuable emissions permits, some of which they may sell? In other words, why should some firms be allowed to profit from their past pollution? One way of modifying option 3 to counter this objection would be to charge a price for the permits when they are first issued. While this would not be as favourable to business as giving out the permits free, it would appear more equitable. If there is a charge for permits, this policy becomes very similar to a tax, with the firms being charged in either case for the polluting they do. Nonetheless, there is an important difference: Under option 3, the government retains more direct and precise control over the amount of pollution that actually takes place.

### Tradeable Permits and Property Rights

Earlier in this chapter, we saw that the problem of pollution can be interpreted as arising from the fact

[5] Why is $T$ the equilibrium price for permits? At this price, $Q_3$ is the quantity of permits firms want. This is exactly equal to the $Q_3$ of permits the government supplies.

that there are no property rights in the resources that make up the environment: clean air and water. In the example of a polluted river, we also explained why simply creating property rights in these resources would not be a practical solution: The transactions costs and administrative complexity of any such scheme would be much too high.

By now, you probably recognize that a system of tradeable pollution permits is, in fact, a version of the kind of property rights solution discussed by Coase, but modified so as to make it less difficult to administer. A permit that gives a firm the right to emit a certain amount of a specific pollutant can be interpreted as a permit to "use up" a certain amount of clean air. Therefore, when the government creates property rights in pollution permits, it is indirectly creating property rights in clean air. Moreover, Coase's suggestion that creation of property rights would tend to have a beneficial effect no matter who initially held them applies to pollution permits: The incentive on firms to reduce pollution, given the market price of permits, would be the same whether they had initially been given to the firms free of charge, or initially sold to them by the government.

Thus far, we have assumed that the government has set as its target a reduction in pollution by one-half, to $Q_3$. Why not by a third, or three-quarters, or some other figure?

## How Far Should Pollution Be Reduced?

In Figure 22-4 we reproduce MCR from Figure 22-3 and also show MCP, the marginal cost of pollution to society. These two curves should not be confused. MCR is the cost of *reducing* pollution—for example, the cost of pollution-control equipment. On the other hand, MCP is the cost of *having* pollution—that is, the cost to us of foul air and contaminated water. As long as there is only a small amount of pollution—at, say, $Q_4$—the marginal cost of having this pollution (the height of MCP) is low. The first units of waste that are dumped into a stream generally break down and are absorbed by the environment. Similarly, the smoke from a campfire in a deserted area has no perceptible effect on the air. However, as pollution builds up, additional emissions become increasingly noxious and damaging; that is, as we move to the right in this diagram, the MCP curve rises.

With these two curves, the best target is to reduce pollution to point $Q_3$, where MCP = MCR. Any other quantity is less desirable, as we can illustrate with the case where pollution is left completely uncontrolled and consequently reaches $Q_1$. For all units of pollution to the right of $Q_3$, MCP is greater than MCR, so it is a mistake to let this pollution continue. To evaluate the social cost of this mistake, consider one typical unit of this excess pollution, say unit $Q_2$. The cost of eliminating this unit of pollution is the height of the MCR curve, as shown by the hollow bar. This is less than the cost of letting this pollution continue (the height of the MCP curve, as shown by both the hollow bar and the black bar). Therefore, the net cost of allowing this unit to continue is the black bar. If we sum the similar costs on all such units through the range $Q_3$ to $Q_1$, the result is the triangular grey area—the loss to society from allowing pollution to continue at its uncontrolled level of $Q_1$ rather than limiting it to $Q_3$.

On the other hand, a policy of cutting pollution back to the left of $Q_3$ also causes a loss. For example, if pollution is reduced to $Q_4$, the cost of the last unit is just the height of the MCP curve above $Q_4$. However, this last unit is exceedingly costly to eliminate (the height of the MCR curve). Eliminating it is, therefore, a mistake. We conclude that the best target, $Q_3$ — ***the optimal amount of pollution*** — can be found only by taking into account both the cost MCP of having pollution, and the cost MCR of reducing it.

Unfortunately, in practice it is not that easy to estimate the target $Q_3$ because of the difficulties in estimating MCP and MCR. For example, in trying to estimate the marginal cost of pollution MCP, we sim-

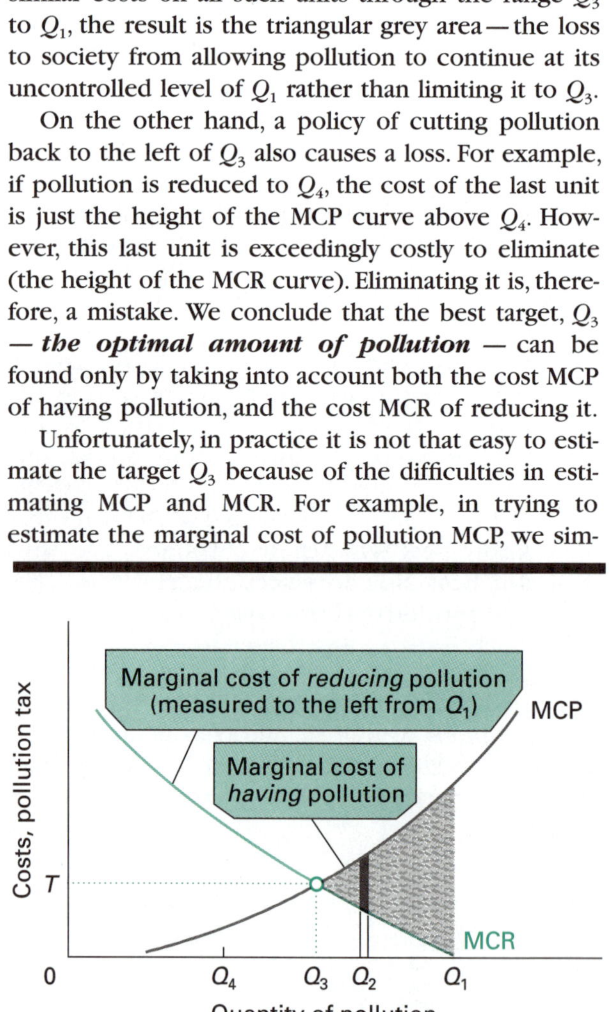


**FIGURE 22-4 Efficiency loss from leaving pollution uncontrolled.**

MCR is reproduced from Figure 22-3. We also show MCP, the environmental cost of additional units of pollution. The best target is to restrict pollution to $Q_3$, where MCR = MCP.

## TOOLS AND TECHNIQUES — BOX 22-2
## Pollution Control: An Historical Perspective

Why are we so concerned now with pollution, while a few decades ago we were almost totally unconcerned? Is the problem worse, or have we just awakened? If it is getting worse, what can we expect 20 or 30 years from now?

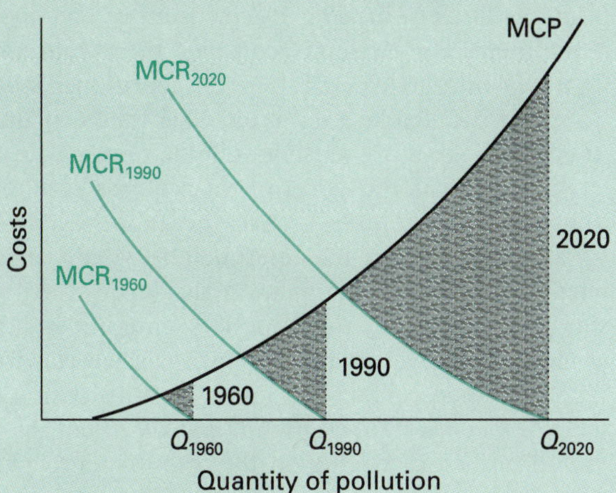


**Pollution in perspective.**
Without controls, unrestricted pollution would have increased (with growing GDP) from $Q_{1960}$ to $Q_{1990}$, and eventually to $Q_{2020}$. The loss to society of leaving pollution unchecked in each of these years would have been the rapidly growing set of triangles marked 1960, 1990, and 2020.

The figure illustrates how the MCR curve shifts to the right as the economy grows. $MCR_{1960}$ cuts the baseline at $Q_{1960}$, the level of pollution that would have occurred had it been left completely unrestricted at that early date. Similarly, the other MCR curves indicate uncontrolled pollution levels $Q_{1990}$ and $Q_{2020}$ at those later dates. The grey triangle marked 1990 shows the loss from a policy of leaving pollution uncontrolled at that time. It is defined just like the grey triangle in Figure 22-4.

Now consider our situation in 1960. At that time, there were fewer factories clustered along any river and fewer cars spewing fumes into the air. Therefore, pollution was less severe. The result of leaving pollution uncontrolled was the relatively small loss shown as the grey triangle marked 1960. In those days, people did not think much about this problem.

Now let us look ahead to the future, to the year 2020. If industrial activity keeps growing, unrestricted pollution would grow to $Q_{2020}$, and the loss from failing to deal with it would be the very large grey triangle 2020. There are several reasons this loss builds up so rapidly. First, as output grows, so too does the unrestricted pollution level, from $Q_{1960}$ to $Q_{1990}$ to $Q_{2020}$. Second, pollution may grow even faster, since more powerful chemicals and other materials may be used as technology changes. Thus, MCR shifts rapidly to the right.

We emphasize that the figure is not a prediction of the future; it is merely a picture of what the future would have looked like *if* we had not taken action—or what it will look like *if* we give up our efforts to control pollution. In this respect, pollution is similar to the public health problem in the nineteenth century. With the increase in urban population, lack of adequate sanitation produced a growing health problem that could equally well have been described by a diagram like the one in this box. The response to this challenge was the public health programs that prevented the "prophecy" in such a diagram from coming true. Similarly, pollution-control legislation can help to ensure that the prophecy in this figure does not come true.

ply do not know with any precision how dangerous many pollutants really are. Furthermore, there are many pollutants, and the damage that any one pollutant does may depend on the presence of other types. For example, asbestos in the air is more likely to cause cancer when other pollutants are present or when people smoke. Similarly, it may not be easy for the government to estimate MCR, the marginal cost of reducing pollution. Estimation of this cost requires detailed knowledge about the production processes of the polluting firms, and the cost of shifting to less-polluting production methods. In this regard, it is interesting to note an additional advantage of tradeable pollution permits. By observing the market price of these permits, the government obtains an estimate of the marginal cost of reducing pollution. To see this, note that when these permits can be bought and sold, polluting firms would keep bidding up the price of permits as long as this price was less than the marginal cost to them of reducing pollution by one more unit. The price of permits would thus rise until it was roughly equal to the marginal cost of reducing pollution by one more unit in every polluting firm.

## An Alternative Policy? Subsidizing Pollution-control Equipment

In the pulp and paper industry, one of the major polluters in Canada, the federal government and the provincial governments in Ontario and Quebec have programs under which they fund capital expenditures for modernization of the industry's anti-pollution equipment. Provincial governments also subsidize pollution-control equipment by paying a large share of the cost of municipal sewage treatment facilities. And, as we have seen, the federal government provides subsidies in the form of tax reductions to private firms that install pollution-control equipment. How effective are these kinds of subsidy schemes as a way of controlling pollution?

In the first place, such subsidies are effective only if the equipment that is installed does a good job of reducing pollution. One of the problems has been that, after the government subsidizes the new equipment, it may pay little or no attention to how efficiently it is operated — that is, how effectively it reduces pollution.

The second problem is that this form of subsidy puts all the emphasis on ***end-of-pipe treatment*** — that is, on the reduction of pollution as it is about to be discharged into the environment. However, if a subsidy is justified for end-of-pipe treatment, it should be similarly justified for *any* reduction in pollution, regardless of how it may be achieved — for example, by the use of less powerful chemicals or cleaner fuels. Such alternatives may be far less costly.

It may be concluded, therefore, that an end-of-pipe subsidy is too narrow an attack on the problem. Firms may not use the lowest-cost method to control pollution but, instead, may switch to the end-of-pipe method solely because it is subsidized. The principle is a simple one. It is better to tell firms *what* to do than to give them detailed instructions on *how* to do it. A regulation made as far back as the eighteenth century B.C. illustrates this principle. Hammurabi, King of Babylonia, set a very simple building code. If a house collapsed and killed an occupant, the builder was put to death. All details for meeting this regulation were left to the builder.

An even narrower approach is a regulation that requires firms to install a *specific kind* of end-of-pipe equipment. For example, consider the requirement that coal-burning electrical utilities install "scrubbers" to clean the smoke they emit. This tends to divert them from the more sensible solution of using cleaner coal; as long as the government requires scrubbers, there is no incentive to use the more expensive, cleaner fuel. In turn, the continued heavy use of dirty coal creates a new problem in the form of a liquid sludge generated by the scrubbers. Thus, reducing air pollution creates water pollution. Again we conclude: The lowest-cost policy is to provide firms with a sufficient incentive to clean up, and let them, in the pursuit of profit, decide on the least expensive *way* of doing it.

# POLLUTION CONTROL IN CANADA: Which Option Does the Government Use?

Surprisingly, the provincial governments in Canada, which are responsible for enforcing our anti-pollution legislation, rely principally on regulatory controls rather than letting the market work with a pollution tax, or tradeable pollution permits. Specific pollution limits are set and enforced for individual firms — a policy, as already noted, that involves large, unnecessary clean-up costs.

Moreover, there is a second problem. Air and water standards are set with little regard for the cost of reducing pollution. Instead, the regulators tend to concentrate on what is *technologically* possible given existing pollution-control knowledge, and some of these measures are extremely expensive. Furthermore, the federal specifications for maximum allowable rates of pollution emission by a plant, which are supposed to be enforced by the provinces, are the same for *all* areas of Canada. The purpose of this uniformity is to discourage a particular province from relaxing its emission standards in order to attract new industry. But, as we have seen, uniform emission standards may be inefficient: They mean that the maximum permissible amount of pollution is the same in Southern Ontario (where air quality is already relatively low because there are many polluting industries) and in Saskatchewan (which still has relatively clean air). This blocks one avenue for reducing the overall pollution problem, namely shifting firms from overloaded, highly polluted areas into regions with low pollution levels (where at least *some* of the pollutants could be "washed away" by natural processes).

Moreover, because some pollution regulations have been severe, many firms have been in violation of air or water standards. Because firms have thought it possible to persuade the governments to be more lenient, they have been expending more of their efforts in fighting the regulations in private and public battles with provincial governments than in trying to find a pollution cure. And, sometimes, the firms have had some success. A classic case is the continuing fight between INCO, the International Nickel Corporation in Sudbury, Ontario, and the Ontario Ministry of the Environment. In 1970, INCO (which is North America's largest single source of sulphur dioxide emission) was ordered to gradually reduce its emissions so that by 1978 they would be no more than 15% of the 1970 levels. During the 1970s, INCO repeatedly sought and obtained relaxation of the standards and extensions of the deadline. As a result, emission levels in 1980 were still about 65% of the 1970 level, and a new ministry guideline was set allowing an emission level for 1982 of 30% (rather than the original 15%) of 1970 levels. Such flip-flops have tended, at a minimum, to erode the credibility of the controls. And they have created the impression that standards have not been set in an even-handed way, but instead have been defined by governments under pressure to make last-minute changes. (Another form of pollution policy that holds great promise is recycling, discussed in Box 22-3.)

## POLLUTION AS A SOURCE OF INTERPROVINCIAL AND INTERNATIONAL CONFLICT

An additional problem arises when pollution spills over political boundaries. For example, a large part of the sulphur dioxide emissions from coal-fired generating stations in Ontario ends up polluting the air over Quebec. Therefore, while most of the *costs* of stricter emission controls will be borne by people in Ontario, a large part of the *benefits* will accrue to people outside the province. Because of this, there may be a need for *federal* legislation to make sure that the government of Ontario takes into account the interests of Quebec residents as well as residents of Ontario when it sets provincial emission standards.

An even more perplexing problem arises when pollution spills over *international* boundaries. For example, chemical pollution of the Great Lakes hurts both Canadians and Americans. If the two governments take account only of the benefits *to their own citizens*, the result will be an inefficiently high level of pollution.

To see the problem arising from this kind of ***transboundary pollution***, consider Figure 22-5, which is similar to Figure 22-4; however, the curve MCR now refers to the marginal cost *to Canadian firms* of reducing pollution, and MCP represents the marginal cost *to Canadians* of having more pollution. The environmental costs that Canadian polluters impose

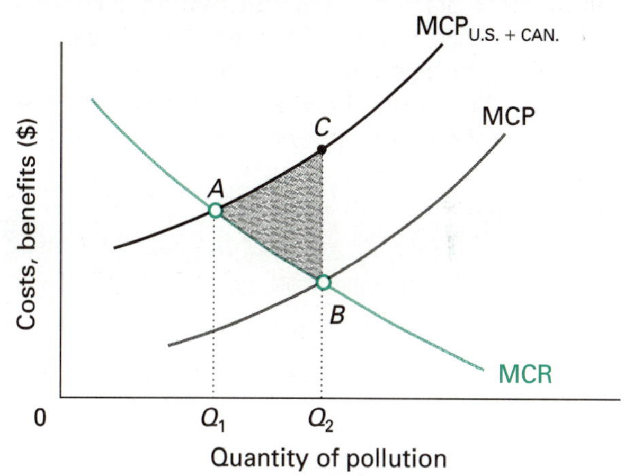


**FIGURE 22-5 The efficiency loss when pollution crosses boundaries.**

This figure is similar to Figure 22-4, except that the marginal cost of having additional pollution from Canadian sources (moving to the right) is borne partly by Canadian residents (MCP), and partly by U.S. residents. The marginal cost of having pollution *taking account of the damage to both countries' residents*, is the curve labelled $MCP_{U.S.+CAN.}$.

If Canadian authorities only take account of the damage to Canadian residents, they will only reduce pollution to $Q_2$. From the viewpoint of both countries together, this leaves an efficiency loss of grey triangle *ABC*. If joint action is possible, pollution will be cut back to $Q_1$, eliminating this efficiency loss.

## APPLICATIONS AND ILLUSTRATIONS BOX 22-3

### Recycling

One of the most promising ways to deal with pollution is to recycle wastes rather than dump them into the environment. Beer cans do not deface the landscape if they are reprocessed and used again. Wastes that are recycled into the production process do not foul our rivers.

The figure illustrates the benefits from recycling by using the concept of material balances. On the left, production draws in the materials it requires. Included are both new materials drawn up through "pipe" *a*, and recycled materials returned to the production process through pipe *c*. These materials pass through the production/consumption process and reappear in different form as "total materials out" on the right side of the diagram. Some of these leftover materials — such as chemical wastes — are the result of production. Others — like beer cans — are residuals from consumption.

This figure provides a framework for thinking about two important issues:

1. As our economic system expands, strains on the environment increase, both because more resources are drawn up through pipe *a*, and because more pollutants are dumped back into the environment through pipe *b*.
2. The pollution problem can be reduced by more recycling, that is, by directing more of the leftover material on the right into pipe *c* rather than pipe *b*. Moreover, any success on this score will provide a further benefit. The more our production/consumption requirements on the left can be satisfied by materials recycled through pipe *c*, the fewer natural resources will have to be drawn from the environment through pipe *a*.

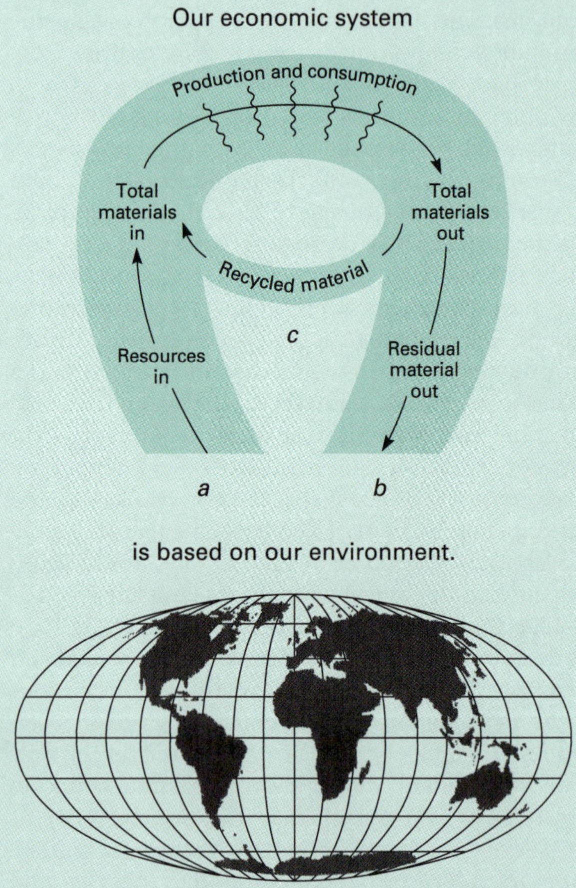


**Recycling and the environment.**
The economic system extracts resources through pipe *a* from the environment, and returns residuals back to it through pipe *b*. Recycling—that is, diverting materials from pipe *b* to pipe *c*—provides two benefits: It reduces environmental damage through pipe *b*, and reduces the depletion of natural resources through pipe *a*.

Although the basic idea is a sensible one, however, turning it into practice is not always easy. In recent years, recycling in the form of Blue Box programs to collect and recycle paper, plastic, glass, and metal have become popular across Canada. The objective of the legislation that created these programs was to reduce the amount of garbage being disposed of in landfills. To that extent, they have worked. However, evidence from Toronto

**BOX 22-3 continued**

suggests that the cost of Blue Box collection is between $200 and $300 per tonne whereas regular garbage collection costs about $50 per tonne. When the revenues raised from selling recycled materials are counted in, the net cost of collecting Blue Boxes is $193 per tonne. Do Blue Box programs make economic sense? There are a number of arguments against them.

First, they do not reduce the amount of garbage households throw out, which would seem to be a worthwhile and more far-reaching objective. The reason is that Blue Box collection is free, as is regular garbage collection in most Canadian towns and cities. (Although people pay for both out of their property taxes, the price of putting out an extra bag of garbage is zero.) That is, there is no incentive to reduce the amount of garbage they produce. User fees, however, would accomplish this as they have in cities like Seattle and Bonn, among others. With the average Ontario resident putting out 2.5 kilograms of garbage daily in 1992, a reduction in waste rather than a splitting of it between regular garbage and Blue Boxes may be a more appropriate objective.

Second, the materials collected in Blue Boxes would not create the same problems in landfills as does regular garbage. Metal cans and bottles, for instance, do not leach into the soil. That is, Blue Box programs deal with the wrong type of garbage, not the kind that causes soil pollution. Rather than recycle these non-toxic materials at great expense, it makes more sense to dispose of them in separate landfills at a lower cost to society.

Third, because these recycling programs are subsidized, they have a distortionary impact on markets. By causing the prices of recycled commodities to be lower than the opportunity cost to society of producing them, they encourage excess consumption of them, thus creating more garbage than otherwise.

Although Blue Box programs are popular, perhaps because they cause people to feel as if they are playing a part in protecting the environment, it would make more sense to legislate user fees for garbage collection and to employ the resources currently being consumed by these programs to undertake initiatives to deal with potentially more dangerous environmental problems.

on American citizens is reflected by the vertical distance between the curve $MCP_{U.S.+Can.}$ and MCP. Taking account of the marginal cost of pollution to both Canadians and Americans, efficiency would require cutting pollution back to $Q_1$. However, if the Canadian government only worries about the costs and benefits to Canadians, it will only aim for point $Q_2$, where the marginal cost of additional pollution *to Canadian citizens* equals the marginal cost of reducing pollution. For the same reason, American regulators may fail to take into account the benefits to Canadians of reduced pollution when they set standards for polluting firms on the U.S. side of the border. As a result of this ***international externality***, both countries will make inadequate efforts to protect the environment.

To overcome this problem, Canada and the United States have negotiated a mutual agreement that specifies limits on allowable effluent discharges from either country. However, these negotiations have not always been smooth. The acid rain problem is a particularly difficult case. While some of Quebec's acid rain problem results from sulphur dioxide emissions in Ontario, most of the acid rain throughout Canada originates with sulphur dioxide emissions in the United States, particularly from coal-burning electric-power plants in the U.S. Midwest. At the same time, little of the damage to the U.S. environment originates in Canada. Thus, in the words of Bruce Forster, formerly of the University of Guelph, the acid rain problem is an "unidirectional international externality." This makes Canada's position in negotiating with the United States very difficult: In attempting to improve the North American environment, we are asking the United States to join us in setting clean-up rules under which Canada will have to bear a relatively small proportion of the cost, but will enjoy a larger proportion of the benefits.

Partly as a result of this problem, the actual negotiations at first went very slowly. In resisting Canadian demands for more direct action, the United States tended to put the burden of proof on Canada: If we expected the Americans to undertake the clean-up for our benefit, the Americans argued, we must first prove to them that they were, in fact, the source of the problem. This has been difficult or even impossible to do because relatively little is known about the extent to which emissions are transferred over long distances (such as from the U.S. Midwest to Canada). The U.S. position on acid rain has infuriated Canadian environmentalists. In their view, there is enough scientific evidence (based in part on computerized models of atmospheric transfer of pollutants) to place the blame squarely on U.S. sources.

Toward the end of the 1980s, American attitudes gradually changed. There were many reasons. One factor was the growing awareness in the United States of the seriousness of the air pollution problem. In 1985, following a suit brought by the conservationist Sierra Club and the governments of several Northeastern states (which also suffer acid rain damage), a U.S. judge ruled that the U.S. Environmental Protection Agency must order Midwestern states to reduce their sulphur dioxide emissions. Moreover, President Bush (who was much more sympathetic to environmental protection than his predecessor Ronald Reagan) was anxious to maintain good relations with Canada during the politically sensitive period when the Canada/United States Free Trade Agreement was being negotiated.

In the end, Bush was able to get a comprehensive package of anti-pollution measures through Congress. With these measures, the flow of acid-rain-causing pollutants from the United States to Canada will be cut by 50% by the year 2000. Following a similar commitment by Canada (which is trying to reach a 50% pollution reduction target by 1994), a clean-air treaty was signed in Ottawa in 1991. (Interestingly, the package that was passed in the United States relies to a considerable extent on tradeable emissions permits of the type discussed earlier.)

In the twenty-first century, carbon dioxide may raise an even greater international problem than acid rain. If it is true, as many scientists believe, that the burning of fossil fuels (oil, coal, and natural gas) is causing an increase in the "greenhouse effect," then the Earth's average temperature may increase by several degrees in the next few decades. This, in turn, could cause drought to occur with increasing frequency in areas that currently receive enough rainfall to support productive agriculture, and the water level in the world's oceans may rise as the polar ice caps melt. To prevent this outcome, a massive conversion from fossil fuels to other forms of energy may be necessary. Huge reforestation projects may also be needed to replace the tropical forests that are now being cut down — forests that have helped to keep the greenhouse effect under control in the past.

Such actions would require an international agreement of unprecedented scope, along with a mechanism for ensuring against cheating. In economic terms, this could be viewed as creating a cartel in the collective interests of all its members. Moreover, it would be a "good cartel" because it would also be acting in the interests of the world as a whole. (Compare this with a standard cartel, such as OPEC, that acts in the interests of its members but not in the interests of the world as a whole.) The cartel would have to have strong enforcement powers because there would be an incentive to cheat; as long as all other countries are cleaning up the world's atmosphere, a small country may try to save costs by avoiding its clean-up responsibilities.

It is far from clear how such an agreement could be negotiated. Finding a way to do this may become one of the major challenges facing the human race in the future.

## ENERGY AND THE ENVIRONMENT

As we saw in the previous chapter, one of the most important natural resources in the global economy is oil. As an efficient and plentiful source of energy, oil has played a fundamental role in powering the industrial development in many countries in the twentieth century. However, the rapid increase in the price of oil in the mid-1970s, and the crises in oil-importing countries when international oil supplies were disrupted, lent force to the argument that we should start preparing for the possibility that in the future, oil might become much less plentiful. To do so, we should strive to further develop existing and potential alternative sources of energy.

There are two major questions to ask about any alternative energy source: (1) What are its costs of production? and (2) What costs does it impose on the environment? The second question has been very important in the case of coal and nuclear energy:

Environmental (or external) costs have deterred the development of these otherwise promising sources of energy.

## Natural Gas

Although burning natural gas produces some carbon dioxide, its overall environmental costs are relatively low. It produces much less air pollution than either coal or oil. Unlike nuclear power, it involves no safety risk or disposal problem. Unlike coal, its extraction from the ground does little damage to the environment.

Fortunately, Canada has large reserves of natural gas, principally in Alberta and British Columbia. (Conventional *oil* reserves in Alberta have been falling steadily, as extraction has outstripped new discoveries. But Alberta's *total* energy reserves have not been falling, because of large new gas discoveries.) The policies in the National Energy Program in the 1970s, which encouraged users to switch to natural gas from other sources of energy, increased Canadian consumption of natural gas. Nevertheless, estimates by the National Energy Board indicate that our gas reserves in the Western provinces are large enough to meet increased Canadian demand and leave room for substantial exports to the United States. In addition, there have been recent finds of natural gas in frontier areas, such as the Arctic Islands and off the coast of Newfoundland; thus, many analysts believe that our reserves will be large enough for our domestic requirements well into the twenty-first century.

## Coal

In the 1970s and early 1980s, the increased price of oil placed coal in a strong position for a comeback from its declining twentieth-century role as an energy source. However, coal's growth has been disappointing because of the problems encountered in both mining and burning it.

### 1. Problems in Mining

Underground mining, as in our Cape Breton coal industry, involves many problems including acid drainage and the risk of black lung disease or fatal accidents underground. Strip mining, which is done mainly in the Western provinces, involves a different problem: It leaves land scarred and unproductive as has happened in the past in southern Saskatchewan. To avoid this, coal producers are now required—often at substantial cost—to reclaim and reconstruct the landscape.

### 2. Problems in Burning Coal in Power Plants

The principal pollutant when coal is burned is sulphur dioxide, which is emitted into the air and eventually comes down in the acid rain that has destroyed life in thousands of lakes in North America and Europe. Moreover, like oil, coal is a major contributor to the carbon dioxide emissions that are causing the greenhouse effect.

## Fighting the Greenhouse Effect: A Carbon Tax?

In the 1990s, as concerns over the greenhouse effect have come to the forefront, there has been increasing support for a simple but potentially effective way of reducing those forms of pollution that contribute most significantly to global warning. Specifically, since the most important of the greenhouse gases is carbon dioxide, environmentalists have argued for a ***carbon tax*** under which different kinds of carbon-based fuels would be taxed, at the point of production, in proportion to the amount of carbon they contain. (For example, under one proposal coal would be taxed at $18 per tonne, while natural gas would be taxed at 48¢ per thousand cubic feet.[6])

A carbon tax would have two kinds of incentive effects. First, by raising the cost of all types of fossil fuels (oil, coal, and natural gas), it would create an added incentive on individuals and firms to reduce their consumption of energy; for the same reason, it would encourage the use of alternative energy sources such as hydroelectricity and nuclear power. Second, it would encourage substitution among different kinds of fossil fuel. In particular, it would penalize coal (which produces a large amount of carbon dioxide per unit of energy it generates), and favour natural gas. (Under a proposal introduced in the U.S. Congress, a tax rate of $30 per tonne of carbon would raise the price of coal by some 80% above current levels, while the price of natural gas would rise by only 20%.)

In comparison with a system of tradeable emissions permits, a carbon tax has the disadvantage that

[6] Roger C. Dower and Mary Beth Zimmerman, *The Right Climate for Carbon Taxes: Creating Economic Incentives to Protect the Atmosphere* (Washington: World Resources Institute, 1992), p. 11.

it does not enable the government to precisely control the amount of pollution that will be emitted. Moreover, it does not encourage the development of technology to reduce the amount of pollution per unit of fuel burned.

However, a carbon tax has one overwhelming advantage. Because the tax would be collected at the point of production, it would be relatively cheap to administer. Furthermore, it would indirectly affect *all* users of fossil fuels, including motorists who burn gas in their cars and homeowners and landlords who burn oil and natural gas for residential heating. If a system of emissions permits were to be used instead, it would be prohibitively expensive to include these users.

As usual, it is difficult to predict if and when a carbon tax will be implemented. Many people continue to believe that the fear of the greenhouse effect is exaggerated, and powerful producer interest groups oppose the tax solution. Nevertheless, because it looks like such a simple and effective idea (and because it would generate substantial revenue for cash-strapped governments), it will almost certainly be widely debated in the 1990s.

## Hydroelectric Power

Hydro power has several advantages: It is perfectly clean and indefinitely renewable. Its only disadvantages are the high initial costs, and its environmental effect. Large hydro projects generally require large dams that change the natural flow of rivers and may put valuable land under water. True, the environmental impact may affect relatively few people if the hydro development is in a wilderness region far from densely populated areas. (An example is the large James Bay project in northern Quebec.) But when the power stations are located in remote wilderness areas, there are high costs of transmitting the power to the distant centres of population. Nevertheless, as the price of energy rises, the capacity to increase Canadian hydro power production through such projects is still there. Some additional hydro power can be produced on a more modest scale by using small dams that have already been built or by exploiting more intensively the rivers close to population centres.

## Nuclear Power

While our capacity to produce nuclear power is increasing, the growth of this form of energy production in the 1970s fell considerably short of earlier expectations. When the rapid expansion of nuclear power began in the mid-1960s, it was hailed as the cheapest of all sources of energy, and — in response to OPEC — the key to reducing North American dependence on offshore oil imports. Yet, by 1990, nuclear power still produced only a small fraction of our energy needs.

The relatively slow growth reflected unexpectedly high plant costs, tough regulations, and some public opposition that became much stronger after the Three Mile Island (3MI) accident near Harrisburg, Pennsylvania, in 1979 and the even more serious accident at Chernobyl in the Soviet Union in 1986. Another concern is: Will a worldwide use of nuclear power contribute to the proliferation of nuclear weapons? And what will we do with nuclear wastes?

Increasingly, the hope that nuclear power will provide a virtually inexhaustible source of energy has been centred on nuclear fusion. Whereas present-day fission splits atoms apart, fusion joins atoms together in a controlled, repeated version of what happens in an uncontrolled way when a hydrogen bomb explodes. It is a miniature copy of what is happening all the time in the sun.

While fusion releases enormous heat, the problem is that it requires enormous heat to accomplish. The first big milestone to watch for in future fusion research is the ***energy break-even point***, where the output of heat energy released by fusion exceeds the input of heat needed to cause the fusion. At this point the process will be able, on balance, to create energy. But that energy will be extremely expensive at first. Therefore, the next step to watch for will be the ***economic break-even point***, where energy output exceeds energy input by enough to make nuclear fusion economically competitive with other forms of energy. (In 1989, there was great excitement for a time after two chemists at the University of Utah held a press conference to announce that they had succeeded in producing a fusion reaction at room temperature. Their announcement held out the hope that it would soon be possible to produce a limitless supply of low-cost energy with virtually no environmental effects. However, other scientists reported that they had been unable to reproduce these results, and it was questioned whether a fusion reaction had, indeed, taken place.)

If and when scientists succeed in developing some form of fusion to the economic break-even point, it would offer great advantages over fission because it would have less external cost. Fusion would be safe, with very little radioactive waste from the fusion process itself; however, there could be waste from the materials surrounding and containing the process, and "heat pollution" could be a problem. But fusion is still a long way off; the best estimate is that it will not become economic until sometime in the next century. In looking ahead along the uncertain path to fusion, we should remember: Thirty years ago there was great optimism about nuclear fission.

## HOW DO WE PROTECT THE ENVIRONMENT?: CONCLUDING OBSERVATIONS

Issues of environmental protection will continue to generate controversy in the 1990s, both at the international level and within Canada. Regulatory authorities will be pressured by environmentalists because they are too lenient and by business because they are too harsh. The continued conflict between government and business in this area provides a further reason for the government to impose fewer of its own regulations and to rely more on the marketplace—that is, replace detailed regulations with a market-oriented system of incentives that requires business to worry about the details. In other words, the government should be spending more of its effort in designing and building "better dams to control pollution" (such as tax incentives or marketable permit systems) and less on "putting a regulatory finger into every leak."

But the biggest advantage of relying on the marketplace is that it allows pollution to be reduced at lower cost. To put the point a different way: It will allow us to use any given percentage of GDP to make far greater reductions in pollution. This is of critical importance, since we are likely to face escalating costs of reducing pollution in the future.

In our criticisms of the government for not always using the most effective pollution-control method, we should not lose perspective. Control should be improved, yes; but relaxed, no. It is important to keep in mind the question, "Where would we be without an agency such as Environment Canada?"

## KEY POINTS

1. Pollution is an example of an external cost—a cost that is borne not by the buyer or seller of a product, but by a third party.
2. Under provincial laws to protect the environment, governments have imposed limits on the physical amounts of pollutants firms can release into our air or water. However, there are two alternative market-oriented systems of control that are more efficient: (a) a tax on polluters or (b) marketable emissions permits. Both are designed to encourage the reduction in pollution by those firms that can do so at the lowest cost. In the United States, authorities have recently been turning to more market-oriented systems.
3. Either a marketable permit system or a tax is superior to another government policy that has been used: subsidizing firms or municipalities for installing pollution-reducing equipment. Because such an "end-of-pipe" subsidy is too narrow an approach to the problem, opportunities to reduce pollution in less costly ways may be missed.
4. Pollution policy is sometimes complicated because pollution moves across political boundaries; the problem becomes especially severe when it crosses an international boundary. Two of the most critical pollution problems in Canada, acid rain and the chemical pollution of the Great Lakes, are affected by transboundary pollution flows; so is the global "greenhouse effect."
5. One of the most difficult future challenges will be to create a "good cartel" whereby each country will act to reduce pollution in the collective interest of improving the environment of all countries. But strong controls will be necessary to prevent member countries from cheating, that is, to prevent countries from cutting corners as they impose costly clean-up measures.
6. To reduce emissions of carbon dioxide, the most important of the "greenhouse gases," a carbon tax has been proposed. A carbon tax would encourage substitution of relatively clean forms of energy (such as natural gas and hydroelectric power) for coal and oil, and the development of other promising sources of energy such as nuclear fusion.

## KEY TERMS

**external cost**
**internal (private) cost**
**social cost**
**pollution as a common-property problem**
**private property rights**
**transactions costs**
**internalizing an externality**
**effluent fee**
**tradeable emissions permits**
**optimal amount of pollution**
**end-of-pipe treatment**
**transboundary pollution**
**international externalities**
**carbon tax**
**energy break-even point**
**economic break-even point**

## PROBLEMS

22-1. If property rights are clearly established, Adam Smith's invisible hand can, in principle, work to eliminate the inefficiency associated with unpriced pollution. (What is the nature of this inefficiency?) The distribution of gains and losses will, however, differ depending on whether the property rights are assigned to the polluter or the pollutee. Explain (using diagrams similar to either Figure 22-2 or Figure 22-3).

22-2. As an alternative to taxing polluters, equivalent efficiency gains may be obtained by subsidizing them to reduce pollution to the efficient level. Analyse this policy option.

22-3. Is it a rational policy goal to seek to eliminate pollution?

22-4. Assess the policy of closing down all polluting firms in a city when the "pollution index" rises above a given level.

22-5. What would you expect to happen to the price of oil if scientists were to announce that the economic break-even point for nuclear fusion had been achieved? In your answer, explain what would happen to the reservation price of oil producers. Would your answer change if scientists announced only that the energy break-even point had been achieved? If so, explain why.

22-6. We have seen that the target rate of pollution is not zero. Do you think that the target rate of crime should be zero? In other words, do you think we should expand crime prevention and hire police until the crime rate is driven toward zero?

CHAPTER

# 23 PUBLIC GOODS AND PUBLIC CHOICE

*Government is a contrivance of human wisdom to provide for human wants.*

*Edmund Burke*

A lighthouse stands at the edge of the rocks, throwing out a beacon to warn ships against disaster. For the ship's captain, crew and passengers, it provides a lifesaving service. Yet even with a role this important, that beam of light cannot be delivered by a free market. Instead, it must be provided by the government.

This is the paradox that will be explained in this chapter: Why can't such an essential service be provided by the same free market that does manage to deliver millions of other products, including such services as psychiatric advice for dogs and cats? What is so special about a lighthouse? Similarly, what is so special about some of the other services the government provides? For example, the government hires the police that patrol our streets. It appoints the judges that preside over our courts. It trains the soldiers who protect us and purchases the military equipment they use. Why does a free market fail in such cases, leaving these goods and services to be delivered by the government?

In the study of such products, it will become evident that externalities are once again the key. However, the kind of externalities that are important now are not external costs, such as pollution, but rather "external or spillover benefits" such as the benefits neighbours get when a homeowner hires a gardener, or the services provided by a lighthouse to ships' captains who had nothing to do with its purchase or sale.

This chapter will show not only that ***external benefits*** resolve the paradox posed by the lighthouse and other goods and services that can't be provided by a free market, but also that external benefits may be important in less dramatic cases where products *can* be provided by a free market. An example is vaccinations. These provide both an internal benefit to purchasers who are protected from the disease and, in addition, an external benefit to others who, as a result of the purchasers being vaccinated, are also less likely to get the disease. Here, a free market does not fail outright. It can provide such services, but in an inefficiently small quantity. In this case, externalities may justify government intervention to encourage the market to deliver more. This is the simpler case, and it will be considered first. This will be followed by an analysis of cases like the lighthouse where externalities dominate, and the only way these "public goods" can be produced is by the government.

Another section in this chapter discusses the role of government in creating regulations to promote health and safety in the workplace, and to ensure the safety of various products consumers buy. Although, as we shall explain, health and safety may not in themselves be "public goods," there is still a role for government in these areas, because the market mechanism may not do a good job of providing information about the health hazards and other risks associated with various jobs or products.

Another major topic in this chapter is ***public choice***. This term refers to the special set of problems that may exist when the government does produce goods or services and makes regulatory decisions. A whole new set of questions arise, such as, "How does the government decide what the public really wants?"

## EXTERNAL BENEFITS: A FREE MARKET PROVIDES TOO LITTLE

If there are any external or spillover effects, whether they be harmful or beneficial, the free market cannot be expected to allocate economic resources efficiently. For example, because the good in Figure 22-2 had an external cost, a free, perfectly competitive market resulted in too much output. Accordingly, we might guess that, if a good has an ***external benefit***, a free market will result in *too little* output.

An *external benefit* is a benefit enjoyed by parties other than those who produce or pay for the good or service that generates the benefit.

Figure 23-1 confirms that this guess is correct. The supporting argument can be stated briefly because it parallels the analysis of external costs. The key is to recognize that instead of the external costs that had to be added to the *supply* curve in Figure 22-2, there are now external benefits that have to be added to the *demand* curve. Specifically, to get the marginal social benefit $MB_S$ in Figure 23-1, we must take the private benefit to the purchaser (MB) as shown by

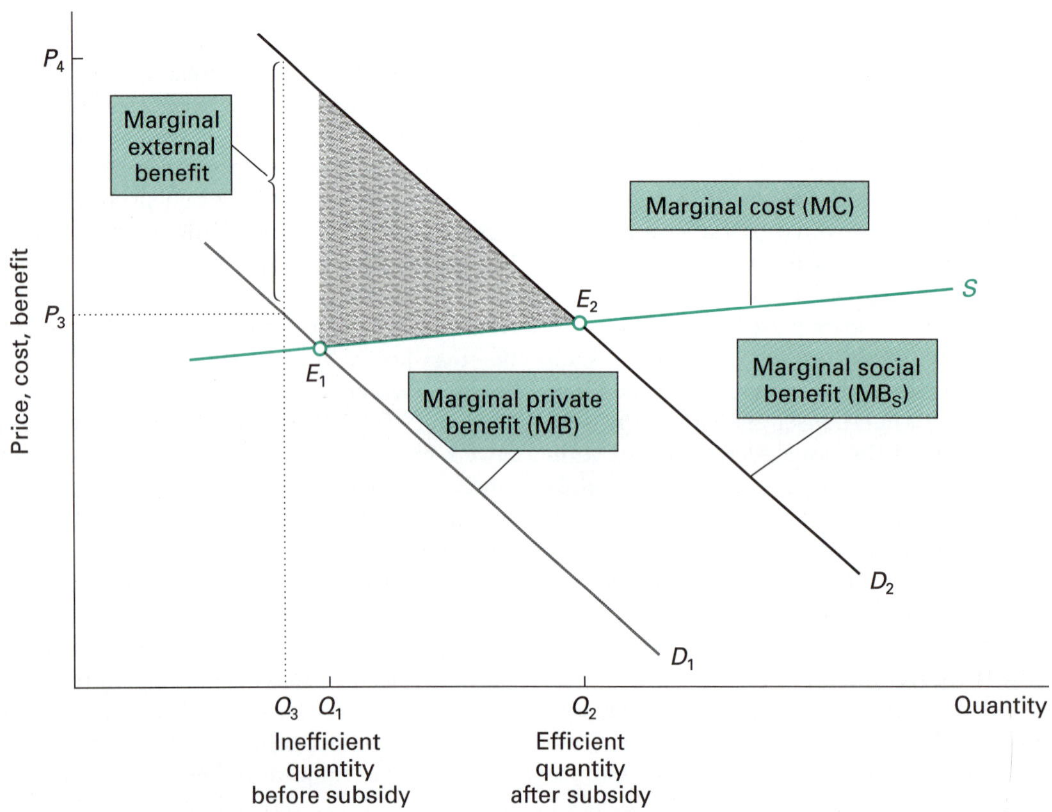


**FIGURE 23-1 Efficiency loss for a product with an external benefit, such as vaccinations.** The height of the market demand $D_1$ shows the marginal internal benefit to those who get vaccinations because they are protected from the disease. The vertical distance between $D_1$ and $D_2$ is the external benefit to others because the disease isn't passed on to them. The sum of these two benefits is the marginal social benefit $MB_S$. Free-market equilibrium is at $E_1$, where marginal cost $S$ is equal to $D_1$, the marginal private benefit (the only benefit taken into account by those who make the decision to get vaccinations). The result is that too little is produced at $Q_1$. To confirm, all units of output between $Q_1$ and $Q_2$ have a benefit (the height of $MB_S$) that would exceed their cost (the height of MC). With this net benefit, they should be produced. Because they are not, there is a net loss shown by the grey triangle.

the height of the demand curve $D_1$, and add to it the marginal external benefit shown by the brace bracket. For example, in the case of vaccinations, both the private benefit MB to those who acquire them and the external benefit to others who become less likely to pick up the disease must be added to calculate the social benefit ($MB_S$) of the shots.

If this marginal social benefit $MB_S$ is equated to the marginal cost MC, the result is an efficient outcome at $E_2$. However, in the absence of government interference, a free competitive market will reach equilibrium at $E_1$ instead, where marginal cost is equal to marginal private benefit. (This is the only benefit taken into account by those buying the vaccinations; thus, it is their demand curve and is marked $D_1$.) With equilibrium at $E_1$ rather than $E_2$, the free market generates too little output — specifically, $Q_1$ rather than $Q_2$, with the resulting efficiency loss shown in grey.

## One Solution: A Subsidy

One way of getting to the efficient equilibrium $E_2$ is to provide buyers with a per-unit subsidy equal to the external benefit bracket, thus shifting the demand curve up from $D_1$ to $D_2$. (Demand shifts in this way because, for example, the individual initially prepared to pay only $P_3$ for unit $Q_3$ is now prepared to pay $P_4$ — that is, the original $P_3$ plus the subsidy received from the government shown by the bracket.) With this shift in demand, a competitive market does the rest. Its new equilibrium is at $E_2$, where supply and new demand $D_2$ intersect. Thus, efficient output $Q_2$ is achieved.

However, such an increase in efficiency alone does not necessarily justify a subsidy or any other form of government intervention. One must also examine the administrative costs of that intervention. Thus, for example, the government does not subsidize each homeowner for hiring a gardener, even though this would provide an external benefit to neighbours. The efficiency gains from such government intervention aren't sufficient to cover the costs of administering such a widespread subsidy program. On the other hand, in the case of many vaccinations, the efficiency gains do outweigh the costs of administration, and a subsidy is justified.[1]

In Figure 23-1 efficiency is achieved by *subsidizing* a product with an external benefit, just as a product with an external cost was *taxed* in Figure 22-2. In either case, the government ***internalizes the externality***. In Figure 22-2, polluting firms that paid the tax were made to "feel internally" the external damage they were causing, so they did less. On the other hand, buyers in Figure 23-1 receive a subsidy that allows them to "enjoy internally" the external benefit they provide; thus, this product is encouraged. In either the tax or subsidy case, private firms or individuals act appropriately because they take external effects into account.

Externalities may sometimes be internalized even without government action, simply as a result of private market forces.

## Encouraging Private Market Transactions to Internalize the Externality

One example of this type of transaction is provided by the private real estate firm that purchases a whole block of houses in a run-down neighbourhood. Its renovation expenditure on each house raises the value of that house and also provides a spillover benefit by raising the value of the other houses in the block as well. Once the firm has renovated all the houses in the block, it has both the internal and external benefits. Specifically, when it sells each house, it will enjoy two types of price increase: (1) the price increase because that particular house has been renovated and (2) the additional price increase because the neighbourhood has improved as a result of the renovations to the other houses. Thus, while the firm may not be able to make a profit by purchasing and renovating a single house, it may be able to do so if it purchases and renovates the whole block, simply because it is able to capture the spillover effects.

As another example, if a firm constructs a ski lift on a mountain, it will be able to sell tow tickets. These receipts will be an internal benefit to the firm. At the same time, the ski lift also will generate an external benefit in the form of greater pleasure for those eating at a nearby restaurant who enjoy watching people ski. The internal benefit to the ski lift company from ticket sales may be insufficient to justify constructing the lift. But suppose the firm can buy the restaurant and, once the ski lift is built, start charging customers more. It thereby captures (internalizes) the external benefit it has created. It now becomes profitable to build the lift. The nation's output of ski lift services is no longer too low. It has now been increased to an

[1] In order to avoid the paperwork and other administrative costs of subsidizing children's vaccinations one at a time, the government often provides them free. This is just another way of subsidizing vaccinations to encourage people to acquire more.

efficient quantity because external benefits have been internalized. They are now being realized by the new, larger firm.

(This suggests another approach to externalities: Allow firms to merge into large enough units so that decision makers will take such spillovers into account. However, this raises a conflict for policy makers. While a case can be made for allowing mergers that internalize externalities, mergers to accumulate market power may not be desirable. The problem is that mergers often do both.)

## Government Action as a Way of Dealing with Externalities

Now let's pursue the issue of positive externalities further by considering a flood-control dam in a river valley. If a single farm family were to build such a dam, they would enjoy an internal benefit since their own crops and buildings would be protected from floods. However, this internal benefit would be small compared with the enormous cost of constructing the dam. As a result, no individual farmer builds it—even though its construction might be easily justified by the large external flood-control benefits it would provide for the thousands of other farmers in the valley. (The benefits to the farmer building the dam would be internal, because he would be buying it; but the benefits to other farmers would be external, because they would not be buying it.)

If the dam is to be built at all, it will have to be built by the government. Thus, we come to the idea of a ***public good***.

# PUBLIC GOODS

The simplest definition of a public good is "anything the government provides." However, this definition is too broad for our purposes for two reasons: (1) It includes all sorts of payments, such as housing subsidies or social assistance payments, that are designed to *transfer* income from one group to another (our discussion of such policies is deferred to Chapter 24); and (2) "Anything the government provides" also includes all sorts of activities that *could* be undertaken by private firms but are provided by the government instead; examples are public bus systems, public health insurance, and postal service. Since we are not interested in such a broad definition, we begin with the narrower idea of goods — such as flood-control dams — that cannot be provided by private firms.

Since the idea of external benefits is important to the definition of a public good, let's look more closely at two previous examples. The first is hiring a gardener. Most of the benefits are internal; that is, they go to the family that hires the gardener to work on its own property. Therefore, the private market works, at least to some degree: Individuals do have gardening done—although the quantity is less than the efficient amount.

Compare this with our example of a flood-control dam in a river valley. There are two important differences in this case. First, as already noted, a free market will not work at all. No dam will be built because there is no individual farmer who will do it. The reason is that the internal benefits of flood control to that individual would be relatively small. Most of the benefits would be external — the protection from floods provided to other farmers in the river valley. Since no individual farmer will do it, any dam that is built will have to be constructed by the government. The second difference is more subtle: Once the government has built the dam, an individual farmer's benefit from it will be the same as if he had built the dam himself. In other words, he cannot be excluded from enjoying its benefits. Indeed, many economists use this characteristic of ***non-excludability*** as their definition of a public good: It provides an individual with a benefit that does not depend on whether or not that person is the actual purchaser. Another illustration is the lighthouse. Once it is built, no sailor can be excluded from using its services. All sailors are protected from the rocks whether or not they helped to pay for the lighthouse.

Another characteristic of a public good is that any one person can enjoy the benefit from it, without thereby reducing the benefit that it can provide to others. That is, there is ***non-rivalry*** among individuals regarding who will get the benefits. (Another way of expressing this idea is to say that the benefit from a public good is *inexhaustible*.)

For example, when you use the light from the lighthouse, the amount available for others is still there undiminished. You haven't used it up. When one farmer uses the flood-control service of a dam, its flood-control benefits remain undiminished for other farmers to enjoy. Compare this to a private good, such as a hamburger. When you use it, it disappears. It is exhausted. Even when you buy a private service, such as an appointment with your dentist, it is temporarily exhausted; she cannot see someone else at the same time.

The benefits of a *public good* can be enjoyed by any one person without diminishing the benefits available to anyone else. That is, there is *non-rivalry* in the enjoyment of its benefits. Moreover, there is *non-excludability*: No one can be excluded from enjoying the benefits.

Before continuing, we should note a couple of qualifications.

1. Some public goods are *local* public goods. That is, their benefits are limited to a particular geographic area, or to the members of particular groups of individuals. For example, the benefits of a lighthouse only extend to ships in the area where it is located; only those who have property along the river benefit from a dam to control floods. In the case of local public goods, non-excludability only extends to residents in the area.
2. Sometimes, a good or project can be classified partly as a public good, partly as a private good. For example, while the protection against flooding that a flood-control dam provides is a public good, a dam may also have other benefits that are not. For example, a dam used to generate electricity may be built by a private firm. The reason is that electricity is not a public good: It can be made available only to those who pay for it, so a private firm can sell it, and finance the building of the dam.

The distinction between a public good and an ordinary private good is shown in Figures 23-2 and 23-3. A private good is illustrated in Figure 23-2. The first two panels show the marginal benefit (demand) of two individual consumers. Each consumer would have to purchase and acquire the good in order to realize this benefit from it. As we saw in Figure 7-1, a horizontal summation of the individual demands (marginal benefits) in panels (a) and (b) provides the total market demand in panel (c) (the marginal social benefit).

In contrast, Figure 23-3 shows a public good, where all individuals can benefit from each unit produced. For example, consumer A gets benefit $a_1$ from the first unit. But this same unit also provides consumer B with benefit $b_1$. Since both individuals benefit from this first unit — both can, for example, see the warning beam from the same lighthouse — the benefit provided by this first unit is $a_1$ plus $b_1$, as shown in panel (c). Thus, for such a public good, marginal social benefit ($MB_S$) is found by *vertically* adding the individual benefits — in contrast to the horizontal addition for a private good.

It is important to recognize that the resulting marginal social benefit ($MB_S$) in Figure 23-3 is not

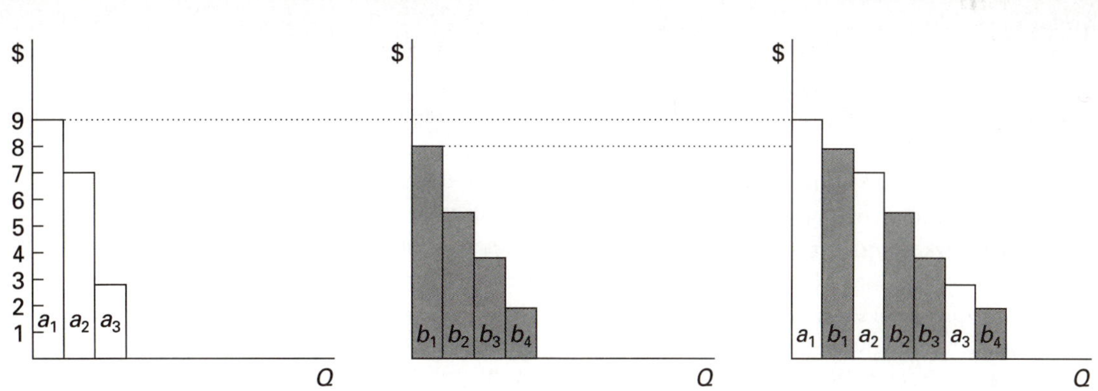


**(a) Consumer A's demand (A's marginal benefit).** **(b) Consumer B's demand (B's marginal benefit).** **(c) Market demand (marginal social benefit).**

**FIGURE 23-2 A private good.**
Individual demands in panels (a) and (b) are horizontally summed to get market demand in panel (c). (At a price of $9, A buys one unit. If the price falls to $8, B also buys a unit. If the price falls to $7, A buys a second unit; and so on.) For such a private good with no external benefits, the market demand curve in panel (c) represents marginal social benefit.

a demand curve. Nobody would buy the first unit if its price were $a_1 + b_1$. However, if it can be produced at this cost or less, the first unit should be produced. Finally, note that Figures 23-2 and 23-3 present only the two extreme cases: a "pure" private good, which provides benefit only to the purchaser, and a "pure" public good, which provides each individual with a level of benefit that does not depend at all on who purchases the good. There are, of course, many intermediate cases where a good provides a benefit to the purchaser and to others as well, but where the level of benefit for each individual does depend on who purchases the good. (If I purchase it, I'll get more benefit from it than if you purchase it.) Such intermediate cases were illustrated earlier in the examples of gardening and vaccinations.

## PROBLEMS IN EVALUATING THE BENEFITS OF A PUBLIC GOOD

Suppose that panel (c) of Figure 23-3 shows the benefits of building a system of flood-control dams on a river. Further suppose that the cost of the first dam would be *K*. Since this is less than its benefit $a_1 + b_1$, this dam should be built. Let us now examine in more detail our earlier claim that this public good can be provided only by the government. Why can't it be provided by private enterprise instead? After all, since the two farmers value it at $a_1 + b_1$, why doesn't some entrepreneur collect this amount from them and build the dam? (The entrepreneur would be collecting more than the cost of the dam and, therefore, could pocket a profit.)

To answer this question, note that any public good has a very large number of consumers; in our example, the two farmers A and B represent thousands of farmers in the valley. Thus, $MB_S$ is the vertical sum, not just of two individual marginal benefit curves but instead of thousands of them—with each individual curve being relatively insignificant. Now suppose that you are one of these individuals and the private entrepreneur who is promoting this project asks you for your valuation of the dam. Specifically, he asks how much you would be willing to pay for its construction.

What would you reply? Clearly, you would have a strong incentive to understate your benefit, because you realize that it is very unlikely that your answer will influence the decision on whether the dam is built. You will either get a dam or not, depending on how the thousands of other farmers in the valley respond. All your reply will do is determine the amount that *you* will be contributing—and it's in your interest to minimize this. So you reply that you believe a flood-control system is exactly what this valley needs, and you believe your neighbours will value it very highly. However, it will provide little value for you; you personally are willing to pay very little for it.

If the dam is built—as you secretly hope—it will cost you very little. Yet you cannot be excluded from enjoying its services: If the dam prevents a flood, your buildings and land will be protected. You get to be a ***free rider***, enjoying the benefits while paying little of the costs. The problem, of course, is that you will not be the only one with an incentive to ride free. Every other individual in the valley also has exactly the same incentive, so that the entrepreneur gets a seriously biased response from everyone.

A *free rider* is someone who cannot be excluded from enjoying the benefits of a project, but who pays nothing (or pays a disproportionately small amount) to cover its costs.

Accordingly, the dam does not get built by the private entrepreneur. It is natural, therefore, to turn to the government, which can solve the free-rider problem by forcing everyone to pay taxes to build the dam.

Although it can collect enough taxes to build the dam, the government still faces the problem of evaluating the benefits of the dam in order to decide whether or not it should be built in the first place. In evaluating the benefits, the government, just like the private entrepreneur, encounters problems: It cannot simply ask people how highly they value the dam. If it were to ask you, and you believe that the government will build the dam without noticeably increasing your taxes, it will be in your interest to *overstate* your valuation in order to increase the chance that the dam will be built. Therefore, even though you previously told the private entrepreneur that the dam is worth almost nothing to you, you now turn around and tell the government it is worth $1 million to you, since you know you won't actually have to pay the $1 million. In short, estimates by individuals of what

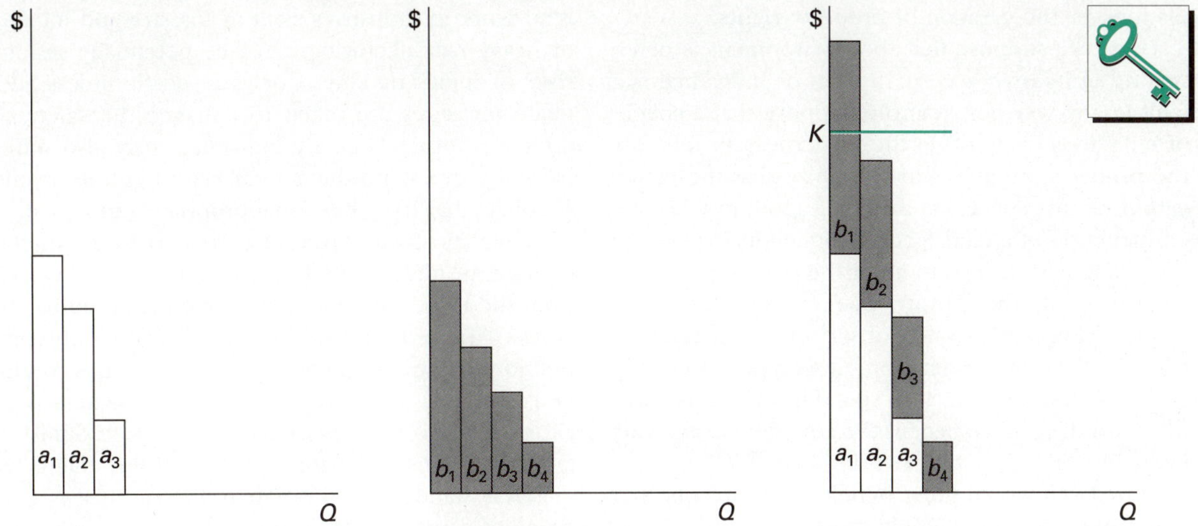


**(a) Consumer A's marginal benefit.**

**(b) Consumer B's marginal benefit.**

**(c) Marginal social benefit $MB_S$.**

**FIGURE 23-3 A public good.**

The individual marginal benefits in panels (a) and (b) are *vertically* summed to get the marginal social benefit in panel (c). Thus $b_1$ is stacked on top of $a_1$ to show that both consumers get a benefit from the first unit.

the dam is worth are unreliable, regardless of who is collecting them.[2]

Another approach is to forget about canvassing people for their views, and instead estimate benefits of the dam in some other way. For example, by examining past records, the government can estimate the value of the crops that are likely to be saved from floods. Such benefits can then be compared with the estimated cost of the dam.

There are, however, two potential problems with such a ***cost-benefit analysis***. First, unless it is treated with care, it may be used simply as an economic justification for projects that the government has already decided to build for political reasons. For example, a dam may have been promised to a key group of voters in the last election campaign. A politically motivated official who has to evaluate this dam and who wants to be able to back up the government's promise may (1) estimate construction costs on the low side and (2) keep adding benefits until the dam is justified. For example, such benefits might include the lives saved by flood control. While any lives saved are an important benefit, a wide range of values can be placed on them. (See Box 23-1.)

Another reason it may be difficult to get an accurate estimate is that the engineers who expect to construct the dam may also be the ones who evaluate its benefits. They may be tempted to estimate the benefits on the high side in order to justify the dam and thus create future income and employment for themselves.

## THE ENVIRONMENT AS A PUBLIC GOOD

The discussion of public goods can be tied into the analysis of environmental and resource protection in Chapters 21 and 22. There, we concluded that in a private market without government intervention, decisions by private firms may seriously damage the

[2] Devising ways to get a better evaluation of public goods has become an important area of inquiry. One imaginative suggestion is to inform people that they will be taxed, but only if their individual valuation tips the scale in favour of building the dam. For such an individual, the tax would be the cost of the dam minus the sum of everyone else's valuation. Putting the question this way makes it less likely that people will provide a wildly inaccurate evaluation. In particular, it would prevent you from making your wild overestimate of a million dollars. Think about it: The more you exaggerate, the more likely it is that your answer will tip the scales in favour of the dam and you will be taxed. In addition, the more you exaggerate, the higher your tax bill could be.

environment or deplete resources, such as fish. The government may limit such damage with taxes, regulations, or the creation of property rights.

However, suppose that the environment is deteriorating of its own accord; no firm or individual is at fault in any way. For example, suppose that a species of wildlife is dying off in the wilderness. In this case, the proper approach is to recognize that the preservation of this species is a public good, just like the construction of a dam. Since no individual values the species highly enough to incur the cost of personally preserving it, the private market generally won't deliver. Although private conservation organizations may act, the ultimate decision on whether to save the species—and how much to spend in the effort—may rest with the government. If the government does act, everyone can enjoy the resulting benefits.

How large would these benefits be? This question is not easy to answer. While most people would put some value on the preservation of a wildlife species, it is very difficult to say how much. As Harvard's Richard Caves has put it: "How highly should we value wombats, if they are so far from civilization that no one will ever see them, let alone eat them?" One answer is that we may place some value on them, even though we may never see them, just as we may place a value on an air-conditioning system even though we may not actually turn it on this year. This phenomenon is described as ***option demand*** — the desire to have an option, whether or not we exercise it. Thus, we may want to keep open the option of seeing a species, or drawing on it for, say, medical research, even though we may never, in fact, exercise this option. Similarly, we may have an option demand for wilderness parks which we may or may not actually visit. Option demand should be taken into account in the evaluation of environmental benefits.

## SAFETY AND HEALTH IN CONSUMER PRODUCTS AND THE WORKPLACE

Protecting the environment is an important role of government because people put a high value on resources such as clean air and water. One reason for this, or course, is that if the air and water are badly polluted, the population will run an increased risk of illness and even a shortened life expectancy. For example, studies have shown that living in a highly polluted urban environment may be as unhealthy as being a heavy smoker, and those who smoke will, on average, die much younger than those who don't.

Individuals' health and safety can also be seriously affected by other factors. For example, many people who work in industries such as forestry and mining, or heavy manufacturing, can face potentially serious risks of injury or illness, or even death, unless adequate measures are taken to enhance the safety of their workplace. Similarly, individuals may also suffer harm if they use products such as drugs or electronic products that have been inappropriately designed.

While most employers are concerned about the conditions under which their labour force works, even the most conscientious may be tempted to cut corners if faced with bankruptcy, or even with competition strong enough to threaten their firm's continued existence. One way they may cut corners is to allow their workplaces to become less safe. Similarly, faced with possible bankruptcy, an airline might let its safety standards deteriorate in the absence of government controls; or a drug company might release a product — its "last hope" — before its testing is completed. If cutting corners is perceived to be the only way to survive, a firm may be prepared to run risks with public health and safety.

This sounds like a problem of externalities, similar to the case of pollution that we discussed in Chapter 22. For example, firms selling products to consumers look at their own costs, but may not look at the risks buyers will face. In hiring labour, a firm examines only its own private costs, but not the risk that employees face in its workplace. Consider, for example, Figure 23-4 where we illustrate the market for a potentially dangerous product (say, farm tractors) for which experience has taught us that users on average run a substantial risk of having accidents that may involve injury or even death. If we can predict the average number of accidents per 1000 tractors sold, say, and if we can somehow come up with an estimate of the average cost that is incurred when such an accident happens, we can compute an average expected "accident cost" for each tractor sold. If we add this cost to the marginal private cost of producing tractors (MC in Figure 23-4(a)), we get the marginal social cost, including the expected accident cost (the $MC_S$ curve in Figure 23-4(a)). As usual, we interpret the demand curve $D$ as the marginal social benefit of tractors (derived from their usefulness in helping produce farm products). If the equilibrium market price is $P_1$, and the number of tractors sold is $Q_1$, we may argue that too many tractors are produced and sold, given their marginal social cost. The efficiency loss from this overuse can be estimated by the familiar grey triangle.

In panel (b) of Figure 23-4, where the demand curve and the MC curve are the same as in panel (a), we illustrate the same situation in a different way. Instead of adding the accident cost to the marginal private cost, we have *subtracted it from the demand curve* (that is, from the original marginal benefit curve). It is easy to see that if the equilibrium price and quantity are $P_1$ and $Q_1$ as before, the efficiency loss measured by the grey triangle in panel (b) must be the same as that in panel (a): The only difference is that in panel (b), we have treated the accident cost as a subtraction from the marginal benefit to farmers, whereas in panel (a) we treated this cost as something to be added to the marginal private cost incurred by those who produce tractors.

By now, however, something may be bothering you about the analogy between a problem such as pollution, and the case of a potentially dangerous product such as that illustrated in Figure 23-4. In particular, you may have noticed an important difference: In the case of a polluting industry such as a pulp mill, the cost of pollution was borne neither by the firm owning the mill, nor by the buyers of its products. In the case of a dangerous product, on the other hand, the cost (in the form of accident risks) is borne by those who buy and use the product. Similarly, in the case of someone who is considering taking a risky job, the potential accident cost is mostly borne by the worker who is being paid to do the risky job. Thus, the risks to health and safety that exist in these cases do not really represent an *external* cost: They are borne by someone who is a party to the transaction (unlike the case of pollution costs, for example, where the cost is borne by "innocent bystanders" like those downstream or downwind who have pollutants dumped on them).[3]

But if these kinds of health and safety hazards do not constitute external costs, is there any reason why

[3] In the case of airline travel, those on the ground who are killed by a crash are innocent bystanders. This is an externality and may provide some justification for government intervention. Hereafter, we keep the analysis simple by avoiding such complications.

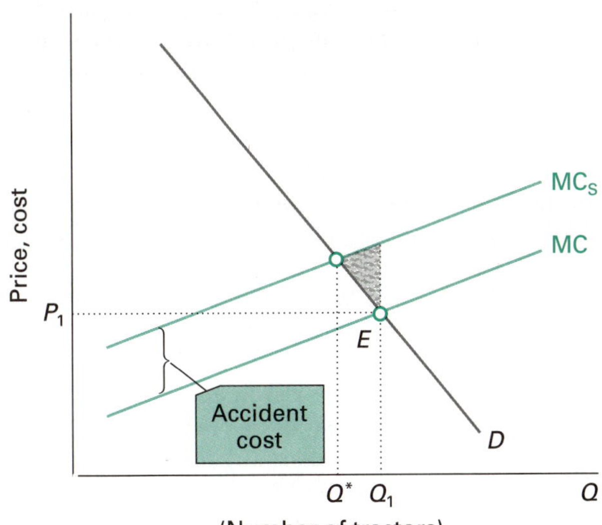


**(a)** The marginal cost of producing tractors is MC. The vertical distance between MC and $MC_S$, the marginal social cost, is the expected costs (injuries and lives lost) from accidents in which drivers are hurt or killed.

If tractor buyers do not take the expected cost of accidents into account, the equilibrium will be at *E*, with $Q_1$ tractors produced. This is larger than the efficient quantity $Q^*$.

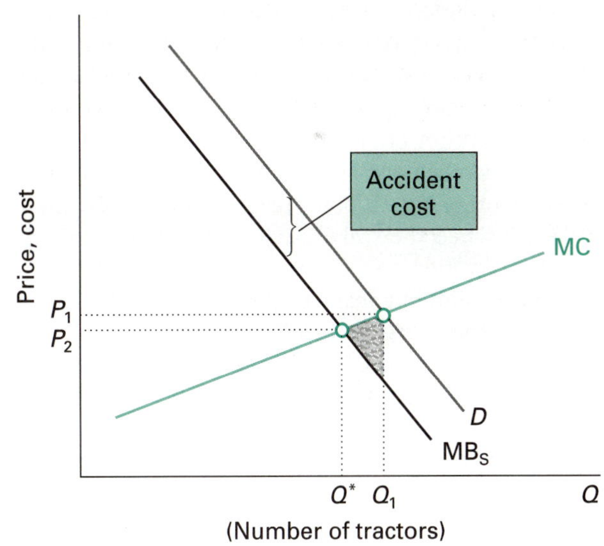


**(b)** An alternative way of taking the expected accident cost into account is to treat it as a subtraction from the marginal benefit *D* of using tractors in farm production. Because the accident cost represented as the vertical distance between the curve *D* and the marginal social benefit curve $MB_S$ in this panel is the same as in panel (a), the efficiency loss that results when the accident cost is not taken into account in the market (the grey triangle) is the same as in panel (a).

**FIGURE 23-4** **The market for a hazardous product.**

private markets would *not* take them into account? For example, if farmers are fully informed about the accident risk when they buy tractors, won't their market demand curve be the same as the marginal *social* benefit curve in Figure 23-4(b), so that the equilibrium market price and quantity will be $P_2$ and $Q^*$, with no triangular efficiency loss? Similarly, if workers have full information about the risk of illness or injury in different workplaces, won't they demand a risk premium as compensation for taking risky jobs? Moreover, if workers and product users are fully informed in this way, won't this give firms a market incentive to produce safer products and create safer working conditions?

The answer to these questions is "yes" in all cases, *provided we can be confident that workers and product buyers are indeed fully informed* about the risks they are taking. However, information of this kind may be costly and difficult to acquire, and hard to evaluate even if you have it. Thus, to the extent that workers and consumers are *not* well informed, there is at least some degree of "market failure." That is, there is a role for government regulation.

Evidence indicates that workers taking risky jobs do, in fact, obtain some compensation by getting paid a higher wage.[4] However, in comparison with the risks involved, the wage differentials in favour of such workers do not appear very large. It is difficult to believe that they completely compensate the workers for the risks they take. The most plausible explanation is that workers often don't realize how serious these risks are when they take the job. (The high turnover rate in risky jobs provides support for this view.) But, when they find out, many conclude that the "risk premium" in their wage is insufficient, and leave.

When workers don't have full information on risk, employers can get away with paying a wage differential that falls short of compensating for risk. In that case, employers make hiring decisions without fully taking into account all costs, including the risks to their employees. The result is too much of this activity—that is, too much hiring in risky jobs. The reason is not an externality, as in the case of "too much pollution." Instead, the problem is that workers have inadequate information about risk.

Thus, a justification for government interference in the marketplace is to improve the information available to workers. For example, the federal government requires firms to label chemicals that are dangerous to handle. In addition, governments also take direct action to reduce risk. For example, they require firms to install safety devices on machinery, and to follow a number of other health and safety standards in the workplace.

## Safety and Health in Consumer Products

Lack of information may also prevent a free market from working efficiently in the provision of consumer goods and services. It's all very well to say that, in the long run, the public will turn away from an airline once they realize it is unsafe, when it has had a series of crashes. The problem is that this information doesn't become available until there is a serious loss of life. In this case, the main problem is again inadequate information. Specifically, information is just too expensive to acquire because it involves loss of life —and this justifies safety regulations imposed by the Department of Transport or the U.S. Federal Aviation Administration. A similar case can be made for the monitoring of new drugs under the federal Food and Drug Act. The public does not have information on which drugs are a health threat. And, by the time it does and takes appropriate action by boycotting the offending producer, it is too late. The damage has been done.

An example was thalidomide, which was banned in the United States. In a number of European countries and in Canada where it was not banned, it caused birth defects (although eventually, it was banned in Canada). While the danger in this case became evident in nine months, for some carcinogens, the danger may take decades to show up. This makes a strong case for government testing of drugs.

Although government drug testing reduces the information problem, it doesn't eliminate it. The reason is that such testing also involves some delay. Regulators in this area are faced with two conflicting objectives: (1) Get a drug out as quickly as possible so that it can begin to save lives, but (2) delay its release for enough safety testing to ensure that it doesn't *take* lives. Faced with this choice, regulators often delay. They will be criticized less for delaying too long — and failing to save lives — than they will be for releasing a drug too soon, in which case its fatal effects may raise a political storm.

(Decisions on new drugs can, of course, be made much more quickly if the drugs have already been tested in other countries, and the test results are avail-

[4] W.K. Viscusi and M.J. Moore, "Workers' Compensation: Wage Effects, Benefit Inadequacies and the Value of Health Losses," *Review of Economics and Statistics*, May 1987, p. 260.

able to the Canadian authorities. But that does not always solve the problem: The average time required for testing and approval of a new drug by the U.S. FDA (Food and Drug Administration) now is roughly five to seven years. And reports of faked test results in private laboratories that have investigated chemicals for the FDA may make Health and Welfare Canada less willing to accept U.S. evidence in approving new drugs.)

### Lack of Information: More Serious for Health than Safety

Ignorance is a greater problem with health risks, such as radiation than with safety risks that are obvious, such as inadequate protection for a worker operating a buzz saw. In the case of safety, the public finds out as soon as accidents happen. In the area of health, it may be decades before people subjected to radiation develop cancer. Obviously, in the extreme case where information becomes available after workers have retired, it cannot influence the wage differentials they demand. Moreover, the longer the delays in contracting a disease, the more difficult it becomes for the public to identify the cause. Is the cancer now developing a result of that radiation 20 years ago, or a result of the thousands of other things that have occurred since?

Since it is more difficult for the public to identify health risks than accident risks, it is appropriate for government control agencies to place more emphasis on risks to health.

### Benefits of Health and Safety Regulations

Whereas most of the costs of health and safety regulations can be expressed in terms of a decrease in GDP or a slower rate of economic growth, their benefits cannot easily be expressed in terms of an increase in GDP. (Benefits such as improved health or safety or a cleaner environment cannot be included in GDP, given present methods of measurement.) Instead, benefits have to be measured in a piecemeal fashion, for one type of regulation at a time.

Past studies estimating such benefits have yielded mixed results. For example, in the early 1980s the Economic Council of Canada estimated the effects of increasingly detailed federal and provincial safety regulations in the workplace. The evidence was disappointing: In spite of the more stringent safety rules (and even though a growing proportion of the labour force was working in the relatively safe service sector), the number of reported work injuries was slightly higher at the end of the 1970s than at the beginning of the decade. The incidence of occupationally induced illness also did not seem to be declining, but this may have been due in part to previous underreporting of such diseases.

On the other hand, some regulations did seem to generate substantial benefits. For example, U.S. and Canadian regulations giving more stringent specifications for the construction of cars to make them safer, together with laws lowering speed limits and making it mandatory for drivers to wear seat-belts, have all contributed to a reduction in auto injuries and fatalities. This is even more impressive because, during the 1970s and 1980s, cars were becoming smaller and lighter—and, for this reason, less safe. Therefore, just preventing the safety record from getting worse represented substantial success.

In brief, the benefits of health and safety regulations have been mixed: disappointing in some areas, but substantial in others. This raises an important question for the future: As proposals are made to introduce new regulations, how should we make the decision on which ones to accept?

## EVALUATING A REGULATION: DOES IT PASS THE COST-BENEFIT TEST?

By now it is clear that a regulation cannot be justified simply because it has a desirable objective, such as improving safety. It must also be *effective* in achieving that objective. Specifically, it should pass a ***cost-benefit test*** to ensure that it provides benefits sufficient to more than offset its costs, including the costs of administering the regulation and the cost to business of complying.

> *Cost-benefit analysis* is an estimate of the costs and benefits of a policy and a comparison of the two. A *cost-benefit test* is the requirement that the benefits of a policy exceed its costs.

Examples of regulations that pass the cost-benefit test include the controls on airline safety imposed by the Department of Transport. However, there have been other regulations that may not have passed this test; in such cases there has been too much regulation. One possible example was the banning of saccharin, a relatively mild carcinogen. The benefit of this ban was to reduce cancer. But its cost included the increase in heart disease in overweight people who were driven back to having to use sugar. (At the time, saccharin was the only available substitute for sugar.) Thus, the ban on saccharin may have saved some lives from cancer but cost others from heart disease; the net effects were unclear.

## Why Cost-benefit Analysis Is Not the Last Word

Cost-benefit analysis is not easy. For example, suppose that, with great difficulty, it has been estimated that the cost of a certain regulation will be $10 million, and its benefit will be the saving of 20 lives. Before these two figures can be compared, it is necessary to put a dollar value on the human lives that will be saved. But how can that be done? Box 23-1 provides some suggestions, along with the reasons that such estimates cannot be very accurate. Thus, the costs and benefits of regulations to protect human life cannot be compared in a very precise way.

Fortunately, however, it still may be possible to identify a desirable policy change, even when only fragmentary evidence is available, as the following example illustrates.

## The Importance of Consistency

In the United States, the federal government has imposed regulations on the use of arsenic that are very costly, and deal with risks that are so remote that the regulations are extremely unlikely to save many lives. Consequently, it has been estimated that each life saved by these regulations has cost $70 million. Clearly, it makes no sense to impose these regulations when there is an alternative way of saving lives—the elimination of railroad level-crossings — that would only cost $100,000 per life.

Note that in this case we can arrive at an important conclusion— even though we have information only on the *cost* of saving a life, but none whatsoever on the benefit of saving a life. Specifically, we can conclude that government policy is inconsistent. It does not make sense to engage in any activity — saving lives or anything else — in an exceedingly expensive way (at $70 million a life) when one can achieve the same objective at far less cost ($100,000 a life).

Moreover, if we have even the roughest sort of estimate of the *benefit* of saving a life — for example, if we know that this benefit falls anywhere in the broad $330,000 to $5 million range cited in Box 23-1 — we can make an even stronger recommendation: Not only should the regulations on arsenic use be abolished, but, in addition, a regulation *should* be imposed to eliminate railroad level-crossings. This switch will save far more lives at the same cost. This example illustrates how it may be possible to make good judgements even though estimates of benefits and costs are very imprecise.

There are many other illustrations of ***regulatory inconsistency***. For example: Why should there be a law that forces people to forgo saccharin because it is a food additive suspected of causing cancer, when there is no ban against natural foods with similar risks of cancer?

# PUBLIC CHOICE: PROBLEMS WITH GOVERNMENT DECISION MAKING

In the last several chapters we have seen that private decision making often has serious flaws; in the face of private market failure, the government may be justified in intervening in the economy. However, this argument is incomplete unless we recognize that government intervention may itself fail, because government decision making also has its own special set of serious flaws.

### 1. The Difficulty in Reversing a Public Expenditure

Some 20 years ago, Chrysler made a costly mistake: It decided that the switch in consumer demand toward smaller, more fuel-efficient cars was just a passing fad. Accordingly, Chrysler continued to produce big cars with large, gas-guzzling engines. As its sales stagnated, however, Chrysler quickly reconsidered, and within a few years was enjoying success with the fuel-efficient K-car models.

A private company such as Chrysler would sooner admit its mistake than lose market share; business executives will admit their mistakes to save their jobs. In the public sector, however, things are different. There, admitting mistakes may *cost* politicians their jobs. For example, if a government drops an expenditure that it introduced earlier, the opposition party

## TOOLS AND TECHNIQUES BOX 23-1

## The Eternal Puzzle: What Is a Human Life Worth?

> Thief (holding a gun): "Your money or your life."
> Jack Benny (pausing): ". . . I'm thinking . . . I'm thinking."

The simple answer to the question in the title is: Any life is worth an infinite amount. The miner trapped underground has a life that is priceless. Yet we don't value our own lives this way. Were they to have infinite value, safety concerns would dominate all others. We would live as close as possible to our workplace and never drive a car, let alone take a trip to earn something as trivial as a few thousand dollars.

Society doesn't place an infinite value on a life either. To illustrate: Lives can be saved by installing crash barriers down the middle of roads. Yet we don't do this on every country road. We simply aren't willing to spend the billions of dollars this would cost. This then raises the critical question: "How much are we willing to spend to save a human life?" This is really just a recasting of the original question: "What is a human life worth?" However, this new question is one that everyone — including even those who philosophically refuse to place a money value on a human life — will recognize should be asked if we want to make a sensible decision on, say, whether a crash barrier should be built or not.

Why not then just ask people: "What would you be willing to pay to save your life?" Unfortunately, we wouldn't be able to get a sensible reply to this question because almost everyone would say "An infinite amount if I could get my hands on it." However, we can estimate how much some people value their lives by observing those who actually "put their lives on the line." Thus, we may ask, for example: "How much more than the average wage must be paid to induce a worker to take a high-risk job like that of a lumberjack?"

Although this is probably the most promising way of evaluating a human life,* several difficulties remain. For example: (1) This estimate includes only the valuation of the person's own life. But isn't an additional value placed on this life by family and friends?† (2) The higher wage paid in high-risk jobs indicates only how the workers who actually take these jobs value their lives. But isn't this far less than the valuation of the vast majority of the population who won't take such risky jobs because they value their lives more highly? (3) How much of the higher wage is compensation for the risk of death, and how much for the risk of injury? The higher wage compensates for both, but only the risk of death is being considered here. (4) These estimates are only meaningful if people taking these jobs understand the risks they are taking; we've already seen that, because of inadequate information, they tend to underestimate these risks.

---

* It is certainly an improvement over one of the early methods that has frequently been used in legal judgements—namely, evaluate a life by asking: "How much would the individual have earned over the rest of his or her lifetime?" This yields a poor measure because it implies that the value of the life of a disabled person is zero. The error is basically the same as the one made in the more extreme statement (in *Technology Review,* July 1981, p. 11) that a clean-air standard for Montana is uneconomic because "some of the people who will die from air pollution are unemployed and, therefore, have no economic value."

† In "Families and the Economic Risks to Life," *American Economic Review,* March 1988, pp. 255–60, Maureen L. Cropper and Frances G. Sussman review previous studies of this question and consider why people seem to put a higher value on their own life if they have beloved dependants than if they do not. Moreover, as noted by John Garen in "Compensating Wage Differentials and the Endogeneity of Job Riskiness," *Review of Economics and Statistics,* February 1988, p. 9, people with wealth and education put a higher value on their own life than those without. They can afford more cars, TVs, and safety. So they "buy safety" by avoiding high-risk jobs.

**BOX 23-1 continued**

Studies that examine how workers act in risky situations provide estimates of the value of a life that range all the way from about $100,000 to over $10 million.** However, almost all fall in the range of $330,000 to just over $5 million. The imprecision of this sort of estimation clearly illustrates how difficult it is to place a value on a human life.

** For a review of such estimates, see Alan E. Dillingham, "The Influence of Risk Variable Definition on Value-of-Life Estimates," *Economic Inquiry*, April 1985, pp. 277–94. He also notes that an alternative method used to estimate the value of a life (or more precisely, how much people are willing to pay to save their own lives) is to examine how much they are willing to pay for consumer goods such as auto air bags and fire detectors that reduce the risk to their lives. See also M. Bailey, *Reducing Risks to Life* (Washington, D.C.: American Enterprise Institute, 1980), p. 26.

may be able to use this "admission of error" to defeat the government in the next election. Furthermore, the taxpayer bears the cost of government expenditures, whether wise or foolish; politicians do not personally pick up the tab. This also makes them less likely to admit a mistake and reverse an expenditure decision. Thus, there may be too much production of public goods.

## 2. Voting Politically for Products Is Not Specific Enough

The Chrysler example suggests another important difference between public and private decision making. When you buy a particular item, you register a clear vote for its production. However, in the public sector, you vote for a dam — at least in theory — by voting for a candidate committed to building it. Unfortunately, in practice it is not this simple. In fact, you may not get to vote on this issue at all. The reason is that in an election, you vote for a candidate who advocates a whole set of policies. Like most other voters, you may vote for this candidate because of her attitude on some other completely unrelated issue, such as minority language rights or whether retail stores should be allowed to open on Sundays, or even because of her personality. Therefore, it is quite possible that the voters who have elected a candidate promising a dam don't really want the dam at all. Instead they may be supporting this candidate *despite* his or her support for the dam.

While the issue is not quite this simple—the public can also express its preferences via campaign contributions, lobbying, and so on—it is nonetheless true that the political process is a relatively poor method for the public to express its preferences on detailed questions. The public does not vote often enough and specifically enough to provide a clear message to the government of who wants what. Compare this with the private market, where communication is much more effective. Each day millions of messages on millions of products are communicated to producers by consumers when they buy — or do not buy — those products.

## 3. Short-run, Crisis-oriented Decision Making

The desire to be re-elected leads politicians to favour policies with costs that are hidden, and benefits that are obvious and will be realized quickly before the next election. Why should they promote policies that the public won't understand, or policies that will provide benefits *after* the next election — and thus may help to re-elect their successors? One of the reasons that elected officials may take this limited short-run view is that a busy public cannot be adequately informed about the hundreds of issues on which the officials must decide. Thus, they tend to put off tough, long-run decisions, and when they finally do take action, it is often in response to a crisis.

However, when officials make decisions that provide short-run benefits at the expense of long-run costs, this is very expensive for future generations who get no vote on this issue. In this sense, no process — not even a democratic one — can ever be a perfectly representative one in which both the present and future generations who will be affected get to vote.

## 4. The Incentive for Politicians to Support "Special-interest" Groups

> The diffuse and inchoate consumer interest has been no match for the sharply focused, articulate and well-financed efforts of producer groups.
>
> Walter W. Heller

In making decisions, our elected representatives have a number of motives. For example, they may honestly be trying to promote the public interest. Frequently, their desire to serve the public is their reason for entering politics in the first place. However, once they enter politics, they can't accomplish anything without being elected. Thus, of necessity, all politicians — no matter how noble — must be concerned with getting elected or re-elected. One of the best ways to get re-elected is to gain the backing of organized constituencies — or "special-interest" groups — who are able to deliver votes and/or financial support. In turn, the best way to get such backing is to support programs that are of great interest to such groups, but of far less concern to the public that has to pay. The special interest of most people is their job; the source of our income is of intense interest to each of us. Politicians, therefore, pay particular attention to people as producers rather than as consumers, as we saw, for example, in our discussion of international trade policy in Chapter 20.

Even for a politician who is prepared to support the public interest, it's not always clear what that may be.

## PROBLEMS IN DEFINING THE "PUBLIC INTEREST"

Majority rule is a basic principle of democracy. Can't we take this simple and well-accepted principle as a straightforward way of determining what is in the public interest? Unfortunately, we often cannot — for several reasons.

### 1. The Problem of the Oppressive Majority

Under majority rule, if 51% of the public want a certain policy they can get it. It doesn't matter how little they value the benefit—as long as they get some benefit. Nor does it matter how heavy the cost of this policy may be to the minority. Thus, it is possible for majority rule to leave society as a whole worse off, with the benefits to the majority falling short of the costs imposed on the minority. This situation is referred to as the problem of an ***oppressive majority***.

To illustrate, consider the following modified version of an example suggested by Gordon Tullock, a leading scholar in the field of political choice. There are 100 farmers in a community. Each requires a small connecting road to get access to a main highway. It is in the interests of 51 of these farmers to vote to have access roads put into their own farms only, using taxes collected from all 100 farmers. However, this will involve a loss to society if the 49 losers who don't get roads suffer a great deal from the tax they have to pay, while the 51 winners who do get roads get a benefit that barely exceeds the tax they pay. Therefore, majority rule may be defective. Like private decision making, it may result in inefficiency — an overall loss to society.[5] (For an example of a case when some Canadians argued that majority rule led to the wrong outcome, see Box 23-2.)

[5] Majority rule can be inefficient not only because such undesirable policies are introduced but also because desirable policies are not introduced. For example, a desirable policy that benefits the minority a great deal may be rejected if it hurts the majority even slightly.

**APPLICATIONS AND ILLUSTRATIONS** **BOX 23-2**

**Public Choice in Action: Canada's Free Trade Election of 1988**

In the autumn of 1988, Canadian voters were called upon to settle one of the most important economic and political questions the nation had faced in a long time: Should Parliament pass the legislation necessary to implement the Free Trade Agreement with the United States? When the Liberal majority in the Senate announced that they wouldn't allow the legislation to pass unless there was a general election first, the Conservative government that had negotiated the agreement decided to go to the polls in November 1988. After an intense campaign, the Conservative party won a majority in Parliament and, in late

**BOX 23-2 continued**

December, the implementing legislation was, in fact, passed. Thus, on 1 January 1989, the Canada/U.S. Free Trade Agreement came into effect.

Because the Conservatives won a majority in Parliament, their policies — such as free trade—prevailed. Nonetheless, it is still interesting to ask: Did this parliamentary victory mean that a majority of Canadians favoured free trade? The answer is: not necessarily. The two parties opposed to the agreement—the Liberals and the NDP — pointed out that together they received 52.3% of the vote; therefore, the majority of Canadians *opposed* the deal. Were *they* right? Again, the answer is: not necessarily.

To see why, consider the following hypothetical example. Suppose that each of the three major parties get 10% of the vote because of (a) party loyalty, regardless of what the issues may be, or (b) other issues unrelated to free trade. (True, free trade dominated the election, but many voters were also influenced by other issues such as each party's stand on day care or cruise missile testing.) Further suppose that small splinter parties attracting protest votes get 4%, while all other voters—that is, 66%—vote solely on free trade and divide evenly on this issue. Thus, 33% vote for free trade and 33% against. Then the Liberals and NDP would get 53% of the popular vote (33% because of free trade, plus the 10% that each party would get because of party loyalty or other issues). In this particular example, it is easy to see that even if a majority of those voting on free trade are in favour of the policy and vote for the Conservatives, it is still possible for the opposing parties—the Liberals and NDP—to win a majority of the votes. To sum up: The Liberal/NDP conclusion that free trade was opposed by a majority of Canadians follows if Canadians voted solely on the free trade issue, without paying any attention to party loyalty or other issues. But if party loyalty or other issues did influence the voting — and they undoubtedly did — then this conclusion does not necessarily follow. Thus, the pattern of voting for *parties* can't tell us how Canadians would have voted on an *issue* (that is, how a referendum would have turned out). All we know for sure is that free trade won in the election because the Conservatives won a parliamentary majority.

However, there were two other interesting things that were evident when the Liberals (the "swing party") decided to oppose free trade. First, this decision to throw their "party loyalty" support against free trade made it more likely that more than 50% of the votes in the upcoming election would go to parties opposing free trade. But this Liberal decision also increased the chances that free trade would *actually win* in the election. The reason is that this decision split the anti-free trade vote between the Liberals and the NDP—and thus made it much more difficult for either of these parties to actually win the election.

Finally, observe that when a party wins a majority of seats in Parliament, this doesn't even mean that a majority of voters support that party, let alone its specific policies. To see why this is true even in a simple two-party system, suppose that a country with two parties, A and B, has 10 ridings with 100 voters in each. Suppose that in nine of the ridings, 51 people vote for the A candidate and 49 for the B candidate, while in the tenth riding, the B candidate receives all 100 votes. The outcome will be that A captures 90% of the seats in the legislature, even though 54% of the population voted for B. Moreover, if there are three parties, it is theoretically possible for one party to win 100% of the seats in the Parliament with just over one-third of the votes. For example, if 36% of the voters in each riding were to support party A (versus 32% for each of the other two parties), then A would win all the seats. While less extreme examples of such problems do arise, they are immediately evident, since the total vote for each party is made public. The real area of obscurity is this: How can we discern how a majority of Canadians feel on a specific issue? While polls may or may not throw some light on the question, it cannot necessarily be answered just by looking at the popular vote each party received.

Is there a better voting procedure than majority rule? The answer is that there are a lot of alternatives, but each has one weakness or another. For example, one could avoid the problem of the oppressive majority by requiring unanimous consent; then no policy could hurt anyone. But this rule is hopeless. By providing a veto to each individual, it paralyses the government. Any policy that damaged even one voter would be vetoed. Rather than searching for a voting system that might conceivably be better than majority rule, a more common and reasonable approach is to protect minorities from an oppressive majority with a constitution, either written or unwritten.

Our example of the oppressive majority illustrates two additional points: (1) The government can redistribute income without transferring any cash. Suppose the 51 farmers who get roads receive more benefits than we have so far assumed. Specifically, suppose their net benefits are roughly equal to the loss borne by the minority. In this case, the minority pays taxes to help finance projects that benefit the majority. The majority receives a large transfer from the minority — even though no cash transfer takes place between the two. (2) Members of a minority have a strong incentive to try to break down the existing majority coalition in order to form a new ruling coalition including themselves. For example, the 49 excluded farmers are likely to try to get 2 farmers to leave the present majority and join them. Then the newly formed coalition can turn the tables on the 49 who were in a majority but now find themselves out of power. Of course, the new coalition may then come under the same pressure from outsiders as the old; there may be a cycle of changing coalition patterns.

## 2. The Voting Paradox: Why Majority Rule May Lead to No Clear Winner

Consider a population of only three individuals faced with a choice among three options, A, B, and C. Table 23-1 shows how each individual ranks each of these options. For example, the first column tells us that individual I prefers option A to option B, and B to C. Which of these options is the will of the majority?

If these individuals choose first between options A and B, a majority (individuals I and III) will vote for A. With A the choice so far, the only remaining question is how it compares with C. In voting between A and C, the majority (individuals II and III) prefer C. So C is the final choice, reflecting the apparent will of the majority.

However, suppose instead that these individuals vote first between B and C. In this case, C is immediately rejected because individuals I and II prefer B. Thus, the preference of the majority isn't clear at all. C may be the final choice or immediately rejected, depending on how the voting is set up.

**TABLE 23-1 The Voting Paradox: Preferences of Three Individuals for Alternative Policies A, B, and C**

| Choice | Individual I | II | III |
|---|---|---|---|
| First choice | A | B | C |
| Second choice | B | C | A |
| Last choice | C | A | B |

Consequently, in a world in which individual preferences differ, an important determinant of the final choice may be the political process itself (in this example, the political decision on which options will be voted on first). Thus, the individual who sets a committee's agenda or controls its voting procedure may be able to control the result.[6]

## 3. Logrolling

***Logrolling*** occurs when several members of Parliament agree: "You vote for my policy, and I'll vote for yours." Table 23-2 shows how it works in a simple case with three voters.

The first row in this table indicates that policy A provides a benefit of 3 to individual I, and a cost of 2 to each of the other two voters.

In a simple majority vote, policies A and B are both defeated; individuals II and III vote against policy A, and I and III vote against B. However, I and II have an incentive to get together first and agree to have II vote for I's pet policy A, if I will vote for II's pet policy B. Because of this logrolling agreement, both policies

[6] This voting paradox, first described over a century ago, was extended by Kenneth Arrow in *Social Choice and Individual Values* (New York: John Wiley, 1951).

**TABLE 23-2 Logrolling: Benefits (+) or Costs (−) of Each Policy to Each Individual**

| | Individual I | II | III |
|---|---|---|---|
| Policy A | +3 | −2 | −2 |
| Policy B | −2 | +3 | −2 |
| Net effect on each individual if *both* policies are passed because of logrolling: | +1 | +1 | −4 |

pass. As shown in the bottom row of this table, individuals I and II both benefit. Indeed, that was the reason that they engaged in logrolling in the first place. However, III loses by even more than the combined gains of I and II. Thus, logrolling hurts the community overall, even though it benefits the groups who engage in it—in our example, individuals I and II.

This is the classic example of logrolling; but there is another possibility. Change the two entries of +3 in Table 23-2 to +5. As before, in the absence of logrolling, neither policy will pass. Logrolling occurs again for exactly the same reason as before, and once again I and II benefit while III loses. The difference this time is that the combined gain of I and II exceeds III's loss. Thus, logrolling results in a net overall benefit for this community. Therefore, logrolling isn't necessarily bad. In some cases, it may be the only way of achieving a socially desirable result.

## THE PROBLEMS OF GOVERNING WITH A BUREAUCRACY

Suppose the public interest on a specific issue is clearly defined, and that Parliament or a provincial legislature has made a decision that in the long run should benefit the province or nation overall. Even in these favourable circumstances, problems may arise because this policy must be introduced and enforced by the appropriate government department — for example, the Department of Transport, the RCMP, or a provincial ministry of health. Each of these departments is a "bureau"; that is, it receives its income from a granting agency (Parliament or a provincial legislature) rather than as a private firm does—from the sale of a product in the marketplace.[7]

### 1. Difficulties in Controlling a Bureau's Performance and Cost

The government bureau typically is a monopolist in the provision of its service to the public. Indeed, the reason the government may have taken over this activity may be that it is a natural monopoly. For precisely this reason it is difficult for Parliament to judge its performance: There is no equivalent private agency providing the same service with which the government bureau might be compared. Another difficulty is that a bureau's output can't be measured. Thus, for example, Agriculture Canada can't be judged the way a private firm would be judged — on the number of bushels of wheat it produces—because it doesn't produce any. (This problem reaches right down through the ranks of a bureau. Difficulties in measuring output make it difficult for senior members in a bureau to evaluate the productivity of their juniors.)

This difficulty in evaluating performance is only one of the reasons a bureau's costs are hard to control. Another reason is that a bureau's officials sometimes feel under pressure at the end of the year to inflate costs by spending any remaining funds in their budget. If they don't, their budget may be cut the next year. Then there are the problems of bureaucratic waste that apply year round and that arise because a bureau is in a different situation than a private firm under pressure to sell its product in the marketplace. The private firm has great incentives to cut costs. These incentives come in the form of both a carrot (the desire to make profits) and a stick (the fear of bankruptcy if costs aren't kept in line). On the other hand, a bureau need not fear going broke. It is, therefore, under far less pressure to keep its costs down. Moreover, because officials in a bureau are not spending their own money, they may lose track of what it is worth. They simply don't "pay attention" in the same way that entrepreneurs do when they have their own money on the line. The result is sometimes substantial waste. For example, in his 1985 Annual Report, Canada's Auditor General cites an expenditure of about $800,000 by the Department of External Affairs to purchase memberships in an exclusive private club in Hong Kong in order to provide recreational opportunities for 34 Canadian diplomats. The Auditor General estimated that membership in a less expensive fitness club could have been bought for less than $25,000.

This and other examples illustrate waste that is the result of a lack of cost controls, leading to technical inefficiency, that is, unnecessarily high costs. Waste may also come about because officials in a bureau have a tendency to be less careful than managers of private firms in estimating the benefits of proposed expenditures. Thus, the Auditor General cites the case of a new airport that was built in the Vancouver region in 1982. When the Canadian Air Traffic Administration (CATA) first proposed the project in the late 1970s, traffic forecasts suggested that the area would need a new airport within a few years because exist-

[7] Departments of large private firms may develop many of the characteristics of a bureaucracy and, if they do, the difference between the operation of a government department and a business is reduced.

ing airports would soon be used to capacity. However, by 1981 it was becoming clear that lower-than-expected traffic volume had essentially eliminated the need for the project: Existing airports had more than enough capacity to handle projected traffic for years to come. Nevertheless, CATA decided to go ahead with the project and, in 1982, the new airport was built—at a cost of $10 million—even though there was no need for it in the foreseeable future.

In the absence of a profit motive, what incentives are there in a bureau? Government officials tend to substitute two other objectives: (1) the public interest (at least as they perceive it) and (2) their own interest, including establishing a public reputation, accumulating the power and perquisites of office, and—often most important — increasing the size of the bureau.[8]

### 2. The Tendency for the Government Bureau and Its Budget to Expand

There are several reasons why a government official might try to increase the size of a bureau. By increasing the number of employees, the official will seem to have more responsibility and thus may gain prestige. More employees may also mean more echelons of management—just as in a private firm—and therefore more jobs at the top; this in turn means improved prospects for promotion. Government officials may also seek more funds in order to serve the public or their constituents better; for example, the more funds going to Agriculture Canada, the more benefits it can provide to Canadian farmers. And the more its constituents are thereby satisfied, the more they will put pressure on Parliament if any attempts are made to cut the bureau's budget.

### 3. Monopoly Inefficiency: Public vs. Private

Both a private monopoly and a monopolized public activity may operate in a technically inefficient way—that is, with unnecessarily high cost. One reason is that both have less incentive than a competitive firm to keep costs down. Moreover, both monopolies can also result in allocative inefficiency — that is, the wrong amount of output. However, this kind of inefficiency appears in two different forms. On the one hand, a private monopoly produces too little output and, therefore, employs too few resources. On the other hand, a public monopoly—a bureau—has natural tendencies to expand. Thus, it often tends to employ too many resources.[9]

## THE PUBLIC VS. THE PRIVATE SECTOR: A REVIEW OF MICROECONOMIC MARKETS

This chapter concludes with a comparison of the various kinds of private markets described in earlier chapters, ranging from perfect competition through monopoly. These are then compared to the market for a public good. Although a complete comparison is beyond the scope of this book, these markets can be better understood by answering the following important question: In each market, how does the cost curve of a single producer compare to its total market demand curve?

In Figure 23-5, this question is answered for four types of markets, panels (a) through (d); the final panel (e) shows public goods, for comparison. In each of the first four cases, starting with perfect competition in panel (a), the type of market depends heavily on how far the firm's average costs continue to fall. To highlight this point, we have assumed that the four products shown are similar in all other respects. For example, total market demand is exactly the same for each, and the average cost AC of each reaches a minimum at the same height, $M$. The only difference in these four products is that, as we move from left to right from panel to panel, AC reaches a minimum at an increasingly large output. Thus, in panel (a), AC reaches a minimum at a very small output $Q_1$, while in panel (d), AC reaches the same minimum height $M$ at such a large level of output—that is, so far to the right—that it cannot even be shown in the diagram.

In the case of perfect competition in panel (a), market demand can be satisfied at minimum cost by a large number of producers. There is little role to be played by the government, since this market is generally efficient when left to its own devices. (We assume here that there are no complications, such as important externalities.)

Panel (b) illustrates the case of natural oligopoly, where market demand can be satisfied at minimum

[8] The objectives and behaviour of officials in a bureau are discussed in detail by Albert Breton and Ronald Wintrobe in *The Logic of Bureaucratic Conduct* (New York: Cambridge University Press, 1982).

[9] In the view of John Kenneth Galbraith, government is too small; compared to private business, it provides too few goods and services. One reason is that the sales of privately produced goods, such as autos, are increased by advertising. However, publicly supplied goods, such as roads, are generally not advertised. Therefore, we overspend on autos but underspend on roads.

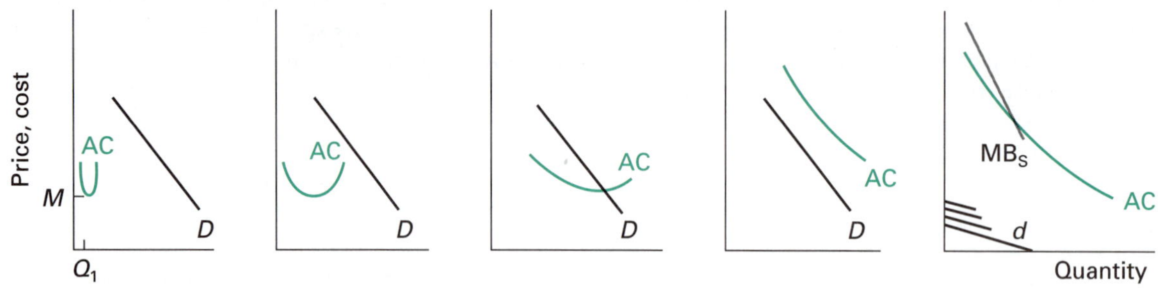


**(a) Perfect competition** (see Figure 13-3(a)).

**(b) Natural oligopoly** (see Figure 13-3(b)).

**(c) Natural monopoly** (see Figure 13-3(c)).

**(d) Non-existent good.**

**(e) Public good** (see Figure 23-3).

**An appropriate government role is to:**

| (a) | (b) | (c) | (d) | (e) |
|---|---|---|---|---|
| Leave the market alone | Enforce competition legislation | Regulate price | Leave the market alone | Provide the good itself |

**FIGURE 23-5** **The relationship between the costs of a single producer and total market demand.**

cost by just a few firms. In such a market, a strong case can be made for the vigorous enforcement of competition laws to prevent collusion or the merger of these firms into a monopoly.

In the case of natural monopoly in panel (c), market demand can be satisfied at lower cost by one firm rather than by more than one. Here, the application of competition legislation to split up a single firm makes little sense, since the split would raise costs. A preferred approach is price regulation, which prevents the firm from charging a high monopoly price, while allowing it to gain the cost advantages of large-scale production.

In panel (d) costs have outrun demand. At no point do *D* and AC overlap, that is, at no point does *D* lie above AC. Therefore, there is no single price a firm can charge and still cover its costs. The product will not even appear on the market.[10]

[10] An exception occurs in the case of the discriminating monopolist. If the gap between *D* and AC is small enough, a discriminating monopolist, such as the dentist in Figure 12-10 may be able to cover her costs if she is able to charge different prices to different buyers. In this special case, the product does appear on the market, and its production can be justified by the benefits it provides to a public that would otherwise have to do without.

Finally, consider panel (e), which shows a public good. In this case, the good is not produced by private firms; there is no standard market demand *D* (as the horizontal sum of individual demands *d*). However, the marginal social benefit $MB_S$ of this good does exist. It is the vertical sum of the individual demand curves. If the $MB_S$ curve overlaps (that is, lies above) the AC curve, it is in the public interest for the government to provide this good.

We conclude by noting that, in some cases, government intervention in the marketplace is not justified. However, in other circumstances, when there is private market failure, a case can be made for such intervention. However, our earlier word of warning should be repeated. Even in cases of private market failure, it should not be assumed that government intervention is a simple, foolproof solution; it may also fail. Recall, for example, the difficulties that arise in bureaucratic decision making, and the problems the government encounters in reversing a bad decision or in controlling its costs. Just because government intervention *could* increase efficiency, doesn't mean that it necessarily will. The government may improve things, or it may make them worse.

## KEY POINTS

1. If a good provides an external benefit, a perfectly competitive market will provide less than the efficient quantity of output. The government can induce the expansion of output to the efficient quantity by subsidizing buyers of this good by the amount of the external benefit. This "internalizes the externality" because buyers then personally enjoy not only the benefit the good provides to themselves, but also an amount equal to the benefit it provides to others.
2. No individual farmer would consider building a flood-control dam, because of its high cost and because the internal benefits he would receive would be trivial compared to the external benefits that would go to thousands of neighbouring farmers. This, then, is the general idea of a public good: It is a good that will not be produced by the private market; if it is to exist at all, it must be produced by the government.
3. A more precise definition is that a public good is one that provides inexhaustible benefits that no one can be excluded from enjoying, regardless of who pays for it. For example, once a flood-control dam has been built, no one can be excluded from enjoying its flood-control services.
4. Building such a dam will be justified if its cost is less than the sum of its benefits to all the public.
5. In practice, there may be major problems in evaluating these benefits. Even if people have a clear idea in their own minds of what the value of the benefits would be, they are unlikely to tell any government official (or, for that matter, any private entrepreneur). Therefore, the alternative approach of cost-benefit analysis is often used. For example, the benefit of flood control is estimated by looking at past records of how often floods have occurred and the damage they have done to crops and buildings.
6. There are two important ways to protect the environment. When it is being damaged by, say, polluting firms, the proper approach is to use one of the policies described in Chapter 22, such as a tax or a system of marketable emissions permits. But when the environment is deteriorating of its own accord — for example, if a wildlife species is becoming extinct — the preservation of the environment may be viewed as a public good. Thus, government protection of the environment is justified if the costs of this protection are less than the benefits it provides to all individuals in society.
7. Whereas anti-pollution regulations are justified because pollution is an external cost, regulations of safety in the workplace and protection of consumers against harmful products are justified because workers and consumers cannot quickly, accurately, and inexpensively acquire information about safety and health risks.
8. A regulation should not be imposed simply because it is pursuing a desirable goal. Instead, any regulation should pass a cost-benefit test. However, estimating costs and benefits is often difficult. Nonetheless, regulatory policy can often be improved with only fragmentary estimates.
9. When the government intervenes in the economy, a number of problems arise. For example, reversing an error is more difficult for the government than for private firms, because politicians fear losing votes if they admit mistakes.
10. By watching what the public buys, private firms can get a clearcut indication of what the public wants. But when the public votes for a candidate who has promised to, say, build a dam, it's not clear whether the public wants the dam or not. It may have voted for the candidate because of his or her views on foreign policy or for other reasons.
11. Politicians often make economic decisions, not so much in the interests of the general public, as in the interests of their specific constituency (or some special-interest group within that constituency). Moreover, they tend to favour policies with a payoff that is obvious and will be realized quickly — in particular, before the next election.
12. There are problems in defining the public interest, since a majority vote may not lead to a clear winning policy. Moreover, a majority vote may, by oppressing a minority, lead to an overall loss to society.

13. There is a natural tendency for a bureau and its budget to expand. One reason is that a bureau typically is not under the same cost-cutting pressures as a private firm which must sell its output on a competitive market.

## KEY TERMS

**external benefit**
**public choice**
**internalizing an external benefit**
**public good**
**non-rivalry**
**non-excludability**
**free rider**
**option demand**
**cost-benefit analysis**
**cost-benefit test**
**regulatory inconsistency**
**oppressive majority**
**voting paradox**
**logrolling**

## PROBLEMS

23-1. (a) Suppose the number of individuals benefiting from the provision of a pure public good increases. Should the supply of the public good therefore be increased too?
(b) If exclusion were possible in the case of public goods, would efficiency be served by practising it?

23-2. If an expressway is to be built into a city, discuss the costs and benefits that you think should be estimated. Explain why preparing such an estimate might be a difficult task.

23-3. Suppose that, instead of the per-unit subsidy to the buyer equal to the bracket in Figure 23-1, the government provides exactly the same subsidy to the seller. Show the effect. Does this subsidy increase output to the efficient quantity? How does this policy compare with the policy of subsidizing the buyer?

23-4. In a free market, the public can refuse to fly on an airline that has had a series of crashes. Why can't the public conclude that the airline is unsafe after one crash? Does this illustrate the difficulty the public may face in acquiring information? Explain why or why not.

23-5. Should a driver who is careless and runs into a railway train be able to sue the auto manufacturer for producing a car that is "an unreasonable safety risk" because it didn't protect him? Should he be able to sue the auto company if he has bumped into another car at very slow speed and his engine has exploded as a consequence? If your answers differ in these two cases, how do you draw the line?

CHAPTER

# 24 GOVERNMENT POLICIES TO REDUCE INEQUALITY: CAN WE SOLVE THE POVERTY PROBLEM?

*If a free society cannot help the many who are poor, it cannot save the few who are rich.*

*John F. Kennedy*

Most of the discussion in earlier chapters has been about the role of government in furthering the objective of economic efficiency. For example, government uses competition laws to try to prevent the inefficiency that results from monopoly; through regulation, it seeks to prevent overuse of natural resources, and to protect the environment; it is efficient for government to subsidize positive externalities and to provide public goods. In this chapter, we return to an issue first raised in Chapter 18: the government's role in promoting equity. Although Canadians may differ on the question of how far we should go in reducing income inequality in general, an overwhelming majority agree that society has a responsibility to protect those at the bottom end of the income scale. Nobody should starve. No child should have to grow up in grinding poverty; nor should the elderly have to suffer deprivation in their declining years. Yet, in 1990, poverty was still a fact of life for about one in eight Canadian families, and one out of three individuals living alone.

The extent and effects of poverty are not as visible in Canada as they are in the United States, where they are depressingly illustrated in the run-down areas in the core of almost every large city, and where it is estimated that more than a third of all children born today will spend part of their childhood in poverty. But while our poverty problem is less apparent, it is very real for the people affected by it. And poverty in North America is difficult to bear not only because it makes it hard for people to get even decent standards of food, housing, and clothing, but also because the poverty of the few contrasts so starkly with the comfort of the many.

This chapter is a study of the poor — the individuals who appeared in the bottom left-hand corner of the Lorenz income curve in Figure 18-1. Who are the poor? Why are they poor? What programs has the government introduced to fight the war on poverty? Should these programs be viewed as a way of cleaning up an economic mess created by the system, or do they create the mess? And finally, can the faults in these programs be cured — and, if so, how?

## POVERTY

The economic definition of poverty is "inadequate income." But this does not mean that poverty is strictly an economic condition. It is often also a state of mind, a condition in which the individual feels helpless and unable to cope. Therefore, poverty is a subject for sociologists and political scientists as well as economists. One of the difficulties encountered in studying poverty is the chicken-or-egg problem: Are people unable to cope because they are poor? Or are they poor because they are unable to cope? Undoubtedly the answer is, "Both." Poverty exists when people have inadequate income with which to buy the necessities of life. In 1991 it was defined, for a family of four in a large city, as an income of $29,601.

## How the Poverty Line Is Defined

The problem in defining the ***poverty line*** — in the statistics, it is called the "low-income cutoff" — is to define what is meant by the necessities of life. For one thing, different families may have different "necessary" expenditures. For some it may be dental care or prescription drugs; for those who must drive to work, it may be the cost of a car. But some necessities must be paid for by every family: decent food and clothing, and a place to live. The importance of spending on food, clothing, and shelter can be seen in studies of family expenditure patterns. They show that the poorer the family, the larger the proportion of the family budget that is spent on these items: As the family becomes poorer, spending on luxury items will decline until all that remains is the cost of food, clothing, shelter, and a small amount of expenditures on other things.

The government defines the poverty line by estimating the income level at which an average family has to spend as much as 56.2% of its budget on food, clothing, and shelter. Because the cost of food and shelter differs between urban and rural areas, the 1991 poverty line for a rural family of four is lower than it is for an urban family: about $20,188 for a rural family versus $29,601 for an urban family. The poverty line is also adjusted for the size of the family unit: For an unattached individual living in an urban area, it was about $14,948 in 1991, but for an urban family of six it was $35,168.

Of course, the poverty line has to be adjusted upward periodically to take inflation into account. And, historically, over the long term it tends to rise for another reason as well: Our concept of poverty keeps shifting up. The poverty income of about $29,601 in 1991 would have been regarded before Confederation as a very handsome income indeed (even after full adjustment is made for inflation). In fact, it would still have been considered a good income as late as the 1930s. So, upward adjustments in the definition of poverty do occur. But beware: If the definition of poverty is made too flexible, the concept becomes meaningless. If, for example, poverty is defined as the income of the bottom one-tenth of the population, there is no hope of curing it: By this definition, one in ten Canadians will always be poor, no matter how much we may raise everyone's income. And the statement that one Canadian family in ten is living in poverty will tell us absolutely nothing about how serious the problem is, or about our success in curing it.

## Who Are the Poor?

As Table 24-1 shows, poverty in the early 1990s was a more serious problem in some Canadian regions than in others. The Prairie provinces and Quebec had the highest percentage of families living in poverty in 1990 — partly because of depressed farm income in that year. The rate for Ontario was less than 10%, substantially below the national average.

Also, from Table 24-2 one can see that some specific kinds of families or individuals have much higher percentages below the poverty line. Often, poverty goes with other problems that make life difficult. Families in which the head of the household is a woman are more than three times as likely to be poor as the average family. And families with three or more children are more than twice as likely to be poor as a couple with no children. Poverty also goes with old age: Almost 45% of the people over the age of 65 who live alone are below the poverty line. For many poor people, the explanation for poverty is simply a lack of jobs. In 1990, some 70% of those who lived alone and had been employed for less than 20 weeks had incomes below the poverty level.

# GOVERNMENT ANTI-POVERTY POLICIES

Programs to combat the problem of poverty have existed in Canada for a long time. Many of the early programs were organized by private charities; small-scale welfare schemes were also set up by local and provincial governments. (In the original British North America Act of 1867, social welfare came exclusively under provincial jurisdiction.) But government spending on programs designed to reduce poverty has been growing steadily over time, especially since the mid-1960s. Between the mid-1960s and the early 1990s, transfer payments by federal and provincial govern-

**TABLE 24-1 Incidence of Low-income Families by Region (Percentage of population in 1990)**

| | |
|---|---|
| Atlantic provinces | 12.7% |
| Quebec | 14.5 |
| Ontario | 9.8 |
| Prairie provinces | 13.5 |
| British Columbia | 11.9 |

*Source:* Statistics Canada, *Income Distribution by Size in Canada, 1990.* Reproduced by permission of the Minister of Supply and Services Canada.

**TABLE 24-2 Incidence of Low Income by Selected Characteristics, 1990**

| | Estimated Percentage below Poverty Line | |
|---|---|---|
| | **Families** | **Unattached Individuals** |
| All families and unattached individuals | 12.1% | 34.1% |
| By age of household head | | |
| 24 and younger | 38 | 53 |
| 25–64 years | 12 | 39 |
| 65 and over | 8 | 44 |
| By sex of household head | | |
| Female | 40 | 39 |
| By marital status of household head | | |
| neither married nor single* | 32 | 37 |
| By weeks worked | | |
| none | 24 | 52 |
| 10–19 weeks | 34 | 69 |
| 20–48 weeks | 13 | 28 |
| 49–52 weeks | 5 | 12 |
| By education of household head | | |
| 0–8 years of school | 17 | 55 |
| some secondary | 17 | 40 |
| By origin of household head | | |
| Canadian born | 11 | 34 |
| non-Canadian born | 15 | 37 |
| By number of children younger than 16 years | | |
| none | 8 | 34 |
| 1 | 17 | — |
| 2 | 15 | — |
| 3 or more | 21 | — |

*Source:* Statistics Canada, *Income Distribution by Size in Canada, 1990.* Reproduced by permission of the Minister of Supply and Services Canada.

*Divorced, separated, widowed.

ments grew by more than ten times in dollar terms, and more than five times when adjusted for inflation.

When the public thinks of anti-poverty programs, it is these government programs — such as Old Age Security, Unemployment Insurance, and social assistance plans — that usually come to mind. But these outlays relieve only the ***symptoms of poverty***: They make it more bearable without providing much hope that the problem will be cured (that is, that the poor will be able to increase their earnings). A more promising long-run approach is to attack the ***causes of poverty***. For example, expenditures on education or training are designed to cure one of the causes of poverty: inadequate human capital. (Although it is usually more promising to attack the causes of a problem than its symptoms, this is not always the case. In extreme cases of "clinical" poverty, where individuals have such a low innate capacity or skill that no amount of training will allow them to earn a living, straight support programs may be the more effective form of assistance.)

## Policies to Reduce the Causes of Poverty

Before turning to the "symptom-relieving" policies, which are aimed at supporting people who are already poor, we consider policies that are intended to reduce the incidence of poverty by attacking its causes.

### 1. Subsidizing Investment in Human Capital

Local governments (with financial contributions from the provinces) subsidize ***investment in human capital*** by paying for the full cost of schooling until the end of high school. Because it is paid for, more individuals will finish high school; high school graduates are less likely to be poor than those with less education. University and community college education is also heavily subsidized by provincial governments. While most students pay part of the cost, the provinces generally have programs to assist community college and university students from low-income families.

For those no longer attending school, the government also supports on-the-job training: For example, under the *National Training Act*, the federal government pays part of the cost of training or retraining people who have lost their old jobs, and who might otherwise end up below the poverty line. Similar programs also exist at the provincial level.

### 2. Dealing With Unemployment and Disability

The most promising government policies to cure unemployment are those designed to keep the economy operating at a high level of output. But this provides no cure for those who cannot work, for example, because they are disabled. To reduce the incidence of disability due to work-related injuries or illness, we have federal and provincial legislation to govern the safety and other conditions in the workplace (discussed in Chapter 23). The incomes of those workers who *do* become disabled are partially protected by provincial Workers' Compensation programs. In addition, provincial health insurance programs provide health care at little or no cost to the user. By making high-quality health care available to everyone, these programs help prevent workers from losing their earning power due to illness.

### 3. Reducing Poverty in One-parent Households

In recent years, some provinces have enacted new laws to improve the enforcement of court orders providing for child support payments following marriage breakdowns. These laws are particularly important because they reduce the incidence of poverty among the rapidly growing number of one-parent (usually single-mother) households. Another area that is especially important for this group is day care: Unless affordable day-care facilities are available, single parents are effectively unable to provide for themselves and their children. Some amount of subsidized day care is provided in most provinces with financial contributions by the federal government, but the number of spaces available is not nearly enough to meet the demand. Although proposals for increasing the amount of subsidized day care have been debated for a long time, progress has been slow, in part because of fears of the potentially high cost to the government, in part because of the disagreement over *how* it should be provided.

### 4. Other Policies

The Canadian Charter of Rights, as well as provincial human rights legislation, represent the implementation of ***policies to eliminate discrimination*** on the basis of race or gender. This is a useful way to attack poverty, since, as we have already seen, discrimination against minorities or women, in rates of pay or in hiring and firing practices, contributes to poverty. Yet another policy has been started by some local governments who have organized special programs to assist welfare recipients to find work.

## POLICIES TO REDUCE THE SYMPTOMS OF POVERTY: GOVERNMENT PROGRAMS TO MAINTAIN INCOMES

Even if it is not possible to cure a disease, it is very important to provide the patient with relief from the symptoms. As a supplement to their efforts at developing long-run cures for poverty (through upgrading human capital, helping one-parent families support themselves, and preventing disability), Canadian governments also provide public assistance programs that keep many families from falling below the poverty line (Table 24-3).

## Social Insurance Programs

Several of the government's transfer programs are *universal*. That is, they are not specifically targeted on the poor: The transfers are made to rich and poor alike. The most important of these general ***social insurance programs*** are ***Old Age Security***, the ***Canada and Quebec Pension Plans***, ***Unemployment Insurance***, and ***provincial health insurance plans***. Even though the transfers under these programs are not restricted to poor people, they play a key role in keeping many individuals and families from falling below the poverty line.

### Old Age Security (OAS)

All Canadian residents over age 65 are eligible for the Old Age Security program, though only those who have been Canadian residents for a sufficiently long time get the full benefit. The OAS comes in the form of a monthly cheque the amount of which is the same

**TABLE 24-3 Major Government Programs to Maintain Income, 1991**

| Program | Total Cost ($ billion) | Government Responsible for Program |
|---|---|---|
| Old Age Security (OAS) | 14.1 | federal |
| Guaranteed Income Supplement (GIS) | 4.3 | federal |
| Canada/Quebec Pension Plan (CPP/QPP) | 12.3 | federal/provincial |
| Family allowances | 2.8* | federal |
| Refundable Child Tax Credit | 2.0* | federal |
| Veterans' pensions | 1.9 | federal |
| Unemployment Insurance (UI) | 12.7 | federal |
| Health care | 40.5 | federal/provincial |
| Social welfare assistance, worker's compensation, and other social welfare services | 11.6 | federal/provincial |
| Total Health and Social Services | 107.2 | |

*Source:* Compiled by the authors from data in Canadian Tax Foundation, *The National Finances, 1991.*

*Note: From 1993, these programs have been replaced by the Child Benefit program.

for all recipients. The amount is indexed to the consumer price index and, therefore, increases from year to year. In 1991 it was $361 per month per recipient.

## The Canada Pension Plan (CPP) and Quebec Pension Plan (QPP)

The CPP, which covers most people in the labour force, provides for retirement benefits to people over 65, with the amount depending on the person's previous earnings. (The CPP may also pay certain other types of benefits, such as health benefits and pensions to surviving spouses and children when a beneficiary dies.) The CPP does not apply to people in Quebec, because Quebec has set up its own government pension plan, the QPP.

The CPP is a contributory plan, which means that it is financed by previous (before-retirement) contributions from workers and their employers. (In 1991, the workers' contribution was fixed at 2.3% of earnings up to a maximum of $632.50 per year. Employers had to contribute the same amount.) The maximum retirement pension (for those who have contributed the maximum amount during their earning years) was roughly $605 per month in 1991. Like the OAS payments, the retirement pensions under CPP are indexed to the consumer price index.

## Unemployment Insurance

Canada's system of government unemployment insurance was started on a fairly modest scale in 1940. However, its scope was greatly expanded in 1971, and it now covers about nine-tenths of our labour force (the remaining 10% are those who are self-employed, such as home repair contractors, lawyers, and others). The program (which is often referred to simply as UI) is designed as an insurance scheme, with employers and workers paying a percentage of the workers' income (6.7% in 1991) into the system, as long as they remain employed. But, as soon as they become unemployed, they receive benefits. Essentially, the weekly benefits are equal to 60% of previous earnings, but cannot be higher than a specified ceiling ($408 per week in 1991).

The number of people drawing UI benefits grew rapidly during the late 1970s and first half of the 1980s, for several reasons:

1. During that period, the economy was operating well below capacity, creating high rates of unemployment.
2. Many new entrants to the labour force were able to find jobs only for short periods of time and then became unemployed.
3. Because of changes in the eligibility rules, it gradually became easier to qualify for UI benefits. One modification was to allow women who are unable to work because of pregnancy to collect benefits. Another was to include some seasonal workers (such as fishermen) in the UI system, so that they became eligible for benefits in the off season.

Although the number of people receiving benefits declined during the economic expansion of the 1980s, it rose again during the severe recession of 1990–1992. In an effort to control the soaring cost of the program, the government introduced somewhat stricter eligibility rules. For example, most people who voluntarily quit their jobs are no longer eligible for benefits.

## Health Insurance

As we have already noted, each province has a health insurance program that provides almost all health care services at little or no cost to almost all of its citizens. (Though some people are allowed to opt out of the program in some provinces, few choose to do so.) While they are still called "insurance" programs, most provinces finance the cost of health care out of their own tax receipts and transfers from the federal government. (Some of the issues in health insurance are discussed in Box 24-1.)

Whereas programs such as Old Age Security and Unemployment Insurance provide cash transfers, health care insurance and programs such as free elementary and secondary education provide ***benefits in kind***, that is, specific goods or services instead of cash.

*Benefits in kind* are transfers, not of cash, but of some good (like drugs) or service (medical care).

### APPLICATIONS AND ILLUSTRATIONS BOX 24-1
### The Rising Cost of Health Care

It is widely recognized that the quality of health care in Canada is as good as anywhere in the world. However, it has become *very* costly. In the early 1990s, we spent almost 10% of GDP on health care.

In Canada, most of the cost of health care is covered by provincial government insurance plans. In the United States, government plans cover only those over age 65 (Medicare) and the poor (Medicaid); the rest of the population is either covered by private plans, or not covered at all. Nevertheless, the U.S. health care system is even more costly than the Canadian one: In the early 1990s, Americans spent well over 13% of their GDP on health care.

One reason health care has become so costly in Canada and the United States is that medical research has now made it possible to save lives in a variety of new ways. But most methods, such as heart transplants, are very expensive. All available lifesaving opportunities cannot be seized unless a larger and larger percentage of the nation's GDP is directed into this effort. One can argue that, with the opening up of new lifesaving opportunities, more of our GDP *should* be spent in this way. However, if we try to capture all of these opportunities, the cost would become extremely high. Therefore, society must have some way of deciding at what point its lifesaving efforts will be limited—that is, at what point funds that could save lives will be cut off. Which patients will be the lucky ones who will live because they get access to the limited number of lifesaving machines and treatments that society can afford? No one likes to make this life-and-death decision on "who will get a seat in the lifeboat" and who will not. For this reason, there are a number of alternative ways of making this decision.

(a) Delay. In 1984, the British National Health Service provided about 110 free heart transplants. However, there was a waiting list of up to a year, during which time most of those in line simply died.

(b) Set an age limit. Unofficially, heart transplants in the United States were, in the past, given only to those less than 50 years of age.

(c) Use chance. Decide on who will live and die in some sort of a doomsday lottery. However, this makes no sense at all, because an Einstein may lose out in such a lottery to a suicidal derelict who places no value on his own life. (For more on this life-or-death choice, see Victor R. Fuchs, *Who Shall Live?* (New York: Basic Books, 1983).)

Because these methods are unsatisfactory or inadequate, the life-or-death decision fre-

**BOX 24-1 continued**

quently has to be made by doctors on the spot—or administrators or committees allocating funds. It's often an agonizing decision. We've seen earlier how difficult it is to put a value on a life. But the task of saying that one *particular* life is worth more than another—and, therefore, is the one that should be saved — is even more difficult. Therefore, whenever possible, those making such decisions understandably argue: Instead of choosing between two lives, let's save them both—if there is any conceivable way we can get the cost covered. This, then, is one reason there is persistent upward pressure on costs.

Another reason is that when most of the bills for a patient's health care are paid for by a government insurance plan (or by private insurance, for that matter), there is little pressure to cut costs. Patients have little or no incentive to seek out low-cost treatment; when your health is at stake you don't go bargain hunting, especially if the government or an insurance company is paying the tab.

Canadian governments have tried a variety of measures to counteract the upward pressure on the costs of health care. Doctors are no longer allowed to set their own fees, but have to charge according to a fee schedule that has been negotiated with the provincial government. (In the mid-1980s, doctors in Alberta and Ontario were allowed to charge their patients in excess of the negotiated schedules ("extra-billing"). However, following the passage of the Canada Health Act, which provided for financial penalties by the federal government for provinces that allowed extra-billing, legislation to ban it was quickly introduced.) While hospitals in Canada are not technically "owned" by provincial governments, they get almost all their operating funds and most of their capital funds directly from the governments. Thus, one way in which provincial governments have been cutting back is by simply giving hospitals smaller budgets.

A number of proposals have been made to increase the efficiency of the health care system by using various forms of financial incentives. A promising alternative that is appearing in the United States is so-called "managed care" of the type provided, for example, by Health Maintenance Organizations (HMOs). HMOs are corporations that own their own hospitals and employ their own doctors. Instead of billing patients directly for the services produced, they provide hospital and physician services, at no direct charge, to people who have enrolled in the HMO plan and pay a fixed fee each year or month. (Such a plan is sometimes referred to as a "prepayment" plan.) Since the income per enrolled patient in an HMO is fixed, the HMO makes more money the *fewer* the services it provides to its patients. In contrast, doctors and hospitals who bill their patients (or their patients' insurance companies) for services rendered, make more money if they provide *more* services. Even though the American Medical Association has long been opposed to HMOs, they have been growing in the United States and they may become more important if the proposals introduced by President Clinton in 1993 to reform the U.S. health care system are actually passed.

Finally, there is evidence from the United States that another explanation for the present high cost of health care may be that some doctors and hospitals have been defrauding the government health insurance plans. A U.S. senate committee investigating the cost of Medicaid found that some doctors would carry out complete physical examinations—with the whole battery of laboratory tests—on essentially healthy people who came to their offices with a minor complaint. Through referrals, a group of specialist doctors may "ping-pong" patients back and forth among themselves. Moreover, Medicaid patients getting a doctor's appointment have sometimes been told to bring their children, too. The doctor can then take a brief look at the children and charge Medicaid the fee for an office visit for each. Attempts to fight this problem of "medifraud" have entailed the creation of costly administrative machinery to supervise the payments made under the plans.

### The OAS and UI Clawback Rules

In trying to reduce the cost of the OAS and UI programs, the federal government has introduced provisions in the Income Tax Act that have the effect of reducing the OAS and UI benefits received by individuals with relatively high incomes. Under these ***benefit clawback*** rules, individuals with taxable income above a base amount are required to pay back a portion (up to 30% in the case of UI, and up to 15% in the case of OAS) of any benefits they have received during the past year, when they pay their income tax. Although the base amounts are relatively high (only individuals with taxable income above $53,215 were required to pay back any part of their OAS benefit in the 1992 taxation year, for example), these provisions have been very controversial. For example, retirees have argued that it is unfair to reduce the benefits for those who already have retired and therefore can't change the amount they receive from their private pension plans. UI beneficiaries, on the other hand, have argued that since everyone pays UI contributions at the same rate, everyone should have the right to collect the benefits at the same rate.

## Targeted Transfer Programs

The government transfer programs described above are programs that are extended to all eligible beneficiaries regardless of income. Thus, while they help many people to escape poverty, they are not specifically designed for this purpose only, because they are not targeted on the poor. The programs described below, by contrast, are directly designed to combat poverty: They are available exclusively to people with low incomes.

### Guaranteed Income Supplement (GIS)

The ***Guaranteed Income Supplement*** is a federal program that is designed to supplement the resources of people over 65 who have little income beyond Old Age Security. The maximum payment to a single person with no income other than OAS was $430 per month in 1991. For those over 65 with other income in addition to OAS, the GIS payments are reduced by 50% of the amount of other income. As we saw earlier, many elderly people in Canada are poor and, in fact, more than half of the people over 65 receive money under the GIS program.

### The Integrated Child Tax Benefit

This program, also known as the ***Child Benefit***, replaced the old system of family allowances in 1993. The family allowance program, also known as the "baby bonus," was a universal program going back as far as 1945. In most provinces, families simply received a flat monthly amount per child. Since 1978, the government had also been providing a tax credit for families with children. Because the credit was "refundable" — that is, the value of the credit was reduced for families with income above a base level — it was in effect a targeted program. The Child Benefit is essentially an enriched version of this credit. In 1993, the basic component was a credit of $1020 per child per year (slightly more for families with three or more children), which was reduced by 5% (2.5% for families with only one child) of family income above $25,921. (Thus, for example, the credit of $2040 for a family with two children would be reduced by $1000 if the family earned $20,000 more than the limit.) To encourage low-income families to earn an income, the credit is increased (by up to $500 per family) when the family's earned income increases in the range from $3750 to $10,000 per year. The Child Benefit is partially indexed: Whenever the rate of price inflation is more than 3% per year, its value will be increased at the rate of inflation less 3%. (For example, if the rate of inflation is 5%, the Child Benefit will increase by 2%.)

### Social Assistance

This program encompasses what most people mean when they speak of somebody "being on welfare." Social assistance programs are the responsibility of the provinces, although municipal authorities may administer the programs at the local level. But the federal government shares in the cost under the ***Canada Assistance Plan***: In the early 1990s, the federal government paid a little less than half of the total amount spent on social assistance. During the 1990–1992 recession, the cost of social assistance programs rose dramatically across Canada, but especially in Ontario, as Figure 24-1 shows.

The amount of assistance a family receives is determined by its *cash deficit* — that is, the amount by which its income falls short of its necessary expenditure on basic food, clothing, shelter, and other essentials. Subject to various administrative limitations, social workers have fairly wide discretion in deciding what expenditures are necessary for the family, and

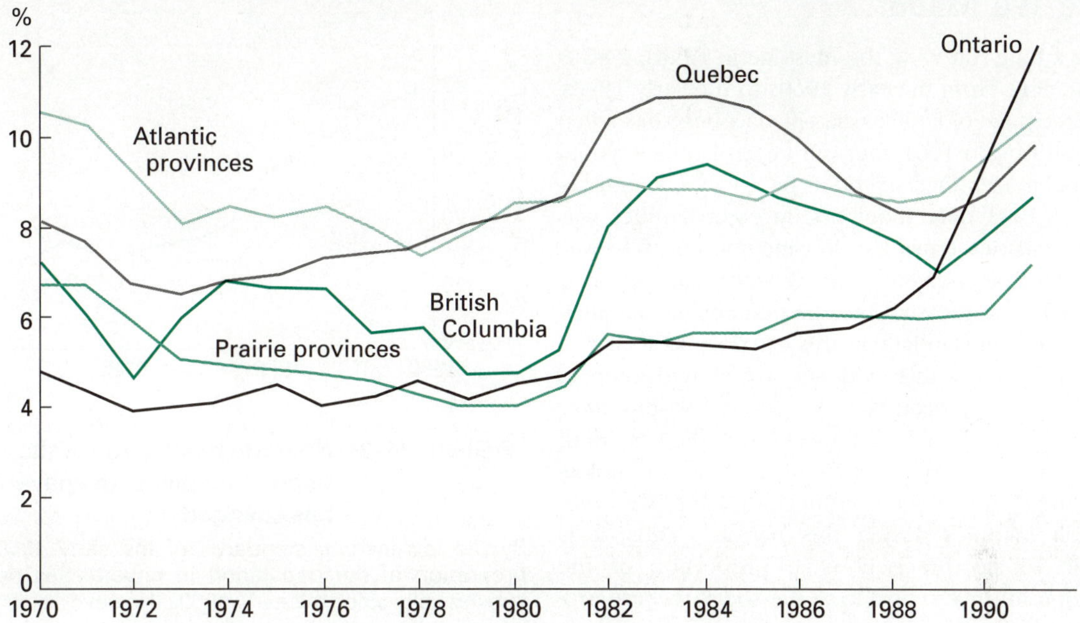


**FIGURE 24-1 Recipients of general social assistance as a percentage of the population.** For most of the 1970s and 1980s, Ontario and the Prairie provinces had the lowest percentages of the population on general social assistance (that is, excluding assistance to recipients in special categories such as single parents).

In the 1982 recession, the number of recipients rose in all parts of Canada, but especially in Quebec and British Columbia. The heavy impact of the 1990–1992 recession on Ontario is dramatically evident in the graph. In 1989, the percentage of the population receiving general social assistance in Ontario was one of the lowest in Canada: By 1991, this percentage had become larger in Ontario than it had been in any other region of Canada in the last two decades.

*Source*: Paul A.R. Hobson and France St-Hilaire, "Fiscal Transfers and the Federal Role in Income Security," mimeo, Institute for Research on Public Policy, 1993.

may arrange payment for specific things that the family would not otherwise be able to afford, such as dental work or the services of a homemaker.

## Other Programs

In addition to the major welfare programs, local and provincial governments have been trying a variety of other ways to give assistance to people with low incomes. For example, several provinces have programs supplementing the federal OAS/GIS payments to needy persons over 65. Both provincial governments and the federal government (through the Canada Mortgage and Housing Corporation) provide subsidized housing to welfare recipients and other people with limited incomes. There are also subsidies to cover part of the cost of care in nursing homes and homes for the aged and, in some provinces, there are programs to ensure that prescription drugs are available at no cost to those who would have difficulty paying for them.

# ASSESSING THE PRESENT WELFARE PACKAGE

The cost of our social welfare programs is very high. In trying to assess whether the money is being well spent, one can consider two different but related questions:

1. How far have the welfare programs taken us toward the fundamental objective of eliminating poverty?
2. Is the current package of social welfare programs efficient? In other words, are we reducing poverty at minimum cost, or could we get the same reduction at a lower cost?

## How Much Progress Have We Made?

Taking a long-run view, the message in Figure 24-2 is encouraging. From the early 1960s to the early 1990s, the percentage of families classified as poor has fallen by two-thirds. In 1961, four out of ten families would have been classified as poor by today's standards, while in 1991 only about one in eight families was below Statistics Canada's "low-income cutoff" level. (If we look at individuals living alone, the progress appears less impressive, but the percentage classified as poor fell substantially in this category as well.)

In interpreting this evidence, we should keep in mind that some reduction in poverty would have occurred even if we had not expanded the system of welfare programs, because factors such as technological change and capital accumulation have been raising real incomes during this period.[1] Thus, it is difficult to say precisely what proportion of the reduction in poverty is due to the social welfare programs. Nevertheless, it is clear that our social welfare system has helped many Canadians escape poverty.

While the statistics are encouraging when we consider the whole period shown in Figure 24-2, it appears that most of the progress was made during the 1960s and 1970s. In the early 1980s, the extent of poverty actually *increased* substantially. This was particularly disturbing when we take into account the fact that during this period, spending on our social welfare programs rose at an unprecedented rate.

The principal explanation for this was undoubtedly the poor performance of the overall economy during the early 1980s; the 1982 recession was the worst since World War II, and unemployment (one of the main factors contributing to poverty) reached record levels. As the economy recovered through the mid-1980s, the percentage of people in poverty decreased once more. Nevertheless, the extent of poverty in 1987 was almost as high as it had been at the beginning of the decade, and when data for 1991/92 become available, they will almost certainly show a substantial increase again.

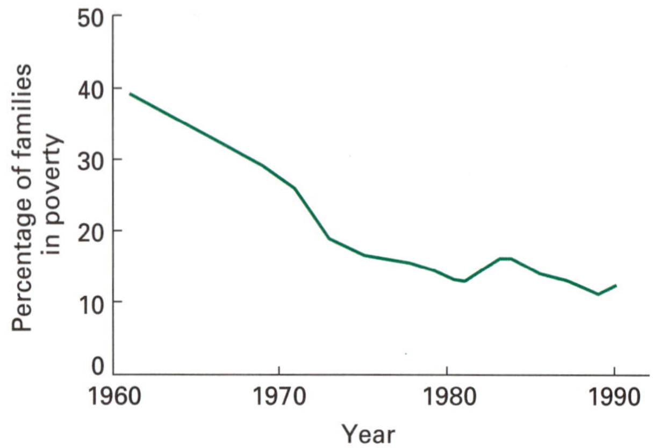


**FIGURE 24-2 How the percentage of the population below the poverty line has changed.**

By the low-income standards of the early 1990s, the proportion of the population in poverty has declined substantially since the early 1960s. However, since 1980, progress has been relatively slow. In the early 1980s, the proportion *increased* substantially.

*Source*: 1961 figure from F. Vaillancourt, *Income Distribution and Economic Security in Canada*, Vol. 1 (Toronto: University of Toronto Press in cooperation with the Royal Commission on the Economic Union and Development Prospects for Canada, 1985), Table 12. 1969–1990 data from Statistics Canada, *Income Distribution by Size in Canada*, various years.

The slow progress in reducing poverty during the 1980s and early 1990s is disappointing. After all, one of the purposes of the social welfare system is to protect Canadians from poverty during economic downturns, and the system has not done a very good job of that in recent years. This brings us to the second question raised above: How efficient is the current system of welfare programs?

## Problems with the Welfare System

Questions about the efficiency of our system of social welfare programs have been raised for a long time, and major proposals for reform date back to the late 1960s. While some critics simply would like to see less spending on social welfare, there are many others who are principally concerned with the possibility of

[1] If we examined the recent income of Canadian families *before taxes and transfers*, we would find as many as one-quarter of them below the poverty line. Taxes and transfers reduce this to about 12%. This sounds like clear evidence that taxes and transfers drastically reduce poverty. But this conclusion does not follow quite so simply. As noted earlier, if transfer payments did not exist, there would be a greater incentive to work. (Without welfare to fall back on, people would feel under more pressure to get a job. With more people working, there would be less than 25% initially below the poverty line.) In other words, because taxes and transfers have the indirect effect of reducing incentives to work, they are less effective in reducing poverty than they initially appear.

changing the *pattern* (rather than the level) of expenditures so as to make more efficient use of the money already being spent. They have two main types of criticism of the present system.

## 1. Perverse Incentives

It is difficult to design a welfare system without creating perverse incentives. To see why, consider for example a hypothetical low-income family in which the wife normally works but is currently unemployed. Suppose she has been told of an opportunity for a temporary job that would allow her to contribute an extra $5000 to the family's income this year. In deciding whether or not to take the job, she has several things to consider. (1) She would not be able to collect unemployment insurance benefits during the period she would be working. (2) If the family is currently living in subsidized low-income housing, where it is required to pay 25% of family income in rent, one-quarter of the wife's extra earnings will simply disappear into higher housing costs. (3) The increase in family income might also make the family ineligible for provincial subsidies such as sales tax or property tax rebates. Suppose the loss in unemployment insurance benefits and the other subsidies would amount to $3500. The family may then ask: If the *net* increase in family earnings would be no more than $1500 — that is, the $5000 gross earnings less $3500 in lost subsidies — is it really worthwhile for her to take this job? Would $1500 be enough to pay for things like day care for the children and help with the housework?

Of the $5000 that the wife in this example would earn by going out to work, only 30% ($1500) represents a benefit; the other 70% (that is, $3500) is offset by lost subsidies. It's just as if the family faced a 70% marginal tax rate on the extra earnings. In fact, this effect is referred to as an ***implicit tax*** built into the social welfare system.

The *implicit tax* built into a welfare program is calculated by examining the loss of benefits or subsidies when a family earns another $1 of income. (If the loss is 70 cents, the implicit tax is 70%.)

As we shall see later, the implicit tax problem is especially severe for people on social assistance; for them, the implicit tax may be as high as 100% or even more.

## 2. Complexity and Inequity

The complexity of the system adds to the cost of the programs. (A simpler system would be less costly to administer.) Worse, the complexity has contributed to introducing many *inequities* in the system. For example, poor families may receive very different levels of income depending on where they live. Some families whose members earn some income from working end up with an income that is no higher (and may even be lower) than families in which no one is working. Furthermore, if we look at the overall impact of the complicated set of transfer programs, we cannot even be sure that we always provide the most help to those who are in the greatest need. For example, according to a calculation in the report of the MacDonald Commission[2] (which contained an extensive discussion of social welfare programs), a family of four in 1985 with one income earner and an income of $100,000 received a combined benefit of $5035 from the family allowance, the refundable child tax credit, and various tax deductions, whereas a similar family with two working adults earning an income of only $25,000 received benefits of only $2240. Thus, the critics charge, one of the shortcomings of our welfare package is that its benefits are not well enough *targeted* on those low-income people who should receive the most help.

According to critics, complexity and undesirable incentive effects make the current system very inefficient. Below, we will discuss two types of reform proposals that are aimed at reducing these problems. The first — a guaranteed minimum income — has the advantage of simplicity. As we shall see, however, it does not resolve the incentive problem. The other — the negative income tax — is designed to deal with both the complexity and incentive problems. While it is unlikely that either of these schemes will ever be adopted as originally proposed, they are nevertheless worth studying because the ideas on which they are based often appear, in modified form, in actual reform proposals.

# A GUARANTEED MINIMUM INCOME: A CURE FOR THE POVERTY PROBLEM?

A scheme that clearly meets the objective of creating a *simpler* system is to eliminate poverty in one stroke

[2] Formally called the Royal Commission on the Economic Union and Development Prospects for Canada.

by having the government guarantee everybody a ***minimum income*** equal to the poverty level. If any family's income were to fall below that level, the government would just cover the shortfall with a direct cash grant. What would this cost? If we add up the shortfall in income for every family currently below the poverty line, we would end up with something less than 2% of GDP. Given what we are already spending, why couldn't we commit ourselves to this sort of relatively modest spending increase, and eliminate poverty once and for all?

Unfortunately, it is not that easy.

## Inefficiencies in a Subsidy Program

One problem is this: A program that raises the income of the poor by $1 billion costs the government (and, therefore, the Canadian taxpayer) far more than $1 billion. Waste occurs because such a program has adverse effects on incentives.

### Disincentives for Those Paying for the Subsidy

The first adverse incentive applies to those who pay the higher taxes necessary to finance this scheme. The heavier the tax rate, the more likely it is that an individual will ask, "Why am I working so hard when the government gets such a large slice of what I earn?" By reducing the reward for working, higher taxes have a negative effect on the incentive to work. Higher tax rates also encourage higher-income individuals to hire accountants or lawyers in a socially unproductive effort to find loopholes to reduce their tax payments. As U.S. economist Arthur Okun has described it: "High tax rates are followed by attempts of ingenious men to beat them, as surely as snow is followed by little boys on sleds."[3]

### Disincentives for Those Receiving the Subsidy

Now let's turn to those at the bottom of the income scale who will receive this subsidy. Here one would expect more substantial incentive effects, for the reasons shown in Figure 24-3. (In this diagram we concentrate on what happens to people at the bottom of the income scale. For simplicity, we disregard any taxes paid now by these people. To simplify further, we use a "round figure" minimum income target of $10,000.) Families are plotted along the horizontal axis according to how much income they originally earn. Thus, family *h* with $8000 earned income is plotted at point *Q* along the horizontal axis. Income after receipt of the subsidy is measured up the vertical axis. If no subsidy were to be paid to family *h*, its "income after" would also be $8000, as shown by the grey bar. In other words, family *h* would be shown by point *F* on the 45° line, where its before and after incomes are equal. Hence, this 45° line may be called the "same-before-and-after" line, or simply the "no-subsidy" line.

But, of course, our minimum income program does pay family *h* a subsidy—specifically, the $2000 coloured bar *FG* that is necessary to raise its income to

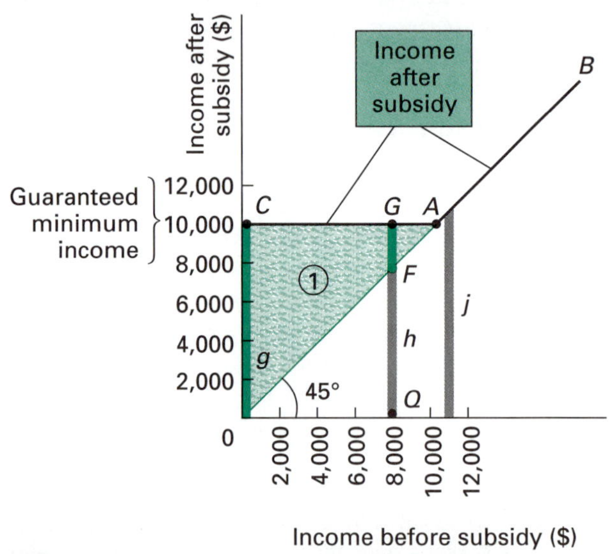


**FIGURE 24-3 Possible disincentive effects of a guaranteed $10,000 minimum income.**

The 45° line 0*AB* is the no-subsidy line. For example, at point *F* on this line, family *h* that earns $8000 (measured left to right) would end up with $8000 (measured up). On the other hand, heavy line *CAB* shows income with the subsidy. Family *h* is paid the $2000 (coloured bar) subsidy necessary to raise it to the guaranteed $10,000 level, while family *g* (which earns no income) must be paid a full $10,000 subsidy. This program erodes the incentive to work: Because *h*'s income will remain at the same $10,000 level, this individual may stop working and thus join *g*.

[3] Arthur M. Okun, *Equality and Efficiency: The Big Tradeoff* (Washington: The Brookings Institution, 1975), p. 97.

the target $10,000 level. Since the income of any other family below the target income is similarly subsidized up to this $10,000 level, the "income-after-subsidy" line is the heavy line *CAB*. Shaded triangle 1 represents the shortfall income gap that the government must fill at an additional cost that we have already noted is likely to run to less than a few percent of our GDP—*provided people continue to work and earn as much after the subsidy as before*.

The problem is that because they are being subsidized, some people will *not* work as hard as before. For example, the father of family *h* may realize: "If I don't work at all, the government will still guarantee us the same $10,000; so why should I work?" And if he stops working, that $8000 of income he earned disappears. The position of that family on the horizontal axis, therefore, shifts all the way to the left, from situation *h* to situation *g*. At this point, nothing is being earned, that family has become totally unproductive, and it must be subsidized by the full $10,000 coloured bar. Therefore, in order to raise this family's income by the original $2000 shortfall, the government ends up paying out $10,000 (which, of course, it had to raise from the public in taxes). This example illustrates what Arthur Okun referred to as "transferring income with a leaky bucket": Although $10,000 has been spent to increase the income of a poor family, it has increased that income by only $2000. The other $8000 has "leaked away" because the family has stopped working. This leakage of the grey bar at *h* also represents the efficiency loss from this policy: The original income this family produced was the $8000 grey bar at *h*, but this is now lost to society because no one in the family works any longer.

## Disincentives that Apply to the Non-poor

Disincentive effects may apply not only to families such as *h* with initial incomes below the $10,000 support level; they may also apply to families such as *j* with incomes above $10,000. Suppose the breadwinner in family *j* has been earning the $10,800 shown, in a boring and unpleasant job. The subsidy program will now offer a tempting option: Go fishing, and receive a $10,000 income from the government. If this happens, family *j* also shifts to the left into position *g*, where it, too, qualifies for the full $10,000 subsidy. So the government has to subsidize not only those with initial incomes below the $10,000 target level, but also some with higher incomes, for whom this program was never intended.

In short, when the government attempts to fill an income gap by such a simple subsidy, its cost may far exceed the initial income shortfall that it set about to cure. The reason is that the subsidy disturbs incentives, and some people stop working. From the viewpoint of the government paying the subsidy, the problem appears in two forms: On the one hand, some poor families such as *h* may absorb more subsidy than expected; on the other hand, a whole new and unexpected group of families such as *j* may appear on the scene, claiming the subsidy. Moreover, when a family such as *j* goes onto the subsidy program, the overall efficiency loss to society is particularly severe. It is the grey bar at *j*—the $10,800 of income that is no longer produced because someone who used to work is now off fishing.

The reason that this policy is so inefficient is that the portion *CA* of the "income-after-subsidy" line is completely horizontal, leaving the poor no incentive to work. That is, *they face an implicit tax of 100%*; they have nothing to show for any additional $1 they earn, because their subsidy is reduced by the same $1.

## The Implicit Tax Under the Cash Deficit Method

Critics have charged that, in terms of their anti-work incentives, provincial social assistance programs are similar to this simple subsidy scheme. Recall that under the cash deficit method, a family's welfare payment is set equal to its shortfall in income. If actual income increases by $1000, the shortfall and, therefore, the welfare payment will be reduced by the same $1000. Since lost welfare benefits are equal to the entire increase in income, this system involves a 100% implicit tax. (But, in practice, because social workers have some discretion over the welfare allowances of recipients, the implicit tax may be a bit less. On the other hand, in some cases it may be more than 100%: For example, when a family's income goes up it may lose not only its social assistance, but also some in-kind subsidies such as free dental care or the right to subsidized public housing. Because of these complications, a precise implicit tax rate is not easy to calculate. But, in a rough and ready way, the guaranteed annual income scheme in Figure 24-3—with its 100% implicit tax—can be used to illustrate some of the problems of the current Canadian system.)

# CONFLICTING VIEWS ON WELFARE

Figure 24-3 illustrates why some observers view welfare as the *cure* for society's failure, while others view it as the *cause* of this failure.

## Economic Failure: Is It Cured or Caused by Welfare?

Proponents of welfare programs point to individuals who are disabled or who simply cannot cope. Because they are unable to succeed economically, they are *initially left at g*. The (coloured bar) welfare benefits raise them up to the minimum income level. In such cases, welfare *solves* a serious social problem.

On the other hand, welfare critics point to individuals who start out at *h* or *j*, and respond to welfare by shifting to *g*. According to this view, welfare payments provide potentially productive people with an incentive to stop producing — to stop earning the grey bar of income at *h* or *j* and instead go on the dole at *g*. In such cases, welfare *creates* a social problem.

In practice, a welfare system has both effects: It solves the poverty problem for people who start at *g*, and it creates a problem by inducing some of the people who start at *h* or *j* to move to *g*. In the Canadian system, what is the relative importance of these two effects? In particular, how much does welfare erode the incentive to work?

So far, no studies are available to give us a definite answer to this question. But studies in the United States seem to show that the negative incentive is not quite as powerful as the discussion so far of Figure 24-3 might suggest. Some families at *h* or *j* don't stop working (don't move to the left). Their (grey bar) productivity is not lost. Moreover, many people start at *g*. In their case, there is no "leak in the bucket" at all: Welfare can't reduce their productivity because they don't produce anything in the first place. On average, U.S. data suggest a moderate response to the reduction in work incentives, implying a "leak" of some 20 to 25 cents for every dollar of welfare expenditures.

Moreover, we must also take into account the losses from collecting the taxes necessary to finance the welfare expenditure, because taxation encourages the search for loopholes and reduces the incentive to work of those who are taxed. Estimates of this excess burden of taxation vary widely, but they seem to suggest that 25% to 35% is the best range for estimating this additional leak, with 30% being perhaps the best single round number. When we add this to the leak that results because the recipients have an incentive to work less, we get a bucket with a leak of roughly 50%. When account is taken of the other costs—such as the administrative costs of running a welfare program—the picture is one of a bucket with somewhat more than a 50% leak.[4]

The hypothetical example in Figure 24-4 illustrates more precisely what we mean by a ***leak in the transfer bucket*** of about 50%. It does *not* mean that the government raises $100 in taxes but only delivers $50 to the poor. To see what happens, begin at line 2 with the $100 the government collects in taxes. Most, but not all of this is delivered to the poor. In our example, we suppose that the government has $10 of administrative costs, so that only $90 can be delivered to the poor. The problem is that about 25% of this — let's say $25 — leaks away. It does not raise the income of the poor at all; it just replaces the income they lose because they work less. (An

[4] Estimating this number is difficult, because it depends on how the government is raising taxes and how it is spending the funds. Nonetheless, a fairly clear, though not precise, picture still emerges. In simulations 1 and 6 in Table 2 of "Welfare Costs per Dollar of Additional Tax Revenue in the United States," *American Economic Review*, June 1984, Charles Stuart estimates that the excess cost of taxation ranges from 7% to 53%. In his judgement, 30% to 40% is the most likely range. In Table 3 of "General Equilibrium Computations of the Marginal Welfare Costs of Taxes in the United States," *American Economic Review*, March 1985, C.L. Ballard, J.B. Shoven, and J. Whalley provide estimates of the marginal excess burden of taxation that range between 17% and 56%, with their best estimate being roughly 33%. With respect to the leak when the funds are spent, because welfare recipients work less, an estimate of 25% is given in S. Danziger, et al., "How Income Transfer Programs affect Work, Savings and the Income Distribution: A Critical Review," *Journal of Economic Literature*, September 1981, pp. 975–1028.

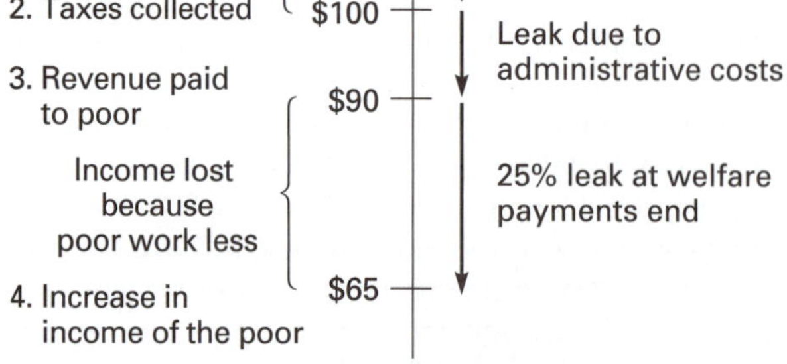


**FIGURE 24-4 Leaks in the transfer bucket.**

extreme example was family *b* in Figure 24-3.) Thus, the income of the poor is increased by only \$65 (\$90 − \$25). Finally, we return to the top of this diagram and see that when the government raises the original \$100 in taxes, this imposes a \$30 excess cost on the economy because, for example, those who are taxed work less. When this \$30 of excess cost is added to the \$100 of taxes, it is costing the Canadian public \$130 to provide a net benefit of \$65 to the poor. It is in this sense that there is a 50% leak.

Such a large leak does not mean that welfare expenditures should necessarily be cut back because of the waste in the transfer process. However, it does illustrate that solving the poverty problem is a more expensive task than was once assumed.

## Non-economic Benefits and Costs

Not surprisingly, economists focus on the economic consequences of programs such as welfare; for example, how much does the "bucket" leak? But we should recognize that many government programs—such as welfare — also have broader effects that go beyond economics.

On the positive side, welfare programs are society's way of stating its commitment to the less fortunate. We would not want to live in a callous nation, which paid no heed to the sick and helpless. By contributing to a humane society, a welfare program can have social gains that go beyond the benefits to the welfare recipients themselves.

Because of the way in which welfare programs are a symbol of society's values, any inequities in the system can be demoralizing. Critics question whether our welfare system has unintended social consequences:

1. One of the reasons some fathers in unstable marriages remain in the home and support their families is the fear of what might happen if they were to leave. If a government welfare program guarantees child support and removes this fear, won't some fathers feel more free to leave?
2. Does welfare encourage a problem it is designed to cure: the "culture of poverty"? Does it encourage dependence and destroy pride and self-respect? Being the breadwinner may be one of the few sources of pride and self-respect for those with low-paying, no-promise jobs. If welfare provides as adequately for their families as they can, does it make them feel like so much excess baggage and destroy their self-respect?

# THE KEY TRADE-OFF: EQUITY VERSUS EFFICIENCY

It all seemed so simple. As we look back over Parts 3, 4, and 5, the following message seemed to be emerging: Where product or factor markets are inefficient, the government should intervene to increase efficiency. (For example, it should intervene to tax polluters or to regulate monopoly price.) If this intervention also has favourable equity effects, so much the better; then there are no conflicts, and the appropriate policy choice is a simple one. (For example, it is easy to endorse ending discrimination in the labour market because this increases efficiency and also transfers income equitably to those who have faced disadvantages in the past because of their race or gender.)

Thus, there are some policies that don't raise a conflict between equity and efficiency. But many others do. For example, attempts to achieve equity by rent controls or interest rate ceilings lead to inefficiency. Providing protection from imports for an industry with a low-paid labour force may be equitable, but it is also inefficient since it is a move away from free trade. Because such policies do raise a conflict between equity and efficiency, they do give rise to the difficult policy choices. Why not design these policies to be efficient, and offset any adverse effects on equity by direct payments from the government?

Unfortunately, it's not so easy after all, because of one weak link in this argument: Direct government transfers may not be very efficient either. In particular, government spending on the poor erodes the incentive to work and reduces total output. So we are still left with the trade-off between the objectives of equity and efficiency: The size of the national pie is reduced if we try to carve it up in a more equitable way. This is not a recommendation that we go back to transferring income by the inefficient market interventions we have criticized in earlier chapters. Not only are they inefficient, but worse yet, as a means of raising the income of the poor, they are often ineffective. (An interest rate ceiling benefits rich borrowers as well as poor and, in fact, may leave many relatively poor borrowers out in the cold completely. As another example, farm price guarantees benefit the rich farmer without lifting many poor farmers out of poverty.)

The message remains: The way to reduce poverty is by direct government policies to aid the poor. But we should be searching for a better way of making these transfers than the simple subsidy programs we have been discussing so far. In particular, we should be seeking a way that is not only equitable—unlike our present welfare system—but one that treats all the poor alike. We also should be seeking a way that is efficient—in other words, that does not destroy the incentive to work.

## THE NEGATIVE INCOME TAX: CAN WE COMBINE EQUITY AND EFFICIENCY?

How can we guarantee families a minimum income (for example, \$10,000) without destroying their incentive to work? This is an essential question, and it is not an easy one to answer. One proposal is the ***negative income tax*** (NIT), which has been advocated by many of those on both the "left" and "right" of the political spectrum who are critical of the present welfare system. To explain this proposal, let's put Figure 24-3 back on the drawing board in Figure 24-5. This new diagram has the same frame of reference as Figure 24-3, except that it is extended to the right to allow us to take account not only of families that receive a subsidy, but also of higher-income families that pay the government a tax. The 45° "same-before-and-after" line *0QB* now represents the "no-subsidy, no-tax" line where families would be if the government neither subsidized nor taxed them.

### Design of a Negative Income Tax

To see how a negative income tax would work, begin by assuming, as before, that the minimum income level is set at \$10,000. Now, rather than subsidizing incomes just up to the line *CA* by filling gap 1 as we did in Figure 24-3, the government instead pays subsidies—that is, "negative taxes"—equal to areas 1 + 2 + 3, thereby bringing incomes up to the line *CQ*. (Beyond an income of \$20,000, a family pays "positive" taxes to the government, as shown by the grey area 4.) Because the "income-after-tax" line *CQH* slopes upward, people have an incentive to work. The more income they earn (the more they move to the right in this diagram), the more income they get to keep (the higher they rise on line *CQ*). By providing this incentive to earn income, we attempt to reduce the leak in the bucket that occurs because people prefer to go on welfare rather than work.

Proponents of the NIT have usually suggested that it should replace all existing welfare programs, including programs such as subsidized housing. If some of these subsidies remain, the poor may get a higher income from these subsidies and the negative income tax than from working. They, therefore, may quit work to draw government benefits.

The NIT should not only improve efficiency. It should also move us toward a greater degree of equity in several ways: (1) It would guarantee a minimum income for all; (2) it would replace the wide variety of existing welfare programs with one consistent policy that would treat all families at the same income level in the same way; and (3) it would also satisfy another equity objective of most Canadians — it would leave those who work with a higher income than those who do not.

At first glance, the NIT illustrated by Figure 24-5 would appear to be a very expensive program, since the subsidy is now area 1 *plus* areas 2 and 3. Specifically, the government now provides an even greater subsidy (areas 1 + 2) to poor families earning less than \$10,000, plus a subsidy of area 3 to families with incomes all the way up to \$20,000. Of course, families earning even higher incomes pay a tax. For example, a family earning \$24,000 pays the \$2000 tax shown as the black bar *t*. Thus, the line *CQH* shows how the government pays coloured subsidies all the way up to point *Q*, and levies the grey tax on incomes above this. (Although this line need not have a constant slope, it does in this simple example. Any family keeps half of any additional income it earns. For example, those with earned incomes of less than \$20,000 get to keep half of any additional income they earn; in other words, they lose half of it, which means they face a 50% implicit tax. At the same time, those at the higher end of the income scale face a 50% regular tax on all their income over \$20,000.)

Another apparent problem with the NIT is that its high cost is not limited to filling new gaps 2 + 3. In addition, the treasury loses the taxes previously collected from many non-poor families with incomes between \$10,000 and \$20,000. Under this program they would pay no tax; instead they would receive a subsidy. Moreover, this program would also reduce the taxes paid by some families with incomes above \$20,000.[5] This was not the objective when we set out to ensure that poor families would have an income of at least \$10,000.

When one takes into account all these considerations, doesn't the NIT come out badly in comparison

[5] To confirm this statement, consider a family with income just barely over \$20,000. In Figure 24-5, it pays a minuscule tax that is less than the tax it used to pay.

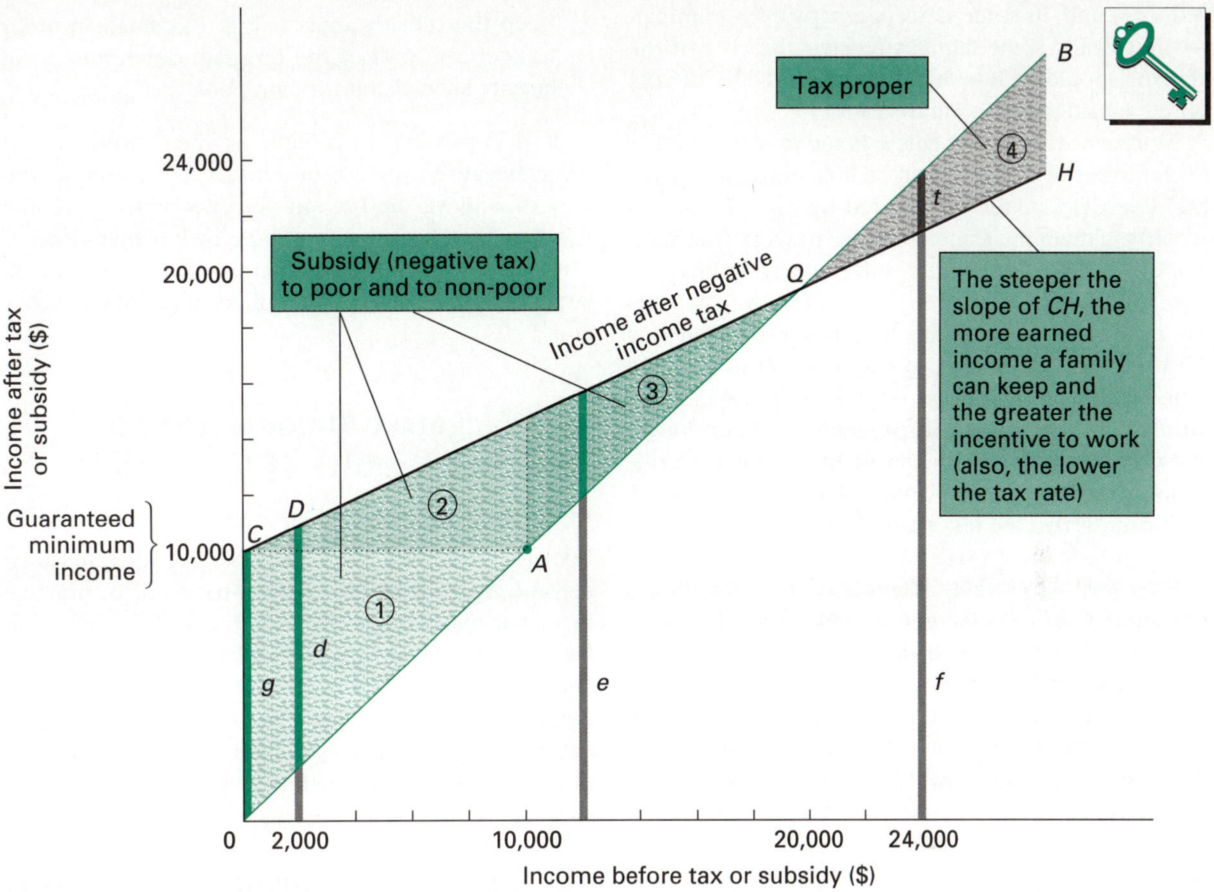


**FIGURE 24-5 How a negative income tax should work. (Compare with Figure 24-3.)**
Family *g* with a zero earned income is paid the coloured bar grant of $10,000. But what do we do with family *d* with $2000 of earned income? If we make the same mistake we made in Figure 24-3 and raise this income up only to that same $10,000 (by an $8000 grant), this will leave that family with no incentive to keep working to earn that $2000. So to provide an incentive to work, we grant this family $9000 instead (as shown by the coloured bar), thus bringing its total up to $11,000 at point *D*. If we continue in this way, always providing a $1000 incentive for families to earn an additional $2000 of income, we move up line *CDQ* to cut-off point *Q* where no subsidy is paid. Moreover, if we continue to allow families to keep half of any additional income they earn, we will tax incomes above this level down from *QB* to *QH*. Thus, grey area 4 shows us how any income above $10,000 is subject to a tax. (For example, family *f* with a $24,000 income pays the $2000 tax *t*). At the same time, areas 1 + 2 + 3 show us how any income below $20,000 is subsidized ("taxed in reverse"). Hence the name: negative income tax.

with the simple subsidy scheme in Figure 24-3? Why would anyone recommend it? The answer is that the NIT *should have a favourable effect on incentives.* The NIT should be a far less leaky bucket than a simple subsidy scheme or than our present welfare system. This point is worth considering in detail.

## Why the Negative Income Tax Should Reduce the Leaks in the "Welfare Bucket"

By allowing families to keep half of any additional income they earn, the negative income tax should induce them to get out and earn more, and thus "move to the right" in Figure 24-5. Since this would reduce—and, in some cases, perhaps even eliminate—the subsidy some families receive, the cost of this scheme should be less than that suggested by the coloured subsidy area in Figure 24-5.

Moreover, the cost of this scheme may be reduced even further by modifications. For example, the "after-tax" line *CQH* might be lowered by, say, $2000. This would maintain the same incentive to work (the same slope of *CQH*), but would substantially reduce the cost (the subsidy areas 1 + 2 + 3). Moreover, by shifting critical point *Q* to the left, it would mean that families with an income in the $16,000 to $20,000 range would no longer receive a subsidy; instead they would pay a tax. Thus, this program would no longer allow so many families to escape taxes. However, one problem would remain. Those at *C* doing no work would now receive less than the $10,000 minimum target.

This problem might be reduced by providing a guaranteed $10,000 income to those who are aged, infirm, or disabled and *cannot* work. If these people can be clearly identified, guaranteeing them a minimum income would result in no inefficiency; it would not affect the amount they work, because they can't work. Such a program would also score high in terms of equity, by providing an adequate safety net for those who cannot do without it. Such a policy—of identifying specific groups with special needs—is called *categorization* or ***tagging***. The big problem is that, in practice, it is difficult to identify exactly who should be tagged as unable to work; it is often difficult to determine who is disabled. While people don't blind themselves to get welfare, some may falsely argue that they have been disabled because, say, of minor backaches that they exaggerate.

## The Negative Income Tax Does Not Resolve All Conflicts

We can now extend this theoretical discussion of the NIT by noting how it gives rise to tension among the following three objectives:

1. Set the minimum income level (*C*) high enough so no one will be left destitute.
2. Give *CQH* enough slope to provide people with a strong incentive to work. (Many would view the slope of *CQH* in Figure 24-5 as being too low and, therefore, providing inadequate incentive to work. Since people can keep only half of any additional income they earn, they all "spend half their time working for the government.")
3. Keep the subsidy areas 1 + 2 + 3 small, in order to keep the cost of the program down and avoid heavily subsidizing the non-poor.

It is impossible to achieve all these objectives at once, because they are in conflict. For example, the way to achieve the second objective is to make line *CQH* steeper. But a greater slope means that either *C* must be lower or subsidy areas 1 + 2 + 3 must be larger. Thus, objective 2 conflicts with objectives 1 and 3.

## The Negative Income Tax in Practice: Results of Controlled Experiments

Because it seemed such an appealing idea, negative income tax schemes have been tried out in practice in actual experiments in both the United States (in New Jersey, and in the cities of Denver and Seattle) and Canada (in Manitoba). In these experiments, a large number of families were subsidized and taxed according to a negative income tax, and the effects on their labour supply and other decisions were studied.

The evidence from the experiments was somewhat mixed. On the one hand, even though the NIT is designed to encourage people to work more, in practice it seemed to make them work somewhat less. The explanation appeared to be that the expected positive work incentive was offset by other influences that encouraged recipients to work less.

For one thing, when people participated in these experimental studies, their rights under the negative income tax were clearly explained to them—in particular, their right to stop working and still continue to receive an income. Another related factor was that people in the experiments did not seem to feel that there was much of a ***stigma*** attached to quitting work and getting the negative income tax benefits. By comparison, many poor people are extremely reluctant to apply for traditional welfare in our present system and will not do so even if they would receive substantial welfare benefits.

An important *positive* finding from the experiments was that almost all of the reduced work time by the young went into increased schooling. The NIT, therefore, did have a positive effect on the accumulation of human capital.

## WHERE DO WE GO FROM HERE?

The evidence from the U.S. experiments suggests that an NIT may be more expensive than originally thought, because it makes more people willing to apply for benefits. On the other hand, one may argue that this is not altogether a bad thing. Many people think it is unfair to have a system where some poor people do not seek assistance because they fear that they will be hassled or because they fear a social stigma: Such a system favours those who don't mind the hassle rather than those most in need.

Thus, although there is less enthusiasm now than in the 1970s for a massive NIT as "the" solution to the welfare problem, there is still considerable support in Canada for the idea that a modified and more limited version of an NIT could have a useful role to play in our system of social welfare programs. Indeed, in Saskatchewan, Quebec, and Manitoba, limited versions of an NIT covering the "working poor" (those who are able to earn *some* income from work, but not enough to get above the poverty line) have already been introduced. In 1985, the wide-ranging report of the MacDonald Commission included a long analysis of Canada's social welfare system: One of its major recommendations was that a range of federal welfare programs should be abolished and replaced by a version of a negative income tax.

Other approaches to designing a welfare system that provides a reasonable protection for poor people without reducing work incentives have recently been considered as well. One suggestion is a ***wage subsidy*** that would increase the take-home pay of low-income workers. (As explained above, the Child Benefit program introduced in 1993 does subsidize the earnings of low-income families with children to some extent.) Because the government subsidy would come to the family via the breadwinner's paycheque, it would eliminate the incentive for the creation of single-parent families, and thus help to break the cycle of welfare dependence. Moreover, by increasing the take-home wage, it would *increase* the incentive to work.

In one recent proposal, it is suggested that a wage subsidy could be used to replace the current minimum wage legislation. Instead of making *employers* pay a minimum wage, the *government* could guarantee that all workers would receive a specific target wage. Employers would then pay whatever the lower market wage may be, while the government would make up the shortfall through a subsidy. Since employers' labour costs would not rise, this policy would avoid the major disadvantage of a minimum wage—namely, the tendency of a minimum wage to raise labour costs and thus induce firms to employ less labour. The government wage subsidy would also ensure that someone working full time would be guaranteed a minimum income, just as in Figure 24-3—with one big difference: Under this target wage, the incentive for individuals is to work more, rather than less, since their welfare payment increases as they work more. Thus, this proposal addresses the poverty problem; but, in doing so, it encourages, rather than discourages, work effort.

One problem is that such a program might be very costly. Furthermore, what should be done when no jobs exist? One answer is that, if the market wage can fall, jobs will exist. Another answer is for the government to hire people as a last resort. However, great care must be taken to avoid earlier "employer-of-last-resort" schemes under which the government would pay a relatively high union wage in such jobs. This would create a perverse incentive for those already in lower-paying, non-union jobs to quit them in order to take the jobs offered by the government.

Whether or not the welfare system involves a wage subsidy, several pressing questions still remain in designing a good welfare system. For example, what can be done to assist women who are caring for their children on their own and who, therefore, cannot work? Expanded child-care facilities may make it possible for them to get into the job market, and various programs may be introduced to assist them in their job search.

Another question is how to ensure that children are supported by their absentee fathers rather than the taxpayers. This means a further tightening up of child support payments. The policy of a target wage provides one way of ensuring that at least some fathers comply. When paying fathers a wage subsidy, the government can first deduct their child support payments.

In the search for a solution to the poverty problem, only one clear conclusion emerges: There are no simple answers. A system that is both efficient and simple to administer and, at the same time, guarantees a decent income for everyone, may just not exist. In an imperfect world, the best we can do is compromise, always trading off one goal against another. But one thing is certain: The search for a better system to fight poverty will remain at the centre of the political debate in Canada, and will continue to be controversial.

## KEY POINTS

1. Poverty is defined as inadequate income to buy the necessities of life. A specific poverty-line figure is determined by finding the income level at which an average family would have to spend as much as 56.2% of its income on food, clothing, and shelter alone. In 1991 the poverty line for a family of four in a large city was about $29,601. In 1991, one in eight Canadian families was still living in poverty. But this was still a big improvement on the figure of about one in three in the early 1960s when the government started many of the present income maintenance programs.
2. As a result of our struggle against poverty, government income transfers have increased by more than ten times when measured in dollars, or by more than five times when adjusted for inflation.
3. In 1991, people in Ontario and British Columbia were less likely to be poor than those living elsewhere in Canada. Older people were more likely to be poor than others. The less an individual is educated, the greater the risk of poverty. Poverty is a particularly serious problem in fatherless families.
4. In the long run, the most promising government anti-poverty policies are those that deal with the causes rather than the symptoms of poverty. These policies include subsidizing investment in human capital (both education and on-the-job training) and eliminating employment discrimination against minorities and women.
5. Government income maintenance programs include Old Age Security and Unemployment Insurance, which are paid to poor and non-poor alike. But there are also many programs, like the Guaranteed Income Supplement to those over 65, and the provincial social assistance plans, that are designed specifically for the poor. The problem with these programs is that when the poor earn more income, there is a reduction in the subsidies they receive (an implicit tax). This reduces their incentive to work, thus lowering the nation's output and level of efficiency.
6. The package of present programs is also inequitable. Some of the poor are not lifted up to the poverty line, while others who qualify under several of the programs may be lifted above it — indeed, in some cases, even above the income earned by some of the people who pay taxes to support the anti-poverty program.
7. Why not, then, replace this present system with a single policy that would lift all the poor up to the same minimum income level? The answer is that the poor, with their incomes thus guaranteed, would have little or no economic incentive left to work. With lost potential output, the economy would operate at a low level of efficiency. Thus, the conflict between greater equality and efficiency persists: As we try to carve up the national pie more equally (by raising the income of the poor), the total size of that pie is reduced.
8. In theory, a negative income tax is a good method of reducing, but not entirely eliminating, this conflict. Under this policy, families would be allowed to keep part of any additional income they earn. This would leave them with an incentive to work. The program would also guarantee every family a minimum income.

## KEY TERMS

**poverty line (low-income cutoff)**
**symptoms of poverty**
**causes of poverty**
**investment in human capital**
**policies to eliminate discrimination**
**social insurance programs**
**Old Age Security**
**Canada Pension Plan (CPP)**
**Quebec Pension Plan (QPP)**
**Unemployment Insurance**
**provincial health insurance plans**
**benefit clawback**
**benefits in kind**
**Guaranteed Income Supplement**
**Child Benefit**
**Canada Assistance Plan**
**implicit tax**
**guaranteed minimum income**
**leak in the transfer bucket**
**negative income tax**
**tagging**
**wage subsidy**
**stigma effect**

# PROBLEMS

24-1. What is meant by an implicit tax rate of 90%? Of 105%? What is the effect of such a tax rate?

24-2. Explain to your bright room-mate (who is taking economics but hasn't yet reached this chapter) exactly what you mean by a "leaky bucket."

24-3. Let's see if we can't reduce the costs to the government of the negative income tax in Figure 24-5. The incentive to work in that diagram is the $500 a family can keep out of each additional $1000 it earns. Now suppose that the amount it can keep is reduced from $500 to $300.

(a) Redraw Figure 24-5 to take this into account.

(b) What has happened to the incentive to work?

(c) What has happened to the implicit tax in this welfare proposal?

(d) Are your answers to (b) and (c) related in any way? If so, how?

(e) What has happened to the total amount of subsidy the government must pay? (Be careful.)

(f) Has this transfer bucket become more or less leaky?

(g) Now regraph this policy, making one further change: Set the poverty level at $8000, rather than $10,000. Again answer questions (b), (c), and (e). What are the pros and cons of the two policies you have graphed?

24-4. Suppose you are designing a negative income tax. Graph your answers to each of the following questions:

(a) What do you consider a reasonable minimum family income (0*C* in Figure 24-5)?

(b) What do you consider to be the maximum reasonable implicit tax rate? How does the slope of *CQ* in your diagram, therefore, compare to *CQ* in Figure 24-5?

(c) From your answers to (a) and (b), calculate the break-even level of income (like the $20,000 at *Q* in Figure 24-5).

(d) Do you think the tax proper (on families to the right of the break-even point *Q*) should be greater or smaller than the implicit tax on families to the left of *Q*?

(e) Explain the possible "public finance problem" in your scheme. In other words, do you think your scheme would make it difficult for the government to collect enough taxes from those to the right of *Q* to cover the cost of subsidizing those to the left of *Q*—and cover other government expenditures as well? As real incomes rise, would this public finance problem become more serious, or less? Would you agree with the view that we should institute a negative income tax someday, with the only question being how soon we can afford it?

# GLOSSARY

This glossary provides references to terms included in the Fourth Editions of both *Macroeconomics* and *Microeconomics*. Therefore, some references will be to terms that do not exist in this volume. Please refer to the companion volume should this occur. Also, not all of these terms appear in the text; some are included here because they occur frequently in readings or lectures.

***ability-to-pay principle.*** The view that taxes should be levied according to the means of the various taxpayers, as measured by their incomes and/or wealth. Compare with *benefit principle*.
***above-normal profit.*** See *economic profit*.
***absolute advantage.*** A country (or region or individual) has an absolute advantage in the production of a good or service if it can produce that good or service with fewer resources than other countries (or regions or individuals). See also *comparative advantage*.
***accelerationist.*** One who believes that an attempt to keep the unemployment rate low by expansive demand policies will cause more and more rapid inflation.
***accelerator principle.*** The principle that investment depends on the change in sales.
***accounts payable.*** Debts to suppliers of goods or services.
***accounts receivable.*** Amounts due from customers.
***action lag.*** The time interval between the recognition that adjustments in aggregate demand policies are desirable and the time when policies are actually changed.
***actual investment.*** Investment as it appears in the GDP accounts; investment including undesired inventory accumulation.
***adaptive expectations.*** The case where agents' expectations regarding the future are determined by what has happened in the recent past.
***adjustable peg system.*** A system whereby countries peg (fix) exchange rates but retain the right to change them in the event of fundamental disequilibrium. (In the adjustable peg system of 1945–1973, most countries fixed the prices of their currencies in terms of the U.S. do[…] period 1950–1962, Canada […]ever, during the rule by allowing its currency […]xception to the
***adjustable rate mortgage.*** [...] *[va]riable rate mortgage*.
***adjustment mechanism.*** See *[inte]rnational adjustment mechanism*.
***ad valorem tax.*** A tax collected as a [p]ercentage of the price or value of a good. Contrast with *specific tax*.
***adverse selection.*** The tendency for thos[e] who know they are at higher risk of loss to buy more insurance than others.
***aggregate demand.*** Total quantity of goods and services that would be bought at various possible average price levels.
***aggregate expenditure.*** Total expenditures on consumer goods and services, government goods and services, (desired) investment, and net exports.
***aggregate supply.*** (1) Total quantity of goods and services that would be offered for sale at various possible average price levels. (2) Potential GDP.
***allocative efficiency.*** Production of the best combination of goods with the lowest-cost combination of inputs.
***annually balanced budget principle.*** The view that government expenditures should be limited each year to no more than government receipts during that year.
***annuity.*** A contract specifying that a constant sum of money will be paid for a specified number of years (the lifetime of the recipient, for example).
***anticombines legislation.*** See *competition policy*.
***anti-dumping duty.*** A duty (tariff) imposed when it has been determined that a foreign exporter has been *dumping* goods in a country's market.
***Anti-Inflation Board.*** Government body charged with overseeing the 1975–1978 price and incomes policy.
***appreciation (depreciation) of a currency.*** In a flexible exchange rate system, a rise (fall) in the price of a currency in terms of another currency or currencies.
***arbitrage.*** A set of transactions aimed at making a profit from inconsistent prices.

**arbitration.** See *compuls*… and *voluntary arbitration.*

**arc elasticity of de**… elasticity of demand between two … demand curve, calculated by the equa… $P_2$ … $\Delta Q$ … $Q$ …ned.

**asset.** Something …

**authorized inv**… **dealer.** Investment dealers who, like ch…anks, may obtain short-term loans from the … Canada. See also *investment dealer.*

**automatic** …**zer.** A feature built into the economy t…ds to reduce the amplitude of fluctuations. …xample, tax collections tend to fall during a …ssion and rise during a boom, slowing the cha… in disposable incomes and aggregate deman… (Th…, they are an automatic fiscal stabilizer.) Anot…r example is the tendency for imports to rise an…all as national income rises and falls; the leakage …to imports also tends to reduce the fluctuatio… in the aggregate demand for Canadian goo… and services.

***average cost pricing.*** Setting the price where the average cost curve (including normal profit) intersects the demand curve.

***average fixed cost.*** Fixed cost divided by the number of units of output.

***average product.*** Total product divided by the number of units of the variable input used.

***average propensity to consume.*** Consumption divided by disposable income.

***average propensity to save.*** Saving divided by disposable income.

***average revenue.*** Total revenue divided by the number of units sold. Where there is a single price, this price equals average revenue.

***average total cost.*** Total (fixed plus variable) cost divided by the number of units produced.

***average variable cost.*** Variable cost divided by the number of units produced.

***balance of payments.*** The summary figure calculated from balance-of-payments credits less balance-of-payments debits, with certain transactions excluded from the calculation. (There are various ways of defining monetary transactions; thus, there are various balance-of-payments definitions. The most common definition, and the one used in this book, excludes official reserve transactions.)

***balance-of-payments accounts.*** A statement of a country's transactions with other countries.

***balance-of-payments surplus (deficit).*** A positive (negative) balance of payments.

***balance of trade (or balance on merchandise account).*** The value of exports of goods minus the value of imports of goods.

***balance sheet.*** The statement of a firm's financial position at a particular time, showing its assets, liabilities, and net worth.

***balanced budget.*** A budget with revenues at least equal to expenditures.

***balanced budget multiplier.*** The change in equilibrium domestic product divided by the change in government spending when this spending is financed by an equivalent change in taxes.

***band.*** The range within which an exchange rate could move without the government's being committed to intervene in exchange markets to prevent further movement. Under the adjustable peg system, governments were obliged to keep exchange rates from moving outside a band (of 1% either side of parity).

***Bank of Canada.*** Canada's *central bank.*

***bank rate.*** The interest rate charged by the Bank of Canada on its loans to the chartered banks.

***bank reserves.*** See *required reserves, target reserves.*

***bank run.*** A situation in which many owners of bank deposits attempt to make withdrawals because of their fear that the bank will be unable to meet its obligations.

***bankruptcy.*** (1) A situation in which a firm (or individual) has legally been declared unable to pay its debts. (2) More loosely, a situation in which a firm (or individual) is unable to pay its debts.

***barrier to entry.*** An impediment that makes it difficult or impossible for a new firm to enter an industry. Examples: patents, economies of scale, accepted brand names.

***barter.*** The exchange of one good or service for another without the use of money.

***base year.*** The reference year, given the value of 100 when constructing a price index or other time series.

***beggar-thy-neighbour policy (or beggar-my-neighbour policy).*** A policy aimed at shifting an unemployment problem to another country. Example: an increase in tariffs.

***benefit-cost analysis.*** See *cost-benefit analysis.*

***benefit principle.*** The view that taxes should be levied in proportion to the benefits that the various taxpayers receive from government expenditures. Compare with *ability-to-pay principle.*

***benefits in kind.*** Benefits not in the form of cash, but in the form of some good (like food) or service (like housing or medical care). Contrast with *unconditional transfers.*

***Bertrand duopoly game.*** A game in which each duopolist finds the best *price* to charge, given the price charged by the other. Compare *Courn*… *duopoly game.*

***bilateral.*** In international trade, … countries only (compare *mult*…

***bilateral monopoly.*** A market structure involving a single seller (monopolist) and a single buyer (monopsonist).
***bill.*** See *Treasury bill.*
***black market.*** A market in which sales take place at a price above the legal maximum.
***blacklist.*** A list of workers who are not to be given jobs because of union activity or other behaviour considered objectionable by employers.
***block grant.*** Grant that may be used in a broad area (such as education), and need not be spent on specific programs (such as reading programs for the handicapped).
***bond.*** *Financial instrument* in the form of a written commitment to pay a scheduled series of interest payments plus the face value (principal) at a specified maturity date.
***book value.*** The book value of a stock is its net worth per share. (It is calculated by dividing the total net worth of the company by the number of its shares outstanding.)
***bourgeoisie.*** (1) In Marxist doctrine, capitalists as a social class. (2) The middle class. (3) More narrowly, shopkeepers.
***boycott.*** A concerted refusal to buy (buyer's boycott) or sell (seller's boycott). A campaign to discourage people from doing business with a particular firm.
***break-even point.*** (1) The output at which costs just equal revenues and therefore profits are zero. (2) The level of disposable income at which consumption just equals disposable income and therefore saving is zero.
***broker.*** One who acts on behalf of a buyer or seller.
***budget deficit.*** The amount by which budgetary outlays exceed revenues.
***budget line (or income line or price line).*** The line on a diagram that shows the various combinations of commodities that can be bought with a given income at a given set of prices.
***budget surplus.*** The amount by which budgetary revenues exceed outlays.
***built-in stabilizer.*** See *automatic stabilizer.*
***burden of (public) debt.*** The burden imposed on the country as a whole in the future of government deficits and debt incurred today.
***burden of tax.*** The amount of the tax ultimately paid by different individuals or groups. (For example, how much does a cigarette tax raise the price paid by buyers, and how much does it lower the net prices received by sellers?) The incidence of the tax.
***Bureau of Competition Policy.*** The government bureau in charge of investigating violations of the Competition Act. Replaced the Restrictive Trade Practices Commission in 1986.
***business cycle.*** The more or less regular upward and downward movement of economic activity over a period of years. A cycle has four phases: recession, trough, expansion, and peak.

***Canada Assistance Plan (CAP).*** A *conditional transfer* plan under which the federal government contributes to provincial and local spending on social welfare assistance to poor individuals and families.
***Canada Savings Bonds (CSBs).*** Federal government bonds issued at attractive rates of interest; CSBs can usually be cashed at face value.
***Canada/United States Free Trade Agreement.*** See *Free Trade Agreement.*
***Canadian Labour Congress (CLC).*** An organization of labour unions with which most of Canada's labour unions are affiliated.
***Canadian Wheat Board.*** A government agency that has a monopoly on the marketing of all wheat, oats, and barley grown in the Prairie provinces.
***cap.*** (1) A limit on the upward adjustment of an indexed wage in response to a rise in the price index; (2) More generally, an upper limit to the amount spent on a specific item.
***CAP.*** See *Canada Assistance Plan, Common Agricultural Policy.*
***capital.*** (1) Real capital: buildings, equipment, and materials used in the productive process that have themselves been produced in the past. (2) Financial capital: either funds available for acquiring real capital *or* financial assets such as bonds or common stock. (3) Human capital: the education, training, and experience that make human beings more productive.
***capital account.*** The account in a country's balance-of-payments accounts that records international *capital flows*, that is, transactions in existing assets.
***capital consumption allowance.*** Depreciation, with adjustments for the effects of inflation on the measurement of capital. Loosely, depreciation.
***capital flows.*** Purchases by foreign residents of Canadian assets (inflow), or by Canadian residents of foreign assets (outflow). Sometimes referred to as capital imports or exports. See also *direct foreign investment, portfolio investment.*
***capital gain.*** The increase in the value of an asset over time.
***capital market.*** A market in which financial instruments such as stocks and bonds are bought and sold.
***capital stock.*** The total quantity of capital.
***capitalism.*** A system in which individuals are permitted to own large amounts of capital, and decisions are made primarily in private markets, with relatively little government interference.
***capitalized value.*** The present value of the income stream that an asset is expected to produce.

***capital-output ratio.*** The value of capital divided by the value of the annual output produced with this capital.

***carbon tax.*** A proposed tax on carbon-based energy sources (coal, oil, and natural gas), to be levied in proportion to the amount of carbon dioxide emitted by each unit (to reduce the *greenhouse effect*).

***cartel.*** A formal agreement among firms to set price and market shares.

***cash reserves.*** See *required reserves*, *target reserves*.

***central bank.*** A banker's bank, whose major responsibility is the control of the money supply. A central bank also generally performs other functions, such as cheque clearing and the inspection of commercial or chartered banks, as well as management of the federal government's debt.

***central planning.*** Centralized direction of the resources of the economy, with the objective of fulfilling national goals.

***certificate of deposit (CD).*** A marketable time deposit.

***ceteris paribus.*** "Other things unchanged." In demand-and-supply analysis, it is common to make the *ceteris paribus* assumption; that is, to assume that none of the determinants of the quantity demanded or supplied is allowed to change, with the sole exception of price.

***chartered bank.*** A privately owned, profit-seeking institution that accepts chequing and savings deposits, makes loans, and acquires other earning assets (particularly bonds and shorter-term debt instruments). There are only about a dozen domestic chartered banks in Canada; the five largest ones have as much as 90% of total chartered bank assets.

***checkoff.*** The deduction of union dues from workers' pay by an employer, who then remits the dues to the union.

***cheque clearing.*** The transfer of cheques from the bank in which they were deposited to the bank on which they were written, with the net amounts due to or from each bank being calculated.

***chequing deposit.*** A deposit against which an order to pay (that is, a cheque) may be written.

***child tax benefit.*** A reduction in the tax payable by families with children. The tax credit is *refundable*, meaning that it is reduced for families with high incomes; it replaces the earlier child tax credit and the family allowance program.

***circular flow of payments.*** The flow of payments from businesses to households in exchange for labour and other productive services and the return flow of payments from households to businesses in exchange for goods and services.

***class struggle.*** In Marxist economics, the struggle for control between the proletariat and the bourgeoisie.

***classical economics.*** (1) In Keynesian economics, the accepted body of macroeconomic doctrine prior to the publication of Keynes's *General Theory*. According to classical economics, a market economy tends toward an equilibrium with full employment; a market economy tends to be stable if monetary conditions are stable; and changes in the quantity of money are the major cause of changes in aggregate demand. Contrast with *Keynesian economics*. (2) The accepted view, prior to about 1870, that value depends on the cost of production. In the late nineteenth century, this was replaced with the "neoclassical" view that value depends on both costs of production (supply) and utility (demand).

***clean float.*** A situation where exchange rates are determined by market forces, without intervention by central banks or governments.

***closed economy.*** An economy where exports and imports are very small relative to national product. In closed-economy models, imports and exports are, for simplicity, assumed to be zero.

***closed shop.*** A business that hires only workers who are already union members. See also *right-to-work law*; contrast with *open shop* and *union shop*.

***cobweb cycle.*** A switching back and forth between a situation of high production and low price and one of low production and high price. A cobweb cycle can occur if there are long lags in production and if producers erroneously assume that price this year is a good indicator of price next year.

***co-determination.*** A system of corporate management in which workers and management jointly decide on the firm's actions, subject to specified rules.

***coincidence of wants.*** Situation in which each of the parties involved in a barter has a product that the other wants.

***collective bargaining.*** Negotiations between a union and management over wages and working conditions.

***collective goods.*** See *pure public good*.

***collusion.*** An agreement among sellers regarding prices and/ or market shares. The agreement may be explicit or tacit.

***Combines Investigation Act.*** See *Competition Act*.

***commercial bank.*** A term used in other countries to describe banks similar to Canada's chartered banks.

***Common Agricultural Policy (CAP).*** The generous program to support the farm sector and subsidize farm exports in the European Community.

***common market.*** See *customs union*.
***common-property resource.*** A resource in which nobody has established property rights and one that can be used by anyone. See also *commons*.
***common stock.*** Each share of common stock represents part ownership in a corporation; and entitles the holder to a share of any profits earned by the corporation. See also *preferred stock*.
***commons.*** Land that is open for use by all or by a large group of people; for example, commonly owned pasture land.
***communism.*** (1) In Marxist theory, the ultimate stage of historical development in which (a) all are expected to work and no one lives by owning capital, (b) exploitation has been eliminated and there is a classless society, and (c) the state has withered away. (2) A common alternative usage: the economic and political systems of China, the former Soviet Union, and other countries such as North Korea and Cuba in which a communist party is in power.
***company union.*** A union dominated by the employer.
***comparable worth.*** See *equal value, work of*.
***comparative advantage.*** If two nations (or cities or individuals) have different opportunity costs of producing a good or service, then the nation (or city or individual) with the lower opportunity cost has a comparative advantage in that good or service. See also *absolute advantage*.
***compensating wage differentials.*** Wage differences that may result if labour views some jobs as less attractive than others. (Employers have to pay a higher wage to fill the unattractive jobs.)
***competition.*** See *perfect competition*.
***Competition Act.*** An act passed by Parliament in 1986 to reform Canada's competition policy and replace the earlier Combines Investigation Act.
***competition policy.*** The laws contained in the Competition Act, and other policies designed to limit monopoly power and discourage business practices that reduce competition in the economy.
***competitive devaluations.*** A round of exchange rate devaluations in which each of a number of countries tries to gain a competitive advantage by devaluing its currency. (Not all can be successful; each must fail to the extent that other countries also devalue.)
***complementary goals.*** Goals such that the achievement of one helps in the achievement of the other. (Contrast with *conflicting goals*.)
***complementary goods.*** Goods that are used together. A rise in the price of one causes a leftward shift in the demand curve for the other. (Contrast with *substitute*.)
***complements in production.*** Goods produced together. A rise in the price of one causes a rightward shift in the supply curve of the other. See also *joint products*.
***compulsory arbitration.*** In a labour dispute, occurs when the government forces both parties to submit their dispute to an arbitrator, who then decides on a binding settlement.
***concentration ratio.*** Usually, the fraction of an industry's total output made by the four largest firms. (Sometimes a different number of firms — such as eight — is chosen in calculating concentration ratios, and sometimes a different measure of size — such as assets — is chosen.) See also *Herfindahl index*.
***conditional transfers.*** Contributions by the federal government to provincial budgets (or by provincial governments to local governments) that are conditional on the amounts spent by the receiving governments. Contrast with *matching grant* and *unconditional transfers*.
***conflicting goals.*** Goals such that working toward one makes it more difficult to achieve the other. (Example: high employment and price stability.)
***conglomerate merger.*** See *merger*.
***consol.*** A government bond that pays a given amount of interest forever; the principal is never repaid.
***conspicuous consumption.*** Consumption whose purpose is to impress others. A term originated by Thorstein Veblen (1857–1929).
***constant dollars (or real dollars).*** A series is measured in constant dollars if it is measured at the prices existing in a specified base year. Such a series has been *deflated* — that is, adjusted to remove the effects of inflation or deflation. Contrast with *current dollars*.
***constant returns (to scale).*** This occurs if an increase of $x$% in all inputs causes output to increase by the same $x$%.
***consumer price index (CPI).*** A weighted average of the prices of goods and services commonly purchased by an average household, as calculated by Statistics Canada.
***consumer surplus.*** The net benefit that consumers get from being able to purchase a good at the prevailing price; the difference between the maximum amounts that consumers would be willing to pay and what they actually do pay. It is approximately the triangular area under the demand curve and above the market price.
***consumption.*** (1) The purchase of consumer goods and services. (2) The act of using goods and services to satisfy wants. (3) The using up of goods (as in capital consumption allowances).
***consumption function.*** (1) The relationship between consumer expenditures and disposable

income. (2) More broadly, the relationship between consumer expenditures and the factors that determine these expenditures.

***contestable market.*** A market with only one or a few producers, whose market power is nevertheless severely limited by the ease with which additional producers may enter.

***continental union.*** A Canadian labour union that is affiliated with a union in the United States (sometimes also called an international union).

***convergence hypothesis.*** (1) The proposition that the differences between communistic and capitalistic societies is decreasing. (2) The proposition that per capita incomes are growing faster in poor countries than in rich ones, so that the difference between them is shrinking.

***convertible bond.*** A bond that can be exchanged for common stock under specified terms and prior to a specified date, at the option of the bondholder.

***cooperative.*** A business owned by the customers that use its services.

***cooperative game.*** A game in which players can communicate and negotiate to try to find a mutually advantageous outcome.

***co-payment.*** The requirement that insured persons pay part of the cost of a loss or an insured service.

***cornering a market.*** Buying and accumulating enough of a commodity to become the single (or at least dominant) seller, and thus acquire the power to resell at a higher price.

***corporation.*** An association of shareholders with a government charter that grants certain legal powers, privileges, and liabilities separate from those of the individual shareholder-owners. The major advantages of the corporate form of business organization are limited liability for the owners, continuity, and relative ease of raising capital for expansion. Contrast with *single proprietorship* and *partnership*.

***correlation.*** The tendency of two variables (such as income and consumption) to move together.

***cost-benefit analysis.*** The calculation and comparison of the costs and benefits of a program or project.

***cost-push inflation.*** Inflation caused principally by increasing costs — in the form of higher prices for labour, materials, and other inputs — rather than by rising demand. Contrast with *demand-pull inflation*.

***cost spillover.*** See *external cost*.

***countercyclical policy.*** (1) Policy that reduces fluctuations in economic activity. (2) Policy whose objective is to reduce fluctuations in economic activity.

***countervailing duty.*** A *tariff* imposed by a country, supposedly to offset a government subsidy to producers in the exporting country.

***countervailing power.*** Power in one group, which has grown as a reaction to power in another group. For example, a big labour union may develop to balance the bargaining power of a big corporation. A term originated by John Kenneth Galbraith.

***Cournot duopoly game.*** A hypothetical situation in which there are only two firms in an industry, and each sets its price on the assumption that the other won't change its price. See also *Nash equilibrium*.

***craft union.*** A labour union whose members have a particular craft (skill or occupation). Examples: an electricians' union, or a plumbers' union. Contrast with *industrial union*.

***crawling peg system.*** A system of exchange rates in which par values would be changed frequently, by small amounts, in order to avoid large changes at a later date.

***credit.*** (1) Borrowed funds. (2) In bookkeeping, an addition to the liabilities and net worth side of a balance sheet, or to the revenue side of an income statement.

***credit crunch.*** A situation of severe credit rationing.

***credit instrument.*** A written promise to pay at some future date.

***credit rationing.*** Allocation of available funds among borrowers when the demand for loans exceeds the supply at the prevailing interest rate.

***credit union.*** A cooperative organization that accepts deposits and extends credit to its members.

***creeping inflation.*** A slow but persistent upward movement of the average level of prices (not more than 2% or 3% per annum).

***cross elasticity of demand.*** The percentage change in the quantity demanded of a good in response to a 1% change in the price of a related good.

***cross-section data.*** Observations taken at the same time. For example, the consumption of different income classes in Canada in 1989.

***cross-subsidization.*** A firm's or agency's use of revenues generated in profitable lines of activity to offset losses in other, less profitable lines of activity.

***crowding out.*** A reduction in private investment demand (or sometimes, net exports) caused when an expansive fiscal policy results in higher interest rates (and, sometimes, appreciation of the country's currency).

***Crown corporation.*** A government-owned corporation, usually one that derives most of its revenue from the sale of goods and services to the public — for example, Canadian National Railways, Hydro-Québec.

***currency.*** (1) Coins and paper money (dollar bills, for instance). (2) In international economics, a

national money, such as the British pound or the Japanese yen.
***current account.*** The account in a country's balance-of-payments accounts that records that country's exports and imports of goods and services, as well as unilateral transfers.
***current dollars.*** A series (like GDP) is measured in current dollars if each observation is measured at the prices that prevailed at the time. Such a series reflects both real changes in GDP *and* inflation (or deflation). Contrast with *constant dollars*.
***current liabilities.*** Debts that are due for payment within a year.
***customs union.*** An agreement among nations to eliminate trade barriers (tariffs, quotas, etc.) among themselves and to adopt common tariffs on imports from non-member countries. Example: the European Community. Compare *free-trade area*.
***cut-throat competition.*** Selling at a price below cost, with the objective of driving competitors out of the market (at which time prices may be raised and monopoly profits reaped).
***cyclically adjusted budget.*** See *full-employment budget*.
***cyclically balanced budget.*** A budget whose receipts over a whole business cycle are at least equal to its expenditures over the same cycle. Unlike an annually balanced budget, a cyclically balanced budget permits the use of countercyclical fiscal policies. Surpluses during prosperity may be used to cover deficits during recessions.

***deadweight loss.*** A cost to someone in the economy (a buyer or a seller) that is not a gain to someone else. The net loss of monopoly, a tax, or an externality. Compare *excess burden of a tax*.
***debasement of currency.*** (1) Reduction of the quantity of precious metal in coins. (2) More broadly, a substantial decrease in the purchasing power of money.
***debit.*** In accounting, an addition to the debit side (the assets side of a balance sheet, or the expenditure side in an income statement) of an account.
***debt-equity swaps.*** In debt rescheduling, an agreement by a lender to accept equity (part ownership) in firms, in exchange for writing off all or part of the original loan.
***debt instrument.*** A written commitment to repay borrowed funds.
***declining industry.*** An industry whose firms make less than normal profits. (Firms will therefore leave the industry.)
***decreasing returns (to scale).*** Occurs if an $x\%$ increase in all inputs results in an increase of output of less than $x\%$.
***deficit.*** The amount by which expenditures exceed revenues. Contrast with *surplus*.
***defined benefit plan.*** A pension plan under which the annual benefits are determined in advance. Compare *money purchase plan*.
***deflation.*** (1) A fall in the average level of prices; the opposite of inflation. (2) The removal of the effects of inflation from a series of observations by dividing each observation with a price index. The derivation of a constant-dollar series from a current-dollar series.
***deflationary bias.*** Such a bias exists in a system if, on average, monetary and fiscal authorities are constrained from allowing aggregate demand to increase as rapidly as productive capacity. (The classical gold standard was criticized on the ground that it created a deflationary bias.)
***deflationary gap.*** See *recessionary gap*.
***demand.*** A schedule or curve showing how much of a good or service would be demanded at various possible prices, *ceteris paribus*.
***demand deposit.*** A bank deposit withdrawable on demand and transferable by cheque.
***demand for money.*** The total amount of money (cash and deposits) that individuals and firms are willing to hold, at different market rates of interest. See also *velocity of money*.
***demand-management policy.*** A change in monetary and/or fiscal policy aimed at affecting aggregate demand.
***demand-pull inflation.*** Inflation caused by excess aggregate demand. Contrast with *cost-push inflation*.
***demand schedule.*** A table showing the quantities of a good or service that buyers would be willing and able to purchase at various market prices, *ceteris paribus*.
***demand shift.*** A movement of the demand curve to the right or left as a result of a change in income or any other determinant of the quantity demanded (with the sole exception of the price of the good).
***demand shifter.*** Anything except its own price that affects the quantity demanded of a good.
***depletion allowance.*** A deduction, equal to a percentage of net taxable income, that certain extractive industries are permitted in calculating taxable profits.
***deposit multiplier.*** See *money multiplier*.
***depreciation.*** (1) The loss in the value of physical capital due to wear and obsolescence. (2) The estimate of such loss in business or economic accounts. (3) The amount that tax laws allow businesses to count as a cost of using plant or equipment.
***depreciation of a currency.*** A decline in the value of a floating currency measured in terms of another currency or currencies. See also *exchange rate*.
***depression.*** An extended period of very high unemployment and much excess capacity. (There is

no generally accepted, precise, numerical definition of a depression. However, none of the economic slumps since World War II has been generally considered a depression.)

***derived demand.*** The demand for an input that depends on the demand for the product or products it is used to make. For example, the demand for flour is derived from the demand for bread.

***desired investment.*** See *investment demand.*

***devaluation.*** In international economics, a reduction of the par value of a currency.

***developing countries.*** See *less developed countries.*

***dictatorship of the proletariat.*** In Marxist economics, the dictatorship that occurs when a revolution has eliminated the capitalist class and power has fallen into the hands of the proletariat.

***differentiated products.*** Similar products that retain some distinctive difference(s); close but not perfect substitutes. Examples: Ford and Chevrolet automobiles, different brands of toothpaste.

***diminishing marginal benefit (utility), law of.*** As a consumer gets more and more of a good, the marginal benefit (utility) of that good will (eventually) decrease.

***diminishing marginal rate of substitution.*** The decreasing (in absolute value) slope of the indifference curve as one moves downward and to the right along it. Closely related to diminishing marginal benefit.

***diminishing returns, law of eventually.*** If technology is unchanged, then the use of more and more units of a variable input, together with one or more fixed inputs, must eventually lead to a declining marginal product for the variable input.

***direct foreign investment.*** Occurs when foreign residents establish or invest in firms in which foreign owners have a controlling interest.

***dirty float.*** See *floating exchange rate.*

***discount rate.*** (1) A term used to denote the rate of interest used to calculate discounted present value. (2) In the United States, the interest charged by the Federal Reserve when lending to commercial banks. See also *bank rate.*

***discounting.*** (1) The process by which the present value of one or more future payments is calculated, using an interest rate. See *present value.* (2) In central banking, lending by the central bank to a chartered bank or authorized investment dealer.

***discouraged worker.*** Someone who wants a job but is no longer looking because work is believed to be unavailable. A discouraged worker is not included in either the labour force or the number of unemployed.

***discretionary policy.*** Policy that is periodically changed in the light of changing conditions. The term is usually applied to monetary or fiscal policies that are adjusted to meet the objectives of high employment and stable prices. Contrast with *monetary rule.*

***discriminating monopoly.*** When the single seller in a market is able to charge different prices to different buyers. (To do so, it must be possible to prevent resale of the good or service.)

***discrimination.*** Charging higher prices or paying different wages to particular groups (such as small retailers, or women) in a market.

***disposable income.*** Income that households have left after the payment of taxes. It is divided among consumption expenditures, the payment of interest on consumer debt, and saving.

***dissaving.*** Negative saving.

***diversification.*** Reducing the risk of large fluctuations in asset value or terms of trade by holding many different assets, or trading with many different partners.

***dividend.*** The part of a corporation's profits paid out to its shareholders.

***dividend tax credit.*** A deduction from the personal income tax payable by someone who has received dividend payments from a Canadian corporation. Intended to offset the income tax already paid by the corporation, to avoid *double taxation* of profits distributed as dividends.

***division of labour.*** (1) The breaking up of a productive process into different tasks, each done by a different worker (for example, on an automobile assembly line). (2) More broadly, specialization according to *comparative advantage.*

***dollar standard.*** An international monetary system in which many international transactions take place in U.S. dollars and many countries hold sizeable fractions of their reserves in dollars. Also, other currencies may be pegged to the U.S. dollar.

***domestic product.*** See *gross domestic product, net domestic product.*

***dominated strategy.*** In game theory, a strategy that leads to a worse outcome for a player than some other strategy, no matter what action is taken by the other player(s).

***double-entry bookkeeping.*** An accounting system in which each transaction results in equal entries on both sides. When double-entry bookkeeping is used, the two sides of the accounts must balance.

***double taxation.*** The taxation of corporate profits first when they are earned and second when they are paid out to shareholders as dividends. Has been effectively eliminated in Canada through the dividend tax credit, but still exists in the United States.

***dual labour market.*** A pair of labour markets, where workers in one market are excluded from taking jobs in the other market.

***dumping.*** The sale of a good at a lower price in a foreign market than in the home market—a form of price discrimination.
***duopoly.*** A market in which there are only two sellers.
***durable goods.*** Consumer goods that can be used for a long period of time (cars, appliances).
***duty.*** See *tariff.*
***dynamic efficiency.*** Efficient change in an economy, particularly the most efficient use of resources over time, the best rate of technological change, and the most efficient rate of growth.
***dynamic wage differential.*** A wage difference that arises because of changing demand or supply conditions in the labour market. It tends to disappear over time as labour moves out of relatively low-wage jobs and into those that pay a relatively high wage.

***EC.*** See *European Community.*
***econometrics.*** The application of statistical methods to economic problems.
***economic efficiency.*** See *allocative efficiency, dynamic efficiency,* and *technological efficiency.*
***economic freedom.*** A situation in which people have the right to choose their own occupations, to enter contracts, and to spend their incomes as they please.
***economic independence.*** A situation in which a nation's economy is controlled by its citizens, with relatively little influence by foreign decision makers.
***economic integration.*** The elimination of tariffs and other barriers between nations. The partial or complete unification of the economies of different countries.
***economic profit.*** Above-normal profit; profit after the opportunity costs of capital have been taken into account.
***economic rent.*** The return to a factor of production in excess of its opportunity cost. See also *rent.*
***economics.*** (1) The study of how people acquire material necessities and comforts, the problems they encounter in doing so, and how these problems can be reduced. (2) Frequently, a narrower definition is used — the study of the allocation of scarce resources to satisfy human wants.
***economies (diseconomies) of scale.*** Occur if an increase of $x$% in the quantity of every input causes the quantity of output to increase by more (less) than $x$% See also *increasing returns to scale.*
***economies of scope.*** Cost advantage resulting from production of several different kinds of goods or services in the same firm.
***economize.*** To make the most of limited resources; to be careful in spending.
***ECU.*** See *European Currency Unit.*
***efficiency.*** The goal of getting the most out of our productive efforts. See also *allocative efficiency, dynamic efficiency,* and *technological efficiency.*
***effluent fee.*** A tax or other levy on a polluting activity, based on the quantity of pollution discharged.
***elastic demand.*** Demand with an elasticity greater than 1 (in absolute value). A fall in price causes an increase in total expenditure on the product in question, because the percentage change in quantity demanded is greater than the percentage change in price.
***elastic supply.*** Supply with an elasticity greater than 1. A supply curve which, if extended in a straight line, would meet the vertical axis.
***elasticity of demand.*** The price elasticity of demand is

$$\frac{\text{Percentage change in quantity demanded}}{\text{Percentage change in price}}$$

Similarly, the income elasticity of demand is

$$\frac{\text{Percentage change in quantity demanded}}{\text{Percentage change in income}}$$

The unmodified term "elasticity" usually applies to price elasticity.
***elasticity of supply.*** The (price) elasticity of supply is

$$\frac{\text{Percentage change in quantity supplied}}{\text{Percentage change in price}}$$

***emission fee.*** See *effluent fee.*
***emissions permit.*** See *tradeable permit.*
***employer of last resort.*** The government acts as the employer of last resort if it provides jobs for all those who are willing and able to work but cannot find jobs in the private sector.
***employment rate.*** The percentage of the labour force employed.
***endogenous variable.*** A variable explained within a theory.
***Engel's Laws.*** Regularities between income and consumer expenditures observed by nineteenth-century statistician Ernst Engel. Most important is the decrease in the percentage of income spent on food as income rises.
***entrepreneur.*** One who organizes and manages production, makes business decisions, and innovates and bears risks.
***envelope curve.*** A curve that encloses, by just touching, a series of other curves. For example, the long-run average cost curve is the envelope of all the short-run average cost curves (each of which shows costs, given a particular stock of fixed capital).
***equal-cost line.*** A line showing different combinations of two productive inputs that can be pur-

chased at a given total cost; similar to a consumer's budget line. Sometimes called iso-cost line.

***equal-output curve.*** See *isoquant.*

***equal-utility curve.*** See *indifference curve.*

***equal value, work of.*** "Equal pay for work of equal value" is a strengthening of the principle "equal pay for equal work" in legislation to eliminate pay discrimination between men and women.

***equalization payments.*** Transfers by the federal government to "have-not" provinces, whose low tax base would make it difficult for them to finance adequate levels of public services without federal assistance.

***equation of exchange.*** MV = *PQ*.

***equilibrium.*** A situation in which there is no tendency for change.

***equity.*** (1) Ownership, or amount owned. (2) Fairness.

***escalated tariff.*** A tariff that is very low (or zero) on unprocessed resources, but rises as goods become more and more highly processed.

***escalator clause.*** A provision in a contract or law whereby a price, wage, or other monetary quantity is increased at the same rate as a specified price index (usually the consumer price index). See also *indexation.*

***Established Programs Financing Act.*** The law that states the amounts to be contributed by the federal government to provincial spending in the areas of health care, post-secondary education, and social assistance.

***estate tax.*** A tax on property owned at the time of death. See also *inheritance tax.*

***Eurodollars.*** Deposits denominated in U.S. dollars but held in banks in countries outside of the United States (such as Canada or the European countries).

***European Community (EC).*** A customs union formed in the 1950s by a number of European nations (Britain became a member in the 1970s). The EC provides for tariff-free trade in goods and services, as well as free flows of investment and a common labour market, among the member nations; its ultimate objective is to move toward some form of political union. Known earlier as European Economic Community (EEC).

***European Currency Unit (ECU).*** An artificial currency used in certain transactions in the European Community; intended to become the basis for a future common European currency.

***European Monetary System (EMS).*** An agreement designed to limit fluctuations in the exchange rates between the currencies of the EC member nations. The ultimate goal is to have a single currency in the EC.

***excess burden of a tax.*** The decrease in efficiency that results when people change their behaviour solely because they want to reduce their tax payments. Compare with *primary burden of tax.*

***excess demand.*** The amount by which the quantity demanded exceeds the quantity supplied at the existing price. A shortage.

***excess reserves.*** (1) Reserves of chartered banks in excess of the legally specified amount, when the banks are subject to a law that prescribes a minimum ratio of reserves to deposits. See also *required reserves.* (2) More generally, reserves in excess of the *target reserves* that the chartered banks want to hold, whether or not they are legally required to do so.

***excess supply.*** The amount by which the quantity supplied exceeds the quantity demanded at the existing price. A surplus.

***Exchange Fund Account (EFA).*** A government account in which Canada's foreign exchange reserves are held.

***exchange rate.*** The price of one national currency in terms of another.

***exchange rate appreciation (depreciation).*** See *appreciation (depreciation) of a currency.*

***exchange risk.*** In international trade, the risk that the profitability of a contract to buy or sell something at a price agreed upon in a foreign currency will be affected by a change in the exchange rate between this foreign currency and the domestic currency.

***excise tax.*** A tax on the sale of a particular good. An *ad valorem tax* is collected as a percentage of the price of the good. A *specific tax* is a fixed number of cents or dollars collected on each unit of the good.

***excludability.*** See *exclusion principle.*

***exclusion principle.*** The basis for distinguishing between public and non-public goods. If those who do not pay for a good can be excluded from enjoying it, then it is not a public good.

***exogenous variable.*** A variable not explained within a theory; its value is considered to be given. Example: investment in the simple Keynesian theory.

***expansion.*** The phase of the business cycle when output and employment are increasing.

***export (X).*** Good or service sold to foreign residents.

***export of capital.*** Acquisition of foreign assets by Canadian residents.

***export-oriented development.*** A generally successful strategy pursued by a number of developing countries under which they have tried to achieve higher economic growth rates by concentrating on production for exports rather than for the home market.

***external cost.*** Cost borne by others. Pollution is an example of an external cost (sometimes called a *spillover cost* or a *neighbourhood cost*). Contrast with *internal cost.*

***externality.*** An adverse or beneficial side effect of production or consumption. Also known as a spillover or third-party effect.

***externally held public debt.*** Government securities held by foreign residents.

***extraterritoriality.*** Attempts by a country to apply its own laws to firms owned by its citizens but operating in another country; for example, the attempts by the U.S. government to enforce its antitrust laws on U.S.-owned firms operating in Canada.

***Fabian socialism.*** Form of socialism founded in Britain in the late nineteenth century, advocating gradual and evolutionary movement toward socialism within a democratic political system.

***face value.*** The stated amount of a loan or bond. The amount that must be paid, in addition to interest, when the bond comes due. The principal.

***factor mobility.*** Ease with which factors can be moved from one use to another, or from one country to another.

***factor of production.*** Resource used to produce a good or service. Land, labour, and capital are the three basic categories of factors of production.

***fair return.*** Return to which a regulated public utility should be entitled.

***fallacy of composition.*** The unwarranted conclusion that something which is true for a single individual, sector, or market is necessarily true for the economy as a whole.

***featherbedding.*** Make-work rules designed to increase the number of workers or the number of hours that must be used to carry out a particular job.

***federal/provincial transfers.*** Transfers of federal government revenue to provincial governments, as equalization payments or as payments under the Established Programs Financing Act.

***fiat money.*** Paper money that is neither backed by nor convertible into precious metals but is nevertheless legal tender. Money that is money solely because the government says that it is.

***final-offer arbitration.*** A procedure in which the arbitrator chooses the offer of one party or the other, without modification.

***final product.*** Product that has been acquired for final use and not for resale or for further processing.

***financial capital.*** Financial assets such as shares, bonds, or bank deposits.

***financial instrument.*** A legal document representing claims or ownership. Examples: bonds, Treasury bills.

***financial intermediary.*** An institution that issues financial obligations (such as demand deposits) in order to acquire funds from the public. The institution then pools these funds and provides them in larger amounts to businesses, governments, or individuals. Examples: chartered banks, trust companies, insurance companies.

***financial market.*** A market in which financial instruments (stocks, bonds, etc.) are bought and sold.

***fine-tuning.*** An attempt to smooth out mild fluctuations in the economy by frequent adjustments in monetary and/or fiscal policies.

***FIRA.*** See *Investment Canada.*

***firm.*** A business organization that produces goods and/or services. A firm may own one or more plants.

***fiscal dividend.*** A budget surplus, measured at the full-employment national product, that is generated by the growth of the productive capacity of the economy. (This term was most commonly used during the 1960s.)

***fiscal drag.*** The tendency for rising tax collections to impede the healthy growth of the aggregate demand that is needed for the achievement and maintenance of full employment. (This term was most commonly used during the 1960s.)

***fiscal policy.*** The adjustment of tax rates or government spending in order to affect aggregate demand. See also *pure fiscal policy.*

***fiscal year.*** A 12-month period selected as the year for accounting purposes.

***Fisher equation.*** See *equation of exchange.*

***fixed asset.*** A durable good, expected to last at least a year.

***fixed cost.*** A cost that does not vary with output.

***fixed exchange rate.*** An exchange rate that is held within a narrow band by the monetary authorities.

***fixed factor.*** A factor of production whose quantity cannot be changed in the short run.

***flat tax.*** A tax with only one rate applying to all income. A proportional tax.

***floating (or flexible) exchange rate.*** An exchange rate that is not pegged by monetary authorities but is allowed to change in response to changing demand or supply conditions. If governments and central banks withdraw completely from the exchange markets, the float is *clean.* (That is, the exchange rate is *freely flexible.*) A float is *dirty* when governments or central banks intervene in exchange markets by buying or selling foreign currencies in order to influence exchange rates.

***focal-point pricing.*** This occurs when independent firms quote the same price even though they do not explicitly collude. They are led by convention, rules of thumb, or similar thinking to the same price. (For example, $59.95 for a pair of shoes.)

***forced saving.*** A situation where households lose control of their income, which is directed into saving even though they would have preferred to consume it. This can occur if the monetary authorities provide financial resources for investment, creating inflation which reduces the purchasing power of households' incomes (and therefore reduces their consumption). Alternatively, forced saving occurs if taxes are used for investment projects (such as dams).

***foreign exchange.*** The currency of another country.

***foreign exchange market.*** A market in which one national currency is bought in exchange for another national currency.

***foreign exchange rate.*** See *exchange rate.*

***foreign exchange reserves.*** Foreign currencies held by the government or central bank.

***foreign investment.*** See *capital flows.*

***Foreign Investment Review Agency.*** See *Investment Canada.*

***forward price.*** A price established in a contract to be executed at a specified time in the future (such as three months from now). See also *futures market.*

***fractional-reserve banking.*** A banking system in which banks keep reserves (generally in the form of currency or deposits in the central bank) equal to only a fraction of their deposit liabilities.

***free enterprise economy.*** One in which individuals are permitted to own large amounts of capital, and decisions are made primarily in markets, with relatively little government interference.

***free good.*** A good or service whose price is zero, because at that price the quantity supplied is at least as great as the quantity demanded.

***free-market economy.*** An economy in which the major questions "What?" "How?" and "For whom?" are answered by the actions of individuals and firms in the marketplace rather than by the government.

***free rider.*** Someone who cannot be excluded from enjoying the benefits of a project, but who pays nothing (or pays a disproportionately small share) to cover its costs.

***free trade.*** A situation in which no tariffs or other barriers exist on trade between countries.

***Free Trade Agreement (FTA).*** A 1988 agreement that provides for elimination of most non-tariff barriers and all tariffs on trade and investment flows between Canada and the United States over a ten-year period, as well as a mechanism to settle some trade disputes between the two countries.

***freedom of entry.*** The absence of barriers that make it difficult or impossible for a new firm to enter an industry.

***free-trade area (or free-trade association).*** A group of countries that agrees to eliminate trade barriers (tariffs, quotas, etc.) within itself, while each country in the group retains the right to set its own tariffs on imports from non-member countries. Compare with *customs union.*

***frictional unemployment.*** Temporary unemployment associated with adjustments in a changing, dynamic economy. It arises for a number of reasons. For example, some new entrants into the labour force take time to find jobs, some with jobs quit to look for better ones, and others are temporarily unemployed by such disturbances as bad weather.

***fringe benefits.*** Benefits other than wages (such as health insurance premiums, subsidized lunches, and employer contributions to employee pension plans) paid as part of the remuneration to employees.

***front-loaded debt.*** A debt on which the payments, measured in constant dollars, are greater at the beginning than at the end of the repayment period. See also *graduated-payment mortgage.*

***full employment.*** (1) A situation in which there is no unemployment attributable to insufficient aggregate demand; that is, where all unemployment is due to frictional causes. (2) A situation where all who want to work can find jobs reasonably quickly.

***full-employment budget (or high-employment budget).*** Full-employment government receipts (that is, the receipts that would be obtained with present tax rates if the economy were at full employment) minus full-employment government expenditures (that is, actual expenditures less expenditures directly associated with unemployment in excess of the full-employment level). Sometimes referred to as cyclically adjusted budget.

***full-employment GDP.*** The GDP that would exist if full employment were consistently maintained. Potential GDP.

***full-employment rate of unemployment.*** See *natural rate of unemployment.*

***full-line forcing.*** See *tied selling.*

***fundamental disequilibrium (in international economics).*** A term used but not defined in the articles of agreement of the International Monetary Fund. The general idea is that a fundamental disequilibrium exists when an international payments imbalance cannot be eliminated without increasing trade restrictions or imposing unduly restrictive aggregate demand policies.

***futures market.*** A market in which contracts are undertaken today at prices specified today for fulfillment at some specified future time. For example, a futures sale of wheat involves the commitment to deliver wheat (say) three months from today at a price set now.

***gains from trade.*** Increase in real income that results from specialization and trade.

***game theory.*** Theory dealing with conflict, in which alternative strategies are formally analysed. Sometimes used in the analysis of duopoly or oligopoly.

***GATT.*** See *General Agreement on Tariffs and Trade.*
***GDP.*** See *gross domestic product.*
***GDP deflator.*** Current-dollar GDP divided by constant-dollar GDP, times 100. Measures the change in prices of goods and services. Also called GDP price deflator.
***GDP gap.*** Amount by which actual GDP falls short of potential GDP.
***GDP price deflator.*** See *GDP deflator.*
***General Agreement on Tariffs and Trade.*** An international organization in which the world's countries have sought to negotiate agreements providing for freer international trade.
***general equilibrium.*** Situation where all markets are in equilibrium simultaneously.
***general equilibrium analysis.*** Analysis taking into account interactions among markets.
***general glut.*** This occurs when excess supply is a general phenomenon. The quantity of goods and services that producers are willing to supply greatly exceeds the quantity buyers are willing and able to purchase.
***general inflation.*** An increase in all prices (sometimes including wages) by the same percent, leaving relative prices unchanged.
***general price level.*** Price level as measured by a broad average, such as the consumer price index or the GDP deflator.
***generalized purchasing power.*** Describes anything that can be used to buy any of the goods and services offered for sale: e.g., money.
***Giffen good.*** A good whose demand curve slopes upward to the right.
***Gini coefficient.*** A measure of inequality derived from the Lorenz curve. It is the "bow" area between the curve and the diagonal line, divided by the entire area beneath the diagonal line. It can range from zero (if there is no inequality and the Lorenz curve corresponds to the diagonal line) to 1 (if there is complete inequality and the Lorenz curve runs along the horizontal axis). See also *Lorenz curve.*
***GIS.*** See *Guaranteed Income Supplement.*
***glut.*** See *general glut.*
***gold point.*** Under the old gold standard, an exchange rate at which an arbitrager can barely cover the costs of shipping, handling, and insuring gold.
***gold standard.*** System in which the monetary unit is defined in terms of gold, the monetary authorities buy and sell gold freely at that price, and gold may be freely exported or imported. If central banks follow the "rule of the gold standard game," they allow changes in gold to be reflected in changes in the money stock.
***gold sterilization.*** A gold flow is sterilized when the central bank takes steps to cancel out the automatic effects of the gold flow on the country's money supply (that is, when the "rule of the gold standard game" is broken).
***good.*** Tangible commodity, such as wheat, a shirt, or an automobile.
***Goods and Services Tax (GST).*** A broadly based sales tax that came into effect in 1991, as a replacement for the existing less broadly based manufacturers' sales tax. Applied as a *value-added tax.*
***graduated-payment mortgage.*** A mortgage on which the money payments rise as time passes, in order to reduce front loading. If the money payments rise rapidly enough to keep real payments constant, then the mortgage is *fully* graduated. See also *front-loaded debt.*
***greenhouse effect.*** The gradual warming of the world's climate that is taking place as a result of the increasing build-up of carbon dioxide and other gases in the Earth's atmosphere.
***greenmail.*** Repurchase, often at a premium price, of its own shares by a "target firm" from another firm or individual (a "shark") who is seeking to acquire a controlling interest in the target firm.
***Gresham's Law.*** Essentially, "Bad money drives out good." More precisely: If there are two types of money whose values in exchange are equal while their values in another use (such as consumption) are different, the more valuable item will be retained for its other use while the less valuable item will continue to circulate as money.
***gross domestic investment ($I_g$).*** Expenditures for new plant, equipment, and new residential buildings, plus the change in inventories.
***gross domestic product (GDP).*** Personal consumption expenditures plus government purchases of goods and services plus gross domestic investment plus net exports of goods and services. The basic measure of aggregate economic activity; it comprises the total value of goods and services produced in Canada, excluding double-counting.
***gross national product (GNP).*** GDP less the return to foreign capital in Canada, net of the return to Canadian-owned capital invested in other countries. Approximately equal to the total value of goods and services produced by *Canadian-owned* factors of production.
***growth.*** An increase in the productive capacity of the economy.
***Guaranteed Income Supplement (GIS).*** Additional federal government payments, over and above *Old Age Security* benefit, to retired people with little or no other income.

***Herfindahl index.*** A measure of concentration. Specifically, the sum of the squared market shares of all the firms.

***high-employment GDP.*** The GDP that would exist if a high rate of employment were consistently maintained. Potential GDP.

***holding company.*** A company that holds a controlling interest in the stock of one or more other companies.

***horizontal merger.*** See *merger*.

***hub and spoke.*** An arrangement where a country (such as the United States) has free trade arrangements with several countries (like Canada and Mexico), but these other countries do not have free trade among themselves.

***human capital.*** Education and training that make human beings more productive.

***hyperinflation.*** Very rapid inflation.

***impact lag.*** The time interval between policy changes and the time when the major effects of the policy changes occur.

***imperfect competition.*** A market in which some buyer(s) or seller(s) is large enough to have a noticeable effect on price.

***implicit (or imputed) cost.*** The opportunity cost of using an input that is already owned by the producer.

***implicit tax.*** Built into a welfare program. The benefits a family loses when it earns another $1 of income. For example, if its benefits are reduced by 46¢, the implicit tax is 46%.

***import (M).*** Good or service acquired from foreign countries.

***import of capital.*** Sale of financial assets to foreign nationals, or establishment by foreign nationals of firms in the domestic country.

***import quota.*** A restriction on the quantity of a good that may be imported.

***import substitution.*** A policy of promoting domestic production of goods that were previously imported.

***incidence of tax.*** The amount of the tax ultimately paid by different individuals or groups. (For example, how much does a cigarette tax raise the price paid by buyers, and how much does it lower the net price received by sellers?)

***income-consumption line.*** The line or curve traced out by the points of tangency between an indifference map and a series of parallel budget (income) lines. It shows how a consumer responds to a changing income when relative prices remain constant.

***income effect.*** Change in the quantity of a good demanded as a result of a change in real income with no change in relative prices. See also *substitution effect*.

***income elasticity of demand.*** See *elasticity of demand*.

***income line.*** See *budget line*.

***income statement.*** An accounting statement that summarizes a firm's revenues, costs, and income taxes over a given period of time (usually a year). A profit-and-loss statement.

***income velocity of money.*** See *velocity of money*.

***incomes policy.*** A government policy (such as wage-price guidelines or wage and price controls) aimed at restraining the rate of increase in money wages and other money incomes. The purpose is to reduce the rate of inflation.

***increasing returns to scale.*** This occurs if an increase of $x$% in all inputs results in an increase in output of more than $x$%. Equivalent to *economies of scale*.

***incremental cost.*** The term that business executives frequently use instead of "marginal cost."

***incremental revenue.*** The term that business executives frequently use instead of "marginal revenue."

***index.*** A series of numbers, showing how an average (of prices, or wages, or some other economic measure) changes over time. Each of these numbers is called an index number. By convention, the index number for the base year is set at 100.

***indexation.*** The inclusion in a contract or law of an automatic adjustment for inflation. A wage contract is *indexed* if it contains an *escalator clause* providing for an automatic increase in the wage in the event of a rise in the average level of prices (as measured, usually, by the consumer price index). The income tax is *indexed* when tax brackets, exemptions, and other provisions of the tax code automatically increase by the same proportion as the increase in the average level of prices.

***indifference curve.*** A curve joining all points among which the consumer is indifferent.

***indifference map.*** A series of indifference curves, each representing a different level of satisfaction or utility.

***indirect tax.*** A tax that is paid when something is purchased. Examples: sales taxes, excise taxes, import duties.

***induced investment.*** Additional investment demand that results from an increase in domestic product.

***industrial union.*** A union open to all workers in an industry, regardless of their specific craft or skill. Contrast with *craft union*.

***industry.*** All producers of a single good or service (or closely related goods or services).

***inelastic demand.*** Demand with an elasticity of less than 1. See *elasticity of demand*.

***inexhaustible benefit.*** A good from which any person can benefit without reducing its ability to benefit others; a property of *pure public goods*.

***infant-industry argument for protection.*** The proposition that new domestic industries with economies of scale or large requirements of human capital need protection from foreign producers until they can become established.

***inferior good.*** A good for which the quantity demanded decreases as income rises, *ceteris paribus*. (Contrast with *normal good.*)

***inflation.*** An increase in the average level of prices.

***inflationary gap.*** The vertical distance by which the aggregate expenditure line is above the 45° line at the full-employment quantity of domestic product.

***information cost.*** See *search cost.*

***infrastructure.*** Loosely, facilities such as transportation, communication, and electricity supply networks that contribute to making a country's economy more productive.

***inheritance tax.*** Tax imposed on a property received from a person who has died. See also *estate tax*.

***injection.*** Demand for a GDP component other than consumption.

***innovation.*** A change in products or in the techniques of production.

***inputs.*** Materials and services used in the process of production.

***interest.*** Payment for the use of money.

***interest parity.*** A situation in which the rates of interest in two countries and the expected change in the exchange rate between their currencies are such that the real return from investing in either country is the same.

***interest rate.*** Interest as a percentage per annum of the amount borrowed.

***interlocking directorate.*** Situation where one or more directors of a company sit on the boards of directors of one or more other companies that are competitors, suppliers, or customers of the first company.

***intermediate product.*** A product intended for resale or further processing.

***internal cost.*** Costs incurred by those who actually produce (or consume) a good. Contrast with *external cost.*

***internalization.*** A measure or process that results in a firm or individual taking into account an external cost (or benefit) of its actions.

***international adjustment mechanism.*** Any set of forces that tends to reduce surpluses or deficits in the balance of payments.

***international investment.*** See *capital flows.*

***international liquidity.*** The total amount of international reserves (foreign exchange, SDRs, etc.) held by the various nations.

***International Monetary Fund (IMF).*** An international organization founded as part of the 1945 Bretton Woods Agreement, with the task of overseeing the world's monetary and exchange rate system. Played a particularly important role in managing the *adjustable peg* system 1945–1973.

***international union.*** See *continental union.*

***interprovincial trade barriers.*** Barriers against trade of goods and services between Canadian provinces.

***inventories.*** Stocks of raw materials, intermediate products, and finished goods held by producers or marketing organizations.

***inventory recession.*** A recession caused to a substantial extent by a reduction in the inventory investment component of aggregate expenditure.

***investment.*** Accumulation of capital.

***Investment Canada.*** An agency set up in the 1970s, as the Foreign Investment Review Agency, by the federal government to regulate and restrict direct foreign investment in Canada. When policy toward foreign investment became less restrictive in the mid-1980s, FIRA was renamed Investment Canada.

***investment dealer.*** A firm that markets common stock, bonds, and other securities. See also *authorized investment dealer.*

***investment demand.*** (Also known as desired investment or *planned investment.*) This is the amount of new plant, equipment, and housing acquired during the year, plus additions to inventories that businesses wanted to acquire. Undesired inventory accumulation is excluded. (If undesired inventory accumulation is included, the result is *actual investment.*)

***investment, domestic (I).*** See *gross domestic investment* and *net domestic investment.*

***investment good.*** A capital good. Buildings, equipment, or inventory.

***investment tax credit.*** A provision in the tax code providing a reduction in taxes to those who acquire capital equipment.

***invisible.*** An intangible; a service (as contrasted with a good).

***"invisible hand."*** Adam Smith's phrase expressing the idea that the pursuit of self-interest by individuals will lead to a desirable outcome for society as a whole.

***iron law of wages.*** The view (commonly held in the nineteenth century) that the high birth rate creates a tendency for the supply of labour to outrun the productive capacity of the economy and the demand for labour. As a consequence, it was an iron law of nature that wages would be driven down to the subsistence level. (Any excess population at that wage would die from starvation, pestilence, or war.)

***iso-cost line.*** See *equal-cost line.*

***isoquant.*** In production theory, a curve showing different combinations of two inputs that are sufficient to produce a given quantity of output.

***joint products.*** Products produced together, as a package. Example: meat and hides. See also *complements in production.*
***joint profit maximization.*** Formal or informal cooperation by oligopolists to pick the price that yields the most profit for the group.

***key currency.*** A national currency commonly used by foreigners in international transactions and by foreign monetary authorities when intervening in exchange markets. Examples: the U.S. dollar, and, historically, the British pound.
***Keynesian economics.*** The major macroeconomic propositions put forward by John Maynard Keynes in *The General Theory of Employment, Interest and Money* (1936): A market economy may reach an equilibrium with large-scale unemployment; steps to stimulate aggregate demand can cure a depression; and fiscal policies are the best way to control aggregate demand. Contrast with *classical economics.*
***kinked demand curve.*** A demand curve that an oligopoly firm faces if its competitors follow any price cut it makes but do not follow any of its price increases. The kink in such a demand curve occurs at the existing price.

***labour.*** The physical and mental talents of human beings, applied to the production of goods and services.
***labour force.*** The number of people employed plus those actively seeking work.
***labour-intensive product.*** A good whose production uses a relatively large quantity of labour and a relatively small quantity of other resources.
***labour participation rate.*** See *participation rate.*
***labour productivity.*** See *productivity of labour.*
***labour theory of value.*** Strictly, the proposition that the sole source of value is labour (including labour "congealed" in capital). Loosely, the proposition that labour is the principal source of value.
***labour union.*** See *union.*
***Laffer curve.*** A curve showing how tax revenues change as the tax rate changes.
***laissez-faire.*** Strictly translated, "let do." More loosely, "leave it alone." An expression used by the French physiocrats and later by Adam Smith, to describe the absence of government intervention in markets.
***land.*** This term is used broadly by economists to include not only arable land but also the other gifts of nature (such as minerals) that come with the land.
***law of diminishing marginal benefit (utility).*** See *diminishing marginal benefit (utility), law of.*
***law of diminishing returns.*** See *diminishing returns, law of eventually.*
***leading indicator.*** An economic variable that reaches a turning point (peak or trough) before the economy as a whole changes direction.
***leakage.*** (1) A withdrawal of potential spending from the circular flow of income and expenditures. (2) A withdrawal of currency from the banking system that reduces the potential expansion of the money stock.
***leakages-injections approach.*** The determination of equilibrium national product by finding the size of the product at which leakages are equal to injections.
***legal monopoly.*** A monopoly resulting from a patent or other legislation.
***legal tender.*** An item that creditors must, by law, accept in payment of a debt.
***less developed countries (LDCs).*** Refers to the world's non-industrialized nations with low *per capita* incomes. Most LDCs are in Africa, Asia, and Latin America.
***leverage.*** The ratio of debt to net worth.
***leveraged buyout.*** The takeover of a target firm using large amounts of borrowed money.
***liability.*** What is owed. See also *limited liability, balance sheet.*
***life-cycle hypothesis.*** The proposition that consumption depends on expected lifetime income (as contrasted with the early Keynesian view that consumption depends on current income).
***limited liability.*** The amount an owner-shareholder of a corporation can lose in the event of bankruptcy. This is limited to the amount paid to purchase shares of the corporation.
***line of credit.*** Commitment by a bank or other lender to stand ready to lend up to a specified amount to a customer on request.
***liquid asset.*** An asset that can be sold on short notice, at a predictable price, with little cost or bother.
***liquidity.*** Ease with which an asset can be sold on short notice, at a predictable price, with little cost.
***liquidity preference.*** The demand for money — that is, the willingness to hold money as a function of the interest rate. See also *demand for money.*
***liquidity preference theory of the interest rate.*** The theory put forward by J.M. Keynes that the interest rate is determined by the willingness to hold money (liquidity preference) and the supply of money (that is, the stock of money in existence). Contrast with *loanable funds theory of interest.*
***liquidity trap.*** In Keynesian theory, the situation in which individuals and businesses are willing to hold all their additional financial assets in the form of money — rather than bonds or other debt instruments — at the existing interest rate. In such circumstances, the creation of additional money by the central bank cannot depress the interest rate further,

and monetary policy cannot be used effectively to stimulate aggregate demand. (All additional money created is caught in the liquidity trap and is held as idle balances.) In geometric terms, the liquidity trap exists where the liquidity preference curve (the demand for money) is horizontal.

***loanable funds theory of interest.*** The theory that the interest rate is determined by the demand for and the supply of funds in the market for bonds and other forms of debt. Contrast with *liquidity preference theory of the interest rate*.

***lockout.*** Temporary closing of a factory or other place of business in order to deprive workers of their jobs. A bargaining tool sometimes used in labour disputes; the employer's equivalent of a strike.

***logarithmic (log) scale.*** See *ratio scale*.

***logrolling.*** In political decision making, a situation where minorities that support certain actions can get them passed by agreeing to vote for each others' preferred actions.

***long position.*** When a speculator or dealer has acquired, or contracted for the future purchase of, an asset which he or she hopes will increase in price. Compare *short position*.

***long run.*** (1) A period long enough for equilibrium to be reached. (2) A period of time long enough for the quantity of capital to be adjusted to the desired level. (3) Any extended period.

***long-run aggregate supply curve.*** The vertical curve in an aggregate supply/aggregate demand diagram above the full-employment level of GDP.

***long-run Phillips curve.*** The curve (or line) traced out by the possible points of long-run equilibrium in a diagram with unemployment and inflation on the axes; that is, the points where people have adjusted completely to the prevailing rate of inflation.

***long-run production function.*** A function describing various combinations of inputs and the maximum output that can be produced with each combination. For a simple firm with only two inputs (labour and capital), the production function can be shown by a two-dimensional table.

***Lorenz curve.*** A curve showing cumulative percentages of income or wealth. For example, a point on a Lorenz curve might show the percentage of income received by the poorest half of the families. (The cumulative percentage of income is shown on the vertical axis. The family with the lowest income is counted first, and then other families are added successively in the order of their incomes. The cumulative percentage of families is on the horizontal axis.) Such a curve can be used to measure inequality; if all families have the same income, the Lorenz curve traces out a diagonal line. See also *Gini coefficient*.

***low-income cutoff.*** The income level below which a family or individual is classified by Statistics Canada as being poor. See also *poverty line*.

***lump-sum tax.*** A tax of a constant amount. The revenues from such a tax do not change when income changes.

***M1.*** The narrowly defined money stock; consisting of the non-bank public's holdings of currency (coins and paper money) plus demand deposits in the chartered banks. Currency held by banks is excluded, as are deposits owned by banks or by the federal government. This was the definition of money used by the Bank of Canada as an indicator of monetary policy from the mid-1970s to the early 1980s.

***M2.*** Defined as M1 *plus* all notice (savings) and personal term deposits in chartered banks. Excludes large term deposits held by corporations; these are included in M3.

***M2+.*** Defined as M2 plus deposits in trust and mortgage loan companies and *caisses populaires*.

***M3.*** Defined as M2 plus non-personal term deposits, *plus* deposits owned by Canadian residents but denoted in foreign currency, in chartered banks.

***macroeconomics.*** The study of the overall aggregates of the economy, such as total employment, the unemployment rate, national product, and the rate of inflation.

***Malthusian problem.*** The tendency for population to outstrip productive capacity, particularly the capacity to produce food. This is the supposed consequence of a tendency for population to grow geometrically (1, 2, 4, 8, etc.) while the means of subsistence grows arithmetically (1, 2, 3, 4, etc.). The pressure of population will tend to depress the wage rate to the subsistence level and keep it there, with the excess population being eliminated by war, pestilence, or starvation. A problem described by Thomas Malthus in his *Essay on the Principle of Population* (1798).

***managed float.*** A dirty float. See *floating exchange rate*.

***margin call.*** The requirement by a lender who holds stocks (or bonds) as security that more money be put up or the stocks (or bonds) will be sold. A margin call may be issued when the price of the stocks (or bonds) declines, making the stocks (or bonds) less adequate as security for the loan.

***margin requirement.*** The minimum percentage that purchasers of stocks or bonds must put up in their own money. For example, if the margin requirement on stock is 60%, the buyer must put up at least 60% of the price in his or her own money and can borrow no more than 40% from a bank or stockbroker.

***marginal.*** The term commonly used by economists to mean "additional." For example: *marginal cost* is the additional cost when one more unit is produced; *marginal revenue* is the addition to revenue when one more unit is sold; *marginal utility* is the utility or satisfaction received from consuming one more unit of a good or service.

***marginal benefit.*** The value (in money terms) that an individual would ascribe to having an additional unit of a good or service; that is, the amount of money the individual would be willing to pay for having an additional unit of the good or service. (An individual's marginal benefit schedule for a good or service is equivalent to the individual's demand curve for that good or service.)

***marginal cost pricing.*** Setting price at the level where MC intersects the demand curve.

***marginal efficiency of investment.*** The schedule or curve relating desired investment to the rate of interest. The investment demand curve.

***marginal physical product.*** The additional output when one more unit of an input is used (with all other inputs being held constant). For example, the *marginal physical product of labour* (often abbreviated to the *marginal product of labour*) is the additional output when one more unit of labour is used.

***marginal product.*** (1) Strictly, the marginal physical product. (2) Sometimes, the value of the marginal physical product.

***marginal product of labour.*** See *marginal physical product.*

***marginal propensity to consume (MPC).*** The change in consumption expenditures divided by the change in disposable income.

***marginal propensity to import (MPM).*** The change in imports of goods and services divided by the change in GDP.

***marginal propensity to save (MPS).*** The change in saving divided by the change in disposable income. 1 − MPC.

***marginal rate of substitution.*** The slope of the indifference curve. The ratio of the marginal utility of one good to the marginal utility of another.

***marginal rate of technical substitution.*** The slope of an *isoquant*. The ratio of the marginal product of one factor of production to the marginal product of another.

***marginal rate of transformation.*** The slope of the *production possibilities curve*. The opportunity cost of one good in terms of another.

***marginal revenue.*** The increase in total revenue from the sale of one more unit.

***marginal revenue product.*** The additional revenue when the firm uses one additional unit of an input (with all other inputs being held constant).

***marginal tax rate.*** The fraction of additional income paid in taxes.

***marginal utility.*** The increase in satisfaction an individual receives from consuming one additional unit of good or service.

***market.*** An institution in which items are bought and sold.

***market economy.*** See *free-market economy.*

***market failure.*** The failure of market forces to bring about the best allocation of resources. For example, when production of a good generates pollution, too many resources tend to go into the production of that good and not enough into the production of alternative goods and services.

***market mechanism.*** The system whereby prices and the interaction of demand and supply help to answer the major economic questions "What will be produced?" "How?" and "For whom?"

***market power.*** The ability of a single firm or individual to influence the market price of a good or service.

***market-power inflation.*** See *cost-push inflation.*

***market share.*** Percentage of an industry's sales accounted for by a single firm.

***market structure.*** Characteristics that affect the behaviour of firms in a market, such as the number of firms, the possibility of collusion, the degree of product differentiation, and the ease of entry.

***marketing board.*** A legally sanctioned producer organization in agriculture; some boards have the right to fix prices and control production of their product.

***Marxist economy.*** One in which most of the capital is owned by the government. (Individuals may of course own small capital goods, such as hoes or hammers, but the major forms of capital—factories and heavy machinery— are owned by the state.) Political power is in the hands of a party pledging allegiance to the doctrines of Karl Marx.

***matching grant.*** A pledge by government or some other donor to match (contribute an equal amount to) the amount raised or spent by another government or a private charity for some specific purpose. Contrast with *conditional transfers* and *unconditional transfers.*

***measure of economic welfare (MEW).*** A comprehensive measure of economic well-being. Per capita real domestic product is adjusted to take into account leisure, pollution, and other such influences on welfare.

***median.*** The item in the middle (that is, half of all items are above the median and half are below).

***mediation (or conciliation).*** In labour disputes, occurs when major negotiations are deadlocked and an impartial outsider is brought in to suggest a settlement.

***medium of exchange.*** Money; any item that is generally acceptable in exchange for goods or services;

any item that is commonly used in buying goods or services.

***mercantilism.*** The theory that national prosperity can be promoted by a positive balance of trade and the accumulation of precious metals.

***merchandise trade surplus.*** The excess of merchandise exports over merchandise imports.

***merger.*** The bringing together of two or more firms under common control through purchase, exchange of common stock, or other means. A *horizontal merger* brings together competing firms. A *vertical merger* brings together firms that are each others' suppliers or customers. A *conglomerate merger* brings together firms that are not related in either of these ways.

***merit good.*** A good or service that the government considers particularly desirable and that it therefore encourages by subsidy or regulation — such as the regulation that children must go to school to get the merit good of education.

***microeconomics.*** The study of individual units within the economy — such as households, firms, and industries — and their interrelationships. The study of the allocation of resources and the distribution of income.

***military-industrial complex.*** A loose term referring to the combined political power exerted by military officers and defence industries; those with a vested interest in military spending.

***minimum efficient scale.*** The amount of output that a firm must produce in order to reach minimum average cost.

***minimum wage.*** The lowest wage that an employer may legally pay for an hour's work.

***mint parity.*** The exchange rate calculated from the official prices of gold in two countries under the gold standard.

***mixed economy.*** An economy in which the private market and the government share the decisions as to what shall be produced, how, and for whom.

***model.*** The essential features of an economy or economic problem, explained in terms of diagrams, equations, or words — or some combination of these.

***monetarism.*** A body of thought that has its roots in classical economics and that rejects much of the teaching of Keynes's *General Theory*. According to monetarists, the most important determinant of aggregate demand is the quantity of money; the economy is basically stable if monetary growth is stable; and the authorities should follow a monetary rule, aiming for a steady growth of the money stock. Many monetarists also believe that the effects of fiscal policy on aggregate demand are weak (unless accompanied by changes in the quantity of money), that the government plays too active a role in the economy, and that the long-run Phillips curve is vertical. (The most famous contemporary monetarist is Milton Friedman.)

***monetary base.*** Currency held by the general public and by chartered banks plus the deposits of chartered banks in the Bank of Canada.

***monetary policy.*** Central bank policies aimed at changing the rate of growth of the money stock; for example, open market operations or changes in required reserve ratios.

***monetary rule.*** The rule, proposed by monetarists, that the central bank should aim for a steady rate of growth of the money stock. Contrast with *discretionary policy*.

***money.*** Any item commonly used in buying goods or services.

***money illusion.*** Strictly defined, people have money illusion if their behaviour changes in the event of a proportional change in prices, money incomes, and assets and liabilities measured in money terms. More loosely, people have money illusion if their behaviour changes when there is a proportional change in prices and money incomes.

***money income.*** Income measured in dollars (or, in another country, income measured in the currency of that country).

***money market.*** The market for short-term debt instruments (such as Treasury bills).

***money multiplier (deposit multiplier).*** The number of dollars by which the money stock can increase as a result of a $1 increase in the reserves of chartered banks.

***money purchase plan.*** A pension plan in which the benefits to the retiree depend on the value of the accumulated assets in the pension fund at the time of retirement. Compare *defined benefit plan*.

***money stock (supply).*** Narrowly, M1. More broadly, M2, M2+, or M3.

***monopolistic competition.*** A market structure with many firms selling a differentiated product, with low barriers to entry.

***monopoly.*** (1) A market in which there is only a single seller. (2) The single seller in such a market. A *natural monopoly* occurs when the average total cost of a single firm falls over such an extended range that one firm can produce the total quantity sold at a lower average cost than could two or more firms. (Compare with *natural oligopoly*.)

***monopoly rent.*** Above-normal profit of a monopoly.

***monopsony.*** A market in which there is only one buyer.

***moral hazard.*** The tendency for people covered by insurance to act in such a way (for example, by being careless) that the expected payout of the insurer increases.

***moral suasion.*** Appeals or pressure by the Bank of Canada intended to influence the behaviour of chartered banks.

***most-favoured-nation clause.*** A clause in a trade agreement that commits a country to impose no greater barriers (tariffs, etc.) on imports from a second country than it imposes on imports from any other country.
***multilateral.*** Involving many countries (compare *bilateral*).
***multinational corporation.*** A corporation that carries on business (either directly or through subsidiaries) in more than one country.
***multiplier.*** The change in equilibrium real national product divided by the change in investment demand (or in government expenditures, tax collections, or exports). In the simplest economy (with a marginal tax rate of zero and no imports), the multiplier is 1 ÷ (the marginal propensity to save). See also *money multiplier.*
***mutual fund.*** A fund whose assets consist of a portfolio of shares in various corporations, and which in turn is owned by individuals who have bought shares (units of ownership) in the fund.

***NAFTA.*** See *North American Free Trade Agreement.*
***Nash equilibrium.*** A situation when no player in a game can improve his or her *payoff* by taking a different action, *given* the actions of the other players.
***national debt.*** See *public debt.*
***National Energy Program (NEP).*** A 1980 program outlining the federal government's policy on pricing and taxation of oil and gas, energy exports, and Canadianization of the energy sector. The NEP was largely abolished by the Conservative government in 1984/85.
***national income.*** The return to all factors of production owned by the residents of a nation.
***national product.*** See *gross national product*, and *net national product.*
***national union.*** A Canadian labour union that is not affiliated with foreign labour unions.
***natural monopoly.*** See *monopoly.*
***natural oligopoly.*** See *oligopoly.*
***natural rate of unemployment.*** The equilibrium rate of unemployment that exists when people have adjusted completely to the existing rate of inflation. The rate of unemployment to which the economy tends when those making labour and other contracts correctly anticipate the rate of inflation. The rate of unemployment consistent with a stable rate of inflation.
***near money.*** A highly liquid asset that can quickly and easily be converted into money. Examples: Canada Savings Bonds, Treasury bills, certificates of deposits.
***negative income tax.*** A reverse income tax, whereby the government makes payments to individuals and families with low incomes. (The lower the income, the greater the payment from the government.)
***neighbourhood cost***. See *external cost.*
***neocolonialism.*** The domination of the economy of a nation by the business firms or government of another nation or nations.
***net domestic investment ($I_n$).*** Gross domestic investment less depreciation.
***net domestic product (NDP).*** Private consumption expenditures plus government purchases of goods and services plus net domestic investment plus net exports of goods and services. Equals GDP minus capital consumption allowances (depreciation).
***net exports.*** Exports minus imports.
***net national product (NNP).*** GNP minus capital consumption allowances (depreciation).
***net official monetary movements.*** Changes in Canada's official foreign exchange reserves. An increase in reserves appears as a positive entry on the debit side of the balance-of-payments accounts, a decrease as a negative debit.
***net worth.*** Total assets less total liabilities. The value of ownership.
***neutrality of money.*** Money is neutral if a change in the quantity of money affects the price level without affecting relative prices or the distribution of income.
***neutrality of taxes.*** (1) A situation where taxes do not affect relative prices. (2) The absence of an excess burden of taxes.
***nominal.*** Measured in money terms. Current-dollar as contrasted to constant-dollar, or real. See also *current dollars.*
***non-competing groups.*** Groups of workers that do not compete with each other for jobs because their training or skills are different.
***non-cooperative game.*** A game in which players act without negotiating or communicating with others.
***non-price competition.*** Competition by means other than price; for example, advertising or product differentiation.
***non-renewable resource.*** Resource of which a finite quantity exists.
***non-tariff barrier.*** Impediment to trade other than tariffs. Example: an import quota.
***normal good.*** A good for which the quantity demanded rises as income rises, *ceteris paribus*. A *superior good.* Contrast with an *inferior good.*
***normal profit.*** The opportunity cost of capital and/or entrepreneurship. (Normal profit is considered a cost by economists but not by business accountants.)
***normative statement.*** A statement about what should be. Contrast with *positive statement.*

***North American Free Trade Agreement (NAFTA).*** An agreement negotiated in 1992 to extend the Canada/United States Free Trade Agreement to include Mexico.
***notice deposit.*** A deposit in a chartered bank or other financial institution for which the institution has the legal right to insist on several days' or weeks' notice before being obliged to allow the depositor to withdraw his or her funds. (Though ordinary savings accounts are legally notice deposits, banks and trust companies routinely waive the notice requirement for small depositors.)

***OAS.*** See *Old Age Security*.
***official settlements surplus.*** See *net official monetary movements*.
***Okun's Law.*** The observation that a change of 2% to 3% in real GDP (compared with its long-run trend) has been associated with a 1% change in the opposite direction in the unemployment rate. (Named after Arthur M. Okun.)
***Old Age Security (OAS).*** A monthly transfer payment by the government to every Canadian or landed immigrant over the age of 65 (provided they meet certain residency requirements).
***oligopoly.*** A market in which there are only a few sellers, who sell either a standardized or differentiated product. A *natural oligopoly* occurs when the average total costs of individual firms fall over a large enough range that a few firms can produce the total quantity sold at the lowest average cost. (Compare with *natural monopoly*.)
***oligopsony.*** A market in which there are only a few buyers.
***OPEC (Organization of Petroleum Exporting Countries).*** A cartel of oil exporters that brought about the large increase in the world price of oil in the 1970s.
***open economy.*** An economy where exports and imports are large relative to domestic national product.
***open market operation.*** The purchase (or sale) of government (or other) securities by the Bank of Canada on the open market (that is, not directly from the issuer of the security).
***open shop.*** A business that may hire workers who are not (and need not become) union members. See also *right-to-work law*; contrast with *closed shop* and *union shop*.
***opportunity cost.*** (1) The alternative that must be forgone when something is produced. (2) The amount that an input could earn in its best alternative use.
***oppressive majority, problem of.*** When a decision that will greatly hurt each member of a minority is taken by a majority even though each member of the majority only benefits a little bit.
***option.*** A contract giving the owner the right to purchase (a *call* option) or sell (a *put* option) an asset at a future date at a specified price.
***option demand.*** The willingness to pay for the option of consuming or benefiting from some good or service in the future, even though it is not certain that it will ever be consumed or used.
***output gap.*** The amount by which output falls short of the potential or full-employment level. The GDP gap.
***overvalued exchange rate.*** A situation in which a country's currency has an official value higher than is warranted by the supply and demand for it in international currency markets.

***panic.*** A rush for safety, historically marked by a switch out of bank deposits into currency and out of paper currency into gold. A run on banks. A *stock-market panic* occurs when there is a rush to sell and stock prices collapse.
***par value.*** (1) Under the IMF adjustable peg system, the officially specified value of the currency in terms of gold or U.S. dollars. (2) A situation in which the Canadian dollar trades for precisely one U.S. dollar in the exchange market.
***paradox of thrift.*** The paradoxical situation, pointed out by Keynes, in which an increase in the desire to save can result in a decrease in the equilibrium quantity of saving.
***paradox of value.*** The apparent contradiction, pointed out by Adam Smith, when an essential (such as water) has a low price while a non-essential (such as a diamond) has a high price.
***Pareto-improvement.*** Making one person better off without making anyone else worse off. (Named after Vilfredo Pareto, 1848–1923.)
***Pareto optimum.*** A situation in which it is impossible to make any Pareto improvement. That is, it is impossible to make any individual better off without making someone else worse off.
***partial equilibrium analysis.*** Analysis of a particular market or set of markets; ignoring feedbacks from other markets.
***participation rate.*** Number of people in the labour force as a percentage of the population of working age.
***partnership.*** An unincorporated business owned by two or more people. Contrast with *single proprietorship* and *corporation*.
***patent.*** Exclusive right, granted by the government to an inventor, to use an invention for a specified time period. (Such a right can be licensed or sold by the patent holder.)
***pay equity.*** See *equal value, work of*.
***payoff.*** In game theory, the gain or loss (often measured in terms of money) that a player would get for a given action by this and all other players. The dif-

ferent possible payoffs are often arranged in a *payoff matrix*.

***payroll tax.*** A tax levied on wages and salaries, or on wages and salaries up to a specified limit. Examples: Unemployment Insurance contributions, Canada/Quebec Pension Plan contributions.

***peak.*** The month of greatest economic activity prior to the onset of a recession; one of the four phases of the business cycle.

***peak-load pricing.*** Setting the price for a good or service higher during periods of heavy demand than at other times. The purpose is to encourage buyers to choose non-peak periods and/or to raise more revenue. Examples: electricity, weekend ski tow.

***pegged exchange rates.*** See *adjustable peg system*.

***penalty rate.*** A central bank lending rate kept consistently above a short-term market rate of interest.

***perfect competition.*** A market with many buyers and many sellers, with no single buyer or seller having any (noticeable) influence over price. That is, every buyer and every seller is a *price taker*.

***perfect price discrimination.*** When a monopolist is able to charge the maximum amount that anyone is willing to pay for each unit sold.

***permanent income.*** Normal income; income that is thought to be normal.

***permanent-income hypothesis.*** The proposition that the principal determinant of consumption is permanent income (rather than current income).

***personal consumption expenditures.*** See *consumption*.

***personal income.*** Income received by households in return for productive services, and from transfers prior to the payment of personal taxes.

***personal saving.*** (1) Loosely but commonly, disposable personal income less consumption expenditures. (2) More strictly, disposable personal income less consumption expenditures less payment of interest on consumer debt.

***Phillips curve.*** The curve tracing out the relationship between the unemployment rate (on the horizontal axis) and the inflation rate or the rate of change of money wages (on the vertical axis). The *long-run Phillips curve* is the curve (or line) tracing out the relationship between the unemployment rate and the inflation rate when the inflation rate is stable and correctly anticipated.

***planned investment.*** Desired investment; *investment demand*; *ex ante* investment.

***plant.*** A physical establishment where production takes place.

***poison pill.*** An action taken by a target firm threatened by a hostile takeover, for the purpose of making itself less attractive as a target.

***policy dilemma.*** This occurs when a policy that helps to solve one problem makes another worse.

***pollution permit.*** See *tradeable permit*.

***pollution tax.*** See *effluent fee*.

***portfolio.*** In the financial literature, a given collection of different assets.

***portfolio investment.*** Purchase by a foreign investor of bonds, stocks, or other Canadian financial assets in corporations or other firms that remain controlled by Canadian owners. (May also refer to purchases by foreigners of Canadian government securities.)

***positive (or descriptive) statement.*** A statement about what is (or was) or about how something works. Contrast with *normative statement*.

***potential output (or potential GDP).*** The GDP that would exist if a high rate of employment were consistently maintained.

***poverty.*** Exists when people have inadequate income to buy the necessities of life.

***poverty line (or poverty standard).*** An estimate of the income needed to avoid poverty. In 1991 Statistics Canada's poverty line (also referred to as the *low-income cutoff*) was approximately $29,601 for a large-city family of four.

***PPC.*** See *production possibilities curve*.

***precautionary demand for money.*** The amount of money that households and businesses want to hold to protect themselves against unforeseen events.

***predatory pricing.*** When a strong firm tries to drive a weaker competitor out of business by selling at a very low price.

***preferences.*** In international trade, a situation where imports from particular countries are given preferred treatment (for example, a lower tariff rate).

***preferred shares (stock).*** Shares (stock) that are given preference over common shares when dividends are paid. That is, specified dividends must be paid on preferred shares before any dividend is paid on common shares.

***premature inflation.*** Inflation that occurs before the economy reaches full employment.

***present value.*** The value now of a future receipt or receipts, calculated using the interest rate, $i$. The present value (PV) of $\$x$ to be received $n$ years hence is $\$x \div (1 + i)^n$.

***price ceiling.*** The legally established maximum price.

***price discrimination.*** The sale of the same good or service at different prices to different customers or in different markets, provided the price differences are not justified by cost differences such as differences in transportation costs.

***price-earnings ratio.*** The ratio of the price of a stock to the annual (after-tax) earnings per share of the stock.

***price elasticity of demand.*** See *elasticity of demand.*
***price elasticity of supply.*** See *elasticity of supply.*
***price index.*** A weighted average of prices, as a percentage of prices existing in a base year.
***price leadership.*** A method by which oligopolistic firms establish similar prices without overt collusion. One firm (the price leader) announces a new price, confident that the other firms will quickly follow.
***price line.*** See *budget line.*
***price maker.*** A monopolist (or monopsonist) who is able to set price because there are no competitors.
***price mechanism.*** See *market mechanism.*
***price searcher.*** A seller (or buyer) who is able to influence price, and who has competitors whose responses can affect the profit-maximizing price. An oligopolist (or oligopsonist).
***price support.*** A commitment by the government to buy surpluses at a given price (the support price) in order to prevent the price from falling below that figure.
***price system.*** See *market mechanism.*
***price taker.*** A seller or buyer who is unable to affect the price and whose market decision is limited to the quantity to be sold or bought at the existing market price. A seller or buyer in a perfectly competitive market.
***price-wage flexibility.*** The ease with which prices and wages rise or fall (especially fall) in the event of changing demand and supply. Contrast with *price-wage stickiness.*
***price-wage stickiness.*** The resistance of prices and wages to a movement, particularly in a downward direction. Contrast with *price-wage flexibility.*
***primary burden of tax.*** The amount of tax collected. Compare with *excess burden of a tax.*
***prime rate of interest.*** (1) A bank's publicly announced interest rate on short-term loans. (2) Historically, the interest rate charged by banks on loans to their most creditworthy customers.
***principal.*** (1) Amount to be repaid, in addition to interest, on a bond or loan (the *face value* of the bond or loan). (2) See *principal-agent problem.*
***principal-agent problem.*** The problem of ensuring that an agent (someone who acts on someone else's, the principal's, behalf) will in fact act in the principal's interest. Example: Corporation managers acting as shareholders' agents; workers acting as their employers' agents.
***prisoner's dilemma.*** A situation where an agreement or action that would benefit both parties in a transaction will not occur because neither party can trust the other to keep the agreement.
***private benefit (cost).*** The benefit (cost) of an action to an individual or firm, not taking into account any *external* benefit or cost. Compare *social benefit (cost).*
***procyclical policy.*** A policy that increases the amplitude of business fluctuations. ("Procyclical" refers to results, not intentions.)
***producer surplus.*** Net benefit that producers get from being able to sell a good at the existing price. Returns to capital and entrepreneurship in excess of their opportunity costs. Rents on capital and entrepreneurship. Measured by the area to the left of the supply curve below the existing price.
***product differentiation.*** See *differentiated products.*
***production function.*** The relationship showing the maximum output that can be produced with various combinations of inputs.
***production possibilities curve (PPC).*** A curve showing the alternative combinations of outputs that can be produced if all productive resources are used. The boundary of attainable combinations of outputs.
***productivity.*** Output per unit of input.
***productivity of labour.*** The *average* productivity of labour is total output divided by the units of labour input. The *marginal* productivity of labour is the additional output when one more unit of labour is added, while all other factors are held constant.
***profit.*** In economics, return to capital and/or entrepreneurship over and above normal profit. In business accounting, revenues minus costs. Also sometimes used to mean profit after the payment of corporate income taxes.
***profit-and-loss statement.*** An accounting statement summarizing a firm's revenues, costs, and income taxes over a given period (usually a year). An income statement.
***progressive tax.*** A tax that takes a larger percentage of income as income rises.
***proletariat.*** Karl Marx's term for the working class, especially the industrial working class.
***property rights.*** The exclusive right to use a good or resource. See also *common-property resource.*
***property taxes.*** Municipal taxes imposed on the basis of the assessed value of residential or commercial property.
***proportional tax.*** A tax that takes the same percentage of income regardless of the level of income.
***proprietors' income.*** The income of unincorporated firms.
***prospectus.*** A statement of the financial condition and prospects of a corporation, presented when new securities are about to be issued.
***protectionism.*** The advocacy or use of high or higher tariffs to protect domestic producers from foreign competition.

***protective tariff.*** A tariff that is intended to protect domestic producers from foreign competition (as contrasted with a revenue tariff, intended to be a source of revenue for the government).
***proxy.*** A temporary written transfer of voting rights at a shareholders' meeting.
***proxy fight.*** A struggle between competing groups in a corporation to obtain a majority vote (and therefore control of the corporation) by collecting proxies of shareholders.
***public choice.*** See *theory of public choice.*
***public debt.*** The debt owed by governments as a result of previous borrowing to finance budget deficits. Most of Canada's public debt is owed to Canadian holders of government debt instruments such as ordinary government bonds, Canada Savings Bonds, or Treasury bills. However, part of it is held by foreign residents.
***public good.*** See *pure public good.*
***public utility.*** A firm that is the sole supplier of an essential good or service in an area and that is regulated by the government.
***pump priming.*** Short-term increases in government expenditures aimed at generating an upward momentum of the economy toward full employment.
***purchase and resale agreement.*** An arrangement by which the Bank of Canada makes short-term loans to investment dealers; by purchasing Treasury bills from the dealers at an agreed price and specifying the price and date at which the dealer has to buy them back, the Bank is in effect making a short-term loan to the dealer.
***purchasing power of money.*** The value of money in buying goods and services. The change in the purchasing power of money is measured by the change in the fraction 1 ÷ the price index.
***purchasing power parity theory.*** The theory that changes in exchange rates reflect and compensate for differences in the rate of inflation in different countries.
***pure fiscal policy.*** Fiscal policy unaccompanied by changes in the money supply.
***pure public good.*** A good (or service) with benefits that people cannot be excluded from enjoying, regardless of who pays for the good. See also *exclusion principle.*

***quantity theory (of money).*** The proposition that velocity is reasonably stable and that a change in the quantity of money will therefore cause nominal domestic product to change by approximately the same percentage.
***quota.*** A numerical limit. For example, a limit on the amount of a good that may be imported, or that a farmer in an industry with a marketing board is allowed to produce.

***Rand Formula.*** A famous arbitration ruling which settled a 1945 strike by Ford workers; it included compulsory contribution of union dues by workers and has had a great deal of influence on Canadian labour relations and labour law since that time.
***random sample.*** A sample chosen from a larger group in such a way that every member of the group has an equal chance of being chosen.
***rate base.*** Allowable capital of a public utility, to which the regulatory agency applies the allowable rate of return.
***rate of interest.*** Interest as a percentage per annum of the amount borrowed.
***rate of return.*** (1) Annual profit as a percentage of net worth. (2) Additional annual revenue from the sale of goods or services produced by plant or equipment, less depreciation and operating costs such as labour and materials, expressed as a percentage of the value of the plant or equipment. See also *yield.*
**ratio (or logarithmic) scale.** A scale in which equal percentage changes are shown as equal distances. For example, the distance from 100 to 200 is equal to the distance from 200 to 400. (Each involves a doubling.)
***rational expectations.*** Expectations based on available information, including information about the policies being pursued by the authorities. If expectations are rational, people do not consistently make the same mistake.
***rationing.*** (1) A method for allocating a good (or service) when the quantity demanded exceeds the quantity supplied at the existing price. (2) More loosely, any method for allocating a scarce resource or good. In this sense, we may speak of the market *rationing by price.*
***Reaganomics.*** The economic program of U.S. President Reagan, including (1) tax cuts, (2) restraint in domestic spending, (3) increases in defence spending, and (4) less regulation.
***real.*** Measured in terms of quantity; adjusted to remove the effects of inflation.
***real capital.*** Buildings, equipment, and other materials, including inventories, used in production, which have themselves been produced in the past.
***real deficit.*** The increase in the real debt of the government. That is, the nominal deficit less the reduction in the real value of outstanding government debt due to inflation.
***real exchange rate.*** An index computed by adjusting the exchange rate between two countries' currencies by the relative inflation rates in the two countries.
***real investment.*** The accumulation of machines and other real capital.
***real quantity of money.*** The nominal quantity of

money adjusted for inflation—that is, deflated by a price index.
***real rate of interest.*** The nominal rate of interest less the expected rate of inflation.
***real wage.*** The quantity of goods and services that a money wage will buy; the nominal (or dollar) wage adjusted for inflation.
***recession.*** A decline in output, income, employment, and trade, usually lasting six months to a year, and marked by widespread contractions in many sectors of the economy.
***recessionary gap.*** The vertical distance by which the aggregate expenditure line is below the 45° line at the full-employment quantity of domestic product.
***recognition lag.*** The time interval between the beginning of a problem and the time when the problem is recognized.
***refundable tax credit.*** A periodic payment by the government to families whose income is expected to be low. If the family's income is higher than expected, part or all of the payment has to be refunded to the government at income tax time. Example: *child tax benefit.*
***regression analysis.*** A statistical calculation of the relationship between two or more variables.
***regressive tax.*** A tax that takes a smaller percentage of income as income rises.
***renewable resources.*** Resources that regenerate themselves, such as fish or timber, so that a certain amount can be harvested each year without depleting the resource.
***rent.*** (1) In economics, any payment to a factor of production in excess of its opportunity cost. (2) A payment by the user of land to the owner. (3) Payments by users to the owners of land, buildings, or equipment.
***repeated game.*** A game that will be played more than once; the best strategy in a repeated game may be different from that in a game played only once.
***replacement-cost depreciation.*** Depreciation based on the current replacement cost of buildings and equipment rather than their original acquisition cost.
***required reserve ratio.*** The fraction of deposit liabilities that a chartered bank is legally obliged to keep in reserves. Under proposed legislative changes, the Bank Act will no longer specify required reserve ratios by the mid-1990s.
***required reserves.*** The reserves that, by law, the chartered banks will have to keep until the mid-1990s under proposed legislative changes. Chartered bank reserves are typically held as currency and deposits with the Bank of Canada.
***resale price maintenance.*** Practice whereby a manufacturer sets the minimum retail price of a product, thereby eliminating price competition among retailers of that product. The practice has long been illegal under Canadian competition legislation, and has recently been made illegal in the United States as well.
***rescheduling of debt.*** The renegotiation of the terms of the debt, to give the debtor more time to repay, and sometimes including a reduction in the interest rate.
***reservation price of a resource.*** The cost of harvesting the resource today plus the amount necessary to compensate for the reduction in the quantity of the resource available in the future.
***resource.*** Basic inputs used in the production of goods and services, namely, labour, land, and capital. See also *factor of production.*
***restrictive agreement.*** Agreement among companies to restrain competition through practices such as price fixing or market sharing.
***Restrictive Trade Practices Commission.*** See *Bureau of Competition Policy.*
***return to capital.*** See *rate of return.*
***revaluation of a currency.*** In international economics, an increase in the par value of a currency.
***revenue sharing.*** See *federal/provincial transfers.*
***revenue tariff.*** See *protective tariff.*
***right-to-work law.*** Law making it illegal to require union membership as a condition of employment. Equivalent to prohibition of *closed shops* and *union shops*. Such laws exist in some states in the United States, but do not exist in Canada. Compare *open shop.*
***risk premium.*** The difference between the yields on two grades of bonds (or other securities) because of differences in their risk. The additional interest or yield needed to compensate the holder of bonds (or other securities) for risk.
***roundabout production.*** The production of capital goods and the use of these capital goods in the production of consumer goods. The production of goods in more than one stage.
***rule.*** See *monetary rule.*
***rule of the gold standard game.*** The understanding that each country would permit its money stock to change in the same direction as the change in its gold stock. That is, if a country's gold stock were to rise, it should allow its money supply to increase, and vice versa.
***rule of 70.*** A rule that tells approximately how many years it will take for something to double in size if it is growing at a compound rate. For example, a deposit earning 2% interest approximately doubles in $70 \div 2 = 35$ years. In general a deposit earning $x$% interest will double in about $70 \div x$ years.
***rules of origin.*** Rules that govern the terms under which goods that have originally been imported into country A from a third country can be re-exported

to country B (with whom A has a trade agreement). See also *trade deflection*.
***run.*** A rush to switch into safer assets; for example, a *run on banks*.

**sales tax.** A tax charged on the sales of goods and services. Similar to an excise tax, but typically collected as a fixed percentage of the sales value of a broad range of goods and services.
***satisficing theory.*** The theory that firms do not try to maximize profits but rather aim for reasonable target levels of profits, sales, and other measures of performance.
***saving.*** See *personal saving*.
***saving function.*** (1) The relationship between personal saving and disposable income. (2) More broadly, the relationship between personal saving and the factors (such as disposable income) that determine saving.
***savings and loan associations.*** American institutions similar to Canadian trust companies.
***Say's Law.*** The discredited view that supply in the aggregate creates its own demand (regardless of the general price level).
***scale economies.*** See *economies of scale*.
***scarcity.*** (1) The inability to satisfy all wants because they exceed what we can produce with our available resources. (2) Loosely, a shortage.
***SDRs.*** See *special drawing rights*.
***search cost.*** The time and money spent in collecting the information necessary to make a decision to buy or sell stocks or any other item.
***seasonal adjustment.*** The removal of regular seasonal movements from a time series.
***second best, theory of the.*** The theory of how to get the best results in remaining markets when one or more markets have defects about which nothing can be done.
***secondary boycott.*** Boycott against a firm to discourage it from doing business with a second firm, in order to exert pressure on the second firm (which may be in a strong position to withstand other forms of pressure).
***secondary reserves.*** Chartered bank holdings of liquid assets (Treasury bills, etc.) that can readily be converted into primary reserves (currency or reserve deposits).
***secular stagnation.*** A situation of inadequate aggregate demand extending over many years. Consequently, large-scale unemployment persists, and it may even become increasingly severe.
***secular trend.*** The trend in economic activity over an extended number of years.
***securities.*** Financial instruments such as shares, Treasury bills, or bonds.
***sell short.*** See *short sale*.
***seniority rules.*** Rules giving preference to those who have been longest on the job. Individuals with seniority are typically the last to be discharged or laid off, and the first to be rehired.
***shareholders' equity.*** The net worth (assets less liabilities) of a firm; the value of shareholders' ownership.
***short position.*** The position of someone who has engaged in *short sales* of some asset. Compare *long position*.
***short run.*** (1) The period before the price level has adjusted to its equilibrium. (2) The period in which the quantity of plant and equipment cannot change. (3) The time period before equilibrium can be re-established. (4) Any brief time period.
***short-run aggregate supply curve.*** An upward-sloping curve showing aggregate output supplied as a function of the average price level. Typically drawn for a given wage rate.
***short-run production function.*** A function or curve describing the relationship between the amount of variable factors used and the amount of output that can be produced, in a situation where the quantity of capital is constant. For the simple case of a firm with just two inputs—capital and one variable factor—the short-run production function is one row in the table that may be used to illustrate the long-run production function.
***short sale.*** A contract to sell something at a later date for a price specified now.
***shortage.*** (1) The amount by which quantity supplied is less than quantity demanded at the existing price. Contrast with *surplus*. (2) Any deficiency.
***shutdown point.*** The point where the MC curve cuts the AVC curve. If the price is below this point, the firm produces nothing.
***single proprietorship.*** A business owned by an individual person. Contrast with *partnership* and *corporation*.
***single-tax proposal.*** The proposal of Henry George (1839-1897) that all taxes be eliminated except one on land. (George argued that all returns to land represent an unearned surplus.)
***slope.*** The vertical rise in a function divided by the horizontal run.
***small, open economy.*** An economy that has substantial international transactions but is too small to have a substantial influence on the prices of the goods and services that are involved in the transactions.
***snake.*** An agreement among some Western European countries to keep their currencies within a narrow band of fluctuation (the snake). Prior to 1973, they allowed their currencies to move jointly in a wider band with respect to the U.S. dollar. (This was called the *snake in the tunnel*.) (Since 1973,

the snake has not been tied to the dollar.) See also *target zone*.
***social assistance.*** Cash payments by local authorities to individuals and families with low incomes; commonly known as "welfare." See also *Canada Assistance Plan*.
***social benefit (cost).*** Benefit (cost) from the viewpoint of society as a whole, including any external cost or benefit. Compare *private benefit (cost)*.
***social insurance.*** Government programs such as Old Age Security, Unemployment Insurance, provincial health insurance plans, etc., which provide payments or services to people in specifed circumstances such as old age, unemployment, or illness. Synonym: social security.
***socialism.*** An economic system in which the means of production (capital equipment, buildings, and land) are owned by the state.
***special drawing rights (SDRs).*** Bookkeeping accounts created by the International Monetary Fund to increase the quantity of international reserves held by national governments. SDRs can be used to cover balance-of-payments deficits.
***specific tax.*** A fixed number of cents or dollars of tax on each unit of the good. Contrast with *ad valorem tax*.
***speculation.*** The purchase (or sale) of an asset in the hope of making a quick profit from a rise (fall) in its price.
***speculative demand for money.*** Money balances held because firms or individuals expect that the prices of bonds and other interest-bearing securities will go down.
***speculator.*** Anyone who buys or sells a foreign currency (or any other asset) in the hope of profiting from a change in its price.
***spillover.*** See *externality*.
***stagflation.*** The coexistence of a high rate of unemployment (stagnation) and inflation.
***standard of value.*** The item (money) in which the prices of goods and services are measured.
***sterilization of balance-of-payments surplus (deficit).*** Operations by the central bank to prevent a balance-of-payments surplus or deficit from causing changes in chartered bank reserves and, hence, in the money supply.
***stickiness.*** When wages and/or prices are slow to adjust to a situation of excess supply or demand in the labour market or product markets.
***store of value.*** An asset that may be used to store wealth through time; an asset that may be used to finance future purchases.
***structural adjustment policies.*** Restrictive policies undertaken by heavily indebted LDCs at the insistence of the International Monetary Fund as a condition for debt relief.
***structural unemployment.*** Unemployment due to a mismatch between the skills or location of the labour force and the skills or location required by employers. Unemployment due to a changing location or composition of jobs.
***subsidy.*** A negative tax.
***subsistence wage.*** Minimum living wage. A wage below which population will decline because of starvation or disease.
***substitute.*** A good or service that satisfies similar needs. Two commodities are substitutes if a rise in the price of one causes a rightward shift in the demand curve for the other. (Contrast with *complementary goods*.)
***substitution effect.*** The change in the quantity of a good demanded because of a change in its price when the real income effect of the change in price has been eliminated. That is, a change in the quantity demanded as a result of a movement along a single indifference curve. See also *income effect*.
***sunspot theory.*** The theory put forward in the late nineteenth century that cycles in sunspot activity cause cycles in agricultural production and, hence, cycles in business activity.
***superior good.*** See *normal good*.
***supply.*** The schedule or curve showing how the price of a good or service influences the quantity supplied, *ceteris paribus*.
***supply of money.*** See *money stock*.
***supply schedule.*** A table showing the quantities of a good or service that sellers would offer at various market prices, *ceteris paribus*.
***supply shift.*** A movement of the supply curve of a good (or service) to the right or left as a result of a change in the price of inputs or any other determinant of the quantity supplied (except the price of the good or service itself).
***supply shifter.*** Anything that affects the quantity of a good or service supplied except its own price.
***supply shock.*** In macroeconomics, some exogenous change (such as a change in the world price of oil) that shifts the aggregate supply curve.
***supply side.*** The view that it is supply factors — such as the quantity of capital and the willingness to work — that are the principal constraints to growth. According to this view, a lack of aggregate demand is not the main constraint.
***support price.*** Agricultural price guaranteed to farmers by the government. (If the market price falls short of the target price, the government pays farmers the difference.)
***surplus.*** (1) The amount by which quantity supplied exceeds quantity demanded at the existing price. Contrast with *shortage*. (2) The amount by which revenues exceed expenditures. Contrast with *deficit*. Any excess or amount left over.
***surplus value.*** In Marxist economics, the amount by which the value of a worker's output exceeds

the wage; the share of output appropriated by capitalists.
***sustainable yield.*** The amount of a renewable resource (such as fish) that can be harvested from a given stock while still leaving next season's stock the same as this season's.
***sympathy strike.*** A strike by a union that does not have a dispute with its own employer, but is trying to strengthen the bargaining position of another striking union.
***syndicate.*** An association of investment bankers to market a large block of securities.

***tacit collusion.*** The adoption of a common policy by sellers without explicit agreement.
***takeoff.*** The achievement of sustained growth, in which capital can be accumulated without depressing the standard of living below its existing level.
***takeover.*** The acquisition, through share purchases, of a controlling interest in a firm by another firm or individual.
***target reserves.*** The reserves in the form of currency or Bank of Canada deposits that a chartered bank tries to maintain as a matter of prudent business practice; typically specified as a percentage of deposit liabilities.
***target zone.*** A zone between the upper and lower limits for the exchange rate between its own and some other currency that a country tries to maintain. See also *snake*.
***tariff.*** A tax on an imported good.
***tax base.*** The total amount of income or sales revenue subject to a specific tax (such as the personal income tax or a provincial sales tax).
***tax-based incomes policy (TIP).*** An incomes policy backed up with tax penalties on violators or tax incentives for those who cooperate.
***tax credit.*** A subtraction from the tax payable. (For example, if a $1000 machine is bought, a 10% investment tax credit means that $100 can be subtracted from the taxes that must be paid to the government.)
***tax deduction.*** A subtraction from taxable income. Suppose an individual pays $1000 in allowable charitable donations. This $1000 can be deducted from taxable income. For someone in the 36% tax bracket, this results in a $360 reduction in taxes. (Note that the tax saving depends on the tax bracket. Thus, a $1000 deduction reduces taxes more for someone in the 36% tax bracket than for a person in a lower bracket. Note also that the $1000 deduction is worth only $360 to this individual, while a $1000 tax credit is worth the full $1000 in tax savings.)
***tax incidence.*** See *incidence of tax*.
***tax neutrality.*** (1) A situation in which taxes do not affect relative prices. (2) A situation in which the excess burden of taxes is zero.
***tax shifting.*** This occurs when the initial taxpayer transfers all or part of a tax to others. (For example, a firm that is taxed may charge a higher price.)
***technological (or technical) efficiency.*** Providing the maximum output with the available resources and technology, while working at a reasonable pace. The avoidance of wasted effort and sloppy management.
***term deposit.*** A deposit in a bank or other financial institution which has a specific term to maturity; a penalty is charged if the depositor wants to cash it in before maturity.
***terms of trade.*** The average price of goods sold divided by the average price of goods bought. Often used to refer to the prices of a country's export and import goods.
***theory of games.*** See *game theory*.
***theory of public choice***. Theory of how government decisions (about spending, regulation, etc.) are made and how they should be made.
***third-party effect***. See *externality*.
***Third World.*** Countries that are neither in the "first" world (the high-income countries of Western Europe and North America, plus a few others such as Japan) nor in the "second" world (the countries of Eastern Europe). Low- and middle-income countries other than those governed by communist parties.
***tied selling.*** Transaction in which purchaser is forced to buy another item or items in the seller's line of products in order to get the one that is really wanted.
***time preference.*** The desire to have goods now rather than in the future. The amount by which goods now are preferred over goods in the future.
***time series.*** A set of observations taken in successive time periods. For example, GDP in 1974, in 1975, in 1976, etc.
***TIP.*** See *tax-based incomes policy*.
***total cost.*** The sum of fixed costs and variable costs.
***total revenue.*** Total receipts from the sale of a product. Where there is a single price, total revenue is the price times the quantity sold.
***trade barriers.*** Tariffs, quotas, and other obstacles to international trade.
***trade deflection.*** When exports from country J (say, Japan) destined for country U (say, the United States) are first exported to country C (say, Canada) and then re-exported from C to U, in order to escape barriers in U against imports from J. See also *rules of origin*.
***trade remedy.*** A U.S. term referring to tariffs and other trade barriers that can be imposed in specified circumstances. Examples: anti-dumping duties, *countervailing duties*.

***tradeable (emissions) permit.*** A permit giving the owner the right to emit a certain amount of a specified pollutant (such as sulphur dioxide), that can be resold to another firm.
***transactions costs.*** The cost, in terms of time and money, of searching for and arranging for the purchase of, an asset or a good or service.
***transactions demand for money.*** The amount of money that firms and individuals want to cover the time between the receipt of income and the making of expenditures.
***transfer of government deposits.*** A technique of monetary control by which the Bank of Canada influences chartered bank reserves by depositing or withdrawing government funds held in the chartered banks.
***transfer payment.*** (1) A payment, usually made by the government to private individuals, for which no good or service is required in return. Examples: Old Age Security or Unemployment Insurance benefits. (2) See *federal/provincial transfers*.
***transmission mechanism.*** The mechanism whereby a recession in one part of the world economy spreads to other countries.
***Treasury bill (T-bill).*** A short-term (less than a year, often three months) debt of the federal government. It carries no explicit interest payment; a purchaser gains by buying a Treasury bill for less than its face value.
***trough.*** The month of lowest economic activity prior to the beginning of a recovery; one of the four phases of the business cycle.
***turning point.*** The trough or peak of a business cycle.
***turnover tax.*** A tax on goods or services (whether they are intermediate or final products) whenever they are sold. Contrast with *value-added tax*.

***unconditional transfers.*** Payments by governments, to individuals or other governments, with no restrictions on how they can be spent. Contrast with *benefits in kind*, *conditional transfers*, *matching grant*.
***underemployed.*** (1) Describes workers who can find only part-time work when they want full-time work. (2) Describes workers who are being paid full time but are not kept busy because of low demand for output.
***underground economy.*** Economic activity unobserved by tax collectors and government statisticians.
***underwrite.*** Guarantee by an investment dealer that the whole new issue of stock will be sold. (An investment dealer unable to sell all the underwritten stock must buy the remainder.)
***undesired inventory accumulation.*** Actual inventory accumulation less desired inventory accumulation.
***undistributed corporate profits.*** After-tax corporate profits less dividends paid.
***unemployment.*** The condition of people who are willing to work but cannot find jobs. More generally, the condition of any underutilized resource.
***Unemployment Insurance (UI).*** A federal program under which contributions are collected from employers and workers, and specified benefits are paid when workers become unemployed.
***unemployment rate.*** The percentage of the labour force unemployed.
***union.*** An association of workers, formed to negotiate over wages, fringe benefits, and working conditions.
***union shop.*** A business where all non-union workers must join the union within a brief period of their employment. Contrast with *closed shop* and *open shop*; see also *right-to-work law*.
***unit elasticity.*** Elasticity of 1. If a demand curve has unit elasticity, total revenue remains unchanged as price changes. (The demand curve is a rectangular hyperbola.) If a supply curve has unit elasticity, it is a straight line that would, if extended, go through the origin.
***unlimited liability.*** Responsibility for debts without limit.
***Uruguay Round.*** The *GATT* negotiations aiming to create a system of freer international trade that began in 1986 but which had not yet been concluded by late 1993.
***utility.*** The ability to satisfy wants.

***value added.*** Value of the product sold less the cost of intermediate products bought from other firms.
***value added tax (VAT).*** A sales tax paid by business firms on their gross sales, but with a provision for a refund of the tax that has been paid on the intermediate goods and services bought as inputs from other firms; thus it is effectively a tax on individual firms' value added. Example: the GST. Contrast with *turnover tax*.
***value of marginal product (VMP).*** Marginal physical product times product price.
***variable costs.*** Any costs that increase as output increases.
***variable rate mortgage.*** A mortgage that has an interest rate that is periodically adjusted in response to changes in the market interest rate.
***velocity of money.*** The average number of times per year that the average dollar in the money stock is spent. There are two principal ways of calculating velocity. (1) *Income velocity* is the number of times the average dollar is spent on final products (that is GDP ÷ M). (2) *Transaction velocity* is the number of times the average dollar is spent on *any* trans-

action (including those for intermediate goods and financial assets). That is, total spending ÷ M.

***vertical merger.*** See *merger.*

***voluntary arbitration.*** In labour disputes, occurs when labour and management submit their conflict to an impartial third party and commit themselves in advance to accepting that third party's decision.

***voluntary export restraints (VERs).*** Agreements negotiated with an exporting country to limit its exports of specified products to another country. Example: Auto exports from Japan to North America in the 1970s and 1980s.

***voting paradox.*** A situation where the choice between several alternatives by majority vote depends on the order in which the alternatives are considered.

***voucher.*** An amount (provided under a government program) that can be used to pay for some specific good or service (such as education) from any one of competing suppliers. A real-world example: U.S. food stamps.

***wage-price controls.*** See *incomes policy.*

***wage-price spiral.*** The process whereby an increase in prices, say, leads to demands for higher wages, the higher wages in turn contribute to still higher prices, and so on.

***wage-price stickiness.*** See *stickiness.*

***welfare program.*** See *social assistance.*

***white knight.*** A "friendly" firm approached by a target firm that is facing the threat of a hostile takeover by another firm; the target firm prefers being taken over by the white knight instead.

***windfall.*** An unexpected increase in profit that accrues to existing producers in an industry as a result of an unforeseen price increase; an example is the increase in the profits of Canadian oil companies as a result of the rapid rise in the producer price of oil during the 1970s.

***withholding tax.*** A tax (generally of about 15%) charged (withheld) by the Canadian government on payments of interest and dividends from Canadian sources to foreign investors.

***workable competition.*** A compromise that limits monopoly power while allowing firms to become big enough to reap economies of scale. A practical alternative to the often unattainable goal of perfect competition.

***World Bank.*** An international bank founded after the 1945 Bretton Woods conference. Its principal activity is to lend money for economic development projects in Third World countries. Affiliated with the International Monetary Fund.

***yellow-dog contract.*** Contract in which an employee agrees not to become a member of a union.

***yield.*** The annual rate of discount that would make the present value of a stream of future payments equal to the price or present value of an asset. Sometimes referred to as internal rate of return.

***zero-base budgeting.*** A budgeting technique that requires items to be justified anew "from the ground up," without regard to how much has been spent on them in the past.

# INDEX


Above-normal profit, 159, 359
perfect competition, 192
rent, 368
Absolute advantage, 392
comparative advantage, 48
Absolute numbers, 26
Abuse of dominant position, 291
Accelerated depreciation
income tax, 93
loopholes, 96
Accounting cost vs. opportunity cost, 158–159
Adjustment costs, 422
Advantages to large size, 287
Adverse selection, 217
Advertising, 274
misleading, 292
non-price competition, 273, 274
*Affluent Society, The*, 7n
Agents, Box 8-1/151
Agricultural products regulation, 85
Agriculture
deficiency payments, 223
elasticity, 118–121
elasticity of demand, 120
General Agreement on Tariffs and Trade, 225
income elasticity of demand, 120
marketing board, 241
price supports, 220–221, 223
rent, 366
support payments, 223
support programs, 223–225
Air Canada privatization, 87
Airline deregulation, 297, Box 14-3/297
Airline industry as natural monopoly, 297
Algebraic techniques, 17–27
Allocative efficiency, 11, 12, 14, 208, Box 12-2/245
average cost pricing, Box 12-2/245
international trade, 14
monopoly, 238
perfectly discriminating monopoly, 254
regulated monopoly, 255
American Federation of Labour, 331
Annuity, 355
Anti-combines law, 263, 285
Anti-dumping, 424
Anti-poverty policy, 504–506
Canada Pension Plan, 507
child tax benefit, 510
disability, 506
discrimination, 506
guaranteed income supplement, 510
health insurance, 508
investment in human capital, 505
old age security, 506
one-parent families, 506
Quebec Pension Plan, 507
social assistance, 510
social insurance programs, 506
unemployment, 506
unemployment insurance, 507
workers' compensation, 506
Anti-trust law, 285
Apple Computer, 31
Arbitration, 348
Assets, 155
Asymmetric information, 304, 344
negotiations, 344
Auto agreement
economies of scale, 51
Average cost, 165
curve, 168
long-run, 168–173
marginal cost, 166
short-run curve, 168
Average cost pricing, Box 12-2/245
allocative efficiency, Box 12-2/245
Average fixed cost, 165
Average product, 167
marginal product, 166–168
total product, 166–168
Average total cost, 165, 173
curve, 173
Average variable cost, 165
Avro Arrow, 31

Baby bonus
taxes, 510
Bailouts, 86
Balance sheet, 155
assets, 155, 156
book value, 157
equity, 155, 157
liabilities, 155, 156
net worth, 155, 156
ownership, 155
Bank deposits, 30
Bank of Canada, 84
Barriers to entry, 263
economies of scale, 263
natural oligopoly, 263
Barriers to trade
Auto Pact, 411
Canada/United States Free Trade Agreement, 411
cultural industry, 411, 412
jobs, 412
national defence, 412
national identity, 412
nationalism, 412
North American Free Trade Agreement, 411

Barter, Fig. 3-1/43
  coincidence of wants, 44
  efficiency, 43
  goods, 43
  indivisibility, 44
  services, 43
Base rate of interest, 357
Bastiat's negative railway, Box 20-1/413
Bastiat, Frederic, Box 20-1/413
Beggar-my-neighbour and international trade, 415
Benefit clawback, 510
Benefits in kind, 508
Bertrand duopoly problem, 280n
Big Bang, 212
Bilateral, 419
Bilateral monopoly, 329, 341–342
Black Death of 1348-1350, 66
Black knight, 303
Black markets, 68, 69
Black Monday, 155
Blue Box programs, Box 22-3/474
Bond market
  inflation, 153
  interest rate, 153
Bonds, 30
  bid price, 153
  convertible. *See* Convertible bonds
  corporation, 148
  face value, 149
  interest, 149
  liquidity, 153
  offer price, 153
  principal, 149
  risk, 153
  risk premium, 153
Bonsor, Norman, 295
Book value, 157
Break-even point, 187
Break-up artists, 304
Broker, 153
Budget line, Fig. 7-9/134, 134
  consumer's equilibrium, 134
  indifference curve, 134
Bureau of Competition Policy, 291
Bureaucracy, 498
  public choice, 498
  public interest, 498
Business accounting, 155–159
  accounting cost. *See* Accounting costs
  opportunity cost. *See* Opportunity cost
Business organization, 145–159
  types, Table 8-2/148
Businesses and circular flow of expenditures and income, 45
Buyer, 44
  market mechanism, 56

Canada Assistance Plan, 84, 510
Canada Pension Plan, 77n, 91, 506, 507
Canada Post, 54
Canada/United States Free Trade Agreement, 389, 420–425
  adjustment costs, 422
  anti-dumping duty, 424
  barriers to trade, 411
  countervailing duty, 424
  dispute settlement mechanism, 424
  economies of scale, 51
  environment, 438
  jobs, 422
  rationalization, 421
  tariff, 288, 421
  trade liberalization, 422
  unemployment, 423
  water resources, 438
Canadair privatization, 87
Canadian Auto Workers, 333
Canadian Broadcasting Corporation, 54, 75
Canadian Labour Congress, 333
Canadian Radio-television and Telecommunications Commission, 84
Canadian Transport Commission
  deregulation, 86
  regulation, 85
Canadian Union of Postal Workers, 333
Canadian Union of Public Employees, 333
Capital
  factor of production, 30
  financial, 30
    *See also* Bonds; Financial capital; Stock
  goods, 30
  investment, 30
  labour, 172
  marginal product, 172
  real, 30
Capital gains
  loopholes, 96
  principal residence, 92
  taxation, 92
Capital goods, 30
  consumer goods, 37–39
  consumption goods, Fig. 2-6/38, Fig. 2-7/39
  growth, 37–39
  production possibilities curve, Fig. 2-6/38
  takeoff, Fig. 2-7/39
Capital imports, 37–38
Capital inflow, 38
Capital intensive, 163
Capitalist economy, 54, 55
Capitalized, 368
Carbon tax, 477
Cartel, 264
  oligopoly, 266
Carter Commission on Taxation, 90
Cash transfer payments, 375
Causes of poverty, 505
Central planning, 54
Certification, 296
*Ceteris paribus* assumption and demand curve, 59
Chartered banks and regulation, 84
Child tax benefit, 510
China and hyperinflation, 11
Choices, 29
  production possibilities curve, 33–35
  scarcity, 29–41
Circular flow in a government economy, Fig. 5-1/76
Circular flow of expenditures and income, Fig. 3-3/45, 45
  businesses, 45
  consumers, 45
  producers, 45
Closed shop, 334
Co-determination, 330
Co-payment, 217

Coincidence of wants in barter, 44
Collective bargaining, 330
Collusion, 264–267
  breakdown of, 267
  cheating, 267
  oligopoly, 266
Collusive agreement, 264, 286, 290
Collusive oligopoly, 266
Combines Investigation Act, 286, 290
Commercial paper, 149
Common medium of exchange, 46
Common stock, 30, 146
  corporation, 148
Common-property, 439
Common-property problem, 465
  property rights, 465
Common-property resource, 443
  conservation, 443
  fee, 443
  limits, 443
  property rights, 443
  taxes, 443
Comparative advantage, 48–49, 392, 394
  absolute advantage, 48
  efficiency, 48–49
  international trade, 389, 392
  opportunity cost, 49, 393
  specialization, 48–49
  tariff, 416
Compensating wage differential, 349
  income distribution, 374
Competition, 257
Competition Act, 84, 285, 290
Competition laws, 263
Competition policy, 285, 286
Competition Tribunal, 291
Competitive equilibrium, Fig. 11-5/211
Competitive market
  efficient output, Fig. 11-2/205
  marginal benefit, Fig. 11-2/205
  marginal cost, Fig. 11-2/205
  prices, 214
Complementary goods as demand shifters, 60
Complements, 115
  cross elasticity of demand, 115
  demand shifters, 60
  elasticity of supply, 108
Compulsory arbitration, 348
Conciliation, 347
Conglomerate merger, 289
Conserving monopolist, Box 21-3/452
Conspiracies, 286
Constant returns, 176
  minimum efficient scale, 177
Constitution
  environment, 462
  environmental standards, 462
  pollution, 462
Consumer goods
  capital goods, 37–39
  growth, 37–39
Consumer prices, Fig. 1-4/10
  *See also* Price
Consumer's equilibrium, 126
  budget line, 134
  income, 135–139
  indifference curve, 130, 134, Fig. 7-10/135, 135
  marginal utility, 135–139
Consumer's surplus, 127
  changes in, 128
  demand curve, Fig. 7-4/127
Consumers in circular flow of expenditures and income, 45
Consumption
  current, 14
  externalities, 88
  future, 14
  growth, 14
  market price, 141
  merit goods, 88
Consumption goods
  capital goods, Fig. 2-6/38; Fig. 2-7/39
  production possibilities curve, Fig. 2-6/38
  takeoff, Fig. 2-7/39
Contestable market, 275
  freedom of entry, 275
Continental unions, 333
Controlling shareholder, 150
Convertible bonds, 149
Corner a market, 220
Corporate reorganization, 305
Corporation, 145
  agents, Box 8-1/151
  bonds, 148
  commercial paper, 149
  common stock, 146, 148
  control, Box 8-1/151
  convertible bonds, 149
  creditors, 146
  debentures, 149
  equity, 146
  financing, 148
  leverage, 152
  liabilities, 146
  limited liability, 146
  line of credit, 153
  notes, 149
  ownership, 146
  preferred stock, 149
  principals, Box 8-1/151
  proxies, Box 8-1/151
  return, 152
  risk, 152
  shares, 146
  taxes, 147
Cost-benefit analysis, 487
Cost-benefit test and regulation, 491
Cost of capital, 354
Cost of foreign capital, 404
Cost-plus pricing and game theory, 273
Costs, 164
  *See also* Average cost; Marginal cost; Total cost
  economies of scale, 176
  envelope curve, 173–175
  implicit, 158
  imputed, 159
  international trade, 178–179
  long run, 168–173
  natural oligopoly, 262–263
  utility, 140
Costs of production. *See* Production costs
Countervailing, 424
Countervailing power, 341
Cournot duopoly game and Nash equilibrium, 278
Cournot, Augustin, 278
Craft unions, 332
Create property rights, 443

Creditors
 corporation, 146
 partnership, 146
 sole proprietorship, 146
Cross elasticity of demand, 115
 complements, 115
 substitutes, 115
Cross-subsidization, 293, 295
Crow's Nest Pass Agreement, 295
Crow's Nest Pass subsidy, 297
Crown corporations, 86–87
 accountability, 86–87
 Atomic Energy of Canada Limited, 86
 bailouts, 86
 Canadair Ltd., 86
 Canadian Broadcasting Corporation, 86
 Canadian National, 86
 economies of scale, 86
 Hydro-Quebec, 86
 monopoly, 86
 natural monopoly, 86
 Petro-Canada, 86
 pioneer enterprise, 86
 privatization, 87
 Via Rail, 86
Cumulative income distribution, 374
Cut-throat competition, 267, 288
Cut-throat pricing, 285
Cycle of price fluctuations, 217
 perfect competition, 217

de Havilland and privatization, 87
Deadweight loss, 208, 210
Debasement of the currency, 47
Debentures, 149
Debt capital, 353
Deductible clause, 217
Deep pockets, 263
Deficits and social costs, 82
Deflation, 10, 47
 efficiency, 12
 price stability, 10
Demand, 56
 curve. *See* Demand curve
 elastic, 102
 elasticity of. *See* Elasticity of demand
 excess, 58
 individual. *See* Individual demands
 inelastic, 102
 market equilibrium, Fig. 4-3/58, 58–59, Table 4-3/59
 market mechanism, 53–71
 market, 123
 monopoly, 231
 perfect competition, 231
 price elasticity of. *See* Elasticity of demand
 schedule, Table 4-1/57
 supply, 53–71, Fig. 4-3/58, Table 4-3/59
 utility, 124
Demand curve, 56, Fig. 4-1/57
 algebraic techniques, 21
 *ceteris paribus* assumption, 59
 consumer's surplus, Fig. 7-4/127
 demand shifters. *See* Demand shifters
 elastic, 102
 elasticity, 104
 income effect, 139, 140
 indifference map, 139–140
 inelastic, 102
 infinitely elastic, 105
 kinked. *See* Kinked demand curve
 labour, 312
 movement along a curve, Fig. 4-7/63
 perfectly elastic, 105
 profit-maximizing point, 234
 real income, 140
 shifts in, Fig. 4-4/59, 59–61
 slope, 105
 substitution effect, 139, 140
 total revenue, 104
 unitary elasticity, 102
Demand curve for labour, 312
Demand for funds in investment, 353–354
Demand for labour
 derived demand, 313
 division of income, 313–314
 shift, 312
Demand schedule, Table 4-1/57
Demand shifters, 60
 complementary goods, 60
 complements, 60
 income, 60
 inferior good, 60
 normal good, 60
 prices, 60
 prices of related goods, 60
 substitutes, 60
 tastes, 60, Fig. 4-5/61
Depreciation, 157, 158
Depression, 9
 unemployment rate, 9
Deregulation, 85, 285, 296
 airline industry, 86, 297
 Canadian Transport Commission, 86
 financial services, 297
 rail transport, 297
Derived demand, 313
Descriptive economics, 40
Destabilizing speculation, 219–220
Difference principle, Box 18-1/379
Diminishing marginal benefit, Fig. 7-3/126, 126
Diminishing marginal rate of substitution
 diminishing marginal utility, 131
 marginal utility, 131
Diminishing marginal utility, 124
 diminishing marginal rate of substitution, 131
Diminishing returns and economies of scale, 178
Direct investment, 401, 407
 foreign ownership, 407
Discriminating monopolist, 249
Discriminating monopoly, 247–249
Discrimination, 420
 European Community, 420
 policies to eliminate, 506
Discriminatory hiring, 321
Diseconomies of scale, 176
Distribution of income, 216
Diversification, 152n, 415
 international trade, 415
 tariff, 415
Dividend tax credit, 147
Dividends and taxes, 147
Division of income, 313–314

Dominated strategy and Nash equilibrium, 278
Doomsday theorists, 437
Double taxation, 147
Downs, Anthony, 113n
Dual labour market, 321
Duopoly, 257, 270
  competition, 257
  market structure, Table 13-3/258
  pricing, 270
Duty and economic policy, 6
Dynamic differentials, 349
Dynamic efficiency, 213–214, 449
  monopoly, 237–238
  non-renewable resource, 449
  perfect competition, 214

Economic break-even point, 478
Economic development
  production possibilities curve, 38
  takeoff, 38
Economic efficiency, 11–12
  *See also* Efficiency
  perfect competition, 203–221
Economic freedom, 14
  economic goals, 7
  market mechanism, 68
Economic goals, 7–14
  complementary, 14
  conflicting, 14
  economic freedom, 7
  economic independence, 7, 14
  economic security, 7
  efficiency, 7, 11–12, 14
  environmental protection, 7, 14
  growth, 7, 13–14
  income distribution, 7, 12–13
  inflation, 14
  pollution, 14
  poverty, 14
  price stability, 7, 10–11
  unemployment, 14
  unemployment rate, 7, 8–10
Economic independence
  economic goals, 7, 14
  efficiency, 14
Economic policy, 6–7
  duty, 6
  government spending, 6
  Great Depression, 7
  international trade, 6
  laissez-faire, 6
  private business, 6
  private market, 6
  regulation, 6
  tariff, 6
  taxation, 6
Economic problem, 4-6, 29
  choices, 29–41
  scarcity, 29–41
Economic profit, 159, 190
  perfect competition, 192
Economic progress, 3
  growth, 4
Economic security, 14
  economic goals, 7
Economic stability
  government role, 89
  regulation, 89
Economic theory, 39–40
Economics, 29
Economies of scale, 49–50, 176–178, 287, 391
  auto agreement, 51
  barriers to entry, 263
  Canada/United States Free Trade Agreement, 51
  constant returns to scale, 176
  costs, 176
  Crown corporations, 86
  diminishing returns, 178
  global economy, 50–51
  international trade, 389, 391–392
  monopoly, 230
  natural monopoly, 230
  natural oligopoly, 263
  specialization, 49
Economies of scope, 249
Economize, 29
Economy and money, Fig. 3-2/44
Education and government expenditures, 80
Efficiency. *See also* Allocative efficiency
  barter, 43
  comparative advantage, 48–49
  deadweight loss, 208
  deflation, 12
  dynamic, 213–214
  economic, 11
  economic goals, 7, 8–10, 11–12, 14
  economic independence, 14
  equity and welfare, 517
  inflation, 12
  interest rate ceiling, 358
  international trade, 392, 395
  invisible hand in labour market, Box 15-1/316
  labour market and invisible hand, Box 15-1/316
  labour unions, 337–338
  long-run, 211
  loss, 208
  marketing board, 242
  minimum wage laws, 320
  monopoly, 237–239
  perfect competition, 203–221
  relative prices, 12
  renewable resource, 457
  short-run, 211
  specialization, 43
  technical, 213–214
  technological, 11, 213–214
  unions, 337
  welfare, 514, 517
Efficiency effect and unions, 335
Efficiency gain, 401, 404
  foreign investment, 404
  international trade, 401
Efficiency loss, 208, 238
  external benefit, 482
  monopoly, 238
Efficient allocation of labour, 315
Efficient output, 206
  competitive market, Fig. 11-2/205
Efficient scale, 194
Effluent fee
  emission permits, 469
  pollution, 468
Effluent tax, 468
Elastic demand. *See* Elasticity of demand
Elasticity
  agriculture, 118–121
  excise taxes, 110
  incidence of taxes, Fig. 6-6/110, 110, 112
  price instability, 118–121
  productivity, 119
  rent control, 112

significance of, 109–113
tax revenue, Fig. 6-7/111, 111, 112
taxes, 110
technology, 119
Elasticity of demand, 101, 102
agriculture, 120
beginning-point problem, 102
cross, 115
demand shifters, 115
elastic, 102
exports, 114
foreign debt, 114
imports, 114
income, 107, 114–115
inelastic, 102
inferior good, 115
infinitely elastic, 105
international trade, 114
luxuries, 106
midpoint formula, Fig. 6-1/103, 103
necessities, 105
normal good, 115
perfectly elastic, 105
revenue, 103
slope, Fig. 6-3/106
slope of demand curve, 105
straight line, Table 6-2/106
substitutability, 105
time, 107
total revenue, 103, Fig. 6-2/104
unitary elasticity, 102
Elasticity of supply, 107
complements, 108
cost of storage, 109
feasibility, 109
joint products, 109
substitutes, 108
time, 108, Fig. 6-5/109
Emission permits, 469
effluent fee, 469
End-of-pipe treatment, 472
pollution, 472
Energy
break-even point, 478
coal, 477
economic break-even point, 478
environment, 476
greenhouse effect, 477
hydroelectric power, 478
natural gas, 477
nuclear power, 478
Energy break-even point, 478
Entrepreneur, 32
Envelope cost curve in long run, Fig. 9-9/175
Envelope curve and costs, 173–175
Environment
Canada/United States Free Trade Agreement, 436, 438
constitution, 462
energy, 476
North American Free Trade Agreement, 427
ozone, 462
private property rights, 465–466
public good, 487–488
regulation, 285, 462
Environmental protection
economic goals, 7, 14
pollution, 14
Environmental regulation, 285
Equal cost curve, 171
Equal pay for equal work, 322
Equal-output curve, 170, Fig. 9-4/171
Equality, 378, Box 18-1/379
free-market distribution of income, 381
Equality of opportunity, 382
Equality of reward, 382
Equilibrium in monopolistic competition, Fig. 13-1/259
Equilibrium price in oligopoly, 264
Equity, 146, 155, 157, 378
efficiency, 517
free-market distribution of income, 382
income distribution, 378
welfare, 517
Equity capital, 353
normal profit, 359
Established Programs Funding, 83
European Community, 419
barrier-free market, 420
common market, 420
customs union, 420
discrimination, 420
preference, 420
Excess burden of tax, Fig. 10-12/198, 198
Excess capacity, 259
Excess employment, 316
Exchange
money, Fig. 3-2/44
specialization, 43–51
Exchange rates, 397
international trade, 396–398
Excise taxes, 81
elasticity, 110
regressive, 92
Expenditures
Canadian federal government, Fig. 1-17/27, Fig. 1-18/27
income and circular flow, Fig. 3-3/45, 45
Exports and elasticity of demand, 114
External benefit, 88, 481, 482
efficiency loss, 482
public good, 482
subsidizing, 483
External cost, 88, 439, 440
pollution, 463, 464
safety in the workplace, 490
External spillover benefits in labour market, 318
External spillover costs in labour market, 318
Externalities, 88, 255n
consumption, 88
labour market, 318
production, 88
Extraterritoriality, 409

Face value, 149
bonds, 149
Factor prices, 66, 359–370
Factors of production
capital, 30
investment, 30
labour, 32
land, 30
markets for, 65
natural resources, 30
resources, 30
Family allowance
government expenditures, 79
taxes, 510
Farm assistance. *See* Agriculture, support programs
Featherbedding, 337

Fee for common-property resource, 443
Final-offer arbitration, 348
Financial capital, 30
  bank deposits, 30
  bonds, 30
  common stock, 30
  stocks, 30
Financial markets, 149–155
  regulation, 150
Firm and market mechanism, 56
Fiscal Equalization Program, 84
Fixed costs, 164
Focal-point pricing and game theory, 273
Foreign debt and elasticity of demand, 114
Foreign exchange market, 397
Foreign exchange rate, 397
Foreign investment, 401–404
  direct investment, 401
  efficiency gain, 404
  net flows, 401
  net inflow, 402
  portfolio investment, 401
Foreign ownership
  control, 407–409
  direct investment, 407
  portfolio investment, 407
Four-firm concentration ratio, 260
Free enterprise economy, 54, 55
Free rider, 486
  public good, 486
*Free to Choose*, 7n
Free-market distribution of income, 378
  equality, 381
  equity, 382
Freedom of entry, 183
  contestable market, 275
Freedom of exit, 183
Freedom to Move policy, 297
Friedman, Milton, 7n
Friedman, Rose, 7n
Frontier, 36
  opportunity possibilities curve, 35–36
Full-line forcing, 292

Gains from trade, 394
Galbraith, John Kenneth, 7n, 69, 71n
Game theory, 270
  cost-plus pricing, 273
  focal-point pricing, 273
  non-price competition, 273
  oligopoly, 269–273
  price leader, 272
  profit-maximizing price, 272
  wage bargaining, 345–346
General Agreement on Tariffs and Trade, 419
  agriculture, 225
  Kennedy Round, 419
  Tokyo Round, 419
  Uruguay Round, 419
General purchasing power of money, 44
General Theory of Employment, Interest and Money, 7
George, Henry, 369
Germany and hyperinflation, 11
Giffen good, 140
Global economy, 50–51
  economies of scale, 50–51
Goods, 30
  barter, 43
  capital, 30
  government expenditures, 77
Goods and Services Tax, 81, 94
  refund, 94
Government
  economic role, 75–96
  public enterprises, 75
  regulation, 75
  spending, 75
  taxation, 75
Government expenditures
  Canadian annual, Fig. 5-2/77
  Canadian total, Fig. 5-3/78
  education, 80
  family allowance, 79
  federal, 79–80, Table 5-1/79
  goods, 77, Fig. 5-4/78
  Great Depression, 76
  growth, 76–79
  Guaranteed Income Supplement, 79
  health care, 80
  laissez-faire, 76
  local, Table 5-2/80, 80
  municipal, 80
  Old Age Security, 79
  perspective of, 76–77
  provincial, Table 5-2/80, 80
  purchases, 77–79
  services, 77, Fig. 5-4/78
  social assistance, 80
  transfer, 77–79
  transfer payments, 77
  unemployment, 76
  unemployment insurance benefits, 79
  welfare programs, 80
  World War II, 76
Government ownership and monopoly, Box 12-2/247
Government policy and monopoly, 242–247
Government receipts. *See* Government revenues
Government regulation. *See* Regulation
Government revenues
  excise taxes, 81
  federal, Table 5-1/79
  income tax, 80
  local, Table 5-2/80
  property taxes, 81
  provincial, Table 5-2/80
  sales taxes, 81
Government spending and economic policy, 6
Government subsidy and marginal cost pricing, Box 12-2/245
Government transfer programs, 510
Government transfers and income distribution, 375
Great Crash of 1929, 154
Great Depression, 89
  economic policy, 7
  government expenditures, 76
  price stability, 10
  tariff, 418, 419
  unemployment rate, 8, 9
Greenhouse effect, 476
  energy, 477
  pollution, 477
Greenmail, 303, 304
Gresham's Law, 47
Gresham, Sir Thomas, 47
Growth, 4, 13–14
  capital goods, 37–39
  capital imports, 37–38

consumer goods, 37–39
consumption, 14
economic goals, 13–14
economic progress, 4
government expenditures, 76–79
production possibilities curve, Fig. 2-4/36, 36
productive capacity, 14
Guaranteed income supplement, 510
Guaranteed minimum income, 513–514

Haymarket Riot, 331
Health regulation, 285, 491
Health care
government expenditures, 80
insurance premiums, 82
payroll taxes, 82
Health in consumer products, 490–491
Health in the workplace, 488–490
Health insurance, 506, 508
benefits in kind, 508
Herfindahl-Hirschman Index, 260
Hidden costs of regulation, 299
Highway Transport Boards and regulation, 85
Holding companies, 150
Homogeneous, 193
Horizontal merger, 289, 302
Households and circular flow of expenditures and income, 45
Hub-and-spoke trading system, 426
Human capital, 32n, 353
education value, 361
income distribution, 373, 374
investment, 361, 505
private return, 362
rent, 363
return, 360–363
salaries, 363
social return, 362
spillover benefits, 361
wages, 363
Hyperinflation, 11
China, 11
Germany, 11
Soviet Union, 11
Imperfect competition, 56
Implicit cost, 158
Implicit tax on welfare, 513, 515
Imports and elasticity of demand, 114
Imputed cost, 159
Income
circular flow, Fig. 3-3/45, 45
consumer's equilibrium, 135–139
demand shifters, 60
elasticity of demand, 107
equal, 12
equitable, 12
expenditures and circular flow, Fig. 3-3/45, 45
marginal utility, 135–139
redistribution, 13
unemployment, 13
Income distribution, 373
cash transfer programs, 375
compensating wage differential, 374
cumulative, 374
discrimination, 374
economic goals, 12–13
equal, 12
equality, 378
equitable, 12, 377–384
equity, 378
family background, 374
free market, 378
government transfers, 375
human capital, 373, 374
income inequality, 376
income tax, 376
inequality slice, 375
innate talent, 373
Lorenz curve, 374
market power, 374
poverty, 12
taxation, 376
taxes, 375
transfer programs, 376
Income effect, 139, 140
demand curve, 140
indifference curve, 140
supply of labour, 327
Income elasticity of demand, 114–115
agriculture, 120
Income inequality, 373–384
income distribution, 376
Income line and indifference curve, 134
Income statement, 155, 157
Income taxes. *See also* Taxes
accelerated depreciation, 93
average tax rate, 81
business income, 82
Canadian-controlled corporations, 81
corporate, 81
federal, 80
federal and provincial, Table 5-3/81
government receipts, 80
income distribution, 376
investment tax credit, 93
marginal tax rate, 81
net income, 82
personal, 81
progressive, 90, 92
progressive tax, 81
provincial, 80
small business corporations, 93
Increased competition, 390
international trade, 390
Indifference curve, Fig. 7-7/130, 130, Box 7-1/133
budget line, 134
consumer's equilibrium, 130, 134, Fig. 7-10/135, 135
diminishing marginal rate of substitution, 131
income effect, 140
income line, 134
indifference map, 132
isoquant, 170
marginal rate of substitution, 131, 132
perfect substitutes, 130
price line, 134
real income, 140
social assistance, 137–139
substitution effect, 140
utility index, 130
willingness to pay, 132
Indifference map, Fig. 7-8/132, 132
demand curve, 139–140
indifference curve, 132
Indirect production, 354
Individual demands, 123
Indivisibility and barter, 44

Industrial unions, 332
Industry and market mechanism, 56
Inelastic demand, 102
Infant subsidy, 416
Inferior good and demand shifters, 60
Infinitely elastic, 105
Inflation, 10
  bond market, 153
  economic goals, 14
  efficiency, 12
  interest, 357
  interest rate, 153
  price stability, 10
  prices, 11
  stock market, 154
  unemployment, 10, 14
  World War II, 10
Information cost, 140
  utility, 140, 141
Inheritance tax, 90
Innate talent and income distribution, 373
Institutional investors, 150
Insurance
  co-payment, 217
  deductible, 217
  moral hazard, 216, 217
Insurance companies, 150
Insurance premiums and health care, 82
Intensity of foreign competition, 288
Interest, 353-359
  annuity, 355
  base rate, 357
  bonds, 149
  cost of capital, 354
  expectation of inflation, 357
  inflation, 357
  rate ceiling, 357-358
  rate of return, 354, 355
  rates, 355
  reward for waiting, 354
  risk, 357
Interest income, 353
Interest rate
  bond market, 153
  inflation, 153
  stock market, 154
Intergovernmental transfers, 82
Internal cost, 440
Internalizing the externality, 467, 483
  public good, 483
International externality, 475
  unidirectional, 475
International trade, 389
  absolute advantage, 392
  allocative efficiency, 14
  beggar-my-neighbour, 415
  comparative advantage, 389, 392
  competition, 290
  costs, 178-179
  diversification, 415
  economic policy, 6
  economies of scale, 389, 391-392
  efficiency, 392, 395
  efficiency gain, 399, 401
  elasticity of demand, 114
  exchange rates, 396-398
  gains from, 398-400
  gains from trade, 394
  increased competition, 389, 390
  intensity of foreign competition, 288
  losers, 400-401
  monopoly, 390
  new products, 391
  oligopoly, 390
  policy debates, 411-431
  quotas, 411
  real income gain, 395
  specialization, 415
  tariff, 288, 411
  technological change, 396
  terms of trade, 394
  trade restrictions, 411
  transfer, 401
  wages, Box 19-1/395
  winners, 400-401
International unions, 333
Investment
  capital, 30
  demand for funds, 353-354
  human capital, 361, 505
Investment goods, 30
Investment in human capital, 505
Investment tax credit
  income tax, 93
  loopholes, 96
Invisible hand, 53, 89, 183, Box 11-1/206, 266, 315, 340
  efficiency, Box 15-1/316
  labour market, Box 15-1/316
  taxation, 89
Iso-cost line, 171
Isoquant, 170, Fig. 9-4/171
  indifference curve, 170
  slope, Fig. 9-6/172, 173

Jevons, William Stanley, 124
Job security, 330, 336-337
Jobs of equal value, 323
Joint products and supply shifters, 62

Kennedy Round, 419
Keynes, John Maynard, 7
Kinked demand curve, 267, 268-269
  oligopoly, 267
Knights of Labour, 331

Labour, 32, 32, 309
  allocation, 315
  capital, 172
  deadweight inefficiency, 318
  demand curve, 312
  factor of production, 32
  marginal physical product, 311
  marginal product, 310
    capital, 172
  marginal productivity, 316
  marginal revenue product, 311
  minimum wage laws, 318
  North American Free Trade Agreement, 413
  opportunity cost, 315
  supply curve, 315
  supply of, 327
  value of the marginal product, 311
  wage rates, 315
Labour intensive, 163
Labour market, 309
  discrimination, 321, 322, 323
  dual, 321
  efficiency, Box 15-1/316
  external spillover benefits, 318
  external spillover costs, 318
  externalities, 318
  imperfect competition, 329-350

invisible hand, Box 15-1/316
Labour unions, 329–338
collective action, 329–331
efficiency, 337–338
historical development, 331–334
market power, 334–337
Laissez-faire
economic policy, 6
government expenditures, 76
market mechanism, 69
regulation, 87
Land, 30
factor of production, 30, 32
Law of diminishing marginal utility, 124
Law of eventually diminishing returns, 168
Leak in the transfer bucket, 516
Legal monopoly, 229
Less developed countries, 4, 429
Leverage, 152
corporation, 152
return, 152
risk, 152
Leveraged buy-out, 302, 304
Liability, 155
corporation, 146
partnership, 146
sole proprietorship, 146
Licensing, 296
Lindbeck, Assar, 112n
Line of credit of corporation, 153
Liquidity, 152
bonds, 153
return, 152
risk, 152
Logarithm, 26
Logrolling, 497
public choice, 497
public interest, 497
Long run, 163
efficiency, 211
short run, 211
Long-run envelope cost curve, Fig. 9-9/175
Long-run market supply curve, 194
Long-run supply, 188–196
Long-run supply curve and production gains, 201
Loopholes, 92, 96
accelerated depreciation, 96
capital gains, 96
corporate income tax rates, 96
investment tax credit, 96
tariff, 96
Lorenz curve, 374
Loss, economic, 159
Low-income cutoff, 504
Luddites, Box 15-2/338
Luxuries and elasticity of demand, 106

Manufacturers sales tax, 94
Marginal benefit, 126, 203
competitive market, Fig. 11-2/205
diminishing. *See* Diminishing marginal benefit
marginal cost, Fig. 11-2/205
maximum utility, 126
prices, 126
utility, 128
Marginal cost, 164, 204
average cost, 166
competitive market, Fig. 11-2/205
marginal benefit, Fig. 11-2/205
marginal product, 168
marginal revenue, 185–186, 234
monopoly, 234
profit maximization, 185–186
resource allocation, 197
Marginal cost pricing, 244
government subsidy, Box 12-2/245
monopoly, 244
Marginal efficiency of investment, 354, 357
Marginal external cost, 442
Marginal physical product, 311
Marginal private cost, 442
Marginal product, 167
average product, 166–168
capital, 172
labour, 172
law of eventually diminishing returns, 168
marginal cost, 168
total product, 166–168
Marginal product of capital and marginal product of labour, 172
Marginal product of labour and marginal product of capital, 172
Marginal productivity of labour, 316
Marginal rate of substitution
diminishing, 131
indifference curve, 131, 132
marginal utility, 131
willingness to pay, 132
Marginal rate of technical substitution, 173
Marginal revenue, 185
marginal cost, 185–186, 234
marginal product of labour, 310
monopoly, 233, 234
perfect competition, 184–185
profit maximization, 185–186
Marginal revenue product, 311
Marginal social cost, 442
Marginal utility, 124
consumer's equilibrium, 135–139
diminishing marginal rate of substitution, 131
income, 135–139
marginal rate of substitution, 131
social assistance, 137–139
Market, 53
perfect competition, 204–206
Market demand, 123
Market demand curve and marketing board, 241
Market equilibrium
demand, Fig. 4-3/58, Table 4-3/59, 58–59
excess demand, 58
excess supply, 58
perfect competition, 209
shortage, 58
supply, Fig. 4-3/58, Table 4-3/59, 58–59
surplus, 58
unique equilibrium, 216
Market for loanable funds, 353
Market mechanism, 55, 66–71
alternatives, 68
black markets, 68

buyer, 56
conservation, 68
demand, 53-71
economic freedom, 68
firm, 56
government price-setting, Fig. 4-9/69
imperfect competition, 55-56
incentive to produce, 66
industry, 56
laissez-faire, 69
limitations, 69-71
monopoly, 69
oligopoly, 69
perfect competition, 55-56
plant, 56
price controls, 68
prices, 55, 68
problems, 69-71
resources, 68
scarcity, 66
side-effects, 69
skills, 66
stability, 69
strengths, 66-68
supply, 53-71
wants, 69
Market power, 56, 231, 232
income distribution, 374
monopoly, 56
natural oligopoly, 262-263
oligopoly, 56
Market price
consumption, 141
search cost, 141
specialization, 141
time cost, 141
Market structure, Table 13-1/258
duopoly, Table 13-3/258
monopolistic competition, Table 13-3/258
monopoly, Table 13-3/258
oligopoly, Table 13-3/258
perfect competition, Table 13-3/258
Marketing board, 241
agriculture, 241
efficiency, 242
market demand curve, 241
quotas, 242
Markets for factors of production, 65
Marshall, Alfred, 108
Marx, Karl, 7, 8
Marxist economy, 54, 55
Maximin criterion, Box 18-1/380
Maximum sustainable yield of renewable resource, 441
Maximum utility and marginal benefit, 126
McRae, James, 295
Mediation, 347
Medium of exchange, 46
Merger, 302
abuse of dominant position, 291
acquiring firm, 302
conglomerate, 289
corporate reorganization, 305
horizontal, 289, 302
monopoly, 229, 238-239
target firm, 303
vertical, 289
Merit goods, 88
consumption, 88
production, 88
Mincer, Jacob, 374
Minimum efficient scale, Fig. 9-10/177, 177
constant returns, 177
natural monopoly, 230
Minimum income, 514
Minimum wage laws, 318
efficiency, 320
teenage unemployment, 320
Misleading advertising, 292
Mixed economy, 54
Monetary economy
buyer, 44
seller, 44
Monetary system, 45-48
common medium of exchange, 46
debasement of the currency, 47
deflation, 47
Gresham's Law, 47
proper quantity of money, 48
quantity of money, 48
uniform money, 47
Money
economy, Fig. 3-2/44
exchange, 43-51, Fig. 3-2/44
general purchasing power, 44
specialization, 43-51
Monopolistic competition, 257
barriers to entry, 259
close substitutes, 258
equilibrium, Fig. 13-1/259
excess capacity, 259
location, 258
market structure, Table 13-3/258
product differentiation, 257
specialty items, 260
substitutes, 258
Monopoly, 55, 229
allocative efficiency, 238, 255
bilateral, 329, 341-342
competition, 257
Crown corporations, 86
demand, 231
discriminating, 247-249
dynamic efficiency, 237-238
economies of scale, 230
efficiency, 237-239
efficiency loss, 238
elasticity of demand, 236-237
government ownership, Box 12-2/247
government policy, 242-247
international trade, 390
legal, 229
marginal cost, 234
marginal cost pricing, 244
marginal revenue, 233, 234
market mechanism, 69
market power, 56
market structure, Table 13-3/258
merger, 229, 238-239
natural, 229
perfect competition, 231
price discrimination, 249
price maker, 233
prices, 233
profit maximization, 236
profits, 235-238
regulation, 242-247
technological efficiency, 237-239
transfer effect, 239-241
two-way, 329
welfare loss, 238
Monopoly inefficiency, 499
public interest, 499

Monopsony, Table 12-3/237, 338
  unions, 340
  wage rates, Box 16-3/339
Moral hazard, 216
  insurance, 216, 217
  perfect competition, 217
Morgenstern, Oskar, 270
Multilateral, 419
Mutual funds, 150

Nash equilibrium, 271n, 279
  Cournot duopoly game, 278
  dominated strategy, 278
National Energy Board
  regulation, 85
National Energy Program, 451
National unions, 333
Natural monopoly, 229, 230, Fig. 12-9/243
  airline industry, 297
  economies of scale, 230
  minimum efficient scale, 230
  natural oligopoly, Fig. 13-3/262
Natural oligopoly, 262
  barriers to entry, 263
  costs, 262–263
  economies of scale, 263
  imported goods, 263
  market power, 262–263
  natural monopoly, Fig. 13-3/262
  perfect competition, Fig. 13-3/262
  predatory pricing, 263
  product differentiation, 263
Natural resource
  common-property, 439
  external cost, 439, 440
  internal cost, 440
  non-renewable, 439
  private cost, 439, 440
  privately owned, 439
  renewable, 439
  rent, 446
  return, 446
  spillover cost, 440
Natural resources, 437–454
Necessities and elasticity of demand, 105
Negative income tax, 518–520
  categorizing, 520
  stigma, 520
  tagging, 520
  wage subsidy, 521
  welfare, 518–520
Negotiations
  asymmetric information, 344
  strikes, 343–345
Net worth, 155
*New Industrial State, The*, 71n
Newly industrialized countries, 429
Non-excludability, 484
Non-price competition
  advertising, 273, 274
  game theory, 273
Non-renewable, 439
Non-renewable resource
  conservation, 447–449
  dynamic efficiency, 449
  oil, 450
  substitution, 449–450
Non-rivalry, 484
Non-tariff barriers, 418, 434
  bureaucracy, 418
  health standards, 418
  quality standards, 418
  quotas, 418
  red tape, 418
Normal good, 140
  demand shifters, 60
Normal profit, 159, 359
  equity capital, 359
  perfect competition, 192
Normative economics, 40
Norris-La Guardia Act, 332
North American Free Trade Agreement, 389
  barriers to trade, 411
  environment, 427
  hub-and-spoke system, 426
  labour, 413
  rules of origin, 427
  tariff, 288, 425
  trade deflection, 427
Notes, 149

Offshore fishery regulation, Box 21-1/444
Oil, 450–454
Old Age Security, 78, 506
  clawback, 510
  government expenditures, 79
  transfer payments, 77
Oligopoly, 55, 230, 260
  cartel, 266
  collusion, 266
  competition, 257
  concentration of an industry, 260
  deep pockets, 263
  equilibrium price, 264
  game theory, 269–273
  international trade, 390
  kinked demand curve, 267
  market mechanism, 69
  market power, 56
  market structure, Table 13-3/258
  marketing, 264
  name-brand, 264
  price searcher, 264
  vicious circle, 264
Oligopsony, 340
Open shop, 334
Opportunity cost, 158, 393
  accounting cost, 158–159
  comparative advantage, 49, 393
  curve, Fig. 2-2/35
  labour, 315
  perfect competition, 192
  production possibilities curve, 33–35, 36
  rent, Box 17-2/364
  supply curve, 315
Opportunity possibilities curve and frontier, 35–36
Oppressive majority, 495
  public choice, 495
  public interest, 495
Optimal amount of pollution, 470
Option demand, 488
Organization of Petroleum Exporting Countries, 267, 281, 450
  cartel, 450
  cheating, 281
  collusion, 281
  production quotas, 282
  residual supplier, 282
Ownership, 155
Ozone. *See* Environment

Parable of the parking lots, Box 14-2/293
Paradox of value, Fig. 7-6/129, 129

Paradox of wealth, 123
Pareto, Vilfredo, Box 11-2/210
Pareto-improvement, Box 11-2/210
Pareto-optimum, Box 11-2/210
Partnership, 145
  agreement, 146
  creditors, 146
  financing, 146
  flexibility, 145, 146
  liabilities, 146
  taxes, 147
  unlimited liability, 146
Patent, 229
Payoff matrix in prisoner's dilemma, 270
Payroll taxes
  health care, 82
  social assistance, 82
  social insurance contributions, 82
  unemployment insurance contributions, 82
Pension funds, 150
Perfect competition, 56, 183
  above-normal profit, 192
  adverse selection, 217
  agricultural price supports, 220–221
  cycle of price fluctuations, 217
  demand, 231
  demand of individual producer, 184
  dynamic efficiency, 214
  economic efficiency, 203–221
  economic profit, 192
  efficiency, 203–221
  entry, 192
  exit, 192
  freedom of entry, 183
  freedom of exit, 183
  government intervention, 215
  homogeneous input, 193
  homogeneous product, 183
  income distribution, 215–216
  long-run supply, 188–196
  marginal revenue, 184–185
  market, 204–206
  market equilibrium, 209
  market structure, Table 13-3/258
  monopoly, 231
  moral hazard, 216, 217
  natural oligopoly, Fig. 13-3/262
  normal profit, 192
  opportunity cost, 192
  perfect information, 183
  perfectly elastic long-run supply, 193–195
  price instability, 218
  price taker, 233
  prices, 214, 217
  profit maximization, 185
  rising long-run supply curve, 195–196
  risk, 217
  short-run supply, 187
  speculation, 218
  standardized product, 183
  supply of labour, 314–315
  technical efficiency, 213
  technological efficiency, 213
  unique equilibrium, 216
Perfectly competitive market, 204–206
Perfectly discriminating monopoly, 253
  allocative efficiency, 254
Perfectly elastic, 105
Petro-Canada privatization, 87
Physical capital, 353
Pioneer enterprise and Crown corporations, 86
Plant, 56
Plurilateral, 419
Poison pill, 304
Policies to eliminate discrimination, 506
Pollution, 465
  command and control, 468
  constitution, 462
  control, 462–463
  controlling, 466–467
  economic goals, 14
  effluent fee, 468
  emission permits, 468–469
  end-of-pipe treatment, 472
  environmental protection, 14
  external cost, 463–464
  greenhouse effect, 476, 477
  optimal amount, 470
  private cost, 464
  property rights, 464–465
  regulation, 462, 472
  regulatory controls, 472
  social costs, 464
  subsidizing control equipment, 472
  taxes, 467, 468
  trans-boundary, 473
  transactions costs, 466
Population of Canada, Fig. 1-16/26
Portfolio investment, 401, 407
  foreign ownership, 407
Positive economics, 40
Poverty, 12, 503–504
  causes, 505
  charity, 504
  economic goals, 14
  government policy, 504
  income distribution, 12
  line, 504
  low-income cutoff, 504
  population percentage living in, Fig. 1-5/13
  standards, Table 1-1/13
  symptoms, 505
  unemployment, 13, 14
  welfare, 504, 516
Poverty line, 504
Predatory pricing, 263, 288
  natural oligopoly, 263
Preferred stock, 149
Prescott, David, 295
Price
  average level, 11
  competitive market, 214
  demand shifters, 60
  inflation, 11
  marginal benefit, 126
  market mechanism, 55, 68
  monopoly, 233
  perfect competition, 214, 217
  rationing device, 215
  relative, 11
  resources, 360
  supply shifters, 62
Price and entry regulation, 293
Price discrimination, 291, 292
  monopoly, 249
Price elasticity of demand, 101
Price elasticity of supply, 107
Price instability and elasticity, 118–121
Price leader and game theory, 272

Price line and indifference curve, 134
Price maker, 233
  monopoly, 233
  price searcher, 264
  price taker, 264
Price of inputs, 182
  *See also* Costs
Price searcher, 264
  oligopoly, 264
  price maker, 264
  price taker, 264
Price stability, 10–11
  deflation, 10
  economic goals, 10–11
  Great Depression, 10
  inflation, 10
Price taker, 183, 233
  perfect competition, 233
  price maker, 264
  price searcher, 264
Price wars, 267
Pricing in duopoly, 270
Primary burden of tax, 198
Principal, 149, Box 8-1/151
  bonds, 149
  corporation, Box 8-1/151
Principal residence
  capital gains, 92
  taxation, 92
Principal/agent problem, 304
Prisoner's dilemma and payoff matrix, 270
Private benefit, 203
Private business and economic policy, 6
Private cost, 203, 440
  pollution, 463
Private good, Fig. 23-2/485
  public good, 485
Private market and economic policy, 6
Private property rights and environment, 465–466
Private property rights, 465
Privately owned, 439
Privately owned resource, 445–447
  reservation price, 445
Privatization, 87
  Air Canada, 87
  Canadair, 87
  Crown corporations, 87
  de Havilland, 87
  Petro-Canada, 87
Problem of the second best, Box 12-1/240
Producers and circular flow of expenditures and income, 45
Product differentiation, 257
  monopolistic competition, 257
  natural oligopoly, 263
Product markets, 65
Production
  externalities, 88
  merit goods, 88
  per capita, Fig. 1-1(a)/4
Production costs, 163–179
  average cost, 165
  average fixed cost, 165
  average total cost, 165
  average variable cost, 165
  capital intensive, 163
  fixed costs, 164
  labour intensive, 163
  long-run, 163
  marginal cost, 164
  short-run, 163
  total cost, 164
  variable costs, 164
Production function in the short run, 166
Production possibilities curve, Fig. 2-1/34, Table 2-1/34
  boundary, 36
  capital goods, Fig. 2-6/38
  capital inflow, 38
  choices, 33–35, 36
  consumption goods, Fig. 2-6/38
  economic development, 38
  growth, Fig. 2-4/36, 36
  opportunity cost, 33–35, 36
  scarcity, 33–35, 36
  single good improvement, Fig. 2-5/37
  unemployment, Fig. 2-3/36
Productivity and elasticity, 119
Profit, 353
  above-normal, 159
  economic, 159
  monopoly, 235–238
  normal, 159
  resource allocation, 197
  resources, 197
Profit maximization, Fig. 10-2/185, Table 10-1/185
  marginal cost, 185–186
  marginal revenue, 185–186
  perfect competition, 185
  total cost, 186–187
  total revenue, 186–187
Profit-and-loss statement. *See* Income statement
Profit-maximizing equilibrium of monopoly, Fig. 12-4/235
Profit-maximizing point, 234
Profit-maximizing price in game theory, 272
Profit-maximizing production decisions, 312
Property rights, 443
  common-property problem, 465
  pollution, 464–465
  tradeable permits, 469–470
Property taxes, 81, 82
Proprietorship. *See* Sole proprietorship
Prospectus, 150
Provincial marketing boards and regulation, 85
Proxies, Box 8-1/151
Public choice, 481
  bureaucracy, 498
  government decision making, 492–495
  logrolling, 497
  oppressive majority, 495
  public good, 481–500
  public interest, 495–498
  special-interest groups, 494–495
  voting paradox, 497
Public enterprise. *See* Crown corporations
Public good, 88, 481–500, Fig. 23-3/487
  definition, 484
  environment, 487–488
  external benefit, 482
  free rider, 486
  inexhaustible, 484
  internalizing the externality, 483
  non-excludability, 484
  non-rivalry, 484

private good, 485
public choice, 481–500
Public interest
bureaucracy, 498
logrolling, 497
monopoly inefficiency, 499
oppressive majority, 495
public choice, 495–498
regulation, 85
voting paradox, 497
Public sector unions, 333
Public Service Alliance of Canada, 333
Public Service Staff Relations Act, 333
Public service strikes, 348–349
Public transit pricing, 255–256

Quality of life regulation, 285
Quebec Pension Plan, 506, 507
Quotas, 411, 434
marketing board, 242

Rand Formula, 332, 334
Rate of return, 354, 355
Ratio, 26
Rationalization, 421
Rationed, 358
Rationing device, 215
Rawls, John, Box 18-1/379
Reaganomics, 95–96
Real capital, 30
Real income, 140
demand curve, 140
indifference curve, 140
Real investment, 32
Real wage rates, 310
Recession, 9
social costs, 82
unemployment rate, 9
Recycling, Box 22-3/474
Regulated industry, 296
Regulated monopoly and allocative efficiency, 255
Regulation, 82–86, 285
agricultural products, 85
Bank of Canada, 84
Canadian Radio-television and Telecommunications Commission, 84
Canadian Transport Commission, 85
certification, 296
chartered banks, 84
consistency, 492
cost-benefit test, 491
demand, 53–71
economic policy, 6
economic stability, 89
efficiency of managers, 87
environment, 285, 462
environmental, 85
government, 75
health, 285, 491
hidden costs, 299
highway transport boards, 85
laissez-faire, 87
licensing, 296
monopoly, 242–247
National Energy Board, 85
offshore fishery, Box 21-1/444
pollution, 462, 472
problems with, 85–86
provincial marketing boards, 85
public enterprises, 53, 54
public interest, 85
quality of life, 285
radio and television, 296
rail transport, 293
reduction, 85
regulation, 53, 54
safety, 285, 491
safety in the workplace, 491
spending, 53
supply, 53–71
taxation, 53, 90
telecommunications, 84
trucking industry, 293, 295
working conditions, 285
Regulatory consistency, 492
Regulatory controls, 285
Relative prices and efficiency, 12
Renewable, 439
Renewable resource
efficiency, 457
maximum sustainable yield, 440, 441
resource rent, 457
sustainable yield, 440, 457
Rent, 363
above-normal profit, 368
agriculture, 366
capitalized, 368–369
economic, 363
human capital, 363
land, 367
mineral deposit, 367
opportunity cost, Box 17-2/364
reservation price, 446
return on a natural resource, 446
taxing, 369–370
Rent control and elasticity, 112
Resale price maintenance, 292
Research and development, 287
Reservation price, 445
privately owned resource, 445
rent, 446
Resource allocation
marginal cost, 197
profits, 197
Resources, 29
factor of production, 30
prices, 360
profits, 197
scarce, 30–33
Return, 152
corporation, 152
leverage, 152
liquidity, 152
risk, 152
stock market, 154
Return on homeowner's equity, 92
Revenue and elasticity of demand, 103
Ricardo, David, 48, 392
Right-to-work laws, 334
Risk, 152
bonds, 153
corporation, 152
interest, 357
leverage, 152
liquidity, 152
perfect competition, 217
return, 152
safety in the workplace, 490
stock market, 154
Risk premium for bonds, 153
Risk-free rate, 357
Robber barons, 292
Robinson-Patman Act, 291
Roundabout production, 354
Rules of origin, 427, Box 20-4/428

Sabotage, 396
Safety regulation, 285, 491
Safety in consumer products, 490–491

Safety in the workplace, 488–490
  external cost, 490
  regulation, 491
  risk, 490
  wages, 490
Salaries and human capital, 363
Sales taxes, 81
  regressive, 92, 94
Scarcity, 30
  choices, 29–41
  production possibilities curve, 33–35
Schumpeter, Joseph, 287
Search cost, 140
  market price, 141
  utility, 140, 141
Securities, 147–155
  *See also* Bonds; Shares; Stock
  buyer, 152
  issuers, 152
Seller, 44
Seniority rules, 330
Services, 30
  barter, 43
  government expenditures, 77
Shares, 146
Shark repellent, 303
Sharks, 303, 304
Shelf space, Box 13-1/265
Short-run, 163
  efficiency, 211
  production function, 166
Short-run costs, Fig. 9-1/165, 165
Short-run market supply curve, 188
Short-run supply
  break-even point, 187
  perfect competition, 187
  shutdown point, 187
Shortage, 58
Shutdown point, 187, 188
Shutdown principle, Box 10-1/190–191
Small business corporations
  income tax, 93
  taxation, 93
Smith, Adam, 6, 50, 53, 89, 123, 128, 183, Box 11-1/206, 266, 315, 340
Social assistance, 510
  aid in kind, 137
  cash assistance, 137
  government expenditures, 80
  indifference curve, 137–139
  marginal utility, 137–139
  payroll taxes, 82
  poverty, 504
  untied cash grant, 137
  utility, 137–139
  voucher, 137
Social benefit, 203
Social cost, 203
  pollution, 464
Social insurance contributions and payroll taxes, 82
Social insurance programs, 506
  Canada Pension Plan, 507
  child tax benefit, 510
  guaranteed income supplement, 510
  health insurance, 508
  old age security, 506
  Quebec Pension Plan, 507
  social assistance, 510
  unemployment insurance, 507
Social welfare, 511
  poverty, 504
*Sociedad Anonima*, 147
*Société Anonyme*, 147
Sole proprietorship, 145
  advantages, 145
  creditors, 146
  disadvantages, 145
  financing, 146
  flexibility, 145, 146
  liabilities, 146
  taxes, 147
  unlimited liability, 146
Soviet Union and hyperinflation, 11
Specialization, 389, 415
  comparative advantage, 48–49
  economies of scale, 49
  efficiency, 43
  exchange, 43–51
  international trade, 415
  market price, 141
  money, 43–51
  tariff, 415
Speculation, 218
  destabilizing, 219–220
  stabilizing, 218–219
Speculators, 218
Spillover benefits, 481
  human capital, 361
Spillover cost, 440
  strikes, 346–347
Stabilizing speculation, 218–219
Star Wars, 29
Stigma, 520
Stock, 30
  common. *See* Common stock
  preferred. *See* Preferred stock
Stock market, 153–155
  broker, 153
  inflation, 154
  interest rate, 154
  return, 154
  risk, 154
  stockbroker, 153
Stockbroker, 153
Strategic Defence Initiative, 29
Strikes, 342–349
  costs, 343
  negotiations, 343–345
  public service, 348–349
  spillover cost, 346–347
Substitutability and elasticity of demand, 105
Substitutes, 115, 360
  cross elasticity of demand, 115
  demand shifters, 60
  elasticity of supply, 108
Substitution effect, 139, 140
  demand curve, 140
  indifference curve, 140
  supply of labour, 327
Supply, 56, 57–58
  demand, 53–71, Fig. 4-3/58, Table 4-3/59
  elasticity, Fig. 6-4/108
    *See also* Elasticity of supply
  excess, 58
  market equilibrium, 58–59, Fig. 4-3/58, Table 4-3/59
  market mechanism, 53–71
  price elasticity. *See* Elasticity of supply
  shifters. *See* Supply shifters
  shifts in, 61–62
Supply curve, Fig. 4-2/57, 58
  labour, 315
  movement along a curve, 63
  opportunity cost, 315
  response to a shift, 62
Supply curve for savings, 356
Supply of labour, 327–328
  income effect, 327
  participation rate, 327

perfect competition, 314-315
substitution effect, 327
Supply schedule, Table 4-2/57, 58
Supply shifters, 61-62
alternative products, 62
complements in production, 62
input costs, 61-62
joint products, 62
prices, 62
prices of related goods, 62
substitutes in production, 62
technology, 62
weather, Fig. 4-6/62, 62
Surplus, 58
Sustainable yield, 440
renewable resource, 457
Symptoms of poverty, 505

Taft-Hartley Act, 334
Takeoff, 38
capital goods, Fig. 2-7/39
consumption goods, Fig. 2-7/39
Takeover battle, 302, 303
Target firm, 302, 303
Tariff, 411, 434
beggar-my-neighbour, 415
bilateral, 419
Canada/United States Free Trade Agreement, 288
Canadian, 418-419
comparative advantage, 416
dependency, 416
diversification, 415
economic policy, 6
Great Depression, 418, 419
imperfect competition, 417
improving terms of trade, 416
infant industries, 416
international trade, 288
loopholes, 96
multilateral, 419
North American Free Trade Agreement, 288, 425
plurilateral, 419
positive externality, 417
scientific, 414
self-sufficiency, 416
specialization, 415
trilateral, 419
voluntary limits, 415
Tax base
broadening, 93
Tax reform, 93
broadening the tax base, 93
deductions, 93, 94
exemptions, 94
flat tax, 93
indexation, 93
marginal rates, 94
rates, 94
tax base, 93
tax brackets, 93
tax credits, 93, 94
tax shelters, 94
Tax revenue and elasticity, Fig. 6-7/111, 111, 112
Taxation. *See* Income taxes; Taxes
Taxes, 78, 89-96
ability to pay, 90
avoidance, 92
baby bonus, 510
benefit principle, 90
burden, 91, 198
capital gains, 92
Carter Commission, 90
child benefit, 510
common-property resource, 443
corporation, 147
dividend tax credit, 147
dividends, 147
double taxation, 147
economic policy, 6
elasticity, 110
equity, 90
evasion, 92
excess burden, 198
family allowance, 510
government, 75
incentives, 89
incidence, Fig. 5-5/91, 91
income distribution, 375, 376
inheritance tax, 90
loopholes, 92
neutrality, 89
partnership, 147
pollution, 467, 468
primary burden, 198
primary function, 75
principal residence, 92
progressive, 90, 92
regressive, 92
regulation, 90
simplicity, 90
small business corporations, 93
social objectives, 89-90
sole proprietorship, 147
Technical efficiency, 213-214
perfect competition, 213
Technological change and international trade, 396
Technological efficiency, 213-214
monopoly, 237-239
perfect competition, 213
Technology
elasticity, 119
supply shifters, 62
Teenage unemployment and minimum wage laws, 320
Telecommunications regulation, 84
Terms of trade in international trade, 394
Theory, 39-40
Theory of the second best, Box 12-1/240, 341n
Tied selling, 292
Time cost and market price, 141
Time series and algebraic techniques, 24
Tokyo Round, 419
Total benefit. *See* Utility
Total cost, 164
profit maximization, 186-187
total revenue, 186-187
Total physical product, 166
Total product, 166
average product, 166-168
marginal product, 166-168
Total revenue
elasticity of demand, 103
profit maximization, 186-187
total cost, 186-187
Trade deflection, Box 20-4/428
Tradeable permits and property rights, 469-470
Trades and Labour Congress of Canada, 331
Transactions costs, 140, 466
pollution, 466
utility, 140
Trans-boundary pollution, 473
Transfer, 401
international trade, 401
Transfer effect, 239
monopoly, 239-241
unions, 335
Transfer payments, 78

government expenditures, 77
Old Age Security, 77
social assistance, 77
unemployment insurance benefits, 77
Transfer price, 315
Transfer programs and income distribution, 376
Transfers in kind, 376
Two-way monopoly, 329
Types of markets, Table 12-3/237

Unconditional grants, 88
Unemployed, 9
Unemployment
economic goals, 14
government expenditures, 76
income, 13
inflation, 10, 14
poverty, 13, 14
production possibilities curve, Fig. 2-3/36
World War II, 10
Unemployment insurance, 77n, 506, 507
clawback, 510
Unemployment insurance benefits
government expenditures, 79
transfer payments, 77
Unemployment insurance contributions as payroll taxes, 82
Unemployment rate, 8–10
Canadian output, Fig. 1-3/9
depression, 9
economic goals, 8–10
Great Depression, 8, 9
recession, 9
time series, Fig. 1-15/25
unemployed, 9
Unfair competition, 288
Unidirectional international externality, 475
Uniform money, 47
Union shop, 334
Unions
closed shop, 334
co-determination, 330
collective bargaining, 330
continental, 333
craft, 332
efficiency, 337
efficiency effect, 335
industrial, 332
international, 333
job security, 330, 336
monopsony, 340
national, 333
open shop, 334
public sector, 333
seniority rules, 330
transfer effect, 335
union shop, 334
Unique equilibrium, 216
Unlimited liability, 146
partnership, 146
sole proprietorship, 146
Uruguay Round, 419, 429
Utility
costs, 140
demand, 124
diminishing marginal, 123–125
index, 130
information cost, 140, 141
marginal, 124
marginal and total, Fig. 7-2/125, Table 7-1/125
marginal benefit, 128
marginal. *See* Marginal utility
search cost, 140, 141
social assistance, 137–139
transactions costs, 140
Utility index, 130

Value added tax, 94
Value of the marginal product, 311
Variable costs, 164
Vertical merger, 289
Viner, Jacob, Box 9-2/175
von Neumann, John, 270
Voting paradox, 497
public choice, 497
public interest, 497

Wage bargaining and game theory, 345–346
Wage rate
labour, 315
monopsony, Box 16-3/339
Wage subsidy, 521
Wages
barriers to entry, 350
compensating wage differential, 349
dynamic differentials, 349
human capital, 363
international trade, Box 19-1/395
real rates, 310
safety in the workplace, 490
subsidy, 521
Wagner Act, 332
Wants, 29
market mechanism, 69
unlimited, 29–30
*Wealth of Nations, The*, 6n, 50
Weather as supply shifters, 62
Welfare, 510, 511
*See also* Social assistance
categorization, 520
complexity, 513
efficiency, 514, 517
equity, 517
implicit tax, 513, 515
inequity, 513
negative income tax, 518–520
non-economic benefits, 517
non-economic costs, 517
perverse incentives, 513
poverty, 504, 516
stigma, 520
subsidy, 514
tagging, 520
wage subsidy, 521
Welfare loss, 238
monopoly, 238
Welfare programs and government expenditures, 80
White knight, 303, 304
Wildcat strikes, 346n
Willingness to pay
indifference curve, 132
marginal rate of substitution, 132
Withholding tax, 404
Work week, Fig. 1-1(b)/4
Workable competition, 292
Workers' compensation, 506
Working conditions regulation, 285
World Bank, 4
World War II
government expenditures, 76
inflation, 10
unemployment, 10

Yellow-dog contracts, 332
Yield. *See* Return

cut here

## STUDENT REPLY CARD

In order to improve future editions, we are seeking your comments on *Microeconomics*, Fourth Edition.

Please answer the following questions and return this form via Business Reply Mail. Your opinions matter. Thank you in advance for sharing them with us!

Name of your college or university: ______________________________

Major program of study: ______________________________

Course title: ______________________________

Were you required to buy this book? ________ yes ________ no

Did you buy this book new or used? ________ new ________ used ($________ )

Do you plan to keep or sell this book? ________ keep ________ sell

Is the order of topic coverage consistent with what was taught in your course?

cut here

fold here

Are there chapters or sections of this text that were not assigned for your course? Please specify:

Were there topics covered in your course that are not included in the text? Please specify:

What did you like most about this text?

What did you like least?

If you would like to say more, we would appreciate hearing from you. Please write to us at the address shown on the reverse of this page.

cut here

fold here

cut here

**Postage will be paid by**

MAIL POSTE

Canada Post Corporation / Société canadienne des postes

**Postage paid** if mailed in Canada

**Port payé** si posté au Canada

**Business Reply**

**Réponse d'affaires**

0183560299 01

0183560299-L1N9B6-BR01

Attn.: Sponsoring Editor
College Division

MCGRAW-HILL RYERSON LIMITED
300 WATER ST
WHITBY ON L1N 9Z9

*tape shut*